Roger Ebert's
Movie Yearbook
2003

Other books by Roger Ebert

An Illini Century

A Kiss Is Still a Kiss

Two Weeks in the Midday Sun: A Cannes
Notebook

Behind the Phantom's Mask

Roger Ebert's Little Movie Glossary

Roger Ebert's Movie Home Companion
annually 1986–1993

Roger Ebert's Video Companion
annually 1994–1998

Questions for the Movie Answer Man

Roger Ebert's Book of Film: An Anthology

Ebert's Bigger Little Movie Glossary

I Hated, Hated, Hated This Movie

The Great Movies

With Daniel Curley
The Perfect London Walk

With Gene Siskel
The Future of the Movies: Interviews with
Martin Scorsese, Steven Spielberg, and
George Lucas

DVD Commentary Tracks
Citizen Kane
Dark City
Casablanca

Roger Ebert's Movie Yearbook 2003

Andrews McMeel Publishing

Kansas City

This book is dedicated
to Robert Zonka, 1928–1985.
God love ya.

Contents

Introduction

In the days after 9/11, there was a debate about whether American tastes in movies would change. Would this event of devastating violence dampen our enthusiasm for thrillers about terrorists and mass destruction? Some movies had their release dates pushed back, and others on the drawing board went into turnaround. Movie critics speculated that a season of kinder, gentler films might be on the way. But a year later, there seems to be no substantial difference in the kinds of movies Americans attend. We still like violence, and we have no trouble with terrorists—although stories like Tom Clancy's *The Sum of All Fears* were rewritten (even before the World Trade attack) to replace Islamic extremists with the evergreen standby, neo-Nazis.

The central event in *The Sum of All Fears* is the destruction of much of Baltimore by a terrorist's nuclear device. There is a shot of a football stadium being vaporized, and then the blast wave spreads out in all directions, in a special-effects shot of startling effectiveness. The director, Phil Alden Robinson, included that shot in TV ads for the film, because he "wanted people to know what they could expect." Apparently it did not deter many; the movie grossed $31 million on its opening weekend and went on to take well over $100 million.

I would have said, on September 12, 2001, that the scenes involving the terrorist destruction of Baltimore would no longer be acceptable to audiences. I would have been wrong. Indeed, by the time the movie opened in the summer of 2002, I found myself giving it a favorable review, writing that while previous movies like *Black Sunday* (also about a terrorist attack on a stadium) worked to exorcise our fears, "this one works instead to give them form."

Yes, you might reply, but didn't 9/11 give them form enough? Do we need fiction to confirm the warnings of fact? No, but we may need fiction to deny the impact of fact. In the closing scenes of *The Sum of All Fears*, while the American president speaks triumphantly in the Rose Garden, the hero and his girlfriend have a picnic on a blanket on the White House lawn, and he produces a ring. This happy ending comes while Baltimore lies destroyed barely forty miles away. "Human nature is a wonderful thing," I wrote. "The reason the ending is happy is because we in the audience assume we'll be the two on the blanket, not the countless who've been vaporized."

That's how all thrillers work: No matter how many people get killed, the audience always survives. One of the endearing things about America is that, as a nation, we have an unshakable confidence and optimism. It may fly in the face of reason, it may be shaken by an event like 9/11, but it is resilient.

In July 2002, I found myself on the jury of the Karlovy Vary Film Festival in the Czech Republic. Some of my fellow jurors were citizens of countries that had been under Soviet rule. When a patriotic Russian film was shown, two of them in particular criticized the festival for including it in the official competition. The movie supplied an upbeat ending to events that were not, in the minds of these jury members, upbeat at all. What the movie called the Soviet "liberation" of Poland, for example, they considered the Soviet occupation.

In our debates, I heard many jury members criticize several entries for being "too Hollywood," by which they meant they were "too well made," "forced a happy ending," or "allow you to sense the crew behind the camera." They resisted movies that took the uncertainties of real life and forced them into the patterns of comforting and predictable fiction.

I had many long and good conversations with my fellow jury member Ibolya Fekete, a director from Hungary. One day she said to me, "In the films of Eastern Europe, the world is not in order. In Hollywood films, the world is in order." I understood. She was shaped by the Soviet occupation to such a degree that to this day she doesn't have e-mail; she has too many memories of her mail being opened and her phone being tapped. The very week of the festival, she received secret security files revealing the extent of Soviet spying on her and her family. In the world she grew up in, the happy ending was not an inevitable part of the story.

We in America have had a good ride for a long time. It has made us expect favorable outcomes. That is part of our charm, part of our fate, and perhaps part of our vulnerability. Our movies reflect that. Even in films with a "sad ending," there is some kind of twist to assure us that life goes on. In the 1970s, briefly, there was a season of American movies with a darker vision, no doubt fueled by our futile efforts in Vietnam. Movies like *Apocalypse Now, Taxi Driver, The Deer Hunter,* and *Coming Home* painted a bleak picture. But that season passed, and with it the ascendancy of directors who functioned as independent artists.

For many years now, Hollywood has conformed almost all its stories to the underlying myth that things will turn out right in the end. Perhaps the happy ending is organic to the movies and to most popular fiction; we may suspect that all will end in sadness, but we will not pay money to have our suspicions confirmed. This is not a good thing or a bad thing, but a fact of our nature. Apparently 9/11 did nothing to alter it.

* * *

Where should you start in compiling a movie library? *For Keeps,* by Pauline Kael, brings together a generous selection from her many previous books of reviews, providing an overview of the career of the most influential of film critics. The greatly revised and expanded new fifth edition of David Thomson's *Biographical Dictionary of Film* is an opinionated, informed, concise summary of hundreds of key careers. The late Ephraim Katz's *Film Encyclopedia* is an invaluable one-volume survey of the world of film. And *Distinguishing Features,* by Stanley Kauffmann, is the latest collection of reviews by the critic whose superb writing and scholarship have distinguished the *New Republic* for decades. Jonathan Rosenbaum's recent book *Movies as Politics* showcases the work of one of the best contemporary critics. David Bordwell's *On the History of Film Style* tells you more about how to look at a movie than any other book I have ever found.

For decades Donald Richie has been an unfailingly literate and perceptive guide to Japanese films. The new *Donald Richie Reader: 50 Years of Writing on Japan*, compiled by Arturo Silva, brings together his film and Japanese writings in a book of remarkably original organization and design.

In March 2002, we lost Billy Wilder, one of the greatest and most inventive of directors. The invaluable book *Conversations with Wilder* is the result of long conversations between the great man and another gifted director, Cameron Crowe *(Almost Famous)*. Like the classic book-length conversation between Hitchcock and Truffaut, it shows two artists talking with love and knowledge about their craft.

For DVD fans, there is no better guide than *Doug Pratt's DVD-Video Guide*. For the critics who shaped today's film criticism, I recommend the collected works of Kael, Kauffmann, Manny Farber, Andrew Sarris, Dwight MacDonald, James Agee, and Graham Greene.

On the Web, to survey many different reviews of a movie, try Rotten Tomatoes (www.rottentomatoes.com) and the Movie Review Query Engine (www.mrqe.com). For parents in search of *detailed* factual information about the contents of movies, supplied without a political or religious agenda, there is no better site than www.screenit.com. The most valuable one-stop movie resource on the Web is the Internet Movie Database (http://www.imdb.com/).

* * *

My muse is my wife, Chaz, a movie lover like myself, who attends most of the screenings and festivals and helps me plow through the mob scenes at Cannes and survive the sneak previews. To her, my love and gratitude.

ROGER EBERT

Acknowledgments

My editor is Dorothy O'Brien, tireless, cheerful, all-noticing. She is assisted by the equally invaluable Julie Roberts. My friend and longtime editor Donna Martin suggested this new approach to the annual volume. The design is by Cameron Poulter, the typographical genius of Hyde Park. My thanks to production editor Christi Clemons-Hoffman, who renders Cameron's design into reality. I have been blessed with the expert and discriminating editing of John Barron, Laura Emerick, Miriam DiNunzio, Teresa Budasi, Jeff Wisser, Darel Jevins, Avis Weatherbee, and Jeff Johnson at the *Chicago Sun-Times*; Sue Roush at Universal Press Syndicate; and Michelle Daniel at Andrews McMeel Publishing. Many thanks are also due to the production staff at *Ebert & Roeper*, and to Marsha Jordan at WLS-TV. My gratitude goes to Carol Iwata, my expert personal assistant, and to Marlene Gelfond, at the *Sun-Times*. And special thanks and love to my wife, Chaz, for whom I can only say: If more film critics had a spouse just like her, the level of cheer in the field would rise dramatically.

ROGER EBERT

Key to Symbols

★★★★ A great film
★★★   A good film
★★   Fair
★   Poor

G, PG, PG-13, R, NC-17:
Ratings of the Motion Picture
Association of America

G   Indicates that the movie is suitable for general audiences

PG   Suitable for general audiences but parental guidance is suggested

PG-13 Recommended for viewers 13 years or above; may contain material inappropriate for younger children

R   Recommended for viewers 17 or older

NC-17 Intended for adults only

141 m. Running time

1999   Year of theatrical release

☞   Refers to "Questions for the Movie Answer Man"

Reviews

A

About a Boy ★ ★ ★ ½
PG-13, 100 m., 2002

Hugh Grant (Will), Nicholas Hoult (Marcus), Rachel Weisz (Rachel), Toni Collette (Fiona), Victoria Smurfit (Suzie), Sharon Small (Christine). Directed by Paul Weitz and Chris Weitz and produced by Jane Rosenthal, Robert De Niro, Brad Epstein, Tim Bevan, and Eric Fellner. Screenplay by Peter Hedges, Chris Weitz, and Paul Weitz, based on the book by Nick Hornby.

Hugh Grant, who has a good line in charm, has never been more charming than in *About a Boy*. Or perhaps that's not quite what he is. "Charming" in the Grant stylebook refers to something he does as a conscious act, and what is remarkable here is that Grant is—well, likable. Yes, the cad has developed a heart. There are times, toward the end of the film, where he speaks sincerely and we can actually believe him.

In *About a Boy*, he plays Will, a thirty-eight-year-old bachelor who has never had a job, or a relationship that has lasted longer than two months. He is content with this lifestyle. "I was the star of the Will Show," he explains. "It was not an ensemble drama." His purpose in life is to date pretty girls. When they ask him what he does, he smiles that self-deprecating Hugh Grant smile and confesses that, well, he does—nothing. Not a single blessed thing. In 1958, his late father wrote a hit song named "Santa's Super Sleigh," and he lives rather handsomely off the royalties. His London flat looks like a showroom for Toys for Big Boys.

Will is the creation of Nick Hornby, who wrote the original novel. This is the same Hornby who wrote *High Fidelity*, which was made into the wonderful John Cusack movie. He depicts a certain kind of immature but latently sincere man who loves Women as a less-demanding alternative to loving a woman. Will's error, or perhaps it is his salvation, is that he starts dating single mothers, thinking they will be less demanding and easier to dump than single girls.

The strategy is flawed: Single mothers invariably have children, and what Will discovers is that while he would make a lousy husband he might make a wonderful father. Of course, it takes a child to teach an adult how to be a parent, and that is how Marcus (Nicholas Hoult) comes into Will's life. Will is dating a single mom named Suzie, whom he meets at a support group named Single Parents Alone Together (SPAT). He shamelessly claims that his wife abandoned him and their two-year-old son, "Ned."

Suzie has a friend named Fiona (Toni Collette), whose son Marcus comes along one day to the park. We've already met Marcus, who is round-faced and sad-eyed and has the kind of bangs that get him teased in the school playground. His mother suffers from depression, and this has made Marcus mature and solemn beyond his years; when Fiona tries to overdose one day, Will finds himself involved in a trip to the emergency room and other events during which Marcus decides that Will belongs in his life whether Will realizes it or not.

The heart of the movie involves the relationship between Will and Marcus—who begins by shadowing Will, finds out there is no "Ned," and ends by coming over on a regular basis to watch TV. Will has had nothing but trouble with his fictional child, and now finds that a real child is an unwieldy addition to the bachelor life. Nor is Fiona a dating possibility. Marcus tried fixing them up, but they're obviously not intended for each other—not Will with his cool bachelor aura and Fiona with her Goodwill hippie look and her "health bread," which is so inedible that little Marcus barely has the strength to tear a bite from the loaf. (There is an unfortunate incident in the park when Marcus attempts to throw the loaf into a pond to feed the ducks, and kills one.)

Will finds to his horror that authentic emotions are forming. He likes Marcus. He doesn't admit this for a long time, but he's a good enough bloke to buy Marcus a pair of trendy sneakers, and to advise Fiona that since Marcus is already mocked at school, it is a bad idea, by definition, for him to sing "Killing Me

Softly" at a school assembly. Meanwhile, Will starts dating Rachel (Rachel Weisz), who turns out to be a much nicer woman than he deserves (she also has a son much nastier than she deserves).

This plot outline, as it stands, could supply the materials for a film of complacent stupidity—a formula sitcom with one of the Culkin offspring blinking cutely. It is much more than that; it's one of the year's most entertaining films, not only because Grant is so good but because young Nicholas Hoult has a kind of appeal that cannot be faked. He isn't a conventionally cute movie child, seems old beyond his years, can never be caught in an inauthentic moment, and helps us understand why Will likes Marcus—he likes Marcus because Marcus is so clearly in need of being liked, and so deserving of it.

The movie has been directed by the Weitz brothers, Paul and Chris, who directed *American Pie*, which was better than its countless imitators, and now give us a comedy of confidence and grace. They deserve some of the credit for this flowering of Hugh Grant's star appeal. There is a scene where Grant does a double take when he learns that *he* has been dumped (usually it is the other way around). The way he handles it—the way he handles the role in general—shows how hard it is to do light romantic comedy, and how easily it comes to him. We have all the action heroes and Method script-chewers we need right now, but the Cary Grant department is understaffed, and Hugh Grant shows here that he is more than a star, he is a resource.

The Adventures of Rocky & Bullwinkle ★ ★ ★
PG, 90 m., 2000

Rene Russo (Natasha), Jason Alexander (Boris), Piper Perabo (Karen Sympathy), Randy Quaid (Cappy Von Trapment), Robert De Niro (Fearless Leader), June Foray (Rocky [voice]), Keith Scott (Bullwinkle [voice]), Keith Scott (Narrator), Janeane Garofalo (Minnie Mogul). Directed by Des McAnuff and produced by Jane Rosenthal and Robert De Niro. Screenplay by Kenneth Lonegran, based on characters developed by Jay Ward.

The original *Rocky & Bullwinkle* TV show was smarter than it needed to be, and a lot of adults sneaked a look now and then. It helped point the way to today's crossover animated shows like *The Simpsons.* Now comes the movie version of the TV show (which was canceled in 1964), and it has the same mixture of dumb puns, corny sight gags and sly, even sophisticated in-jokes. It's a lot of fun.

The movie combines the animated moose and squirrel with live action—and even yanks three of the characters (Natasha, Boris, and Fearless Leader) out of the TV set and into the real world (where they're played by Rene Russo, Jason Alexander, and Robert De Niro, explaining, "We're attached to the project").

The breathless narrator portentously explains: "Expensive animation characters are converted to even more expensive movie stars!" The narrator (Keith Scott), of course, always seemed to stand outside the action and know that *R&B* was only a cartoon (at one point he complains he has been reduced to narrating the events of his own life). And the movie is also self-aware; when someone (I think maybe Fearless L) breathlessly announces, "There has never been a way to destroy a cartoon character until now!" he's asked, "What about Roger Rabbit?"

The plot involves a scheme by Fearless Leader to win world domination by hypnotizing everyone with RBTV (Really Bad TV). Only Rocky and Bullwinkle have long years of experience at foiling the evil schemes of Fearless, Natasha, and Boris, and as they fumble their way to a final confrontation we also get a coast-to-coast road movie (cheerfully acknowledged as a cliché by the narrator).

The movie has a lot of funny moments, which I could destroy by quoting, but will not. (Oh, all right: At one point Rocky cries, "We have to get out of here!" and Bullwinkle bellows: "Quick! Cut to a commercial!") As much fun as the wit is the film's overall sense of well-being; this is a *happy* movie and not the desperate sort of scratching for laughs we got in a cartoon retread like *The Flintstones in Viva Rock Vegas.* It's the sort of movie where De Niro parodies his famous "Are you talking to me?" speech with such good-natured fun that instead of groaning, we reflect—well, everyone else has ripped it off, so why shouldn't he get his own turn?

The movie is wall-to-wall with familiar faces, including Janeane Garofalo as a studio executive, Randy Quaid as the FBI chief, Whoopi Goldberg as a judge, John Goodman as a cop, Billy Crystal as a mattress salesman, James Rebhorn as the president, and Jonathan Winters in three roles. Rene Russo makes a persuasive Natasha, all red lipstick, seductive accent, and power high heels, and De Niro's patent leather hair and little round glasses will remind movie buffs of Donald Pleasance.

But the real discovery of the movie is its (human) lead, a twenty-three-year-old newcomer named Piper Perabo, who plays an FBI agent. She has fine comic timing, and is so fetching she sort of stops the clock. Like Renee Zellweger in *Jerry Maguire*, she comes more or less out of nowhere (well, a couple of obscure made-for-videos) and becomes a star right there before our eyes.

Comedy is such a fragile art form. *The Adventures of Rocky & Bullwinkle* isn't necessarily any more brilliant or witty or inventive than all the other recent retreads of classic cartoons and old sitcoms. But it feels like more fun. From time to time I'm reminded of George C. Scott's Rule No. 3 for judging movie acting: "Is there a joy of performance? Can you tell that the actors are having fun?" This time, you can. There's a word for this movie, and that word is jolly.

An Affair of Love ★ ★ ★ ½
R, 80 m., 2000

Nathalie Baye (Elle), Sergi Lopez (Lui). Directed by Frederic Fonteyne and produced by Patrick Quinet, Rolf Schmid, and Claude Waringo. Screenplay by Philippe Blasband.

She takes an ad in a sex paper. There is something she has always wanted to do with a man, and now, in her forties, she has decided it will never happen unless she acts boldly. He answers the ad. They meet in a café. They are presentable and ordinary—nice people, we sense. They agree to go to a hotel, and the room door closes. We never find out what happens between them in the room. It is what they were both looking for. When they are asked, after the affair is over, if it was "good," we can see from their faces that it was.

An Affair of Love is a story about "He" and "She," two adults who have a strong desire and act on it. It is about the desiring itself, not about what they desire. That makes it more intriguing than if we knew their secret—and sexier. We are reminded of the great scene in *Belle de Jour* where Catherine Deneuve plays a housewife who works afternoons in a brothel. A client opens a little box and shows her what is inside. Whatever it is, she refuses his request—she wants nothing to do with it. What is in the box is the same thing that is behind the room door in this movie, and in the briefcase in *Pulp Fiction*—a void to tantalize our imaginations.

But the movie is not simply about sex. If it were, it would have to play fair and reveal the secret. It is about these people. Gradually, shyly, they get to know each other. We see right away that Lui likes Elle. Eventually she grows very fond of him too. Because they have a deal (they will meet as strangers, they will be anonymous, they will rendezvous only to fulfill their mutual desire), it takes a long while before the personal feels free to replace the impersonal. Once a week they do something (literally) beyond our wildest imaginations, but eventually they gather the courage to consider the ultimate next step: having ordinary sex.

The affair is over when the movie begins. That much is made clear immediately. Elle and Lui speak to an unseen interviewer about their memories of the experience. Their memories do not always agree. That is the way, sometimes. They recall events that violated their privacy—the collapse of an old man in the hotel, for example. When they tried to help him, they fell into their everyday roles, and that added too much information, endangering the fantasy.

The actors are Nathalie Baye and Sergi Lopez. She is about ten years older than he is, but age is not relevant: From the looks on their faces they are lucky to have found someone alive at the same time who wants to do what they do. There are times, during the affair, when they seem tired, not physically, but mentally, the way you get when all your desires are answered at once. Their minds are accustomed to wishing for their fantasy, but not to dealing with it. They must hardly be able to sleep.

Will they live happily ever after? Since the

movie opens by telling us they did not, we wonder—why not? In answering this question, the writer-director, Frederic Fonteyne, makes a movie about love and sex that is wiser and more useful than the adolescent fantasies enacted by adults in Hollywood pictures. How does the old saying go? "Be careful what you wish for, because you might get it."

Their relationship is not about liking each other, this movie observes, and it is not about sex or orgasm. It is about having a part of you that has been your precious secret since you can first remember, a part you thought you could never share, and finding someone whose own secret part is a match for your own. The discovery of this other person forces you to catch your breath as the two of you, together, regard what stands for truth and beauty in your lives. You are not in love with the other person, so much as the two of you share a tenderness because each knows how hard the other has looked, and how hopeless the search seemed at times.

That's why it is so essential that the movie never reveal their secret. Any answer at all to our curiosity would be a disappointment—except for one. And that is the one answer we already have, and no movie can know.

The Affair of the Necklace ★ ★

R, 120 m., 2001

Hilary Swank (Jeanne de la Motte Valois), Simon Baker (Retaux de Vilette), Adrien Brody (Nicolas de la Motte), Joely Richardson (Marie Antoinette), Jonathan Pryce (Cardinal da Rohan), Christopher Walken (Cagliostro), Brian Cox (Minister Breteuil). Directed by Charles Shyer and produced by Broderick Johnson, Andrew A. Kosove, Redmond Morris, and Shyer. Screenplay by John Sweet.

Fed up with historical dramas, Jack Warner is said to have snarled at his producers: "Don't give me any more pictures where they write with feathers." He could have had *The Affair of the Necklace* in mind. This is the kind of movie that used to be called a bodice-ripper, and still could, if only more bodices were ripped. It tells the story of a scandal that prepares the way for the French Revolution, and involves a silly girl who thinks she can outsmart the car-

dinal, the royal jeweler, Marie Antoinette—and Cagliostro, the leader of the Illuminati, played by Christopher Walken. One look at Cagliostro and she should know she's in over her head.

The movie stars Hilary Swank as Jeanne St. Remy de Valois, who after her marriage of convenience becomes Jeanne de la Motte Valois. The operative name is "Valois." It is her family name, and she was orphaned as a child after her parents were involved in schemes against the crown. She dreams of restoring the glory of her family name and returning to the family house where she spent her childhood, and to do this she unfolds a scheme of audacious daring.

She knows that Cardinal Louis de Rohan (played by Jonathan Pryce in a congenial state of sin) wishes to be prime minister. She convinces him that Marie Antoinette will be more favorably disposed toward his cause if he presents the queen with a fabulous necklace containing 647 diamonds. She gets the money from the cardinal, obtains the necklace from the royal jeweler, keeps it for herself, uses it to repurchase her family home, and forges letters from the queen to the cardinal to cover the deception. What was she thinking? That the queen had so many necklaces she would never be able to account for one more or less? And that the cardinal would never dare refer directly to the transaction?

This kind of skullduggery (a word actually used in the film) would be more appropriate in the hands of an actress who includes devious scheming among her specialties—a Helena Bonham Carter, say, or Catherine Zeta-Jones. Hilary Swank, who was so wonderful in her Oscar-winning work in *Boys Don't Cry* (1999), exudes truthworthiness, which is the wrong quality for this assignment. She also embodies a certain plucky vulnerability, when what is wanted for Jeanne Valois is the Monica Lewinsky gene, the ability to imagine herself in the embrace of the great. Above all, she needs a kind of Bette Davis imperiousness. Hilary Swank, I fear, believes we should feel sorry for Jeanne. So does Charles Shyer, who directed this movie and sends Swank on the wrong assignment. *The Affair of the Necklace* only works if it understands Jeanne is one villain among many, not a misguided heroine.

The supporting cast offers incidental pleasures. Joely Richardson is an imperious, silly Marie Antoinette, able to deceive herself but not often deceived by anyone else. Jonathan Pryce makes the cardinal into a venal and greedy schemer, and Christopher Walken, as always, inspires hope when he walks into a scheme. Adrien Brody plays Jeanne's first, ineffectual, husband, and Simon Baker plays the ladies' man who plays Jeanne the way she is trying to play the crown.

But the storytelling is hopelessly compromised by the movie's decision to sympathize with Jeanne. We can admire someone for daring to do the audacious, or pity someone for recklessly doing something stupid, but when a character commits an act of stupid audacity, the admiration and pity cancel each other, and we are left only with the possibility of farce.

Agnes Browne ★ ★ ½

R, 92 m., 2000

Anjelica Huston (Agnes Browne), Marion O'Dwyer (Marion Monks), Ray Winstone (Mr. Billy), Arno Chevrier (Pierre), Niall O'Shea (Mark Browne), Ciaran Owens (Frankie Browne), Roxanna Williams (Cathy Browne), Carl Power (Simon Browne), Mark Power (Dermot Browne), Gareth O'Connor (Rory Browne). Directed by Anjelica Huston and produced by Jim Sheridan, Arthur Lappin, Huston, and Greg Smith. Screenplay by John Goldsmith and Brendan O'Carroll, based on the novel *The Mammy* by O'Carroll.

Agnes Browne is an Irish housewife with six sons and a daughter and her husband dead since ten minutes past four this afternoon, giving a piece of her mind to the government clerk who wants to see a certificate before paying out the poor man's death benefits. She doesn't make much money with her fruit and vegetable cart in a street market, but she's got her pride and her friends, and her children all wear matching sweaters to the funeral—even if they match because they all came from the same charity agency.

Agnes (Anjelica Huston) is like the lucky twin of Angela McCourt, the heroine of *Angela's Ashes*. Things are grim but not bleak, and at least there's no drunken husband in the picture (one of her youngest is so overcome at the funeral he holds two oranges up to block his eyes). She's best friends with Marion (Marion O'Dwyer), who runs the next cart in the market, and if she's not overly smart at least she's observant and thoughtful.

Anjelica Huston might seem like an unlikely actress to play her, and to direct *Agnes Browne*, but reflect that her father, the director John Huston, maintained a country home (almost a castle, really) in Ireland during her childhood, and that she grew up feeling as Irish as American. Her accent can't be faulted, and neither can her touch for detail: not the realistic details of *Angela's Ashes*, but the pop fiction details of what's essentially a warmhearted soap opera.

The supporting characters come on-screen all but wearing descriptive labels on cords around their necks. Consider Mister Billy, played by Ray Winstone, an actor so good at being mean that two of England's best actors (Tim Roth and Gary Oldman) both cast him as an abusive father in their first movies. Mister Billy is the neighborhood loan shark, a man who hands you the cash and expects you to pay interest on it for the rest of your life.

Agnes has to borrow from him to finance her husband's funeral, and when she's able to pay him back in a lump sum, his eyes narrow with disappointment. When her son Frankie finds a trade and needs to buy tools, Mister Billy is there with another loan, and sinister intentions.

Some days are sunny, some cloudy in Agnes's life. She is flattered to be asked out on a date by the French baker Pierre (Arno Chevrier), and saddened when Marion gets bad news about a medical exam. And always in the back of her head is a dream, which, her aim being modest, is to meet Tom Jones. Whether she marries Pierre or meets Jones, as well as the state of Marion's health and the outcome of Frankie's loan, I will leave you to discover.

This is a modest but likable film, and Anjelica Huston plays a heroine who makes us smile. But it's skimpy material, and I'm not sure why Huston was attracted to it; her first film as a director, *Bastard Out of Carolina* (1996), a story about child abuse, was fiercer and more passionate. *Agnes Browne* is not consequential enough to inspire a visit to a theater, but as a video rental it's not a bad idea.

A.I. Artificial Intelligence ★ ★ ★
PG-13, 145 m., 2001

Haley Joel Osment (David), Jude Law (Gigolo Joe), Frances O'Connor (Monica Swinton), Brendan Gleeson (Lord Johnson-Johnson), Sam Robards (Henry Swinton), William Hurt (Professor Hobby), Jake Thomas (Martin Swinton). Directed by Steven Spielberg and produced by Kathleen Kennedy, Spielberg, and Bonnie Curtis. Screenplay by Spielberg and Ian Watson, based on the short story "Supertoys Last All Summer Long" by Brian Aldiss.

Greatness and miscalculation fight for screen space in Steven Spielberg's *A.I. Artificial Intelligence,* a movie both wonderful and maddening. Here is one of the most ambitious films of recent years, filled with wondrous sights and provocative ideas, but it miscalculates in asking us to invest our emotions in a character that is, after all, a machine.

"What responsibility does a human have to a robot that genuinely loves?" the film asks, and the answer is: None. Because the robot does not genuinely love. It only genuinely seems to love. We are expert at projecting human emotions into nonhuman subjects, from animals to clouds to computer games, but the emotions reside only in our minds. *A.I.* evades its responsibility to deal rigorously with this trait, and goes for an ending that wants us to cry but had me asking questions just when I should have been finding answers.

At the center of the movie is an idea from Brian Aldiss's 1969 short story, "Supertoys Last All Summer Long," about an advanced cybernetic pet that is abandoned in the woods. When real household animals are abandoned, there is the sense that humans have broken their compact with them. But when a manufactured pet is thrown away, is that really any different from junking a computer? (I hope Buzz Lightyear is not reading these words.) From a coldly logical point of view, should we think of David, the cute young hero of *A.I.,* as more than a very advanced gigapet? Do our human feelings for him make him human?

Stanley Kubrick worked on this material for fifteen years, before passing it on to Spielberg, who has not solved it either. It involves man's relationship to those tools that so closely mirror our own desires that we confuse them with flesh and blood; consider that Charles Lindbergh's autobiography, *We,* is about himself and an airplane. When we lose a toy, the pain is ours, not the toy's, and by following an abandoned robot boy rather than the parents who threw him away, Spielberg misses the real story.

The film opens with cerebral creepiness, as Professor Hobby (William Hurt) presides at a meeting of a company that makes humanoid robots (or "mechas"). We are in the future; global warming has drowned the world's coastlines, but the American economy has survived thanks to its exploitation of mechas. "I propose that we build a robot that can love," Hobby says. Twenty months later, we meet Monica and Henry (Frances O'Connor and Sam Robards), a married couple whose own child has been frozen until a cure can be devised for his disease. The husband brings home David (Haley Joel Osment), a mecha who looks as lifelike and lovable as—well, Haley Joel Osment.

"There's no substitute for your own child!" sobs Monica, and Henry tries to placate her: "I'll take him back." Cold, but realistic; David is only a product. Yet he has an advanced chip that allows him to learn, adapt, and "love," when Monica permanently "imprints" him. In some of the most intriguing passages in the film, Spielberg explores the paradoxes that result, as David wins their love and yet is never—quite—a real boy. He doesn't sleep, but he observes bedtime. He doesn't eat, but so fervent is his desire to belong that he damages his wiring by ingesting spinach (wouldn't a mecha be programmed not to put things into its mouth?). David is treated with cruelty by other kids; humans are frequently violent and resentful against mechas. Why? Maybe for the same reason we swear at computers.

Events take place that cause David's "mother" to abandon him in the woods, opening the second and most extraordinary section of the movie, as the little mecha, and Teddy, his mecha pet bear, wander lost through the world, and he dreams of becoming a real boy and earning Monica's love. He knows *Pinocchio* from his bedtime reading, and believes that the Blue Fairy might be able to make him real. David and Teddy are befriended by Gigolo Joe (Jude Law), a love mecha living the life of a hustler. There is a sequence at a Flesh Fair, not unlike a WWF event, at which humans cheer as damaged mechas are destroyed grotesquely. Eventually, after a harrowing escape, they arrive at Rouge City, where a wizard tells David where to look for the Blue Fairy.

It's here that *A.I.* moves into its most visionary and problematical material, in spectacular scenes set in a drowned New York. There are secrets I won't reveal, but at one point David settles down to wait a very long time for the Blue Fairy, and the movie intends his wait to be poignant, but for me it was a case of a looping computer program—not a cause for tears, but a cause for rebooting. In the final scenes, David is studied in a way I will not reveal; it is up to us to determine who, or what, his examiners are.

The movie is enormously provocative, but the story seems to skew against its natural grain. It bets its emotional capital on David and his desire to be a real boy, but it's the old wood-carver Geppetto, not the blockhead puppet, who is the poignant figure in *Pinocchio*. The movie toys with David's nature in the edgy party scenes, but then buys into his lovability instead of balancing on the divide between man and machine. Both of the closing sequences—the long wait and an investigation—are unsuccessful. The first goes over the top. The second raises questions it isn't prepared to answer. There are a couple of possible earlier endings that would have resulted in a tougher movie.

Haley Joel Osment and Jude Law take the acting honors (and, of course, Hurt is perfect at evoking the professor). Osment, who is on-screen in almost every scene, is one of the best actors now working. His David is not a cute little boy but a cute little boy *mecha;* we get not the lovable kid from *The Sixth Sense* but something subtly different. The movie's special effects are awesome. The photography by Janusz Kaminski reflects Spielberg's interest in backlighting, bright whites, and the curiously evocative visible beams of flashlights. The effects seamlessly marry the real with the imaginary.

A.I. is audacious, technically masterful, challenging, sometimes moving, ceaselessly watchable. What holds it back from greatness is a failure to really engage the ideas it introduces.

The movie's conclusion is too facile and sentimental, given what has gone before. It has mastered the artificial, but not the intelligence.

Aimee & Jaguar ★ ★ ★
NO MPAA RATING, 125 m., 2000

Maria Schrader (Felice Schragenheim [Jaguar]), Juliane Kohler (Lilly Wust [Aimee]), Johanna Wokalek (Ilse), Heike Makatsch (Klarchen), Elisabeth Degen (Lotte), Detlev Buck (Gunther Wust), Inge Keller (Lilly [today]), Kyra Mladeck (Ilse [today]), Margit Bendokat (Mrs. Jager). Directed by Max Farberbock and produced by Gunter Rohrback and Hanno Huth. Screenplay by Farberbock and Rona Munro, based on the book by Erica Fischer.

Felice is Jewish and a lesbian, in Berlin in 1943—which means she is walking around with a suspended sentence of death. She takes incredible chances. She works for an underground resistance group, and her daytime job is as the assistant to the editor of a Nazi newspaper ("What would I do without you?" he asks). Her strategy is to hide in plain view; her boldness is a weapon. Then she falls in love with Lilly.

Lilly (Juliane Kohler) is the mother of four. Her husband is away at the front. The first time we see her, she is at a Beethoven concert with a German officer—not her husband. She cheats. He cheats, even with their nanny. It is wartime. One night at a club Lilly is swept up by Felice (Maria Schrader) and her friends; she's too naive at first to know they are lesbians, and doesn't figure out Felice is Jewish until she is finally told. Why would you suspect that of an employee of the Nazis?

Aimee & Jaguar (those were Lilly and Felice's pet names for each other) is based on a true story. Lilly Wust is alive even today, at eighty-five, and is the subject of a book that inspired the film. Felice almost certainly died in the concentration camps; her death was hastened because Lilly heedlessly tried to visit her there, calling the wrong kind of attention. War is a time for desperate and risky love affairs, but theirs was so dangerous it was like an act of defiance against the laws, the state, the world, all set against them.

It is pretty clear that Germany is losing the

war, that the end is not far away; the bombs rain on Berlin, and through her underground sources Felice knows even better than her editor of the German defeats. The movie suggests that a few Jews who did escape identification were able to survive in a sort of shadowland. Early in the film, a German woman in a rest room sells food stamps to women she knows (or assumes) are Jewish, and later other Germans know Felice's secret but do not reveal it. They support a genocidal state, but are unwilling to take personal action. There is even a subtle and delicately written scene suggesting that the editor of the Nazi paper realizes Felice is not what she seems, and chooses not to know.

For Lilly, love with Felice is a revelation. At first she doesn't even realize her new friend is a lesbian, and when Felice kisses her she reacts with horror. On reflection, she is not so horrified at all, and soon they are lovers. There is a sex scene in the movie, not graphic in its visual details but startling in its intensity, that is one of the most truthful I have seen. Most lovers in the movies are too in command; the actors fear the embarrassment of lost control. A person having an orgasm can look funny, even ridiculous, to an outsider, which is why you won't find many movie stars who really want to fake it all that well. When Lilly and Felice make love, there is a trembling, a fear, a loss of control that colors all the scenes that follow.

Maria Schrader plays Felice with a kind of doomed and reckless bravery. She must know her days are numbered. She cannot get away with her deception forever, and when she is caught, she will not be just any Jew, but one who penetrated to the center of the Nazi establishment—who partied with those who had condemned her to death. She is initially attracted to Lilly as sort of a lark; it might be fun to take this officer's wife, this mother of four little Aryans, and conquer her. Then they are both surprised by love.

There is a moment in the film when it appears that the nightmare is ending. A report spreads of Hitler's death after the failed assassination plot by some of his officers. No one knows quite how to respond; Felice is too cautious to reveal her feelings, but among Berliners in general there is the unstated feeling that the war was lost anyway, and might as well

end. Then Hitler goes on the radio to declare himself untouched, and for Felice his voice is a death sentence: She will not get another pass, she senses. "I'm Jewish, Lilly," she tells her lover. Lilly looks at her in surprise, and then asks, "How can you love me?" It is the crucial moment of the movie.

Aimee & Jaguar has some holes in its storytelling that raise questions. How can Lilly's husband return from the fighting seemingly at will? Was Felice hired by the newspaper without any personal documentation? These questions do not matter. What matters is that at a turning point in her life, Felice is given a chance to escape Germany, and stays. Maybe she didn't have a choice. This is the kind of story that has to be true; as fiction, it would not be believable.

Ali ★ ★
R, 157 m., 2001

Will Smith (Muhammad Ali), Jamie Foxx (Drew "Bundini" Brown), Jon Voight (Howard Cosell), Mario Van Peebles (Malcolm X), Ron Silver (Angelo Dundee), Jeffrey Wright (Howard Bingham), Michael Bentt (Sonny Liston), Candy Ann Brown (Odessa Clay), Giancarlo Esposito (Ali's Dad). Directed by Michael Mann and produced by Paul Ardaji, A. Kitman Ho, James Lassiter, Mann, and Jon Peters. Screenplay by Eric Roth and Mann, based on the story by Gregory Allen Howard, Stephen J. Rivele, and Christoper Wilkinson.

Ali is a long, flat, curiously muted film about the heavyweight champion. It needs more of the flash, fire, and humor of Muhammad Ali and is shot more in the tone of a eulogy than a celebration. There is little joy here. The film is long and plays longer because it permits itself sequences that are drawn out to inexplicable lengths, while hurrying past others that should have been dramatic high points. It feels like an unfinished rough cut that might play better after editing.

Consider, for example, a training sequence set in Zaire, after Ali travels there for the Rumble in the Jungle. He begins his morning run, which takes him past a panorama of daily life. All very well, but he runs and runs and runs, long after any possible point has been made—

and runs some more. This is the kind of extended scene you see in an early assembly of a film, before the heavy lifting has started in the editing room.

The film considers ten years in the life of Ali, from 1964, when he won the heavyweight championship as Cassius Clay, to 1974, when as Muhammad Ali he fought in the Rumble. This is the key decade in Ali's life, interrupted for three years when he was barred from boxing because of his refusal to be drafted.

Although many mistakenly believe he refused to serve because of guidance from the Nation of Islam, the film makes it clear that he took his stand on principle, and it cost him both his title and his religion; the Nation disapproved of his decision and suspended him. By the time the U.S. Supreme Court ruled 8–0 in his favor, he had lost what should have been his prime years as a young fighter. When he went into the ring against George Foreman in Zaire, he was thirty-two, the champion twenty-four.

Michael Mann's story of these ten years is told in the style of events overheard—this isn't a documentary, but it seems to lack a fiction's privileged access to its hero. Key scenes play out in enigmatic snippets of dialogue. We work to make connections. We see Ali's wives, but don't feel we know them; they fade in and out of focus like ghosts. The screenplay by Eric Roth and Mann seems reluctant to commit to a point of view, and leaves us to draw our own conclusions. During some scenes you can almost sense it shrugging. Ali remains an enigma.

This is despite what is actually a good job of acting by Will Smith in the title role. He has bulked up and looks convincing in the ring, but the key element of his performance is in capturing Ali's enigmatic, improvisational personality. He gets the soft-spoken, kidding quality just right, and we sense Ali as a man who plays a colorful public role while keeping a private reserve. There are times when he grows distant from even those close to him, and they look at him as if into a mystery.

The real problem with Smith's performance is the movie it finds itself in. Smith is the right actor for Ali, but this is the wrong movie. Smith is sharp, fast, funny, like the Ali of trash-talking fame, but the movie doesn't unleash that side of him or his character. Ali was not only the most famous man of his time, but had

fun with his fame. I can't claim any special insights, but I did once spend a day with him, and I saw a man enormously entertained by life, twinkling with bemusement, lowering the tinted glass window of his Rolls limousine so that pedestrians could do a double take when they saw it was the Champ. Smith could play that man, but *Ali* doesn't know or see him; it sees Ali as more meditative and subdued—as sad, sometimes, when sadness is the last thing you feel when you risk everything on principle. The film feels under a cloud.

Among the many key players in his life—his wives, his trainer Angelo Dundee, his right-hand man Bundini Brown, his mentor Malcolm X, his father, his leader Elijah Muhammad—Ali's most authentic relationship in the film seems to be with the sportscaster Howard Cosell. Played by Jon Voight in a performance that captures his theatrical weirdness and forthright honesty, Cosell comes across as a man who slipped into TV before the cookie cutting began. His voice, his toupee, his sublime self-assurance are all here, along with a tender, almost paternal regard for Ali, a man he clearly loves and worries about. Ali responds in kind, and Smith is able to suggest that in a world that surrounded him with toadies, bootlickers, and yes-men, Ali turned to Cosell almost in relief at being able to hear the truth, plainly spoken. Jamie Foxx is also engaging and appealing as Bundini, the self-destructive mascot who sold the Champ's belt "and put it into my arm."

The fight scenes are convincing and well staged. Smith looks at home in the ring. But the unique thing about the life of Muhammad Ali is precisely that it was not just about the fighting. More than any other heavyweight champion and few athletes in any sport, Ali changed the subject: His life was not about boxing, but about a black man who dared to triumph in American society without compromise, apology, or caution.

Those who called him a coward for refusing to fight in the war will learn here that he'd been offered a sweetheart deal by the army; all he had to do was go along, be inducted, not play the angry black rebel, and he'd be entertaining the troops and defending his title and getting nowhere close to combat. To turn down that deal and the heavyweight title, and to lose the blessing of the Nation of Islam in the process, was to show himself as a brave man entirely governed by ethics.

"No Viet Cong ever called me nigger," Ali famously said, and the movie makes it clear that the American establishment was terrified of a black uprising in the tumultuous Vietnam era, and that J. Edgar Hoover, whose G-men tracked and tricked Martin Luther King and Ali, was one of the great villains of his time.

The movie includes scenes involving King and Malcolm X, but doesn't really deal with them (you find out more in Spike Lee's *Malcolm X*). After King is shot, Ali watches a city burn, but curiously has no dialogue. We wait for issues to be clarified, for points to be made, for the movie to punch up what is important, but the dramatic high points slowly slip back down into a miasma of unfocused and undisciplined footage. The visual look of the picture mirrors its lack of energy; the colors are subdued, the focus often a little soft. *Ali* looks like a movie that was never properly prepared and mounted, that got away from its makers in the filming, that has been released without being completed.

All the Pretty Horses ★ ★ ★ ½
PG-13, 117 m., 2000

Matt Damon (John Grady Cole), Henry Thomas (Lacey Rawlins), Lucas Black (Jimmy Blevins), Rubén Blades (Don Hector Rocha y Villarel), Penelope Cruz (Alejandra), Robert Patrick (John Grady's Father), Bruce Dern (Judge), Sam Shepard (Banker), Miriam Colon (Alfonsa). Directed and produced by Billy Bob Thornton. Screenplay by Ted Tally, based on the novel by Cormac McCarthy.

Billy Bob Thornton's *All the Pretty Horses* is an elegiac Western about two young cowboys, and then a third, who ride from Texas into Mexico in search of what may be left of the Old West. The movie is really as simple as that. It touches on adventure and romance, but isn't really about them. It's about the mythic idea of heading south on a good horse, with a change of clothes, some camp gear, and a gun, and seeing what happens. It takes place in 1949. A few years later, its heroes would have headed down Route 66 in a Chevy convertible.

The movie stars Matt Damon and Henry Thomas as John Grady Cole and Lacey Rawlins, and they're followed on the trail by a kid named Jimmy Blevins (Lucas Black), who is riding more horse than the other two can convince themselves he paid for. He wants to come along and they let him, although one observes he is going to get them into trouble and is right.

In Mexico they get involved in a misunderstanding, or maybe it isn't, about stealing horses that requires them to leave in a hurry. The kid knows it's his fault and does the right thing, keeping to the trail in front of the pursuers, while John and Lacey lose themselves in the sagebrush.

Following no particular plan, they end up on a ranch owned by Don Hector Rocha y Villarel (Rubén Blades), who values his private airplane but not nearly as much as he values his daughter, Alejandra (Penelope Cruz). John breaks some wild mustangs for Don Hector, and discusses fine points of horse breeding, on which the two men find themselves in agreement. Don Hector gives them a job, and John and Alejandra are attracted to each other like those two little Scotty dogs with the magnets in them.

Thornton cares about the story, I think, but he's not distracted by it. The real subject of his movie is the *feeling* of being young, on horseback, in a foreign country, in trouble, and in love. *All the Pretty Horses* reminds me, in a strange way, of *George Washington*, another new movie. The two films have nothing in common except for how much they want to fix in the memory the way it was to be at that place, at that time: They use dialogue as if it were music, to establish a mood.

Listen carefully to the opening scenes of *All the Pretty Horses*. Something interesting is going on. The dialogue, by Ted Tally, is put in the foreground of the sound track instead of being surrounded by the ambience. It remains at the same volume from scene to scene. It overlaps a little strangely—anticipating or tarrying—so that we understand the words are not being illustrated by the pictures, but are evoking them. Indoors, outdoors, the presence of the dialogue dominates the track, and natural noises and music are in the background. Thornton goes to a more naturalistic sound style later in the film, but at the beginning he seems to be reminding us that this is a memory being told.

It is a tribute to Damon's performance that even in love scenes or when he fights for his life in prison, he never seems to be the "hero," but is more like a guy this stuff is happening to. Henry Thomas and Lucas Black (from Thornton's earlier film *Sling Blade*) also do a good job of not being "characters" and just being there. Tally's dialogue never gives them too much to say. They figure it out and we figure it out without a lot of words.

That same economy of language works in two lovely supporting performances, by Miriam Colon as Alfonsa, the eagle-eyed aunt of Alejandra, and Bruce Dern, as a judge on the Texas side. "I won't have her unhappy or gossiped about," the aunt warns John. She warns him away from her niece—and later warns him off again, when the stakes are higher. She's not made into a standard old shrew, but is wise, self-possessed, and knows very well what trouble she is trying to avert. The Dern character has a key scene in a courtroom, but the next scene is in a sense the most important in the movie, because what John really wants is to confess and have his sins forgiven, and the judge knows that.

You can see how this movie could have been jacked up into a one-level action picture, but what makes it special is how Thornton modulates the material. Even the prison knife-fight scenes aren't staged as action confrontations, but as quick, desperate, and strangely intimate. This is the kind of movie it's best to see on a big screen, where the size of the sky and the colors of the land can do their work. It's as if the events are bigger than the people— as if John Grady Cole will never again be such a reckless damn fool kid as he was during this year, and will always sort of regret that.

Almost Famous ★ ★ ★ ★

R, 124 m., 2000

Patrick Fugit (William Miller), Billy Crudup (Russell Hammond), Frances McDormand (Elaine Miller), Kate Hudson (Penny Lane), Jason Lee (Jeff Bebe), Philip Seymour Hoffman (Lester Bangs), Zooey Deschanel (Anita Miller), Michael Angarano (Young William), Noah Taylor (Dick Roswell). Directed by Cameron Crowe and produced by Crowe and Ian Bryce. Screenplay by Crowe.

Oh, what a lovely film. I was almost hugging myself while I watched it. *Almost Famous* is funny and touching in so many different ways. It's the story of a fifteen-year-old kid, smart and terrifyingly earnest, who through luck and pluck gets assigned by *Rolling Stone* magazine to do a profile of a rising rock band. The magazine has no idea he's fifteen. Clutching his pencil and his notebook like talismans, phoning a veteran critic for advice, he plunges into the experience that will make and shape him. It's as if Huckleberry Finn came back to life in the 1970s and instead of taking a raft down the Mississippi got on the bus with the band.

The kid is named William Miller in the movie; he's played by Patrick Fugit as a boy shaped by the fierce values of his mother, who drives him to the concert that will change his life, and drops him off with the mantra, "Don't do drugs!" The character and the story are based on the life of Cameron Crowe, the film's writer-director, who indeed was a teenage *Rolling Stone* writer, and who knows how lucky he was. Crowe grew up to write and direct *Say Anything* (1989), one of the best movies ever made about teenagers; in this movie, he surpasses himself.

The movie is not just about William Miller. It's about the band and the early 1970s, when idealism collided with commerce. The band he hooks up with is named Stillwater. He talks his way backstage in San Diego by knowing their names and hurling accurate compliments at them as they hurry into the arena. William wins the sympathy of Russell Hammond (Billy Crudup), the guitarist, who lets him in. Backstage, he meets his guide to this new world, a girl who says her name is Penny Lane (Kate Hudson). She is not a groupie, she explains indignantly, but a Band Aide. She is, of course, a groupie, but she has so much theory about her role it's almost like sex for her is a philosophical exercise.

William's mom, Elaine (Frances McDormand), is a college professor who believes in vegetarianism, progressive politics, and the corrupting influence of rock music. Banning the rock albums of her older daughter Anita

(Zooey Deschanel), she holds up an album cover and asks Anita to look at the telltale signs in Simon and Garfunkel's eyes: "Pot!" Anita, who had played the lyrics "I Walked Out to Look for America," leaves to become a stewardess.

William walks out too, in a way. He intends to be away from school for only a few days. But as Russell and the rest of Stillwater grow accustomed to his presence, he finds himself on the bus and driving far into the Southwest. Along the way, he observes the tension between Russell and Jeff Bebe (Jason Lee), the lead singer, who thinks Russell is getting more attention than his role definition deserves: "I'm the lead singer and you're the guitarist with mystique."

William has two guardian angels to watch over him. One is Penny Lane, who is almost as young as he is, but lies about her age. William loves her, or thinks he does, but she loves Russell, or says she does, and William admires Russell, too, and Russell maintains a reserve that makes it hard to know what he thinks. He has the scowl and the facial hair of a rock star, but is still only in his early twenties, and one of the best moments in the movie comes when William's mom lectures him over the phone about the dangers to her son: "Do I make myself clear?" "Yes, ma'am," he says, reverting to childhood.

William's other angel is the legendary rock critic Lester Bangs (Philip Seymour Hoffman), then the editor of *Creem:* "So you're the kid who's been sending me those articles from your school paper." He ignores the kid's age, trusts his talent, and shares his credo: "Be honest, and unmerciful." During moments of crisis on the road, William calls Lester for advice.

Lester Bangs was a real person, and so are Ben Fong Torres and Jann Wenner of *Rolling Stone,* played by look-alike actors. The movie's sense of time and place is so acute it's possible to believe Stillwater was a real band. As William watches, the band gets a hit record, a hotshot producer tries to take over from the guy who's always managed them, they switch from a bus to an airplane, and there are ego wars, not least when a T-shirt photo places Russell in the foreground and has the other band members out of focus (there's a little *Spinal Tap* here).

Almost Famous is about the world of rock,

but it's not a rock film; it's a coming-of-age film about an idealistic kid who sees the real world, witnesses its cruelties and heartbreaks, and yet finds much room for hope. The Penny Lane character is written with particular delicacy, as she tries to justify her existence and explain her values (in a milieu that seems to have none). It breaks William's heart to see how the married Russell mistreats her. But Penny denies being hurt. Kate Hudson has one scene so well acted it takes her character to another level. William tells her, "He sold you to Humble Pie for 50 bucks and a case of beer." Watch the silence, the brave smile, the tear, and the precise spin she puts on the words, "What *kind* of beer?" It's not an easy laugh. It's a whole world of insight.

What thrums beneath *Almost Famous* is Cameron Crowe's gratitude. His William Miller is not an alienated bore, but a kid who had the good fortune to have a wonderful mother and great sister, to meet the right rock star in Russell (there would have been wrong ones), and to have the kind of love for Penny Lane that will arm him for the future and give him a deeper understanding of the mysteries of women. Looking at William—earnestly grasping his tape recorder, trying to get an interview, desperately going to Lester for advice, terrified as Ben Fong Torres rails about deadlines, crushed when it looks like his story will be rejected—we know we're looking at a kid who has the right stuff and will go far. Someday he might even direct a movie like *Almost Famous.*

Note: Why did they give an R rating to a movie perfect for teenagers? ☞

Along Came a Spider ★ ★
R, 105 m., 2001

Morgan Freeman (Detective Alex Cross), Monica Potter (Agent Jezzie Flannigan), Michael Wincott (Gary Soneji), Jay O. Sanders (Detective Kyle Craig), Dylan Baker (Mayor Carl Monroe), Raoul Ganeev (Agent Charles Chakley), Billy Burke (Agent Michael Devine), Penelope Ann Miller (Katherine Rose Dunne). Directed by Lee Tamahori and produced by David Brown and Joe Wizan. Screenplay by Marc Moss, based on a novel by James Patterson.

A few loopholes I can forgive. But when a plot is riddled with them, crippled by them, made implausible by them, as in *Along Came a Spider*, I get distracted. I'm wondering, since Dr. Alex Cross is so brilliant, how come he doesn't notice yawning logical holes in the very fabric of the story he's occupying?

Dr. Cross (Morgan Freeman) is a District of Columbia police detective, a famous forensic psychologist whose textbook is quoted by other cops. As the movie opens, he loses his partner in one of those scenes where you're thinking, gee, I didn't know the police had *that* kind of technology. A woman cop has a small camera concealed on her being, which takes a TV signal of the killer, who is driving a car, and relays it to Cross in a helicopter, causing us to wonder if there is a way to arrest this guy at less taxpayer expense.

After this chase, Cross goes into a depression and passes the time building model boats— until his phone rings and it's another diabolical killer, who once again has devised an elaborate cat-and-mouse game for the detective to play. No killers in Washington ever just want to murder somebody; they're all motivated by the desire to construct elaborate puzzles for Cross.

No one is better than Morgan Freeman at being calm and serious and saying things like, "He's really after somebody else." Freeman was brilliant at unraveling the diabolical pattern in *Seven* (1995), and the success of that movie inspired the splendid *Kiss the Girls* (1997), where he first played Cross, the hero of six novels by James Patterson. In *Girls*, he intuited that the madman wasn't killing his victims but collecting them. Now comes another criminal who has read way too many James Patterson novels.

I will tread carefully to avoid revealing surprises, since the movie socks us with one every five minutes, counting on our astonishment to distract us from implausibilities. The film opens with a strangling and a kidnapping at an exclusive private school. The kids have parents so important that the Secret Service has agents permanently assigned. Because the hostage is the daughter of a senator, Cross finds himself working with Agent Jezzie Flannigan (Monica Potter), who found time for a career despite a lifetime of explaining to people how her name is spelled.

The school's students have computer monitors at every desk, and are challenged by their teacher to see who can find Charles Lindbergh's home page in the fewest possible clicks. (Answer: Go to Google, type in "Lindbergh," get 103,000 results, discover he doesn't have a home page.) Most kids their age are already busy creating viruses to bring the economy to its knees. Why such a lamebrained exercise? Dr. Cross figures it out.

The correct Lindbergh page, which he finds immediately out of 103,000 possibilities, has been put up by the kidnapper (or come to think of it, has it?), and includes a live cam shot with resolution so high Cross can read the name on a bottle of pills. This clue, plus the kidnapper's insistence on communicating through Cross, gets him on the case, partnered with Agent Flannigan.

Kiss the Girls, directed by Gary Fleder, had a palpable sense of time and place; deep, moist, shadowy, ominous woodlands figured heavily. *Along Came a Spider*, directed by Lee Tamahori (of the great *Once Were Warriors*), is also thick with atmosphere, and evokes the damp, wet gloom of a chilly season. As Cross and Flannigan follow leads, we also see the kidnapper and his victim, and are filled with admiration for her imagination; she is able to escape, set fires, swim toward shore, and perform other feats far more difficult than a Google search.

But then . . . well, there's not much more I can say without giving away astonishing surprises. The film contains two kinds of loopholes: (1) those that emerge when you think back on the plot, and (2) those that seem like loopholes at the time, and then are explained by later developments which may contain loopholes of their own.

Of Morgan Freeman as a movie actor, no praise is too high. Maybe actors should be given Oscars not for the good films they triumph in, but for the weak films they survive. The focus of his gaze, the quiet authority of his voice, make Dr. Cross an interesting character even in scenes where all common sense has fled. And the look and texture of the film are fine; Tamahori and cinematographer Matthew F. Leonetti have created a convincing sense of place (to be sure, they shot their Virginia exteriors in British Columbia, but, hey, that's a place too). Michael Wincott makes a satisfactory bad guy, especially when his mastermind schemes start blowing up in his face.

But, man, are you gonna be talking when you come out of this movie! Saying things like "but why . . ." and "if she . . ." and "wouldn't he . . ." and "how come . . ." as you try to trace your way back through the twisted logic of the plot. Here's a sample question: Dr. Cross mentions a $12 million ransom and later explains that the person he was talking to should have known it was $10 million but never said anything. And I'm thinking, should that person have even known about the ransom at all? Well, maybe, if . . . but I dunno. There are places in this movie you just can't get to from other places in this movie.

The Amati Girls ★

PG, 91 m., 2001

Cloris Leachman (Dolly), Mercedes Ruehl (Grace), Dinah Manoff (Denise), Sean Young (Christine), Lily Knight (Dolores), Paul Sorvino (Joe), Lee Grant (Aunt Spendora), Edith Field (Aunt Loretta), Cassie Cole (Carla), Marissa Leigh (Laura), Doug Spinuzza (Armand), Mark Harmon (Lawrence). Directed by Anne De Salvo and produced by James Alex, Melanie Backer, Steven Johnson, Michael I. Levy, and Henry M. Shea Jr. Screenplay by De Salvo.

A lot of saints are mentioned in *The Amati Girls,* including Christopher, Lucy, Cecelia, Theresa (the Little Flower), and the BVM herself, but the movie should be praying to St. Jude, patron saint of lost causes. Maybe he could perform a miracle and turn this into a cable offering, so no one has to pay to see it.

The movie's a tour of timeworn clichés about family life, performed with desperation by a talented cast. Alone among them, Mercedes Ruehl somehow salvages her dignity while all about her are losing theirs. She even manages to avoid appearing in the shameless last shot, where the ladies dance around the kitchen singing *Doo-wah-diddy, diddy-dum, diddy-dum.*

The movie is about a large Italian-American family in Philadelphia. Too large, considering that every character has a crisis, and the story races from one to another like the guy on TV who kept all the plates spinning on top of the poles. This family not only has a matriarch (Cloris Leachman) but her superfluous sister (Lee Grant) and their even more superfluous sister (Edith Field). There are also four grown daughters, two husbands, two hopeful fiancées, at least three kids, and probably some dogs, although we never see them because they are no doubt hiding under the table to avoid being stepped on.

The adult sisters are Grace (Ruehl), who is married to macho-man Paul Sorvino ("No Padrone male will ever step foot on a ballet stage except as a teamster"); Denise (Dinah Manoff), who is engaged to Lawrence (Mark Harmon) but dreams of show biz (she sings "Kiss of Fire" to demonstrate her own need for St. Jude); Christine (Sean Young), whose husband, Paul (Jamey Sheridan), is a workaholic; and poor Dolores (Lily Knight), who is retarded. Denise and Christine think Grace is ruining her life with guilt because when she was a little girl she ran away and her mother chased her and fell, which of course caused Dolores to be retarded.

Sample subplot. Dolores decides she wants a boyfriend. At the church bingo night, she sits opposite Armand (Doug Spinuzza), who, we are told "has a head full of steel" after the Gulf War. This has not resulted in Armand being a once-normal person with brain damage, but, miraculously, in his being exactly like Dolores. At the movies, after they kiss, he shyly puts his hand on her breast, and she shyly puts her hand on his.

You know the obligatory scene where the reluctant parent turns up at the last moment for the child's big moment onstage? No less than two fathers do it in this movie. Both Joe (Sorvino) and Paul have daughters in a ballet recital, and not only does Joe overcome his loathing for ballet and even attend rehearsals, but Paul overcomes his workaholism and arrives backstage in time to appear with his daughter.

The movie has one unexpected death, of course. That inspires a crisis of faith, and Dolores breaks loose from the funeral home, enters the church, and uses a candlestick to demolish several saints, although she is stopped before she gets to the BVM. There are also many meals in which everyone sits around long tables and talks at once. There is the obligatory debate, recycled from *Return to Me,* about who is better, Frank Sinatra or Tony Bennett. And an irritating editing twitch: We are shown the outside of every location before we cut inside. There is also one priceless conversation, in which Lee Grant explains to Cloris Leachman that her hair is tinted "copper bamboo bronze." For Cloris, she suggests "toasted desert sunrise." The Little Flower had the right idea. She cut off her hair and became a Carmelite.

Amelie ★ ★ ★ ½
R, 115 m., 2001

Audrey Tautou (Amelie Poulain), Mathieu Kassovitz (Nino Quicampoix), Rufus (Raphael Poulain), Yolande Moreau (Madeleine Wallace), Arthus De Penguern (Hipolito [The Writer]), Urbain Cancellier (Collignon [The Grocer]), Dominique Pinon (Joseph), Maurice Benichou (Bretodeau [The Box Man]), Claude Perron (Eva [The Stripteaser]). Directed by Jean-Pierre Jeunet and produced by Claudie Ossard. Screenplay by Guillaume Laurant and Jeunet. In French with English subtitles.

Jean-Pierre Jeunet's *Amelie* is a delicious pastry of a movie, a lighthearted fantasy in which a winsome heroine overcomes a sad childhood and grows up to bring cheer to the needful and joy to herself. You see it, and later when you think about it, you smile.

Audrey Tautou, a fresh-faced waif who looks like she knows a secret and can't keep it, plays the title role, as a little girl who grows up starving for affection. Her father, a doctor, gives her no hugs or kisses, and touches her only during checkups—which makes her heart beat so fast he thinks she is sickly. Her mother dies as the result of a successful suicide leap off the towers of Notre Dame, a statement that reveals less of the plot than you think it does.

Amelie grows up lonely and alone, a waitress in a corner bistro, until one day the death of Princess Diana changes everything. Yes, the shock of the news causes Amelie to drop a bottle cap, which jars loose a stone in the wall of her flat, which leads her to discover a rusty old box in which a long-ago boy hoarded his treasures. And in tracking down the man who was that boy and returning his box, Amelie finds her life's work: She will make people happy.

But not in any old way. So, she will amuse herself (and us) by devising the most extraordinary stratagems for bringing about their happiness.

I first began hearing about *Amelie* last May at the Cannes Film Festival, where there was a *scandale* when *Amelie* was not chosen for the official selection. "Not serious," sniffed the very serious authorities who decide these matters. The movie played in the commercial theaters of the back streets, where audiences vibrated with pleasure. It went on to win the audience awards at the Edinburgh, Toronto, and Chicago festivals, and I note on the Internet Movie Database that it is currently voted the twelfth best film of all time.

I am not sure *Amelie* is better than *Fargo* (No. 64) or *The General* (No. 85), but I know what the vote reflects: immediate satisfaction with a film that is all goodness and cheer—sassy, bright, and whimsical, filmed with dazzling virtuosity, and set in Paris, the city we love when it sizzles and when it drizzles. Of course this is not a realistic modern Paris, and some critics have sniffed about that, too: It is clean, orderly, safe, colorful, has no social problems, and is peopled entirely by citizens who look like extras from *An American in Paris.* This is the same Paris that produced Gigi and Inspector Clouseau. It never existed, but that's okay.

After discovering the box and bringing happiness to its owner, Amelie improvises other acts of kindness: painting word-pictures of a busy street for a blind man, for example, and pretending to find long-lost love letters to her concierge from the woman's dead husband, who probably never mailed her so much as a lottery ticket. Then she meets Nino (the director Mathieu Kassovitz), who works indifferently in a porn shop and cares only for his hobby, which is to collect the photos people don't want from those automated photo booths and turn them into collages of failed facial expressions.

Amelie likes Nino so much that one day when she sees him in her café, she dissolves. Literally. Into a puddle of water. She wants Nino, but some pixie quirk prevents her from going about anything in a straightforward manner, and success holds no bliss for her unless it comes about through serendipity. There must be times when Nino wonders if he is being blessed or stalked.

Jean-Pierre Jeunet has specialized in films of astonishing visual invention but, alas, impenetrable narratives *(Delicatessen, The City of Lost Children)*. He worked for Hollywood as the director of *Alien Resurrection* (1997), placing it, I wrote, "in what looks like a large, empty hangar filled with prefabricated steel warehouse parts." With *Amelie* he has shaken loose from his obsession with rust and clutter, and made a film so filled with light and air it's like he took the cure.

The film is filled with great individual shots and ideas. One of the best comes when Amelie stands high on the terrace of Montmartre and wonders how many people in Paris are having orgasms at that exact instant, and we see them, fifteen in all, in a quick montage of hilarious happiness. It is this innocent sequence, plus an equally harmless childbirth scene, that has caused the MPAA to give the movie an undeserved R rating (in Norway it was approved for everyone over eleven).

It is so hard to make a nimble, charming comedy. So hard to get the tone right, and find actors who embody charm instead of impersonating it. It takes so much confidence to dance on the tightrope of whimsy. *Amelie* takes those chances, and gets away with them.

American Movie ★ ★ ★ ★
R, 104 m., 2000

Mark Borchardt (Filmmaker), Mike Schank (Friend/Musician), Uncle Bill (Mark's Uncle), Monica Borchardt (Mark's Mom), Cliff Borchardt (Mark's Dad), Chris Borchardt (Mark's Brother), Alex Borchardt (Mark's Brother), Ken Keen (Friend), Joan Petrie (Mark's Girlfriend). A documentary directed by Chris Smith and produced by Sarah Price.

If you've ever wanted to make a movie, see *American Movie,* which is about someone who wants to make a movie more than you do. Mark Borchardt may want to make a movie more than anyone else in the world. He is a thirty-year-old odd-job man from Menomonee Falls, Wisconsin, who has been making movies since he was a teenager, and dreams of an epic about his life, which will be titled *Northwestern,* and be about "rust and decay."

Mark Borchardt is a real person. I have met him. I admire his spirit, and I even admire certain shots in the only Borchardt film I have seen, *Coven*. I saw it at the 1999 Sundance Film Festival—not because it was invited there, but because after the midnight premiere of *American Movie* there wasn't a person in the theater who didn't want to stay and see Mark's thirty-five-minute horror film, which we see him making during the course of the documentary.

American Movie is a very funny, sometimes very sad, documentary directed by Chris Smith and produced by Sarah Price, about Mark's life, his friends, his family, his films, and his dreams. From one point of view, Mark is a loser, a man who has spent his adult life making unreleased and sometimes unfinished movies with titles like *The More the Scarier III*. He plunders the bank account of his elderly Uncle Bill for funds to continue, he uses his friends and hapless local amateur actors as his cast, he enlists his mother as his cinematographer, and his composer and best friend is a guy named Mike Schank who after one drug trip too many seems like the twin of Kevin Smith's Silent Bob.

Borchardt's life is a daily cliff-hanger involving poverty, desperation, discouragement, and die-hard ambition. He's behind on his child support payments, he drinks too much, he can't even convince his ancient Uncle Bill that he has a future as a moviemaker. Bill lives in a trailer surrounded by piles of magazines that he possibly subscribed to under the impression he would win the Publishers' Clearing House sweepstakes. He brightens slightly when Mark shows him the portrait of an actress. "She wants to be in your movie, Bill!" Bill studies the photo: "Oh, my gorsh!" But when Mark tells him about great cinema, what he hears is "cinnamon." And when Bill fumbles countless takes while trying to perform the ominous last line of *Coven* and Mark encourages him to say it like he believes it, Bill answers frankly, "I *don't* believe it."

Smith's camera follows Borchardt as he discusses his theories of cinema (his favorite films: *Night of the Living Dead* and *The Seventh Seal*). We watch as Mark and Bill go to the bank so Bill can grudgingly sign over some of his savings. He is at cast meetings, where one local actor (Robert Jorge) explains in a peeved British accent that *Coven* is correctly pronounced

"CO-ven." Not according to Mark, who says *his* film is pronounced "COVE-n." "I don't want it to rhyme with 'oven'!"

Some of the scenes could work in a screwball comedy. One involves an actor being thrown headfirst through a kitchen cabinet. To capture the moment, Mark recruits his long-suffering Swedish-American mother, Monica, to operate the camera, even though she complains she has shopping to do. He gets on the floor behind his actor, who finds out belatedly that Mark's special-effects strategy is simply to ram the actor's head through the door. The first time, the actor's head bounces off. Mark prepares for take two. One reason to see *Coven* is to appreciate that shot knowing what we know now. For another shot, Mark lies flat on the frozen ground to get low-angle shots of his friends, dressed in black cloaks. "Look menacing!" he shouts. That's hard for them to do, since their faces are invisible.

If Mark's mother is supportive, his father stays out of sight, sticking his head around a doorway occasionally to warn against bad language. Mark has two brothers, who are fed up with him; one says he would be "well suited to factory work," and the other observes, "His main asset is his mouth."

And yet Mark Borchardt is the embodiment of a lonely, rejected, dedicated artist. No poet in a Paris garret has ever been more determined to succeed. To find privacy while writing his screenplays, he drives his old beater to the parking lot of the local commuter airport, and composes on a yellow legal pad. To support himself, he delivers the *Wall Street Journal* before dawn and vacuums the carpets in a mausoleum. He has inspired the loyalty of his friends and crew members, and his girlfriend observes that if he accomplishes 25 percent of what he hopes to do, "that'll be more than most people do."

Every year at Sundance young filmmakers emerge from the woodwork, bearing the masterpieces they have somehow made for peanuts, enlisting volunteer cast and crew. Last year's discovery was not *Coven* but *The Blair Witch Project*. It cost $25,000 and so far has grossed $150 million. One day Mark Borchardt hopes for that kind of success. If it never comes, it won't be for lack of trying.

American Outlaws ★
PG-13, 94 m., 2001

Colin Farrell (Jesse James), Scott Caan (Cole Younger), Ali Larter (Zee Mimms), Gabriel Macht (Frank James), Gregory Smith (Jim Younger), Harris Yulin (Thaddeus Rains), Will McCormack (Bob Younger), Kathy Bates (Ma James), Timothy Dalton (Allan Pinkerton). Directed by Les Mayfield and produced by James G. Robinson and Bill Gerber. Screenplay by Roderick Taylor and John Rogers.

For years there have been reports of the death of the Western. Now comes *American Outlaws*, proof that even the B Western is dead. It only wants to be a bad movie, and fails. Imagine the cast of *American Pie* given a camera, lots of money, costumes and horses, and told to act serious and pretend to be cowboys, and this is what you might get.

The movie tells the story of the gang formed by Jesse James and Cole Younger after the Civil War—a gang which, in this movie, curiously embodies the politics of the antiglobalization demonstrators in Seattle, Sweden, and Genoa. A railroad is a-comin' through, and they don't want it. When the railroad hires Pinkertons to blow up farms, and Jesse and Frank's mother is blowed up real good, the boys vow revenge. They will steal the railroad's payroll from banks, and blow up tracks.

It is curious that they are against the railroad. In much better movies like *The Claim*, the coming of the railroad is seen by everybody as an economic windfall, and it creates fortunes by where it decides to lay its tracks. For farmers, it was a lifeblood—a fast and cheap way to get livestock and crops to market. But the James farm is one of those movie farms where nothing much is done. There are no visible herds or crops, just some chickens scratching in the dirt, and Ma James (Kathy Bates) apparently works it by herself while the boys are off to war. Her hardest labor during the whole movie is her death scene.

Jesse James is played by Colin Farrell, who turned on instant star quality in the Vietnam War picture *Tigerland* (2001) and turns it off here. That this movie got a theatrical push and *Tigerland* didn't is proof that American distribution resembles a crap shoot. Scott Caan plays

Jesse's partner, Cole Younger, Gabriel Macht is Frank James, and Jim and Bob Younger are played by Gregory Smith and Will McCormack. Farrell here seems less like the leader of a gang than the lead singer in a boy band, and indeed he and the boys spend time arguing about their billing. Should it be the James Gang? The James-Younger Gang? The Younger-James Gang? (Naw, that sounds like there's an Older James Gang.) There was a great American film about the James-Younger Gang, Philip Kaufman's *The Great Northfield, Minnesota, Raid* (1972), and this movie crouches in its shadow like the Nickelodeon version.

According to *American Outlaws*, Jesse James was motivated not by money but by righteous anger (and publicity—all the boys liked being famous). After getting his revenge and knocking over countless banks, what he basically wants to do is retire from the gang and get himself a farm and settle down with pretty Zee Mimms (Ali Larter). His delusion that the most famous bank robber in America—the perpetrator, indeed, of "the first daylight bank robbery in American history"—could peacefully return to the farm is an indication of his grasp of reality, which is limited.

While we are musing about how many nighttime robberies there had been in American history, we meet the villains. The railroad is owned by Thaddeus Raines (Harris Yulin), who lectures about "the righteousness of progress," and the hired goons are led by Allan Pinkerton (Timothy Dalton), who spends most of the movie looking as if he knows a great deal more than he is saying, some of it about Jesse James, the rest about this screenplay.

There is some truth to the story; the James home really was bombed by the Pinkertons, although Ma didn't die, she only lost an arm. But there's little truth in the movie, which makes the James-Younger Gang seem less like desperadoes than ornery cutups. The shootouts follow the timeless movie rule that the villains can't aim and the heroes can't miss. Dozens of extras are killed, countless stuntmen topple forward off buildings, but the stars are treated with the greatest economy, their deaths doled out parsimoniously according to the needs of the formula screenplay.

Should cruel mischance lead you to see this movie, do me a favor and rent Kaufman's *The*

Great Northfield, Minnesota, Raid and then meditate on the fact that giants once walked the land in Hollywood. The style, class, and intelligence of a Western like that (in an era which also gave us *The Wild Bunch*) is like a rebuke to *American Outlaws*. What happened to the rough-hewn American intelligence that gave us the Westerns of Ford, Hawks, and Peckinpah? When did cowboys become teen pop idols?

American Pie 2 ★ ★ ★
R, 100 m., 2001

Jason Biggs (Jim), Shannon Elizabeth (Nadia), Alyson Hannigan (Michelle), Chris Klein (Oz), Natasha Lyonne (Jessica), Thomas Ian Nicholas (Kevin), Tara Reid (Vicky), Seann William Scott (Stifler), Mena Suvari (Heather), Eugene Levy (Jim's Dad). Directed by J. B. Rogers and produced by Warren Zide, Craig Perry, and Chris Moore. Screenplay by Adam Herz, based on a story by David H. Steinberg and Herz.

This may seem crushingly obvious, but here goes: The problem with a sequel like *American Pie 2* is that it's about the same characters and the elements of surprise and discovery are gone. In the first movie, Stifler's mom appeared unexpectedly like a gift from above. In this movie, she has become a standing joke (except to Stifler). In the first movie, Jim didn't know that he and Nadia were making love in streaming video on the Internet. In this one, there's a sequence where strangers pick up a sex scene on their CB radios, and we're thinking: this year's version of Internet broadcast.

That said, I had a good time at *American Pie 2*, maybe because the characters are broad comic types, well played; because the movie feels some sympathy for their dilemmas; and because it's obsessed with sex. Also because it has Jim's dad (Eugene Levy), the world's most understanding and supportive parent, meet his son in the emergency room during the most embarrassing and humiliating evening of the kid's life (and remember, this is the kid who made love on the Internet), and tell him, "I'm proud of you, son."

I will not tell you why Jim is in the emergency room. There's a lot I can't tell you about the movie because it's filled with turnabouts, sight gags, and horrifying sexual adventures. Also a lot of sex lore, as that three is the magic number in sexual histories: When a woman tells you how many men she has slept with, you should multiply by three, and when a man tells you, you should divide by three.

The cast of *American Pie* is back for this sequel, no doubt because their original contracts provided for it, and just as well: The first film cost $11 million and grossed more than $150 million worldwide. Now they've graduated from high school, just finished their first year of college, and decided to spend the summer by renting a place on the lake at Grand Haven, Michigan. And the party's on.

Jim (Jason Biggs) is first among equals in the cast. His experience on the Internet, his first sexual encounter, left him badly shaken, and a prom night experience was a fiasco. His current girlfriend invites him to have "friendly good-bye sex" before the school term ends, but he observes gloomily that they've never had "friendly hello sex." When he learns that Nadia (Shannon Elizabeth), the Internet girl, is heading back for the summer, in desperation he enlists Michelle (Alyson Hannigan) to give him lessons. She's the strange but lovable girl he took to the prom, and is a good sport, even strapping her brassiere around a pillow so he can practice unfastening it with one hand.

The movie's longest comic sequence is not exactly its best. It involves three of the guys being trapped inside the house they're painting by its two residents, who they think are lesbians. The girls agree to put on a show, if the guys will do everything to each other that they want to see the girls doing to each other. Some of this works, some loses the right note, and it goes on too long. A subtler and funnier way could have been found to indicate the guys' homophobic feelings. A scene in which Jim is mistaken for a retarded trombone player doesn't play well, either.

One nice thing about the movie is that the girls are portrayed as equal opportunity predators, and not simply as objectified sex objects. Heather (Mena Suvari), for example, suggests phone sex to her boyfriend, and we consider for the first time the detumescent effect of call-waiting.

I laughed at *American Pie 2*, yes, but this is either going to be the last *Pie* movie or they're going to have to get a new angle. I'd hate to see the freshness of the series grind down into the repetition of the same formula to wring a few more dollars out of the brand name. One hopeful sign that the filmmakers can learn and grow is that the sequel does not contain a single pie, if you know what I mean.

Note: I am informed it does indeed contain one pie, although not to the same purpose.

American Psycho ★ ★ ★
R, 100 m., 2000

Christian Bale (Patrick Bateman), Willem Dafoe (Donald Kimball), Jared Leto (Paul Allen), Reese Witherspoon (Evelyn Williams), Samantha Mathis (Courtney Rawlinson), Chloe Sevigny (Jean), Justin Theroux (Timothy Price), Matt Ross (Luis Carruthers). Directed by Mary Harron and produced by Edward R. Pressman, Chris Hanley, and Christian Halsey Solomon. Screenplay by Guinevere Turner and Harron, based on the novel by Bret Easton Ellis.

It's just as well a woman directed *American Psycho*. She's transformed a novel about bloodlust into a movie about men's vanity. A male director might have thought Patrick Bateman, the hero of *American Psycho*, was a serial killer because of psychological twists, but Mary Harron sees him as a guy who's prey to the usual male drives and compulsions. He just acts out a little more.

Most men are not chain-saw killers; they only act that way while doing business. Look at the traders clawing each other on the floor of the stock exchange. Listen to used-car dealers trying to dump excess stock on one another. Consider the joy with which one megacorp raids another, and dumps its leaders. Study such films as *In the Company of Men, Glengarry Glen Ross, Boiler Room,* or *The Big Kahuna*. It's a dog-eat-dog world, and to survive you'd better be White Fang.

As a novel, Bret Easton Ellis's 1991 best-seller was passed from one publisher to another like a hot potato. As a film project, it has gone through screenplays, directors, and stars for years. It was snatched up for Oliver Stone, who planned to star Leonardo Di Caprio, before ending up back in Harron's arms with Christian Bale in the lead. (To imagine this material

19

in Stone's hands, recall the scene in Ken Russell's *The Music Lovers* where Tchaikovsky's head explodes during the 1812 Overture, then spin it out to feature length.)

Harron is less impressed by the vile Patrick Bateman than a man might have been, perhaps because as a woman who directs movies she deals every day with guys who resemble Bateman in all but his body count. She senses the linkage between the time Bateman spends in the morning lovingly applying male facial products, and the way he blasts away people who annoy him, anger him, or simply have the misfortune to be within his field of view. He is a narcissist driven by ego and fueled by greed. Most of his victims are women, but in a pinch a man will do.

The film regards the male executive lifestyle with the devotion of a fetishist. There is a scene where a group of businessmen compare their business cards, discussing the wording, paper thickness, finish, embossing, engraving, and typefaces, and they might as well be discussing their phalli. Their sexual insecurity is manifested as card envy. They carry on grim rivalries expressed in clothes, offices, salaries, and being able to get good tables in important restaurants. It is their uneasy secret that they make enough money to afford to look important, but are not very important. One of the film's running jokes is that Patrick Bateman looks so much like one of his colleagues (Jared Leto) that they are mistaken for each other. (Their faces aren't really identical, but they occupy empty space in much the same way.)

The film and the book are notorious because Bateman murders a lot of people in nasty ways. I have overheard debates about whether some of the murders are fantasies ("Can a man really aim a chain saw that well?"). All of the murders are equally real or unreal, and that isn't the point: The function of the murders is to make visible the frenzy of the territorial male when his will is frustrated. The movie gives shape and form to road rage, golf course rage, family abuse, and some of the scarier behavior patterns of sports fans.

You see why Harron has called the film "feminist." So it is—and a libel against the many sane, calm, and civilized men it does not describe. But it's true to a type, all right. It sees Bateman in a clear, sharp, satiric light, and it

despises him. Christian Bale is heroic in the way he allows the character to leap joyfully into despicableness; there is no instinct for self-preservation here, and that is one mark of a good actor. When Bateman kills, it is *not* with the zeal of a villain from a slasher movie. It is with the thoroughness of a hobbyist. Lives could have been saved if instead of living in a high-rise, Bateman had been supplied with a basement, a workbench, and a lot of nails to pound.

An American Rhapsody ★ ★ ★
PG-13, 102 m., 2001

Nastassja Kinski (Margit), Scarlett Johansson (Suzanne [at fifteen]), Tony Goldwyn (Peter), Agi Banfalvy (Helen), Zoltan Seress (George), Zsuzsa Czinkoczi (Teri), Balazs Galko (Jeno). Directed by Eva Gardos and produced by Colleen Camp and Bonnie Timmermann. Screenplay by Gardo.

An American Rhapsody is told from the point of view of a fifteen-year-old American girl, but in a way it's more her mother's story. The girl is named Suzanne, and until the age of six she was raised in her native Hungary by two foster parents she loved dearly. Then, the way she understands it at the time, she's stolen away from them and put on an airplane to join her "real" family in America.

As she grows older, she understands more: Her parents, Margit and Peter, escaped Hungary with her older sister at the height of the Stalin horror. Babies were not allowed to be brought along, so they left the infant Suzanne with her grandmother—who, after being arrested, passed her on to the older childless couple. Stalin dies, the grandmother is released from jail, she reclaims Suzanne for a "day's visit," and puts her on the plane to America.

These are two versions of the same events, and they have much different emotional loads. Little Suzanne is happy to have her own room in a Los Angeles bedroom suburb, but she misses the only people she has ever known as her parents. The wound remains. As she grows older, she coexists with her father (Tony Goldwyn), but has an uneasy truce with her mother (Nastassja Kinski). We meet her at fifteen, in the full flood of adolescent rebellion

Suzanne (Scarlett Johansson) is a budding Valley Girl, with a best friend, a boyfriend, and a habit of smoking cigarettes when she's out of sight of her parents. Her mother is protective of her to a degree approaching panic. When she sees the girl kissing her boyfriend, she yanks her away, puts bars on her bedroom window, and a dead bolt on the door. The way Suzanne responds to imprisonment is direct and extreme, and has the advantage of getting everyone's attention.

Suzanne is allowed to return to Hungary to meet again with her grandmother, Helen (Agi Banfalvy), and her foster parents, Teri (Zsuzsa Czinkoczi) and Jeno (Balazs Galko). She learns things about her mother's childhood that help her understand, if not fully accept, her mother's extreme protectiveness.

Along the way what we get is a view of the way unhealthy states create unhealthy citizens, and the way evil at the top can poison even the trust between a mother and a daughter. *An American Rhapsody* was written and directed by Eva Gardos, who is the model for Suzanne. It is her story. Her mother's story is told obliquely, but it is her mother who really suffered, who is the victim more than the daughter.

Nastassja Kinski, in one of her most affecting performances, does much to convey the turmoil going on in her soul, but has the handicap of being offscreen much of the time, or seen through her daughter's eyes. She wears fresh American dresses and keeps her home spotless and enjoys prosperity, but it must at times all seem like a mirage to her—to this survivor of World War II, this victim of sudden violence, this refugee from Stalinism and worse. There is good reason to be protective of a child, but at some point childhood is over and life will collect its dues one way or another, and parents who deny that are practicing a form of insanity.

Scarlett Johansson, so good in *Ghost World*, plays Suzanne in a sort of a glower; immersed in the culture celebrated by the Beach Boys, she wants to be a California Girl and have fun, fun, fun, and her mother treats her like a bomb about to explode. I appreciated the way Johansson created this character not as a colorful victim, but as an ordinary teenage girl who retreats into secrecy and passive hostility. She wisely sees that Suzanne is not meant to be a rebel with or without a cause, but more like the bystander at a sad historical accident.

We can understand why Eva Gardos wants to tell her own story (we all do), but at the end of the day she had it easy compared to her mother. I suppose the film, in a way, is about how she comes to realize that. The American children of immigrants from anywhere will probably find moments they recognize in this movie.

America's Sweethearts ★ ★
PG-13, 100 m., 2001

Julia Roberts (Kiki Harrison), Billy Crystal (Lee Phillips), Catherine Zeta-Jones (Gwen Harrison), John Cusack (Eddie Thomas), Hank Azaria (Hector), Stanley Tucci (Dave Kingman), Christopher Walken (Hal Weidmann), Seth Green (Danny Wax), Alan Arkin (Wellness Guide). Directed by Joe Roth and produced by Susan Arnold, Billy Crystal, and Donna Roth. Screenplay by Crystal and Peter Tolan.

America's Sweethearts recycles *Singin' in the Rain* but lacks the sassy genius of that 1952 musical, which is still the best comedy ever made about Hollywood. Both movies open with profiles of famous couples whose onscreen chemistry masks an offscreen split. Both have canny studio heads and eager-beaver assistants. Both have plain little wallflowers who suddenly blossom. Both climax with sneak previews that are fraught with disaster. One difference is that a Hedda Hopper–style gossip columnist, in the earlier picture, is replaced by a whole junket-load of freeloading journalists in this one.

Here's a quick casting key. The movie stars Julia Roberts in the Debbie Reynolds role, Catherine Zeta-Jones as Jean Hagen, John Cusack as Gene Kelly, Billy Crystal as Donald O'Connor, and Stanley Tucci as Millard Mitchell (the studio head). Added to the mix are two grotesque caricatures—one funny (Christopher Walken's auteur director), one overdone (Hank Azaria's Spanish lover). Both movies are about a troubled megamillions production that could save, or sink, the studio.

In principle, there's nothing wrong with returning to a classic for inspiration. But *Singin'*

21

in the Rain unreeled with effortless grace, and America's Sweethearts lacks inner confidence that it knows what it is and where it's going. The opportunities are here for a classic comedy, but the fangs never sink in and the focus isn't sharp enough.

I was especially disappointed by the junket scene; in this season of fake critics and phony quotes, the time was ripe for savage satire, but this movie goes way too easy on the junket blurbsters. They've been invited to a remote desert location for the premiere of a movie that may not even exist; the studio P.R. ace (Crystal) claims he can distract them from the missing movie by convincing them the stars are in love again. While it's true that most junketeers care more about celeb gossip than the movies themselves, the movie goes too easy on them. One can imagine a scene, modeled on real life, where Crystal writes quotes praising the unseen movie and asks the freebie hounds to sign up for them, and they eagerly line up to claim their blurbs so they can get to the open bar and the complimentary buffet.

Julia Roberts and Catherine Zeta-Jones play sisters, Kiki and Gwen. Gwen is the sleek and famous beauty. Kiki has always been sixty pounds overweight, her sister's lapdog and gofer. John Cusack is Eddie, Gwen's costar, as they say, on-screen and off. But Gwen has been lured away by the oily charms of Hector (Azaria), a Latin lover with a lisp and too much jewelry, and Eddie has gone ballistic, attacking them with his motorcycle before being bundled off to a rehab center run by "wellness guide" Alan Arkin.

Meanwhile, Hal Weidmann (Christopher Walken) is the mad-dog auteur who has directed Eddie and Gwen in their latest epic (for solitude while editing his film, he has purchased the Unibomber's cabin and erected it in his backyard). The studio head gnashes his teeth with frustration: Hal has spent $86 million and shown him only twenty seconds of titles, along with a note: "We could also do these in blue."

These early scenes are promising. But then . . . well, I think the problem is that years of read-my-lips filmmaking have drained Hollywood of the quick intelligence of the screwball comedy. It's obvious that Kiki the wallflower has slimmed down into a beauty,

that Gwen is a tiresome egomaniac, that Hector's days are numbered, that Eddie must realize that Kiki, not Gwen, is the sister he has always loved. But in the romantic scenes, there's too much earnestness and not enough rapid-fire cynicism. The movie forgets it's a comedy at times, and goes for conviction and insight when it should be running in the opposite direction.

The movie moves from a bright beginning and a passable middle to a disastrous closing act, when Hal Weidmann helicopters in with the long-awaited print of his masterpiece. The scenes showing the premiere of this movie don't work for a number of reasons, including their lack of a proper comeuppance for Gwen. Remember the unmasking and humiliation of the Jean Hagen character in Singin' in the Rain and compare it with the unfocused, dull-edged result of this screening.

Part of the problem is with the movie-within-a-movie itself—the masterpiece Hal unveils. We get the idea behind what he's trying to do, but America's Sweethearts never lets him do it. There are no scenes in Hal's movie that pay off on their own and really skewer the stars sitting in the audience. We want revenge and payoff time, and we get a muddled sequence that eventually degenerates into a routine series of shots tying up the loose ends.

You can't blame the actors (although you might blame the casting for Azaria, who doesn't seem plausible as a movie star or a lover). Julia Roberts is sweet and lovable, Catherine Zeta-Jones is chilly and manipulative, John Cusack is desperately heartsick, and Billy Crystal is, as we'd expect, convincing as the wise-guy publicist. But the screenplay, by Crystal and Peter Tolan, is all over the map, and director Joe Roth should have ordered rewrites and a new ending. Isolated scenes work but don't add up. Godard said the way to criticize a movie is to make another movie. Even while you're watching America's Sweethearts, it gets shouldered aside by Singin' in the Rain.

Amores Perros ★ ★ ★ ½
R, 153 m., 2001

Emilio Echevarria (El Chivo), Gael Garcia Bernal (Octavio), Goya Toledo (Valeria), Alvaro Guerrero (Daniel), Vanessa Bauche (Susana),

Jorge Salinas (Luis), Laura Almela (Julieta), Marco Perez (Ramiro). Directed and produced by Alejandro Gonzalez Inarritu. Screenplay by Guillermo Arriaga.

Amores Perros arrives from Mexico trailing clouds of glory—it was one of this year's Oscar nominees—and generating excitement on the Internet, where the fanboys don't usually flip for foreign films. It tells three interlinked stories that span the social classes in Mexico City, from rich TV people to the working class to the homeless, and it circles through those stories with a nod to Quentin Tarantino, whose *Pulp Fiction* had a magnetic influence on young filmmakers. Many are influenced but few are chosen: Alejandro Gonzalez Inarritu, making his feature debut, borrows what he can use but is an original, dynamic director.

His title translates as *Love's a Bitch,* and all three of his stories involve dogs who become as important as the human characters. The film opens with a disclaimer promising that no animals were harmed in the making of the film. That notice usually appears at the ends of films, but putting it first in *Amores Perros* is wise, since the first sequence involves dog fights and all three will be painful for softhearted animal lovers to sit through. Be warned.

"Octavio and Susana," the first segment, begins with cars hurtling through city streets in a chase and gunfight. The images are so quick and confused, at first we don't realize the bleeding body in the backseat belongs to a dog. This is Cofi, the beloved fighting animal of Octavio (Gael Garcia Bernal), a poor young man who is helplessly in love with Susana (Vanessa Bauche), the teenage bride of his ominous brother, Ramiro (Marco Perez). Flashbacks show how Cofi was shot after killing a champion dog; now the chase ends in a spectacular crash in an intersection—a crash that will involve all three of the movie's stories.

In the second segment, "Daniel and Valeria," we meet a television producer (Alvaro Guerrero) who has abandoned his family to live with a beautiful young model and actress (Goya Toledo). He's rented a big new apartment for her; Valeria's image smiles in through a window from a billboard. But then their happiness is marred when Valeria's little dog chases a ball into a hole in the floor, disappears under the floorboards, and won't return. Is it lost, trapped, or frightened? "There are thousands of rats down there," they warn each other.

Then Valeria is involved in the same crash; we see it this time from a different angle, and indeed it comes as a shock every time it occurs. Her leg is severely injured, and one complication leads to another—while the dog still snuffles under the floor, sometimes whining piteously, sometimes ominously silent. This sequence surely owes something to the great Spanish director Luis Buñuel, who made some of his best films in Mexico, and whose *Tristana* starred Catherine Deneuve as a beauty who loses her leg. The segment is sort of dark slapstick—morbid and ironic, as the romance is tested by the beauty's mutilation and by the frustration (known to every pet owner) of a dog that *will not* come when it is called.

From time to time during the first two segments, we've seen a street person, bearded and weathered, accompanied by his own pack of dogs. The third segment, "El Chivo and Maru," stars the famous Mexican actor Emilio Echevarria, who, we learn, is a revolutionary turned squatter, and supports himself by killing for hire. He is approached by a man who wants to get rid of his partner, and is inspired to add his own brutal twist to this murder scheme. The three stories have many links, the most interesting perhaps that El Chivo has rescued the wounded dog Cofi and now cares for it.

Amores Perros at 153 minutes is heavy on story—too heavy, some will say—and rich with character and atmosphere. It is the work of a born filmmaker, and you can sense Inarritu's passion as he plunges into melodrama, coincidence, sensation, and violence. His characters are not the bland, amoral totems of so much modern Hollywood violence, but people with feelings and motives. They want love, money, and revenge. They not only love their dogs but also desperately depend on them. And it is clear that the lower classes are better at survival than the wealthy, whose confidence comes from their possessions, not their mettle.

The movie reminded me not only of Buñuel but also of two other filmmakers identified with Mexico: Arturo Ripstein and Alejandro Jodorowsky. Their works are also comfortable with the scruffy underbelly of society, and involve the dangers when jealousy is not given room to breathe. Consider Jodorowsky's great *Santa Sangre*, in which a cult of women cut off their own arms to honor a martyr. *Amores Perros* will be too much for some filmgoers, just as *Pulp Fiction* was and *Santa Sangre* certainly was, but it contains the spark of inspiration. ☞

Angela's Ashes ★ ★ ½
R, 145 m., 2000

Emily Watson (Angela), Robert Carlyle (Malachy [Dad]), Michael Legge (Older Frank), Ciaran Owens (Middle Frank), Joe Breen (Young Frank), Ronnie Masterson (Grandma Sheehan), Pauline McLynn (Aunt Aggie), Liam Carney (Uncle Pa Keating), Eanna MacLiam (Uncle Pat), Andrew Bennett (Narrator). Directed by Alan Parker and produced by Parker, Scott Rudin, and David Brown. Screenplay by Parker and Laura Jones, based on the book by Frank McCourt.

Frank McCourt's book *Angela's Ashes* is, like so much of Irish verbal history, suffering recollected in hilarity. I call it verbal history because I know from a friend of his that the stories so unforgettably told in his autobiography were honed over years and decades, at bars and around dinner tables and in the ears of his friends. I could have guessed that anyway, from the easy familiarity you hear in his voice on the audiobook he recorded, the quickening rhythm of humor welling up from the description of grim memories. Some say audiobooks are not "real" books, but in the case of *Angela's Ashes* the sound of the author's voice transforms the material with fondness and nostalgia. McCourt may have had a miserable childhood, but he would not trade it in for another—or at least would not have missed the parts he retells in his memories.

That whole sense of humor is mostly missing from Alan Parker's film version of *Angela's Ashes*, which reminded me of Mark Twain's description of a woman trying to swear: "She knows the words, but not the music." The film is so faithful to the content of the book that it reproduces scenes that have already formed in my imagination. The flooded downstairs in the Limerick home, the wretched family waiting for a father who will never come home with money for eggs and bacon, the joy of flying down the street on a post office bicycle—all of these are just as I pictured them. What is missing is the tone. The movie is narrated by Andrew Bennett, who is no doubt a good actor and blameless here, but what can he do but reproduce the words from the page without McCourt's seasoning of nostalgia? McCourt's voice tells us things he has seen. Bennett's voice tells of things he has heard about.

The result is a movie of great craft and wonderful images, lacking a heart. There must have been thousands of childhoods more or less like Frank McCourt's, and thousands of families with too many children, many of them dying young, while the father drank up dinner down at the pub and the mother threw herself on the mercy of the sniffy local charities. What made McCourt's autobiography special was expressed somehow beneath the very words as he used them: These experiences, wretched as they were, were not wasted on a mere victim, but somehow shaped him into the man capable of writing a fine book about them. There is in *Angela's Ashes* a certain lack of complaint, a sense in which even misery is treasured, as a soldier will describe his worst day of battle with the unspoken subtext: "But I survived, and I love to tell the story, because it is the most interesting thing that has ever happened to me."

The movie stars Emily Watson and Robert Carlyle as Angela and Malachy McCourt, Frank's parents. It is impossible to conceive of better casting of Angela, and although other actors (Tim Roth, Gary Oldman) might have done about as good a job as Carlyle, how much can be done with that poor man who has been made shifty-eyed, lying, and guilty by the drink? We do not even blame him as he leaves his family to starve while he pours their money into the pockets of the manufacturers of Guinness Stout: Clearly, he would not drink if it were at all within his control. But he is powerless over alcoholism, and it has rendered him not a man but simply the focus of the family's bad luck.

What is touching is the way Frank, and soon his younger brother Malachy, treasure those few moments when Dad was too abashed or impoverished to drink, and lavished some attention on them. Consider my favorite sequence, in which the boys' shoes are letting in the rain, and Dad nails tire rubber to the soles. At school, flopping along on their little Michelin snowshoes, they're laughed at by the other kids, until the Christian brother who teaches the class reprimands them all, and points up dramatically to the crucifix on the schoolroom wall: "You don't see our Blessed Savior sportin' shoes!"

It is the "sportin'" that does it, that makes it work, that reveals McCourt's touch. The possibility that the dying Christ would, could, or even desired to "sport" shoes turns the whole sentence and the whole anecdote around, and it becomes not the story of schoolroom humiliation, but a rebuke to those classmates so foolish as to be sportin' shoes themselves. In the mechanics of that episode is the secret of the whole book, and although it comes across well in the film, so many of the similar twists, ironies, and verbal revenges are missed. The film lacks the dark humor with which the Irish like to combine victory with misfortune (as in the story of the man who cleverly fed his horse less and less every day, until "just when he finally had the horse trained to eat nothing— the horse died!").

Frank is played at various ages by Joe Breen (young), Ciaran Owens (middle), and Michael Legge (older). He comes across as determined to make his own way and get out of Limerick and back to New York where he was born, and there are scenes of him picking up spilled coal from the road as a little boy, impressing the brothers with his essay "Jesus and the Weather," getting his first job, falling in love, and coming home drunk the first time ("Jesus!" cries his mother. "It's your father you've become!").

The grim poverty of the lane in Limerick where the family lived for much of the time is convincingly re-created by Parker and production designer Geoffrey Kirkland, although Parker is much too fond of a shot in which Frank and Malachy splash deliberately through every puddle they can find, indoors and out, season after season and year after year. Surely they would eventually learn to keep their feet dry? And although we know from the book that the flooded downstairs was "Ireland" and the dry upstairs was "Italy," was the family so

entirely without resources that a plank could not be found to make a bridge from the door to the stairs?

What is wonderful about *Angela's Ashes* is Emily Watson's performance, and the other roles are convincingly cast. She has the kind of bitterness mixed with resignation that was forced on a woman in a country where marriage to a drunk was a life sentence, and it was a greater sin to desert him than to let him starve her children. At one point, Dad leaves to seek work in England, complaining that she has "refused her wifely duties." His husbandly duties, of course, consisted of fathering more children to starve and die, and buying rounds like a big shot down at the pub.

Angel Eyes ★ ★ ★
R, 104 m., 2001

Jennifer Lopez (Sharon), Jim Caviezel (Catch), Terrence Howard (Robby), Sonia Braga (Mrs. Pogue), Jeremy Sisto (Larry), Victor Argo (Mr. Pogue), Shirley Knight (Elanora Davis). Directed by Luis Mandoki and produced by Mark Canton and Elie Samaha. Screenplay by Gerald DiPego.

Jennifer Lopez is the real thing, one of those rare actresses who can win our instinctive sympathy. She demonstrates that in *Angel Eyes*, playing a tough cop who does everything she can to wall out the world, and yet always seems worthy of trust and care. The film's story involves the cop's skittish, arm's-length relationship with a man named Catch (Jim Caviezel), whose walls are higher than her own.

Who is this Catch, anyway? He walks the streets in a long overcoat, head down, lonely, depressed, looking like one of the angels in *Wings of Desire*. Once a week he brings groceries to a shut-in named Nora (Shirley Knight). The first time he sees Sharon, the Lopez character, he stops and stares at her through a restaurant window—not with lust or curiosity, but as if he's trying to repair some lost connection.

Lopez constructs Sharon, not out of spare parts from old cop movies, but in specific terms. She is a good cop from a technical point of view—firm, confident, brave. She wants to do well and punish evil, and only gradually do we learn that her orientation toward this career may have been formed early, when she called the cops on her abusive father (Victor Argo) as he beat up her mother (Sonia Braga). Her father has disowned her for that, her brother is still mad about it, and even her mother defends the man. He never did it again, after all, she argues, to which Sharon replies that perhaps he would have if she hadn't acted. Fighting other lawbreakers may be her way of proving she was right in the first place.

The movie, directed by Luis Mandoki, has intriguing opening scenes. Is this a thriller? A supernatural movie? Who do the angel eyes belong to? An angel? Or does Catch only come on like a guardian angel, while reserving secrets of his own? We are still asking these questions during a stretch of the film where Sharon is staring at a gun in her face, and her life is saved by . . . Catch.

They talk. It is like a verbal chess game. Catch doesn't simply answer questions, he parries them; his responses redefine the conversation, as an unexpected move changes the logic on the board. She invites him home. He pokes through drawers. She likes him. She begins to kiss him. He doesn't want to be kissed. They settle into a cat-and-mouse rhythm in which one and then the other flees, and one and then the other pursues. She follows him to his apartment. It is empty except for a futon. "This is it," he says. "I live here. I walk around town. That's it, except for how I feel about you."

But how does he feel about her? *Angel Eyes* is a complex, evasive romance, involving two people who both want to be inaccessible. It's intriguing to see their dance of attraction and retreat. Meanwhile, secrets about both their family situations emerge; credit the screenwriter, Gerald DiPego, for not resolving the standoff with the father with an easy payoff.

There are lots of movies about cops because their lives lend themselves to excitement in a movie plot. They get involved with bad guys. They see action. They spend a lot of time drinking coffee in diners because a booth in a diner provides an ideal rationale for a face-to-face two-shot that doesn't look awkward or violate body language. For these and other reasons *Angel Eyes* is a cop movie, but its real story doesn't involve the police; it involves damaged lives and the possibility that love can heal.

Jim Caviezel, who has been in movies for ten years, emerged in *The Thin Red Line* (1998) and then played Dennis Quaid's son in *Frequency*—the one who contacts his father with a radio signal that travels back in time. Here he has an elusive, dreamy quality, using passivity as a mask for sharp, deep emotions. Since he apparently has no desire to meet anyone, why is he so attracted to Sharon? The answer has been waiting for us since the opening scene.

Lopez has a hard assignment here, remaining plausible in action scenes and touchy, slippery dialogue scenes. She and Caviezel play tricky notes, and so do the other actors, especially Victor Argo as a stubborn, hard man and Sonia Braga as his conflicted wife. The screenplay doesn't let them off the hook. And notice what simplicity and conviction the veteran Shirley Knight brings to her role, never straining for an effect, never punching up false emotions, embodying acceptance. This is a surprisingly effective film.

Note: Because Angel Eyes *steps so surely for so long, I suspect the movie's very last seconds were dictated over the director's dead body. The movie arrives at exactly the right note at the end, and then the sound track bursts prematurely into David Gray singing "Sail Away With Me Honey" and shatters the mood. I know Hollywood believes every audience must be patronized with an upbeat ending, but this movie has earned its final silence, and deserves it. Couldn't the screen have at least decently faded to black before the jarring music crashes in?*

The Anniversary Party ★ ★ ★
R, 115 m., 2001

Alan Cumming (Joe Therrian), Jennifer Jason Leigh (Sally Therrian), Gwyneth Paltrow (Skye Davidson), John Benjamin Hickey (Jerry Adams), Parker Posey (Judy Adams), Kevin Kline (Cal Gold), Jennifer Beals (Gina Taylor), Phoebe Cates (Sophia Gold), Jane Adams (Clair Forsyth), John C. Reilly (Mac Forsyth), Mina Badie (Monica Rose), Denis O'Hare (Ryan Rose), Michael Panes (Levi Panes). Directed by Alan Cumming and Jennifer Jason Leigh and produced by Cumming, Leigh, and Joanne Sellar. Screenplay by Cumming and Leigh.

The Anniversary Party is a long night's journey

into day with a group of Hollywood types—actors, directors, photographers, agents—and a couple of neighbors who are invited over. The occasion is a get-back-together party for Joe and Sally Therrian (Alan Cumming and Jennifer Jason Leigh), he a writer-director, she an actress who hears time's winged chariot drawing near. It's their sixth anniversary, although they've lived apart for most of the past year; the issues between them involve his infidelity, sometime bisexuality and drug use, and his decision not to cast his wife in a role obviously inspired by her. He believes that, in her late thirties, she's too old to play herself. (I am reminded of Margaret Cho's documentary *I'm the One That I Want*, where she describes the CBS sitcom producer who told her she was too fat to play herself, and should be a little less Chinese-y.)

This is not an original idea for a movie. I can think of a dozen movies about all-night parties at which painful truths are revealed. What makes *The Anniversary Party* intriguing is how close it cuts to the bone of reality—how we're teased to draw parallels between some of the characters and the actors who play them. Cumming is not a stranger to sexual ambiguity, Leigh is indeed in her thirties (although, unlike her character, at the top of her form), and look at some of the others.

Kevin Kline plays an actor who is no longer the first choice to play romantic leading men. Phoebe Cates, his real-life wife, plays an actress who has retired from acting to be a mother and wife. Gwyneth Paltrow plays the rising young star who gets multimillion-dollar paychecks, and has been cast in Joe's new movie. Other stars play recognizable types. Jennifer Beals is a savvy photographer who once slept with Joe. John Benjamin Hickey is the couple's business manager, and Parker Posey is his motormouth wife. Michael Panes plays Levi Panes (no coincidence, I assume), Sally's best pal and court jester. John C. Reilly is the director who desperately needs a hit, and is troubled because Sally is sleepwalking through her role in his new movie. Jane Adams is his neurotic, anorexic wife, in the throes of postpartum depression; she looks typecast, until you see her as a robust country schoolteacher in *Songcatcher*, and realize it's just acting. The next-door neighbors, happy to be invited to a party with so many stars, are played by Denis O'Hare and Mina Badie.

In the earlier days of this genre, the characters got drunk in order to blurt out what they were really thinking (see such examples as *Long Day's Journey Into Night* and *The Boys in the Band*). The truth serum this time is the drug ecstasy, brought along by the Paltrow character and inspiring an orgy of truth-telling, sexual cheating, and other reasons they're going to hate themselves in the morning. The movie doesn't use the drug simply as a story element, but knows it is dangerous and weaves it into a subtle thread of material about addiction and recovery; unless you watch carefully, you may miss the alcoholic who chooses this night to have a relapse.

The appeal of the film is largely voyeuristic. We learn nothing we don't already more or less know, but the material is covered with such authenticity and unforced, natural conviction that it plays like a privileged glimpse into the sad lives of the rich and famous. We're like the neighbors who are invited. Jennifer Jason Leigh and Alan Cumming cowrote and codirected, and are confident professionals who don't indulge their material or themselves. This isn't a confessional home movie, but a cool and intelligent look at a lifestyle where smart people are required to lead their lives according to dumb rules.

The movie was shot with a digital camera. Yes, you can tell. (Critics who say it looks as good as film are like friends who claim you don't look a day older.) It doesn't have the richness and saturation of film, but on the other hand, it does capture a spontaneity that might have been lost during long setups for lighting and camera (the shooting schedule was only four weeks). There are perfect uses for digital, and a movie like this is one of them. Leigh and Cumming and their cinematographer, the veteran John Bailey, wisely prefer the discipline of classic cinematography to the dizziness of handheld, and treat their little camera as if it were a big one. (Every digital camera should come with a warning label: "Just because you can move this around a lot doesn't mean you have to.")

I mentioned that some of the actors seem to be playing themselves. It might be more correct to say they are playing characters who we think of as being like themselves. Paltrow, for example, is not a mock-humble diva, but a smart pro who grew up in the industry and probably eavesdropped on parties like this from the top of the stairs. The tone we get from the whole movie reflects that knowingness: Being invited to a party like this (and leading these lives) is not the gold at the end of the rainbow, but what you get instead of the rainbow.

AntiTrust ★ ★
PG-13, 108 m., 2001

Ryan Phillippe (Milo Hoffman), Tim Robbins (Gary Winston), Rachael Leigh Cook (Lisa Calighan), Claire Forlani (Alice Poulson), Yee Jee Tso (Teddy Chin), Tygh Runyan (Larry Banks), Ned Bellamy (Phil Grimes), Douglas McFerran (Bob Shrot), Zahf Hajee (Desi). Directed by Peter Howitt and produced by Keith Addis, David Nicksay, and Nick Wechsler. Screenplay by Howard Franklin.

They might have been able to make a nice little thriller out of *AntiTrust*, if they'd kept one eye on the Goofy Meter. Just when the movie is cooking, the needle tilts over into Too Goofy and breaks the spell. What are we to make of a brainy nerd hero who fears his girlfriend is trying to kill him by adding sesame seeds to the Chinese food, and administers himself a quick allergy test at a romantic dinner by scratching himself with a fork and rubbing on some of the brown sauce? Too goofy.

The movie uses a thinly disguised fictional version of Bill Gates as its hero—so thinly, I'm surprised they didn't protect against libel by having the villain wear a name tag saying, "Hi! I'm not Bill!" This billionaire software mogul, named Gary Winston, is played by Tim Robbins as a man of charm, power, and paranoia. "Anybody working in a garage can put us out of business," he frets, and he's right. Cut to a garage occupied by Milo Hoffman (Ryan Phillippe) and his best buddy, Teddy Chin (Yee Jee Tso), who are on the edge of a revolutionary communications breakthrough.

Winston's company, which seems a *whole* lot like Microsoft, is working toward the same goal. In fact, Winston claims his new Synapse global communications system will, and I quote, "link every communications device on the planet." Too goofy. In order to discourage his competitors, Winston has announced a release date for his new software while it is still being written (details like this are why the company seems a whole lot like Microsoft).

He needs a software breakthrough, and he thinks Milo and Teddy can provide it. He invites them up for a tour of his company's campus in the Pacific Northwest. Teddy declines: He hates the megacorp and believes code should be freely distributed. Milo accepts, and before he goes is visited by an agent from the (pre-Bush) Department of Justice (Richard Roundtree), who is preparing an antitrust case against Winston. "If you see something up there that hits you the wrong way, do the right thing," the agent says, offering Milo, who stands on the brink of untold millions, a salary much higher than you can earn at McDonald's.

Milo takes the junket to the software campus, and is shown around by cool young software dudes and a sexy software babe named Lisa (Rachel Leigh Cook), whose vibes suggest she likes him. Then he gets a tour of Winston's palatial high-tech lakeside home, which even includes computers that sense when you're in a room and play your favorite music while displaying your favorite art on the digital wall screens. "Bill Gates has a system like this," says Milo, just as we were thinking the exact same words. "Bill who?" says Winston. "His is primitive."

Milo decides to go to work for the megacorp, and is flattered by all the personal attention he gets from Winston, a friendly charmer who has a habit of dropping around even in the middle of the night. At one point when Milo is stuck, Winston hands him a disk with some code on it that "might help," just as a TV set in the background is reporting a news story about the death of a gifted software programmer. Hmmm.

Milo's girlfriend from his garage days was the loyal and steadfast Alice Poulson (Claire Forlani), who comes to visit and smells a rat in Lisa. And sure enough the little software vixen gets her talons in Milo and begins to seduce him away from Alice, although if Milo were not such a nerd and had seen a few thrillers in between programming worldwide communications, he would be able to predict her secret agenda as easily as we can.

There's a moment in the movie you should savor, if you see it. Teddy continues to work back in the garage, and has a breakthrough he summarizes as, "It's not in the box. It's in the band." Soon after, Teddy is beaten senseless in what is disguised as a racist attack. Soon after that, Winston tells Milo: "It's not in the box. It's in the band." Milo's delusions collapse as he realizes Winston will kill for code, and to eliminate the competition. This is a realization we have long since arrived at, but for Winston it is earth-shattering, as we can see because the movie's editing goes into hyperdrive. There's a berserk montage of remembered dialogue, jagged images, tiling cameras, echo chamber effects, everything but a woo-woo-woo alarm horn. Too goofy. In Ingmar Bergman's *Persona*, when one character realizes the other one isn't nice, the film itself seems to break. In *AntiTrust* it's like the projector explodes.

The movie then degenerates into fairly conventional thriller material, like chases, deadly stalkings through dark interior spaces, desperate sesame-seed allergy tests, and so on. At the end we are left with an argument that software code should not be copyrighted because "human knowledge belongs to the world." Stirring sentiments, although it is unlikely that a free digital version of this movie will be posted on the Net anytime soon.

Apocalypse Now Redux ★ ★ ★ ★
R, 197 m., 2001

Marlon Brando (Kurtz), Robert Duvall (Kilgore), Martin Sheen (Willard), Frederic Forrest (Chef), Dennis Hopper (Photographer), Aurore Clement (Roxanne), Laurence Fishburne (Clean), Albert Hall (Chief), Harrison Ford (Colonel Lucas). Directed by Francis Ford Coppola and produced by Coppola and Kim Aubry. Screenplay by John Milius and Coppola.

More than ever it is clear that Francis Ford Coppola's *Apocalypse Now* is one of the great films of all time. It shames modern Hollywood's timidity. To watch it is to feel yourself lifted up to the heights where the cinema can take you, but so rarely does. The film is a mirror reflecting our feelings about the war in Vietnam, in all their complexity and sadness. To those who wrote me defending the banality of *Pearl Harbor*, I wrote back: "See *Apocalypse Now* and reflect on the difference."

The movie comes to us now in a new version, forty-nine minutes longer than the original. The most unexpected thing about *Apocalypse Now Redux* may not be the restored footage, however, but the new Technicolor dye-transfer prints. An expert on prints, Jeff Joseph, tells me: "This is essentially a reworking of the old three-strip Technicolor process. Instead of the chemical development of colors, color dyes are transferred to the film directly, resulting in the stunning 'Technicolor' look of the '40s and '50s: lush, gorgeous, bright, sharp, and vivid, with deep, rich, true blacks."

The physical look of the film is therefore voluptuous and saturated. This is what would be at risk with digital projection. Coppola also pushes the envelope with the remastered sound track, and I was reminded of the film's world premiere at Cannes in 1979, when the old Palais was so filled with light and sound that I felt enveloped; the helicopters in the famous village assault could first be heard behind me, and then passed overhead, and yes, there were people who involuntarily ducked. To be able to come home from the hellish production conditions on the Philippines locations with a film of such technical mastery is miraculous.

The story concerns a journey upriver by Captain Willard (Martin Sheen), who commands a patrol boat to penetrate behind enemy lines and discover the secret redoubt of the almost mythical Colonel Kurtz (Marlon Brando)—one of the army's most decorated soldiers, now leading his own band of tribesmen. The story is based on Joseph Conrad's *Heart of Darkness*, but replaces the implacable mystery of the upper reaches of the Congo with the equally unfathomable mystery of the American venture in Vietnam. When you get to the bottom of who Kurtz has become and what he is thinking, you can see how the war transformed the original American idealism.

The movie consists of a series of set pieces. The most famous is the assault on the village, opening with the helicopter loudspeakers blasting Wagner at the terrified students and teachers, and continuing with Lieutenant Kilgore (Robert Duvall) and his swashbuckling bravado on the beach ("I love the smell of napalm in the morning"). Other sequences are also in the permanent memory of moviegoers: the drugged monotony of the river journey, the sudden gunfire that kills everyone on the sampan, the Playboy Playmates entertaining the troops, the dreamlike final approach to Kurtz's compound, the shadowed Kurtz and his bleak aphorisms, and the giggling assent of the stoned photographer (Dennis Hopper), who is the Fool to his Lear.

To the majesty of these scenes in their progression to Kurtz's words "the Horror," Coppola has now added forty-nine minutes, most of them devoted to a visit by the crew to a French plantation, a colonial leftover that somehow survives. At dinner the Americans and French discuss the colonial history of Vietnam, and Willard's eyes meet those of Roxanne (Aurore Clement), a widow who will spend the night in his arms. Other new footage includes dialogue and byplay on the boat, a second encounter with the Playmates, and additional dialogue by Kurtz.

In a note released with the film, Coppola emphasizes that this new material was not simply shoehorned into the original version of the film, but that *Redux* is "a new rendition of the movie from scratch." He and his longtime editor Walter Murch "re-edited the film from the original unedited raw footage—the dailies," he says, and so possibly even some of the shots that look familiar to us are different takes than the ones we saw before. The 1979 version "terrified" him, he says, because it was "too long, too strange and didn't resolve itself in a kind of classic big battle at the end." Facing financial disaster, he shaped it for the "mainstream audience of its day," and twenty years later, seeing it again, he found it "relatively tame."

To consider *Apocalypse Now* mainstream or tame in either form is a bizarre judgment for Coppola to pass on his picture, but then he has a history of incautious and inexplicable remarks about it, going back to the infamous Cannes press conference where he confessed he had "problems with the ending," and many critics thought he was talking about the Kurtz episode, and not (as he was) the closing titles.

My own feeling is that the original cut was neither mainstream nor tame, but epic filmmaking on a scale within the reach of only a few directors—Tarkovsky, Lean, Eisenstein,

Kurosawa. The new version therefore triggered my suspicion. I was happy to see the additional footage, and indeed had seen it before, in outtake form. Did the movie require it?

Some of the footage enters seamlessly into the work and disappears, enriching it. That would include the river footage and some moments with the photographer. The new Brando footage, including some more pointed analysis of the war, is a valuable addition. The Playmate footage simply doesn't work; it was left out of the original because a typhoon prevented him from completing its filming, Coppola says, but "Walter found a way to get in and out of the sequence." Perhaps, but no reason to be there.

It is the French plantation sequence that gives me the most pause. It is long enough, I think, that it distracts from the overall arc of the movie. The river journey sets the rhythm of the film, and too much time on the banks interrupts it (there is the same problem with the feuding families in *Huckleberry Finn*). Yet the sequence is effective and provoking (despite the inappropriate music during the love scene). It helps me to understand it when Coppola explains that he sees the French like ghosts; I questioned how they had survived in their little enclave, and accept his feeling that their spirits survive as a cautionary specter for the Americans.

Longer or shorter, *Redux* or not, *Apocalypse Now* is one of the central events of my life as a filmgoer. To have it in this beautiful print is a luxury. This new version will make its way to DVD and be welcome there, but the place to see it is in a movie theater, sitting not too far back, your eyes and ears filled with its haunting vision. Now this is a movie.

Atlantis: The Lost Empire ★ ★ ★ ½
PG, 95 m., 2001

With the voices of: Michael J. Fox (Milo), James Garner (Rourke), Cree Summer (Princess Kida), Don Novello (Vinny), Phil Morris (Dr. Sweet), Claudia Christian (Helga), Jacqueline Obradors (Audrey), John Mahoney (Preston Whitmore), Corey Burton (Moliere), Jim Varney (Cookie), Florence Stanley (Mrs. Packard), Leonard Nimoy (King of Atlantis). Directed by Gary Trousdale and Kirk Wise and produced by Don Hahn.

Screenplay by Tab Murphy, based on a story by Wise, Trousdale, Joss Whedon, Bryce Zabel, Jackie Zabel, and Murphy.

Disney's *Atlantis: The Lost Empire* is an animated adventure movie with a lot of gusto and a wowser of a climax. It's an experiment for the studio. Leaving behind the song-and-dance numbers and the cute sidekicks, Disney seems to be testing the visual and story style of anime—those action-jammed animated Japanese movies that occupy shelves in every video store, meaning someone must be renting them.

The movie is set in 1914, a favorite period for stories like this, because technology was fairly advanced while people could still believe that a sunken continent or lost world or two might have gone overlooked. Just as the *Jurassic Park* movies owe something (actually, a lot) to Arthur Conan Doyle's *The Lost World*, so does *Atlantis* spring from the old Edgar Rice Burroughs novels about a world in the center of Earth. (There is also discussion on the Web about how it springs even more directly from a 1989 Japanese anime named *Nadia: The Secret of Blue Water*.)

All stories like this require a rich, reclusive billionaire to finance an expedition to the lost corners of Earth, and *Atlantis* has Preston Whitmore (voice by John Mahoney), who lives Citizen Kane–style behind vast iron gates in a mysterious citadel, and puts together a team to go to the bottom of the sea.

Whitmore summons the linguist Milo Thatch (voice by Michael J. Fox) to join the expedition; he knew Milo's grandfather, and trusts an ancient notebook in which the old man perhaps recorded the secret of Atlantis. Milo himself has spent much time trying to convince Smithsonian scientists of the possibility of a sunken continent; he works at the institute—as a janitor.

The diving team, which uses a sub Captain Nemo would have envied, is led by the rough-and-ready Rourke (James Garner) and includes a mixed bag of adventurers, including Vinny the explosives man (Don Novello), who has voluptuous ambitions for blowing up stuff real good; Moliere the Mole (Corey Burton), the digging expert; Rourke's first mate Helga (Claudia Christian), a scheming vamp;

Audrey the mechanic (Jacqueline Obradors); Doctor Sweet (Phil Morris); Cookie the cook (the late Jim Varney); and Mrs. Packard (Florence Stanley), who chain-smokes while handling communications.

You will note among this crew no dancing teacups, even though the movie was directed by Gary Trousdale and Kirk Wise, who made the wonderful *Beauty and the Beast* for Disney. Perhaps that's because of the influence of a comic-book artist named Mike Mignola, previously unknown to me but described by my colleague Elvis Mitchell as the creator of an underground comic character named Hellboy; his drawing style may have something to do with the movie's clean, bright, visual look, which doesn't yearn for the 3-D roundness of *Toy Story* or *Shrek,* but embraces the classic energy of the comic-book style. You especially see that in the movie's spectacular closing sequence—but I'm getting ahead of the story.

Atlantis is protected by fearsome robotic sea leviathans, which all but destroy the expedition before Rourke, Milo, and the crew succeed in penetrating a volcano and reaching the ocean floor in their sub, where Milo is befriended by Princess Kida (Cree Summer). The submerged land is ruled by her father the king (Leonard Nimoy), who wants to banish the outsiders, but Kida has eyes for Milo in a subplot owing more than a little to *The Little Mermaid.*

Atlantis itself seems desperately in need of fresh blood—not for population (since the residents are 1,000 years old and going strong) but for new ideas, since the land has fallen into apathy and disrepair. Princess Kida is kind of a reformist, nudging her father to get off his throne and organize some public works projects.

Now about that closing sequence. If you recall the ballroom scene in *Beauty and the Beast,* you will remember the exhilarating way directors Trousdale and Wise liberated their characters not only from gravity but from the usual rules of animation, so that they careered thrillingly through the air. Multiply that several times, and you get the excitement of a final battle that brings to animated life the kind of explosive energy we sense imprisoned in the printed KA-BOOM!s, KERRR-ASSHHHH!es, and THUNK!s of those full-page drawings in action comic books, where superheroes battle for control of the universe.

The story of *Atlantis* is rousing in an old pulp science fiction sort of way, but the climactic scene transcends the rest, and stands by itself as one of the great animated action sequences. Will the movie signal a new direction for Disney animation? I doubt it. The synergy of animated musical comedies is too attractive, not only for entertainment value but also for the way they spin off hit songs and stage shows. What *Atlantis* does show is a willingness to experiment with the anime tradition—maybe to appeal to teenage action fans who might otherwise avoid an animated film. It's like *20,000 Leagues Under the Sea* set free by animation to look the way it dreamed of looking.

B

Baby Boy ★ ★ ★ ½
R, 129 m., 2001

Tyrese Gibson (Jody), Omar Gooding (Sweetpea),
A. J. Johnson (Juanita), Taraji P. Henson (Yvette),
Snoop Dogg (Rodney), Tamara LaSeon Bass
(Peanut), Ving Rhames (Melvin). Directed
and produced by John Singleton. Screenplay
by Singleton.

John Singleton's *Baby Boy* is a bold criticism of young black men who carelessly father babies, live off their mothers, and don't even think of looking for work. It is also a criticism of the society that pushes them into that niche. There has never been a movie with this angle on the African-American experience. The movie's message to men like its hero is: Yes, racism has contributed to your situation—but do you have to give it so much help with your own attitude?

In the opening sequence, we meet Jody (Tyrese Gibson), a twenty-year-old who has children by two women and still lives in his room in his mother's house. He drives his girlfriend Yvette (Taraji P. Henson) home from a clinic where she has just had an abortion. She is understandably sad and in pain, a little dopey from pills. She doesn't want to talk. In that case, says Jody, she won't mind if he borrows her car. He does, and uses it to visit his other girlfriend.

That scene will not come as a shock to Mary A. Mitchell, the *Chicago Sun-Times* columnist who has written a series of sad, angry articles about absentee fathers and "man-sharing" in the black community, where drugs, crime, and prison have created a shortage of eligible men. Her columns are courageous; the African-American community prefers to present a positive front and keep its self-criticism behind closed doors. She takes heat for what she writes. Now Singleton, too, dares to take a hard look at his community. Ten years ago, in *Boyz N the Hood*, he told a brilliant story about young men in a movie made by a young man. Now he returns to the same neighborhood, South Central in Los Angeles. His characters are a little older, and he is older, too, and less forgiving.

Baby Boy doesn't fall back on easy liberal finger-pointing. There are no white people in this movie, no simplistic blaming of others; the adults in Jody's life blame him for his own troubles, and they should. At some point, as Jody's mother, Juanita (A. J. Johnson), tells him again and again, he has to grow up, move out, get a job, and take care of his family.

Jody doesn't even bother to answer, except to accuse her of not loving him. He likes the life he leads, and doesn't consider employment as an option. He sponges off of two women: his mother, and Yvette, who has a job. Also in the picture is Peanut (Tamara Laseon Bass), the mother of his other child. But it's Yvette he loves. Still, he plays around, and she knows it and in a certain way accepts it, although she gets mad when she can never drive her own car, which she's making payments on. She screams that he lies to her, and his answer is a logical masterpiece: "I'm out in these streets telling these ho's the truth. I lie to you because I care about you."

All would be well if Jody could keep on sleeping in his childhood bedroom (where he still builds model cars), eat his mother's cooking, drive Yvette's car, sleep with his women, and hang with his boys—especially his best friend, Sweetpea (Omar Gooding). But Yvette is fed up. Sweetpea is getting involved with dangerous gang types. Yvette's old boyfriend (Snoop Dogg) is out of prison and hanging around. And at home, most disturbingly, his mother has a new boyfriend named Melvin (Ving Rhames), who has no patience with him. Melvin has spent ten years in the slammer, is determined to go straight, has a landscaping business, and moves in and marks his territory. Jody knows things are different when he finds Melvin stark naked in the kitchen, scrambling eggs for Juanita. "I was like you, Jody," he says. "Young, dumb, and out of control."

Juanita herself is a piece of work, a still-youthful woman who loves her backyard garden and tries patiently, over and over, to cut through Jody's martyrdom and evasion. When he complains to her that Yvette has locked him out, she levels: "What would *you* do if Yvette f——— around on you, took your car, and left you in a hot house all day with a baby?" An excellent question. Yvette answers it, in a way, by stealing back her own car, so the "baby boy" is reduced to riding his childhood bicycle around the neighborhood.

When John Singleton burst on the scene with *Boyz N the Hood*, he brought the freshness of direct, everyday experience to movies about black Americans. He was still in his mid-twenties, fresh out of South Central, already a legend for the way, at sixteen, he started hanging around the USC film school—volunteering as a gofer until the dean concluded, "We might as well make him a student, since he acts like he is one anyway." Singleton comes from the same background as his characters, knows them, sees aspects of himself and his friends in them. Like many self-made men, he is impatient with those, like Jody, who do not even try.

He has a gift for finding good actors. *Boyz* was Cuba Gooding Jr.'s first movie. Here we meet Cuba's brother Omar, also gifted. Tyrese Gibson, already known as a singer, model, and music video DJ, is a natural, unaffected actor who adds a spin of spoiled self-pity to Jody. Taraji P. Henson has some of the most difficult scenes as Yvette, who does love her man, but despairs of him, and is tired to the bone of working, child care, and caring, too, for Jody, the twenty-year-old "baby boy." And there is a wonderful rapport between A. J. Johnson and Ving Rhames as the mother and her ex-con boyfriend; they have an exuberant sex life, feel they deserve a second chance at happiness, and have lived long enough and paid enough dues to be impatient with Jody's knack for living off the land.

Baby Boy has a trailer that makes it look like a lot of fun—like a celebration of the lifestyle it attacks. I was reminded of the trailer for *Boyz N the Hood*, which seemed to glorify guns and violence, although the movie deplored them. I asked Singleton about it at the time, and he said, "Maybe some kids will see the trailer and come to see the movie, and leave with a lot of ideas they didn't have before." Maybe so. I have a notion the Yvettes of the world are going to love this movie, and march their Jodys in to see it.

Bad Company ★ ★
PG-13, 111 m., 2002

Anthony Hopkins (Gaylord Oakes), Chris Rock (Jake Hayes), Garcelle Beauvais-Nilon (Nicole), Gabriel Macht (Seale), Peter Stormare (Adrik Vas), Kerry Washington (Julie), John Stattery (Roland Yates). Directed by Joel Schumacher and produced by Jerry Bruckheimer and Mike Stenson. Screenplay by Jason Richman, Michael Browning, Gary Goodman, and David Himmelstein.

Hard on the heels of *The Sum of All Fears*, here's Jerry Bruckheimer's *Bad Company*, another movie about an American city threatened by the explosion of a stolen nuclear device. This one is an action comedy. There may come a day when the smiles fade. To be sure, the movie was made before 9/11 (and its original autumn 2001 release was delayed for obvious reasons), but even before 9/11 it was clear that nuclear terrorism was a real possibility. While *The Sum of All Fears* deals in a quasi-serious way with the subject (up until the astonishingly inappropriate ending), *Bad Company* is more lighthearted. Ho, ho.

The nuclear device is really only the Maguffin. It could be anything, as long as bad guys want it and good guys fight to keep them from it. The movie's a collision among three durable genres: Misfit Partners, Fish Out of Water, and Mistaken Identity. After an opening scene in which the Chris Rock character is killed, we learn that he had a twin brother named Jake Hayes; the babies were separated at birth and never knew about each other. The first was adopted by a rich family, went to Ivy League schools, and joined the CIA. Jake is a ticket scalper and chess hustler who's in love with a nursing student (Kerry Washington).

One problem with the movie, directed by Joel Schumacher, is that it jams too many prefabricated story elements into the running time. Consider the training sequence, in which Rock has nine days to perfect the mannerisms and absorb the knowledge of his dead brother. Odd that most of the coaching sessions have him learning to recognize fine vintages of wine and evaluate ancient cognacs; is he going to be dining with the terrorists? Meanwhile, he's apparently expected to learn to speak Czech from a dictionary tossed onto his bunk.

His minder at the CIA is Gaylord Oakes (Anthony Hopkins), a spookily calm veteran operative whose plan is to substitute this twin for the other in a sting operation designed to buy a stolen nuclear device. When another would-be buyer enters the picture, the film descends into a series of chase scenes, which are well enough done, but too many and too long.

Hopkins plays his character right down the middle, hard-edged and serious. Rock has some effective scenes played straight, but at other times he goes into a nonstop comic monologue that is funny, yes, but unlikely; when he's being shot at, how can he think of all those one-liners? The movie's strategy is to make every sequence stand on its own, with no thought to the overall tone of the film, so that we go from the deadly serious to something approaching parody.

Of the plot I can say nothing except that it exists entirely at the whim of the stunts, special effects, chases, and action. The two competing teams of would-be evil bomb buyers function entirely to supply an endless number of guys who fire machine guns a lot but hardly ever hit anything. The motive for blowing up New York is scarcely discussed. And could I believe my eyes? Here in 2002—another Red Digital Readout counting down to zero, just when I thought that was one cliché that had finally outlived its viability.

As for the girls, well, Kerry Washington is sweet and believable as Rock's girlfriend, but a Bruckheimer movie is not the place to look for meaningful female performances. No doubt there was a nice payday, but meanwhile, Washington's fine performance in *Lift,* the shoplifting film from Sundance 2001, goes unheralded. Even more thankless is the role by Garcelle Beauvais-Nilon as a CNN correspondent who was the girlfriend of the first twin, and spots this one because he kisses differently. She disappears entirely from the film after an ironically appropriate slide down a laundry chute. (By the way: During the shoot-out in that hotel, how come not a single guest or employee is ever seen?)

I won't tell you I didn't enjoy parts of *Bad Company,* because I did. But the enjoyment came at moments well separated by autopilot action scenes and stunt sequences that outlived their interest. As for the theme of a nuclear device that might destroy New York, I have a feeling that after this generation of pre-9/11 movies plays out, we won't be seeing it much anymore.

Baise-Moi ★

NO MPAA RATING, 77 m., 2001

Raffaela Anderson (Manu), Karen Bach (Nadine), Delphine MacCarty (La Colocataire), Lisa Marshall (Karla), Estelle Isaac (Alice), Herve P. Gustave (Martin), Marc Rioufol (L'architecte), Ouassini Embarek (Radouan). Directed by Virginie Despentes and Coralie Trinh Thi and produced by Philippe Godeau. Screenplay by Despentes and Trinh Thi, based on the novel by Despentes.

Baise-Moi is (a) a violent and pornographic film from France about two women, one a rape victim, the other a prostitute, who prowl the countryside murdering men. Or, *Baise-Moi* is (b) an attempt to subvert sexism in the movies by turning the tables and allowing the women to do more or less what men have been doing for years—while making a direct connection between sex and guns, rather than the sublimated connection in most violent movies.

I pose this choice because I do not know the answer. Certainly most ordinary moviegoers will despise this movie—or would, if they went to see it, which is unlikely. It alternates between graphic, explicit sex scenes, and murder scenes of brutal cruelty. You recoil from what's on the screen. Later, you ask what the filmmakers had in mind. They are French, and so we know some kind of ideology and rationalization must lurk beneath the blood and semen.

The film has been written and directed by Virginie Despentes, based on her novel; she enlisted Coralie Trinh Thi, a porno actress, as her codirector (whether to help with the visual strategy or because of her understanding of the mechanical requirements of on-screen sex, it is hard to say). The movie's central characters, Manu and Nadine, are played by Raffaela Anderson and Karen Bach, who act in hardcore films, and some of the men are also from the porno industry. This is, in fact, the kind of film the director in *Boogie Nights* wanted to make—"porn, but artistic"—although he would have questioned the box-office appeal of the praying mantis approach to sex, in which the male is killed immediately after copulation.

As it happens, I saw a Japanese-American coproduction named *Brother* not long after seeing *Baise-Moi*. It was written and directed by Takeshi Kitano, who starred under his acting name, Beat Takeshi. Kitano under any name is the Japanese master of lean, violent, heartless action pictures, and in this one the plot is punctuated every five minutes or so by a bloodbath in which enemies are shot dead. Many, many enemies. We're talking dozens. The killings are separated in *Brother* by about the same length of time as those in *Baise-Moi*, or the sex acts in a porno film. Obviously all three kinds of film are providing payoffs by the clock. Would *Brother* be as depressing as *Baise-Moi* if all the victims had sex before they were gunned down? I don't know, but I'm sure *Baise-Moi* would be perfectly acceptable if the women simply killed men, and no sex was involved. At some level it seems so . . . cruel . . . to shoot a man at his moment of success.

A case can be made that *Baise-Moi* wants to attack sexism in the movies at the same time it raises the stakes. I'm not interested in making that argument. Manu and Nadine are man-haters, and clinically insane, and not every man is to blame for their unhappiness—no, not even if he sleeps with them. An equally controversial new American movie named *Bully* is also about stupid, senseless murder, but it has the wit to know what it thinks about its characters. *Baise-Moi* is more of a bluff. The directors know their film is so extreme that most will be repelled, but some will devise intellectual defenses and interpretations for it, saving them the trouble of making it clear what they want to say. I can't buy it. Ernest Hemingway, who was no doubt a sexist pig, said it is moral if you feel good after it, and immoral if you feel bad after it. Manu and Nadine do not feel bad, and that is immoral.

Bait ★ ★ ★
R, 110 m., 2000

Jamie Foxx (Alvin Sanders), David Morse (Edgar Clenteen), Doug Hutchison (Bristol), Kimberly Elise (Lisa Hill), David Paymer (Agent Wooly), Mike Epps (Stevie Sanders), Nestor Serrano (Agent Boyle), Jamie Kennedy (Agent Blum). Directed by Antoine Fuqua and produced by Sean Ryerson. Screenplay by Tony Gilroy, Andrew Scheinman, and Adam Scheinman.

Bait is a deadpan action comedy with a little Hitchcock, a little Bond, and a lot of attitude. It's funny and clever, and it grows on you, especially with the tension between Jamie Foxx's trash-talking thief and David Morse's monomaniac federal agent. It's one of those movies where you start out thinking you've seen it all before, and the longer it runs, the less you've seen before. There's even an effective use of the exhausted old Red Digital Readout gambit.

The movie opens with the high-tech robbery of $42 million in bullion from the Federal Gold Reserve in New York. Two guards are executed. The mastermind is Bristol (Doug Hutchison), a genius computer hacker but a poor judge of men, who unwisely entrusts the getaway truck to a slob partner who drives off without him. The feds nab the partner, and he's interrogated by the hard-boiled U.S. agent Clenteen (David Morse). The guy keeps asking for a doctor, but Clenteen doesn't get the message until another agent (David Paymer) comments, "I don't think he's kidding."

The getaway driver is dead. That leaves both the feds and the hacker desperate to find out where the gold is hidden. One man may know: Alvin Sanders (Jamie Foxx) shared the same prison cell with the dead man, and may have learned something. Clenteen devises a diabolical scheme. He will implant Alvin with a miniature audio and tracking chip, allowing agents to eavesdrop on every word and follow every move. He'll be bait to lure Bristol—and then the feds will pounce.

This is all setup for a movie that is funny in an oblique, underplayed sort of way. It's kidding itself but doesn't always admit it. It doesn't go for obvious laughs, like a Martin Lawrence movie might have, but uses Foxx's wisecracking, ad-lib style to create Alvin as a character who gets more complicated the more time we spend with him. In his opening scenes, as Alvin bungles the theft of a shipment of prawns, I was writing "condescending" in my notes: He was coming across as a broad, urban stereotype, not too smart. Then it became clear than Alvin uses his persona as a shield, a weapon of humor to protect and deflect. By the end of the movie, when he sets up his own sting to find out who's following him, we're not surprised.

A lot of the best scenes involve federal agents in a monitoring post, eavesdropping on Alvin's life, his conversations, his problems with his girlfriend (Kimberly Elise), and the trouble his brother (Mike Epps) gets him in. This isn't reality TV but reality radio; the agents start to like Alvin—all except for the hard-edged Clenteen, who was born without a sense of humor. Alvin's brother involves him in a stolen car scam, and the feds panic that their bait will be back in jail before he can catch the fish. They try to control his life without letting him know they exist, arranging for him to come into money—in scenes that Foxx milks for all they're worth.

Hutchison, as Bristol, the computer genius and killer thief, does an effective John Malkovich number. He's calm, until he shrieks; calculated, until he cracks; all business, until he gets involved in a bizarre scheme involving kidnapping, bombs, torture, and a racetrack sequence that owes more than a little to Hitchcock (and something to the Marx Brothers' *A Day at the Races*).

In my review of *The Watcher*, I was complaining about killers who spend more time devising elaborate booby traps for the cops than in committing their crimes. Now I forgive Bristol for the same practice. It's all in how you do it—in the style. And while Keanu Reeves's killer in *The Watcher* seemed interested only in playing mind games with James Spader's FBI man, Bristol, here, has a more realistic motivation—he wants his $42 million.

Some will argue that the climax at the racetrack is preposterous. They will be right. The secret hiding place for the gold also raises a lot of questions—like, how easy would it actually be to put it there? Those are not the kinds of questions that are relevant to a film like this. It's over the top, an exercise in action comedy that cuts loose from logic and enjoys itself. And it's intriguing the way the Foxx character conceals his thinking even from the audience at times—how he is more than he seems, and finds it prudent to keep that fact to himself.

The Ballad of Ramblin' Jack ★ ★ ★
NO MPAA RATING, 112 m., 2000

A documentary directed by Aiyana Elliott and produced by Elliott, Paul Mezey, and Dan Partland. Screenplay by Elliott and Dick Dahl.

Ramblin' Jack Elliott is beloved by those who know him and his work, but because of disputes with record companies, breakups with managers, and his ramblin' ways, not many people do. His importance to the larger music world is as the link between Woody Guthrie and Bob Dylan. He was Guthrie's protégé, was at his bedside during his illness, sang his songs in the Village during the early folk revival, and was imitated by Dylan right down to the harmonica in the neck brace. Arlo Guthrie, who may have a bone to pick, says: "There wouldn't be no Bob Dylan without Ramblin' Jack Elliott."

The Ballad of Ramblin' Jack is a documentary made by his daughter, Aiyana, who is thirtyish and observes, "I can't remember ever having an actual conversation with my dad." Making the film was perhaps a way to get to know him better, but it doesn't work that way; Elliott has a knack for ramblin' right off topic, and when he takes his daughter on a drive in Mendicino to visit "the house where we came closest to being a family," he can't find it. At another point he explains that a birthday call was six days late because "I couldn't find a phone."

If he was not a good dad, he was at least an excellent rambler, often booking himself from gig to gig. I saw him first at the University of Illinois YMCA in the early 1960s, playing to a small roomful of folkies, and then again in Chicago's Old Town during the folk revival. He was more a personality than a great singer; it wasn't so much what he did as what he stood for, and even his own sister, noting that he learned to play the guitar while a rodeo cowboy, adds, "He should have taken singing lessons." Yet Elliott won a Grammy in 1995, and was given the National Medal of Arts in 1998 by President Clinton.

Elliott was born Elliott Charles Adnopoz, son of a Brooklyn doctor, in 1931. He ran away from home to join the rodeo, and has been rambling ever since. Elliott arguably provided Dylan with more than an insight into the music of Woody Guthrie: "What Dylan really took from Ramblin' Jack were lessons on how to configure a complete persona out of a mundane middle-class Jewish upbringing," writes Henry Cabot Beck of Film.com.

As Dylan turned into one of the biggest stars of the early 1960s, Elliott "didn't even notice at first" that his act had been copied (and, in all fairness, improved upon—not to mention the additional dimension of Dylan's songwriting). Real hurt came later, at a 1967 Guthrie tribute concert; Dylan was the headliner, Elliott at first was not even invited. By then Elliott's career was ramblin' out of control, and the film quotes an early manager, Harold Leventhal, who says: "I respected his talent but he was too disorganized. [With Jack], if there's a plan, it comes from whatever wife he happens to be with."

For Aiyana Elliott, daughter by the fourth wife, all of this is just the historical backdrop to a life during which her father was briefly glimpsed between rambles. He was on the road, or had signed on to crew a sailboat, or had turned up with a new girlfriend, and it was no fun "having the world's greatest rambler as your dad." Her documentary is an effort to pin down Elliott, but he is unpinnable, and her specific questions get answers that drift off into free association. His concerts, we gather, were much the same way: "He never knew what the program would be, and there wasn't even a song list taped to the guitar. Sometimes he'd start a song without even deciding on the key." Old footage from a Johnny Cash TV show shows Cash looking on quizzically as Elliott tunes, and tunes, and tunes.

The movie reminded me of another recent documentary, *Pop and Me*, about a father and son who embark on a round-the-world trip during which they plan to get to know each other better, and find that wherever they go, their relationship has preceded them. Some parents are elusive, and some children are never going to get closure, and *The Ballad of Ramblin' Jack* hovers intriguingly between homage and revenge.

Bamboozled ★ ★

R, 135 m., 2000

Damon Wayans (Pierre Delacroix), Savion Glover (Manray/Mantan), Jada Pinkett-Smith (Sloan Hopkins), Tommy Davidson (Womack/Sleep 'n' Eat), Michael Rapaport (Dunwitty), Mos Def (Big Black Africa). Directed by Spike Lee and produced by Lee and Jon Kilik. Screenplay by Lee.

"You've been hoodwinked. You've been had. You've been took. You've been led astray, led amok. You've been bamboozled."

So said Malcolm X, as quoted by Spike Lee in the production notes to *Bamboozled,* his perplexing new film. To Malcolm, the bamboozlers were white people in general, but in Lee's films they're the television executives, black and white, who bamboozle themselves in the mindless quest for ratings. The film is a satirical attack on the way TV uses and misuses African-American images, but many viewers will leave the theater thinking Lee has misused them himself.

That's the danger with satire: To ridicule something, you have to show it, and if what you're attacking is a potent enough image, the image retains its negative power no matter what you want to say about it. *Bamboozled* shows black actors in boldly exaggerated blackface for a cable production named "Mantan—The New Millennium Minstrel Show." Can we see beyond the blackface to its purpose? I had a struggle.

The movie stars Damon Wayans as Pierre Delacroix, a Harvard graduate who is a program executive at a cable TV network. He works under a boss who is, in his own eyes, admirably unprejudiced: Dunwitty (Michael Rapaport) says Delacroix's black shows are "too white," and adds: "I have a black wife and two biracial kids. Brother man—I'm blacker than you."

Well, Delacroix isn't very black; his accent makes him sound like Franklin Pangborn as a floorwalker. But he's black enough to resent how Dunwitty and the network treat him (when he's late to a meeting, his boss says he's "pulling a Rodman"). In front of his office, he often passes two homeless street dancers, Manray (Savion Glover) and Womack (Tommy Davidson). Fed up with the news that he's not black enough, Delacroix decides to star them in a blackface variety show set in a watermelon patch on an Alabama plantation.

The new show shocks and offends many viewers, but turns into an enormous hit, sending the plot into twists and terrorist turns that are beside the issue. The central questions any viewer of *Bamboozled* has to answer are How do I feel about the racist images I'm seeing? and Is Spike Lee making his point?

I think he makes his point intellectually; it's quite possible to see the film and understand his feelings. In conversation Lee wonders why black-themed shows on TV are nearly always comedies; why are episodic dramas about blacks so rare? Are whites so threatened by blacks on TV that they'll only watch them being funny? An excellent question. And when Lee says the modern equivalent of a blackface minstrel show is the gangsta-rap music video, we see what he means: These videos are enormously popular with white kids, just as minstrel shows were beloved by white audiences, and for a similar reason: They package entertainment within demeaning and negative black images.

Lee's comments are on target, but is his film? I don't think so. Lee's spin on a gangsta-rap video or an African-American domestic comedy might be radically revealing. And what about execs rewriting scenes and dialogue according to their narrow ideas? (Margaret Cho's concert doc *I'm the One that I Want* tells of executives at CBS asking for rewrites to make the Korean-American comedian "less ethnic.")

To satirize black shows on TV, Lee should have stayed closer to what really offends him; I think his fundamental miscalculation was to use blackface itself. He overshoots the mark. Blackface is so blatant, so wounding, so highly charged, that it obscures any point being made by the person wearing it. The makeup is the message.

Consider the most infamous public use of blackface in recent years. Ted Danson appeared in blackface at a Friar's Club roast for his then-girlfriend Whoopi Goldberg. The audience sat in stunned silence. I could feel the tension and discomfort in the room. In his defense, Danson said the skit had been dreamed up and written by Whoopi. One of his lines was about how he'd invited Whoopi home to dinner and his parents had asked her to clean up the kitchen after the meal. Not funny when Danson said it. If Whoopi had said it about herself, it would have been funny, with an edge. But if Whoopi had said it while wearing blackface? Not funny. After Danson's flop, comedian Bobcat Goldthwait summed up the mood: "Jesus Christ, Ted, what were you thinking of? Do you think black people think blackface is funny in nineteen ninety and [bleeping] three?"

No, and white people don't, either. Blacks in blackface eating watermelon and playing characters named Sleep 'n' Eat, Rufus, and Aunt Jemima fail as satire and simply become—well, what they seem to be: crude racist caricatures.

I think Spike Lee misjudged his material and audience in the same way Whoopi Goldberg did, and for the same reason: He doesn't find a successful way to express his feelings, angers, and satirical points. When Mel Brooks satirizes Nazis in the famous "Springtime for Hitler" number in *The Producers*, he makes Hitler look like a ridiculous buffoon. But what if the musical number had centered on Jews being marched into gas chambers? Not funny. Blackface is over-the-top in the same way—people's feelings run too strongly and deeply for such exaggerated satire to be effective. The power of the racist image tramples over the material and asserts only itself.

Bandits ★ ★
PG-13, 123 m., 2001

Bruce Willis (Joe), Cate Blanchett (Kate), Billy Bob Thornton (Terry), Troy Garity (Harvey), Rocky La Rochelle (Tomales Bank Manager), Jaye K. Danford (Alamo Bank Manager), Anthony Burch (Phil), Norman Fessler (Alamo Bank Hostage). Directed by Barry Levinson and produced by Michael Birnbaum, Michele Berk, Levinson, Paula Weinstein, Ashok Amritraj, David Hoberman, and Arnold Rifkin. Screenplay by Harley Peyton.

Bandits is a movie so determined to be clever and whimsical that it neglects to be anything else. That decision wouldn't be fatal if the movie had caved in and admitted it was a comedy, but no, it also wants to contain moments of pathos, suspense, and insight, and it's too flimsy to support them. It's an anthology of unrelated tones; individual scenes may play well, but seem unaware of the movie they're in. And the love triangle never decides if it's romance or romantic comedy. If the movie won't commit, why should we?

It's rare for a movie to have three such likable characters and be so unlikable itself. Bruce Willis and Billy Bob Thornton star as "America's most famous bank robbers," and Cate Blanchett is Kate, the executive's wife who starts as their hostage and becomes their lover. Yes, both of them (or neither of them; the PG-13 movie is cagey about what happens in between those knocks on the motel room doors). She can't choose. She likes Joe (Willis) because he's brave, strong, and handsome, and Terry (Thornton) because he's sensitive and cute.

Thornton's character is the jewel—a neurotic, fearful hypochrondiac who is lactose intolerant, hears a ringing in his ears, suffers from psychosomatic paralysis, and has a phobia about antique furniture. (You never know what's real and what they're making up in the movies; Billy Bob Thornton has a real-life phobia about antique furniture, in fact, and almost had a meltdown once during a visit to Johnny Cash's antique-filled home.)

The plot: The partners break out of prison after Joe steals a cement truck, and there's a nice shot of it plowing its way through suburban backyards. Terry comes up with the idea of taking bank managers hostage in their homes the night before a job, so they can get into the bank before business hours in the morning. They steal a lot of loot, become celebrities, and stay on the loose for an amazing length of time, considering their driver, lookout, and "outside man" is Joe's moronic cousin Harvey (Troy Garity), who dreams of being a stuntman.

The movie, directed by Barry Levinson and written by Harley Peyton (*Twin Peaks*), is told in a flashback and actually begins with the news that the two men have been shot dead after a failed hostage situation. Cut to a tabloid TV show whose host got an exclusive interview shortly before the final shoot-out; Joe and Terry narrate their career, try to justify themselves, and say Kate was an innocent hostage and not a fellow criminal. Eventually the film works its way back to the fatal robbery it began with and to the classic line, "The suspects are in a shoot-out with themselves."

The film has laughs sprinkled here and there. I liked the way the confused Terry asks Joe, "What's on our mind?" And the way Kate's preoccupied husband, a self-involved hotshot, goes on TV to tell the kidnapped woman: "I'm going to Spain next week. If the kidnappers want to reach me, they can get in touch with my people." And I liked the jolly little fireplug of a bank manager who is delighted to meet the "Sleepover Bandits" in person, but cannot take them seriously.

Problem is, the movie doesn't commit to any of the several directions where it meanders. Is the romantic triangle poignant, or a gimmick? Do the guys joke and make small talk during robberies because this is a comedy, or because they are pathological narcissists? The flashback structure is an annoyance, and by the time it is justified, it's too late: We've already been annoyed. One of the joys of Barry Levinson's *Wag the Dog* (1997) was the way he juggled tones, moving from satire to suspense to politics. This time it's the audience that feels juggled.

Baran ★ ★ ★ ½
PG, 94 m., 2002

Hossein Abedini (Latif), Zahra Bahrami (Baran), Mohammad Amir Naji (Memar), Hossein Rahimi (Soltan), Gholam Ali Bakhshi (Najaf). Directed by Majid Majidi and produced by Majidi and Fouad Nahas. Screenplay by Majidi.

What are they like, over there in Iran? Are they all glowering fanatics, stewing in resentment of America? What's your mental image? When a land is distant, unknown, and labeled as an enemy, it's easy to think in simple terms. No doubt Iranians are as quick to think evil about us as we are to think evil about them. The intriguing thing about an Iranian movie like *Baran* is that it gives human faces to these strangers. It could be a useful learning tool for those who have not traveled widely, who never see foreign films, who reduce whole nations to labels.

The movie is a romantic fable about a construction worker. His name is Latif, and he labors on a building site not far from the border with Afghanistan. All of the labor here is manual, including hauling fifty-pound bags of cement up a series of ramps. Latif doesn't actually work very hard, since he is Iranian and most of the labor is being done by underpaid refugees from Afghanistan. Latif is the tea boy, bringing hot cups to the workers and drinking more than his own share.

We learn at the beginning of the movie that millions of Afghans have poured into Iran as refugees. Since it is illegal to hire them, they work secretly for low wages, like undocumented

Mexicans in America. Many are fleeing the Taliban for the comparatively greater freedom and prosperity of Iran, a distinction that may seem small to us, but not to them. (The title cards carrying this information were already in place when the film debuted at the 2001 Montreal and Toronto festivals, and were not added post-9/11.)

One day there is an accident on the site. A man named Najaf injures his leg, and that is a catastrophe because he has five children to feed in the squatters' camp where his family lives. Najaf sends his son Rahmat to take his place, but the son is small, slight, and young, and staggers under the burden of the concrete sacks. So Memar, the construction boss, who pays low wages but is not unkind, gives Rahmat the job of tea boy and reassigns Latif to real work.

Latif is lazy, immature, resentful. He trashes the kitchen in revenge, and makes things hard for Rahmat. Yet at the same time he finds something intriguing about the new tea boy, and eventually Latif discovers the secret: The boy is a girl. So desperate for money was Rahmat's family that in a society where women are strictly forbidden from mixing with men on a job like this, a deception was planned. In keeping the secret, Latif begins his journey to manhood and tolerance.

The outlines of *Baran*, as they emerge, seem as much like an ancient fable as a modern story. Middle Eastern society, so insistent on the division between men and women, has a literature filled with stories about men and women in disguise, passing through each other's worlds. The vast gulf between Latif and Rahmat is dramatized by the way they essentially fall in love without exchanging a single word. Meanwhile, watching conditions on the work site and seeing raids by government agents looking for illegal workers, we get an idea of Iran's ground-level economy.

My description perhaps makes the film sound grim and gray, covered with a silt of concrete dust. Not at all. It is the latest work by Majid Majidi, whose *Children of Heaven* (1997) was a heartwarming fable about a brother and sister who lose a pair of sneakers and try to hide this calamity from their parents. The director uses natural colors and painterly compositions to make even the most spartan

locations look beautiful, and as Stephanie Zacharek of Salon.com observes: "Majidi uses sunlight, a completely free resource if you can time your filmmaking around it, as a dazzling special effect."

What happens between Rahmat and Latif I will leave you to discover. There are many surprises along the way, one of the best involving a man Latif meets during a long journey—an itinerant shoemaker, who has thoughtful observations about life. *Baran* is the latest in a flowering of good films from Iran, and gives voice to the moderates there. It shows people existing and growing in the cracks of their society's inflexible walls.

Barenaked in America ★ ★ ★
NO MPAA RATING, 90 m., 2000

Featuring the band members of Barenaked Ladies: Ed Robertson, Steven Page, Jim Creeggan, Kevin Hearn, and Tyler Stewart. Directed by Jason Priestley and produced by Cheryl Teetzel and Susanne Tabata.

If you knew a lot about movies but nothing about a band named Barenaked Ladies, you might reasonably assume that *Barenaked in America* was a spoof—a *Spinal Tap*-style mockumentary aimed at the popular image of Canadians as people who are awfully nice. While most band documentaries wade through sex, drugs, and rock 'n' roll, this one has no sex, no drugs, and the kind of rock 'n' roll that reminds one of their fans of "something I'd hear at a dorm party."

It's groundbreaking when the lead singer comes out in chinos and a dress shirt with the buttons stretching over his tummy. But the movie becomes even stranger when the camera goes aboard the tour bus. What do the band members do on the bus? Play euchre. Yes, euchre. "Euchre is a Canadian thing," one of the sidemen says. "I don't know if Americans have ever heard of it." Oh, and I almost forgot: There is sex on the bus, but it doesn't involve groupies and orgies. A couple of the guys giggle about sneaking out in the morning to dispose of used Kleenex.

Barenaked Ladies is a real band, and a popular one. It has a lot of fans, and one reason for its appeal is that they're the Slim Whitman of rock bands: When they sing a song it sounds like you could do it too, about as well as they can. You couldn't; there's a lot of musicianship buried in their deceptively square stage act, but it sounds like you could.

The Ladies started as street buskers in Toronto, selling cassettes of their work. They came to the attention of MuchMusic, that cable channel that looks like a multicultural and countercultural MTV. They haven't done a single thing to glitz up their act or to appear as anything other than what they are: nice Canadian boys having fun. When Jim Creegan, the bass player, gets a vocal solo, what song does he choose? "Itsy Bitsy Spider." Another one of their songs is about a farmer who loves Anne Murray. Then there's tape of an Anne Murray Christmas special on which the Barenaked Ladies sing "God Rest Ye, Merry Gentlemen."

Steve Page, the chubby one, is the lead singer. Ed Robertson, with the dyed blond goatee and cropped hair, is the other front man. Just before the tour started, they lost their longtime lead singer and keyboardist Kevin Hearn, who was diagnosed with leukemia. Midway through the tour Kevin is feeling good enough to join them onstage, but it is somehow typical of the Barenaked Ladies that management supplies him with an electronic keyboard that's "covered with cigarette welts, with a lot of keys that have turned yellow and don't work." Also onstage, in addition to bass, drums, and backup guitar, are occasional French horn and accordion players.

The documentary, directed by Jason Priestley, arrives in Boston, where the Ladies fill an enormous arena with their fans. We get the usual sound bites outside the hall, but not the usual opinions: "They look like guys you'd see working at the Gap," one fan says.

The Rolling Stones once figured in a documentary where someone was literally murdered by Hells Angels in front of the stage. There are dangers in being a Barenaked Lady too. When the band plays its hit "If I Had a Million Dollars," fans throw Kraft dinners onto the stage. Those boxes have sharp edges, Steve observes, and it can hurt if one hits you.

Bartleby ★ ★ ½
PG-13, 82 m., 2002

David Paymer (The Boss), Crispin Glover (Bartleby), Glenne Headly (Vivian), Joe Piscopo (Rocky), Maury Chaykin (Ernie), Seymour Cassel (Frank Waxman), Carrie Snodgress (Book Publisher), Dick Martin (Mayor). Directed and produced by Jonathan Parker. Screenplay by Parker and Catherine DiNapoli, based on the story "Bartleby the Scrivener" by Herman Melville.

The mass of men lead lives of quiet desperation.
—Thoreau

The life work of the employees in the Public Record Office can be easily described: They take enormous quantities of printed documents they have no interest in, and they file them. They are surrounded by the monument to their labor: lots of file cabinets. No wonder they go mad. Vivian distracts herself by flirting. Rocky pretends he has the inside line on everything. For Ernie, changing the toner cartridge in a Xerox machine is an invitation to disaster. Their boss patiently oversees their cheerless existence trying not to contemplate the devastating meaningless of the office.

One day a new employee is hired. His name is Bartleby. The boss asks him to do something. "I would prefer not to," Bartleby says. That becomes his reply to every request. He would prefer not to. He would prefer not to work, not to file, not to obey, not to respond, *not* to. What he prefers to do is stand in the center of the office with his neck cocked at an odd angle, staring at the ceiling.

The boss is checkmated. Bartleby is not doing bad work; he isn't working at all. His refusal to work subverts the entire work ethic of the organization. Everyone in the office—Vivian, Rocky, Ernie, and the boss himself—would prefer not to work. But that way madness lies. Our civilization is founded on its ability to get people to do things they would prefer not to do.

Bartleby is set in the present day in a vast, monolithic office building that crouches atop a hill like an Acropolis dedicated to bureaucracy. It is based on "Bartleby the Scrivener," a famous story published in 1856 by Herman Melville, who not only wrote *Moby-Dick*, but also labored for many empty years as a clerk in a customs house. Although the story is nearly 150 years old, it is correct to observe, as A. O. Scott does in the *New York Times*, that Melville anticipated Kafka—and Dilbert. This kind of office work exists outside time.

David Paymer plays the boss, a sad-eyed man who has a private office of his own, its prestige undermined by the fact that his window directly overlooks a Dumpster. Glenne Headly is Vivian, who flirts because if a man shows interest in her, that may be evidence that she exists. Joe Piscopo is Rocky, who dresses flamboyantly to imply he is not as colorless as his job. Maury Chaykin is the hopeless nebbish Ernie, who elevates strategic incompetence to an art form.

And Crispin Glover is Bartleby. The teen star of the eighties appears here like a ghost, pale and immobile, arrested by some private grief or fear. When he says, "I would prefer not to," it doesn't sound like insubordination, rebellion, or resistance, but like a flat statement of fact—a fact so overwhelming it brings all possible alternatives to a dead halt.

The film has been directed by Jonathan Parker; he adapted the Melville story with Catherine DiNapoli. It's his first work, and a promising one. I admire it and yet cannot recommend it, because it overstays its natural running time. The Melville short story was short because it needed to be short—to make its point and then stop dead without compromise or consideration. *Bartleby* is short for a feature film, at eighty-two minutes, but might have been more successful at fifty or sixty minutes. Too bad there seems to be an unbreakable rule against features that short, or short subjects that long. In a perfect world, *Bartleby* would establish the office and its workers, introduce Bartleby, develop response to the work, and stop. Side stories, such as Vivian's attraction to the city manager (Seymour Cassel), would not be necessary.

And yet there is a kind of uncompromising, implacable simplicity to *Bartleby* that inspires admiration. In a world where most movies are about exciting people doing thrilling things, here is a film about a job that is living death, and a man who prefers not to do it. My friend McHugh worked his way through college at Acme Pest Control of Bloomington, Indiana. One day while he was crawling under a house with a spray gun, a housewife invited him into the kitchen for a lemonade. As he drank it, while covered in cobwebs and mud, she told her son, "Study your lessons hard, Jimmy, or you'll end up like him." Or like Bartleby.

Battlefield Earth ½★

PG-13, 117 m., 2000

John Travolta (Terl), Barry Pepper (Jonnie Goodboy Tyler), Forest Whitaker (Ker), Kim Coates (Carlo), Richard Tyson (Robert the Fox), Michael MacRae (District Manager Zete), Michael Byrne (Parson Staffer), Sean Hewitt (Heywood). Directed by Roger Christian and produced by Elie Samaha, Jonathan D. Krane, and John Travolta. Screenplay by Corey Mandell and J. D. Shapiro, based on the novel by L. Ron Hubbard.

Battlefield Earth is like taking a bus trip with someone who has needed a bath for a long time. It's not merely bad; it's unpleasant in a hostile way. The visuals are grubby and drab. The characters are unkempt and have rotten teeth. Breathing tubes hang from their noses like ropes of snot. The sound track sounds like the boom mike is being slammed against the inside of a fifty-five-gallon drum. The plot . . .

But let me catch my breath. This movie is awful in so many different ways. Even the opening titles are cheesy. Sci-fi epics usually begin with a stab at impressive titles, but this one just displays green letters on the screen in a type font that came with my Macintosh. Then the movie's subtitle unscrolls from left to right in the kind of "effect" you see in home movies.

It is the year 3000. The race of Psychlos have conquered Earth. Humans survive in scattered bands, living like actors auditioning for the sequel to *Quest for Fire*. Soon a few leave the wilderness and prowl through the ruins of theme parks and the city of Denver. The ruins have held up well after 1,000 years. (The books in the library are dusty but readable, and a flight simulator still works, although where it gets the electricity is a mystery.)

The hero, named Jonnie Goodboy Tyler, is played by Barry Pepper as a smart human who gets smarter thanks to a Psychlo gizmo that zaps his eyeballs with knowledge. He learns Euclidean geometry and how to fly a jet, and otherwise proves to be a quick learner for a caveman. The villains are two Psychlos named Terl (John Travolta) and Ker (Forest Whitaker).

Terl is head of security for the Psychlos, and has a secret scheme to use the humans as slaves to mine gold for him. He can't be reported to his superiors because (I am not making this up), he can blackmail his enemies with secret recordings that, in the event of his death, "would go straight to the home office!" Letterman fans laugh at that line; did the filmmakers know it was funny?

Jonnie Goodboy figures out a way to avoid slave labor in the gold mines. He and his men simply go to Fort Knox, break in, and steal it. Of course it's been waiting there for 1,000 years. What Terl says when his slaves hand him smelted bars of gold is beyond explanation. For stunning displays of stupidity, Terl takes the cake; as chief of security for the conquering aliens, he doesn't even know what humans eat, and devises an experiment: "Let it think it has escaped! We can sit back and watch it choose its food." Bad luck for the starving humans that they capture a rat. An experiment like that, you pray for a chicken.

Hiring Travolta and Whitaker was a waste of money, since we can't recognize them behind pounds of matted hair and gnarly makeup. Their costumes look purchased from the Goodwill store on Tatoine. Travolta can be charming, funny, touching, and brave in his best roles; why disguise him as a smelly alien creep? The Psychlos can fly between galaxies, but look at their nails: Their civilization has mastered the hyperdrive but not the manicure.

I am not against unclean characters—at least now that the threat of Smell-O-Vision no longer hangs over our heads. Lots of great movies have squalid heroes. But when the characters seem noxious on principle, we wonder if the art and costume departments were allowed to run wild.

Battlefield Earth was written in 1980 by L. Ron Hubbard, the founder of Scientology. The film contains no evidence of Scientology or any other system of thought; it is shapeless and senseless, without a compelling plot or characters we care for in the slightest. The director,

Roger Christian, has learned from better films that directors sometimes tilt their cameras, but he has not learned why.

Some movies run off the rails. This one is like the train crash in *The Fugitive*. I watched it in mounting gloom, realizing I was witnessing something historic, a film that for decades to come will be the punch line of jokes about bad movies. There is a moment here when the Psychlos' entire planet (home office and all) is blown to smithereens, without the slightest impact on any member of the audience (or, for that matter, the cast). If the film had been destroyed in a similar cataclysm, there might have been a standing ovation.

The Beach ★ ★
R, 119 m., 2000

Leonardo DiCaprio (Richard), Tilda Swinton (Sal), Virginie Ledoyen (Francoise), Guillaume Canet (Etienne), Robert Carlyle (Daffy), Paterson Joseph (Keaty), Lars Arentz Hansen (Bugs). Directed by Danny Boyle and produced by Andrew MacDonald. Screenplay by John Hodge, based on the book by Alex Garland.

The Beach is a seriously confused film that makes three or four passes at being a better one, and doesn't complete any of them. Since Leonardo DiCaprio is required to embody all of its shifting moods and aims, it provides him with more of a test than a better film might have; it's like a triathlon where every time he sights the finish line, they put him on a bicycle and send him out for another fifty miles.

The early scenes deliberately evoke the opening of *Apocalypse Now*, with its sweaty close-ups, its revolving ceiling fans, and its voice-overs by DiCaprio trying to sound like Martin Sheen. In a fleabag hotel in Bangkok, a fellow traveler (Robert Carlyle) tells him of an island paradise, hard to find but worth the trip. Will his journey borrow from a Joseph Conrad novel (*Victory*, say) as *Apocalypse Now* borrowed from *Heart of Darkness*?

No such luck, DiCaprio's character, named Richard, recruits a French couple in the next room, and as they set out for the legendary island, the movie abandons Conrad and *Apocalypse* and borrows instead from *The Blue Lagoon* on its way to a pothead version of *Lord of the Flies.* This is the kind of movie where the heroes are threatened by heavily armed guards in a marijuana field, and that's less alarming than when they jump off a ledge into a deep pool. Later they'll go swimming in glowing clouds of plankton, and Richard will face a shark in one-on-one combat.

Many of the scenes look, frankly, like time-fillers. Richard and his new French friends Francoise (Virginie Ledoyen) and Etienne (Guillaume Canet) arrive safely at a sort of retro hippie commune, where the pot is free, the bongos beat every night, and all is blissful on the beach, watched over by the stern eye of Sal (Tilda Swinton), the community's leader. It's paradise, Richard tells us—except for his lust for Francoise. So will this become a love triangle? No, because Francoise, once enjoyed, is forgotten, and besides, Etienne only wants her to be happy. Those French. A later encounter with Sal is more like plumbing than passion, and both sex scenes are arbitrary—they aren't important to the characters or the movie.

But then many of the sequences fall under the heading of good ideas at the time. Consider, for example, a strange interlude in which Richard becomes the hero of a video game, stomping through the landscape in computerized graphics. There is an echo here from *Trainspotting,* a better film by the same director, Danny Boyle, in which special effects are used to send the hero on a plunge into the depths of the world's filthiest toilet. There the effects worked as comic exaggeration; here they're just goofy.

What is important, I guess, is Richard's evolution from an American drifter in the Orient into a kind of self-appointed Tarzan, who takes to the jungle and trains himself, well aware that a movie so pointless and meandering will need contrived violence to justify the obligatory ending. In a paroxysm of indecision, the film's conclusion mixes action, existential resignation, the paradise-lost syndrome, and memories of happier days, the last possibly put in for studio executives who are convinced that no matter how grim a movie's outcome, it must end on a final upbeat. Watching *The Beach* is like experiencing a script conference where only sequences are discussed—never the whole film.

What is it about, anyway? There are the elements here for a romantic triangle, for a man-against-the-jungle drama, for a microcosm-of-civilization parable, or for a cautionary lesson about trying to be innocent in a cruel world. The little society ruled over by Sal is a benevolent dictatorship—you can be happy as long as you follow the rules—and that's material for satire or insight, I guess, although the movie offers none.

There is one extraordinary development. One of the commune guys is bitten by a shark, and when his anguished screams disturb the island idyll of the others, Sal simply has him moved out of earshot. This event suggests the makings of another, darker movie, but it's not allowed to pay off or lead to anything big.

Maybe that's because the whole film is seen so resolutely through Richard's eyes, and the movie doesn't want to insult its target demographic group or dilute DiCaprio's stardom by showing the character as the twit that he is. In a smarter film Richard would have been revealed as a narcissistic kid out of his depth, and maybe he would have ended up out in the woods where his screams couldn't be heard.

Beautiful ★
PG-13, 113 m., 2000

Minnie Driver (Mona Hibbard), Joey Lauren Adams (Ruby), Hallie Kate Eisenberg (Vanessa), Kathleen Turner (Verna Chickle), Leslie Stefanson (Joyce Parkins), Bridgette Wilson (Miss Texas), Kathleen Robertson (Miss Tenessee), Ali Landry (Belindy [Miss American Miss]). Directed by Sally Field and produced by John Bertolli and B. J. Rack. Screenplay by Jon Berstein.

Beautiful should have gone through lots and lots more rewrites before it was imposed on audiences. It's a movie with so many inconsistencies, improbabilities, unanswered questions, and unfinished characters that we have to suspend not only disbelief but intelligence.

The movie tells the story of Mona, a girl who dreams of becoming a beauty queen, and grows up to become obsessed with her dream. Her life is not without difficulties. As a child from Naperville, Illinois, she is graceless, wears braces, chooses costumes Miss Clarabell would not be seen in, cheats, and is insufferably self-centered. As an adult, played by Minnie Driver, she gets rid of the braces, but keeps right on cheating, until by the time she becomes Miss Illinois she has survived her fourth scandal.

Sample scandal. A competitor in a pageant plans to twirl a fire baton. Mona paints the baton with glue so the girl's hand gets stuck to it, and then dramatically races onstage to save the girl with a fire extinguisher. Don't they press criminal charges when you do things like that?

As a girl, Mona is best pals with Ruby, a girl who for no good reason adores her. As an adult, Ruby (now played by Joey Lauren Adams) works as a nurse but inexplicably devotes her life to Mona's career. Mona has had a child out of wedlock, but because beauty contestants aren't supposed to have kids, Ruby even agrees to pose as the little girl's mom.

Why? Why does Ruby devote her entire life to Mona and become a surrogate mother? Search me. Because the plot makes her, I guess. Mona has parents of her own, a mother and a stepfather who are sullen, unhelpful, drink too much, and spend most of their time being seen in unhelpful reaction shots. The screenplay is no help in explaining their personalities or histories. They're props.

Mona's daughter, Vanessa (Hallie Kate Eisenberg), is at least a life source within the dead film, screaming defiantly in frustration because Mona keeps forgetting to take her to her soccer games. She suspects Mona is her real mom, and seems fed up being used as a pawn (at one point she gets on the phone to order some foster parents).

And what about Joyce Parkins (Leslie Stefanson), a TV reporter who hates Mona? She knows Mona has a child and is planning to break the story, but no one who has watched television for as long as a day could conceivably believe her character or what she does. Consider the big Miss American Miss pageant, where Joyce keeps telling her viewers she's about to break a big scandal. She is obviously not on the same channel as the pageant, so she must be on another channel. What are that channel's viewers watching when Joyce is not talking? Joyce, I guess, since she addresses them in real time whenever she feels like it. The staging is so inept she is actually seen

eavesdropping on the pageant by placing her ear near to a wall. No press gallery? Not even a portable TV for her to watch?

As for Mona herself, Minnie Driver finds herself in an acting triathlon. Mona changes personalities, strategies, and IQ levels from scene to scene. There is no way that the Mona of the heartrending conclusion could develop from the Mona of the beginning and middle of the film, but never mind: Those Monas aren't possible, either. They're made of disconnected pieces, held together with labored plot furniture. (I was amazed at one point when people told Mona what the matter with her was, and then she went home and lay down on the sofa and we got flashback voice-overs as memories of the accusing voices echoed in her head. That device was dated in 1950.)

Driver would have been miscast even if the screenplay had been competent. She doesn't come across like the kind of person who could take beauty pageants seriously. Oddly enough, Joey Lauren Adams (the husky-voiced would-be girlfriend from *Chasing Amy*) could have played the beauty queen—and Driver could have played the pal.

And what about Ruby, the nurse played by Adams? She can't be at the big pageant because she's in jail accused of deliberately killing an elderly patient at a nursing home by giving her an overdose of pills. This would be too gruesome for a comedy if anything were done with it, but the death exists only as a plot gimmick—to explain why Ruby can't be there. The filmmakers have no sense of proportion; Ruby could just as easily have been stuck in a gas station with a flat tire and provided the same reaction shots (watching TV) in the climax. Why kill the sweet old lady?

Now consider. Mona has been involved in four scandals. She scarred one of her competitors for life. Her roommate and manager is in jail charged as an Angel of Death. A TV newswoman knows she has a secret child. What are the odds *any* beauty pageant would let that contestant onstage? With this movie, you can't ask questions like that. In fact, you can't ask any questions. This is Sally Field's first film as a director. The executives who greenlighted it did her no favors. You can't send a kid up in a crate like this.

Beautiful Creatures ★ ½
R, 88 m., 2001

Rachel Weisz (Petula), Susan Lynch (Dorothy), Iain Glen (Tony), Maurice Roeves (Ronnie McMinn), Alex Norton (Hepburn), Pauline Lynch (Sheena), Tom Mannion (Brian McMinn). Directed by Bill Eagles and produced by Simon Donald and Alan Wands. Screenplay by Donald.

I spent last week at the Conference on World Affairs at the University of Colorado, Boulder, where one of my fellow panelists created a stir by standing up and shouting that the women on his panel were "man-haters," and he was fed up and wasn't going to take it anymore.

He would have had apoplexy if he'd seen *Beautiful Creatures*, from Scotland. Here is a movie about two of the most loathsome women in recent cinema, and the movie thinks the male characters are the villains. It gets away with this only because we have been taught that women are to be presumed good and men are to be presumed evil. Flip the genders in this screenplay, and there would not be the slightest doubt that the characters named Petula and Dorothy are monsters.

Consider, for example, the setup. Dorothy (Susan Lynch) has been unwise enough to shack up with a boyfriend who is not only a junkie but also a golfer. This makes her a two-time loser. She pawns his golf clubs. He gets revenge by throwing her brassiere in boiling water, dyeing her dog pink, and stealing her money, which is from the pawned golf clubs. Any golfer (or junkie) will tell you that at this point, they are approximately morally even.

Dorothy leaves the house and comes upon a disturbance in the street. Petula (Rachel Weisz) is being beaten by Brian (Tom Mannion). Why is he doing this? Because the movie requires this demonstration of typical male behavior. Dorothy is already mad, and now she loses it. She slams Brian with a pipe to the back of the head, and the two women, instantly bonding, carry his unconscious body to Dorothy's flat, where they share a joint while Brian dies in the bathtub. "You just get sick listening to all that gonna (bleeping) kill you stuff," Dorothy explains.

Imagine a scene where a man slams a woman with a pipe, and then joins her boyfriend in dragging the body into the bathtub and sharing a joint while she dies. Difficult. Even more difficult in a comedy, which, I neglected to mention, *Beautiful Creatures* intends to be. But I don't want to get mired in male outrage. Men are more violent than women, yes, and guilty of abuse, yes, although the percentage of male monsters is incalculably higher in the movies than in life. Like Thelma and Louise, Dorothy and Petula commit crimes that are morally justifiable because of their gender. We even like them for it. They have to conceal the death, for example, because "no one would believe" they had not committed murder. My own theory is that any jury in Scotland would believe their story that the man was violent and Dorothy had come to the defense of a sister.

The movie, set in Glasgow and one of the many offspring of *Trainspotting*, uses local color for a lot of its gags. Instead of picketing *The Sopranos*, Italian-Americans should protest the new wave of films from Scotland, which indicate Scots make funnier, more violent, more eccentric, and more verbal gangsters than they do. Films and TV shows that portray ethnic groups as interesting and colorful are generally a plus, since those viewers dumb enough to think every story is an "accurate portrait" are beyond our help anyway.

The plot. The dead man has a brother who is a rich bad guy. The women cut off the corpse's finger and send it with a ransom demand. A detective (Alex Norton) comes to investigate, gets in on the scheme, and alters it with designs of his own. Meanwhile, the junkie boyfriend turns up again, and one thing leads to another. You know how it is.

There is some dark humor in the movie, of the kind where you laugh that you may not gag. And the kind of convoluted plotting that seems obligatory in crime films from Scotland (consider *Shallow Grave*). I am not really offended by the movie's gender politics, since I am accustomed to the universal assumption in pop (and academic) culture that women are in possession of truth and goodness and men can only benefit from learning from them. In fact, if the movie had been able to make me laugh, I might have forgiven it almost anything.

A Beautiful Mind ★ ★ ★ ★
PG-13, 129 m., 2001

Russell Crowe (John Forbes Nash Jr.), Ed Harris
(William Parcher), Jennifer Connelly (Alicia
Nash), Paul Bettany (Charles), Adam Goldberg
(Sol), Austin Pendleton (Thomas King), Vivien
Cardone (Marcee), Judd Hirsch (Helinger),
Christopher Plummer (Dr. Rosen). Directed by
Ron Howard and produced by Brian Grazer
and Howard. Screenplay by Akiva Goldsman,
based on the book by Sylvia Nasar.

The Nobel Prize winner John Forbes Nash Jr.
still teaches at Princeton and walks to campus
every day. That these commonplace statements nearly brought tears to my eyes suggests the power of *A Beautiful Mind,* the story
of a man who is one of the greatest mathematicians, and a victim of schizophrenia. Nash's
discoveries in game theory have an impact on
our lives every day. He also believed for a time
that the Russians were sending him coded messages on the front page of the *New York Times.*

A *Beautiful Mind* stars Russell Crowe as Nash,
and Jennifer Connelly as his wife, Alicia, who
is pregnant with their child when the first
symptoms of his disease become apparent. It
tells the story of a man whose mind was of
enormous service to humanity while at the
same time betraying him with frightening
delusions. Crowe brings the character to life
by sidestepping sensationalism and building
with small behavioral details. He shows a man
who descends into madness and then, unexpectedly, regains the ability to function in the
academic world. Nash has been compared to
Newton, Mendel, and Darwin, but was also
for many years just a man muttering to himself in the corner.

Director Ron Howard is able to suggest a
core of goodness in Nash that inspired his
wife and others to stand by him, to keep hope,
and, in her words in his darkest hour, "to believe that something extraordinary is possible."
The movie's Nash begins as a quiet but cocky
young man with a West Virginia accent, who
gradually turns into a tortured, secretive paranoid who believes he is a spy being trailed by
government agents. Crowe, who has an uncanny ability to modify his look to fit a role,

always seems convincing as a man who ages
forth-seven years during the film.

The early Nash, seen at Princeton in the late
1940s, calmly tells a scholarship winner, "There
is not a single seminal idea on either of your
papers." When he loses at a game of Go, he
explains: "I had the first move. My play was
perfect. The game is flawed." He is aware of his
impact on others ("I don't much like people,
and they don't much like me") and recalls that
his first-grade teacher said he was "born with
two helpings of brain and a half-helping of
heart."

It is Alicia who helps him find the heart. She
is a graduate student when they meet, is attracted to his genius, is touched by his loneliness, is able to accept his idea of courtship
when he informs her, "Ritual requires we proceed with a number of platonic activities before we have sex." To the degree that he can be
touched, she touches him, although often he
seems trapped inside himself; Sylvia Nasar,
who wrote the 1998 biography that informs
Akiva Goldsman's screenplay, begins her book
by quoting Wordsworth about "a mind forever
voyaging through strange seas of thought
alone."

Nash's schizophrenia takes a literal, visual
form. He believes he is being pursued by a federal agent (Ed Harris), and finds himself in
chase scenes that seem inspired by 1940s crime
movies. He begins to find patterns where no
patterns exist. One night he and Alicia stand
under the sky and he asks her to name any object, and then connects stars to draw it. Romantic, but it's not so romantic when she
discovers his office thickly papered with countless bits torn from newspapers and magazines
and connected by frantic lines into imaginary
patterns.

The movie traces his treatment by an understanding psychiatrist (Christopher Plummer), and his agonizing courses of insulin
shock therapy. Medication helps him improve
somewhat—but only, of course, when he takes
the medication. Eventually newer drugs are
more effective, and he begins a tentative re-
entry into the academic world at Princeton.

The movie fascinated me about the life of
this man, and I sought more information,
finding that for many years he was a recluse,

wandering the campus, talking to no one, drinking coffee, smoking cigarettes, paging through piles of newspapers and magazines. And then one day he paid a quite ordinary compliment to a colleague about his daughter, and it was noticed that Nash seemed better.

There is a remarkable scene in the movie when a representative for the Nobel committee (Austin Pendleton) comes visiting, and hints that Nash is being "considered" for the prize. Nash observes that people are usually informed they have won, not that they are being considered: "You came here to find out if I am crazy and would screw everything up if I won." He did win, and did not screw everything up.

The movies have a way of pushing mental illness into corners. It is grotesque, sensational, cute, funny, willful, tragic, or perverse. Here it is simply a disease, which renders life almost but not quite impossible for Nash and his wife, before he becomes one of the lucky ones to pull out of the downward spiral.

When he won the Nobel, Nash was asked to write about his life, and he was honest enough to say his recovery is "not entirely a matter of joy." He observes: "Without his 'madness,' Zarathustra would necessarily have been only another of the millions or billions of human individuals who have lived and then been forgotten." Without *his* madness, would Nash have also lived and then been forgotten? Did his ability to penetrate the most difficult reaches of mathematical thought somehow come with a price attached? The movie does not know and cannot say.   ☞

Beautiful People ★ ★ ★
R, 107 m., 2000

Charlotte Coleman (Portia Thornton), Charles Kay (George Thornton), Rosalind Ayres (Nora Thornton), Roger Sloman (Roger Midge), Heather Tobias (Felicity Midge), Danny Nussbaum (Griffin Midge), Siobhan Redmond (Kate Higgins), Gilbert Martin (Jerry Higgins). Directed by Jasmin Dizdar and produced by Ben Woolford. Screenplay by Dizdar.

A man boards a London bus, locks eyes with another man, and immediately starts to fight with him. Thrown off the bus, they chase each other through the streets and eventually end up in adjacent hospital beds, still ready to fight. One is a Croat, one is a Serb, and so they hate each other.

Ah, but hate is not limited to Bosnians. In the next bed is the Welsh firebomber, a man who torched the holiday cottages of twenty English weekenders before burning himself on the face. Elsewhere in *Beautiful People* we see three skinheads attacking a black kid, and a foreigner who is mistaken for a thief while trying to return a wallet, and the beat goes on even at the breakfast tables of the ruling class: "God!" says the wife of a government official, "Antonia Fraser is so bloody Catholic."

Beautiful People, written and directed in London by the Bosnian filmmaker Jasmin Dizdar, is about people who hate because of tribal affiliation, which is a different thing than hating somebody you know personally and have good reasons to despise. One of its interlocking stories involves a pregnant Bosnian woman who wants an abortion because her baby, the product of a rape, "is my enemy."

The movie loops and doubles back among several stories and characters, like Robert Altman's *Short Cuts* or Paul Thomas Anderson's *Magnolia*. The insights in one story cast light on the problems of another, and sometimes the characters meet—as when a young woman doctor falls in love with a patient, and brings him home to meet her stuffy family. Nor are the moral judgments uncomplicated. Although she explodes when her family condescends to the man, the fact remains that he speaks only about six words of English, and so her own affection for him is condescending too.

The most involving story involves a young heroin addict named Griffin (Danny Nussbaum), who has always been a trial for his parents ("Remember sixth form," his father asks, "when all of the teachers went on strike because no one wanted to teach him?"). As part of an involved attempt to attend a football match, Griffin stumbles onto an airfield, falls asleep on an air freight pallet, and is dropped by parachute into Bosnia as part of an airlift of UN aid supplies.

This has the aroma of an urban legend to it, like the scuba diver who was scooped up by a fire-fighting airplane and dumped onto a forest fire. In *Beautiful People,* it works like one of those fairy tales where a naughty child gets his comeuppance by trading places with one less fortunate. Here what happens is that Griffin, dazed and withdrawing, stumbles around the war zone and ends up behaving rather well.

There is another character stumbling there, too: a BBC war correspondent who loses his mind in the chaos of blood and suffering. Shipped home, he tries to check himself into a hospital to have his leg amputated; he has "Bosnian Syndrome," a doctor whispers, and perhaps he feels guilty to have two legs when so many do not.

I have made the film sound grim. Actually it is fairly lighthearted, under the circumstances; like *Catch-22,* it enjoys the paradoxes that occur when you try to apply logic to war. Consider the sequence where the foreigner walks into a café, annoys a British woman with his friendliness, and then, after she stalks out, he sees she has forgotten her billfold. He runs after her, is mistaken for a madman, and is injured in traffic. Another urban legend? Not if you saw the story only last week about a black taxi passenger in Chicago whose innocent presence so terrified his immigrant driver that the cabbie careened at top speed down one-way streets looking for a cop.

Why are we so suspicious of one another? It may be a trait hard-wired by evolution: If you're not in my tribe, you may want to eat my dinner or steal my mate. The irony about those two Bosnian patients, fighting each other in the London hospital, is that they're the only two people in the building who speak the same language. So to speak.

Beauty and the Beast ★ ★ ★ ★
G, 94 m., revised 2002

With the voices of: Paige O'Hara (Belle), Robby Benson (Beast), Richard White (Gaston), Jerry Orbach (Lumiere), David Ogden Stiers (Cogsworth), Angela Lansbury (Mrs. Potts), Jesse Corti (LeFou). Directed by Gary Trousdale and Kirk Wise and produced by Don Hahn. Art direction by Brian McEntee. Animation screenplay by Linda Woolverton.

With *The Little Mermaid* (1989) and *Beauty and the Beast* (1991), Disney in two strokes reinvented the animated feature and the movie musical. Both genres were languishing in the 1980s—musicals seemed like a lost art—and these two films brought them to a new kind of life. All the big animated hits since *(The Lion King, Aladdin, Toy Story, Monsters, Inc., Shrek)* descend from that original breakthrough, which blasted animated films out of the kiddie-film category and saw them, as Walt Disney originally saw them, as popular entertainments for all ages.

The Little Mermaid was the film that reminded audiences how entertaining animation could be, and *Beauty and the Beast* was the breakthrough—the first animated film to win an Oscar nomination in the Best Picture category. Disney itself groups the film with *Snow White* and *Pinocchio* as one of its three best. Now *Beauty* is back, in a new version so vibrant it's like experiencing the film anew. For its engagements on giant IMAX screens around the country, the movie has received a frame-by-frame restoration (since even the tiniest blemish isn't tiny on an IMAX screen). The sound track has been prepped for IMAX's seventy-four-speaker surround sound. And there's even new footage.

"Human Again," the added footage, is not a "deleted scene" that has been added to this rerelease in the spirit of countless recent "director's cuts." Although a scene is occasionally dropped from an animated film, the preplanning that goes into them, and the labor-intensive nature of the work, make it rare for scenes to be fully animated and then cut. What Disney started with was an original song by Howard Ashman and Alan Menken, written for the *Beauty and the Beast* score but then dropped from the screenplay. The song was put back in for the Broadway stage version of *Beauty,* was a hit, and belatedly won a place in the movie. It has now been animated for the first time.

The new scene stars three of the Beast's household servants, who fell under the same curse as their master, and were transformed into (hardly inanimate) objects. Lumiere (voice by Jerry Orbach) is a candelabra, Cogsworth (David Ogden Stiers) is the clock, and Mrs. Potts (Angela Lansbury) is the teapot (Chip, of course, is her son, the teacup). Joined by a chorus line of other household utensils, products, and tools, they sing in anticipation of being restored to human form if the Beast makes his deadline and falls in love with Belle before the last petal falls from the enchanted rose.

Sitting in front of the IMAX screen, I was reminded again that the giant format is a major part of the experience. There is a theory that quick cuts in such a large format tend to disorient the audience, and many IMAX films move in a stately manner from one static composition to another, but the quick pace of *Beauty* presented no problems. To be sure, the picture was not originally filmed with IMAX cameras, but this restoration is not a blowup of an existing 35mm print; it's a digital re-creation of it for the bigger screen.

Disney pioneered this form of giant-screen rerelease with its *Fantasia 2000* (1999). Seeing *Beauty and the Beast* again this way, I began to daydream about other classics that could be showcased on IMAX. The year 2001 came and went without a proper national rerelease of *2001: A Space Odyssey,* and although Francis Ford Coppola's *Apocalypse Now Redux* got somewhat more exposure, imagine it on the giant screen. As the average American movie screen grows smaller and smaller, as palaces are phased out for multiplexes, why isn't IMAX the natural home for the great Hollywood epics?

Bedazzled ★ ★
PG-13, 93 m., 2000

Brendan Fraser (Elliot Richards), Elizabeth Hurley (The Devil), Frances O'Connor (Alison Gardner), Orlando Jones (Dan), Miriam Shor (Carol), Paul Adelstein (Bob), Toby Huss (Jerry). Directed by Harold Ramis and produced by Ramis and Trevor Albert. Screenplay by Ramis, Peter Tolan, and Larry Gelbart.

Watching *Bedazzled,* I was reminded of the ancient newspaper legend about the reporter sent to cover the Johnstown Flood. "God stood on a mountaintop," he wrote, "and saw what his flood waters had wrought." His editor cabled back: "Forget flood. Interview God." Why was I remembering this old story? Because, in the new comedy *Bedazzled,* Brendan Fraser falls in love with Frances O'Connor and, to win her, sells his soul to the devil, who

is played by Elizabeth Hurley. Forget girl, I'm thinking. Seduce Satan.

Not that Hurley is that good a Satan—just that she's the ranking babe in this movie. As Satan, she seems too composed and collected. A certain zaniness is required; Satan must have been quite a madcap to leave heaven in order to spend eternity as a troublemaker. In the original *Bedazzled* (1967), Peter Cook played Satan and Raquel Welch played Lust, one of the seven deadly sins. That seven-to-one ratio between Satan's evil genius and its sinful building blocks is, I think, about right.

The new movie has been directed by Harold Ramis from a screenplay that uses the 1967 film more as inspiration than source. It is lacking in wickedness. It doesn't smack its lips when it's naughty. When its hero sells his soul to the devil, what results isn't diabolical effrontery, but a series of contract negotiations and consumer complaints.

The movie stars Brendan Fraser as Elliot, an office nerd whose goofy grin and effusive banalities send his coworkers into hiding. For three years he has dreamed of the lovely Alison (Frances O'Connor, splendid in *Mansfield Park*), who barely notices him. Then he meets the devil with a red dress on: This is Hurley, who offers him the standard contract, seven wishes for his soul. What always goes wrong with these deals is that the human words his request in the wrong way, and the sneaky devil tricks him. This is bad business. Since Satan wants to win souls, he (or she) should deliver magnificently on every promise, so that by number four or five the satisfied customers are telling their friends, and Satan is getting pass-along business.

Fraser is a wonderful comic actor—better than he gets the credit for, because he creates funny characters instead of exploding in what is intended as funny behavior. Here he finds himself reincarnated (or remodulated, or whatever the process is called) as a Colombian drug lord, a bucktoothed New Age nice guy, an NBA star, Abraham Lincoln, and so on. He's often very funny; I liked the courtside interview after an NBA game where he drips buckets of sweat.

The problem with his seven wishes and their associated interludes is that they're not funny enough, consistently enough. The double-

51

cross after every wish works like a punch line that comes before the joke. He requests, we see what went wrong, and then the movie lingers too long while developing the situation.

Why not some twists and U-turns? What if Elliot figured out how to word the perfect wish? ("You, as Satan, already know what would really make me happy. I want you to grant it unconditionally, without loopholes.") There's a hint of that in the scene where he asks to be made the world's most sensitive man, and finds himself in an alternative universe where Alison loves him, but is bored by how sensitive he is: "I want a life with a man who will ignore me and take me for granted and only pretend to be interested in me to get in my pants."

Funny, but the movie never reaches escape velocity, and Elizabeth Hurley is too calm to be the devil. She lacks abandon, risk, and maniacal self-amusement. She doesn't crank it up enough. I was reminded of another old story, about the time Jack L. Warner heard that Ronald Reagan was thinking of running for president. "That can't be right," he said. "Ronald Reagan for best friend. Jimmy Stewart for president." Walking out of the screening, I was thinking: Elizabeth Hurley for girlfriend, Courtney Love for Satan.

Before Night Falls ★ ★ ★ ½
R, 143 m., 2001

Javier Bardem (Reinaldo Arenas), Olivier Martinez (Lazaro Gomez Carilles), Andrea Di Stefano (Pepe Malas), Johnny Depp ("Bon Bon"/Lieutenant Victor), Sean Penn (Cuco Sanchez), Michael Wincott (Herberto Zorilla Ochoa), Najwa Nimri (Fina Correa), Vito Maria Schnabel (Teenage Reinaldo). Directed by Julian Schnabel and produced by Jon Kilik. Screenplay by Cunningham O'Keefe, Lazaro Gomez Carilles, and Schnabel, based on the memoirs of Reinaldo Arenas.

Born into crushing poverty in pre-Castro Cuba, young Reinaldo Arenas was told by a teacher than he had a gift for poetry. When his father heard this news, he slammed his fist down on the table and beat the boy. That more or less sets the pattern for Arenas's life: He tries to exercise his gifts as a poet and a

novelist, and society slaps him down. It doesn't help that he's a homosexual.

Arenas believed the great betrayal in his life was by Fidel Castro. As a teenager, Reinaldo hitchhiked to the hills and joined the revolution, but once Castro came to power he showed little sympathy for artists and none for homosexuals. Arenas was an outcast and for seven years a prisoner in Cuba—until 1980, when he took advantage of the boat exodus for criminals, gays, the mentally ill, and others considered unfit to be Cubans. Ten years later, in Manhattan, dying of AIDS, he committed suicide, using pills and (just to be sure) a plastic "I Love NY" bag over his head.

Before Night Falls tells the story of Arenas's life through the words of his work and the images of Julian Schnabel's imagination. Schnabel, the painter, makes his screen a rich canvas of dream sequences, fragmented childhood memories, and the wild Cuban demimonde inhabited by Arenas and others who do not conform. There is no sequence more startling than one where Arenas stumbles onto a ragtag commune of refuseniks and finds that in the roofless ruin of an old cathedral they are building a hot-air balloon with which they hope to float to Florida. The balloon actually makes one brief flight. Did this episode actually happen? I would like to think that it did.

This is Schnabel's second film, and his second about an artist who is also a moody, difficult outcast. The first film was *Basquiat* (1996), about Jean Michel Basquiat, the Manhattan graffiti artist who rose briefly from homelessness to fame before sinking into madness. Arenas describes a similar trajectory. For both men, joy seems to come primarily at those moments when they are actually creating. Sex (for Arenas) and drugs (for Basquiat) are a way to avoid work, loneliness, and pain, but they lead to trouble, not release. Arenas claimed to have slept with 5,000 men by the age of twenty-five. That is not the record of a man who finds sex satisfying, but of one who does not.

Arenas is played by Javier Bardem, a Spanish actor with a specialty in macho heterosexuality (if you doubt me, see *Jamon, Jamon*). He doesn't play Arenas as a gay man so much as a man whose body fits like the wrong suit of clothes. We accept Arenas as gay in the movie because the story says he is, and because there are after all no rules about how a homosexual should look or behave—but there is somehow the feeling that the movie's Arenas is not gay from the inside out, but has chosen the lifestyle as part of a compulsion to defy Castro in every way possible. The film contains two more-convincing homosexual characters, both played by Johnny Depp: Lieutenant Victor, a sleek, tight-trousered military officer, and "Bon Bon," a flamboyant transvestite who struts through Castro's prisons and proves incredibly useful by smuggling out one of Arenas's manuscripts, concealing it in that place where most of us would be most inconvenienced by a novel, however brilliant.

What is most heroic about Arenas is his stubbornness. He could make his life easier with a little discretion, a little cunning, a little tact, and even a small ability to tell the authorities what they want to hear. There must have been a lot of gay men in Cuba who didn't make their lives as impossible as Arenas did. Consider the character of Diego, in *Strawberry and Chocolate,* the 1993 movie by the great Cuban director Tomas Gutierrez Alea. The movie is set in 1979, Diego is clearly gay, and yet he lives more or less as he wants to, because he is clever and discreet.

There is a little something of the spoiled masochist about Arenas. One would not say he seeks misery, but he wears it like a badge of honor, and we can see his mistakes approaching before he does. This is not a weakness in the film but one of its intriguing strengths: Arenas is not presented as a cliché, as the heroic gay artist crushed by totalitarian straightness, but as a man who might have been approximately as unhappy no matter where he was born. That angle between Arenas and his society is perhaps what inspired his work. Trapped on the margin, he wrote in spite of everything, and the anguish of creation was a source of energy. One is reminded a little of the Marquis de Sade, as portrayed in *Quills.* It was never simply what they wrote, but that, standing outside convention, taunting the authorities, inhabiting impossible lives, they wrote at all.

Behind Enemy Lines ★ ½
PG-13, 93 m., 2001

Owen Wilson (Burnett), Gene Hackman (Reigart), Joaquim de Almeida (Piquet), Vladimir Mashkov (Tracker), David Keith (O'Malley), Olek Krupa (Lokar), Eyal Podell (Kennedy), Gabriel Macht (Stackhouse). Directed by John Moore and produced by John Davis. Screenplay by David Veloz and Zak Penn, based on a story by Jim Thomas and John Thomas.

The premiere of *Behind Enemy Lines* was held aboard the aircraft carrier USS *Carl Vinson.* I wonder if it played as a comedy. Its hero is so reckless and its villains so incompetent that it's a showdown between a man begging to be shot, and an enemy that can't hit the side of a Bosnian barn. This is not the story of a fugitive trying to sneak through enemy terrain and be rescued, but of a movie character magically transported from one photo opportunity to another.

Owen Wilson stars as Burnett, a hotshot navy flier who "signed up to be a fighter pilot—not a cop on a beat no one cares about." On a recon mission over Bosnia, he and his partner, Stackhouse (Gabriel Macht), venture off mission and get digital photos of a mass grave and illegal troop movements. It's a Serbian operation in violation of a fresh peace treaty, and the Serbs fire two missiles to bring the plane down. The plane's attempts to elude the missiles supply the movie's high point.

The pilots eject. Stackhouse is found by Tracker (Vladimir Mashkov), who tells his commander, Lokar (Olek Krupa), to forget about a big pursuit and simply allow him to track Burnett. That sets up the cat-and-mouse game in which Burnett wanders through open fields, stands on the tops of ridges, and stupidly makes himself a target, while Tracker is caught in one of those nightmares where he runs and runs but just can't seem to catch up.

Back on the USS *Vinson*, Admiral Reigart (Gene Hackman) is biting his lower lip. He wants to fly in and rescue Burnett, but is blocked by his NATO superior, Admiral Piquet (Joaquim de Almeida)—who is so devious he substitutes NATO troops for Americans in a phony rescue mission, and calls them off just when Burnett is desperately waving from a pickup area.

Admiral Piquet, who sounds French, is played by a Portuguese actor.

The first-time director is John Moore, who has made lots of TV commercials, something we intuit in a scene where Reigart orders Burnett to proceed to another pickup area, and Burnett visualizes fast-motion whooshing tracking shots up and down mountains and through valleys before deciding, uh-uh, he ain't gonna do that.

What Burnett does do is stroll through Bosnia like a bird-watcher, exposing himself in open areas and making himself a silhouette against the skyline. He's only spotted in the first place because when his buddy is cornered, he's hiding safely but utters a loud involuntary yell and then starts to run up an exposed hillside. First rule of not getting caught: No loud involuntary yells within the hearing of the enemy.

This guy is a piece of work. Consider the scene where Burnett substitutes uniforms with a Serbian fighter. He even wears a black ski mask covering his entire face. He walks past a truck of enemy troops, and then what does he do? Why, he *removes the ski mask,* revealing his distinctive blond hair, and then he *turns back toward the truck* so we can see his face, in case we didn't know who he was. How did this guy get through combat training? Must have been a social promotion to keep him with his age group.

At times Burnett is pursued by the entire Serbian army, which fires at him with machine guns, rifles, and tanks, of course never hitting him. The movie recycles the old howler where hundreds of rounds of ammo miss the hero, but all he has to do is aim and fire, and—pow! another bad guy jerks back, dead. I smiled during the scene where Admiral Reigart is able to use heat-sensitive satellite imagery to look at high-res silhouettes of Burnett stretched out within feet of the enemy. Maybe this is possible. What I do not believe is that the enemies in this scene could not spot the American uniform in a pile of enemy corpses.

Do I need to tell you that the ending involves a montage of rueful grins, broad smiles, and meaningful little victorious nods, scored with upbeat rock music? No, probably not. And of course we get shots of the characters and are told what happened to them after the story was over—as if this is based on real events. It may have been inspired by the adventures of air force pilot Scott O'Grady, who was rescued after being shot down over Bosnia in 1995, but based on real life, it's not. ☞

Behind the Sun ★ ★
PG-13, 94 m., 2002

Jose Dumont (Father), Rodrigo Santoro (Tonio), Rita Assemany (Mother), Ravi Ramos Lacerda (Pacu), Luis Carlos Vasconcelos (Salustiano), Flavia Marco Antonio (Clara), Everaldo De Souza Pontes (Old Blind Man). Directed by Walter Salles and produced by Arthur Cohn. Screenplay by Karim Ainouz and Sergio Machado.

Behind the Sun describes a blood feud elevated to the dignity of tragedy. It takes place in a rural area of Brazil, but it could be set instead in the Middle East, in Bosnia, in India, in Africa, in any of those places where people kill each other because of who their parents were.

Religion, which is often cited as a justification for these killings, is just a smoke screen for tribalism. The killings spring out of a universal human tendency to dislike anyone who is not like we are.

The movie takes place in 1910. Two families live on either side of a cane field. The Ferreiras are richer, live in a sprawling villa, have an extended family. The Breves are poorer, humble, hardworking. Since time immemorial there has been a feud between these two families, springing from some long-forgotten disagreement over land. Over time a set of ground rules has grown up: First a Ferreira man (or a Breves man) kills a Breves (or a Ferreira) man, and then the tables are turned.

If it amounted only to that, all the Breves and Ferreiras would be dead, or one side would have won. Certain customs somewhat slow the pace of the killing. When someone has been killed, his bloodstained shirt is left out in the sun to dry, and there is a truce until the red has turned yellow. Despite the predictable timetable that would seem to operate, the next victim is somehow always unprepared, as we see when a young Breves stalks his quarry one night after a shirt has turned yellow.

We meet the Kid (Ravi Ramos Lacerda), youngest son of the Breves family, who knows that since his adored older brother Tonio (Rodrigo Santoro) has killed a Ferreira, it is only a matter of time until the blood fades and Tonio is killed. While the ominous waiting period continues, a troupe of itinerant circus performers passes through, and the Kid meets the ringmaster and his sultry fire-eating star. They give him a picture book about the sea, which, wouldn't you know, encourages him to dream about a world different from the one he knows.

The circus itself offers an alternative vision, not that the cheerless sugar cane feud doesn't make anything look preferable. Tonio meets the fire-breather and is thunderstruck by love, and there is the possibility that, yes, he might run away with the circus. More than this I dare not reveal, except to hint that the age-old fate of the two families must play out under the implacable sun.

Behind the Sun is a good-looking movie, directed by Walter Salles, who was much praised for his 1998 Oscar nominee *Central Station,* also about a young boy whose life is scarred by the cruelty of his elders. It has some of the simplicity and starkness of classical tragedy, but what made me impatient was its fascination with the macho blood lust of the two families. Since neither family has evolved to the point where it can see the futility of killing and the pointlessness of their deadly ritual, it was hard for me to keep from feeling they were getting what they deserved. Sure, I hoped Tonio would get the girl and the Kid would see the ocean, but these are limited people and we can care about them only if we buy into their endless cycle of revenge and reprisal. After a certain point no one is right and no one is wrong, both sides have boundless grievances, and it's the audience that wants to run away with the circus.

The Believer ★ ★ ★
R, 98 m., 2002

Ryan Gosling (Danny Balint), Summer Phoenix (Carla Moebius), Theresa Russell (Lina Moebius), Billy Zane (Curtis Zampf), A. D. Miles (Guy Danielson), Joshua Harto (Kyle), Glenn Fitzgerald (Drake), Garret Dillahunt (Billings). Directed by Henry Bean and produced by Susan Hoffman and Christopher Roberts. Screenplay by Bean.

Censors feel *they* are safe with objectionable material, but must protect others who are not as smart or moral. The same impulse tempts the reviewer of *The Believer.* Here is a fiercely controversial film about a Jew who becomes an anti-Semite. When I saw it at Sundance 2000, where it won the Grand Jury Prize, I wrote, "Some feared the film could do more harm than good." I shared those fears. The film's hero is so articulate in his retailing of anti-Semitic beliefs that his words, I thought, might find the wrong ears. I understand the film, I was saying—but are you to be trusted with it?

Certainly the movie has been a hot potato. After a screening at the Simon Weisenthal Center inspired audience members to protest it, no major distributor would pick it up. Showtime scheduled it for a cable showing, which was canceled in the aftermath of 9/11. Then it was finally shown in the spring, and now has theatrical distribution from small Fireworks Pictures. In the meantime, to its Sundance awards it has added Independent Spirit Awards for best screenplay and best first feature (both to director Henry Bean), best actor (Ryan Gosling), and best supporting actress (Summer Phoenix). Few doubt it is a good film. But do we really need a movie, right now, about a Jewish neo-Nazi?

I am not the person to answer that question for you. You have to answer it for yourself. The film's anti-Semitism is articulate but evil, and the conflict between what the hero says and what he believes (or does not want to believe) is at the very center of the story.

Gosling's character, named Danny Balint, is based on a real person. The *Jerusalem Report* writes: "The film has its roots in a true story. Daniel Burros was a nice Jewish boy from Queens who somehow went from being his rabbi's star pupil to a hotheaded proponent of the long-defunct Third Reich. After a stint in the army, he became involved with the American Nazi Party and the Ku Klux Klan. In 1965, following Burros's arrest at a KKK event in New York City, the *New York Times* disclosed that he was Jewish. Hours after the paper hit the stands, Burros took his own life."

In the film, Danny is seen as a bright young yeshiva student who gets into impassioned arguments with his teachers. Why must Abraham sacrifice his son Isaac? What kind of a God would require such an act? "A conceited bully,"

Danny decides. As a young man, Danny rejects his Orthodox upbringing, confronts Jews on the street and in subway cars, beats and kicks one, and expresses contempt for a race which, as he sees it, did not fight back during the Holocaust. Eventually he falls into the orbit of a neo-Nazi organization run by Theresa Russell and Billy Zane, who are impressed by his rhetoric but want him to dial down on the subject of Judaism: "It doesn't play anymore."

For Danny, anti-Semitism and the self-hate it implies is the whole point; he is uninterested in the politics of fascism. For Danny, the weakness of Jews is what he sees as their willingness to be victims, and after a court assigns him to an encounter group with Holocaust survivors, he bluntly asks one why he didn't fight back. Israelis, he believes, are not Jews because they own their own land and defend it, and therefore have transcended their Jewishness. You can see this reasoning twisting back into his own unhappy soul; he objects to Abraham taking instructions from God, and he objects to taking instructions from his church. His values involve his muscles, his fighting ability (both physical and rhetorical), his willingness to confront. In some kind of sick way, he attacks Jews, hoping to inspire one to beat him up.

Ryan Gosling (who, incredibly, was a Mouseketeer contemporary of Britney Spears), is at twenty-two a powerful young actor. He recently starred in *Murder by Numbers* as one of two young killers resembling Leopold and Loeb in their desire to demonstrate their superiority by committing a perfect crime. In *The Believer,* he reminds us of Edward Norton in *American History X,* another movie about a bright, twisted kid who is attracted to the transgressive sickness of racism. The movie is not very convincing in its portrayal of the fascist group (Zane and Russell seem less like zealots than hobbyists), but his personal quest is real enough.

When he involves himself in a raid on a temple, there is a revealing paradox: He resents the skinheads who come along with him because they don't understand the traditions they are attacking. What good is it to desecrate the Torah if you don't know what it is? He knows, and we begin to understand that he cares, that he accepts Judaism in the very core of his soul, and that his fight is against himself.

The ending of *The Believer,* if not exactly open, is inconclusive, and this is the kind of movie where you need to budget in time afterward for a cup of coffee and some conversation. The movie is better at portraying Danny's daily reality than at making sense of his rebellion (if sense can be made), but perhaps the movie plus the discussion can add up to a useful experience. Although his film needs more clarity and focus, Henry Bean has obviously taken a big chance because of his own sincere concerns. And if the wrong people get the wrong message—well, there has never been any shortage of wrong messages. Or wrong people.

Best in Show ★ ★ ★ ½
PG-13, 90 m., 2000

Jennifer Coolidge (Sherri Ann Ward Cabot), John Michael Higgins (Scott Donlan), Michael Hitchcock (Hamilton Swan), Eugene Levy (Gerry Fleck), Jane Lynch (Christy Cummings), Michael McKean (Stefan Vanderhoof), Catherine O'Hara (Cookie Fleck), Parker Posey (Meg Swan), Fred Willard (Buck Laughlin), Christopher Guest (Harlan Pepper). Directed by Christopher Guest and produced by Karen Murphy. Screenplay by Guest and Eugene Levy.

I am a dog lover, but I am not a dog fancier. I can understand people who dote on their dogs, but I cannot understand dog shows, which make dogs miserable while bringing out the worst traits of their owners. Dogs were not put on Earth to pose, prance, sit, point, and have their coats shampooed. They were created to chew shoes, bark at cars, have accidents on the rug, and get their tummies scratched.

That's why I approve of *Best in Show,* a wickedly funny mocumentary by Christopher Guest that makes fun of a Philadelphia dog show with every instrument in the satirist's arsenal, from the skewer to the mallet. Built around the improvisational techniques of Second City, the movie is consistently just plain funny and sometimes ascends to a kind of crazed genius. Consider Parker Posey's rage and loathing, for example, as she assaults a store clerk who cannot supply a Busy Bee dog toy. Her dog has lost its toy and is fretting, and the way she screams, "Busy Bee! Busy Bee!" you'd think she was looking for emergency snakebite remedy.

The movie introduces several dogs and their owners, who are seen in their homes and then followed to the Mayflower Kennel Club's dog show, where a telecast of the event includes color commentary by Buck Laughlin (Fred Willard). Bearing certain points of similarity to Joe Garagiola, Buck is genial, chatty, weirdly misinformed, and easily lost in the overgrown byways of his mind. He wonders aloud if a bribe would help to sway the judges, confuses Columbus with the Pilgrims, comments knowingly on a dog's attempt to hump the leg of its owner, and speculates that the bloodhound's chances might improve if he wore a little Sherlock Holmes hat and had a pipe in his mouth.

Harlan Pepper, the bloodhound's owner (played by Guest) is single, and that seems appropriate: Don't ask me why, but bloodhounds, even female bloodhounds, have always seemed like bachelors to me. The other dogs belong to couples (and a threesome) who seem in some cases to be more inbred than their animals.

Consider Gerry and Cookie Fleck, from Florida, and their Norwich terrier, Winky. Eugene Levy and Catherine O'Hara, who play the Flecks, obviously have need of a dog to deflect their attentions from each other. Gerry, for example, was born with two left feet. Literally. And Cookie's mating habits are infamous among her fellow dog owners; one of the running jokes is Gerry's perplexed look as one man after another seems to know his wife far better than he should.

Parker Posey's character met her mate (Michael Hitchcock) when their eyes locked as they visited Starbucks shops across the street from each other. Their conversations seem to be conducted largely by using the names of retail products: "We are so lucky," she observes, "to have been raised among catalogs."

The bountifully siliconed Sherri Ann Ward Cabot (Jennifer Coolidge), not light-years in difference from Anna Nicole Smith, cuddles with her geriatric millionaire husband ("We could not talk or talk forever and still find things to not talk about"), but seems to have a complex and perhaps rewarding relationship with Christy Cummings (Jane Lynch), the lesbian dominatrix they've hired to train their poodle. Stefan Vanderhoof (Michael McKean)

and Scott Donlan (John Michael Higgins) are a gay couple whose twin shih tzus are the apples of their eyes.

With this film Christopher Guest nails down his command of the comedy mocumentary, a genre he helped to invent by cowriting and starring in *This Is Spinal Tap* (about a rock band coming apart at the seams) and by writing, directing, and starring in *Waiting for Guffman* (about a small town hiring an allegedly hotshot Broadway director for its 150th anniversary pageant). *Guffman* starred many of the same actors (Guest, Levy, Willard, O'Hara, Hitchcock, and Posey), and in both films some of their dialogue seems based on improvisations, especially as conversations veer into revealing detours.

Just as *Guffman* ended with the ill-fated pageant, *Best in Show* ends with the dog show itself, depending on the built-in structure of the competition to bring all of the owners and their stories together at the same time. Satires have a way of running out of steam, but the suspense of the judging process keeps the energy high, even apart from an assist by the dog who attacks a judge, inspiring Buck's most appreciative play-by-play commentary.

Beyond the Mat ★ ★ ★
R, 92 m., 2000

With Mick "Mankind" Foley, Terry Funk, "Jake the Snake" Roberts, "Stone Cold" Steve Austin, Coco BWare, The Rock, Chyna, Vince McMahon, and others. A documentary directed by Barry Blaustein and produced by Brian Grazer, Ron Howard, Michael Rosenberg, Barry Bloom, and Blaustein. Screenplay by Blaustein.

Beyond the Mat is the wrestling documentary that Vince McMahon had barred from advertising on his World Wrestling Federation programs. Why? Because it shows an old pro maintaining on crack cocaine, and children weeping at ringside while their daddy is beaten bloody? Not at all. Because he doesn't have a cut of the profits.

Even if you've never watched a professional wrestling match on television, you've probably heard the words "Mr. McMahon" just while surfing past the channel. Here he explains why the WWF is like the Muppets: "They're both family owned, and they both have real human beings playing characters.'"

Uh-huh. We see him interviewing Darren Drozdov, a former pro football player who wants to wrestle and has a unique skill: He can vomit "on command." McMahon gives him a ring name, "Puke," and envisions a scenario: "After you've regurgitated on your opponent or the referee . . ." Drozdov is sent to the minor leagues for seasoning, and calls his mother with the good news.

Other subjects of the documentary have been around a long time. Terry Funk is over fifty, has been wrestling forever, and hears the doctor forecast a lifetime of pain from his wrecked knees. Then he climbs into the ring again. He can hardly walk, but during the match he seems to come to life, giving audiences the show they expect.

It is a show, yes. *Beyond the Mat* makes no secret of the fact that every match is scripted, and that the outcomes are not in doubt. But we knew that. What I didn't fully realize, until I saw this film, is how real the show is. Just because you script a guy being thrown out of the ring doesn't mean it's painless when he bounces off a table and onto the floor. You can't bleed unless you're cut. And sometimes things go wrong; a wire cage mesh breaks and a wrestler falls maybe twenty feet to the mat. That hurts. Last year a wrestler named Owen Hart fell seventy feet and was killed when his harness failed while he was being lowered into a ring.

Mick "Mankind" Foley comes across as one of the nicest guys in the film, a family man with small children who's a gentle teddy bear when he's not in the ring. He explains to his kids how it's all carefully planned, how his opponent doesn't really hate him, and then the two preschoolers sit at ringside as their daddy is handcuffed and beaten with a chair. He starts to bleed. They start to cry. "Close your eyes," their mother says, before finally taking them out of the room. They watch in the dressing room as a medic applies first aid to Foley's cuts and checks for a concussion.

Later, the filmmakers show Foley their footage of his kids crying, and he is sobered. He vows never to let them watch a fight again. We sense the care in his voice, but we also wonder: What were they doing ringside in the first place? What do kids know about scripts?

Beyond the Mat was written and directed by Barry Blaustein, a onetime *Saturday Night Live* writer and successful film producer, mostly of Eddie Murphy projects *(Coming to America, Boomerang, The Nutty Professor)*. He confesses to being a TV wrestling fan all his life. There's real pain when he meets one of his old heroes, "Jake the Snake" Roberts, once a superstar, now reduced to barnstorming the back roads for small change.

Roberts opens up in an extraordinary way to the camera. He talks about an unhappy childhood, a mother who was thirteen when she married. He has shaky relationships with his own family, and when Blaustein arranges a meeting with his estranged daughter at the Ramada, she's so nervous she wants to bring along two friends. A fight promoter says Jake demands crack before doing a show, and Jake agrees he's had drug problems.

What we wonder is, how can you be a pro wrestler and not use drugs? A working wrestler performs twenty-six to twenty-seven days in a month—twice on weekends. It's not all on TV. There are bus and plane trips to far-flung arenas, where even on a good day (no serious injuries) their bodies are slammed around in a way that might alarm a pro football player. Have you ever heard of a pro wrestler being suspended for drug use? Do they even check for drugs? Only asking.

Beyond the Mat isn't a slick documentary; some of it feels like Blaustein's home movie about being a wrestling fan. But it has a hypnotic quality. Those who oppose boxing because of its violence acknowledge that it is at least a supervised sport, with rules and safeguards. Wrestling is not a sport but a spectacle, in which weary and wounded men, some obviously not in the best of shape, injure each other for money.

At one point we see two wrestlers set each other on fire and then throw each other on barbed wire. There are ways to do this in which you do not get burned severely or lacerated—much. But it's not simple trickery, and what goes on in the ring clearly really does hurt, sometimes a lot. After a bloody match, two wrestlers slap each other on the back, and explain, "The more you hurt each other, the more money you make, so the more you like each other." Not capitalism's finest hour.

Big Bad Love ★ ★
R, 111 m., 2002

Arliss Howard (Leon Barlow), Debra Winger (Marilyn), Paul Le Mat (Monroe), Rosanna Arquette (Velma), Angie Dickinson (Mrs. Barlow), Michael Parks (Mr. Aaron). Directed by Arliss Howard and produced by Debra Winger. Screenplay by James Howard and Arliss Howard, based on stories by Larry Brown.

It all comes down to whether you can tolerate Leon Barlow. I can't. *Big Bad Love* can, and is filled with characters who love and accept him even though he is a full-time, gold-plated pain in the can. Leon is a college graduate (no doubt of creative writing classes) who has adopted a Good Old Drunk persona that wavers between the tiresome and the obnoxious. The movie has patience with his narcissistic self-pity. My diagnosis: Send Barlow to rehab, haul him to some AA meetings, and find out in a year if he has anything worth saying.

I know there are people in real life who smoke as much as Barlow (Arliss Howard) does, but at today's cigarette prices he is spending $400 a month on cigarettes and almost as much on the manuscripts he ships out to literary magazines. His bar bill is beyond all imagining. The first thing you learn as a poor writer is to cut back on the overhead. Here at H & R Ebert ("Budget Control for Unpublished Drunks"), we could pare $25,000 a year from his costs just by cutting out his bad habits.

Barlow smokes more or less all the time. He becomes a character whose task every morning is to get through sixty to eighty cigarettes that day. Everything else is a parallel activity. He lives in a colorfully rundown house in rural Mississippi—the sort that passes for genteel poverty in the movies and is priced at $300,000 and up, with land, in the real-estate ads. He pounds away on his Royal typewriter as if engaged in a mano-a-mano with Robert E. *(Conan the Barbarian)* Howard in *The Whole Wide World.* Since he is a man without a glimmer of awareness of his own boorishness, one wonders what he writes. Epic fantasy, perhaps?

Like many drunks, he is enabled by his loved ones (or, as is often the case, his former loved ones). His ex-wife, Marilyn, well played by Debra Winger (Arliss Howard's real-life wife), has divorced him but still has a soft spot for the crazy lug. His buddy Monroe (Paul Le Mat) loves him, maybe because you protect your drinking buddy just like you protect your drinking money. Monroe's old lady, Velma (Rosanna Arquette), has a fate that was preordained when she was christened Velma, a name that summons up Raymond Chandler novels and long-suffering girlfriends. Velma sees more than she lets on, but is stuck in her sexpot act.

The movie's basic problem is that it has no distance on Barlow—no way to criticize him. The screenplay, written by Arliss Howard and James Howard, based on stories by the Mississippi writer Larry Brown, lets Barlow get away with murder. We all have a tendency to go easy on ourselves, and *Big Bad Love* is unaware that its hero is a tiresome jerk. Larry Brown writes about "hard-bitten, hard-drinking, hard-living male characters," according to a Website about his work, and is a "bad-boy novelist." One suspects that the movie lacks perspective on Barlow because Brown is, in some respects, Barlow.

Because a movie must be about something more than smoking, drinking, and talking as if you are the best-read drunk in town, *Big Bad Love* delivers two tragedies, both foreshadowed, right on time. It also involves some visual touches, such as an indoor rainstorm, that may perplex audiences not familiar with the work of Tarkovsky.

Arliss Howard is not a bad actor or a bad director, but in this film he shows himself an unreliable judge of character. Leon Barlow could be saved by an emergency transfusion of irony, or even a film that is cheerfully jaundiced about him. But the martyr act doesn't work. Here is a man who wants us to like him because of his marriage that did not work, his stories that do not sell, and his children that he is not doing a very good job of parenting. Then we are asked to pity him because of all the cigarettes he must smoke and all the booze he has to drink, and because they make him feel so awful in the morning. He's a familiar type, imprisoned by self-monitoring: How am I doing? How do I feel? How long can I continue to abuse myself and those around me? In the movie, he's blessed by people who can see through the facade to the really great guy inside. All I could see was a cry for help.

Big Eden ★ ★
PG-13, 118 m., 2001

Arye Gross (Henry Hart), Eric Schweig (Pike Dexter), Tim DeKay (Dean Stewart), George Coe (Sam Hart), Louise Fletcher (Grace Cornwell), Nan Martin (Widow Thayer), Veanne Cox (Mary Margaret). Directed by Thomas Bezucha and produced by Jennifer Chaiken. Screenplay by Bezucha.

Big Eden tells a story of gay love in a small Montana town whose citizens are so accepting of homosexuality that the old coots around the cracker barrel at the general store rush to the window to monitor the progress of a triangle involving the local hunk, the artist feller from New York, and a tall, silent Indian. Earlier, the Widow Thayer, who failed to fix up the New Yorker with the local girls, discovers her error and throws a party so he can meet the local boys.

This is the same Montana that's next door to Wyoming, where a gay man named Matthew Shepard was murdered not long ago. Or rather, it is not the same Montana, but some kind of movie fantasy world in which all the local folk know and approve of the fact that Henry Hart (Arye Gross) is gay; by the end of the film, they're ready to use crowbars on the door to Henry's closet. This is the kind of movie small town with no ordinary citizens; everyone has a speaking role, and they all live in each other's pockets, know each other's business, and have jobs that allow them to drop into the general store and each other's kitchens with the frequency of neighbors on a sitcom.

That's not to say the movie doesn't have a lot of sweetness and warmth. Until the plot becomes intolerably cornball, there's charm in the story of how the withdrawn Henry returns to Big Eden after his granddad (George Coe) has a stroke. He's welcomed by Grace (Louise Fletcher), the local teacher, and learns immediately that "Dean is back in town." That would be Dean Stewart (Tim DeKay), Henry's hunky best friend in high school, and the object of an unrequited crush that spans the decades. Now Dean is divorced, and smiling at Henry during Sunday church services.

Grandpa starts to mend, Henry helps Grace in the local school, and the Widow Thayer is hired to cook meals for the two men. But Widow Thayer is a fearsomely bad cook, and soon the wonderfully named Pike Dexter (Eric Schweig) is secretly preparing gourmet meals from recipes on the Internet, and feeding the widow's swill to his dog. Pike is an Indian who runs the general store, despite painful shyness and a deep reluctance to say more than three words at a time.

We think the plot may involve local homophobia. But no: Everybody in this town is pro-gay. Then we think perhaps Henry and Dean will fall in love. They seem headed in that direction until a scene so awkwardly written and acted that it seems to have been pounded into the plot with sledgehammers (you'll know the scene I mean; ask yourself exactly how and why it justifies Henry's later anger, in another awkward scene). Finally it turns out that Henry's future lies in the arms of Pike, whose life changes the day he checks *The Joy of Cooking* out of his own lending library. (The movie misses a golden opportunity; Pike should have selected *The Settlement Cook Book,* with its cover motto, "The way to a man's heart is through his stomach.")

There are things in the movie that are very good. I admired George Coe's work in a difficult role (listen to his reading of the line, "God has done a good job here"). I liked Louise Fletcher's unforced intelligence and goodwill. Ayre Gross plays a character who at times is willfully obtuse, but it would be fatal to be more open—since the moment he acknowledges his gayness, the plot, which depends on him being the least liberated person in town, would collapse.

I had real troubles, I must admit, with the coots who gather at the general store. I doubt that in the real world all six of these bewhiskered, pipe-puffing, jeans-wearing, cowboy-hatted old cowboys would be cheerleaders for a gay romance. I also found Pike's character a puzzle. In the opening scenes he seems either retarded or mentally ill, but by the end love has conquered all and repaired it. The last scene is painfully overdone; a shy "like to dance?" and a fade-out would have worked a lot better than the current ending. When you lay it on too thick, the audience is distracted by implausibility rather than identifying with the characters.

Whether Henry will find happiness in Big Eden we can only wonder. Some may think him courageous to abandon his art career in Manhattan to join the circle of Pike's admirers around the cracker barrel. I think it is a prudent decision. Based on the one example of Henry's painting that we see, his artistic talents are best suited to designing gift-wrap paper.

Big Fat Liar ★ ★ ★
PG, 87 m., 2002

Frankie Muniz (Jason Shepherd), Paul Giamatti (Marty Wolf), Amanda Bynes (Kaylee), Amanda Detmer (Monty), Donald Faison (Frank). Directed by Shawn Levy and produced by Brian Robbins and Michael Tollin. Screenplay by Dan Schneider and Robbins.

Big Fat Liar takes the smartest fourteen-year-old fibber in Michigan and pairs him up against the dumbest thirty-something fibber in Hollywood. Jason Shepherd is an eighth-grader who lies about almost everything, so when a movie producer steals his homework and turns it into a movie, naturally Jason's parents and teacher don't believe him. So he enlists his girlfriend Kaylee, and goes to Hollywood to confront the creep and prove he was telling the truth. (Naturally, he lies to cover up his absence from home.)

This premise, which sounds like something a fourteen-year-old might have dreamed up, becomes a surprisingly entertaining movie—one of those good-hearted comedies like *Spy Kids* where reality is put on hold while bright teenagers outsmart the best and worst the adult world has to offer. It's ideal for younger teens, and not painful for their parents.

Jason is played by Frankie Muniz (who was wonderful in *My Dog Skip*), Kaylee is Amanda Bynes, a TV actress making her film debut, and the reprehensible Marty Wolf, Hollywood sleazo supremo, is played by Paul Giamatti with the kind of teeth-gnashing venom the Beagle Boys used against Uncle Scrooge.

Marty, the "Wolfman," has indeed stolen Jason's eighth-grade story, which fell from his backpack into Wolf's limousine, for reasons too complicated to explain. The story, which is autobiographical, involves, of course, an eighth-grader who tells so many lies that no one believes him when he tells the truth. Marty is astonished when confronted in his studio office by the kid, who doesn't want money or even a share of ownership, but just for the guy to call his dad and admit, yes, it's true, I stole your kid's story. Marty laughs incredulously: That'll be the day.

The story is an excuse to take the kids on a tour of Hollywood, starting with the Universal back lot, which, like all back lots in movies, is jammed with countless extras dressed as Romans, aliens, cowboys, biblical figures, and can-can dancers. Jason and Kaylee get onto the lot via the Universal tour, and hide out in the wardrobe and props department, which has everything they need for their skulduggery.

Marty Wolf is such a seven-letter word that Jason quickly wins the sympathy of two key allies: his limo driver, Frank (Donald Faison), and his secretary, Monty (Amanda Detmer). Frank has reason for revenge. He was a hopeful actor until Marty wrote "loser" on his composite and sent it to every casting director in town. Monty does, too: She gets blamed for the Wolfman's every mistake.

A lot of the funniest scenes involve Giamatti, who is the target of so many practical jokes by the two kids that his life becomes miserable. The best: They fill his swimming pool with blue dye, so that on the day of his big meeting with the studio chief, he looks like an understudy for the Blue Man Group. His broad humor here is dramatically different from his needy, imploding documentary producer in Todd Solondz's *Storytelling*.

The movie's charm is that it has confidence in this goofy story, and doesn't push it too hard. Muniz and Bynes have an easy prepubertal relationship (she's a lot taller, of course). It's based on wisecracks and immunity from the problems of the real world, where Hollywood might be a lot more dangerous for fourteen-year-olds. Giamatti's slow burn alternates with his fast burn and his explosive rages, and his comeuppance at the end is entirely appropriate in movie terms. And certain lines have a charm of their own, as when the kids send the Wolfman (now bright blue) not to the studio head's house as he expects, but to a birthday party, where the little guests joyfully cry, "Hey, it's the clown! Let's hurt him!"

The Big Kahuna ★ ★ ★ ½
R, 90 m., 2000

Kevin Spacey (Larry), Danny DeVito (Phil), Peter Facinelli (Bob). Directed by John Swanbeck and produced by Elie Samaha, Kevin Spacey, and Andrew Stevens. Screenplay by Roger Rueff.

There are two religions in America, one spiritual, one secular. The first worships in churches, the second at business conventions. Clergy of both religions wear dark suits and ties (or roman collars). They exchange a lot of business cards. *The Big Kahuna* is about an uneasy confrontation between these two systems of faith.

True believers are similar whatever their religion. Their theology teaches: We know the right way. We are saved. We support one another and strive to convert the heathen. Those who come with us will know the kingdom of heaven—or will be using the best industrial lubricant. Adherents of both religions often meet in hotels, attend "mixers," and participate in "workshops" at which the buried message is: The truth is in this room.

The Big Kahuna is about a tool and die industry convention in a Wichita hotel. In a "hospitality suite" on an upper floor, three men wait uneasily. Their company sells industrial lubricants. Their entire convention depends on landing the account of a man named Dick Fuller, referred to as the Big Kahuna. The men are Larry (Kevin Spacey), Phil (Danny DeVito), and Bob (Peter Facinelli). Larry and Phil have been comrades for a long time—road warriors who do battle at conventions. Bob is a young man, new to the firm, at his first convention. Larry is edgy, sardonic, competitive. Phil is more easygoing. Phil is the backslapper; Larry is the closer. "I feel like I've been shaking somebody's hand one way or another all of my life," Phil says.

The film mostly takes place within that one hotel room. Yes, it is based on a play. I like that. I like the fact that it is mostly dialogue among three people on one set. That is the way to tell this story. Why does every filmed play trigger movie critics into a ritual discussion of whether (or how, or if) the play has been "opened up"? Who cares? What difference would it make if the movie set some scenes in the coffee shop

and others in the park across the street? The story is about these three guys and what they say to one another. Keeping it in one room underlines their isolation: They are in the inner sanctum of their religion.

The movie, directed by John Swanbeck and written by Roger Rueff, is sharp-edged, perfectly timed, funny, and thoughtful. Spacey and DeVito are two of the smartest actors in the movies, filled with the joy of performance, and they exchange their dialogue with the precision of racquetball players, every volley redefining the game. They talk about business strategy, sales goals, the cutthroat world of industrial lubricants, the mystical power of the Big Kahuna to transform their lives. There is not one word about the technical side of lubricants; they couldn't care less. Lubricants are the Maguffin. They could be selling auto parts, ladies' ready-to-wear, or kitchen gizmos.

Bob, the kid, is softer and more unformed. He hasn't been broken in (or down) by life on the road. It appears that the Big Kahuna did not visit their suite. But in the small hours of the morning, during a postmortem, Larry and Phil discover that the great man was indeed in the room, wearing someone else's name tag— and that Bob talked to him for hours. What did they talk about? The Big Kahuna was depressed by the death of his dog.

That leads to a larger discussion, about a topic close to Bob's heart—his personal savior, Jesus Christ. Bob believes in Jesus like Larry and Phil believe in sales. "We talked about Christ," he says, quietly and simply, filled with enormous self-satisfaction. "About *Christ?*" screams Larry. "Did you mention what line of industrial lubricant Jesus uses?"

Those who are not true believers may be left cold by this film. For those who link their lives to a cause, it may have a real resonance. The tricky thing may be realizing that the two systems are interchangeable. If Larry and Phil believed in Jesus, and Bob wanted to land the big contract, the dialogue could stay about the same, because the story is about their personalities, not their products.

Now here's a funny thing. This movie premiered last January at Sundance. A lot has been written about it since then. You can read about the actors, the dialogue, the convention, the Kahuna, the industrial lubricants. But you can search the reviews in vain for any mention of Jesus Christ. Most of the reviewers seem to have forgotten that Bob is born-again. Maybe it never registered. From their secular viewpoint, what they remember is that Bob had the Kahuna in the palm of his hand and blew the deal, but they don't remember why.

That underlines how, once you sign onto a belief system, you see everything through that prism, and anything outside of it becomes invisible. *The Big Kahuna* is remarkable in the way it shows the two big systems in conflict. Of course, there is such a species as the Christian businessman, who has his roots in a strain of the Protestant ethic. He believes that prospering and being saved go hand in hand. Maybe Bob was onto something. Maybe he had the right approach to Dick Fuller. Maybe that's why Fuller is the Big Kahuna.

Big Momma's House ★ ★
PG-13, 99 m., 2000

Martin Lawrence (Malcolm), Nia Long (Sherry), Paul Giamatti (John), Jascha Washington (Trent), Terrence Howard (Lester), Anthony Anderson (Nolan), Ella Mitchell (Big Momma). Directed by Raja Gosnell and produced by David T. Friendly and Michael Green. Screenplay by Darryl Quarles and Don Rhymer.

Any movie that employs an oven mitt and a plumber's friend in a childbirth scene cannot be all bad, and I laughed a lot during *Big Momma's House*. I also spent a certain amount of time staring at the screen in disbelief. While it's true that comedy can redeem bad taste, it can be appalling when bad taste thinks it is being redeemed by comedy and is wrong. The movie's opening toilet scene, featuring the biggest evacuation since we pulled out of Vietnam, is a grisly example.

Martin Lawrence stars in the movie as Malcolm, an FBI agent who is a master of disguise. A vicious bank robber named Lester (Terrence Howard) escapes from prison, and Malcolm and his partner John (Paul Giamatti) conduct a surveillance on Lester's girlfriend Sherry (Nia Long), who may know where $2 million in loot has been concealed. Sherry, afraid of Lester, flees with her child to the Georgia home of her grandmother, Big Momma (Ella Mit-

chell). And when Big Momma is called out of town, Malcolm disguises himself as the 350-pound juggernaut, deceives Sherry, and infiltrates the case from within, while his partner keeps watch from the house across the street.

This is all essentially an attempt by Lawrence to follow Eddie Murphy's disguise as a fat guy in *The Nutty Professor,* and credit should also go to Robin Williams in *Mrs. Doubtfire.* The whole enterprise has been ratcheted down several degrees in taste, however; while Murphy's funniest scene involves vast explusions of intestinal gas, Big Momma's noisy visit to the bathroom is scary, not funny.

Martin Lawrence is a gifted actor, and with clever makeup, padding, and sass he creates a fake Big Momma who doesn't look completely like a drag queen, although she comes close. It's doubtful her granddaughter, neighbors, and would-be boyfriend would be fooled. But we go along with the gag, since the plot is no more than a flimsy excuse for Big Momma to behave in a way that most 350-pound grandmothers in their sixties would find impossible.

We see Big Momma playing a pickup basketball game, including a reverse dunk that ends with her hanging from the hoop. Big Momma in karate class, throwing the instructor around the room. Big Momma in church, letting some four-letter words slip into her testimony and covering up with a quick segue to "Oh, Happy Day!"

The funniest scene involves a pregnant neighbor in the throes of childbirth—which is how Malcolm the FBI agent finds out Big Momma is a midwife. The zany editing of the childbirth scene makes it work, and the appearance of the oven mitt is the high point of the film. Other scenes are not handled so well; when Big Momma's sexy granddaughter climbs into bed with her, for example, Malcolm has a physiological reaction not entirely explained by his flashlight. This is a recycling of the classic bed scene between Steve Martin and John Candy in *Planes, Trains and Automobiles* ("Those aren't pillows!"), not handled nearly as well.

The movie's one of those ideas that seems increasingly labored as the plot drags on. A little of Big Momma is funny enough, but eventually we realize Martin Lawrence is going to spend virtually the entire movie in drag (he appears as Malcolm only long enough to stir up a sweet romance with Sherry). The problem is that Lawrence's gifts come packaged with his face and voice: Present him as Big Momma all the time, and you lose his star power. It's the same problem John Travolta presents in *Battlefield Earth*. We don't go to a big star's movie to see him as an unrecognizable character. The movie has some big laughs, yes, but never reaches takeoff velocity.

The Big Tease ★ ★
R, 86 m., 2000

Craig Ferguson (Crawford Mackenzie), Frances Fisher (Candy Harper), Mary McCormack (Monique Geingold), David Rasche (Stig Ludwiggssen), Chris Langham (Martin), Donal Logue (Eamonn), Isabella Aitken (Mrs. Beasie Mackenzie), Kevin Allen (Gareth Trundle). Directed by Kevin Allen and produced by Philip Rose. Screenplay by Sacha Gervasi and Craig Ferguson.

In the theory of comedy, more attention should be paid to the time between the laughs. It's easy enough to get a laugh in a movie, but tricky and difficult to build comic momentum, so that underlying hilarity rolls over from one laugh to the next and the audience senses it's looking at a funny movie instead of a movie with funny moments.

The Big Tease is a movie with a lot of laughs, but they come one at a time. It doesn't build, and by the time we get to the big payoff it's kind of dragging. I could describe moments and lines to you and you'd probably laugh, but sitting there in the audience, you want it to roll, and it meanders.

The film stars Craig Ferguson, a gifted comic actor from Glasgow (and *The Drew Carey Show*), as a gay hairdresser named Crawford Mackenzie—by his own admission the finest hairdresser, indeed, in Scotland. When an invitation arrives from the World Freestyle Hairdressing Championship in Los Angeles, he vibrates with excitement: Here at last is his chance to compete against the big names in hairdressing. Accompanied by a documentary film crew, he flies off to L.A., only to discover belatedly that he has been invited, not to compete, but to sit in the audience (between

Daniel Day-Lewis and Carrot Top), and is expected to pay all his own bills.

He's crushed, but not defeated. With the now-desperate doc crew following him around and lending him that air of vague importance bestowed by any camera, he invades the sanctum of the legendary Stig Ludwiggssen (David Rasche), defending hairdressing champion, a Norwegian twit with an accent that casts doubt on his Norwegian or any other origins. Rasche is wonderful in the role, conveying that towering self-importance so often displayed by the giants of inconsequential fields; having once overheard Jose Eber when he was mad at a rental car agent, I can even speculate that Rasche's portrait is not particularly exaggerated.

To be considered for the competition, Crawford needs a union card. His quest for one occupies the middle passages of the movie. At one point he is reduced to grooming the animal costumes at a theme park. He thinks his fellow Scotsman Sean Connery might come to the rescue (perhaps he will remember the time Crawford groomed his hairpiece), and confronts Connery's publicist, played by Frances Fisher with dead-on accuracy.

Whether he gets his card, and what happens at the bizarre hairdressing finals, I leave it to you to discover. I found Ferguson likable as the hairdresser out of water, and enjoyed Fisher, Rasche, and Mary McCormack as the head of the competition. But somehow *The Big Tease* never quite attains takeoff velocity. Maybe it needed to position itself a little closer to the ground and go for the comedy of observation rather than exaggeration. I trust, anyway, that the final competition is an exaggeration. If it is anywhere at all close to real life, just the telecast of the real thing would have been funny enough.

Big Trouble ★ ★ ½
PG-13, 84 m., 2002

Tim Allen (Eliot Arnold), Rene Russo (Anna Herk), Stanley Tucci (Arthur Herk), Tom Sizemore (Snake), Patrick Warburton (Walter), Zooey Deschanel (Jenny Herk), Dennis Farina (Henry Algott), Omar Epps (Seitz), Heavy D (Greer), Jason Lee (Puggy), Janeane Garofalo (Monica Romero), Ben Foster (Matt Arnold). Directed by Barry Sonnenfeld and produced by Tom Jacobson, Barry Josephson, and Sonnenfeld. Screenplay by Robert Ramsey and Matthew Stone, based on the novel by Dave Barry.

Big Trouble is based on a novel by Dave Barry, and I have no trouble believing that. The genius of Dave Barry is that he applies a logical and helpful analysis to a situation that can only be worsened by such intervention. It is impossible, for example, to explain to a policeman why he is wasting his time on your illegal left turn while real criminals go free. Or to the IRS agent that Enron is robbing billions from widows and orphans while he ponders your business-related need to buy lots of CDs. Or to your wife why it is pointless to do the dishes on a daily basis when you can save hot water by letting them accumulate for a week in the dishwasher—which, being airtight, will not stink up the kitchen if you slam it right after adding more dishes.

All of these positions, which make perfect sense, only infuriate the cop, tax man, spouse, etc., by applying logic to a situation they have invested with irrational passion. As a sane voice in a world gone mad, Barry alone sees clearly. The Dave Barry figure in *Big Trouble*, I think, is Puggy (Jason Lee), a man who when he first addresses the camera seems to be Jesus, until he starts munching Fritos between his words of wisdom, observing, "You really can't beat these when they're fresh." Puggy is a homeless man who was living in the rainy north inside a cardboard box, when an article in *Martha Stewart's Living* inspired him to move to sunny southern Florida.

He is the film's omniscient narrator, not because he knows everything in a godlike way, but because he lives outdoors and happens to be ideally positioned during an evening when most of the film's other characters meet at the luxury home of Arthur Herk (Stanley Tucci), who is "one of the few Floridians who actually did vote for Pat Buchanan." (Saddened by the inability of many Republicans to express even token pity about the Jewish senior citizens whose mistaken votes for the Great Foamer tilted the election, I am always happy to have this event recalled.)

Arthur Herk is . . . ah, but if I begin a plot

synopsis, we will be here all day, and I have already squandered three paragraphs with fancy writing. There is a plot in *Big Trouble*, quite a logical one actually, with all the threads tied into neat knots at the end, but to explain it would leave you banging your forehead against the newspaper and crying, "Why must I know this?" It might be simpler to describe the characters and let you discover their interactions for yourself.

Herk is a rich man who owes money to the wrong people and wants to buy a bomb. Rene Russo is his wife, Anna, who no longer remembers why she married this jerk. Zooey Deschanel is their daughter Jenny, who is the target of Matt Arnold (Ben Foster), a school classmate who needs to squirt her with a one-gallon water gun. Tim Allen is Eliot Arnold, Matt's father, who was the two-time Pulitzer Prize–winning columnist of the *Miami Herald* until he kicked in the computer screen of an editor who gave him idiotic assignments while refusing to meet his eyes. (It would seem to the casual moviegoer that Eliot Arnold is the Dave Barry figure in the movie, since he closely resembles the author, but no, it's Puggy.)

Then there are Dennis Farina and Jack Kehler as two hit men assigned to kill Arthur Herk. And Janeane Garofalo and Patrick Warburton as two cops who answer a call to the Herk home. And Lars Arenta-Hansen and Daniel London, who have a nuclear bomb they can sell to Arthur Herk. And Omar Epps and Heavy D as FBI agents on the trail of the bomb sellers. And Sofia Vergara as Nina, the Herks's maid, whom Arthur wants to have sex with. She despises Herk, but instantly lusts for Puggy—another clue he is the Dave Barry character. And Tom Sizemore and Johnny Knoxville as Snake and Eddie, who try to stick up the bar where the bomb dealers meet Arthur Herk while the FBI stakes it out. (Sample dialogue: "Snake, let's get the hell out of here. I think I hear one of them silent alarms.") There is also a toad whose spit is hallucinogenic.

The film has been directed by Barry Sonnenfeld, who made *Get Shorty*. It's not in that class—indeed, it seems so crowded that it sometimes feels like the casting call for an eventual picture not yet made—but it has its charms. It's the kind of movie you can't quite recommend because it is all windup and not much of a pitch, yet you can't bring yourself to dislike it. A video or airplane or cable movie. Originally scheduled for an autumn opening, it was pulled from the release schedule after 9/11 because it involves terrorists and a nuclear bomb. But these are terrorists and bombs from a simpler and more innocent time. The movie is a reminder of an age when such plots were obviously not to be taken seriously. It is nice to be reminded of that time.

Billy Elliot ★ ★ ★
R, 110 m., 2000

Jamie Bell (Billy), Julie Walters (Mrs. Wilkinson), Gary Lewis (Dad), Jamie Draven (Tony), Nicola Blackwell (Debbie), Stuart Wells (Michael), Adam Cooper (Billy [aged 25]), Jean Heywood (Grandmother). Directed by Stephen Daldry and produced by Greg Brenman and John Finn. Screenplay by Lee Hall.

Billy Elliot is the flip side of *Girlfight*. While the recent American film is about a girl who wants to be a boxer and is opposed by her macho father but supported by her brother, this new British film is about a boy who wants to be a ballet dancer but is opposed by his macho father and brother. Both films feature supportive adults who encourage the dreams, both oppose rigid gender definitions, both end in a big fight/dance. *Girlfight* is tougher, *Billy Elliot* sweeter. I suppose that's appropriate.

The movie takes place in 1984 in a British coal mining town, where Billy (Jamie Bell) trudges off to boxing lessons for which he is ill equipped. Life at home is tense because his father (Gary Lewis) and brother Tony (Jamie Draven) are striking miners. One day, at the other end of the village hall, he sees ballet lessons being taught by a chain-smoking disciplinarian (Julie Walters), and his eyes grow large. Soon he is shyly joining her class, the only boy in a crowd of tutus.

Billy's father equates male ballet dancers with homosexuality, but Billy doesn't seem to be gay, a fact he discovers to his sudden embarrassment during a pillow fight with his friend Debbie (Nicola Blackwell). Billy's best friend, Michael (Stuart Wells), is gay, however—a cross-dresser who reaches the high point of

his young life by putting on one of the tutus. Michael is attracted to Billy, who doesn't reciprocate, but seems unusually sophisticated about the implications for a boy his age.

The movie is sort of awkwardly cobbled together, and there are big shifts in character without much explanation. Billy's dad, a supporter of the strike, not only begins to understand his son's dream, but actually becomes a strike breaker to get money for Billy to attend an important audition. I can believe a coal miner supporting his son's dancing dreams, but anyone who believes he would become a scab to raise the money doesn't know much about union miners.

Still, the movie is as much parable and fantasy as it is realistic. The character of the transvestite Michael in particular seems based more on wishful thinking than on plausible reality; would a gay boy of his age in this neighborhood of this town in 1984 be quite so sure of himself? Julie Walters, a 1984 Academy nominee for *Educating Rita*, is spirited and colorful as the ballet teacher, and Gary Lewis is somehow convincing as the dad even when the screenplay requires him to make big offscreen swings of position. Jamie Bell is an engaging Billy, earnest and highspirited, and a pretty good dancer too.

The movie was directed by Stephen Daldry, a well-known stage director, and photographed by Brian Tufano, who has one shot that perfectly illustrates the difference between how children and adults see the world. Billy's friend Debbie is walking along a fence, clicking a stick against the boards. She doesn't notice that she is suddenly walking in front of a line of cops, called up against the striking miners and carrying plastic shields; she clicks on those too.

Note: Once again, we are confronted by a movie that might be ideal for teenagers about Billy Elliot's age, but it has been slapped with the R rating. While kids will gladly sneak into R-rated movies they hope will be violent or scary, the R barrier only discourages them from films that could be helpful or educational. In the case of Billy Elliot, *the movie contains only mild violence and essentially no sex, and the R is explained entirely by the language, particularly the f-word. The filmmakers believe that is a word much used by British coal miners, and I am sure they are correct.*

There are two solutions to the linkage of the f-word and the R rating: (1) The MPAA should concede the melancholy fact that every teenager has heard this and most other nasty words thousands of times, or (2) filmmakers should sacrifice the f-word in order to make their films more available to those under seventeen.

Birthday Girl ★ ★
R, 93 m., 2002

Nicole Kidman (Nadia/Sofia), Ben Chaplin (John Buckingham), Vincent Cassel (Yuri), Mathieu Kassovitz (Alexei), Stephen Mangan (Bank Manager). Directed by Jez Butterworth and produced by Eric Abraham, Steve Butterworth, and Diana Phillips. Screenplay by Jez Butterworth and Tom Butterworth.

Anyone who orders a mail-order bride over the Internet deserves more or less who he gets. The bride may or may not be looking forward to a lifetime as a loving and devoted spouse, but she is certainly looking forward to an air ticket, a visa, and citizenship in a Western democracy. Would-be husbands who do not understand this probably believe that beautiful women gladly offer themselves sight unseen to men merely because they have mastered such skills as logging on, typing, and possessing a credit card.

Yet hope springs eternal. John Buckingham (Ben Chaplin), a bank teller in a small British town, is a lonely guy who clicks forlornly on the photos of Russian mail-order brides and finally orders Nadia, who says she is tall, blonde, speaks English, and is a nonsmoker. When, at the airport, Nadia turns out to look exactly like Nicole Kidman, you would think John might be satisfied. But no: She is tall, all right, but she is a chain-smoker, speaks no English, and throws up out the car window. He tests her language skills in a brief conversation: "Are you a giraffe?" "Yes."

John calls the marriage agency to complain. He wants to return Nadia and get himself a nonsmoking English speaker. Nadia keeps smiling, discovers his secret horde of porn magazines and videos, and cheerfully reenacts some of the scenarios she finds there. Soon John is beginning to reevaluate his consumer complaint.

So goes the setup for *Birthday Girl,* a comedy that starts out lightheartedly and makes some unexpected turns, especially after Nadia's two alleged cousins arrive from Russia. Yuri and Alexei, played by those two hard-edged French actors Vincent Cassel and Mathieu Kassovitz, reminded me of Emil and Oleg, the two Russians who turn up in *15 Minutes,* with the difference that they are not quite as ambitious and sinister; it appears at first they are basically after a free lunch.

There is a curious problem with *Birthday Girl,* hard to put your finger on: The movie is kind of sour. It wants to be funny and a little nasty, it wants to surprise us and then console us, but what it mostly does is make us restless. Strange, how the personalities of characters can refuse to match the work laid out for them by the script. I did not much like anyone in the movie, not even poor John Buckingham, and as for Nadia, she has to go through so many twists and turns that finally we don't know what to believe, nor do we much care.

The movie's downfall is to substitute plot for personality. It doesn't really know or care about the characters, and uses them as markers for a series of preordained events. Since these events take us into darker places than we expect, and then pull us back out again with still more arbitrary plotting, we lose interest; these people do not seem plausible, and we feel toyed with. Even the funny moments feel like nothing more than—well, the filmmakers inventing funny moments.

Black and White ★ ★ ★
R, 100 m., 2000

Bijou Phillips (Charlie), Power (Rich Bower), Scott Caan (Scotty), Ben Stiller (Mark Clear), Allan Houston (Dean), Claudia Schiffer (Greta), Mike Tyson (Himself), Brooke Shields (Sam), Robert Downey Jr. (Terry), Stacy Edwards (Sheila), Gaby Hoffmann (Raven), Jared Leto (Casey), Marla Maples (Muffy), Kim Matulova (Kim), Joe Pantoliano (Bill King). Directed by James Toback and produced by Michael Mailer, Daniel Bigel, and Ron Rotholz. Screenplay by Toback.

Like James Toback himself, his new film is in your face, overflowing with ideas, outrageous in its connections, maddening, illogical, and fascinating. Also like its author, it is never boring. Toback is the brilliant wild child of indie cinema, now a wild man in his fifties, whose films sometimes seem half-baked, but you like them that way: The agony of invention is there on the screen.

Black and White is one of those Manhattan stories where everyone knows each other: rich kids, ghetto kids, rappers, Brooke Shields, the district attorney, a rogue cop, a gambler, a basketball star, Mike Tyson, recording executives. They're all mixed up in a story about race, sex, music, bribery, fathers, sons, murder, and lifestyles. What's amazing is how it's been marketed as a film about white kids who identify with black lifestyles and want to be black themselves. There's a little of that, and a lot more other stuff. It's a crime movie as much as anything.

The sex has gotten the most attention; the opening scene, of a threesome in Central Park, had to be recut three times to avoid an NC-17 rating (you can see the original version, murkily, on the Web). We meet Charlie (Bijou Phillips), the rich girl who "wants to be black" and also adds, later: "I'm a little kid. Kids go through phases. When I grow up, I'll be over it. I'm a kid from America."

True, the racial divide of years ago is blurred and disappearing among the younger siblings of Generation X. The characters in this movie slide easily in and out of various roles, with sex as the lubricant. Toback's camera follows one character into a situation and another out of it, gradually building a mosaic in which we meet a black gangster named Rich (hip-hop producer Power), a rap group (Wu-Tang Clan), a basketball guard named Dean (real-life Knick Allan Houston), his faithless Ph.D. candidate girlfriend (Claudia Schiffer), a crooked cop (Ben Stiller), a documentary filmmaker (Brooke Shields), the husband everyone but she knows is gay (Robert Downey Jr.), and heavyweight champ Mike Tyson, playing himself, and improvising some of the best scenes.

The story, which involves bribery, murder, and blackmail, I will leave for you to discover. Consider the style. Toback has observed that for musicians like Wu-Tang Clan, their language is their art form, so he didn't write a lot of the dialogue in the movie. Instead, he plugged actors into situations, told them where they had to go, and let them improvise. This leads to an electrifying scene where Downey makes a sexual advance on Mike Tyson ("In the dream, you were holding me . . ."), and Tyson's reaction is quick and spontaneous.

But now compare that with another scene where Brooke Shields makes a pass at Tyson. Downey is one kind of an actor, Shields another. Downey is in character, Shields is to some degree playing herself, and Tyson is completely himself. What we are watching in the second scene is Brooke Shields the celebrity playing a character who is essentially herself, acting in an improvised scene. So the scene isn't drama; it's documentary: cinema verité of Shields and Tyson working at improvisation. It's too easy to say the scene doesn't work because Shields is not quite convincing: It *does* work because she's not quite convincing. Toback's films have that way of remaining alive and edgy, and letting their rough edges show.

The plot is sometimes maddening. Without revealing too much, I will say that a great deal hinges on the policeman (Stiller) being able to count on a chain of events he could not possibly have anticipated. He needs to know that the basketball player will tell his girlfriend something, that she will tell another person, and that the other person will eventually try to hire as a killer the very person who suits the cop's needs. Unlikely.

Against untidiness like that, Toback balances passages of wonderful invention. Downey has a scene where he tries to tell Shields he is gay. Tyson ("I'm a man who has made too many mistakes to be known for his wisdom") has a scene where he gives advice to a friend who wants to know if he should have someone killed. Toback plays the manager of a recording studio who brushes off a rap group that wants to hire space, but the next day is happy to talk to their white manager (wary of the shootings associated with some rap artists, he explains, "What I cannot afford is a corpse in my lobby"). And to balance Charlie's rich white girl play-acting ("I want to be black") is a more sensible black girl ("I'm from the 'hood and I don't want to live there. I go back and see my friends and they wanna get out").

Black and White is not smooth and well-oiled, not fish, not fowl, not documentary, not quite fiction, and not about any single theme you can pin down. Those points are all to its credit.

Black Hawk Down ★ ★ ★ ★
R, 143 m., 2002

Josh Hartnett (Eversmann), Ewan McGregor (Grimes), Tom Sizemore (McKnight), Eric Bana (Hoot), William Fichtner (Sanderson), Ewen Bremner (Nelson), Sam Shepard (Garrison), Gabriel Casseus (Kurth), Kim Coates (Wex). Directed by Ridley Scott and produced by Jerry Bruckheimer and Scott. Screenplay by Ken Nolan and Steve Zaillian, based on the book by Mark Bowden.

Ridley Scott's *Black Hawk Down* tells the story of a U.S. military raid that went disastrously wrong when optimistic plans ran into unexpected resistance. In Mogadishu, Somalia, in October 1993, eighteen Americans lost their lives, seventy more were wounded, and within days President Bill Clinton pulled out troops that were on a humanitarian mission. By then some 300,000 Somalians had died of starvation, and the U.S. purpose was to help deliver UN food shipments. Somalian warlords were more interested in protecting their turf than feeding their people—an early warning of the kind of zeal that led to September 11.

The movie is single-minded in its purpose. It wants to record as accurately as possible what it was like to be one of the soldiers under fire on that mission. Hour by hour, step by step, it reconstructs the chain of events. The plan was to stage a surprise raid by helicopter-borne troops, joined by ground forces, on a meeting of a warlord's top lieutenants. This was thought to be such a straightforward task that some soldiers left behind their canteens and night vision gear, expecting to be back at the base in a few hours. It didn't work out that way.

What happened is that enemy rockets brought down two of the helicopters. The warlord's troops gathered quickly and surrounded the U.S. positions. Roadblocks and poor communications prevented a support convoy from approaching. And a grim firefight became a war of attrition. The Americans gave better than they got, but from any point of view the U.S. raid was a catastrophe. The movie's im-

plied message was that America on that day lost its resolve to risk American lives in distant and obscure struggles, and that mind-set weakened our stance against terrorism.

The engagement itself seems to have degenerated into bloody chaos. Ridley Scott's achievement is to render it comprehensible to the audience. We understand, more or less, where the Americans are, and why, and what their situation is. We follow several leading characters, but this is not a star-driven project and doesn't depend on dialogue or personalities. It is about the logistics of that day in October, and how training did help those expert fighters (Army Rangers and Delta Force) to defend themselves as well as possible when all the plans went wrong and they were left hanging out to dry.

His longest day begins with a briefing by Major General William F. Garrison (Sam Shepard), who explains how intelligence has discovered the time and location of a meeting by lieutenants of the warlord Mohamed Farah Aidid. A taxi with a white cross on its roof will park next to the building to guide the airborne troops, who will drop down on ropes, be joined by ground forces, secure the building, and take prisoners. The problem with this plan, as Garrison discovers in steadily more discouraging feedback, is that the opposition is better armed, better positioned, and able to call on quick reinforcements.

We follow several stories. A man falls from a helicopter and is injured when he misses his descent rope. A pilot is taken prisoner. Desperate skirmishes unfold in streets and rubble as darkness falls. The Americans are short on ammo and water, facing enemies not particularly shy about exposing themselves to danger.

Black Hawk Down doesn't have heroic foreground figures like most war movies. The leading characters are played by stars who will be familiar to frequent moviegoers, but may be hard to tell apart for others. They include Josh Hartnett, much more convincing here than in *Pearl Harbor*, as a staff sergeant in command of one of the raiding teams; Ewan McGregor as a Ranger specialist whose specialties are paperwork and coffee making until he is pressed into service; Tom Sizemore as a veteran who provides steady counsel for younger troops; and William Fichtner as a fighter who seems to have internalized every shred of training, and embodies it instinctively.

The cinematography by Slawomir Idziak avoids the bright colors of upbeat combat movies, and its drab, dusty tones gradually drain of light as night falls. The later scenes of the movie feel chilly and forlorn; the surrounded troops are alone and endangered in the night. The screenplay by Ken Nolan and Steve Zaillian, working from a book by Mark Bowden, understands the material and tells it so clearly and efficiently that we are involved not only in the experience of the day but also in its strategies and unfolding realities.

Films like this are more useful than gung ho capers like *Behind Enemy Lines*. They help audiences understand and sympathize with the actual experiences of combat troops, instead of trivializing them into entertainments. Although the American mission in Somalia was humanitarian, the movie avoids speechmaking and sloganeering, and at one point, discussing why soldiers risk their lives in situations like this, a veteran says, "It's about the men next to you. That's all it is." ☞

Blade II ★ ★ ★ ½
R, 110 m., 2002

Wesley Snipes (Blade), Kris Kristofferson (Whistler), Ron Perlman (Reinhardt), Luke Goss (Nomak), Leonor Varela (Nyssa), Matt Schulze (Chupa), Norman Reedus (Scud). Directed by Guillermo del Toro and produced by Peter Frankfurt and Patrick Palmer. Screenplay by David S. Goyer.

Blade II is a really rather brilliant vomitorium of viscera, a comic book with dreams of becoming a textbook for mad surgeons. There are shots here of the insides of vampires that make your average autopsy look like a slow afternoon at Supercuts. The movie has been directed by Guillermo del Toro, whose work is dominated by two obsessions: war between implacable ancient enemies, and sickening things that bite you and aren't even designed to let go.

The movie is an improvement on *Blade* (1998), which was pretty good. Once again it stars Wesley Snipes as the Marvel Comics hero who is half-man, half-vampire. He was raised from childhood by Whistler (Kris Kristofferson), a vampire hunter who kept Blade's vampirism in check, and trained him to fight the nosferatus. Time has passed, Whistler has been captured by vampires and floats unconscious in a storage tank while his blood is harvested, and Blade prowls the streets in his lonely war.

One night, acrobatic creatures with glowing red eyes invade Blade's space and engage in a violent battle that turns out to be entirely gratuitous, because after they remove their masks to reveal themselves as vampires—a ferocious warrior and a foxy babe—they only want to deliver a message: "You have been our worst enemy. But now there is something else on the streets worse than you!" This reminded me of the night in O'Rourke's when McHugh asked this guy why he carried a gun and the guy said he lived in a dangerous neighborhood and McHugh said it would be safer if he moved.

The Vampire Nation is under attack by a new breed of vampires named Reapers, who drink the blood of both humans and vampires, and are insatiable. Blade, who is both human and vampire, is like a balanced meal. If the Reapers are not destroyed, both races will die. This news is conveyed by a vampire leader whose brain can be dimly seen through a light blue, translucent plastic shell, more evidence of the design influence of the original iMac.

Blade and Whistler (now rescued from the tank and revived with a "retro-virus injection") join the vampires in this war, which is not without risk, because of course if the Reapers are destroyed, the vampires will turn on them. There is a story line, however quickly sketched, to support the passages of pure action, including computer-aided fight scenes of astonishing pacing and agility. Snipes once again plays Blade not as a confident superhero, but as a once-confused kid who has been raised to be good at his work and uncertain about his identity. He is attracted to the vampire Nyssa (Leonor Varela), but we sense a relationship between a creature of the night and Blade, known as the Daywalker, is sooner or later going to result in arguments over their work schedules.

The Reapers are the masterpieces of this movie. They all have what looks like a scar down the center of their chins. The first time we see one, it belongs to a donor who has turned up at a blood bank in Prague. This is not the kind of blood bank you want to get your next transfusion from. It has a bug zapper hanging from the wall, and an old drunk who says you can even bring in cups of blood from outside and they'll buy them.

The chin scar, it turns out, is not a scar but a cleft. These Reapers are nasty. They have mouths that unfold into tripartite jaws. Remember the claws on the steam shovels in those prize games at the carnival, where you manipulated the wheels and tried to pick up valuable prizes? Now put them on a vampire and make them big and bloody, with fangs and mucous and viscous black saliva. And then imagine a tongue coiled inside with an eating and sucking mechanism on the end of it that looks like the organ evolution forgot— the sort of thing diseased livers have nightmares about. Later they slice open a Reaper's chest cavity and Blade and Whistler look inside.

Blade: The heart is surrounded in bone!
Whistler: Good luck getting a stake through it!

Del Toro's early film *Cronos* (1993) was about an ancient golden beetle that sank its claws into the flesh of its victims and injected an immortality serum. His *Mimic* (1997) was about a designer insect, half-mantis, half-termite, that escapes into the subway system and mutates into a very big bug. Characters would stick their hands into dark places and I would slide down in my seat. His *The Devil's Backbone* (2001), set in an orphanage at the time of the Spanish civil war, is a ghost story, not a horror picture, but does have a body floating in a tank.

Still in his thirties, the Mexican-born director doesn't depend on computers to get him through a movie and impress the kids with fancy fight scenes. He brings his creepy phobias along with him. You can sense the difference between a movie that's a technical exercise *(Resident Evil)* and one steamed in the dread cauldrons of the filmmaker's imagination.

Blood Simple: 2000 Director's Cut ★ ★ ★ ★

R, 97 m., 2000

John Getz (Ray), Frances McDormand (Abby), Dan Hedaya (Julian Marty), M. Emmet Walsh (Loren Visser), Samm-Art Williams (Meurice), Deborah Neumann (Debra), Raquel Gavia (Landlady), Van Brooks (Man from Lubbock). Directed by Joel Coen and produced by Ethan Coen. Screenplay by Joel Coen and Ethan Coen.

The genius of *Blood Simple* is that everything that happens seems necessary. The movie's a blood-soaked nightmare in which greed and lust trap the characters in escalating horror. The plot twists in upon itself. Characters are found in situations of diabolical complexity. And yet it doesn't feel like the film is just piling it on. Step by inexorable step, logically, one damned thing leads to another.

Consider the famous sequence in which a man is in one room and his hand is nailed to the windowsill in another room. How he got into that predicament, and how he tries to get out of it, all makes perfect sense when you see the film. But if you got an assignment in a film class that began with a close-up of that hand snaking in through the window and being nailed down, how easy would it be to write the setup scenes?

This was the first film directed by Joel Coen, produced by Ethan Coen, and cowritten by the brothers. Their joint credits have since become famous, with titles like *Miller's Crossing, Raising Arizona, Barton Fink,* and the incomparable *Fargo.* Sometimes they succeed and sometimes they fail, but they always swing for the fences, and they are masters of plot. As I wrote in my original review of *Blood Simple:* "Every individual detail seems to make sense, and every individual choice seems logical, but the choices and details form a bewildering labyrinth." They build crazy walls with sensible bricks.

What we have here is the fifteenth anniversary "director's cut" of *Blood Simple,* restored and rereleased. Its power remains undiminished: It is one of the best of the modern *film noirs,* a grimy story of sleazy people trapped in a net of betrayal and double cross. When it uses clichés like The Corpse that Will Not Die, it raises them to a whole new level of usefulness. The Coens are usually original, but when they borrow a movie convention, they rotate it so that the light shines through in an unexpected way.

How exactly is this a "director's cut"? It runs ninety-seven minutes. The original film had the same running time. The term "director's cut" often means the director has at last been able to restore scenes that the studio or the MPAA made him take out. The Coens have kept all the original scenes in *Blood Simple,* and performed a little nip and tuck operation, tightening shots of dialogue they think outstayed their usefulness. It is a subtle operation; you will not notice much different from the earlier cut. The two running times are the same, I deduce, because the brothers have added a tongue-in-cheek preface in which a film restoration expert introduces the new version and claims that it takes advantage of technological breakthroughs made possible since the original came out in 1985.

Blood Simple was made on a limited budget, but like most good films seems to have had all the money it really needed. It is particularly blessed in its central performances. Dan Hedaya plays the unshaven owner of a scummy saloon who hires a private eye to kill his wife and her lover. The wife (Frances McDormand) is having an affair with one of the bartenders (John Getz). The detective is played by that poet of sleaze, M. Emmet Walsh. He takes the bar owner's money and then kills the bar owner. Neat. If he killed the wife, he reasons, he'd still have to kill the bar owner to eliminate a witness against him. This way, he gets the same amount of money for one killing, not two.

Oh, but it gets much more complicated than that. At any given moment in the movie there seems to be one more corpse than necessary, one person who is alive and should be dead, and one person who is completely clueless about both the living and the dead. There is no psychology in the film. Every act is inspired more or less directly by the act that went before, and the motive is always the same: self-preservation, based on guilt and paranoia.

Blood Simple is comic in its dark way, and obviously wants to go over the top. But it doesn't call attention to its contrivance. It is easy to do a parody of *film noir,* but hard to do good *film noir,* and almost impossible to make a film that works as suspense and exaggeration at the same time. *Blood Simple* is clever in the way it makes its incredulities seem necessary.

In my 1985 review, I tried to explain that: "It keys into three common nightmares: (1) You clean and clean but there's still blood all over

the place; (2) you know you have committed a murder, but you're not sure how or why; (3) you know you've forgotten a small detail that will eventually get you into a lot of trouble." Those feelings are so elemental that the movie involves us even though we know the Coens are laughing as they devise their fiendish complications. In a strange way, the contrivances also help excuse the blood and gore. If you are squeamish, here is the film to make you squeam.

Blow ★ ★ ½
R, 119 m., 2001

Johnny Depp (George Jung), Penelope Cruz (Mirtha), Franka Potente (Barbara), Paul Reubens (Derek Foreal), Ray Liotta (Fred Jung), Jacque Lawson (Biker), Cliff Curtis (Pablo Escobar), Ethan Suplee (Tuna), Rachel Griffiths (Ermine Jung). Directed by Ted Demme and produced by Demme, Denis Leary, and Joel Stillerman. Screenplay by David McKenna and Nick Cassavetes, based on the book by Bruce Porter.

Blow stars Johnny Depp in a biopic about George Jung, a man who claims that in the late 1970s he imported about 85 percent of all the cocaine in America. That made him the greatest success story in drugs, an industry that has inspired more movies than any other. So why is he such a sad sack? Why is his life so monotonous and disappointing? That's what he'd like to know. The last shot in the film shows the real George Jung staring out at us from the screen like a man buried alive in his own regrets.

The story begins in a haze of California dreamin' for George, who escapes West from an uninspiring Massachusetts childhood, a relentless mother (Rachel Griffiths), and a father (Ray Liotta) who doesn't want to deal with bad news about his son. In the Los Angeles environs of Manhattan Beach, George smokes pot, throws Frisbees, meets stewardesses, and engages in boozy plans with his friend Tuna (Ethan Suplee), who asks him, "You know how we were wondering how we were gonna get money being that we don't want to get jobs?"

The brainstorm: Import marijuana from Mexico in the customs-free luggage of their stewardess pals and sell it to eager students at eastern colleges. This is a business plan waiting to be born, and soon George is wealthy, although not beyond his wildest imaginings. His first love is a stewardess named Barbara (Franka Potente, from *Run, Lola, Run*) and it's fun, fun, fun, and her daddy never takes her T-Bird away.

These opening chapters in the life of George Jung tell a story of small risk and great joy, especially if your idea of a good time is having all the money you can possibly spend and hopelessly conventional ideas about how to spend it. How big a house can you live in? How many drugs can you consume? George never actually planned to become a drug dealer and is a little bemused at his good luck. Even a 1972 bust in Chicago seems like a minor bump in the road (speaking in his own defense, he tells the judge, "It ain't me, babe").

Back on the streets, George finds clouds obscuring the California sun. Barbara dies unexpectedly (i.e., not because of drugs), and his success attracts the interest of a better class of narcotics cop. He becomes a fugitive, and it is his own mother who rats on him with the cops, even while his father is beaming at what might seem to be his success.

In Danbury Prison, he tells us, "I went in with a bachelor's of marijuana and came out with a doctorate in cocaine." As the 1970s roll on, the innocence of pot has been replaced by the urgency of cocaine. Soon George is making real money as a key distributor for his new friend Pablo Escobar (Cliff Curtis) and the Medellin drug cartel of Colombia. It's with their cocaine that he racks up his record market share. And there is a new woman, Mirtha (Penelope Cruz), sexy as hell, but a real piece of work in the deportment department. At one point she gets him arrested by throwing a tantrum in their car.

The Colombians, of course, are heavy-hitters, and George tries to protect his position by concealing the identity of his key California middleman, a onetime hairdresser named Derek Foreal (Paul Reubens). But the Colombians want to know that name really bad, and meanwhile George might be asking, is a rich man under the shadow of sudden death measurably happier than a man with a more mundane but serene existence?

This is not, alas, a question that occurs to George Jung. Indeed, not many questions occur to him that are not directly related to getting, spending, and sleeping with. The later chapters of his life grow increasingly depressing. He was never an interesting person, never had thoughts worth sharing or words worth remembering, but at least he represented a colorful type in his early years: the kid who smokes a little weed, finds a source, starts to sell, and finds himself with a brand-new pair of roller skates. By his middle years, George is essentially just the guy the Colombians want to replace and the feds want to arrest. No fun.

The dreary story of his final defeats is a record of backstabbing and broken trusts, and although there is a certain poignancy in his final destiny, it is tempered by our knowledge that millions of lives had to be destroyed by addiction so that George and his onetime friends could arrive at their crossroads.

That's the thing about George. He thinks it's all about him. His life, his story, his success, his fortune, his lost fortune, his good luck, his bad luck. Actually, all he did was operate a tollgate between suppliers and addicts. You wonder, but you never find out, if the reality of those destroyed lives ever occurred to him.

The movie, directed by Ted Demme and written by David McKenna and Nick Cassavetes (from an as-told-to book by Bruce Porter), is well made and well acted. As a story of the rise and fall of this man, it serves. Johnny Depp is a versatile and reliable actor who almost always chooses interesting projects. The failure is George Jung's. For all the glory of his success and the pathos of his failure, he never became a person interesting enough to make a movie about. The appearance of Ray Liotta here reminds us of Scorsese's *GoodFellas*, which took a much less important criminal and made him an immeasurably more interesting character. And of course Al Pacino's *Scarface* has so much style he makes George Jung look like a dry-goods clerk. Which essentially he was. Take away the drugs, and this is the story of a boring life in wholesale.

The Blue Angel ★ ★ ★ ½
NO MPAA RATING, 106 m., 1929 (rereleased 2001)

Emil Jannings (Professor Immanuel Rath), Marlene Dietrich (Lola Lola), Kurt Gerron

(Kiepert, the Magician), Rosa Valetti (Guste, His Wife), Hans Albers (Mazeppa, the Strong Man), Reinhold Bernt (The Clown), Eduard von Winterstein (The Headmaster), Hans Roth (The Caretaker), Rolf Muller (Angst [Rath's Pupil]). Directed by Josef von Sternberg and produced by Erich Pommer. Screenplay by Robert Liebmann, Karl Vollmoeller, and Carl Zuckmayer, based on the novel *Professor Unrat* by Heinrich Mann.

The Blue Angel will always have a place in film history as the movie that brought Marlene Dietrich to international stardom. At the time it was made, at the birth of the sound era in 1929, it was seen as a vehicle for Emil Jannings, the German actor who had just won the first Academy Award for Best Actor (for both *The Last Command* and *The Way of All Flesh*) after starring in such silent landmarks as *The Last Laugh* and *Faust*. Dietrich's overnight stardom inspired distributors to recut the film, ending it with one of her songs instead of his pathetic closing moments, and this restored version shows the entire film for the first time in years.

Even then there is a choice to be made. Jannings and his director, Josef von Sternberg, had established themselves in the silent era, when films knew no language barriers, and they shot the film in both English and German. This is the English version, with Dietrich and Jannings fluent (the Swiss Jannings claimed, falsely, that he had been born in Brooklyn), but many prefer the German version because the actors feel more at home with the dialogue.

Whatever its language, *The Blue Angel* looks and feels more like a silent film, with its broad performances that underline emotions. Von Sternberg, who was raised in Europe and America and began his career in Hollywood, was much influenced by German expressionism, as we see in early street scenes where the buildings tilt toward each other at crazy angles reminiscent of *The Cabinet of Dr. Caligari*. He was a bold visual artist who liked shots where the actors shared space with foreground props and dramatic shadows, and he makes the dressing room beneath the stage of the Blue Angel nightclub into a haunting psychic dungeon.

Lotte Eisner observes in *The Haunted Screen*, her study of German expressionism, that Stern-

berg was more at ease with sound than many of his contemporaries (this was his second talkie), and was perhaps the first director to deal with how offstage sounds alter as doors are opened and closed. Sound itself was seen as self-sufficient in the earlier days, but von Sternberg was already modulating it, tilting it toward realism.

His story involves the fall and humiliation of Professor Immanuel Rath (Jannings), a respected high school professor who one day confiscates a postcard showing Lola Lola (Dietrich), the dancer at a local nightclub. Visiting the club to reprimand any students he might find there, the professor falls under the spell of Dietrich, who looks fleshier and more carnal than she later appeared. Soon he is lost. He marries her (in a showbiz wedding of grotesque toasts and whispered gossip), goes on the road, and returns to his hometown some years later as a bit player in her stage show—the stooge of a magician who produces eggs from the professor's nose and cracks them on the old man's head.

Jannings specialized in roles where he was humiliated; *The Last Laugh*, where he plays a proud hotel doorman who loses his position, is the most famous. His performance in *The Blue Angel* is odd; he plays a high school teacher and is presumably intelligent, yet his thoughts and actions seem slowed-down and laborious, as if he's puzzling things out as he goes along. Dietrich had made seven silent films before this one, but seems to adapt easily to the quickened pace of talkies, and of course her stardom depended on sound; her singing of "Falling in Love Again" in this film established it as her trademark. (Three years later, in von Sternberg's *Shanghai Express*, she would utter that masterpiece of understatement, "It took more than one man to change my name to Shanghai Lily.")

The puzzle throughout *The Blue Angel* is why Lola Lola marries the sad, besotted professor. It appears they have a sex life, at least for one night, although it is not appealing to imagine its nature. There are times when she seems fond of him, times when she is indifferent, times when she is unfaithful, and yet she has a certain stubborn affection for this pathetic figure. Perhaps he acts as a front for her shadow life of discreet prostitution; perhaps, in a world that regards her as a tramp, she values the one man who idealizes her.

Dietrich, in any event, never seemed to embody romance; the sexual identity she offered, in film after film, was that of a predator, disillusioned by men, satisfying her physical needs but indifferent to their providers. She seems to have all of the equipment of a woman except for the instruction manual, and it's interesting that Dietrich is a favorite role for female impersonators, in movies like *The Damned* and in life; if you are a man who wants to play a woman, Dietrich meets you halfway.

The Blue Angel lumbers a little on its way to a preordained conclusion, but is intriguing for its glimpses of backstage life in shabby German prewar vaudeville, and for Dietrich's performance, which seems to float above the action as if she's stepping fastidiously across gutters. The final humiliation of the professor is agonizing and protracted, and Siegfried Kracauer, in his study *From Caligari to Hitler*, found it one more example of the way German movies mirrored their society in humiliating intellectuals and glorifying the physical. You can glimpse the sadomasochism of the Nazi pose in the strange relationship of Professor Rath and Lola Lola.

Boiler Room ★ ★ ★ ½
R, 119 m., 2000

Giovanni Ribisi (Seth), Vin Diesel (Chris), Nia Long (Abby), Nicky Katt (Greg), Scott Caan (Richie), Ron Rifkin (Seth's Father [Marty]), Jamie Kennedy (Adam), Taylor Nichols (Harry Reynard), Ben Affleck (Jim). Directed by Ben Younger and produced by Suzanne Todd and Jennifer Todd. Screenplay by Younger.

Boiler Room tells the story of a nineteen-year-old named Seth who makes a nice income running an illegal casino in his apartment. His dad, a judge, finds out about it and raises holy hell. So the kid gets a daytime job as a broker with a Long Island bucket shop that sells worthless or dubious stock with high-pressure telephone tactics. When he was running his casino, Seth muses, at least he was providing a product that his customers wanted.

The movie is the writing and directing debut of Ben Younger, a twenty-nine-year-old who says he interviewed a lot of brokers while writing the screenplay. I believe him. The movie hums with authenticity, and knows a lot about the cultlike power of a company that promises to turn its trainees into millionaires, and certainly turns them into efficient phone salesmen.

No experience is necessary at J. P. Marlin: "We don't hire brokers here—we train new ones," snarls Jim (Ben Affleck), already a millionaire, who gives new recruits a hard-edged introductory lecture, crammed with obscenities and challenges to their manhood. "Did you see *Glengarry Glen Ross*?" he asks them. He certainly has. Mamet's portrait of high-pressure real-estate salesmen is like a bible in this culture, and a guy like Jim doesn't see the message, only the style. (Younger himself observes that Jim, giving his savage pep talks, not only learned his style from Alec Baldwin's scenes in *Glengarry* but also wants to *be* Baldwin.)

The film's narrator is Seth Davis (Giovanni Ribisi), an unprepossessing young man with a bad suit who learns in a short time to separate suckers from their money with telephone fantasies about hot stocks and IPOs. Everybody wants to be a millionaire *right now*, he observes. Ironically, the dream of wealth he's selling with his cold calls is the same one J. P. Marlin is selling him.

In the phone war room with Seth are several other brokers, including the successful Chris (Vin Diesel) and Greg (Nicky Katt), who exchange anti-Jewish and Italian slurs almost as if it's expected of them. At night the guys go out, get drunk, and sometimes get in fights with brokers from other houses. The kids gambling in Seth's apartment were better behaved. We observe that both gamblers and stockbrokers bet their money on a future outcome, but as a gambler you pay the house nut, while as a broker you collect the house nut. Professional gamblers claim they do not depend on luck but on an understanding of the odds and prudent money management. Investors believe much the same thing. Of course, nobody ever claims luck has nothing to do with it unless luck has something to do with it.

The movie has the high-octane feel of real life, closely observed. It's made more interesting because Seth isn't a slickster like Michael Douglas or Charlie Sheen in *Wall Street* (a movie these guys know by heart), but an uncertain, untested young man who stands in the shadow of his father the judge (Ron Rifkin) who, he thinks, is always judging him. The tension between Seth and the judge is one of the best things in the film—especially in Rifkin's quiet, clear power in scenes where he lays down the law. When Seth refers to their relationship, his dad says: "Relationship? What relationship? I'm not your girlfriend. Relationships are your mother's shtick. I'm your father."

A relationship does grow in the film, however, between Seth and Abby (Nia Long), the receptionist, and although it eventually has a lot to do with the plot, what I admired was the way Younger writes their scenes so that they actually share hopes, dreams, backgrounds, and insecurities instead of falling into automatic movie passion. When she touches his hand, it is at the end of a scene during which she empathizes with him.

Because of the routine racism at the firm, Seth observes it must not be a comfortable place for a black woman to work. Abby points out she makes $80,000 a year and is supporting a sick mother. Case closed, with no long, anguished dramaturgy over interracial dating; they like each other, and have evolved beyond racial walls. Younger's handling of their scenes shames movies where the woman exists only to be the other person in the sex scene.

The acting is good all around. A few days ago I saw Vin Diesel as a vicious prisoner in the space opera *Pitch Black,* and now here he is, still tough, still with the shaved head, but now the only guy at the brokerage that Seth really likes and trusts enough to appeal to. Diesel is interesting. Something will come of him.

Boiler Room isn't perfect. The film's ending is a little too busy; it's too contrived the way Abby doesn't tell Seth something he needs to know; there's a scene where a man calls her by name and Seth leaps to a conclusion when in fact that man would have every reason to know her name; and I am still not sure exactly what kind of a deal Seth was trying to talk his father into in their crucial evening meeting. But those are all thoughts I had afterward. During the movie I was wound up with tension and involvement, all the more so because the characters are all complex and guilty, the good as well as the bad, and we can understand why everyone in the movie does what they do. Would we? Depends.

Book of Shadows: Blair Witch 2 ★ ★
R, 90 m., 2000

Kim Director (Kim Director), Jeffrey Donovan (Jeffrey Donovan), Erica Leerhsen (Erica Leerhsen), Tristen Skyler (Tristen Skyler), Stephen Turner (Stephen Turner). Directed by Joe Berlinger and produced by Bill Carraro, Daniel Myrick, and Eduardo Sanchez. Screenplay by Berlinger and Dick Beebe.

To direct a sequel to their phenomenal *Blair Witch Project,* Daniel Myrick and Eduardo Sanchez made an unexpected choice: Joe Berlinger, codirector of the documentaries *Paradise Lost: The Child Murders at Robin Hood Hills* and *Paradise Lost 2: Revelations.* Those two films make a persuasive case that three innocent young men from Arkansas are in prison, one on death row, because of local hysteria over teenagers who wear black and listen to heavy metal music. Meanwhile, a person who seems to be the real killer all but confesses on camera.

The movies are deadly serious because they make the case that injustice is being done. Lives are at stake. I wondered earlier why Berlinger would want to make a fiction film on witchcraft and black magic, but suspended judgment: He is one of the best documentarians around. But now that I've seen *Book of Shadows: Blair Witch 2,* I'm disturbed.

The movie shows no special insight that made it necessary for Berlinger to direct it. It's a muddled, sometimes atmospheric, effort that could have come from many filmmakers. At the same time, because of loaded characters and dialogue, *BW2* supplies ammunition to those who think the Arkansas prisoners are guilty. I can imagine a preacher thundering from his pulpit: "This Berlinger comes down here and makes a couple of propaganda films making us look bad, and then what does he do? Make a film glorifying black magic and witches."

If the film had argued against the mind-set that essentially framed the West Memphis Three, that would be one thing. But it doesn't. This is not one of Joe Berlinger's proudest days.

But what about the movie itself—apart from Berlinger's involvement? It opens promisingly as a documentary about the effect that the first movie had on the (fictional) town of Burkittsville, Maryland, where the Blair Witch was rumored to haunt the nearby woods. Tourists have descended on the town, locals are on eBay selling twig sculptures like those in the movie, and the exasperated local sheriff patrols the woods with a bullhorn, shouting, "Get out of these woods and go home! There is no goddamned Blair Witch!"

We meet a group of witch fanciers who have signed up for an overnight tour in the woods. The Blair Witch Hunt, as it is called, is led by a tour guide (Jeff Donovan) who, we will learn, is a former mental patient, now cured, apparently. Others include Erica, a witch who practices wicca, which is the white-magic form of witchcraft; Stephen and his girlfriend, the pregnant Tristen, who are writing a book on the hysteria caused by the film; and Kim, who dresses in black and says, in an oblique reference to the *Paradise Lost* movies, "Where I come from, people believe because I dress in black I'm some kind of killer." (In keeping with the *BW* pseudorealistic approach, all of the actors play characters who have their names.)

The group plunges into the woods, where they begin to argue about their different approaches to the experience. I liked Erica's cautionary wiccan lore: "The first rule of wicca is, do no harm, because whatever you do will come back to you threefold." This sounds like *Pay It Forward* in reverse. Soon they have a confrontation with another tour group, which leads to an unconvincing shoving match. The other group is advised to seek out Coffin Rock, with fatal results, and eventually the sheriff gets involved and the movie intercuts interrogation scenes as the Witch Hunt group are quizzed by the law.

Like the first movie, this one has two visual styles (but not nearly as much of that handheld photography that forced some patrons to recycle their popcorn bags). Most of it is in 35mm. The rest is video footage shot by the protagonists. The 35mm footage may or may not accurately reflect how the characters remember what happened; the video footage may or may not be an objective record of some of the same events. And . . . is there really a Blair Witch? The answer, if any, may come in *BW3*, now being prepared by Myrick and Sanchez.

Book of Shadows: Blair Witch 2 is not a very lucid piece of filmmaking (and contains no Book of Shadows). I suppose it seems clear enough to Berlinger, who cowrote it and helped edit it, but one viewing is not enough to make the material clear, and the material is not intriguing enough, alas, to inspire a second viewing. The characters are not strongly and colorfully established, there is no persuasive story line, and what planet does that hey-rube sheriff come from? He breaks the reality with every appearance.

The Blair Witch Project was perhaps one of a kind. Its success made a sequel inevitable, but this is not the sequel, I suspect, anyone much wanted. The opening scenes—the documentary showing the townspeople affected by the first film—is a more promising approach, because instead of trying to cover similar ground, it goes outside the first film and makes its own stand.

Bootmen ★ ½
R, 95 m., 2000

Adam Garcia (Sean Ikden), Sam Worthington (Mitchell Ikden), Sophie Lee (Linda), William Zappa (Walter), Richard Carter (Gary), Susie Porter (Sara), Dein Perry (Anthony). Directed by Dein Perry and produced by Hilary Linstead. Screenplay by Steve Worland.

Bootmen is the story of a young dancer and his friends who revisit the clichés of countless other dance movies in order to bring forth a dance performance of clanging unloveliness. Screwing metal plates to the soles of their work boots, they stomp in unison on flat steel surfaces while banging on things. Imagine Fred Astaire as a punch-press operator.

The movie has been adapted by director Dein Perry from his own performance piece, which he might have been better advised to make into a concert film. It takes place in Australia, where Sean (Adam Garcia) dreams of becoming a dancer. His salt-of-the-earth father, a steelworker, opposes the plan. Sean cannot face life without dance in Newcastle, a steel town, despite the charms of the fragrant Linda (Sophie Lee), a hairdresser who has given him to understand that he might someday, but not yet, enjoy her favors. He flees to Sydney to pursue his career, leaving behind his brother Mitchell, who basks in the old man's favor by adopting a reasonable occupation and stealing cars for their parts.

In Sydney, Sean encounters a hard-nosed choreographer (William Zappa), a staple of dance movies, who is not easy to impress. Sean is too talented to be dismissed, but at rehearsals he angers the star (Dein Perry himself) because the star's girlfriend likes his looks, and Sean gets fired. It is one of the oddities of this movie about dance that almost everyone in it is not merely straight but ferociously macho; it's as if the Village People really did work eight hours a day as linemen, Indian chiefs, etc. I am not suggesting that all, or most, or many dancers are gay, but surely one has heard that some are?

Sean returns disillusioned but undefeated to Newcastle, where Mitchell meanwhile has gotten the lonely Linda drunk, plied her with morose theories about Sean's long absence, and bedded her during an alcoholic lapse of judgment on her part (Mitchell has no judgment). Sean arrives in the morning, discovers that Mitchell and Linda have sailed into waters that Linda had assured him would remain uncharted pending their own maiden voyage, and becomes so depressed that we realize we have reached the Preliminary Crisis as defined in elementary screenwriting outlines.

Now what? It remains only for the steel mills to close so that Sean can realize that the millworkers should be retrained as computer experts. But there are no computers. Why not have a benefit? Sean gathers his friends and says, in other words, "Say, gang! Let's rent the old steel mill, and put on a show!" He trains his buddies in the art of synchronized stomping so that the town can turn out to watch them clang and bang. Judging by the crowd they attract, and estimating $10 a ticket, they raise enough money for approximately two computers, but never mind; cruel fate will quickly turn these recycled steelworkers into unemployed dot-com workers, so the fewer, the better.

Is there a scene near the end of the performance where the once-bitter dad enters, sees that his son is indeed talented, and forgives all? Is Linda pardoned for her lapse of faithfulness? Do Mitchell and Sean realize that even though Mitchell may have slept with the woman Sean loves it was because Mitchell had too much to drink, something that could happen in any family? Do the townspeople of Newcastle give a lusty ovation to the performance? Is there an encore? Veteran moviegoers will walk into the theater already possessing the answers to these and many other questions.

Borstal Boy ★ ★
NO MPAA RATING, 93 m., 2002

Shawn Hatosy (Brendan Behan), Danny Dyer (Charlie), Eva Birthistle (Liz), Michael York (Warden), Robin Laing (Jock), Mark Huberman (Mac). Directed by Peter Sheridan and produced by Arthur Lappin and Pat Moylan. Screenplay by Nye Heron and Sheridan, based on the book by Brendan Behan.

For a dozen years of my life, I gazed into the face of Brendan Behan almost nightly. There was an enormous photograph of him on the wall of O'Rourke's Pub on North Avenue, and it didn't take a lip-reader to guess which word began with his upper teeth posed on his lower lip. Drunk and disheveled, he must have been in a late stage of his brief and noisy progress through life. He wrote that to be drunk in Ireland in his youth was not a disgrace but a sign of status, because it showed you had enough money to pay for the drink. By that measurement, Behan was a millionaire.

Still beloved and read by those who remember him, the boy-o has long since faded from his time of great celebrity, when he enlightened talk shows with his boisterous proletarian philosophy. The recent equivalent of his risky performances as a late-night chat star would be Farrah Fawcett crossed with Andrew Dice Clay. He also wrote some good plays and the classic memoir *Borstal Boy*, and died at forty-one—which was old age, considering how he lived.

That is the Behan I remember. The Behan of *Borstal Boy* (Shawn Hatosy) is another person altogether, an idealistic young lad who naively goes to England on a mission for the IRA, is arrested, sent to juvenile prison ("borstal") and there learns to love those he thinks he hates, including the English (through the warden's daughter) and "queers" (through his prison pal Charlie). After being discharged as a presumably pacified bisexual, he returns to Ireland and the movie ends quickly, before having to deal with the facts that he once again took up arms for the IRA, shot a cop, was sent back to prison, and (despite marriage to the saintly Beatrice) found love most reliably in the arms of the bottle.

Is the Brendan Behan of *Borstal Boy* simply the young man before alcoholism rewrote his script? I haven't read the book in years, but my strongest memory is of Behan's defiance—of his unshakable belief that carrying bombs to Liverpool and shooting cops was not criminal because he was a soldier at war. That has been the policy of the IRA from the beginning, that they are not terrorists but soldiers or prisoners of war. It is the same today with terrorists, with the difference that things were ever so much more innocent in the 1950s, so that the borstal warden (Michael York) could see Brendan as a lad with a good heart who just needed a chance to settle down and think things through.

The story hinges on parallel love affairs, both depending on a permissiveness one is a little startled to find in an English juvenile prison in the 1950s. Young Brendan makes best friends with his fellow prisoner Charlie (Danny Dyer), a young sailor who is "openly gay" (says Stephen Holden of the *New York Times*), although I believe being openly gay in those days, when it was against the law, was more a matter of sending signals to those who knew them and staying prudently in the closet otherwise. Certainly Brendan is slow to catch on, both to Charlie's homosexuality and to the promptings of his own heart. He is more obviously attracted to Liz (Eva Birthistle), the warden's daughter.

My guess is that the likelihood of a borstal boy being allowed to spend quality time with the warden's daughter is approximately the same as his chances of making friends with an "openly gay" prisoner, which is to say less likely than being invited to tea with the queen.

Of course, Liz and Charlie may come directly from the pages of the book and I have simply forgotten them. But my problem with *Borstal Boy* isn't so much with the facts as with the tone. If this is an accurate portrait of Brendan Behan at sixteen, then *Borstal Boy* makes the same mistake *Iris* does—gives us these writers before (and in the case of *Iris,* after) the years in which they were the people they became famous for being. True, Behan's book is *about* that period in his life, but written with a gusto and rudeness that's lacking in Peter Sheridan's well-mannered film.

Yes, I know I've defended *A Beautiful Mind* against charges that it left out seamy details from the earlier years of John Forbes Nash, but the difference is, *A Beautiful Mind* focused intently on the central story, which is that he was a schizophrenic whose work won the Nobel Prize. Does anyone much think the central story of Brendan Behan is that he was a bisexual sweetheart before he took to drink? The photo on the wall at O'Rourke's shows him forming the first letter of the first word of his response to that theory.

Bounce ★ ★ ★
PG-13, 102 m., 2000

Ben Affleck (Buddy Amaral), Gwyneth Paltrow (Abby), Natasha Henstridge (Mimi), Johnny Galecki (Buddy's Secretary), Jennifer Grey (Mrs. Guererro), Tony Goldwyn (Greg), Joe Morton (Jim), David Paymer (Lawyer), Alex D. Linz (Scott). Directed by Don Roos and produced by Michael Besman and Steve Golin. Screenplay by Roos.

Bounce begins with flights delayed at Chicago's O'Hare airport. One guy gives another guy his boarding pass, the plane crashes, the other guy dies. The survivor is Buddy (Ben Affleck), an alcoholic ad executive from Los Angeles, whose boozing now spirals out of control, until he joins AA and finds that one of the twelve steps involves making amends to those he harmed with his drinking. So he pays a call on Abby (Gwyneth Paltrow), the widow of the man who died in the crash.

Strictly speaking, Buddy has no amends to make. He was doing the other guy a favor. It wasn't his fault that the flight crashed. But he tracks down Abby, discovers she's a real-estate agent, and arranges for her to get a commission on a building his agency was going to buy anyway. Then she asks him to a Dodgers game, and before you know it they're in love and he's bonding with her kids.

The problem, of course, is that he hasn't told her he's responsible in some cosmic, fateful way for her husband's death. He means to, but he puts it off. Lovers with untold secrets are a familiar movie situation, seen earlier this year in *Return to Me* when Minnie Driver can't tell David Duchovny his late wife's heart was transplanted into her chest.

Bounce builds toward a big revelation scene, of course, and when it comes, it has to be perfectly aimed and well acted because both actors are on thin ice. The moment of truth in *Bounce* is not quite right. The revelation is delayed a few scenes beyond its natural place in the film, and we grow restless; we enjoy the suspense only up to a point. Buddy moistens his lips, clears his throat, and coughs nervously and *still* doesn't tell Abby, and it begins to feel like the movie's playing with us.

There have been hints that the secret may not be revealed verbally. A videotape was made at the airport, and because all props are brought onstage for a reason, we know sooner or later that the tape, showing Buddy with the dead guy, will be seen again. Thinking ahead, I began to wonder how director Don Roos would use the tape. I guessed that maybe before Abby had a chance to look at the tape, the two would share a moment of tenderness and then one of the kids would pop the tape into the VCR and the truth would start playing, unnoticed at first, in the background. Stage this correctly and you might have one of those scenes an audience remembers for a long time.

Incredibly, Roos keeps Abby offstage for the moment of revelation. We don't see her when she learns the truth, and she's not there when he sees the tape. What a missed opportunity. *Bounce* has a strong setup, good characters, intelligent dialogue, and attractive characters, but it loses its way in technique. In movies with this story structure, all depends on the precise timing of the delay and the revelation, and *Bounce* misses. Not by a lot, but by enough.

I liked the movie anyway. I liked it because of the convincing way the relationship got started. And because Buddy's gay secretary (Johnny Galeckie) isn't afraid to talk back to him—about alcoholism and Abby. And because of the way Buddy got closer to the kids. And because Paltrow dials down her beauty and becomes a convincing widow. And because I *wanted* them to become lovers, which means they sold me on themselves.

The Bourne Identity ★ ★ ★
PG-13, 118 m., 2002

Matt Damon (Jason Bourne), Franka Potente (Marie Kreutz), Chris Cooper (Ted Conklin), Clive Owen (The Professor), Brian Cox (Ward Abbott), Adewale Akinnuoye-Agbaje (Wombosi). Directed by Doug Liman and produced by Patrick Crowley, Richard N. Gladstein, and Liman. Screenplay by Tone Gilroy and William Blade Herron, based on the novel by Robert Ludlum.

The Bourne Identity is a skillful action movie about a plot that exists only to support a skillful action movie. The entire story is a setup for the martial arts and chases. Because they are done well, because the movie is well crafted and acted, we give it a pass. Too bad it's not about something.

Well, perhaps it is. Perhaps it is about the amoral climate in spy agencies like the CIA. There are no good guys in the movie—certainly not the hero, played by Matt Damon, who is a trained assassin—and no bad guys, either. Even the people who want to kill Damon are only doing their jobs. Just as the guardians of the Navaho windtalkers in another movie are told to kill their charges rather than let them fall into enemy hands, so is Bourne, or whatever his name is, targeted for death after he fails to assassinate an African leader. (There's a good possibility he would also be targeted if he had succeeded.)

As the movie opens, a fisherman on a boat out of Marseilles spots a body floating in what is obviously a studio back-lot tank. Hauled aboard, the body turns out to be alive, to have two bullet wounds, and to have a capsule embedded under the skin that contains the code to a Swiss bank account. The friendly fisherman gives the rescued man (who doesn't remember who he is) money to take the train to Switzerland, and he is welcomed in that nation and withdraws a fortune from a bank despite lacking a name or any form of personal identification.

Indeed, he finds out who he may be by looking inside the red bag from the bank, where he finds several passports, one saying his name is Bourne. Determined to find out his real name and why he was floating in the Mediterranean, Bourne pays $10,000 to a gypsy named Marie (Franka Potente from *Run, Lola, Run*) to drive him to Paris. Meanwhile, the movie cuts to CIA headquarters in Virginia, where we meet Bourne's handler, Conklin (Chris Cooper), and his boss, Abbott (Brian Cox). Bourne was thought to be dead. Now that he is alive, he must be killed, and the assignment goes to several assassins, including the Professor (Clive Owen), who is as highly trained as Bourne.

I forgot to say that Bourne is trained. Is he ever. He speaks several languages, is a formidable martial artist, has highly trained powers of observation and memory, knows all the spy tricks, and is a formidable driver. We see that during a sensational chase scene through the streets of Paris, much of it through narrow alleys, down flights of steps, and against traffic.

There comes a point at which we realize there will be no higher level to the screenplay, no greater purpose than to expend this kinetic energy. The movie's brutally cynical happy ending reveals that it doesn't take itself seriously. And we catch on (sooner than Marie) that the girl stays in the picture only because—well, there has to be a girl to provide false suspense and give the loner hero someone to talk to.

I kind of enjoyed *The Bourne Identity*. I had to put my mind on hold, but I was able to. I am less disturbed by action movies like this, which are frankly about nothing, than by action movies like *Windtalkers*, which pretend to be about something and then cop out. Doug Limon, the director of *Bourne*, directs the traffic well, gets a nice wintry look from his locations, absorbs us with the movie's spycraft, and uses Damon's ability to be focused and sincere. The movie is unnecessary, but not unskilled.　　☞

Boys and Girls ★ ★
PG-13, 100 m., 2000

Freddie Prinze Jr. (Ryan), Claire Forlani (Jennifer), Jason Biggs (Hunter), Heather Donahue (Megan), Amanda Detmer (Amy). Directed by Robert Iscove and produced by Sue Baden-Powell, Harvey Weinstein, and Bob Weinstein. Screenplay by the Drews (Andrew Lowery and Andrew Miller).

Boys and Girls is about a boy and a girl who meet when they are both about twelve and carry on a love-hate relationship for the next ten years, until they finally sleep with each other, with disastrous results. It is clear they're in love, but after that night of bliss a great chill forms between them, and she doesn't understand why.

I thought I did understand why. The other day on the radio, Terry Gross was interviewing Jeffrey Eugenides, the author of *The Virgin Suicides*. In that novel, now made into a movie by Sofia Coppola, a boy and a girl have sex in the middle of the football field on prom night—and the next morning, when she awakes, she is alone. Trip, the boy, is the narrator, and tells us: "I liked her a lot. But out there on the football field, it was different."

Terry Gross gently grilled Eugenides about that passage. She was interested, she said, because Trip's behavior was—well, not atypical of boys after sexual conquests, and a lot of women, courted and then dumped, were curious about that cruel male pattern. Eugenides declined to analyze Trip's behavior. He'd known people like Trip, he said, and he thought it was just the sort of thing Trip would do.

I have a theory to explain such postcoital disillusionment: Boys cannot deal with their dreams made flesh. He has idealized a woman who now turns out to be real, who engages in the same behavior as ordinary women, who allows herself to be despoiled (so he thinks) by his lust, which he has been taught to feel guilty about. He flees in shame and self-disgust. Boys get over this, which is the good news, but by losing their idealism about women, which is the bad news.

This is an excellent theory, but *Boys and Girls* does not use it. Instead, confusing the sexes, it supplies the boy with a motive for his behavior that in the real world would more likely come from a girl. He cut off contact between them, he says, because it was the greatest moment of his life, and he knew then that she was his true love, and when she said it had perhaps been "a mistake," and that they should move on and go back to being "best friends," nothing had ever hurt him more. Of course, she was just trying to say what she thought he wanted to hear, because she really loved him, but . . .

Their dilemma is fueled by the movie convention in which the characters say the wrong things and do not say the right things, and remain baffled by a situation long after it has become clear to us. But then Ryan and Jennifer (for those are their names) are not quick studies anyway. It takes them ten years and countless Meet Cutes before they finally break down and have their first kiss. They specialize in that form of sex most maddening for the audience, "coitus postponus."

They're both awfully nice people. They're played by Freddie Prinze Jr. and Claire Forlani as good and sweet and honest and sensitive, and we like them a lot. We also like his best friend (Jason Biggs) and hers (Amanda Detmer). Perky Heather Donahue, survivor of the *Blair Witch*, gets good screen time as his interim girlfriend. They are so lovable that we earnestly wish they'd grow up and develop more interesting and complex personalities. We are reminded of the theory that American society prolongs adolescence far beyond its natural life span. If these characters were French and engaging in the same dialogue and behavior, we would guess their age at about thirteen.

I was amused by their college majors. He is a structural engineer, as we can see in scenes that invariably show him studying balsa-wood models of bridges with a perplexed expression. After his junior year, the models do not collapse any more, so he must be learning something. She studies Latin. Why? "Because I plan to do postgraduate work in Italy." In the Vatican City, I hope.

Boys and Girls is soothing and harmless, gentle and interminable. It is about two people who might as well fall in love, since fate and the plot have given them nothing else to do and no one else to do it with. Compared to the wisdom and wickedness of *High Fidelity,* this is such a slight movie. It's not that I don't like it. It's that I don't care.

Bread and Roses ★ ★ ★ ½
R, 106 m., 2001

Pilar Padilla (Maya), Adrien Brody (Sam), Elpidia Carrillo (Rosa), Jack McGee (Bert),

George Lopez (Perez), Alonso Chavez (Ruben), Monica Rivas (Simona). Directed by Ken Loach and produced by Rebecca O'Brien. Screenplay by Paul Laverty.

If you work in a building with janitors, how much do they get paid? Is it enough to decently support a family? Have you given any thought to the question? I haven't. Ken Loach's *Bread and Roses,* a drama about a janitorial strike in Los Angeles, made me think. It suggests that the people who manage your building pay the janitors as little as they possibly can, and pass the savings on to your employers. Here is a statistic: In 1982, union janitors in Los Angeles were paid $8.50 an hour. In 1999, nonunion janitors were paid $5.75. Do they have a health plan? Don't make me laugh.

Under the trickle-down theory, if the boss makes millions and the janitor makes $5.75, in the long run we all benefit. How does this work in practice? A simple illustration will suffice. When both parents have to moonlight in underpaid jobs, that gives their children an opportunity to get in trouble on the streets, leading to arrests, convictions, and millions of dollars pumped into the economy through the construction of new prisons and salaries for their guards. Right now America has a larger percentage of its population in prison than any other Western nation, but that is not good enough.

Bread and Roses tells its story through the eyes of Maya (Pilar Padilla), an illegal immigrant newly arrived in Los Angeles. Her sister Rosa (Elpidia Carrillo) gets her a job in a sleazy bar, but Rosa is a good girl and doesn't like it: "I want to work with you cleaning the offices." Rosa gets Maya hired in a high-rise, where she has to kick back her first month's salary. Maya meets Sam (Adrien Brody), an organizer for the janitor's union, who is trying to sign up the workers in the building.

For some of my readers, the key words in the previous paragraph were "illegal immigrant." Why, they are thinking, should such a person have a job in America at all, let alone complain about the low wages? This attitude is admirable in its idealism, but overlooks the fact that the economy depends on workers who will accept substandard wages. The man who hires Maya certainly knows she is illegal.

That man's boss, as they say, "knows but doesn't know." The man above him doesn't know and doesn't care—he's only interested in delivering janitorial services to the building management at the lowest possible price.

If the janitors were paid a decent wage plus health benefits, there would be no shortage of American citizens to take the jobs, so it is better this way, especially since the illegal workers have no rights and are easily intimidated. If the Mexican border were sealed, Los Angeles would be a city without janitors, gardeners, car washes, and maids. And in Michigan, who would pick the fruit?

Sam the organizer encourages Maya and her friends to organize for the union within the building—secretly, of course. Rosa, the sister, is not so enthusiastic: "We could all lose our jobs, and then who would pay the bills?" There is a juicy scene where the striking janitors invade a housewarming by a big Hollywood agency which has just taken offices in the building. Do the star clients know their agents are exploiting the workers? (Credit here to Ron Perlman and other actors who play recognizable extras.)

Sam is played by Brody as a complex character, filled with anger but also with a streak of zany street comedian. He's trapped in the middle, since the union's bosses, like all bosses, are basically establishment. When his boss argues that a strike might cost the union too much money, Sam snaps back: "No more $40 million to give the Democrats." Sam and Maya are drawn to one another, and there is a shy little love scene, but Ken Loach is not the kind of director to confuse his real story with the love story; he knows that no matter what happens between Sam and Maya, the janitors are still underpaid and the strike is still dangerous. That same stubborn integrity prevents him from giving the movie a conventional happy ending. Just think. If he had directed *Pearl Harbor,* it would have ended sadly.

Loach is left-wing but realistic. The best scene in *Bread and Roses* argues against Sam, Maya, and the union. It is a searing speech by Rosa, delivered by Elpidia Carrillo with such force and shaming truth that it could not have been denied the Oscar—if the Academy voters in their well-cleaned buildings ever saw movies like this. Rosa slices through Maya's idealism with hard truths, telling her sister that she worked as a prostitute to pay for Maya's education, and indeed slept with the supervisor to get Rosa her job. "I've been whoring all my life, and I'm tired," she says. Now she has a sick husband and kids to feed and they take priority over the union and the college-boy organizer.

The more you think about it, the more this movie's ending has a kind of nobility to it. Loach, who has always made films about the working class *(Riff-Raff, My Name Is Joe, Ladybird, Ladybird),* is too honest to believe in easy solutions. Will the union get its contract? Will Maya and Sam live happily ever after? Will the national minimum wage ever be a living wage? Will this movie change anything, or this review make you want to see it? No, probably not. But when you come in tomorrow morning someone will have emptied your wastebasket.

Bread and Tulips ★ ★ ★ ½
PG-13, 115 m., 2001

Licia Maglietta (Rosalba), Bruno Ganz (Fernando), Giuseppe Battiston (Costantino), Marina Massironi (Grazia), Antonio Catania (Mimmo), Felice Andreasi (Fermo), Vitalba Andrea (Ketty), Tatiana Lepore (Adele), Ludovico Paladin (Eliseo). Directed by Silvio Soldini and produced by Daniele Maggioni. Screenplay by Doriana Leondeff and Soldini.

It's all in the casting. Silvio Soldini's *Bread and Tulips* tells a story that seems born to be remade in Hollywood with Sandra Bullock or Julia Roberts, but look at Licia Maglietta and tell me what you see. Not a classic beauty, not a "movie star," but a fortyish dreamer who's just a little overweight, with the kind of sexiness that makes you think of bread baking, clean sheets, and that everything is going to be all right. Maglietta is the secret of this film's romantic charm because we like her so much.

We like her, and we like the dignified and sad waiter Fernando (Bruno Ganz), and we like her friend Grazia (Marina Massironi), who is a "holistic beautician and masseuse," and we like the sweet old florist Fermo (Felice Andreasi), and we like the plump, perspiring Costantino (Giuseppe Battiston) who is the plumber and amateur detective hired to track her down.

We like them to begin with, and we like them more because they occupy an obscure corner of Venice, that city above all others that encourages us to yield to our romantic impulses. We like them, and so did the David Di Donatello Awards, the Italian version of the Oscars, which showered *Bread and Tulips* with Davids for Best Picture, Actor, Actress, Supporting Actor, Supporting Actress, Director, and three more besides. The Italians say this is their favorite movie in years, and they are not without reason.

Licia Maglietta plays Rosalba, a housewife who is taken utterly for granted by her family. When she loses an earring down the drain at a highway rest stop, her husband and teenage children board their tourist bus and it pulls away without anyone even missing her. Rosalba's husband calls on his cell phone; he's mad at her—because, of course, it was her fault that they didn't miss her. Rosalba impulsively hitches a ride with a friendly woman, and later, more impulsively, hitches another ride—to Venice, where she has never been. Suddenly this has turned into *her* vacation.

In the serene city she meets characters who are not likely to exist in real life—but here is the point, they're *played* as if they were. With a few lira in her handbag, she visits a lonely little restaurant near the train station, and meets Fernando, a waiter played by Bruno Ganz with a sad countenance and dignified charm. The cook is sick, but Fernando prepares a cold dish for her and serves it as if she were a queen. One thing leads to another, not in an obvious way, and soon she has a job with the florist, is living in an extra room of Fernando's flat, and has made friends with Grazia, whose profession may extend beyond massage, or at least liberally define it.

Bruno Ganz is the actor who will be forever remembered as the angel in *Wings of Desire*—the angel whose love and sympathy for mankind caused him to turn in his wings and take his chances in the physical universe. Here he's something of an angel, too—a melancholy one. When Rosalba unexpectedly knocks on his door on the second day, he has to take down the noose from his ceiling before he can let her in. He has no carnal designs on his houseguest, and she is too abashed at her rebellion to even think in those terms, but they are both

confronted with the inescapable fact that their souls match.

The movie intercuts events in Venice with a human comedy involving Mimmo (Antonio Catania), Rosalba's husband, who has long enjoyed the favors of a mistress but is now dismayed to find that she refuses to perform Rosalba's domestic tasks in her absence. Rosalba has sent him postcards that announce she is safe in Venice, but they are vague about the possibility of her return. Mimmo enlists the services of Costantino, the plumber, who fancies himself a detective and goes off to Venice to track her down; his mission provides first a guided tour of Venice and then experiences of his own in applied holism.

I am aware that stories like this have been told before. Venice has been put on earth as an opportunity for underappreciated women of a certain age to make one more roll of the romantic dice. The film is haunted by Katharine Hepburn's adventures in *Summertime,* and by films as unlike as *Blume in Love, Wings of the Dove, Only You,* and *Everyone Says I Love You.* But I don't require the story to be original. I am not at the movies for lonely-hearts tips. I require the characters to be strange and wonderful, romantic and quirky, and above all lovable. It may be that a relationship like the one here between Rosalba and Fernando is impossible in real life. All the more reason for this movie.

Bride of the Wind ½★
R, 99 m., 2001

Sarah Wynter (Alma Mahler), Jonathan Pryce (Gustav Mahler), Vincent Perez (Oskar Kokoschka), Simon Verhoeven (Walter Gropius), Gregor Seberg (Franz Werfel), Dagmar Schwarz (Anna Moll), Wolfgang Hubsch (Karl Moll), August Schmolzer (Gustav Klimt), Francesca Becker (Maria). Directed by Bruce Beresford and produced by Lawrence Levy and Evzen Kolar. Screenplay by Marilyn Levy.

"I'm not just any widow! I'm Mahler's widow!"
—Alma Mahler

She must have been a monster. The Alma Mahler depicted in *Bride of the Wind* is a woman who prowls restlessly through the beds of the famous, making them miserable while displaying no charm of her own. Whether this was the case with the real woman I do not know. But if she was anything like the woman in this movie, then Gustav Mahler, Gustav Klimt, Oskar Kokoschka, Walter Gropius, and Frank Werfel should have fled from her on sight.

Bride of the Wind, which tells her story, is one of the worst biopics I have ever seen, a leaden march through a chronology of Alma's affairs, clicking them off with the passion of an encyclopedia entry. The movie has three tones: overwrought, boring, laughable. Sarah Wynter, who plays Alma, does not perform the dialogue but recites it. She lacks any conviction as a seductress, seems stiff and awkward, and should have been told that great women in turn-of-the-century Vienna didn't slouch.

We first meet her going to a ball her father has forbidden her to attend. He is stern with her when she returns. So much for her adolescence. We move on to a dinner party where she flirts with the artist Klimt (August Schmolzer), who labors over one-liners like, "Mahler's music is much better than it sounds." She insults Mahler (Jonathan Pryce) at dinner, offending and fascinating him, and soon the older man marries her.

She has affairs throughout their marriage. She cheats with the architect Gropius (Simon Verhoeven), who unwisely writes a love letter to Alma but absentmindedly addresses it to Gustav—or so he says. "You drove me to him," she pouts to her husband. Mahler is always going on about his music, you see, and thinks himself a genius. Well, so does Gropius. The screenplay shows the egos of the men by putting big, clanging chunks of information in the dialogue. Sample:

"You've been very kind, Herr Gropius."
"Dancing is one of the two things I do well."
"And what is the other?"
"I am an architect."

Since Alma already knows this, the movie misses a bet by not having her ask, winsomely, "Is there a ... third ... thing you at least do not do badly?"

There is. Another affair is with the sculptor and painter Oskar Kokoschka (Vincent Perez),

who goes off to fight the war, is shot through the head, and bayoneted after falling wounded. In what the movie presents as a dying vision, he imagines Alma walking toward him. Since his head is flat on the ground, she walks toward him sideways, rotated ninety degrees from upright. But, of course, a vision stands upright no matter what position one's head is in, or dreams would take place on the ceiling.

Oskar's mother posts herself outside Alma's house with a pistol, seeking revenge for her son's death. "I was never popular with mothers," Alma sighs. She becomes involved with the writer Werfel. Just when we are wondering if Oskar's mother is still lying in ambush outside the gates, Kokoschka himself returns a year later—alive!—and surprises her in her drawing room. "It's not every man who is shot in the head, bayoneted, and lives to tell about it," he observes. Then he sees she is pregnant and rejoices that she decided to have his baby after all, instead of an abortion. "But it has been a year," Alma tells him. "Think, Oskar! A year."

The penny falls. He stalks away, disgusted either at the fact that she is bearing another man's child, or that he cannot count. I meanwhile am thinking that when one is reported dead in action, it is only common good manners to wire ahead before turning up unexpectedly at a lover's house. Ben Affleck makes the same mistake in *Pearl Harbor*.

Bride of the Wind was directed by Bruce Beresford, who has made wonderful films (*Tender Mercies, Crimes of the Heart, The Fringe Dwellers, Driving Miss Daisy*). At a loss to explain this lapse, I can only observe that another of his filmed biographies, *King David* (1985), was also very bad. Maybe there is something about a real-life subject that paralyzes him.

If Sarah Wynter is not good as Alma Mahler, the other actors seem equally uneasy—even the usually assured Pryce and Perez. Something must have been going wrong on this production. Even that doesn't explain the lack of Bad Laugh Control. Filmmakers need a sixth sense for lines that might play the wrong way. For example: After Alma has slept with as many Viennese artists as she can manage without actually double-booking, she quarrels with the latest. Her winsome little daughter, Maria (Francesca Becker), whines, "Is he going to leave us? Are you going to send him away?"

Alma replies, "What made you think that?" Wrong answer. At the end of the movie there are titles telling us what happened to everyone; Gropius moved to America and went on to become a famous architect, etc. We are not surprised to learn that little Maria went on to be married five times.

Bridget Jones's Diary ★ ★ ★ ½
R, 95 m., 2001

Renée Zellweger (Bridget Jones), Colin Firth (Mark Darcy), Hugh Grant (Daniel Cleaver), Honor Blackman (Penny), Crispin Bonham-Carter (Greg), Gemma Jones (Bridget's Mum), Jim Broadbent (Bridget's Dad), James Callis (Tom), Embeth Davidtz (Natasha). Directed by Sharon Maguire and produced by Tim Bevan, Jonathan Cavendish, and Eric Fellner. Screenplay by Richard Curtis, Andrew Davies, and Helen Fielding, based on the novel by Fielding.

Glory be, they didn't muck it up. *Bridget Jones's Diary,* a beloved book about a heroine both lovable and human, has been made against all odds into a funny and charming movie that understands the charm of the original, and preserves it. The book, a fictional diary by a plump, thirty-something London office worker, was about a specific person in a specific place. When the role was cast with Renée Zellweger, who is not plump and is from Texas, there was gnashing and wailing. Obviously the Miramax boys would turn London's pride into a Manhattanite, or worse.

Nothing doing. Zellweger put on twenty-something pounds and developed the cutest little would-be double chin, as well as a British accent that sounds reasonable enough to me. (*Sight & Sound,* the British film magazine, has an ear for nuances and says the accent is "just a little too studiedly posh," which from them is praise.)

As in the book, Bridget arrives at her thirty-second birthday determined to take control of her life, which until now has consisted of smoking too much, drinking too much, eating too much, and not finding the right man, or indeed much of any man. In her nightmares, she dies fat, drunk, and lonely, and is eaten by Alsatian dogs. She determines to monitor her daily intake of tobacco and alcohol units, and her weight, which she measures in stones. (A stone is fourteen pounds; the British not only have pounds instead of kilos but stones on top of pounds, although the other day a London street vendor was arrested for selling bananas by the pound in defiance of the new European marching orders; the next step is obviously for Brussels to impound Bridget's diary.)

Bridget's campaign proceeds unhappily when her mother (who "comes from the time when pickles on toothpicks were still the height of sophistication") introduces her to handsome Mark Darcy (Colin Firth), who is at a holiday party against his will and in a bad mood and is overheard (by Bridget) describing her as a "verbally incontinent spinster." Things go better at work, where she exchanges saucy e-mails with her boss, Daniel Cleaver (Hugh Grant). His opener: "You appear to have forgotten your skirt." They begin an affair, while Darcy circles the outskirts of her consciousness, still looking luscious but acting emotionally constipated.

Zellweger's Bridget is a reminder of the first time we became really aware of her in a movie, in *Jerry Maguire* (1996), where she was so cute and vulnerable we wanted to tickle and console her at the same time. Her work in *Nurse Betty* (2000) was widely but not sufficiently praised, and now here she is, fully herself and fully Bridget Jones, both at once. A story like this can't work unless we feel unconditional affection for the heroine, and casting Zellweger achieves that; the only alternate I can think of is Kate Winslet, who comes close but lacks the self-destructive puppy aspects.

The movie has otherwise been cast with dependable (perhaps infallible) British comic actors. The first time Hugh Grant appeared on-screen, I chuckled for no good reason at all, just as I always do when I see Christopher Walken, Steve Buscemi, Tim Roth, or Jack Nicholson—because I know that whatever the role, they will infuse it with more than the doctor ordered. Grant can play a male Bridget Jones (as he did in *Notting Hill*), but he's better as a cad, and here he surpasses himself by lying to Bridget about Darcy and then cheating on her with a girl from the New York office. (An "American stick insect," is what Bridget tells her diary.)

Colin Firth on the other hand must unbend

to become lovable, and when we do finally love him, it's largely because we know what an effort it took on his part. *Bridget Jones's Diary* is famously, if vaguely, patterned after Jane Austen's *Pride and Prejudice;* Firth played Mr. Darcy in the BBC's 1995 adaptation of the novel, and now plays another Darcy here. I didn't see the TV version but learn from the critic James Berardinelli that Firth "plays this part exactly as he played the earlier role, making it evident that the two Darcys are essentially the same."

It is a universal rule of romantic fiction that all great love stories must be mirrored by their low-comedy counterpoints. Just as Hal woos Katharine, Falstaff trifles with Doll Tearsheet. If Bridget must choose between Mark and Daniel, then her mother (Gemma Jones) must choose between her kindly but easy-chair-loving husband (Jim Broadbent) and a dashing huckster for a TV shopping channel.

The movie strings together one funny set-piece after another, as when Bridget goes in costume to a party where she *thought* the theme was "Tarts & Vicars." Or when she stumbles into a job on a TV news show and makes her famous premature entrance down the fire pole. Or when she has to decide at the beginning of an evening whether sexy underwear or tummy-crunching underwear will do her more good in the long run. Bridget charts her own progress along the way, from "tragic spinster" to "wanton sex goddess," and the movie gives almost unreasonable pleasure as it celebrates her bumpy transition.

Bring It On ★ ★
PG-13, 95 m., 2000

Kirsten Dunst (Torrance Shipman), Eliza Dushku (Missy Pantone), Gabrielle Union (Isis), Jesse Bradford (Cliff), Nicole Bilderback (Whitney), Clare Kramer (Courtney), Ian Roberts (Choreographer). Directed by Peyton Reed and produced by Marc Abraham and Thomas A. Bliss. Screenplay by Jessica Bendinger.

I jump! You can look but don't you hump. I'm major. I roar. I swear I'm not a whore.

We cheer as we lead. We act like we're on speed. Hate us 'cause we're beautiful—but we don't like you either. We're cheerleaders! We are cheerleaders!

Those are lyrics from the opening musical number of *Bring It On*—yet another example of the most depressing trend of the summer of 2000, the cynical attempt by Hollywood to cram R-rated material into PG-13–rated movies. This is done not to corrupt our children, but (even worse) with complete indifference to their developing values. The real reason is more cynical: Younger teenagers buy a lot of tickets and are crucial if a movie hopes to "win the weekend." The R rating is a penalty at the box office. So movies that were born to be R, like *Gone in 60 Seconds, Coyote Ugly,* and *Bring It On,* are trimmed to within a millimeter of the dividing line and released as PG-13, so that any child tall enough to push its dollars through the ticket window is cheerfully admitted, with or without an adult.

Bring It On shows every evidence of beginning life as a potentially funny, hard-edged R-rated comedy. There's raunchy language, a half-nude locker-room scene, jokes about sex, and those startling cheerleader songs. I smiled at the songs; I might have enjoyed the movie if it had developed along the lines of *Animal House* or *American Pie.* Instead, we get a strange mutant beast, half Nickelodeon movie, half R-rated comedy. It's like kids with potty-mouth playing grown-up.

The movie stars Kirsten Dunst *(The Virgin Suicides)* and Gabrielle Union *(She's All That)* as the captains of two opposing cheerleader squads, one from an affluent San Diego suburb (which apparently contains no parents) and the other from a mostly black high school in East Compton. Dunst is the new captain of her team, which is the defending national champion cheerleading squad even though it supports a team barely able to stumble into the field. Union visits their practice one day to reveal that their previous captain had stolen all of their winning routines from East Compton. This year that will make a difference, she says, because East Compton is going to the nationals.

In desperation, Dunst breaks the rules

and hires a professional choreographer (Ian Roberts), who shouts at them like a drill sergeant but has the moves of a Chippendale's dancer. As he puts them through new routines, we get subplots involving the standard characters in all teenage movies, including the cool guy who is somebody's brother, the snotty teacher, and the bitchy girl who gets her comeuppance. There's the usual suspense about whether the heroine will end up with the guy she likes, despite massive attacks of Idiot Plot misunderstandings.

This movie wants it all. In addition to the sex comedy, the romance, the cheerleading intrigue, and the condescending treatment of the black school, there's also the big climax at the cheerleading competition, so that a movie that has exhausted every possible high school cliché can now recycle all the obligatory plot gimmicks involving the Big Game. Will our team, which used the illegal choreographer, win or lose? In a movie with a memory, it might lose, but short-term memory loss is a symptom of movies like this, and the choreographer, who was illegal to make a quick plot point, is long forgotten by the time the movie gets to the finals.

Bring It On contains within it the seeds of a sharp and observant high school satire, maybe something in the same league (although not as high in the standings) as *Election* or *Rushmore*. I'll bet anything Jessica Bendinger's original screenplay was a lot smarter than the dumbed-down PG-13 version we get here. The movie as it now stands is too juvenile and insipid for older teenagers and has way too much language and sex for kids thirteen and below.

As an entry in the PG-13 category, it's not as appalling as *Coyote Ugly*, which basically instructs young girls that there's money to be made in the bimbo business. But it illustrates the same point: The MPAA's rating system, having first denied American moviegoers any possibility of a workable adult category, is now busily corrupting the PG-13 rating. The principle seems to be: As long as we act sanctimonious by creating a climate in which legitimate adult films cannot be made, we can get away with maximizing the box office by opening up the PG-13. The MPAA in the summer of 2000 reveals itself as more willing to peddle smut to children than to allow adults to make their own choices.

The Broken Hearts Club ★ ★ ★
R, 91 m., 2000

Zach Braff (Benji), Dean Cain (Cole), Andrew Keegan (Kevin), Nia Long (Leslie), John Mahoney (Jack), Mary McCormack (Anne), Matt McGrath (Howie), Timothy Olyphant (Dennis), Ben Weber (Patrick), Billy Porter (Taylor), Justin Theroux (Marshall). Directed by Greg Berlanti and produced by Mickey Liddell and Joseph Middleton. Screenplay by Berlanti.

"I'm twenty-eight years old and all I'm good at is being gay," complains Marshall (Justin Theroux), one of the gay friends who hang out together in *The Broken Hearts Club*. To cheer himself up, he should rent *The Boys in the Band* (1970), and find out how much better gay men are at being gay than they used to be. The new movie acts like a progress report; instead of angst, Freudian analysis, despair, and self-hate, the new generation sounds like the cast of a sitcom, trading laugh lines and fuzzy truisms. The earlier movie half-suggested it was impossible to be gay and happy. That possibility would not occur to the *Broken Hearts* characters.

The movie takes place in the predominately gay area of West Hollywood, where its heroes hang out in coffee shops, restaurants, clubs, and each other's homes. Most of the principals are not sleeping with one another, although some are, and others are not sleeping with anyone. Mostly, they talk, and the movie listens. What it discovers is that gay men, like straight men, spend an extraordinary amount of time thinking about sex. And that they can be insecure, unfaithful, lonely, and deceptive (when an actor recycles lines from an audition to make a touching breakup speech, his ex asks, "Are you reading that off of your hand?").

Life centers around the Broken Hearts, a restaurant run by the fatherly Jack (John Mahoney), who also sponsors a softball team. Many of the characters are members of the team, and there's a funny scene where the handsome Cole (Dean Cain, from *Lois & Clark: The New Adventures of Superman*) steps up to the plate and gets the phone number of the opposing catcher between strikes. Mostly, though, dates don't come that easily, and Patrick (Ben Weber) complains, "Gay men in L.A. are 10s looking for an 11. On a good night, and if the other guy's drunk enough, I'm a 6."

What's striking about the movie is the ordinariness of its characters and what they talk about. This is a rare gay-themed movie that relaxes. Historically, many movies about gays have had a buried level of—I dunno, call it muted hysteria, anxiety, impending doom. It's the *Kiss of the Spider Woman* syndrome, with characters dramatizing what they see as their own current or impending tragedies. *The Broken Hearts Club* is not about neurosis, resentment, AIDS, or secrecy, and the humor can be described as sarcastic rather than bitchy. The big difference between this picture and your regular guy movie is that there aren't any girls (except for a lesbian sister and her lover). There are no complaints about parents. One guy says his mother was a sixties love child: "In high school, she caught me smoking pot and all she said was, 'I hope you didn't pay market.'"

The lighthearted tone is set right at the beginning, as a group of friends play a game to see who can act the straightest the longest before one reveals an OGT (Obviously Gay Trait). We are introduced to the definition of "meanwhile," which is a word introduced into any conversation when an interesting sex object walks by. One of the characters lands a date with a handsome J. Crew model, then drops him because he doesn't like the Carpenters. There's a debate: "Who would you kick out of bed? Morley Safer or Mike Wallace?" This is exactly the way straight guys talk, except they substitute Cameron Diaz and Jennifer Lopez. (Answer: "I'd kick them both out of bed for Ed Bradley, circa 1980.")

All, of course, is not banter. There's tension between Patrick and Leslie (Nia Long), the girlfriend of his sister (Mary McCormack). There's bitterness about "gym bunnies" and their obsessions with "sex and protein shakes." There are moments of truth, involving a romance threatened by roving-eye syndrome, and the movie is so eager to get to an obligatory funeral scene that we can diagnose the doomed character almost from his entrance.

The writer-director, Greg Berlanti, one of the creators of *Dawson's Creek,* has mastered his screenplay workshops and knows just when to introduce the false crisis, the false dawn, the real crisis, and the real dawn.

But the movie is so likable we go with it on its chosen level. It's almost the *point* of *The Broken Hearts Club* that it doesn't crank up the emotion. It insists on the ordinariness of its characters, on their everyday problems, on the relaxed and chatty ways they pass their time. The movie's buried message celebrates the arrival of gays into the mainstream. That key line ("I'm twenty-eight years old and all I'm good at is being gay") is like an announcement liberating gay movies from an exclusive preoccupation with sexuality. *The Broken Hearts Club* is good at things other than being a gay movie. There you are.

Brother ★ ★
R, 114 m., 2001

Beat Takeshi (Yamamoto), Omar Epps (Denny), Claude Maki (Ken), Masaya Kato (Shirase), Susumu Terajima (Kato), Royale Watkins (Jay), Lombardo Boyar (Mo), Ren Osugi (Harada). Directed by Takeshi Kitano and produced by Masayuki Mori and Jeremy Thomas. Screenplay by Kitano.

The actor Beat Takeshi is a Japanese original, but if you made a list of the American stars he resembles, it would start with Clint Eastwood. The director Takeshi Kitano is also a Japanese original, but if you made a list of the Western filmmakers he resembles, it would reach from Sergio Leone to Jim Jarmusch, with Eastwood somewhere in the middle. But there is no one in Hollywood quite like the two of them put together, and, of course, they are the same man, using two names to separate his many jobs on the set.

Kitano, for so we will call him, is revered in Japan as an auteur of hard-boiled, minimalist action. His films consist of periods of quiet in which you can feel violence coiling out of sight, and then sudden explosions of mayhem. He is a weathered, deadpan, wary-looking man, a yakuza Jack Webb. He usually wears dark glasses, rarely has much to say, and occasionally barks out an amazed little laugh at what life has to offer him. When part of his face was paralyzed in a motorcycle accident, it became part of his lore that you couldn't tell which side, because he never moved his facial muscles anyway.

Brother is Kitano's deliberate attempt to enter the American market, in a movie set in Los Angeles and essentially in English, although Kitano, unlike Jackie Chan, doesn't pretend fluency. Many of the movie's key situations depend on who speaks English or Japanese, and why—although one enemy dies right after Kitano tells him, in perfect English, "I understand 'dirty Jap.'"

As the movie opens, Yamamoto, Kitano's character, has had to leave Japan suddenly after a gang war has gone against him. In Los Angeles, he teams up with a half-brother (Claude Maki), his African-American partner Denny (Omar Epps), and others in a drug ring. Yamamoto is the catalyst in many situations, simplifying them with the sudden elimination of those he disagrees with. Soon the gang is riding high, and has its own headquarters with a private basketball court (a tattooed yakuza complains when the blacks won't pass the ball to him).

Kitano is as much an existentialist as a action hero, however, and his crime movies (like *Sonatine*) rarely end with victory for himself and his friends. He is more in love with doom-laden irony, with grand gestures in defeat. His final scene in *Brother* owes more to the defiant last gestures of 1930s Warner Bros. gangsters than to simpleminded modern action pictures that end after all the enemies have been eliminated.

What's fascinating about Kitano is the way he pounces. He specializes in moments of action almost too fast to see (here he resembles Eastwood as The Man With No Name—and Eastwood, of course, was ripping off Mifune in *Yojimbo*). An opponent will say the same thing, there will be a flash of action, and he'll have chopsticks stuck halfway up his nose. A pause for the realization to sink in, and then the sudden blow to push them the rest of the way in. All over in a moment.

Brother is a typical Kitano film in many ways, but not one of his best ones. Too many of the killing scenes have a casual, perfunctory tone: lots of gunfire, a row of enemies lies dead, the plot moves on. Finally so many people are dead

that the movie looks more like a shooting gallery or a video game than a stylized crime parable. Kitano, both Beat and Takeshi, is a name that belongs on the list of anyone who wants to be familiar with the key players in modern world cinema, but don't start with *Brother*. Rent *Sonatine* or *Fireworks*, and then double back.

Brotherhood of the Wolf ★ ★ ★
R, 146 m., 2002

Samuel Le Bihan (Fronsac), Vincent Cassel (Jean-Francois), Mark Dacascos (Mani), Monica Bellucci (Sylvia), Emilie Dequenne (Marianne), Jeremie Renier (Thomas de'Apcher), Jacques Perrin (Old Thomas). Directed by Christophe Gans and produced by Samuel Hadida and Richard Grandpierre. Screenplay by Stephane Cabel. In French with English subtitles.

Brotherhood of the Wolf plays like an explosion at the genre factory. When the smoke clears, a rough beast lurches forth, its parts cobbled together from a dozen movies. The film involves quasi-werewolves, French aristocrats, secret societies, Iroquois Indians, martial arts, occult ceremonies, sacred mushrooms, swashbuckling, incestuous longings, political subversion, animal spirits, slasher scenes, and bordellos, and although it does not end with the words "based on a true story," it is.

The story involves the Beast of Gevaudan that, in 1764, terrorized a remote district of France, killing more than sixty women and children, and tearing out their hearts and vitals. I borrow these facts from Patrick Meyers of TheUnexplainedSite.com, who reveals that the Beast was finally found to be a wolf. Believe me, this information does not even come close to giving away the ending of the movie.

Directed by Christophe Gans, *Brotherhood of the Wolf* is couched in historical terms. It begins in 1794, at the time of the Revolution, when its narrator (Jacques Parrin), about to be carried away to the guillotine, puts the finishing touches on a journal revealing at last the true story of the Beast. Although a wolf was killed and presented to the court of the king, that was only a cover-up, he says, as we flash back to . . .

Well, actually, the Beast attacks under the

opening credits, even before the narrator appears. For the first hour or so we do not see it, but we hear fearsome growls, moans, and roars, and see an unkempt but buxom peasant girl dragged to her doom. Enter Gregoire de Fronsac (Samuel Le Bihan), an intellectual and naturalist, recently returned from exploring the St. Lawrence Seaway. He is accompanied by Mani, an Iroquois who speaks perfect French and perfect tree (he talks to them). Mani is played by Mark Dacascos, a martial arts expert from Hawaii whose skills might seem out of place in eighteenth-century France, but no: Everyone in this movie fights in a style that would make Jackie Chan proud.

Fronsac doubts the existence of a Beast. Science tells us to distrust fables, he explains. At dinner, he passes around a trout with fur, from Canada, which causes one of the guests to observe it must really be cold for the fish there, before Fronsac reveals it is a hoax. The Beast, alas, soon makes him a believer, but he sees a pattern: "The Beast is a weapon used by a man." But what man? Why? How? Charting the Beast's attacks on a map, he cleverly notices that all of the lines connecting them intersect at one point in rural Gevaudan. Fronsac and Mani go looking.

The local gentry include Jean-Francois (Vincent Cassel), who has one arm, but has fashioned a rifle he can brace in the crook of his shoulder. It fires silver bullets (this is also a historical fact). His sister Marianne (Emilie Dequenne) fancies Fronsac, which causes Jean-Francois to hate him, significantly. Also lurking about, usually with leaves in her hair, is the sultry Sylvia (Monica Bellucci), who travels with men who might as well have "Lout" displayed on a sign around their necks, and likes to dance on tabletops while they throw knives that barely miss her.

I would be lying if I did not admit that this is all, in its absurd and overheated way, entertaining. Once you realize that this is basically a high-gloss werewolf movie (but without a werewolf), crossed with a historical romance, a swashbuckler, and a martial arts extravaganza, you can relax. There is, of course, a deeper political message (this movie is nothing if not inclusive), and vague foreshadowings of fascism and survivalist cults, but the movie uses its politics only as a plot convenience

Brotherhood of the Wolf looks just great. The photography by Dan Laustsen is gloriously atmospheric and creepy; he likes fogs, blasted heaths, boggy marshes, moss, vines, creepers, and the excesses of eighteenth-century interior decorating. He has fun with a completely superfluous scene set in a bordello just because it was time for a little skin. The Beast, when it finally appears, is a most satisfactory Beast indeed, created by Jim Henson's Creature Shop. There are times when its movements resemble the stop-motion animation of a Ray Harryhausen picture, but I like the oddness of that kind of motion; it makes the Beast weirder than if it glided along smoothly.

The one thing you don't want to do is take this movie seriously. Because it's so good-looking, there may be a temptation to think it wants to be high-toned, but no: Its heart is in the horror-monster-sex-fantasy-special-effects tradition. "The Beast has a master," Fronsac says. "I want him." That's the spirit.

The Brothers ★ ★ ★
R, 103 m., 2001

Morris Chestnut (Jackson Smith), D. L. Hughley (Derrick West), Bill Bellamy (Brian Palmer), Shemar Moore (Terry White), Tamala Jones (Sheila West), Gabrielle Union (Denise Johnson), Julie Benz (Jesse Caldwell), Jenifer Lewis (Louise Smith), Clifton Powell (Fred Smith). Directed by Gary Hardwick and produced by Darin Scott and Paddy Cullen. Screenplay by Hardwick.

The Brothers is another movie about black guys who have been friends since childhood and how wedding bells are breaking up that old gang of theirs. This is getting to be a genre; I was reminded of *The Wood* (1999). What makes this one interesting is the way one couple actually deals with the crisis that threatens to keep them apart, instead of saying all the wrong things at the wrong times in traditional Idiot Plot fashion.

An early scene, of course, shows the friends playing basketball together. This is obligatory, showing how they cling to the innocence of those earlier days before romance and responsibility cluttered their lives. We meet Jackson the pediatrician (Morris Chestnut), Brian the lawyer (Bill Bellamy), Terry the executive (Shemar Moore), and Derrick the teacher (D. L. Hughley), who married young and regrets it. Now there's a crisis: Terry announces that he's going to get married.

The others, of course, oppose this decision, especially the married Derrick, whose marriage is approaching a crisis stage because of his wife's refusal to engage in oral sex. Derrick takes this as a personal affront—as proof she doesn't love him—and the arguments they have on this subject are among the movie's more tedious.

Jackson is a fervent opponent of premature marriage; they are, after all, young urban professionals, the cream of the crop, and deserve to play the field for a few more years. Then he meets a freelance photographer named Denise (Gabrielle Union), and is thunderstruck by love. Their relationship redeems the movie, because it involves real issues, and not simply plot points that are manipulated to keep them apart until it's time to push them together.

At first, Jackson and Denise seem too good to be true. They were made for each other. They're happy not simply in romantic montages, but even in dialogue sequences where we sense a meeting of the minds. Then Jackson finds out something from Denise's past, which I will not reveal, except to say that Denise is blameless, and that Jackson has all the information he needs to realize this. (In an Idiot Plot, she would be blameless, but Jackson would be kept in the dark by contortions of the screenplay.)

No, it's not information Jackson needs, but a better understanding of himself, and of his troubled relationship with his divorced parents. And as he works on that, there is a strong scene where Denise tries to reason with him. She is persuasive and logical and emotional; she's arguing for her own happiness as well as his. This is precisely the kind of scene I yearn for in Idiot Plots, where the characters should say something but never do. She gives it her best shot, and so when Jackson stubbornly sticks to his wrongheaded position, it's about the characters, not the screenplay mechanics.

Gabrielle Union you may recall from *Bring It On* (2000), the dueling cheerleader comedy. This movie demonstrates how teenager come-

dies can obscure real talent. The cast is generally good, but writer-director Gary Hardwick doesn't give them the scenes that Chestnut and Union get. There is, for example, an awkward scene in a restaurant; the lawyer (Bellamy) brings in a white date (Julie Benz) who is a karate expert, and they run into a black woman judge who is one of his former girlfriends. There is a fight, which is stagy, artificial, and leads to race-based dialogue from the lawyer that seems out of character.

Even the divorced parents of the Morris Chestnut character get good scenes (his whole family seems to be in a better movie than the others). His mother, Louise (Jenifer Lewis), and his father, Fred (Clifton Powell), have had their good and bad times; their son resents the father and sides with the mother, and doesn't see their marriage with an adult's sense of complexity. It's interesting how he has to deal with his parents in order to learn how to deal with the woman he loves, and both parents have well-written scenes.

As for the others, well, the less said about the marriage in crisis over oral sex, the better. There might be useful or entertaining things to say about such a dilemma, but this movie doesn't find them. The subplot about Terry's approaching marriage is pretty standard sitcom stuff. And so on. The movie's a mixed bag, but worth seeing for the good stuff, which is a lesson in how productive it can be to allow characters to say what they might actually say.

Bully ★ ★ ★

NO MPAA RATING, 112 m., 2001

Brad Renfro (Marty Puccio), Rachel Miner (Lisa Connelly), Nick Stahl (Bobby Kent), Bijou Phillips (Ali Willis), Michael Pitt (Donny Semenec), Kelli Garner (Heather Swaller), Daniel Franzese (Derek Dzvirko), Leo Fitzpatrick (Hit Man). Directed by Larry Clark and produced by Chris Hanley, Don Murphy, and Fernando Sulichin. Screenplay by Zachary Long and Roger Pullis, based on the book *Bully: A True Story of High School Revenge* by Jim Schutze.

Larry Clark's *Bully* calls the bluff of movies that pretend to be about murder but are really about entertainment. His film has all the sadness and shabbiness, all the mess and cruelty and thoughtless stupidity of the real thing. Based on a real incident from 1993, it tells the story of a twisted high school bully and a circle of friends who decide to kill him. But this is not about the evil sadist and the release of revenge; it's about how a group of kids will do something no single member is capable of. And about the moral void these kids inhabit.

Clark moved to the Hollywood, Florida, suburb where the actual murder took place, and sees it as a sterile expanse of identikit homes, strip malls, and boredom, where the kids drift from video arcades to fast-food hangouts, and a car means freedom. There is no doubt a parallel universe in this same suburb, filled with happy, creative, intelligent people and endless opportunities—there always is— but these kids are off that map. They are stupid by choice, not necessity; they have fallen into a slacker subculture that involves leading their lives in a void that can be filled only by booze, drugs, sex, and the endless, aimless analysis of their pathetic emptiness.

The movie is brilliantly and courageously well acted by its young cast; it's one of those movies so perceptive and wounding that there's no place for the actors to hide, no cop-out they can exercise. Their characters bleed with banality and stupid, doped reasoning. Their parents are not bad and, for the most part, not blamed; their children live in a world they do not understand or, in some cases, even see.

We meet Marty Puccio (Brad Renfro) and Bobby Kent (Nick Stahl). For as long as Marty can remember, Bobby has picked on him, and we see it as a daily ordeal: the ear twisting, the hard punches, the peremptory orders ("Get back in the car now!"), the demands that he go where he doesn't want to go and do what he doesn't want to do. In a key scene, Bobby takes him to a gay strip club and makes him dance on the stage while patrons stuff bills into his shorts. Marty is not gay. Bobby may be; certainly his relationship with Marty is sublimated S&M.

Marty and Bobby meet Lisa and Ali (Rachel Miner and Bijou Phillips). Bobby eventually rapes both girls. He also likes to watch Marty and Lisa in the backseat. He is, we sense, evil to the core; something has gone very wrong in his life, and maybe it was engendered by the authoritarian style of his father, who likes to dominate people under the guise of only doing what's right for them.

The movie establishes these kids in a larger circle of friends, including the tall, strong, and essentially nice Donny (Michael Pitt), the anything-goes Heather (Kelli Garner), and Derek (Daniel Franzese), along for the ride. It watches as they drift from coffee shops to malls to each other's cars and bedrooms, engaged in an endless loop of speculation about the only subject available to them, their lives. The leadership in this circle shifts according to who has a strongly held opinion; the others drift into line. A consensus begins to form that Bobby deserves to be killed. At one point, Lisa simply says, "I want him dead."

It's chilling, the way the murder is planned so heedlessly. The kids decide they don't know enough to do it themselves and need to hire a "hit man." This turns out to be Leo Fitzpatrick (from Clark's powerful first film, *Kids*), who is essentially a kid himself. The conspirators vaguely think his family is "Mafia," although his qualifications come into question when he worries that car horns will bother the neighbors; eventually we get the priceless line, "The hit man needs a ride."

The details of the murder are observed unblinkingly in a scene of harrowing, gruesome sadness. It is hard, messy work to kill someone. Once the body is disposed of, the arguments begin almost immediately: Everybody had a hand in the assault, but nobody actually can be said to have delivered the fatal blow, and we watch incredulously as these kids cave in to guilt, remorse, grief, blaming each other, and the irresistible impulse to tell an outsider what happened.

Clark's purpose in the film is twofold. He wants to depict a youth culture without resources, and to show how a crowd is capable of actions its members would never commit on their own. In *Kids* (1995) and in this film, the adult society has abandoned these characters— done little to educate or challenge them, or to create a world in which they have purpose. One of Bobby's sins, which I neglected to mention, is that he is still in high school and plans to go to college; the others live with fast-food jobs and handouts from parents, and Ali has a revealing line: "I was married once, for about three weeks. I have a little boy, but it's no big deal—my parents take care of him." *Kids* takes place in Manhattan and *Bully* in south Florida, but these kids occupy essentially the same lives, have the same parents, share the same futures.

It may be that *Bully* helps to explain the high school shootings. We sense the chilling disconnect between an action and its consequences, the availability of firearms, the buildup of teenage resentments and hatreds, the moral vacuum, the way they can talk themselves into doing unthinkable things, and above all, the need to talk about it. (So many high school shooters leave diaries and Web pages, and tell their friends what they plan to do.) Yes, Bobby Kent is a bully (and one of the most loathsome characters I've seen in a movie). But he dies not for his sins, but because his killers are so bored and adrift, and have such uncertain ideas of themselves.

Larry Clark is obviously obsessed by the culture of floating, unplugged teenagers. Sometimes his camera seems too willing to watch during the scenes of nudity and sex, and there is one particular shot that seems shameless in its voyeurism (you'll know the one). But it's this very drive that fuels his films. If the director doesn't have a strong personal feeling about material like this, he shouldn't be making movies about it. Clark is not some objectified outside adult observer, making an after-school special, but an artist who has made a leap into this teenage mindscape. Some critics have attacked him as a dirty old man with a suspect relationship to his material; if this film had been directed by a twenty-five-year-old, some of these same critics might be hailing it. I believe *Bully* is a masterpiece on its own terms, a frightening indictment of a society that offers absolutely nothing to some of its children— and an indictment of the children, who lack the imagination and courage to try to escape. Bobby and his killers deserve one another.

The Business of Strangers ★ ★ ★

R, 83 m., 2001

Stockard Channing (Julie Styron), Julia Stiles (Paula Murphy), Frederick Weller (Nick Harris). Directed by Patrick Stettner and produced by Susan A. Stover and Robert H. Nathan. Screenplay by Stettner.

The Business of Strangers starts as a merciless dissection of a high-powered business executive, turns into a confrontation between two styles of being a tough woman, and ends as an upmarket version of a Pam Grier revenge melodrama. It keeps you watching.

The movie centers on two performances that are closely observed in their details and nuances. Stockard Channing plays Julie Styron, a road warrior for a software company, who is divorced, childless, curt, dismissive, and paranoid. When she hears that the boss is flying in to have dinner with her, she immediately assumes she's being fired and instructs her secretary to copy all her files and messenger them to her house.

She's having a bad day. Her tech person turned up forty-five minutes late and blew an important presentation. That would be Paula Murphy (Julia Stiles), a Dartmouth grad who considers this "only a money job," is "really" a writer, and has a lot of tattoos, including a spider on the back of her neck and what looks like the Chrysler logo centered on her chest. (Why do some women believe tattoos enhance their breasts? Aren't they bringing coals to Newcastle?)

"As far as I'm concerned, she's fired," Julie says into her cell phone, ignoring Paula, who is standing next to her. As the older woman gets into her limo, the younger one calls her "uberfrau," but by that night in the hotel bar they find that they get along just fine as drinkers.

The third character in Patrick Stettner's original screenplay is Nick Harris (Frederick Weller), an executive headhunter, who flies in on a false alarm when Julie thinks she's being fired, and stays overnight after all of their flights are canceled. He's tall, slick, saturnine, and uses a lot of hair products.

The movie for at least its first hour is simply a very close study of how road warriors live. Their briefcases, their cell calls, their flight schedules, their hotel rooms, their use of the hotel bar and restaurant, their alienation and loneliness. Yet there is something uncoiling beneath this surface, based on the fact that Paula is a woman who doesn't like to be messed with, and Julie messed with her more than she realizes.

At first this manifests itself in daring one-upmanship, as when Julie offers to buy Paula a drink, Paula specifies a brand of cognac, the waiter says, "That's $20 a shot," Paula says,

"Make it a double," and Julie says she'll have the same thing. Later, after three or four more stiff drinks, Paula uses an elevator full of men to play a mind game—whispering to Julie about unusual sexual practices. Only gradually do we understand that Paula is challenging Julie, as when they're in the sauna and she asks, "Is this what a hot flash is like?" Julie responds with a description of her first hot flash, but that isn't why Paula asked.

What happens later in the film would not be fair to reveal. But I can express my ambivalence about it. Although the climactic scenes in the film have a certain weird fascination, I am not sure they're in character—maybe not for Paula, and certainly not for Julie, unless she's more drunk than she seems. The movie, having started with acute psychological observation, moves beyond realism into melodrama, and although some audiences will be fascinated (I was, to a degree), I think we lose something in the transfer.

Here's the paradox: If the first half of the film hadn't been so good, I might not question the second half so much. Channing and Stiles are so accurate in the way they create their two recognizable types that, well, the types are enough. We're fascinated by the dynamic between the two women, both smart and hard-edged, both obscurely wounded, both seeing themselves in the other. We like the way the younger woman goes after the older one ("Your best friend is your secretary. That's pathetic"). We want *this* to be the story, and when *The Business of Strangers* veers off into a series of manufactured plot developments, we're not sure we like it as much. Either way, it's a good movie, and Stockard Channing and Julia Stiles are the right choices for these roles. They zero in on each other like heat-seeking missiles.

But I'm a Cheerleader ★ ★ ★
R, 81 m., 2000

Natasha Lyonne (Megan), Clea DuVall (Graham), Cathy Moriarty (Mary Brown), RuPaul Charles (Mike), Bud Cort (Peter), Mink Stole (Nancy), Michelle Williams (Kimberly). Directed by Jamie Babbit and produced by Andrea Sperling and Leanna Creel. Screenplay by Brian Wayne Peterson.

The danger signals are clear. Megan eats tofu, listens to Melissa Etheridge songs, and has pillowcases decorated with Georgia O'Keeffe's gynecological flowers. She is obviously a lesbian. Another clue: When she kisses her boyfriend, she fantasizes about her fellow cheerleaders. Since kissing her boyfriend is something like having her tonsils cleaned by Roto-Rooter, her fantasies can be explained, but not excused.

Her friends and parents stage an intervention. Yes, it is not too late for Megan (Natasha Lyonne) to be reprogrammed. An organization named True Directions is called in. And one afternoon an astonished Megan is confronted by the evidence of her orientation, and encouraged by Mike (RuPaul Charles), the reprogrammer, to seek the path back to the straight life.

Megan is thunderstruck. It has never occurred to her that she is a lesbian, although indeed she may be. *But I'm a Cheerleader* is about her sudden transition from pom-poms to indoctrination, from high school silliness to a desert camp ruled by the fierce and unsmiling Mary Brown (Cathy Moriarty). The movie seeks the general tone of a John Waters film, although Waters might have been ruder and more polished. Director Jamie Babbit goes more for the raucous and the slapstick, and succeeds, mostly; some of the jokes don't work, but satire is always chancy, and best when it's closest to life.

There are, I am informed, actually camps like this, where gay teenagers are slammed back into the closet. The people who run them may not be as deeply into denial as Mary Brown (whose son, Rock, has moves with a weed whacker that would only be envied at Chippendale's). I don't know what luck such outfits have; people are inclined to be who they think they are and to change, if at all, only voluntarily.

Life at True Directions is draconian. Long lists of regulations are issued. Inmates attend compulsory meetings based on twelve-step programs where they analyze their "addiction." And there are classes devoted to implanting gender behavior, as when the girls practice at diapering baby dolls and the boys chop logs. Mary's lessons in vacuuming look oddly rhythmic, and Mike's car-repair classes are ripe with double entendres ("add a little more oil and shove it in and out"). The staff of True Directions is more sex-obsessed than the patients.

Megan's best friend at True Directions becomes a girl named Graham (Clea DuVall) who's going through the motions to please the staff and helps Megan figure out if she is or isn't homosexual. Other key characters include the residents of a gay "free house" not far away, where True Directions prisoners can find shelter. And there's a nearby gay bar, good for illicit midnight excursions. Everyone in the neighborhood seems preoccupied with homosexuality in one way or another.

But I'm a Cheerleader is not a great, breakout comedy, but more the kind of movie that might eventually become a regular on the midnight cult circuit. It feels like an amateur-night version of itself, awkward, heartfelt, and sweet. Natasha Lyonne, with her lower lip in a perpetual pout, is a likable heroine—not too smart, not too rebellious, more confused than troubled. And Cathy Moriarty brings great comic resolve to her role: She'd be a good drill instructor in the lesbian marines.

Butterfly ★ ★ ★
R, 97 m., 2000

Fernando Fernan Gomez (Don Gregorio), Manuel Lozano (Moncho), Uxia Blanco (Rosa), Gonzalo Uriarte (Ramon), Alexis De Los Santos (Andres), Jesus Castejon (D. Avelino), Guillermo Toledo (Otis), Elena Fernandez (Carmina), Tamar Novas (Roque). Directed by Jose Luis Cuerda. Screenplay by Rafael Azcona, based on the collection of short stories *Que Me Quieres, Amor* by Manuel Rivas.

Butterfly takes place during that brief moment in Spain between the formation of the Republic and the civil war. A history lesson will be necessary for most viewers, and the movie provides it, explaining that the old order of church, military, and monarchy was overthrown by a new leftist government, legally elected, which was then challenged by the right.

The war that followed was like a rehearsal for World War II, with Hitler testing his Luftwaffe and Russia supplying the communist side. The story was more complicated, because the Russians also fought for control of the left against the democratic socialists and the anar-

chists; Orwell's *Homage to Catalonia* tells the whole story from the point of view of an observer who was left-wing but anticommunist.

The point is that freedom flickered briefly before being crushed by big players on the world stage, who ushered in Franco and decades of dictatorship. People dared to admit their real religious beliefs (or lack of them), and to prefer democracy to the king. And in a village in Galicia, a seven-year-old boy is preparing for his first day of school.

His name is Moncho (Manuel Lozano), and he is frightened because his older brother sometimes comes home after being beaten. In class, when the teacher calls him to the front of the room, Moncho pees his pants and flees. But then the teacher comes calling. He is a kindly old man named Don Gregorio (Fernando Fernan Gomez), who explains he would never beat anyone. He coaxes the boy back into class, and gently introduces him to the world and its wonders. He gives him two presents in particular: *Treasure Island,* by Stevenson, and a butterfly net. Together, the old man and the boy study nature.

The boy's father is a tailor. Moncho's home life is happy, and enlivened by his older brother's enthusiastic interest in the opposite sex. There are, however, scandalous secrets in the village, which lend an ironic twist to one of the subplots. But in general, life is good—until the fascist uprising changes their lives forever.

Butterfly is based on the short stories of Manuel Rivas, and indeed ends like a short story, with a single word that colors everything that went before. Because the film marches so inexorably toward its conclusion, it would be unfair to hint at what happens, except to say that it provides a heartbreaking insight into the way that fear creates cowards.

Fernando Fernan Gomez, who plays the teacher, had the title role in *The Grandfather,* a 1998 Spanish film that got an Oscar nomination and won Gomez the Goya Award as Spain's best actor of the year. I found it a little too sentimental; *Butterfly,* while not lacking in sentiment, excuses it by being seen through the eyes of a naive child, and dilutes it with nostalgia and regret. The film's ending poses a hard question for the viewer: Would we behave more bravely than the characters on the screen do? We are fortunate to live in easy times.

C

Captain Corelli's Mandolin ★ ★
R, 127 m., 2001

Nicolas Cage (Captain Antonio Corelli), Penelope Cruz (Pelagia), John Hurt (Dr. Iannis), Christian Bale (Mandras), David Morrissey (Captain Gunther Weber), Irene Papas (Drosoula), Patrick Malahide (Colonel Barge), Aspasia Kralli (Mrs. Stamatis), Gerasimos Skiadaressis (Stamatis). Directed by John Madden and produced by Tim Bevan, Eric Fellner, Mark Huffam, and Kevin Loader. Screenplay by Shawn Slovo, based on the novel by Louis de Bernieres.

Perhaps *Captain Corelli's Mandolin* would have worked with subtitles. That way we would have had Greek, Italian, and German actors flavoring the story with the sound of their languages, and perhaps more local quirkiness too. In this film there is a scene where something is said in English pronounced with one accent, and a character asks, "What did he say?" and he is told—in English pronounced with another accent.

The story takes place on a small Greek island that serves as a microcosm for the Second World War, and as the backdrop for scenes of battle and romance. Its love story coexists with the war much more intelligently than the romance in *Pearl Harbor*, but it has a similar lack of passion: The lovers seem to be acting on assignment, rather than being compelled by passion.

I am increasingly suspicious of love at first, or even second, sight, because it inevitably means the two lovers stare fixedly at each other as if something Extremely Important has just happened, and the music tells us they have fallen in love—and the screenplay takes it as a given, and doesn't do the heavy lifting and tell us how, and why, and with what words, and for what reasons. To be required to love by the needs of a genre formula is no kind of fun.

The lovers in *Captain Corelli's Mandolin* are a Greek girl named Pelagia (Penelope Cruz) and the Italian Captain Corelli (Nicolas Cage). She is the daughter of the village physician, Dr. Iannis (John Hurt). Raised by her father and educated by him in literature and medi-

cine, she is smarter than the other village women, and when, earlier, she falls in love with the muscular, handsome Mandras (Christian Bale), her father warns her: "I would expect you to marry a foreigner." Greek men, he explains, expect to be dominant in a marriage, and "he is not your equal."

Mandras enlists in the Greek army to fight for freedom, ships out, and in the best-selling novel by Louis de Bernieres, has detailed and harrowing adventures that the movie avoids through a general downgrading of his role. Corelli arrives at the head of an invading "force"—a handful of Italian soldiers who sing opera and spend a lot of time at the beach with friendly prostitutes. When the mayor of the town is asked to surrender, he stands on his dignity, requiring a German officer to accept his surrender, as he doesn't take the Italians seriously. (He would rather surrender to the German officer's dog than to an Italian, he explains helpfully.)

The most delicate and fetching passages in the novel involve the stages by which Pelagia falls in love with Corelli, despite her engagement to Mandras, her dislike of foreigners, and her father's watchful eye. Then there are some effective scenes in which the Italians try to follow Mussolini's lead in surrendering, and the Germans respond. The novel's touching passages about Corelli's long secret stay in the Iannis house are, alas, compressed so painfully they lose all their meaning.

What we get is kind of a condensed version of some of the sights and sounds of the novel, without the heart, the spirit, and the juicy detail. The movie seems to exist on some sort of movie stage, and not in the real world. Curious, because it looks right. Dr. Iannis's house and its surrounding hillside looked uncannily like the scene I imagined while reading the novel, and the locations have a color the characters lack.

All except for one of them. Mandras's mother is played by the fierce Irene Papas, great spirit of the Greek cinema, now seventy-two. Her presence, and even some of her brief scenes, are a reminder that the Greeks are a little stormier and more unforgiving than some Mediterranean peoples. Penelope Cruz is Spanish, and with all the best intentions plays a Greek girl more motivated by sentiment than passion. Cage is American, and plays an Italian man for whom what is really important about love is that he is adored and forgiven by this enemy woman. A Greek and an Italian might have played these characters like romantic kickboxers.

There is a moment when the Irene Papas character sees Pelagia and Corelli dancing in the town square, and realizes Pelagia has betrayed her son Mandras (who is away fighting for freedom) with this foreign enemy. In the movie, the Papas character looks sorrowful and turns away. In life, I have a feeling, she would have come after the doctor's daughter with her teeth bared.

Cast Away ★ ★ ★
PG-13, 140 m., 2000

Tom Hanks (Chuck Noland), Helen Hunt (Kelly Frears), Christopher Noth (Jerry Lovett), Nick Searcy (Stan), Lari White (Bettina Peterson), Viveka Davis (Pilot Gwen), Lauren Birkell (Lauren Madden). Directed by Robert Zemeckis and produced by Tom Hanks, Jack Rapke, Steve Starkey, and Zemeckis. Screenplay by William Broyles Jr.

Tom Hanks does a superb job of carrying *Cast Away* all by himself for about two-thirds of its running time, but isn't much helped by additional characters in the opening and closing sequences. Here is a strong and simple story surrounded by needless complications, and flawed by a last act that first disappoints us and then ends on a note of forced whimsy.

Hanks plays Chuck Noland, a time-obsessed Federal Express executive who troubleshoots all over the world, arranging hurry-up package transfers in Moscow before flying off to solve problems in Asia. Helen Hunt plays his fiancée, Kelly Frears, who tries her best to accept a man ruled by a beeper. She comes from clock-watching stock, and for Christmas gives Chuck her grandfather's railroad watch.

Noland hitches a ride on a FedEx flight across the Pacific, which is blown off course before crashing after an onboard explosion. That seems like two catastrophes when one would have done, but director Bob Zemeckis

uses the storm for scenes of in-flight fear, wisely following Hitchcock's observation that from a suspense point of view, an explosion is over before you get your money's worth.

Noland survives the crash and floats in a life raft to a deserted island. And . . . am I telling too much of the story? I doubt it, since the trailers and commercials for this movie single-mindedly reveal as much of the plot as they can, spoiling any possible suspense. Not only do they tell you he gets off the island, they tell you *what happens then*. What am I to do? Pretend you haven't seen the ad, or discuss what we all know happens?

The early scenes are essentially busywork. Exotic locales like Moscow add a little interest to details about Noland's job. An airport farewell to the fiancée is obligatory, including the inevitable reassurances about how Chuck will be right back and they'll have a wonderful New Year's Eve. Then the crash.

The movie's power and effect center on the island. Chuck the time-and-motion man finds himself in a world without clocks, schedules, or much of a future. There's something wonderfully pathetic about the way he shouts "Hello? Anybody?" at the sand and trees. Those are his last words for a time, as he tries to remember childhood lessons about fire-making and shelter construction. Then there's a four-year flash-forward and we see the formerly plump Chuck as a gaunt, skinny survivor. (Zemeckis shut down the movie while Hanks lost weight.)

I find it fascinating when a movie just watches somebody doing something. Actual work is more interesting than most plots. Chuck splits coconuts, traps fish, builds fires, and makes use of the contents of several FedEx boxes that washed up with him (too bad nobody was mailing K rations). And he paints a face on a volleyball and names it Wilson—a device which, not incidentally, gives him an excuse for talking out loud. Hanks proves here again what an effective actor he is, never straining for an effect, always persuasive even in this unlikely situation, winning our sympathy with his eyes and his body language when there's no one else on the screen.

I liked every scene on the island and wanted more of them. There's a lovely moment when he squats on the ground, contemplating a crate that has washed up, and the shot is composed as an homage to *2001*, Hanks's favorite film. I also liked the details of his escape. A shot of the giant bow of an ocean tanker, looming over his raft, could have been the setup for the movie to end. But no. As the trailers incredibly reveal, he returns home, where . . .

Well, I can't bring myself to say, just on the chance you're still reading and don't know. Let's say that the resolution of an earlier story strand is meant to be poignant and touching, but comes across flat and anticlimactic. And that the smile at the end of the film seems a little forced.

I would have preferred knowing much less about *Cast Away* on my way into the theater. Noland's survival should be an open question as far as the audience is concerned. You might assume that the 20th Century–Fox marketing department gave away the secrets over the dead body of director Zemeckis, but no: Zemeckis apparently *prefers* to reveal his surprises in the trailers. He got a lot of flak earlier this year when the ads for his previous film, *What Lies Beneath*, let you know Harrison Ford was the bad guy, there was a ghost, etc. At that time he was quoted by David Poland's Web column:

> We know from studying the marketing of movies, people really want to know exactly everything that they are going to see before they go see the movie. It's just one of those things. To me, being a movie lover and film student and a film scholar and a director, I don't. What I relate it to is McDonald's. The reason McDonald's is a tremendous success is that you don't have any surprises. You know exactly what it is going to taste like. Everybody knows the menu.

A strange statement, implying as it does that Zemeckis is a movie lover, student, and scholar but that he doesn't market his movies for people like himself. This is all the more depressing since he usually makes good ones.

Catfish in Black Bean Sauce ★ ½
PG-13, 111 m., 2000

Paul Winfield (Harold Williams), Mary Alice (Dolores Williams), Chi Muoi Lo (Dwayne), Lauren Tom (Mai), Kieu Chinh (Thanh), Sanaa Lathan (Nina), Tyler Christopher (Michael), Tzi Ma (Vinh), Wing Chen (Samantha). Directed and produced by Chi Muoi Lo. Screenplay by Lo.

Here's a first draft for a movie that could have been extraordinary. The story materials are rich and promising, but the film is a study in clumsy construction, dead-end scenes, murky motivation, and unneeded complications. Still, at its heart, *Catfish in Black Bean Sauce* has a compelling story to tell, and there are scenes that come to life enough to show us what we're missing.

The movie is about two Vietnamese war waifs being raised by an African-American couple. Harold Williams (Paul Winfield) encountered them while working in an adoption center, and he and his wife, Dolores (Mary Alice), raised them and love them. Dwayne (played by the writer-director, Chi Muoi Lo) fully accepts them as his parents, but his older sister, Mai (Lauren Tom), still searches for their birth mother.

Dwayne's life is further complicated. His girlfriend Nina (Sanaa Lathan, from *Love and Basketball*) seems to like him more than he likes her. His roommate Michael (Tyler Christopher) is dating a Chinese girl named Samantha (Wing Chen) who may be a Chinese boy named Sam. Does Dwayne like Michael more than Nina?

The screenplay is constructed like a sitcom, with dramatic entrances and exits, lots of punch lines, and quiet moments interrupted by bombshells. At one point Dwayne blurts out, "Will you marry me?" to Nina, whose answer is interrupted by Mai's sudden entrance: "I've found Ma!"

The imminent arrival of their long-lost mother, Thanh (Kieu Chinh), puts the family in an uproar; Dolores and Harold didn't even know Mai was still looking for her. But note how filmmaker Lo is too clever by half: Instead of a carefully written airport scene showing the tensions involved, he throws in an irrelevant fantasy sequence involving a cowboy oil man.

Mai is married to a Vietnamese-American infomercial ham—an excuse for unnecessary comic infomercials, of course. She has prepared a guest bedroom for Thanh, who prefers instead to stay with Dwayne and Michael, who hardly have room for her. Meanwhile, Dolores prepares a Chinese-African dinner, which offers countless cross-cultural possibilities, most of them blown in an awkward sequence where Thanh pulls out a bottle of Vietnamese sauce, they all try it, and their reaction shots are so impenetrable we can't tell if it's too hot, too nasty, or simply an insult to Dolores's cooking.

Lo obviously has a lot of material he wants to consider, but the subplot of the transsexual Samantha is a blind alley. Given the drama at the heart of this story, who cares about Dwayne's roommate's girlfriend? There is a well-written and acted conversation between Dwayne and Michael (who argues that his love for Samantha does not make him gay), but this really works only if Dwayne is jealous, and the movie doesn't seem to know if he is or not. Certainly he is sullen and uncommunicative around Nina, the woman he allegedly loves; the movie lacks a single scene to suggest why Nina puts up with this slug.

Paul Winfield, Mary Alice, and Kieu Chinh provide the anchors for the picture—three adults whose feelings and identities are clearly established. But even here Lo bypasses perceptive dramatic scenes for concocted sitcom payoffs, including a false health crisis and a hair-pulling wrestling match on the floor between the two mothers that is wrong in every atom.

All of the material is here for another, better picture. *Catfish in Black Bean Sauce* was obviously shot quickly on a low budget, and lacked anyone willing to tell Lo his screenplay was simply not ready to be filmed. It stands as a missed opportunity. A wiser course might have been to show it to potential investors as a sketch for a more evolved production, with a better screenplay, more insights into the characters, and less deadwood.

Cats and Dogs ★ ★ ★
PG, 87 m., 2001

Jeff Goldblum (Professor Brody), Elizabeth Perkins (Carolyn Brody), Alexander Pollock (Scott Brody). With the voices of: Tobey Maguire (Lou), Alec Baldwin (Butch), Sean Hayes (Mr. Tinkles), Susan Sarandon (Ivy), Joe Pantoliano (Peek), John Lovitz (Calico), Michael Clarke Duncan (Sam), Charlton Heston (The Mastiff). Directed by Lawrence Guterman and produced by Andrew Lazar, Chris Defaria, Warren Zide, and Craig Perry. Screenplay by John Requa and Glenn Ficarra.

Dogs are man's best friend, and that makes cats insanely resentful, in *Cats and Dogs,* a family comedy that uses every trick in the book to turn its dogs and cats into talking, scheming warriors. This movie probably has more special effects in it than *Lara Croft Tomb Raider,* although you don't notice them so much because you think you're looking at real animals even when you're not.

The movie reveals that cats and dogs have been at war since time immemorial, and in recent decades have escalated into high-tech battle technology, just like humans. Early in the film, a shepherd named Butch (voice by Alec Baldwin) trots into a doghouse, pushes a button, and is transported to a secret underground canine war room worthy of Dr. Strangelove. Later in the film, in a scene that is inexplicably even funnier than it should be, Ninja cats parachute to Earth wearing night-vision goggles.

The current battle in the long-running pet war involves the Brody family, and especially Professor Brody (Jeff Goldblum), whose research may eradicate man's allergies to dogs. The cats think that would be a very bad idea, and have mobilized on two fronts: (1) They want to sabotage Brody's research, and (2) in a lab of their own, they are developing a plan to make all humans allergic to all dogs.

Assigned to guard the Brody family is the inexperienced little beagle puppy Lou (voice of Tobey Maguire). He gets the job through a mix-up, and is briefed by Butch and introduced to the secrets of the canine war machine. Leading the opposition is the waspish cat Mr. Tinkles (voice of Sean Hayes) and his assistant Calico (voice of Jon Lovitz).

Warner Bros. says dozens of cats and dogs were used in the filming of the movie, but that doesn't even begin to suggest the result, which combines real animals with realistic puppets and computer-generated effects. The dogs and cats talk a lot, with perfect lip-synch, and they do things we somehow doubt any animals, however well trained, could really do. So advanced are the special-effects techniques that the filmmakers even combine animated faces with real animal bodies with such uncanny skill that after a while you give up trying to find the seams.

One of the movie's most enjoyable in-jokes is the way some of the animals actually look a little like the humans doing their voices. Not a lot—that would spoil the illusion—but subtly. Baldwin and Maguire are fairly easy to identify behind the ears and whiskers, and look for Susan Sarandon, Michael Clarke Duncan, Joe Pantoliano, and (as the general, of course) Charlton Heston.

This has been a year for inventive family movies. In addition to the animated features like *Atlantis* and *Shrek,* there have been three live-action films: *Spy Kids, Dr. Dolittle 2,* and now *Cats and Dogs.* I'd make *Cats and Dogs* a strong second on that list, for the remarkably convincing animals, the wild action and, not least, the parachuting Ninja cats. You really have to see them. Know how something will get you started giggling?

The Cat's Meow ★ ★ ★
PG-13, 110 m., 2002

Kirsten Dunst (Marion Davies), Cary Elwes (Thomas Ince), Edward Herrmann (William Randolph Hearst), Eddie Izzard (Charlie Chaplin), Joanna Lumley (Elinor Glyn), Jennifer Tilly (Louella Parsons). Directed by Peter Bogdanovich and produced by Kim Bieber and Carol Lewis. Screenplay by Steven Peros.

William Randolph Hearst did, or did not, get away with murder on board his private yacht *Oneida* on November 15, 1924. If he did, there is no question he was powerful enough to cover it up. Hearst was the carnivorous media tycoon of the age, proprietor of newspapers, magazines, radio stations, wire services, movie production companies, a private castle, and his mistress Marion Davies, an actress of great but perhaps not exclusive charms. He was above the law not so much because of clout or bribery but because of awe; the law enforcement officials of the day were so keenly aware of their inferior social status that they lacked the nerve to approach him. The silent movies of the time are filled with scenes in which cops arrest a millionaire, discover who he is, respectfully tip their hats to him, and apologize.

On that day in 1924, the Hollywood pro-

ducer Thomas Ince possibly died, or was murdered, on board the *Oneida.* Or perhaps not. According to one story, he was shot dead by Hearst through an unfortunate misunderstanding; Hearst mistook him for Charlie Chaplin, and thought Chaplin was having an affair with Davies. Other theories say Hearst accidentally stuck Ince with a hat pin, precipitating a heart attack. Or that Ince drank some bad rotgut. There is even the possibility that Ince died at home. There was no autopsy, so the official cause of death was never determined. No guests on the yacht were ever questioned; indeed, no one can agree about who was on the yacht during its cruise.

In Hollywood at the time, whispers about Ince's death and Hearst's involvement were easily heard, and the story told in Peter Bogdanovich's *The Cat's Meow* is, the film tells us, "the whisper heard most often." Bogdanovich is not much interested in the scandal as a scandal. He uses it more as a prism through which to view Hollywood in the 1920s, when the new medium had generated such wealth and power that its giants, like Chaplin, were gods in a way no later stars could ever be. Hearst (Edward Herrmann) liked to act the beneficent host, and on the *Oneida* for that cruise were the studio head Ince (Cary Elwes), the stars Davies (Kirsten Dunst) and Chaplin (Eddie Izzard), the British wit Elinor Glyn (Joanna Lumley), and an ambitious young gossip columnist named Louella Parsons (Jennifer Tilly). There were also various stuffed shirts and their wives, and a tame society doctor.

In this company Hearst is an insecure loner, an innocent barely the equal of the life of sin he has chosen for himself. He has the *Oneida* bugged with hidden microphones, and scarcely has time to join his guests because he needs to hurry away and eavesdrop on what they say about him in his absence. Davies knows about the microphones and knows all about Willie; she was a loyal mistress who loved her man and stood by him to the end. Whether she did have an affair with Chaplin is often speculated. According to this scenario, she may have, and Willie finds one of her brooches in Chaplin's stateroom (after tearing it apart in a scene mirroring Kane's famous destruction of Susan's bedroom in the Welles picture).

Bogdanovich has an exact way of conveying the forced and metronomic gaiety on the yacht, where guests are theoretically limited to one drink before dinner, Marion Davies has to order the band to play the Charleston to cover awkward silences, every guest has a personal agenda, and at night, as guests creep from one stateroom to another and deck planks creak, they seem to be living in an English country house mystery—*Gosford Yacht.*

Apart from its theory about the mistaken death of Ince and its cover-up, the movie's most intriguing theory is that Louella Parsons witnessed it, which might explain her lifetime contract with the Hearst papers. In the exquisite wording of a veiled blackmail threat, she tells the tycoon: "We're at the point in our careers where we both need real security." Since she was making peanuts and he was one of the richest men in the world, one can only admire the nuance of "our careers."

The film is darkly atmospheric, with Edward Herrmann quietly suggesting the sadness and obsession beneath Hearst's forced avuncular chortles. Dunst is as good, in her way, as Dorothy Comingore in *Citizen Kane* in showing a woman who is more loyal and affectionate than her lover deserves. Lumley's zingers as Glyn cut right through the hypocritical grease. Tilly, we suspect, has the right angle on Parsons's chutzpah.

There is a detail easy to miss toward the end of the film that suggests as well as anything what power Hearst had. After the society doctor ascertains that Ince, still alive, has a bullet in his brain, Hearst orders the yacht to moor at San Diego, and then dispatches the dying producer by private ambulance—not to a local hospital, but to his home in Los Angeles! Hearst is on the phone to the future widow, suggesting a cover story, long before the pathetic victim arrives home.　　　☞

The Caveman's Valentine ★ ★ ★

R, 105 m., 2001

Samuel L. Jackson (Romulus), Colm Feore (Leppenraub), Ann Magnuson (Moira), Damir Andrei (Arnold), Aunjanue Ellis (Lulu), Tamara Tunie (Sheila), Peter MacNeill (Cork), Jay Rodan (Joey/No Face). Directed by Kasi Lemmons and produced by Danny DeVito, Michael Shamberg, Stacey Sher, Elie Samaha, and Andrew Stevens. Screenplay by George Dawes Green, based on his novel.

The detective in *The Caveman's Valentine* is a raving lunatic on his bad days, and a homeless man on a harmless errand on his good ones. Once he was a brilliant pianist, a student at Julliard. Now he lives in a cave in a park. His dreadlocks reach down to his waist, and his eyes peer out at a fearsome world. You'd be fearful, too, if your enemy lived at the top of the Chrysler Building and attacked you with deadly rays.

Romulus Ledbetter is one of Samuel L. Jackson's most intriguing creations, a schizophrenic with sudden sharp stabs of lucid thought and logical behavior, whose life is changed one day when the frozen body of a young man is found outside his cave in a city park. The police believe the man, a transient, froze to death. Romulus thinks he knows better. And his desire to unmask the real killer draws him out of his cave and into a daring foray into the New York art world.

Romulus is not without connections. His daughter, Lulu (Aunjanue Ellis), is a policewoman. But she is hardly convinced by his first suspect: his enemy in the Chrysler Building. By the time he discards that hypothesis and zeroes in on a fashionable photographer named Leppenraub (Colm Feore), it's too late for anyone to take him seriously—if they ever could have in the first place.

The challenge for Jackson and his director, Kasi Lemmons, is to make Romulus believable both as the caveman and as a man capable of solving a murder. Too much ranting and raving, and Romulus would repel the audience. Too much logic, and we don't buy him as mentally ill. Even the clothes and the remarkable hair have to be considered; this is not a man you would want to sit next to during a three-day bus trip, but, on the other hand, he doesn't tilt over into repellent grunge (like the aliens in *Battlefield Earth*). It's remarkable the way Jackson begins with the kind of character we'd avert our eyes from, and makes him fascinating and even likable.

This is Lemmons's second film; after her remarkable debut *Eve's Bayou* (1997), she repeats her accomplishment in fleshing out a story with intriguing supporting characters. Chief among these is Leppenraub, a gay photographer who savors S and M imagery, and his employee/lover Joey (Jay Rodan), who makes digital videos. If Leppenraub killed the dead young man, did Joey film it? Romulus is able to enter the photographer's world through an unlikely route, involving a bankruptcy lawyer who befriends him, cleans him up, and enlists him as a pianist at a party. At one of Leppenraub's openings, the dreadlocked caveman looks at the photographs with the clear eye of the mad but logical, and says exactly what he thinks.

Is this a reach, suggesting that the caveman and the photographer could find themselves in the same circles? Not in the art world, where unlikely alliances are forged every day; the movie *Basquiat* is about an artist who made the round trip from the streets to the galleries. It's also plausible, if unlikely, that the cleaned-up Romulus, an exciting man with an electric presence, could attract the sexual attention of Leppenraub's sister, Moira (Ann Magnuson), who seduces him because she likes to shock, she likes to try new things, and she likes the guy (of course, she doesn't know his whole story).

The actual solution to the murder mystery was, for me, the least interesting part of the movie. *The Caveman's Valentine* is based on a crime novel by George Dawes Green, who also wrote the screenplay, and like many procedurals it has great respect for clues, sudden insights, logical reasoning, holes in stories, and all the beloved devices of the detection genre. Although the detective in this case may be completely original, his method (under the madness) is traditional. At the end all is settled and solved, but I agree with Edmund Wilson in his famous essay on detective novels when he concluded, essentially, "so what?"

The solution simply allows the story to end. The engine that makes the story live is in the life of Romulus: in how he survives, how he thinks, how people see in him what they are looking for. To watch Samuel L. Jackson in the role is to realize again what a gifted actor he is, how skilled at finding the right way to play a character who, in other hands, might be unplayable. I think the key to the whole performance is in his walk. It's busy and bustling, as if he's late for an appointment that he's rather looking forward to. He seems absorbed in his thoughts and plans, a busy man, with the jam-packed calendar of the mad.

Cecil B. Demented ★ ½
R, 88 m., 2000

Melanie Griffith (Honey Whitlock), Stephen Dorff (Cecil B. Demented), Alicia Witt (Cherish), Adrian Grenier (Lyle), Larry Gilliard Jr. (Lewis), Maggie Gyllenhaal (Raven), Jack Noseworthy (Rodney), Mike Shannon (Petie), Harriet Dodge (Dinah), Ricki Lake (Libby). Directed by John Waters and produced by John Fiedler, Joe Caracciolo Jr., and Mark Tarlov. Screenplay by Waters.

My best guess is that John Waters produced the talent shows in his high school. There's always been something cheerfully amateurish about his more personal films—a feeling that he and his friends have dreamed up a series of "skits" while hanging out together. *Cecil B. Demented* takes this tendency to an almost unwatchable extreme, in a home movie that's like a bunch of kids goofing off.

To be sure, he has real stars in the picture; Melanie Griffith stars *as* a Hollywood star, and Stephen Dorff plays the cult leader who kidnaps her as part of his guerrilla assault on mainstream cinema. But they're used more as exhibits than performers (Look! It's Melanie Griffith!). The movie has a radical premise, as Weathermen-type movie lovers try to destroy dumb commercial films, but it is pitched at the level of a very bad sketch on *Saturday Night Live*.

Cinema guerrilla Cecil B. Demented (Dorff) and his cult group kidnap Griffith, who will be forced to star in their own film. Their targets include the Maryland Film Commission, the big shots who produced Griffith's own new film, and *Gump Two*, a sequel to *Forrest Gump*, which is being shot in Baltimore. Some of this stuff is funny in concept (when they attack the director's cut of *Patch Adams*, that's good for a laugh, although the scene itself isn't).

And Griffith, as a spoiled star named Honey Whitlock, gets into the spirit. She makes the life of her assistant (Ricki Lake) miserable, she makes impossible demands, she sends back a limousine that's the wrong color (not fiction;

I once actually saw Ginger Rogers do this), and she is not a good sport when it comes to eating Maryland seafood ("I'm not interested in some kind of meal you have to beat with a mallet while wearing some stupid little bib, while families of mutants gawk in your face").

But the story and dialogue are genuinely amateur night, and there are times when you can almost catch the actors giggling, like kids in a senior class sketch. It's been like that in a lot of Waters's movies, from the raunchy early sleazoids like *Pink Flamingos*, through his transitional phase *(Polyester)* to his studio productions *(Hairspray, Cry-Baby, Serial Mom)*. Now he seems to have returned to his middle period again, if such a thing is possible.

Cecil B. Demented got its title, Waters says, because that's what he was called in an early review. Like Ed Wood (but inevitably at a higher level of artistry), he seems to enjoy the actual process of making films: He likes to go to the set, have actors say "Action!" and see everyone have a good time. Sometimes, in this film, that geniality works against him; the actors are having a better time than we are.

Too much of the movie feels like the kind of film where you're supposed to say, "Look! There's . . ." and fill in the name of a faded TV personality. Patricia Hearst, who appeared in Waters's funny *Cry-Baby*, is back, for example, to add ironic weight to a story about a kidnap victim who identifies with her captors. How entertaining is that really supposed to be?

Waters has always embraced a tacky design look in his films, and here a lot of the sets seem decorated by stuff everybody brought from home. Old movie posters are plastered on the walls, the cult hangs around in what looks like a rec room, and there are movie in-jokes everywhere. (Cult members have the names of their favorite directors tattooed on their arms.)

Cecil also tells us, "I don't believe in phony life-affirming endings." He sure doesn't. The ending of *Cecil B. Demented* may be phony, but it's not life-affirming. One wonders if the script simply says, "Everyone runs around like crazy."

There will, however, always be a (small) corner of my heart filled with admiration for John Waters. He is an anarchist in an age of the cautious, an independent in an age of studio

creatures, a man whose films are homemade and contain no chemicals or preservatives. Even with *Cecil B. Demented*, which fails on just about every level, you've got to hand it to him: The idea for the film is kind of inspired. When this kid gets out of high school he's going to amount to something. You wait and see.

The Cell ★ ★ ★ ★
R, 108 m., 2000

Jennifer Lopez (Catherine Deane), Vince Vaughn (Agent Novak), Vincent D'Onofrio (Carl Stargher), Marianne Jean-Baptiste (Dr. Miriam Kent), Jake Weber (Agent Ramsey), Dylan Baker (Henry West), Patrick Bauchau (Lucien Baines), Gerry Becker (Dr. Cooperman), James Gammon (Teddy Lee), Catherine Sutherland (Anne Marie Vicksey), Jake Thomas (Young Stargher), Pruitt Taylor Vince (Dr. Reid). Directed by Tarsem and produced by Julio Caro and Eric McLeod. Screenplay by Mark Protosevich.

The Cell is a bizarre mixture of science fiction and serial murders, mind games and pop psychology, wild images and haunting special effects. It's a thriller and a fantasy, a police movie and a venture into the mind of a killer so perverse he could see Hannibal Lecter and raise him. For all of its visual pyrotechnics, it's also a story where we care about the characters; there's a lot at stake at the end, and we're involved. I know people who hate it, finding it pretentious or unrestrained; I think it's one of the best films of the year.

Jennifer Lopez stars, as Catherine Deane, a social worker who has a knack for establishing rapport with troubled clients. She is recruited for a project in which experimental technology is used to establish a link between her mind and that of a little boy locked inside a coma. Can she coax him out? The opening images, of black stallions and desert vistas, show her riding across the sands in a flowing white dress, and then finding the little boy in a landscape filled with stark Dali trees, and almost making contact, before . . .

The director, named Tarsem, uses this story to establish the mind-sharing methodology. The mind-trips take place in a sci-fi laboratory, with earnest scientists peering through plate-glass windows at their eerie subjects, who are suspended in midair wearing virtual reality gear. We meet the millionaire parents of the little boy, learn about his problems, and get to know Catherine, who is played by Lopez as quiet, grave, and confident.

In a parallel story, the FBI finds the body of the latest victim of a serial killer who drowns his captives and then makes them up to look like dolls. Vince Vaughn plays an agent named Novak, who believes the killer has a ritual he goes through—a ritual that means his latest victim has only hours to live before a clockwork mechanism brings about her death. Using slim clues and brilliant lab work, the FBI is able to capture the killer, a vile man named Carl Stargher (Vincent D'Onofrio). But how to get him to reveal where his latest captive is hidden? The FBI turns to Catherine Deane and the scientists in charge (Marianne Jean-Baptiste, Dylan Baker, and Pruitt Taylor Vince), who warn that she risks psychic harm by venturing into Stargher's unwholesome subconscious.

The screenplay, by Mark Protosevich, is ingenious in the way it intercuts three kinds of stories. On one level *The Cell* is science fiction about virtual reality, complete with the ominous observation that if your mind thinks it's real, then it is real, and it could kill you. On another level the movie is a wildly visionary fantasy in which the mind-spaces of Stargher and Deane are landscapes by Jung out of Dali, with a touch of the Tarot deck, plus light-and-sound trips reminiscent of *2001*. On the third level, the movie is a race against time, in which a victim struggles for her life while the FBI desperately pieces together clues; these scenes reminded me of *The Silence of the Lambs*. The intercutting is so well done that at the end there is tension from all three directions, and what's at stake is not simply the life of the next victim, but also the soul of Carl Stargher, who lets Catherine get glimpses of his unhappy childhood.

Stargher's sexual practices are also suggested, somewhat obliquely. Like the predators in *Seven, The Silence of the Lambs,* and *Hannibal,* Stargher is a creature of neo-S&M, a seriously twisted man whose libido needs such complicated tending it hardly seems worth the trouble. We are left with a few technical questions (how

did he embed the hooks in his own back?), but a movie like this is more concerned with suggesting weirdness than explaining it.

The Cell is one of those movies where you have a lot of doubts at the beginning, and then one by one they're answered, and you find yourself seduced by the style and story. It plays fair all the way through—it develops its themes and delivers on them, instead of copping out like *Hollow Man* by making a U-turn into a slasher film. It's not often the imagination and the emotions are equally touched by a film, but here I was exhilarated by the boldness of the conception while still involved at a thriller level.

I don't seek out advance information about movies because I like to go in with an open mind. Walking into the screening of *The Cell,* I knew absolutely nothing about the plot or premise, but a TV producer in New York made a point of telling me how much she hated it, and various on-line correspondents helpfully told me how bad they thought it was. Did we see the same movie?

We live in a time when Hollywood shyly ejects weekly remakes of dependable plots, terrified to include anything that might confuse the dullest audience member. The new studio guidelines prefer PG-13 cuts from directors, so we get movies like *Coyote Ugly* that start out with no brains and now don't have any sex, either. Into this wilderness comes a movie like *The Cell,* which is challenging, wildly ambitious, and technically superb, and I dunno: I guess it just overloads the circuits for some people.

Tarsem (he dropped his surname, Duamdwar) is a first-time director who comes to movies via music videos and commercials (indeed his title sequence in the desert looks like it could lead into a beer ad as easily as a psychological fantasy). He must have seized this project with eager ambition. Like other emerging directors (Spike Jonze, David O. Russell, Paul Thomas Anderson) he likes to take big chances; he reminds me of how Spike Lee and Oliver Stone came lunging out of the starting gate.

Tarsem is an Indian, like M. Night Shyamalan of *The Sixth Sense,* and comes from a culture where ancient imagery and modern technology live side by side. In the 1970s, Pauline Kael wrote, the most interesting directors were Altman, Scorsese, and Coppola, because they were Catholics whose imaginations were enriched by the church of pre-Vatican II, while most other Americans were growing up on Eisenhower's bland platitudes. Now our whole culture has been tamed by marketing and branding, and mass entertainment has been dumbed down. It is possible the next infusion of creativity will come from cultures like India, still rich in imagination, not yet locked into malls.

The Center of the World ★ ★ ★ ½
NO MPAA RATING, 86 m., 2001

Peter Sarsgaard (Richard Longman), Molly Parker (Florence), Carla Gugino (Jerri), Balthazar Getty (Brian Pivano). Directed by Wayne Wang and produced by Peter Newman and Wang. Screenplay by Ellen Benjamin Wong (pseudonym for Wang, Paul Auster, and Siri Hustvedt).

Sex isn't the subject of *The Center of the World.* It's the arena. The subject is making money, and the movie is about two people who hate their jobs. Richard (Peter Sarsgaard) is a computer whiz whose company is about to go public and make him a millionaire. Florence (Molly Parker) is a lap dancer in a strip club, but technically not a prostitute. You can be aroused by her, but you can't touch her. Richard is the same way. He skips a meeting with investors, and disappears as his company floats its IPO. You can profit from his skills, but you can't have him.

Here are two people who want to succeed only on their own terms. The big difference between them, as she points out, is "money. You have it and I don't." As a sex worker, her strategy is to get the client's money without giving herself. She meets Richard in a coffee shop. He finds out where she works, turns up, and buys a lap dance. He's fascinated. He asks her to go to Las Vegas for a weekend. She says she's not that kind of person. "I can compensate you," he says. "Compensate" is a revealing word in this context. He offers her $10,000. She says he'll have to observe her rules. He agrees.

He may actually be happy to agree. She's

spared him from performance anxiety. He gets the intrigue, the excitement, the mystique, and her full attention, and avoids physical and psychological risk. Nice deal. Good for her, too, because she needs money but doesn't think of herself as a prostitute (she's "really" a drummer in a rock band). Wayne Wang says his film was inspired by the strip clubs of the Silicon Valley. They bring together men who have too much money and no interest in relationships with women who have too little money and no interest in relationships.

Sex supplies the stakes. It's the currency of the microeconomy created for a weekend by Richard and Flo. She manufactures sex, he consumes it, and cash flow is generated. When she goes a little further than her guidelines permit, that's like Alan Greenspan lowering interest rates. The casual observer may think the weekend is all about sex; more evolved viewers will notice that the sex is not very fulfilling, very original, or very good; what is fascinating are the mind games. They're like negotiations. Flo is the better negotiator, but then of course she's the market-maker.

In theory, a prostitute and her client form a closed system, in which everything in their private lives, even their real names, may be kept secret. Because Richard and Flo met socially before entering into their agreement, information leaked out. She knows he's about to make millions of dollars, although all she wants is $10,000. The commitment involved in getting the millions would interfere with her idea of herself. We in the audience get more information because we eavesdrop during their private moments; he deals by e-mail with partners who are enraged that he stiffed the investors and (they hear) is in Vegas with a hooker on the company's biggest day. She calls a Vegas friend named Jerri (Carla Gugino), who gives her technical advice; she tells Jerri she "kinda likes" the guy.

Now look at their sex. Her rules permit action only between 10 P.M. and 2 A.M. The rest of the time, they sightsee, visit restaurants, play video games. The sex in theory will not involve intercourse. They have connecting rooms. At 10 P.M. she throws open the doors, dressed dramatically in "erotic" clothes that are pretty routine. She does advanced versions of a lap dance. He wants to go further. "You want real?" she asks. "I'll show you real." What she shows him is real, all right, but scant consolation for an onlooker.

At one point they practice something called "fire and ice," which involves ice cubes and hot sauce, and has been compared by credulous reviewers with the most famous scene in *Last Tango in Paris*. The difference is, in *Last Tango* something was really happening between two unpaid and involved participants; in *The Center of the World*, it's erotic showbiz. (Show me a sexual practice that involves ice cubes and hot sauce, and I will show you a sexual practice that would be improved without them.) The movie has also been compared to *Leaving Las Vegas*, but couldn't be more different. That was about agony and redemption, and the hooker was a healing angel. This movie is about two entrepreneurs.

The suspense in *The Center of the World* is not about whether Flo and Richard will have real sex. The suspense involves whether they'll start to like each other. He tells her he's in love, but guys always say that. She kinda likes him, but having started off in this way, can she ever have sex with him that will not seem, in some way, like a subtle extension of prostitution? To this intrigue is added another level when Jerri, the friend, visits their suite with a story of being beaten up. Is Richard being scammed by the two women?

In a scenario like this, it's impossible to figure out what's real. Does Richard love Flo, or the erotic illusion she creates, or the freedom from responsibility she makes possible? Does Flo like Richard, or his money, or the gamesmanship of dancing closer to the flame? When they spontaneously find themselves turned on outside the four-hour time zone, is that real, or does it feed off the excitement of breaking the rules? The situation is complicated because all of their interruptus brinksmanship has been a turn-on. They're only human.

If you understand who the characters are and what they're supposed to represent, the performances are right on the money. Flo is not supposed to be a sexy tart, and Richard is not supposed to be a lustful client. They're sides of the same coin, and very much alike. You want real? This movie shows you real. For Richard and Flo, real is a weekend in Vegas trying to figure out what they really want, and how much they're willing to sell off in order to buy it.

Center Stage ★ ★ ★
PG-13, 113 m., 2000

Amanda Schull (Jody), Ethan Stiefel (Cooper Neilson), Peter Gallagher (Jonathan Reeves), Sascha Radetsky (Charlie), Shakiem Evans (Erik), Zoe Saldana (Eva Rodriguez), Donna Murphy (Juliette [Teacher]), Susan Mary Pratt (Maureen), Ilia Kulik (Sergei). Directed by Nicholas Hytner and produced by Laurence Mark. Screenplay by Carol Heikkinen.

Center Stage follows a group of young ballet students through their first year of advanced training at the fictional American Ballet Academy in New York. They had to be very good to get in. Only three will be chosen at the end of the year to join the company. They work hard, but when they are not actually dancing, they are a lot like freshmen in any college; they survive romances, they party, they gossip, they despair and dream, and they smoke too much.

Dancers do tend to smoke a lot. It's bad for their wind, but they think it helps them to lose weight. The movie knows that and a lot of other things about the world of ballet; it feels like an inside job. It isn't so perceptive about its characters, who tend to fall into recognizable types (the ingenue, the rebel, the girl who's too fat, the girl who is pushed by her mother). Here it's similar to *Fame*, but not as electrifying. But if you look at *Center Stage* as another example of the school movie of the week, with auditions taking the place of the senior prom, you realize it's a lot smarter and more perceptive—and it's about something.

It is about the union of hard work and artistic success. To be a world-class ballet dancer is to be an athlete of the highest order, and if you look at ballet as a sport, it has many Michael Jordans and the NBA had only one. The movie casts real dancers in many of the roles, and that provides an obvious standard of excellence that gives the movie an underlying authenticity.

Ethan Stiefel, considered by many to be the best male dancer in the world, plays Cooper, the lead—the star of the company, who has just lost his girlfriend to Jonathan (Peter Gallagher), the company's head. He becomes attracted to Jody (Amanda Schull), one of the new students, and in a predictable progression invites her into his bed and into the new ballet he is creating.

Predictable, yes, but not with all the soap-opera payoffs we might fear. The movie uses the materials of melodrama, but is gentle with them; it's oriented more in the real world, and doesn't jack up every conflict and love story into an overwrought crisis. That restraint is especially useful in creating the character Eva Rodriguez (Zoe Saldana), the class rebel, who talks back to the teacher (Donna Murphy), comes late to rehearsals, has a bad attitude—and yet actually has the best attitude of all, because she dances out of her love for dance, not because of ambition or duty.

Some of the other students are not so lucky. One has been pushed into dancing by her mother. One has a body-image problem. And so on. But a lot of these kids are pretty normal, apart from their demanding profession. In a dance club, Sergei (Ilia Kulik), from Russia, tries to pick up two women. They both want to know what he does. He says he's a ballet dancer, and they turn away. With the next woman, he has more luck. "Mafia," he explains.

The movie doesn't force it, but it has the pleasures of a musical. It ends with two big ballet numbers, wonderfully staged and danced, and along the way there are rehearsals and scenes in a Broadway popular dance studio that have a joy and freedom. Film is a wonderful way to look at dance, because it gets you closer and varies the point of view, but since the death of the Hollywood musical there hasn't been enough of it. *Center Stage* has moments of joy and moments of insight, and is about both human nature and the inhuman demands of ballet.

Chalk ★ ★ ★

NO MPAA RATING, 135 m., 2000

Edwin Johnson (Watson), Johnnie Reese (Jones), Kelvin Han Yee (T.C.), Don Bajema (Dorian James), Denise Concetta Cavaliere (Lois), John Tidwell (Johnnie), Destiny Costa (Wanda). Directed by Rob Nilsson and produced by Rand Crook and Ethan Sing. Screenplay by Don Bajema and Nilsson.

Rob Nilsson's *Chalk* opens with half an hour of murky, grungy scene-setting in a San Francisco pool hall. Out of this miasma, the story gradually wells up; without quite realizing when it happens, we pass from passive witnesses to active watchers. What purpose does the shapeless opening serve? Perhaps to immerse us in the movie's world, to provide a passage from one reality to another.

The story, once its outlines have become clear, involves a black man in his sixties named Watson (Edwin Johnson), who runs a pool hall with his two sons. He spent time in Japan, we learn, where he perhaps fathered Jones (Johnnie Reese), who is half-Asian. His other son is the adopted Korean-American T.C. (Kelvin Han Yee), who walked into the pool hall one day.

Jones wants to set up a high-stakes pool game between T.C. and a man named Dorian James (Don Bajema), who is a ranking professional. T.C. hesitates. He has choked before, and there are hints that Jones hopes T.C. will fail again. Then T.C. discovers that Watson is dying, and decides to take the $10,000 match and prove himself to his adoptive father. Filling out the canvas is Lois (Denise Concetta Cavaliere), T.C.'s girlfriend, who works as the bartender in the pool hall.

As I describe this plot you are perhaps thinking of *The Hustler* or *The Color of Money*, but *Chalk* feels nothing like those films. It is more like a movie extruded from the world in which it is set. Information about its making is essential to understanding its feeling. It was directed by Nilsson, a fiercely independent filmmaker whose earlier titles include *Northern Lights* (1979), about a farmer-labor strike in Minnesota, and *On the Edge* (1986), with Bruce Dern's great performance as an outlaw runner who makes one last great effort.

Around 1990, Nilsson moved to San Francisco and started a filmmaking workshop in the Tenderloin area, recruiting street people and marginal survivors as his actors and technicians. Only two of the actors in *Chalk* are professionals (Johnson and Bajema). The others do not play themselves, precisely, but their characters are informed by people they know and where they live.

The visual style, with Mickey Freeman as cinematographer, is deliberately stylized; *Chalk* looks like *film noir* seen through a glass darkly, with backlit highlights. Although Nilsson's hero is Cassavetes, the film does not feel improvised, but more as if the video camera waited patiently for the right moments.

Much of the dialogue is half-heard, elliptical, allusive. A few conversations play out at length. One of the best has T.C. talking with a pool hustler who lives in his van and remembers when he had, and lost, a mobile home: "Pool players don't make as much as volleyball players—even dart players. If you're not in the top 10, forget about it." He gives T.C. advice on how to beat Dorian James, if indeed Dorian can be beaten.

The other conversation is between Dorian and his girlfriend Wanda (Destiny Costa), and it involves his request that she do something particularly painful to him as part of his preparation for the match. Their talk is desultory; he asks, she refuses, they fight, embrace, rest, talk quietly, and he brings up the subject again. We sense depths of loneliness and insecurity.

The $10,000 match, which occupies perhaps the last forty-five minutes of the film, is for the first player to win seven games. The movie makes the progress of the games clear, and yet doesn't dwell on them, because the real contest is between the players. During two of the games, Freeman's camera adopts the fast-moving, tabletop "ball eye view" approach used by Scorsese in *The Color of Money*, maybe just to show that he can. After the match is settled, there is another payoff, quick, painful, and brutal, which we didn't see coming.

Chalk is not the kind of movie many people will appreciate at first viewing. You have to understand who Nilsson and his actors are, and give some thought to the style to appreciate it. It is not just one more *Hustler* clone, that's for sure, but a plunge into the hermetic world these characters have created and inhabit. There may be a world outside the pool hall, but when T.C. goes to the beach one day, he's like a fish out of water. And inside the hall, old errors, ancient drug habits, and deep psychic wounds make happiness, we realize, impossible.

Changing Lanes ★ ★ ★
R, 100 m., 2002

Ben Affleck (Gavin Banek), Samuel L. Jackson (Doyle Gipson), Toni Collette (Michelle), Sydney Pollack (Delano), William Hurt (Doyle's Sponsor), Amanda Peet (Cynthia), Kim Staunton (Valerie Gipson), Dylan Baker (Fixer). Directed by Roger Michell and produced by Scott Rudin. Screenplay by Chap Taylor and Michael Tolkin.

"One wrong turn deserves another," say the ads for *Changing Lanes*. Yes, both of the movie's dueling hotheads are in the wrong—but they are also both in the right. The story involves two flawed men, both prey to anger, who get involved in a fender bender that brings out all of their worst qualities. And their best. This is not a dumb formula film about revenge. It doesn't use rubber-stamp lines like, "It's payback time." It is about adults who have minds as well as emotions, and can express themselves with uncommon clarity. And it's not just about the quarrel between these two men, but about the ways they have been living their lives.

The story begins with two men who need to be in court on time. Gavin Banek (Ben Affleck) needs to file a signed form proving that an elderly millionaire turned over control of his foundation to Banek's law firm. Doyle Gipson (Samuel L. Jackson) needs to show that he has loan approval to buy a house for his family; he hopes that will persuade his fed-up wife to stay in New York and not move with the kids to Oregon. Banek and Gipson get into a fender bender. It's not really anybody's fault.

Of course they are polite when it happens: "You hurt?" Nobody is. Banek, who is rich and has been taught that money is a solution to human needs, doesn't want to take time to exchange insurance cards and file a report. He hands Gipson a signed blank check. Gipson, who wants to handle this the right way, doesn't want a check. Banek gets in his car and drives away, shouting, "Better luck next time!" over his shoulder, and leaving Gipson stranded in the middle of the expressway with a flat tire.

Gipson gets to court twenty minutes late. The case has already been settled. In his absence, he has lost. The judge isn't interested in his story. Banek gets to court in time, but discovers that he is missing the crucial file folder with the old man's signature. Who has it? Gipson.

At this point, in a film less intelligent and ambitious, the vile Banek would pull strings to make life miserable for the blameless Gipson. But *Changing Lanes* doesn't settle for the formula. Gipson responds to Banek's rudeness by faxing a page from the crucial file to Banek with "Better luck next time!" scrawled on it. Banek turns to his sometime mistress (Toni Collette), who knows a guy who "fixes" things. The guy (Dylan Baker) screws with Gipson's credit rating so his home mortgage falls through. Gipson finds an ingenious way to counterattack. And so begins a daylong struggle between two angry men.

Ah, but that's far from all. *Changing Lanes* is a thoughtful film that by its very existence shames studio movies that have been dumbed down into cat-and-mouse cartoons. The screenplay is by Chap Taylor, who has previously worked as a production assistant for Woody Allen, and by Michael Tolkin, who wrote the novel and screenplay *The Player* and wrote and directed two extraordinary films, *The Rapture* and *The New Age*. The writers, rookie and veteran, want to know who these men are, how they got to this day in their lives, what their values are, what kinds of worlds they live in. A dumb film would be about settling scores after the fender bender. This film, which breathes, which challenges, which is excitingly alive, wants to see these men hit their emotional bottoms. Will they learn anything?

Doyle Gipson is a recovering alcoholic. His AA meetings and his AA sponsor (William Hurt) are depicted in realistic, not stereotyped terms. He's sober, but still at the mercy of his emotions. As he stands in the wreckage of his plans to save his marriage, his wife (Kim Staunton) tells him, "This is the sort of thing that always happens to you—and never happens to me unless I am in your field of gravity." And his sponsor tells him, "Booze isn't really your drug of choice. You're addicted to chaos." At one point, seething with rage, Gipson walks into a bar and orders a shot of bourbon. Then he stares at it. Then he gets into a fight that he deliberately provokes, and we realize that at

some level he walked into the bar not for the drink but for the fight.

Gavin Banek leads a rich and privileged life. His boss (Sydney Pollack) has just made him a partner in their Wall Street law firm. It doesn't hurt that Banek married the boss's daughter. It also doesn't hurt that he was willing to obtain the signature of a confused old man who might not have known what he was signing, and that the firm will make millions as a result. His wife (Amanda Peet) sees her husband with blinding clarity. After Banek has second thoughts about the tainted document, Pollack asks his daughter to get him into line, and at lunch she has an extraordinary speech.

"Did you know my father has been cheating on my mother for twenty years?" she asks him. He says no, and then sheepishly adds, "Well, I didn't know it was for twenty years." Her mother knew all along, his wife says, "but she thought it would be unethical to leave a man for cheating on his marriage, after she has enjoyed an expensive lifestyle that depends on a man who makes his money by cheating at work." She looks across the table at her husband. "I could have married an honest man," she tells him. She did not, choosing instead a man who would go right to the edge to make money. You don't work on Wall Street if you're not prepared to do that, she says.

And what, for that matter, about the poor old millionaire whose foundation is being plundered? "How do you think he got his money?" Pollack asks Affleck. "You think those factories in Malaysia have day-care centers?" He helpfully points out that the foundation was set up in the first place as a tax dodge.

Such speeches are thunderbolts in *Changing Lanes*. They show the movie digging right down into the depths of the souls, of the values of these two men. The director, Roger Michell, has made good movies, including *Persuasion* and *Notting Hill*, but this one seems more like Neil LaBute's *In the Company of Men*, or Tolkin's work. It lays these guys out and X-rays them, and by the end of the day, each man's own anger scares him more than the other guy's. This is one of the best movies of the year. ☞

Charlie's Angels ½★
PG-13, 92 m., 2000

Cameron Diaz (Natalie), Drew Barrymore (Dylan), Lucy Liu (Alex), Bill Murray (Bosley), Sam Rockwell (Eric Knox), Kelly Lynch (Vivian Wood), Tim Curry (Roger Corwin), John Forsythe (Voice of Charlie). Directed by McG and produced by Leonard Goldberg, Drew Barrymore, and Nancy Juvonen. Screenplay by Ryan Rowe, Ed Solomon, and John August.

Charlie's Angels is eye candy for the blind. It's a movie without a brain in its three pretty little heads, which belong to Cameron Diaz, Drew Barrymore, and Lucy Liu. This movie is a dead zone in their lives, and mine.

What is it? A satire? Of what? Of satires, I guess. It makes fun of movies that want to make fun of movies like this. It's an all-girl series of mindless action scenes. Its basic shot consists of Natalie, Dylan, and Alex, the angels, running desperately toward the camera before a huge explosion lifts them off their feet and hurls them through the air and smashes them against windshields and things—but they survive with injuries only to their makeup.

Why, I am asking, is this funny? I am thinking hard. So much money and effort was spent on these explosions that somebody must have been convinced they had a purpose, but I, try as I might, cannot see them as anything other than action without mind, purpose, humor, excitement, or entertainment.

The movie's premise will be familiar to anyone who ever watched the original TV show. I never watched the show, and the plot was familiar even to me. A disembodied voice (John Forsythe) issues commands to the three babes who work for his detective agency, and they perform his missions while wearing clothes possibly found at the thrift shop across the street from Coyote Ugly.

Barrymore, Diaz, and Liu represent redhead, blonde, and brunette respectively (or, as my colleague David Poland has pointed out, T, A, and Hair). Sad, isn't it, that three such intelligent, charming, and talented actresses could be reduced to their most prominent component parts? And voluntarily too. At the tops of their careers, they *chose* to make this movie (Barrymore even produced it). They volunteered for what lesser talents are reduced to doing.

The cast also contains Bill Murray, who likes to appear unbilled in a lot of his movies, and picked the wrong one to shelve that policy. He is winsome, cherubic, and loopy, as usual, but the movie gives him nothing to push against. There's the curious feeling he's playing to himself. Sam Rockwell plays a kidnapped millionaire, Tim Curry plays a villain, and . . . why go on?

In the months to come there will be several movies based on popular video games, including one about "Tomb Raiders" and its digital babe, Lara Croft. *Charlie's Angels* is like the trailer for a video game movie, lacking only the video game and the movie.

Charlotte Gray ★ ★
PG-13, 123 m., 2002

Cate Blanchett (Charlotte Gray), Billy Crudup (Julien Lavade), Rupert Perry-Jones (Peter), Michael Gambon (Levarde), Anton Lesser (Benech), Ron Cook (Mirabel). Directed by Gillian Armstrong and produced by Sarah Curtis and Douglas Rae. Screenplay by Jeremy Brock, based on the novel by Sebastian Faulks.

Consider now Cate Blanchett, a wondrous actress. Born in Melbourne in 1969, honored for her stage work in Australia, a survivor of U.S. TV-like *Police Rescue*, she made her first film in 1997 (*Paradise Road*, about female prisoners of war in the Pacific) and then arrived immediately at stardom in the title role of *Elizabeth* (1998), winning an Oscar nomination.

In the four years since then she has played in an astonishing range of roles: as a calculating Londoner in *An Ideal Husband*, as a strong-willed nineteenth-century gambler from the Outback in the wonderful *Oscar and Lucinda*, as an Italian-American housewife from New Jersey in *Pushing Tin*, as a rich society girl in *The Talented Mr. Ripley*, as a gold-digging Parisian showgirl in *The Man Who Cried*, as an Appalachian redneck with psychic powers in *The Gift*, as the woman who convinces both Billy Bob Thornton and Bruce Willis they love her in *Bandits*, as Galadriel in *Lord of the Rings*, as a lanky-haired Poughkeepsie slattern in *The Shipping News*, and now as a British woman who parachutes into France and fights with the Resistance in *Charlotte Gray*. Oh, and also in 2001 she had a baby.

Name me an actress who has played a greater variety of roles in four years, and I'll show you Meryl Streep. Were you counting Blanchett's accents? British, Elizabethan English, Edwardian English, Scots, Australian, French, American southern, midwestern, New England, New Joisey. And she has the kind of perfect profile they used in the "Can You Draw This Girl?" ads. She can bring as much class to a character as Katharine Hepburn, and has a better line in sluts.

While I was watching *Charlotte Gray*, I spent a lot of time thinking about Blanchett's virtues, because she, Billy Crudup, and Michael Gambon were performing life support on a hopeless screenplay. This is a movie that looks great, is well acted, and tells a story that you can't believe for a moment. I have no doubt that brave British women parachuted into France to join the Resistance; indeed, I have seen a much better movie about just such a woman—*Plenty* (1985), starring, wouldn't you know, Meryl Streep. It's just that I don't think such women were motivated primarily by romance. After *Pearl Harbor*, here is another movie where World War II is the backdrop for a love triangle.

Blanchett plays the title character, a Scottish woman in London who speaks perfect French and meets a young airman named Peter (Rupert Perry-Jones) at a publisher's party. They fall instantly in love, they have a one-night stand, he's shot down over France, and (she hears and believes) finds shelter with the Resistance. Charlotte allows herself to be recruited into British Special Operations, goes through training, and is dropped into France—near where Peter is thought to be. She is going to—what? Rescue him? Comfort him in her arms? Get him back to Britain? The movie doesn't spell this out very well.

In France, she comes into contact with a Resistance group led by Julien (Billy Crudup), a Communist, whose father, Levarde (Michael Gambon), disapproves of his son's politics, but keeps quiet because he hates the Nazis. Soon Charlotte is taken along on a raid that underlines the screenplay's basic problem, which is her utterly superfluous presence.

Crudup and his men hide in a ditch, blow up a Nazi train, are chased and nearly killed by Nazi soldiers. The next morning, Charlotte is told: "You did a good job last night." Why? How? What did she accomplish but tag along on a mission she had nothing to do with, watch the men blow up the train, and run for her life? A stranger, not needed, why was she taken along in the first place? This is the Resistance version of the practice of taking a girl along with you on a hunting trip so she can admire you shooting the big bad birds.

Soon Charlotte and Julien are drifting into unacknowledged love, while a subplot involves the fate of two local Jewish children whose parents have been shipped to the camps. Charlotte touches base with a dyspeptic local contact who seems to exist primarily to raise doubts about himself, and . . . but see for yourself, as the plot thickens. One question you might ask: How wise is it for Julien, an important Resistance fighter who wants to remain unnoticed, to shout curses at arriving Nazi troops? Another is: How important is that final letter Charlotte risks her life to type?

Blanchett, Crudup, and Gambon stand above and somehow apart from the absurdities of the screenplay. Their presence in their characters is convincing enough that we care about them and hope they survive—if not the war, at least the screenplay. The movie was directed by Gillian Armstrong, usually so good (*My Brilliant Career*, the overlooked and inspired *Oscar and Lucinda*). This time she excels in everything but her choice of material.

It is Cate Blanchett's fate to be born into a time when intelligence is fleeing from mainstream movies. The script for *Plenty* was based on a great play by David Hare. *Charlotte Gray* is based on a best-selling novel by Sebastian Faulks, unread by me, and on the basis of this movie, not on my reading list. Next Blanchett appears in *Heaven*, based on a screenplay by the late Krzysztof Kieslowski and directed by Tom Tykwer *(Run Lola Run, The Princess and the Warrior)*. Good career move.

Chelsea Walls ★ ★ ★
R, 109 m., 2002

Rosario Dawson (Audrey), Vincent D'Onofrio (Frank), Kris Kristofferson (Bud), Robert Sean

Leonard (Terry), Natasha Richardson (Mary), Uma Thurman (Grace), Steve Zahn (Ross), Tuesday Weld (Geta), Mark Webber (Val), Jimmy Scott (Skinny Bones). Directed by Ethan Hawke and produced by Alexis Alexanian, Pamela Koffler, Christine Vachon, and Gary Winick. Screenplay by Nicole Burdette, based on her play.

A rest stop for rare individuals.
—Motto of the Chelsea Hotel

Chelsea Walls is the movie for you if you have a beaten-up copy of the Compass paperback edition of Kerouac's *On the Road* and on page 124 you underlined the words, "The one thing that we yearn for in our living days, that makes us sigh and groan and undergo sweet nauseas of all kinds, is the remembrance of some lost bliss that was probably experienced only in the womb and can only be reproduced (though we hate to admit it) in death." If you underlined the next five words ("But who wants to die?"), you are too realistic for this movie.

Lacking the paperback, you qualify for the movie if you have ever made a pilgrimage to the Chelsea Hotel on West 23rd Street in New York, and given a thought to Dylan Thomas, Thomas Wolfe, Arthur C. Clarke, R. Crumb, Brendan Behan, Gregory Corso, Bob Dylan, or Sid and Nancy, who lived (and in some cases died) there. You also qualify if you have ever visited the Beat Bookshop in Boulder, Colorado, if you have ever yearned to point the wheel west and keep driving until you reach the Pacific Coast Highway, or if you have never written the words "somebody named Lawrence Ferlinghetti."

If you are by now thoroughly bewildered by this review, you will be equally bewildered by *Chelsea Walls*, and had better stay away from it. Ethan Hawke's movie evokes the innocent spirit of the Beat Generation fifty years after the fact, and celebrates characters who think it is noble to live in extravagant poverty while creating Art and leading untidy sex lives. These people smoke a lot, drink a lot, abuse many substances, and spend either no time at all or way too much time managing their wardrobes. They live in the Chelsea Hotel because it is cheap, and provides a stage for their psychodramas.

Countless stories have been set in the Chelsea. Andy Warhol's *Chelsea Girls* (1967) was filmed there. Plays have between written about it, including one by Nicole Burdette that inspired this screenplay. Photographers and painters have recorded its seasons. It is our American Left Bank, located at one convenient address. That Ethan Hawke would have wanted to direct a movie about it is not surprising; he and his wife, Uma Thurman, who could relax with easy-money stardom, have a way of sneaking off for dodgy avant-garde projects. They starred in Richard Linklater's *Tape* (2001), about three people in a motel room, and now here is the epic version of the same idea, portraying colorful denizens of the Chelsea in full bloom.

We meet Bud (Kris Kristofferson), a boozy author who uses a typewriter instead of a computer, perhaps because you can't short it out by spilling a bottle on it. He has a wife named Greta (Tuesday Weld) and a mistress named Mary (Natasha Richardson), and is perhaps able to find room for both of them in his life because neither one can stand to be around him all that long. He tells them both they are his inspiration. When he's not with the Muse he loves, he loves the Muse he's with.

Val (Mark Webber) is so young he looks embryonic. He buys lock, stock, and barrel into the mythology of bohemia, and lives with Audrey (Rosario Dawson). They are both poets. I do not know how good Audrey's poems are because Dawson reads them in close-up—just her face filling the screen—and I could not focus on the words. I have seen a lot of close-ups in my life but never one so simply, guilelessly erotic. Have more beautiful lips ever been photographed?

Frank (Vincent D'Onofrio) is a painter who thinks he can talk Grace (Uma Thurman) into being his lover. She is not sure. She prefers a vague, absent lover, never seen, and seems to know she has made the wrong choice but takes a perverse pride in sticking with it. Ross (Steve Zahn) is a singer whose brain seems alarmingly fried. Little Jimmy Scott is Skinny Bones, a down-and-out jazzman. Robert Sean Leonard is Terry, who wants to be a folk singer. The corridors are also occupied by the lame and the brain-damaged; every elevator trip includes a harangue by the house philosopher.

Has time passed these people by? Very likely. Greatness resides in ability, not geography, and it is futile to believe that if Thomas Wolfe wrote *Look Homeward, Angel* in Room 831, anyone occupying that room is sure to be equally inspired. What the movie's characters are seeking is not inspiration anyway, but an audience. They stay in the Chelsea because they are surrounded by others who understand the statements they are making with their lives. In a society where the average college freshman has already targeted his entry-level position in the economy, it's a little lonely to embrace unemployment and the aura of genius. To actors with a romantic edge, however, it's very attractive: No wonder Matt Dillon sounds so effortlessly convincing on the audiobook of *On the Road*.

Hawke shot the film for $100,000 on digital video, in the tradition of Warhol's fuzzy 16mm photography. Warhol used a split screen, so that while one of his superstars was doing nothing on the left screen, we could watch another of his superstars doing nothing on the right screen. Hawke, working with Burdette's material, has made a movie that by contrast is action-packed. The characters enjoy playing hooky from life and posing as the inheritors of bohemia. Hawke's cinematographers, Tom Richmond and Richard Rutkowski, and his editor, Adriana Pacheco, weave a mosaic out of the images, avoiding the temptation of a simple realistic look: The film is patterned with color, superimposition, strange exposures, poetic transitions, grainy color palettes.

Movies like this do not grab you by the throat. You have to be receptive. The first time I saw *Chelsea Walls*, in a stuffy room late at night at Cannes 2001, I found it slow and pointless. This time I saw it earlier in the day, fueled by coffee, and I understood that the movie is not about what the characters do, but about what they are. It may be a waste of time to spend your life drinking, fornicating, posing as a genius, and living off your friends, but if you've got the money, honey, take off the time.

Cherish ★ ★ ★

R, 99 m., 2002

Robin Tunney (Zoe), Tim Blake Nelson (Deputy Bill), Brad Hunt (D.J.), Liz Phair (Brynn), Jason Priestley (Andrew), Nora Dunn (Bell), Lindsay Crouse (Therapist), Ricardo Gil (Max). Directed by Finn Taylor and produced by Mark Burton and Johnny Wow. Screenplay by Taylor.

In most locked-room mysteries, the death takes place inside the room and the hero tries to figure out how it was done. *Cherish* is a variation on the theme: The death takes place outside the room, and then the heroine is locked into it, and has to find the killer without leaving. Throw in a love story, a touch of *Run, Lola, Run*, and a lot of Top 40 songs, and you have *Cherish*, a lightweight charmer with a winning performance by Robin Tunney.

She plays Zoe, the kind of clueless office worker that her coworkers subtly try to avoid (I was reminded of the Shelley Duvall character in Altman's *Three Women*). She has a hopeless crush on coworker Andrew (Jason Priestley), and that leads her one night to a nightclub and to a fateful encounter with a masked man who enters her car, steps on the accelerator, mows down a cop, and then flees on foot.

Zoe is arrested for drunken vehicular homicide and several other things, and given little hope by her attorney, who gets the case continued in hopes that the heat will die down. The court orders her confined to a walk-up San Francisco apartment, with a bracelet on her ankle that will sound alarms if she tries to leave. In charge of the bracelet program: a nerdy technician named Daly (Tim Blake Nelson, from *O Brother, Where Art Thou?*), who tries his best to keep everything on a businesslike footing.

By limiting Zoe to her apartment, the movie creates the opportunity to show her fighting boredom, testing the limits of the bracelet, and making friends with Max (Ricardo Gil), the gay dwarf who lives downstairs. It also allows her, through quite a coincidence to be sure, to get a lead on that masked man who is the real cop-killer. But since absolutely no one believes her story about the masked man in the first place (and since her Breathalyzer test was alarming), it's up to her to gather evidence and nail the perp—all, apparently, without straying from her apartment.

How the movie manages to exploit and side-step her limitations is a lot of the fun. It's good, too, to see Zoe growing and becoming more real, shedding the persona of office loser. And although as a general rule I deplore movies that depend on chase scenes for a cheap third act, I concede that in a locked-room plot, a chase scene of any description is a tour de force.

Robin Tunney has a plucky charm that works nicely here; it's quite a shift from her best movie, the overlooked *Niagara, Niagara* (1997), where she played a runaway with Tourette's; and she needed considerable pluck, to be sure, to play the mother of the Antichrist in *End of Days* (1999). Here she brings a quiet goofiness to the role, which is a much better choice than grim heroism or calm competence or some of the other speeds she could have chosen. Tim Blake Nelson is a case study as the kind of man who looks at a woman as if desperately hoping to be handed an instruction manual. And I liked the fire and ingenuity of Ricardo Gil, as the little man downstairs.

Chicken Run ★ ★ ★ ½
G, 85 m., 2000

Mel Gibson (Rocky), Miranda Richardson (Mrs. Tweedy), Tony Haygarth (Mr. Tweedy), Julia Sawalha (Ginger), Jane Horrocks (Babs), Lynn Ferguson (Mac), Imelda Staunton (Bunty), Benjamin Whitrow (Fowler), Timothy Spall (Nick), Phil Daniels (Fetcher). Directed by Peter Lord and Nick Park and produced by Lord, Park, and David Sproxton. Screenplay by Karey Kirkpatrick.

Mrs. Tweedy isn't fooling. Despite her twee British name, she's not a nice little old lady chicken farmer. She means business. Early in *Chicken Run*, she singles out a chicken who hasn't been laying its daily egg, and condemns it to the chopping block. Since this is an animated film, we expect a joke and a close escape. Not a chance. The chicken gets its head chopped off, the other chickens hear the sickening thud of the ax—and later, in case there's the slightest shred of doubt about what happened, we see chicken bones.

So it truly is a matter of life and death for the chickens to escape from the Tweedy Chicken Farm in *Chicken Run*, a magical new animated film that looks and sounds like no other. Like the otherwise completely different *Babe*, this is a movie that uses animals as surrogates for our hopes and fears, and as their chickens run through one failed escape attempt after another, the charm of the movie wins us over.

The film opens as a spoof on the World War II prison pictures like *The Great Escape* and *Stalag 17* (the most important location in the movie is Hut 17). Most of the chickens are happy with captivity and free meals ("Chicken feed! My favorite!"), but one named Ginger has pluck, and tries one escape attempt after another, always being hurled into the coalhole for a week as her punishment. Her cause grows more urgent when Mrs. Tweedy (voice by Miranda Richardson) decides to phase out the egg operation and turn all of her chickens into chicken pies.

Ginger (voice by Julia Sawalha) has tried everything: tunnels, catapults, disguises, deceptions. Mr. Tweedy (Tony Haygarth) is sure the chickens are mapping intelligent escape plans, but can't convince his wife, who is sure they are too stupid. Then a godsend arrives: Rocky the Flying Rooster (Mel Gibson), an American bird who is on the run from a circus. Surely he can teach the chickens to fly and they can escape that way?

Maybe, maybe not. There are many adventures before we discover the answer, and the most thrilling follows Ginger and Rocky through the bowels of the chicken pie machine, in an action sequence that owes a little something to the runaway mine train in *Indiana Jones and the Temple of Doom*. There are tests of daring and skill in the escape plan, but also tests of character, as the birds look into their souls and discover hidden convictions.

In a more conventional movie, the plot would proceed on autopilot. Not in *Chicken Run*, which has a whimsical and sometimes darker view of the possibilities. One of the movie's charms is the way it lets many of the characters be true eccentrics (it's set in England in the 1950s and sometimes offers a taste of those sly old Alec Guinness comedies). Characters like the Royal Air Force veteran rooster with a sneaky secret exist not to nudge the plot along but to add color and texture: This movie about chickens is more human than many formula comedies.

The movie is the first feature-length work by the team of Peter Lord and Nick Park, who've won three Oscars (Park) and two Oscar nominations (Lord) for the work in Claymation, a stop-action technique in which Plasticine is minutely changed from shot to shot to give the illusion of 3-D movement. Park is the creator of the immortal Wallace and Gromit, the man and his dog who star in *The Wrong Trousers* and *A Close Shave*.

Here, they bring a startling new smoothness and fluid quality to their art. Traditional Claymation tweaks and prods the clay between every shot; you can almost see the thumbprints. Their more sophisticated approach here is to start with Plasticine modeled on articulated skeletons, and clothe the models with a "skin" that gives them smoothness and consistency from shot to shot. The final effect is more like *Toy Story* than traditional Claymation.

What I like best about the movie is that it's not simply a plot puzzle to be solved with a clever escape at the end. It is observant about human (or chicken) nature. A recent movie like *Gone in 60 Seconds* is the complete slave of its dim-witted plot and fears to pause for character development, lest the audience find the dialogue slows down the action. *Chicken Run*, on the other hand, is not only funny and wicked, clever and visually inventive, but . . . kind and sweet. Tender and touching. It's a movie made by men, not machines, and at the end you don't feel wrung out or manipulated, but cheerful and (I know this sounds strange) more hopeful.

Chocolat ★ ★ ★
PG-13, 121 m., 2000

Juliette Binoche (Vianne Rocher), Victoire Thivisol (Anouk Rocher), Johnny Depp (Roux), Alfred Molina (Comte de Reynaud), Hugh O'Conor (Pere Henri), Lena Olin (Josephine Muscat), Peter Stormare (Serge Muscat), Judi Dench (Amande Voizin), John Wood (Guillaume Blerot), Leslie Caron (Madame Audel), Carrie-Anne Moss (Caroline Claimont). Directed by Lasse Hallstrom and produced by David Brown, Kit Golden, and Leslie Holleran. Screenplay by Robert Nelson Jacobs, based on the novel by Joanne Harris.

Chocolat is about a war between the forces of paganism and Christianity, and because the pagan heroine has chocolate on her side, she wins. Her victory is delayed only because, during Lent, a lot of the locals aren't eating chocolate. The movie takes place "once upon a time" in a small French village where utter tranquillity, by which is meant stagnancy, has reigned since time immemorial, until "a sly wind blew in from the north," bringing with it Vianne (Juliette Binoche), who opens the chocolate shop, after which nothing is ever again the same.

The movie is charming and whimsical, and Binoche reigns as a serene and wise goddess. Like Catherine Deneuve's, her beauty is not only that of youth but will carry her through life, and here she looks so ripe and wholesome that her very presence is an argument against the local prudes. Whether her character has deeper agendas, whether she is indeed a witch, as some believe, or a pagan priestess as she seems to hint, is left unresolved by the movie— but anyone who schedules a Fertility Celebration up against Easter Sunday is clearly picking a fight.

The town is ruled by Count de Reynaud (Alfred Molina), whose wealth and books do not console him for the absence of his countess, who is allegedly visiting Venice but may just have packed up and moved out. The count styles himself as the local arbiter of morals, even writing the sermons that Father Henri (Hugh O'Conor) delivers from the pulpit while the complacent aristocrat's lips move contentedly in unison.

There are troubles in the town, quickly confided to Vianne, who consoles Josephine (Lena Olin) after she is beaten by her husband, Serge (Peter Stormare). It is a convention in such stories that husbands tend toward wife-beating, and a quiet argument is made for the superior state of Vianne, who is the unmarried mother of Anouk (Victoire Thivisol) and thus harbors no potential brute beneath her roof. She does, however, have an interest in the opposite sex, represented by Roux (Johnny Depp), who anchors his houseboat in the nearby river and shocks the bourgeoisie with its communal lifestyle.

Vianne's chocolates contain magic ingredients, like the foods in *Like Water for Chocolate*, and soon her shop is a local healing center. One confection seems to work like Viagra, while others inspire love, not lust, and inspire an old man (John Wood) to screw up his courage and confess to a local widow (Leslie Caron) that he has adored her forever. Even Amande (Judi Dench), Vianne's opinionated old landlady, melts under the influence and ends her long hostility to her daughter (Carrie-Anne Moss).

Chocolat was directed by Lasse Hallstrom (*Cider House Rules, My Life as a Dog, What's Eating Gilbert Grape*). It's the sort of movie you can enjoy as a superior fable, in which the values come from children's fairy tales but adult themes have been introduced. It goes without saying in such stories that organized religion is the province of prudes and hypocrites, but actually *Chocolat* is fairly easy on the local establishment—they're not evil people, although they resent outsiders like the Depp character; they're more like tranquil sleepwalkers who wake up and smell the coffee, or in this case the chocolate. Even the count is converted, and is shocked when he finds that his reckless language has inspired a local dimwit to set a dangerous fire.

I enjoyed the movie on its own sweet level, while musing idly on the box-office prospects of a film in which the glowing, life-affirming local Christians would prevail over glowering, prejudiced, puritan, and bitter druidworshipers. That'll be, as John Wayne once said, the day.

Chopper ★ ★ ★
NO MPAA RATING, 90 m., 2001

Eric Bana (Chopper), Simon Lyndon (Jimmy Loughnan), Kenny Graham (Keith Read), Dan Wyllie (Bluey), David Field (Keithy George), Vince Colosimo (Neville Bartos), Kate Beahan (Tanya). Directed by Andrew Dominik and produced by Michele Bennett. Screenplay by Dominik, based on books by Mark Brandon Read.

It is not agreed how "Chopper" Read got his nickname. Some say it was because he chopped off the toes of his enemies. Others believe it was because he had his own ears chopped off, or because he had his teeth capped in metal. He is Australia's most infamous prisoner, a best-selling author, a vicious killer, a seething mass of contradictions. *Chopper* tells his story with a kind of fascinated horror.

Is everyone in Australia a few degrees off from true north? You can search in vain through the national cinema for characters who are ordinary or even boring; everyone is more colorful than life. If England is a nation of eccentrics, Australia leaves it at the starting line. Chopper Read is the latest in a distinguished line that includes Ned Kelly, Mad Max, and Russell Crowe's Hando in *Romper Stomper*. The fact that Chopper is real only underlines the point.

Since the real Chopper is again behind bars, the film depends entirely on its casting, and in a comedian named Eric Bana the filmmakers have found, I think, a future star. He creates a character so fearsome and yet so clueless and wounded that we can't tell if the movie comes to praise or bury him. There is a scene in the movie where Chopper is stabbed by his best friend, and keeps right on talking as if nothing has happened; his nonchalance is terrifying. And another where he shoots a drug dealer and then thoughtfully drives him to the emergency room. Bana's performance makes the character believable—in fact, unforgettable. We feel we're looking at a hard man, not at an actor playing one.

As the film opens, Chopper is in prison watching himself on television. He seems curiously conflicted about what he sees—as if the Chopper on TV has been somehow constructed by others and then installed inside his skin. The writer-director Andrew Dominik and producer Michele Bennett, who met Chopper Read while preparing the film, sensed the same thing. "After we'd passed some time with him," says Bennett, "we could see that he was waiting to gauge our reaction before he proceeded. We did offer to show him the script, but he declined, remarking, 'Anything I say would be fiddling. I want to know what you think of me,' so we didn't pursue it. He pretends that he doesn't care how he's perceived by others, but I suspect he really does."

That's how he comes across as a film—as a man who seems to stand outside himself and watch what Chopper does. He's as fascinated by himself as we are, and isolated from his actions. Even pain doesn't seem to penetrate. He looks down at blood pouring from his body as if someone else has been wounded, and then up at his attacker as if expressing regret that it should have come to this.

The movie wisely declines to offer a psychological explanation for Chopper's violent amorality. But it provides a clue in the way he stands outside criminal gangs and has no associates; he is not a "criminal," if that word implies a profession, but a violent psychopath who is seized by sudden rages. There is a startling moment in the film, during a brief stretch on the streets between prison sentences, when he revisits old haunts and old friends and seems genial and conciliatory—until his mad-dog side leaps out in uncontrolled fury. The earlier niceness was not an act to throw people off their guard, we sense; he really was feeling friendly, and did not necessarily anticipate the sudden rush of rage.

Eric Bana's performance suggests he will soon be leaving the comedy clubs of Australia and turning up as a Bond villain or a madman in a special-effects picture. He has a quality no acting school can teach and few actors can match: You cannot look away from him. The performance is so . . . strange. The parts you remember best are the times when he seems disappointed in others, or in himself, as if filled with sadness that the world must contain so much pain caused to or by him. Of course in creating this Chopper, he may simply be going along with the original Chopper's act, and the real Chopper Read with his TV interviews and best-sellers may be a performance too. Whatever the reality, Chopper is a real piece of work, and so is Bana.

Note: Chopper Read speaks in an unalloyed Australian accent that may be difficult for some North American audiences; he's no toned-down mid-Pacific Crocodile Dundee. I understood most of what he was saying. And when you don't catch the words, you get the drift.

Chuck & Buck ★ ★ ★
R, 95 m., 2000

Mike White (Buck), Chris Weitz (Chuck), Lupe Ontiveros (Beverly), Beth Colt (Carlyn), Paul Weitz (Sam), Maya Rudolph (Jamila), Mary Wigmore (Diane), Paul Sand (Barry), Gino Buccola (Tommy), Directed by Miguel Arteta and produced by Matthew Greenfield. Screenplay by Mike White.

Buck's mother coughs, and dies. That releases

him from his childhood, which has lasted well into his twenties. He invites his boyhood friend Chuck to come to the funeral. Chuck, a music executive from L.A., arrives with his fiancée, Carlyn. Buck grins at Chuck confidingly. "You . . . wanna go see my room?" he asks. This line, early in *Chuck & Buck*, sets up the tone of the movie. Buck is stuck at the age of twelve or thirteen; Chuck has grown up, and now finds himself stalked by a weirdo who still wants to be his junior high school buddy.

This surface story would be enough for most movies, but *Chuck & Buck* has subterranean depths, and is a study in how we handle embarrassing situations—or don't handle them. Buck (Mike White, the film's author) is a gawky case of arrested development, who stands too close and doesn't know when to stop talking and never realizes when he's not welcome. He's had only one valued relationship in his life, with Chuck (Chris Weitz), and assumes it has been the same with Chuck. "I noticed there aren't any pictures of me around," he says on his first visit to Chuck's house.

How did he get invited to visit Chuck and Carlyn (Beth Colt)? At his mother's funeral, she unwisely asked him to visit them if he was ever in L.A., and a few days later, he was in L.A. Buck visits Chuck at his office, tails him to lunch, turns up everywhere, sucking on his little Tootsie Pops down to the fudge surprise. Chuck tells him bluntly to get lost. But it's not that simple. Chuck bears some of the responsibility for Buck's feelings, and he knows it.

Freed of his long captivity in his mother's house, Buck finds more than Chuck to interest him in Los Angeles. He discovers a little fringe theater, writes an autobiographical play named *Frank & Hank*, and convinces Beverly, the stage manager (Lupe Ontiveros), to direct it. In the theater scenes, White and his director, Miguel Arteta, avoid obvious traps and take the movie to another level. It would be easy to turn Buck into a comic figure and surround him with caricatures, but the movie allows all of the people at the theater to be as real as they might actually be, and to deal with Buck as the case study he so manifestly is.

Ontiveros, as Beverly, takes one look at Buck and clocks him as one of the countless odd jobs who circle show business like flies. She agrees to direct his play for $25 an hour, firm, cash, and guarantees it one performance. One of the actresses finishes a rehearsal and flatly declares, "I'm not inviting my agent." An actor named Sam (Paul Weitz, Chris's brother), clueless and not very swift, takes his role with utter seriousness. He asks Buck up to his apartment, complains about a neighbor "who won't let me hold parties in the hall," smoothly rebuffs Buck's advance without batting an eye, and thinks Buck would make a great neighbor since he wouldn't object to the parties.

All of these supporting characters give *Chuck & Buck* the texture that makes it more than just a psychological stalker movie. By treating Buck as real people might plausibly treat him, they prevent us from seeing him as a comic figure. He really is this sad, strange person, and that realization sets up the final events in the movie, which wouldn't work otherwise.

What is the movie about? It seems to be about buried sexuality or arrested development, but it's also a fascinating study of behavior that violates the rules. Most of us operate within a set of conventions and instincts that lead us through conversations and relationships. We know precisely how close we are to one another, and our behavior reflects that. Some people, through ignorance or hostility, don't observe the rules. How should we handle them? Chuck may have grown up normally while Buck got stuck behind, but in their own personal war, Buck has all the best moves.

Cinema Paradiso: The New Version
★ ★ ★ ½
R, 170 m., 2002

Salvatore Cascio (Salvatore [Young]), Marco Leonardi (Salvatore [Teenager]), Agnese Nano (Elena [Teenager]), Jacques Perrin (Salvatore [Adult]), Brigitte Fossey (Elena [Adult]), Philippe Noiret (Alfredo), Leopoldo Trieste (Father Adelfio). Directed by Guiseppe Tournatore and produced by Mino Barbera, Franco Cristaldi, and Giovanna Romagnoli. Screenplay by Tournatore.

When *Cinema Paradiso* won the Academy Award as Best Foreign Film in 1990, it was an open secret that the movie the voters loved was not quite the same as the one director Guiseppe Tournatore made. Reports had it that Harvey Weinstein, the boss at Miramax, had trimmed not just a shot here or there, but a full fifty-one minutes from the film. Audiences loved the result, however, and the movie is consistently voted among the 100 best movies of all time at the Internet Movie Database.

Now comes a theatrical release of *Cinema Paradiso: The New Version,* with an ad campaign that promises, "Discover what really happened to the love of a lifetime." Considering that it was Miramax that made it impossible for us to discover this in the 1990 version, the ad is sublime chutzpah. And the movie is now so much longer and covers so much more detail that it almost plays as its own sequel.

Most of the first two hours will be familiar to lovers of the film. Little Salvatore (Salvatore Cascio), known to one and all as Toto, is fascinated by the movies and befriended by the projectionist Alfredo (Philippe Noiret). After a fire blinds Alfredo, Toto becomes the projectionist, and the Cinema Paradiso continues as the center of village life, despite the depredations of Father Adelfio (Leopoldo Trieste), who censors all of the films, ringing a bell at every kissing scene.

The new material of the longer version includes much more about the teenage romance between Salvatore (Marco Leonardi) and Elena (Agnese Nano)—a forbidden love, since her bourgeoisie parents have a better match in mind. And then there is a long passage involving the return of the middle-aged Salvatore (Jacques Perrin) to the village for the first time since he left to go to Rome and make his name as a movie director. He contacts the adult Elena (Brigitte Fossey), and finds out for the first time what really happened to a crucial rendezvous, and how easily his life might have turned out differently. (His discoveries promote the film to an MPAA rating of R, from its original PG.)

Seeing the longer version is a curious experience. It is an item of faith that the director of a film is always right, and that studios who cut films are butchers. Yet I must confess that the shorter version of *Cinema Paradiso* is a better film than the longer. Harvey was right. The 170-minute cut overstays its welcome, and continues after its natural climax.

Still, I'm happy to have seen it—not as an alternate version, but as the ultimate exercise in viewing deleted scenes. Anyone who loves the film will indeed be curious about "what really happened to the love of a lifetime," and it is good to know. I hope, however, that this new version doesn't replace the old one on the video shelves; the ideal solution would be a DVD with the 1990 version on one side and the 2002 version on the other.

The Circle ★ ★ ★ ½
NO MPAA RATING, 91 m., 2001

Mariam Palvin Almani (Arezou), Nargess Mamizadeh (Nargess), Fereshteh Sadr Orfani (Pari), Monir Arab (Ticket Seller), Elham Saboktakin (Nurse), Fatemeh Naghavi (Mother), Mojhan Faramarzi (Prostitute). Directed and produced by Jafar Panahi. Screenplay by Kambozia Partovi.

Few things reveal a nation better than what it censors. In America, the MPAA has essentially eliminated adult sexuality from our movies, but smiles on violence and films tailored for the teenage toilet-humor market. Now consider *The Circle,* a film banned in Iran. There is not a single shot here that would seem offensive to a mainstream American audience— not even to the smut-hunting preacher Donald Wildmon. Why is it considered dangerous in Iran? Because it argues that under current Iranian law, unattached women are made to feel like hunted animals.

There is no nudity here. No violence. No drugs or alcohol, for sure. No profanity. There is a running joke that the heroines can't even have a cigarette (women cannot smoke in public). Yet the film is profoundly dangerous to the status quo in Iran because it asks us to identify with the plight of women who have done nothing wrong except to be female. *The Circle* is all the more depressing when we consider that Iran is relatively liberal compared to, say, Afghanistan under the Taliban.

Jafar Panahi's film begins and ends with the same image, of a woman talking to someone in authority through a sliding panel in a closed door. In the opening shot, a woman learns that her daughter has given birth to a girl when the ultrasound promised a boy; she fears angry reprisals from the in-laws. In the closing shot,

a woman is in prison, talking to a guard. In closing the circle, the second shot suggests that women in strict Muslim societies are always in prison in one way or another.

The film follows a series of women through the streets of a city. We follow first one and then another. We begin with two who have just been released from prison—for what crime, we are not told. They want to take a bus to a city where one of them hopes to find a safe harbor. But they have no money and lack the correct identification. They run through the streets and down back alleys at the sight of policemen, they crouch behind parked cars, they ask a ticket-seller to give them a break and sell them a ticket though they have no ID. At one point it's fairly clear that one of the women prostitutes herself (offscreen) to raise money to help the other. Men all over the world are open-minded about exempting themselves from the laws prohibiting other men from frequenting prostitutes.

If you have no ID, you cannot leave town. If you have no ID, you cannot live in a town. Your crime, obviously, is to be a woman living outside the system of male control of women; with a husband or a brother to vouch for you, you can go anywhere, sort of like baggage. The argument is that this system shows respect for women, just as Bantustans in South Africa gave Africans their own land, and American blacks in Jim Crow days did not have to stand in line to use white rest rooms. There is a universal double-speak in which subjugation is described as freedom.

We meet another woman, who has left her little daughter to be found by strangers. She hides behind a car, her eyes filled with tears; as a single mother she cannot care for the girl, and so dresses her up to look nice, and abandons her. We meet another woman, a prostitute, who is found in the car of a man and cannot prove she is related to him. She is arrested; the man seems to go free. Has there ever been a society where the man in this situation is arrested and the woman goes free? The prostitute at least gets to smoke on the prison bus (not when she wants to, but after the men light up, so the smoke will not be noticed).

The movie is not structured tautly like an American street thriller. There are handheld shots that meander for a minute or two, just following women as they walk here or there. The women seem aimless. They are. In this society, under their circumstances, there is nowhere they can go and nothing they can do, and almost all of the time they have to stay out of doors. They track down rumors: A news vendor, for example, is said to be "friendly" and might help them. From time to time, a passing man will say something oblique, like "Can I help you?" but that is either casual harassment or a test of availability.

The Iranian censors may ban films like *The Circle*, but it got made, and so did the recent *The Day I Became a Woman*, about the three ages of women in such a society. One suspects that videotapes give these films wide private circulation; one even suspects the censors know that. I know a director from a communist country where the censor had been his film school classmate. He submitted a script. The censor read it and told his old friend, "You know what you're really saying, and I know what you're really saying. Now rewrite it so only the audience knows what you're really saying."

The Claim ★ ★ ★ ½
R, 120 m., 2001

Peter Mullan (Daniel Dillon), Sarah Polley (Hope Dillon), Wes Bentley (Donald Dalglish), Milla Jovovich (Lucia), Nastassja Kinski (Elena Dillon), Julian Richings (Bellanger), David Lereaney (Saloon Actor), Sean McGinley (Sweetley). Directed by Michael Winterbottom and produced by Andrew Eaton. Screenplay by Frank Cottrell Boyce, based on the novel *The Mayor of Casterbridge* by Thomas Hardy.

In the town of Kingdom Come, winter is more of a punishment than a season. High in a pass of the Sierra Nevada, its buildings of raw lumber stand like scars on the snow. The promise of gold has drawn men here, but in the winter there is little to do but wait, drink, and visit the brothel. The town is owned and run by Mr. Dillon, a trim Scotsman in his forties who is judge, jury, and (if necessary) executioner.

I dwell on the town because the physical setting of Michael Winterbottom's *The Claim* is central to its effect. Summer is a season for work, but winter is a time for memory and regret. Mr. Dillon (Peter Mullan) did something

years ago that was wrong in a way a man cannot forgive himself for. He lives in an ornate Victorian house, submits to the caresses of his mistress, settles the affairs of his subjects, and is haunted by his memories.

Two women arrive in Kingdom Come. One is a fading beauty named Elena (Nastassja Kinski), dying of tuberculosis. The other is her daughter, about twenty, named Hope (Sarah Polley). They have not journeyed to Kingdom Come to forgive Mr. Dillon his trespasses. It becomes clear who they are, but the movie is not about that secret. It is about what happened twenty years ago, and what, as a result, will happen now.

To the town that winter also comes Donald Dalglish (Wes Bentley), a surveyor for the railroad. Where the tracks run, wealth follows. What they bypass will die. Dalglish is young, ambitious, and good at business. He attracts the attention of Lucia (Milla Jovovich), who is not only Mr. Dillon's comfort but the owner of the brothel. She kisses him boldly on the lips in full view of a saloon-full of witnesses, sending a message to Mr. Dillon: If he doesn't want to keep her, others will. Dalglish is not indifferent, but he is more intrigued by the strange young blonde woman, Hope, who stands out in this grimness like the first bud of spring.

The past comes crashing down around them all—and then the future arrives to finish them off. Mr. Dillon's fate, which he fashions for himself, is all the more complex because he has done great evil but is in some ways a good man. Nor is Dalglish morally uncomplicated. In the hard world they inhabit, no one can afford to act only on a theoretical basis.

The Claim is parsimonious with its plot, which is revealed on a need-to-know basis. At first, we're not even sure who is who; dialogue is half-heard, references are unclear, the townspeople know things we discover only gradually. The method is like Robert Altman's in *McCabe and Mrs. Miller*, and Antonia Bird's in the underrated 1999 Western *Ravenous* (a movie that takes place in about the same place and time as this one). Like strangers in town, we put the pieces together for ourselves.

The movie is so rooted in the mountains of the American West that it's a little startling to learn *The Claim* is based on Thomas Hardy's

1886 British novel *The Mayor of Casterbridge*. Winterbottom filmed *Jude*, a version of Hardy's *Jude the Obscure*, in 1996. By transmuting Hardy into a Western here, he has not made a commercial decision (Westerns are not as successful these days as British period pictures), but an artistic one, perhaps involving his vision of Kingdom Come, a town which is like a stage waiting for this play.

Winterbottom is a director of great gifts and glooms. His *Butterfly Kiss* (also 1996) starred Amanda Plummer in a great performance as a kind of homeless flagellant saint. Here he tells the story of another kind of self-punishing character, and Peter Mullan's performance is private and painful, as a man whose first mistake is to give away all he has, and whose second mistake is to try to redeem himself by giving it all away again. Mullan *(My Name Is Joe)* is like a harder, leaner, younger (but not young) Paul Newman, coiled up inside, handsome but not depending on it, willing to go to any lengths to do what he must. Intriguing, how he makes a villain sympathetic, in a movie where the relatively blameless Dalglish seems corrupt.

A movie like this rides on its cinematography, and Alwin H. Kuchler evokes the cold darkness so convincingly that Kingdom Come seems built on an abyss. Like the town of Presbyterian Church in *McCabe and Mrs. Miller*, it is a folly built by greed where common sense would have steered clear. There are two great visual scenes, the arrival of the railroad and the moving of a house, one exercising public will, the other private will. And an ending uncannily like *McCabe and Mrs. Miller*'s, although for an entirely different reason.

Winterbottom is a director comfortable with ambiguity. In movies like *Wonderland* (1999), *Welcome to Saravejo* (1997), and others, he's reluctant to corner his characters into heroism or villainy. In the original Hardy novel, the Dillon character, named Henchard, is a drunk who pays so well for his sins that he seems more like Job than a sinner being punished. Dillon, who was also a drunk, tells the woman he has wronged, "I don't drink anymore. I want you to know that." For his time and place, he has grown into a hard but not bad man, and when he has a citizen horsewhipped, the man explains that the town would have lynched him—the whipping saved his life. The strength of *The Claim* is that Dillon and Dalglish are on intersecting paths; Dillon is getting better, while Dalglish started out good and is headed down.

Claire Dolan ★ ★ ★ ½
NO MPAA RATING, 95 m., 2000

Katrin Cartlidge (Claire), Colm Meaney (Roland), Vincent D'Onofrio (Elton). Directed by Lodge Kerrigan and produced by Ann Ruark. Screenplay by Kerrigan.

"I'm here for you," Claire Dolan tells one of her clients. "I can't get you out of my head," she whispers to another over the telephone. "You're not like other men," she tells a third. He is exactly like other men. All men are like other men when they visit a prostitute. "What do you want?" she says. "You can tell me."

Lodge Kerrigan's *Claire Dolan* is a film about a woman whose knowledge about men encompasses everything except how to trust them and find happiness with them. She is a Manhattan prostitute, mid-priced, who presents herself as a quiet, almost shy woman dressed in understated good taste. She has none of the flamboyance of the typical movie hooker, is not voluptuous, looks her clients straight in the eye while lying to them about how much she's missed them. Some guys like that. Makes them think they're doing the poor deprived girl a favor.

Claire is played by Katrin Cartlidge (the sister-in-law in *Breaking the Waves*) as a woman whose profession has given her an instinctive knowledge about how to deal with some men. There is a scene in the movie where she is seated in a bar, bothering no one, not looking for attention. Two men walk up. "I'm not looking for company," she says. "That's not your decision," says the first man, who is aggressive and menacing. She seems in danger. She looks up at the man who is looming over her, his aggression pulsing in his face. Then she looks at his sidekick, who hangs back. "I prefer him," she says. "He's better-looking than you. Would you let him go first?"

The scene is no longer than my description of it. It is just about perfect. She has changed the subject. She understands the tension that must exist between two men who have agreed to harass a woman. Beneath their relationship is a fear of women, which links to sexual insecurity; she has castrated the first by preferring the second, and called the bluff of the second by depriving him of his leader. The men are stopped cold, and skulk away.

Much of the movie consists of Claire Dolan's business dealings. Her clients are white-collar guys in offices and hotel rooms. They believe her praise. Maybe it's what they're really paying her for. She isn't very enthusiastic during sex—sometimes she seems repelled or indifferent—but the men don't notice or care. When she doesn't follow the script, though, they have a way of turning vicious.

Her pimp, who has known her since she was a child in Dublin, is Roland (Colm Meaney, his neat little lips swimming in a face so broad he looks like Humpty-Dumpty). He addresses her with formal politeness. We see he is strong and vicious, but with Claire he has an enigmatic relationship based on buried mutual history, which perhaps involves her dying mother, and perhaps involves money he has loaned her for the mother's care (the movie is wisely vague). They work well together, Roland tells a taxi driver who thinks he loves her, because she was born to be a prostitute, likes it, and will always be one.

Whether that statement is true is the movie's central question. The taxi driver is named Elton (Vincent D'Onofrio). They spend some monosyllabic time together, make love successfully and then unsuccessfully, and agree to have a child. "We can make this work," she says. "All right," he says. They cannot make it work, because he cannot understand her profession or her pimp; he shadows her, and even goes to the extreme of hiring a new girl in the pimp's stable in order to vicariously understand how it might be between Claire and a client.

If a movie like this had a neat ending, the ending would be a lie. We do not want answers, but questions and observations. The film is bleak about sex. It avoids the common Hollywood assumption that hookers love sex (many producers apparently believe the same lies Claire tells her clients). It is the second film by writer-director Lodge Kerrigan, whose *Clean, Shaven* was a portrait of a schizophrenic. In both films he accepts the challenge of central characters who do not let us know what they're thinking. We have to look and listen and decide for ourselves. I think Claire Dolan will make a good mother. I think she can make it work. Not with Elton, but by herself, which is the only way she can live and not have to lie.

Clockstoppers ★ ★ ½
PG, 90 m., 2002

Jesse Bradford (Zak Gibbs), French Stewart (Dr. Earl Dopler), Paula Garces (Francesca De La Cruz), Michael Biehn (Henry Gates), Robin Thomas (Dr. George Gibbs), Gariyaki Mutambirwa (Danny Meeker). Directed by Jonathan Frakes and produced by Gale Anne Hurd and Julia Pistor. Screenplay by Rob Hedden, J. David Stem, and David N. Weiss.

In an early scene of *Clockstoppers*, a student in a college physics class is unable to complete the phrase, "Einstein's Theory of . . ." And just as well, too, since any time-manipulation movie has to exist in blissful ignorance of Einstein's theory. Not that it can't be done, at least in the movies. *Clockstoppers* has a new twist: The traveler doesn't travel through time but stays right where he is and lives faster. This is closer to Einstein's Theory of Amphetamines.

Dr. George Gibbs (Robin Thomas) has invented a way for a subject to live much faster than those around him, so that they seem to stand in place while he whizzes around. He is like the mayfly, which lives a lifetime in a day—and that is precisely the trouble. The system works well, but experimenters age so quickly that they return looking worn and wrinkled, like Keir Dullea in *2001*, who checks into that alien bedroom, doesn't check out. Gibbs needs to iron out a few kinks.

Before he can perfect his discovery, intrigue strikes. His teenage son, Zak (Jesse Bradford), is informed by the friendly Dr. Earl Dopler (French Stewart) that Gibbs has been kidnapped into hyperspace by the evil and scheming millionaire Henry Gates (Michael Biehn). Dopler is named after the Effect. I have no idea how they came up with the name of Gates.

Zak has just met the beautiful Francesca De La Cruz (Paula Garces), a pretty student from Venezuela, at his high school, and they find themselves teamed on a mission to venture into hyperspace, rescue his father, outsmart Gates, and return without becoming senior citizens. (That's if hyperspace is the same place as speeded-up-time-space, and frankly the movie lost me there.) To assist in their mission they use a gun that fires marbles filled with liquid nitrogen, which burst on impact and instantly freeze their targets. That this gun is not fatal is a fact the movie wisely makes no attempt to explain.

Clockstoppers has high energy, bright colors, neat sets, and intriguing effects as the speeded-up characters zip around. There is a time when Zak outsmarts characters who are merely speeded-up by speeding up while *in* speed-space, or whatever it's called, so that he whizzes around the whizzers while emitting a kind of pulsing glow.

The movie has been produced by Nickelodeon, and will no doubt satisfy its intended audience enormously. It does not cross over into the post-Nickelodeon universe. Unlike *Spy Kids* or *Big Fat Liar*, it offers few consolations for parents and older brothers and sisters. It is what it is, efficiently and skillfully, and I salute it for hitting a double or maybe a triple. I also like the dialogue of Dr. ("Don't blow your RAM") Dopler. No one can be altogether uninteresting who makes a verb out of "ginzu."

Note: At one point the characters pass a high-security checkpoint and have to submit to a retinal scan. In a subtle bow to the Americans With Disabilities Act, the retinal scan device is at waist level.

The Closer You Get ★ ★
PG-13, 92 m., 2000

Niamh Cusack (Kate), Sean McGinley (Ian), Ian Hart (Kieran), Ewan Stewart (Pat), Sean McDonagh (Sean), Cathleen Bradley (Siobhan), Pat Shortt (Ollie), Deborah Barnett (Ella). Directed by Aileen Ritchie and produced by Uberto Pasolini. Screenplay by William Ivory, based on a story by Herbie Wave.

See enough of its movies and a nation's cinema can tell you something about the nation involved. It may be right, it may be wrong, but there it is. I now assume, for example, that everyone in Australia is a little strange, and half of them are bizarre eccentrics. The French, they are worried all the time. Americans live trapped inside the clichés of genre fiction, and so do the Canadians, only they are nicer, unless they are in David Cronenberg films.

And the Irish are sweet, cheerful folk who live in each other's pockets, settle things by communitywide debate, gang up men against women, and visit home briefly between pubs. They are also blessed with great verbal alacrity, and there would be a great many more of them if the women were not so opinionated and the men so baffled by women with opinions.

This picture has nothing to do with the Irish I have met during half a dozen visits to the Emerald Isle, who are likely to be successful professionals benefiting from a booming economy and a standard of living higher than England's. But the Irish have no one but themselves to blame for their screen image, except in the case of *The Closer You Get*, which was produced by an Italian.

Umberto Pasolini earlier made *The Full Monty*, which made millions of dollars with its heartfelt and bawdy comedy about six unemployed Englishmen who became male strippers. Now he has moved to the west of Ireland, to county Donegal, upon whose sainted strands late one night I once kissed a publican's red-haired daughter.

She was, I must admit, a good deal like Siobhan (Cathleen Bradley), the heroine of *The Closer You Get*, who will stand for no nonsense from Kieran (Ian Hart), the local butcher—who is both her employer and her obvious mate, if he were not so daft he doesn't realize it. "Siobhan is a hard case," Kieran laments, by which he means that she is disinclined to conduct both sides of their courtship while he slips out for a few pints with his mates.

This is a town starved for entertainment. The priest livens things up by mounting loudspeakers on the bell tower and playing tapes of the bells from St. Peter's in Rome. (Then he starts a film society and books *The Ten Commandments*, but is sent 10 instead.) The local lads, despairing of the standoffish women in town, chip in to buy an ad in the *Miami Herald* to invite American women to their annual dance. The local women retaliate by inviting a band of alarmingly swarthy and hirsute Spaniards, who make the pale Donegal locals look like they've spent too much time in the cellar counting the root vegetables.

Everyone in *The Closer You Get* is nice, and Ian Hart's butcher is especially likable, with his brown hair dyed platinum in a failed attempt to look hip. But the movie is too thin and low-key to generate much comic energy. Compared to *Waking Ned Devine,* it's dilute and transparent. And I doubt many contemporary Irish young people are this naive and shy. It's a sweet film, mildly pleasant to watch, but it's not worth the trip or even a detour.

The Closet ★ ★ ½
R, 85 m., 2001

Daniel Auteuil (Francois Pignon), Gerard Depardieu (Felix Santini), Thierry Lhermitte (Guillaume), Michele Laroque (Mlle. Bertrand), Michel Aumont (Belone), Jean Rochefort (Kopel), Alexandra Vandernoot (Christine). Directed by Francis Veber and produced by Alain Poire. Screenplay by Veber.

Francois Pignon is the most boring employee at the condom factory, a meek accountant who seems so unnecessary that he's told he'll be fired after twenty years of loyal service. That figures. His wife divorced him two years earlier, his son despises him as a nobody, and at work they snicker about what a nerd he is.

Pignon returns to his depressing bachelor apartment, finds a kitten on the balcony, gives it a saucer of milk, and hears a knock at the door. It is his new neighbor, an older man who is looking for the kitten—and sees immediately that Francois is miserable. "Give me a drink," he says. "I'm lonelier than you are."

Pignon is played by Daniel Auteuil, the sad-eyed, crooked-nose star of some of the best French films of recent years *(The Widow of St. Pierre, The Girl on the Bridge).* His neighbor is Belone (Michel Aumont), large, expansive, sympathetic. Soon Pignon is pouring out his story. Belone listens and comes up with a way for Francois to keep his job: He must pretend to be gay. That way, the condom company will be terrified of bad publicity if it fires him.

The Closet is a new French comedy that turns the tables on *La Cage aux Folles.* That was about a gay man trying to appear straight; this is about a straight, conservative, timid man who is transformed in the eyes of the world when he seems to be gay. Belone, who is gay himself, uses his computer to fabricate photographs that seem to show Pignon being very friendly with a leather-clad gay man, and mails it to coworkers at the factory. The news spreads instantly, and Pignon's office mates now interpret his inhibited behavior as just a cover-up.

The movie is a box-office hit in France, not least because it has four top actors in unusual roles. Gérard Depardieu, the most macho of French actors, plays Santini, a homophobe who stops gay-bashing and tries to befriend Pignon. Jean Rochefort, is the magisterial boss of the company. And Thierry Lhermitte is the troublemaker who inflames Depardieu's fears by telling him he'll be fired for his political incorrectness. To understand this casting in Hollywood terms, think of Auteuil, Depardieu, Rochefort, and Lhermitte as Tom Hanks, Brendan Fraser, Michael Douglas, and Kevin Pollack. (Given the success of the Hollywood remake of *La Cage aux Folles,* we may actually be seeing casting like this before long.)

At least two of Pignon's coworkers are intrigued by the revelations about his sexuality. Ms. Bertrand (Michele Laroque), his superior, found him boring when he was straight but sexy now that he's gay, and wants to seduce him. And the rugby-playing Santini, who picked on Pignon when he thought he was a sissy, tries to save his own job by taking the accountant out to lunch and being nice to him—suspiciously nice, some might think.

The movie passes the time pleasantly and has a few good laughs (the loudest is when Pignon rides in a gay pride parade wearing a crown that looks like a jolly giant condom). But the screenplay relies too much on the first level of its premise and doesn't push into unexpected places. Once we get the setup, we can more or less anticipate the sitcom payoff, and there aren't the kinds of surprises, reversals, and explosions of slapstick that made *La Cage aux Folles* so funny. In the rating system of the Michelin guide, it's worth a look, but not a detour or a journey.

Collateral Damage ★ ★ ★
R, 115 m., 2002

Arnold Schwarzenegger (Gordon Brewer), Elias Koteas (CIA Agent Peter Brandt), Francesca Neri (Selena Perrini), Cliff Curtis (Claudio "The Wolf" Perrini), John Leguizamo (Felix Ramirez), John Turturro (Sean Armstrong). Directed by Andrew Davis and produced by David Foster, Peter MacGregor-Scott, and Steven Reuther. Screenplay by David Griffiths and Peter Griffiths.

Collateral Damage is a relic from an earlier (if not kinder and gentler) time, a movie about terrorism made before terrorists became the subject of our national discourse. "You Americans are so naive," says the movie's terrorist villain. "You see a peasant with a gun, you change the channel. But you never ask why a peasant needs a gun." Well, we still don't wonder why the peasant needs the gun (we think we should have the gun), but we're not so naive anymore.

The movie stars Arnold Schwarzenegger as Brewer, a Los Angeles fireman who sees his wife and son killed by a terrorist bomb. Vowing revenge, he flies to Colombia, escapes several murder attempts, survives an improbable trip down a waterfall, penetrates guerrilla territory, kills a lot of people, and blows up a lot of stuff. He is your typical Los Angeles fireman if the fire department sent all of its men through Delta Force training.

To review this movie in the light of 9/11 is not really fair. It was made months earlier, and indeed its release date was postponed in the aftermath of the attack. That has escaped the attention of the Rev. Brian Jordan, a priest who, according to the Associated Press, ministers to workers at Ground Zero. "Making the main character a firefighter who becomes a vigilante is an insult to the firefighters who became heroes after the terrorist attacks," he says. He adds that the film discriminates against Colombians; his fellow protesters said the movie will "cement stereotypes that Colombians are drug traffickers and guerrillas, rather than hardworking, educated people."

Jordan added that he has not seen the film. His criticism is therefore theoretical. He believes making a firefighter a vigilante in a movie made before the attacks is an insult now that the attacks have taken place. Would it have been an insult even if the attacks had not taken place? Why is it an insult? Should a firefighter not feel like avenging the murder of his family? As to the film's view of Colombia, since the guerrillas are shown as drug traffickers and enemies of the government, it seems clear they are not considered the majority of Colombians. The AP, which would not run the review of a critic who had not seen the film, felt Jordan was sufficiently qualified to attack it sight unseen. We await his further insights once he has seen it.

My guess is that the average firefighter, like the average American moviegoer, might sort of enjoy the movie, which is a skillfully made example of your typical Schwarzenegger action film. The Arnold character is uncomplicated, loyal, brave, and resourceful, and does only six or seven things that are impossible in the physical universe. The villains, it is true, give a bad name to Colombian guerrillas and drug traffickers. The only ambiguity comes in the person of a government agent played by Elias Koteas, who first refuses to share information with the FBI, and then appears to be an FBI agent himself. It's the kind of movie where you don't give that a passing thought.

I kept expecting a subtext in which the CIA or other American agencies were involved in skulduggery in Colombia, but no: The plot leads us to believe there may be a double agent on our side, but that's a blind alley. Instead, all leads up to a climax involving the planned destruction of a Washington skyscraper, which is creepy and disturbing given our feelings about 9/11, but traditional in movies made earlier—when terrorism plots were standard in the movies. You may not want to attend *Collateral Damage* because of 9/11, but it hardly seems fair to attack it for not knowing then what we all know now.

That leaves me with a couple of tactical questions. There is an air attack on a guerrilla base where the fireman is being held captive. How can they be sure their rockets won't kill him? Or do they want to kill him? And there is a neatly timed rendezvous involving a terrorist and a man on a motorcycle that leads us to wonder, thinking back through the plot, how this plan could have been made. There are also some coincidences that are a little too neat, like how a fire ax saves lives in the first scene and then, at the end, becomes the fireman's handy and symbolic tool for creating one of those booby traps where you wonder how in the hell he could have figured that one out.

There will not be any more action stories like this for a long time. We're at the end of the tunnel, the light is out, the genre is closed. *Collateral Damage* may stir unwanted associations for some viewers. Others may attend it with a certain nostalgia, remembering a time when such scenarios fell under the heading of entertainment.

The Color of Paradise ★ ★ ★ ½
PG, 90 m., 2000

Mohsen Ramezani (Mohammad), Hossein Mahjub (Hashem), Salime Feizi (Granny). Directed by Majid Majidi and produced by Mehdi Karimi. Screenplay by Majidi.

Words appear on a black screen: "To the glory of God." I was reminded of Catholic grade school, where every page of homework began at the top with our childish handwriting: "JMJ"—for Jesus, Mary, and Joseph. Was I dedicating my arithmetic to heaven, or requesting a miracle?

There is no doubt in the mind of Majid Majidi, the Iranian writer and director of *The Color of Paradise*. His work feels truly intended for God's glory, unlike so much "religious art" that is intended merely to propagandize for one view of God over another. His film looks up, not sideways. In this and his previous film, the luminous Oscar nominee *Children of Heaven*, he provides a quiet rebuke to the materialist consumerism in Western films about children. (Both films have subtitles, but they're not too difficult for any child who can read.)

The Color of Paradise is about a blind boy. Quick and gentle, in love with knowledge, acutely attuned to the world around him, Mohammad loves his lessons at a school for the blind. He is loved at home by his grandmother and his two sisters. But his father, Hashem, does not love him. Hashem is a widower, ambitious to marry into a prosperous family, and he fears the possession of a blind son will devalue him in the marriage market.

As the film opens, the school term is over, and the other boys have been picked up by their parents. Mohammad waits alone outside his school, for a father who does not come. There is a remarkable sequence in which he hears the peep of a chick that has fallen from its nest. The boy finds the chick, gently takes it in his hand, and then climbs a tree, listening for the cries of the lost one's nest-mates. He replaces the bird in its nest. God, who knows when a sparrow falls, has had help this time from a little blind boy.

The father finally arrives, and asks the headmaster if Mohammad can stay at the school over the vacation term. The answer is no. Hashem reluctantly brings the boy home with him, where his grandmother and sisters welcome him. Mohammad is under no illusions about his father's love. Local children attend a school. Mohammad has all the same books, in Braille, and begs to be allowed to attend. In class, he knows the answers—but his father forbids him to continue at the school, possibly hoping to keep his existence a secret. Eventually the boy is apprenticed to a blind carpenter, who will teach him how to build cabinets by touch. This might be a good job for some, but not for Mohammad, who is eager to compete in the world of the seeing.

For all of its apparent melodrama, *The Color of Paradise* is not an obvious or manipulative film. It is too deliberately simple. And it is made with delicacy and beauty. The sound track is alive with natural sounds of woodpeckers, songbirds, insects and nature, voices and footfalls. A blind person would get a good idea of the locations and what is happening—as Mohammad does. The performance by young Mohsen Ramezani, as the boy, is without guile; when he cries once in frustration, we do not see acting, but raw grief.

The ending, after a sequence in which the boy is in great danger, will strike some as contrived. Certainly it is not subtle by our cynical Western standards. If Hollywood told this story, the father would have a change of heart. In Iran, heaven intervenes more directly—as if God, having tested Mohammad as much as he dares, has the change of heart Himself.

The Color of Paradise is a family film that shames the facile commercialism of a product like *Pokemon* and its value system based on power and greed. Because they do not condescend to young audiences, Majidi's films, of

127

course, are absorbing for adults as well, and there is a lesson here: Any family film not good enough for grown-ups is certainly not good enough for children.

Company Man ½★
PG-13, 81 m., 2001

Douglas McGrath (Allen Quimp), Sigourney Weaver (Daisy Quimp), John Turturro (Crocker Johnson), Anthony LaPaglia (Fidel Castro), Ryan Phillippe (Rudolph Petrov), Denis Leary (Fry), Woody Allen (Lowther), Alan Cumming (General Batista). Directed by Peter Askin and Douglas McGrath and produced by Guy East, Rick Leed, John Penotti, and James W. Skotchdopole. Screenplay by Askin and McGrath.

Company Man is the kind of movie that seems to be wearing a strained smile, as if it's not sure we're getting the jokes. If it could, it would laugh for us. It's an arch, awkward, ill-timed, forced political comedy set in 1959 and seemingly stranded there.

Astonishing, that a movie could be this bad and star Sigourney Weaver, John Turturro, Anthony LaPaglia, Denis Leary, Woody Allen, Alan Cumming, and Ryan Phillippe. I am reminded of Gene Siskel's classic question, "Is this movie better than a documentary of the same actors having lunch?" In this case, it is not even better than a documentary of the same actors ordering room service while fighting the stomach flu.

In addition to the cast members listed above, the movie stars Douglas McGrath, its author and codirector, who is a low-rent cross between Jack Lemmon and Wally Cox and comes across without any apparent comic effect. He plays Allen Quimp, rhymes with wimp, a grammar teacher from Connecticut whose wife (Weaver) frets that he needs a better job. To get her and his own family off his back, he claims to be a CIA agent, and that leads, through a series of events as improbable as they are uninteresting, to his involvement in the defection of a Russia ballet star (Phillippe) and his assignment to Cuba on the eve of Castro's revolution.

His contact agent there is Fry, played by Denis Leary, who looks appalled at some of the scenes he's in. Example: As Fry denies that a revolutionary fever is sweeping the island, a man with a bottle full of gasoline approaches them and borrows a light from Quimp. Soon after, the man runs past in the opposite direction and they pass (without noticing—ho, ho) a burning auto. And not any burning auto, but an ancient, rusty, abandoned hulk filled with phony gas flames obviously rigged and turned on for the movie. How does it help the revolution to restage ancient auto fires?

But never mind. Fry introduces Quimp to Lowther (Woody Allen), the CIA's man in charge, who also denies a revolution is under way, while turning aside to light his cigarette from a burning effigy of Batista (ho, ho). The mystery of what Woody Allen is doing in this movie is solved in a two-name search on the Internet Movie Database, which reveals that McGrath cowrote the screenplay for Allen's *Bullets Over Broadway.* Now Allen is returning the favor, I guess.

Well, that was a funny movie, and the same search identifies McGrath as the writer-director of *Emma* (1996), a nice little comedy with Gwyneth Paltrow. So he is obviously not without talent—except in this movie. Maybe the mistake was to star himself. He doesn't have the presence to anchor a comedy; all those jokes about Quimp the nonentity ring true, instead of funny.

As bad movies go, *Company Man* falls less in the category of Affront to the Audience and more in the category of Nonevent. It didn't work me up into a frenzy of dislike, but dialed me down into sullen indifference. It was screened twice for the Chicago press, and I sat through the first thirty minutes of the second screening, thinking to check it against a different crowd. I heard no laughter. Just an occasional cough, or the shuffling of feet, or a yawn, or a sigh, like in a waiting room.

The Contender ★ ★ ★ ★
R, 126 m., 2000

Joan Allen (Laine Hanson), Gary Oldman (Shelly Runyon), Jeff Bridges (President Jackson Evans), Christian Slater (Reginald Webster), Sam Elliott (Kermit Newman), William Petersen (Jack Hathaway), Saul Rubinek (Jerry Toliver), Philip Baker Hall (Oscar Billings), Mike Binder (Lewis

Hollis). Directed by Rod Lurie and produced by Marc Frydman, Douglas Urbanski, Willi Baer, and James Spies. Screenplay by Lurie.

The Contender, a thriller about the first woman nominated to be vice president, hinges on a question from her past: Did she more or less willingly participate in group sex while she was in college? "That's Hanson getting gang-banged," an investigator says, smacking his lips over an old photo from a sorority party. If it really is, she's going to have trouble getting congressional confirmation.

The movie is frankly partisan. Its sentiments are liberal and Democratic, its villains conservative and Republican. When I asked its star, Jeff Bridges, if the plot was a veiled reference to Monicagate, he smiled. "Veiled?" he said. "I don't think it's so veiled." The difference between Senator Laine Hanson (Joan Allen) and President Bill Clinton is that when zealots start sniffing her laundry, she simply refuses to answer their questions. "It's none of your business," she tells GOP Representative Shelly Runyon (Gary Oldman), whose inquiring mind wants to know.

As the movie opens, an incumbent vice president has died in office. It is universally assumed that a man will be named to replace him, and a leading candidate is Senator Jack Hathaway (William Petersen), who has recently made headlines as a hero. While he was on a fishing trip, a car plunged off a bridge near his boat and he dove into icy waters in an unsuccessful attempt to save the woman trapped inside. It is an adventure like this, not a lifetime of service, that the image-mongers like, but the senator's misfortune is that his rescue attempt failed. "A girl died and you let it happen," he's told sorrowfully by presidential advisers, and President Jackson Evans (Jeff Bridges) consoles him cryptically: "You're the future of the Democratic Party, and you always will be."

The president wants to make history by appointing a woman, and Senator Hanson looks like the best choice. She is happily married, has a young child, and when we first see her is having robust sex (on a desktop) with her husband. Runyon, the Oldman character, doubts any woman should be trusted with the nuclear trigger: What if she has her period or

something? He is delighted with evidence she may have been the life of the party on campus.

The movie's story of confirmation hearings, backstage politics, and rival investigations unfolds as a political thriller based on suspense and issues. Senator Hanson flatly refuses to answer any questions about her sexual past, and for a time it looks as if the president may have to dump her as a nominee. Is she really taking an ethical stand, or covering up something? There is a remarkable scene between Hanson and Runyon, who have lunch together in a private club, the Republican shoveling down his meal and talking with his mouth full as if he would like to chew on her too.

The movie was written and directed by Rod Lurie, a former Los Angeles film critic who is the son of the political cartoonist Ranan Lurie. He grew up with politics discussed at every meal, he says; his first movie, *Deterrence,* starred Kevin Pollack as a president faced with a nuclear crisis. I liked the way that film dealt with issues and ideas, but *The Contender* is a leap forward, more assured, more exciting, more biting.

Most American movies pretend there are no parties; even in political movies, characters rarely reveal their affiliations. *The Contender* does take sides, most obviously in the character of the GOP congressman Runyon, who is played by Oldman as an unprincipled power broker with an unwholesome curiosity about other people's sex lives. Whether you are in sympathy with the movie may depend on which you found more disturbing: the questions of the Starr commission or Clinton's attempts to avoid answering them. Full disclosure: I could imagine myself reacting as Clinton did, but to ask Starr's questions would have filled me with self-disgust.

Joan Allen is at the center of the movie, in one of the strongest performances of the year. Some actresses would have played the role as too sensual, others as too cold; she is able to suggest a woman with a healthy physical life who nevertheless has ethical standards that will not bend. She would rather lose the vice presidency than satisfy Runyon's smutty curiosity, and through her the movie argues that we have gone too far in our curiosity about private behavior.

Jeff Bridges plays the president as a man who got elected by seeming a great deal more affable and down-home than he really is. He's forever ordering food and pressing it upon his guests, in gestures that are not so much hospitality as decoys. His top aides, played by Sam Elliott and Saul Rubinek, have a terse shorthand that shows they understand the folksy act but aren't deceived by it. And Christian Slater has a slippery role as a freshman Democratic congressman who is prepared to barter his vote for a seat on Runyon's committee.

And what about Runyon, in Gary Oldman's performance? Oldman is one of the great actors, able to play high, low, crass, noble. Here he disappears into the character, with owly glasses, a feral mouth, and curly locks teased over baldness. He plays the kind of man who, in high school, would rather know who was sleeping with the cheerleaders than sleep with one himself. There are two revealing scenes involving his wife, who knows him better than anyone should have to.

Of course, if he is right about Hanson, then he is not a bad man—merely an unpleasant one. But even if he is right he is wrong, because he opposed the nominee because she is a woman; her shady past is only a means of attacking her. This is one of those rare movies where you leave the theater having been surprised and entertained, and then start arguing. *The Contender* takes sides and is bold about it. Most movies are like puppies that want everyone to pet them.

Corky Romano ½★
PG-13, 86 m., 2001

Chris Kattan (Corky Romano), Peter Falk (Pops Romano), Vinessa Shaw (Kate Russo), Peter Berg (Paulie), Fred Ward (Leo Corrigan), Chris Penn (Peter), Richard Roundtree (Howard Shuster). Directed by Rob Pritts and produced by Robert Simonds. Screenplay by David Garrett and Jason Ward.

Corky Romano continues the *Saturday Night Live* Jinx, which in recent years has frustrated the talented members of the TV program in their efforts to make watchable movies. It's a desperately unfunny gangster spoof, starring Chris Kattan as the kid brother in a Mafia family, so trusting and naive he really does believe his father is in the landscaping business.

This is the third time the jinx has claimed Kattan as a victim, after *A Night at the Roxbury* (1998) and this year's *Monkey Bone,* two films that will be among the first to go when Blockbuster destroys 25 percent of its VHS tape inventory, and will not be leading the chain's list of DVD replacement titles.

Now when I use the words "desperately unfunny," what do I mean? Consider one of Corky's earlier scenes, where we see him as an assistant veterinarian. Clumsy beyond belief, he knocks over everything in a room full of ailing animals, and a snake crawls up his pants and eventually, inevitably, emerges from his fly.

I submit as a general principle that it is not funny when a clumsy person knocks over *everything* in a room. The choreography makes it obvious that the character, in one way or another, is deliberately careening from one collision to another. It always looks deliberate. Indeed, it looks like a deliberate attempt to force laughs instead of building them. One movie where it does work is *The Mummy,* where Rachel Weisz knocks over a bookcase and a whole library tumbles over domino-style. But there an original accident builds and builds beyond her control; Corky Romano's approach would be to reel around the room knocking over every bookcase individually.

In the movie, Corky's father is played by Peter Falk. True, Falk is one of the first guys you'd think of for the role, but they should have kept thinking. He has played similar roles so many times that he can sleepwalk through his dialogue; a completely unexpected casting choice might have been funnier. Corky has two very tough brothers (Peter Berg and Chris Penn) who doubt their father's plan, which is that the youngest son should infiltrate the FBI in order to destroy the evidence against the old man.

That brings Corky into contact with Howard Schuster (Richard Roundtree), the local FBI chief, who is given the thankless comic task of never knowing more than he needs to know in order to make the wrong decision. There's also Vinessa Shaw as an FBI agent who goes undercover as a sexy nurse. Or maybe she's a sexy agent who goes undercover as a nurse. Such a thin line separates the two concepts.

Corky Romano is like a dead zone of comedy. The concept is exhausted, the ideas are tired, the physical gags are routine, the story is labored, the actors look like they can barely contain their doubts about the project.

Cotton Mary ★ ★
R, 125 m., 2000

Greta Scacchi (Lily MacIntosh), Madhur Jaffrey (Cotton Mary), Sakina Jaffrey (Rosie), James Wilby (John MacIntosh), Prayag Raaj (Abraham), Laura Lumley (Theresa), Sarah Badel (Mrs. Evans), Joanna David (Mrs. Smythe), Gemma Jones (Mrs. Davids), Neena Gupta (Blossom). Directed by Ismail Merchant and produced by Nayeem Hafizka and Richard Hawley. Screenplay by Alexandra Viets.

Ismail Merchant's *Cotton Mary* centers on the stories of two women: an Anglo-Indian who wants to be white, and a white British woman who wants to brood and sulk and be left alone. We don't like either character, but what we can't understand is the British woman's sullen passivity and indifference to her household; a faithful servant is fired, her husband has an affair, a crazy woman takes charge of her new baby, and she hardly seems to notice. The film wants to make larger points, but succeeds only in being a story of derangement.

The British Raj shut down in 1947, and Indians took over their own country for the first time in centuries. But many people of British descent, born there, considered it home and stayed after independence. The best portrait of that time I've read is Paul Scott's *Staying On*, the novel that followed his masterful *Raj Quartet. Cotton Mary* is like a lurid reduction of material set in a similar time and place, without the human insights—either in the story or between the characters.

As the story opens, a British woman named Lily (Greta Scacchi) has given birth, but has no milk. Mary (Madhur Jaffrey), a nurse at the hospital, takes the sickly child to her sister Blossom (Neena Gupta), who lives in a poorhouse and serves as a wet nurse. Lily hardly seems to notice. When she finally asks, "Mary, how do you feed the baby?" and is told, "Mother's milk, madam," that seems to satisfy her. She is maddeningly incurious.

Mary insinuates herself into the household, which is run by the aged family servant Abraham (Prayag Raaj). Soon she plots to convince Lily to fire Abraham (who can clearly see Cotton Mary is mad) and replace him with her own candidate, the cousin of a cousin. Abraham is the most convincing and touching character in the movie; when Lily tells him to go home, he protests, "But madam, this is my home." The newly hired cousin is a drunk; Lily sees him staggering around the garden, pulling up plants, and does nothing.

Lily's husband, John (James Wilby), a reporter for the BBC World Service, is absent much of the time covering alarming portents, and when he returns it is to have an affair with Mary's shapely friend Rosie (Sakina Jaffrey). But this affair is more obligatory than necessary, and supplies little more than a perfunctory sex interest. Meanwhile, the household goes to pieces while Cotton Mary dreams ominously of having white babies.

What is the point of this movie? To show that some Anglo-Indians identified with the departing British? Of course they did. When British men first arrived in India as soldiers and traders, they engaged in widespread liaisons and marriages with Indian women, and that custom ended only with the arrival of large numbers of British women, who introduced racism into the mix; similar feelings were mirrored on the Indian side. The Raj provided a privileged place for Anglo-Indians, but when the British departed, mixed-race people like Cotton Mary were left without a safety net. This story could be told more poignantly if Mary were not so clearly bonkers that her race is beside the point.

As for Lily, is she suffering from postpartum depression, or is she so clueless because the story requires her to notice almost nothing around her? A competent person would have treasured Abraham and left instructions for Mary to be barred from the house, and then there would have been no story. I think of the old couple in *Staying On,* and their lifelong loyalty to one another—their friendship with the manager of the nearby hotel, and their clockwork firing of their faithful servant (who refuses to be fired), and the loneliness of the local Anglican church, surrounded by the gravestones of ghosts whose descendants have all gone back to England. That is a story. *Cotton Mary* is a soap opera.

The Count of Monte Cristo ★ ★ ★
PG-13, 118 m., 2002

Guy Pearce (Fernand Mondego), James Caviezel (Edmond Dantes), Richard Harris (Faria), Dagmara Dominczyk (Mercedes), Luis Guzman (Jacobo), Henry Cavill (Albert Mondego), James Frain (Villefort), Albie Woodington (Danglars). Directed by Kevin Reynolds and produced by Gary Barber, Roger Birnbaum, and Jonathan Glickman. Screenplay by Jay Wolpert, based on the novel by Alexandre Dumas.

The Count of Monte Cristo is a movie that incorporates piracy, Napoleon in exile, betrayal, solitary confinement, secret messages, escape tunnels, swashbuckling, comic relief, a treasure map, Parisian high society, and sweet revenge, and brings it in at under two hours, with performances by good actors who are clearly having fun. This is the kind of adventure picture the studios churned out in the Golden Age—so traditional it almost feels new.

James Caviezel stars, as Edmond Dantes, a low-born adventurer betrayed by his friend Fernand Mondego (Guy Pearce). Condemned to solitary confinement on the remote prison island of Chateau d'If, he spends years slowly growing mad and growing his hair, until one day a remarkable thing happens. A stone in his cell floor moves and lifts, and Faria (Richard Harris) appears. Faria has even more hair than Dantes, but is much more cheerful because he has kept up his hope over the years by digging an escape tunnel. Alas, by digging in the wrong direction, he came up in Dantes's cell instead of outside the walls, but *c'est la vie.*

"There are 5,119 stones in my walls," Dantes tells Faria. "I have counted them." Faria can think of better ways to pass the time. Enlisting Dantes in a renewed tunneling effort, Faria also tutors him in the physical and mental arts; he's the Mr. Miyagi of swashbuckling. Together, the men study the philosophies of Adam Smith and Machiavelli, and the old man tutors the younger one in what looks uncannily like martial arts, including the ability to move with blinding speed.

This middle section of the movie lasts long enough to suggest it may also provide the end, but no: The third act takes place back in soci-ety, after Faria supplies Dantes with a treasure map, and the resulting treasure finances his masquerade as the fictitious Count of Monte Cristo. Rich, enigmatic, mysterious, he fascinates the aristocracy and throws lavish parties, all as a snare for Mondego, while renewing his love for the beautiful Mercedes (Dagmara Dominczyk).

The story, of course, is based on the novel by Alexandre Dumas, unread by me, although I was a close student of the *Classics Illustrated* version. Director Kevin Reynolds redeems himself after *Waterworld* by moving the action along at a crisp pace; we can imagine Errol Flynn in this material, although Caviezel and Pearce bring more conviction to it, and Luis Guzman is droll as the count's loyal sidekick, doing what sounds vaguely like eighteenth-century stand-up ("I swear on my dead relatives—and even the ones that are not feeling so good . . .").

The various cliffs, fortresses, prisons, treasure isles, and chateaus all look suitably atmospheric, the fight scenes are well choreographed, and the moment of Mondego's comeuppance is nicely milked for every ounce of sweet revenge. This is the kind of movie that used to be right at home at the Saturday matinee, and it still is.

Coyote Ugly ★ ★
PG-13, 101 m., 2000

Piper Perabo (Violet Sanford), Adam Garcia (Kevin O'Donnell), Maria Bello (Lil), Melanie Lynskey (Gloria), Izabella Miko (Cammie), Bridget Moynahan (Rachel), Tyra Banks (Zoe), John Goodman (Dad). Directed by David McNally and produced by Jerry Bruckheimer and Chad Oman. Screenplay by Gina Wendkos.

Coyote Ugly is a cliff-hanger in which Piper Perabo ventures into a Jerry Bruckheimer production and escapes more or less untouched. The film stars her as one of a group of heedless wenches who dance on a bar and pour straight shots down the throats of the seething multitude. In a movie of this sort, it is inevitable that the song "I Will Survive" will sooner or later be performed by drunken pals. Next week's opening, "The Replacements," makes us wait an hour to hear it. *Coyote Ugly* takes no chances and puts it under the opening titles. Do you get the feeling these movies are assembled from off-the-shelf parts?

There is a story beloved in movie lore about the time Howard Hawks asked John Wayne to appear in *Rio Lobo*. Wayne had already starred in Hawks's *Rio Bravo* and *El Dorado*, which were essentially the same picture. So was *Rio Lobo*. "Shall I send over the script?" asked Hawks. "Why bother?" asked the Duke. "I've already been in it twice."

Does Jerry Bruckheimer have the same nagging feeling of déjà vu as he compares each new screenplay to those that have gone before? I wonder if he suspects his movie may not be original, as he contemplates a story about a girl from New Jersey who dreams of being a songwriter, moves to Manhattan, meets a guy, gets a job, and has a heartrending reconciliation with her dad, all in a movie that ends (yes, it really does) with the final line, "What do you do when you realize all your dreams have come true?"

Bruckheimer and his director bring superb technical credits to this wheezy old story, and they add wall-to-wall music to make it sound like fun. But you can only pump up the volume so far before it becomes noise. I don't ask for startling originality in a movie like *Coyote Ugly*. I don't object to the scene in which the heroine and her guy neck in a convertible and regard the lights on a Manhattan bridge. I am not even surprised that the hero drives a classic car (no characters in Bruckheimer movies drive cars less than twenty-five years old unless they are parents or gangsters). I don't even mind the obligatory dialogue, "It's payback time!" All I ask is that I be surprised a couple of times. Give me something I can't see coming, and make it more unexpected than a beloved character getting hit by a car instead of having a heart attack.

In the movie, Piper Perabo, who has big-time star power, plays Violet, a working-class girl from South Amboy, New Jersey, who packs up and moves to a cheap apartment in Chinatown (where she meets not a single Chinese person), and gets a job in Coyote Ugly, a bar that would be the result if you took the bar in *Cocktail* and performed reckless experiments on its DNA.

It's the kind of bar you would fight to get out of—and you'd have to. Customers are jammed so tightly together the fire marshal can barely wedge his way into the room. They are offered no mixed drinks, no wine, just "Jim, Jack, Johnny Red, Johnny Black, and Jose—all my favorite friends," according to Lil (Maria Bello), the sexy blonde who owns the club. "You can have it any way you want it as long as it's in a shot glass."

Violet auditions for her job, which consists of dancing on top of the bar, pouring drinks, dumping ice on customers who get into fights, and spraying the others every so often with the soda gun. These are skilled dancers. They can do Broadway routines on a slippery bar top, while drunks grab at their ankles. Every once in a while, just for variety, they pour booze on the bar and set it on fire. Many of the movie's shots are high-angle, looking down at the customers, their mouths upturned and gulping like gasping fish. Illuminated by garish neon, they bear an uncanny resemblance to Hieronymus Bosch's paintings of the damned roasting in hell.

After a shaky start Violet becomes a hit at the bar, while trying to place tapes of her songs around town. She has stage fright, you see, and can't sing her own songs because she's afraid to sing in front of an audience, although she will obviously do almost anything else.

She meets Kevin (Adam Garcia), an awfully nice Australian short-order cook, who encourages her, and even bribes a guy to give her an audition by trading his precious Spiderman comic. They would no doubt have steamy sex except that Bruckheimer, a student of straws in the wind, knows this is the summer when PG-13, not his old favorite R, is the coveted rating. (His *Gone in 60 Seconds* was also PG-13, which may explain why Angelina Jolie was missing from most of the picture.) *Coyote Ugly* finally leads up to the questions: (1) Does she find the courage to sing? (2) Do they stay together after their Idiot Plot misunderstanding? and (3) Do all of her dreams come true?

There is a reason to see the movie, and that reason is Piper Perabo, whom I first noticed in *The Adventures of Rocky and Bullwinkle*, writing that she was "so fetching she sort of stops the clock." She has one of those friendly Julia

Roberts smiles, good comic timing, ease and confidence on the screen, and a career ahead of her in movies better than this one. Lots better.

Crazy/Beautiful ★ ★ ★
PG-13, 95 m., 2001

Kirsten Dunst (Nicole Oakley), Jay Hernandez (Carlos Nunez), Joshua Feinman (Football Player), Bruce Davison (Tom Oakley), Lucinda Jenney (Courtney Oakley), Taryn Manning (Maddy), Keram Malicki-Sanchez (Foster). Directed by John Stockwell and produced by Rachel Pfeffer, Harry J. Ufland, and Mary Jane Ufland. Screenplay by Phil Hay and Matt Manfredi.

She's a wild child, a drinker, a truant, sexually bold, deliberately reckless. He's a model student, serious, responsible, who wants to attend Annapolis. She's the daughter of a liberal white congressman. He's the son of a hardworking Mexican-American woman. She goes after him because he's a hunk. He likes her but is frightened by her wildness, which is against his nature. Will she lead him into trouble, or will he help her grow up and quiet her demons? *Crazy/Beautiful,* which is about these questions, is an unusually observant film about adolescence.

The movie stars Kirsten Dunst and Jay Hernandez as Nicole and Carlos. Both actors are natural and unaffected—they level with their characters, instead of trying to impress us. They're students at a magnet high school in Pacific Palisades; she lives in Malibu, he lives in the barrio, and when she gets him into trouble and he's assigned to detention, he's angry: "I'm bussed two hours both ways. If I wanted to screw up, I'd do it in my own school, and get a lot more sleep." Nicole is self-destructive and parties with the wrong crowd; perhaps because Carlos uses his intelligence and has goals, he represents not just a cute guy but a self that she lost along the way.

Of course they are in love. Hormones take over when you're seventeen. But even during sex he's worried by her behavior. She brings him home, they get into bed, he insists on a condom, and then he sees her father wandering by the pool outside her window. He's alarmed, but she laughs: "That's my dad. He

doesn't care. I can do anything. We're using a condom—he'd be so proud. And a person of color in his daughter's bed!"

Actually, it isn't quite that simple, and her father, Tom (Bruce Davison), is a good man who is written without resorting to the usual stereotypes about well-meaning but clueless adults. At one point he forbids Carlos to see his daughter—for the boy's own good, since he considers his daughter irredeemable, a lost cause. There are times when we agree.

Both characters find elements in the other they envy. "You don't care about what people think, and when I'm with you I don't care about what people think," says Carlos, who actually cares a great deal. Nicole works hard on her reputation for trouble, but there's a part of her that mourns, "I wish I wasn't the child that everybody learned what not to do from."

One of Nicole's problems is that her mother is dead, and her father's second wife has given him a perfect little child that they both dote on. The mother is obsessed by the tiniest rash on her child, but indifferent to the entire scope of Nicole's life. Carlos has problems at home, too, but of a different nature: His father is absent, and he carries the burden of his family's hopes. His mother and older brother are fiercely protective of him and hostile to Nicole, partly because she is white, even more because she is obviously trouble.

Crazy/Beautiful, directed by John Stockwell, written by Phil Hay and Matt Manfredi, is like a tougher, less-sentimental mirror version of *Save the Last Dance.* In that one, a white girl attends a black boy's inner-city high school, but in both films there are cultural differences, resentment because of color, a feeling of star-crossed loves, and the sense that each can help the other.

Crazy/Beautiful is tougher, and would have been tougher still, I understand, if the studio hadn't toned it down to get the PG-13 rating. It was originally intended to include drug use and irresponsible sex, and play as a cautionary message—but the R rating would have limited it to those over seventeen, and these days, alas, the warnings need to come a little sooner. As it stands, the movie sets up real tension between Nicole's self-destructive behavior and Carlos's responsible nature. And because of the real conviction that Dunst and Hernandez bring to the roles, we care about them as people, not case studies.

The Crew ★ ½
PG-13, 88 m., 2000

Richard Dreyfuss (Bobby Bartellemeo), Burt Reynolds (Joey "Bats" Pistella), Dan Hedaya (Mike "The Brick" Donatelli), Seymour Cassel (Tony "Mouth" Donato), Carrie-Anne Moss (Detective Olivia Neal), Jennifer Tilly (Ferris), Lainie Kazan (Pepper Lowenstein), Jeremy Piven (Detective Steve Menteer). Directed by Michael Dinner and produced by Barry Sonnenfeld and Barry Josephson. Screenplay by Barry Fanaro.

Hot on the heels of *Space Cowboys*, which was about four astro-codgers, here comes *The Crew*, about four mobster-codgers. Go with the cowboys. One difference between the two movies is that *Space Cowboys* develops quirky characters and tells a story that makes it necessary for the old friends to have a reunion, while *The Crew* is all contrivance and we don't believe a minute of it.

Of course, *The Crew* wants only to be a comedy, not a bittersweet coda to *Wise Guys*. But even at that it fails, because we don't buy the opening premise, which is that four onetime heavy-duty mobsters would all retire to the same seedy residential hotel on South Beach in Miami, there to tick down their days lined up in wicker chairs on the porch, watching the dollies go by. This is a situation that shouts out Plot, not Life, and everything that happens to them seems generated from overconfident chuckles in the screenwriting process.

The retired mobsters are Bobby Bartellemeo, Joey "Bats" Pistella, Mike "The Brick" Donatelli, and Tony "Mouth" Donato (Bobby violently rejected a nickname in his youth and never got another). In the same order, they're played by Richard Dreyfuss, Burt Reynolds, Dan Hedaya, and Seymour Cassel. After this movie and *Mad Dog Time* (1996), which reached a kind of grandeur as one of the worst films of all time, Dreyfuss and Reynolds should instruct their agents to reject all further mob "comedies" on sight. The later stages of their careers cannot withstand another one.

The plot has to do with plans to upgrade their fleabag hotel into yet another art-retro South Beach yuppie playpen. The old guys like where they live and want to preserve it, so they dream up a cockamamie scheme in which they steal a corpse from the morgue (Hedaya has a part-time job among the stiffs) and bring it back to the hotel, where they plan to shoot it and make it look like a murder, except that, as "Bats" complains, the old guy "looks like the pope." And so he does—Pope Pius XII, who was several popes ago, back when young "Bats" was no doubt taking a livelier interest in the church.

One thing leads to another. Turns out the corpse is in fact the ancient father of a current Miami crime lord. The old guy had Alzheimer's, wandered away from the nursing home, died anonymously, and it was just their bad luck to make the wrong choice at the morgue. Their pseudo-whack of the old dead guy is imprudently revealed by "Mouth" to a nightclub stripper named Ferris (Jennifer Tilly), whose stepmother turns out to be Pepper Lowenstein (Lainie Kazan), known to the mafia-codgers from the deli she used to run in New York, back in their carefree youth when they were blowing up trucks. Into the mix come two local detectives (Carrie-Anne Moss and Jeremy Piven), and one of them has an unexpected link to the past too.

And so on. Somehow it all needs to be more desperate, or more slapstick, or have more edge, or turn up the heat in some other way. Lainie Kazan's presence suggests one obvious idea: Why not a comedy about four Mafia widows in Miami Beach? *The Crew* unfolds as a construction, not a series of surprises and delights. Occasionally a line of dialogue or two will float into view, providing a hint of the edge the whole movie might have had. (My favorite: A gun dealer, happily selling them a shotgun with no background check, adds, "Don't thank me—thank the Republicans.")

Comparing this to *Space Cowboys*, I realize how much more heft and dimension the cowboys had. Attention was paid to making them individuals, instead of just rattling off attributes and body types. And Clint Eastwood, who directed that movie, is a better filmmaker than Michael Dinner, who seems too content and not hungry enough—too complacent that his material will sell itself. There is also the fact that Eastwood, James Garner, Tommy Lee Jones, and Donald Sutherland have built up good-will and screen authority by avoiding movies like *The Crew* instead of making them.

Crime and Punishment in Suburbia ★ ★ ★
R, 98 m., 2000

Monica Keena (Roseanne Skolnik), Ellen Barkin (Maggie Skolnik), Michael Ironside (Fred Skolnik), Vincent Kartheiser (Vincent), James DeBello (Jimmy), Jeffrey Wright (Chris), Blake C. Shields (Moznick), Conchata Ferrell (Bella). Directed by Rob Schmidt and produced by Pamela Koffler, Larry Gross, and Christine Vachon. Screenplay by Larry Gross.

Crime and Punishment in Suburbia is no doubt "flawed"—that favorite moviecrit word—and it suffers from being released a year after the similar *American Beauty*, even though it was made earlier. But it is the kind of movie that lives and breathes; I forgive its short-comings because it strives, and because it contains excellent things. To lean back and dismiss this movie, as most critics have done, is to show ingratitude. A messy but hungry film like this is more interesting than cool technical perfection.

The story is a dark, juicy melodrama involving the kinds of things that happen only in soap operas and in real life. Imagine *American Beauty* told from the point of view of the cheerleader. Her name is Roseanne (Monica Keena), and she is popular in school, where she dates the quarterback of the football team. But there is a cloud in her eyes, an inner failure to believe in herself. At home, where the dinner table creates an eerie echo of *American Beauty*, we see that her stepfather (Michael Ironside) is a pathetic drunk and her mother (Ellen Barkin) is fed up—not that her mother is a saint, either.

All of this is observed by a classmate named Vincent (Vincent Kartheiser), who silently sits behind her in the movies, who lurks across the street from her house, who takes her picture with a telephoto lens, and fits the profile of a stalker. But there is more to Vincent. He is a complicated boy with an angelic face, and a mom who looks at him and says, "It's gonna be so interesting to see what you're like after you get out of this stage." Taking a clue from the movie's title, we wonder if he represents Raskolnikov, the hero of Dostoyevsky's novel. But director Rob Schmidt and writer Larry Gross have borrowed little other than the title and the workings of guilty emotions from *Crime and Punishment*. Vincent seems inspired more by the angels in *Wings of Desire*, who keep secret watch over their humans, want to help them, and finally descend to the physical level so they can touch and heal them.

Roseanne needs healing. She needs some-body who *sees* her—not the popular blonde cheerleader but the girl whose home life is hell and whose boyfriend is painfully limited. She needs a boy she can sing with, but she's never heard the song. Monica Keena does a great deal with Roseanne, a character who is herself an actress—pretending to be a daughter, a girl-friend, a cheerleader, all the time screaming inside.

Save the rest of the review for later if you plan to see the movie. One night the defiant mother goes out drinking with her girlfriend and picks up a bartender (Jeffrey Wright) who is probably nicer than she deserves. Her hus-band suspects an affair, finds them at the yo-gurt stand, and starts a fight. The scandals sink Roseanne at school, where the rumor machine whispers that her mother has left home to live with a black pimp. Black, yes; pimp, no. One drunken night the self-pitying stepfather (it is one of Ironside's best perfor-mances) forces himself on Roseanne. She con-vinces her quarterback (James DeBello) that they must murder him.

The attack echoes Raskolnikov's experience with the messiness of murder. The wrong per-son ends up charged with the crime because of circumstantial evidence. And the movie arrives at last at its Dostoyevskian component, as guilt eats away at the true killers. Some peo-ple are just not made to get away with murder; their freedom seems wrong to them. Now it is time for Vincent to come forward in his es-sential goodness, like Sonia (who was an in-spiration and affront to Raskolnikov), and offer redemption, which is what Sonia did.

The movie is rated R. It's a funny thing. Many of the PG-13 movies aimed at teenagers (*Coyote Ugly*, for example) seem corrupt and without value. Many of the R-rated movies about teenagers (like this film, *Welcome to the Dollhouse*, and *Almost Famous*) seem ideal for thoughtful teenagers. The MPAA counts the beans but never tastes the soup. Make a worthless movie but limit the nudity and language, and get a PG-13. Make a movie where the characters live with real problems and try to figure out what to do, and god forbid our children should be exposed to such an experience.

The Crimson Rivers ★ ★ ★ ½
R, 105 m., 2001

Jean Reno (Pierre Niemans), Vincent Cassel (Max Kerkerian), Nadia Fares (Fanny Ferreira), Laurent Avare (Remy Caillois), Jean-Pierre Cassel (Dr. Bernard Cherneze), Karim Belkhadra (Captaine Dahmane), Dominique Sanda (Sister Andree). Directed by Mathieu Kassovitz and produced by Alain Goldman. Screenplay by Kassovitz and Jean-Christophe Grange, based on the novel by Grange.

If the makers of the next Hannibal Lecter picture don't hire Mathieu Kassovitz to direct it, they're mad. His new thriller *The Crimson Rivers* is a breathtaking exercise in the macabre, a gruesome thriller with quirky cops and a killer of Lecterian complexity, and even when the movie is perfect nonsense it's so voluptuous that you're grateful to be watching it anyway. This is the work of a natural filmmaker.

The film begins with parallel stories involving two cops, who eventually meet. One is Niemans (Jean Reno), a famed investigator from Paris, such a lone wolf that when he's asked about his unit, he says, "I'm the unit." The other is Kerkerian (Vincent Cassel), a provincial policeman. Niemans is investigating the murder of a man who is found hanging 150 feet in the air in the fetal position, blinded, his hands amputated. Kerkerian is investigating the desecration of a tomb containing a child whose mother said she was killed by the devil.

The investigations are in a spectacularly forlorn valley in the French Alps, where a famous university clings to the slopes. The children of its teachers go to school here, and eventually become professors themselves; there are hints of problems with inbreeding. The university

dean is the "mayor of the valley," and he haughtily tells Niemans: "We all live in perfect harmony. To accuse one of us is to accuse all of us, including me."

Niemans has nobody he wants to accuse. The murder is baffling. "The hands and eyes are the body parts that belong to us alone," the surgeon tells him after the autopsy, adding that in his opinion the victim was tortured for hours. Plodding through his investigation, morose, inward, afraid of dogs, Niemans meets Kerkerian and then meets him again. Why do their two cases seem to lead to the same places?

The movie is as good-looking as any film this year. It is cold, wet, and gray, like *The Silence of the Lambs*, and its mountain fastness doesn't look like a place for a ski holiday, but like a place where you could be lost and never found. Kassovitz's camera gives us the sensation of these peaks and altitudes by moving with uncanny grace through high, empty spaces: There was one shot that had me frankly baffled about where the camera could possibly be positioned.

Notice, too, the way an innocuous visit to a university library somehow becomes a venture into the research room of hell. The room is architecturally beautiful (so is the university—Guernon, in Modane-Avrieux), but Kassovitz and his cinematographer, Thierry Arbogast, somehow light it and move through it so that every innocent student seems to glance up from satanic studies. The entire university—the grounds, the labs, the dean's office—has this unwholesome quality, and if you could figure out how Kassovitz does it you'd learn something about the craft of filmmaking, because he starts with a picture postcard.

The two cops establish a grumpy, monosyllabic relationship, based on the isolationist Niemans's gradual realization that Kerkerian is not a complete fool. There is a moment when they visit a grubby little rental apartment where somehow Kassovitz conjures suspense out of thin air. And a scene where Niemans and a local woman mountaineer lower themselves down a sheer ice face to find a ten-year-old sample of acid rain needed as a clue. They find another clue: a second victim.

All of this, alas, eventually yields a solution to the mystery. Along the way we have been much too interested in current developments to bother formulating our own hypothesis. When the answer comes, it comes all in a package, like one of Sherlock Holmes's wrapups for the admiring Watson. The dialogue is such a rush, indeed, that I was reminded of Russ Meyer's analysis of *Vixen*: "I put all the socially redeeming stuff in one speech at the end, so the audience knows when that comes on, it's safe to leave."

What Kassovitz may be doing here, consciously or not, is demonstrating that we go to a mystery thriller for the windup, not the delivery. All the fun is in the atmosphere, the setup, the surprises, and murky sense of danger. The whodunit part is usually either (a) too predictable, or (b) so unpredictable it's a cheat. Joseph Conrad said he didn't like popular adventure stories because they were all based on accidents—random adventures, not generated by the nature of the characters. For almost all of its length, *The Crimson Rivers* is anchored by the natures of Niemans and Kerkerian, as tested by criminal events. Kassovitz holds off telling us whodunit as long as possible, and then grits his teeth like a runner who finds a puddle at the finish line. Look at this movie and tell me this director shouldn't have a date with Hannibal Lecter. ☞

Crocodile Dundee in Los Angeles ★ ★
PG, 95 m., 2001

Paul Hogan (Mick Dundee), Linda Kozlowski (Sue Charlton), Jere Burns (Arnan Rothman), Jonathan Banks (Milos Drubnik), Aida Turturro (Jean Ferraro), Paul Rodriguez (Diego), Alec Wilson (Jacko), Serge Cockburn (Mikey Dundee). Directed by Simon Wincer and produced by Paul Hogan and Lance Hool. Screenplay by Matthew Berry and Eric Abrams.

I don't want to see a movie about Crocodile Dundee; I just want to hang out with him. Anyone who can rassle crocodiles and be that nice must know the secret of life. If he knew the secret of making movies, there'd be no stopping the bloke.

Crocodile Dundee in Los Angeles is a movie about a genial man and his sweet wife and nice son, and how they leave the Outback and fly to L.A. and foil an international smuggling ring. I've seen audits that were more thrilling.

The movie recycles the formula of the original *Crocodile Dundee* movie from 1986, and the 1988 sequel. Together those two titles rang up a worldwide gross in the neighborhood of $610 million for Paul Hogan. Good on ya, mate! The only mystery about the third movie, more intriguing than anything in its plot, is why there was a thirteen-year delay before the next title in such a lucrative series.

Paul Hogan is just plain a nice guy. He's low-key and folksy, and hardly ever gets mad, and has such a studied naïveté regarding life in the big city that he not only comes from the Outback but must live in a soundproof hole out there. Like the hero of *Memento* he seems to suffer from short-term memory loss, which is why in movie after movie he can expose himself to would-be muggers, or walk into gay bars without realizing it.

In *Crocodile Dundee in Los Angeles*, he lives in a town with a population of twenty with his partner, Sue (Linda Kozlowski), who met him in the first movie when she was a New York TV reporter. He runs Outback safaris, traps crocodiles, and picks his son, Mikey, up after school. Sue, whose father is an international press baron, is happy to live so far from town, as indeed she might be, considering that Croc does the dishes and only occasionally puts an animal trap in to soak with the china. Now her father asks her to fill in for a deceased reporter in his Los Angeles bureau, and that leads Sue and Croc to stumble over a scheme in which money-losing movies are made in order to cover up a scam.

The movie is pokey and the jokes amble onscreen, squat down on their haunches, and draw diagrams of themselves in the dust. But enough Croc-bashing. Truth in journalism compels me to report that *Crocodile Dundee* is at least genial family entertainment, quite possibly of interest to younger audiences, and entirely lacking in the vomitous content of such other current films as *See Spot Run, Joe Dirt,* and *Freddy Got Fingered.*

Since the studios are advertising those excremental exercises in places where kids develop a desire to see them, it is good, after they see *Spy Kids,* to have an innocent and harmless entertainment like *Crocodile Dundee in Los Angeles* as another choice. It may not be brilliant, but who would you rather your kids took as role models: Crocodile Dundee, David Spade, or Tom Green? It is a melancholy milestone in our society when parents pray, "Please, God, let my child grow up to admire a crocodile rassler," but there you have it.

The Crocodile Hunter: Collision Course
★ ★ ★
PG, 90 m., 2002

Steve Irwin (Steve Irwin), Terri Irwin (Terri Irwin), Magda Szubanski (Brozzie), Kenneth Ransom (Vaughan Archer), Lachy Hulme (Robert Wheeler), David Wenham (Sam Flynn), Aden Young (Ron Buckwhiler), Kate Beahan (Jo Buckley). Directed by John Stainton and produced by Judy Bailey, Arnold Rifkin, and Stainton. Screenplay by Holly Goldberg Sloan and Stainton.

There are scenes in *The Crocodile Hunter: Collision Course* where Steve Irwin jumps into rivers at night and wrestles crocodiles bare-handed, while his wife, Terri, helps him tie their jaws shut and haul them onto the boat. In another movie you would question the possibility of such scenes.

But there is something about this one that argues they are true: a certain straightforward, matter-of-fact approach that suggests Steve has been wrestling crocodiles all his life. And he has; according to his bio, Steve's dad, Bob, who ran the Queensland Reptile and Fauna Park in Australia, "taught the young Steve everything there was to know about reptiles—even teaching his nine-year-old how to jump in and catch crocodiles in the rivers of North Queensland at night!"

How, I am wondering, *do* you teach a nine-year-old to jump in and catch crocodiles in the rivers of North Queensland at night? Is rehearsal possible, or do you just get a lot of theory and then jump in? Is it child abuse to tell your nine-year-old to wrestle crocodiles, or only tough love? I urgently await a film titled *Young Steve: The Education of a Croc Hunter.*

Studying the bio more closely, I realize that many of its sentences end with an exclamation point. In the movie, nearly every sentence uttered by Irwin does, although supporting players are allowed periods and question marks. Half of his sentences have only one word:

"Crikey!" He says this frequently while handling the dangerous creatures of the outback, which he likes to get real close to, so they can snap at him during his lectures.

There is a plot to this movie, which I hardly need to mention, since it's irrelevant to the experience. A secret communications satellite falls to Earth and its black box is gobbled up by a croc, and two rival U.S. intelligence agencies send teams to the outback to retrieve it. Meanwhile, Steve and Terri don't realize it's in the stomach of the croc they plan to move to another river system.

Forget the plot. The movie is really about Steve and Terri taking us on a guided tour of the crocs, snakes, deadly insects, and other stars of the outback fauna. Steve's act is simplicity itself. He holds a deadly cobra, say, by its tail and looks straight at the camera and explains that the cobra has enough venom to kill him one hundred times over. The cobra twists and tries to strike at Steve's bare leg. He jerks it away. Crikey! Steve's monologues about the incredible danger he's in do sometimes run a bit long, but he has the grace to interrupt them to slap at flies that are biting him.

Later we meet a "bird-eating" spider whose fangs contain venom that would kill Steve, I dunno, a thousand times over, and he pokes it with a stick to make it display its fangs, and it almost bites Steve's thumb. Crikey! Then he shows us the spider's nest, and sticks his finger down it and yanks it back as if he's been bitten. Crikey! But he was only fooling, mate.

The movie is entertaining exactly on the level I have described it. You see a couple of likable people journeying though the outback, encountering dangerous critters and getting too close for comfort, while lecturing us on their habits and dangers and almost being killed by them. The stunts are not faked, and so there is a certain fascination. Steve and Terri are not exactly developed as deeply realized characters, and only on their Website did I discover they were married in 1992 and in 1998 gave birth to little Bindi Sue Irwin, who is now four, and started in as a baby by wrestling tiny gecko lizards. Crikey.

Crossroads ★ ½
PG-13, 90 m., 2002

Britney Spears (Lucy), Zoe Saldana (Kit), Anson Mount (Ben), Taryn Manning (Mimi), Justin Long (Henry), Dan Aykroyd (Lucy's Dad), Kim Cattrall (Lucy's Mom). Directed by Tamra Davis and produced by Ann Carli. Screenplay by Shonda Rhimes.

I went to *Crossroads* expecting a glitzy bimbo fest and got the bimbos but not the fest. Britney Spears's feature debut is curiously low key and even sad. Yes, it pulls itself together occasionally for a musical number, but even those are so locked into the "reality" of the story that they don't break loose into fun.

The movie opens with three eighth-graders burying a box filled with symbols of their dreams of the future. Four years later, on high school graduation day, the girls are hardly on speaking terms, but they meet to dig up the box, tentatively renew their friendship, and find themselves driving to California in a convertible piloted by a hunk.

Lucy (Spears) hopes to find her long-indifferent mother in Arizona. Kit (Zoe Saldana) wants to find her fiancé in Los Angeles; he has become ominously vague about wedding plans. Mimi (Taryn Manning) is pregnant, but wants to compete in a record company's open audition. Spoiler warning! Stop reading now unless you want to learn the dismal outcome of their trip, as Lucy's mom informs her she was a "mistake," Kit's fiancé turns out to have another woman *and* to be guilty of date rape, and Mimi, who was the rape victim, has a miscarriage.

I'm not kidding. *Crossroads*, which is being promoted with ads showing Britney bouncing on the bed while lip-synching a song, is a downer that would be even more depressing if the plot wasn't such a lame soap opera.

This is the kind of movie where the travelers stop by the roadside to yell "Hello!" and keep on yelling, unaware that there is no echo. Where Britney is a virgin at eighteen and enlists her lab partner to deflower her. Where when that doesn't work out she finds herself attracted to Ben (Anson Mount), the guy who's giving them the ride, even though he is alleged to have

killed a man. Where the apparent age difference between Spears and Mount makes it look like he's robbing the cradle. (In real life, he's twenty-nine and she's twenty, but he's an experienced twenty-nine and she's playing a naive eighteen-year-old.)

Of the three girls, Mimi has the most to do. She teaches Kit how to land a punch, tells the others why she doesn't drink, and deals almost casually with her miscarriage. Kit is a slow study who takes forever to figure out her fiancé has dumped her. And Spears, as Lucy, seems to think maybe she's in a serious Winona Ryder role, but with songs.

"What are you writing in that book?" Ben asks her. "Poems," she says. He wants her to read one for him. She does. "Promise not to laugh," she says. He doesn't, but the audience does. It's the lyrics for her song "I'm Not a Girl, Not Yet a Woman." Didn't anyone warn her you can't introduce famous material as if it's new without risking a bad laugh? Later, Ben composes music for the words, and he plays the piano while she riffs endlessly to prove she has never once thought about singing those words before.

The movie cuts away from the payoffs of the big scenes. We get the foreplay for both of Britney's sex scenes, but never see what happens. Her big meeting with her mother lacks the showdown. We can be grateful, I suppose, that after Mimi falls down some stairs after learning that Kit's fiancé is the man who raped her, we are spared the details of her miscarriage and cut to her later in the hospital. Perhaps study of the live childbirth scene in the Spice Girls movie warned the filmmakers away from obstetric adventures in this one.

Like *Coyote Ugly*, a movie it resembles in the wardrobe department, *Crossroads* is rated PG-13 but is going on 17. Caution, kids: It can be more dangerous to get a ride in a convertible with a cute but ominous guy than you might think (see *Kalifornia*).

And you can't always support yourself by tips on Karaoke Night. When the girls sing in a karaoke contest, a three-gallon jug is filled with bills which, after they're piled in stacks on the bar, are enough to pay for car repairs and the rest of the trip. Uh-huh. Curious thing about that karaoke bar: It has a position on the stage with an underlight and one of those poles that strippers twine around. You don't see those much in karaoke clubs.

Crouching Tiger, Hidden Dragon ★ ★ ★ ★
PG-13, 119 m., 2000

Chow Yun Fat (Li Mu Bai), Michelle Yeoh (Yu Shu Lien), Zhang Ziyi (Jen Yu), Chang Chen (Lo), Lung Sihung (Sir Te), Cheng Pei Pei (Jade Fox), Li Fa Zeng (Governor Yu), Gao Xian (Bo). Directed by Ang Lee and produced by Bill Kong, Hsu Li Kong, and Lee. Screenplay by James Schamus, Wang Hui Ling, and Tsai Kuo Jung, based on the novel by Wang Du Lu.

The best martial arts movies have nothing to do with fighting and everything to do with personal excellence. Their heroes transcend space, gravity, the limitations of the body, and the fears of the mind. In a fight scene in a Western movie, it is assumed the fighters hate each other. In a martial arts movie, it's more as if the fighters are joining in a celebration of their powers.

To be sure, people get killed, but they are either characters who have misused their powers, or anonymous lackeys of the villain. When the hero stands in the center of a ring of interchangeable opponents and destroys them one after another, it's like a victory for the individual over collectivism—a message not lost in the Asian nations where these movies are most loved. The popularity of strong heroines is also interesting in those patriarchal societies.

Ang Lee's Crouching Tiger, Hidden Dragon is the most exhilarating martial arts movie I have seen. It stirred even the hardened audience at the 8:30 A.M. press screening at Cannes. There is a sequence near the beginning of the film involving a chase over rooftops, and as the characters run up the sides of walls and leap impossibly from one house to another, the critics applauded, something they rarely do during a film, and I think they were relating to the sheer physical grace of the scene. It is done so lightly, quickly, easily.

Fight scenes in a martial arts movie are like song-and-dance numbers in a musical: After a certain amount of dialogue, you're ready for one. The choreography of the action scenes in Crouching Tiger was designed by Yuen Wo-Ping, whose credits include The Matrix, and who understands that form is more important than function. It's not who wins that matters (except to the plot, of course); it's who looks most masterful.

There's also a competition to find unlikely settings for martial arts scenes. In Legend of Drunken Master, the recently rereleased Jackie Chan movie, a bed of glowing coals is suspended in the air next to an elevated factory railway. Why? So Chan can fall into them. In Crouching Tiger, Hidden Dragon, Ang Lee and Yuen Wo-Ping give us a scene of startling daring and beauty when two protagonists cling to the tops of tall, swaying trees and swing back and forth during a swordfight.

Watching this scene, I assumed it was being done with some kind of computer trickery. I "knew" this because I "knew" the actors were not really forty feet in the air holding onto those trees. I was wrong. Everything we see is real, Lee told me. Computers were used only to remove the safety wires that held the actors. "So those were stunt people up there?" I asked, trying to hold onto some reserve of skepticism. "Not for the most part," he said. "Maybe a little stunt work, but most of the time you can see their faces. That's really them in the trees." And on the rooftops too, he told me.

The film stars Chow Yun Fat and Michelle Yeoh—she a veteran martial arts star who has extraordinary athletic abilities (as Jackie Chan and many of the other stars of the genre also do). Two other key characters are played by Zhang Ziyi (as Jen Yu) and Cheng Pei Pei (as Jade Fox). Long rehearsal and training went into their scenes, but what's unusual about Crouching Tiger, Hidden Dragon is the depth and poetry of the connecting story, which is not just a clothesline for action scenes, but has a moody, romantic, and even spiritual nature.

The story involves Li Mu Bai (Chow Yun Fat), a warrior who has vowed to avenge the death of his master. He has for many years been in love with Yu Shu Lien (Michelle Yeoh), and she with him, but their personal feelings wait upon vengeance and upon their attempts to recapture Green Destiny, a sword that once

141

belonged to Li Mu Bai's master. That brings Yu Shu Lien into contact with the governor's daughter, Jen Yu (Zhang Ziyi), who has a secret I will leave you to discover. The other major character, Jade Fox (Cheng Pei Pei), stands between the heroes and their dreams.

This story, like all martial arts stories, is at some level just plain silly, but Ang Lee *(The Ice Storm, Sense and Sensibility)* and his longtime collaborator James Shamus (who wrote the screenplay with Wang Hui Ling and Tsai Kuo Jung) are unusually successful in bringing out the human elements, especially the unrealized love between the Chou Yun Fat and Michelle Yeoh characters. There are times when they're together that you forget about the swords and are just watching a man and a woman, tenderly cherishing the unspoken bond between them. Zhang Ziyi's character, the governor's daughter, is also intriguing because she chafes at the rules that limit her and realizes a secret fantasy life.

There are those, I know, who will never go to a martial arts movie, just as some people hate Westerns and Jack Warner once told his producers, "Don't make me any more movies where the people write with feathers." But like all ambitious movies, *Crouching Tiger, Hidden Dragon* transcends its origins and becomes one of a kind. It's glorious, unashamed escapism, and surprisingly touching at the same time. And they're really up there in those trees.

Croupier ★ ★ ★
NO MPAA RATING, 91 m., 2000

Clive Owen (Jack Manfred), Kate Hardie (Bella), Alex Kingston (Jani de Villiers), Gina McKee (Marion), Nicholas Ball (Jack's Father). Directed by Mike Hodges and produced by Jonathan Cavendish. Screenplay by Paul Mayersberg.

You have to make a choice in life: Be a gambler or a croupier.

So believes Jack Manfred, the hero of *Croupier*, whose casino job places him halfway between the bosses and the bettors, so he can keep an eye on both. He is a cold, controlled man, at pains to tell us, "I do not gamble." True enough, he does not gamble at casino games of chance,

but in his personal life he places appalling bets, and by the end of the film is involved with three women and a scheme to defraud the casino.

Manfred (Clive Owen) wants to be a writer, and narrates his own story in the third person, as if he's writing it. With his slicked-back black hair, symmetrical good looks, and cold detachment, he's a reminder of Alain Delon's professional killer in *Le Samourai*—a man who wants to stay aloof and calculate the odds, but finds himself up to the neck in trouble anyway. There's the hint that this is a pattern, and that at one time he did gamble, obsessively.

The key figure in Jack's life is his father (Nicholas Ball), who was indeed a gambler, a Jack-the-lad who womanized, drank, gambled, and ran roughshod over Jack's early years. Jack's secret is that his hard, calculating facade has been hammered together as a shield over the little boy inside.

Jack's father, now in South Africa, lines up a job for him at the roulette wheels of a London casino. Jack never gambles, but he does deal, and is a skilled card manipulator (we imagine his dad teaching the boy to shuffle). The movie knows its way around casinos, and particularly observes how the dealers, with their strange hours and surreal jobs, tend to date each other instead of outsiders ("incest," the screenplay calls it). He observes dispassionately as punters line up to try their luck, and the movie notices what complete indifference the dealers have for their clients: Whether they win or lose, the work shift is exactly as long.

Jack has a girlfriend named Marion (Gina McKee), who is a store detective. "I want to marry a writer, not a (bleeping) croupier," she tells him. During the course of the story he also has liaisons with a dealer named Bella (Kate Hardie) who works on his shift. And he meets the glamorous Jani de Villiers (Alex Kingston), a casino client from South Africa— wild, reckless, in debt, a sexual predator who wants to hook him on a scheme to cheat the casino. Jack is just detached enough from his job, just enough of a mechanic intrigued by the intricacies of the plot, to be interested.

The movie was directed by Mike Hodges, whose *Get Carter* (1971) is one of the best of the hard-boiled British crime movies. It was written by Paul Mayersburg (*The Man Who Fell to Earth, Eureka*), who must have done his research, since the casino scenes feel real: This isn't an unconvincing movie casino (even though it was built on a set in Germany), but a convincing portrayal of one of those smaller London operations where the plush and the gilt and the tuxedos on the gorillas at the door don't quite cover the tarnish.

The plot is more than we bargained for. I will not hint at the details, which lead to an unexpected and satisfactory but not entirely convincing ending. The point of the movie is not the plot but the character and the atmosphere; Hodges is bemused by Jack Manfred, who thinks he can stand outside his own life, control it, figure the odds, and turn it into a novel.

The choice of Clive Owen as the star is a good one. He's got the same sort of physical reserve as Sean Connery in the *Bond* pictures; he doesn't give himself wholly to the action, but seems to be keeping a part of his mind outside of it, measuring and calculating. This is not just a strategy but essential to his personality. We sense that his father had a way of catching him off balance, and that he vowed that when he grew up he would never be fooled again. If he ever did grow up.

Crush ★ ★ ★
R, 115 m., 2002

Andie MacDowell (Kate), Imelda Staunton (Janine), Anna Chancellor (Molly), Kenny Doughty (Jed), Bill Paterson (Rev. Gerald Farquar-Marsden). Directed by John McKay and produced by Lee Thomas. Screenplay by McKay.

If I were reviewing *Crush* in England, I would work the name of Joanna Trollope into the first sentence, and my readers would immediately be able to identify the terrain. Trollope, a best-seller who is often quite perceptive and touching, writes at the upper range of the category just below serious fiction. She is a good read for those, like myself, who fantasize about living prosperously in the Cotswolds in an old but comfortably remodeled cottage not far from the village green, the churchyard, the tea shop, the bookstore, and the rail line to London, while growing involved in a web of imprudent adulterous sex. (As a happily married man, you understand, I do not want to *perform* adulterous imprudent sex, only to be involved in a web with such entertaining neighbors.)

This is not England. Few North Americans read Joanna Trollope, and fewer still respond to key words in her vocabulary such as "Aga." An Aga cookstove is so expensive and versatile it does everything but peel the potatoes, and its presence in a kitchen tells you so much about the occupants that in the Brit book review pages, the phrase "Aga romance" perfectly categorizes a novel.

Crush is an Aga romance crossed with modern retro-feminist soft porn, in which liberated women discuss lust as if it were a topic and not a fact. We begin by meeting the three heroines, who are forty-something professionals who meet once a week to (1) drink gin, (2) smoke cigarettes, (3) eat caramels, and (4) discuss their lousy love lives. My advice to these women: stop after (3).

The characters: Kate (Andie MacDowell) is the American headmistress of the local upscale school, Janine (Imelda Staunton) is a physician, and Molly (Anna Chancellor) is the police chief. That these three professional women at their age would all still be smoking can be explained only by a movie that does not give them enough to do with their hands. One day Kate goes to a funeral, is immeasurably moved by the music, and meets the organist. His name is Jed (Kenny Doughty), and he was once a student of hers. She is between fifteen and eighteen years older, but their conversation drifts out of the church and into the churchyard, and soon they are performing the old rumpy-pumpy behind a tombstone while the mourners are still stifling their sobs.

This is, you will agree, an example of lust. In a rabbit, it would be simple lust. In a headmistress, it is reckless lust. (In a twenty-five-year-old organist, it is what comes from pumping the foot pedals for thirty minutes while observing Andie MacDowell.) The movie cannot leave it at lust, however, because then it would be a different movie. So it elevates it into a Love That Was Meant to Be, in which the two lovers overcome differences of age, class, and grooming, and determine to spend their lives together. Because they are attractive people and we like them, of course we identify with their foolishness and feel good when romance triumphs.

A sixth sense tells us, however, that romance has triumphed a little too early in the movie. The only way for *Crush* to get from its romantic triumph to the end of the film is to supply setbacks, and does it ever. I will not reveal what episodes of bad judgment, bad karma, and plain bad luck lead to the ultimate bittersweet denouement, and will distract myself from the temptation by telling you that the pastor of the local church is named the Rev. Gerald Farquar-Marsden, a name to rival Catsmeat Potter-Pirbright.

The movie does its best to work us over, with second helpings of love, romance, tragedy, false dawns, real dawns, comic relief, two separate crises during marriage ceremonies, and the lush scenery of the Cotswolds (or, as the Website refers to the district, "Cotswold"). It's the kind of world where romance begins in tombs among the headstones, or vice versa, and almost immediately requires engraved invitations. Jed is described as being twenty-five years old and Kate is described as being forty "cough," but Andie MacDowell is the definition of a dish, and Jed, just by being a church organist, is mature for his age. Besides, what is an age difference of fifteen or even eighteen years when my old friend Betty Dodson, at seventy-two, is in the third year of a steamy romance with a twenty-five-year-old? You can look it up at Salon.com, under "sex."

The Cup ★ ★ ★
G, 94 m., 2000

Orgyen Tobgyal (Geko), Neten Chokling (Lodo), Jamyang Lodro (Orgyen), Lama Chonjor (Abbot), Godu Lama (Old Lama), Thinley Nudi (Tibetan Layman), Kunsang (Cook Monk), Kunsang Nyima (Palden), Pema Tshundup (Nyima), Dzigar Kongtrul (Vajra Master). Directed by Khyentse Norbu and produced by Malcolm Watson and Raymond Steiner. Screenplay by Norbu.

In the courtyard of their monastery, dressed in traditional robes, their heads shaven, young monks play a game of soccer, kicking around a Coke can. This image, near the beginning of

The Cup, symbolizes its cheerful truce between the sacred and the mundane. The movie is a lighthearted comedy with serious undertones about the Chinese campaign against the traditions of Tibet.

The film takes place at a Tibetan monastery in exile in India, which from time to time receives Tibetan children whose parents have smuggled them past the border guards so that they can be raised in the ancient Buddhist teachings. And so they are, in a monastery which seems a little like any boarding school for irrepressible kids. "We shave our heads so that girls will not find us attractive," one explains to another, sighing that it doesn't work in the opposite direction.

The monastery is overseen by an abbot (Lama Chonjor), who is old and holy and deep and revered, and human, with a twinkle in his eye. He knows that the ancient ways in which he was raised are now in collision with the modern world, and so he is not altogether astonished when a fourteen-year-old student named Orgyen (Jamyang Lodro) stirs up desire among his fellow students to watch the World Cup finals on TV.

Why is this match so important? Because the World Cup itself is an obsession for most males in most of the world, of course, but especially because the final is between France and Brazil, "and France supports the cause of Tibet."

The abbot's assistant (Orgyen Tobgyal) is not an unreasonable man, and agrees to take the request to the holy man, who after due thought agrees. But official permission is only the first of many hurdles for the young monks, who now must raise the money to rent a television set and a satellite dish, and transport both to the monastery. Their attempts are told against a backdrop of daily life and human (and sacred) comedy in the monastery.

In addition to the Coke can, we see a lot of soccer magazines, studied by the students at least as intently as their sacred texts. And we get a real sense for these monks as human beings whose calling does not set them aside from contemporary society so much as give them a distinctive position in it. Often Tibetan monks are portrayed in the movies as distant and almost inhuman: automatons of worship. These are men and boys for whom

Buddhism is a religion, a calling, a profession, and a reasonable way to live. Perhaps Westerners are too much in awe of the spirituality they encounter, and it took an insider to see the humanity involved.

The Cup, which is the first feature film ever made in Bhutan, was directed by Khyentse Norbu, a lama who must have learned a lot about filmmaking while serving as Bernardo Bertolucci's assistant during the filming of *Little Buddha*. The film has a distinctly Western feel in its timing and character development; it's not an inaccessible exercise in impenetrable mysteries, but a delightful demonstration of how spirituality can coexist quite happily with an intense desire for France to defeat Brazil.

The movie was a runner-up for the Audience Award at the Toronto Film Festival in 1999, and was also a hit at Sundance in 2000, where I met Khyentse Norbu, and was struck by his poise and a certain distance he kept from those around him; his body language seemed to suggest he was interested in more evolved questions than what films Miramax was picking up. Then I learned that in addition to being a lama and a director, he is also considered to be the incarnation of the nineteenth-century saint Jamyang Khyentse Wangpo. And I thought: Of course. So many sinners have directed films that it is only fair for a saint to have a chance.

The Curse of the Jade Scorpion ★ ★ ½
PG-13, 103 m., 2001

Woody Allen (C. W. Briggs), Dan Aykroyd (Chris Magruder), Elizabeth Berkley (Jill), Helen Hunt (Betty Ann Fitzgerald), Brian Markinson (Al), Wallace Shawn (George Bond), David Ogden Stiers (Voltan), Charlize Theron (Laura Kensington). Directed by Woody Allen and produced by Letty Aronson. Screenplay by Allen.

Woody Allen's *The Curse of the Jade Scorpion* takes place in an insurance office not unlike the one in *Double Indemnity*, where the very woodwork and the reassuring bulk of the filing cabinets seem to guarantee the company's solidity. But after the company's fraud investigator and its efficiency expert are hypnotized by a nightclub charlatan, none of the company's clients are safe.

In *Double Indemnity*, Billy Wilder's classic *noir*, Fred MacMurray was an investigator who betrayed his company after a slinky seductress (Barbara Stanwyck) lured him into a scheme to murder her husband for profit. The comic angle in Allen's approach is that C. W. Briggs, the investigator (Allen himself), is an obsessive-compulsive perfectionist, and the slinky sex bomb, Betty Ann Fitzgerald (Helen Hunt), is his archenemy (although that doesn't discourage him from asking her out). When "Fitz" has her wits about her, she describes C.W. with an impressive array of insults ("mealymouthed little creep," "inchworm," "snoopy little termite," "squirming little trapped rat"). They hate each other. "I love where you live," she tells him. "A grimy little rat hole. I find it strangely exciting standing here in a grungy hovel with a myopic insurance investigator." Then the hypnotic trigger is pulled, and they think they're in love.

To this inspiration Allen adds another; they have separate cue words, so that one can be under the hypnotic spell while the other isn't. And then he surrounds them with dependable comic types. Dan Aykroyd is Magruder, the cost-cutting boss who has brought in Fitz. Elizabeth Berkley is Jill, the curvy secretary he's having an affair with. And Charlize Theron is Laura Kensington, a rich kid who is attracted to C.W. when she catches him in midtheft, but is helpless in the face of the hypnotic depth bomb.

David Ogden Stiers plays Voltan the hypnotist, a great convenience to the story, because all he has to do is telephone C.W., utter a magic word into the telephone, and order him to do whatever he wishes—in this case, to break into houses C.W. himself has burglar-proofed, and steal precious diamonds.

All of this sounds like the setup for a wicked screwball comedy, but somehow *Curse of the Jade Scorpion* never quite lifts off. The elements are here, but not the magic. There are lines that you can see are intended to be funny, but they lack the usual Allen zing. Allen is as always a master of the labyrinthine plot (his characters turn up in the wrong place at the right time, and vice versa, with inexhaustible ingenuity), but we never much care how things turn out.

That said, there are pleasures in the film that have little to do with the story. Its look and feel are uncanny; it's a tribute to a black-and-white era, filmed in color, and yet the colors seem burnished and aged. No *noir* films were shot in color in the 1940s, but if one had been, it would have looked like this. And great attention is given to the women played by Hunt, Berkley, and Theron; they look not so much like the women in classic *film noir* as like the women on *film noir* posters—their costumes and styles elevate them into archetypes. Hunt in particular has fun with a wisecracking dame role that owes something, perhaps, to Rosalind Russell in *His Girl Friday.*

Woody Allen's characters depend on self-deprecating, double-reverse ironic wit for their appeal, and C.W. doesn't seem to have an infallible ear for it. (Example: He says that she went to Harvard but he went to driving school; that's first-level and Allen usually gets to second or third.) He should be invulnerable in a verbal exchange, but here sometimes he seems brought to a halt by Fitz. He's funny in the nightclub hypnosis scene, when he slumps like a puppet with loose strings, but later he seems wide of the target. The movie is a pleasure to watch, the craft is voluptuous to regard, but *The Curse of the Jade Scorpion* lacks the elusive zing of inspiration.

Note: The two hypnotic triggers are "Madagascar" and "Constantinople." Did Allen miss comic opportunity by not making them "Istanbul" and "Constantinople"? Like all of his films, Jade Scorpion *is scored with jazz and pop classics of the period, and I imagine a scene where C.W. and Fitz both hear the famous song "Istanbul (not Constantinople)," and are inadvertently launched into loveland without the participation of Voltan.*

CyberWorld 3D ★ ★ ★

NO MPAA RATING, 48 m., 2000

With the voices of: Jenna Elfman (Phig), Matt Frewer (Frazzled), Robert Smith (Buzzed, Wired), Dave Foley (Hank the Technician). An animated film with material from several sources. Linking sequences directed by Colin Davies and Elaine Despins. Produced by Steve Hoban and Hugh Murray. Screenplay by Charlie Rubin, Hoban, and Murray.

CyberWorld 3D, shown in the giant-screen IMAX format, is remarkable not only for what it shows us, but for the wider world of 3-D animation it predicts. It looks better than most other 3-D films I've seen—clearer, brighter, more convincing. And it uses new software and technology to take existing flat animation, from such sources as the movie *Antz* and *The Simpsons* TV show, and process it into convincing 3-D.

This is not a makeshift transfer, but a fundamental reuse of the original material; everything in this movie looks made from scratch for 3-D, even though only about half of it really was. What the movie is telling us is that many animated films can be reconfigured into 3-D while retaining the elements of drawing and visual style that made them distinctive in the first place (indeed, *Shrek,* a 2001 animated feature from DreamWorks, will be retrofitted for the IMAX 3-D screen after its conventional theatrical run).

Like the recent retread of Disney's *Fantasia 2000* and earlier IMAX 3-D efforts, *CyberWorld 3D* takes advantage of the squarish six-story screen to envelop us in the images; the edges of the frame don't have the same kind of distracting cutoff power they possess in the smaller rectangles of conventional theaters. Then IMAX adds its custom-made headsets, which flicker imperceptibly so we see first out of one eye, then the other, while tiny speakers next to our ears enhance the reality of the surround sound. I have been watching 3-D since *Bwana Devil* (1952), and not until I saw it in IMAX did I consider it anything other than a shabby gimmick.

How does *CyberWorld 3D* take a 2-D source like *The Simpsons* TV show and convert it into 3-D? With animation, it's more direct than it seems. Begin with the fundamental method of 3-D, which is to shoot each image twice, with cameras spaced slightly apart, just as our eyes are. Project both images on the screen, and view them through glasses that create the illusion they are one 3-D image instead of (take the glasses off) two slightly out-of-register 2-D images. Our eye-mind system is tricked by the stereoscopic illusion into reading the two flat images as one image with depth.

Now move on to the building blocks of animation. While live action's POV resides in the camera, animation has a virtual camera—

the point of view supplied by the animator. Using new software developed by Intel and IMAX, filmmakers are able to break the animation materials down into separate elements and reshoot them, in a sense, from two points of view, allowing the separation necessary for 3-D. It's more complicated than that, but the effect is astonishing.

More than one kind of animation is used in *CyberWorld 3D*. The separate self-contained segments are animated with the new system, which takes existing film and gives it three dimensions. They float within a linking story that has been done with conventional computer-generated 3-D. This story stars a sprightly young girl named Phig (voice by Jenna Elfman), who takes us on a tour of a vast, high-tech virtual space where the individual segments seem to reside inside self-contained modules. Open one portal and find the Simpsons; open another, and find a thrilling futuristic city with sky trains, and so on.

Phig, meanwhile, is harassed by three cyber nuisances named Frazzled (voice by Matt Frewer), Buzzed (Robert Smith), and Hank the Technician (Dave Foley). This linking story is as inane as IMAX can make it; there's an unwritten rule that the hosts or other narrative devices of IMAX films condescend to the audience. Phig is shallow and silly, but she does at least figure in some wondrous animation, as when she glides through the interior space, has a vertiginous fall, and eventually journeys down a black hole.

CyberWorld 3D gathers several impressive stand-alone works of animation; to describe every one would be beside the point. It's more of a demo than a stand-alone work, and lacks even the unifying concept of *Fantasia 2000*. No matter; the point is to show us what can be done with recycled traditional animation in the IMAX 3-D process, and the demonstration is impressive. I'm looking forward to the IMAX version of *Shrek* and, eventually, classics like *Snow White and the Seven Dwarfs*. The only animation that's probably IMAX-proof is *South Park*, which is 2-D and proud of it.

D

Dancer in the Dark ★ ★ ★ ½
R, 160 m., 2000

Bjork (Selma), Catherine Deneuve (Kathy),
David Morse (Bill), Peter Stormare (Jeff),
Joel Grey (Oldrich Novy), Vincent Paterson
(Samuel), Cara Seymour (Linda), Jean-Marc
Barr (Norman). Directed by Lars von Trier
and produced by Vibeke Windelov.
Screenplay by von Trier.

Some reasonable people will admire Lars von Trier's *Dancer in the Dark,* and others will despise it. An excellent case can be made for both positions.

The film stars Bjork, the Icelandic pop star, as Selma, a Czech who has immigrated to America, has a small son, works as a punch-press operator, is going blind, and is saving her money for an operation to prevent her son from going blind too. To supplement her income she fastens straight pins to cards for a fraction of a penny per card. She keeps her money in a candy box. If I told you the movie was set in 1912 and starred Lillian Gish, you might not have the slightest difficulty in accepting this plot; whether you would like it, of course, would depend on whether you could make the leap of sympathy into the world of silent melodrama.

But the movie is set not in 1912 but in 1964. People still went blind, but plots had grown more sophisticated by then—and even more so by 2000, when this film won the Cannes Film Festival. Since it is impossible to take the plot seriously on any literal level, it must be approached, I think, as a deliberate exercise in soap opera. It is valid to dislike it, but not fair to criticize it on the grounds of plausibility, because the movie has made a deliberate decision to be implausible: The plot is not a mistake but a choice.

Bjork and her son live in a house trailer behind the home of Bill, a local cop (David Morse), who is in thrall to his materialistic wife. He earns, she spends. She thinks he has a big inheritance, and "it makes her proud," he confides in Bjork, to see him visiting his safety deposit box. In fact, the box is empty. The cop likes or loves Bjork or something (he is too gormless to be sure), but betrays her trust. This leads to a deadly confrontation between them, which is stretched out like one of those silent scenes where a victim staggers, speaks, staggers, speaks some more, falls down, curses the fates, tries to climb up, laments, falls over again, etc. Either you see this for what it is, von Trier deliberately going for effect, or it seems silly. Maybe it seems silly anyway, but you can admire his nerve.

Selma is followed everywhere by Jeff (Peter Stormare, from the chipper scene in *Fargo*). He wants to be her boyfriend. She's not looking for a boyfriend right now. It is important to note that both Selma and Jeff are simple-minded. Today we would call them retarded; in 1912 they would have been about as smart as many characters in melodrama. Selma also has a good friend named Kathy (Catherine Deneuve—yes, Catherine Deneuve), who figures out Selma is going blind and wants to help her but is defeated by her stubbornness.

The movie begins with Selma rehearsing for a leading role in a local production of *The Sound of Music.* It is interrupted by several song-and-dance numbers. Most of the film is shot in fairly drab digital video, but the musical numbers have brighter colors. They're set in locales like the factory floor and a railroad bridge. Against their jolly notes must be set the remarkably graphic death that closes the movie.

The first press screening at Cannes was at 8:30 A.M. That's the screening where all the real movie people attend—the critics, festival heads, distributors, exhibitors, film teachers, other directors, etc. (the evening black-tie audience is far more philistine). After the screening, the auditorium filled with booing and cheering—so equal in measure that people started booing or cheering *at* one another.

I sat in my seat, ready to cheer or boo when I made up my mind. I let the movie marinate, and saw it again, and was able to see what von Trier is trying to do. Having made a "vow of chastity" with his famous Dogma 95 statement, which calls for films to be made more simply with handheld cameras and available light, he is now divesting himself of modern fashions in plotting. *Dancer in the Dark* is a brave throwback to the fundamentals of the cinema—to heroines and villains, noble sacrifices and dastardly betrayals. The relatively crude visual look underlines the movie's abandonment of slick modernism.

Dancer in the Dark is not like any other movie at the multiplex this week, or this year. It is not a "well-made film," is not in "good taste," is not "plausible" or, for many people, "entertaining." But it smashes down the walls of habit which surround so many movies. It returns to the wellsprings. It is a bold, reckless gesture. And since Bjork has announced she will never make another movie, it is a good thing she sings.

The Dangerous Lives of Altar Boys ★ ★ ½
R, 105 m., 2002

Kieran Culkin (Tim Sullivan), Jena Malone (Margie Flynn), Emile Hirsch (Francis Doyle), Vincent D'Onofrio (Father Casey), Jodie Foster (Sister Assumpta), Jake Richardson (Wade), Tyler Long (Joey Scalisi). Directed by Peter Care and produced by Meg LeFauve, Jay Shapiro, and Jodie Foster. Screenplay by Jeff Stockwell, based on the book by Chris Furhman.

There were times when *The Dangerous Lives of Altar Boys* evoked memories of my own Catholic school days—not to confirm the film, but to question it. There is a way in which the movie accurately paints its young heroes, obsessed with sex, rebellion, and adolescence, and too many other times when it pushes too far, making us aware of a screenplay reaching for effect. The climax is so reckless and absurd that we can't feel any of the emotions that are intended.

Yet this is an honorable film with good intentions. Set in a small town in the 1970s, it tells the story of good friends at St. Agatha's School, who squirm under the thumb of the strict Sister Assumpta (Jodie Foster) and devise elaborate plots as a rebellion against her. At the same time, the kids are growing up, experimenting with smoking and drinking, and learning more about sex than they really want to know.

The heroes are Tim Sullivan (Kieran Culkin) and Francis Doyle (Emile Hirsch). We look mostly through Francis's eyes, as the boys and two friends weave a fantasy world out of a comic book they collaborate on called *The Atomic Trinity,* with characters like Captain Asskicker and easily recognized caricatures of Sister Assumpta and Father Casey (Vincent D'Onofrio), the distracted, chain-smoking pastor and soccer coach who seems too moony to be a priest.

The movie has a daring strategy for representing the adventures of the Trinity: It cuts to animated sequences (directed by Todd McFarlane) that cross the everyday complaints and resentments of the authors with the sort of glorified myth-making and superhero manufacture typical of Marvel comics of the period. (These sequences are so well animated, with such visual flair and energy, that the jerk back to the reality sequences can be a little disconcerting.) The villainess in the book is Sister Nunzilla, based on Sister Assumpta right down to her artificial leg.

Does the poor sister deserve this treatment? The film argues that she does not, but is unconvincing. Sister Assumpta is very strict, but we are meant to understand that she really likes and cares for her students. This is conveyed in some of Jodie Foster's acting choices, but has no payoff, because the kids apparently don't see the same benevolent expressions we sometimes glimpse. If they are not going to learn anything about Sister Assumpta's gentler side, then why must we?

The kids are supposed to be typical young adolescents, but they're so rebellious, reckless, and creative that we sense the screenplay nudging them. Francis feels the stirrings of lust and (more dangerous) idealistic love inspired by his classmate Margie Flynn (Jena Malone), and they have one of those first kisses that makes you smile. Then she shares a family secret that is, I think, a little too heavy for this film to support, and creates a dark cloud over all that follows.

If the secret is too weighty, so is the ending. The boys have been engaged in an escalating series of pranks, and their final one, involving plans to kidnap a cougar from the zoo and transport it to Sister Assumpta's living quarters, is too dumb and dangerous for anyone, including these kids, to contemplate. Their previous stunt was to steal a huge statue of St. Agatha from a niche high on the facade of the school building, and this seems about as far as they should go. The cougar business is trying too hard, and leads to an ending that doesn't earn its emotional payoff.

Another hint of the overachieving screenplay is the running theme of the boys' fascination with William Blake's books *Songs of Innocence* and *Songs of Experience*. I can believe that boys of this age could admire Blake, but not these boys. And I cannot believe that Sister Assumpta would consider Blake a danger. What we sense here is the writer, Jeff Stockwell, sneaking in material he likes even though it doesn't pay its way. (There's one other cultural reference in the movie, unless I'm seeing it where none was intended: Early in the film, the boys blow up a telephone pole in order to calculate when it will fall, and they stand just inches into the safe zone. I was reminded of Buster Keaton, standing so that when a wall fell on him, he was in the exact outline of an open window.)

The movie has qualities that cannot be denied. Jena Malone *(Donnie Darko, Life as a House)* has a solemnity and self-knowledge that seems almost to stand outside the film. She represents the gathering weather of adulthood. The boys are fresh and enthusiastic, and we remember how kids can share passionate enthusiasms; the animated sequences perfectly capture the energy of their imaginary comic book. Vincent D'Onofrio muses through the film on his own wavelength, making of Father Casey a man who means well but has little idea what meaning well would consist of. If the film had been less extreme in the adventures of its heroes, more willing to settle for plausible forms of rebellion, that might have worked. It tries too hard, and overreaches the logic of its own world.

Note: The movie is rated R, consistent with the policy of the flywheels at the MPAA that any movie involving the intelligent treatment of teenagers must be declared off-limits for them.

Dark Blue World ★ ★

R, 114 m., 2002

Ondrej Vetchy (Franktisek Slama), Krystof Hadek (Karel Vojtisek), Tara Fitzgerald (Susan), Charles Dance (Colonel Bentley), Oldrich Kaiser (Machaty), Linda Rybova (Hanicka), Lukas Kantor (Tamtam), Hans-Jorg Assmann (Dr. Blaschke). Directed by Jan Sverak and produced by Eric Abraham and Jan Sverak. Screenplay by Zdenek Sverak.

Dark Blue World recycles some of the aerial combat footage shot for *Battle of Britain* (1969), and indeed, some of the same old-fashioned war movie clichés, like the faithful dog pining for its master. Told mostly in English, it's the story of two Czech pilots who escape their Nazi-occupied homeland, go to England, and enlist in the RAF to fight the Germans. Returning to Czechoslovakia after the war, one is rewarded for his pains by being jailed (exposure to British values might cause him to question communism). He finds that former S.S. men are his guards.

The Czech scenes are bookends for the heart of the story, which intercuts aerial dogfights with a love triangle in which both pilots have romances with the same English woman. Susan (Tara Fitzgerald) is minding a houseful of orphans in the countryside, and befriends Karel (Krystof Hadek). They fall in the wartime equivalent of love (her husband is missing in action), and Karel proudly introduces her to his friend Franktisek (Ondrej Vetch). Alas, not long after, he feels embittered and betrayed.

With *Pearl Harbor* fresh in my mind, here is yet another movie in which World War II supplies a backdrop for a love triangle. And not even a convincing, psychologically complex love triangle, but one imposed upon us by the requirements of the screenplay: The participants are attractive and sweet and we like them, but they get shuffled around for pragmatic reasons.

The aerial footage is good. It should be; in many cases, those are real planes, really in the air. Some of the shots come from the 1969 Harry Saltzman production, and well do I remember visiting a British airfield near Newmarket to see the actual Spitfires and other real planes purchased or rented for *Battle of Britain*. I even met Battle of Britain aces Douglas Bader, Ginger Lacey, and Group Captain Peter Townsend, although I inform you at this late date primarily because that old memory is more interesting than this movie.

The director, Jan Sverak, works from a screenplay by his father, Zdenek Sverak. They also made the splendid *Kolya* (1997), in which

Zdenek starred as an ideologically untrustworthy cellist who is bounced from the philharmonic, marries a woman to save her from being returned to Russia, and (when she skips town) ends up in an uneasy but eventually heartwarming relationship with her five-year-old son. *Kolya* was as emotionally authentic and original as *Dark Blue World* is derivative and not compelling.

The movie's open and close will be significant in Czechoslovakia, where communism turned out to be preferable only to Nazism, which isn't saying much. As the German doctor observes in the prison hospital: "I'll bet back in England you never thought they'd welcome you back with such a sad song."

Dark Days ★ ★ ★ ½
NO MPAA RATING, 84 m., 2000

A documentary directed and produced by Marc Singer.

"Nobody in his right mind would come down here," says one of the cave dwellers of *Dark Days*. That is the advantage of living in the railroad tunnels below New York City. You don't get attacked by kids, hassled by cops, or ripped off in homeless shelters. You're on your own.

Marc Singer's film shows an extraordinary world that exists below the streets of Manhattan. In the perpetual darkness of the tunnels, people make their homes. They build shacks out of cardboard and lumber, and fill them with furniture dragged down from above. Tapping into city lines, they have light and water, and many have stoves, refrigerators, and TV sets.

One thinks of documentaries about life at the bottom of the sea, where giant worms live in the warmth of sulfur vents. Life is opportunist and finds its way everywhere, and there is something Darwinian about these tunnel dwellers, who have found a niche where they can survive. They are not, they emphasize, "homeless."

Singer heard about the tunnel people on a news broadcast. He went looking for them, and then came back to film them. Eventually, making *Dark Days* became his obsession; he spent all of his money on it, until he was homeless. It is a film about people who have fallen through the cracks, but still share most of the same ambitions and hopes as the rest of us.

Many of the tunnel people keep cats to fight the rats. Others bait traps with lye. Rats and cold are the big problems, and having your stuff stolen. On the plus side, people look out for each other, and there is a guy named Tito who has become something of a cook: "Until I was in rehab, I never liked eggplant. Now it's the chef's special."

Some show Singer photos of their pets, but more rarely of their families. Old memories still hurt. One recalls his first hit of cocaine, and how much he liked it. "But I never got back to that first high. I made a mess of myself." His wife issued an ultimatum: the drugs, or me. He took the drugs.

Dee is a woman who also has a crack problem. She was in jail when she saw on TV that her two kids were burned in a fire. Now she lives in the tunnels. One of her neighbors has a chain-link enclosure for his dogs: "It's hard to keep a place clean with dogs," he observes.

The dwellers journey to the surface for food and treasure. "Kosher restaurants are the best," one says, "because the food isn't all mixed up with coffee grounds." They look for cans and bottles that can be redeemed. Sometimes they find things they can sell: "Gay porno is the best."

Watching this movie, I was reminded of George Orwell's *Down and Out in Paris and London,* his memoir of eighteen months spent living in abject poverty. What he learned, he said, was that tramps were not tramps out of choice, but necessity. Hard luck and bad decisions had led to worse luck and fewer choices, until they were stuck at the bottom. To call a homeless person lazy, he said, was ignorant, because the homeless must work ceaselessly just to stay alive. To tell them to get a job is a cruel joke, given their opportunities. *Dark Days* is the portrait of men and a few women who stubbornly try to maintain some dignity in the face of personal disaster. You could call them homemakers.

The Day I Became a Woman ★ ★ ★ ½
NO MPAA RATING, 78 m., 2001

Fatemeh Cheragh Akhtar (Hava [Young Girl]), Hassan Nabehan (Boy [Her Friend]), Shahrbanou Sisizadeh (Mother), Ameneh Pasand (Grandmother), Shabnam Toloui (Ahoo [Bicyclist]), Cyrus Kahouri Nejad (Ahoo's Husband), Mahram Zeinal Zadeh (Osman), Nourieh Mahiguirian (Rival Cyclist), Azizeh Seddighi (Hourfa [Old Woman]), Badr Irouni Nejad (Young Boy). Directed by Marziyeh Meshkini and produced by Makhmalbaf Film House. Screenplay by Mohsen Makhmalbaf. In Farsi with English subtitles.

The Day I Became a Woman links together three stories from Iran—the three ages of women—involving a girl on the edge of adolescence, a wife determined not to be ruled by her husband, and a wealthy widow who declares "whatever I never had, I will buy for myself now."

All three of the stories are told in direct and simple terms. They're so lacking in the psychological clutter of Western movies that at first we think they must be fables or allegories. And so they may be, but they are also perfectly plausible. Few things on the screen could not occur in everyday life. It is just that we're not used to seeing so much of the *rest* of everyday life left out.

The first story is about Hava, a girl on her ninth birthday. As a child she has played freely with her best friend, a boy. But on this day she must begin to wear the chador, the garment which protects her head and body from the sight of men. And she can no longer play with boys. Her transition to womanhood is scheduled for dawn, but her mother and grandmother give her a reprieve, until noon. They put an upright stick in the ground, and tell her that when its shadow disappears, her girlhood is over. She measures the shadow with her fingers, and shares a lollypop with her playmate.

The second episode begins with an image that first seems surrealistic, but has a pragmatic explanation. A group of women, all cloaked from head to toe in black, furiously pedal their bicycles down a road next to the sea. A ferocious man on horseback pursues one of the women, Ahoo, who is in the lead. This is a women's bicycle race, and Ahoo's husband does not want her to participate. He shouts at her, at first with solicitude (she should not pedal with her bad leg) and then with threats (a bike is "the devil's mount," and he will divorce her). She pedals on as the husband is joined by other family members, who finally stop her forcibly.

The third story begins like an episode from a silent comedy, as a young boy pushes a wheelchair containing an old woman, who is alert as a bird. She directs him into stores where she buys things—a refrigerator, a TV, tables and chairs—and soon she is at the head of a parade of boys pushing carts filled with consumer goods. We learn she inherited a lot of money and plans to spend it while she can, on all the things she couldn't buy while she was married. The scene concludes with a Felliniesque image I will not spoil for you; it is the film's one excursion out of the plausible and into the fantastic, but the story earns it.

The Day I Became a Woman is still more evidence of how healthy and alive the Iranian cinema is, even in a society we think of as closed. It was directed by Marziyeh Meshkini, and written by her husband, Mohsen Makhmalbaf (whose own *Gabbeh*, from 1996, found a story in the tapestry of a rug). It is a filmmaking family. Their daughter, Samira, directed *The Apple* in 1998, and last year her *Blackboards* was an official selection at Cannes (not bad for a twenty-year-old). Unlike the heroines of this film, the women of the Makhmalbaf family can think about the day they became directors. In fact, Iranian women have a good deal more personal freedom than the women of many other Islamic countries; the most dramatic contrast is with Afghanistan.

One of the strengths of this film is that it never pauses to explain, and the characters never have speeches to defend or justify themselves (the wife in the middle story just pedals harder). The little girl will miss her playmate, but trusts her mother and grandmother that she must, as they have, modestly shield herself from men who are not family members. Only the old grandmother, triumphantly heading her procession, seems free of the system—although she, too, has a habit of pulling her shawl forward over her head, long after any man could be seduced by her beauty; the gesture is like a reminder to herself that she is a woman and must play by the rules.

Death to Smoochy ½★

R, 105 m., 2002

Robin Williams (Rainbow Randolph), Edward Norton (Sheldon Mopes [Smoochy]), Danny DeVito (Burke), Jon Stewart (Stokes), Catherine Keener (Nora), Harvey Fierstein (Merv Green), Vincent Schiavelli (Buggy Ding Dong). Directed by Danny DeVito and produced by Andrew Lazar and Peter MacGregor-Scott. Screenplay by Adam Resnick.

Only enormously talented people could have made *Death to Smoochy.* Those with lesser gifts would have lacked the nerve to make a film so bad, so miscalculated, so lacking any connection with any possible audience. To make a film this awful, you have to have enormous ambition and confidence, and dream big dreams.

The movie, directed by Danny DeVito (!), is about two clowns. That violates a cardinal rule of modern mass entertainment, which is that everyone hates clowns almost as much as they hate mimes. (*Big Fat Liar,* a much better recent showbiz comedy, got this right. When the clown arrived at a birthday party, the kids joyfully shouted, "Hey, it's the clown! Let's hurt him!") Most clowns are simply tiresome (I exempt Bozo). There are, however, two dread categories of clowns: clowns who are secretly vile and evil, and clowns who are guileless and good. *Death to Smoochy* takes no half-measures, and provides us with one of each.

We begin with Rainbow Randolph, played by Robin Williams, an actor who should never, ever play a clown of any description, because the role writes a license for him to indulge in those very mannerisms he should be striving to purge from his repertoire. Rainbow is a corrupt drunk who takes bribes to put kids on his show. The show itself is what kiddie TV would look like if kids wanted to see an Ann Miller musical starring midgets.

The good clown is Smoochy (Edward Norton), a soul so cheerful, earnest, honest, and uncomplicated you want to slap him and bring him back to his senses. Sample helpful Smoochy song for kids: "My Stepdad's Not Bad, He's Just Adjusting." Both of these clowns wear the kinds of costumes seen at the openings of used-car lots in states that doubt the possibility of evolution. Rainbow is convoluted, but Smoochy is so boring that the film explains why, on a long bus ride, you should always choose to sit next to Mrs. Robinson, for example, rather than Benjamin.

Enter the film's most engaging character, a TV producer named Nora (Catherine Keener), who, like Rachel Griffiths, cannot play dumb and is smart enough never to try. She's taking instructions from the network boss (Jon Stewart, who might have been interesting as one of the clowns). They're trapped in an inane subplot involving two bad guys, Burke (DeVito) and Merv Green (played by the gravel-voiced Harvey Fierstein, who, as he puts on weight, is becoming boulder-voiced). There is also Vincent Schiavelli as a former child star, now a crackhead.

The drama of the two clowns and their battle for the time slot is complicated by Rainbow Randolph's attempts to smear Smoochy by tricking him into appearing at a neo-Nazi rally. One wonders idly: Are there enough neo-Nazis to fill a thundering convention center? Do they usually book clowns? The answer to the second question may be yes.

The movie ends by crossing an ice show with elements of *The Manchurian Candidate.* It involves an odd sexual predilection: Nora has a fetish for kiddie show hosts. It has a lesbian hit-squad leader with a thick Irish brogue. It uses four-letter language as if being paid by the word. In all the annals of the movies, few films have been this odd, inexplicable, and unpleasant

The Debut ★ ★ ★

NO MPAA RATING, 89 m., 2002

Dante Basco (Ben Mercado), Bernadette Balagtas (Rose Mercado), Tirso Cruz III (Roland Mercado), Gina Alajar (Gina Mercado), Eddie Garcia (Lolo Carlos), Joy Bisco (Annabelle), Darion Basco (Augusto), Dion Basco (Rommel), Fe de Los Reyes (Alice). Directed by Gene Cajayon and produced by Lisa Onodera. Screenplay by Cajayon and John Manal Castro.

There is a moment in *The Debut* where a white man, who has married into a Filipino-American family, solemnly informs a dinner party of Filipinos that they are "not considered Asians, but Malays." He doesn't realize how offensive and condescending it is for an outsider to tell people about themselves, but there is another reason to put the dialogue in this first-ever Filipino-American film: Most Americans don't know that. And now, knowing it, they don't know what a Malay is. And unless they've been in the Philippines, they don't have much idea of the heritage of the islands, where the cultures of the Pacific and Spain intersect with America. And they don't know that Tagalog is the national language, coexisting with English. And that the Philippine film industry is one of the few outside the United States and India to possess more than 50 percent of its own market.

Given the health of the film industry and the availability of English, it's surprising that it took so long for this first Filipino-American feature to be born. It joins a group of films about second-generation immigrants, standing between the traditions of their parents and their own headlong dive into American culture. *Maryam* is about an Iranian-American teenage girl in conflict with strict Iranian parents. *ABCD* and *American Desi* are about Indian-Americans. *Real Women Have Curves* is about a Mexican-American teenager whose mother opposes her college plans. *Bread and Roses* is about a Mexican-American strike leader whose sister opposes her. *Mi Familia* is a multi-generational story about Mexican-Americans, and *The Joy Luck Club* is a Chinese-American version. For that matter, *Stolen Summer* has an Irish-American dad who wants his son to follow him into the fire department instead of going to college.

The films have elements in common: A bright young person who dreams of personal fulfillment. Parents who worked hard to support their families in a new land, and now want to dictate the choices of their children. A father who is stern, a mother who is a mediator. And with surprising frequency, a stiff, unyielding older man, a grandfather or "sponsor," who is like the ghost at the family feast. The message of all of the movies: The older generation must bend and let the kids follow their dreams. That's not surprising, since the kids make the films, and all of these filmmakers must have had parents who thought they were crazy to dream of becoming movie directors. *The Debut* is familiar in its story arc, but fresh in its energy and lucky in its choice of ac-

tors. Filmed on a low budget, it looks and plays like an assured professional film, and its young leads are potential stars. The story involves a high school student named Ben Mercado (Dante Basco), who works in a comic-book store and in the opening scene is selling his comics collection to help pay his way into Cal Arts.

He wants to be a graphic artist. His father, Roland (Tirso Cruz III), a postman, has other plans for Ben, who has won a pre-med scholarship to UCLA. The boy will be a doctor, period. Everything comes to a head at the eighteenth birthday party of Ben's sister Rose (Bernadette Balagtas), the "debut" of the title.

Ben has assimilated by always keeping a certain distance between his friends and his family. His best buddies are an Anglo and a Mexican-American, who are curious about Ben's home life, but keep getting shuffled aside. When they mention the inviting cooking aromas, Ben takes that as a criticism of the way his home smells. On the night of Rose's party, Ben has made plans to meet a pretty Anglo girl at a high school party, and is torn between the two events (unlike his friends, who have more fun at Rose's party).

The movie involves some melodrama when Ben meets Rose's pretty Filipino-American friend Annabel (Joy Bisco) and it's love at first sight; Annabel is breaking up with a tough boyfriend who, in the modern equivalent of male possessiveness, wants her to wear a pager. In a scene at a burger joint, there's casual racism in jibes that Filipinos eat dogs, and Ben is called a "Chink." "I'm not Chinese," he murmurs, and we realize one reason for the white man's gauche line about Malays is to get information into the screenplay that Filipinos would hardly tell one another.

The outcome of all of this is not hard to anticipate, but the setting is new, and the birthday party provides an excuse for traditional songs and dances (as well as for a virtuoso performance of hip-hop turntabling, an art where Filipino-Americans often win U.S. contests). In Dante Basco, Bernadette Balagtas, and Joy Bisco the movie has likable, convincing young actors with marquee potential, and all of the major roles are filled with capable pros. There is one surprise. In most movies about artists, the artwork never looks as good as the movie thinks it does. But when Ben shows his father his portfolio, we see he does have the talent to realize his dream of writing graphic novels. Or maybe even go into animation and make some real dough.

The Deep End ★ ★ ★ ½
R, 99 m., 2001

Tilda Swinton (Margaret Hall), Goran Visnjic (Alek Spera), Jonathan Tucker (Beau Hall), Peter Donat (Jack Hall), Josh Lucas (Darby Reese), Raymond J. Barry (Carlie Nagle), Tamara Hope (Paige Hall), Jordon Dorrance (Dylan Hall), Margo Krindel (Jackie). Directed and produced by Scott McGehee and David Siegel. Screenplay by McGehee and Siegel, based on the book *The Blank Wall* by Elisabeth Sanxay Holding.

The Deep End uses relentless ingenuity to dig its heroine into deeper and deeper holes—until finally, when she seems defeated by the weight of her problems, it's equally ingenious in digging her out again. This is one of those plots like *Blood Simple* where one damn thing leads to another—although it has an entirely different tone, because the heroine is a completely ordinary woman we begin to care about.

Tilda Swinton stars as Margaret, a mother of three who lives in a handsome home on the shores of Lake Tahoe. Her husband is an admiral, away at sea. She lives with her kids and her querulous, distant father-in-law. She's worried about the oldest son, Beau (Jonathan Tucker), who is seventeen and has started to run with dangerous company.

The movie's opening shot shows her visiting a gay club in Reno to ask a thirty-year-old man named Darby (Josh Lucas) to stay away from her son; while they were both drunk, Beau crashed the car they were driving. Darby is handsome, but in a way that makes us mistrust him because he uses his looks so obviously. He's got a gambling problem, apparently, and offers to stay away—for $5,000.

The movie shows a quiet delicacy in dealing with Margaret's feelings about her son's recently revealed homosexuality. It wisely doesn't make his sexuality the subject of the story; she gently tries to approach the subject once, he roughly avoids it, and that's all they really say. What she sees is a good child, a talented musician with a scholarship on the way, who has been temporarily dazzled by Darby.

We also see a household filled with silences. Margaret is lonely and isolated, maintains a distance from her father-in-law, performs motherly duties for her children, but seems vaguely worried most of the time. One reason the movie works is because she's so practiced at keeping secrets. That reserve, linked to a strong will, sets up the *noir* plot. If she weren't so capable and secretive . . . but she is.

When Darby visits Beau late one night, the two men fight in a boathouse, and after Beau stalks away, the drunken Darby stumbles, falls, and kills himself. The next morning, Margaret finds the body, assumes her son killed Darby, and sets about trying to conceal the corpse. Scott McGehee and David Siegel, the writer-directors, are merciless in creating one difficulty after another—the problem of the car keys, for example—and there is a long, sustained sequence in which we follow Margaret as she does her best.

Then a man comes knocking on the door. This is Alek Spera (Goran Visnjic). He thinks he has incriminating information and wants $50,000 to keep quiet and destroy some evidence. What is intriguing here, and elsewhere, is that we know more about the actual death than anyone in the movie, and *The Deep End* creates that kind of suspense Hitchcock likes, in which an innocent person is wrongly accused, looks guilty, tries to cope, and lacks essential information.

The movie is based on a 1947 crime novel named *The Blank Wall,* by Elisabeth Sanxay Holding (it was filmed in 1949 by Max Ophuls as *The Reckless Moment,* with James Mason and Joan Bennett). This version changes the gender of the child and adds homosexuality, but relishes the freedom of 1940s melodrama to pile on complications and dark coincidences. When the film played at Sundance and Cannes, some critics complained that the later developments were simply too implausible. But there are times at the movies when we have to cut loose from plausibility and enjoy the ride; this movie would not be better if the ending were more believable, because there is a part of us that enjoys melodrama stretched to the limit.

155

What's skillful, too, is the way McGehee and Siegel go for broke in the plot but keep the performances reined in. Tilda Swinton is the key. She is always believable as this harassed, desperate, loving mother. She projects a kind of absorption in her task; she juggles blackmail, murder, bank loans, picking up the kids after school—it's as if the ordinary tasks keep her sane enough to deal with the dangers that surround her. Swinton's career has included one extraordinary movie after another. In *Orlando*, she was a man who became a woman and lived for four centuries. In *Love Is the Devil,* the Francis Bacon story, she presided over London's most notorious drinking club. In Tim Roth's *The War Zone* she was a pregnant wife in a family harboring dark secrets. And you may remember her in *The Beach* as the imperious leader of the tropical commune Leonardo DiCaprio stumbles across. Her American housewife here is, in a way, a bigger stretch than most of those; she is believable and touching.

The Deep End is the kind of crime movie where the everyday surroundings make the violence seem all the more shocking and gruesome. Nobody much wants to really hurt anybody, and in a nice twist even one of the villains doesn't have much heart for the task, but once the machinery of death and deception has been set into motion, it carries everyone along with it. It's intense and involving, and it doesn't let us go.

Deterrence ★ ★ ★

R, 101 m., 2000

Kevin Pollak (Walter Emerson), Timothy Hutton (Marshall Thompson), Sheryl Lee Ralph (Gayle Redford), Sean Astin (Ralph), Bajda Djola (Harvey), Mark Thompson (Gerald Irving), Michael Mantell (Taylor Woods), Kathryn Morris (Lizzie Woods), Clotilde Courau (Katie). Directed by Rod Lurie and produced by Marc Frydman and James Spies. Screenplay by Lurie.

Not long before election day 2008, the president of the United States is making a campaign tour through Colorado when a sudden snowstorm traps him in a roadside diner. Alarming news arrives: Saddam Hussein's son has sent Iraqi troops into Kuwait, and 80 percent of America's troops are far away, committed in the Sea of Japan. What to do? Drop the bomb, obviously.

Or at least threaten to. That's the strategic tactic tried by President Walter Emerson, played by Kevin Pollak as a man who wasn't elected to the highest office but got there through a combination of unforeseen events. He doesn't look very presidential, and he's not terrifically popular with the voters, but the office makes the man, they say, and Emerson rises to the occasion with terrifying certitude: Yes, he is quite prepared to drop the first nuclear weapon since Nagasaki.

This story unfolds in a classic closed-room scenario. The storm rages outside, no one can come or go, and the customers and staff who were already in the diner get a front-row seat for the most momentous decision in modern times. Although the president cannot move because of the weather, he can communicate, and he negotiates by telephone and speaks to the nation via a camera from the cable news crew that's following him around.

Watching the film, I found a curious thing happening. My awareness of the artifice dropped away, and the film began working on me. The situation, it is true, has been contrived out of the clichés of doomsday fiction. The human relationships inside the diner are telegraphed with broad strokes (and besides, wouldn't the Secret Service clear the room of onlookers while the president was conducting secret negotiations with heads of state?). There is a ludicrous moment when the president steps outside into the storm with his advisers to tell them something we're not allowed to hear. And the ending is more or less inexcusable.

And yet the film works. It really does. I got caught up in the global chess game, in the bluffing and the dares, the dangerous strategy of using nuclear blackmail against a fanatic who might call the bluff. With one set and low-rent props (is that an ordinary laptop inside the nuclear briefcase "football"?), *Deterrence* manufactures real suspense and considers real issues.

The movie was written and directed by Rod Lurie, the sometime film critic of *Los Angeles* magazine. On the basis of this debut, he can give up the day job. He knows how to direct, although he could learn more about rewriting. What saves him from the screenplay's implausibilities and dubious manipulation is the strength of the performances.

Kevin Pollak makes a curiously convincing third-string president—a man not elected to the office, but determined to fill it. He is a Jew, which complicates his Middle East negotiations and produced a priceless theological discussion with the waitress (Clotilde Courau). He is advised by a chief of staff (Timothy Hutton) and his national security adviser (Sheryl Lee Ralph), who are appalled by his nuclear brinkmanship, and who are both completely convincing in their roles. The screenplay gives them dialogue of substance; the situation may be contrived, but we're absorbed in the urgent debate that it inspires.

I mentioned the ending. I will offer no hints, except to say that it raises more questions than it answers—questions not just about the president's decisions, but about the screenwriter's sanity. *Deterrence* is the kind of movie that leaves you with fundamental objections. But that's after it's over. While it's playing, it's surprisingly good.

The Devil's Backbone ★ ★ ★
R, 106 m., 2001

Marisa Paredes (Carmen), Eduardo Noriega (Jacinto), Federico Luppi (Casares), Fernando Tielve (Carlos), Irene Visedo (Conchita), Inigo Garces (Jaime). Directed by Guillermo del Toro and produced by Agustin Almodovar and Bertha Navarro. Screenplay by del Toro, Antonio Trashorras, and David Munoz.

Ghosts are more interesting when they have their reasons. They should have unfinished affairs of the heart or soul. Too many movies use them simply for shock value, as if they exist to take cues from the screenplay. *The Devil's Backbone*, a mournful and beautiful new ghost story by Guillermo del Toro, understands that most ghosts are sad, and are attempting not to frighten us but to urgently communicate something that must be known so that they can rest.

The film takes place in Spain in the final days of the civil war. Franco's fascists have the upper hand, and in a remote orphanage the children of left-wing families await the end. An enormous crucifix has been put on display to disguise the institution as a Catholic school, and the staff is uneasily prepared to flee. In the courtyard, a huge unexploded bomb rests, nose down, like a sculpture. "They say it's switched off," says one of the kids, "but I don't believe it. Put your head against it. You can hear it ticking."

A young boy named Carlos (Fernando Tielve) has been brought to the school in a car riding across one of those spaghetti Western landscapes. He is assigned Bed No. 12— "Santi's bed," the children whisper. Santi is a boy who died and whose ghost is sometimes seen, sometimes heard sighing. Carlos learns the ways of the school, its rules, the boys who will be his friends and his enemies.

The most ominous presence is Jacinto (Eduardo Noriega), a former student who is now the janitor. The orphanage is run by Dr. Casares (Federico Luppi), elderly and self-absorbed, and by Carmen (Marisa Paredes), who has a wooden leg. There is also Conchita (Irene Visedo), the sexy maid; Jacinto sleeps with her, but also goes through the motions of courting Carmen because he suspects she has gold hidden somewhere on the grounds and he wants it.

This information unfolds gradually, as Carlos discovers it. He also begins to see the ghost, a sad, gray, indistinct figure who seems associated with a deep water tank in the basement. There's a creepy sequence in which the other boys dare Carlos to make a forbidden nighttime expedition to the kitchen to bring back water; he is venturing into the world of the orphanage's dread secrets.

What happens, and why, must remain a secret. The Mexican director, del Toro, is a master of dark atmosphere, and the places in his films seem as frightening as the plots. He is only thirty-seven; he began with *Cronos* (1994), the story of an antique dealer who invents a small, elegant golden beetle that sinks its claws into the flesh and imparts immortality. In 1997, he made a Hollywood film, *Mimic*, starring Mira Sorvino and Jeremy Northam, which trapped them in a subway system with a fearsome bug that mutates out of control. That makes it sound dumb, but it was uncanny in its ability to transcend the creature genre, to create complex characters and an incredible interior space (an abandoned subway station).

157

Now this film. Del Toro is attracted by the horror genre, but not in thrall to it. He uses the golden beetle, the mimic insects, the school ghost, not as his subjects but as the devices that test the souls of his characters. Here he uses buried symbolism that will slip past American audiences not familiar with the Spanish civil war, but the impotent school administrators and the unexploded fascist bomb do not need footnotes, nor does the grown child of the Left (Jacinto), who seduces the younger generation while flattering the older for its gold. Carlos, I suppose, is the Spanish future, who has a long wait ahead. Such symbols are worthless if they function only as symbols; you might as well hand out name tags. Del Toro's symbols work first as themselves, then as what they may stand for, so it doesn't matter if the audience has never heard of Franco, as long as it has heard of ghosts.

Any director of a ghost film is faced with the difficult question of portraying the ghost. A wrong step, and he gets bad laughs. The ghost in *The Devil's Backbone* is glimpsed briefly, is heard sighing, is finally seen a little better as a dead boy. What happens at the end is not the usual action scene with which lesser ghost films dissipate their tension, but a chain of events that have a logic and a poetic justice. *The Devil's Backbone* has been compared to *The Others*, and has the same ambition and intelligence, but is more compelling and even convincing.

Diamond Men ★ ★ ★ ½
NO MPAA RATING, 100 m., 2002

Robert Forster (Eddie Miller), Donnie Wahlberg (Bobby Walker), Bess Armstrong (Katie Harnish), Jasmine Guy (Tina), George Coe (Tip Rountree), Jeff Gendelman (Brad), Douglas Allen Johnson (John Ludwig), Kristin Minter (Cherry). Directed and produced by Daniel M. Cohen. Screenplay by Cohen.

Robert Forster has a note of gentle sadness in some of his roles, revealing a man who has lived according to a code, not always successfully. Whether that is true of his acting career, I cannot say, but it is often true of his characters. Here is an actor who has been bringing special qualities to his work as long as I have been a critic, in early movies like John Huston's *Reflections in a Golden Eye* (1967) and Haskell Wexler's *Medium Cool* (1969), and recent ones like Quentin Tarantino's *Jackie Brown* (1997) and Joe Mantegna's *Lakeboat* (2000). But for the most part he has been relegated to exploitation movies like *Maniac Cop 3* and *Original Gangstas*.

Now here he is in his best performance, in *Diamond Men*, as a man in his fifties who is about to lose the job he loves. Forster plays Eddie Miller, a diamond salesman who has long traveled the mid-sized cities of Pennsylvania, selling to the owners of jewelry stores. He has a heart attack, recovers, and is told that he is no longer "insurable" to drive around with $1 million in stock in his car. His boss introduces him to Bobby Walker (Donnie Wahlberg), a brash kid whose sales experience is limited mostly to pretzels. Eddie is to train Bobby to take over his route.

He takes on the kid because he has no choice. There is a generation gap. Eddie likes jazz; Bobby likes heavy metal. Eddie keeps a low profile: "I stay at out-of-the-way motels, I eat in quiet restaurants, I don't talk about what I do." Bobby is a party animal who has a girl in every town, or hopes to. Eddie winces as Bobby tries to sell diamonds, and fails. "How do you do it?" Bobby asks the older man. "What's the magic word? I never ever saw a diamond until a week ago. I'm afraid of them." Eddie, who has nurtured his clients for years and plays them skillfully, tries to explain: "When they say 'no,' they're looking for a way to say 'yes.'"

Bobby is not a bad kid. He's in over his head, but he wants to learn. And he wants Eddie to have more fun. Eddie's wife, we learn, died of cancer; Forster's reading as he remembers her is an exercise in perfect pitch: "She didn't want to go into a facility because . . . well, you know. And I don't blame her." Bobby takes it as his personal assignment to get Eddie laid, and after various schemes fail because Eddie is too old to attract the barflies Bobby recruits, Bobby takes Eddie to the Altoona Riding Club, which is a discreet rural brothel run by Tina (Jasmine Guy).

Here, too, Eddie strikes out: He doesn't *want* to get laid. He wants to check into that obscure motel and find that quiet restaurant. Finally Tina suggests Katie (Bess Armstrong), who is, she explains, a secretary who lost her job and needs money but doesn't want to go all the way. That's fine with Eddie. Katie treats him politely, calls him "Edward," and administers a gentle massage, and so moved is Eddie that he invites her to dinner. Really, to dinner. A quiet restaurant.

The story, written and directed by Daniel M. Cohen (himself a former diamond salesman), seems to be shaping up as a buddy movie with a good woman at the end of the road. But Cohen has laid the preparations for a series of unexpected developments, which I will not reveal. The movie keeps surprising us. First it's about salesmen, and then it's about lonely men, and then it's about sex, and then it's about romance, and then it's about crime. It reinvents itself with every act.

Among its gifts is a quick perception of human nature. Eddie is a thoroughly good man, honest and hardworking. Bobby sees work as an unpleasant necessity. Katie is a character study, a woman who has so surrounded her occupation (hooker) with her beliefs (yoga, inner truth, meditation, transcendence) that sex is like a by-product of redemption. As in *Jackie Brown,* where he had a lovely, subtle, almost unstated courtship with the Pam Grier character, Forster plays a man for whom romance sometimes seems like more trouble than it's worth. There is truth in the wary way he regards the women Bobby finds for him.

Diamond Men is the kind of movie the American distribution system is not set up to handle. It does not appeal to teenagers. It doesn't fit into an easy category, but moves from one to another. It has actors who, by playing many different kinds of characters, have never hardened into brand names. It has fun with a crime plot and a twist at the end, but stays true to its underlying direction. It looks and listens to its characters, curious about the unfolding mysteries of the personality. It is a treasure.

Diamonds ★

PG-13, 89 m., 2000

Kirk Douglas (Harry), Dan Aykroyd (Lance), Corbin Allred (Michael), Lauren Bacall (Sin-Dee), Kurt Fuller (Moses), Jenny McCarthy (Sugar), Mariah O'Brien (Tiffany), June Chadwick (Roseanne). Directed by John Asher and produced by Patricia T. Green. Screenplay by Allan Aaron Katz.

Diamonds is a very bad movie and a genuinely moving experience. As the story of three generations of menfolk who go looking for long-lost diamonds and find hookers with hearts of gold, it is unbearable dreck. As a demonstration of Kirk Douglas's heart and determination, it is inspiring.

Douglas suffered a stroke years ago, which left his speech impaired, a problem which the film addresses directly by showing him, in his first scene, doing speech therapy with a videotape. This therapy (or other therapy and a lot of determination) must have worked, because Douglas's speech is easily understandable (as clear, indeed, as Robert De Niro's stroke victim in *Flawless*). And the Kirk Douglas personal style is unaffected: He was always one of the cocky, high-energy stars, the life force made lithe and springy.

Diamonds feels like it was conceived as a showcase for Douglas at eighty-three, and so it is, but what a dreary story and unconvincing characters he has been surrounded with. Dan Aykroyd plays his son, and Corbin Allred plays his fifteen-year-old grandson. We get phoned-in scenes involving a lack of communication between them and learn that Aykroyd believes it's time for his old man to give up his independence and move into a retirement home.

Nothing doing! says Douglas, playing a former boxing champion named Harry who still likes to duke it out (there are flashbacks of him in the ring, lifted from his 1949 film *Champion*). He wants to live independently, and tells his son and grandson about some diamonds that he was given decades ago to throw a fight in Reno. The diamonds are still hidden inside the walls of the house of a man named Duff the Muff, he says, and they should all three go to Nevada and recover them. As a plot premise, this would look thin in an Adam Sandler movie.

The men travel south from Canada in the obligatory vintage convertible, its top down to make it easier to shoot all three passengers. Harry might get pneumonia in the winter weather, but nobody thinks of that—and besides, the old guy is feisty enough to get smart with the border guards. In Nevada, when their diamond search experiences a setback, they all end up at a brothel, where the young grandson draws Jenny McCarthy and Kirk Douglas gets the warmhearted madam, played by Lauren Bacall, who seems right at home as the nurturing angel, as indeed she should, having nursed the ailing John Wayne character back to life, so to speak, in *The Shootist* twenty-five years ago.

The scenes in the brothel are mostly unforgivable, especially the byplay between Allred and McCarthy, who is reminded of the high school sweetheart she left behind. The climax involving the diamonds is so wheezy that we could meet during our lunch hours and pep it up. Characters so simple in plots so tired with dialogue so banal are not easily found; it is painful to watch actors speaking dialogue that is clearly inferior to the thoughts that must be running through their minds at the very same time.

But tribute must be paid to Kirk Douglas. I remember meeting him over several days in 1969, while writing a profile for *Esquire* magazine. I was almost bowled over by his energy, his zest for life, his superb physical condition. He could hardly sit still. He bounded from his chair to the side of a desk to a yoga position on the floor, talking rapid-fire about his career and hopes, and I have never forgotten what determination and joy he seemed to gather into every day of living. You can see that same quality in *Diamonds*, and seeing it is a way to enjoy the film—alas, the only way.

Dinner Rush ★ ★ ★
R, 98 m., 2002

Danny Aiello (Louis Cropa), Edoardo Ballerini (Udo Cropa), Sandra Bernhard (Jennifer), Vivian Wu (Nicole), Mark Margolis (Fitzgerald), Mike McGlone (Carmen), Kirk Acevedo (Duncan), Summer Phoenix (Marti), John Corbett (Ken). Directed by Bob Giraldi and produced by Louis DiGiaimo and Patti Greaney. Screenplay by Rick Shaughnessy and Bryan Kalata.

"Unbelievable. Only in New York can a double murder triple your business."

So it is observed in *Dinner Rush*, a movie set in one of those Italian restaurants that the customers are tickled to believe is mob-connected even though it isn't, because it makes it more thrilling that way. (Rosebud, the Chicago eatery, had billboards saying, "We serve the whole mob.") The story unfolds during one long night at an Italian place in Tribeca that is undergoing an identity crisis. The owner, Louis (Danny Aiello), likes traditional Italian fare. His son Udo (Edoardo Ballerini) is into nouvelle, or nuovo, cuisine, and boasts: "Sausage and peppers is not on my menu."

Louis is in despair. He wants to turn the place over to his son, but not if it means abandoning dishes that make you think of bread sticks and red-and-white checkerboard tablecloths. There are other problems. A man has been murdered, and the identity of his killers may be known to Louis. And two men have come into the restaurant, taken a table, called Louis over, and informed him, "We're not leaving here until we're partners in the business." Louis says they can have the book he runs, but not the restaurant. Never the restaurant. They don't leave.

It's a busy night. The party at one long table is presided over by Fitzgerald (Mark Margolis), a gravel-voiced snob who talks slooow-ly so the cretins of the world can understand him. He runs an art gallery and is treating a visiting Greek artist. The entertainment consists of insulting his waitress (Summer Phoenix) and the maitresse d' (Vivian Wu). At another table, Sandra Bernhard plays a food critic as if she considers the performance personal revenge on every theater and movie critic who has ever said a word against her.

So there's a crisis in management and a crisis in the dining room. A third crisis is unfolding in the kitchen, where Duncan (Kirk Acevedo), the only cook who will still make Louis "salsiccia e peperoni," is deep in debt to a bookmaker. Louis, who takes bets but is a reasonable man, tells Duncan's bookmaker: "Stop taking his action. The kid's a pathological gambler. He needs help, not another bookmaker."

There are enough plots here to challenge a Robert Altman, specialist in interlocking stories, but the director, Bob Giraldi, masters the complexities as if he knows the territory. He does. He owns the restaurant, which in real life is named Giraldi's. His center of gravity is supplied by Danny Aiello, who plays his cards close to his vest—closer than we suspect—and like a man who has been dealing with drunks for a very, very long time, doesn't get worked up over every little thing. He talks to his accountant and the visiting gangsters as if they're in the same business.

Like *Big Night*, a film it resembles, *Dinner Rush* has a keen appreciation for the intricacies of a restaurant. In front, everybody is supposed to have a good time. In the kitchen, the chef is a dictator and the workers are galley slaves. Udo has a scene right at the start where he makes one thing clear: Do it his way or get out. The scenes in the kitchen show the bewildering speed with which hard and exact work is accomplished, and Giraldi is able to break these scenes down into details that edit together into quick little sequences; not surprising, since he has directed hundreds of commercials.

In a plot like this, there isn't a lot of time to establish characters, so the actors have to bring their characters into the film with them. They do. The gangsters walk in menacing. Mark Margolis has a manner that makes Fitzgerald hateful on sight. Bernhard and her long-suffering companion play out nightly private dramas over the work of the city's chefs. And Aiello suggests enormous depths of pride, sympathy, worry, and buried anger.

The last scenes are fully packed, with developments that come one after another, tempting critics to complain it's all a little too neat. Maybe, but then you wouldn't want those story strands left dangling, and to spend any more time on them would be laboring the point: Like a good meal, this movie is about the progression of the main courses and not about the mints at the door.

Dinosaur ★ ★ ★
PG, 84 m., 2000

Voices of: Alfre Woodard (Plio), Ossie Davis (Yar), Max Casella (Zini), Hayden Panettiere (Suri), D. B. Sweeney (Aladar), Samuel E. Wright (Kron), Peter Siragusa (Bruton), Julianna Margulies (Neera), Joan Plowright (Baylene), Della Reese (Eema). Directed by Ralph Zondag and Eric Leighton and produced by Pam Marsden. Screenplay by John Harrison and Robert Nelson Jacobs, based on an original screenplay by Walon Green.

If a film had been made in the Jurassic age, it might have looked a lot like *Dinosaur.* The movie is startling in its impact. Against a backdrop of nature that is clearly real, we see dinosaurs that are scarcely less real. We feel the same sense of wonder that was stirred by *Jurassic Park.* These great beasts ruled the earth much longer than we have, their unlikely bodies sketched out in exaggerated Darwinian strokes.

The visual look of *Dinosaur* is a glimpse of wonders to come. The movie sends the message that computer animation is now sophisticated enough to mimic life itself in full motion, with such detail that the texture of reptilian skin seems as real as a photograph in *National Geographic.* The problem, as always, is to match the artistry with the technique.

The film opens with a little short story about an egg. The egg is first glimpsed in the nest of an iguanodon, which is fairly friendly looking, as dinosaurs go. Predators attack the parents and disturb the nest, and then the egg is snatched by a scampering little critter that runs away with it. There's a fight for possession, the egg drops into a stream, is swallowed and then disgorged by a river monster, is snatched up by a flying creature, and finally dropped from the sky to land in the habitat of lemurs.

Lemurs are, of course, about as cute as mammals can get. There were not any lemurs looking like this at the time of the dinosaurs, but never mind: The movie does a little overlapping of its eras to expand the cast, and to give the mammals in the audience a point of identification. The egg hatches, a mother lemur takes the baby iguanodon into its arms, and then . . . she speaks.

I can't tell you how disappointed I was to hear that voice. I guess I had forgotten that this movie wasn't going to be a reckless leap into the distant past, but a fairy tale in which the dinosaurs are human in all but outer form. They not only talk, they also have personalities, and they argue, plan, scheme, and philosophize, just like humans. They even have human values; when one of the leaders says it's going to be "survival of the fittest" on a long desert trek, he comes across as cold and heartless. If there is one thing I think I know about dinosaurs, it's that sentimentality for the underdog played no part in their decision making.

I wonder why I was disturbed by the sound of dinosaurs with human voices. I know that cartoons can speak. I expect them to. When the dinosaurs spoke in *The Land Before Time*, that was fine with me. But *Dinosaur* looked so real that it didn't play like an animated film for me—it felt more like a nature documentary. There is a continuum reaching from Mickey Mouse to *Jurassic Park*, and at some point on that continuum the animals stop wisecracking and start eating one another. *Dinosaur* feels too evolved for cute dialogue.

Why are we as a species so determined to impose our behavior on creatures that are manifestly not human, and all the more wondrous for not being so? Why must we make the past more "accessible" by translating it into the terms of the present? At one point during the desert trek, simians climb aboard a dinosaur for a free ride, and it complains, "Just what I need—a monkey on my back." A dinosaur, even one that spoke English, would be unlikely to know what that line implied—and so will the kids in today's audience.

I don't know if Disney has a house rule about which animals can speak and which cannot, but guidelines seem to be emerging. The rule is, if you are a predatory carnivore, you don't talk, but if you are a pacifist, a vegetarian, or cute, you do. In *Tarzan* the apes spoke, but the leopards didn't. In *Dinosaur*, all of the creatures speak except for the vicious carnotaurs. A Faustian bargain seems to be at work: If you are an animal in a Disney picture, you can speak, but only if you are willing to sacrifice your essential nature.

All of this is of limited interest, I know, to the hordes clamoring to see this movie. Most younger kids probably assume that dinosaurs *can* speak, because they hear them speaking on TV every day. Even adults will probably not wonder if dinosaurs really roared. I enjoyed the movie as sheer visual spectacle, and I felt a certain awe at sequences like the meteor

shower or the discovery of water beneath a parched lake bed. I was entertained, and yet I felt a little empty-handed at the end, as if an enormous effort had been spent on making these dinosaurs seem real, and then an even greater effort was spent on undermining the illusion.

The Dish ★ ★ ★ ½
PG-13, 101 m., 2001

Sam Neill (Cliff Buxton),Kevin Harrington (Ross "Mitch" Mitchell), Tom Long (Glenn Latham), Patrick Warburton (Al Burnett), Genevieve Mooy (May McIntyre), Tayler Kane (Rudi Kellerman), Bille Brown (Prime Minister), Roy Billing (Mayor Bob McIntyre), Eliza Szonert (Janine Kellerman), Lenka Kripac (Marie McIntyre). Directed by Rob Sitch and produced by Michael Hirsh, Santo Cilauro, Tom Gleisner, Jane Kennedy, and Sitch. Screenplay by Cilauro, Gleisner, Kennedy, and Sitch.

In a sheep pasture outside the little town of Parkes in New South Wales stands the pride and joy of Australian astronomy, a radio telescope the size of a football field. Most days it eavesdrops on the stars. In 1969, it gets a momentous assignment: Relaying the television signals from the Moon that will show Neil Armstrong's one small step for man, one giant leap for mankind.

Parkes is agog. This is the town's shining hour. *The Dish*, a smiling human comedy, treats the Moon walk not as an event 240,000 miles away, but as a small step taken by every single member of mankind, particularly those in Parkes. Resigned to thinking of themselves as provincials in a backwater, they're thrilled and a little humbled by their role on the world stage. True, NASA is relying on its primary telescope in Goldstone, California, and Parkes is only the backup—but still!

Mayor Bob McIntyre and his wife, Maisie (Roy Billing and Genevieve Mooy), nervously prepare for visits from the prime minister and the U.S. ambassador. Out at the telescope, Cliff Buxton (Sam Neill), the imperturbable, pipe-smoking scientist in charge of the telescope, steadies his team. There's Glenn (Tom Long), the soft-spoken mathematician, Mitch (Kevin

Harrington), in charge of keeping the equipment humming, and Al (Patrick Warburton), the American observer from NASA, whose black horn-rims and foursquare demeanor make him seem like Clark Kent. Patrolling the parameters of the site, prepared to repel foreign invaders and curious sheep, is Rudi the security guard (Tayler Kane), whose sister, Janine (Eliza Szonert), is in love with Mitch and effortlessly penetrates Rudi's defenses.

Since we all know Neil Armstrong and his shipmates returned safely from the Moon, *The Dish* can't develop suspense over the outcome of the mission. But it's a cliffhanger anyway, through the ingenious device of making the movie more about Parkes than about the Moon. The movie is "inspired by fact" (very loosely, I suspect), but who can remember if the historic TV signals were relayed by Parkes or Goldstone? Since we've met the locals in Parkes, we're as eager as they are to have it be them.

But it won't be simple. Director and cowriter Rob Sitch (whose *The Castle* is one of the funniest comedies of recent years) intercuts the drama of the approaching Moon walk with the drama of the momentous visit to Parkes by the prime minister and the ambassador. At the observatory, embarrassing technical problems pop up when the town blows a fuse. And at a crucial moment, high gusts of wind threaten to topple the telescope right over onto the sheep.

Sitch laces the Moon walk and the local plots together so effortlessly that it would be unfair to describe his plot developments. I will be vague, then, in mentioning the visit by the U.S. ambassador, who arrives at the telescope at a particularly delicate moment, but leaves satisfied that he has at least heard Neil Armstrong speaking from the Moon. There is also the inspired solution to another crisis, when Parkes "loses" the spacecraft after a power outage, and Glenn tries to find it with frantic mathematical calculations before the team hits upon a solution of stunning simplicity.

The Dish is rich in its supporting characters. I like the mayor's daughter Marie (Lenka Kripac), who has moved on from the sunny, idealistic 1960s and already embodies the sullen, resentful 1970s. I like the way Mayor Bob and his wife so cheerfully and totally dote on each other—and the way she tries to get him to use the upscale name "May" for her, when he's been calling her "Maisie" as long as he can remember. And the way Rudi the security guard is in fact the town's greatest security threat.

With *The Dish* and *The Castle*, Sitch and his producing partner Michael Hirsh have made enormously entertaining movies. Perhaps just as important, they've made good-hearted movies. Recent Hollywood comedy has tilted toward vulgarity, humiliation, and bathroom humor. Sometimes I laugh at them, even a lot; but I don't feel this good afterward. *The Dish* has affection for every one of its characters, forgives them their trespasses, understands their ambitions, doesn't mock them, and is very funny. It placed second for the People's Choice Award at the 2000 Toronto Film Festival—after *Crouching Tiger, Hidden Dragon*. That's about right.

Disney's The Kid ★ ★ ★
PG, 101 m., 2000

Bruce Willis (Russ Duritz), Spencer Breslin (Rusty Duritz), Emily Mortimer (Amy), Lily Tomlin (Janet), Jean Smart (Deirdre Lafever), Chi McBride (Kenny), Daniel Von Bargen (Sam Duritz), Dana Ivey (Dr. Alexander), Susan Dalian (Giselle). Directed by Jon Turteltaub and produced by Turteltaub, Christina Steinberg, and Hunt Lowry. Screenplay by Audrey Wells.

Bruce Willis is developing a nice little sideline, costarring with children in films with supernatural elements. After *The Sixth Sense* in the summer of 1999, here is *Disney's The Kid*, which (despite the Disney trademark in the title) is not really a kid's picture but aimed more or less at the *Sixth Sense* audience. It's a sweet film, unexpectedly involving, and shows again that Willis, so easily identified with action movies, is gifted in the areas of comedy and pathos: This is a cornball plot, and he lends it credibility just by being in it.

He plays Russ Duritz, a Los Angeles "image consultant" who needs a lot of consulting on his own image. He's rude, abrasive, dismissive, angry. Trapped next to a TV anchorwoman on a plane, he first tries to ignore her, then delivers a devastating critique of her hair, eyebrows, makeup, clothes, voice, and the horse she rode in on. In the office, he tyrannizes his assistant (Lily Tomlin), who survives only because of a tough, humorous shell.

Strange things begin to happen. If *The Sixth Sense* was about a kid who keeps seeing dead people, this one is about a guy who is dead inside and keeps seeing a kid. A pudgy little kid, who leads him into a diner that later seems to have disappeared. The kid eventually allows himself to be cornered. They compare distinguishing characteristics, and Russ is forced to the amazing conclusion that this kid is *himself*, a few days before his own eighth birthday.

I don't know about you, but I would be able to recognize myself at eight without looking for scars and markings. Still, maybe Russ, so sleek and groomed, doesn't want to remember that he was once a pudgy little pushover. The kid, called Rusty (Spencer Breslin), is lovable and direct, and seems to know what's going on in a way old Russ doesn't. (Clue: The movie could have been called *Ebenezer Willis and the Ghost of Childhood Past*.) Together, the boy and the man share memories and revisit the scenes of childhood defeats, and the adult begins to understand why he is so cold to his father, to the world, and to himself.

The movie was directed by Jon Turteltaub *(While You Were Sleeping)* and written by Audrey Wells *(The Truth About Cats and Dogs)*, and has that nice mixture of sentiment and comedy that both of those movies found. I like Rusty's attitude as he confronts the full horror of growing up. At one point, quizzing Russ about his life, he discovers that Russ doesn't even have a dog.

"No dog? I grow up to be a guy with no dog?"

Russ admits that he does.

"What do I do?" the kid asks.

"You're an image consultant," says the adult.

The kid takes inventory. "So . . . I'm forty, I'm not married, I don't fly jets, and I don't have a dog? I grow up to be a loser!"

The movie reveals more supernatural dimensions as it goes along. At first it appears to simply be about a visit from Russ's childhood self. Then, through shadowy mechanisms, the boy and man are able to revisit and even revise scenes from the past, and particularly a crucial playground fight involving a bully and a scheme

to tie firecrackers around the neck of a three-legged dog named Tripod.

The movie's quick-fix psychology argues that Rusty grew up to be sour old Russ because he didn't stand up for his rights on the playground. This time, after Russ takes Rusty to train under a client who is a professional boxer, Rusty does a better job of defending himself, which does *not* simply change the future (as in *Back to the Future*), but more obscurely allows Russ to learn the same lesson at forty that Rusty now learns at eight.

The problem here is that this lesson is the same old macho John Wayne BS in which the secret of being a happy man is to learn to fight. That's the same lesson preached in *The Patriot*. Both movies dismiss the possibility that men can think and reason their way out of difficulty, and they teach that the answer lies in revenge, assisted by fighting skills. Both movies, otherwise so dissimilar, have plots that absolutely depend on these values. (*The Patriot*, to be fair, provides powerful motivation after a British monster kills one of the hero's sons and prepares to hang another, which is even worse than mistreating poor Tripod, although PETA might not think so.) When will a mainstream, big-budget, mass-market movie argue that one can use intelligence instead of violence to settle a dilemma? To quote John Wayne, "That'll be the day."

These observations aside, *Disney's The Kid* is warmhearted and effective, a sweet little parable that involves a man and a boy who help each other become a better boy and a better man (there are parallels, of course, with *Frequency*). I smiled a lot, laughed a few times, left feeling good about the movie. I am still mystified by the title. If Disney added the studio name to *The Kid* to avoid confusion with the 1921 Charlie Chaplin classic starring Jackie Coogan—well, I'm surprised they believe that many people remember it, and a little touched.

Divine Secrets of the Ya-Ya Sisterhood ★ ½
PG-13, 116 m., 2002

Sandra Bullock (Sidda), Ellen Burstyn (Vivi), Fionnula Flanagan (Teensy), James Garner (Shep

Walker), Ashley Judd (Younger Vivi), Shirley Knight (Necie), Maggie Smith (Caro), Angus MacFadyen (Connor). Directed by Callie Khouri and produced by Bonnie Bruckheimer and Hunt Lowry. Screenplay by Khouri and Mark Andrus, based on the novels by Rebecca Walls.

Divine Secrets of the Ya-Ya Sisterhood has a title suggesting that the movie will be cute and about colorful, irrepressible, eccentric originals. Heavens deliver us. The Ya-Ya Sisterhood is rubberstamped from the same mold that has produced an inexhaustible supply of fictional southern belles who drink too much, talk too much, think about themselves too much, try too hard to be the most unforgettable character you've ever met, and are, in general, insufferable. There must be a reason these stories are never set in Minnesota. Maybe it's because if you have to deal with the winter it makes you too realistic to become such a silly goose.

There is not a character in the movie with a shred of plausibility, not an event that is believable, not a confrontation that is not staged, not a moment that is not false. For their sins the sisterhood should be forced to spend the rest of their lives locked in a Winnebago camper. The only character in the movie who is bearable is the heroine as a young woman, played by Ashley Judd, who suggests that there was a time before the story's main events when this creature was palatable.

The heroine is Vivi, played by Ellen Burstyn in her sixties, Judd in her thirties and, as a child, by a moppet whose name I knoweth not. Yes, this is one of those movies that whisks around in time, as childhood vows echo down through the years before we whiplash back to the revelations of ancient secrets. If life were as simple as this movie, we would all have time to get in shape and learn Chinese.

As the film opens, four little girls gather around a campfire in the woods and create the Ya-Ya Sisterhood, exchanging drops of their blood, no doubt while sheriff's deputies and hounds are searching for them. Flash forward to the present. Vivi's daughter Sidda (Sandra Bullock) is a famous New York playwright, who tells an interviewer from *Time* magazine that she had a difficult childhood, mostly because of her mother. Whisk down to Louisiana, where

Vivi reads the article and writes the daughter forever out of her life—less of a banishment than you might think, since they have not seen each other for years and Vivi doesn't even know of the existence of Sidda's Scottish fiancé, Connor (Angus MacFadyen).

Connor seems cut from the same mold as Shep Walker (James Garner), Vivi's husband. Both men stand around sheepishly while portraying superfluous males. No doubt their women notice them occasionally and are reminded that they exist and are a handy supply of sperm. Shep's role for decades has apparently been to beam approvingly as his wife gets drunk, pops pills, and stars in her own mind. Both men are illustrations of the impatience this genre has for men as a gender; they have the presence of souvenirs left on the mantel after a forgotten vacation.

Anyway. We meet the other adult survivors of the Ya-Ya Sisterhood: Teensy (Fionnula Flanagan), Necie (Shirley Knight), and Caro (Maggie Smith). Why do they all have names like pet animals? Perhaps because real names, like Martha, Florence, or Esther would be an unseemly burden for such featherweights. Summoned by Vivi so that she can complain about Sidda, Teensy, Necie, and Caro fly north and kidnap Sidda, bringing her back to Louisiana so that they can show her that if she really knew the secrets of her mother's past, she would forgive her all shortcomings, real and imagined. Since the central great mystery of Vivi's past is how she has evaded rehab for so long, this quest is as pointless as the rest of the film.

Why do gifted actresses appear in such slop? Possibly because good roles for women are rare, for those over sixty precious. Possibly, too, because for all the other shortcomings of the film, no expense has been spared by the hair, makeup, and wardrobe departments, so that all of the women look just terrific all of the time, and when Vivi is distraught and emotional, she looks even more terrific. It's the kind of movie where the actresses must love watching the dailies as long as they don't listen to the dialogue.

The movie is a first-time directing job by Callie Khouri, author of *Thelma and Louise*. She seems uncertain what the film is about, where it is going, and what it hopes to prove apart from the most crashingly obvious clichés of light women's fiction. So inattentive is the screenplay that it goes to the trouble of providing Vivi with two other children in addition to Sidda, only to never mention them again. A fellow critic, Victoria Alexander, speculates that the secret in Vivi's past may have been that she drowned the kids, but that's too much to hope for.   ☞

Dogtown and Z-Boys ★ ★ ★
PG-13, 89 m., 2002

Themselves: Jay Adams, Tony Alva, Bob Biniak, Paul Constantineau, Shogo Kubo, Jim Muir, Peggy Oki, Stacy Peralta, Nathan Pratt, Wentzle Ruml, and Allen Sarlo. Directed by Stacy Peralta and produced by Agi Orsi. Screenplay by Peralta and Craig Stecyk.

Dogtown and Z-Boys, a documentary about how the humble skateboard became the launch pad for aerial gymnastics, answers a question I have long been curious about: How and why was the first skateboarder inspired to go aerial, to break contact with any surface and do acrobatics in midair? Consider that the pioneer was doing this for the very first time over a vertical drop of perhaps fifteen feet to a concrete surface. It's not the sort of thing you try out of idle curiosity.

The movie answers this and other questions in its history of a sport that grew out of idle time and boundless energy in the oceanfront neighborhood between Santa Monica and Venice. Today the area contains expensive condos and trendy restaurants, but circa 1975 it was the last remaining "beachfront slum" in the Los Angeles area. Druggies and hippies lived in cheap rentals and supported themselves by working in hot-dog stands, tattoo parlors, head shops, and saloons.

Surfing was the definitive lifestyle, the Beach Boys supplied the sound track, and tough surfer gangs staked out waves as their turf. In the afternoon, after the waves died down, they turned to skateboards, which at first were used as a variation of roller skates. But the members of the Zephyr Team, we learn, devised a new style of skateboarding, defying gravity, adding acrobatics, devising stunts. When a drought struck the area and thousands of swimming pools were drained, they invented

vertical skateboarding on the walls of the empty pools. Sometimes they'd glide so close to the edge that only one of the board's four wheels still had a purchase on the lip. One day a Z-boy went airborne, and a new style was born—a style reflected today in Olympic ski acrobatics.

I am not sure whether the members of the Zephyr Team were solely responsible for all significant advances in the sport, or whether they only think they were. *Dogtown and Z-Boys* is directed by Stacy Peralta, an original and gifted team member, still a legend in the sport. Like many of the other Z-boys (and one Z-girl), he marketed himself, his name, his image, his products, and became a successful businessman and filmmaker while still surfing concrete. His film describes the evolution of skateboarding almost entirely in terms of the experience of himself and his friends. It's like the vet who thinks World War II centered around his platoon.

The Southern California lifestyle in general, and surfing and skateboarding in particular, are insular and narcissistic. People who live indoors have ideas. People who live outdoors have style. Here is an entire movie about looking cool while not wiping out. Call it a metaphor for life. There comes a point when sensible viewers will tire of being told how astonishing and unique each and every Z-boy was, while looking at repetitive still photos and home footage of skateboarders, but the film has an infectious enthusiasm, and we're touched by the film's conviction that all life centered on that place, that time, and that sport.

One question goes unanswered. Was anyone ever killed? Maimed? Crippled? There is a brief shot of someone on crutches, and a few shots showing skateboarders falling off their boards, but since aerial gymnastics high over hard surfaces are clearly dangerous and the Z-boys wear little or no protective gear, what's the story?

That most of them survived is made clear by info over the end credits, revealing that although one Zephyr Team member is in prison and another was "last seen in Mexico," the others all seem to have married, produced an average of two children, and found success in business. To the amazement, no doubt, of their parents.

Domestic Disturbance ★ ½
PG-13, 88 m., 2001

John Travolta (Frank Morrison), Vince Vaughn (Rick Barnes), Teri Polo (Susan Morrison Barnes), Matthew O'Leary (Danny Morrison), Steve Buscemi (Ray Coleman), Chris Ellis (Detective Warren), Nick Loren (Officer Foxx), Charles E. Bailey (Streetwalker). Directed by Harold Becker and produced by Becker, Donald De Line, and Jonathan D. Krane. Screenplay by Lewis Colick, William S. Comanor, and Gary Drucker.

John Travolta plays a nice guy better than just about anybody else, which is why it's hard to figure out why his seemingly intelligent wife would divorce him, in *Domestic Disturbance*, to marry Vince Vaughn, who plays a creep better than just about anybody else. Maybe that's because it's not until the wedding day that her new husband's best friend turns up, and it's Steve Buscemi, who plays the creep's best friend absolutely better than anybody else.

All of this is a setup for a child-in-terror movie, in which a child is the eyewitness to a brutal murder and the incineration of the body. Then the kid sees his father hammered to within an inch of his life, his mother beaten until she has a miscarriage, and himself as the unwitting cause of an electrocution. I mention these details as a way of explaining why the flywheels at the MPAA Ratings Board gave the movie a PG-13 rating. Certainly it doesn't deserve an R, like *Amelie* or *Waking Life*.

The movie is a paid holiday for its director, Harold Becker. I say this because I know what Becker is capable of. This is the same director who made *The Onion Field*, *The Boost*, and *Sea of Love*. If this is the best screenplay he could find to work on, and it probably was, all I can do is quote Norman Jewison at this year's Toronto Film Festival: "You wouldn't believe the shit the studios want you to make these days."

Sad, because there are scenes here showing what the film could have been, if it hadn't abandoned ambition and taken the low road. Travolta plays Frank Morrison, a boatbuilder and all-around nice guy—so nice he's even optimistic about the approaching marriage of his ex-wife, Susan (Teri Polo). Frank's son, Danny (Matthew O'Leary), is a little dubious about this new guy, so Frank even takes the three of them on a fishing trip together. But Danny is still upset, and has a habit of lying, running away, and not turning up for basketball games. He's Trying To Tell Them Something.

The fiancé is Rick Barnes (Vaughn), new in town, who has made a lot of money and is about to be honored by the chamber of commerce. But when his old buddy Ray (Buscemi) turns up uninvited at the wedding, Rick's eyes narrow and his pulse quickens and it is only a matter of time until the domestic drama turns into a domestic monster movie. You know it's a bad sign when you're Frank, the understanding ex-husband, standing around at the reception, and Ray tells you your ex-wife "must know some pretty good tricks to make old Rick settle down."

Suspense builds, not exactly slowly, in scenes involving an ominous game of catch. Then there's a scene that flies in the face of all logic, in the way the child is made to be an eyewitness to murder. The physical details are so unlikely they seem contrived even in a thriller. All leads up to a final confrontation so badly choreographed that I was not the least bit surprised when the studio called to say the Chicago critics had seen "the wrong last reel," and would we like to see the correct reel on Monday? I agreed eagerly, expecting revised footage—but, no, the only problem was the earlier reel was lacking the final music mix.

Music is the last thing wrong with that reel. Apparently the filmmakers saw no problem with the way a key character enters on cue, at a dead run, without any way of knowing (from outside) where to run to, or why. No problem with a fight scene so incomprehensibly choreographed it seems to consist mostly of a chair. And no problem with a spectacularly inappropriate speech at a crucial moment (it's the one beginning, "Too bad . . ."). This speech provides additional information that is desperately unwanted, in a way that inspires only bad laughs from the audience, just when you want to end the movie without any more stumbles.

Donnie Darko ★ ★ ½
R, 122 m., 2001

Jake Gyllenhaal (Donnie Darko), Mary McDonnell (Rose Darko), Holmes Osborne

(Eddie Darko), Jena Malone (Gretchen Ross), Drew Barrymore (Ms. Pomeroy), Daveigh Chase (Samantha Darko), Patrick Swayze (Jim Cunningham), Katharine Ross (Dr. Thurman), Noah Wyle (Dr. Monnitoff). Directed by Richard Kelly and produced by Adam Fields and Sean McKittrick. Screenplay by Kelly.

There is a kind of movie that calls out not merely to be experienced but to be solved. The plot coils back on itself in intriguing mind-puzzles, and moviegoers send bewildering e-mails to one another explaining it. First came *Mulholland Dr.*, which has inspired countless explanations, all convincing, none in agreement, and now here is *Donnie Darko*, the story of a teenage boy who receives bulletins about the future from a large and demonic rabbit.

The film stars Jake Gyllenhaal, from *October Sky*, as Donnie Darko, a high school student whose test scores are "intimidating," whose pose is to be likable and sardonic at once, and who occasionally forgets to take his medication, for unspecified but possibly alarming reasons. He is seeing a psychiatrist (Katharine Ross), who uses hypnosis to discover that he has a nocturnal visitor who leads him on sleepwalking expeditions. One of these trips is fortunate, because while he's out of the house a 747 jet engine falls directly through his bedroom.

The movie is grounded solidly in a leafy suburban setting, where the neighbors gather behind police lines while a big flatbed truck hauls the engine away and the FBI questions the Darko family. There is much unexplained. For example, no airline is reporting that an engine is missing from one of its jets. Where did the engine come from? Donnie has no more idea than anyone else, and we follow him through high school days with an English teacher (Drew Barrymore) who is sympathetic, and a gym teacher who requires the class to locate imaginary experiences on a "lifeline" between Fear and Love. When Donnie suggests what the gym teacher can do with her lifeline, he and his parents are called in for a conference with the principal—and one of the movie's charms is that they are not shocked but amused.

Donnie comes from a happy enough home. His mother (Mary McDonnell) is sensible and cheerful, and his father (Holmes Osborne) is imperturbable. An older sister announces at dinner that she will vote for Dukakis (it is autumn 1988), and a younger sister is a sly instigator, but *Donnie Darko* doesn't go the well-traveled route of making its hero the tortured victim of an unhappy home. Donnie even gets a girlfriend (Jena Malone) during the course of the movie.

Yet disturbing undercurrents are gathering. Donnie's nocturnal rabbit-wizard informs him the end of the world is near. Donnie becomes able to see time lines in front of his family—semitransparent liquid arrows that seem to lead them into the future. He becomes fascinated by the theory of wormholes, and discovers that a key book, *The Philosophy of Time Travel*, was written by a neighbor, Roberta Sparrow—known to the neighborhood as Grandma Death, and now, at 100, reduced to endless round trips to her mailbox for a letter that never comes.

This setup and development is fascinating, the payoff less so. I could tell you what I think happens at the end, and what the movie is about, but I would not be sure I was right. The movie builds twists on top of turns until the plot wheel revolves one time too many and we're left scratching our heads. We don't demand answers at the end, but we want some kind of closure; Keyser Soze may not explain everything in *The Usual Suspects*, but it *feels* like he does.

Richard Kelly, the first-time writer-director, is obviously talented—not least at creating a disturbing atmosphere out of the materials of real life. His mysterious jet engine is a masterstroke. He sees his characters freshly and clearly, and never reduces them to formulas. In Jake Gyllenhaal he finds an actor able to suggest an intriguing kind of disturbance; the character is more curious than frightened, more quixotic than eccentric, and he sets a nice tone for the movie. But somehow the control fades in the closing scenes, and our hands, which have been so full, close on emptiness. *Donnie Darko* is the one that got away. But it was fun trying to land it.

Don't Say a Word ★ ★ ½
R, 110 m., 2001

Michael Douglas (Dr. Nathan Conrad), Sean Bean (Patrick B. Koster), Brittany Murphy (Elisabeth Burrows), Sky McCole Bartusiak (Jessie Conrad), Guy Torrey (Martin J. Dolen), Jennifer Esposito (Detective Sandra Cassidy), Oliver Platt (Dr. Sachs). Directed by Gary Fleder and produced by Arnon Milchan, Arnold Kopelson, and Anne Kopelson. Screenplay by Anthony Peckham and Patrick Smith Kelly, based on the book by Andrew Klavan.

Don't Say a Word is one of those movies where a happy professional couple suddenly find their lives threatened by depraved outsiders. Like airline owner Mel Gibson in *Ransom* and Dr. Harrison Ford in *Frantic,* psychiatrist Michael Douglas has to discover if he possesses the basic instincts to fight to the death for the ones he loves.

The movie turns this into a race against the clock when kidnappers take his eight-year-old daughter and give him a five P.M. deadline. To do what? To pry a six-digit number from the memory of a mental patient. And that's not all. For the second half of the movie, there are four parallel plots, involving Douglas working over the patient, his wife struggling to defend herself with her leg in a cast, his daughter trying to outsmart the kidnappers, and a woman detective stumbling over the crime during a related investigation.

Plotting this dense is its own reward. We cast loose from the shores of plausibility and are tossed by the waves of contrivance. I like thrillers better when they put believable characters in possible situations (*The Deep End,* with Tilda Swinton, was accused of implausibility but is *cinema verité* compared to this). But I also have a sneaky affection for Douglas thrillers where he starts out as a sleek, rich businessman and ends up with an ax in his hand. Who else can start out so well groomed and end up as such a mad dog?

The movie was directed by Gary Fleder, whose *Kiss the Girls* (1997) was taut and stylish. Here again he shows a poetic visual touch, cutting between cozy domestic interiors and action scenes shot in gritty grays and blues.

The look of his pictures shows the touch of an artist, and he has a fondness for character quirks that flavors the material. Consider Douglas's fellow psychiatrist, played by Oliver Platt, who has his own reasons for immediate results.

The bank robbery opening the movie is recycled from countless similar scenes, but then the movie makes a twist and the plot keeps piling it on. What's remarkable is how certain performances, especially Brittany Murphy's as the mental patient and Sky McCole Bartusiak's as the kidnapped girl, find their own rhythm and truth in the middle of all that urgency.

Some might wonder (actually, I might wonder) why the villain can wait ten years and then give Douglas only eight hours to work with his patient. Or at the way Murphy's character is sane and insane to suit the conveniences of the plot (a glib explanation doesn't account for what should be the lingering effects of drugs). And the police detective (Jennifer Esposito) is pushing it when she arrives in the nick of time. Sean Bean, as the villain who wants his "property," is as malevolent as he can be without suffering serious dental damage.

Douglas has made roles like this his own, and redeems them by skirting just barely this side of overacting—which is about where a character in this plot should be positioned. Shame that his subtler and more human work in movies like *Wonder Boys* is seen by smaller audiences than his fatal/basic/instinct/attraction/disclosure movies.

The end of *Don't Say a Word* does descend, as so many thrillers do, to a species of a chase. But the final locations are darkly effective, and I liked the way the villain arrives at a spectacular end. But the movie as a whole looks and occasionally plays better than it is. There is a point, when the wife is struggling with her leg cast and crutches and the daughter is cleverly signaling her whereabouts and Douglas is trying to perform instant psychiatry at an emergency room tempo, and flashbacks accompany the time-honored Visit to the Scene of the Previous Trauma, when it just all seemed laid on too thick. There is a difference between racing through a thriller and wallowing in it.

Double Take ★
PG-13, 88 m., 2001

Orlando Jones (Daryl Chase), Eddie Griffin (Freddy Tiffany), Gary Grubbs (T. J. McCready), Daniel Roebuck (Agent Norville), Sterling Macer Jr. (Agent Gradney), Benny Nieves (Martinez), Garcelle Beauvais (Chloe Kent), Vivica A. Fox (Shari). Directed by George Gallo and produced by David Permut and Brett Ratner. Screenplay by Gallo, based on *Across the Bridge* by Graham Greene.

Double Take is the kind of double-triple-reverse movie that can drive you nuts because you can't count on *anything* in the plot. Characters, motivations, and true identities change from scene to scene at the whim of the screenplay. Finally, you weary of trying to follow the story. You can get the rug jerked out from under you only so many times before you realize the movie has the attention span of a gnat, and thinks you do too.

Orlando Jones stars as Daryl Chase, a businessman who becomes the dupe of a street hustler named Freddy Tiffany (Eddie Griffin). The movie opens with Daryl as the victim of a complicated briefcase-theft scam, which turns out not to be what it seems, and to involve more people than it appears to involve. Freddy is at the center of it, and Daryl soon learns that Freddy will be at the center of everything in his life for the rest of the movie.

Who is this guy? He seems to have an almost supernatural ability to materialize anywhere, to know Daryl's secret plans, to pop up like a genie, and to embarrass him with a jive-talking routine that seems recycled out of the black exploitation pictures of the 1970s. The movie's attitudes seem so dated, indeed, that when I saw a computer screen, it came as a shock: The movie's period feels as much predesktop as it does pretaste.

Freddy embarrasses Daryl a few more times, including during a fashion show, where he appears on the runway and shoulders aside the models. Meanwhile, Daryl discovers he is under attack by mysterious forces, for reasons he cannot understand, and to his surprise Freddy turns out to be an ally. The obnoxious little sprite even helps him out of a dangerous spot in a train station by changing clothes with

him, after which the two men find themselves in the dining car of a train headed for Mexico. The switch in wardrobe of course inspires a switch in personalities: Freddy orders from the menu in a gourmet-snob accent, while Daryl is magically transformed into a ghetto caricature who embarrasses the waiter by demanding Schlitz Malt Liquor.

And so on. Wardrobes, identities, motivations, and rationales are exchanged in a dizzying series of laboriously devised "surprises," until we find out that nothing is as it seems, and that isn't as it seems, either. It's not that we expect a movie like this to be consistent or make sense. It's that when the double-reverse plotting kicks in, we want it to be funny, or entertaining, or anything but dreary and arbitrary and frustrating.

The movie was directed by George Gallo, who wrote the much better *Midnight Run* and here again has latched onto the idea of a nice guy and an obnoxious one involved in a road trip together. One of his problems is with Eddie Griffin. Here is a fast-thinking, fast-talking, nimble actor who no doubt has good performances in him, but his Freddy Tiffany is unbearable—so obnoxious he approaches the fingernails-on-a-blackboard category. You know you're in trouble when your heart sinks every time a movie's live wire appears on the screen. I realized there was no hope for the movie, because the plot and characters had alienated me beyond repair. If an audience is going to be entertained by a film, first they have to be able to stand it.

Down to Earth ★
PG-13, 87 m., 2001

Chris Rock (Lance Barton), Regina King (Suntee), Mark Addy (Cisco), Eugene Levy (Keyes), Frankie Faison (Whitney), Jennifer Coolidge (Mrs. Wellington), Greg Germann (Sklar), Chazz Palminteri (Mr. King). Directed by Chris Weitz and Paul Weitz and produced by Sean Daniel, James Jacks, and Michael Rotenberg. Screenplay by Elaine May, Warren Beatty, Chris Rock, Lance Crouther, Ali LeRoi, and Louis C.K.

Down to Earth is an astonishingly bad movie, and the most astonishing thing about it comes in the credits: "Written by Elaine May, Warren Beatty, Chris Rock, Lance Crouther, Ali LeRoi, and Louis C.K." These are credits that deserve a place in the Writer's Hall of Fame, right next to the 1929 version of *The Taming of the Shrew* ("screenplay by William Shakespeare, with additional dialogue by Sam Taylor").

Yes, Chris Rock and his writing partners have adapted Elaine May's Oscar-nominated 1978 screenplay for *Heaven Can Wait* (Warren Beatty falls more in the Sam Taylor category). It wasn't broke, but boy, do they fix it.

The premise: Lance Barton (Rock) is a lousy stand-up comic, booed off the stage during an amateur night at the Apollo Theater. Even his faithful manager, Whitney (Frankie Faison), despairs for him. Disaster strikes. Lance is flattened by a truck, goes to heaven, and discovers from his attending angel (Eugene Levy) that an error has been made. He was taken before his time. There is a meeting with God, a.k.a. "Mr. King" (Chazz Palminteri), who agrees to send him back to Earth for the unexpired portion of his stay.

The catch is, only one body is available: Mr. Wellington, an old white millionaire. Lance takes what he can get and returns to Earth, where he finds a sticky situation: His sexpot wife (Jennifer Coolidge) is having an affair with his assistant, who is stealing his money. Meanwhile, Lance, from his vantage point inside Mr. Wellington, falls in love with a young African-American beauty named Suntee (Regina King).

Let's draw to a halt and consider the situation as it now stands. The world sees an old white millionaire. So does Suntee, who has disliked him up until the point where Lance occupies the body. But we in the audience see Chris Rock. Of course, Rock and Regina King make an agreeable couple, but we have to keep reminding ourselves he's a geezer, and so does she, I guess, since soon they are holding hands and other parts.

The essential comic element here, I think, is the disparity between the two lovers, and the underlying truth that they are actually a good match. Wouldn't that be funnier if Mr. Wellington looked like . . . Mr. Wellington? He could be played by Martin Landau, although, come to think of it, Martin Landau played an old white millionaire who got involved with

Halle Berry and Troy Beyer in *B.A.P.S.* (1997), and don't run out to Blockbuster for *that* one.

The real problem with Mr. Wellington being played by an old white guy, even though he is an old white guy, is that the movie stars Chris Rock, who is getting the big bucks, and Chris Rock fans do not want to watch Martin Landau oscillating with Regina King no matter *who* is inside him. That means that in the world of the movie everyone sees an old white guy, but we have, like, these magic glasses, I guess, that allow us to see Chris Rock. Well, once or twice we sort of catch a glimpse of the millionaire, in reflections and things, but nothing is done with this promising possibility.

The story then involves plots against and by Mr. Wellington, plus Lance's scheming to get a better replacement body, plus Suntee being required to fly in the face of emotional logic and then fly back again, having been issued an emotional round-trip ticket. If I were an actor, I would make a resolution to turn down all parts in which I fall in and out of love at a moment's notice, without logical reason, purely for the convenience of the plot.

Chris Rock is funny and talented, and so I have said several times. I even proposed him as emcee for the Academy Awards (they went for an old white millionaire). This project must have looked promising, since the directors are the Weitz brothers, Chris and Paul Weitz, fresh from *American Pie*. But the movie is dead in the water.

Dr. Dolittle 2 ★ ★ ★
PG, 88 m., 2001

Eddie Murphy (Dr. John Dolittle), Jeffrey Jones (Joseph Potter), Kevin Pollak (Jack Riley), Steve Irwin (Himself), Kyla Pratt (Maya Dolittle), Raven-Symone (Charisse Dolittle), Kristen Wilson (Lisa Dolittle). With the voices of: Norm Macdonald (Lucky), Lisa Kudrow (Ava), Steve Zahn (Archie), and Molly Shannon. Directed by Steve Carr and produced by John Davis and Joseph Singer. Screenplay by Larry Levin, based on the stories of Hugh Lofting.

Dr. Dolittle 2 is a cute, crude, and good-hearted movie about a doctor who can talk to the animals—and listen, too, often to them loudly passing gas. It combines the charm of the 1998

movie with the current Hollywood obsession with intestinal tracts, resulting in a movie that kids, with their intense interest in digestive details, may find fascinating.

Eddie Murphy stars as a famous veterinarian who now runs his own animal clinic (complete with twelve-step therapy groups for ownerless dogs). His home life is almost more demanding than his work: His daughter Charisse (Raven-Symone) is sixteen and starting to date, and his wife (Kristen Wilson) is remarkably patient with a house full of pets and a yard full of animals, including a raccoon who comes to summon the doctor to an emergency.

The crisis: A forest is about to be leveled by a plump, sneering enemy of the ecology (Jeffrey Jones), and the animals, led by a Godfather-style beaver, hope Dolittle can help. The forester is represented by a slick attorney (Kevin Pollack), and Dolittle recruits his lawyer wife to defend his case in court.

Much depends on the fact that the land is the habitat of a female bear, member of a protected species. But since she can't reproduce all by herself, the villain's lawyer argues, what's the use of preserving her habitat? Dolittle, thinking fast, recruits a male performing bear from a circus. Can the bear be persuaded to perform those functions that a male bear in the wild does naturally? When the bear proves shy, Dolittle turns into an animal sex counselor.

All of this is helped immeasurably by the doctor's ability to speak to the animals (who all speak the same language—English, curiously enough). There are no nasty animals in the movie, except for a crocodile who does his dirty work just offscreen, and the bear is so accommodating he actually visits Dolittle in a rustic restaurant, enters the toilet, and seems familiar with the function, if not the limitations, of a toilet seat. The bear, in fact, is one of the funniest elements in the movie; it is about as happy to be in the forest as Woody Allen would be.

There's also a sequence, perhaps inspired by a scene in *The Edge*, where the bear creeps out onto a precariously balanced log to try to grab some honey and prove himself a man, or bear. Will the bear master the intricacies of the reproductive process? Will Dr. and Mrs. Dolittle accept a measly compromise offer of ten acres?

The story takes an unexpected twist when the animals of the world go on strike and shut down Sea World.

Dr. Dolittle 2 is not the kind of movie that rewards deep study, and it's an easy assignment for Murphy, whose work in the *Nutty Professor* movies is much more versatile (and funnier). As the PG rating suggests, this is a movie aimed at younger audiences, who are likely to enjoy the cute animals, the simple plot, the broad humor, and Dolittle's amazingly detailed explanation (to the bear) of how a bear's elimination system shuts itself down during hibernation.

Driven ★ ★ ½
PG-13, 109 m., 2001

Sylvester Stallone (Joe Tanto), Til Schweiger (Beau Brandenburg), Kip Pardue (Jimmy Bly), Burt Reynolds (Carl Henry), Estella Warren (Sophia Simone), Cristian de la Fuente (Memo Moreno), Gina Gershon (Cathy Moreno), Robert Sean Leonard (DeMille Bly), Stacy Edwards (Lucretia "Luc" Jones). Directed by Renny Harlin and produced by Elie Samaha, Sylvester Stallone, and Harlin. Screenplay by Stallone, based on a story by Stallone and Harlin.

Whether they admit it or not, many fans go to auto races to see crashes, and they'll see a lot of them in *Driven*. Cars slam into walls, tumble upside down, come apart in midair, land in water, explode in flames, fall on top of other cars and disintegrate. So serious are these crashes that one of the movie's heroes injures his ankle. No one is killed, I guess. There is a horrible multicar pileup in the final race, but it serves only to clear the field for the movie's stars and is never referred to again.

Most of the crashes are apparently done with special effects, and there are subtle moments when you can tell that: A car in midair will jerk into split-second freeze-frames, or pieces of sheet metal will fly toward us more slowly than in real life. But we get our money's worth; the races consist of quick cutting between long shots of real races, close-ups of narrowed eyes behind face masks, close-ups of feet pushing the pedal to the metal, POV shots of the track (sometimes in a blur or haze), the crashes, and the finish lines.

Director Renny Harlin, an expert at action, has made better pictures (*Die Hard 2, Cutthroat Island*), but delivers the goods here and adds a wall-to-wall music track that pumps up the volume. He cuts almost as quickly in the dialogue scenes; his camera, often handheld, circles the actors and sometimes he cuts after every line of dialogue. The music continues. *Driven* is a movie by, for, and about the attention deficit disordered.

Sylvester Stallone stars and wrote the screenplay, which was originally inspired by his desire to make a biopic about the Brazilian racing great Ayrtan Senna, who was killed in 1994. The first drafts may have contained bio, but the final draft is all pic, and the characters are off the shelf. Stallone plays a hotshot retired driver whose comeback problems are quickly dealt with ("What about the fear?" "The fear is gone"). Burt Reynolds is the wheelchair-bound owner of a racing team. Til Schweiger plays the defending champion from Germany. Kip Pardue plays a rookie phenom, in a role once penciled in for Leonardo DiCaprio. And Robert Sean Leonard is the phenom's brother, required to utter the thankless dialogue: "I saw this eight-year-old goofy-looking kid on a go-kart come from three laps behind to beat kids twice his age." Think about that. Three laps on a go-kart track. At Captain Mike's Go-Kart Track in Sawyer, Michigan, where I practice the sport, you don't even get enough time to *fall* that far behind.

The movie is rated PG-13, and so the women, like the drivers, have to act with their eyes, lips, and shoulders. The gorgeous Canadian supermodel Estella Warren plays Sophia, who is dumped by the champ, dates the rookie, and is taken back by the champ. She has lips that could cushion a nasty fall and swimmer's shoulders that look great except in that off-the-shoulder dress that makes them look wider than Stallone's. Gina Gershon plays the mean girl who used to date Stallone and dumped him for another driver ("He's a younger, better you," she explains). Gershon has sexy lips too, but goes for sneers, pouts, and curls—she's doing a self-satire. Then there's a journalist played by Stacy Edwards who will

follow the team for the season. "She's doing an exposé on male dominance in sports," explains Reynolds, only smiling a little, as if to himself, at this line.

It's tough to fit all these relationships in between the races, but Harlin uses an interesting device. Not only does Reynolds communicate with his team members by headset, but so do the girls; there are times when three people are shouting advice at a guy doing 195 miles per hour. The Edwards character nevertheless disappears so inexplicably from the story (apart from reaction shots) that when she's there at the end, Stallone (who has been holding hands with her) says, "Glad you stuck around."

The movie is so filled with action that dramatic conflict would be more than we could handle, so all of the characters are nice. There are no villains. There is a shoving match over the girl, but no real fights, and afterward a character actually apologizes.

One of the action sequences is noteworthy. The phenom, mad at the girl, steals a race car from an auto show in Chicago and hits 195 miles per hour through the Chicago Loop with Stallone chasing him in another race car. Although this high-speed chase is tracked by helicopters, so inefficient are the Chicago police that after the kid pulls over, Stallone has time to give him the first trophy he ever won *and* deliver a lecture about faith and will—and *still* we don't even hear any sirens in the background from the Chicago police—perhaps because, as students of geography will observe, the two characters are now in Toronto.

I mentioned that all of the characters are nice (except for Gershon, who sticks to bitchiness in a stubborn show of integrity). The feel-good ending is a masterpiece even in a season where no audience can be allowed to exit without reassurance. There's an endless happy-happy closing montage at a victory celebration, with hugs and champagne, and all the characters smile at all the other characters, and outstanding disagreements are resolved with significant little nods.

Drowning Mona ★ ★
PG-13, 91 m., 2000

Danny DeVito (Chief Rash), Bette Midler (Mona Dearly), Neve Campbell (Ellen), Jamie Lee Curtis (Rona), Casey Affleck (Bobby), William Fichtner (Phil Dearly), Marcus Thomas (Jeff Dearly), Kathleen Wilhoite (Lucinda), Peter Dobson (Feege). Directed by Nick Gomez and produced by Al Corley, Bart Rosenblatt, and Eugene Musso. Screenplay by Peter Steinfeld.

Everyone in Verplanck, New York, drives a Yugo. An older Yugo, since the car hasn't been manufactured since its country went out of business. We learn that Verplanck was selected as a test market when the Yugo was being introduced to the United States. That explains why everyone was driving them then. After we meet the local residents, we understand why they're driving them now: They can't afford to replace them.

As the movie opens, a local woman named Mona Dearly (Bette Midler) speeds down a country road and directly into the Hudson River when her brakes fail. It is a measure of the local intelligence that when the car and driver are dragged to shore some hours later, the doctor checks her pulse. "She's dead," he confirms to Chief Rash (Danny DeVito), who nods grimly and begins a murder investigation.

Lucinda (Kathleen Wilhoite), the local garage mechanic, checks out the death vehicle and confirms his suspicions: The car was rigged. All four brake drums were tampered with, the brake fluid was drained, and the perp also drained some other fluids just to be on the safe side. Now Rash has to decide who killed Mona Dearly.

Almost everyone in town is a suspect. As played in flashbacks by Midler, Mona is a ferocious harridan who may have hacked off her own son's hand just because he was trying to snatch her beer. There are, to be fair, other theories about how Jeff (Marcus Thomas) lost his hand, although in every scenario he was reaching for a beer. Jeff might have wanted to kill her. Or perhaps the murderer was her husband, Phil (William Fichtner), who is having an affair with Rona (Jamie Lee Curtis), a waitress at the local diner (who is also having an

affair with Jeff, so maybe she killed Mona just because she was tired of hearing about her from both men).

Or maybe Bobby (Casey Affleck), Jeff's landscaping partner, killed her to save the embarrassment of having her create a scene at his wedding to Ellen (Neve Campbell), Chief Rash's daughter. The possibility upsets Ellen, who explains, in some of the movie's best dialogue: "I can't marry a murderer. That's not who I am. That's not what I'm about."

It helps to understand that everyone in Verplanck is dim to one degree or another, except for the Rash family. The chief is not rash, but fairly levelheaded as he patiently sorts his way through a case that seems to reduce itself to a series of bar fights dimly remembered by drunks. No one in the movie is particularly vicious (well, Jeff's no prize), and the urgency of the case is undermined by the general agreement that Verplanck is calmer and happier now that Mona's gone.

The movie was directed by Nick Gomez, who in *Laws of Gravity* and *New Jersey Drive* brought a Cassavetes touch to working-class crime and confusion. The characters this time could be lightened up and dumbed-down versions of the confused drunks in *Laws of Gravity,* their social lives centered on bars, their center of gravity the bartender. These are the kind of people who don't like to be thrown out of bars because it's a loss of valuable drinking time.

My problem was that I didn't care who killed Mona Dearly, or why, and didn't want to know anyone in town except for Chief Rash and his daughter. The Jamie Lee Curtis character looks like she has some colorful insights to share, but isn't given the dialogue to do it—she's more of a plot marker than a person.

She does figure, however, in a quiet little in-joke. Ever notice how a lot of movie smokers seem to have just lighted their cigarettes? Hers are always burned down precisely half an inch, and then we see her lighting a new one from the old one, and realize, yeah, she only smokes them for the first two puffs. A very quiet little in-joke indeed, but I mention it anyway, so the filmmakers will know their work was not in vain.

Dr. Seuss' How the Grinch Stole Christmas ★ ★

PG, 102 m., 2000

Jim Carrey (The Grinch), Jeffrey Tambor (Mayor of Whoville), Taylor Momsen (Cindy Lou Who), Christine Baranski (Martha May Who-Vier), Molly Shannon (Betty Lou Who), Anthony Hopkins (Narrator), Josh Ryan Evans (Eight-Year-Old Grinch), Jeremy Howard (Dru Lou Who), Frankie Ray (Who). Directed by Ron Howard and produced by Brian Grazer and Howard. Screenplay by Jeffrey Price and Peter S. Seaman, based on the book by Dr. Seuss.

The Grinch who stole Christmas has a reason for growing up to be so bitter. As a child, he was picked on for being green and having hair all over his body and having a beard. Show me the child who would not pick on such a classmate and I will show you Baby Jesus. But if *Dr. Seuss' How the Grinch Stole Christmas* had only worked on that angle some more, had drummed up a little more sympathy for the Grinch, maybe we wouldn't want to pick on him too.

This is a movie that devotes enormous resources to the mistaken belief that children and their parents want to see a dank, eerie, weird movie about a sour creature who lives on top of a mountain of garbage, scares children, is mean to his dog, and steals everyone's Christmas presents. Yes, there's a happy ending, and even a saintly little girl who believes the Grinch may not be all bad, but there's not much happiness before the ending, and the little girl is more of a plot device than a character.

The Grinch is played by Jim Carrey, who works as hard as an actor has ever worked in a movie, to small avail. He leaps, he tumbles, he contorts, he sneers, he grimaces, he taunts, he flies through the air and tunnels through the garbage mountain, he gets stuck in chimneys and blown up in explosions, and all the time ...

Well, he's not Jim Carrey. After John Travolta and Robin Williams were paid many millions to appear inside unrecognizable makeup in *Battlefield Earth* and *Bicentennial Man*, did it occur to anyone that when audiences go to a movie with a big star, they buy their tickets in the hopes of being able to *see* that star? Carrey has hidden behind invented faces before, in *The Mask*, for example, but his Grinch, with his pig-snout nose and Mr. Hyde hairdo, looks more like a perverse wolf man than the hero of a comedy.

The movie uses gigantic sets and lots of special effects and trick photography to create Whoville, which is inside a snowflake, and where all the Whos live in merry jollity, preparing for Christmas. The Grinch lives in a cave on the garbage mountain that towers over the town, brooding and gnashing and remembering old wounds and childhood hurts. Eventually the happiness below is so unbearable to him that he descends on the town and steals all the Christmas presents, and only the touching faith of little Cindy Lou Who (Taylor Momsen) redeems him.

But the general outlines of the story, expanded here, will be familiar from Dr. Seuss. What is strange is how the inspiration of his drawings has been expanded almost grotesquely into a world so unattractive and menacing. Red is the dominant color in the palate—not Santa red, but a kind of grungy, brownish red, so much of it we yearn to slake our eyes on green or blue. The film seems shot through a subtle filter that just slightly blurs everything, and the result is not cheerful. All of the characters, as I have mentioned, have noses that look like atrophied upturned pig snouts, which is nice if you like atrophied upturned pig snouts, but not if you don't.

The balance is off. There should be more scenes establishing sympathy for the Grinch, fewer scenes establishing his meanness, more scenes to make the townspeople seem interesting, a jollier production design, and a brighter look overall. I am not a mind reader and cannot be sure, but I think a lot of children are going to look at this movie with perplexity and distaste. It's just not much fun. Adults may appreciate Carrey's remarkable performance in an intellectual sort of way and give him points for what was obviously a supreme effort, but the screenplay doesn't give the Grinch any help. Of course, I may be wrong. As the Grinch himself observes, "One man's toxic sludge is another man's potpourri." Or vice versa, I'm afraid.

Dr. T and the Women ★ ★ ★
R, 122 m., 2000

Richard Gere (Dr. T), Helen Hunt (Bree),
Farrah Fawcett (Kate), Laura Dern (Peggy),
Shelley Long (Carolyn), Tara Reid (Connie),
Kate Hudson (Dee Dee), Liv Tyler (Marilyn).
Directed by Robert Altman and produced by
Altman and James McLindon. Screenplay
by Anne Rapp.

Robert Altman would never admit this, but I believe Doctor T, the gynecologist in his latest film, is an autobiographical character. Played by Richard Gere with tact, sweetness, and a certain weary bemusement in the face of female complexity, Dr. T works for and with women, and sometimes dares to love them. So with Altman, who is more interested in women than any other great director, with the exception of Ingmar Bergman.

In a time when almost all movies revolve around men, Altman alone gives more than equal time to his female characters. He has built whole films (*Brewster McCloud, Three Women*) around a woman like Shelley Duvall, whose face and presence fascinated him when he discovered her as a waitress in a Texas coffee shop. Many of his best films, like *Nashville; Come Back to the Five and Dime, Jimmy Dean, Jimmy Dean;* and *Cookie's Fortune,* are dominated by female characters. And in *Dr. T and the Women,* he creates a galaxy of Dallas women—old, young, wonderful, crabby, infatuated, independent—and surrounds his hero with them. When you hear that Dr. T is a gynecologist played by Richard Gere, you assume he is a love machine mowing down his patients. Nothing could be further from the truth.

The Altman character Dr. T most resembles is the hapless frontier businessman played by Warren Beatty (like Gere a Hollywood sex symbol) in *McCabe and Mrs. Miller.* Desperately wanting to do the right thing, not sure he knows what that is, baffled by a woman who does not seem to need him, McCabe, like Dr. T, is that rare creature, a male hero who does not represent the director's need to dominate. Altman in his personal life is inseparable from his wife, Katherine, and surrounds himself with women as writers, producers, and colleagues. At a time when most movies have no interesting roles for women, actresses seek his sets like the promised land.

Yet *Dr. T* has been accused of misogynism—the hatred of women. How can this be? It is a comedy with sneaky, dark undertones about the shopping classes of Dallas—rich women who (Altman explains) live in a city with no river, shore, or mountains, and are forced to seek solace in upscale malls. They dress expensively, they are perfectly groomed and made up, they drive luxury cars, they buy, they lunch. "Work" is their word for plastic surgery, not labor. To make a film about them is not the impulse of a misogynist, but of a documentarian. They exist. Altman rather loves some of them. So does Dr. T.

This is Richard Gere's nicest role. He works hard as a gynecologist. He cares about his patients. Listen as he counsels one who is upset about the approach of menopause. See how he lets one smoke on the examination table, because she must. He trusts his nursing staff, which is a bulwark against the unceasing parade of women in his waiting room; he loves and is faithful to his wife, Kate (Farrah Fawcett), and he cares for his daughters. One, Dee Dee (Kate Hudson), is something like a Dallas Cowgirl, and is engaged to be married. The other, Connie (Tara Reid), is a guide at the Conspiracy Museum, pointing out the X on the pavement where JFK was shot.

One day Kate goes shopping with her chic friends, and something cracks. She wanders through the mall, shedding clothes (in front of the Godiva store), ending up nude in a fountain. She is institutionalized. A psychiatrist explains she suffers from the "Hestia Complex," a complaint affecting "affluent upper-class women who have pretty much all they need." She is too fortunate and too loved, and has cracked up because she cannot understand why she deserves her good fortune.

This diagnosis has enraged certain feminist critics of the film, who see it reflecting hostility toward women. But why? We have had countless films about men abusing women (Fawcett starred in one of them), but let there be one film in which women suffer from affluence, idleness, and too much love, and it is an attack on the sex. I find the movie's purpose ironic and satirical, not hateful, and certainly Dr. T continues to love his wife and to visit her, although his visits seem to make her worse, not better.

It is only after Kate seems likely to be institutionalized indefinitely that Dr. T begins to see another woman, at first without really meaning to cheat. She is Bree (Helen Hunt), the new golf pro at his country club, and she has a tactful frankness about what she wants. She invites him over for dinner, and there is a tables-turned quality about the way Dr. T is the "date," given a drink, and left to stand around and smile, while Bree shows off by slapping the steaks on the grill.

Because this is an Altman film, there are a lot of other major roles; he is too expansive to be limited by the tunnel vision of most screenplays, and with his writer, Anne Rapp, he juggles several story lines. Sometimes characters in the backgrounds of shots are involved in entirely other plots than those in the foreground. One of these is Carolyn (Shelley Long), the nurse who runs Dr. T's office and imagines herself as his wife. There is also screen time for Dr. T's two daughters, so different in the ways they turned out—there is something revealing about her materialist culture that Dee Dee is clearly prepared, even at her tender age, to make a marriage of convenience.

What holds the stories and the characters together is the decency of Dr. T, and Gere seems wholly comfortable with the role. He plays a good man of modest requirements and dutiful conscience, plugging away, trying to get his job done, trying not to be driven mad by Freud's unanswerable question, "What do women want?" Because this is a comedy, he even finds the answer, sort of.

Duets ★ ★ ½
R, 113 m., 2000

Maria Bello (Suzi Loomis), Andre Braugher (Reggie Kane), Paul Giamatti (Todd Woods), Huey Lewis (Ricky Dean), Gwyneth Paltrow (Liv), Scott Speedman (Billy), Angie Dickinson (Blair). Directed by Bruce Paltrow and produced by Kevin Jones, Paltrow, and John Byrum. Screenplay by Byrum.

Duets has little islands of humor and even perfection, floating in a sea of missed marks and murky intentions. There must have been a lot of scenes that everybody was happy with on the set that day, but they don't add up—the movie is all over the map. Its fundamental error is to try to squeeze bittersweet heartbreak and goofy social satire into the same story. Just when the movie gets the rhythm, it steps on its own feet.

The screenplay by John Byrum weaves together the stories of three couples, all destined to meet at a $5,000 karaoke contest in Omaha. All three stories involve ancient movie formulas: (1) the daughter who wants to bond with her long-lost father, (2) the black guy and white guy from different worlds who become best friends, and (3) the slut with a good heart who redeems the aimless guy who lacks faith in himself. Combine these three relationships with the payoff of a big contest that only one couple can win, and you have an exercise in recycling.

Still, if the movie had found one tone and stayed with it, the material might have worked better—there's a lot of isolated stuff to like in this movie. The fatal miscalculation is to make one of the stories (the black guy and white guy) deeper and more somber than the others, so the film is forever plunging into gloom and then trying to get the grin back on its face.

Paul Giamatti is touching and, at first, funny as a sales executive who gets fed up with his brutal workload, walks out on his family, and hits the road. He meets Andre Braugher, an ex-con with a violent past, and in some weird way they bond during a karaoke night in a bar on the highway to nowhere. I liked the way that both of these characters were literally transformed once they stepped into the karaoke spotlight.

We also meet Huey Lewis as a professional karaoke hustler (he bets he can out-sing anyone in the house, and can), and Gwyneth Paltrow, as the daughter he never knew. He's a rolling stone, but she wants him to stay put long enough for her to get to know him. The third couple is another karaoke pro (Maria Bello) who hands out sexual favors like she's presenting her credit card, and a taxi driver (Scott Speedman) who dropped out of studies for the priesthood and now has no focus in his life.

The surprise among these actors is Huey Lewis, who has worked in other movies (notably

Robert Altman's *Short Cuts*) but here generates an immediate interest in his first scene—we watch him conning a karaoke champ, and savor the timbre of his voice and the planes of his face. The camera likes him. At the end of the movie, a high point will be his karaoke duet with Paltrow (who can sing amazingly well). Watch his taunting grin as he gets a rise out of his target with insults about karaoke.

But about that world of karaoke: I believe the film when it tells me there are regulars on the karaoke circuit who travel from town to town, going for the prize money. Yes, and hustlers like the Lewis character, who is like a pool shark of an earlier age, getting the bartender to hold the money and then blowing away the competition. I believe it, and yet the songs sung by the characters seem to belong in a different kind of a movie. In a musical, it's expected that characters sing the songs all the way through, but in a drama they should be only an element in a larger idea of a scene; when the drama stops cold so a song can be performed, the song is fun, but the movie's pacing suffers.

There's another curious thing that happens. The karaoke finals upstage the dramatic payoffs. The real karaoke world doesn't want to stay in the background, but edges into the spotlight with its intrinsic interest. In the big $5,000 contest, there's a fat kid in a Hawaiian shirt who comes onstage. We never see him again and he has no spoken dialogue, but he stops the show because he is, in a touching way, so fascinating. I'm sure Bruce Paltrow, the film's director, left him in for the same reason I'm writing about him—because he had a haunting quality. But a movie is in trouble when you start thinking that a documentary about that kid and the other karaoke regulars would be more interesting than the resolution of the three pairs of formula stories.

Dungeons & Dragons ★ ½
PG-13, 105 m., 2000

Justin Whalin (Ridley), Marlon Wayans (Snails), Thora Birch (Empress Savina), Zoe McLellan (Marina), Kristen Wilson (Norda), Lee Arenberg (Elwood), Bruce Payne (Damodar), Jeremy Irons (Profion). Directed by Courtney Solomon and produced by Thomas M. Hammel, Kia Jam, and Solomon. Screenplay by Topper Lilien and Carroll Cartwright.

Dungeons & Dragons looks like they threw away the game and photographed the box it came in. It's an amusing movie to look at, in its own odd way, but close your eyes and the dialogue sounds like an overwrought junior high school play. The movie tells the story of a power struggle in the mythical kingdom of Izmer, where a populist empress wants power for the common man but an elitist member of the ruling caste plans a coup. High marks for anyone who can explain the role that dragons play in the Izmerian ecology.

The plot does not defy description, but it discourages it. Imagine a kingdom that looks half the time like a towering fantasy world of spires and turrets, castles and drawbridges—and the other half like everyone is standing around in the wooded area behind Sam's Club on the interstate. Imagine some characters who seem ripped from the pages of action comics and other characters who look like their readers. Imagine arch, elevated medievalese alternating with contemporary slang. The disconnects are so strange that with a little more effort they could have become a style.

Empress Savina (Thora Birch) rules in a land where the Mages run everything and the commoners do all the work. She fights for equality, but a scheming Mage named Profion (Jeremy Irons—yes, Jeremy Irons) wants to wrest power from her. This will involve obtaining a magic scepter, which I think (this is a little obscure) is powered by a gem known as the Dragon's Eye. Plugging the eye into the scepter will allow Profion to command the kingdom's dragons, overthrow the empress, and retain power for himself and his fellow Mages.

Meanwhile (there are a lot of meanwhiles in this film), enter two thieves, Ridley (Justin Whalin) and Snails (Marlon Wayans). Ridley is a cross between action hero and mall rat; Snails tilts more toward Stepin Fetchit ("Be careful!" Ridley is always telling Snails, and then he'll turn and bang his head on a beam). Soon they accumulate three sidekicks: Marina (Zoe McLellan), who knows a lot of magic, Elwood the dwarf (Lee Arenberg), and Norda (Kristen Wilson), whose breastplate is a metallic salute to the guns of Navarone.

These five bumble about in undistinguished settings and then occasionally venture into sets so hallucinatory in their medieval Gothery that they look stolen from another movie. Their archenemy is Damodar (Bruce Payne), the sadistic shaven-headed enforcer for Profion, whose ears contain long snaky Roto Rooter–type things that spring out on flexible arms and suck out people's brains and stuff.

And then there are the dragons. What, I asked myself, is their nature? Are they intelligent? Loyal? Obedient? Do they wait for eons in dungeons until they are needed? Do they eat? Reproduce? At one point Profion releases one from its lair, but he hasn't fitted his scepter with the correct missing part, and so the dragon attacks and breathes fire and has to be skewered by a falling gate. (Its blood flows into a river that begins to burn, just like the Cuyahoga before the cleanup.)

The dragons apparently exist in order to materialize in the sky and flap ominously above Izmer until they are vaporized by magic. What use they are in war is hard to figure. How would the Mages enjoy life if the dragons burned down Izmer? These and other questions percolate during a great deal of swordplay, interrupted by shouted dire imprecations from Jeremy Irons, who has not had so much fun since Juliette Binoche decided she had to ravish him right then and there in *Damage*.

E

East Is East ★ ★ ★
R, 96 m., 2000

Om Puri (George Khan), Linda Bassett
(Ella Khan), Jordan Routledge (Sajid Khan),
Archie Panjabi (Meenah Khan), Emil Marwa
(Maneer Khan), Chris Bisson (Saleem Khan),
Jimi Mistry (Tariq Khan), Raji James (Abdul
Khan). Directed by Damien O'Donnell and
produced by Leslee Udwin. Screenplay by
Ayub Khan-Din, based on his play.

George Khan is like that performer on the old
Ed Sullivan show, who tried to keep plates
spinning simultaneously on top of a dozen
poles. He runs from one crisis to another, desperately trying to defend his Muslim worldview in a world that has other views. George is
a Pakistani immigrant to England, living in
Manchester in 1971 with his British wife and
their unruly herd of seven children, and his
plates keep falling off the poles.

As the movie opens, George glows proudly
as his oldest son goes through the opening
stages of an arranged marriage ceremony. The
bride enters, veiled, and as she reveals herself
to her future husband we see that she is quite
pretty—and that the would-be husband is
terrified. "I can't do this, Dad!" he shouts, bolt-
ing from the hall. George is humiliated.

George is played by Om Puri, as a mixture
of paternal bombast and hidebound conservatism. His wife, Ella (Linda Bassett), has worked
by his side for years in the fish-and-chips shop
at the corner of their street of brick working-
class row houses. After their oldest son flees,
they are left with a houseful, including a
neighborhood ladies' man, a shy son, a would-
be artistic type, a jolly daughter, and little
Sajid, the youngest, who never, ever takes off
his jacket with its fur-trimmed parka. There is
even a son who agrees with his father's values.

Puri plays George Kahn as the Ralph
Cramden of Manchester. He is bluff, tough,
big, loud, and issues ultimatums and pronouncements, while his long-suffering wife
holds the family together and practices the art
of compromise. His own moral high ground
is questionable: He upholds the values of the
old country, yet has moved to a new one,

taken a British wife although he left a Muslim
wife behind in Pakistan, and is trying to raise
multiracial children through monoracial eyes.

There's rich humor in his juggling act. His
family is so large, so rambunctious, and so
clearly beyond his control that it has entirely
escaped his attention that little Sajid has never
been circumcised. When this lapse is discovered, he determines it is never too late to right
a wrong, and schedules the operation despite
the doubts of his wife and the screams of Sajid.
And then there is the matter of the marriages
he is trying to arrange for his No. 2 and No. 3
sons—oblivious of the fact that one of the
boys is deeply in love with the blond daughter
of a racist neighbor who is an admirer of Enoch
("Rivers of blood") Powell, the anti-immigra-
tion figurehead (who has been confused in
some reviews, perhaps understandably, with
the 1930s fascist leader Oswald Mosley).

Of course the neighbor would have apoplexy if he discovered his daughter was dating
a brown boy. And George would have similar
feelings, although more for religious reasons.
One purpose of the rules and regulations of
religions is to create in their followers a sense
of isolation from nonbelievers, and what
George is fighting, in 1971 Britain, is the seduction of his children by the secular religion
of pop music and fashion.

East Is East is related in some ways to *My
Son, the Fanatic,* another recent film starring
Om Puri as an immigrant from Pakistan. In
that one, the tables are turned: Puri plays a
taxi driver who has drifted away from his religion and falls in love with a prostitute, while
his son becomes the follower of a cult leader
and invites the man into their home.

In both films, the tilt is against religion and
in favor of romance on its own terms, but then
all movie love stories argue for the lovers. Two
Oscar winners, *Titanic* and *Shakespeare in
Love,* were both stories of romance across class
lines, and *American Beauty* and *Boys Don't Cry*
were about violating taboos; it could be that
movie love stories are the most consistently subversive genre in the cinema, arguing always for
personal choice over the disapproval of parents, church, ethnic groups, or society itself.

If there is a weakness in *East Is East*, it's that

Om Puri's character is a little too serious for the comedy surrounding him. He is a figure of deep contradictions, trying to hold his children to a standard he has eluded his entire life. Perhaps the real love story in the movie is the one we overlook, between George and his wife, Ella, who has stood by him through good times and bad, running the fish shop and putting up with his nonsense. When he blusters that he will bring over his first wife, who understands his thinking, Ella tells him, "I'm off if she steps foot in this country!" But he's bluffing. His own life has pointed the way for his children. It's just that he can't admit it, to them or himself.

Note: This is a provocative film for useful discussions between parents and children. The R rating is inexplicable.

East-West ★ ★ ½
PG-13, 121 m., 2000

Sandrine Bonnaire (Marie), Oleg Menchikov (Alexei), Catherine Deneuve (Gabrielle), Sergei Bodrov Jr. (Sacha), Ruben Tapiero (Serioja [Seven]), Erwan Baynaud (Serioja [Fourteen]). Directed by Regis Wargnier and produced by Yves Marmion. Screenplay by Rustam Ibragimbekov, Sergei Bodrov, Louis Gardel, and Wargnier.

If the Soviet Union had made honorable use of the idealism it inspired in the West, it might have survived and been a happier place today. Marxism seduced and betrayed some of the best minds of its time. The executioner was Stalin. One of his cruel tricks, after the end of World War II, was to invite Russians in exile to return to the motherland—and then execute many of them, keeping the rest as virtual prisoners of the state.

East-West tells the fictional story of one couple who returned. Marie (Sandrine Bonnaire) is French; she married Alexei (Oleg Menchikov), a doctor, in Paris. He is eager to return and help in the rebuilding of Russia, and she loves him and comes along. Their disillusionment is swift and brutal. They see arriving passengers treated like criminals, sorted into groups, and shipped away into a void where many disappeared.

Alexei is spared because the state needs doctors, but the couple is lodged in a boarding-house where the walls are thin and many of their neighbors seem to be, in one way or another, informers. Marie is suspect because she speaks French and therefore, given the logic of the times, could be a spy. The old woman who once owned the house also speaks French, comforts Marie, is informed on, and dies—possibly not of natural causes.

The film, directed by Regis Wargnier (*Indochine*), tells its story not in stark, simple images, but with the kind of production values we associate with historical epics. The music by Patrick Doyle is big and sweeping, as if both the score and the visuals are trying to elevate a small story to the stature of, say, *Dr. Zhivago.* But Marie is not Lara Zhivago. She is a materialist Parisian who isn't a good sport about sharing spartan facilities, who complains to a husband who is doing his best, who unilaterally does things that endanger them both.

Not that she is a bad woman. She has the kind of strong-willed independence that would be safe enough, and effective, in the West. She is simply slow or reluctant to see that such behavior in Russia is suicidal. Her husband, born and raised in Russia, preaches patience and stealth, not techniques she is familiar with.

East-West shows physical deprivation, but makes it clear that its characters are starving mostly for the clear air of freedom. It shows a system that is unjust and brutal, but made barely livable because the ordinary humans who enforce it are prey to universal human feelings. Good people tend to want to do good things no matter what their duty commands them. Both Marie and Alexei find friends in the bureaucracy, and both find romantic friends, too; Marie's is a swimmer whose ability may be the key to their freedom.

Toward the end of the film there is a set piece worthy of a vintage thriller. A famous left-wing French actress named Gabrielle (Catherine Deneuve) arrives on tour, is made aware of the plight of the couple, and tries to help them. Her plan depends on an intuitive knowledge of how Soviet guards will react to foreign visitors; the payoff is suspenseful.

And yet the movie as a whole lacks the conviction of a real story. It is more like a lush morality play, too leisurely in its storytelling, too sure of its morality. I remember *The Inner Circle* (1992), by Andrei Konchalovsky, which starred Tom Hulce as Stalin's movie projectionist, a nonentity who through his job was able to see the dark side of the great man. It is told matter-of-factly, more in everyday detail and less in grand gestures. *East-West* has too large a canvas for its figures.

The Edge of the World ★ ★ ★
NO MPAA RATING, 81 m., 1937 (rereleased 2000)

John Laurie (Peter Manson), Belle Chrystall (Ruth Manson), Eric Berry (Robbie Manson), Kitty Kirwan (Jean Manson), Finlay Currie (James Gray), Niall MacGinnis (Andrew Gray), Grant Sutherland (The Catechist), Campbell Robson (The Laird). Directed by Michael Powell and produced by Joe Rock. Screenplay by Powell.

Michael Powell was one of the greatest British directors—the best in the land after Alfred Hitchcock decamped to Hollywood—and his major films stand like bedrock in film history: *The Red Shoes, The Life and Death of Colonel Blimp, Black Narcissus, The Thief of Bagdad, A Matter of Life and Death, Peeping Tom.*

Powell was a quixotic individualist whose works also include films far from the mainstream, strange works like *A Canterbury Tale,* about a pervert who takes advantage of wartime blackouts to pour glue into women's hair. When I taught a class on Powell at the University of Chicago, the students applauded all of his films but one, *Tales of Hoffmann,* a mannered operatic production they found unbearable, walking out to discuss it mournfully in the hallway.

His two-volume autobiography is the best ever written by a director: *A Life in Movies* and *Million Dollar Movie.* His life paralleled the development of the cinema. Born in 1905, he died in 1990 still deeply involved in the cinema as a consultant to Scorsese, Coppola, and other successors. He began in silent films, made talkie thrillers he was indifferent to, and reached "the turning point of my life in art" with *The Edge of the World* (1937), the first of his films that he "wanted to make." It has long been unavailable, but has now returned in a restored 35mm print which made its way through art theaters on its way to video.

It is a strange, haunting, beautiful film, shot on location on the spare Scottish island of Foula, in the cold North Sea. Like Robert Flaherty's documentary of Irish islanders, *Man of Aran,* made three years earlier, it tells the story of a dying way of life. But it was risky to mention Flaherty's film to Powell, who rejected comparisons: "He hasn't got a story," he tells a friend in his autobiography, "just a lot of waves and seaweed and pretty pictures. This is a *drama!* An *epic!* About people!"

The inhabitants of Foula have supported themselves since time immemorial by fishing, and by the wool from their prized sheep herds. Now modern trawlers are grabbing the fishing market, and it is time for these rugged islanders to weigh their future—should they move to the mainland? The story involves two young men, Andrew and Robbie, and Robbie's twin sister, Ruth. Ruth and Andrew are engaged to be wed. The two men and their fathers stand on opposite sides of the question of evacuating the island, and there is a "parliament" at which all the island men sit in a circle and discuss the issue. Andrew and Robbie decide to settle it more simply: They will have a race to the top of a 1,300-foot sea cliff.

One is killed, which leads to the estrangement of the two families and more complications when it becomes evident that Ruth is pregnant. But the story is not told as ham-handed melodrama; all of the characters respect one another, and the daily struggle to win a living from the hard land has made them stalwart and brave.

Watching the movie, I made a note about Powell's extraordinary close-ups of faces. Then in his book I found he went to extraordinary lengths, when money and time were running out, to get those close-ups, many shot from small boats in rising seas: "Why didn't I trick these shots in the studio? It was the faces. Islanders have an inner strength and repose that other men and women do not have, and it shows in their faces."

The film's location shooting creates a palpable sense of the time and place. No set designer would dare build a church as small as the one on Foula, where the congregation crams in shoulder-to-shoulder, and inches separate the first pew from the pulpit (one parishioner tells the dour preacher about his sermon, "One hour and fifteen minutes. Let them beat that in Edinburgh if they can!"). Small touches, like a kitten in an old lady's lap, and chickens foraging for their dinner in farmyards, seem unplanned.

The reception of this film allowed Powell to sign a contract with Alexander Korda, then the most powerful British producer, and soon he would begin his long association with the screenwriter Emeric Pressburger (they signed their productions "The Archers," and their trademark was an arrow striking a bull's-eye). Their films together made glorious use of Technicolor and theatricality, so striking that the opening credits of Kenneth Branagh's new *Love's Labour's Lost* pay obvious homage to them.

This first "serious" film by Powell doesn't seem to predict his career. You can't imagine the maker of this film going on to make *The Red Shoes*. What it does show, though, is a voluptuous regard for visual images. The cliff-climbing scenes are especially dramatic, and, watching them, I realized that in most climbing scenes the climbers seem heroic. Here they seem tiny and endangered. It is the cliff that seems heroic, and that is probably the right way around.

8½ Women ★ ★ ★
R, 120 m., 2000

John Standing (Philip Emmenthal), Matthew Delamere (Storey Emmenthal), Vivian Wu (Kito), Shizuka Inoh (Simato), Barbara Sarafian (Clothilde), Kirina Mano (Mio), Toni Collette (Griselda), Amanda Plummer (Beryl). Directed by Peter Greenaway and produced by Kees Kasander. Screenplay by Greenaway.

Having met Peter Greenaway, I find it easier to understand the tone of his films. Not a lighthearted man, he is cerebral, controlled, so precise in his speech he seems to be dictating. "He talks like a university lecturer," I wrote after meeting him in 1991, "and gives the impression he would rather dine alone than suffer bores at his table." Yet there is an aggressive, almost violent, streak of comedy in his makeup; one can imagine him, like Hitchcock, springing practical jokes.

Consider a scene in *8½ Women*, his new film. It takes place in a staid Swiss cemetery. His hero, Philip Emmenthal (John Standing),

is a billionaire who has just lost his beloved wife. He arrives at the services dressed in a white summer suit, because his wife disliked dark clothing. He is informed that a black suit is absolutely required by the bylaws.

Enraged, defiant, stubborn, Philip grimly strips down until he is standing naked on the gravel; observing the letter of the law, he demands even black underwear. He is surrounded by minions who lend him their own clothing—a black shirt, black tie, pants, coat, even underwear ("it looks like a swimming suit," its wearer explains, "and I was hoping to go swimming later"). His decision has forced his employees to strip as well, and now, dressed in black, he walks a few feet to one side and we see what we could not see before—that the preacher and all of the mourners were waiting nearby, in full view of everything.

Now how is this funny? Trying to imagine other kinds of comedies handling the material, I ran it through Monty Python, Steve Martin, and Woody Allen before realizing it has its roots in Buster Keaton—whose favorite comic ploy was to overcome obstacles by applying pure logic and ignoring social conventions or taboos. Keaton would have tilted it more toward laughs, to be sure; Greenaway's humor always seems dour, and masks (not very well) a lot of hostility. But, yes, Keaton.

One possible approach to *8½ Women*, I think, is to view it as a slowed-down, mannered, tongue-in-cheek silent comedy, skewed by Greenaway's anger and desire to manipulate. The movie's title evokes memories of the ways Greenaway numbers, categorizes, sorts, and orders the characters in his other films. His titles *Drowning by Numbers* and *A Zed and Two Noughts* show the same sensibility; he distances himself from the humanity of his characters by treating them like inventory.

Here, however, real emotion is allowed to fight its way onto the screen. Philip is in genuine mourning for his dead wife ("Who will hold and comfort me now she's gone?"), and his hopelessness moves his son, Storey (Matthew Delamere). There is a scene, offscreen but unmistakably implied, in which they have incestuous sex, perhaps as a form of mutual comfort, and many scenes in which Greenaway, so interested in male nudity, has them naked in front of mirrors and each other. This is not the nudity of sexuality, but of disclosure; a billionaire stripped of his clothes (and his Rolls-Royces and chateaus and servants) is just, after all, a naked man with flat feet and a belly.

Father and son have been involved in a scheme to take over a series of pachinko parlors in Kyoto, Japan. Pachinko is an addictive form of pinball, much prized by the Japanese. They meet a woman who has gambled away most of her family's money on pachinko, and are surprised to discover that her father and her fiancé both suggest she sleep with Storey (or Philip) to work off the debt. (This does not represent a loss of honor, the translator explains, because the Emmenthals are not Japanese, thus do not count.)

This woman becomes one of the first of eight and a half women the father and son move into their Geneva mansion, in an attempt to slake their grief with the pleasures of the flesh. All of the women are willing participants, for reasons of their own—the one in the bizarre body brace, the one unhappy unless she is pregnant, an amputee who only counts as a half, and so on. Greenaway deliberately does not build or shoot any of the movie's many sex scenes in a revealing or erotic way; they are always about power, manipulation, control.

Apart from the father's real scenes of grief, the film is cold and distant. It shows its bones as well as its skin; some of its shots are superimposed on pages from the screenplay that describes them. It is not possible to "like" this film, although one admires it, and is intrigued. Greenaway does not much require to be liked (is my guess), and what he is doing here has links to deep feelings he reveals only indirectly. At two times in the film, father and son watch Fellini's 8½, particularly the scene where the hero gathers all of the women in his life into the same room and tries to tame and placate them. After the second viewing, the father asks the son, "How many film directors make films to satisfy their sexual fantasies?" "Most of them," his son replies. This one for sure.

Eight Legged Freaks ★ ★ ★
PG-13, 99 m., 2002

David Arquette (Chris McCormack), Kari Wuhrer (Sheriff Sam Parker), Scott Terra (Mike Parker), Scarlett Johansson (Ashley Parker), Doug E. Doug (Harlan), Eileen Ryan (Gladys). Directed by Ellory Elkayem and produced by Dean Devlin and Roland Emmerich. Screenplay by Jesse Alexander, Elkayem, and Randy Kornfield.

Eight Legged Freaks may be the movie that people were hoping for when they went to see *Men in Black II.* They no doubt walked into the theater hoping for laughs, thrills, wit, and scary monsters, and they backed their hopes with something like $133 million over twelve days. It is depressing to contemplate that many people spending that much money on a limp retread that runs out of gas long before it's over. Now here is *Eight Legged Freaks,* which has laughs, thrills, wit, and scary monsters, and is one of those goofy movies like *Critters* that kids itself and gets away with it.

The movie is about spiders, but it doesn't make the mistake of *Arachnophobia* (1990), which was about little spiders. Research shows that small insects don't play on the big screen. See also *The Swarm* from 1978, which, despite its Oscar for the beekeeper's uniforms, failed to excite audiences with its clouds of little buzzing dots. No, these spiders are built along the lines of the one Woody Allen encountered in *Annie Hall;* the females are as big as a Buick, and even the jumpers are as big as a dirt bike. I am reminded of the bird-eating spider in *Crocodile Hunter.*

The movie takes place in bankrupt Prosperity, Arizona, which the mayor wants to sell lock, stock, and barrel to a company that will fill its abandoned mines with toxic wastes. Outside of town, an eccentric spider lover (an unbilled Tom Noonan) lives surrounded by glass tanks containing hundreds of exotic species. An ever-reliable fifty-five-gallon drum, that standby of all toxic waste movies, spills into a nearby river and makes the grasshoppers grow so big they're like "spider steroids." Soon a spider escapes and bites the collector, who of course thrashes around in such methodical agony that he overturns every single glass case, releasing all of his spiders, who soon start dining on dirt bikers, etc.

The movie stars David Arquette as a local boy who has returned after ten years and still has a crush on cute Sheriff Sam Parker (Kari Wuhrer). Her son, Mike (Scott Terra), is the owl-eyed little friend of the spider man; her daughter, Ashley (Scarlett Johansson), seems superfluous at first but becomes indispensable in scenes involving a stun gun and, of course, lots of spiders. Little Mike has learned a lot about spiders from his dead friend, and becomes the local expert.

The town is populated mostly by kooks, whose paranoia is led and fed by Harlan (Doug E. Doug); he runs a radio station from his mobile home and warns of alien attacks. The townsfolk are fed up with the mayor, whose get-rich-quick schemes have included a mall and an ostrich farm, but the mall provides a convenient locale for a last-ditch stand (like in *Dawn of the Dead*), and the ostriches disappear gratifyingly when hauled under by giant trap-door spiders.

The movie's director, Ellory Elkayem, has a sure comic touch; he first handled this material in a short subject that played at the Telluride Film Festival and then was hired by Dean Devlin and Roland Emmerich, of *Godzilla* fame, to direct the feature. I like the way he keeps the characters likable and daffy and positions the spiders just this side of satire. The arachnids make strange nonspidery gurgles and chirps, are capable of double takes, and are skilled at wrapping their victims in cocoons to be devoured later.

The movie contains creepy but reliable clichés (sticking your hand into dark places), funny dialogue ("Please! Not the mall!"), and bizarre special effects, as when a spider slams a cat so hard against plasterboarding that its face can be seen on the other side in bas-relief. The chase scene with jumping spiders and dirt bikes adds a much-needed dimension to the boring sport of dirt bike racing. And I liked the way the cute sheriff dismisses her daughter's spider ravings as "media-induced paranoid delusional fantasies." Meanwhile, a love story blossoms, sort of.

I am not quite sure why the basement of the widow Gladys (Eileen Ryan) would lead directly into a mine shaft, or how the exoskeleton of a spider is strong enough to pound through a steel wall, or how, once again, the hero is able to outrun a fireball. But I am not much bothered. *Eight Legged Freaks* is clever and funny, is amused by its special effects, and leaves you feeling like you've seen a movie instead of an endless trailer.

Elling ★ ★ ★
R, 89 m., 2002

Per Christian Ellefsen (Elling), Sven Nordin (Kjell Bjarne), Marit Pia Jacobsen (Reidun Nordsletten), Jorgen Langhelle (Frank Asli), Per Christensen (Alfons Jorgensen), Hilde Olausson (Gunn), Ola Otnes (Hauger), Eli Anne Linnestad (Johanne), Cecilie A. Mosli (Cecilie Kornes). Directed by Petter Naess and produced by Dag Alveberg. Screenplay by Axel Hellstenius, based on a novel by Ingvar Ambjornsen.

Here are two men, both around forty, with no desire to cope with the world: Elling, who lived all of his life as a mama's boy and had to be hauled by the police out of a cupboard, where he was crouched and trembling, after his mother's death. And Kjell Bjarne, who has been institutionalized so long it is the only world he knows—although he fantasizes endlessly about nubile women in other worlds. Elling is assigned as Kjell's roommate in a care home, and two years later they are moved into an apartment in Oslo and given a shot at independent living.

Elling, the deadpan Norwegian comedy that tells their stories, was nominated for an Oscar in 2002 in the Best Foreign Film category. It's the kind of story that in the wrong hands would be cloying and cornball, but director Petter Naess has the right hands. He gives the movie edge and darkness, is unsentimental about mental illness, makes his heroes into men instead of pets, and still manages to find a happy ending.

Elling (Per Christian Ellefsen) is slight, fastidious, fussy, and extremely reluctant to go outdoors. Kjell Bjarne (Sven Nordin) is burly, unkempt, goes for days without a bath, and knows a certain amount about the world, mostly by hearsay. When their social worker Frank (Jorgen Langhelle) tells them they must leave the apartment to buy food and eat in restaurants, Elling is incredulous: What's the use of putting the Norwegian welfare state to all the expense of renting them a nice flat if they are expected to leave it?

The movie is narrated by Elling, who depends on Kjell Bjarne (always referred to by both names) and is threatened when Reidun, an upstairs neighbor, pregnant and drunk, gets Kjell's attention. Yet Elling is a fiercely honest man who tells both Kjell and Reidun (Marit Pia Jacobsen) that the other is in love. Then he ventures out into the night to poetry readings, having written down some words about Reidun's fall on the stairs and realized, as he puts it, "My God, Elling, all your life you have walked the Earth not knowing you were a poet!"

At a reading he befriends an old man who turns out to be a famous poet and to own a wonderful car, a 1958 Buick Century hardtop. Kjell Bjarne can fix the car, and soon the four of them are heading for the poet's country cottage for a weekend at which matters of love and identity will be settled, not without difficulties, not least when Kjell Bjarne discovers that Reidun is prepared to sleep with him but does not suspect he has been wearing the same underwear for more than a week.

In a subtle, half-visible way, *Elling* follows the movie formula of other movies about mentally impaired characters (the picnic outing is an obligatory scene). But *Elling* has no lessons to teach, no insights into mental illness, no labels, no morals. It is refreshingly undogmatic about its characters, and indeed Elling and Kjell may not be mentally ill at all—simply unused to living in the real world. The humor comes from the contrast between Elling's prim value system, obviously reflecting his mother's, and Kjell Bjarne's shambling, disorganized, good-natured assault on life. If Felix and Oscar had been Norwegian, they might have looked something like this.

The Emperor's New Clothes ★ ★ ★
PG, 105 m., 2002

Ian Holm (Napleon/Eugene Lenormand), Iben Hjejle (Pumpkin), Tim McInnerny (Dr. Lambert), Tom Watson (Gerard), Nigel Terry (Montholon), Hugh Bonneville (Bertrand), Murray Melvin (Antommarchi), Eddie Marsan (Marchand), Clive Russell (Bommel). Directed by Alan Taylor and produced by Uberto Pasolini. Screenplay by Kevin Molony, Taylor, and Herbie Wave, based on the novel *The Death of Napoleon* by Simon Leys.

Napoleon did not die on the island of St. Helena in 1821. That was Eugene Lenormand, who looked a lot like him. *The Emperor's New Clothes*, a surprisingly sweet and gentle comedy, tells how it happened. Lenormand is smuggled

onto St. Helena to act as a double for the emperor, who is smuggled off as a cargo hand on a commercial ship ("A position above decks would have been more appropriate"). The theory is, he will arrive in Paris, the impostor will reveal his true identity, and France will rise up to embrace the emperor.

"So many have betrayed me," Napoleon announces grandly at the outset of this adventure. "I place my trust in only two things now: my will, and the love of the people of France." He forgets that he has also placed his trust in Eugene Lenormand—a poor man who grows to enjoy the role of Napoleon, is treated well by his British captors, dines regularly, and refuses to reveal his real identity: "I have no idea what you're talking about."

Both Napoleon and Lenormand are played by Ian Holm (Bilbo Baggins from *The Lord of the Rings*), that invaluable British actor who actually looks so much like Napoleon he has played him twice before, in *Time Bandits* (1981) and on a 1974 TV miniseries. Another actor might have strutted and postured, but Holm finds something melancholy in Bonaparte's fall from grace.

To begin with, the escape ship goes astray, lands at Antwerp instead of a French port, and Napoleon has to use his limited funds for a coach journey with an unscheduled stop at the battlefield of Waterloo—where he can, if he wants, buy souvenirs of himself. Finally in Paris, he goes to see a loyalist named Truchaut, who will engineer the unveiling. Truchaut, alas, has died, and so confidentially has he treated his secret that not even his widow, Pumpkin (Iben Hjejle, from *High Fidelity*), knows the story.

She has no sympathy with this madman who claims to be Napoleon. There is no shortage of those in Paris. But after he injures himself she calls a doctor and grows tender toward this little man, and insightful: "I think you've been in prison." During his convalescence, Napoleon comes to treasure the pleasant young widow, and learns of a guild of melon-sellers who are barely making a living. Planning their retail sales like a military campaign, he dispatches melon carts to the key retail battlefields of Paris, greatly increasing sales.

The story, inspired by Simon Leys's 1992 novel *The Death of Napoleon*, could have gone in several directions; it's not hard to imagine the

Monty Python version. But Holm, an immensely likable actor, seems intrigued by the idea of an old autocrat finally discovering the joys of simple life. The director, Alan Taylor, avoids obvious gag lines and nudges Bonaparte gradually into the realization that the best of all worlds may involve selling melons and embracing Pumpkin.

Of course, there must have been countless people in Paris at that time who could have identified Napoleon—but how could he have gotten close enough to them? The government was hostile to him. The British insisted they had the emperor locked up on St. Helena. And at home, Pumpkin wants no more of his foolish talk: "You're not Napoleon! I hate Napoleon! He has filled France with widows and orphans! He took my husband. I won't let him take you."

For Napoleon, this last adventure is a puzzling one: "I have become a stranger to myself." But who knows who we are, anyway? We affix names and identities to ourselves to provide labels for the outside world. When the labels slip, how can we prove they belong to us? Like a modern victim of identity theft, Napoleon has had his name taken away and is left as nothing. Well, not nothing. Pumpkin loves him. And the melon merchants are grateful.

The Emperor's New Groove ★ ★ ★
G, 78 m., 2000

With the voices of: David Spade (Emperor Kuzco), John Goodman (Pacha), Eartha Kitt (Yzma), Patrick Warburton (Kronk), Wendie Malick (Pacha's Wife, Chicha). Directed by Mark Dindal and produced by Randy Fullmer. Screenplay by David Reynolds, based on the story by Chris Williams and Dindal.

In animation circles the word "cartoon" is frowned upon because it makes people think of a film that is 6 minutes long and stars Bugs Bunny, rather than a film that is 100 minutes long and grosses $200 million. I've trained myself to refer to "animated features," but now here comes Disney's *The Emperor's New Groove,* and the only word for it is "cartoon."

I mean that as a compliment. *Groove* is not an animated musical telling an archetypal fable about mermaids, lions, or brave young Chinese girls. It's a goofy slapstick cartoon, with the attention span of Donald Duck. The plot is a transparent excuse to string together the sight gags, and the characters are slapped together, too, although they wisely look like the actors who voice them, so in a way we know them already.

Consider the Emperor Kuzco, who rules over a mythical kingdom somewhere in South America. He's voiced by David Spade, and he's a lot like the characters Spade often plays, a laconic, cynical wiseguy fascinated by himself. A little of Spade goes a long way, but here the animation provides enough distance so that I actually found myself enjoying Kuzco, even if his name does sound like a discount store.

Kuzco makes the mistake, early in the film, of firing an aged crone named Yzma (Eartha Kitt), who vows revenge. Her sidekick is Kronk (Patrick Warburton, from *Seinfeld*), a cook who would truly like to be an evil accomplice but simply cannot focus his mind on the task; he's distracted by his first love, cooking. One of the running gags is Yzma's attempt to whip Kronk into a frenzy of villainy, and his own genial disinterest in her plots.

Kuzco spends his days in ill will. He has recently displaced a village, and now has his eye on a nice hilltop site for his summer palace "Kuzcotopia"—a hill currently occupied by the jolly peasant Pacha (John Goodman), his pregnant wife, Chicha (Wendie Malick), and their children. Kuzco orders them banished, not long before Yzma slips him a potion that is intended to kill him but, through a miscalculation, merely turns him into a llama.

The life of a llama does not by its nature lend itself to being lived by a smart-ass emperor, something Kuzco quickly discovers. He slinks away into the jungle, which is fearsome and frightening, especially at night, and although he has always been into self-pity he now finds real-life inspiration for his tears. Enter Pacha, who is a really nice guy and helps the llama even after he finds out the animal is occupied by the emperor who wanted to displace his family. Their relationship, which continues Spade's long-running tradition of picking fat guys as movie costars, is unusual among Disney pictures because the lead is the jerk and the sidekick is the hero.

That's the plot, more or less. It would be thin if this were the typical uplifting Disney fable, but it isn't. *The Emperor's New Groove* seems to have been made over in a corner of the Disney lot by animators who just wanted to laugh a lot and wear funny hats. The film's director is Mark Dindal, who worked on the visuals of *The Little Mermaid* and *Aladdin,* but whose most relevant credit is a 1997 Warner Bros. animated feature named *Cats Don't Dance.* It didn't do much business, perhaps because audiences look for the Disney trademark on most animation, but I liked its visual aliveness and its cheeky storytelling quality.

He brings the same quality to *The Emperor's New Groove*—he wants to be silly in the moment and trust the movie to take care of itself. His style here has been compared to the classic Chuck Jones and Tex Avery cartoons at Warner Bros., where sentimentality is avoided, wisecracks are valued, and the animators sneak social and media satire in between the gags.

The Emperor's New Groove began life, I understand, as quite a different kind of movie— a portentous, ambitious Disney feature along the lines of *Mulan* or *Pocohantas.* Apparently that vein didn't yield gold, and some of the original footage was junked while other scenes were retracked and the original musical score was largely shelved. I don't know what the earlier version would have been like, but this version is a zany tonic, more upbeat and funnier than the lugubrious *Grinch.*

The movie doesn't have the technical polish of a film like *Tarzan,* but is a reminder that the classic cartoon look is a beloved style of its own. When the Looney Tunes trademark came on the screen at the kiddie matinee of long ago, the kiddies would cheer in unison because they knew they were going to have unmitigated fun. *The Emperor's New Groove* evokes the same kind of spirit.

The Endurance ★ ★ ★ ½
G, 93 m., 2002

A documentary of Sir Ernest Shackleton's 1914–1916 expedition to Antarctica. Directed by George Butler and produced by Butler, Caroline Alexander, and Louise Rosen. Screenplay by Alexander and Joseph Dorman, based on the book by Alexander.

Footage from a remarkable silent documentary has been combined with new photography, music, and a narration to produce an even more remarkable sound documentary, *The Endurance,* the story of Ernest Shackleton's doomed 1914 expedition to the South Pole. The expedition failed when its ship, the *Endurance,* became trapped in ice and eventually broke up and sank. It was then that the heroism of Shackleton and his twenty-eight-man crew proved itself, as they survived a long polar winter and a hurricane while eventually finding rescue through an 800-mile journey in a lifeboat.

Shackleton's expedition was not necessarily noble, but its failure created the opportunity for legend. The South Pole had already been reached by the Norwegian Roald Amundsen, who outraced Robert Falcon Scott in 1911–12, in a competition that ended in Scott's death. Shackleton's plan was to cross Antarctica via the pole, and claim it for England; explorers of his generation were inflamed by visions of daring conquests.

What made Shackleton's adventure so immediate to later generations was that he took along a photographer, Frank Hurley, who shot motion picture film and stills (and entered the sinking *Endurance* to rescue it). That film was the basis of *South* (1916), a silent documentary that was restored and rereleased in 2000. It was not a sophisticated film; Hurley employed the point-and-shoot approach to cinematography, but his simple shots spoke for themselves: men with frost on their beards, dogs plowing through snow, the destruction of the *Endurance* in the ice. Above all they underlined the might of nature and the impudence of men; we are surprised by how small the *Endurance* is, and how the crew members seem like dots of life in a frozen world.

That footage has now been used by the documentarian George Butler (*Pumping Iron*) as the basis for *The Endurance,* a new documentary based on Caroline Alexander's book about the expedition. The narration is by Liam Neeson. The old black-and-white footage, retaining all of its power, is intercut with new color footage of the original locations, including Elephant Island, where the *Endurance* crew wintered in the endless night, crouching inside shelters for six months.

Determining that his expedition would have to rescue itself, Shackleton set forth in the lifeboat with six men to try to cross 800 miles of open sea and reach a whaling port at South Georgia Island. That they survived this journey of seventeen days is extraordinary. Then they had to find the courage to face what they found on the island: "A chaos of peaks and glaciers that had never been crossed." Exhausted, without adequate food or water, they trekked for three more days through this landscape to find the village and bring rescue back to the men who were left behind.

Amazingly, not a single life was lost. When the *Endurance* crew returned to England, it was at the height of World War I; instead of being greeted as heroes, they were suspected of malingering. Some volunteered for the army, and died in the trenches.

The physical toll of polar exploration has taken a psychic price as well from many of its survivors. The best book about Polar ordeals is *The Worst Journey in the World* by Apsley Cherry-Garrard, a member of Scott's expedition, who walked by himself over hundreds of miles of ice to study penguin behavior. In later life he was a broken shell of the confident young man who set out with Scott. *The Endurance* interviews surviving descendants of Shackleton's expedition, including Peter Wordie, the son of James Wordie, who says of his father: "He would never let us read his diaries."

Enemy at the Gates ★ ★ ★
R, 131 m., 2001

Jude Law (Vassili), Joseph Fiennes (Danilov), Ed Harris (Konig), Rachel Weisz (Tania), Bob Hoskins (Khrushchev), Ron Perlman (Koulikov), Gabriel Marshall-Thomson (Sacha), Eva Mattes (Mother Filipov), Matthias Habich (General von Paulus). Directed by Jean-Jacques Annaud and produced by Annaud and John D. Schofield. Screenplay by Annaud and Alain Godard.

Enemy at the Gates opens with a battle sequence that deserves comparison with *Saving Private Ryan*, and then narrows its focus until it is about two men playing a cat-and-mouse game in the ruins of Stalingrad. The Nazi is sure he is the cat. The Russian fears he may be the mouse.

The movie is inspired by true events, we're told, although I doubt real life involved a love triangle; the film might have been better and leaner if it had told the story of the two soldiers and left out the soppy stuff. Even so, it's remarkable, a war story told as a chess game where the loser not only dies, but goes by necessity to an unmarked grave.

This is a rare World War II movie that does not involve Americans. It takes place in the autumn of 1942 in Stalingrad, during Hitler's insane attack on the Soviet Union. At first it appeared the Germans would roll over the ragged Russian resistance, but eventually the stubbornness of the Soviets combined with the brutal weather and problems with supply lines deliver Hitler a crushing defeat and, many believe, turn the tide of the war.

We see the early hopelessness of the Soviet cause in shots showing terrified Russian soldiers trying to cross a river and make a landing in the face of withering fire. They are ordered to charge the Germans across an exposed no-man's-land, and when half are killed and the others turned back, they are fired on by their own officers, as cowards. This is a sustained sequence as harrowing, in its way, as Spielberg's work.

One of the Russians stands out. His name is Vassili (Jude Law), and we know from the title sequence that he is a shepherd from the Urals, whose marksmanship was learned by killing wolves that preyed on his flock. In the heat of battle, he kills five Germans, and is noticed by Danilov (Joseph Fiennes), the political officer assigned to his unit. As Russian morale sinks lower, Danilov prints a leaflet praising the heroic shepherd boy.

We learn that Vassili is indeed a good shot, but has little confidence in his own abilities (in the opening sequence, he has one bullet to use against a wolf, and misses). Danilov encourages him, and as the battle lines solidify and both sides dig into their positions, Vassili continues to pick off Germans and star in Danilov's propaganda. Even Nikita Khrushchev (Bob Hoskins, looking uncannily like the real thing), the leader of the Soviet defense of Stalingrad, praises the boy and the publicity strategy.

As German resolve falters, they bring in their own best sniper, a sharpshooter named

Konig (Ed Harris), a Bavarian aristocrat who in peacetime shoots deer. He is older, hawk-faced, clear-eyed, a professional. His assignment is to kill Vassili and end the propaganda. "How will you find him?" he's asked. "I'll have him find me."

The heart of the movie is the duel between the two men, played out in a blasted cityscape of bombed factories and rubble. The war recedes into the background as the two men, who have never had a clear glimpse of each other, tacitly agree on their ground of battle. The director, Jean-Jacques Annaud, makes the geography clear—the open spaces, the shadows, the hollow pipes that are a way to creep from one point to another.

The duel is made more complicated when Vassili meets Sacha (Gabriel Marshall-Thomson), a boy of seven or eight who moves like a wraith between the opposing lines and is known to both snipers. Through Sacha, Vassili meets his neighbor Tania (Rachel Weisz), a Jewish woman whose parents were killed by the Nazis. Vassili falls in love with Tania—and so does Danilov, and this triangle seems like a plot device to separate the scenes that really interest us.

Sacha is a useful character, however. As a child of war he is old beyond his years, but not old enough to know how truly ruthless and deadly a game he is involved in. His final appearance in the film brings a gasp from the audience, but fits into the implacable logic of the situation.

Annaud (*Quest for Fire, In the Name of the Rose, Seven Years in Tibet*) makes big-scale films where men test themselves against their ideas. Here he shows the Nazi sniper as a cool professional, almost without emotion, taking a cerebral approach to the challenge. The Russian is quite different; his confidence falters when he learns who he's up against, and he says, simply, "He's better than me." The strategy of the final confrontation between the two men has a kind of poetry to it, and I like the physical choices that Harris makes in the closing scene.

Is the film also about a duel between two opposing ideologies, Marxism and Nazism? Danilov, the propagandist, paints it that way, but actually it is about two men placed in a situation where they have to try to use their intelligence and skills to kill each other. When Annaud focuses on that, the movie works with rare concentration. The additional plot stuff and the romance are kind of a shame.

Enigma ★ ★ ★
R, 117 m., 2002

Dougray Scott (Tom Jericho), Kate Winslet (Hester Wallace), Jeremy Northam (Wigram), Saffron Burrows (Claire Romilly), Nikolaj Coster-Waldau ("Puck" Pukowski), Tom Hollander (Logie), Corin Redgrave (Admiral Trowbridge), Matthew MacFadyen (Cave). Directed by Michael Apted and produced by Mick Jagger and Lorne Michaels. Screenplay by Tom Stoppard, based on a book by Robert Harris.

World War II may have been won by our side because of what British code-breakers accomplished at a countryside retreat named Bletchley Park. There they broke, and broke again, the German code named Enigma, which was thought to be unbreakable, and was used by the Nazis to direct their submarine convoys in the North Atlantic. Enigma was decoded with the help of a machine, and the British had captured one, but the machine alone was not enough. My notes, scribbled in the dark, indicate the machine had 4,000 million trillion different positions—a whole lot, anyway—and the mathematicians and cryptologists at Bletchley used educated guesses and primitive early computers to try to penetrate a message to the point where it could be tested on Enigma.

For those who get their history from the movies, *Enigma* will be puzzling, since *U-571* (2000) indicates Americans captured an Enigma machine from a German submarine in 1944. That sub is on display at the Museum of Science and Industry in Chicago, but no Enigma machine was involved. An Enigma machine *was* obtained, not by Americans but by the British ship HMS *Bulldog*, when it captured U-110 on May 9, 1941.

Purists about historical accuracy in films will nevertheless notice that *Enigma* is not blameless; it makes no mention of Alan Turing, the genius of British code-breaking and a key theoretician of computers, who was as responsible as anyone for breaking the Enigma code. Turing was a homosexual, eventually hounded into suicide by British laws, and is replaced here by a fictional and resolutely heterosexual hero named Tom Jericho (Dougray Scott). And just as well, since the hounds of full disclosure who dogged *A Beautiful Mind* would no doubt be asking why *Enigma* contained no details about Turing's sex life.

The movie, directed by the superb Michael Apted, is based on a literate, absorbing thriller by Robert Harris, who portrays Bletchley as a hothouse of intrigue in which Britain's most brilliant mathematicians worked against the clock to break German codes and warn North Atlantic convoys. As the film opens, the Germans have changed their code again, making it even more fiendishly difficult to break (from my notes: "150 million million million ways of doing it," but alas I did not note what "it" was). Tom Jericho, sent home from Bletchley after a nervous breakdown, has been summoned back to the enclave because even if he is a wreck, maybe his brilliance can be of help.

Why did Jericho have a breakdown? Not because of a mathematical stalemate, but because he was overthrown by Claire Romilly (Saffron Burrows), the beautiful Bletchley colleague he loved, who disappeared mysteriously without saying good-bye. Back on the job, he grows chummy with Claire's former roommate, Hester Wallace (Kate Winslet), who may have clues about Claire even though she doesn't realize it. Then, in a subtle, oblique way, Tom and Hester begin to get more than chummy. All the time Wigram (Jeremy Northam), an intelligence operative, is keeping an eye on Tom and Hester, because he thinks they may know more than they admit about Claire—and because Claire may have been passing secrets to the Germans.

Whether any of these speculations are fruitful, I will allow you to discover. What I like about the movie is its combination of suspense and intelligence. If it does not quite explain exactly how decryption works (how could it?), it at least gives us a good idea of how decrypters work, and we understand how crucial Bletchley was—so crucial its existence was kept a secret for thirty years. When the fact that the British had broken Enigma finally became known, histories of the war had to be rewritten; a recent biography of Churchill suggests, for example, that when he strode boldly on the rooftop of the Admiralty in London, it was because secret Enigma messages assured him there would be no air raids that night.

The British have a way of not wanting to seem to care very much. It seasons their thrillers. American heroes are stalwart, forthright, and focused; Brits like understatement and sly digs. The tension between Tom Jericho and Wigram is all the more interesting because both characters seem to be acting in their own little play some of the time, and are as interested in the verbal fencing as in the underlying disagreement. It is a battle of style. You can see similar fencing personalities in the world of Graham Greene, and, of course, it is the key to James Bond.

Kate Winslet is very good here, plucky, wearing sensible shoes, with the wrong haircut—and then, seen in the right light, as a little proletarian sex bomb. She moves between dowdy and sexy so easily it must mystify even her. Claire, when she is seen, is portrayed by Saffron Burrows as the kind of woman any sensible man *knows* cannot be kept in his net—which is why she attracts a masochistic romantic like Tom Jericho, who sets himself up for his own betrayal. If it is true (and it is) that *Pearl Harbor* is the story of how the Japanese staged a sneak attack on an American love triangle, at least *Enigma* is not about how the Nazis devised their code to undermine a British love triangle. That is true not least because the British place puzzle solving at least on a par with sex, and like to conduct their affairs while on (not as a substitute for) duty.

Enough ★ ½
PG-13, 115 m., 2002

Jennifer Lopez (Slim), Billy Campbell (Mitch), Juliette Lewis (Ginny), Russell Milton (Alex), Tessa Allen (Gracie), Dan Futterman (Joe), Chris Maher (Phil), Noah Wyle (Robbie), Fred Ward (Jupiter). Directed by Michael Apted and produced by Rob Cowan and Irwin Winkler. Screenplay by Nicholas Kazan.

Enough is a nasty item masquerading as a feminist revenge picture. It's a step or two above *I Spit on Your Grave*, but uses the same structure, in which a man victimizes a woman for the first half of the film, and then the woman turns the tables in an extended sequence of graphic violence. It's surprising to see a director like Michael Apted and an actress like Jennifer Lopez associated with such tacky material.

It is possible to imagine this story being told in a good film, but that would involve a different screenplay. Nicholas Kazan's script makes the evil husband (Billy Campbell) such an unlikely caricature of hard-breathing, sadistic testosterone that he cannot possibly be a real human being. Of course there are men who beat their wives and torture them with cruel mind games, but do they satirize themselves as the heavy in a B movie? The husband's swings of personality and mood are so sudden, and his motivation makes so little sense, that he has no existence beyond the stereotyped Evil Rich White Male. The fact that he preys on a poor Latino waitress is just one more cynical cliché.

The story: Jennifer Lopez plays Slim, a waitress in a diner where she shares obligatory sisterhood and bonding with Ginny (Juliette Lewis), another waitress. A male customer tries to get her to go on a date, and almost succeeds before another customer named Mitch (Billy Campbell) blows the whistle and reveals the first man was only trying to win a bet. In the movie's headlong rush of events, Slim and Mitch are soon married, buy a big house, have a cute child, and then Slim discovers Mitch is having affairs, and he growls at her: "I am, and always will be, a person who gets what he wants." He starts slapping her around.

Although their child is now three or four, this is a Mitch she has not seen before in their marriage. Where did this Mitch come from? How did he restrain himself from pounding and strangling her during all of the early years? Why did she think herself happy until now? The answer, of course, is that Mitch turns on a dime when the screenplay requires him to. He even starts talking differently.

The plot (spoiler warning) now involves Slim's attempts to hide herself and the child from Mitch. She flees to Michigan and hooks up with a battered-wife group, but Mitch, like the hero of a mad slasher movie, is always able to track her down. Along the way Slim appeals for help to the father (Fred Ward) who has never acknowledged her, and the father's dialogue is so hilariously over the top in its cruelty that the scene abandons all hope of working seriously and simply functions as haywire dramaturgy.

Slim gets discouraging advice from a lawyer ("There is nothing you can do. He will win."). And then she gets training in self-defense from a martial arts instructor. Both of these characters are African-American, following the movie's simplistic moral color-coding. The day when the evil husband is black and the self-defense instructor is white will not arrive in our lifetimes.

The last act of the movie consists of Slim outsmarting her husband with a series of clever ploys in which she stage-manages an escape route, sets a booby trap for his vehicle, and then lures him into a confrontation where she beats the shinola out of him, at length, with much blood, lots of stunt work, breakaway furniture, etc. The movie, in time-honored horror movie tradition, doesn't allow Mitch to really be dead the first time. There is a plot twist showing that Slim can't really kill him—she's the heroine, after all—and then he lurches back into action like the slasher in many an exploitation movie, and is destroyed more or less by accident. During this action scene Slim finds time for plenty of dialogue explaining that any court will find she was acting in self-defense.

All of this would be bad enough without the performance of Tessa Allen as Gracie, the young daughter. She has one of those squeaky, itsy-bitsy piped-up voices that combines with babyish dialogue to make her more or less insufferable; after the ninth or tenth scream of "Mommy! Mommy!" we hope that she will be shipped off to an excellent day-care center for the rest of the story.

Jennifer Lopez is one of my favorite actresses, but not here, where the dialogue requires her to be passionate and overwrought in a way that is simply not believable, maybe because no one could take this cartoon of a story seriously. No doubt she saw *Enough* as an opportunity to play a heavy, dramatic role, but there is nothing more dangerous than a heavy role in a lightweight screenplay, and this material is such a melodramatic soap opera that the slick production values seem like a waste of effort. ☞

Erin Brockovich ★ ★
R, 126 m., 2000

Julia Roberts (Erin Brockovich), Albert Finney (Ed Masry), Aaron Eckhart (George), Marg Helgenberger (Donna Jensen), Cherry Jones (Pamela Duncan), Peter Coyote (Kurt Potter), Scotty Leavenworth (Matthew), Gemmenne De La Pena (Katie). Directed by Steven Soderbergh and produced by Danny DeVito, Michael Shamberg, and Stacey Sher. Screenplay by Susannah Grant.

Erin Brockovich is *Silkwood* (Meryl Streep fighting nuclear wastes) crossed with *A Civil Action* (John Travolta against pollution), plus Julia Roberts in a plunging neckline. Roberts plays a real-life heroine who helped uncover one of the biggest environmental crimes in history. But her performance upstages the story; this is always Roberts, not Brockovich, and unwise wardrobe decisions position her character somewhere between a caricature and a distraction.

I know all about the real Erin Brockovich because I saw her on *Oprah*, where she cried at just the right moment in a filmed recap of her life. She was a divorced mom of three with few employment prospects, who talked her way into a job at a law firm, began an investigation on her own initiative, and played a key role in a pollution suit that cost Pacific Gas and Electric a $333 million settlement.

There is obviously a story here, but *Erin Brockovich* doesn't make it compelling. The film lacks focus and energy, the character development is facile and thin, and what about those necklines? I know that the real Brockovich liked to dress provocatively; that's her personal style and she's welcome to it. But the Hollywood version makes her look like a miniskirted hooker, with her bras that peek cheerfully above her necklines.

Oh, the movie tries to deal with the clothes. "You might want to rethink your wardrobe a little," her boss (Albert Finney) tells her. She inelegantly replies, "I think I look nice, and as long as I have one ass instead of two, I'll wear what I like." Yeah, fine, after she's already lost her own personal injury suit by flashing cleavage on the witness stand and firing off four-letter words. When she dresses the same way to go door-to-door in a working-class neighborhood where industrial chemicals have caused illness, we have to wonder whether, in real life, she was hassled or mistrusted.

Whether she was or wasn't, the costume design sinks this movie. Julia Roberts is a sensational-looking woman, and dressed so provocatively, in every single scene, she upstages the material. If the medium is the message, the message in this movie is sex.

That's all the more true because the supporting characters are not vivid or convincing. Albert Finney is one of the most robust and powerful actors in the movies, but here, as a personal injury lawyer named Ed Masry, he comes across like an office manager at H & R Block. He's dampened; there's no fire in his performance, and when he complains that the cost of the lawsuit may bankrupt him, all we can think about is the infinitely greater impact of John Travolta's similar dialogue in *A Civil Action*.

Erin has a kind of relationship with her next-door neighbor, George, a Harley fan who becomes a baby-sitter for her children. George is played by Aaron Eckhart, who was so dominant in *In the Company of Men*, but here, wearing a twirpy John Ritter beard that he doesn't seem comfortable with, he's a shallow cipher. The couple can't even have convincing arguments because there's not enough between them in the first place.

Seeing the details of Brockovich's home life, her relationship with her kids and friends, the way she talks, the way she postures, we're always aware that there's a performance going on. Streep was so much more convincing in the somewhat similar role of Karen Silkwood. We understand that Pacific Gas and Electric has polluted groundwater and is apparently responsible for death and disease, but it never emerges as much of a villain, and in the pallid confrontations with their attorneys there's none of the juice that Robert Duvall's company attorney brought to *A Civil Action*.

Steven Soderbergh, who directed, has blown a great opportunity to make the movie that the real Erin Brockovich calls for. Susannah Grant's by-the-numbers screenplay sees the characters as markers on a storyboard rather than flesh-and-blood humans. Scenes with members of the suffering families genuflect in the direction of pathos, but are cut and dried.

193

It doesn't feel like we're seeing Erin Brockovich share the pain, but like we're seeing Julia Roberts paying a house call (again, we remember the power of *A Civil Action*).

Erin Brockovich has a screenplay with the depth and insight of a cable-TV docudrama, and that won't do for a 126-minute "major production." Maybe it's not that the necklines are distracting. Maybe it's just that the movie gives us so little to focus on that they win by default.

An Everlasting Piece ★ ★ ★
R, 109 m., 2000

Barry McEvoy (Colm), Brian F. O'Byrne (George), Anna Friel (Bronagh), Billy Connolly (The Scalper). Directed by Barry Levinson and produced by Louis DiGiaimo, Mark Johnson, Levinson, Jerome O'Connor, and Paula Weinstein. Screenplay by Barry McEvoy.

Anecdotes are polished in Ireland until they haven't a word to spare, with the listeners nodding at the familiar lines they've heard a hundred times. Some of the scenes in *An Everlasting Piece* have the feel of tales rehearsed in pubs for years. The scene, for example, where the hero's mother and his sister open the door and find his brother passed out drunk on the lawn. They haul him in, strip him of his wet clothes, and drop him facedown on the sofa. But when his face is revealed, of course it isn't the brother at all.

My guess is that Barry McEvoy, who wrote the movie and stars in it, didn't dream that up. I have a feeling it actually happened to somebody. The whole movie feels like that, even the dramatic parts—not in the details but in the tone. It's about two barbers in a prison for the insane, one Catholic, one Protestant, who go into the hairpiece business in Northern Ireland and find that hairpieces, like everything else in that unhappy land, have a way of getting mixed up with sectarian politics.

The lads are Colm (McEvoy) and George (Brian F. O'Byrne), and Colm got his job because his girlfriend, Bronagh (Anna Friel), works in the prison. The work is steady, although the conditions leave something to be desired, as when one prisoner tries to bite off

Colm's ear. Then they hear of a prisoner named the Scalper (Billy Connolly), so called because he tried too hard to create a market for his wares, who before his imprisonment was the only retailer of hairpieces in Northern Ireland.

There is now obviously a market that needs to be served, and Colm and George call their new company the Piece People, with George selling to Protestants, Colm selling to Catholics, and either one willing to be less than frank about his religion if it means making a sale. They hope to have the market to themselves, but a rival firm, Toupee or Not Toupee, sets up in business, and they get involved in a desperate sales competition to sell thirty pieces by the end of the year.

The movie is light on plot and heavy on incident, including several sales calls on peculiar or difficult clients, and a run-in with the IRA, whose leader doesn't know whether to shoot them or buy a piece from them. When the piece is later found at the scene of an IRA crime, the police come calling, and the Piece People seem to face a choice between jail and kneecapping.

The movie, wicked and cheeky, was directed by Barry Levinson (*Diner, Rain Man, Wag the Dog*), who has set four pictures in his hometown of Baltimore and now seeks the same kind of local color in Belfast, even if the details are different. He apparently decided to make the movie after coming across the original screenplay by McEvoy, a journeyman actor who based his own character, he says, on his father.

The movie has the ring of old, beloved, and partially but not entirely true stories. One detail is unexpectedly from life. Colm's home is shown in the middle of a vacant lot in Belfast, a wasteland bisected by a "peace wall" between the Protestant and Catholic sections, with a wire mesh fence to protect the home from firebombs. This house actually exists, I understand, and so of course do the conditions in Northern Ireland, where people try to go about their daily business while troops patrol the streets and a bitter struggle continues.

The key scene in *An Everlasting Piece* is a conversation between Colm and George as they contemplate selling hairpieces to a roomful of British soldiers who have lost their hair through stress. Colm, the Catholic, explains to his friend that he welcomes this sale to the enemy as a "gesture," which he can make although his friend cannot. Why not? "Because we're right and you're wrong," Colm explains, undercutting somewhat the benevolence of the gesture and leaving George trying to puzzle out the logic.

Everybody's Famous ★ ½
R, 92 m., 2001

Josse De Pauw (Jean Vereecken), Werner De Smedt (Willy van Outreve), Eva van der Gucht (Marva Vereecken), Thekla Reuten (Debbie), Victor Low (Michael Jansen), Gert Portael (Chantal Vereecken). Directed by Dominique Deruddere and produced by Loret Meus and Deruddere. Screenplay by Deruddere.

Everybody's Famous opens at a dreary talent contest at which the plump, desperate Marva demonstrates that she cannot sing, and could not deliver a song if she could. The judges, including the local mayor, hold up Olympic-style paddles scoring her with twos and threes, and we feel they're generous. But Jean, Marva's father, remains fanatically convinced that his daughter is talented and has a future—this despite the thankless girl's rudeness toward her old man.

Poor Jean (Josse De Pauw) is a good man, endured by his patient wife, Chantal (Gert Portael), treasured by his best friend, Willy (Werner De Smedt), and chained to the night shift at a factory where he has to inspect endless lines of bottles for hours at a time. At home, he joins his family in admiring the concerts of a pop singer named only Debbie (Thekla Reuten), who wears an incandescent blue polyester wig.

One day a bolt of coincidence joins Debbie and Jean. He finds an opportunity to kidnap her, and does, enlisting Willy to help him. His ransom demand: Debbie's manager (Victor Low) must record and release a song that Jean has written and that Marva (Eva van der Gucht) must sing.

This sets into motion a plot that begins with the same basic situation as *The King of Comedy*, where the Robert De Niro character kidnapped a TV host played by Jerry Lewis,

but the difference here is that *Everybody's Famous* is cheerful and optimistic, and if by the end everybody is not famous at least everybody has gotten what they want in life.

Three of the characters—the mother, the best friend, and the pop star—are so bland they're essentially place-holders. Josse De Pauw does what he can with the lead role, as a simple, good-hearted man who can't even get a goodnight kiss from the daughter he has sacrificed everything for. Victor Low seems like a very low-rent pop impresario, especially considering he can get a song scored, recorded, and on the charts in about twenty-four hours. But Eva van der Gucht brings some pouting humor to the role of the untalented daughter, whose costumes look like somebody's idea of a cruel joke, and who is bluntly told that she sings with a complete absence of emotion.

The big scene at the end involves one of those TV news situations that never happen in real life, where a reporter and camera materialize at a crucial point and are seemingly at the pleasure of the plot. And there's a surprise during a televised talent show, which will not come as that much of a surprise, however, to any sentient being.

The movie, from the Flemish community of Belgium, was one of this year's Oscar nominees for Best Foreign Film, leading one to wonder what films were passed over to make room for it. It is as pleasant as all get-out, sunny and serendipitous, and never even bothers to create much of a possibility that it will be otherwise. By the time the police spontaneously applaud a man they have every reason to believe is holding a hostage, the movie has given up any shred of plausibility and is simply trying to be a nice comedy. It's nice, but it's not much of a comedy.

Evolution ★ ★ ½
PG-13, 103 m., 2001

David Duchovny (Ira Kane), Orlando Jones (Harry Block), Ted Levine (Dr. Woodman), Julianne Moore (Allison Reed), Seann William Scott (Wayne Green), Dan Aykroyd (Governor Lewis), Wayne Duvall (Dr. Paulson), Michael Bower (Danny Donald), Wendy Braun (Nurse Tate). Directed by Ivan Reitman and produced by Daniel Goldberg, Joe Medjuck, and Reitman. Screenplay by David Diamond, David Weissman, and Don Jakoby.

I can't quite recommend *Evolution*, but I have a sneaky affection for it. It's not good, but it's nowhere near as bad as most recent comedies; it has real laughs, but it misses real opportunities. For example, by giving us aliens who are sort of harmless, it sets up a situation where the heroes should be trying to protect them. But no. Everybody wants to kill them, apparently because the national psyche has reverted to the 1950s, when all flying saucers were automatically fired on by the army.

Ivan Reitman, who directed the film, also made *Ghostbusters*, and there are times when you can see that he remembers his earlier success all too well. Both movies have vast gaseous monsters, although only this one, keenly alert to the bodily orifice du jour, gives us "Help! I'm Trapped Up the Alien's Sphincter!" jokes. I have days on the movie beat when I don't know if I'm a critic or a proctologist.

As the film opens, a would-be fireman (Seann William Scott) is practicing by rescuing an inflatable doll from a burning shack, when a flaming meteor crashes nearby. Harry Block (Orlando Jones), a scientist from nearby Glen Canyon Community College, is called to investigate and brings along his friend, science instructor Ira Kane (David Duchovny). They discover the meteor has "punched through" to an underground cavern, where it is oozing strange sluglike little creatures.

Kane and Bloch have a nice double-act together; like the characters in *Ghostbusters* they talk intelligently and possess wit and irony, and are not locked into one-liners. Jones even gets a laugh out of a significant nod, which is not easy in a movie with this decibel level. I also liked the way they came up with a popular drugstore item as a weapon against the invaders.

The alien creatures have the amazing ability to evolve in brief generations into whatever the screenplay requires: flying dinosaurs, creepy-crawlies, savage reptiles, even a sad-eyed ET clone that has an *Alien* tooth-monster hiding down its throat. The army is called in, led by Dr. Woodman (Ted Levine), a soldier-scientist who worked with Ira Kane once before ("he's

a dangerous disgrace"). Turns out Ira inoculated platoons of soldiers with a substance with such side effects as diarrhea, blindness, facial paralysis, and hair loss. The army named this tragic syndrome after Kane; I found myself thinking of funnier names for it, starting with the Bald Runs.

Dr. Woodman's assistant is Allison Reed (Julianne Moore), whose character trait is that she falls over everything. She is, however, funny in other ways, and sides with the two community college guys when her boss tries to freeze them out of the investigation. Meanwhile, the evolving creatures take on weird manifestations while the Mother of All Creatures is expanding down there in that cavern, generating all manner of strange offspring, while preparing to make an appearance in the grand finale.

The aliens are clever and bizarre movie creatures, designed by special-effects wizard Phil Tippett, who applied "the basic theory of panspermia," according to the press notes, which I always study after movies like this. It will come as news to panspermists that pansperm can evolve into amphibians, reptiles, birds, and mammals within a week; *Evolution* parts company with the basic theory almost before the publicist can get it into the notes, but never mind: One does not attend this movie for scientific facts. That is what the *Star Trek* movies are for.

Would it surprise you if I said that after ninety minutes of preparation, we discover that the entire movie has been leading up to a moment when the Orlando Jones character finds himself occupying the business end of a giant alien's digestive tract? Not if you have a sense of fair play. Earlier in the movie, a little alien crawls under Jones's skin and lodges in *his* intestines, inspiring emergency measures by a doctor who cries, "There's no time for lubricant!"—inspiring Jones to utter the best line in the movie, "There's *always* time for lubricant!"

The Exorcist (2000 Version) ★ ★ ★ ½ (1973 Version) ★ ★ ★ ★
R, 132 m., 2000

Linda Blair (Regan), Ellen Burstyn (Chris MacNeil), Jason Miller (Father Karras), Max von Sydow (Father Merrin), Lee J. Cobb (Detective Kinderman), Kitty Winn (Sharon),

Jack MacGowran (Burke), Rev. William O'Malley (Father Joe Dyer). Directed by William Friedkin and produced by William Peter Blatty. Screenplay by Blatty, based on his novel.

I want to write about William Friedkin's *The Exorcist*, and instead find myself faced with the film's "director's cut." Here is one of the great horror films, and it has been subjected to editorial tinkering—no doubt to justify the advertising line, "The version you've never seen." No, and you don't need to, either.

I've revisited *The Exorcist* over the years and found it effective every time. Because it's founded on characters, details, and a realistic milieu, the shocks don't date; they still seem to grow from the material. In the early 1990s, I joined Owen Roizman, the film's cinematographer, in a shot-by-shot analysis of the film over four days at the Hawaii Film Festival. As we dissected it I gained an appreciation of the craft of the film—how it embeds the sensational material in an everyday world of misty nights, boozy parties, and housekeeping details, chats in a laundry room, and the personal lives of the priests. The movie is more horrifying because it does not seem to want to be. The horror creeps into the lives of characters preoccupied with their lives: Father Karras with his mother and his faith, Father Merrin with his work and health, Chris MacNeil with her career and marriage.

The movie also gains power because it takes its theology seriously—for a movie, anyway. *The Exorcist* was able to create a convincing portrait of priests at work, of their private lives, their fears and temptations. Instead of hurrying to exorcism as a cinematic stunt, it pauses for Father Karras (Jason Miller) to tell Regan's mother, Chris (Ellen Burstyn), that the best way to obtain an exorcism would be to take a time machine back to the sixteenth century. Exorcism has been replaced by modern discoveries about mental illness, he says, and we note he is a psychiatrist.

Above all, the movie's power came from the shocking nature of the victim—a sweet-faced young girl, who is poked and prodded by medical science, examined by fearsome machines, and gruesomely possessed by her evil visitor. There has been much discussion over the years about whether Linda Blair, the actress, was ex-

ploited by the film; she has said she was not, and the most fearsome scenes were accomplished with special effects and doubles, while the foul dialogue was dubbed by Mercedes McCambridge.

The Exorcist was and is a brilliant horror film, one with an archetypal ability to reach and disturb us. It will survive as long as people care about well-made movies. But now we are faced with this new version, some twelve minutes longer than the original. The restored material doesn't come as a surprise; some of it has been seen as outtakes on earlier video releases, and all of it has been much discussed by Friedkin and William Peter Blatty, the film's author and producer. Blatty has often said that Friedkin's original cut of about 140 minutes was "perfect." But the studio forced him to trim it to two hours. Friedkin defended the shorter version, saying his trims helped the pacing. This new version seems more like a "producer's cut" than a "director's cut." Although Friedkin endorses it, it reflects Blatty's long-standing preferences.

Having seen the new version and reviewed my laser disc of the original version, I noticed four areas of difference between the 1973 and 2000 versions. One change is probably useful, the second neutral, the third pointless, the fourth catastrophic. There may be other changes I missed, including some flash-frames of satanic faces, but here's what stood out:

1. Early in the film, Regan, the possessed girl, is subjected to invasive testing and a spinal tap, with lots of queasy close-ups of needles and fluids. This scene provides a preliminary medical explanation for Regan's behavior and sets up the later bedtime dialogue between mother and daughter about "what the doctor said"—dialogue that is unsupported in the 1973 version. It's useful.

2. The priests Karras and Merrin (Max von Sydow) have a talk on the stairs after the first round of exorcism, and Merrin suggests the true satanic target may not be the girl but those around her—the devil wants them to despair. The scene is interesting from a theological point of view, but interrupts the momentum.

3. We see the "spider walk," an infamous scene much discussed by *Exorcist* buffs where Regan is seen walking downstairs upside down, crab-style. This shot strikes me as a distracting

stunt, and since it exists in isolation from the scenes around it, feels gratuitous.

4. The original ending of *The Exorcist* shows Regan and her mother leaving their house for the last time. "She doesn't remember any of it," her mother tells Father Dyer (Reverend William O'Malley). Regan greets him politely, focuses on his Roman collar, and suddenly hugs him. They get in the car, which begins to pull away, and then stops so that Chris can give the priest Father Merrin's medal, found in Regan's room. His hand closes over it. The car drives away. The priest looks down the fatal stairs below Regan's bedroom window. He turns away. Music and fade-out.

In the new version, after Chris gives Dyer the medal, he gives it back to her, and her hand closes over it. This is an unnecessary extra beat, but nothing compared to what follows. As the car drives away, Dyer looks down the stairs, walks toward the house, and encounters Kinderman (Lee J. Cobb), the police detective. They have a conversation about movies—some nonsense about a version of *Wuthering Heights* starring Jackie Gleason and Lucille Ball. Hello? An ending that struck the perfect closing note has been replaced by one that jars and clangs and thumbs its nose at the film.

While these scenes may have various rationales in the minds of Friedkin and Blatty, they have one obvious rationale in the thinking at the studio: They provide an excuse for the theatrical rerelease and will help sell the video, even to those who already own the earlier version. That is not good enough. If the changes don't make the film better, they should not have been made. If I were showing *The Exorcist* to a friend, I would show the 1973 version without the slightest hesitation. I hope Warner Bros. doesn't suppress it in favor of this marketing ploy.

Note: Friedkin took strong exception to my remarks about marketing opportunities as one of the reasons for this version. See the Answer Man exchange.

The Eyes of Tammy Faye ★ ★ ★
PG-13, 79 m., 2000

A documentary produced and directed by Randy Barbato and Fenton Bailey.

"When she was born," her aunt recalls, "she had perfectly manicured fingernails." She still does. She also has eyelashes so firmly attached that she never removes them: "They have to sort of wear out. When one falls off, I replace it." Tammy Faye, once the evangelizing queen of a global satellite network, now "living in virtual exile in a gated community in Palm Springs," is the subject of *The Eyes of Tammy Faye*, a new documentary by Fenton Bailey and Randy Barbato.

Her saga is well known. How she and first husband, Jim Bakker, began as traveling evangelists, parlayed a puppet show into TV stardom, created three TV networks, were the first Christian broadcasters with their own satellite, and built the theme park Heritage USA near Charlotte, North Carolina—while Jim, according to the courts, was defrauding his viewers of millions. He went to prison, is now on parole and remarried. After their divorce ("we're still friends"), Tammy married Roe Messner, who oversaw construction on Heritage USA. Alas, he was convicted of bankruptcy fraud, and spent two years in prison, being released in early 1999.

All movies about women like this are required by law to contain the words, "She's a survivor." But John J. Bullock, the gay cohost of her most recent talk show, *John J. and Tammy Faye*, puts a new spin on it: "She's a survivor. After the Holocaust, there will be roaches, Tammy Faye, and Cher."

When Jim and Tammy were on the air in the 1980s, I confess to watching them, not because I was saved, but because I was fascinated. They were like two little puppets—Howdy Doody and Betty Boop made flesh. Tammy Faye cried on nearly every show, and sang with the force of a Brenda Lee, and when she'd do her famous version of "We're Blest," yes, dear reader, I would sing along with her.

The documentary reveals that she was a bundle of nerves in those days, as Jim withdrew into an obsession with Heritage USA empire-building (and brooded, no doubt, over his infamous one-night stand with Jessica Hahn). Tammy became addicted to pills, and her attention sometimes seemed to drift; directors Bailey and Barbato plundered the video archives to find moments like the one where Jim says, "Now Tammy's going to sing for us," and

Tammy is discovered wandering at the back of the set, gazing at a prop and saying, "I'm looking at this boat."

But she did have chemistry and a natural TV presence, and narrator RuPaul Charles points out that she'd do two or three shows in a row, entirely ad-lib, completely comfortable without a script.

RuPaul? Yes, the famous drag queen is the film's narrator, and a subtext of *The Eyes of Tammy Faye* is that unlike most Christian televangelists (especially her nemesis Jerry Falwell) she has always been friendly with gays. Old videotape shows her commiserating with an HIV-positive preacher at a time when mainstream shows still shunned the topic of AIDS, and she chose the gay Bullock as the cohost on her comeback attempt. (One segment shows him pulling a brassiere out of her purse and waving it over his head, claiming it's his.)

Codirectors Bailey and Barbato are also openly gay, and there was a hint in some of their remarks after the Sundance premiere of the film that they got into this project because they saw Tammy Faye as a camp icon. So she is, as in a sequence where she explains the amazing contents of her makeup kit ("I don't know what this is," she confesses about one product). But she is also, we sense, a woman of great generosity of spirit, and a TV natural: The star she most reminds me of is Lucille Ball.

Was she in on the scams? She was never charged, never brought to trial. In the doc she walks through the ruins of Heritage USA, which has been padlocked for ten years ("I'd love to give this place a good coat of paint"), and the Palm Springs home she and Jim shared at the end. She lived in comfort, and still does. But the movie tacitly implies she didn't do anything criminal, that what you saw on TV was the real Tammy Faye, all of her, with no hidden edges or secrets. In terms of broadcast hours, she lived more of her life on live TV than perhaps anyone else in history. She was like Jim Carrey in *The Truman Show*—only in on the secret.

F

Faithless ★ ★ ★ ½
R, 142 m., 2001

Lena Endre (Marianne), Erland Josephson (Bergman), Krister Henriksson (David), Thomas Hanzon (Markus), Michelle Gylemo (Isabelle), Juni Dahr (Margareta), Philip Zanden (Martin Goldman), Therese Brunnander (Petra Holst). Directed by Liv Ullmann and produced by Kaj Larsen. Screenplay by Ingmar Bergman.

The island is Faro, where Ingmar Bergman lives, and the house is Bergman's house, and the beach is where he walks, and the office is where he works, and we can see a shadowy 16mm film projector in the background, and remember hearing that the Swedish Film Institute sends him weekly shipments of films to watch. And the old man in the film is named "Bergman," although we don't learn that essential piece of the jigsaw until the final credits.

Or perhaps the house and its office are a set. And perhaps "Bergman" is partly Ingmar Bergman and partly the director's fictional creation. And surely, we think, he has a DVD player by now. *Faithless*, a film made from his screenplay and directed by Liv Ullmann, is intriguing in the way it dances in and out of the shadow of Bergman's autobiography. We learn in his book *The Magic Lantern*, for example, that in 1949 he was involved in an affair something like the one in this film—but we sense immediately that *Faithless* is not a memoir of that affair, but a meditation on the guilt it inspired.

Bergman, the son of a Lutheran bishop, has in his eighties forsaken the consolations of religion but not the psychic payments that it exacts. His film feels like an examination of conscience, and he's hard on himself. It's with a start we realize that Ullmann is also one of his former lovers, that they have a child together, and that in her vision he has clearly been forgiven his trespasses.

The movie is about a messy affair from "Bergman's" past, and it is about the creative process. As it begins, the old man (Erland Josephson) has writing paper on the desk before him, and is talking with an actress (Lena Endre). It becomes clear that this actress is not physically present. The dialogue suggests the director has enlisted this woman, or her memory, to help him think through a story he is writing. But she is also the woman the story is about. And she sometimes seems to be reading her story from his notes—as if he created her and she exists only in his words.

The woman is named Marianne. She is married to Markus (Thomas Hanzon), a symphony conductor, often away on tours. They have a daughter of eight or nine, Isabelle (Michelle Gylemo). David (Krister Henriksson) is Markus's best friend. One night while Markus is away David asks Marianne if he may sleep with her. She laughs him off, but then agrees they can share the same bed as brother and sister. Soon they have hurtled into a passionate affair, unforeseen and heedless.

It is clear that David is "Bergman" at an earlier age. He is a film director with vague projects in mind, he has long been attracted to Marianne, and he is, let us say, a louse. What becomes clear during the course of the film is that Markus is no saint either, and that he uses his daughter as a hostage in the unpleasantness that results.

Ullmann has a sure sense for the ways people behave in emotional extremity. *Faithless* is not made of soap opera sincerity, but from the messiness of people who might later wish they had behaved differently. When Markus surprises the naked David in bed with Marianne, he projects not jealous anger, but a kind of smarmy "gotcha!" triumph (for their part, they giggle nervously).

It is David who feels sexual jealousy; when Marianne returns from Markus with the news she has regained custody of her child, David thinks "something doesn't sound right," and cross-examines her until he forces out a description of how Markus raped her as the cost of custody. (This rape, described but not seen, has the same kind of reality in the mind's eye as the monologue about the boys on the beach in *Persona*.)

At one point in the film, "Bergman" reaches out and tenderly touches the cheek of David, and Ullmann has said this is the old man forgiving the young man, even though the old man can never forgive himself.

Ingmar Bergman has had his name on films for nearly sixty years. Some are among the best ever made. In old age he has grown more inward and personal, writing versions of his autobiography, usually to be directed by close friends. The films shot on Faro are in a category by themselves: chamber films, spare, chilly, with grateful interiors warmed by fires or candles. In *Faithless*, scenes in Stockholm and Paris show cozy interiors, boudoirs, restaurants, theaters, cafés. And then all is reduced to the spare, stark office—almost a monk's cell—where "Bergman" sits and remembers, summons his muses, and writes.

The Family Man ★ ★ ½
PG-13, 124 m., 2000

Nicolas Cage (Jack Campbell), Tea Leoni (Kate Reynolds), Jeremy Piven (Arnie), Don Cheadle (Cash), Makenzie Vega (Annie), Josef Sommer (Lassiter). Directed by Brett Ratner and produced by Marc Abraham, Tony Ludwig, Alan Riche, and Howard Rosenman. Screenplay by David Diamond and David Weissman.

It's a funny thing about supernatural movies. The black characters are always the ones with all the insights into the occult, but they rarely get to be the occulted. Consider Whoopi Goldberg in *Ghost*, Will Smith in *The Legend of Bagger Vance*, and now Don Cheadle in *The Family Man*. They're all on good terms with the paranormal, but act only as guides for Demi Moore, Matt Damon, Nicolas Cage, et al. They're always the medium but never the message.

In *The Family Man*, Cage plays Jack Campbell, a businessman who is ruled by his career. He has no personal life to speak of, works on Christmas Eve, and doesn't even bother to return a phone message from Kate Reynolds (Tea Leoni), his girlfriend from college. In 1987, we learn, Jack flew off for a year in London even though Kate tearfully begged him to stay. She feared if he left they'd never get married, and she was right.

Now, through the paranormal intervention of a taxi driver (Cheadle) who acts as his guide, or portal, or something, Jack goes to sleep as a wealthy bachelor and awakens in a parallel time-track where apparently he did fly back

from London, marry Kate, and father a six-year-old and a baby. He also now has a dog, which is slobbering all over him.

The heart of the movie is his gradual realization that his other life has somehow disappeared, that he's now a family man, that he has been granted the opportunity to experience all that he missed by putting his career ahead of personal goals. I always wonder, in movies like this, why the hero has been transferred into the alternate life but has retained the original memories—but, of course, if he had the alternate memories he wouldn't know anything had happened.

Tea Leoni *(Deep Impact, Flirting with Disaster)* is lovable as the wife, and does a good job of covering the inevitable moments when she *must*, we think, realize that a stranger is inhabiting her husband's body. The story takes a sitcom turn as Jack finds out he works for his father-in-law as a tire salesman, and tries to talk his way back into the big money in Manhattan.

I liked the movie, liked Cage, liked Leoni, smiled a lot, and yet somehow remained at arm's length, because I was having a parallel-life experience of my own. I kept remembering a movie named *Me Myself I*, which came out in spring 1999 and did a more persuasive and thoughtful job of considering more or less the same plot. In that one, Rachel Griffiths is a workaholic writer who through supernatural intervention is transported into married life with the guy she loved fifteen years ago. She suddenly has three children, etc. The two movies even share a plot point: One of the kids is observant and knows this is not their real parent. "When's Mommy gonna be home?" asks her son; "You're not really daddy, are you?" asks his daughter.

Why similar movies get made at the same time is a good question. Demi Moore's *Passion of Mind* was about a character shuttling nightly between two lives. And of course another wellspring of *The Family Man* is *It's a Wonderful Life*, except that this time the dark version is reality and the warm family world is the fantasy—or whatever it is.

One problem with the underlying plot is, how do you dispose of the family in the alternative world after the supernatural visitor learns his lesson? *Me Myself I* handled that neatly with actual contact between the two versions of the heroine. *The Family Man* doesn't find a satisfactory resolution: Not that it's crucial, but it would have been nice. The movie is sweet, light entertainment, but could have been more.

The Fast and the Furious ★ ★ ★
PG-13, 101 m., 2001

Vin Diesel (Dominic Toretto), Paul Walker (Brian), Jordana Brewster (Mia Toretto), Michelle Rodriguez (Letty), Rick Yune (Johnny Tran), Beau Holden (Ted Gessner). Directed by Rob Cohen and produced by Neal H. Moritz. Screenplay by Ken Li, Gary Scott Thompson, Erik Bergquist, and David Ayer.

The Fast and the Furious remembers summer movies from the days when they were produced by American-International and played in drive-ins on double features. It's slicker than films like *Grand Theft Auto*, but it has the same kind of pirate spirit—it wants to raid its betters and carry off the loot. It doesn't have a brain in its head, but it has some great chase scenes, and includes the most incompetent cop who ever went undercover.

According to the "In a World" Guy, who narrates the trailer, the movie takes place "In a world . . . beyond the law." It stars Vin Diesel, the bald-headed, mug-faced action actor who looks like a muscular Otto Preminger. He plays Toretto, a star of the forbidden sport of street racing who rockets his custom machine through Los Angeles at more than 100 mph before pushing a button on the dashboard and *really* accelerating, thanks to a nitrous oxide booster. He also runs a bar where his sister Mia (Jordana Brewster) serves "tuna salad on white bread, no crusts" every day to Brian (Paul Walker), who looks a little like white bread, no crusts himself.

Brian hangs out there because he wants to break into street racing, and because he likes Mia. Toretto's gang is hostile to him, beats him up, disses him, and he comes back for more. He ends up winning Toretto's friendship by saving him from the cops. The races involve cars four abreast at speedway speeds down city streets. This would be difficult in Chicago, but is easy in Los Angeles, because, as everybody knows, L.A. has no traffic and no cops.

Actually, Brian is a cop, assigned to investigate a string of multimillion-dollar truck hijackings. The hijackers surround an eighteen-wheeler with three Honda Civics, shoot out the window on the passenger side, fire a cable into the cab, and climb into the truck at high speeds. This makes for thrilling action sequences when it works, and an even more thrilling action sequence when it doesn't, in a chase scene that approaches but does not surpass the climax of *The Road Warrior*.

During the chases, we observe that there is *no* other traffic on the highway—just the trucks and the Hondas. Anyone who has ever driven a Honda next to an eighteen-wheeler will know that a Humvee is the wiser choice, but never mind. And only a hopeless realist would observe that leaping through the windshield of a speeding truck is a dangerous and inefficient way of stealing VCRs. In Chicago, the crooks are more prudent, and steal from parked trucks, warehouses, and other unmoving targets. Toretto should try it.

Anyway, Brian at first seems just like a guy who wants to race, but is revealed as a cop in an early scene, although not so early the audience has not guessed it. He works for a unit that has its undercover headquarters in a Hollywood house, and as he enters it his boss says, "Eddie Fisher built this house for Elizabeth Taylor in the 1950s." I am thinking: (1) This is almost certainly true or it would not be said in a movie so stingy with dialogue, and (2) Is this the first time Brian has seen his unit's office?

One of the nice things about the movie is the way it tells a story and explains its characters. It's a refreshing change from such noplot, all-action movies as *Gone in 60 Seconds*. We learn a little about Toretto's father and his childhood, and we see Brian and Mia falling in love—although I think in theory you are not supposed to date the sister of a guy you are undercover to investigate. Michelle Rodriguez, the star of the underappreciated boxing movie *Girlfight*, costars as a member of the hijack gang, and gets to land one solid right on a guy's jaw, just to keep her credentials.

The Fast and the Furious is not a great movie, but it delivers what it promises to deliver, and knows that a chase scene is supposed to be about something more than special effects. It has some of that grandiose, self-pitying dialogue we've treasured in movies like this ever since *Rebel Without a Cause.* "I live my life a quarter-mile at a time," Toretto tells Brian. "For those ten seconds, I'm free." And, hey, even for the next thirty seconds, he's decelerating.

Fast Food, Fast Women ★ ½
R, 95 m., 2001

Anna Thomson (Bella), Jamie Harris (Bruno), Louise Lasser (Emily), Robert Modica (Paul), Lonette McKee (Sherry-Lynn), Victor Argo (Seymour), Angelica Torn (Vitka), Austin Pendleton (George). Directed by Amos Kollek and produced by Hengameh Panahi. Screenplay by Kollek.

There's nothing wrong with *Fast Food, Fast Women* that a casting director and a rewrite couldn't have fixed. The rewrite would have realized that the movie's real story involves a sweet, touching romance between two supporting characters. The casting director would have questioned the sanity of using Anna Thomson in the lead role.

The sweet love story stars Louise Lasser in her best performance, as Emily, a widow who finds Paul (Robert Modica) through a personals ad. Their courtship is complicated by pride and misunderstanding, and by way too many plot contrivances. The lead role involves Thomson as Bella, a waitress who is said to be thirty-five.

A gentleman does not question a lady about her age, but Thomson was playing adult roles twenty years ago, has obviously had plastic surgery, and always dresses to emphasize her extreme thinness and prominent chest, so that we can't help thinking she's had a boob job.

Faithful readers will know I rarely criticize the physical appearance of actors. I would have given Thomson a pass, but the movie seems to be inviting my thoughts about her character, since Lasser's character has one big scene where she confesses she's not really as young as she claims, and another where she wonders if she should have her breasts enlarged—and then Thomson's character asks the taxi driver, "Aren't I voluptuous enough?" It's unwise to have one character being honest about issues when we're supposed to overlook the same questions raised by another character.

The movie takes place in one of those movie diners where everybody hangs out all day long and gets involved in each other's business. Bella rules the roost, pouring coffee for Paul and his pal Seymour (Victor Argo). The diner has so many regulars, it even has a regular hooker, Vitka (Angelica Torn), who stutters, so that guys can't tell she's asking them if they feel like having a good time. We learn that for years Bella has been having an affair with the married George (Austin Pendleton), who claims to be a Broadway producer, but whose shows sound like hallucinations. He spends most of their time together looking away from her and grinning at a private joke.

Bella meets a cab driver named Bruno (Jamie Harris), who has become the custodian of two children, leading to more misunderstandings that threaten to derail their future together. And then Bruno meets Emily, Seymour falls for Wanda, a stripper in a peep show, and there comes a point when you want to ask Amos Kollek, the writer-director, why the zany plot overkill when your real story is staring you in the face? (You want to ask him that even before the zebras and the camels turn up, and long before the unforgivable "happy ending.")

Lasser and Modica, as Emily and Paul, are two nice, good, lovable people who deserve each other, and whenever the movie involves their story, we care (even despite some desperate plot contrivances). Lasser's vulnerability, her courage, and the light in her eyes all bring those scenes to life, as does Paul's instinctive courtesy and the way he responds to her warmth. There's the movie. If it has to pretend to be about Bella, Kollek as the director should at least have been able to see the character more clearly—clearly enough to know the audience cannot believe she is thirty-five, and thinks of her whenever anyone else mentions plastic surgery.

The Fast Runner ★ ★ ★ ★
NO MPAA RATING, 172 m., 2002

Natar Ungalaaq (Atanarjuat), Sylvia Ivalu (Atuat), Peter-Henry Arnatsiaq (Oki), Lucy Tulugarjuk (Puja), Madeline Ivalu (Panikpak), Paul Qulitalik (Qulitalik), Eugene Ipkarnak (Sauri, the Chief), Pakkak Innushuk

(Amaqjuaq). Directed by Zacharias Kunuk and produced by Paul Apak Angilirq, Norman Cohn, and Zacharias Kunuk. Screenplay by Paul Apak Angilirq.

We could begin with the facts about *The Fast Runner*. It is the first film shot in Inuktitut, the language of the Inuit peoples who live within the Arctic Circle. It was made with an Inuit cast, and a 90 percent Inuit crew. It is based on a story that is at least 1,000 years old. It records a way of life that still existed within living memory.

Or we could begin with the feelings. The film is about romantic tensions that lead to tragedy within a small, closely knit community of people who depend on one another for survival, surrounded by a landscape of ice and snow. It shows how people either learn to get along under those circumstances, or pay a terrible price.

Or we could begin with the lore. Here you will see humans making a living in a world that looks, to us, like a barren wasteland. We see them fishing, hunting, preparing their kill, scraping skins to make them into clothing, tending the lamps of oil that illuminate their igloos, harvesting the wild crops that grow in the brief summertime, living with the dogs that pull their sleds.

Or we could begin with the story of the film's production. It was shot with a high-definition digital video camera, sidestepping the problems that cinematographers have long experienced while using film in temperatures well below zero. Its script was compiled from versions of an Inuit legend told by eight elders. The film won the Camera d'Or, for best first film, at Cannes, and was introduced at Telluride by the British stage director Peter Sellars; telling the story of its origin, he observed, "In most cultures, a human being is a library."

We could begin in all of those ways, or we could plunge into the film itself, an experience so engrossing it is like being buried in a new environment. Some find the opening scene claustrophobic. It takes place entirely inside an igloo, the low lighting provided only by oil lamps, most of the shots in close-up, and we do not yet know who all the characters are. I thought it was an interesting way to begin: to plunge us into this community and share its warmth as it

shelters against the cold, and then to open up and tell its story.

We meet two brothers, Amaqjuaq (Pakkak Innushuk), known as the Strong One, and Atanarjuat (Natar Ungalaaq), known as the Fast Runner. They are part of a small group of Inuit including the unpleasant Oki (Peter-Henry Arnatsiaq), whose father is the leader of the group. There is a romantic problem. Oki has been promised Atuat (Sylvia Ivalu), but she and Atanarjuat are in love. Just like in Shakespeare. In the most astonishing fight scene I can recall, Atanarjuat challenges Oki, and they fight in the way of their people: They stand face to face while one solemnly hits the other, there is a pause, and the hit is returned, one blow after another, until one or the other falls.

Atanarjuat wins, but it is not so simple. He is happy with Atuat, but eventually takes another wife, Puja (Lucy Tulugarjuk), who is pouty and spoiled and put on Earth to cause trouble. During one long night of the midnight sun, she is caught secretly making love to Amaqjuaq, and banished from the family. It is, we gather, difficult to get away with adultery when everybody lives in the same tent.

Later there is a shocking murder. Fleeing for his life, Atanarjuat breaks free, and runs across the tundra—runs and runs, naked. It is one of those movie sequences you know you will never forget.

At the end of the film, over the closing titles, there are credit cookies showing the production of the film, and we realize with a little shock that the film was made now, by living people, with new technology. There is a way in which the intimacy of the production and the 172-minute running time lull us into accepting the film as a documentary of real life. The actors, many of them professional Inuit performers, are without affect or guile: They seem sincere, honest, revealing, as real people might, and although the story involves elements of melodrama and even soap opera, the production seems as real as a frozen fish.

I am not surprised that *The Fast Runner* has been a box-office hit in its opening engagements. It is unlike anything most audiences will ever have seen, and yet it tells a universal story. What's unique is the patience it has with its characters: The willingness to watch and listen as they reveal themselves, instead of pushing them to the front like little puppets and having them dance through the story. *The Fast Runner* is passion, filtered through ritual and memory.

Fat Girl ★ ★ ★ ½

NO MPAA RATING, 83 m., 2001

Anais Reboux (Anais), Roxane Mesquida (Elena), Libero De Rienzo (Fernando), Arsinee Khanjian (Mother), Romain Goupil (Father), Laura Betti (Fernando's Mother), Albert Goldberg (The Killer), Claude Sese (Police Officer), Marc Samuel (Inspector). Directed by Catherine Breillat and produced by Fredy Lagrost and Jean-Francois Lepetit. Screenplay by Breillat.

Young love is idealized as sweet romance, but early sexual experiences are often painful and clumsy and based on lies. It is not merely that a boy will tell a girl almost anything to get her into bed, but that a girl will pretend to believe almost anything because she is curious too. *Fat Girl* is the brutally truthful story of the first sexual experiences of a fifteen-year-old sexpot and her pudgy twelve-year-old sister.

The movie was written and directed by Catherine Breillat, a French woman who is fascinated by the physical and psychological details of sex. Her characters may talk of love, but rarely feel it, and are not necessarily looking for it: Her women, as well as men, have a frank curiosity about what they can do, and what can be done, with their bodies. Her previous film, the notorious *Romance*, was about a sexually unsatisfied woman who goes on a deliberate quest for better sex—and if that sounds like a porn film, *Romance* is not about ecstasy but about plumbing, sweating, hurting, lying and loathing.

Fat Girl, seemingly more innocent, at times almost like one of those sophisticated French movies about an early summer of love, turns out to be more painful and shocking than we anticipate. It is like life, which has a way of interrupting our plans with its tragic priorities. True, Anais (Anais Reboux) achieves a personal milestone, but at what a cost.

The movie takes place in a summer resort area. Anais and her sexy fifteen-year-old sister, Elena (Roxane Mesquida), are vacationing with their mother (Arsinee Khanjian). Their father (Romain Goupil) is a workaholic for whom the family is just one more item on his to-do list. Elena attracts the attention of the local boys, and her overweight kid sister looks on with smoldering jealousy: Anais at twelve is smarter and in certain ways more grown-up. She is eager for a sexual experience, although she has little idea what that would entail (in one sad-sweet scene in a swimming pool, she imagines a romantic rivalry for her affections between . . . a pier and a ladder). In another scene, she eats a banana split in the backseat while watching Elena necking in the front.

Fernando (Libero De Rienzo) comes sniffing around. He is older, a law student, also on vacation. Elena finds his attention flattering. He speaks of love, is vague about the future, insistent about his demands. What Breillat sees clearly is that Elena is not an innocent who is deceived by his lies, but a curious girl with high spirits who wants to believe. Yes, she says she wants to keep her virginity (Anais wants to lose hers). But virginity and purity for Elena are two very different things. Like a lover in a Latin farce, Fernando climbs in through the bedroom window one night, and the "sleeping" Anais watches as Elena and Fernando have sex. What do they do? There is no doubt a French phrase for the words "everything but."

Breillat has no false sentimentality about women, no feeling that men are pigs. Sentiment and piggishness are pretty equally distributed between the sexes in her movies. Consider a sequence in which Fernando steals one of his mother's rings and gives it to Elena, not quite saying what he promises by it. And then how Fernando's mother calls on Elena's mother to get the ring back. We discover that the ring is part of a little collection Fernando's mother has, of jewelry given to her by lying men; if she had a sense of humor, she would see the irony in how it has been passed on.

The private scenes between Anais and Elena are closely observed. The girls say hateful and insulting things to each other, as young adolescents are likely to do, but they also share trust and affection, and talk with absolute frankness about what concerns them. Elena's dalliance with Fernando ends unhappily, but then of course, in a way she knew it would.

Anais is left raging with jealousy that she is still a virgin, and she is at least more realistic about life than Elena: When she loses her virginity, she says, it will be without love, to a man she hardly knows, because she just wants to get it out of the way and move on.

The film has a shocking ending, which Breillat builds to with shots that are photographed and edited to create a sense of menace. This ending leaves the audience stunned, and some will be angered by it. But consider how it works in step with what went before, and with the drift of Breillat's work. This is not a film softened and made innocuous by timid studio executives after "test screenings." There is a jolting surprise in discovering that this film has free will, and can end as it wants, and that its director can make her point, however brutally. And perhaps only with this ending could Anais's cold, hard, sad logic be so unforgivingly demonstrated.

Fellini Satyricon ★ ★ ★ ★
R, 129 m., 1970 (rereleased 2001)

Martin Potter (Encolpio), Hiram Keller (Ascilto), Max Born (Gitone), Salvo Randone (Eumolpo), Mario Romagnoli (Trimalcione), Magali Noel (Fortunata), Capucine (Trifena), Alain Cuny (Lica), Fanfulla (Vernacchio). Directed by Federico Fellini and produced by Alberto Grimaldi. Screenplay by Fellini and Bernardino Zapponi, based on the book by Petronius.

"I am examining ancient Rome as if this were a documentary about the customs and habits of the Martians."
—Fellini in an interview, 1969

Fellini Satyricon was released in 1970, and I was ready for it: "Some will say it is a bloody, depraved, disgusting film," I wrote in a fever. "Indeed, people by the dozens were escaping from the sneak preview I attended. But *Fellini Satyricon* is a masterpiece all the same, and films that dare everything cannot please everybody." Today I'm not so sure it's a masterpiece, except as an expression of the let-it-all-hangout spirit of the 1970 world that we both then occupied. But it is so much more ambitious and audacious than most of what we see today that simply as a reckless gesture, it shames

these timid times. Films like this are a reminder of how machine-made and limited recent product has become.

The movie is based on a book that retold degenerate versions of Roman and Greek myth. Petronius's *Satyricon,* written at the time of Nero, was lost for centuries and found in a fragmented form, which Fellini uses to explain his own fragmented movie; both book and film end in midsentence. Petronius was a sensualist who celebrated and mocked sexual decadence at the same time. So does Fellini, who observes that although the wages of sin may be death, it's nice work if you can get it.

The movie was made two years after the Summer of Love—it came out at about the same time as the documentary *Woodstock*—and it preserves the postpill, pre-AIDS sexual frenzy of that time, when penalty-free sex briefly seemed to be a possibility (key word: seemed). The characters in the Fellini film may be burned alive, vivisected, skewered, or crushed, but they have no concerns about viruses, guilt, or psychological collapse. Like most of the characters in ancient myth, indeed, they have no psychology; they act according to their natures, without introspection or the possibility of change. They are hard-wired by the myths that contain them.

The film loosely follows the travels and adventures of several characters, notably the students Encolpio (Martin Potter) and Ascilto (Hiram Keller), as they fight over the favors of the comely slave boy Gitone (Max Born). Gitone is won by Ascilto, who sells him to the repulsive actor Vernacchio (Fanfulla), whose performances include mutilation of prisoners. True to the nature of the film, Gitone doesn't mind such treatment and indeed rather enjoys the attention, but the story moves on, presenting a series of masters and slaves in moments of grotesque drama and lurid fantasy. It is all phantasmagoria, said Pauline Kael, who hated the film, and wrote, "Though from time to time one may register a face or a set or an episode, for most of the time one has the feeling of a camera following people walking along walls."

Well, yes and no. There are scenes that are complete playlets, as when a patrician couple free their slaves and then commit suicide, or when a dead rich man's followers gather on the seashore to consider his final request that his body be eaten. These moments pop out from the fresco as they must have popped out of Petronius, but Fellini is unconcerned with beginnings, middles, and ends, and wants us to walk through the film as through a gallery in which an artist tries variations on a theme. This would increasingly be his approach in the films that followed; set against this ancient Rome is the fragmented modern city in *Fellini Roma*, which is a series of episodes in search of a destination, and lacks the structure of his great Roman film, *La Dolce Vita* (1959).

Does *Satyricon* work? Depends. Certainly the visuals are rich (Kael's wall-image doesn't do justice to their grungy, spermy, tactile fertility). Is there anyone we care about as we watch the film? We share the joy during a couple of sexual romps, and are touched by the suicides of the patricians, but—no, we don't care about them, because they seem defined not by their personalities but by their mythical programming. Like the figures in Keats's "Ode on a Grecian Urn," they are forever caught in the act of demonstrating their natures, without prologue or outcome.

In no other Fellini film do we see a more abundant demonstration of his affection for human grotesques (although *Fellini Casanova* comes close). I visited the set of this film one day, on the coast near Rome, when he was shooting the funeral of the man who wanted to be cannibalized. We were surrounded by dwarfs and giants, fat people and beanpoles, hermaphrodites and transvestites, some grotesquely painted or costumed, some deformed by nature or choice. "People ask, where did you find these faces?" Fellini said. "None of them are professional actors; these faces come from my private dreams. I opened a little office in Rome and asked funny-looking people to come in. Did you know Nero had a hang-up on freaks? He surrounded himself with them." And so does Fellini, perhaps because ordinary-looking extras would bring too much normality into his canvas.

What is the sum of all this effort? A film that deals in visual excess like no other, showing a world of amorality, cruelty, self-loathing, and passion. Did Fellini see his *Satyricon* as a warning to modern viewers, an object lesson? Not at all, in my opinion. He found an in-

stinctive connection between Petronius and himself—two artists fascinated by deviance and excess—and in the heady days of the late 1960s saw no reason to compromise. *Fellini Satyricon* is always described as a film about ancient Rome, but it may be one of the best films about the Summer of Love—not celebrating it, but displaying the process of its collapse. What is fun for a summer can be hard work for a lifetime.

15 Minutes ★ ★ ★
R, 120 m., 2001

Robert De Niro (Eddie Flemming), Edward Burns (Jordy Warsaw), Kelsey Grammer (Robert Hawkins), Karel Roden (Emil Slovak), Oleg Taktarov (Oleg Razgul), Melina Kanakaredes (Nicolette Karas), Vera Farmiga (Daphne Handlova). Directed by John Herzfeld and produced by Keith Addis, David Blocker, Herzfeld, and Nick Wechsler. Screenplay by Herzfeld.

I want to know if you think this is possible. Two creeps videotape themselves committing murder, and then attempt to sell the video to a reality news show for $1 million. They plan to beat the murder charges with an insanity plea, adding that they were abused as children.

I think it is possible. I heard about a documentary at Sundance this year where a fraternity boy videotaped his friend in a sex act that the woman claimed was rape. The video, later sold to the press by law enforcement officials, is included in the documentary, so you can decide for yourself.

What kind of person would do something like that? (I refer both to the fictional murder plot and to the rape footage.) The kind of person, I imagine, who appears on the Jerry Springer show, a program I study for signposts on our society's descent into barbarism. When you say these people have no shame, you have to realize that "shame" is a concept and perhaps even a word with which they are not familiar. They will eagerly degrade themselves for the fifteen minutes of fame so famously promised them by Andy Warhol.

15 Minutes is a cynical, savage satire about violence, the media, and depravity. It doesn't have the polish of *Natural Born Killers* or the wit of *Wag the Dog*, but it's a real movie, rough edges and all, and not another link from the sausage factory. A couple of the early reviews have called it implausible. They doubt that real killers would sell their footage to TV and then watch it in a Planet Hollywood, hoping to be spotted and arrested. See, that's the funny thing. I think there are people who would.

The movie stars Robert De Niro as a Manhattan detective who has become a celebrity, Edward Burns as a fire inspector, and Kelsey Grammer as a cross between Springer and Geraldo Rivera. Working the other side of the street are Karel Roden and Oleg Taktarov as Emil and Oleg, one Czech, one Russian, who fly into Kennedy airport and are robbing an electronics store within hours of getting off the plane. Emil dreams of becoming rich and famous through violence, and Oleg videotapes his efforts—at first just for fun, later as part of a scheme. Emil loves America because "no one is responsible for what they do!" and Oleg idolizes Frank Capra, the poet of the little man who shoves it to the system.

The movie, written and directed by John Herzfeld, is the work of a man intoxicated by characters and locations. His previous film, *2 Days in the Valley* (1997), was the same way, filled with characters who spinned into each other and bounced apart like pinballs. His movie may overachieve, may weary sometimes as it hurries between plotlines, but I prefer this kind of energy and ambition to a plodding exercise in action clichés. Herzfeld has something he wants to say.

His premise depends on Emil and Oleg being perfectly amoral idiots, shaped in their homelands by overdoses of American TV and movies. Since their countries are saturated with U.S. entertainment, and since the most popular exports are low-dialogue action shows, this is not a stretch. Is their view of America hopelessly brutal and unrealistic? Yes, but it is the view we export for study abroad.

They shoot, slash, burn, and pillage their way through Manhattan, attacking former friends, call girls, and bystanders. Meanwhile, Burns, as the fire inspector, finds evidence that a fire was set to conceal a murder, and De Niro engages in a little jockeying for position in the media spotlight because he wants credit for the investigation. His publicity efforts are helped by his friendship with Grammer, a star of reality TV, and by his affair with a TV reporter (Melina Kanakaredes).

Emil and Oleg are really the center of the movie. They reminded me of Dick Smith and Perry Hickock from *In Cold Blood*, except the vicious amorality of the 1968 movie no longer seems so totally alien to the society surrounding it; programs like Grammer's *Top Story* are based on, feed on, depend on there being people like these.

The movie is far from unflawed. I have a private theory that half the time you see a character tied to a chair, the screenwriter ran out of ideas. Some of the getaways are unlikely. The ending is on autopilot. But there's an absolutely sensational scene where Burns tries to help a woman escape from a burning apartment; it's the best work along these lines since *Backdraft*. And poignant personal moments for De Niro that keep his character from simply being a publicity hound. And performances by Karel Roden and Oleg Taktarov that project the kind of flat, empty-headed, blank-faced evil that is so much scarier than evil by people who think about what they're doing.

Some movies, however good, seem to be simply technical exercises. Others, even if flawed, contain the seed of inspiration. John Herzfeld has not made a great movie yet, but on the basis of his first two, he might. He cares, he strives, he's not content. While you're watching the movie, you question details and excesses. Afterward, you admire it for the passion of its attack, and the worthiness of its targets.

The Fighter ★ ★ ★
NO MPAA RATING, 91 m., 2002

With Arnost Lustig and Jan Wiener. A documentary directed by Amir Bar-Lev and produced by Bar-Lev, Jonathan Crosby, and Alex Mamet.

The Fighter is named after one of its two subjects, Jan Wiener, seventy-seven years old, who describes himself as a "professor, wilderness guide, and old fart," and adds: "But I still can connect." We see him pounding a punching bag to prove it. His friend is Arnost Lustig, seventy-two. Both of them were born in Czechoslovakia and now live in America. The story of Wiener's escape from the Nazis, how he flew for the RAF against Germany, how he returned to his homeland and was imprisoned by the Communists as a spy, has inspired more than one movie. Lustig has long planned to write a book about it, and the two old men set off on a trip to the places of their youth and their war.

Following them is Amir Bar-Lev, an American documentary filmmaker, born in Israel, who could hardly have anticipated what would happen. *The Fighter* could have been just a travelogue about two old-timers reliving their wartime memories. Even a heroic story can slow in the retelling. But *The Fighter* picks up surprising energy, as old wounds are reopened and the two men express strong opinions that may be unforgivable. What unfolds on-screen is remarkable: The passions and arguments of the past are resurrected in the present.

At first the trip goes smoothly. Both men are fit and quick, not slowed by the ravages of age. Both teach at universities. They retrace Wiener's steps as he recalls the collapse of Czechoslovakia (he and other pilots never dreamed the Nazis would roll in so decisively). In a scene of stunning power, he visits the house where his parents committed suicide rather than be captured by the Nazis. He recalls his father saying: "Tonight I am going to kill myself. That is the only freedom we have left." He remembers how it happened, his father telling him, "I have taken the pills. Hold my hand." And then, says Wiener, sitting in the same chair he sat in all those years ago, "he was asleep."

They visit Terezienstadt, a model concentration camp set up by the Nazis to fool a Swiss Red Cross inspection team (the notorious Nazi documentary *The Fuhrer Gives a City to the Jews* was filmed there). Lustig was a prisoner there, and remembers how the prisoners were terrified to speak to the inspectors, and how food and comforts disappeared along with the Swiss. Together, the two men retrace the route of Wiener's escape, ending in Italy, where a compassionate Italian cop did not betray him to the Nazis. He later became a POW in Italy, later still a pilot for the British.

After the war their lives diverged. Wiener returned home to Czechoslovakia only to be

suspected of spying and sentenced to prison. Lustig became a Communist official until he became disillusioned and left for America. The old friends met again in the United States.

And so the story might end, gripping, fascinating, happily—but then they have a fight. There is a disagreement over why the Italian cop spared Wiener. Another one over why Lustig could have survived Nazism only to become a Communist. Filming shuts down for three days during this impasse, and when it begins again it is clear that the old men are friends no longer. We understand that for them the war is a wound that has not healed, and that it led to decisions that cannot be explained. We stand a little outside: No one who was not there knows for sure what he would have done. Suddenly, we are not in the past but in the present, seeing real emotions, not remembered ones. In this movie the war is not quite over. For those who survived it, maybe it will never be.

Note: The 2002 feature Dark Blue World *also tells a story about a Czech pilot who flies for the British.*

The Filth and the Fury ★ ★ ★ ½
R, 105 m., 2000

A documentary directed by Julien Temple and produced by Anita Camarata and Amanda Temple.

At the height of their fame, the Sex Pistols inspired a London city councilor to observe, "Most of these guys would be much improved by sudden death." In a decade when England was racked by unemployment, strikes, and unrest, its season of discontent had a sound track by the Pistols. They sang of "Anarchy in the U.K.," and their song "God Save the Queen (She Ain't No Human Being)" rose to No. 1 on the hit charts—but the record industry refused to name it. In *The Filth and the Fury,* a hard-edged new documentary about the Pistols, we see a Top 10 chart with a blank space for No. 1. Better than being listed, Johnny Rotten grinned.

The saga of the Sex Pistols is told for the third time in *The Filth and the Fury.* Not bad for a band that symbolized punk rock but lasted less than two years, fought constantly, insulted the press, spit on their fans, were banned from

TV, were fired by one record company twenty-four hours after being signed, released only one album, pushed safety pins through noses and earlobes to more or less invent body piercing, broke up during a tour of the United States, and saw front man Sid Vicious accused of murdering his girlfriend and dying of a drug overdose.

Director Julien Temple based his *Great Rock and Roll Swindle* (1980) on a version of the Pistols story supplied by Malcolm McLaren, their infamously self-promoting manager, and now, twenty years later, Temple tells the story through the eyes and in the words of the band members themselves. In between came Alex Cox's *Sid & Nancy* (1986), with Gary Oldman's shattering performance as the self-destructive Sid Vicious.

It wasn't what the band stood for. It was what they stood against. "Attack, attack, attack," says lead singer Johnny Rotten in the film. Now once again John Lydon, he appears along with guitarist Steve Jones, drummer Paul Cook, McLaren, original band member Glen Matlock (deposed by Vicious), and even Vicious himself, in an interview filmed a year before his death. The surviving members are backlit so we cannot see their faces, which would have provided a middle-aged contrast to the savage young men on the screen; McLaren talks from behind a rubber bondage mask like those he and girlfriend Vivienne Westwood sold in their boutique Sex, on Kings' Road.

McLaren claimed the Sex Pistols were entirely his invention, and painted himself as a puppet master. Lydon, who calls him "the manager" throughout the film, says, "There was never a relationship between the manager and me except he stole my ideas and used them as his own." The truth probably resides in between.

I had a glimpse of the Sex Pistols in 1977, when McLaren hired Russ Meyer to direct them in a movie, and Meyer hired me to write it (McLaren and Rotten were fans of our *Beyond the Valley of the Dolls*). I wrote a screenplay in Los Angeles with McLaren feeding me background and ideas. Then Meyer and I flew to London to meet with Rotten, Vicious, Cook, and Jones. (Meyer, wary of McLaren's trademark bondage pants, insisted on sitting on the

aisle: "If we have to evacuate, he'll get those goddamned straps tangled up in the seats.")

I remember a surrealistic dinner involving Rotten, Meyer, and myself ("We won the Battle of Britain for you," Meyer sternly lectured Rotten, while I mused that America was not involved in the Battle of Britain and Rotten was Irish). Rotten seemed amused by the fact that Meyer was unintimidated by his fearsomely safety-pinned facade. As we drove him home, he complained bitterly that McLaren had the band on a salary of £8 a week, borrowed £5 from Meyer, and had us stop at an all-night store so he could buy a six-pack of lager and cans of pork and beans.

The truth is, no one made much money off the Pistols, although McLaren made the most. The plug was pulled on our film, *Who Killed Bambi?* after a day and a half of shooting, when the electricians walked off the set after McLaren couldn't pay them. Meyer had presciently demanded his own weekly pay in advance every Monday morning.

The catch-22 with punk rock, and indeed with all forms of entertainment designed to shock and offend the bourgeoisie, is that if your act is *too* convincing, you put yourself out of business, a fact carefully noted by today's rappers as they go as far as they can without going too far.

The Sex Pistols went too far. They never had a period that could be described as actual success. Even touring England at the height of their fame, they were booked into clubs under false names. They were hated by the establishment, shut down by the police, and pilloried by the press ("The Filth and the Fury" was a banner headline occupying a full front page of the *Daily Mirror*). That was bad enough. Worse was that their own fans sometimes attacked them, lashed into a frenzy by the front line of Rotten and Vicious, who were sometimes performers, sometimes bearbaiters.

Rotten was the victim of a razor attack while walking the streets of London; McLaren not only failed to provide security, he wouldn't pay taxi fares. Vicious was his own worst enemy, and if there was one thing that united the other three band members and McLaren, it was hatred for Sid's girlfriend, Nancy Spungen, who they felt was instrumental in his drug addiction. "Poor sod," today's John Lydon says of his dead bandmate.

To see this film's footage from the '70s is to see the beginning of much of pop and fashion iconography for the next two decades. After the premiere of *The Filth and the Fury* at Sundance, I ran into Temple, who observed: "In the scenes where they're being interviewed on television, they look normal. It's the interviewers who look like freaks." Normal, no. But in torn black T-shirts and punk haircuts, they look contemporary, unlike the dated polyestered, wide-lapeled, and blow-dried creatures interviewing them.

England survived the Sex Pistols, and they mostly survived England, although Lydon still feels it is unsafe for him to return there. He now has an interview program on VH-1 and the Web. Cook and Jones lead settled lives. McLaren still has bright ideas. Vivienne Westwood has emerged as one of Britain's most successful designers, and poses for photographs in which she has a perfect resemblance to Mrs. Thatcher. And as for Sid, my notes from the movie say that while the Pistols were signing a record deal in front of Buckingham Palace and insulting the queen, Sid's father was a Grenadier Guard on duty in front of the palace. Surely I heard that wrong?

Final ★ ★
R, 111 m., 2002

Denis Leary (Bill), Hope Davis (Ann), J. C. MacKenzie (Todd), Jim Gaffigan (Dayton), Jim Hornyak (Orderly), Maureen Anderman (Supervisor), Marin Hinkle (Sherry), Madison Arnold (Bill's Father), Caroline Kava (Bill's Mother). Directed by Campbell Scott and produced by Gary Winik, Alexis Alexanian, Mary Frances Budig, Steve Dunn, and Campbell Scott. Screenplay by Bruce McIntosh.

In a mental hospital in Connecticut, a patient defends his paranoid fantasies against a psychiatrist who gently tries to bring him back to reality. He says it is the year 2399, that he has been cyrogenically frozen for 400 years, and that he has been thawed and awakened so that his organs can be harvested. She says he was in a serious truck accident, was in a coma, and is

now being treated to remove his delusions. While they discuss this rather basic disagreement, it becomes clear they are gradually falling in love.

Campbell Scott's *Final* is a movie told mostly through dialogue. It lacks the life and humor of his wonderful *Big Night,* codirected with Stanley Tucci, and burrows into its enigmatic situation with cheerless intensity. Only the innate energy of its actors, Denis Leary and Hope Davis, keep it on its feet. Both are very good—Leary at trying to talk his way out of what looks like a trap he has set for himself, and Davis at remaining professionally responsible even while getting emotionally involved, if that is possible. She cares for him.

Then the plot takes a turn that I will not even begin to reveal, and we have to reevaluate the meaning of their relationship, their characters, their situation. By even mentioning the turn, I know I will get protests from readers who complain that they would have never known there was going to be a turn if I hadn't revealed it, etc., but really, what is a critic to do? Stop writing after the first two paragraphs and completely misrepresent the film? *Final* is "difficult to discuss without giving away the surprise that pops up halfway through," A. O. Scott observes in the first sentence of his *New York Times* review, thereby giving away the surprise that there *is* a surprise. You see what I mean.

So, yes, there is a surprise. I will have nothing to say about it. You will have to deal with it on your own. But if you should see *Final* and start to analyze it, ask yourself these questions: Why is the therapy necessary in the first place? Why are this patient and this psychiatrist even talking? What do they have to accomplish? Unless my logic is flawed (and if it is, other audience members are going to make the same mistake), the entire movie is a red herring.

That doesn't mean it lacks certain virtues. The movie, shot on video by Dan Gillham, creates a convincing space around the characters; the institution seems real enough, if underpopulated, and the claustrophobia it brings on helps define the relationship. Although the screenplay by Bruce McIntosh suffers from that plausibility gap, the characters of course don't know this and establish a rapport so nuanced and subtle it deserves a better story. Maybe one without a surprise.

Final Destination ★ ★ ★
R, 90 m., 2000

Devon Sawa (Alex Browning), Ali Larter (Clear Rivers), Kerr Smith (Carter Horton), Kristen Cloke (Valerie Lewton), Daniel Roebuck (Agent Weine), Chad E. Donella (Tod Waggner), Seann William Scott (Billy Hitchcock). Directed by James Wong and produced by Glen Morgan, Warren Zide, and Craig Perry. Screenplay by Jeffrey Reddick, Morgan, and Wong.

Final Destination observes the time-honored formula of the Dead Teenager Movie: It begins with a lot of living teenagers, and dooms them. But the movie, made by two veterans of *The X Files* TV series, is smarter and more original than most DTMs. It has mordant humor, Rube Goldberg death traps, and sophomoric but earnest discussions of fate. Also an opening sequence that assures this film will never, ever, be shown on an airplane.

The movie begins with a high school class boarding a plane for a class trip to Paris. Alex (Devon Sawa), one of the students, has a vision, vivid and terrifying, of the plane exploding in flight. He jumps up to get off, has a fight with another student, and ends up being ejected along with five other students and a teacher. Then the airplane takes off and, you guessed it, explodes in midair.

This scenario is, of course, in the worst possible taste in view of the real-life fate of TWA flight 800, also bound for Paris with students aboard. I will observe that and not belabor it. The explosion is a setup for the rest of the movie, in which it appears that the survivors may also be marked for death—and that Alex is psychic and can foresee their deaths.

Can he really? That's where the movie gets interesting, since instead of using his eerie precognitions as a gimmick, the movie allows the characters to talk urgently about their feelings of doom and helplessness. The film in its own way is biblical in its dilemma, although the students use the code word "fate" when what they are really talking about is God. In their own terms, in their own way, using teen-

age vernacular, the students have existential discussions.

Final Destination isn't all dialogue, however, and there's a weird disconnection between the words and the action. One after another, the characters die, almost always because of a bizarre chain of connected events. To describe them would be to spoil the fun—if that's what it is—as lightning, natural gas, knives, trains, laundry cords, power lines, and flying metal shards are choreographed by fate (or You Know Who).

Why must these students die? Well, everybody does. Why should they be the exception? As the movie opens, they're filled like most teenagers with a sense of their own immortality, and gradually their dilemma wears them down.

The movie is neither quite serious nor quite ironic; sometimes it's funny, but in a creepy way rather than in the breezier style of the *Scream* movies. The very last shot, set in Paris but filmed in Canada (during a last-minute reshoot in January), is a shaggy dog trick. I laughed, I guess, but the movie really deserves better. My guess is the original ending was more considered, but New Line was afraid of it.

The director is James Wong. He and cowriter Glen Morgan worked on *The X-Files, 21 Jump Street,* and *Millennium.* They haven't made a great or distinguished film, but, working within a tired genre with a talented cast, they've brought unusual substance and impact to the DTM. The vision of the airplane crash is remarkably scary, and other scenes, like a car stopped on railroad tracks, work even though they're clichés—because of the dialogue and the motivations of the characters.

Final Destination will no doubt be a hit and inspire the obligatory sequels. Like the original *Scream,* this movie is too good to be the end of the road. I have visions of my own. I foresee poor Alex making new friends and then envisioning *their* deaths as they embark on ocean liners, trains, buses, and dirigibles. It's a funny thing about Hollywood: It can't seem to get enough of dead teenagers. Talk about biting the hand that feeds you.

Final Fantasy: The Spirits Within
★ ★ ★ ½
PG-13, 105 m., 2001

Voices of: Ming-Na (Dr. Aki Ross), Alec Baldwin (Gray Edwards), Steve Buscemi (Neil), Peri Gilpin (Jane Proudfoot), Ving Rhames (Ryan), Donald Sutherland (Dr. Sid), James Woods (General Hein). Directed by Hironobu Sakaguchi and produced by Jun Aida, Chris Lee, and Akio Sakai. Screenplay by Al Reinert, Sakaguchi, and Jeff Vintar.

Other movies have been made entirely on computers, but *Final Fantasy: The Spirits Within* is the first to attempt realistic human characters. Not Shrek with his trumpet ears, but the space soldier Gray Edwards, who looks so much like Ben Affleck that I wonder if royalties were involved. The movie, named after a famous series of video games, creates Planet Earth, circa 2065, where humans huddle beneath energy shields and wraithlike aliens prowl the globe.

The film tells a story that would have seemed traditional in the golden age of Asimov, van Vogt, and Heinlein. But science-fiction fans of that era would have wept with joy at the visuals, and they grabbed me too. I have a love of astonishing sights, of films that show me landscapes and cityscapes that exist only in the imagination, and *Final Fantasy* creates a world that is neither live-action nor animation, but some parallel cyber universe.

The characters live in that cyberspace too. Not for an instant do we believe that Dr. Aki Ross, the heroine, is a real human. But we concede she is *lifelike*, which is the whole point. She has an eerie presence that is at once subtly unreal and yet convincing; her movements (which mirror the actions of real actors) feel about right, her hair blows convincingly in the wind, and the first close-up of her face and eyes is startling because the filmmakers are not afraid to give us a good, long look—they dare us not to admire their craft. If Aki is not as real as a human actress, she is about as real as a Playmate who has been retouched to a glossy perfection.

The story involves a struggle by Aki and a band of Deep Eyes (futuristic human warriors) to defend the survivors of an alien invasion of Earth. Humans live inside energy shields that protect some of the largest cities, and they venture out cautiously, armored and armed, to do battle with the aliens, who look like free-form transparent monster nightmares; I was reminded of the water creature in *The Abyss*. The aliens can infect humans with their virus, or essence, and Aki (Ming-Na) thinks she can defeat them by channeling the eight "spirit waves" of Earth—or Gaia, the planetary soul.

Her allies include Gray (Alec Baldwin), the leader of the Deep Eyes troop, and Dr. Sid (Donald Sutherland), her wise old teacher. Her other teammates include the pilot Neil (Steve Buscemi) and the fighters Ryan (Ving Rhames) and Jane Proudfoot (Peri Gilpin). Leading the forces of evil is General Hein (James Woods), who wants to blast the aliens with his high-tech orbiting space cannon.

Those who find a parallel between Hein's cannon and George W. Bush's missile shield will find it easy to assign Aki and her friends to the environmentalists; they believe Earth's mantle sits above a Gaia-sphere containing the planet's life force, and that if the cannon destroys it, not only the aliens but all human life will die. One of Aki's early expeditions is to find, rescue, and tend a tiny green growing thing that has survived in the wasteland caused (I think) when a giant meteorite crashed into Earth and released the aliens it contained.

The aliens are strange creatures, made stranger still by the film's inconsistency in handling them. Without revealing one major secret about their essence, I can ask how they seem to be physical and conceptual both at once. They defeat a human not by physically attacking him, but by absorbing his life essence. Yet they can be blasted to smithereens by the weapons of the Deep Eyes. Maybe the human weapons are not conventional, but operate on the aliens' wavelength; either I got confused on that point, or the movie did.

Enough about the plot, which is merely the carrier for the movie's vision. The reason to see this movie is simply, gloriously, to look at it. Aki has dream scenes on another planet, where a vast, celestial sphere half fills the sky. We see New York City in 2065, ruined, ghostlike, except for the portions under the protective dome. There are action sequences that only vaguely obey the laws of gravity, and yet seem convincing because we have become familiar with the characters who occupy them: shots like the one where we look straight up at Aki standing on the surface of a shimmering lake. The corridors and machines composing the infrastructure of the protective dome surpass any possible real-world sets.

Final Fantasy took four years to create. A computer animation team, half-Japanese, half-American, worked in Hawaii with director Hironobu Sakaguchi; they shot many of the physical movements and then rotoscoped them, and artists were assigned to specialize in particular characters. The most realistic are probably Dr. Sid and Ryan. It all comes together into a kind of amazing experience; it's as if you're witnessing a heavy-metal story come to life.

Is there a future for this kind of expensive filmmaking ($140 million, I've heard)? I hope so, because I want to see more movies like this, and see how much further they can push the technology. Maybe someday I'll actually be fooled by a computer-generated actor (but I doubt it). The point anyway is not to replace actors and the real world, but to transcend them—to penetrate into a new creative space based primarily on images and ideas. I wouldn't be surprised if the Star Wars series mutated in this direction; George Lucas's actors, who complain that they spend all of their time standing in front of blue screens that will later be filled with locations and effects, would be replaced by computerized avatars scarcely less realistic.

In reviewing a movie like this, I am torn between its craft elements and its story. The story is nuts-and-bolts space opera, without the intelligence and daring of, say, Spielberg's *A.I.* But the look of the film is revolutionary. *Final Fantasy* is a technical milestone, like the first talkies or 3-D movies. You want to see it whether or not you care about aliens or space cannons. It exists in a category of its own, the first citizen of the new world of cyberfilm.

Finding Forrester ★ ★ ★
PG-13, 133 m., 2000

Sean Connery (William Forrester), Rob Brown (Jamal Wallace), F. Murray Abraham (Professor Crawford), Michael Nouri (Dr. Spence), Anna Paquin (Claire), Busta Rhymes (Terrell), Joey Buttafuoco (Security Guard), Michael Pitt (Coleridge), Stephanie Berry (Janice).

Directed by Gus Van Sant and produced by Sean Connery, Laurence Mark, and Rhonda Tollefson. Screenplay by Mike Rich.

Movies about writers are notoriously hard to do, since writing by its nature is not cinematic. *Finding Forrester* evades that problem by giving us a man who wrote one good novel a long time ago, and now writes no more: He has turned into a recluse afraid to leave his own apartment. This is William Forrester (Sean Connery), who keeps an eye on his Bronx neighborhood by using binoculars from his upper-floor window. "The man in the window" attracts the attention of black teenagers playing basketball on a court below, and that leads to the turning point in the life of Jamal Wallace (Rob Brown).

Jamal is a brilliant student who has no one to share his brilliance with. At school he conceals his learning because, as an adult observes, "Basketball is where he gets his acceptance." He gets C's when his SAT scores show him to be an A student, and he stars on the high school team. One night on a dare he sneaks into Forrester's apartment, is startled by the old writer, and begins a strange friendship. Jamal gets someone to read his writings. Forrester gets someone to lure him out of his hibernation.

Finding Forrester was directed by Gus Van Sant, written by Mike Rich, and bears some similarity to Van Sant's *Good Will Hunting* (1997), also about a working-class boy with genius. The stories are really quite different, however, not least because Connery's character is at least as important as Brown's, and because the movie has some insights into the dilemma of a smart black kid afraid his friends will consider him a suck-up.

The movie contains at least two insights into writing that are right on target. The first is William's advice to Jamal that he give up waiting for inspiration and just start writing. My own way of phrasing this rule is: The Muse visits during composition, not before. The other accurate insight is a subtle one. An early shot pans across the books next to Jamal's bed, and we see that his reading tastes are wide, good, and various. All of the books are battered except one, the paperback of Joyce's *Finnegans Wake*, which looks brand-new and has no creases on its spine. That's the book everyone buys but nobody reads.

The scenes between the old man and the teenager are at the heart of the movie, and it's a pleasure to watch the rapport between Connery, in his fiftieth year of acting, and Brown, in his first role. Forrester gives the kid all kinds of useful advice about being a writer, including the insight, "Women will sleep with you if you write a book." That's something Jamal might have figured out for himself, but Forrester is even more encouraging: "Women will sleep with you if you write a *bad* book."

Jamal gets a scholarship to a private academy (his SAT is high enough that it's not an athletic scholarship, although the board certainly hopes he'll play). On its faculty is the embittered Crawford (F. Murray Abraham), coincidentally an old enemy of Forrester's, who simply doesn't believe an African-American basketball player from the Bronx can write at Jamal's level. That sets up the crisis and the payoff, which will remind some viewers of *Scent of a Woman*.

I was reminded of another movie, a great one, named *The Loneliness of the Long Distance Runner* (1962). In both that movie and this one, a disadvantaged young man simply refuses to perform like a trained seal because he knows that will be a lethal blow against his adult tormentors. In a movie where sports supplies an important theme, Jamal's crucial decision supplies the best insight in the story about his journey between two worlds.

The Five Senses ★ ★ ★
R, 105 m., 2000

Molly Parker (Anna Miller), Mary-Louise Parker (Rona), Gabrielle Rose (Ruth), Elize Frances Stolk (Amy Lee Miller), Nadia Litz (Rachel), Daniel MacIvor (Robert), Philippe Volter (Richard), Clinton Walker (Carl), Marco Leonardi (Roberto), Brendan Fletcher (Rupert). Directed by Jeremy Podeswa and produced by Podeswa and Camelia Frieberg. Screenplay by Podeswa.

"You can smell love," says Robert. "If anyone I used to be in love with still loves me, I can tell." He makes dates with former lovers to sniff them across a café table, and meanwhile

Richard, an eye doctor who is going deaf, hires a hooker to listen to music with him. Ruth the massage therapist still has her touch with her clients, but is out of touch with her daughter Rachel. Rachel allows a little girl to wander out of her sight and get lost. Rona is great at decorating cakes, but they don't taste good.

The Five Senses tells interlocking stories about people who are losing their senses, and fear they are losing themselves in the process. But to state the film's subject that directly is to miss the way the writer-director, Jeremy Podeswa, intercuts the stories. He doesn't insist on the senses and the danger of their loss, but allows the fears of his characters to emerge in stories that have weight of their own. Like *Magnolia* and *Short Cuts*, the real subject of the movie is loneliness.

The lost child provides the central story. While Ruth (Gabrielle Rose) massages Anna (Molly Parker), Ruth's young teenage daughter Rachel (Nadia Litz) is assigned to take Anna's young daughter to the park. There Rachel meets Rupert (Brendan Fletcher), a boy about her age, who invites her to follow a couple into the woods. Fascinated by indistinct views of the couple making love, Rachel forgets the little girl, who wanders away and is lost. The search for the girl occupies much of the film, although Podeswa gives the audience a clue that the girl may be safe. In its labyrinthine way, the story curls back to Rachel and Rupert, who play a game with makeup and wigs that may, ironically, help them get better in touch with themselves ("It's like looking at you inside out," Rachel tells him).

There is bittersweet humor in some of the other stories. The bad cake baker, Rona (Mary-Louise Parker), has fallen in love with a chef during a trip to Italy. Roberto (Marco Leonardi) follows her back to Toronto, moves in, cooks delicious dishes, makes love, is happy. But Rona cannot believe her good luck and fears Roberto is simply after money or a passport. Against this lighter comedy stands the sadness of Richard (Philippe Volter), the eye doctor, who is consciously collecting a library of remembered sounds against the day when he goes deaf.

Love has its way of finding paths around problems, and that is the discovery of Robert (Daniel MacIvor), a bisexual housecleaner

215

who works for a couple whose house he cannot quite figure out. She is a perfume designer, and one day when she lets him sniff a new perfume, everything suddenly becomes clear.

A story like *The Five Senses* sounds like a gimmick, but Podeswa has a light touch when dealing with the senses and a sure one when telling his stories. The evolution of Rachel, the angry young girl, is especially touching; as we find out more about her problems and the reasons she can't communicate with her mother, we begin to care. She's a lot more than just the girl who lost the child in the park. And the missing child's mother, Anna, is more than simply a cliché of a grief-stricken parent. She deals with the loss with her mind as well as her feelings, does not necessarily blame Ruth's daughter, finds herself depending on Ruth, and prays in a way that is particularly touching.

Interwoven stories like this can have a particular effect on me. Most movies tell linear plots in which the hero moves from A to B, accompanied by human plot devices. They can be very involving, but I also like the messiness of movies that cut from one story to another, showing how lives can intersect and separate. Some people find these kinds of movies contrived. I think it is just the opposite. A to B stories are obviously plots. Stories like this one show that life goes on all around, and over and beneath, and inside, the artifice of plot.

The Flintstones in
Viva Rock Vegas ½★
PG, 90 m., 2000

Mark Addy (Fred Flintstone), Stephen Baldwin (Barney Rubble), Kristen Johnston (Wilma Slaghoople), Jane Krakowski (Betty O'Shale), Thomas Gibson (Chip Rockefeller), Joan Collins (Pearl Slaghoople), Alex Meneses (Roxie), Alan Cumming (Gazoo/Mike Jagged). Directed by Brian Levant and produced by Bruce Cohen. Screenplay by Deborah Kaplan, Harry Elfont, Jim Cash, and Jack Epps Jr.

The Flintstones in Viva Rock Vegas has dinosaurs that lumber along crushing everything in their path. The movie's screenplay works sort of the same way. Think of every possible pun involving stones, rocks, and prehistoric

times, and link them to a pea-brained story that creaks and groans on its laborious march through unspeakably obvious, labored, and idiotic humor.

This is an ideal first movie for infants, who can enjoy the bright colors on the screen and wave their tiny hands to the music. Children may like it because they just plain like going to the movies. But it's not delightful or funny or exciting, and for long stretches it looks exactly like hapless actors standing in front of big rocks and reciting sitcom dialogue.

The story isn't a sequel to *The Flintstones* (1994) but a prequel, recalling those youthful days when Fred and Wilma Flintstone first met and fell in love. Fred is portrayed this time by Mark Addy, the beefiest of the guys in *The Full Monty*. His best pal, Barney Rubble, is played by Stephen Baldwin, who recites his lines as if he hopes Fred will ask him to come out and play, but is afraid he won't. As the movie opens Fred and Barney have gotten jobs at the rock quarry, and have settled down to a lifetime of quarrying rocks, which their world does not seem to need any more of, but never mind.

Meanwhile, in a parallel plot, Wilma Slaghoople (Kristen Johnston) resists the schemes of her mother (Joan Collins) to get her to marry the millionaire Chip Rockefeller (get it?). Fleeing the rich neighborhood, she ends up working in a drive-in restaurant ("Bronto King") with Betty O'Shale (Jane Krakowski), and soon the two of them have met Fred and Barney. There's instant chemistry, and the two couples grind off to a weekend in Rock Vegas. The jealous Chip (Thomas Gibson) is waiting there to foil romance and get his hands on the Slaghoople fortune. His conspirator is a chorus-line beauty named Roxie (Second City grad Alex Meneses), whose boulders are second to none. The Vegas sequence is livened by a soundtrack rendition of "Viva Las (and/or Rock) Vegas" by Ann-Margret.

Another story line involves Gazoo (Alan Cumming), an alien who arrives in a flying saucer. He looks exactly like a desperate measure to flesh out an uninteresting plot with an uninteresting character. The movie would be no better and no worse without Gazoo, which is a commentary on both Gazoo and the movie, I think.

The pun, it has been theorized, is the lowest form of humor. This movie proves that theory wrong. There is a lower form of humor: jokes about dinosaur farts. The pun is the second lowest form of humor. The third lowest form is laborious plays on words, as when we learn that the Rock Vegas headliners include Mick Jagged and the Stones.

Minute by weary minute the movie wends its weary way toward its joyless conclusion, as if everyone in it is wearing concrete overshoes, which, come to think of it, they may be. The first film was no masterpiece, but it was a lot better than this. Its slot for an aging but glamorous beauty queen was filled by Elizabeth Taylor. This time it is Joan Collins. As Joan Collins is to Elizabeth Taylor, so *The Flintstones in Viva Rock Vegas* is to *The Flintstones*.

Focus ★ ★ ★
PG-13, 106 m., 2001

William H. Macy (Lawrence Newman), Laura Dern (Gertrude Newman), David Paymer (Mr. Finkelstein), Meat Loaf Aday (Fred). Directed by Neal Slavin and produced by Robert A. Miller and Slavin. Screenplay by Kendrew Lascelles and Arthur Miller, based on the novel by Miller.

Focus is a parable about Lawrence Newman, a meek office manager who hasn't had a day of trouble in his life until he gets a new pair of glasses and everyone, even his own mother, decides he "looks Jewish." In Brooklyn in 1944, even during a war against Nazism, anti-Semitism runs deep and help-wanted ads specify "Christians only." Newman's neighbor, the bully Fred (Meat Loaf Aday), scowls at Finkelstein's convenience store on the corner and tells Newman, "That Yid is moving in all of his relatives." Newman is supposed to nod in agreement, and you can see that Fred is watching closely for his reaction.

Newman is not Jewish, or particularly Christian (he is played by William H. Macy, who is often cast as a gentile everyman). He's a secular nerd, a little man who is precise in his habits and exact in his work, and has never married. His job is to oversee a room full of women typists and hire replacements. He hires a woman named Kipinski, and his boss complains, "We can't have her kind here." Soon he is being shifted to a new job in a remote office, apparently because with his new glasses he makes the wrong impression.

Focus doesn't reach for reality; it's a deliberate attempt to look and feel like a 1940s social problems picture, right down to the texture of the color photography. The movie is based on a novel by Arthur Miller, which he says was written during a period of disillusionment with the stage; angered by American anti-Semitism even during the war against Hitler, he wrote it in a white heat. It's a didactic warning that it *can* happen here.

Well, of course it can. Tribalism is deeply ingrained in the American culture, and even though we are all outsiders we look with fear on *other* outsiders. The truest words in the movie are spoken by Finkelstein (David Paymer), at a time when a native Nazi group is trying to intimidate everyone on the block: "For God's sake, don't you see what they're doing?! There's hundreds of millions of people in this country, and a couple of million Jews. It's you they want, not me! They are a gang of devils, and they want this country." This is an insight into the methods of the far right, which uses scapegoats and prejudice to lure people out of the middle and into their corner. They need the Jews, because without them how can they create anti-Semitism? Hatred of another group is what binds their group together. That process feeds nicely on the sick impulses of xenophobics.

Frightened for his job, Newman turns down a job applicant named Gertrude Hart (Laura Dern) because her name "sounds Jewish." She's more world-wise than he is, and knows exactly what he's doing. Later, after being shifted away from his position of twenty years, Newman resigns in anger, and can't get hired elsewhere because he looks "too Jewish"—until he is hired at a Jewish firm by . . . Miss Hart. He apologizes to her, they begin to talk, and soon are married, with Fred next door eyeing the new bride suspiciously.

Fred puts Newman to an acid test, pressuring him to attend a meeting of the Union Crusaders, a neo-Nazi group that feeds off the rantings of a right-wing radio broadcaster. (Father Charles Coughlin, the anti-Semitic priest who had a national following, is the model.) "Either you go to the meeting or we get out now," Gertrude tells him. He goes, but is thrown out for displaying insufficient enthusiasm. ("I never applaud," he lamely explains as he's being hustled to the door.)

The purpose of the movie is to take a man who might be willing to go along with anti-Semitic values, and show him what it's like to be discriminated against as a Jew. The climax of this experience comes late one night in Finkelstein's store, when the merchant asks him, "What do you see when you look at me?" The problem in all societies throughout history, the opening for all prejudice, is that we don't look at all. We look away, or at our prejudices, or we allow the worst among us to look on our behalf, and accept their reports.

40 Days and 40 Nights ★ ★ ★
R, 93 m., 2002

Josh Hartnett (Matt Sullivan), Shannyn Sossamon (Erica), Maggie Gyllenhaal (Samantha), Emmanuelle Vaugier (Susie), Keegan Connor Tracy (Mandy), Vinessa Shaw (Nicole), Paulo Costanzo (Ryan), Adam Trese (John), Monet Mazur (Candy). Directed by Michael Lehmann and produced by Tim Bevan, Eric Fellner, and Michael London. Screenplay by Rob Perez.

Matt is weary of sex. Weary of himself as a sex partner. Weary of the way he behaves around women, weary of the way women make him behave, and weary of his treacherous ex-girl. So weary that he swears off sex for Lent in *40 Days and 40 Nights*. On the scale of single guy sacrifice, this is harder than not drinking but easier than asking for directions.

Matt (Josh Hartnett) is a nice guy who is disgusted by his predatory sexual nature—at the way his libido goes on autopilot when he sees an attractive woman. The breakup with Nicole (Vinessa Shaw) is the final straw. She loved him, dumped him, still excites him, and no wonder; as Bagel Man, who makes morning deliveries to the office, observes, "She's so hot you need one of those cardboard eclipse things just to look at her." Matt gets some support from his brother John (Adam Trese), who is studying to be a priest and offers advice that is more practical than theologically sound,

but nobody else in Matt's life believes he can go forty days without sex. Certainly not a coworker (Monet Mazur), who gives him her phone number on a photocopy of her butt.

Then Matt meets Laundromat Girl. She is sweet, pretty, smart, and something clicks. He tries to keep his distance and end the conversation before his dreaded instincts click in, but a week later he's back in the Laundromat and so is she. Her name is Erica (Shannyn Sossamon), and soon they are engaged in a courtship that proceeds, from her point of view, rather strangely. On their first real date, when the moment comes for their first kiss, they grow closer and quieter and then he gives her a high-five. What's up with this guy?

40 Days and 40 Nights was directed by Michael Lehmann, who has a sympathy for his characters that elevates the story above the level of a sexual sitcom. He uses humor as an instrument to examine human nature, just as he did in the wonderful, underrated *The Truth About Cats and Dogs*. Amazing, what a gulf there is between movies about characters governed by their genitals, and this movie about a character trying to govern his genitals.

The world seems to conspire against him. The movie's single funniest scene involves dinner with his parents, where his father, who has just had a hip replacement, is delighted to show him a checklist of sexual positions still workable even while he is wearing the cast. The second funniest scene involves a roommate who bursts into Matt's flat with an ultraviolet lamp to check for telltale secretions on the sheets.

Then Matt discovers to his horror that his coworkers have not only got up an office pool on how long he can go without sex, but also have put the pool on a Website. Matt looks at the site in disbelief: "You're selling banner ads?" When Erica sees the site, there's hell to pay.

Josh Hartnett shows here a breezy command of his charming, likable character. It is a reminder of his talent and versatility. After an actor stars in a movie that's widely disparaged, as Hartnett did with *Pearl Harbor,* there is an unfair tendency to blame the film on him. The same thing happened to Kevin Costner after *The Postman.* Actors we liked fall out of favor, as if they didn't work just as hard, and hope as much, for their flops as for their hits. Walking into this movie, I heard *Pearl Harbor* jokes ("40 days that will live in infamy"), but during the film the screenplay kicked in and the next stage of Hartnett's career was officially declared open.

40 Days and 40 Nights does observe the plot conventions of a standard comedy, requiring Erica to persist in unreasonably obtuse behavior far beyond its logical time span, but the details are fresh and writer Rob Perez's dialogue about sex has more complexity and nuance than we expect. And a romantic scene involving flower blossoms is unreasonably erotic. The ending, alas, goes astray, for reasons I cannot reveal, except to suggest that Nicole's entire participation is offensive and unnecessary, and that there was a sweeter and funnier way to resolve everything.

Note: Not even under the end titles does the movie use the Muddy Waters classic 40 Days and 40 Nights. *In an age when every song title seems to be recycled into a movie, what were they thinking of?*   ☞

42 Up ★ ★ ★ ★
NO MPAA RATING, 139 m., 2000

A documentary series directed and produced by Michael Apted.

Give me the child until he is seven, and I will show you the man.

—Jesuit saying

In 1964, a British television network began an intriguing experiment. They would interview a group of seven-year-olds, asking them what they wanted to do in life and what kind of a future they envisioned. Then these same subjects would be revisited every seven years to see how their lives were turning out. It was an intriguing experiment, using film's unique ability to act as a time machine—"the most remarkable nonfiction film project in the history of the medium," wrote Andrew Sarris.

Now here is *42 Up*, the sixth installment in the series. I have seen them all since *14 Up*, and every seven years the series measures out my own life too. It is impossible to see the films without asking yourself the same questions—

without remembering yourself as a child and a teenager, and evaluating the progress of your life.

I feel as if I know these subjects, and indeed I do know them better than many of the people I work with every day, because I know what they dreamed of at seven, their hopes at fourteen, the problems they faced in their early twenties, and their marriages, their jobs, their children, even their adulteries.

When I am asked for career advice, I tell students that they should spend more time preparing than planning. Life is so ruled by luck and chance, I say, that you may end up doing a job that doesn't even exist yet. Don't think you can map your life, but do pack for the journey. Good advice, I think, and yet I look at *42 Up* and I wonder if our fates are sealed at an early age. Many of the subjects of the series seemed to know at seven what they wanted to do and what their aptitudes were, and they were mostly right. Others produce surprises, and keep on producing them right into middle age.

Michael Apted could not have predicted that his future would include a lifelong commitment to this series. He was a young man at the beginning of his career when he worked as a researcher on *7 Up*, choosing the fourteen subjects who would be followed. He became the director of *14 Up*, and has guided the series ever since, taking time off from a busy career as the director of feature films (*Coal Miner's Daughter, Gorillas in the Mist*). In his introduction to a new book about the series, he says he does not envy his subjects: "They do get notoriety and it's the worst kind of fame—without power or money. They're out in the street getting on with their lives and people stop them and say, 'Aren't you that girl?' or 'Don't I know you?' or 'You're the one,' and most of them hate that."

The series hasn't itself changed their lives, he believes. "They haven't got jobs or found partners because of the film, except in one case when a friendship developed with dramatic results."

That case involves Neil, who for most longtime followers of the series has emerged as the most compelling character. He was a brilliant but pensive boy, who at seven said he wanted to be a bus driver, so he could tell the passengers what to look for out the windows; he saw himself in the driver's seat, a tour guide for the lives of others. What career would you guess for him? An educator? A politician?

In later films he seemed to drift, unhappy and without direction. He fell into confusion. At twenty-eight, he was homeless in the Highlands of Scotland, and I remember him sitting outside his shabby house trailer on the rocky shore of a loch, looking forlornly across the water. He won't be around for the next film, I thought: Neil has lost his way. He survived, and at thirty-five was living in poverty on the rough Shetland Islands, where he had just been deposed as the (unpaid) director of the village pageant; he felt the pageant would be going better if he were still in charge.

The latest chapter in Neil's story is the most encouraging of all the episodes in *42 Up*, and part of the change is because of his fellow film subject Bruce, who was a boarding school boy, studied math at Oxford, and then gave up a career in the insurance industry to become a teacher in London inner-city schools. Bruce has always seemed one of the happiest of the subjects. At forty, he got married. Neil moved to London at about that time, was invited to the wedding, found a job through Bruce, and today—well, I would not want to spoil your surprise when you find the unlikely turn his life has taken.

Apted says in his introduction to the book *42 Up* (The New Press, $16.95) that if he had the project to do again, he would have chosen more middle-class subjects (his sample was weighted toward the upper and working classes), and more women. He had a reason, though, for choosing high and low: The original question asked by the series was whether Britain's class system was eroding. The answer seems to be: yes, but slowly. Sarris, writing in the *New York Observer*, delivers this verdict: "At one point, I noted that the upper-class kids, who sounded like twits at 7 compared to the more spontaneous and more lovable lower-class kids, became more interesting and self-confident as they raced past their social inferiors. It was like shooting fish in a barrel. Class, wealth, and social position did matter, alas, and there was no getting around it."

None of the fourteen have died yet, although three have dropped out of the project (some drop out for a film and are back for the next one). By now many have buried their parents. Forced to confront themselves at seven, fourteen, twenty-one, twenty-eight, and thirty-five, they seem mostly content with the way things have turned out. Will they all live to forty-nine? Will the series continue until none are alive? This series should be sealed in a time capsule. It is on my list of the ten greatest films of all time, and is a noble use of the medium.

Frailty ★ ★ ★ ★
R, 100 m., 2002

Bill Paxton (Dad), Matthew McConaughey (Fenton Meiks), Powers Boothe (Agent Wesley Doyle), Matthew O'Leary (Young Fenton Meiks), Jeremy Sumpter (Young Adam Meiks), Luke Askew (Sheriff Smalls), Derk Cheetwood (Agent Griffin Hull), Blake King (Eric). Directed by Bill Paxton and produced by David Blocker, David Kirschner, and Corey Sienega. Screenplay by Brent Hanley.

Heaven protect us from people who believe they can impose their will on us in this world, because of what they think they know about the next. *Frailty* is about such a man, a kind and gentle father who is visited by an angel who assigns him to murder demons in human form. We are reminded that Andrea Yates believed she was possessed by Satan and could save her children by drowning them. *Frailty* is as chilling: The father enlists his two sons, who are about seven and ten, to join him in the murders of victims he brings home.

This is not, you understand, an abusive father. He loves his children. He is only following God's instructions: "This is our job now, son. We've got to do this." When the older son, terrified and convinced his father has gone mad, says he'll report him to the police, his father explains, "If you do that, son, someone will die. The angel was clear on this." The pressure that the children are under is unbearable and tragic, and warps their entire lives.

Frailty is an extraordinary work, concealing in its depths not only unexpected story turns but also implications, hidden at first, that make it even deeper and more sad. It is the first film directed by the actor Bill Paxton, who also plays the father, and succeeds in making "Dad" not a villain but a sincere man lost within his delusions. Matthew McConaughey plays one of his sons as a grown man, and Powers Boothe is the FBI agent who is investigating the "God's Hand" serial murders in Texas when the son comes to him one night, with the body of his brother parked outside in a stolen ambulance.

The movie works in so many different ways that it continues to surprise us right until the end. It begins as a police procedural, seems for a time to be a puzzle like *Usual Suspects*, reveals itself as a domestic terror film, evokes pity as well as horror, and reminded me of *The Rapture,* another film about a parent who is willing to sacrifice a child in order to follow the literal instructions of her faith.

As the film opens, Matthew McConaughey appears in the office of FBI agent Wesley Doyle (Powers Boothe), introduces himself as Fenton Meiks, and says he knows who committed the serial killings that have haunted the area for years. His story becomes the narration of two long flashbacks in which we see Paxton as the elder Meiks, and Matthew O'Leary and Jeremy Sumpter as young Fenton and Adam. Their mother is dead; they live in a frame house near the community rose garden, happy and serene, until the night their father wakes them with the news that he has been visited by an angel.

The film neither shies away from its horrifying events nor dwells on them. There is a series of ax murders, but they occur offscreen; this is not a movie about blood, but about obsession. The truly disturbing material involves the two boys, who are played by O'Leary and Sumpter as ordinary, happy kids whose lives turn into nightmares. Young Adam simply believes everything his father tells him. Fenton is old enough to know it's wrong: "Dad's brainwashed you," he tells Adam. "It's all a big lie. He murders people and you help him."

The construction of the story circles around the angel's "instructions" in several ways. The sons and father are trapped in a household seemingly ruled by fanaticism. There is, however, the intriguing fact that when Dad touches his victims, he has graphic visions of their sins—he can see vividly why they need to be

killed. Are these visions accurate? We see them, too, but it's unclear whether through Dad's eyes or the movie's narrator—if that makes a difference. Whether they are objectively true is something I, at least, believe no man can know for sure about another. Not just by touching him, anyway. But the movie contains one shot, sure to be debated, that suggests God's hand really is directing Dad's murders.

Perhaps only a first-time director, an actor who does not depend on directing for his next job, would have had the nerve to make this movie. It is uncompromised. It follows its logic right down into hell. We love movies that play and toy with the supernatural, but are we prepared for one that is an unblinking look at where the logic of the true believer can lead? There was just a glimpse of this mentality on the day after 9/11, when certain TV preachers described it as God's punishment for our sins, before backpedaling when they found such frankness eroded their popularity base.

On the basis of this film, Bill Paxton is a gifted director; he and his collaborators, writer Brent Hanley, cinematographer Bill Butler, and editor Arnold Glassman, have made a complex film that grips us with the intensity of a simple one. We're with it every step of the way, and discover we hardly suspect where it is going.

Note: Watching the film, I was reminded again of the West Memphis Three (www.wm3.org), those three Arkansas teenagers convicted of the brutal murder of three children. One faces death and the other two long sentences. The documentaries Paradise Lost *(1992) and* Paradise Lost 2: Revelations *(2000) make it clear they are probably innocent (a prime suspect all but confesses on-screen), but the three are still in jail because they wore black, listened to heavy metal music, and were railroaded by courts and a community convinced they were Satanists—which must have been evidence enough, since there wasn't much else, and the boys could prove they were elsewhere.* ☞

Freddy Got Fingered no stars
R, 93 m., 2001

Tom Green (Gord Brody), Rip Torn (Jim Brody), Harland Williams (Darren), Julie Hagerty (Julie Brody), Marisa Coughlan (Betty), Eddie Kaye

Thomas (Freddy). Directed by Tom Green and produced by Larry Brezner, Lauren Lloyd, and Howard Lapides. Screenplay by Green and Derek Harvie.

It's been leading up to this all spring. When David Spade got buried in crap in *Joe Dirt,* and when three supermodels got buried in crap in *Head Over Heels,* and when human organs fell from a hot-air balloon in *Monkey Bone* and were eaten by dogs, and when David Arquette rolled around in dog crap and a gangster had his testicles bitten off in *See Spot Run,* and when a testicle was eaten in *Tomcats,* well, somehow the handwriting was on the wall. There had to be a movie like *Freddy Got Fingered* coming along.

This movie doesn't scrape the bottom of the barrel. This movie isn't the bottom of the barrel. This movie isn't below the bottom of the barrel. This movie doesn't deserve to be mentioned in the same sentence with barrels.

Many years ago, when surrealism was new, Luis Buñuel and Salvador Dali made a film so shocking that Buñuel filled his pockets with stones to throw at the audience if it attacked him. Green, whose film is in the surrealist tradition, may want to consider the same tactic. The day may come when *Freddy Got Fingered* is seen as a milestone of neosurrealism. The day may never come when it is seen as funny.

The film is a vomitorium consisting of ninety-three minutes of Tom Green doing things that a geek in a carnival sideshow would turn down. Six minutes into the film, his character leaps from his car to wag a horse penis. This is, we discover, a framing device—to be matched by a scene late in the film where he sprays his father with elephant semen, straight from the source.

Green plays Gord Brody, a twenty-eight-year-old who lives at home with his father (Rip Torn), who despises him, and his mother (Julie Hagerty), who wrings her hands a lot. He lives in a basement room still stocked with his high school stuff, draws cartoons, and dreams of becoming an animator. Gord would exhaust a psychiatrist's list of diagnoses. He is unsocialized, hostile, manic, and apparently retarded. Retarded? How else to explain a sequence where a Hollywood animator tells him to "get inside his animals," and he skins a stag

and prances around dressed in the coat, covered with blood?

His romantic interest in the movie is Betty (Marisa Coughlan), who is disabled, and dreams of rocket-powered wheelchairs and oral sex. A different kind of sexual behavior enters the life of his brother, Freddy, who gets the movie named after him just because, I suppose, Tom Green thought the title was funny. His character also thinks it is funny to falsely accuse his father of molesting Freddy.

Tom Green's sense of humor may not resemble yours. Consider, for example, a scene where Gord's best friend busts his knee open while skateboarding. Gord licks the open wound. Then he visits his friend in the hospital. A woman in the next bed goes into labor. Gord rips the baby from her womb and, when it appears to be dead, brings it to life by swinging it around his head by its umbilical cord, spraying the walls with blood. If you wanted that to be a surprise, then I'm sorry I spoiled it for you.

Frequency ★ ★ ★ ½
PG-13, 117 m., 2000

Dennis Quaid (Frank Sullivan), Jim Caviezel (John Sullivan), Andre Braugher (Satch DeLeon), Elizabeth Mitchell (Julia Sullivan), Noah Emmerich (Gordo Hersch), Shawn Doyle (Jack Shepard), Jordan Bridges (Graham Gibson), Melissa Errico (Samantha Thomas), Daniel Henson (Johnny Sullivan [Six]). Directed by Gregory Hoblit and produced by Hawk Koch, Hoblit, Bill Carraro, and Toby Emmerich. Screenplay by Emmerich.

I know exactly where the tape is, in which box, on which shelf. It's an old reel-to-reel tape I used with the tape recorder my dad bought me in grade school. It has his voice on it. The box has moved around with me for a long time, but I have never listened to the tape since my dad died. I don't think I could stand it. It would be too heartbreaking.

I thought about the tape as I was watching Gregory Hoblit's *Frequency.* Here is a movie that uses the notion of time travel to set up a situation where a man in 1999 is able to talk to his father in 1969, even though his father died when the man was six. The movie harnesses this notion to a lot of nonsense, including a double showdown with a killer, but the central idea is strong and carries us along. There must be something universal about our desire to defeat time, which in the end defeats us.

The father in 1969 is named Frank Sullivan (Dennis Quaid). He is a fireman, and he dies heroically while trying to save a life in a warehouse fire. The son in 1999 is named John Sullivan (Jim Caviezel), and he has broken with three generations of family tradition to become a policeman instead of a fireman. One night he's rummaging under the stairs of the family house where he still lives, and finds a trunk containing his dad's old ham radio. The plot provides some nonsense about sunspots and the northern lights, but never mind: What matters is that the father and the son can speak to each other across a gap of thirty years.

The paradox of time travel is familiar. If you could travel back in time to change the past in order to change the future, you would already have done so, and therefore the changes would have resulted in the present that you now occupy. Of course, the latest theories of quantum physics speculate that time may be a malleable dimension, and that countless new universes are splitting off from countless old ones all the time—we can't see them because we're always on the train, not in the station, and the view out the window is of this and this and this, not that and that.

But *Frequency* is not about physics, and the heroes are as baffled as we are by the paradoxes they get involved in. Consider a scene where the father uses a soldering iron to burn into a desk the message: "I'm still here, Chief." His son sees the letters literally appearing in 1999 as they are written in 1969. How can this be? If they were written in 1969, wouldn't they have already been on the desk for thirty years? Not at all, the movie argues, because every action in the past *changes* the future into a world in which that action has taken place.

Therefore—and here is the heart of the story—the son, knowing what he knows now, can reach back in time and save his father's life by telling him what he did wrong during that fatal fire. And the father and son can exchange information that will help each one fight a serial killer who, in various time-line configurations, is active now, then, and in between, and

threatens both men and, in some configurations, the fireman's wife. How do the voices know they can trust each other? The voice in the future can tell the voice in the past exactly what's going to happen with the Amazing Mets in the '69 Series.

Are you following this? Neither did I, half the time. At one point both the father and the son are fighting the same man at points thirty years separated, and when the father shoots off the 1969 man's hand, it disappears from the 1999 version of the man. But then the 1999 man would remember how he lost the hand, right? And therefore would know—but, no, not in this time line he wouldn't.

There may be holes and inconsistencies in the plot. I was too confused to be sure. And I don't much care, anyway, because the underlying idea is so appealing—that a son who doesn't remember his father could talk to him by shortwave and they could try to help each other. This notion is fleshed out by the father's wife (Elizabeth Mitchell), who must also be saved by the time-talkers, by partners in the fire and police department, and so on. By the end of the movie, the villain (Shawn Doyle) is fighting father and son simultaneously, and there is only one way to watch the movie, and that is with complete and unquestioning credulity. To attempt to unravel the plot leads to frustration if not madness.

Moviegoers seem to like supernatural stories that promise some kind of escape from our mutual doom. *Frequency* is likely to appeal to the fans of *The Sixth Sense, Ghost,* and other movies where the characters find a loophole in reality. What it also has in common with those two movies is warmth and emotion. Quaid and Caviezel bond over the radio, and we believe the feelings they share. The ending of the movie is contrived, but then of course it is: The whole movie is contrived. The screenplay conferences on *Frequency* must have gone on and on, as writer Toby Emmerich and the filmmakers tried to fight their way through the maze they were creating. The result, however, appeals to us for reasons as simple as hearing the voice of a father you thought you would never hear again.

From Hell ★ ★ ★
R, 137 m., 2001

Johnny Depp (Frederick Abberline), Heather Graham (Mary Kelly), Ian Holm (Sir William Gull), Katrin Cartlidge (Dark Annie), Robbie Coltrane (Peter Godley), Bryon Frear (Robert Best). Directed by Albert Hughes and Allen Hughes and produced by Don Murphy and Jane Hamsher. Screenplay by Terry Hayes and Rafael Yglesias, based on the graphic novel by Alan Moore and Eddie Campbell.

"One day men will say I gave birth to the twentieth century."
—dialogue by Jack the Ripper

I'd like to think Darwin has a better case, but I see what he means. The century was indeed a stage for the dark impulses of the soul, and recently I've begun to wonder if Jack didn't give birth to the twenty-first century, too. Twins.

During ten weeks in autumn 1888, a serial killer murdered five prostitutes in the White-chapel area of London. The murders were linked because the Ripper left a trademark, surgically assaulting the corpses in a particularly gruesome way. "I look for someone with a thorough knowledge of human anatomy," says Inspector Abberline of Scotland Yard. An elementary knowledge would have been sufficient.

The story of Jack the Ripper has been fodder for countless movies and books, and even periodic reports that the mystery has been "solved" have failed to end our curiosity. Now comes *From Hell*, a rich, atmospheric film by the Hughes brothers *(Menace II Society)*, who call it a "ghetto film," although knowledge of film, not the ghetto, is what qualifies them.

Johnny Depp stars as Inspector Frederick Abberline, an opium addict whose smoke-fueled dreams produce psychic insights into crime. The echo of Sherlock Holmes, another devotee of the pipe, is unmistakable, and *From Hell* supplies its hero with a Watsonoid sidekick in Peter Godley (Robbie Coltrane), a policeman assigned to haul Abberline out of the dens, gently remind him of his duty, protect him from harm, and marvel at his insights. Depp plays his role as very, very subtle comedy—so droll he hopes we think he's serious.

The movie feels dark, clammy, and exhilarating—it's like belonging to a secret club where you can have a lot of fun but might get into trouble. There's one extraordinary shot that begins with the London skyline, pans down past towers and steam trains, and plunges into a subterranean crypt where a Masonic lodge is sitting in judgment on one of its members. You get the notion of the robust physical progress of Victoria's metropolis, and the secret workings of the Establishment. At a time when public morality was strict and unbending, private misbehavior was a boom industry. Many, perhaps most, rich and pious men engaged in private debauchery.

The Hughes brothers plunge into this world, so far from their native Detroit, with the joy of tourists who have been reading up for years. Their source is a 500-page graphic novel (that is, transcendent comic book) by Alan Moore and Eddie Campbell, and some of their compositions look influenced by comic art, with its sharp obliques and exaggerated perspectives. The movie was shot on location with the medieval streets of Prague doubling for London, and production designer Martin Childs goes for lurid settings, saturated colors, deep shadows, a city of secret places protected by power and corruption.

We meet some of the prostitutes, particularly Mary Kelly (Heather Graham), who is trying to help her sisters escape from the dominance of the pimps. We see Abberline and Kelly begin a romance that probably would have been a lot more direct and uncomplicated at that time than it is in this movie. We see members of Victoria's immediate family implicated in whoring and venereal mishaps, and we meet the queen's surgeon, a precise and, by his own admission, brilliant man named Sir William Gull (Ian Holm).

The investigation is interrupted from time to time by more murders, graphically indicated, and by forms of official murder, like lobotomy. Sir William is an especially enthusiastic advocate of that procedure, reinforcing my notion that every surgeon of any intelligence who practiced lobotomy did so with certain doubts about its wisdom, and certain stirrings of curious satisfaction.

Watching the film, I was surprised how consistently it surprised me. It's a movie "catering to no clear demographic," *Variety* reports in its review, as if catering to a demographic would be a good thing for a movie to do. Despite its Gothic look, *From Hell* is not in the Hammer horror genre. Despite its Sherlockian hero, it's not a Holmes and Watson story. Despite its murders, it's not a slasher film. What it is, I think, is a Guignol about a cross section of a thoroughly rotten society, corrupted from the top down. The Ripper murders cut through layers of social class designed to insulate the sinners from the results of their sins.

G

George Washington ★ ★ ★ ★
NO MPAA RATING, 89 m., 2001

Candace Evanofski (Nasia), Donald Holden (George), Curtis Cotton III (Buddy), Eddie Rouse (Damascus), Paul Schneider (Rico Rice), Damian Jewan Lee (Vernon), Rachael Handy (Sonya), Jonathan Davidson (Euless), Janet Taylor (Ruth). Directed by David Gordon Green and produced by Green, Sacha W. Mueller, and Lisa Muskat. Screenplay by Green.

There is a summer in your life that is the last time boys and girls can be friends until they grow up. The summer when adolescence has arrived, but has not insisted on itself. When the stir of arriving sexuality still makes you feel hopeful instead of restless and troubled. When you feel powerful instead of unsure. That is the summer *George Washington* is about, and all it is about. Everything else in the film is just what happened to happen that summer.

This is such a lovely film. You give yourself to its voluptuous languor. You hang around with these kids from the poor side of town, while they kill time and share their pipe dreams. A tragedy happens, but the movie is not about the tragedy. It is about the discovery that tragedies can happen. In the corresponding summer of my life, a kid tried to be a daredevil by riding his bicycle up a ramp, and fell off and broke his leg, and everybody blamed that when he got polio. I tell you my memory instead of what happens in this film, because the tragedy in the film comes so swiftly, in the midst of a casual afternoon, that it should be as surprising to you as to the kids.

The movie takes place in a rusting industrial landscape, which the weeds are already returning to nature. It is in North Carolina. We meet some black kids, between ten and thirteen, and a few white kids. They're friends. They are transparent to one another. They are facts of life. You wake up every morning and here they are, the other kids in your life. They are waiting to grow up. There are some adults around, but they're not insisted upon. Some of them are so stranded by life they kill time with the kids. Nothing better to do.

Buddy (Curtis Cotton III) has a crush on Nasia (Candace Evanofski). She leaves him for George (Donald Holden). This is all momentous because it is the first crush and the first leaving of their lives. Buddy asks for one last kiss. "Do you love me?" asks Nasia. Buddy won't say. He wants the kiss voluntarily. No luck. George has his own problems: The plates in his skull didn't meet right, and he wears a football helmet to protect his skull. "When I look at my friends," Nasia muses, "I know there's goodness. I can look at their feet, or when I hold their hands, I pretend I can see the bones inside."

George fears for his dog because his Uncle Damascus (Eddie Rouse) doesn't like animals. "He just don't like to get bothered," says Aunt Ruth (Janet Taylor). "Do you remember the first time we made love to this song?" Damascus asks Ruth. "We were out in that field. You buried me in that grass." "Why is it," Ruth asks him, "every time you start talkin', you sound like you gonna cry?"

The heat is still, the days are slow, there is not much to do. A kid with freckles gets in trouble in the swimming pool and George jumps in to save him, even though he's not supposed to get his head wet. Then George starts wearing a cape, like a superhero. Buddy wears a Halloween dinosaur mask while he stands in a rest room, which is one of their hangouts, and delivers a soliloquy that would be worthy of Hamlet, if instead of being the prince of Denmark, Hamlet had been Buddy. Buddy disappears. Nasia thinks he ran away "because he still has his crush on me." Others know why Buddy disappeared but simply do not know what to do with their knowledge. Vernon (Damian Jewan Lee) has a soliloquy beginning with the words "I wish," that would be worthy of Buddy, or Hamlet.

The film has been written and directed by David Gordon Green. The cinematography, by Tim Orr, is the best of the year. The mood and feel of the film has been compared to the work of Terence Malick, and Green is said to have watched *The Thin Red Line* over and over while preparing to shoot. But this is not a copy of Malick; it is simply in the same key. Like Malick's *Days of Heaven*, it is not about plot, but about memory and regret. It remembers a summer that was not a happy summer, but there will never again be a summer so intensely felt, so alive, so valuable.

Getting to Know You ★ ★ ★
NO MPAA RATING, 96 m., 2000

Heather Matarazzo (Judith), Zach Braff (Wesley), Michael Weston (Jimmy), Bebe Neuwirth (Trix [Judith's Mom]), Mark Blum (Darrell [Judith's Dad]), Bo Hopkins (Officer Caminetto, Tristine Skyler (Irene), Christopher Noth (Sonny), Jacob Reynolds (Lamar Pike Jr.). Directed by Lisanne Skyler and produced by Laura Gabbert and George LaVoo. Screenplay by Tristine Skyler and Lisanne Skyler, based on stories by Joyce Carol Oates.

The work of Joyce Carol Oates is populated with characters who live in a lonely landscape, filled with hurt and shame. She has written so much about them, and knows them so well, that we are at a loss to understand the springs of her invention; she reminds me of a story I read long ago about a man who was telepathic, and went mad because he could not drown out the incoming pain and cries for help.

Getting to Know You is a film based on several of Oates's stories, held together by the linking device of some people waiting in a small bus station: a sixteen-year-old girl named Judith, her brother Wesley, a boy named Jimmy who hangs around the station, a security guard, and some others. Judith and Wesley (Heather Matarazzo and Zach Braff) have clung together in the wreckage of their parents' alcoholic marriage; Jimmy is a kid who makes up stories about himself and about the strangers he sees in the bus station, and in a way he represents Oates.

The kids' parents are Trix (Bebe Neuwirth) and Darrell (Mark Blum), two drinkers and ballroom dancers who live in a world of their own. In a flashback, the kids sit on a staircase, peering down at their parents drifting across a living room that has become, in their minds, a ballroom. Going through old family photo albums, they notice that the pictures stop at about the time they were born. Now, we learn, Trix is in an institution, maybe with wet brain, and when Judith calls her dad, he doesn't want her to call anymore—he has "canceled all debts."

When the bus arrives, Wesley will be off to college, and then Judith will be going to a foster home. Wesley spends most of the movie buried in textbooks, obviously determined to learn his way out of despair. Judith starts talking to Jimmy, who singles out people in the bus station and tells her stories about them. He says the security guard (Bo Hopkins), for example, left the police force after his partner was killed on a day off in what may have been an unnecessary way.

A movie like this runs the risk of feeling cut up and episodic, but director Lisanne Skyler, who cowrote the screenplay with her actress sister Tristine, makes the episodes vivid. One stars Tristine and Chris Noth in the story of a girl who meets a gambler in an Atlantic City casino. He wins $75,000 and is charming, expansive, blessed, and it's love for a night. Then he's drawn back to the tables, and his sad need to lose draws shadows over his face, and she is frightened. Another story involves a scrawny, deep-voiced boy named Lamar Jr. (Jacob Reynolds), and his dad, and an ax.

Heather Matarazzo is at the center of the film, her first major role since *Welcome to the Dollhouse* (1995). The camera likes to regard her; she has a repose and inwardness that attracts our attention. Like Lili Taylor or Shelley Duvall, she is not conventionally pretty, although she glows and is more entrancing than the teen-mag beauties who pass for stars in Friday night specials. Her character Judith takes a . . . care with life. When she touches something, you can't tell if she doesn't want to harm it, or is afraid of being burned. She is poised on the edge of a life when things like she's heard about today could happen to her.

The history of this film is intriguing. It played first on the Sundance Channel, and is now going out theatrically. Another good film, *Panic,* also went to cable after winning a warm reception in festivals. Mass distribution is so dominated by 3,000-screen f/x extravaganzas that smaller films get lost in the noise, and perhaps the cable exposure will act like a sneak preview, as people tell each other about the film they discovered and admired. Movies about people are being drowned out these days by movies about things, which can give you insights about yourself only if you are a cyborg. Here is a film about people.

Ghost Dog: The Way of the Samurai ★ ★ ★

R, 116 m., 2000

Forest Whitaker (Ghost Dog), Henry Silva (Ray Vargo), Richard Portnow (Handsome Frank), Tricia Vessey (Louise Vargo), John Tormey (Louie), Cliff Gorman (Sonny Valerio), Victor Argo (Vinny). Directed by Jim Jarmusch and produced by Jarmusch and Richard Guay. Screenplay by Jarmusch.

It helps to understand that the hero of *Ghost Dog* is crazy. Well, of course he is. He lives in a shack on a rooftop with his pigeons. He dresses like a homeless man. "He has no friends and never talks to anybody," according to the mother of the little girl in the movie. Actually, he does talk: to the little girl and to a Haitian ice-cream man. The Haitian speaks no English and Ghost Dog speaks no French, so they simply speak in their own languages and are satisfied with that. What's your diagnosis?

Ghost Dog (Forest Whitaker) is a killer for the mob. He got into this business because one day a mobster saved his life—and so, since he follows "The Way of the Samurai," he must dedicate his life to his master. The mobster is named Louie (John Tormey). He orders hits by sending Ghost Dog messages by carrier pigeon. The Dog insists on being paid once a year, on the first day of autumn. When the mob bosses want Ghost Dog rubbed out, they're startled to discover that Louie doesn't know his name or where he lives; their only contact is the pigeons.

It seems strange that a black man would devote his life to doing hired killing for a group of Italian-American gangsters after having met only one of them. But then it's strange, too, that Ghost Dog lives like a medieval Japanese samurai. The whole story is so strange, indeed, that I've read some of the other reviews in disbelief. Are movie critics so hammered by absurd plots that they can't see how truly, profoundly weird *Ghost Dog* is? The reviews treat it matter-of-factly: Yeah, here's this hit man, he lives like a samurai, he gets his instructions by pigeon, blah, blah . . . and then they start talking about the performances and how the director, Jim Jarmusch, is paying homage to Kurosawa and *High Noon*.

But the man is insane! In a quiet, sweet way, he is totally unhinged and has lost all touch with reality. His profound sadness, which permeates the touching Whitaker performance, comes from his alienation from human society, his loneliness, his attempt to justify inhuman behavior (murder) with a belief system (the samurai code) that has no connection with his life or his world. Despite the years he's spent studying "The Way of the Samurai," he doesn't even reflect that since his master doesn't subscribe to it, their relationship is meaningless.

I make this argument because I've seen *Ghost Dog* twice, and admired it more after I focused on the hero's insanity. The first time I saw it, at Cannes, I thought it was a little too precious, an exercise in ironic style, not substance. But look more deeply, and you see the self-destructive impulse that guides Ghost Dog in the closing scenes, as he sadly marches forth to practice his code in the face of people who only want to kill him (whether he survives is not the point).

Jarmusch is mixing styles here almost recklessly, and I like the chances he takes. The gangsters (played by colorful character actors like Henry Silva, Richard Portnow, Cliff Gorman, and Victor Argo), sit in their clubhouse doing sub-Scorsese while the Louie character tries to explain to them how he uses an invisible hit man. Ghost Dog meanwhile mopes sadly around the neighborhood, solemnly recommending *Rashomon* to a little girl ("you may want to wait and read it when you're a little older"), and miscommunicating with the ice-cream man. By the end, Whitaker's character has generated true poignance.

If the mobsters are on one level of reality and Ghost Dog on another, then how do we interpret some of the Dog's killings, particularly the one where he shoots a man by sneaking under his house and firing up through the lavatory pipe while the guy is shaving? This is a murder that demands Inspector Clouseau as its investigator. Jarmusch seems to have directed with his tongue in his cheek, his hand over his heart, and his head in the clouds. The result is weirdly intriguing.

Ghosts of Mars ★ ★ ★
R, 98 m., 2001

Ice Cube (Desolation Williams), Natasha Henstridge (Melanie Ballard), Jason Statham (Jericho Butler), Clea DuVall (Bashira Kincaid), Pam Grier (Helena), Joanna Cassidy (Whitlock), Richard Cetrone (Big Daddy Mars), Duane Davis (Uno). Directed by John Carpenter and produced by Sandy King. Screenplay by Larry Sulkis and Carpenter.

John Carpenter's *Ghosts of Mars* is a brawny space opera, transplanting the conventions of Western, cop, and martial arts films to the Red Planet. As waves of zombified killers attack the heroes, action scenes become shooting galleries, and darned if in the year 2176 they aren't still hurling sticks of dynamite from moving trains. All basic stuff, and yet Carpenter brings pacing and style to it, and Natasha Henstridge provides a coolheaded center.

As the film opens, a ghost train pulls into Chryse City, so named for a flat plain north of the Martian equator. No driver is at the helm, and only one passenger is on board. She is Melanie Ballard (Henstridge), a cop who headed a detail to an outlying mining town named Shining Canyon to bring back a killer named Desolation Williams (Ice Cube). Called up before a tribunal in the matriarchal Martian society, she tells her story, and most of the action is in flashback.

The mining camp seems empty when the cops arrive. Henstridge is joined by Helena (Pam Grier), Bashira (Clea DuVall), Jericho (Jason Statham), and Uno (Duane Davis). They start finding bodies. Desolation is still in jail, proving he could not be the killer, and eventually a survivor named Whitlock (Joanna Cassidy) tells the story of how the miners found the entrance to a long-buried tunnel. It led to a door that, when merely touched, crumbled into dust and released, yes, the ghosts of Mars. They possessed humans and turned them into killing machines, to take, she says, "vengeance on anyone who tries to lay claim to their planet."

That's the setup. The payoff is a series of well-staged action sequences, made atmospheric by the rusty red atmosphere that colors everything. At one point the cops barricade themselves inside the mining camp's police station, which will remind Carpenter fans of his early feature, *Assault on Precinct 13*. There is also something about the ghoulish way the possessed miners lurch into action that has a touch of the *Living Dead* movies.

These ghouls or zombies or ghost-creatures are not, however, slow. They're pretty fast in the martial arts scenes, especially their leader, Big Daddy Mars (Richard Cetrone). But like all similar movie creatures, they're just a little slower than the heroes. They keep coming but never quite catch up.

Natasha Henstridge has come full circle. Her movie career began in *Species* (1995), where she played Sil, an alien who looked like Natasha Henstridge part of the time, and like gloppy puke-monsters the rest of the time. Now she's fighting the aliens, and for most of the movie is partnered with Desolation, the Ice Cube character, played by Mr. Cube with solid authority.

Ghosts of Mars delivers on its chosen level and I enjoyed it, but I wonder why so many science-fiction films turn into extended exercises in Blast the Aliens. *Starship Troopers* was another. Why must aliens automatically be violent, angry, aggressive, ugly, mindless, and hostile? How could they develop the technology to preserve their spirits for aeons, and exhibit no civilized attributes? And, for that matter, if Earth creatures came along after, oh, say, 300 million years of captivity and set you free, would you be mad at them?

These are all questions for another movie. This one does have one original touch. After Melanie is possessed by a ghost, Desolation administers a fix from her stash, and the drug, whatever it is, inspires the alien to get out of her body fast. It is encouraging to learn that the ancient races of our solar system learned to just say no to drugs. ☞

Ghost World ★ ★ ★ ★
R, 111 m., 2001

Thora Birch (Enid), Scarlett Johansson (Rebecca), Steve Buscemi (Seymour), Brad Renfro (Josh), Illeana Douglas (Roberta), Bob Balaban (Enid's Dad), Teri Garr (Maxine). Directed by Terry Zwigoff and produced by Lianne Halfon, John Malkovich, and Russell

Smith. Screenplay by Daniel Clowes and Zwigoff, based on the comic book by Clowes.

There's a small tomb in Southwark Cathedral that I like to visit when I am in London. It contains the bones of a teenage girl who died three centuries ago. I know the inscription by heart:

> *This world to her*
> *Was but a tragic play.*
> *She came, saw, dislik'd,*
> *And passed away.*

I thought of those words while I was watching *Ghost World,* the story of an eighteen-year-old girl from Los Angeles who drifts forlorn through her loneliness, cheering herself up with an ironic running commentary. The girl is named Enid, she has just graduated from high school, and she has no plans for college, marriage, a career, or even next week. She's stuck in a world of stupid, shallow phonies, and she makes her personal style into a rebuke.

Unfortunately, Enid is so smart, so advanced, and so ironically doubled back upon herself that most of the people she meets don't get the message. She is second-level satire in a one-level world, and so instead of realizing, for example, that she is mocking the 1970s punk look, stupid video store clerks merely think she's twenty-five years out of style.

Enid is played by Thora Birch, from *American Beauty,* and in a sense this character is a continuation of that one—she certainly looks at her father the same way, with disbelief and muted horror. Her running mate is Rebecca (Scarlett Johansson). There's a couple like this in every high school: the smart outsider girls who are best friends for the purpose of standing back-to-back and fighting off the world. At high school graduation, they listen to a speech from a classmate in a wheelchair, and Enid whispers: "I liked her so much better when she was an alcoholic and drug addict. She gets in one stupid car crash and suddenly she's Little Miss Perfect."

But now Rebecca is showing alarming signs of wanting to get on with her life, and Enid is abandoned to her world of thrift shops, strip malls, video stores, and 1950s retro diners. One day, in idle mischief, she answers a personal ad in a local paper, and draws into her net a pa-

thetic loner named Seymour (Steve Buscemi). At first she strings him along. Then, unexpected, she starts to like him—this collector who lives hermetically sealed in a world of precious 78 rpm records and old advertising art.

By day, Seymour is an insignificant fried chicken executive. By night, he catalogs his records and wonders how to meet a woman. Why does Enid like him? "He's the exact opposite of all the things I hate." Why does he like her? Don't get ahead of the story. *Ghost World* isn't a formula romance where opposites attract and march toward the happy ending. Seymour and Enid are too similar to fall in love; they both specialize in complex personal lifestyles that send messages no one is receiving. Enid even offers to try to fix up Seymour, but he sees himself as a bad candidate for a woman: "I don't want to meet someone who shares my interests. I hate my interests."

Seymour resembles someone I know, and that person is Terry Zwigoff, who directed this movie. It's his first fiction film. Zwigoff earlier made two docs, the masterpiece *Crumb* (1995), about the comic artist R. Crumb, and *Louie Bluie,* about the old-timey Chicago string band Martin, Bogan, and the Armstrongs. He looks a little like Buscemi, and acts like a Buscemi character: worn down, dubious, ironic, resigned. Zwigoff was plagued by agonizing back pain all during the period when he was making *Crumb,* and slept with a gun under his pillow, he told me, in case he had to end his misery in the middle of the night. When Crumb didn't want to cooperate with the documentary, Zwigoff threatened to shoot himself. Crumb does not often meet his match, but did with Zwigoff.

Both Zwigoff and his character Seymour collect old records that are far from the mainstream. Both are morose and yet have a bracing black humor that sees them through. Seymour and Enid connect because they are kindred spirits, and it's hard to find someone like that when you've cut yourself off from mankind.

The movie is based on a graphic novel by Daniel Clowes, who cowrote the screenplay with Zwigoff. It listens carefully to how people talk. Illeana Douglas, for example, has a perfectly observed role as the art teacher in Enid's summer makeup class, who has fallen for political correctness hook, line, and sinker, and praises art not for what it looks like but for what it "represents." There are also some nice moments from Teri Garr, who plays the take-charge girlfriend of Enid's father (Bob Balaban).

One scene I especially like involves a party of Seymour's fellow record collectors. They meet to exchange arcane information, and their conversations are like encryptions of the way most people talk. This event must seem strange to Enid, but see how she handles it. It's Seymour's oddness, his tactless honesty, his unapologetic aloneness, that Enid responds to. He works like the homeopathic remedy for angst: His loneliness drives out her own.

I wanted to hug this movie. It took such a risky journey, and never stepped wrong. It created specific, original, believable, lovable characters, and meandered with them through their inconsolable days, never losing its sense of humor. The Buscemi role is one he's been pointing toward during his entire career; it's like the flip side of his alcoholic barfly in *Trees Lounge*, who also becomes entangled with a younger girl, not so fortunately.

The movie sidesteps the happy ending Hollywood executives think lobotomized audiences need as an all-clear to leave the theater. Clowes and Zwigoff find an ending that is more poetic, more true to the tradition of the classic short story, in which a minor character finds closure that symbolizes the next step for everyone. *Ghost World* is smart enough to know that Enid and Seymour can't solve their lives in a week or two. But their meeting has blasted them out of lethargy, and now movement is possible. Who says that isn't a happy ending?

The Gift ★ ★ ★
R, 110 m., 2001

Cate Blanchett (Annie Wilson), Giovanni Ribisi (Buddy Cole), Keanu Reeves (Donnie Barksdale), Greg Kinnear (Wayne Collins), Hilary Swank (Valerie Barksdale), J. K. Simmons (Sheriff Pearl Johnson), Michael Jeter (Defense Attorney), Gary Cole (David Duncan). Directed by Sam Raimi and produced by James Jacks, Tom Rosenberg, and Robert G. Tapert. Screenplay by Billy Bob Thornton and Tom Epperson.

Psychics and hairdressers have three things in common: They can appoint themselves, they can work out of their homes, and they don't have a lot of overhead—a Tarot deck, shampoo, candles, scissors, incense, mousse. It helps if they have a reassuring manner, because many of their clients want to tell their troubles and receive advice.

Poor neighborhoods have a lot of women working as beauticians or soothsayers. If you're a woman with few options, no husband, and a bunch of kids, you can hang out the shingle and support yourself. The advice dispensed by these professionals is often as good as or better than the kind that costs $200 an hour, because it comes from people who spent their formative years living and learning. The problems of their clients are not theoretical to them.

Consider Annie Wilson (Cate Blanchett), the heroine of *The Gift*. Her husband was killed in an accident a year ago. She has three kids. She gets a government check, and supplements it by reading cards and advising clients. She doesn't go in for mumbo jumbo. She takes her gift as a fact of life; her grandmother had it, and so does she. She looks at the cards, she listens to her clients, she feels their pain, she tries to dispense common sense. She is sensible, courageous, and good.

She lives in a swamp of melodrama; that's really the only way to describe her hometown of Brixton, Georgia, which has been issued with one example of every standard Southern Gothic type. There's the battered wife and her redneck husband; the country club sexpot; the handsome school principal; the weepy mama's boy who is afeared he might do something real bad; the cheatin' attorney; the salt-of-the-earth sheriff; and various weeping willows, pickup trucks, rail fences, country clubs, shotguns, voodoo dolls, courtrooms, etc. When you see a pond in a movie like this, you know that sooner or later it is going to be dragged.

With all of these elements, *The Gift* could have been a bad movie, and yet it is a good one, because it redeems the genre with the characters. Cate Blanchett's sanity and balance as Annie Wilson provide a strong center, and the other actors in a first-rate cast go for the realism in their characters, instead of being tempted by the absurd. The movie was directed by Sam Raimi and written by Billy Bob

Thornton and Tom Epperson. They know the territory. Raimi directed Thornton in *A Simple Plan* (1998), that great movie about three buddies who find a fortune and try to hide it; and Thornton and Epperson wrote *One False Move* (1991), about criminals on the run and old secrets of love.

The Gift begins by plunging us into the daily lives of the characters, and then develops into a thriller. One of Annie's kitchen-table clients is Valerie Barksdale (Oscar winner Hilary Swank), whose husband, Donnie (Keanu Reeves), beats her. Another is Buddy Cole (Giovanni Ribisi), who is haunted by nightmares and is a seething basket case filled with resentment against his father. Annie advises Valerie to leave her husband before he does more harm, and then Keanu Reeves has two terrifying scenes—one threatening her children, the other a midnight visit where he uses the voodoo doll as a prop.

Social interlude: Annie attends a country club dance, where she has a flirty conversation with the school principal (Greg Kinnear). He's engaged to Jessica King (Katie Holmes), a sultry temptress (i.e., country club slut) who Annie accidentally sees having a quickie with another local man. Not long after, Jessica disappears, and Sheriff Pearl Johnson (J. K. Simmons), frustrated by an absence of clues, appeals to Annie for some of her "hocus-pocus."

Annie has a dream that leads the law to Donnie Barksdale's pond, where the dead body is found, and Donnie looks like the obvious killer, but Annie's visions don't stop, and we are left (1) with the possibility that the murder may have been committed by several other excellent candidates, and (2) with suspicion falling on the psychic herself.

The movie is ingenious in its plotting, colorful in its characters, taut in its direction, and fortunate in possessing Cate Blanchett. If this were not a crime picture (if it were sopped in social uplift instead of thrills), it would be easier to see the quality of her work. By the end, as all hell is breaking loose, it's easy to forget how much everything depended on the sympathy and gravity she provided in the first two acts. This role seems miles away from her Oscar-nominated *Elizabeth* (1998), but after all isn't she once again an independent woman

surrounded by men who want to belittle her power, seduce her, frame her, or kill her? A woman who has to rely on herself and her gifts, and does, and is sufficient.

Girlfight ★ ★ ★ ½
R, 122 m., 2000

Michelle Rodriguez (Diana), Jaime Tirelli (Hector), Ray Santiago (Tiny), Paul Calderon (Sandro), Santiago Douglas (Adrian), Louis Guss (Don), J. P. Lipton (Mr. Price). Directed by Karyn Kusama and produced by Sarah Green, Martha Griffin, and Maggie Renzi. Screenplay by Kusama.

After the screening of *Girlfight* at Cannes, I was talking to the two leads: Michelle Rodriguez, who plays Diana, a troubled Brooklyn girl who solves some of her problems by training to become a boxer, and Santiago Douglas, who plays her boyfriend and (improbably but with much suspense) her rival in the ring.

"There was a blooper in the big fight," Rodriguez told me. "He hit me by mistake. Really hit me."

"Don't start," said Douglas.

"I got mad and I jumped at him. So I had to leave the ring and just compose myself and just breathe."

"When I hit Michelle," Douglas said, "it wasn't a mistake. She'd won all of her fights in the story so far. I realized there was no fear in her eyes. She was overconfident."

"You did that on *purpose?*" said Michelle.

"I did."

There was a little silence, while Rodriguez absorbed that information, and I began to understand why, under the craft and drama of *Girlfight,* there was a certain real feeling of danger and risk.

Rodriguez told me she trained as a boxer for the movie, and enjoyed it, but finally, "I had to stop the boxing because your ego flies all over the place, and I started to actually welcome the challenge of someone in the street stepping up to me."

Yes, and that would fit, because Michelle Rodriguez is ideally cast in the movie, not as a hard woman or a muscular athlete, but as a spirited woman with a temper, and fire in her eyes. We need that for the picture to work.

Consider one of her first scenes. Diane gets in an argument over a boy in the hallways at high school. It's her fourth fight this semester. She's threatened with expulsion. In her eyes we can see resentment and outrage—the world is against her.

Later she's at the gym where her brother Tiny (Ray Santiago) takes lessons without much enthusiasm. A sparring partner hits Tiny with a sucker punch, and Diana jumps in the ring and clocks him. And likes the feeling.

Girlfight looks like a sports picture, but it's really more of a character study, in which boxing is the way that Diana finds direction in her life. She and Tiny live at home with their dad (Paul Calderon). Old angers simmer about the death of their mother. It's a traditionally macho Latin household in which Tiny's boxing lessons are paid for even though he has no interest in the sport. Diana does, and eventually her brother gives her his boxing money: "I'm a geek. I'll do something constructive with my time."

At the gym Diana meets Adrian, who seems to be going with another girl but maybe not. They go to dinner. She says she likes boxing. "It's a dangerous sport," he says. "I didn't make the cheerleading team," she says, and the tone of her voice says more.

Yes, the movie leads up to the obligatory big fight. But what is proven in the fight settles more about the characters and their relationships than it does about the plot. This is a story about a girl growing up in a macho society and, far from being threatened by its values, discovering she has a nature probably more macho than the men around her. Since the movie (written, directed, and produced by women) is deeply aware of that theme, it's always about more than boxing.

Karyn Kusama was named Best Director at Sundance for *Girlfight* (which also won the Grand Jury Prize), and she wisely realizes many of the changes in the story have to be embodied in the performances (it would be fatal to spell out the themes in dialogue). Rodriguez, a newcomer, seems to have a natural affinity for the camera. Her Diana hungers, she cares, she is easily wounded and quick to defend herself, and all of those qualities are simply there in every scene; they don't need to be underlined, because Rodriguez brings them along.

"Making this movie was good for me," Rodriguez told me that day in Cannes. "I learned discipline. I'm a very irresponsible person with a short attention span. I learned to dedicate myself to something." Was she talking about herself, or her character? The movie is stronger because that's such a close call.

Girl, Interrupted ★ ★ ½
R, 125 m., 2000

Winona Ryder (Susanna), Angelina Jolie (Lisa), Clea Duvall (Georgina), Brittany Murphy (Daisy), Elisabeth Moss (Polly), Jared Leto (Tobias Jacobs), Whoopi Goldberg (Valerie [nurse]), Jeffrey Tambor (Dr. Potts), Vanessa Redgrave (Dr. Wick). Directed by James Mangold and produced by Douglas Wick and Cathy Konrad. Screenplay by Mangold, Lisa Loomer, and Anna Hamilton Phelan, based on the book by Susanna Kaysen.

In the spring of 1967, while everyone else in her senior class seems to be making plans for college, Susanna consumes a bottle of aspirin and a bottle of vodka. "My hands have no bones," she observes. Soon, with a push from her family, she has committed herself to Claymoore, an upscale psychiatric institution. The diagnosis? "Borderline personality disorder," say the shrinks. A supervising nurse played by Whoopi Goldberg offers her own diagnosis: "You are a lazy, self-indulgent little girl who is driving herself crazy."

Winona Ryder plays Susanna Kaysen, whose real-life memoir tells of how she lost two years of her life by stumbling onto the psychiatric conveyor belt. Although mental illness is real and terrifying, the movie argues that perfectly sane people like Susanna can become institutionalized simply because once they're inside the system there is the assumption that something must be wrong with them. Goldberg's nurse has seen this process at work and warns Susanna: "Do not drop anchor here."

But Susanna fits easily into the cocoon of Claymoore, where the other women include a rebel misfit named Lisa (Angelina Jolie), a roommate named Georgina (Clea Duvall) who would like to live in the land of Oz, the burn victim Polly (Elisabeth Moss), and the deeply troubled Daisy (Brittany Murphy). The staff is headed by a bureaucrat (Jeffrey Tambor) and an intelligent but detached psychiatrist (Vanessa Redgrave).

The film unfolds in an episodic way, like the journal it's based on. Themes make an appearance from time to time, but not consistently; the film is mostly about character and behavior, and although there are individual scenes of powerful acting, there doesn't seem to be a destination. That's why the conclusion is so unsatisfying: The story, having failed to provide itself with character conflicts that can be resolved with drama, turns to melodrama instead.

One problem is the ambivalent nature of Susanna's condition ("ambivalent" is one of her favorite words). She isn't disturbed enough to require treatment, but she becomes strangely absorbed inside Claymoore, as if it provides structure and entertainment she misses on the outside. Certainly Lisa is an inspiration, with her cool self-confidence masking deep wounds. Instead of being in a women's dorm at college, Susanna is in a women's dorm at Claymoore, where her subject of study is herself. Susanna is not therefore a captive of an evil system, but someone seduced by a careless one, and there is the temptation to suspect she deserves what she gets.

Even a feminist argument with her psychiatrist (Redgrave) lacks power. They argue over the definition of promiscuity; Susanna points out that women are labeled promiscuous after much less sexual experience than men. Susanna has indeed slept in one day with both her boyfriend and an orderly, but under the circumstances is that promiscuity or opportunism?

Jared Leto plays her boyfriend, Toby, whose number is up in the draft lottery. He wants them to run away to Canada. She is no longer much interested in steering her future into their relationship, and prefers her new friends in Claymoore. "Them?" says Toby. "They're eating grapes off of the wallpaper." Susanna chooses solidarity: "If they're insane, I'm insane." Wrong. They're insane and she isn't, and that deprives the film of the kind of subterranean energy that fueled its obvious inspiration, *One Flew Over the Cuckoo's Nest.*

Two reasons to see the film: Winona Ryder and Angelina Jolie. Their characters never really get a plot to engage them, and are subjected to a silly ending, but moment to moment they

are intriguing and watchable. Jolie is emerging as one of the great wild spirits of current movies, a loose cannon who somehow has deadly aim. Ryder shows again her skill at projecting mental states; one of her gifts is to let us know exactly what she's thinking, without seeming to. Their work here deserves a movie with more reason for existing.

The Girl on the Bridge ★ ★ ★ ½
R, 92 m., 2000

Daniel Auteuil (Gabor), Vanessa Paradis (Adele), Claude Aufaure (Suicide Victim), Bertie Cortez (Kusak), Giorgios Gatzios (Barker), Demetre Georgalas (Takis), Catherine Lascault (Irene), Mireille Mosse (Miss Memory). Directed by Patrice Leconte and produced by Christian Fechner. Screenplay by Serge Frydman.

The hero of *The Girl on the Bridge* hangs around bridges in Paris, looking for girls who are about to jump. Then he offers them a deal. Suicide is a permanent solution to a temporary problem, so perhaps they will consider working for him. He is a knife thrower. There is always the possibility he will miss. If he doesn't, they get an interesting job with lots of travel. If he does hit them, well, what do they have to lose?

This logic proves persuasive to Adele (Vanessa Paradis), who signs on with Gabor (Daniel Auteuil). Well, not immediately; first she jumps, or perhaps slips, into the water, and he has to jump in and save her life. That will get a girl's attention. They travel from one venue to another, at first in the south of France, as he straps her to a cork backdrop and hurls knives at her. There are variations. He straps her to a spinning wheel. Sometimes he is blindfolded, or she is concealed beneath a sheet. They are booked on cruise ships, where the rocking of the waves adds a risk factor.

Gabor complains that his eyes are failing him ("past forty, knife throwing becomes erratic"), but he is really very good, a skill revealed by the fact that this film is not a short subject. If he is good at knives, she is good at roulette, and in the casinos in the towns where they appear she has an extraordinary run of good luck. His luck has turned good, too; they're making better money, finding better bookings, and they become so closely in synch they can even hear each other's thoughts.

The Girl on the Bridge was directed by Patrice Leconte, a French filmmaker whose work includes *Monsieur Hire* (1989), *The Hairdresser's Husband* (1990), and *Ridicule* (1996). He is fascinated by the hoops that his characters will jump through in their search for sexual fulfillment. Monsieur Hire is a bald little man of solemn visage who is a voyeur. He meekly worships the woman in the apartment across the way, who is not oblivious to his attentions, but his haplessness is his undoing. *The Hairdresser's Husband,* on the other hand, is about a man who became fixated in adolescence on hairdressers, and wants only to be present while the woman of his dreams cuts hair. Now comes the knife thrower.

Leconte's movies almost always involve a deep, droll humor (it is hard to see in *Monsieur Hire,* but it is there). He's amused by human nature. His characters in *The Girl on the Bridge* aren't oblivious to the humor in their situation; their love and luck seem to depend on earning their living by seeing how close they can come to disaster. Much of their appeal comes from the human qualities of the performers. Auteuil, he of the crooked nose and mournful countenance, is a man who can hardly believe good fortune, and Paradis is a woman who can see that during many of her orgasms the joke is on her.

The movie begins by taking an absurd situation rather seriously, and then lets the seriousness melt away; by the time the lovers have voluntarily gotten themselves into a rowboat in the middle of the ocean, we are almost in Looney Tunes territory.

Leconte's own adolescent fixation seems to be with exotic Turkish harem music, which he gets around to with amazing frequency in his movies. In *The Hairdresser's Husband,* so great was the husband's exuberance that he would sometimes put Turkish music on the phonograph and dance about the shop. In *The Girl on the Bridge,* the lovers work through the French and Italian Rivieras, and then move on by sea to Istanbul—perhaps for no better reason than so Leconte can slip his favorite music onto the sound track.

What's best about the movie is its playfulness. Occupations like knife throwing were not uncommon in silent comedy, but modern movies have become depressingly mired in ordinary lifestyles. In many new romantic comedies, the occupations of the characters don't even matter, because they are only labels; there's a setup scene in an office, and everything else is after hours. Here knife throwing explains not only the man's desperation to meet the woman, but the kind of woman he meets, and the way they eventually feel about each other. Dr. Johnson said that the knowledge that you will be hanged in the morning concentrates the mind wonderfully. There is nothing like being partners in a knife-throwing act to encourage a man and a woman to focus on their relationship.

Gladiator ★ ★
R, 150 m., 2000

Russell Crowe (Maximus), Joaquin Phoenix (Commodus), Connie Nielsen (Lucilla), Oliver Reed (Proximo), Richard Harris (Marcus Aurelius), Derek Jacobi (Gracchus), Djimon Hounsou (Juba), David Schofield (Falco). Directed by Ridley Scott and produced by Douglas Wick, David Franzoni, and Branko Lustig. Screenplay by Franzoni, John Logan, and William Nicholson.

Maximus: *I'm required to kill—so I kill. That's enough.*
  Proximo: *That's enough for the provinces, but not for Rome.*

A foolish choice in art direction casts a pall over Ridley Scott's *Gladiator* that no swordplay can cut through. The film looks muddy, fuzzy, and indistinct. Its colors are mud tones at the drab end of the palate, and it seems to have been filmed on grim and overcast days. This darkness and a lack of detail in the long shots helps obscure shabby special effects (the Coliseum in Rome looks like a set from a computer game), and the characters bring no cheer: They're bitter, vengeful, depressed. By the end of this long film, I would have traded any given gladiatorial victory for just one shot of blue skies. (There are blue skies in the hero's dreams of long-ago happiness, but that proves the point.)

The story line is *Rocky* on downers. The

hero, a general from Spain named Maximus (Russell Crowe), is a favorite of emperor Marcus Aurelius (Richard Harris). After Maximus defeats the barbarians, Marcus names him protector of Rome. But he is left for dead by Marcus's son, a bitter rival named Commodus (the name comes from the Latin for "convenient" and not what you're thinking). After escaping and finding that his wife and son have been murdered, Maximus finds his way to the deserts of North Africa, where he is sold as a slave to Proximo (the late Oliver Reed), a manager of gladiators. When Commodus lifts his father's ban on gladiators in Rome, in an attempt to distract the people from hunger and plagues, Maximus slashes his way to the top, and the movie ends, of course, with the Big Fight.

This same story could have been rousing entertainment; I have just revisited the wonderful *Raiders of the Lost Ark,* which is just as dim-witted but twelve times more fun. But *Gladiator* lacks joy. It employs depression as a substitute for personality, and believes that if the characters are bitter and morose enough, we won't notice how dull they are.

Commodus (Joaquin Phoenix) is one of those spoiled, self-indulgent, petulant Roman emperors made famous in the age of great Roman epics, which ended with *Spartacus* (1963). Watching him in his snits, I recalled Peter Ustinov's great Nero, in *Quo Vadis* (1951), collecting his tears for posterity in tiny crystal goblets. Commodus has unusual vices even for a Caesar; he wants to become the lover of his older sister Lucilla (Connie Nielsen), whose son he is raising as his heir.

The ethical backbone of the story is easily mastered. Commodus wants to be a dictator, but is opposed by the Senate, led by such as Gracchus (Derek Jacobi). The senators want him to provide sewers for the city's Greek district, where the plague is raging, but Commodus decides instead on a season of games. Proximo arrives with his seasoned gladiators from Africa, who prove nearly invincible, and threaten the emperor's popularity. The moral lesson: It is good when gladiators slaughter everyone in sight, and then turn over power to the politicians.

The Coliseum productions play like professional wrestling. Events are staged to re-create famous battles, and after the visitors wipe out the home team, a puzzled Commodus tells his aide, "My history's a little hazy—but shouldn't the barbarians *lose* the battle of Carthage?" Later, an announcer literally addresses the crowd in these words: "Caesar is pleased to bring you the only undefeated champion in Roman history—the legendary Tiger!"

The battle sequences are a pale shadow of the lucidly choreographed swordplay in *Rob Roy* (1995); instead of moves we can follow and strategy we can appreciate, Scott goes for muddled close-ups of fearsome but indistinct events. The crowd cheers, although those in the cheaper seats are impossible to see because of the murky special effects.

When Maximus wins his first big fight, it's up to Commodus to decide whether he will live or die. "Live! Live!" the fans chant, and Commodus, bowing to their will, signals with a "thumbs up." This demonstrates that Commodus was not paying attention in Caesar School, since the practice at the Coliseum at that time was to close the thumb in the fist to signal life; an extended thumb meant death. Luckily, no one else in the Coliseum knows this either.

Russell Crowe is efficient as Maximus; bearded, taciturn, brooding. His closest friend among the gladiators is played by Djimon Hounsou, who played the passionate slave in *Amistad.* Since protocol requires him to speak less than Maximus, he mostly looks ferocious, effectively. Connie Nielsen shows the film's most depth as the sister. Phoenix is passable as Commodus, but a quirkier actor could have had more fun in the role. Old pros Harris, Jacobi, and Reed are reliable; Scott does some fancy editing and a little digital work to fill the gaps left when Reed died during the production.

Gladiator is being hailed by those with short memories as the equal of *Spartacus* and *Ben Hur.* This is more like *Spartacus Lite.* Or dark. It's only necessary to think back a few months to Julie Taymor's *Titus* for a film set in ancient Rome that's immeasurably better to look at. The visual accomplishment of *Titus* shames *Gladiator,* and its story is a whole heck of a lot better than the *Gladiator* screenplay, even if Shakespeare didn't make Titus the only undefeated champion in Roman history.

The Glass House ★ ★
PG-13, 101 m., 2001

Diane Lane (Erin Glass), Leelee Sobieski (Ruby Baker), Stellan Skarsgard (Terry Glass), Rita Wilson (Grace Baker), Bruce Dern (Lawyer), Michael O'Keefe (Dave Baker), Trevor Morgan (Rhett Baker). Directed by Daniel Sackheim and produced by Heather Zeegen. Screenplay by Wesley Strick.

The Glass House brings skilled technique to a plot that's a foregone conclusion. Since it's clear from early in the film what must have happened and why, it's a film about waiting for the characters to catch up to us. The movie's trailer doesn't help, with its comprehensive betrayal of the movie's key secrets. It should even be a secret that this is a thriller—we should walk in thinking it's about kids surviving the loss of their parents. No chance of that.

The film opens with one of those irrelevant shock buttons that have become annoying in recent years—five or ten minutes that have nothing to do with the rest of the story, but fool us with misleading footage. In this case, there's a horror scene, and then we see it's a film, and then we see the heroine and her friends watching it—and, yes, they're cute as they giggle at their own reactions, but openings like this are empty stylistic exercises. Once was a time when the well-made film used its opening scenes to dig in, not just spin its wheels.

The movie was directed by the TV veteran Daniel Sackheim, who worked on *ER, X Files, Law and Order,* and other series that are smarter than this. It stars Leelee Sobieski, one of the best young actresses, as Ruby Baker, who with her little brother Rhett (Trevor Morgan) is orphaned when their parents die in a car crash. The family lawyer (Bruce Dern) explains that the parents had arranged for their close friends Erin and Terry Glass to be their guardians in the case of tragedy, and soon the kids are moving into the Glasses' big glass house (uh-huh), which is luxurious, although Ruby and Rhett are a little too old to be sharing the same bedroom.

It's a detail like that we find annoying. Why would the Glasses, who have acres of living space on their Malibu hilltop, put the kids into one room? Given the Glasses' long-term plans, why not make the kids as happy as possible?

There's a kind of thriller in which the events unfold as they might in real life, and we have to decide which way to take them—and another kind of thriller, this kind, where the events unfold as a series of ominous portents, real and false alarms, and music stingers on the sound track. The first kind of thriller is a film; the second is a technical exercise.

What makes *The Glass House* sad is that resources have been wasted. Diane Lane and Stellan Skarsgard, as the Glasses, are so good in the dialed-down "realistic scenes" that we cringe when they have to go over the top and make everything so very absolutely clear for the slow learners in the audience. Sobieski is fine, too—as good an upscale Los Angeles high school student as Kirsten Dunst in the recent *crazy/beautiful,* but in a genre exercise that strands her instead of going someplace interesting and taking her along.

It was good to see Bruce Dern again. He's one of those actors, like Christopher Walken, who you assume on first glance has a secret evil agenda. Here he's the family lawyer the kids can or can't trust, and is wise enough to play the character absolutely straight, with no tics or twitches, so that he keeps us wondering—or would, if Wesley Strick's screenplay wasn't one of those infuriating constructions where the key outside characters turn up at the wrong times, believe the wrong people, and misinterpret everything.

Speaking of turning up, Sobieski's character turns up at too many right times. How fortunate that she drops in on Mr. Glass's office just at the right moment to eavesdrop, unobserved, on crucial dialogue. And how unfortunate that she seems to be proving the Glasses right and herself wrong when a social worker walks in on a crucial moment and, of course, misinterprets it.

If you want to see a great movie about a couple of kids endangered by a sinister guardian, rent *Night of the Hunter.* Watching *The Glass House* has all the elements for a better film, but doesn't trust the audience to keep up with them. Having criticized the Strick screenplay, I should in fairness observe that the way it usually works is, the writer puts in the smart stuff and then it comes out in the story conferences with executives who figure if they don't understand it, nobody will.

The Gleaners and I ★ ★ ★ ★
NO MPAA RATING, 82 m., 2001

A documentary by Agnes Varda.

In our alley we see men searching through the garbage for treasure. *The Gleaners and I* places them in an ancient tradition. Since 1554, when King Henry IV affirmed the right of gleaning, it has been a practice protected by the French constitution, and today the men and women who sift through the Dumpsters and markets of Paris are the descendants of gleaners who were painted by Millet and van Gogh.

Gleaners traditionally follow the harvest, scavenging what was missed the first time around. In Agnes Varda's meditative new film we see them in potato fields and apple orchards, where the farmers actually welcome them (tons of apples are missed by the first pickers, because the professionals work fast and are not patient in seeking the hidden fruit). Then we meet urban gleaners, including an artist who finds objects he can make into sculpture, and a man who has not paid for his food for more than ten years.

Everybody seems to know this practice is protected by law, but no one seems to know quite what the law says. Varda films jurists standing in the fields with their robes and law books, who say gleaning must take place between sunup and sundown, and she shows oyster-pickers in rubber hip boots, who say they must come no closer than ten, or twenty, or twelve, or fifteen yards of the oyster beds, and cannot take more than eight, or twenty, or ten pounds of oysters—not that anybody is weighing them.

In a provincial city, Varda considers the case of young unemployed people who overturned the Dumpsters of a supermarket after the owner drenched the contents with bleach to discourage them. Perhaps both parties were violating the law; the young people had the right to glean, but not to vandalize. But as she talks to the young layabouts in the town square, we realize they don't have the spirit of the other gleaners, and in their own minds see themselves as getting away with something instead of exercising a right. They have made themselves into criminals, although the French law considers gleaning a useful profession.

The true gleaner, in Varda's eyes, is a little noble, a little idealistic, a little stubborn, and deeply thrifty. We meet a man who gleans for his meals and to find objects he can sell, and follow him back to a suburban homeless shelter where for years he has taught literature classes every night. We look over the shoulders of him and his comrades as they find perfectly fresh tomatoes left after a farmer's market. Varda and her cinematographer find a clock without hands—worthless, until she places it between two stone angels in her house, and it reveals a startling simplicity of form.

Agnes Varda, of course, is a gleaner herself. She is gleaning the gleaners. And in what appears to be a documentary, she conceals a tender meditation about her own life, and life itself. Who is this woman? I have met her, with her bangs cut low over her sparkling eyes in a round and merry face, and once had lunch in the house she shared with her late husband, the director Jacques Demy *(The Umbrellas of Cherbourg)*. The house itself was in the spirit of gleaning: not a luxury flat for two famous filmmakers, but a former garage, with the bays and rooms around a central courtyard parceled out, one as a kitchen, one as Jacques's office, one a room for their son, Mathieu, one Agnes's workroom, etc.

Varda is seventy-two and made her first film when she was twenty-six. She was the only woman director involved in the French New Wave, and has remained truer to its spirit than many of the others. Her features include such masterpieces as *One Sings, the Other Doesn't, Vagabond,* and *Kung Fu Master* (which is not about kung fu but about love). Along the way she has made many documentaries, including *Uncle Yanco* (1968), about her uncle who lived on a houseboat in California and was a gleaner of sorts, and *Daguerreotypes* (1975), about the other people who live on her street. Her *A Hundred and One Nights* (1995) gleaned her favorite moments from a century of cinema.

In *The Gleaners and I,* she has a new tool— a modern digital camera. We sense her delight. She can hold it in her hand and take it anywhere. She is liberated from cumbersome equipment. "To film with one hand my other hand," she says, as she does so with delight. She shows how the new cameras make a personal essay possible for a filmmaker—how she can walk out into the world and, without the risk of a huge budget, simply start picking up images as a gleaner finds apples and potatoes.

"My hair and my hands keep telling me that the end is near," she confides at one point, speaking confidentially to us as the narrator. She told her friend Howie Movshovitz, the critic from Boulder, Colorado, how she had to film and narrate some scenes while she was entirely alone, because they were so personal. In 1993, she directed *Jacquot de Nantes*, the story of her late husband, and now this is her story of herself, a woman whose life has consisted of moving through the world with the tools of her trade, finding what is worth treasuring.

Glitter ★ ★
PG-13, 103 m., 2001

Mariah Carey (Billie Frank), Max Beesley (Julian Dice), Da Brat (Louise), Tia Texada (Roxanne), Valarie Pettiford (Lillian Frank), Isabel Gomes (Young Billie), Padma Lakshmi (Sylk), Terrence Howard (Timothy Walker), Ann Magnuson (P.R. Woman). Directed by Vondie Curtis-Hall, produced by Laurence Mark. Screenplay by Kate Lanier, based on a story by Cheryl L. West.

Glitter is not *The Mariah Carey Story*, but it's tempting to try to read it that way. The movie is based not on Carey's life but on a kind of mirror image, in which she has a black mother and a white father instead of the other way around, and is taken under the wing of a club DJ instead of a record executive. Her character, named Billie Frank (after the two great vocalists?), makes all the usual stops on the rags-to-riches trail, but the movie rushes past them. We're in the strange position of knowing everything that's going to happen and wishing it would take longer.

Young Billie (Isabel Gomes) is first seen in a smoky dive, invited up onstage to join her mother, Lillian (Valarie Pettiford), in a duet. Soon after, Lillian falls asleep while smoking and burns the house down, and we are left to conclude she is a junkie, although the movie is so reticent it only confirms this years later, with a report that Lillian is now clean and sober. Billie is shipped off to an orphanage, where she makes instant friends (a black, a

white, and a Puerto Rican), identifies herself as "mixed" and—well, that's it for the orphanage.

Fast-forward to grown-up Billie, now played by Carey, who is a backup singer behind the untalented protégé of a would-be record producer (Terrence Howard). She ghosts the other singer's voice and is spotted by a DJ named Dice (Max Beesley), who buys her contract from the would-be producer for $100,000, but unwisely neglects to make the payment.

Dice guides her into a record contract, a hit single, and so on, before undergoing a sudden, unexplained personality change; he seems to become Mr. Hyde purely as a plot device. The closing several scenes of the movie are a blinding whirl of developments, jammed so close together that there's barely time for Billie to get tragic news before she rushes onto the stage of Madison Square Garden and then into the arms of her long-lost mother.

You can see, here and there, what the movie was aiming at. It makes some sly digs at self-important music video directors, has an affectionate cameo by Ann Magnuson as a hyper publicist, and does a good job of showing how a young talent attracts friends, enemies, leeches, and hangers-on. Always steadfast are Billie's two backup singers, Louise (Da Brat) and Roxanne (Tia Texada), who seem to spend twenty-four hours a day in their apartment so they are always available to take her calls, see her on TV, listen to her song on the radio, and take her in when she needs a home. Those girls should get out more.

Carey sings a lot, well, in footage that would be at home in a concert video. Her acting ranges from dutiful flirtatiousness to intense sincerity; she never really lets go. The title *Glitter* is perhaps intended to evoke *Sparkle* (1976), which was grittier, livelier, and more convincing. The name "Billie" evokes *Lady Sings the Blues* (1972), which was miles better. And for a biopic of a singer's hard road to the top, the touchstone is *What's Love Got to Do With It* (1993), where Angela Basset took the seemingly impossible assignment of playing Tina Turner and triumphed.

One problem with *Glitter* is that it doesn't step up and offer itself as Mariah Carey's real story, and yet is so afraid of being taken that way that it goes easy on the details anyway. Was being a mixed-race child as much of a nonissue in Carey's childhood as it is in this movie? Billie searches for her birth mother, and yet there's a scene so confusingly handled that we're not sure if she sees her on the street one night or not. We're given a triumphant concert in Madison Square Garden, but it's unlikely she could even sing under the circumstances shown. And the film is lacking above all in joy. It never seems like it's fun to be Billie Frank.

The Golden Bowl ★ ★ ★
R, 130 m., 2001

Nick Nolte (Adam Verver), Kate Beckinsale (Maggie Verver), Uma Thurman (Charlotte Stant), Jeremy Northam (Prince Amerigo), Anjelica Huston (Fanny Assingham), James Fox (Bob Assingham). Directed by James Ivory and produced by Ismail Merchant. Screenplay by Ruth Prawer Jhabvala, based on the novel by Henry James.

There are four good people in *The Golden Bowl* and four bad people, making, in all, four characters. The genius of Henry James's greatest novel is that these four people have placed themselves in a moral situation that alters as you rotate them in your view. If you come to the movie without reading the book, you may find yourself adrift; it's not easy to know who to like when everyone is a sinner, and all have their reasons.

The story involves two marriages, with the same dreadful secret hidden at the heart of both of them. Adam Verver (Nick Nolte), an American billionaire, has been traveling in Europe with his daughter, Maggie (Kate Beckinsale), buying things. Having grown rich on the backs of his workers (he frets about their long hours), he now vows to brighten their lives by filling a museum with his treasures, which they can admire while he no doubt feels virtuous. Having purchased innumerable statues, houses, and paintings, he finds it time to buy Maggie a husband. Prince Amerigo (Jeremy Northam) seems a good investment: He is handsome and refined, and his old Italian family occupies the Pallazzo Ugolini in Florence. The prince needs Verver's money, and will provide a title for his grandson; Maggie is swayed by his charm.

There is a complication, which is revealed in the very first scene of the movie. The prince was long involved in an affair with Charlotte Stant (Uma Thurman), Maggie's best friend. Since the story takes place in 1902, when such affairs could ruin reputations, it has been a secret—even from Maggie. The prince is prepared to marry Maggie for her father's money, and also because she is lithe and fragrant. But where does that leave poor Charlotte?

In her drawing room in London, Fanny Assingham (Anjelica Huston) thinks she knows the answer. She's one of those middle-aged American exiles, much beloved by James, who lurks at the center of a web of social connections, waiting for twitches. She boldly suggests that the widower billionaire Verver is the perfect match for Charlotte. That will mean that the father and daughter will be married to former lovers, a fact known to Mrs. Assingham, who can live with it.

Now, does that make Charlotte and the prince dishonest? Yes, they share a secret. But both the prince and Charlotte must, because they are poor, marry money. They are marrying people who want them. Perhaps they are making a sacrifice—especially if they behave themselves, which they are determined to do. Or are Maggie and her father dishonest, since she is marrying to please her father and he is marrying her best friend to please his daughter? No one at the altar is blameless. But no one is marrying for love, except Maggie, whose definition of love is too specialized to be entirely idealistic.

Soon the two couples settle into a routine that satisfies Maggie and Mr. Verver, who dote on each other and spend all of their time together, to the dissatisfaction of their mates. Charlotte complains that her husband and his daughter are always together. "What becomes of me when they're so happy?" she asks the prince. "And what becomes of you?" Soon enough the two former lovers find themselves at a house party in the country without their spouses, and one thing apparently leads to another (it is difficult to be sure with James, since no novelist ever used the word "intercourse" more frequently without quite making it clear what he meant by it).

It is not sexual infidelity that causes trouble, however, but the slight shade of suspicion—

and then a darker shade, when a golden bowl in an antique shop provides Maggie with absolute proof that the prince and Charlotte knew each other before they had, presumably, met. Now comes the diabolical unfolding of James's plan, since at no time do the four people ever openly discuss what each one of them privately knows. Instead, wheels of unspoken priorities grind mercilessly, and Charlotte, in my opinion, becomes the character we have most reason to pity.

The Golden Bowl would seem to be an ideal project for director James Ivory, producer Ismail Merchant, and screenwriter Ruth Prawer Jhabvala; they specialize in literary adaptations, and previously collaborated on James's *The Europeans* and *The Bostonians*. But here they've taken on the most difficult of James's novels—a story told largely through what remains unsaid. James has not made it easy for the modern moviegoer who expects good and evil to be clearly labeled and lead to a happy ending. His villain is a system based on wealth and class, which forces the poor to deal on the terms of the rich and then sometimes spits them out anyway—or, in Charlotte's case, buries her alive. That James spent his career chronicling people like these characters does not mean he loved them, and in a novel like *The Ambassadors* you can hear him cheering as a female version of Verver is frustrated in her desire to control her son.

I admired this movie. It kept me at arm's length, but that is where I am supposed to be; the characters are, after all, at arm's length from one another, and the tragedy of the story is implied but never spoken aloud. It will help, I think, to be familiar with the novel, or to make a leap of sympathy with the characters; they aren't dancing through a clockwork plot, but living their lives according to rules which, once they accept them, cannot ever be broken.

Gone in 60 Seconds ★ ★
PG-13, 119 m., 2000

Nicolas Cage (Memphis Raines), Delroy Lindo (Detective), Giovanni Ribisi (Kip Raines), Robert Duvall (Otto Halliwell), Angelina Jolie ("Sway" Wayland), Christopher Eccleston (Raymond Calitri), T. J. Cross (Mirror Man), William Lee Scott (Toby), Scott Caan (Tumbler), James Duval (Freb), Will Patton (Atley Jackson). Directed by Dominic Sena and produced by Jerry Bruckheimer and Mike Stenson. Screenplay by Scott Rosenberg.

Gone in 60 Seconds is like a practice game between the varsity and the reserves. Everybody plays pretty well, but they're saving up for Saturday. First team is Nicolas Cage, Delroy Lindo, and Robert Duvall. Second team is Giovanni Ribisi, Will Patton, and Angelina Jolie, who gets second billing but not much playing time. There are lots of subs who come off the bench for a play or two. This is the kind of movie that ends up playing on the TV set over the bar in a better movie.

Nicolas Cage plays Memphis Raines, who used to be the greatest car thief in Los Angeles ("I didn't do it for the money. I did it for the cars"). Now he has retired to the desert to run a gas station and go-cart track. He retired because his mom asked him to. She was afraid his younger brother Kip (Ribisi) would become a thief too. Kip became a thief anyway. Kip steals a car, recklessly leads the cops to a chop shop, and angers a vile crime lord named Raymond (Christopher Eccleston), who, according to a line Robert Duvall successfully says out loud without laughing, is "a jackal tearing at the soft belly of our fair city."

Memphis learns about Kip's screwup from one of his old crew members. He visits Raymond to try to set things right, but Raymond has Kip handcuffed inside a car and threatens to crush him and sell him as scrap metal. Memphis can save him by stealing fifty hard-to-find cars. Memphis recruits an old pal (Duvall); together they assemble a very large team in a very long and boring sequence that produces so many car thieves we can't keep them all straight. It looks like they sent out contracts to a lot of actors and were surprised when they all said yes.

The pros try to steal the fifty cars. Delroy Lindo, as the cop, knows who they are and what they plan to do, but wants to catch them at it. He intuits that the key theft will be of a 1967 Shelby GT 350 Mustang, a car Memphis both loves and fears. "He'll save that for the last," says Lindo, planning to nab him in the act. This decision means that forty-nine cars will *already* have been stolen before Memphis

241

moves on the Mustang. I am reminded of the line from *Fargo* when Marge tells her deputy, "I'm not sure I agree with you a hundred percent on your police work there, Lou."

There isn't much time for character development. Cage walks on-screen with his character already established from *The Rock* and *Con Air*. Duvall is . . . Duvall. Angelina Jolie's rare appearances are reminders she is still in the picture. After the confusions of the recruitment scenes and the puzzlement about who all these guys are, it's a relief when the movie goes on autopilot with a fabulous chase sequence and an obligatory final confrontation inside a flame and steam factory.

We have discussed flame and steam factories before. They are cavernous industrial locations with flame and steam in the background and no people around. The moment I saw the first shower of sparks, I predicted that Memphis and Raymond would eventually be climbing around on high catwalks while shooting at one another, that Memphis would inevitably cling to a catwalk by his fingers, and that Raymond would fall to his death. See how well your own predictions turn out.

The chase sequence is fine. Memphis hurtles the Mustang down city streets and alleys and hits 160 mph in a drainage ditch, outsmarting a police helicopter by taking the tunnel under the airport while the copter is waved away from commercial airspace. There is a stunt jump that would have made Evel Knievel famous, and dead. All of this is done in weirdly underlit, saturated dark colors; the movie desperately yearns to be in sepiatone, and some of its skies are so dark you're looking for the twister.

Movies like this are what they are. *Gone in 60 Seconds* is a prodigious use of money and human effort to make a movie of no significance whatever, in which the talents of the artists are subordinated to the requirements of the craftsmen. Witnessing it, you get some thrills, some chuckles, a few good one-liners, and after 119 minutes are regurgitated by the theater not much the worse for wear.

Good Housekeeping ★ ★ ★
R, 90 m., 2002

Bob Jay Mills (Don), Petra Westen (Donatella),

Tacey Adams (Marion), Al Schuermann (Joe), Zia (Chuck), Andrew Eichner (Don Jr.), Maeve Kerrigan (Tiffany). Directed by Frank Novak and produced by Mark G. Mathis. Screenplay by Novak.

I watch the guests on *Jerry Springer* with the fascination of an ambulance driver at a demo derby. Where do these people come from? Their dialogue may be "suggested," but their lives are all too evidently real, and they have tumbled right through the safety net of taste and self-respect and gone spiraling down, down into the pit of amoral vulgarity. Now comes *Good Housekeeping*, a film about how the people on *Springer* live when they're not on camera.

No, it's not a documentary. It was written and directed by Frank Novak, otherwise a trendy Los Angeles furniture manufacturer, who regards his white trash characters with deadpan neutrality. How is the audience expected to react? Consider this dialogue:

Don: "Maybe if we cut her in half we could get her in there."

Chuck: "We can't cut her in half!"

Don: "So what are you? Mr. Politically Correct?"

Don and Chuck are brothers. Don (Bob Jay Mills) uneasily shares his house with his wife, Donatella (Petra Westen), while Chuck (credited only as Zia) sleeps with his girlfriend Tiffany (Maeve Kerrigan) in Don's car. Things are not good between Don and Donatella, and he uses two-by-fours and plasterboard to build a wall that cuts the house in two ("She got way more square feet than I got," he tells the cops during one of their frequent visits). Realizing he has forgotten something, Don cuts a crawl hole in the wall so that Don Jr. (Andrew Eichner) can commute between parents. Soon Donatella's new lesbian lover Marion (Tacey Adams) is poking her head through the hole to discuss the "parameters" Don is setting for his son.

Donatella is a forklift operator. Don is self-employed as a trader of action figures, with a specialty in Pinhead and other Hellraiser characters. When Chuck tries to sell him a Sad-Eye Doll, he responds like a pro: "Couldn't you Swap-Meet it? I'm not gonna put that on my table and drag down my other merch." Don Jr.

has less respect for action figures, and occasionally saws off their heads.

Terrible things happen to the many cars in this extended family, both by accident and on purpose. One of the funniest sequences shows a big blond family friend, desperately hungover, methodically crunching into every other car in the driveway before she runs over the mailbox. Don lives in fear of Donatella running him down, and at one point discusses his defense with a gun-show trader (Al Schuermann) who scoffs, "You would use a .38 to defend yourself?" He comes back with real protection against vehicular manslaughter: a shoulder-mounted rocket launcher.

Marion, the well-mannered lesbian lover, is the source of many of the film's biggest laughs because of the incongruity of her crush on Donatella. She watches Donatella smoke, eat, talk, and blow her nose all at the same time, and her only reaction is to eat all the more politely, in the hope of setting an example. Marion is an accountant at the factory where Donatella works; she dresses in chic business suits, has smart horn-rimmed glasses and a stylish haircut, and plunges into Springerland with an arsenal of liberal clichés. At one point, after a nasty domestic disturbance, she tries to make peace by inviting Don out to brunch. "There's no way the cops can make you go to brunch," Don's beer-bellied buddies reassure him.

It is perhaps a warning signal of incipient alcoholism when the family car has a Breathalyzer permanently attached to the dashboard. Yet Don is not without standards, and warns his brother against making love in the car because "I drive Mom to church in it." Family life follows a familiar pattern. Most evenings end with a fight in the yard, and Novak and his cinematographer, Alex Vandler, are skilled at getting convincing, spontaneous performances out of their unknown actors; many scenes, including the free-for-alls, play with the authenticity of a documentary.

Just as mainstream filmmakers are fascinated by the rich and famous, so independent filmmakers are drawn to society's hairy underbelly. *Good Housekeeping* plunges far beneath Todd Solondz's territory and enters the suburbs of John Waters's universe in its fascination for people who live without benefit of education, taste, standards, hygiene, and shame. Indeed, all they have enough of are cigarettes, used cars, controlled substances, and four-letter words. The movie is, however, very funny, as you peek at it through the fingers in front of your eyes.

Note: Good Housekeeping *has had its ups and downs. It won the grand jury prize at Slamdance 2000, was the only U.S. film chosen for Critic's Week at Cannes that year, and was picked up for distribution by the Shooting Gallery—which alas went out of business, leaving the film orphaned.*

Gosford Park ★ ★ ★ ★
R, 137 m., 2002

Eileen Atkins (Mrs. Croft), Bob Balaban (Morris Weissman), Alan Bates (Jennings), Charles Dance (Lord Stockbridge), Stephen Fry (Inspector Thompson), Michael Gambon (Sir William McCordle), Richard E. Grant (George), Derek Jacobi (Probert), Kelly Macdonald (Mary Maceachran), Helen Mirren (Mrs. Wilson), Jeremy Northam (Ivor Novello), Clive Owen (Robert Parks), Ryan Phillippe (Henry Denton), Maggie Smith (Constance, Countess of Trentham), Kristin Scott Thomas (Lady Sylvia McCordle), Emily Watson (Elsie). Directed by Robert Altman and produced by Altman, Bob Balaban, and David Levy. Screenplay by Julian Fellowes, based on an idea by Altman and Balaban.

Robert Altman's *Gosford Park* is above all a celebration of styles—the distinct behavior produced by the British class system, the personal styles of a rich gallery of actors, and his own style of introducing a lot of characters and letting them weave their way through a labyrinthine plot. At a time when too many movies focus every scene on a $20 million star, an Altman film is like a party with no boring guests. *Gosford Park* is such a joyous and audacious achievement it deserves comparison with his very best movies, such as *M*A*S*H, McCabe and Mrs. Miller, Nashville, The Player, Short Cuts,* and *Cookie's Fortune.*

It employs the genre of the classic British murder mystery, as defined by Agatha Christie: Guests and servants crowd a great country house, and one of them is murdered. But *Gosford Park* is a Dame Agatha story in the same sense that *M*A*S*H* is a war movie, *McCabe* is a Western, and *Nashville* is a musical: Altman uses the setting, but surpasses the limitations and redefines the goal. This is no less than a comedy about selfishness, greed, snobbery, eccentricity, and class exploitation, and Altman is right when he hopes people will see it more than once; after you know the destination, the journey is transformed.

The time is November 1932. Sir William McCordle (Michael Gambon) and Lady Sylvia McCordle (Kristin Scott Thomas) have invited a houseful of guests for a shooting party. They include Sir William's sister Constance, the Countess of Trentham (Maggie Smith), who depends on an allowance he is constantly threatening to withdraw. And Lady Sylvia's sister Louisa (Geraldine Somerville), who like Sylvia had to marry for money (they cut cards to decide who would bag Sir William). And Louisa's husband, Commander Anthony Meredith (Tom Hollander). And their sister Lavinia (Natasha Wightman), married to Raymond, Lord Stockbridge (Charles Dance). And the Hollywood star Ivor Novello (Jeremy Northam). And Morris Weissman (Bob Balaban), a gay Hollywood producer who has brought along his "valet," Henry Denton (Ryan Phillippe).

Below stairs we meet the butler Jennings (Alan Bates), the housekeeper Mrs. Wilson (Helen Mirren), the cook Mrs. Croft (Eileen Atkins), the footman George (Richard E. Grant), and assorted other valets, maids, grooms, and servers. When the American Henry comes to take his place at the servants' table and says his name is Denton, Jennings sternly informs him that servants are addressed below stairs by the names of their masters, and he will be "Mr. Weissman" at their table—where, by the way, servants are seated according to the ranks of their employers.

It has been said that the most enjoyable lifestyle in history was British country house life in the years between the wars. That is true for some of the people upstairs in this movie, less true of most of those downstairs. Altman observes exceptions: Some of the aristocrats, like Lady Constance, are threatened with financial ruin, and others, like Novello, have to sing for their supper; while below stairs, a man like Jennings is obviously supremely happy to head the staff of a great house.

The classic country house murder story begins with perfect order, in which everyone up and down the class ladder fits securely into his or her place—until murder disrupts that order and discloses unexpected connections between the classes. That's what happens here, when one of the characters is poisoned and then stabbed, suggesting there are two murderers to be apprehended by Inspector Thompson (Stephen Fry).

Half of those in the house have a motive for the murder, but the investigation isn't the point, and Altman has fun by letting Thompson and his assistant Constable Dexter (Ron Webster) mirror the relative competence of the upper and lower classes in the house. Thompson, like the aristocrats, sets great store by his title and dress (he puffs a pipe that will be recognized by anyone who knows the name Monsieur Hulot). Dexter, like the servants, just gets on with it, doggedly pointing out clues (footprints, fingerprints on a tea cup, a secret door) that Thompson ignores.

The cast of *Gosford Park* is like a reunion of fine and familiar actors (I have not yet even mentioned Derek Jacobi, Kelly Macdonald, Clive Owen, Emily Watson, and James Wilby). This is like an invitation for scene-stealing, and Maggie Smith effortlessly places first, with brittle comments that cut straight to the quick. When Novello entertains after dinner with one song, and then another, and then another, and shows no sign of stopping, Smith crisply asks, "Do you think he'll be as long as he usually is?" and then stage-whispers, "Don't encourage him."

Altman has a keen eye and ear for snobbery. Note the way that when Mr. Weissman introduces himself, Lady Sylvia asks him to repeat his name, and then she repeats it herself. Just that, but she is subtly underlining his ethnicity. And the way Constance puts Novello in his place by mentioning his most recent film and observing, ostensibly with sympathy, "It must be rather disappointing when something flops like that."

The screenplay by Julian Fellowes, based on an idea by Altman and Balaban, is masterful in introducing all of the characters and gradually making it clear who they are, what they've done, and what it means. Like guests at a big party, we are confused when we first arrive:

Who are all these people? By the end, we know. No director has ever been better than Altman at providing the audience with bearings to find its way through a large cast. The sense of place is also palpable in this film; the downstairs and attics were entirely constructed on sound stages by production designer Steven Altman, Altman's son, who also supervised the real country house used for the main floors. Andrew Dunn's photography is sumptuous upstairs, while making the downstairs look creamy and institutional. The editor, Tim Squyres, must have been crucial in keeping the characters in play.

Gosford Park is the kind of generous, sardonic, deeply layered movie that Altman has made his own. As a director he has never been willing to settle for plot; he is much more interested in character and situation, and likes to assemble unusual people in peculiar situations and stir the pot. Here he is, like Prospero, serenely the master of his art.　　☞

Gossip ★ ★
R, 90 m., 2000

James Marsden (Derrick), Lena Headey (Jones), Norman Reedus (Travis), Kate Hudson (Naomi Preston), Joshua Jackson (Beau Edson), Marisa Coughlan (Sheila), Edward James Olmos (Detective Curtis), Sharon Lawrence (Detective Kelly), Eric Bogosian (Professor Goodwin). Directed by Davis Guggenheim and produced by Jeffrey Silver and Bobby Newmyer. Screenplay by Gregory Poirier and Theresa Rebeck.

Gossip stays in the game until the bottom of the ninth, and then blows it. The trick ending is a kick in the teeth. The movie tells a story worth telling, and then cops out with an ironic gimmick that's like a sneer at the craft of storytelling. *Usual Suspects* had the grace to earn its surprise ending, but *Gossip* pulls a 180 just for the hell of it. Chop off the last two or three minutes, fade to black, and you have a decent film.

The premise is promising. We meet three college roommates who decide to start a rumor just to see how far it will go. They spread the news that a couple had sex in an upstairs bedroom at an off-campus party. Problem is, the

rich girl in the bedroom was drunk and passed out. She hears the gossip, assumes it's true, and brings rape charges against her date. And then it gets a lot more complicated than that, until simply telling the truth won't mend things anymore.

The story takes place on the kind of campus that would be designed by the ad agency for Bennetton. The roommates are Jones (Lena Headey), independent and smart, who seems to cast herself in a real-time version of *Murder, She Wrote*, Derrick (James Marsden), a ladies' man with easy charm and something wrong inside, and Travis (Norman Reedus), who creates strange art out of graphics and photographs, and has trouble expressing himself. The roomies share a luxurious loft, where they spend more time drinking than Nick and Nora Charles in the *Thin Man* movies. My guess is that less booze and at least some drugs would be involved with characters like these, but it's glug, glug, glug, scene after scene.

The film is heavy on style, and knows what it's doing. Cinematographer Andrzej Bartkowiak *(Speed, Species)* deepens the colors and photographs the actors like models, which works because great though he makes them look, they can still act. Jones is the catalyst. She agrees to spread the rumor, and then develops a conscience when the gossip goes wrong. She also gets to perform the obligatory high school yearbook scene, in which secrets from the past are obligingly revealed.

As the seriousness of the situation escalates, the student charged with rape (Joshua Jackson) is led away in handcuffs, and his date (Kate Hudson) hits the bottle as if she were Dorothy Malone in a 1950s weeper. Edward James Olmos knocks on the door and introduces himself as the detective on the case, and he's good at his role, brushing aside Derrick's alibis and self-assurance as if shooing a fly. Eric Bogosian has a juicy role as one of those showboat professors who conducts lectures like a talk show and is filled with a deep appreciation of himself.

And then the movie self-destructs. The material was here, in Gregory Poirier and Theresa Rebeck's screenplay, for a movie that had something interesting to say about date rape and gossip. But it all derails in a self-indulgent exercise, as director Davis Guggenheim ducks responsibility to the story and gives us a cop-out instead. I really got into this film. If I hadn't, maybe the ending wouldn't have annoyed me so much.

Go Tigers! ★ ★ ★
R, 103 m., 2001

Featuring Dave Irwin, Danny Studer, Ellery Moore, and the rest of the team. A documentary directed by Ken Carlson and produced by Sidney Sherman and Carlson. Screenplay by Carlson.

I don't know if Massillon, Ohio, has the best high school football team in the country, but since the annual Massillon-McKinley rivalry is the only prep game that carries Vegas odds, doesn't that tell you something? *Go Tigers!* is a documentary about a town of 33,000 so consumed by football it makes South Bend and Green Bay look distracted.

The film was directed by Ken Carlson, a Massillon native and, it must be said, a Tiger booster. He raises an eyebrow at the widespread local practice of holding boys back to repeat the eighth grade, whether they need to or not, because they'll be older and bigger as high school seniors. He listens to a couple of kids observe that if you aren't into football you're an automatic outsider ("I can't wait to get out of this dump"). But the movie argues that Massillon lives for football, that it creates identity and pride, and on the evidence I would have to agree.

Consider a town where a live tiger cub is the team mascot (and cringe as it plants a friendly paw on a small child). Where the "Tiger Lady" fills her house so full of tiger paraphernalia that there is scant room for her husband, jammed into his chair in a corner. Where the high school band has mayoral permission to march and play anywhere within the city limits on the day of the McKinley game (it marches through department stores, cafeterias, and the library). Where more fans attend the games than at many (maybe most) colleges. Where there are so many assistant coaches one specializes in strength and fitness.

Massillon is a steel town, working class and moderately prosperous, and one of the things we notice (the movie doesn't make a point of it) is that there seems to be racial harmony.

Possibly the team is such a strong binding and unifying force that it rolls over the divisive feelings that might exist in another town. The Tigers are a secular religion. And mainstream religion gets in the act, too, with a Jewish speaker at the breakfast on the day of the big game, followed by a Catholic mass, the Lord's Prayer in the locker room, and other evocations to the Almighty (Massillon has lost to McKinley the last four years, inspiring a certain urgency).

We meet two of the team's cocaptains, Dave Irwin and Ellery Moore. Like other Massillon players going back four generations, they see football as their ticket to college scholarships. Irwin, the quarterback, is a gifted passer, and during the 1999 season (shown in the film) throws seventeen touchdown passes in nine games before the McKinley game, whose outcome I will leave for you to discover. He works part-time as a drill press operator, and shortly before the big game injures the index finger of his passing hand. So much is at stake: If he loses that finger, he can look forward to the drill press instead of college.

It looks like Massillon would be fun to live in if you're a football fan (one good player from nearby Petty transfers just to get in on the action). To *not* be a football fan in Massillon would be a lonely and unrewarding enterprise. Underlying tension is created because the local schools face severe budget cuts unless a tax levy passes. Opponents argue that the football program is so expensive it drives up the budget—but it seems more likely that the better the team does, the more likely the voters are to approve the levy. "I've seen more good come from that pigskin than from a lot of schoolbooks," observes one local sage. If it gets the kids into college, he may have a point.

Note: The movie has an R rating because its high school kids talk and drink beer exactly like high school kids.

Goya in Bordeaux ★ ★
R, 98 m., 2000

Francisco Rabal (Goya), Jose Coronado (Goya as a Young Man), Dafne Fernandez (Rosario), Maribel Verdu (Duchess of Alba), Eulalia Ramon (Leocadia), Joaquin Climent (Moratin), Cristina Espinosa (Pepita Tudo), Jose Maria Pou (Godoy). Directed by Carlos Saura and

produced by Andres Vincent Gomez.
Screenplay by Saura.

Lushly photographed and grandly conceived, Carlos Saura's *Goya in Bordeaux* never comes alive. It is an homage to the great Spanish painter, but we must come to the film already fascinated by Francisco Goya; if we do not, the film will not convince us. It is too much a study and an exercise, not enough a living thing.

The film opens with an extraordinary image: a cow's carcass, dragging itself to a scaffold and then hoisted up so that we can regard animal flesh and meditate that thus are we all. Then the details of muscle and fat begin to run like paint, until they reveal the ruined face of an old man. This is Goya on his deathbed.

The old man rises up, confused. Where is he? Who brought him here? He wanders from his bed, and a shift in the lighting reveals the walls of his room as a scrim. We can see him through the walls, and then find him wandering bewildered in the street, until he is found and taken home by his daughter, Rosario. For the rest of the film he will relate his memories to Rosario, and we will see many of them in flashback, as well as his nightmares and fantasies.

The cinematographer is Vittorio Storaro, who has worked with Saura frequently. *Tango* (1999) is a recent collaboration, the story of a man trying to make a film in Argentina, caught in a labyrinth of love, politics, and music. *Goya in Bordeaux* is as good-looking but not as fruitful.

Goya has fled to France, we gather, because of troubles at home, linked to the fate of the woman of his dreams, Cayetano, Duchess of Alba (Maribel Verdu). She unwisely opposed Queen Maria Luisa and paid with her life; now Goya, in exile, likes the scenery and the wine but misses his villa in Madrid.

As Rosario sits by his side, her attention sometimes drifting (as ours does), Goya recalls his earlier years, his experiments with paint and lighting, the illness that made him deaf. Played as an old man by Francisco Rabal and in middle age by Jose Coronado, he finds it difficult to draw a line between his work and his life. Cayetano emerges from a painting to cast a shadow over him, one that eventually will mark his life's end. Other death's-head specters also emerge from his canvases, or his memories of them, to haunt his dreams.

There are better films about how a painter works (Rivette's *La Belle Noiseuse* from 1991 is incomparable), and better films about old men remembering their lives. Goya, younger and older, shuffles through morose regrets and rueful memories. He does not seem to have created his paintings so much as become their innocent victim. This is not a stand-alone film so much as a visual aid to the study of Goya; I could imagine an old 16mm projector clacking away in the back of art appreciation class.

Grass ★ ★
R, 80 m., 2000

A documentary directed and produced by Ron Mann. Narrated by Woody Harrelson. Screenplay by Solomon Vesta.

It is agreed by reasonable people that one of the results of antidrug laws is to support the price of drugs and make their sale lucrative. If drugs were legalized, the price would fall, and the motive to promote them would fade away. Since anyone who wants drugs can already get them, usage would be unlikely to increase. Crime would go down when addicts didn't have to steal to support their habits, and law enforcement would benefit from the disappearance of drug-financed bribery, payoffs, and corruption.

All of this is so obvious that the opposition to the legalization of drugs seems inexplicable— unless you ask who would be hurt the most by the repeal of drug laws. The international drug cartels would be put out of business. Drug enforcement agencies would be unnecessary. Drug wholesalers and retailers would have to seek other employment. If it is true (as often charged) that the CIA has raised money by dealing in drugs, it would lose this source of funds free from congressional accounting. Who would *benefit* if drugs were legalized? The public—because both drug usage and its associated crimes would diminish.

Despite the logic of this argument, few political candidates have had the nerve to question the way that our drug laws act as a price support system, and encourage drug usage. *Grass*, a new documentary by Ron Mann, traces the history of the laws against one drug—marijuana—back to their origins in anti-Mexican prejudice at the turn of the century, and forward through periods when marijuana was seen as part of the Red conspiracy. When New York Mayor Fiorello LaGuardia commissioned a study of the weed, his commission found the "sociological, psychological, and medical" threat of the substance was "exaggerated." He called for its decriminalization. So, many years later, did President Jimmy Carter—until he had to lay low after an aide was nabbed on cocaine charges.

Other presidents, of course, have enthusiastically supported antidrug laws (Nixon going so far as to swear in Elvis Presley in the war against narcotics). *Grass* traces much of our national drug policy to one man, Harry J. Anslinger, the first drug czar, who like J. Edgar Hoover, created a fiefdom that was immune to congressional criticism.

Grass is not much as a documentary. It's a cut-and-paste job, assembling clips from old and new antidrug films, and alternating them with prodrug footage from the Beats, the flower power era, and so on. The narration by prohemp campaigner Woody Harrelson is underlined by the kind of lurid graphics usually seen on 1940s coming attractions trailers.

The film is unlikely to tell many of its viewers anything they don't already know, and unlikely to change our national drug policy. The situation will continue indefinitely, corrupting politicians and whole nations with billions of dollars of illegal profits. Those who use drugs will continue to do so. Others will abstain, die, or find a way to stop, just as they do now. Prohibition proved that when the government tries to come between the people and what the people want to do, laws are not effective; statistically, Prohibition coincided with a considerable increase in drinking.

Am I in favor of drugs? Not at all. Drug abuse has led to an epidemic of human suffering. Grass seems relatively harmless, but I have not known anyone who used hard drugs and emerged undamaged. Still, in most societies throughout human history, drug use has been treated realistically—as a health problem, not a moral problem. Have our drug laws prevented anyone from using drugs? Apparently not. Have they given us the world's largest

prison population, cost us billions of dollars, and helped create the most violent society in the First World? Yes. From an objective point of view—what's the point?

Greenfingers ★ ★
R, 90 m., 2001

Clive Owen (Colin Briggs), Helen Mirren (Georgina Woodhouse), David Kelly (Fergus Wilks), Warren Clarke (Governor Hodge), Danny Dyer (Tony), Adam Fogerty (Raw), Paterson Joseph (Jimmy), Natasha Little (Primrose Woodhouse). Directed by Joel Hershman and produced by Travis Swords, Daniel J. Victor, and Trudie Styler. Screenplay by Hershman.

Greenfingers is a twee little British comedy in which hardened prisoners became gifted gardeners and are allowed to enter their prize flowers in the Hampton Court Garden Show. Their entry, a garden that seems to bloom in a junkyard, is no more bizarre than entries I've seen in the Chelsea Flower Show.

The movie populates this story with standard types: the salvageable murderer, the elderly lifer with a secret, the ferocious bouncer, the punk kid, the Caribbean guy. There is a warden who glows and beams and nods as approvingly as a Wodehousian vicar, and a formidable gardening expert (Helen Mirren). Would it amaze you to learn that the expert comes supplied with a comely daughter who catches the eye of the salvageable murderer?

If you follow little British TV comedies on PBS, many of the cast members will be familiar to you—especially the priceless David Kelly, who took the immortal nude motorcycle ride in *Waking Ned Devine*. The lead is Clive Owen, who made an impression in the breakthrough thriller *Croupier*. Mirren's Georgina Woodhouse, the garden lady, wears big hats and is a TV star and is based, we assume, on British media types not familiar over here; she has some fun with the distance between vast wealth and celebrity on the one hand and domestic and gardening skills on the other, and we wonder if the name Martha Stewart might not sometimes pass through her mind.

The film is set in an "open prison" in the Cotswolds, where long-term convicts with good behavior records are trusted to work on a farm or in craft shops. When the Owen character accidentally raises a patch of double violets, the warden decides he has a green thumb—or fingers, in this case—and assigns him to cultivate a garden, with the mixed lot of other prisoners as his assistants. Soon they're studying horticulture books and creating a prize garden that inspires Miss Woodhouse to suggest an entry in the big garden show.

It's not that I disliked the movie. It has nothing in it to dislike—or to like very much. It's relentlessly pleasant and good-tempered, positive and eager to amuse, as it goes through the various obligatory stages of such stories. We know, for example, that the prisoners will succeed at gardening, but that there'll be some kind of setback to their hopes. That the officials at the Hampton Court show will include snobs who do not want to admit prisoners. That a young man and a young woman are written into movies like this for the express purpose of falling in love. And that the story will not end on the gallows.

It's as if this current round of small British (and Irish and Welsh and Scots) comedies started strong, with titles like *The Full Monty, The Commitments, The Snapper,* and *Ned Devine* and then started to lose energy about the time of *Saving Grace* (2000) and is now, for the time being, out of gas. The wellsprings of the genre are the Ealing comedies of the 1950s, with Peter Sellers, Terry Thomas, and others as dotty eccentrics; *Local Hero, Gregory's Girl,* and *Comfort and Joy* are interim high points. *Greenfingers* is amusing enough to watch and passes the time, but it's the kind of movie you're content to wait for on your friendly indie cable channel.

Groove ★ ★

R, 86 m., 2000

Lola Glaudini (Leyla), Hamish Linklater (David), Denny Kirkwood (Colin), MacKenzie Firgens (Harmony), Vince Riverside (Anthony), Rachel True (Beth), Steve Van Wormer (Ernie), Nick Offerman (Sergeant), Ari Gold (Cliff). Directed by Greg Harrison and produced by Danielle Renfrew. Screenplay by Harrison.

Groove provides a cleaned-up, innocuous version of the rave scene, showing it as a life-affirming voyage of discovery instead of what it often is, a stop-and-shop ticket to troubles with Ecstasy. Like drug movies from the 1960s, it's naive, believing that the problems of the straight life can be solved by dropping out and tuning in. It somehow manages not to have any of its characters actually say, "After that night, nothing was ever the same again," but I have a feeling they're thinking it.

The movie opens with a raid on an abandoned warehouse by the rave-master Ernie (Steve Van Wormer), who is seeking a venue for his next rave. Ernie sees himself as a sort of public servant; he charges only $2 a head because he *believes* in raves. When he is asked, toward dawn, why he risks arrest on all sorts of charges, he explains he does it for "the nod." The nod? Yes, the nod he gets at least once every party from someone who tells him, "Thanks, man. I feel like I really needed this."

If that's a tad simpleminded as a rationale for the zealous promotion of a drug-soaked venue, consider one of the film's self-proclaimed amateur narcotics experts, who offers advice like, "Never take drugs on an empty stomach." These characters are living in a neverland of idealism and bliss, and I look forward to other rave movies to document what must be the underside of their dream.

The movie's characters are barely sketched. We meet an experienced raver named Colin (Denny Kirkwood), who convinces his straight-arrow brother David (Hamish Linklater) to attend a rave against his own better judgment. David meets a woman named Leyla (Lola Glaudini) at the party and gets past her somewhat forbidding exterior to discover he likes her. She gives him Ecstasy and advises him to "drink a lot of water," although I am not sure if the water intake is associated with the drug use, or is simply her ingrained mantra (she seems like one of those women who never goes anywhere without two liters of Evian, and lectures you on the ominous threat of dehydration). By dawn David and Leyla have arrived at an understanding that, I hope for their sake, will allow them to move in together and quit the rave singles scene.

What is a rave, anyway, but an all-night party where you get high and dance? And what is very new about that? What sets raves apart from disco parties, be-ins, beer blasts, and all the earlier manifestations of the same thing is that they've become professionalized; word is spread on the Internet, and with his $2 admissions Ernie has somehow been able to afford a series of famous DJs, who trundle their turntables and vinyl on and off the scene without ever inspiring the curiosity of the filmmaker, Greg Harrison. We see a lot of them, but learn little about them—but then the film itself is very thin, with dance and music sequences stretched out to cover the lack of dramatic substance.

I liked the music. I would rather have the movie's sound track than see it again—or at all. I know that every generation goes through its rites of passage, and having partied until the dawn more than a time or two myself, I am in sympathy. But the filmmaker has a different responsibility than his subjects. While their job is to be young, get high, meet a sexual partner, and possibly find someone they can stand to live with, the job of the director is to see beyond these immediate goals. I don't ask that he take a long-term view. Even a taste of the middle distance would do.

H

Hamlet ★ ★ ★
R, 111 m., 2000

Ethan Hawke (Hamlet), Kyle McLachlan (Claudius), Diane Venora (Gertrude), Sam Shepard (Ghost), Bill Murray (Polonius), Liev Schreiber (Laertes), Julia Stiles (Ophelia), Karl Geary (Horatio), Steve Zahn (Rosencrantz), Dechen Thurman (Guildenstern). Directed by Michael Almereyda and produced by Andrew Fierberg and Amy Hobby. Screenplay by Almereyda, based on the play by William Shakespeare.

I've seen Hamlet as an intellectual,
And I've seen Hamlet as an ineffectual,
And I've seen Hamlet as a homosexual,
And I've seen Hamlet ev'ry way but textual....
—"I've Seen Shakespeare," by Weeden, Finkle, and Fay

And now the melancholy Dane is a Manhattan techno-nerd, closeted with his computers, his video-editing gear, and his bitter thoughts. His father's company, the Denmark Corp., has made the front page of *USA Today* after a boardroom takeover by the scheming Claudius. Hamlet's mother has married the usurper. And the ghost of Hamlet's father appears on security cameras and materializes in a form transparent enough for Hamlet to see the Pepsi machine behind him.

Michael Almereyda's *Hamlet*, with Ethan Hawke as the prince and Bill Murray as Polonius, is both a distraction and a revelation. Sometimes the modern setting works against the material, sometimes it underlines it, and at all times it proves that *Hamlet* no more belongs in medieval Denmark than anywhere else. However it is staged, wherever it is set, it takes place within Hamlet's mind.

There are few thoughts worth having about life, death, and existence that *Hamlet* does not express in the fewest and most memorable words. "To be, or not to be" is the central question of human life, and Shakespeare asked it 400 years before the existentialists, and better than the Greeks. If man is the only animal that knows he must die, *Hamlet* is the distillation of that knowledge. This twenty-first-century

Hamlet, with its concealed microphones, answering machines, videotapes, and laptops, is as much Shakespeare's as Olivier's in medieval dress was, or Burton's in business suits, or Branagh's in nineteenth-century Blenheim Castle, or Mel Gibson's in a Scottish castle. It is Shakespeare because it respects his language, just as Baz Luhrmann's *Romeo + Juliet* (1996) was not because it did not.

Ethan Hawke plays Hamlet as a restless, bitter neurotic, replaying his memories on video machines and doing dry runs of his big speeches on a PixelVision camera he aims at himself. "To be, or not to be" is sketchily seen on Hamlet's own video, and finally reaches its full ironic flower in the "Action" corridor of a Blockbuster store. When Polonius (Murray) asks his daughter Ophelia (Julia Stiles) to sound out Hamlet, he supplies her with a concealed tape recorder—and Hamlet discovers the bug. When Hamlet denounces Ophelia, there is a reprise on her answering machine. The play within a play is Hamlet's own video production, presented in a screening room.

Kyle McLachlan and Diane Venora play Claudius and Gertrude, as reasonable as any modern materialist parents or stepparents (indeed, Gertrude is so modern she might be literature's first corporate wife). They are a couple comfortable in their affluence, content in their compromises, annoyed as much as disturbed by Hamlet's whingeing. He has had every opportunity, and now look at him, holed up with his resentments and driving his girlfriend crazy. Even Hawke's wardrobe strikes the right note: He wears an ugly knit ski hat that looks a little like a Norse helmet and a lot like the deliberately gauche clothes that teenagers choose to show they reject such middle-class affectations as taste.

Bill Murray is a good choice as Polonius, although Almereyda should have simply let him deliver his great speech to Laertes ("Neither a borrower nor a lender be . . .") without so much unnecessary business on the sound track. Liev Schreiber, as Laertes, is the well-meaning brother of Ophelia, helpless to intervene because his common sense provides no strategy for dealing with madness. Steve Zahn and Dechen Thurman, as Rosencrantz and

Guildenstern, are the neighborhood layabouts, and it is a nice touch when Hamlet hacks into their laptop, changing their instructions so they, not he, will be murdered.

I like the way the material has truly been "adapted" to its modern setting without the language being adulterated. Yes, the play has been shortened (Branagh's *Hamlet* is one of the rare uncut versions, and runs 238 minutes). But it demonstrates how Shakespeare, who in a way invented modern English, has so dominated it ever since that his meanings are always broadly clear to us, even despite unfamiliar usages.

The purpose of this staging of the play is not simply to tart up *Hamlet* in modern dress, but to see him as the young man he was (younger than almost all of the great actors who have played him)—a seething bed of insecurities, guilt, unformed resolution, lust, introspection, and self-loathing. It was his misfortune that he was able to express his feelings so clearly that, once stated, they could not be evaded.

He marches here as he marched in Shakespeare's mind, toward an ending to life that settles nothing, that answers no questions, that contains victory for no one and confusion for all. The ultimate irony of Shakespeare's final scene, in which the dead king's successor steps over the bloody corpses and prepares for business as usual, is richly ironic in this modern corporate setting. Executives are eviscerated, their wives go down with them, their children die in grand, senseless gestures, new management comes in, and the stock price goes up. It happens every day.

Hanging Up ★ ★
PG-13, 99 m., 2000

Meg Ryan (Eve), Diane Keaton (Georgia), Lisa Kudrow (Maddy), Walter Matthau (Lou), Adam Arkin (Joe), Cloris Leachman (Pat). Directed by Diane Keaton and produced by Laurence Mark and Nora Ephron. Screenplay by Delia and Nora Ephron, based on the book by Delia Ephron.

"I live half my life in the real world and half on the telephone," Delia Ephron's father once told her. He was Henry Ephron (1911–1992), the successful writer of such comedies as *Desk Set* and *Daddy Longlegs*. He was always on the phone with his daughters, and they were al-

ways on the phone with one another, and now we have *Hanging Up*, a movie inspired by his last days, in which Walter Matthau plays the father as a man who probably should have lived more of his life in the real world.

The movie is based on Delia's 1995 novel, has been adapted by Delia and her sister Nora, and directed by Diane Keaton, who stars with Meg Ryan and Lisa Kudrow. It is so blonde and brittle, so pumped up with cheerful chatter and quality time, so relentless in the way it wants to be bright about sisterhood and death, that you want to stick a star on its forehead and send it home with a fever.

Lou, the Matthau character, is in the hospital dying of one of those diseases that only leaves you with enough strength for one-liners. He's been in show business for centuries. He wants constant reassurance from his daughters, who are racing in three different directions and keep in touch through an amazing number of telephones. The oldest, Georgia (Diane Keaton), runs her own magazine, which is named *Georgia* and is apparently a cross between *George* and *Lear*. The middle daughter, Eve (Meg Ryan), is a party planner and mother. The youngest, Maddy (Lisa Kudrow), is an actress on a soap opera that she takes at least as seriously as any of its fans. They love telephone round-robins, where one will tell something to the second, who immediately has to tell the third.

The film is really more about the lifestyles of the women than about their parting from their father, and he sort of understands this; this family has been raised as if it's on a stage, putting on a performance for the world, and the show must go on. There is a moment when Eve recruits Georgia to speak at an event she is coordinating, and Georgia starts talking about her sick father, and does something that can only be described as faking real tears. Yes, she is snuffling on demand, for dramatic purpose, at a key moment in her remarks—but just because you can turn an emotion on and off at will doesn't mean it isn't real. Of course, the attitudes she is expressing are really Eve's ("You take my life and you use it"), but borrowed real emotion is still real, right?

Delia Ephron and her sister Nora have lived in worlds not unlike this film, and so, of course, have Keaton, Ryan, and Kudrow. There are moments of sharp observation, as when we sense that these pretty, chic women dress for their meetings with one another at least as carefully as a boxer tapes his wrists. The best scenes are the ones in which the daughters are performing as themselves—projecting the images they use in order to carve out psychic space within the family. Georgia must be dominant because oldest. Eve must be accommodating and commonsensical because middle. Maddy must be dotty because youngest. If the movie hadn't been based on *Hanging Up,* it could have been based on Gail Sheehy's *Passages.*

The peculiar thing about the Matthau character is that he doesn't seem to be sick so much as waiting in a hospital bed for his dialogue to arrive. This is not a movie about true dying heartbreak (for that, see *Unstrung Heroes,* Keaton's wonderful 1995 film, much wiser about death and about the children it leaves behind). *Hanging Up* is more about continuing the legend of the irascible but lovable old man into the grave, if necessary.

Matthau is of course an invaluable actor, lined and weathered, a perfect fit, a catcher's mitt that has seen us through many a good season. Matthau has himself been very ill, and could no doubt have drawn on that experience for enough cries and whispers to furnish a Bergman movie. But he's read the script and understands it, and doesn't embarrass himself by providing more authenticity than the material can carry.

And the movie doesn't really want to be all that heartbreakingly true. It's a facile comedy of manners, a story in which the three daughters have somehow been taught by their upbringing to put a consistent face on everything. Their incessant telephoning is like a way of staying in tune. There are a couple of other characters in the film, an Iranian doctor and his salt-of-the-earth mother, who at first seem inexplicable, until you realize they function as a reality check. They're phoning in from the real world.

Hannibal ★ ★ ½
R, 131 m., 2001

Anthony Hopkins (Hannibal Lecter), Julianne Moore (Clarice Starling), Ray Liotta (Paul Krendler), Frankie R. Faison (Barney), Giancarlo Giannini (Pazzi), Francesca Neri (Signora Pazzi), Zeljko Ivanek (Dr. Cordell Doemling), Hazelle Goodman (Evelda Drumgo). Directed by Ridley Scott and produced by Dino De Laurentiis and Martha De Laurentiis. Screenplay by David Mamet and Steven Zaillian, based on the novel by Thomas Harris.

Ridley Scott's *Hannibal* is a carnival geek show elevated in the direction of art. It never quite gets there, but it tries with every fiber of its craft to redeem its pulp origins, and we must give it credit for the courage of its depravity; if it proves nothing else, it proves that if a man cutting off his face and feeding it to his dogs doesn't get the NC-17 rating for violence, nothing ever will.

The film lacks the focus and brilliance of *The Silence of the Lambs* for a number of reasons, but most clearly because it misplaces the reason why we liked Hannibal Lecter so much. He was, in the 1991 classic, a good man to the degree that his nature allowed him to be. He was hard-wired as a cannibal and mass murderer, true, but that was his nature, not his fault, and in his relationship with the heroine, FBI Agent Clarice Starling, he was civil and even kind. He did the best he could. I remember sitting in a restaurant with Anthony Hopkins as a waitress said, "You're Hannibal Lecter, aren't you? I wish my husband was more like you."

Hopkins returns here as Lecter, although Jodie Foster has been replaced by Julianne Moore as Clarice. We do not miss Foster so much as we miss her character; this Clarice is drier, more cynical, more closed-off than the young idealist we met ten years ago. A decade of law enforcement has taken the bloom off her rose. She is credited, indeed, by the *Guinness Book* as having killed more people than any other female FBI agent, although like all cops in movies, she still doesn't know what to say when her boss demands her badge and her gun. (Suggestion: "I ordered the D.C. police to stand down, and they opened fire anyway.")

Exiled to a desk job, she soon finds herself invited back to the chase by Lecter himself, who writes her from Florence, where he is now a wealthy art curator. On his trail is another millionaire, Mason Verger, who wants revenge. Verger was a child molester assigned to Dr.

Lecter for therapy, which Lecter supplied by drugging him and suggesting he cut off his face and feed it, as mentioned, to the dogs. Now horribly disfigured, with no eyelids or lips, he remembers: "It seemed like a good idea at the time." (Verger is played with repellent ooze by an uncredited and unrecognizable star; search the end credits.)

A Florence policeman named Pazzi (Giancarlo Giannini) suspects that the curator is actually Hannibal Lecter, and decides to shop him to Verger for a $3 million reward. This turns out to be a spectacularly bad idea, he realizes, as he ends up spilling his guts for Lecter. Giannini has always had sad eyes, never sadder than in his big scene here.

But do we like Lecter on the loose? It was the whole point of *Silence* that he could never hope to escape. Clarice descended seven flights of stairs and passed through seven locked doors before arriving at the Plexiglas wall that contained his shackled body. Only his mind was free to roam and scheme; the only way he could escape was to think himself out. In *Hannibal*, Lecter can move freely, and that removes part of the charm. By setting him free to roam, the movie diminishes his status from a locus of evil to a mere predator. He can escape from traps seemingly at will, but that misses the point. He is never more sympathetic here than when he's strapped to a cruciform brace and about to be fed, a little at a time, to wild boars. His voice at that point sounds a note of pity for his tormentors, and we remember the earlier Lecter.

Having read the Harris novel, I agreed with earlier reviewers who doubted it could be filmed in its original form. What is amazing is that Ridley Scott, with screenwriters David Mamet and Steven Zaillian, has kept most of the parts I thought would have to go. Verger's muscle-bound lesbian dominatrix sister is missing, along with her electric eel, and the very ending of the novel is gone, perhaps to spare Clarice irreversible humiliation in case there is a sequel. But the face-eating and voracious boars are still here, along with the man whose skull is popped open so that nonessential parts of his brain can be sliced off and sautéed for his dinner.

Many still alive will recall when a movie like this could not be contemplated, let alone filmed

and released. So great is our sophistication that we giggle when earlier generations would have retched. The brain-eating scene is "special effects," the face-eating is shot in deep shadow and so quickly cut that you barely see the dogs having their dinner, and Julianne Moore explains in interviews that the story is a fable of good and evil (although she cautions that she "actually talked to my shrink about it").

I cannot approve of the movie, not because of its violence, which belongs to the Grand Guignol tradition, but because the underlying story lacks the fascination of *The Silence of the Lambs*. Lecter on the loose loses power, Clarice is harder and less likable, the story unsuccessfully joins its depravity with its police procedural details, and the movie is too bold in its desire to shock (*Silence* somehow persuaded us the shocks were forced upon it).

Still, I'm left with admiration for Scott's craft in pulling this off at all, and making it watchable and (for some, I'm sure) entertaining. The Mason Verger character is a superb joining of skill and diabolical imagination, Julianne Moore's agent is probably an accurate portrait of how Clarice would have changed in ten years, and Anthony Hopkins makes Lecter fascinating every second he is on the screen. The old cannibal still has his standards. "He said that whenever possible," his former jailer Barney recalls, "he preferred to eat the rude—the free-range rude." ☞

Happy Accidents ★ ★ ★
R, 110 m., 2001

Marisa Tomei (Ruby Weaver), Vincent D'Onofrio (Sam Deed), Nadia Dajani (Gretchen), Tovah Feldshuh (Lillian), Holland Taylor (Therapist), Richard Portnow (Trip), Sean Gullette (Mark), Cara Buono (Bette), Anthony Michael Hall (Famous Actor). Directed by Brad Anderson and produced by Susan A. Stover. Screenplay by Anderson.

Sam tells Ruby he has back-traveled in time from May 8, 2439—starting in Dubuque, Iowa, "on the Atlantic Coast." Guys have used weirder pickup lines. Ruby has heard them. She's a "fixer," an emotional codependent who seems to attract the losers, the needy, and the fetishists. In some ways, Sam is the most normal guy she's dated. *Happy Accidents* is their love story.

Ruby (Marisa Tomei) is deep in analysis. She repeats after her therapist, "I am willing to find a balance between my own needs and my concern for others." Sam (Vincent D'Onofrio) is not who she needs to meet at this stage in her recovery. He explains that mankind has survived two ice ages, that most humans are clones created by corporations, and that his parents are "anachronists" who live in a reservation and practice the officially discouraged practice of reproducing through sex. He found a photo of Ruby, he says, and felt compelled to travel through time to find her, love her, and save her from certain death.

Uh-huh. And yet there is something strangely convincing about Sam. D'Onofrio has played some odd characters in his time (notably Robert E. Howard, the creator of Conan the Barbarian, in *Whole Wide World*). This time, given an astonishing background, he plays the character persuasively and realistically; if a man came back from 2439, he might act something like this. Indeed, if an otherwise absolutely normal man of the present time *thought* he came back from 2439, he might act like this in all details other than the time-travel business.

It is Ruby who seems from another time. The first time we meet her, she's working as a directory assistance operator and is fired for inappropriate verbal interactions with the customers. Her shrink thinks maybe she has some kind of a need to look for trouble, and thinks Sam is trouble with a capital T. Yet Sam and Ruby fall in love. And although it would seem in the nature of things that there is no way for Sam to prove that his story is on the level, things do sometimes oddly turn out as if he might possibly be telling the truth. (The camera allows us to see, as he sees, coffee running backward out of his cup and up into the pot, in what is possibly an example of Residual Temporal Drag Syndrome.)

Whether or not he is really from 2439, I will not say. *Happy Accidents* isn't really about that anyway. It's about the collision of these two personalities, and the catalyst of love. Brad Anderson, the writer-director, chose wisely in casting Tomei and D'Onofrio because they can both look normal one moment and then have a strange light in their eyes a second later.

Watch the way Tomei screws up her mouth in unhappiness at an art gallery opening. See how D'Onofrio seems absolutely, convincingly, bottom-line credible—and then pushes just a smidgen further.

Happy Accidents is essentially silliness crossed with science fiction. The actors make it fun to watch. And Anderson is good with the supporting roles, including Tovah Feldshuh as Ruby's mother, Lillian, who advises her to seize the moment (Lillian's husband was an alcoholic, and she learned too late that she liked him better when he was drinking). There is also a cameo for Anthony Michael Hall that is the best thing in its line since Marshall McLuhan stepped out from behind the movie poster in *Annie Hall*.

Hardball ★ ★ ½
R, 106 m., 2001

Keanu Reeves (Conor O'Neill), Diane Lane (Elizabeth Wilkes), DeWayne Warren (G-Baby), John Hawkes (Ticky), Bryan Hearne (Andre), Julian Griffith (Jefferson), Michael B. Jordan (Jamal), Alan Ellis Jr. (Miles), Kristopher Lofton (Clarence). Directed by Brian Robbins and produced by Tina Nides, Robbins, and Michael Tollin. Screenplay by John Gatins, based on the book *Hardball: A Season in the Projects* by Daniel Coyle.

Hardball tells the story of a compulsive gambler whose life is turned around by a season of coaching an inner-city baseball team. That sounds like a winning formula for a movie, and it might be, if the story told us more about gambling, more about the inner city, and more about coaching baseball. But it drifts above the surface of its natural subjects, content to be a genre picture. We're always aware of the formula—and in a picture based on real life, we shouldn't be.

Keanu Reeves stars as Conor O'Neill, whose life revolves around sports bars and the point spread on the post-Jordan Bulls. True, betting on the Bulls is just about the only way to develop interest in the team these days, but compared to movies like *The Gambler* and *California Split*, *Hardball* uses gambling just for motivation and atmosphere; we never feel the urgency and desperation of a man deeply in debt to bad people. Oh, we see a man *acting* urgent and desperate, but the juice isn't there. Consider the scene where O'Neill negotiates a weekly payment plan with a collector; they could be working out the installments on a car.

O'Neill turns to a friend in the investment business for a loan, and the friend makes him an offer: 500 bucks a week to coach a kids' baseball team in the Chicago Housing Authority league. This is not something O'Neill wants to do, but he needs the money. We meet the kids (one too small, one with birth certificate problems, one with asthma, etc.) and of course they're a bunch of unmotivated losers, and of course by the end of the movie they will be champions, because the formula demands it. (It would take more imagination than this movie has to show the kids and the coach redeemed by a losing season.)

There's little detail about who these kids really are and what kinds of homes they come from. A few dialogue scenes with worried parents, and that's it. Toward the end, in a truly heartbreaking scene where an older kid cradles the body of a younger one who has been shot in a drive-by, there's genuine emotion that makes us realize how much was missing earlier.

As the coach, O'Neill mostly addresses the kids as a group, not individually. His dialogue consists of the announcement of plot points (he likes them, he doesn't, he's quitting, he's staying, he's taking them to a Cubs game, they have to believe in themselves). There is not, as nearly as I can remember, a single one-on-one scene in which he tells a kid anything specific about baseball strategy. For that matter, does he know anything about baseball? In many scenes he just lines them up and hectors them, and they look like kids patiently watching some crazy white guy work out his issues.

There's a low-key love story involving Diane Lane as Elizabeth, who teaches some of the kids and keeps an eye on O'Neill because she would like him if (can you see this coming?) he could learn to like himself. I liked the freshness of a moment when O'Neill breaks into a conversation to say, "You like me! You just looked at me a certain way and I could see you liked me." The rhythm of the formula was broken for a moment, and it felt nice.

The movie is based on the book *Hardball: A Season in the Projects* by Daniel Coyle, based on life. I doubt the book, unread by me, is as inauthentic as the movie; the screenplay shows signs of having been tilted in the direction of the basic Hollywood workshop story structure in which we get a crisis because it's time for one. And Keanu Reeves seems subdued in the role—so glum and distant we wonder why we should care if he doesn't. He retails some of his dialogue with excessive hand movements, as if trying to guide his sentences in for a landing.

There was controversy when the movie was made because the dialogue included various words that would be used by most kids on any baseball team. I think I spotted a couple of times when an eight-letter word was dubbed in for its seven-letter synonym. Why bother? Kids talk this way. We might as well face it.

Harrison's Flowers ★ ★ ½
R, 122 m., 2002

Andie MacDowell (Sarah Lloyd), David Strathairn (Harrison Lloyd), Elias Koteas (Yeager Pollack), Adrien Brody (Kyle Morris), Brendan Gleeson (Marc Stevenson), Alun Armstrong (Samuel Bruceck). Directed by Elie Chouraqui and produced by Chouraqui and Albert J. Cohen. Screenplay by Chouraqui, Michael Katims, Isabel Ellsen, and Didier LePecheur.

I am pleased we have women in our fighting forces, since they are so much better at war than men. *Harrison's Flowers* is about an American wife who journeys to the Balkans to rescue her husband from a hotbed of genocide. In *Charlotte Gray,* a British woman parachuted behind German lines in France to rescue her boyfriend. I can just about believe that Charlotte Gray could deceive the Germans with her perfect French, but that Sarah Lloyd could emerge alive from the Balkans hell is unlikely; much of the movie's fascination is with the way Croatians allow this woman and her new friends to wander through the killing zones intact.

I doubt, for that matter, that a Los Angeles fireman could fly to Colombia in *Collateral Damage* and single-handedly outfight guerrillas and drug empires, but that is an Arnold Schwarzenegger picture and not supposed to be realistic. *Harrison's Flowers* is not based on fact but plays like one of those movies that is, and the scenes of carnage are so well staged and convincing that they make the movie's story even harder to believe. Strong performances also work to win us over, wear us down, and persuade us to accept this movie as plausible. Who we gonna believe, the screenplay or our lyin' eyes?

Andie MacDowell stars, in another reminder of her range and skill, in what is essentially an action role. She plays Sarah Lloyd, mother of two, wife of the celebrated war photographer Harrison (David Strathairn). In an obligatory scene that triggers an uh-oh reflex among experienced filmgoers, he tells his boss he wants to retire and is persuaded to take One Last Job. Off he flies to the early days of the war in the Balkans to investigate "ethnic cleansing," which was I think a term not then quite yet in use. He is reported dead, but Sarah knows he's still alive: "Something would have happened inside if he were dead."

She watches TV obsessively, hoping for a glimpse of Harrison among POWs, and takes up chain-smoking, which is the movie symbol for grief-stricken obsession and is dropped as soon as it's no longer needed. Because of a hang-up call in the middle of the night and other signs, she decides to fly to the Balkans to find Harrison. A more reasonable spouse might reason that since (a) her husband is reliably reported dead, and (b) she has no combat zone skills, (c) she should stay home with her kids so they will not become orphans, but no.

The war scenes have undeniable power. Violence springs from nowhere during routine moments and kills supporting characters without warning. Ordinary streets are transformed instantly into warscapes. Sarah joins up with three of Harrison's photographer friends who accompany her quest: pill-popping, wisecracking Morris (Adrien Brody), shambling, likable Stevenson (Brendan Gleeson), and bitter, existentialist Yeager Pollack (Elias Koteas). (If any of them are killed, can you predict from the character descriptions which order it will happen in?) They commandeer cars and jeeps, and essentially make a tour of the war zone, while bullets whiz past their ears and unspeakable horrors take place on every side.

They are protected, allegedly, by white flags and large letters proclaiming "TV" on the sides of their cars. But there is a scene where troops are methodically carrying out an ethnic massacre, and the photographers wander in full view at the other end of the street: Does their status as journalists render them invisible? At one point, Sarah wears fatigues, which (I learn from an article by a war correspondent) is the last thing she should do. Civilian clothes mark her as a noncombatant; camouflage marks her as a target even before her gender is determined.

Whether Sarah finds her husband I will leave you to discover. Whether, when she is in a burning building, the flames shoot up everywhere except precisely where she needs to be, you already know. There is a way in which a movie like this works no matter what. Andie MacDowell is a sympathetic actress who finds plausible ways to occupy this implausible role. Brendan Gleeson is a comforting force of nature, and Adrien Brody's work is a tour de force, reminding me of James Woods in *Salvador* in the way he depends on attitude and cockiness to talk his way through touchy situations. Watch the way he walks them all through a roadblock. I don't believe it can be done, but I believe he did it.

As for the war itself, the movie exhibits the usual indifference to the issues involved. Although it was written and directed by Elie Chouraqui, a Frenchman, it is comfortably xenophobic. Most Americans have never understood the differences among Croats, Serbs, and Bosnians, and this film is no help. (I am among the guilty, actually mislabeling the bad guys in my review of *Behind Enemy Lines,* another film set in the region.) All we need to know is: The Americans are tourists in a foreign war involving ruthless partisans with fierce mustaches. Why are those people killing one another? Why is the war being fought? With those crazy foreigners, who knows? The New Jersey housewife wants to return her man to the arms of his family and the peace of his greenhouse. The movie's buried message is that domestic order must be restored. Just like in Shakespeare.

Harry Potter and the Sorcerer's Stone
★ ★ ★ ★
PG, 152 m., 2001

Daniel Radcliffe (Harry Potter), Rupert Grint (Ronald Weasley), Emma Watson (Hermione Granger), Tom Felton (Draco Malfoy), Richard Harris (Albus Dumbledore), Maggie Smith (Professor Minerva McGonagall), Alan Rickman (Professor Severus Snape), Ian Hart (Professor Quirrell), Robbie Coltrane (Gamekeeper Rubeus Hagrid), Julie Walters (Mrs. Weasley), Harry Melling (Dudley Dursley), Warwick Davis (Professor Flitwick), Zoe Wanamaker (Madame Hooch). Directed by Chris Columbus and produced by David Heyman. Screenplay by J. K. Rowling and Steven Kloves, based on the novel by Rowling.

Harry Potter and the Sorcerer's Stone is a red-blooded adventure movie, dripping with atmosphere, filled with the gruesome and the sublime, and surprisingly faithful to the novel. A lot of things could have gone wrong, and none of them have: Chris Columbus s movie is an enchanting classic that does full justice to a story that was a daunting challenge.

The novel by J. K. Rowling was muscular and vivid, and the danger was that the movie would make things too cute and cuddly. It doesn't. Like an *Indiana Jones* for younger viewers, it tells a rip-roaring tale of supernatural adventure, where colorful and eccentric characters alternate with scary stuff like a three-headed dog, a pit of tendrils known as the Devil's Snare, and a two-faced immortal who drinks unicorn blood. Scary, yes, but not too scary—just scary enough.

Three high-spirited, clear-eyed kids populate the center of the movie. Daniel Radcliffe plays Harry Potter, he with the round glasses, and like all of the young characters, he looks much as I imagined him, but a little older. He once played David Copperfield on the BBC, and whether Harry will be the hero of his own life in this story is much in doubt at the beginning. Deposited as a foundling on a suburban doorstep, he is raised by his aunt and uncle as a poor relation, then summoned by a blizzard of letters to become a student at Hogwarts School, an Oxbridge for magicians.

Our first glimpse of Hogwarts sets the tone for the movie's special effects. Although computers can make anything look realistic, too much realism would be the wrong choice for *Harry Potter,* which is a story in which everything, including the sets and locations, should look a little made-up. The school, rising on ominous Gothic battlements from a moonlit lake, looks about as real as Xanadu in *Citizen Kane,* and its corridors, cellars, and Great Hall, although in some cases making use of real buildings, continue the feeling of an atmospheric book illustration.

At Hogwarts, Harry makes two friends and an enemy. The friends are Hermione Granger (Emma Watson), whose merry face and tangled curls give Harry nudges in the direction of lightening up a little, and Ronald Weasley (Rupert Grint), all pluck, luck, and untamed talents. The enemy is Draco Malfoy (Tom Felton), who will do anything, and plenty besides, to be sure his house places first at the end of the year.

The story you either already know or do not want to know. What is good to know is that the adult cast, a who's who of British actors, play their roles more or less as if they believed them. There is a broad style of British acting, developed in Christmas pantomimes, that would have been fatal to this material; these actors know that, and dial down to just this side of too much. Watch Alan Rickman drawing out his words until they seem ready to snap, yet somehow staying in character.

Maggie Smith, still in the prime of Miss Jean Brodie, is Professor Minerva McGonagall, who assigns newcomers like Harry to one of the school's four houses. Richard Harris is Headmaster Dumbledore, his beard so long that in an Edward Lear poem birds would nest in it. Robbie Coltrane is the gamekeeper, Hagrid, who has a record of misbehavior and a way of saying very important things and then not believing that he said them.

Computers *are* used, exuberantly, to create a plausible look in the gravity-defying action scenes. Readers of the book will wonder how the movie visualizes the crucial game of Quidditch. The game, like so much else in the movie, is more or less as I visualized it, and I was reminded of Stephen King's theory that writers practice a form of telepathy, placing ideas and images in the heads of their readers.

(The reason some movies don't look like their books may be that some producers don't read them.)

If Quidditch is a virtuoso sequence, there are other set pieces of almost equal wizardry. A chess game with life-size, deadly pieces. A room filled with flying keys. The pit of tendrils, already mentioned, and a dark forest where a loathsome creature threatens Harry but is scared away by a centaur. And the dark shadows of Hogwarts's library, cellars, hidden passages, and dungeons, where an invisibility cloak can keep you out of sight but not out of trouble.

During *Harry Potter and the Sorcerer's Stone*, I was pretty sure I was watching a classic, one that will be around for a long time, and make many generations of fans. It takes the time to be good. It doesn't hammer the audience with easy thrills, but cares to tell a story and to create its characters carefully. Like *The Wizard of Oz, Willy Wonka and the Chocolate Factory, Star Wars,* and *E.T.,* it isn't just a movie but a world with its own magical rules. And some excellent Quidditch players. ☞

Hart's War ★ ★ ★
R, 125 m., 2002

Bruce Willis (Colonel William McNamara), Colin Farrell (Lieutenant Tommy Hart), Terrence Howard (Lieutenant Lincoln Scott), Vicellous Shannon (Lieutenant Lamar Archer), Cole Hauser (Staff Sergeant Bedford), Marcel Iures (Commandant Visser), Linus Roache (Captain Peter Ross). Directed by Gregory Hoblit and produced by David Foster, Hoblit, David Ladd, and Arnold Rifkin. Screenplay by Billy Ray and Terry George, based on the novel by John Katzenbach.

"Your colonel is throwing you to the wolves," the Nazi commandant of a POW camp tells the young American lieutenant. It looks that way. A white racist American has been murdered, a black officer is charged with the crime, and Lieutenant Tommy Hart (Colin Farrell) has been assigned to defend him in a court-martial. The Nazi has permitted the trial as a gesture (he is a Yale man, not uncivilized, likes jazz). But Colonel William McNamara (Bruce Willis), the senior officer among the American prisoners, doesn't seem much interested in justice.

Because the movie is told mostly from Hart's point of view, we lack crucial pieces of information available to McNamara, and as these are parceled out toward the end of the film, the meaning of the events shifts. But one underlying truth does not change: Racism during World War II in America and in the army was a reality that undercut duty, patriotism, and truth.

As the movie opens, Hart has been captured, interrogated, and sent to Stalag VI in Belgium. He is a senator's son, destined for a desk job. At the POW camp he is cross-examined by Willis, who senses he's lying about the interrogation, and assigns him to a barracks otherwise filled with enlisted men. It's a problem of space, Willis explains, and a few days later the officers' barracks is again too crowded to accommodate two black air corps pilots who have been shot down: Lieutenant Lincoln Scott (Terrence Howard) and Lieutenant Lamar Archer (Vicellous Shannon).

Bunking with black men does not sit well with Vic Bedford (Cole Hauser), a staff sergeant who calls the pilots "flying bellhops." Soon a tent spike, which could be used as a weapon, is found under Archer's mattress, and he's summarily shot by the Nazis without a trial. Since it is pretty clear that Bedford planted the spike, no one is very surprised not long after when the man is found dead with Scott standing over his body.

A clean-cut case of murder, right? Not according to Hart, who believes this is another setup and demands that a trial be held. Colonel McNamara is not enthusiastic about the idea, but the Nazi commandant is, and soon a court-martial is under way with Hart (who has no legal experience) as the defense attorney.

All of this is absorbing, if of course manipulative, but what makes it more intriguing is the sense that something else is going on underneath the action—that McNamara's motives may be more complicated than we know. One hitch is that both the dead man and his alleged killer left the barracks by a secret route at night, a route that cannot be revealed without jeopardizing the other American prisoners. So Hart agrees to a cover story about how his man left the barracks, and then, in a scene

259

built on devastating logic, has to stand mute while the phony cover story is used against his client.

Colin Farrell, the young star of Joel Schumacher's powerful but hardly released *Tigerland* (2000), is a twenty-five-year-old Dublin native obviously destined for stardom. He does a good job with the conflicted, anguished Lieutenant Hart, and Bruce Willis brings instinctive authority to the colonel. Marcel Iures, a Romanian actor, is sharp-edged and intriguing as the Nazi commandant; when he gets condolences on the death of his son in battle, he muses, "I killed my share of English and French soldiers in the first war. They had fathers too." There is a shade of the Erich von Stroheim character in *Grand Illusion* here, the suggestion of a German whose military ideas do not depend on that little twerp Hitler.

But for all the interest in these performances, *Hart's War* would be just another military courtroom drama if it were not for the work by Terrence Howard as Lincoln Scott, the man on trial. He expects no justice from an American court-martial. He enlisted in the air corps, trained at Tuskegee, wanted to serve his nation, and has seen racism and contempt from whites in uniform. He makes one statement that is chilling because we know it was true: German POWs held in the Deep South were allowed to attend movies and eat in restaurants that were off limits to blacks, even those in uniform. "If I wanted to kill a cracker," Scott says, "I could have stayed at home in Macon."

The movie worked for me right up to the final scene, and then it caved in. Bowing to ancient and outdated convention, director Gregory Hoblit and writers Billy Ray and Terry George put the plot through an awkward U-turn so that Willis can end up as a hero. How and why he does so is ingenious, yes, but the ending gives the impression it is a solution when it is only a remedy. And I would have liked it better if the far-off bugle had been playing under a black character at the end and not a white one. It's as if the movie forgot its own anger.

Head Over Heels ★ ½
PG-13, 91 m., 2001

Monica Potter (Amanda Pierce), Freddie Prinze Jr. (Jim Winston), Shalom Harlow (Jade), Ivana Milicevic (Roxana), Sarah O'Hare (Candi), Tomiko Fraser (Holly), Raoul Ganeev (Harold). Directed by Mark S. Waters and produced by Julia Dray and Robert Simonds. Screenplay by Ron Burch and David Kidd.

Head Over Heels opens with fifteen funny minutes and then goes dead in the water. It's like they sent home the first team of screenwriters and brought in Beavis and Butt-Head. The movie starts out with sharp wit and edgy zingers, switches them off, and turns to bathroom humor. And not funny bathroom humor, but painfully phony gas-passing noises, followed by a plumbing emergency that buries three supermodels in a putrid delivery from where the sun don't shine. It's as if the production was a fight to the death between bright people with a sense of humor and cretins who think the audience is as stupid as they are.

Monica Potter and Freddie Prinze Jr. star, in another one of those stories where it's love at first sight and then she gets the notion that he's clubbed someone to death. The two characters were doing perfectly well being funny as *themselves*, and then the movie muzzles them and brings in this pea-brained autopilot plot involving mistaken identities, dead bodies, and the Russian mafia.

Why? I wanted to ask the filmmakers. Why? You have a terrific cast and the wit to start out well. Why surrender and sell out? Isn't it a better bet, and even better for your careers, to make a whole movie that's smart and funny, instead of showing off for fifteen minutes and then descending into cynicism and stupidity? Why not make a movie you can show to the friends you admire, instead of to a test audience scraped from the bottom of the IQ barrel?

Monica Potter is radiant as Amanda, an art restorer at the Museum of Modern Art. She has been betrayed by a boyfriend, and vows to focus on her job. "I love art better than real life," she says, because the people in paintings "stay in love forever." True of the Grecian urn, perhaps, if not of Bosch, but never mind; her latest challenge is to restore a priceless Titian, which the curator hauls into the room with his fingers all over the paint, banging it against the doorway.

Moving out from her faithless boyfriend, she finds a $500-a-month room (i.e., closet) in a vast luxury apartment occupied by "the last four nonsmoking models in Manhattan" (Shalom Harlow, Ivana Milicevic, Sarah O'Hare, and Tomiko Fraser). And then she falls head over heels in love with a neighbor, Jim (Prinze), who walks a big dog that knocks her over and sets up a conversation in which she says all of the wrong things. That's the dialogue I thought was so funny.

In a film with more confidence, the comedy would continue to be based on their relationship. This one prefers to recycle aged clichés. She thinks she sees him club someone to death. We know he didn't, because—well, because (a) it happens in silhouette, so the movie is hiding something, and (b) Freddie Prinze is not going to play a *real* club-murderer, not in a movie with a cute dog. Idiot Plot devices prevent either one of them from saying the two or three words that would clear up the misunderstanding. Meanwhile, the exhausted screenwriters haul in the Russian mafia and other sinister characters in order to make this movie as similar as possible to countless other brain-dead productions.

As my smile faded and I realized the first fifteen minutes were bait-and-switch, my restless mind sought elsewhere for employment. I focused on Amanda's job, art restoration. Her challenge: An entire face is missing from a grouping by Titian. She "restores" it by filling the gap with, yes, Freddie Prinze's face and head, complete with a haircut that doesn't exactly match the Renaissance period.

But never mind. Give the movie the benefit of the doubt. Maybe one of those Renaissance geniuses like Michelangelo invented Supercuts clippers at the same time he invented bicycles and submarines. What's really odd is that the face is not in the style of Titian, but in the style of Norman Rockwell. Obviously it was only with the greatest restraint that Amanda was able to prevent herself from adding a soda fountain to the background.

Now what about that eruption of unspeakable brown stuff that coats the supermodels as they hide behind a shower curtain in a bathroom? Why was that supposed to be funny? The scene betrays a basic ignorance of a fundamental principle of humor: It isn't funny when innocent bystanders are humiliated. It's funny when they humiliate themselves. For example, *Head Over Heels* would be funny if it were about the people making this movie.

Heartbreakers ★ ★ ★
PG-13, 123 m., 2001

Sigourney Weaver (Max), Jennifer Love Hewitt (Page), Ray Liotta (Dean Cumanno), Jason Lee (Jack), Gene Hackman (William B. Tensy), Anne Bancroft (Gloria Vogal/Barbara), Nora Dunn (Miss Madress). Directed by David Mirkin and produced by John Davis and Irving Ong. Screenplay by Robert Dunn, Paul Guay, and Stephen Mazur.

Heartbreakers is *Dirty Rotten Scoundrels* plus Gene Hackman as W. C. Fields, plus Jennifer Love Hewitt and Sigourney Weaver walking into rooms wearing dresses that enter about a quarter of an inch after they do. I guess that's enough to recommend it. It's not a great comedy, but it's a raucous one, hardworking and ribald, and I like its spirit.

Weaver and Hewitt play Max and Page, a mother-and-daughter con team. Their scam: Max (Weaver) marries a rich guy and then surprises him in a compromising position with Page (Hewitt), after which there's a big divorce settlement. This has worked thirteen times, according to Max, whose latest victim is Dean (Ray Liotta), a chop-shop owner who falls for what my old buddy Russ Meyer would describe as Hewitt's capacious bodice.

Hewitt spends the entire film with her treasures on display, maybe as product placement for the Wonder Bra, and for that matter, Heather Graham is identically costumed in *Say It Isn't So*. The moviegoers of America owe something, possibly gratitude, to Erin Brockovich, the most influential movie style-setter since Annie Hall.

Weaver and Hewitt attack their roles with zeal, but the movie doesn't really start humming until Hackman enters. He plays William B. Tensy, a chain-smoking tobacco zillionaire who lives on the water in Palm Beach with a draconian housekeeper (Nora Dunn) and lots of ashtrays. He believes everyone, especially children, should take up smoking, and has a cigarette in his mouth at all times except when violently choking with bronchial spasms, which is frequently.

My guess is that Hackman decided to take the role when he hit on the approach of playing Tensy as W. C. Fields. There is nothing in the role as written that suggests Fields, but everything in the role as played, including Hackman's recycling of Fields's wardrobe from the famous short *The Golf Specialist* (1930).

Weaver seems tickled by the sheer awfulness of Tensy, a man most women would cross not only the room but perhaps the state to avoid. With the Liotta character she was within the guidelines of traditional farce, but with Hackman she's working without a net: What strategy *can* a woman adopt in dealing with such an astonishing combination of the gauche and the obnoxious? Their relationship concludes with a sight gag involving, of course, cigarette smoke; I wouldn't dream of revealing one more thing about it.

Weaver's approach to Tensy is a devious one; she pretends to be Russian, which leads into a precarious situation when she's called up on the stage in a Russian nightclub and expected to sing; her response to this emergency is inspired. Not so brilliant is another strategy she and her daughter use. In restaurants, they sneak broken glass onto their salads and then complain loudly, refusing to pay. Nice, but wiser if they'd eat some of the salad course before complaining; by dropping the glass immediately, they defeat the purpose.

Anyway. While Max courts the disgusting Tensy, Hewitt, as Page, is developing a relationship with Jack (Jason Lee), the owner of a Palm Beach bar. She's torn between falling in love with him and fleecing him, especially after she learns he's been offered 3 million bucks for his bar and its waterfront property. This is the moment that will get the biggest laughs in Palm Beach, where the last time this much ocean frontage went for $3 million was when Roxanne Pulitzer was taking trumpet lessons. That both Jack and Page are dumb enough to be dazzled by the offer is a hint that they may be made for each other.

The movie has been directed by David

Mirkin, who made the sly and charming *Romy and Michele's High School Reunion* (1997). *Heartbreakers* is not as sly and has no ambition to be charming, but in a season of dreary failed comedies it does what a comedy must: It makes us laugh. ☞

Hearts in Atlantis ★ ★ ★ ½
PG-13, 101 m., 2001

Anthony Hopkins (Ted Brautigan), Anton Yelchin (Bobby Garfield), Hope Davis (Liz Garfield), Mika Boorem (Carol Gerber), Will Rothhaar (Sully), David Morse (Adult Bobby Garfield), Alan Tudyk (Monte Man), Tom Bower (Len Files), Celia Weston (Alana Files). Directed by Scott Hicks and produced by Kerry Heysen. Screenplay by William Goldman, based on the book by Stephen King.

Hearts in Atlantis weaves a strange spell made of nostalgia and fear. Rarely does a movie make you feel so warm and so uneasy at the same time, as Stephen King's story evokes the mystery of adolescence, when everything seems to be happening for the very first time.

Set in 1960, the movie tells the story of an eleven-year-old named Bobby (Anton Yelchin) whose father left when he was five, whose mother (Hope Davis) seems too distracted to love him, whose life centers on his best friend, Sully (Will Rothhaar), and Carol Gerber (Mika Boorem), with whom he will share a first kiss by which he will judge all the others. As is often the case in King stories, the period is re-created through an intense memory of cars, radio shows, clothes, baseball mitts— material treasures in an uncertain world.

Then a man comes as a boarder in the upstairs apartment at Bobby's house. This is Ted Brautigan (Anthony Hopkins). "I never trust a man who carries his possessions in grocery bags," says Bobby's mother, as Ted stands on the curb without much in the way of possessions. Bobby is often home alone (his mother is much distracted by her office job), and Ted offers root beer, conversation, and even a dollar a day to read him the paper. Then he reveals a more shadowy assignment for Bobby: keeping a lookout for Low Men, who are seeking Ted because they want to use his gift. By now Bobby does not have to be told that Ted can sometimes foresee the future; Bobby has the same ability, but muted.

"One feels them first at the back of one's eyes," Ted tells Bobby, and we note how Anthony Hopkins takes this line, which could come from a cheap horror film, and invests it with nuance. The Low Men themselves are as symbolic as real. In the King story it's hinted they may come from another world or time, and in the movie they may be FBI agents who want to use Ted's powers for the government, but it hardly matters; in either version, they are the hard realities of an adult world that takes the gifted and the unconforming and either uses them or destroys them.

Scott Hicks and Piotr Sobocinski, who directed and photographed the movie, have wisely seen that atmosphere is everything in *Hearts of Atlantis*. They evoke a shady lower-middle-class neighborhood in a town of hills and trees, and the sleepy Sunday 1950s feel of the newspaper, root beer, Chesterfields, and a game on the radio. In this world Bobby grows up. He is threatened by an older neighborhood bully, he is in love with Carol Gerber, he is in awe of Ted. When Bobby's mother gives him an adult library card for his birthday, it is Ted who advises him which authors bear reading.

There are wonderful set pieces in the film. One of the best is the way Ted tells Bobby the story of the great Chicago Bears running back Bronco Nagurski, who came out of retirement, old and hurt, and seemed to carry the whole Chicago team on his back as he marched down the field in a last hurrah. Another is a visit to a pool hall in a neighboring town, where Ted wants to place a bet, and Bobby meets a woman who knew his father.

The movie ends as childhood ends, in disillusionment at the real world that lies ahead. Bobby's mother is cruelly divested of her illusions, and later lashes out at the innocent Ted, and then the Low Men come, as they always do. But Bobby's summer had to end, and at least he experienced the best of all possible kisses.

A movie like this is kind of a conjuring act. Like a lot of Stephen King's recent work, it is not a horror story so much as an everyday story with horror lurking in the margins. It's not a genre movie, in other words, but the story of characters we believe in and care

about. Anton Yelchin is not just a cute kid but a smart and wary one, and Mika Boorem is not just the girl down the street but the kind of soul who inspires the best in others. And Anthony Hopkins finds just the tired, truthful note for Ted Brautigan—who knows the worst about men and fears for his future, but still has enough faith to believe it will do a kid good to read the right books.

Note: So should you therefore read the book after seeing the movie? I would recommend the audiobook; William Hurt's reading is one of the best audio performances I have ever heard.

Hedwig and the Angry Inch ★ ★ ★
R, 95 m., 2001

John Cameron Mitchell (Hansel/Hedwig), Miriam Shor (Yitzhak), Michael Pitt (Tommy Gnosis), Andrea Martin (Phyllis Stein), Alberta Watson (Hedwig's Mother), Ben Mayer-Goodman (Hansel [six years old]), Stephen Trask (Skszp), Theodore Liscinski (Jacek). Directed by John Cameron Mitchell and produced by Pamela Koffler, Katie Roumel, and Christine Vachon. Screenplay by Mitchell, based on the musical by Mitchell and Stephen Trask.

Hedwig and the Angry Inch occupies an almost extinct movie category: It's an original rock musical—indeed, according to its maker, a "postpunk neo–glam-rock musical," a category almost as specialized as the not dissimilar *Beyond the Valley of the Dolls*, which was a "camp-rock horror musical." Filmed with ferocious energy and with enough sexual variety to match late Fellini, it may be passing through standard bookings on its way to a long run as the midnight successor to *The Rocky Horror Picture Show*.

Hedwig began life in 1997 as an off-Broadway musical, and now arrives as a movie with its cult status already established. It tells the story of an East German boy named Hansel who grows up gay, falls in love with a U.S. master sergeant, and wants to go to America with him. The master sergeant explains that, as Hansel, that will be impossible, but if the lad undergoes a sex-change operation, they can get married and then the passport will be no problem ("To walk away, you gotta leave something behind").

Hansel becomes Hedwig (John Cameron

Mitchell) in a botched operation that leaves a little too much behind (thus the title), and she soon finds herself abandoned in a Kansas trailer park. She turns tricks at a nearby military base, becomes a baby-sitter for the general, and meets the general's son, Tommy Gnosis (Michael Pitt). They're lovers, until Tommy discovers the secret of Hedwig's transsexualism and abandons her—quickly becoming a rock star on the basis of songs stolen from Hedwig.

All of this we discover in flashback. The movie opens with Hedwig on a national tour with her own band ("The Angry Inch"). Her itinerary makes her into a virtual stalker of Tommy Gnosis, with the difference that while Tommy plays stadiums, Hedwig plays behind the salad bar of a fast-food chain called Bilgewater's. The customers look on in disbelief, and would be even more disbelieving if they could study the lyrics and discover that the songs (by Stephen Trask and Mitchell) add up to an Aristotelian argument about gender and wholeness.

John Cameron Mitchell electrifies the movie with a performance that isn't a satire of glam-rock performers so much as an authentic glam-rock performance. The movie may have had a limited budget, but the screen is usually filled with something sensational, including a trailer home that transforms itself in an instant into a stage. Michael Pitt's performance as Tommy is all the more astonishing if you've recently seen him, as I did, playing Donny, the overgrown tough kid, in *Bully*.

This material could have been glib and smug, but it isn't. There's some kind of pulse of sincerity beating below the glittering surface, and it may come from Mitchell's own life story. He was raised in Berlin as the son of the general in charge of the U.S. military garrison there. (The defense secretary at the time was Dick Cheney; did they discuss their gay children?) The fall of the Berlin Wall must have made an impression on young John Cameron Mitchell, as did also the wild nightlife scene in Berlin, and in a way the movie is about a collision between those two inspirations.

The filmmaking is as free-form as such movies as *Pink Floyd the Wall*. There's an animated sequence to illustrate one of the songs, and a bouncing ball for a sing-along; the musical numbers spill out from behind the salad bar to become as exuberant as something from MGM. Hedwig stands astride the material, sometimes literally, and it's interesting that the character is presented as someone whose sex change was not eagerly sought, but seemed to be a necessary by-product of love. Does Hedwig really want to be a boy or a girl? And what about Yitzhak (Miriam Shor), who may be her boyfriend, although the movie doesn't say for sure. Strange, how the movie seems to be loud, flashy, and superficial, and yet gives a deeper dimension to its characters.

Heist ★ ★ ★ ½
R, 107 m., 2001

Gene Hackman (Joe Moore), Danny DeVito (Mickey Bergman), Delroy Lindo (Bobby Blane), Sam Rockwell (Jimmy Silk), Rebecca Pidgeon (Fran), Ricky Jay (Pinky Pincus), Patti LuPone (Betty Croft), Jim Frangione (D. A. Freccia). Directed by David Mamet and produced by Art Linson, Elie Samaha, and Andrew Stevens. Screenplay by Mamet.

David Mamet's *Heist* is about a caper and a con, involving professional criminals who want to retire but can't. It's not that they actually require more money. It's more that it would be a sin to leave it in civilian hands. Gene Hackman plays a jewel thief who dreams of taking his last haul and sailing into the sunset with his young wife (Rebecca Pidgeon). Danny DeVito is the low-rent mastermind who forces him into pulling one last job. Hackman complains he doesn't need any more money. DeVito's wounded reply is one of the funniest lines Mamet has ever written: "Everybody needs money! That's why they call it money!"

Hackman plays Joe Moore, a thief whose real love is building and sailing boats. His crew includes Bobby Blane (Delroy Lindo) and Pinky Pincus (Ricky Jay); his wife, Fran (Pidgeon), is a groupie who has confused danger with foreplay. They pull off a big job, with one hitch: Moore is caught on a security camera. Time to haul anchor and head for Caribbean ports—but not according to Mickey Bergman (DeVito), who pressures Joe into pulling one last job and insists he take along his feckless nephew Jimmy Silk (Sam Rockwell). Jimmy is the kind of hothead who carries a gun because he lives in a dangerous neighborhood, which would be safer if he moved.

The plot moves through labyrinthine levels of double cross. Mamet loves magic, especially sleight of hand (his favorite supporting actor, Ricky Jay, is a great card artist), and the plot of *Heist,* like those of *The Spanish Prisoner* and *House of Games,* is a prism that reflects different realities depending on where you're standing. It also incorporates a lot of criminal craft, as in the details of the diamond robbery that opens the movie, and the strategy for stealing gold bars from a cargo plane at the end.

When the movie played at the Venice, Toronto, and Chicago festivals, some critics disliked the details I enjoyed the most. We learn from *Variety* that "some late-reel gunplay could have benefited enormously from more stylish handling." This is astonishingly wrongheaded. Does *Variety* mean it would have preferred one of those by-the-numbers high-tech gunfights we're weary of after countless retreads? "Stylish handling" in a gunfight is for me another way of saying the movie's on autopilot.

What I like about the "late-reel" gunplay in *Heist* is the way some of the shooters are awkward and self-conscious; this is arguably the first gunfight of their lives. And the way DeVito dances into the path of the bullets hysterically trying to get everybody to stop shooting ("Let's talk this over!"). The precision with which Hackman says, "He isn't gonna shoot me? Then he hadn't oughta point a gun at me. It's insincere." And the classical perfection of this exchange:

"Don't you want to hear my last words?"
"I just did."

I am also at a loss to understand why critics pick on Rebecca Pidgeon. Yes, she has a distinctive style of speech that is well suited to Mametian dialogue: crisp, clipped, colloquial. Mamet loves to fashion anachronisms for her ("You're the law west of the Pecos"). She is not intended as a slinky *film noir* seductress, but as a plucky kid-sister type who can't quite be trusted. Mamet goes to the trouble of supplying us with style and originality, and is criticized because his films don't come from the cookie cutter.

Hackman, of course, is a dab hand at tough, grizzled veterans. ("Dab hand"—that could be a Pidgeon line.) He and Lindo inhabit their characters so easily they distract from the plot twists by the simple sincerity with which they confront them. Their world-wise dialogue is like a magician's patter, directing our attention away from the artifice. And DeVito is one of the most consistently entertaining actors in the movies, with an energy that makes his dialogue vibrate. "I've just financialized the numbers," he explains. He is not a bad man in this movie. Just an unprincipled greedy-guts with dangerous associates.

Close attention may reveal a couple of loopholes in the plot. One wonders why the Pidgeon character would do what she does after the truck crashes. Whether we can be sure that her last revelation is, indeed, her last revelation. And the film ends with a character who gives us a little smile that seems wrong, because he is smiling at the audience and not at what has happened. Unless, of course, he knows the last revelation is not the last revelation.

Heist is the kind of caper movie that was made before special effects replaced wit, construction, and intelligence. This movie is made out of fresh ingredients, not cake mix. Despite the twists of its plot, it is about its characters. Consider the exchanges between Lindo and Hackman: They have a shorthand that convinces us they've worked together for a very long time and are in agreement on everything that matters. Most modern caper movies convince us the characters met this morning on the set. ☞

Here on Earth ★ ★
PG-13, 97 m., 2000

Chris Klein (Kelley), Leelee Sobieski (Samantha), Josh Hartnett (Jasper), Bruce Greenwood (Earl Cavanaugh), Annette O'Toole (Jo Cavanaugh), Michael Rooker (Malcolm Arnold), Annie Corley (Betsy Arnold). Directed by Mark Piznarski and produced by David T. Friendly. Screenplay by Michael Seitzman.

When we see the sweet advertising art for *Here on Earth,* we suspect this may be another movie about angels walking among us, and it is—but these are human angels, not heavenly ones. It is about characters so generous, understanding, forgiving, and just doggone nice that they could have been created by Norman Rockwell, just as their town seems to have been.

The movie begins, however, on a sour note, as a snotty prep school boy named Kelley (Chris Klein) gets a new Mercedes convertible from his rich dad, and takes some friends slumming at the diner in the nearby small town. He gets smart with Samantha, the waitress (Leelee Sobieski), and has words with her boyfriend, Jasper (Josh Hartnett). That leads to a drag race during which Kelley and Jasper crash their cars into a gas pump and burn down the gas station and the diner, which are owned by Samantha's parents.

Kelley has come across up until this point as an arrogant brat. Sure, he's the class valedictorian, but he doesn't care about stuff like that. All he cares about is expanding the family fortune. So maybe it will teach him a lesson when the judge orders Kelley and Jasper to help rebuild the diner during the summer ahead. And maybe Samantha is right to see something good hidden beneath his cynical defiance. Consider the scene where he sneaks through the woods to eavesdrop on the substitute valedictorian's speech (he's been banned from graduation), and she tiptoes behind him and watches as he gives his own speech to the trees and the birds. It's a sweet scene. Unlikely in its logistics, but sweet.

Kelley isn't easy to like ("My probation doesn't say anything about sitting around and spitting out watermelon seeds with you people"). But as the summer meanders along, the boys get tans and develop muscles, and Samantha and Kelley fall in love, while good-hearted Jasper looks on helplessly. Read no further if you don't want to know . . . that Samantha, alas, has received bad news from her doctor. The cancer has spread from her knee to her liver, nothing can be done, and besides, "So I lived another year or two. It's not worth it."

Not worth it? When you're young and smart and in love? I would personally endure a good deal of pain just to live long enough to read tomorrow's newspaper. But Samantha fades away, another victim of Ali MacGraw's Disease (first identified many years ago in *Love Story*), which makes you more beautiful the sicker you get.

By now the film has become fairly unbelievable. Jasper is telling Kelley that although it kills him to see the woman he loves in the arms of another man, whatever makes her happy is all he wants for her. And Kelley is softening up and telling his rich dad that money isn't the only thing in life, and that you can be just as happy with a poor girl as a rich one.

But then comes a scene that clangs with a harsh false note. (Once again: Spoiler warning.) While Samantha bravely faces death and nobly smiles upon all around her, Kelley, the rat, suddenly announces he "has a life to get back to," and leaves town. This seems to be an utterly unmotivated act, but actually it has a splendid motivation: He has to leave so that he can come back. The plot requires a crisis before the dawn. The fact that his action is unconvincing and inexplicable doesn't bother the filmmakers, any more than it bothers the saintly and forgiving Samantha.

Leelee Sobieski is really very good in this movie. Still only nineteen, she was wonderful in *A Soldier's Daughter Never Cries* and *Eyes Wide Shut*, and in lesser movies like *Deep Impact* and *Never Been Kissed*. I didn't see her TV version of *Joan of Arc*, but with her deep, grave voice and unforced presence, I have a feeling she was equal to the role. The cast is filled with other winning actors: Klein and Hartnett, and Bruce Greenwood and the undervalued Annette O'Toole as Samantha's parents. But they need a little more reality to kick against. *Here on Earth* slides too easily into its sentimentality; the characters should have put up more of a struggle.

High Crimes ★ ★ ★
PG-13, 115 m., 2002

Ashley Judd (Claire Kubik), Morgan Freeman (Charles Grimes), James Caviezel (Tom Kubik), Adam Scott (Lieutenant Terrence Embry), Amanda Peet (Jackie Grimaldi), Michael Gaston (Major Waldron), Tom Bower (FBI Agent Mullins), Jesse Beaton (Ramona Phillips). Directed by Carl Franklin and produced by Arnon Milchan, Janet Yang, and Jesse B'Franklin. Screenplay by Yuri Zeltser and Cary Bickley, based on the novel by Joseph Finder.

Although I believe Ashley Judd could thrive in more challenging roles, and offer *Normal Life* (1996) as an example, her career seems to tilt toward thrillers, with the occasional comedy. She often plays a strong, smart woman who is in more danger than she realizes. Although her characters are eventually screaming as they flee brutal killers in the long tradition of Women in Danger movies, the setups show her as competent, resourceful, independent.

High Crimes is a movie like that. Judd plays Claire Kubik, a high-profile defense attorney for a big firm. When her ex-soldier husband (Jim Caviezel) is arrested by the FBI, charged with murder, and arraigned before a military tribunal, she defiantly says she will defend him herself. And because she doesn't know her way around military justice, she enlists a lawyer named Grimes (Morgan Freeman) as co-counsel. Grimes is that dependable character, a drunk who is on the wagon but may (i.e., will) fall off under stress.

This is the second movie Judd and Freeman have made together (after *Kiss the Girls* in 1997). They're both good at projecting a kind of southern intelligence that knows its way around the frailties of human nature. Although Freeman refers to himself as the "wild card" in the movie, actually that role belongs to Caviezel, whose very identity is called into question by the military charges. "Is your name Tom Kubik?" Claire asks her husband at one point. She no longer knows the answer.

The plot involves a massacre in a Latin American village and a subsequent cover-up. Did Claire's husband gun down innocent civilians, or was he framed by a scary marine vet and his straight-arrow superior? Does the military want justice or a cover-up? We are not given much reason to trust military tribunals—evidence the screenplay was written before 9/11—and the Freeman character intones the familiar refrain, "Military justice is to justice as military music is to music."

And yet . . . well, maybe there's more to the story. I wouldn't dream of revealing crucial details. I do like the way director Carl Franklin and writers Yuri Zeltser and Cary Bickley, working from Joseph Finder's novel, play both ends against the middle, so that the audience has abundant evidence to believe two completely conflicting theories of what actually happened. In the very season of the DVD release of *Rashomon*, which is the template for stories with more than one convincing explanation, here's another example of how Kurosawa's masterpiece continues to inspire movie plots.

High Crimes works to keep us involved and make us care. Although Freeman's character may indeed start drinking again, it won't be for reasons we can anticipate (of course, like all heroic movie drunks, he retains the exquisite timing to sober up on demand). The unfolding of various versions of the long-ago massacre is handled by Franklin in flashbacks that show how one camera angle can refute what another angle seems to prove. And if we feel, toward the end, a little whiplashed by the plot manipulations, well, that's what the movie promises and that's what the movie delivers.

As for Miss Judd. From the first time I saw her, in *Ruby in Paradise* (1993), I thought she had a unique sympathy with the camera, an ability that cannot be learned but only exercised. In the years since then, she has often been better than her material—or do her advisers choose mainstream commercial roles for her as the safest course? When she strays out of genre, as she did in *Smoke, Heat, Normal Life,* and *Simon Birch,* she shows how good she is. Of course, she's good in *High Crimes,* too, and involves us more than the material really deserves. But this is the kind of movie any studio executive would green light without a moment's hesitation—always an ominous sign.

High Fidelity ★ ★ ★
R, 120 m., 2000

John Cusack (Rob), Iben Hjejle (Laura), Todd Louiso (Dick), Jack Black (Barry), Lisa Bonet (Marie), Catherine Zeta-Jones (Charlie), Joan Cusack (Liz), Tim Robbins (Ian). Directed by Stephen Frears and produced by Tim Bevan and Rudd Simmons. Screenplay by D. V. Devincentis, Steve Pink, John Cusack, and Scott Rosenberg, based on the book by Nick Hornby.

In its unforced, whimsical, quirky, obsessive way, *High Fidelity* is a comedy about real people in real lives. The movie looks like it was easy to make—but it must not have been, because movies this wry and likable hardly ever get made. Usually a clunky plot gets in the way, or the filmmakers are afraid to let their characters seem too smart. Watching *High Fidelity*,

I had the feeling I could walk out of the theater and meet the same people on the street—and want to, which is an even higher compliment.

John Cusack stars as Rob, who owns a used-record store in Chicago and has just broken up with Laura, his latest girlfriend. He breaks up a lot. Still hurting, he makes a list of the top five girls he's broken up with, and cackles that Laura didn't make it. Later he stands forlornly on a bridge overlooking the Chicago River and makes lists of the top five reasons he misses her.

The key design elements in Rob's apartment are the lumber bookshelves for his alphabetized vinyl albums. He has two guys working for him in his store. Each was hired for three days a week, but both come in six days a week, maybe because they have no place else to go. These guys are the shy, sideways Dick (Todd Louiso) and the ultraconfident Barry (Jack Black). They are both experts on everything, brains stocked with nuggets of information about popular culture.

Rob is the movie's narrator, guiding us through his world, talking directly to the camera, soliloquizing on his plight—which is that he seems unable to connect permanently with a girl, maybe because his attention is elsewhere. But on what? He isn't obsessed with his business, he isn't as crazy about music as Dick and Barry, and he isn't thinking about his next girl—he's usually moping about the last one. He seems stuck in the role of rejected lover, and never likes a girl quite as much when she's with him as after she's left.

Laura (Iben Hjejle) was kind of special. Now she has taken up with an unbearably supercilious, ponytailed brainiac named Ian (Tim Robbins), who comes into the store to "talk things over" and inspires fantasies in which Rob, Dick, and Barry dream of kicking him senseless. "Conflict resolution is my job," he offers helpfully. Whether Ian is nice or not is of no consequence to Rob; he simply wants Laura back.

The story unspools in an unforced way. Barry and Dick involve Rob in elaborate debates about music minutiae. They take him to a nightclub to hear a new singer (Lisa Bonet). Rob gets advice from Laura's best friend (Joan Cusack), who likes him but is fed up with his emotional dithering. Rob seeks out former girlfriends like Charlie (Catherine Zeta-Jones), who tells him why she left him in more detail than he really wants to hear. Rob decides that his ideal girl would be a singer who would "write songs at home and ask me what I thought of them—and maybe even include one of our private little jokes in the liner notes."

High Fidelity is based on a 1995 novel by Nick Hornby, a London writer, and has been directed by Stephen Frears, also British. Frears and his screenwriters (D. V. Devincentis, Steve Pink, Cusack, and Scott Rosenberg) have transplanted the story to Chicago so successfully that it feels like it grew organically out of the funky soil of Lincoln Avenue and Halsted, Old Town and New Town, Rogers Park and Hyde Park, and Wicker Park, where it was shot—those neighborhoods where the workers in the alternative lifestyle industry live, love, and labor.

This is a film about, and also for, not only obsessed clerks in record stores, but the video store clerks who have seen all the movies, and the bookstore employees who have read all the books. Also for bartenders, waitresses, greengrocers in health food stores, kitchen slaves at vegetarian restaurants, the people at GNC who know all the herbs, writers for alternative weeklies, disc jockeys on college stations, salespeople in retro-clothing shops, tattoo artists and those they tattoo, poets, artists, musicians, novelists, and the hip, the pierced, and the lonely. They may not see themselves, but they will recognize people they know.

The Cusack character is someone I have known all my life. He is assembled out of my college friends, the guys at work, people I used to drink with. I also recognize Barry, the character played by Jack Black; he's a type so universal it's a wonder he hasn't been pinned down in a movie before: a blowhard, a self-appointed expert on all matters of musical taste, a monologuist, a guy who would rather tell you his opinion than take your money. Jack Black is himself from this world; he's the lead singer of the group Tenacious D, and it is a measure of his acting ability that when he does finally sing in this movie, we are surprised that he can.

The women I recognize too. They're more casual about romance than most movie characters, maybe because most movies are simpleminded and pretend it is earthshakingly important whether this boy and this girl mate forever, when a lot of young romance is just window-shopping and role-playing, and everyone knows it. You break up, you sigh, you move on. The process is so universal that with some people, you sigh as you meet them, in anticipation.

I am meandering. All I want to say is that *High Fidelity* has no deep significance, does not grow exercised over stupid plot points, savors the rhythms of these lives, sees how pop music is a sound track for everyone's autobiography, introduces us to Rob and makes us hope that he finds happiness, and causes us to leave the theater quite unreasonably happy.

Himalaya ★ ★ ★

NO MPAA RATING, 104 m., 2001

Thinlin Lhondup (Tinle), Gurgon Kyap (Karma), Karma Wangiel (Passang/Tsering), Lhakpa Tsamchoe (Pema), Karma Tenzing Nyima Lama (Norbou). Directed by Eric Valli and produced by Jacques Perrin and Christophe Barratier. Screenplay by Olivier Dazat and Valli.

Himalaya tells the story of a village that since time immemorial has engaged in a winter trek to bring salt to its people and send out goods to be traded. The journeys are conducted by yak caravans. For many years the old chief, Tinle, led the treks, but he retired in favor of his son. Now his son is dead, his body brought back to the village by Karma, who wants to take his place at the head of the caravans.

Tinle (Thinlin Lhondup) is not so sure. He is half-convinced Karma (Gurgon Kyap) has something to do with the death of the son. And he believes the position of honor should remain within his own family. He goes to visit another son, who is a monk in a Buddhist monastery. This son wants to stay where he is. So Tinle defiantly says he will come out of retirement and lead the next caravan. And Karma says, no, he will lead it instead.

So begins *Himalaya*, a film of unusual visual beauty and enormous intrinsic interest. Set in the Dolpo area of Nepal, it has been directed by Eric Valli, a photographer who has lived in Nepal for years, filmed it for *National Geographic*, and made documentaries about it. Now in this fiction film he uses conflict to build his story, but it's clear the narrative is mostly an excuse; this movie is not so much about what its characters do, as about who they are.

It is astonishing to think that lives like this are still possible in the twenty-first century. We are less surprised when we see such treks reflecting modern realities—as in *A Time for Drunken Horses* (2000), about the Kurdish people of Iran, who use mule caravans to transport contraband truck tires into Iraq. We suspect that the story of *Himalaya* re-creates a time that has now ended, but no: Such caravans still exist, and were the subject of *The Saltmen of Tibet*, a 1997 documentary by Ulrike Koch.

Much of the film is simply pictorial, as Karma and Tinle make rival journeys, and Tinle ominously squints at the clear sky and foresees snow. There is one passage of pure suspense, as part of a narrow mountain path slips away, and the yaks and their masters have to traverse a dangerous stretch; we are reminded of similar situations involving trucks in *The Wages of Fear* and *Sorcerer*.

The actors are not experienced and sometimes simply seem to be playing men very much like themselves, but we are not much concerned with subtle drama here. The real movie takes place in our minds, as we think about these people who share the planet with us right now, and yet lead unimaginably different lives. Would it be a trial or a blessing to be a member of a community like this? That would depend, I imagine, on whether your view of the world has expanded to encompass more than villages and salt journeys. There must be something deeply satisfying about knowing your place in an ancient social structure, and fitting into it seamlessly. So I thought as I watched this film, although it did not make me want to lead a yak caravan.

Hollow Man ★ ★

R, 114 m., 2000

Elisabeth Shue (Linda McKay), Kevin Bacon (Sebastian Caine), Josh Brolin (Matthew Kensington), Kim Dickens (Sarah Kennedy), Greg Grunberg (Carter Abbey), Joey Slotnick (Frank Chase), Mary Jo Randle (Janice Walton),

William Devane (Dr. Kramer). Directed by Paul Verhoeven and produced by Douglas Wick and Alan Marshall. Screenplay by Andrew W. Marlowe.

Hollow Man deserves a niche in the Underachievement Hall of Fame right next to *Jack Frost*. That was the movie, you will recall, where a dead father came back as a snowman, and all he could think of to do was advise his kid about a bully at school. Now we get a scientist who becomes invisible, and all he can become is a mad slasher. Does Paul Verhoeven, who directed *Hollow Man,* have such a low opinion of his audience that he thinks all we want is to see (or not see) the invisible man go berserk?

Although the movie will be compared with the 1933 Claude Rains classic, a better parallel is with *The Fly,* David Cronenberg's 1986 film about a scientist who tests his theories on himself and becomes trapped in the nature of the creature he becomes. That film was charged with curiosity. *Hollow Man* uses the change simply as a stunt: Scientist becomes invisible, becomes sex fiend, goes berserk, attacks everyone.

Have today's audiences lost all interest in anything except mayhem, or does Hollywood only think they have? *Hollow Man* stars Kevin Bacon, who in *Flatliners* (1990) was one of a group of medical students who dared to see how close they could come to death and still return to tell the story. That was a film with genuine curiosity. Now he plays Dr. Sebastian Caine, a scientist who perfects an invisibility formula, tests it on animals, and then injects it into himself. But then *Hollow Man* can think of nothing more interesting for him to do than spy on his girlfriend and assault his neighbor.

Too bad. Really too bad, because the movie is supported by some of the most intriguing special effects I've seen. Early in the film, a chemical is pumped into the bloodstream of an invisible gorilla, and we see it racing up an artery to the heart and then fanning out into the circulatory system while the body remains invisible: It's like a road map of the veins. Later we see both the gorilla and the scientist as they gradually lose layers of visibility and then slowly regain them; the intermediate stages are like those see-through pages in high school biology textbooks (exactly like them, even to the see-through genitals).

These effects are astonishing. The movie also has fun with the attempts of the characters to make the invisible visible: They spray him with fire-fighting chemicals, turn on the sprinkler system, splash blood around. All very ingenious, but by then the movie is just a slasher film with a science gimmick.

Why, I'm wondering, would the Pentagon spend a fortune on a secret underground lab to invent this process anyway? It's clear that the invisible man can be sensed by motion and heat detectors. That makes him vulnerable to any security system. Yes, he could sneak into secret meetings, but isn't it cheaper to use spies or electronic bugs? Logical quibbles are out of place in this movie, anyway. It ends with a fireball exploding up an elevator shaft until the flames lick the ankles of the fleeing heroine; a superheated jet of hot gas should reasonably be pushed above the visible flames, incinerating her, but not in this movie.

The heroine, by the way, is Dr. Linda McKay—played by Elisabeth Shue, who won an Oscar nomination for *Leaving Las Vegas.* Here both she and Kevin Bacon do what they can with their roles, which isn't much. The screenplay builds in some jealousy between Dr. Caine, who is McKay's former lover, and Josh Brolin, as her current squeeze. Apparently the invisibility process makes Bacon more animalistic, so that when he spies them together, he goes berserk. Anything will do as the excuse for a twenty-five-minute action sequence in which the monster chases the scientist around the lab like someone who has spent a lot of time studying *The Thing.*

At some kind of mechanical level I suppose the movie works. But it brings nothing to the party except the most simplistic elements. Paul Verhoeven is the director of *RoboCop, Total Recall,* and *Basic Instinct,* films with imagination and wit. *Hollow Man* follows his *Starship Troopers,* in which mankind ventures to the stars in order to squish bugs. Here's a guy who needs an injection of idealism.

Hollywood Ending ★ ★ ½
PG-13, 114 m., 2002

Woody Allen (Val Waxman), Tea Leoni (Ellie), George Hamilton (Ed), Debra Messing (Lori), Mark Rydell (Al Hack), Tiffani Thiessen (Sharon Bates), Treat Williams (Hal), Barney Cheng (Translator). Directed by Woody Allen and produced by Letty Aronson. Screenplay by Allen.

Val Waxman is a movie director going through a slow period in his career. Maybe it's more like a slow decade. He left his last movie project, explaining, "I quit over a big thing." What was that? "They fired me." Then he gets a big break: Galaxie Studios has just green-lighted *While the City Sleeps*, and his ex-wife has convinced the studio head that Val, despite his laundry list of psychosomatic anxieties and neurotic tics, is the right guy to direct it.

Woody Allen's new comedy, *Hollywood Ending*, quickly adds a complication to this setup: Waxman goes blind. It may all be in his mind, but he can't see a thing. For his ever-smiling agent, Al Hack (Mark Rydell), this is insufficient cause to leave the project. Al says he will glide through the picture at Waxman's elbow, and no one will ever notice. When the studio demurs at the agent being on the set, Al and Val recruit another seeing-eye man: the business student (Barney Cheng) who has been hired as the translator for the Chinese cinematographer. The translator says he'll blend right in: "I will practice casual banter."

Further complications: Waxman's ex-wife, Ellie (Tea Leoni), is now engaged to Hal (Treat Williams), the head of Galaxie Studios. Waxman casts his current squeeze, Lori (Debra Messing), to star in the movie, but while Lori is away at a spa getting in shape, costar Sharon (Tiffani Thiessen) moves on Waxman. In his dressing room, she removes her robe while explaining that she is eager to perform sexual favors for all of her directors (Waxman, who cannot see her abundant cleavage, helpfully suggests she advertise this willingness in the *Directors Guild* magazine).

What is Val Waxman's movie about? We have no idea. Neither does Waxman, who agrees with every suggestion so he won't have to make any decisions. He's not only blind but apparently has ears that don't work in stereo, since he can't tell where people are standing by the sound of their voices, and spends much of his time gazing into space. No one notices this, maybe because directors are such gods on movies that they can get away with anything.

The situation is funny, and Allen of course populates it with zingy one-liners, orchestrated with much waving of the hands (he's a virtuoso of body language). But somehow the movie doesn't get over the top. It uses the blindness gimmick in fairly obvious ways, and doesn't bring it to another level—to build on the blindness instead of just depending on it. When Waxman confesses his handicap to the wrong woman—a celebrity journalist—because he thinks he's sitting next to someone he can trust, that's very funny. But too often he's just seen with a vacant stare, trying to bluff his way through conversations.

Why not use the realities of a movie set to suggest predicaments for the secretly blind? Would Val always need to take his translator into the honey wagon with him? Could there be tragic misunderstandings in the catering line? Would he wander unknowingly into a shot? How about the cinematographer offering him a choice of lenses, and he chooses the lens cap? David Mamet's *State and Main* does a better job of twisting the realities of a movie into the materials of comedy.

Because Allen is a great verbal wit and because he's effortlessly ingratiating, I had a good time at the movie even while not really buying it. I enjoyed Tea Leoni's sunny disposition, although she spends too much time being the peacemaker between the two men in her life and not enough time playing a character who is funny in herself. George Hamilton, as a tanned studio flunky, suggests a familiar Hollywood type, the guy who is drawing a big salary for being on the set without anybody being quite sure what he's there for (he carries a golf club to give himself an identity—the guy who carries the golf club). And Mark Rydell smiles and smiles and smiles, as an agent who reasons that anything he has 10 percent of must be an unqualified good thing. As Waxman's seeing eyes, Barney Cheng adds a nice element: Not only is Waxman blind, but he is being given an inexact description of the world through the translator's English, which is always slightly off-track.

I liked the movie without loving it. It's not great Woody Allen, like *Sweet and Lowdown* or *Bullets Over Broadway,* but it's smart and sly, and the blindness is an audacious idea. It also has moments when you can hear Allen editorializing in the dialogue. My favorite is this exchange:

"He has made some very financially successful American films."

"That should tell you everything you need to know about him."

Holy Smoke! ★ ★ ½
R, 114 m., 2000

Kate Winslet (Ruth Barron), Harvey Keitel (P. J. Waters), Julie Hamilton (Miriam [Mum]), Tim Robertson (Gilbert [Dad]), Sophie Lee (Yvonne), Dan Wyllie (Robbie), Paul Goddard (Tim), George Mangos (Yani), Pam Grier (Carol). Directed by Jane Campion and produced by Jan Chapman. Screenplay by Anna and Jane Campion.

Holy Smoke! begins as a movie about the deprogramming of a cult member and ends with the deprogramming of the deprogrammer. It's not even a close call. The cult member is Ruth (Kate Winslet), an Australian who has gone to India and allied herself with a guru. And the deprogrammer is Harvey Keitel, summoned by Ruth's parents; he stalks off the plane like his no-nonsense fix-it man in *Pulp Fiction* and then starts falling to pieces. The movie leaves us wondering why the guru didn't become Ruth's follower too.

The film isn't really about cults at all, but about the struggle between men and women, and it's a little surprising, although not boring, when it turns from a mystic travelogue into a feminist parable. The director is Jane Campion *(The Piano),* who wrote the screenplay with her sister Anna. Like so many Australian films (perhaps even a majority), *Holy Smoke!* suggests that everyone in Australia falls somewhere on the spectrum between goofy and eccentric, none more than characters invariably named Mum and Dad. Parents are totally unhinged beneath a facade of middle-class conventionality; their children seem crazy but like many movie mad

people are secretly saner than anyone else. Campion's first film, *Sweetie,* was an extreme example; *Holy Smoke!* reins in the strangeness a little, although to be sure there's a scene where Keitel wanders the Outback wearing a dress and lipstick, like a passenger who fell off *Priscilla, Queen of the Desert.*

Ruth, the Winslet character, journeys to India and falls under the sway of a mystic guru. Her parents trick her into returning, and hire P. J. Waters (Keitel) to fly over from America and deprogram her. At this point I was hoping perhaps for something like *Ticket to Heaven* (1981), the powerful Canadian film about the struggle for a cult member's mind. But no. The moment Ruth and P.J. face off against each other, their struggle is not over cult beliefs but about the battle between men and women. And P.J., with his obsolete vocabulary of sexual references, is no match for the strong-willed young woman who overwhelms him mentally, physically, and sexually.

Winslet and Keitel are both interesting in the film, and indeed Winslet seems to be following Keitel's long-standing career plan, which is to go with intriguing screenplays and directors and let stardom take care of itself. That may mean he doesn't get paid $20 million a picture, but $20 million roles, with rare exceptions, are dog's bones anyway—because they've been chewed over and regurgitated by too many timid executives. A smaller picture like this, shot out of the mainstream, has a better chance of being quirky and original.

And quirky it is, even if not successful. Maybe it's the setup that threw me off. Ruth comes onscreen as one kind of person—dreamy, escapist, a volunteer for mind-controlling beliefs—and then turns into an articulate spokeswoman for Jane and Anna Campion's ideas. It's also a little disappointing that the film didn't penetrate more deeply into the Indian scenes, instead of using them mostly just as setup for the feminist payoff. And it's difficult to see how the Ruth at the end of the film could have fallen under the sway of the guru at the beginning. Not many radical feminists seek out male gurus in patriarchal cultures.

Home Movie ★ ★ ★

NO MPAA RATING, 65 m., 2002

As themselves: Linda Beech, Francis Mooney, Diana Peden, Ed Peden, Darlene Satrinano, Ben Skora, Bill Tregle, Bob Walker. A documentary film directed by Chris Smith and produced by Barbara Laffey and Susane Preissler.

The five homes in Chris Smith's *Home Movie* are no doubt strange and eccentric. Not everyone would choose to live on a houseboat in alligator country, or in a missile silo, or in a tree house, or in a house modified for the comfort of dozens of cats, or in a house that looks like Rube Goldberg running berserk.

But what is a normal house, anyway? In *The Fast Runner*, we see a civilization that lives in igloos. In *Taiga*, we visit the yurt dwellers of Outer Mongolia. Their homes are at least functional, economical, and organic to the surrounding landscape. It's possible that the most bizarre homestyles on Earth are those proposed by Martha Stewart, which cater to the neuroses of women with paralyzing insecurity. What woman with a healthy self-image could possibly dream of making those table decorations?

The five subjects of *Home Movie* at least know exactly why they live where they do and as they do, and they do not require our permission or approval. There is Bill Tregle, whose Louisiana houseboat is handy for his occupation of trapping, selling, and exhibiting alligators. He catches his dinner from a line tossed from the deck, has electric lights, a microwave and a TV powered by generator, pays no taxes, moves on when he feels like it, and has decorated his interior with the treasures of a lifetime.

Or consider the Pedens, Ed and Diana, who live in a converted missile silo. The concrete walls are so thick that they can have "tornado parties," and there's an easy commute down a buried tunnel from the living space to the work space. True, they had to build a greenhouse on the surface to get some sun or watch the rain, because otherwise, Diana observes, it's too easy to stay underground for days or weeks at a time. Their living room is the silo's former launch center: interesting karma.

Linda Beech speaks little Japanese, yet once starred on a Japanese soap opera. Now she lives in the Hawaiian rain forest, in a tree house equipped with all the comforts of home. To be sure, family photos tend to mildew, but think of the compensations, such as her own waterfall, which provides hydroelectric power for electricity, and also provides her favorite meditation spot, on a carefully positioned "water-watching rock." She can't imagine anyone trying to live without their own waterfall.

Bob Walker and Francis Mooney have dozens of cats. They've renovated the inside of their house with perches, walkways, and tunnels, some of them linking rooms, others ending in hidey-holes. They speculate about how much less their house is worth today than when they purchased it, but they're serene: They seem to live in a mutual daze of cat-loving. The cats seem happy too.

Ben Skora lives in a suburb of Chicago. His house is an inventor's hallucination. Everything is automatic: the doors, which open like pinwheels, the toilets, the lights, the furniture. The hardest task, living in his house, must be to remember where all the switches are and what they govern. He also has a remote-controlled robot that is a hit at shopping malls. The robot will bring him a can of pop, which is nice, although the viewer may reflect that it is easier to get a can out of the refrigerator than build a robot to do it for you. Skora's great masterwork is a ski jump that swoops down from his roof.

Are these people nuts? Who are we to say? I know people whose lives are lived in basement rec rooms. Upstairs they have a living room with the lamps and sofas still protected with the plastic covers from the furniture store. What is the purpose of this room? To be a Living Room Museum? What event will be earth-shaking enough to require the removal of the covers? Do they hope their furniture will appreciate in value?

There is no philosophy, so far as I can tell, behind Chris Smith's film. He simply celebrates the universal desire to fashion our homes for our needs and desires. Smith's previous doc was the great *American Movie*, about the Wisconsin man who wanted to make horror movies, and did, despite all obstacles. Perhaps the message is the same: If it makes you happy and allows you to express your yearnings and dreams, who are we to enforce the rules of middle-class conformity?

273

The House of Mirth ★ ★ ★ ½
PG, 140 m., 2000

Gillian Anderson (Lily Bart), Eric Stoltz
(Lawrence Selden), Dan Aykroyd (Gus Trenor),
Eleanor Bron (Mrs. Peniston), Terry Kinney
(George Dorset), Anthony LaPaglia (Sim
Rosedale), Laura Linney (Bertha Dorset),
Jodhi May (Grace Stepney), Elizabeth
McGovern (Carrie Fisher). Directed by Terence
Davies and produced by Olivia Stewart.
Screenplay by Davies, based on the novel
by Edith Wharton.

Like the Edith Wharton novel that inspired it,
Terence Davies's *The House of Mirth* conceals
rage beneath measured surface appearances.
This is one of the saddest stories ever told
about the traps that society sets for women.
Perhaps its characters fear that if they ever
really spoke their thoughts, their whole house
of cards, or mirth, would tumble down. And
so they speak in code, and people's lives are
disposed of with trivial asides and brittle wit.

The movie tells the story of Lily Bart (Gillian
Anderson), a respectable member of New York
society in her late twenties, who keenly feels it
is time for her to be married. Is there nothing
else she can do? Apparently not; her upbringing has equipped her for no trade except mat-
rimony, and even Lawrence Selden (Eric Stoltz),
her best friend, observes dispassionately: "Isn't
marriage your vocation? Isn't that what you
were brought up for?"

Lily is alone in the world except for a rich
maiden aunt, whom she expects to inherit
from. She lives in a world of lunches and teas,
house parties and opening nights, where she is
no longer a fresh face: "I've been about too
long. People are getting tired of me." But her
life is not unpleasant until a chain of events
destroys her with the thoroughness and indifference of a meat grinder.

She goes to tea at Selden's house, and is seen
leaving by Mr. Rosedale (Anthony LaPaglia).
He knows only bachelors live in the building.
For a woman to go unaccompanied to a man's
rooms is not proof she is a tramp, but might
as well be. Mr. Rosedale guesses something of
Lily's financial situation, and makes her an
offer she refuses. So, in a different way, does
Gus Trenor (Dan Aykroyd), playing one of

those rich men who offer investment advice to
desirable women as if they have only benevolence on their minds.

Lily's social world includes George and
Bertha Dorset (Terry Kinney and Laura Linney). Bertha flaunts her infidelities, and George
is too timid, or well-mannered, to rise to the
bait. She all but insists Lily accompany them
on their yacht in the Mediterranean, and then
gets herself out of a tight spot by a subterfuge
against Lily so cruel and unfair it almost rips
the fabric of the film. After that, Lily is all but
done for, although her descent is gradual.

"Men have minds like moral flypaper,"
Lily's plain cousin Grace observes. "They will
forgive a woman almost anything except the
loss of her good name." As Lily finds her credit
in society running out, she turns to the resources she has left—or thinks she has—and
we see finally that she is defeated. She is prepared for two things in life, to be a rich man's
wife, or to do piecework at poverty wages. The
vise that closes on her in the final scenes is
inexorable.

And yet she could have prevented her fate.
There is the matter of a debt to Gus Trenor.
We modern viewers are thinking that she need
not repay it, that he is a louse and she can save
herself, but that is not the sort of thing that
would occur to Lily Bart. Nor can she accept a
liaison of convenience with Mr. Rosedale. She
cannot keep a job as a rich woman's companion because her reputation is wanting. Everyone knows the truth about her—that she is
not a bad woman but an admirable one—and
yet no one will act on it, because perceptions
are more important than reality. What finally
defeats Lily Bart is her own lack of imagination, her inability to think outside the envelope she was born within.

Gillian Anderson seems an unexpected
choice as Lily. Apparently Terence Davies saw
a still of her in *The Mighty* (1998) and made
her his first choice. Her success on *The X-Files*
might seem to disqualify her, but Anderson's
talent has many notes, and I liked the presence
she brought to Lily Bart. It would be wrong, I
think, to cast the role as a fragile flower; Lily is
a strong, healthy, and competent woman who
has everything she needs to lead a long and
happy life except (1) a husband, or (2) a society that provides for independent women.

Edith Wharton, a sharp and unforgiving chronicler of New York society, knew that, and knew that her own independence was based on her self-employment as a novelist. It is ironic that Virginia Woolf, in *A Room of One's Own*, writes about Jane Austen and other earlier women writers as finding the only profitable and challenging female occupation that could be undertaken in a drawing room, and Wharton was still illustrating that a century later.

The House of Mirth will be compared with Scorsese's *The Age of Innocence*, also based on a Wharton novel. The two directors focus on different sides of Wharton's approach. Wharton as a writer was a contemporary of her great friend Henry James, and also of the rising group of realists like Theodore Dreiser. *The Age of Innocence* is a Jamesian novel, but *The House of Mirth* is more like Dreiser, like an upper-class version of *Sister Carrie*, in which a woman's life is defined by economic determinism. (If Lily had read *Sister Carrie*, indeed, it might have given her some notions about how to survive.) The movie will seem slow to some viewers, unless they are alert to the raging emotions, the cruel unfairness, and the desperation that are masked by the measured and polite words of the characters.

Human Nature ★ ★ ★
R, 96 m., 2002

Tim Robbins (Nathan Bronfman), Patricia Arquette (Lila Jute), Rhys Ifans (Puff), Miranda Otto (Gabrielle), Robert Forster (Nathan's Father), Mary Kay Place (Nathan's Mother), Rosie Perez (Louise). Directed by Michel Gondry and produced by Anthony Bregman, Ted Hope, Spike Jonze, and Charlie Kaufman. Screenplay by Kaufman.

Is human life entirely based on sex, or is that only what it seems like on cable television? *Human Nature*, a comedy written and produced by the writer and director who made us the great gift of *Being John Malkovich*, is a study of three characters at war against their sexual natures.

Lila (Patricia Arquette) fled to the woods at the age of twenty, after hair entirely covered her body. She becomes a famous reclusive nature writer, a very hairy Annie Dillard, but finally returns to civilization because she's so horny. Puff (Rhys Ifans) is a man who was raised as an ape, thinks he's an ape, and is cheerfully eager on all occasions to act out an ape's sexual desires. And Nathan (Tim Robbins) was a boy raised by parents so strict that his entire sexual drive was sublimated into the desire to train others as mercilessly as he was trained.

With these three characters as subjects for investigation, *Human Nature* asks if there is a happy medium between natural impulses and the inhibitions of civilization—or if it is true, as Nathan instructs Puff, "When in doubt, don't ever do what you really want to do." The movie involves these three in a ménage à trois that is (as you can imagine) very complicated, and just in order to be comprehensive in its study of human sexual behavior, throws in a cute French lab assistant (Miranda Otto).

None of which gives you the slightest idea of the movie's screwball charm. The writer, Charlie Kaufman, must be one madcap kinda guy. I imagine him seeming to wear a funny hat even when he's not. His inventions here lead us down strange comic byways, including Disneyesque song-and-dance numbers in which the hairy Arquette dances nude with the cute little animals of the forest. (Her hair, like Salome's veil, prevents us from seeing quite what we think we're seeing, but the MPAA's eyeballs must have been popping out with the strain.)

Early scenes show poor Nathan as a boy, at the dinner table with his parents (Robert Forster and Mary Kay Place), where every meal involves as much cutlery as a diplomatic feast, and using the wrong fork gets the child sent to his room without eating. As an adult, Nathan dedicates his life to training white mice to eat with the right silver, after the male mouse politely pulls out the female mouse's chair for her.

Then he gets a really big challenge, when the ape-man (Ifans) comes into his clutches. Nicknaming him Puff, Nathan keeps him in a Plexiglas cage in his lab, and fits Puff with an electrified collar that jolts him with enough juice to send him leaping spasmodically into the air every time he engages in sexual behavior, which is constantly. Lila, the hairy girl, meanwhile has turned herself over to a sympathetic electrologist (Rosie Perez), who fixes her up with Nathan—who does not know she is covered with hair and, if he did, would be sure it was bad manners.

The movie has nowhere much to go and nothing much to prove, except that Stephen King is correct and if you can devise the right characters and the right situation, the plot will take care of itself—or not, as the case may be. Ifans is so dogged in the determination of his sex drive, despite the electrical shocks, that when the professor sets his final examination at a Hooters-type place, we're grinning before he gets inside the door.

The movie is the feature debut of Michel Gondry, who directed a lot of Bjork's videos and therefore in a sense has worked with characters like these before. His movie is slight without being negligible. If it tried to do anything more, it would fail and perhaps explode, but at this level of manic whimsy, it is just about right. You had better go alone, because in any crowd of four there will be three who find it over their heads, or under their radar. They would really be better off attending *National Lampoon's Van Wilder,* unless you want to go to the trouble of having them fitted with electric collars.

Human Resources ★ ★ ★
NO MPAA RATING, 100 m., 2000

Jalil Lespert (Frank), Jean-Claude Vallod (Father), Chantal Barre (Mother), Veronique de Pandelaere (Sylvie), Michel Begnez (Olivier), Lucien Longueville (Chief Executive), Danielle Melador (Mrs. Arnoux), Pascal Semard (Head of Human Resources). Directed by Laurent Cantet and produced by Caroline Benjo and Carole Scotta. Screenplay by Cantet and Gilles Marchand.

"This is my machine," the father tells his son. He explains its workings. It rotates like this, he says, and then he adds a part, he pushes a lever, and the machine performs a function. "I can do 700 an hour," he says with quiet satisfaction. He has been doing it for thirty years. His body is permanently stooped as if bowing to the machine. He seems hypnotized by continuity: As long as he stays here, doing this, he is alive and serves a function.

His son has broken out of the family's class.

He has gone to college, and now has returned to their small French town as a trainee in the personnel division. The night before his first job interview, his father fearfully briefs him to respect his boss and to play down his own opinion. The father's spirit has long since been broken down into timid subservience.

Human Resources, written and directed by Laurent Cantet, follows the son during his first weeks on the job, gradually revealing itself as an angry and unforgiving look at the way factories can treat employees as machines, and sometimes scrap them. More class-conscious than an American film would be, it shows the son torn between tempting management opportunities and his sense of fairness. He begins to realize that "human resources" is not a benevolent term, but belongs on the same list with "raw materials resources." Humans are simply an element in a production flow chart.

Management is thinking of scaling back. Frank (Jalil Lespert), the son, is involved in the discussions, and suggests a questionnaire that might help employees feel they have input. Mrs. Arnoux (Danielle Melador), the Communist shop steward, is having none of it. She chairs an angry meeting, but her very anger discredits her, and her warnings aren't heeded. Then Frank, poking around on his boss's computer, discovers his questionnaire has been used as a rationale for layoffs, and his dad will be one of those to be fired.

The film is not really driven by specific plot elements. It's not so much about what management does and how the workers fight back as it is about feelings. Consider, for example, that the father (Jean-Claude Vallod) will not strike even after he learns he is going to be fired. He doggedly marches back to his machine like an animal that has learned only one trick. On his days off, he works on another machine in his garage—he seems to have no identity without a machine to give his life a symbiotic partner.

In the town, Frank finds a barrier growing between himself and old friends. There's a shoving match in a bar. He is seen as a sellout. At the same time, he sees through the efforts of his bosses to recruit him to their view. Most of those being fired would have qualified for retirement in a few years, but now won't. That's a particularly vile and common misuse of "human resources," not just in France. When Frank's dad is offered a pension, however, Frank sees the irony: The factory has so broken his father than the old man cannot live without serving his machine. A pension has nothing to do with it.

And yet—Frank doesn't feel merely pity for his father. He also feels shame. Moving up on the class ladder has separated him from his father's tunnel vision, and to his educated eyes, the old man seems pathetic. He is a man almost robbed of speech, of imagination, and when he cries, his wife finds that a wonder rather than a shame.

American films are hardly ever about work, especially hard work, factory work. The most common employment areas in American movies are probably law enforcement, crime, medicine, the law, prostitution, and bartending. The movies have no curiosity about people who get up every day and go out to work hard and earn a living. *Human Resources* is a valuable, heartbreaking film about the way those resources are plugged into a system, drained of their usefulness, and discarded.

Human Traffic ★ ★
R, 84 m., 2000

John Simm (Jip), Lorraine Pilkington (LuLu), Shaun Parkes (Koop), Nicola Reynolds (Nina), Danny Dyer (Moff), Dean Davies (Lee). Directed by Justin Kerrigan and produced by Allan Niblo and Emer McCourt. Screenplay by Kerrigan.

"Act like an adult. Be fake."

So says one of the feckless heroes of *Human Traffic*, a sad comedy about druggies in Wales. This movie is about how he and his friends are already acting like adults. They're right that many adults are fakes, but some adults at least know when they're faking it. These kids are clueless.

They know how to take drugs and feel good. That doesn't require cleverness. When they don't take drugs they don't feel good, partly because of withdrawal, partly because they lack any other avenue to happiness. They possess, for the time being, youth. It is their only capital, and when it is spent, they will lead the rest of their lives empty-handed. They're sheep marching into the slaughter of middle age.

The film takes place in Cardiff, and is mostly about five friends who have jobs of stultifying boredom. They live for the weekends, when they can go out to rave clubs, use ecstasy, heroin, and whatever else they can get their hands on, and pretend for forty-eight hours that they are free. They have high spirits, and their speech possesses the style and wit that can still be heard in those pockets of verbal invention (Ireland is another) where conversation is an art form.

They are, in fact, likable. That's why their comedy is so sad. There must, we think, be something more for them than this dead-end lifestyle. The movie remembers how at a certain age, hanging out with your friends, feeling solidarity against the nine-to-five world, creates a fierce inner joy. They laugh at each other's self-destructiveness. It is funny to get wasted, to almost overdose, to do reckless things, to live dangerously, to flirt with crime and drugs. Why is it funny? Because they're getting away with it. The odds don't apply to them. They're immune. Fate has said they can put unknown substances into their systems and survive. Fate, of course, is a practical joker with a nasty streak, but tell them that.

The director of the film, Justin Kerrigan, is twenty-five. He sees his story from the inside. It's based on his friends. There is no perspective, no angle: He sympathizes with his characters. But he's already escaped their fate. He isn't working in a fast-food outlet at minimum wage. He's a movie director.

I was reminded of Mark Borchardt, the subject of the tragicomic documentary *American Movie*, who dropped out at thirteen or fourteen and started drinking with his friends in the basements of their houses. "I was always watching them, always fascinated by them," he remembers, and today, at thirty-four, while he still plays the same role, he does it on the *Letterman* show, while his friends are still in the basement, or the ground.

Human Traffic is narrated as a pseudo-documentary; the characters take us on a tour of their world, but the real narrator is the director, who could not make the film if he lived as his heroes do. The characters have names, and there is a plot—a plot and a half, in fact. I could name them (all right: Jip, Lulu, Koop, Nina, and Moff). I could describe the plot.

But every weekend has its own plot, and every plot has its own unhappy ending, which is known as Monday morning.

Stories like this can transcend. *Trainspotting* had a certain charm. *SLC Punk* had more wit and fewer drugs. *Kicking and Screaming* was enlightening because it showed that kids of about the same age, given a chance at a decent education, were more interesting and better at entertaining themselves. For the characters in *Human Traffic*, these weekends are as good as it's going to get.

"There is definitely more to their relationships than just going out, taking drugs, and having a good time," says Nicola Reynolds, an actress in the film. "They are strong, strong friendships. The more you go through things together, the more you bond those relationships." Uh-huh. You know the difference between a real friend and a party friend? You have a flat tire. The real friend goes outside in the rain and helps you change it. The party friend says, "Bummer," and buys you a drink.

The Hurricane ★ ★ ★ ½
R, 125 m., 2000

Denzel Washington (Rubin Carter), Vicellous Reon Shannon (Lesera Martin), Deborah Kara Unger (Lisa Peters), Liev Schreiber (Sam Chaiton), John Hannah (Terry Swinton), Dan Hedaya (Della Pesca), Debbie Morgan (Mae Thelma), Clancy Brown (Lieutenant Jimmy Williams), David Paymer (Myron Beldock), Harris Yulin (Leon Friedman), Rod Steiger (Judge Sarokin), Garland Whitt (John Artis). Directed by Norman Jewison and produced by Armyan Bernstein, John Ketcham, and Jewison. Screenplay by Bernstein and Dan Gordon, based on *The 16th Round* by Rubin "Hurricane" Carter and *Lazarus and the Hurricane* by Sam Chaiton and Terry Swinton.

The key moment in *The Hurricane*, which tells the story of a boxer framed for murder, takes place not in a prison cell but at a used-book sale in Toronto. A fifteen-year-old boy named Lesera spends twenty-five cents to buy his first book, the autobiography of the boxer Rubin "Hurricane" Carter. As he reads it, he becomes determined to meet the boxer and support his fight for freedom, and that decision leads to redemption.

The case and cause of Hurricane Carter are well known; Bob Dylan wrote a song named "The Hurricane," and I remember Nelson Algren's house sale when the Chicago novelist moved to New Jersey to write a book about Carter. Movie stars and political candidates made the pilgrimage to Carter's prison, but his appeals were rejected and finally his case seemed hopeless.

This film tells his story—the story of a gifted boxer (Denzel Washington) who was framed for three murders in Patterson, New Jersey, and lost nineteen years of his life because of racism, corruption, and—perhaps most wounding—indifference. In the film, the teenage boy (Vicellous Reon Shannon), who is from New Jersey, enlists his Canadian foster family to help Carter, and they find new evidence for his defense attorneys that eventually leads to his release. The villain is a cop named Pesca (Dan Hedaya), who essentially makes it his lifelong business to harm Carter.

Norman Jewison's film starts slowly, with Carter's early years and his run-ins with Pesca. In my notes I wrote: "If this is going to be the story of a persecuting cop, we need to know him as more than simply the instrument of evil"—as a human being rather than a plot convenience. We never do. Pesca from beginning to end is there simply to cause trouble for Carter. Fortunately, *The Hurricane* gathers force in scenes where Carter refuses to wear prison clothing, and learns to separate himself mentally from his condition. Then young Lesera enters the picture, and two people who might seem to be without hope find it from one another.

This is one of Denzel Washington's great performances, on a par with his work in *Malcolm X*. I wonder if *The Hurricane* is not Jewison's indirect response to an earlier controversy. Jewison was preparing *Malcolm X* with Washington when Spike Lee argued that a white man should not direct that film. Jewison stepped aside, Lee made a powerful film with Washington—and now Jewison has made another. Washington as Hurricane Carter is spare, focused, filled with anger and pride. There is enormous force when he tells his teenage visitor and his friends, "Do not write me. Do not visit me. Find it in your hearts to not weaken me with your love."

But the Canadians don't obey. They move

near to Trenton State Prison, they meet with his lead defense attorneys (David Paymer and Harris Yulin), they become amateur sleuths who help take the case to the New Jersey Supreme Court in a do-or-die strategy. It always remains a little unclear, however, just exactly who the Canadians are, or what their relationship is. They're played by Deborah Kara Unger, Liev Schreiber, and John Hannah, they share a household, they provide a home for Lesera, a poor African-American kid from a troubled background, and we wonder: Are they a political group? An unconventional sexual arrangement?

I learn from an article by Selwyn Raab, who covered the case for the *New York Times,* that they were in fact a commune. Raab's article, which appeared the day before the film's New York opening, finds many faults with the facts in *The Hurricane.* He says Carter's defense attorneys deserve much more credit than the Canadians. That Carter was not framed by one cop with a vendetta, but victimized by the entire system. That Carter's codefendant, John Artis (Garland Whitt), was a more considerable person than he seems in the film. That events involving the crime and the evidence have been fictionalized in the film. That Carter later married the Unger character, then divorced her. That Lesera broke with the commune when it tried for too much control of his life.

News travels fast. Several people have told me dubiously that they heard the movie was "fictionalized." Well, of course it was. Those who seek the truth about a man from the film of his life might as well seek it from his loving grandmother. Most biopics, like most grandmothers, see the good in a man and demonize his enemies. They pass silently over his imprudent romances. In dramatizing his victories, they simplify them. And they provide the best roles to the most interesting characters. If they didn't, we wouldn't pay to see them.

The Hurricane is not a documentary but a parable, in which two lives are saved by the power of the written word. We see Carter's concern early in the film that the manuscript of his book may be taken from his cell (it is protected by one of several guards who develop respect for him). We see how his own reading strengthens him; his inspirations include Malcolm X. And we see how his book, which he hoped would win his freedom, does so—not because of its initial sales, readers, and reviews, but because one kid with a quarter is attracted to Hurricane's photo on the cover. And then the book wins Lesera's freedom too.

This is strong stuff, and I was amazed, after feeling some impatience in the earlier reaches of the film, to find myself so deeply absorbed in its second and third acts, until at the end I was blinking at tears. What affects me emotionally at the movies is never sadness, but goodness. I am not a weeper, and have only really lost it at one film *(Do the Right Thing),* but when I get a knot in my throat it is not because Hurricane Carter is framed, or loses two decades in prison, but that he continues to hope, and that his suffering is the cause for Lesera's redemption.

That is the parable Norman Jewison has told, aiming for it with a sure storyteller's art and instinct. The experts will always tell you how a movie got its facts wrong (Walter Cronkite is no doubt correct that Oliver Stone's *JFK* is a fable). But can they tell you how they would have made the movie better? Would *The Hurricane* have been stronger as the story of two selfless lawyers doing pro bono work for years? And a complex network of legal injustice? And a freed prisoner and a kid disillusioned with a commune? Maybe. Probably not.

I

I Am Sam ★ ★
PG-13, 133 m., 2002

Sean Penn (Sam Dawson), Michelle Pfeiffer (Rita), Dakota Fanning (Lucy Dawson), Dianne Wiest (Annie), Doug Hutchison (Ifty), Stanley DeSantis (Robert), Brad Silverman (Brad), Joseph Rosenberg (Joe), Richard Schiff (Turner), Laura Dern (Randy). Directed by Jessie Nelson and produced by Marshall Herskovitz, Nelson, Richard Solomon, and Edward Zwick. Screenplay by Kristine Johnson and Nelson.

"Daddy, did God mean for you to be like this, or was it an accident?"

That's little Lucy Dawson, asking her father why he isn't quite like other people. She's a bright kid and figures out the answer herself, and when a classmate at grade school asks, "Why does your father act like a retard?" she explains, "He is."

I Am Sam stars Sean Penn as Lucy's dad, Sam, who has the IQ of a seven-year-old but is trying to raise the daughter he fathered with a homeless woman. The mother disappeared right after giving birth (her farewell words: "All I wanted was a place to sleep"), and now Sam is doing his best to cope, although sometimes Lucy has to help him with her homework. Eventually Lucy decides to stop learning so she won't get ahead of her dad. "I don't want to read if you can't," she tells him.

Sam loves the Beatles (his favorite is George). He named his daughter after "Lucy in the Sky With Diamonds," and has learned most of life's lessons from Beatles songs. The lesson *I Am Sam* wants to teach us is, "All you need is love." This is not quite strictly true. Sam loves his daughter more than anyone else, and she loves him, but it will take more than love for him to see her through grade school and adolescence and out into the world. Since the movie does not believe this, it has a serious disagreement with most of the audience.

Sean Penn does as well as can be expected with Sam, but it is painful to see an actor of his fire and reach locked into a narrow range of emotional and intellectual responses. Not long ago a veteran moviegoer told me that when he sees an actor playing a mentally retarded person, he is reminded of a performer playing "Lady of Spain" on an accordion: The fingers fly, but are the song or the instrument worthy of the effort? The kind of performance Sean Penn delivers in *I Am Sam*, which may look hard, is easy compared, say, to his amazing work in Woody Allen's *Sweet and Lowdown*. As Robert Kohner observes in his *Variety* review: "In a way, Edward Norton's turn in *The Score*, in which his thief used a mental handicap as a disguise, gave the trade secret away when it comes to this sort of performance."

The movie sets up the Department of Children and Family Services and its attorney as the villains when they take Lucy away from Sam and try to place her with a foster family. The heroine is a high-velocity Beverly Hills lawyer named Rita (Michelle Pfeiffer), who takes Sam's case on a pro bono basis to prove to the other people in her office that she's not a selfish bitch. This character and performance would be perfect in an edgy comedy, but they exist in a parallel universe to the world of this film.

Sam has the kinds of problems that come up in story conferences more than in life. For example, he's sitting in a diner when an attractive young woman smiles at him. He smiles back. She comes over and asks him if he would like to have a good time. He says he sure would. Then a cop pounces and arrests him for frequenting a prostitute. Back at the station, the cop admits, "This is the first time in nineteen years I actually believe a guy who says he didn't know she was a hooker." Hey, it's the first time in history that a man has been arrested on sex charges for talking to a woman in a diner before any clothes have come off, money has changed hands, or services have been discussed.

The movie climaxes in a series of courtroom scenes, which follow the time-honored formulas for such scenes, with the intriguing difference that this time the evil prosecutor (Richard Schiff) seems to be making good sense. At one point he turns scornfully to the Pfeiffer character and says, "This is an anecdote for you at some luncheon, but I'm here every day. You're out the door, but you know who I see come back? The child." Well, he's right, isn't he?

The would-be adoptive mother, played by Laura Dern, further complicates the issue by not being a cruel child-beater who wants the monthly state payments, but a loving, sensitive mother who would probably be great for Lucy. Sam more or less understands this, but does the adoptive mother? As the film ends, the issue is in doubt.

I Am Sam is aimed at audiences who will relate to the heart-tugging relationship between Sam and Lucy (and young Dakota Fanning does a convincing job as the bright daughter). Every device of the movie's art is designed to convince us Lucy must stay with Sam, but common sense makes it impossible to go the distance with the premise. You can't have heroes and villains when the wrong side is making the best sense.

Ice Age ★ ★ ★
PG, 88 m., 2002

Denis Leary (Diego the Saber-Toothed Tiger), John Leguizamo (Sid the Sloth), Ray Romano (Manfred the Mammoth), Goran Visnjic (Soto the Saber-Toothed Tiger), Jack Black (Zeke), Tara Strong (Roshan), Cedric the Entertainer (Rhino). Directed by Chris Wedge and produced by Lori Forte. Screenplay by Peter Ackerman, Michael Berg, and Michael Wilson.

Ice Age is a pleasure to look at and scarcely less fun as a story. I came to scoff and stayed to smile. I confess the premise did not inspire me: A woolly mammoth, a saber-toothed tiger, and a sloth team up to rescue a human baby and return it to its parents. Uh-huh. But the screenplay is sly and literate, and director Chris Wedge's visual style so distinctive and appealing that the movie seduced me.

The film takes place during a southward migration of species during a great ice age. Such migrations took place over millennia and were not the pre-Cambrian equivalent of going to Florida for the winter months, but no matter: As the ice packs advance, the animals retreat. There is no time to lose. Baby mammoths, playing in a tar pit, are told by their parents to hurry up: "You can play Extinction later."

We meet Manfred the Mammoth (voice by Ray Romano) and Sid the Sloth (John Legui-

zamo). Of course they can speak. (It is the humans, they believe, who have not yet mastered language.) When Sid and Manfred come upon a small, helpless human child, they decide to protect it and return it to its parents—even though those same parents, they know, have developed weapons for killing them. Along the trail they are joined by Diego the Saber-Toothed Tiger (Denis Leary), who has a hidden agenda. They are potentially each other's dinners, and yet through Sid's insouciance and Manfred's bravery in saving Diego from certain death, they bond and become friends.

It is true that altruism is a positive evolutionary trait; a species with individuals willing to die for the survival of the race is a species that will get somewhere in the Darwinian sweepstakes. But listen closely. When Diego the Saber-Toothed Tiger asks Manfred the Mammoth why he saved him, Manfred replies, "That's what you do as a herd." Yes, absolutely. But herds are by definition made up of members of the same species (and tigers are not herd animals anyway). If Manfred's philosophy were to get around in the animal kingdom, evolution would break down, overpopulation would result, there would be starvation among the nonvegetarians, and it would be an ugly picture. Much of the serenity and order of nature depends on eating the neighbors.

Ice Age does not preach Darwinian orthodoxy, however, but a kinder, gentler worldview: Ice Age meets New Age. And the philosophy scarcely matters anyway, since this is an animated comedy. Enormous advances have been made in animation technology in recent years, as computers have taken over the detail work and freed artists to realize their visions. But few movies have been as painterly as *Ice Age*, which begins with good choices of faces for the characters (note the tiger's underslung jaw and the sloth's outrigger eyes). The landscape is convincing without being realistic, the color palate is harmonious, the character movements include little twists, jiggles, hesitations, and hops that create personality. And the animals blossom as personalities.

That's because of the artwork, the dialogue, and the voice-over work by the actors; the filmmakers have all worked together to really see and love these characters, who are not "cartoon animals" but as quirky and individual as human actors, and more engaging than most.

I would suggest the story sneaks up and eventually wins us over, except it starts the winning process in its very first shots, showing a twitchy squirrel desperately trying to bury an acorn in an icy wilderness. We follow the progress of this squirrel all through the picture, as a counterpoint to the main action, and he is such a distinctive, amusing personality I predict he'll emerge as the hero of a film of his own. ☞

I Dreamed of Africa ★ ★
PG-13, 112 m., 2000

Kim Basinger (Kuki Gallmann), Vincent Perez (Paolo Gallmann), Liam Aiken (Emanuele [Seven]), Garrett Strommen (Emanuele [Seventeen]), Eva Marie Saint (Franca), Daniel Craig (Declan Fielding), Lance Reddick (Simon), Connie Chiume (Wanjiku). Directed by Hugh Hudson and produced by Stanley R. Jaffe and Allyn Stewart. Screenplay by Paula Milne and Susan Shilliday, based on the book by Kuki Gallmann.

It's strange to see *I Dreamed of Africa* at a time when the papers are filled with stories of white farmers being murdered in Zimbabwe. Here is the story of an Italian couple who move to the highlands of Kenya in 1972, buy a ranch near the Great Rift Valley, and lead lives in which the Africans drift about in the background, vaguely, like unpaid extras. Is it really as simple as that? The realities of contemporary Africa are simply not dealt with.

A shame, since Kuki Gallmann is a real woman and still lives on Ol Ari Nyiro, a 100,000-acre ranch in Kenya that she has made into a showcase farm and a wildlife conservancy. I know this because of her Web page (www.gallmannkenya.org); the movie never makes it very clear how the Gallmanns support themselves—it's not by working, apparently. Paolo is away for days at a time, hunting and fishing with his friends, and Kuki doesn't seem deeply engaged with the land, either (her attempt to create a dirt dam begins when she inadvertently pulls down a barn, and ends with the tractor stuck in the mud).

The real Kuki Gallmann must have arrived at an accommodation with Africa and Africans,

and with the Kenyan government. The Kuki in the movie has a few brief conversations in Swahili with her farm foreman and laborers, but devotes most of her attention to the landscape, which is indeed breathtaking (the film was shot on the ranch and in South African game preserves). The only social commentary we get, repeated three times, is, "Things have a different rhythm here."

Kuki is played by Kim Basinger, who is ready to do more than the screenplay allows. She is convincing throughout, especially in a scene where trouble strikes her son, Emanuele (Garrett Strommen)—her panic is real, but so is her competence as she tries to deal with the emergency. Her frustration with her husband, Paolo (Vincent Perez), is also real, but mundane (frustrated at his extended hunting trips and general irresponsibility, she throws a handful of pasta at him).

Her life is interrupted from time to time by visits from her mother (Eva Marie Saint), who begs her to return to Italy, but no, she belongs to the land, learns from experience, and tries to bring good out of the tragedies in her life by becoming a conservationist and a leader in the fight against poaching.

All admirable. But Hugh Hudson's film plays curiously like a friendly documentary of her life, especially with the voice-over narration that sounds like it belongs in an idealistic travelogue. There is a lack of drama and telling detail. When events happen, they seem more like set pieces than part of the flow. Consider the big storm that blows up, toppling the windmill and blowing the thatch from the ranch house roof. It strikes, it is loud and fierce, and then it is over, and after one more shot, it is forgotten. An entry in a diary, growing from nothing, leading to nothing, but occupying screen time. As is the scene where Kuki, Paolo, and her mother drive a Range Rover down a rough road and it gets stuck in the mud (that happens to her a lot). What to do? They get out and walk home. The film doesn't even show them arriving there.

Watching *I Dreamed of Africa*, I was reminded that one often meets people who have led fascinating lives, but only rarely people who can tell fascinating stories. The events don't make the story; the storytelling does. Russell Baker or Frank McCourt can make human sagas out of everyday memories. Generals who have led thousands into battle can write memoirs of stultifying dullness. Kuki Gallmann has led a fascinating life, yes, but either she's not remembering the whole truth, or she should have made up more. The film doesn't sing with urgency and excitement, and we attend it in the same way we listen politely to the stories of a hostess who must have really been something in her day.

The Importance of Being Ernest
★ ★ ★
PG, 100 m., 2002

Rupert Everett (Algernon Moncrieff), Colin Firth (Jack Worthing), Reese Witherspoon (Cecily Cardew), Judi Dench (Lady Bracknell), Frances O'Connor (Gwendolen Fairfax), Tom Wilkinson (Dr. Chasuble), Anna Massey (Miss Prism), Edward Fox (Lane). Directed by Oliver Parker and produced by Uri Fruchtmann and Barnaby Thompson. Screenplay by Parker, based on the play by Oscar Wilde.

Be careful what you ask for; you might get it. Recently I deplored the lack of wit in *Star Wars: Episode II—Attack of the Clones*, which has not one line of quotable dialogue. Now here is *The Importance of Being Earnest*, so thick with wit it plays like a reading from *Bartlett's Familiar Quotations*. I will demonstrate. I have here the complete text of the Oscar Wilde play, which I have downloaded from the Web. I will hit "page down" twenty times and quote the first complete line from the top of the screen:

"All women become like their mothers. That is their tragedy. No man does. That's his."

Now the question is, does this sort of thing appeal to you? Try these:

"Really, if the lower orders don't set us a good example, what on earth is the use of them?"

"To lose one parent, Mr. Worthing, may be regarded as a misfortune. To lose both looks like carelessness."

It appeals to me. I yearn for a world in which every drawing room is a stage, and we but players on it. But does anyone these days know what a drawing room is? The Universal Studios theme park has decided to abolish its characters dressed like the Marx Brothers and Laurel and Hardy because "a majority of people no longer recognize them." I despair. How can people recognize wit who begin with only a half-measure of it?

Oscar Wilde's *The Importance of Being Earnest* is a comedy constructed out of thin air. It is not really about anything. There are two romances at the center, but no one much cares whether the lovers find happiness together. Their purpose is to make elegant farce out of mistaken identities, the class system, mannerisms, egos, rivalries, sexual warfare, and verbal playfulness.

Oliver Parker's film begins with music that is a little too modern for the period, circa 1895, following the current fashion in anachronistic movie scores. It waltzes us into the story of two men who are neither one named Ernest and who both at various times claim to be. Jack Worthing (Colin Firth) calls himself Jack in the country and Ernest in town. In the country, he is the guardian of the charming Miss Cecily Cardew (Reese Witherspoon), who is the granddaughter of the elderly millionaire who adopted Jack after finding him as an infant in a handbag he was handed in error at the cloakroom in Victoria Station. When Jack grows bored with the country, he cites an imaginary younger brother named Ernest who lives in London and must be rescued from scrapes with the law.

This imaginary person makes perfect sense to Jack's friend Algernon Moncrieff (Rupert Everett), who lives in town but has a fictitious friend named Bunbury who lives in the country and whose ill health provides Algernon an excuse to get out of town. I have gone into such detail about these names and alternate identities because the entire play is constructed out of such silliness, and to explain all of it would require—well, the play.

In town Jack is much besotted by Gwendolen Fairfax (Frances O'Connor), daughter of the formidable Lady Bracknell (Judi Dench), Algernon's aunt, who is willing to consider Jack as a suitor for the girl but nonplussed to learn that he has no people—none at all—and was indeed left in a bag at the station. Thus her remark about his carelessness in losing both parents.

Algernon in the meantime insinuates himself into the country estate where young Cecily is being educated under the watchful eye of Miss Prism (Anna Massey), the governess; eventually all of the characters gather at the manor house, Woolton, where there's some confusion since Algernon has taken the name Ernest for his visit and proposed to Cecily, so that when Cecily meets Gwendolen, they both believe they are engaged to Ernest, although Cecily, of course, doesn't know that in town Gwendolen knows Jack as Ernest.

But now I have been lured into the plot again. The important thing about *The Importance* is that all depends on the style of the actors, and Oliver Parker's film is well cast. Reese Witherspoon, using an English accent that sounds convincing to me, is charming as Jack's tender ward, who of course falls for Algernon. She is a silly, flighty girl, just right for Algernon, for whom romance seems valuable primarily as a topic of conversation. Frances O'Connor is older and more sensuous as Gwendolen, and gently encourages the shy Jack to argue his case ("Mr. Worthing, what have you got to say to me?"). Judi Dench keeps a stern eye on the would-be lovers and a strong hand on the tiller.

The Importance of Being Earnest is above all an exercise in wit. There is nothing to be learned from it, no moral, no message. It adopts what one suspects was Wilde's approach to sex— more fun to talk about than to do. As Algernon observes, romance dies when a proposal is accepted: "The very essence of romance is uncertainty." Wilde takes this as his guide. When the play's uncertainties have all been exhausted, the play ends. The last line ("I've now realized for the first time in my life the vital importance of being earnest") takes on an interesting spin if we know that "earnest" was a vernacular term for "gay" in 1895. Thus the closing line may subvert the entire play, although not to the surprise of anyone who has been paying attention.

Innocence ★ ★ ★ ★

NO MPAA RATING, 94 m., 2001

Julia Blake (Claire), Charles "Bud" Tingwell (Andreas), Terry Norris (John), Kristien Van Pellicom (Young Claire), Kenny Aernouts (Young Andreas). Directed and produced by Paul Cox. Screenplay by Cox.

Here is the most passionate and tender love story in many years, so touching because it is not about a story, not about stars, not about a plot, not about sex, not about nudity, but about *love itself.* True, timeless, undefeated love. *Innocence* tells the story of two people who were lovers in Belgium as teenagers and discover each other, incredibly, both living in Adelaide, Australia, in their late sixties. They meet for tea and there is a little awkward small talk and then suddenly they realize that all the old feelings are still there. They are still in love. And not in some sentimental version of love for the twilight years, but in mad, passionate, demanding, forgiving, accepting love.

Paul Cox's *Innocence* is like a great lifting up of the heart. It is all the more affirming because it is not told in grand, phony gestures, but in the details of the daily lives of these two people. Life accumulates routines, obligations, habits, and inhibitions over the years, and if they are going to face their feelings then they're going to have to break out of long, safe custom and risk everything.

Their names are Claire (Julia Blake) and Andreas (Charles "Bud" Tingwell). Both actors are respected in Australia, both unknown in North America, which is all the better, because the purity of this story would be diffused by the presence of familiar faces (perhaps, for example, *The Bridges of Madison County* would have seemed riskier without the familiarity of Clint Eastwood and Meryl Streep). Andreas is a retired music teacher. His wife died thirty years ago. Claire has long been married to John (Terry Norris), in a marriage she thinks, in that bittersweet phrase, will see her out. Both Claire and Andreas have children, friends, people who count on their predictability. How, for example, does Andreas's housekeeper of many years feel when she discovers (as a housekeeper must) that he is sleeping with someone?

Not that sleeping with someone is that easy. In the movies, characters fall into bed with the casual ease of youth or experience, and no film ever stops to consider that questions of modesty, fear, or shyness might be involved. Paul Cox is a director who never loses sight of the humor even in the most fraught situations, and there is a moment in the film that is just about perfect, when Claire and Andreas find themselves at last unmistakably alone in a bedroom, and she says: "If we're going to do this—let's do it like grown-ups. First, close the curtains. Then, close your eyes."

Innocence has no villains. The treatment of John, Claire's husband, is instructive. He is not made into a monster who deserves to be dumped. He is simply a creature of long habit, a man who is waiting it out, who wears the blinders of routine, who expects his life will continue more or less in the same way until accident or illness brings it to a close. When Claire decides to tell him about Andreas ("I'm too old to lie"), his reaction is a study in complexities, and Paul Cox knows human nature deeply enough to observe that in addition to feeling betrayed, disappointed, and hurt, John also feels—well, although he doesn't acknowledge it, somehow grateful for the excitement. At last something unexpected has happened in the long slow march of his life.

The casting of Blake and Tingwell must have been a delicate matter. It is necessary for them to look their age (unlike aging Hollywood stars who seem stuck at forty-five until they die). But they must not seem dry and brittle, as if left on the shelf too long. Both of them seem touchable, warm, healthy, alive to tenderness and humor. And there is a sweet macho stubbornness in Tingwell's Andreas, who refuses to accept the world's verdict that he must be over "that sort of thing" at "his age." He is not over it, because, as he writes her in the letter that brings them together, he always imagined them on a journey together, and if she is still alive then the possibility of that journey is alive. If sixty-nine is a little late to continue what was started at nineteen—what is the alternative?

Many things happen in the movie that I have not hinted at. You must share their discoveries as they happen. By the end, if you are like me, you will feel that something transcendent has taken place. This is the kind of film that makes critics want to reach out and shake their readers. Andrew Sarris, for example, who usually maintains a certain practiced objectivity, writes: "The climax of the film is accompanied by a thrilling musical score that lifts the characters to a sublime metaphysical level such as is seldom attained in the cinema." Then he goes on to call *Innocence* a "film for the ages." You see what I mean.

For myself, *Innocence* is a song of joy and hope, and like its characters it is grown up. Here is a movie that believes love leads to sex, made at a time when movies believe that sex leads to love. But sex is only mechanical unless each holds the other like priceless treasure, to be defended against all of the hazards of the world. This movie is so wise about love it makes us wonder what other love stories think they are about.

Insomnia ★ ★ ★ ½
R, 118 m., 2002

Al Pacino (Will Dormer), Robin Williams (Walter Finch), Hilary Swank (Ellie Burr), Martin Donovan (Hap Eckhart), Maura Tierney (Rachel), Jonathan Jackson (Randy Stetz). Directed by Christopher Nolan and produced by Broderick Johnson, Paul Junger Witt, Andrew A. Kosove, and Edward McDonnell. Screenplay by Hillary Seitz, Nikolaj Frobenius, and Erik Skjoldbjaerg.

He looks exhausted when he gets off the plane. Troubles are preying on him. An investigation by Internal Affairs in Los Angeles may end his police career. And now here he is in—where the hell is this?—Nightmute, Alaska, land of the midnight sun, investigating a brutal murder. The fuels driving Detective Will Dormer are fear and exhaustion. They get worse.

Al Pacino plays the veteran cop, looking like a man who has lost all hope. His partner, Hap Eckhart (Martin Donovan), is younger, more resilient, and may be prepared to tell the Internal Affairs investigators what they want to know—information that would bring the older man down. They have been sent up north to help with a local investigation, flying into Nightmute in a two-engine prop plane that skims low over jagged ice ridges. They'll be assisting a local cop named Ellie Burr (Hilary Swank), who is still fresh with the newness of her job.

Insomnia, the first film directed by Christopher Nolan since his famous *Memento* (2001), is a remake of a Norwegian film of the same name, made in 1998 by Erik Skjoldbjaerg. That was a strong, atmospheric, dread-heavy film, and so is this one. Unlike most remakes, the Nolan *Insomnia* is not a pale retread, but a re-examination of the material, like a new production of a good play. Stellan Skarsgard, who starred in the earlier film, took an existential approach to the character; he seemed weighed down by the moral morass he was trapped in. Pacino takes a more physical approach: How much longer can he carry this burden?

The story involves an unexpected development a third of the way through, and then the introduction of a character we do not really expect to meet, not like this. The development is the same in both movies; the character is much more important in this new version, adding a dimension I found fascinating. Spoilers will occur in the next paragraph, so be warned.

The pivotal event in both films, filmed much alike, is a shoot-out in a thick fog during a stakeout. The Pacino character sets a trap for the killer, but the suspect slips away in the fog, and then Pacino, seeing an indistinct figure loom before him, shoots and kills Hap—his partner from L.A. It is easy enough to pin the murder on the escaping killer, except that one person knows for sure who did it: the escaping killer himself.

In the Norwegian film, the local female detective begins to develop a circumstantial case against the veteran cop. In a nice development in the rewrite (credited to original authors Nikolaj Frobenius and Erik Skjoldbjaerg, working with Hillary Seitz), the killer introduces himself into the case as sort of Pacino's self-appointed silent partner.

The face of the killer, the first time we see it, comes as a shock, because by now we may have forgotten Robin Williams was even in the film. He plays Walter Finch, who does not really consider himself a murderer, although his killing was cruel and brutal. These things happen. Everyone should be forgiven one lapse. Right, detective? Pacino, sleepless in a land where the sun mercilessly never sets, is trapped: If he arrests Finch, he exposes himself and his own cover-up. And the local detective seems to suspect something.

Unusual for a thriller to hinge on issues of morality and guilt, and Nolan's remake does not avoid the obligatory Hollywood requirement that all thrillers must end in a shoot-out. There is also a scene involving a chase across floating logs, and a scene where a character is trapped underwater. These are thrown in as—what? Sops for the cinematically impaired, I suppose. Only a studio executive could explain why we need perfunctory action, just for action's sake, in a film where the psychological suspense is so high.

Pacino and Williams are very good together. Their scenes work because Pacino's character, in regarding Williams, is forced to look at a mirror of his own self-deception. The two faces are a study in contrasts. Pacino's is lined, weary, dark circles under his eyes, his jaw slack with fatigue. Williams has the smooth, open face of a true believer, a man convinced of his own case. In this film and *One Hour Photo,* which played at Sundance 2002, Williams reminds us that he is a considerable dramatic talent—and that, while over the years he has chosen to appear in some comedic turkeys (*Death to Smoochy* leaps to mind), his serious films are almost always good ones.

Why Christopher Nolan took on this remake is easy to understand. *Memento* was one of a kind; the thought of another film based on a similar enigma is exhausting. *Insomnia* is a film with a lot of room for the director, who establishes a distinctive far-north location, a world where the complexities of the big city are smoothed out into clear choices. The fact that it is always daylight is important: The dilemma of this cop is that he feels people are always looking at him, and he has nowhere to hide, not even in his nightmares.   ☞

In the Bedroom ★ ★ ★ ★
R, 130 m., 2001

Tom Wilkinson (Matt Fowler), Sissy Spacek (Ruth Fowler), Nick Stahl (Frank Fowler), William Mapother (Richard Strout), Marisa Tomei (Natalie Strout), William Wise (Willis Grinnel), Celia Weston (Katie Grinnel), Karen Allen (Marla Keyes). Directed by Todd Field and produced by Field, Ross Katz, and Graham Leader. Screenplay by Robert Festinger and Field, based on a short story by Andre Dubus.

Todd Field's *In the Bedroom* only slowly reveals its real subject, in a story that has a shocking reversal at the end of the first act, and then looks more deeply than we could have guessed into the lives of its characters. At first it seems to be about a summer romance. At the end, it's about revenge—not just to atone for a wound, but to prove a point. The film involves love and violence, and even some thriller elements, but it is not about those things. It is about two people so trapped in opposition that one of them must break.

The story opens in sunshine and romance. Frank Fowler (Nick Stahl) is in love with Natalie Strout (Marisa Tomei). He'll be a new graduate student in the autumn. She is in her thirties, has two children, is estranged from Richard (William Mapother), who is a rich kid and an abusive husband. Frank's parents are worried.

"This is not some sweetie from Vassar you can visit on holidays," his mother tells him. "You're not in this alone."

"We're not serious, Mom," Frank says. "It's a summer thing."

"I see," says his mother. She sees clearly that Frank really does love Natalie—and she also sees that Frank's father may be vicariously enjoying the relationship, proud that his teenage son has conquered an attractive woman.

Ruth Fowler (Sissy Spacek) is a choral director at the local high school. Her husband, Matt (Tom Wilkinson), is the local doctor in their Maine village. On the local social scale, they are a step above the separated Natalie and her husband, whose money comes from the local fish business. Is she a snob? She wouldn't think so. The Fowlers pride themselves on being intelligent, open-minded, able to talk about things with their son (who does not want to talk about anything with them). We sense that their household accommodates enormous silences; that the parents and their son have each retreated to a personal corner to nurse wounds.

Then something happens. A review should not tell you what it is. It changes our expectations for the story, which turns out to be about matters more deeply embedded in the heart than we could have imagined. The film unfolds its true story, which is about the marriage of Matt and Ruth—about how hurt and sadness turns to anger and blame. There are scenes as true as movies can make them, and even when the story develops thriller elements, they are redeemed, because the movie isn't about what happens, but about why.

In the Bedroom is the first film directed by Todd Field, an actor *(Eyes Wide Shut, The Haunting)*, and one of the best-directed films this year. It's based on a story by the late Andre Dubus, the Massachusetts-based writer who died in 1999, and who worked with Field on the adaptation before his death. It works with indirection; the events on the screen are markers for secret events in the hearts of the characters, and the deepest insight is revealed, in a way, only in the last shot.

Every performance has perfect tone: Nick Stahl as the man who is half in love with a woman and half in love with being in love; Marisa Tomei, who is wiser than her young lover, and protective toward him, because she understands better than he does the problems they face; William Mapother as the abusive husband, never more frightening than when he tries to be conciliatory and apologetic; William Wise and Celia Weston as the Grinnels, the Fowlers' best friends.

And Sissy Spacek and Tom Wilkinson. They know exactly what they're doing, they understand their characters down to the ground, they are masters of the hidden struggle beneath the surface. Spacek plays a reasonable and civil wife and mother who has painful issues of her own; there is a scene where she slaps someone, and it is the most violent and shocking moment in a violent film. Wilkinson lives through his son more than he admits, and there is a scene where he surprises Frank and Natalie alone together, and finds a kind of quiet relish in their embarrassment. When Matt and Ruth lash out at each other, when the harsh accusations are said aloud, we are shocked but not surprised; these hard notes were undertones in their civilized behavior toward each other. Not all marriages can survive hard times.

Most movies are about plot, and chug from one stop to the next. Stephen King, whose book *On Writing* contains a lot of good sense, argues for situation over plot, suggests that if you do a good job of visualizing your characters, it is best to put them into a situation and see what happens, instead of chaining them to a plot structure. Todd Field and Andre Dubus use the elements of plot, but only on the surface, and the movie's title refers not to sex but to the secrets, spoken, unspoken, and dreamed, that are shared at night when two people close the door after themselves. ☞

In the Mood for Love ★ ★ ★
PG, 97 m., 2001

Tony Leung (Chow Mo-wan), Maggie Cheung (Su Li-zhen), Rebecca Pan (Mrs. Suen), Lai Chin (Mr. Ho), Siu Ping-lam (Ah Ping), Cin Tsi-ang (The Amah). Directed and produced by Wong Kar-wai. Screenplay by Wong.

They are in the mood for love, but not in the time and place for it. They look at each other with big damp eyes of yearning and sweetness, and go home to sleep by themselves. Adultery has sullied their lives: His wife and her husband are having an affair. "For us to do the same thing," they agree, "would mean we are no better than they are."

The key word there is "agree." The fact is, they do not agree. It is simply that neither one has the courage to disagree, and time is passing. He wants to sleep with her and she wants to sleep with him, but they are both bound by the moral stand that each believes the other has taken.

You may disagree with my analysis. You may think one is more reluctant than the other. There is room for speculation, because whole continents of emotions go unexplored in Wong Kar-wai's *In the Mood for Love,* a lush story of unrequited love that looks the way its songs sound. Many of them are by Nat King Cole, but the instrumental "Green Eyes," suggesting jealousy, is playing when they figure out why her husband and his wife always seem to be away at the same times.

His name is Mr. Chow (Tony Leung). Hers is Su Li-zhen (Maggie Cheung). In the crowded Hong Kong of 1962, they have rented rooms in apartments next to each another. They are not poor; he's a newspaper reporter, she's an executive assistant, but there is no space in the crowded city and little room for secrets.

Cheung and Leung are two of the biggest stars in Asia. Their pairing here as unrequited lovers is ironic because of their images as the usual winners in such affairs. This is the kind of story that could be remade by Tom Hanks and Meg Ryan, although in the Hollywood version there'd be a happy ending. That would

kind of miss the point and release the tension, I think; the thrust of Wong's film is that paths cross but intentions rarely do. In his other films, like *Chungking Express,* his characters sometimes just barely miss connecting, and here again key things are said in the wrong way at the wrong time. Instead of asking us to identify with this couple, as an American film would, Wong asks us to empathize with them; that is a higher and more complex assignment, with greater rewards.

The movie is physically lush. The deep colors of *film noir* saturate the scenes: reds, yellows, browns, deep shadows. One scene opens with only a coil of cigarette smoke, and then reveals its characters. In the hallway outside the two apartments, the camera slides back and forth, emphasizing not their nearness but that there are two apartments, not one.

The most ingenious device in the story is the way Chow and Su play-act imaginary scenes between their cheating spouses. "Do you have a mistress?" she asks, and we think she is asking Chow, but actually she is asking her husband, as played by Chow. There is a slap, not as hard as it would be with a real spouse. They wound themselves with imaginary dialogue in which their cheating partners laugh about them. "I didn't expect it to hurt so much," Su says, after one of their imaginary scenarios.

Wong Kar-wai leaves the cheating couple offscreen. Movies about adultery are almost always about the adulterers, but the critic Elvis Mitchell observes that the heroes here are "the characters who are usually the victims in a James M. Cain story." Their spouses may sin in Singapore, Tokyo, or a downtown love hotel, but they will never sin on the screen of this movie, because their adultery is boring and commonplace, while the reticence of Chow and Su elevates *their* love to a kind of noble perfection.

Their lives are as walled in as their cramped living quarters. They have more money than places to spend it. Still dressed for the office, she dashes out to a crowded alley to buy noodles. Sometimes they meet on the grotty staircase. Often it is raining. Sometimes they simply talk on the sidewalk. Lovers do not notice where they are, do not notice that they repeat themselves. It isn't repetition, anyway—it's reassurance. And when you're holding back and speaking in code, no conversation is boring, because the empty spaces are filled by your desires.

Intimacy ★ ★ ★
NO MPAA RATING, 119 m., 2001

Mark Rylance (Jay), Kerry Fox (Claire), Timothy Spall (Andy), Alastair Galbraith (Victor), Philippe Calvario (Ian), Marianne Faithfull (Betty), Susannah Harker (Susan), Rebecca Palmer (Pam), Fraser Ayres (Dave). Directed by Patrice Chereau and produced by Jacques Hinstin and Patrick Cassavetti. Screenplay by Chereau and Anne-Louise Trividic, based on the stories "Intimacy" and "Night Light" by Hanif Kureishi.

Intimacy is a movie in which a man and a woman meet for short, brutal, anonymous sex every Wednesday afternoon. They want to keep it to that: no names, no small talk.

After the screening at Sundance 2001, I ran into Kristina Nordstrom, who runs the Women Filmmakers Symposium in Los Angeles.

"Of course no woman would be attracted to sex like that," she said.

"Why not?"

"The sex in the movie all involves the bottom of the ninth inning. A woman would be turned off by a man who doesn't spend time being tender and sweet, and showing that he cares for her. There's no foreplay. She walks in, they rip off each other's clothes, and a few seconds later they're in a frenzy. Any woman would know that this movie was directed by a man."

A man might know that too. The film, which is brave but not perceptive, stars Mark Rylance as Jay, a former musician, a divorced husband and father, who now works as a barman and lives in a barely furnished London hovel. In an early scene, he is angry about an assistant hired to work with him behind the bar, because the new man is not a professional bartender but is an actor between jobs. The rage wells up because Jay fit that description himself until he left behind music six years ago and masochistically buried himself behind the bar.

The woman is named Claire (Kerry Fox). How they met we do not learn. At first she's simply a woman who turns up at his door every Wednesday afternoon to relieve an urgent physical need. They tear off each other's clothes

and have passionate sex on the floor of a messy room. Then they part. She is so single-minded she courageously avoids the line we know every other woman on Earth would have eventually said: "I could help you fix up this place."

Their arrangement of raw sex begins to go wrong when he follows her one day. He discovers her real life, as a housewife, mother, and actress who is playing Laura in a London fringe theater production of *The Glass Menagerie* (a door in a pub is helpfully labeled "Toilets and Theater"). At one performance, he sits next to her husband, Andy (Timothy Spall), and son. Andy is a taxi driver, jovial with strangers. One day Jay asks Andy, "What would you think of a mother who has it off on the sly and then goes back home in the evenings as if nothing has happened?"

He *wants* Andy to know. He all but tells him about the affair. He reveals that he meets a woman every Wednesday afternoon. His eyes burn with intensity: Is Andy getting the message? Andy gets it, but keeps his thoughts to himself.

Apparently Jay needs more than anonymous sex. The film at first suggests that he wants contact, that he is dying of loneliness. But the material, based on stories by the London writer Hanif Kureishi and directed by Patrice Chereau, tilts in a different direction. We see, I think, that what Jay really wants is revenge—revenge against women and against a happy marriage.

Much depends on what went on in Jay's failed marriage. We see him bathing his two small sons, looking like a doting father, and then his wife asks him if he loves them, and he is unable to answer. This may be the most important moment in the movie. If he did love them, would he enter Claire's personal life so violently? Would he attack their marriage, having met her own son? His anger toward women is terrifying.

Andy, the taxi driver, has a surprising scene, too, finally telling Claire what he really thinks of her. We find his issues revolve not around sex but around honesty. And there are scenes at an amateur acting workshop Claire teaches where the line between acting and reality is the real subject; it has not occurred to her, in the workshop or in life, that the point of acting is not to reproduce reality but to improve upon it.

Intimacy is a raw, wounding, powerfully

acted film, and you cannot look away from it. Its flaws are honestly come by, in the service of a failed search for truth. Its failure, I think, is an inability to look hard enough at what really drives Jay. His long, antagonistic relationship with a gay colleague might provide an answer, particularly since his taste for quick, anonymous sex seems to reflect a cruising sensibility.

Does he hate women because his inability to accept his homosexuality forces him to use them as substitutes for the partners he would prefer? Only a theory, suggested but not proven by the film. But *Intimacy* stays shy of any theory. It lets Jay off the hook, lets him retreat into the safe haven of loneliness and alienation. It should demand more of Jay, should insist on knowing him better. We leave the film with the conviction that the story is not over—that Jay is finished with Claire, but not with himself.

Invisible Circus ★ ½
R, 98 m., 2001

Jordana Brewster (Phoebe), Christopher Eccleston (Wolf), Cameron Diaz (Faith), Blythe Danner (Gail), Patrick Bergin (Gene), Camilla Belle (Young Phoebe), Isabelle Pasco (Claire), Moritz Bleibtreu (Eric). Directed by Adam Brooks and produced by Julia Chasman and Nick Wechsler. Screenplay by Brooks, based on the book by Jennifer Egan.

Adam Brooks's *Invisible Circus* finds the solution to searing personal questions through a tricky flashback structure. There are two stories here, involving an older sister's disappearance and a younger sister's quest, and either one would be better told as a straightforward narrative. When flashbacks tease us with bits of information, it has to be done well, or we feel toyed with. Here the mystery is solved by stomping in thick-soled narrative boots through the squishy marsh of contrivance.

Jordana Brewster stars as Phoebe, eighteen years old in 1976. In the summer of 1969, she tells us in her narration, her sister Faith went to Europe and never came back. The story was that Faith (Cameron Diaz) killed herself in Portugal. Phoebe doesn't buy it. After a heart-to-heart with her mother (Blythe Danner),

Phoebe sets off on a quest to solve the mystery, message, meaning, method, etc., of Faith's disappearance.

The search begins with Wolf (Christopher Eccleston), Faith's old boyfriend, now engaged and living in Paris. Since Wolf knows all the answers, and that's pretty clear to us (if not to Phoebe), he is required to be oblique to a tiresome degree. And there is another problem. In any movie where a lithesome eighteen-year-old confronts her older sister's lover, there is the inescapable possibility that she will sleep with him. This danger, which increases alarmingly when the character is named Wolf, is to be avoided, since the resulting sex scene will usually play as gratuitous, introducing problems the screenplay is not really interested in exploring. I cringe when a man and a woman pretend to be on a disinterested quest, and their unspoken sexual agenda makes everything they say sound coy.

Wolf and Faith, we learn, were involved in radical 1960s politics. Faith was driven by the death of her father, who died of leukemia caused by giant corporations (the science is a little murky here). Phoebe feels her dad always liked Faith more than herself. What was Dad's reason? My theory: Filial tension is required to motivate the younger sister's quest, so he was just helping out.

The movie follows Faith, sometimes with Wolf, sometimes without, as she joins the radical Red Army, becomes an anarchist, is allowed to help out on protest raids, fails one test, passes another, and grows guilt-ridden when one demonstration has an unexpected result. Phoebe traces Faith's activities during an odyssey/travelogue through Paris, Berlin, and Portugal, until we arrive at the very parapet Faith jumped or fell from, and all is revealed.

I can understand the purpose of the film, and even sense the depth of feeling in the underlying story, based on a novel by Jennifer Egan. But the clunky flashback structure grinds along, doling out bits of information, and it doesn't help that Wolf, as played by Eccleston, is less interested in truth than in Phoebe. He is a rat, which would be all right if he were a charming one.

There is a better movie about a young woman

who drops out of sight of those who love her and commits to radical politics. That movie is *Waking the Dead* (2000). It has its problems, too, but at least it is unclouded by extraneous sex, and doesn't have a character who withholds information simply for the convenience of the screenplay. And its Jennifer Connelly is much more persuasive than Cameron Diaz as a young woman who becomes a radical; she enters a kind of solemn holy trance, unlike Diaz, who seems more like a political tourist.

I Remember Me ★ ★ ★
NO MPAA RATING, 74 m., 2001

Featuring Kim A. Snyder, Michelle Akers, Blake Edwards, Stephen Paganetti. A documentary directed, produced, and written by Kim A. Snyder.

I now believe in Chronic Fatigue Syndrome. I was one of many who somehow absorbed the notion that it was an imaginary illness. I am ashamed of myself. At the Hamptons Film Festival, I met Kim A. Snyder, who was working as an assistant producer on a Jodie Foster film when she contracted CFS in 1995. For the last five years, while still battling the disease herself, she directed *I Remember Me*, a documentary that does what the Centers for Disease Control in Atlanta shamefully failed to do: connects the dots.

Snyder begins in Lake Tahoe, where the disease struck hundreds of people. She talks to Dr. Daniel L. Peterson, who first started treating CFS patients there in 1984, has had seven who committed suicide because of the disease, and has no doubt it is real. She also talks to a spokesperson for the nearby Incline Village Visitors' Bureau, who says CFS is promoted by "quack doctors and mostly overweight women." This person succeeds in becoming the living embodiment of the mayor in *Jaws*, who doesn't want anyone to believe there's a shark.

Yes, Dr. Peterson sighs, investigators from the CDC in Atlanta looked into the Lake Tahoe outbreak: "They came out here and skied and looked at a few charts." The conclusion was that Chronic Fatigue Syndrome was psychosomatic or hysterical or misdiagnosed. We are reminded that until the 1950s multiple sclerosis was also considered a hysterical condition.

Kim Snyder is an investigative journalist who does her own detective work. She identifies many earlier outbreaks with the same symptoms as CFS, and goes to Punta Gorda, Florida, to visit five women who had the disease forty years ago. Investigators visiting their community at the time concluded it was a real disease and not an imaginary condition, and said so in a report—which the women never saw. Snyder shows one woman the report on camera. She expresses her anger; this report would have informed her she was not, as many assured her, going crazy.

Snyder interviews two famous CFS sufferers: the film director Blake Edwards, who has continued to work during remissions in a fifteen-year struggle with the disease, and the Olympic gold medalist soccer player Michelle Akers, who walked off a field one day and collapsed.

But her most touching is the depressing visit to the bedside of Stephen Paganetti, a high school senior in Connecticut. He has been on his back in bed for years. The slightest exercise exhausts him. He is fed through tubes. Determined to attend his high school graduation, he's taken there by ambulance and wheeled in on a gurney. Few of his classmates had come to see him imprisoned in his bedroom; one says, "You get better—and we'll talk!" They give him a quilt they have all contributed patches to. Just what a high school kid wants for his graduation. By the end of filming, Stephen is still suffering, and indeed fewer than 20 percent of CFS sufferers get better, Snyder says.

The movie claims the disease strikes as many women as HIV. There has been recent progress. Robert J. Suhadolnik, a biochemist at Temple University, has identified a blood enzyme that acts as a marker of CFS, after many doctors claimed it had no physical symptoms. A whistle blower at the Centers for Disease Control has revealed to government accountants that $13 million was illegally diverted from CFS study to other diseases. Yet TV comics still joke about the disease as a form of laziness. Ironic, isn't it, that Kim Snyder wasn't too lazy to make this film—while the CDC and the medical establishment are only now stirring into action.

Iris ★ ★
R, 90 m., 2002

Judi Dench (Iris Murdoch), Jim Broadbent (John Bayley), Kate Winslet (Young Iris Murdoch), Hugh Bonneville (Young John Bayley). Directed by Richard Eyre and produced by Robert Fox and Scott Rudin. Screenplay by Eyre and Charles Wood.

I must look into myself and ask why I disliked *Iris* so intensely. Was it entirely a complaint against the film, or was it also a protest against the fate that befell the great novelist? There is no modern writer whose work I admire more than Iris Murdoch's, and for that mind to disappear in Alzheimer's is so sad that perhaps I simply refused to accept a film about it. Perhaps. Or perhaps it is true that the movie fails to do her justice—simplifies the life of one whose work was open to such human complexities.

Iris Murdoch (1919–1999) was one of the most important and prolific British novelists of her century, and wrote and taught philosophy as well. She wrote twenty-eight novels (between books, she said, she "took off for about half an hour"). Her novels involved "the unique strangeness of human beings," played against philosophical ideas. There were also touchstones that her readers looked forward to: a lonely child, a magus, an architectural oddity, an old friendship sorely tested, adulteries and unexpected couplings, intimations of the supernatural, theoretical conversations, ancient feuds. Her novel *The Sea, The Sea* won the Booker Prize and is a good place to start.

For years I looked forward to the annual Murdoch. Then her final novel arrived, shorter than usual, and at about the same time the dread news that she had Alzheimer's. "I feel as if I'm sailing into darkness," she said, a line used in the movie. After her death, her husband, John Bayley, wrote two books about her, dealing frankly and compassionately with her disease.

The film *Iris*, directed by the London stage director Richard Eyre and written by Eyre and the playwright Charles Wood, is literate, fair, and well acted, but is this particular film necessary? It moves between the young and old Iris, painting her enduring relationship with Bayley while at the same time suggesting her openness to affairs and sexual adventures. As a young woman she is played by Kate Winslet, as an older woman by Judi Dench (Bayley is played by Hugh Bonneville and Jim Broadbent). We see her high spirits and fierce intelligence at the beginning, and the sadness at the end. What is missing is the middle.

What Iris Murdoch basically did is to write books. It is notoriously difficult to portray a writer, because what can you show? The writer writing? It isn't the writing that makes a writer interesting—it's the having written. In Murdoch's case, that would suggest that instead of making a film of her life, it might be a good idea to make a film of one of her books. Only one Murdoch novel has ever been made into a film (the undistinguished *A Severed Head*, 1971). Her stories are rich in characters, conflict, and sexual intrigue, and I'm surprised more haven't been filmed.

Instead of honoring the work, *Iris* mourns the life. It's like a biopic of Shakespeare that cuts back and forth between his apprentice days and his retirement in Stratford. Alzheimer's is especially tragic because it takes away the person while the presence remains. The character of Bayley, meanwhile, is presented as a befuddled and ineffectual man who contends with the baffling Murdoch, young and old, accepting her infidelity at the beginning and giving her love and support at the end. Yes, but there is much more to Bayley. He is one of the most brilliant of literary critics, whose essays grace the *New York Review of Books* and the *Times Literary Supplement*, but on the basis of this film you would think of him, frankly, as a fond old fool.

Because the film is well acted and written with intelligence, it might be worth seeing despite my objections. I suspect my own feelings. Perhaps this is so clearly the film I did not want to see about Iris Murdoch that I cannot see the film others might want to see. Stanley Kauffmann's case in praise of the film in *The New Republic* is persuasive, but no: I cannot accept this Iris. The one in my mind is too alive, too vital, too inspiring.

The Iron Ladies ★ ★
NO MPAA RATING, 104 m., 2001

Chaichan Nimpoonsawas (Jung), Sahaparp Virakamin (Mon), Giorgio Maiocchi (Nong), Gokgorn Benjathikul (Pia), Jessdaporn Pholdee (Chai), Ekachai Buranapanit (Wit), Siridhana Hongsophon (Coach Bee). Directed by Yongyoot Thongkongtoon and produced by Visute Poolvoralaks. Screenplay by Visuthichai Boonyakarinjana, Jira Maligool, and Thongkongtoon.

The Iron Ladies would have been a fearless statement for gay pride if it had been released in, oh, say, 1960. Its attitudes are so dated it plays like a float in a Gay and Lesbian Pride Parade, featuring drag stereotypes of the past. That the movie is fun is undeniable. That it is bad is inarguable.

The film is about a Thai volleyball team made up of gays, transvestites, a transsexual, and one allegedly straight member (ho, ho). Locked out of volleyball courts, scorned by the league, the victims of cheating and pigheaded officials, they fight their way to the national finals. Think of *The Mighty Ducks*, with a slight adjustment in spelling.

That gays can excel at volleyball is beyond question. That they can play their best game only when wearing a lot of makeup is questionable. That they must win by shocking their homophobic opponents with flouncing, flaunting, flamboyant behavior and limp-wristed serves is offensive—especially in Thailand, where transsexuality and transvestism are minor tourist industries.

The story arc of the movie is familiar to anyone who has ever seen a formula sports film about an underdog team. Every act seems recycled from the archives. We see the early setbacks. The recruitment of a team of misfits, losers, and reluctant heroes. The key player who needs a lot of convincing. The coach with personal issues of her own (she may be a lesbian, but the movie refuses to commit). The sports authorities who want to ban the team. The early victories. The setbacks. Capturing the popular imagination. The big game. The crisis. The realization that the team can win only by returning to its True Nature (that is, gobs of foundation, lots of lipstick).

It's a good thing *The Iron Ladies* is about a gay team, because if this team were straight, the film would be an exercise in formula. The characters redeem the material by giving us somewhere else to look. It is, alas, too shy to look very hard. Judging by this movie, gay volleyball players have no sex lives at all, and don't even smooch a little in public. The Iron Ladies make admirable role models for celibacy in drag.

I found myself intrigued, however, by the matter-of-fact Coach Bee (Siridhana Hongsophon). Her performance is so utterly without spin, style, or affect that it could be lifted intact from a documentary. She is utterly convincing as—a volleyball coach. It's as if a real coach is being filmed with a hidden camera. There is no attempt to "perform," no awareness of punch lines, no artificial drama. Just a flat, straight-ahead, no-nonsense coaching job. It is either one of the most convincing performances I have ever seen, or no performance at all.

At the end of the film, we see newsreel footage of the real Iron Ladies, who are indeed a gay Thai volleyball team, and did indeed become national favorites. I understand that the story of the film is adjusted only slightly from real life (although greatly adjusted, I suspect, from real sex lives). This is the kind of movie you kind of enjoy, in a dumb way, with half your mind on hold, wishing they'd tell you more about some of the characters—especially Pia (Gokgorn Benjathikul), the glamorous transsexual. There's something sexy about the way she says, "Your serve." 🖅

Iron Monkey ★ ★ ★
PG-13, 85 m., 2001

Donnie Yen (Wong Kei-Ying), Rongguang Yu (Dr. Yang/Iron Monkey), Jean Wang (Orchid Ho), Yee Kwan Yan (Hiu Hing), James Wong (Governor Cheng), Hou Hsiao (Disfigured Swordsman), Sze-Man Tsang (Young Wong Fei-Hung), Sai-kun Yam (Hin Hung), Shun-Yee Yuen (Master Fox), Fai Li (Witch). Directed by Woo-ping Yuen and produced by Hark Tsui. Screenplay by Tai-Muk Lau, Cheung Tan, Pik-yin Tang, and Hark.

The enormous popularity of *Crouching Tiger, Hidden Dragon* has inspired Miramax to test the market for other upmarket martial arts movies, and its resident kung-fu fan, Quentin Tarantino, has gone plunging back into the stacks of classics to "present" a beautifully restored version of *Iron Monkey*. This 1993 film, produced by the action master Hark Tsui, is seen in all its 35mm glory.

The film includes a young version of Wong Fei-Hung, whose adult exploits were chronicled in *The Legend of Drunken Master*, a 1994 Jackie Chan film released in 2000 by Miramax's Dimension division. Wong was a nineteenth-century folk hero who ranged the Chinese countryside doing, one suspects, very few of the things he is seen doing in this film. (For that matter, in *Iron Monkey* he is played by Sze-Man Tsang, a girl.) One of his specialties was "drunken fighting," in which, by pretending to be drunk, he could loosen himself up enough to be a better fighter.

Here we see twelve-year-old Wong Fei-Hung traveling with his father, Wong Kei-Ying (Donnie Yen), when they are caught in a dragnet set to snare the Iron Monkey, a mysterious Robin Hood figure. Hauled before the provincial governor, Wong Kei-Ying is charged with being the Iron Monkey, but then the real Monkey materializes in the court. The governor tells Wong Kei-Ying his son will be held captive until he captures the Iron Monkey.

Since such a standoff would have the movie's two heroes fighting each other, obviously unacceptable, we see young Wong Fei-Hung escaping, which frees his father to partner with the Iron Monkey, who is actually Dr. Yang (Rongguang Yu), a freelance idealist who fights for the poor against the rich. They find a common enemy in an evil monk.

The story is essentially a clothesline for a series of spectacular action scenes, culminating, as *Drunken Master* did, with one involving fire. This one is pretty spectacular, as the fighters balance on tall wooden poles over an inferno, battering each other with blazing battering rams while leaping from one precarious perch to another. At one point the two allies are balanced one on top of the other on one shaky pole, and at another point they're balanced on either end of a shaky horizontal pole (this scene may have inspired a similar predicament involving ladders in the recent *The Musketeer;*

Western movies are stealing martial arts stunts with shameless abandon).

Iron Monkey is a superior example of its genre without transcending it. The Jackie Chan movie benefited from our knowledge that Chan does most of his own stunts, and *Crouching Tiger* was not simply action scenes but also a poetic story, told with great visual beauty. This movie is great-looking, slick and highly professional, but stops at that. Donnie Yen has great moves, but how many of them are real?

What you can see, watching *Iron Monkey*, is what martial arts fans have been telling me via e-mail ever since *Crouching Tiger* came out: Its scenes of characters running across rooftops and floating in air were far from original, and had been well established in movies like this one. The technique of using invisible wires to "fly" the characters is not new (on the Web, in fact, it has a name: "wire-fu"). The reason *Crouching Tiger, Hidden Dragon* is a better movie is not in the technology but in the art; it incorporates the stunt and action techniques but is not satisfied with them, and aims higher, while a film like *Iron Monkey* is basically aimed at audiences who want elaborate fight sequences and fidget at the dialogue in between. It's for the fans, not the crossover audience. ☞

Isn't She Great? ★

R, 95 m., 2000

Bette Midler (Jacqueline Susann), Nathan Lane (Irving Mansfield), Stockard Channing (Florence Maybelle), David Hyde Pierce (Michael Hastings), John Cleese (Henry Marcus), John Larroquette (Maury Manning), Amanda Peet (Debbie). Directed by Andrew Bergman and produced by Mike Lobell. Screenplay by Paul Rudnick, based on an article by Michael Korda.

Perhaps it's appropriate that Jacqueline Susann's biopic has been written by Paul Rudnick, whose alter ego, "Libby Gelman-Waxner," waxes witty and bitchy in her *Premiere* magazine column every month. It was Truman Capote who said on a talk show that Jackie Susann "looks like a truck driver in drag," but whenever that image swims into view, it somehow seems to have the Gelman-Waxner byline attached.

Susann became famous writing potboilers

about the sex and drug lives of the stars. Identifying the real-life models for her thinly veiled characters grew into a parlor game, and her *Valley of the Dolls* became the best-selling novel of all time. She also became famous for revolutionizing book retailing; Susann and her agent husband, Irving Mansfield, turned the book tour into a whistle-stop of America, and there was scarcely a bookseller, interviewer, or indeed shipping dockworker who didn't get the Susann treatment.

So tireless was her publicity that she even talked to me, at a time when I was twenty-three years old and had been on the *Sun-Times* for ten minutes. Jackie, Irving, and I had lunch at Eli's the Place for Steak, although all I can recall of the conversation is that she said, "I'm like Will Rogers. I never met a dog I didn't like." Full disclosure: Three years later I wrote the screenplay for the parody *Beyond the Valley of the Dolls,* and a few years after that, the Fox studio was sued by Mansfield on the grounds that the film diminished his wife's literary reputation. (Had I been called to testify, I would have expressed quiet pride in whatever small part I had played in that process.)

Susann's life would seem to be the perfect target for the Libby Gelman-Waxner sensibility; who better to write about the woman whose prose one reader described as "like overhearing a conversation in the ladies' room." My hopes soared when I learned that Andrew Bergman, who made the wacky comedies *Honeymoon in Vegas* and *Soapdish,* would be directing—and that John Cleese would play her publisher. I was hoping for satire, but they've made a flat and peculiar film that in its visual look and dramatic style might be described as the final movie of the 1950s.

Maybe that was the purpose. Maybe the whole look, feel, and sensibility of *Isn't She Great?* is part of the joke. It's a movie that seems to possess the same color scheme and style sense as *Valley of the Dolls,* but, alas, without Jackie's dirty mind. So devout is this story that when Irving (Nathan Lane) walks out on Jackie (Bette Midler), we don't even find out why he really left. Jackie would have given us the scoopola.

And when they get back together again, is it with tearful recriminations and shocking ac-

cusations? Not at all. There is a tree in Central Park that they hold precious, because to them it represents God, and one day when Jackie visits the tree Irving is there already talking to God. To prove how much he loves her, on this and another occasion, he even wades into the Central Park lagoon. I think, although the movie isn't clear, that Irving left her not because of another person, but because the diamond brooch he bought for Jackie at the height of her success was upstaged by the diamond necklace given by her publisher. As her agent, shouldn't his gift be only 10 percent as expensive as her publisher's?

Money brings up another point: their lifestyle. Once Jackie makes it big time, they have a lot of money. But even before then, they live in Mansfield's lavishly expensive Manhattan apartment, reproduced on one of those spacious Hollywood sets where people make dramatic entrances and exits and the interior decorators have taste as vague as their budgets. Where did Mansfield get the money to live like this? When they first meet, he drops names like Perry Como and Frank Sinatra, but it turns out he represents their distant relatives.

Never mind. Factual accuracy is not what we're looking for anyway. What we want, I think, is the portrait of a funny trash-talker, not a secular saint who bravely bore the birth of an autistic son (visited on weekends in a luxury care center) and later battled cancer. Bette Midler would seem to be the right casting choice for Jackie, but not for this Jackie, who is not bright enough, vicious enough, ambitious enough, and complicated enough to be the woman who became world-famous through sheer exercise of will. Stockard Channing, who plays Jackie's boozy best friend, does a better job of suggesting the Susann spirit.

Jackie Susann deserved better than *Isn't She Great?* A woman who writes *Valley of the Dolls* shouldn't be punished with a biopic that makes her look only a little naughtier than Catherine Cookson. There's a scene here where Jackie and Irving visit with Jackie and Aristotle on the Onassis yacht. Consider for a moment what Susann could have done with that. Then look at the tepid moment where Ari sighs fondly,

"Perhaps I married the wrong Jackie." Uh-huh. Here is a movie that needed great trash, great sex, and great gossip, and at all the crucial moments Susann is talking to a tree.

Italian for Beginners ★ ★ ★
R, 112 m., 2002

Anders W. Berthelsen (Andreas), Ann Eleonora Jorgensen (Karen), Anette Stovelbaek (Olympia), Peter Gantzler (Jorgen Mortensen), Lars Kaalund (Hal-Finn), Sara Indrio Jensen (Giulia), Elsebeth Steentoft (Kirketjener), Rikke Wolck (Sygeplejerske). Directed by Lone Scherfig and produced by Ib Tardini. Screenplay by Scherfig.

What a masterstroke it was for Lars von Trier to invent the Dogma movement! Every review of a Dogma film must begin with the announcement that it is a Dogma film, and then put it to the Dogma test to see if it conforms. Von Trier's name is often mentioned more prominently than the name of the film's actual director. He exacts a tax on our attention to the film. Since most people reading reviews don't know what Dogma is and don't care, this discussion puts them off the movie. Wise Dogma directors should no more trumpet their affiliation than should a movie begin with an announcement of the film stock it was shot on.

I say this because *Italian for Beginners* is a charming Danish comedy, and the fact that it's a Dogma film has little to do with its appeal. Yes, like all Dogma films, it's shot on video, on location, with only music found at the source—but so what? You see how Dogma changes the subject. What is appealing about it, the freshness and quirkiness of its characters and their interlinked stories, has nothing to do with Dogma—although, of course, lower costs may have helped it get made.

The movie takes place near Copenhagen, mostly in a small complex that includes a sports facility, a restaurant, a hair salon, and a nearby church. New to the church is Pastor Andreas (Anders W. Berthelsen), taking the place of a former pastor who took his ideas about services a little too seriously (he pushed the organist off the balcony). Short tempers seem to run in this little community; we meet Hal-Finn (Lars Kaalund), manager of the restaurant, who treats his job like a military command and is hilariously rude to customers who have bad manners.

Ordered to get a haircut, he meets the hairdresser Karen (Ann Eleonora Jorgensen). Everyone seems to cross paths in Karen's salon, including Pastor Andreas, who stops in for a haircut and has to dispense emergency spiritual advice to Olympia (Anette Stovelbaek), a bakery employee who gets a crush on Andreas.

Giulia (Sara Indrio Jensen) is an Italian waitress in the restaurant. It is not beside the point that she is Italian. Jorgen (Peter Gantzler), the manager of the complex, likes her so much he signs up for Italian classes. The Italian teacher suddenly drops dead, and Hal-Finn, who finds himself with some free time, decides to take over the class, which he teaches as if he is instructing Cub Scouts on fire-building techniques.

The movie gradually reveals certain unsuspected connections between some of the characters, and allows romances to bloom or fade among others, and all comes to a head during a class trip to Venice, which they all take more or less in desperation. The film has been written and directed by Lone Scherfig, who has a real affection for her characters, and likes to watch them discovering if happiness can be found in the absence of crucial social skills.

Because it comes attached to the Dogma label, I suppose we assume going into it that *Italian for Beginners* will test our taste or our patience. The film only wants to amuse. It's a reminder that Dogma films need not involve pathetic characters tormented by the misuse of their genitalia, but can simply want to have a little fun. This is the sort of story American independent filmmakers also like to tell, right down to the setting in a restaurant—which, like a bar or an apartment in a sitcom, is convenient because all the characters can drop in without explanation. I was surprised how much I enjoyed *Italian for Beginners*, and made a mental note not to get all hung up on the Dogma movement in my review.

It All Starts Today ★ ★ ★
NO MPAA RATING, 117 m., 2001

Philippe Torreton (Daniel), Maria Pitarresi (Valeria), Nadia Kaci (Samia), Veronique Ataly (Mrs. Lienard), Nathalie Becue (Cathy),

Emmanuelle Bercot (Mrs. Tievaux), Francoise Bette (Mrs. Delacourt), Lambert Marchal (Remi). Directed by Bertrand Tavernier and produced by Alain Sarde and Frederic Bourboulon. Screenplay (in French, with English subtitles) by Dominique Sampiero, Tiffany Tavernier, and Bertrand Tavernier.

Daniel, the kindergarten teacher in *It All Starts Today*, finds himself doing a lot more than teaching. He is also expected to be a social worker, child abuse investigator, hot lunch provider, political activist, fund-raiser, administrator, son, and lover, and now his girlfriend wants him to become a father as well. Philippe Torreton plays the role with a kind of desperate energy, relaxing only with the kids in the schoolroom and one night when he dances at a birthday party.

There is not much good cheer in the town where he teaches, a depressed mining village in the very area of France that inspired Zola's great exposé of mine conditions, *Germinal*. Today the typical miner is more like Daniel's dad, a broken figure who shuffles through the living room with his oxygen tank strapped to his back. Unemployment is widespread, government funds are lacking, and the mayor complains that schools and social services eat up his budget.

Not that the services are that good. Early in the film, Daniel locks out a social worker (Nadia Kaci) after she hangs up on him. Later they get to be friends and bend a few rules to make things happen. But what can they do about the pathetic mother who pushes her baby carriage into the schoolyard to pick up her preschooler, collapses on the asphalt, and then runs away, leaving behind both her baby and her little girl?

"She reeked of red wine," another teacher tells Daniel (the French would note the color). He visits her home, to find that the power has been turned off. It is winter, and cold. It's against the law to turn off a customer's power in the winter, but the power company gets around that by turning it off in the autumn. This woman, her kids, and her dispirited husband have no money, no hope, no plans.

The movie is a tender and passionate protest, not without laughter, by Bertrand Tavernier—a director who is not only gifted

but honorable, and who since his debut with the wonderful *The Clockmaker* in 1973 has never put his hand to an unworthy film. He works all over the map, from the fantasy of *Death Watch* to the politics of *The Judge and the Assassin* to the character study *A Week's Vacation* to the jazz biopic *'Round Midnight* to the heartbreaking *Daddy Nostalgia* and the angry *L.627*, about the impossibility of being an effective drug cop.

It All Starts Today has most in common with *L.627*. Both films are about talented professionals who are hamstrung by the French bureaucracy and driven to despair by the untidy lives of their citizen clients. The screenplay, written by Tavernier with his daughter Tiffany and a schoolteacher named Dominique Sampiero, works by looking at everyday challenges. What is Daniel to say, for example, when the schoolyard woman and her husband explain that their son has stopped coming to school because it is just too much effort for them to set the alarm and get him out of bed? Irresponsible? Or would you also be defeated by months without heat and light?

The movie sketches Daniel's run-ins with a world that seems determined to make it impossible for him to be a good kindergarten teacher. He is considered a troublemaker, but what can he do? Consider the insufferable school inspector who advises him not to "move among groups" while teaching. "What should I do about the other three groups?" Daniel asks. "Make them self-reliant," advises the inspector, who obviously knows little about the self-reliance skills of two- to five-year-olds.

Maria Pitarresi plays Daniel's girlfriend, a sculptor with a young son who resents him. Her character seems a little unlikely, especially when she dreams up the school fete that ends the film, with classrooms filled with sand and Berber tents made from sheets, and a schoolyard filled with a maze of brightly colored bottles. As the town band plays and the children dance, we're aware that the upbeat ending changes absolutely nothing about the grim prospects for these kids when they someday look for work in this dying region. They'll end up paralyzed in front of the TV, like their parents. No wonder two of the students are named Starsky and Hutch.

Ivans xtc. ★ ★ ★ ★
NO MPAA RATING, 94 m., 2002

Danny Huston (Ivan Beckman), Peter Weller (Don West), Lisa Enos (Charlotte White), Adam Krentzman (Barry Oaks), Alex Butler (Brad East), Morgan Vukovic (Lucy Lawrence), Tiffani-Amber Thiessen (Marie Stein), James Merendino (Danny McTeague), Caroleen Feeney (Rosemary). Directed by Bernard Rose and produced by Lisa Enos. Screenplay by Rose and Enos, based on *The Death of Ivan Ilyich* by Leo Tolstoy.

There is much sadness but little mourning at the funeral of Ivan Beckman. All agree he brought about his own death. He had few close friends. It is said he died from cancer. Insiders whisper, "The cancer is a cover story." You know you have lived your life carelessly when cancer is your cover story.

Ivans xtc., a remarkable film by Bernard Rose, stars Danny Huston, the rich-voiced, genial, tall son of John Huston, as a powerful Hollywood agent whose untidy personal life becomes a legend. Cocaine was the solution to his problems, which were caused by cocaine. He is headed for a shipwreck anyway when the diagnosis of lung cancer comes, but instead of looking for medical help he bulldozes ahead with cocaine, denial, and call girls.

The film opens with his funeral. There is a fight between a writer fired from a new movie and the star (Peter Weller) who fired him. Their disagreement cannot wait upon death. In voice-over, we hear the voice of the dead agent, who says that at the end, "the pain was so bad I took every pill in the house." And he tried, he says, "to find one simple image to get me through it."

Then we flash back through his life, as Ivan appears on-screen, one of those charming but unknowable men who have perfect courtesy, who lean forward with the appearance of great attention, and whose minds seem to be otherwise involved. As it happens, that is precisely the impression I had of John Huston on the three or four occasions when I met him: He was a shade too courteous, too agreeable, too accommodating, leaning forward too attentively from his great height, and I felt that he was playing a nice man while thinking about other things.

Danny Huston plays Ivan Beckman as the sort of man who believes he cannot be touched. Who has been given a pass. To whom all things come because they must, and for whom addictions like cocaine do not bring the usual ravages. I am told that if you have enough money for enough cocaine you can hold out like that for quite a while, which is not good, because you are building up a deficit in your mind and body that eventually cannot be repaid.

When Ivan doesn't return phone calls, when he doesn't appear at the office, when clients can't find him, he doesn't get in the same kind of trouble that a less legendary agent might experience, because—well, that's Ivan. When his girlfriend Charlotte (Lisa Enos) can't find him, and then discovers he was partying with hookers—well, who did she think he was when she started going out with him? Surely she heard the stories? Surely this doesn't come as news? When his bosses grow restless at his irresponsibility—hey, he has the big client list. If the clients like him, then the agency must.

The diagnosis of cancer comes like a telegram that should have been delivered next door. It is the final, irrefutable reply to his feeling of immunity. There are two painful scenes where he tries, in one way or another, to deal with this news. One comes in a meeting with his father, whose ideas have made him a stranger. One comes during a party with two call girls, who are happy with the money, happy with the cocaine, happy to be with Ivan Beckman, and then increasingly unhappy and confused as their services are needed, not to pretend, but to be real. You cannot hire someone to really care about you.

The movie is allegedly inspired by *The Death of Ivan Ilyich* by Leo Tolstoy. I say "allegedly," because Bernard Rose has charged that the powerful Creative Artists Agency tried to prevent the film, seeing it as a transparent version of the life of Jay Moloney, an agent who at one time (I learn from a news story) represented Leonardo DiCaprio, Steven Spielberg, Bill Murray, Uma Thurman, Tim Burton—and Rose himself. Fired from CAA in 1996 because of cocaine, the story says, he moved to the Caribbean and killed himself in 1999.

Well, the story could be based on a lot of lives. The parabola of serious addiction often looks a lot the same. If the victim has more money, the settings are prettier. The tragedy of Ivan Beckman is that he doesn't know how to call for help, and has no one to call if he did. It is important to recognize that he is not a bad man. He can be charming, does not wish to cause harm, is grateful for company, and, as such people like to say, "If I'm hurting anybody, I'm only hurting myself." It is not until too late that he discovers how much it hurts.

Note: The story of the making of Ivans xtc. *is the story of how a lot of movies can now be made, according to Bernard Rose, its director.*

Because of its controversial subject matter and because the Hollywood establishment has no wish to fund the thinly veiled story of the death of one of its own, the movie could not find conventional financing.

"So we went ahead and filmed it anyway," *Rose told me after the film's screening at Cannes 2001. "We got a 24-fps digital video camera, and we shot it in our own homes, and the crew was the cast and the cast was the crew and we took care of catering by calling for carryout."*

Rose, forty-two, is the British-born director of a number of commercial hits, notably Candyman *(1992) and* Immortal Beloved *(1995), and he is known for the power of his visual imagery. In* Paperhouse *(1988), he created a real landscape based on a child's imaginary drawings. In* Immortal Beloved, *a boy runs through the woods at night and plunges into a lake, floating on his back as the camera pulls back to show him surrounded by the reflections of countless stars.*

Ivans xtc., *made on a $500,000 budget, did not support or require such images. Produced by Lisa Enos, who also stars in it, it was directed by Rose on high-def video, which looks—appropriate, I think, is the word. Some shots are beautiful, others are functional, and there are no shots that do not work.*

"We finished the movie, we took it to Artisan Entertainment, and we made a deal," he said. "A 50-50 split of all the proceeds from dollar one. It was made so cheaply that we'll make out and so will they."

Does he wish he'd had film? "It's no use saying you'd rather have film, because this project on film could not have existed."

J

Jackpot ★ ★
R, 100 m., 2001

Jon Gries (Sunny Holiday), Garrett Morris (Lester Irving), Daryl Hannah (Bobbi), Peggy Lipton (Janice), Ricky Trammell (Candy Singer), Allen Fawcett (KJ Number One), Patrick Bauchau (Sevon Voice/Santa Claus), Adam Baldwin (Mel James), Rosie O'Grady (Sweet Dreams Singer), Rick Overton (Roland), Anthony Edwards (Tracy). Directed by Michael Polish and produced by Mark Polish and Michael Polish. Screenplay by Mark Polish and Michael Polish.

Sailing in a big pink Chrysler boat from one sad saloon to another, Sunny Holiday and Lester Irving travel the highways of the West, seeking fame. Sunny (Jon Gries) is the singer, Lester (Garrett Morris) is his manager. Their plan: By gradually building a constituency among karaoke fans, Sunny will position himself for his big breakthrough into the world of pop music. "Our winnings total ... thousands," Sunny assures an interviewer. One of his prizes looks more like a Waring blender (Lester, as manager, gets 15 percent, and keeps the lid).

Jackpot is the new movie by the Polish brothers, directed by Michael, coproduced and cowritten by Mark. Their first film, *Twin Falls Idaho* (1999), was a virtuoso dark melodrama about conjoined twins approaching an inescapable separation. This one feels more like when the pianist noodles on the keyboard before breaking into the melody. All the pieces are in place—the characters, the seedy milieu, the look and tone—but we never get to the nod inviting the drums and bass to come in. It's all warm-up, no pitch.

Yet you can tell these guys have a feel for film. This is a sophomore lapse on the way to a real career. There are moments that zing. One comes when Sunny seduces Janice (Peggy Lipton), who lives in a trailer near his motel. First they sleep together. Then he spills his coffee. Then he goes out to his car to get a gallon jug of industrial soap. "None of those big chain stores carry this kind of power," he assures her. Then he tries to sell her the soap. Lesser filmmakers would have stopped there. Not the Polish brothers. "You screwed me once. Why are you trying to screw me again?" asks Janice, in words to that effect.

Sunny and Lester have a relationship like George and Lennie in *Of Mice and Men,* except that both of them are more like Lennie. They travel through life side by side, the fortyish white man and sixtyish black man, toward success that always remains out there on the horizon. Sunny dresses like a caller at a Saturday night square dance, Lester like an unsuccessful undertaker. Lester prays before every competition, and gives advice (no matter how bad things are going, never, ever just walk off the stage).

Sunny has abandoned a wife and child for this quest. Bobbi (Daryl Hannah) waits at home during what she calls his "fantasy tour," raising their baby and waiting for child support. It's her pink Chrysler. She reports it stolen. Sunny does religiously send her a $1 lottery ticket every week, which if it was a winner (he points out) would more than make up for the missing support payments, but somehow for Bobbi this is not enough.

The film has a nice way of getting into scenes. I like the way Sunny and Lester are discovered sitting at the counter of a diner, an empty seat between them, caught in midflow of a conversation they have been having for months. And the way Sunny's brother Tracy (Anthony Edwards) turns up to defend and support him. And the way the fans in the karaoke bars have to think the contestants are stars—because if they're not, what does that make the fans?

In its mastery of its moments, *Jackpot* has charm, humor, and poignancy. What it lacks is necessity. There's a sense in which we're always waiting for it to kick in. If we saw *Duets,* the 2000 Gwyneth Paltrow and Huey Lewis movie, we know this world of competitive karaoke. *Jackpot* is not so much about the karaoke as about the relationship between Sunny and Lester. But do they have a relationship, or it is a double act, so long in rehearsal that all the lines are set? Somebody has to break out if anything is to happen. *Jackpot* was made by twins, and both of their films are about two men joined at the hip, either literally or figuratively. Maybe it's time for them to go in for the operation.

Note: I learn on the Web that the film was photographed with Sony's new Cine Alta digital video camera, the same one George Lucas is using for the next Star Wars movie. I don't know whether the movie's look (described by Elvis Mitchell as "left on the dashboard faded") is the result of the camera, or of cinematographer M. David Mullen—more Mullen's choice, I assume, or Star Wars fans are going to be plenty displeased. It's right for this film, but it's not ready for prime time.

Jason X ½★
R, 93 m., 2002

Kane Hodder (Jason Voorhees), Lexa Doig (Rowan), Lisa Ryder (Kay-Em 14), Chuck Campbell (Tsunaron), Jonathan Potts (Professor Lowe), Peter Mensah (Sergeant Brodski), Melyssa Ade (Janessa), Todd Farmer (Dallas), Melody Johnson (Kinsa). Directed by James Isaac and produced by Noel Cunningham and Isaac. Screenplay by Victor Miller and Todd Farmer.

"This sucks on so many levels."
—Dialogue from *Jason X*

Rare for a movie to so frankly describe itself. *Jason X* sucks on the levels of storytelling, character development, suspense, special effects, originality, punctuation, neatness, and aptness of thought. Only its title works. And I wouldn't be surprised to discover that the name *Jason X* is copyrighted © 2002, World Wrestling Federation, and that Jason's real name is Dwayne Johnson. No, wait, that was last week's movie. *Jason X* is technically *Friday the 13th, Part 10*. It takes place centuries in the future, when Earth is a wasteland and a spaceship from Earth II has returned to the Camp Crystal Lake Research Facility and discovered two cryogenically frozen bodies, one of them holding a machete and wearing a hockey mask.

The other body belongs to Rowan (Lexa Doig), a researcher who is thawed out and told it is now the year 2455: "That's 455 years in the future!" Assuming that the opening scenes take place now, you've done the math and come up with 453 years in the future. The missing two years are easily explained: I learn from the Classic Horror Website that the

movie was originally scheduled to be released on Halloween 2000, and was then bumped to March 2001, summer 2001, and Halloween 2001 before finally opening on the sixteenth anniversary of Chernobyl, another famous meltdown.

The movie is a low-rent retread of the *Alien* pictures, with a monster attacking a spaceship crew; one of the characters, Dallas, is even named in homage to the earlier series. The movie's premise: Jason, who has a "unique ability to regenerate lost and damaged tissue," comes back to life and goes on a rampage, killing the ship's plentiful supply of sex-crazed students and staff members. Once you know that the ship contains many dark corners and that the crew members wander off alone as stupidly as the campers at Camp Crystal Lake did summer after summer, you know as much about the plot as the writers do.

With *Star Wars Episode II: Attack of the Clones* opening, there's been a lot of talk lately about how good computer-generated special effects have become. On the basis of the effects in *Jason X* and the (much more entertaining) *Scorpion King*, we could also chat about how bad they are getting. Perhaps audiences do not require realistic illusions, but simply the illusion of realistic illusions. Shabby special effects can have their own charm.

Consider a scene where the spaceship is about to dock with *Solaris*, a gigantic mother ship, or a city in space, or whatever. Various controls go haywire because Jason has thrown people through them, and the ship fails to find its landing slot and instead crashes into *Solaris*, slicing off the top of a geodesic dome and crunching the sides of skyscrapers (why *Solaris* has a city-style skyline in outer space I do not presume to ask).

This sequence is hilariously unconvincing. But never mind. Consider this optimistic dialogue by Professor Lowe (Jonathan Potts), the greedy top scientist who wants to cash in on Jason: "Everyone OK? We just overshot it. We'll turn around." Uh-huh. We're waiting for the reaction from *Solaris* Air Traffic Control when a dull thud echoes through the ship and the characters realize *Solaris* has just exploded. Fine, but how could they hear it? Students of *Alien* will know that in space, no one can hear you blow up.

The characters follow the usual rules from Camp Crystal Lake, which require the crew members to split up, go down dark corridors by themselves, and call out each other's names with the sickening certainty that they will get no reply. Characters are skewered on giant screws, cut in half, punctured by swords, get their heads torn off, and worse. A veteran pilot remains calm: "You weren't alive during the Microsoft conflict. We were beating each other with our own severed limbs."

There is one good effects shot, in which a scientist's face is held in supercooled liquid until it freezes, and then smashed into smithereens against a wall. There is also an interesting transformation, as the onboard regenerator restores Jason and even supplies him with superhero armor and a new face to replace his hockey mask and ratty army surplus duds. I left the movie knowing one thing for sure: There will be a *Jason XI*—or, given the IQ level of the series, *Jason X, Part 2.*

Jay and Silent Bob Strike Back ★ ★ ★
R, 95 m., 2001

Kevin Smith (Silent Bob), Jason Mewes (Jay Phat Buds), Shannen Doherty (Rene Mosier), Renee Humphrey (Tricia "The Dish" Jones), Ben Affleck (Holden McNeil/Himself), James Van Der Beek (Himself/Bluntman), Jason Biggs (Himself/Chronic), Matt Damon (Himself/Will Hunting), Jason Lee (Banky Edwards). Directed by Kevin Smith and produced by Laura Greenlee and Scott Mosier. Screenplay by Smith.

The Movie Answer Man got a question earlier this year about whether movie characters know about other movie characters and movies. *Jay and Silent Bob Strike Back* is like an answer to that question. It is becoming clear that the film universe of Kevin Smith is interconnected, that characters from one movie can expect to run into characters from another—like Faulkner's Yoknapatawpha County, Smithland has a permanent population, even though we may not meet all of them in every movie.

The connecting threads, apparently, are Jay and Silent Bob, who we met in Smith's first movie, *Clerks,* where they were permanently stationed outside a convenience store, ostensibly pot dealers, more accurately waiting for

something to happen. They moved inside in *Mallrats,* had their lives ripped off to make a comic book in *Chasing Amy,* and risked salvation in *Dogma.* Having visited all of Smith's other movies, they are now given their own, in which characters and stars from the earlier pictures return the favor.

Consider the metaphysics. Ben Affleck and Matt Damon appear as themselves in this movie, making a sequel to their movie *Good Will Hunting,* and then we go into the fourth dimension and begin to suspect wormholes in the plot, because they also starred in *Dogma,* in which Chris Rock played an angel—and now he turns up in *Jay and Silent Bob* as the director of *Bluntman and Chronic,* which is the movie based on the lives of Jay and Silent Bob, which is an adaptation of the comic book created in *Chasing Amy.* And before he appears as himself, Affleck appears as Holden, his *Chasing Amy* character, and introduces Jay and Silent Bob to the Internet.

And look—isn't that Joey Lauren Adams, from *Chasing Amy*? And hey—wasn't Ben Affleck one of the comic artists in *Chasing Amy*? And while Affleck does not play his *Chasing Amy* character in *Jay and Silent Bob,* Jason Lee, the cocreator of the Bluntman comic, does, turning up in this one to warn Jay and Silent Bob that the comic is being made into a movie by Miramax. And Miramax is the studio releasing this movie, which . . .

Jay and Silent Bob will be seen as a self-indulgence by Kevin Smith to those outside the circle of his films—and by those within it as Kevin Smith's indulgence to them. And don't get me started on whether it's plenary or temporal. This is one of those movies where the inmates take over the asylum, by which I mean that the director was obviously unrestrained by any timid notions of "reaching the biggest possible audience," and allowed to make an in-joke of epic proportions. Like the Monty Python movies, it depends for full enjoyment on your encyclopedia knowledge of the world that generated it.

The story begins more or less at birth, as we discover that Jay (Jason Mewes) and Silent Bob (Kevin Smith) were deposited as infants in front of the convenience store in *Clerks* and have more or less been there ever since. Now a restraining order has encouraged them to budge, and in a comic-book store they run into Banky Edwards (Jason Lee), who based his *Bluntman and Chronic* comic on them, and now informs them it's been sold to Miramax.

> Jay: Miramax? I thought they only made classy pictures like *The Piano* or *The Crying Game.*
> Banky: After they made *She's All That,* everything went to hell.

Jay and Silent Bob decide to hitchhike to the coast, and encounter George Carlin as a hitchhiker who tells them of the one thing guaranteed to get you a ride, and Carrie Fisher as a nun who represents an exception to Carlin's advice. Then they get a ride from four animal activist babes (Shannon Elizabeth, Eliza Dushku, Ali Larter, and Jennifer Smith), who pose as friends but want to exploit them in the theft of a monkey.

Once in Los Angeles, we and they go through the looking-glass into a world where director Gus Van Sant, Affleck, and Damon appear as themselves on the set of *Good Will Hunting,* and Chris Rock is the race-card-playing director of the *Bluntman* movie, which stars James Van Der Beek and Jason Biggs as Jay and Silent Bob. And Silent Bob finally arrives at the monologue we patiently await in every picture, and reveals himself to be as least as articulate as Chris Matthews.

The charm of a Kevin Smith movie is that it assumes you do not enter the theater as a blank slate. *Chasing Amy* assumes a little knowledge of the world of serious comic books and collectors, *Dogma* required you to know something about Catholic theology, and *Jay and Silent Bob* has moments like the one where the Affleck character defines the Internet for Jay: "It's a place used the world over where people can come together to bitch about movies and share pornography together." This is a much more sophisticated idea of the Net than we find in high-tech cyberthrillers, where the Net is a place that makes your computer beep a lot.

Whether you will like *Jay and Silent Bob* depends on who you are. Most movies are made for everybody. Kevin Smith's movies are either made specifically for you, or specifically not made for you. If you read this review without a smile or a nod of recognition, I would recommend *Rush Hour II,* which is for everybody or nobody, you tell me.

Note: The Gay and Lesbian Alliance Against Discrimination has chosen the wrong target in attacking Jay and Silent Bob for alleged antigay material. GLAAD should give audiences credit for enough intelligence to know the difference between satire and bigotry. Smith agreed to add a disclaimer to the end of the movie saying "the use of antigay slurs in real life is not acceptable," as if this will (a) come as news, or (b) act as a wake-up call for those who use them. But he refused to apologize for his film, which describes Jay and Silent Bob as "hetero life-partners," and said in a statement: "I'm not sorry, because I didn't make the jokes at the expense of the gay community. I made jokes at the expense of two characters who neither I nor the audience have ever held up to be paragons of intellect. They're idiots." ☞

Jesus' Son ★ ★ ★ ½
R, 110 m., 2000

Billy Crudup (FH), Samantha Morton (Michelle), Denis Leary (Wayne), Jack Black (Georgie), Will Patton (John Smith), Greg Germann (Dr. Shanis), Holly Hunter (Mira), Dennis Hopper (Bill). Directed by Alison Maclean and produced by Elizabeth Cuthrell, Lydia Dean Pilcher, and David Urrutia. Screenplay by Cuthrell, Urrutia, and Oren Moverman, based on stories by Denis Johnson.

Thinking at first I am seeing still one more road movie about a druggie, I find I am wrong. *Jesus' Son* surprises me with moments of wry humor, poignancy, sorrow, and wildness. It has a sequence as funny as any I've seen this year, and one as harrowing, and it ends in a bittersweet minor key, as it should, because to attach this story to a big climax would be a lie, if not a crime. Like all good films, it is not for everybody (only bad films are for everybody).

The story revolves around the time and place of Iowa City, circa 1971, although the hero does a lot of traveling all over the country, and in his own memories. His name is FH, which is short for guess what, and in the beginning he is one of those college town layabouts with no plans and not many problems. One day on a bench he meets Michelle. They talk a little and he asks, "Do I kiss you now?"

Later, she asks him, "You ever seen anybody shoot up before?" He has not, but soon heroin is running his life.

But this is not a drug movie like any you've seen. It doesn't glamorize drugs or demonize them, but simply remembers them from the point of view of a survivor. FH (Billy Crudup) narrates the story, sometimes doubling back to fill in gaps or add overlooked details. He isn't a hero or an antihero, just a fairly clueless guy with good intentions who gets muddled by the drug lifestyle—which creates a burden the mind is not really designed to endure.

The movie's director is Alison Maclean, a New Zealander whose screenplay (by Elizabeth Cuthrell, David Urrutia, and Oren Moverman) is based on short stories by the American Denis Johnson. Some will complain that the episodes jostle too loosely against one another (it's "a barbiturate-driven version of *Pulp Fiction,* in which the guns misfire and the cars don't have brakes," writes *Salon*'s Andrew O'Hehir, in a negative but somehow affectionate review). I think short stories are right for a story about druggies. Their lives are too episodic to add up to a novel; the highs and lows settle out into disconnected adventures and anecdotes, separated by voids and blackouts.

The thing about FH and Michelle (Samantha Morton) is that they love each other, in a fashion, but are inhabiting a lifestyle that has too many distractions for any kind of continuity. Drugs or love: You sort of have to choose one or the other, because you can't pay attention to both. Their romance, when it is working, has a kind of tenderness that grows out of their suffering. They are so screwed up that when the movie lingers on the sight of them kissing, we realize with a stir that their kissing is direct and needy, not movie-stylized. They aren't putting on a show for the camera, but feeding at each other's lips.

Samantha Morton you will remember from Woody Allen's *Sweet and Lowdown,* where she played a mute. Here she plays a woman who is more or less the result of the situation she's gotten herself into: If you are going to use drugs and don't have infinite money, you are going to have to make some compromises. Crudup is a good partner for her, coming in under her radar, ready for whatever she has in mind.

But the movie is not just about (or even re-

ally about) FH and Michelle. It's episodic, and there are moments that stand out like sharp memories in a confused time. Like the fat kid who races after their car and runs into the pole. Or the naked woman parasailing. "That's my wife," says FH's newfound barroom buddy Wayne (Denis Leary). No further explanation. They spend an afternoon stripping the copper wires out of an empty house. "How much money do you think we can make from this?" FH asks. "Enough to go to bed drunk tonight," says Wayne.

FH eventually gets a job as an orderly in a hospital, and that leads to a sequence that combines the gruesome and the comic as memorably as the needle to the heart in *Pulp Fiction.* A patient comes in with a knife sticking out of his eye socket. The ER nurse tells him, "We better get you lying down." I liked the way the man's condition is diagnosed: "Patient complains of knife in head." FH's fellow orderly is Jack Black (the larger of the two clerks in *High Fidelity*). When a doctor hesitates, he knows what to do.

The last third of the film is one bemusement and perplexity after another. FH goes into rehab, and gives a shave to a patient (Dennis Hopper) whose sentences summarize decades. He has a little romance with a woman (Holly Hunter) who just plain has bad luck with her husbands. He gets a job as the editor of a newsletter at an old folks' home. ("This job includes a lot of touching," he's told. "We want to see you touching the patients.") He falls in love with the overheard voice of a Mennonite woman, singing in her shower—and observes the complexities of the situation where her husband tells him, "Take what you need."

The movie's title is not intended to be a literal description of FH ("Jesus' Son" is a line from a Lou Reed song), but I see what it's getting at: A lot of great men have sons who plug away at the family business but just don't have the knack. FH's story is not a cautionary tale, a parable, or a fable. It is just what happened to him. He's not a bad guy. He should play more of an active role in his life, instead of just letting it happen to him. And when he's asked if he's ever seen anybody shoot up before, he should ask himself if he hasn't been getting along more or less okay without having had that experience.

Jimmy Neutron: Boy Genius ★ ★ ★
G, 90 m., 2001

Debi Derryberry (Jimmy Neutron), Candi Milo (Cindy Vortex), Rob Paulsen (Carl Wheezer), Martin Short (Ooblar), Patrick Stewart (King Goobot). Directed by John A. Davis and produced by Davis, Albie Hecht, and Steve Oedekerk. Screenplay by Davis, David N. Weiss, J. David Stem, and Oedekerk.

The animated comedy *Jimmy Neutron: Boy Genius* takes place in those carefree years right before puberty strikes kids down with zits and self-consciousness. "We don't like girls yet, do we, Jimmy?" asks fearful Carl Wheezer, the hero's best friend. "No, no, not yet," Jimmy reassures him. But he broods about what is on the horizon: "Hormones over which we have no control will overpower our better judgment."

Jimmy Neutron, sometimes called "Nerdtron" by his jeering classmates on the school bus, is a boy inventor who pilots his own rocket plane and is seen, as the movie opens, trying to launch a satellite before breakfast. He makes Tom Swift look slow. His dog, for example, is not a mammal but a robot named Goddard (after the father of rocketry). When Goddard makes a mess, it consists of nuts and bolts.

At home, Jimmy has inventions to brush his teeth and comb his hair. During show-and-tell at school, he unveils a device that will shrink people, and inadvertently shrinks his teacher, who is attacked by the worm in her apple. Jimmy also has a communicator capable of picking up signals from space, and becomes convinced he has been contacted by an advanced civilization. "I don't care how advanced they are," his mother says. "If your father and I haven't met them, they're strangers."

A crisis strikes. Alien spaceships suck up all of the adults in town. At first the kids celebrate, but after eating too much popcorn and candy and drinking forbidden coffee, they're as green in the morning as the lads on the Island of Lost Boys in *Pinocchio.* Jimmy enlists the other kids in an expedition to find the alien planet and rescue the parents.

Their space travel is conceived by the filmmakers in a way that is not only charming but kind of lovely. Jimmy converts some of the rides in an amusement park into spaceships, and we see a Ferris wheel, an octopus ride, and a merry-go-round journeying across the field of stars. In another inspired conceit, they stop for the night on an asteroid, build a campfire, and frighten each other with campfire ghost stories.

Jimmy Neutron: Boy Genius is a Nickelodeon production, frankly aimed at grade-schoolers. It doesn't have the little in-jokes that make *Shrek* and *Monsters, Inc.* fun for grown-ups. But adults who appreciate the art of animation may enjoy the look of the picture, which is a kind downsized *Toy Story* with a lot of originality in the visual ideas. All movies for kids currently pay intense attention to bodily functions, and it is progress of a sort, I suppose, that Jimmy Neutron's rude noise of choice is merely the belch.

Joe Dirt ★ ½
PG-13, 93 m., 2001

David Spade (Joe Dirt), Brittany Daniel (Brandy), Dennis Miller (Zander Kelly), Adam Beach (Kicking Wing), Christopher Walken (Clem), Jaimie Pressly (Jill), Kid Rock (Robby), Erik Per Sullivan (Little Joe Dirt), Carson Daly (Himself). Directed by Dennie Gordon and produced by Robert Simonds. Screenplay by David Spade and Fred Wolf.

I wrote the words *Joe Dirt* at the top of my notepad and settled back to watch the new David Spade movie. Here is the first note I took: "Approx. 6 min. until first cow fart set afire." *Joe Dirt* doesn't waste any time letting you know where it stands.

This is the kind of movie where the hero finds two things that have fallen from the skies—a meteor and an atomic bomb—and both turn out to be a case of mistaken identity. Yes, the meteor is actually a large chunk of frozen treasure from an airplane lavatory, and the bomb is actually a large human waste storage unit.

We professional movie critics count it a banner week when only one movie involves eating, falling into, or being covered by excrement (or a cameo appearance by Carson Daly). We are not prudes. We are prepared to laugh. But what these movies, including *Joe Dirt,* often do not understand is that the act of being buried in crap is not in and of *itself* funny.

Third-graders might think so (they're big on fart jokes, too), but trust me: When Joe Dirt thinks he has an atom bomb until the cap gets knocked off and a geyser of brown crud pours out, and he *just stands there* while it covers him—that's not funny. Especially since we know he's only standing there to be sure we get the joke. Otherwise, he would move to avoid being entirely covered. Wouldn't you? (Direct quote from the press release, in connection with a scene where Spade is nearly eaten by an alligator: "David Spade performed his own stunts with the animatronic reptile. Trapped in a tangle of cable while lodged in the beast's mouth, he joked to the crew that he hoped he'd never have to get a job at a zoo." To which I can only add, "What? And leave show business?!")

Spade plays Joe Dirt, who is white trash. The movie uses that expression constantly, even observing at one point that his facial hair has grown in "white trash style" without the need for trimming. Joe's haircut is one of those 1970s mullet jobs; we learn it's not real hair but a wig supplied by his parents to cover a crack in his infant head that exposed his brain (Note: This is also supposed to be funny). The wig is a rare gift from his parents, who apparently abandoned him at the Grand Canyon when he was eight and happily playing in a garbage can.

Joe's origins and adventures are related many years later, when he happens into the studio of a talk jock played by Dennis Miller, whose own facial hair makes him look uncannily like the BBC's recent computer reconstruction of historical Jesus. Little Joe has been on his own ever since he was eight, he says, wandering the country as kind of a low-rent Forrest Gump, stumbling into interesting people and strange experiences. Where Forrest might meet a president, however, Joe is more likely to accidentally find himself in the gondola of a hot-air balloon in the shape of a tooth.

The movie's production notes further inform us: "Spade says this is the first time he has ever played a character that is likable. 'It's a big switch for me,' he says." I think he may still have his first likable character ahead of him. Joe Dirt is so obviously a construction

that it is impossible to find anything human about him; he is a concept, not a person, and although Spade arguably looks better in the mullet wig than he does with his trademark mop-top, he still has the same underlying personality. Here is a man born to play the Peter Lorre role.

The movie has a very funny moment. (Spoiler alert!) It involves Christopher Walken, an actor with so much identity and charisma that his mere appearance on a screen generates interest in any audience (and gratitude and relief from this one). He plays a character named Clem, who has good reasons for not wanting to appear on television. Eventually he reveals that he has gone underground with a new identity and is now Gert B. Frobe.

Note: The movie's PG-13 rating is one more plaque on the Jack Valenti Wall of Shame. The press kit quotes Spade on the movie: "Honestly, I think it's kind of good for kids. I mean, here's a guy that's just trying to be a good guy. He's not mean to people, and he's not sarcastic, and he's not a jerk." That could be an apology for the mean, sarcastic jerks he's played up until now, but probably not.

Joe Gould's Secret ★ ★ ★ ½
R, 108 m., 2000

Ian Holm (Joe Gould), Stanley Tucci (Joe Mitchell), Hope Davis (Therese Mitchell), Sarah Hyland (Elizabeth Mitchell), Hallee Hirsh (Nora Mitchell), Celia Weston (Sarah), Patrick Tovatt (Harold Ross), Susan Sarandon (Alice Neel). Directed by Stanley Tucci and produced by Elizabeth W. Alexander, Tucci, and Charles Weinstock. Screenplay by Howard A. Rodman, based on *Professor Seagull* and *Joe Gould's Secret* by Joseph Mitchell.

The secret of *Joe Gould's Secret* is that it is not Joe Gould's secret at all. It is Joe Mitchell's secret. Joe Gould is easy to understand, because like many madmen he is consistent from day to day—stuck in the rut of his delusions. But Joe Mitchell is a hard case, a man who hides his elusive nature behind a facade of shyness and courtly southern manners. Stanley Tucci's lovingly crafted film pretends to be about Joe Gould, and all the time its real subject is hidden right there before us in plain view.

Joseph Mitchell was a writer for the *New Yorker* in its glory days, in the 1930s and 1940s, when Harold Ross was the editor and the staff included Robert Benchley and E. B. White. He wrote stories about the people of the city, characters he encountered or heard about. One of them was Joe Gould, a bearded bohemian who marched through the streets of Greenwich Village clutching his tattered portfolio and demanding donations to the "Joe Gould Fund."

Gould claimed to be writing an oral history of New York, a million-word record of the daily conversations of the citizens, and had collected many patrons who believed him. "Gimme a bowl of soup—I don't have all day," he announces, marching into a restaurant the first time Mitchell sees him. He gets his soup. Max Gordon of the Village Vanguard donates to the "fund," and so does the poet e. e. cummings. In the film, the painter Alice Neel (Susan Sarandon) tells Mitchell: "I have always felt that the city's unconscious is trying to speak to you through Joe Gould."

Gould (Ian Holm) is a man of swiftly changing emotional weather. He can be sweet, perceptive, philosophical, and then burst out in sudden rage. The first time he has a conversation with Joe Mitchell (Stanley Tucci), he gets right to the heart of the matter. "Say 'I may marry Mary,'" he orders Mitchell, and then, after listening to the writer's accent, asks, "How did your father feel when you didn't want to go into the tobacco industry?" He has correctly clocked Mitchell as a refugee from a southern tobacco state, who became a writer against his father's wishes.

In another scene, Mitchell brings home watermelon for his wife and daughters, and cuts it on a piece of newspaper. "My father always said this was the only thing a newspaper was good for," he recalls. "And what did you say?" his wife asks the writer. He replies evenly, "I said not a thing."

There are clues to the film's real subject all through the movie. Mitchell's opening narration observes that Joe Gould felt at home among the city's outcasts and homeless, cranks and crazies. Mitchell says he did, too, and adds, "As time went on, I would find that this was not the only thing we had in common." What else they had in common is saved for the movie's end title, and suddenly illuminates the whole film.

Stanley Tucci is a director and actor with an openhearted generosity for his characters; he loves and forgives them. His first film, *Big Night,* codirected with Campbell Scott, was a perfect little masterpiece about an Italian restaurant run with too many ideals and not enough customers. Here he's made a chamber piece of quiet scenes, acutely heard dialogue, and subterranean emotional shifts. Ian Holm's role as Joe Gould is the flashy one, and some viewers will be fooled into thinking the film is about Gould. But he isn't the one who changes. He is himself from beginning to end, repeating the same notes, sometimes touchingly, sometimes maddeningly.

The movie is about Joe Mitchell, a man who avoids confrontation with such determination that he even hesitates to finish a sentence, lest it not be to his interrogator's liking. He pauses and backtracks, stammers and corrects himself, qualifies every word, and phrases everything with elusive southern courtesy. Joe Gould enters his life like a cautionary tale. Toward the end of the film, at a Greenwich Village party, Mitchell finds himself describing the book he plans to write, and we realize (if he does not) that he is describing a version of Joe Gould's oral history. Indeed, most of Mitchell's *New Yorker* articles did what Gould claimed to do; Mitchell wandered the city, stumbling bemusedly on people and their stories.

There is a dark, deep, and sad undercurrent in the movie. There is a whole story to be extracted from Mitchell's hints about himself. We sense it from the opening moments. It tantalizes us as the subtext of most of the scenes. Where is he headed? At the movie's very end we learn that one additional piece of information about Joseph Mitchell, and everything becomes clear. Tucci and Howard A. Rodman, who wrote the screenplay, based it on Mitchell's two articles about Gould, but they discovered something unwritten in those articles that gave them the clue to this movie. Some have said the film is too quiet and slow. There is anguish here that makes *American Beauty* pale by comparison.

Joe Somebody ★ ½
PG, 98 m., 2001

Tim Allen (Joe Scheffer), James Belushi (Chuck Scarett), Julie Bowen (Meg Harper), Patrick Warburton (Mark McKinney), Greg Germann (Jeremy Callahan), Kelly Lynch (Callie Scheffer), Hayden Panettiere (Natalie Scheffer). Directed by John Pasquin and produced by Kenneth Atchity, Matthew Gross, Anne Kopelson, Arnold Kopelson, and Brian Reilly. Screenplay by John Scott Shepherd.

Joe Somebody plays like an after-school special with grown-ups cast in the kids' roles. It's a simple, wholesome parable, crashingly obvious, and we sit patiently while the characters and the screenplay slowly arrive at the inevitable conclusion. It needs to take some chances and surprise us. Everybody in the movie is kinda nice (except for the bully), and the principal—I mean, the boss—is patient while they learn their lessons and Joe finds out he really is somebody when the smart girl smiles at him.

Tim Allen is likable as the hero named Joe, but is likable enough? He's a Milquetoast video guy at a marketing agency, divorced, lonely, with nothing much to talk about, who makes up stuff to say to the cute Meg (Julie Bowen) when he runs into her in the office, because his real life is too boring to contemplate. The most exciting point in the day is when he staples his sleeve to the wall.

He dotes on his daughter, Natalie (Hayden Panettiere), and takes her along on Bring Your Daughter to Work Day. But in the company parking lot for employees with ten years or more of service, he is cut off by a big SUV driven by the bully (Patrick Warburton), who is not only rude and reckless but also doesn't even have ten years of service. When Joe protests, he is slapped and knocked down in front of his daughter, and decides, thinking it over, that he won't take her to work that day after all.

We feel really bad for him. He seems on the edge of tears. His spirit is crushed, he enters into a depression, and then he decides to get even. Enter Chuck Scarett (James Belushi), a martial arts instructor who is, I think, intended to remind us of Steven Seagal (and who looks rather more sleek and fit than Seagal himself has recently). Chuck has an an-

cient and obligatory role as the coach who will take the underdog and turn him into a contender. And Joe demands a rematch with the bully.

This pays the unexpected dividend of making his stock rise at the office, although his boss's reasons for promoting him are suitably devious. He even has more to talk about with Meg now, although she looks at his changes with concern, and we are reminded of the schoolmarm in a Western who gets worried when the farmer takes to carrying a rifle.

What happens, and how and why, will be perfectly clear to any sentient moviegoer as soon as the plot lays down its tracks. There are few experiences more disheartening (at the movies, anyway) than a film that suffers from preordination. By the end of *Joe Somebody*, we are faced with the dismal prospect of being denied a climax which, if it occurred, would be just as predictable as its substitute.

Joe Somebody is Tim Allen's third film directed by John Pasquin; they worked together on TV's *Home Improvement*. Their previous movies were *The Santa Clause* (1994) and *Jungle2Jungle* (1997). The first was mediocre, the second was aggressively awful, and now we get this movie, well-meaning but pretty thin soup.

I agree with all the sentiments in *Joe Somebody*, and indeed I can see them being cobbled into a parable of considerable power, especially if Joe were played by somebody who really seemed to have a capacity for violence. But Tim Allen plays Joe as a guy who never really changes, while the screenplay desperately tells us he does. And when the girl seems to turn away—isn't that what the girl always does in these plots, so that later she can turn back again?

John Q. ★ ½
PG-13, 118 m., 2002

Denzel Washington (John Q.), Robert Duvall (Grimes), James Woods (Dr. Turner), Anne Heche (Rebecca Payne), Ray Liotta (Monroe), Shawn Hatosy (Mitch), Kimberly Elise (Denise), Keram Malicki-Sanchez (Freddy), Daniel E. Smith (Mike). Directed by Nick Cassavetes and produced by Mark Burg and Oren Koules. Screenplay by James Kearns.

John Q. is the kind of movie *Mad* magazine prays for. It is so earnest, so overwrought, and so wildly implausible that it begs to be parodied. I agree with its message—that the richest nation in history should be able to afford national health insurance—but the message is pounded in with such fevered melodrama, it's as slanted and manipulative as your average political commercial.

The film stars Denzel Washington as John Q. Archibald, a Chicago factory worker whose apparently healthy son collapses during a Little League game. John Q. and his wife, Denise (Kimberly Elise), race the kid to an emergency room, where his signs are stabilized, and then a cardiologist (James Woods) explains that young Mike's heart is three times normal size.

There are two options: a heart transplant, or optimizing Mike's "quality of life" during the "months . . . weeks . . . days" left to him. Joining the doctor is appropriately named hospital administrator Rebecca Payne (Anne Heche), who already knows the Archibalds have no money and argues for the "quality of life" choice.

John Q. thinks he's covered by insurance, but no: His company switched to a new HMO that has a $20,000 ceiling, and since John has been downsized to twenty hours a week, he's lucky to have that much coverage. Payne demands a $75,000 down payment on the $250,000 operation, and explains the harsh realities of life for "cash patients." John Q. considers taking the kid to County Hospital, but is urged by a friendly hospital employee to stay right there at the ominously named Crisis of Hope Memorial Hospital.

The TV ads helpfully reveal that John Q. exhausts all his options and eventually pulls a gun and takes hostages, demanding that his son be put at the top of the list of eligible recipients. (He wouldn't be jumping the queue because the Heche character explains Mike is so sick he would automatically be the first recipient—if the money were available.)

The hostages are your usual cross section of supporting roles: a gunshot victim, a battered woman and her violent boyfriend, a pregnant mother who has "started to dilate!" and so on. Plus Dr. Turner. The cops surround the building, and veteran negotiator Grimes (Robert Duvall) tries to build a relationship with John Q.,

while hotshot police chief Monroe (Ray Liotta) grandstands for the TV cameras—displaying sixteen stars on his uniform, four each on both collars and both lapels. Any more and he'd be Tinker Bell.

The underlying situation here is exactly the same as in *Dog Day Afternoon* (1975), an infinitely smarter hostage picture. What *John Q.* lacks is the confidence to allow its characters to act intelligently. Chief Monroe is almost hilariously stupid. Consider this. A local TV station somehow manages to tap the police feed from the hospital's security cameras, and broadcasts live video and sound of John Q. inside the hospital. Monroe smuggles a sniper into the hospital who has John Q. in his sights. John Q. is in the act of having an emotional and heartbreaking telephone conversation with his little boy when Monroe, who is (a) unaware of the TV feed, or (b) too dumb to live, orders the marksman to fire.

Does John Q. die? That's a question you find yourself asking a lot during this film. To avoid spoilers, I won't go into detail, but there is a moment when the movie just plain cheats on the question of John Q.'s status, and I felt conned.

There are passages where the actors transcend the material. John Q.'s farewell to his son is one. Kimberly Elise's relationship with her husband is well handled. But in a sense special honors should go to James Woods and Robert Duvall for achieving what they can with roles so awkwardly written that their behavior whipsaws between good, evil, and hilarious. Anne Heche is deep sixed by her role, which makes her a penny-pinching shrew and then gives her a cigarette to smoke just in case we missed that she's the villain. The Grim Reaper would flee from this woman.

Josie and the Pussycats ½★

PG-13, 95 m., 2001

Rachael Leigh Cook (Josie McCoy), Tara Reid (Melody Valentine), Rosario Dawson (Valerie Brown), Parker Posey (Fiona), Alan Cumming (Wyatt Frame), Gabriel Mann (Alan M. Mayberry), Paulo Costanzo (Alexander Cabot), Missi Pyle (Alexandra Cabot). Directed by Harry Elfont and Deborah Kaplan and produced by Tony DeRosa-Grund, Tracey E. Edmonds, Chuck

Grimes, and Marc E. Platt. Screenplay by Elfont and Kaplan.

The heroines of *Josie and the Pussycats* are not dumber than the Spice Girls, but they're as dumb as the Spice Girls, which is dumb enough. They're a girl band recruited as they're crossing the street by a promoter who wants to use their songs as a carrier for subliminal messages. The movie is a would-be comedy about prefab bands and commercial sponsorship, which may mean that the movie's own plugs for Coke, Target, Starbucks, Motorola, and Evian are part of the joke.

The product placement for Krispy Kreme doughnuts is, however, an ominous development, since it may trigger a war with Dunkin' Donuts, currently the most visible product placer in the movies. With Krispy and Dunkin' dukin' it out, there may soon be no doughnut-free movies not actually featuring gladiators.

The movie, based on a comic book from the Archie stable, stars Rachel Leigh Cook as Josie McCoy, its lead singer; Tara Reid as Melody Valentine, the bubble-brained blonde; and Rosario Dawson as Valerie Brown. None of these women have families, friends, or employers, apparently, and are free to move randomly through the plot as a unit without ever calling home. After a prologue in which a previous prefab boy band disappears in a plane crash, a nefarious record producer named Wyatt Frame (Alan Cumming, the gay villain du jour) hires them on first sight, without hearing them sing a note, to be his newest promotion.

The prologue has some vaguely *Spinal Tap* overtones (I liked the detail that its members wear headsets at all times, not just onstage). But *Josie* ignores bountiful opportunities to be a satire of the Spice Girls and other manufactured groups, and gets dragged down by a lame plot involving the scheme to control teen spending with the implanted messages. (The movie calls them "subliminal." Since they're sound waves, they're actually "subaural," but never mind; the Pussycats would probably think subaural was a kind of foreplay.)

One curiosity about the movie is its stiff and sometimes awkward dialogue; the words don't seem to flow, but sound as if the actors are standing there and reciting them. The movie's market on verbal wit is cornered by Cumming, in the Richard E. Grant role, who has one (1) funny moment in which he demonstrates how very well trained the boy band is. The rest of the time, he has the thankless task of acting as if he is funny in a plot that is not funny.

The music is pretty bad. That's surprising, since Kenneth (Babyface) Edmunds is one of the producers, and knows his way around music. Maybe it's *supposed* to sound like brainless preteen fodder, but it's not good enough at being bad to be funny, and stops merely at the bad stage.

Parker Posey has one of those supporting roles from hell, where she has to make her entrance as a cliché and then never even gets to play with the conventions of her role. She's Cummings's boss, one of the masterminds of the nefarious subaural marketing scheme, and since she is, in fact, a funny and talented actress with wicked timing, her failure to make anything of this role is proof there's nothing for her to work with. Also drifting aimlessly through the plot is a character named Alexandra Cabot (Missi Pyle), who at least has the best explanation for why she's in the movie, as well as the movie's second (2nd) funny line of dialogue. "Why are you here?" she's asked, and replies with serene logic, "I'm here because I was in the comic book."

Joy Ride ★ ★ ★ ½
R, 96 m., 2001

Steve Zahn (Fuller), Paul Walker (Lewis), Leelee Sobieski (Venna), Jessica Bowman (Charlotte), Stuart Stone (Danny), Basil Wallace (Car Salesman), Brian Leckner (Officer Keeney). Directed by John Dahl and produced by J. J. Abrams and Chris Moore. Screenplay by Clay Tarver and Abrams.

There is a kind of horror movie that plays so convincingly we don't realize it's an exercise in pure style. *Halloween* is an example, and John Dahl's *Joy Ride* is another. Both films have an evil, marauding predator who just keeps on coming, no matter what, and always seems to know what the victims will do next. *Joy Ride* adds the detail that we never see the villain. We only hear his voice and see his truck.

The film is anchored by convincing characters in a halfway plausible setup. Paul Walker *(The Fast and the Furious)* plays Lewis, a college student who has pretended for years to be the best friend of Venna (Leelee Sobieski) when actually he wants to be her boyfriend. He's at school in California, she's in Boulder, Colorado, and after a sudden inspiration he offers to drive them both back East for the holidays.

True to the *Ebert's Little Glossary* entry that explains that all movie heroes on cross-country journeys drive gas-guzzling classics, Lewis buys a 1971 Chrysler Newport (most of the cars since 1980 look nerdy). Ordinarily the Newport would be a convertible; it needs to be a hardtop this time, so they can be trapped inside.

Lewis makes a detour along the way—to Salt Lake City, where his feckless brother Fuller (Steve Zahn, with a "What? Me worry?" expression) needs to be bailed out on drunk charges. Then it's on to Boulder, while we have lots of time to wonder why the movie spends so much time repeating that Venna goes to Boulder, Boulder, Boulder—only to show us an absolutely flat, neocolonial campus with no mountains in the background. This evens the score, I guess, for the mountains that *were* in the background in *Rumble in the Bronx.*

No matter. The plot has already tightened its screws. Fuller, who has a gift for attracting trouble, and another gift for seeking it out when it doesn't come to him, talks Lewis into buying a $40 citizen's band radio ("kind of a prehistoric Internet"), and then eggs him into imitating a woman's voice on the air. As Candy Cane, Lewis makes a date with a trucker named Rusty Nail. "She" says she'll be in Room 17 of a roadside motel—which, Lewis and Fuller know, will be occupied by a customer who's a particularly obnoxious racist. The practical jokers are next door in Room 18.

The device of the never-seen enemy is particularly effective here, as Rusty Nail pounds on the door of the neighbor, there are some indistinct voices, and then a long silence. Later, when the guy in Room 17 is found in the middle of the road in a coma and Fuller is talking to the police, he says he heard a noise like—well, you have to hear Zahn performing it. He somehow finds a note of realistic goofiness; he's funny, but you believe he's like this all the time.

The movie then settles into a series of high-tension action scenes as Rusty Nail, driving an enormous semi, tracks the Chrysler down the back roads of the Plains states. It is a convention in road movies that the heroes never take the interstate and always find ramshackle gas stations that in real life have been bankrupt for years; the atmosphere of menace is further underlined by the obligatory redneck bar with the menacing drunks who threaten the girl (Zahn's character defuses this situation with a brilliant improvisation).

It will be impossible for critics to review this movie without mentioning Steven Spielberg's TV debut film, *Duel* (1971), and it does admittedly feature an implacable foe in a big truck, but the details are all different and original, and John Dahl *(Red Rock West, The Last Seduction)* is a master of menace in everyday life. His writers, Clay Tarver and J. J. Abrams, find the details and pacing to make the unlikely into the inevitable.

It's puzzling at first how Rusty Nail, whose truck would seem to be hard to hide, is apparently able to follow them everywhere and know what they're doing; my guess is, when he tells them to "look in the trunk" and they find their CB radio there, he's rigged it so he can eavesdrop on them. That would also explain some (but not all) of his info about Venna's roommate Charlotte (Jessica Bowman). Also, other truckers could be spotting for him, and every semi in the background looks ominous.

One sequence was both effective and distracting at the same time. The truck pursues the three characters through a cornfield at night, its powerful searchlight looking for suspiciously waving stalks, and there is a great shot of the heroes running toward the camera with the truck right on top of them. At moments like this, I always wonder why they don't jump out of the way and run in the opposite direction, since it's a big operation to turn a rig like that around in a cornfield.

Quibbles. *Joy Ride* is a first-rate pure thriller, an exercise that depends on believable characters and the director's skill in putting the pieces together. The final motel sequence, in which everything breathlessly and bloodily comes together, is relentlessly well crafted. You want to be scared and have a few laughs and not have your intelligence insulted? Here you go. ☞

Jump Tomorrow ★ ★ ★
PG, 96 m., 2001

Tunde Adebimpe (George), Hippolyte Girardot (Gerard), Natalia Verbeke (Alicia), James Wilby (Nathan), Patricia Mauceri (Consuelo), Isiah Whitlock Jr. (George's Uncle), Kaili Vernoff (Heather Leather), Gene Ruffini (Old Man), Abiola Wendy Abrams (Sophie). Directed by Joel Hopkins and produced by Nicola Usborne. Screenplay by Hopkins.

People are always asking George to smile, and he tries to oblige, with a self-conscious twitch of the lips that reveals less happiness than wariness. What is he afraid of? Of smiling, I think. George (Tunde Adebimpe) is a serious, dutiful Nigerian who always wears glasses and usually wears a suit and needs to learn to listen to his heart.

We meet him at the airport in Buffalo, where he plans to meet his bride-to-be; it is an arranged marriage with a Nigerian woman his family has known for years. Alas, she arrived on yesterday's plane, and finding no one to meet her, has already gone on to Niagara, where the wedding is to take place. George's uncle (Isiah Whitlock Jr.) is apoplectic: The marriage makes good "sense," and George is blowing it.

That's the setup for the low-key screwball comedy *Jump Tomorrow*, which takes a 1930s Hollywood formula and recasts it with unexpected types. At the airport, George meets Alicia (Natalia Verbeke), a Latina who flirts with him and tells him about a party that night. And he meets Gerard (Hippolyte Girardot), a disconsolate Frenchman who has just proposed marriage and been slammed down.

George is not a demonstrative man, but for some reason he inspires others to enlist in his cause. He ends up at Alicia's party with Gerard, and by the end of the evening it is clear to Gerard, if not to George, that George is in love with Alicia. Gerard sees George as an assignment from heaven: If Gerard cannot find happiness in love, perhaps he can help George find it. He offers to drive George to Niagara. Along the way they encounter Alicia and her unpromising British boyfriend Nathan (James Wilby). Everyone ends up in Gerard's car (license plate: AMOUR), their romantic futures in doubt.

The title of *Jump Tomorrow* refers to helpful advice for potential suicides. It may also refer to taking a big romantic leap. The movie has been written and directed by Joel Hopkins, a recent graduate of the NYU film school, whose short subject *Jorge* starred the same character and was a hit on the festival and on-line circuits. The movie doesn't have an unkind thought in its head. It's all sweetness and understated charm, and after a while even George begins to grow on us.

That is a slow process, because Tunde Adebimpe plays the character as a man who values probity above all else, and has an instinctive loathing for instinctive gestures. If he were happy-go-lucky, the movie would lose much of its charm; the buried question is whether this sober, severe young man is capable of a grand romantic gesture. The movie plays with ethnic stereotypes by having the Gallic Gerard and the Latin Alicia as his emotional prods; the Englishman Nathan is as uptight as George, but while George's personality is a challenge, Nathan's is a trial.

Is there a market for a movie like this? It doesn't punch out its comic points but lets the story gradually reveal them. It takes us time to like George. The plot unfolds with the gradual richness of something by Eric Rohmer, who has the whole canvas in view from the beginning but uncovers it a square inch at a time. By the end of *Jump Tomorrow* I was awfully fond of the picture. Is that enough for a first-run admission, or should you wait until it turns up on one of the indie cable channels? You tell me.

Jurassic Park III ★ ★ ★
PG-13, 91 m., 2001

Sam Neill (Dr. Alan Grant), William H. Macy (Paul Kirby), Tea Leoni (Amanda Kirby), Alessandro Nivola (Billy Brennan), Trevor Morgan (Eric Kirby), Michael Jeter (Udesky), John Diehl (Cooper), Bruce A. Young (Nash), Laura Dern (Ellie). Directed by Joe Johnston and produced by Kathleen Kennedy and Larry Franco. Screenplay by Peter Buchman, Alexander Payne, and Jim Taylor, based on characters created by Michael Crichton.

This movie does a good job of doing exactly

what it wants to do. *Jurassic Park III* is not as awe-inspiring as the first film or as elaborate as the second, but in its own B-movie way it's a nice little thrill machine. One of its charms is its length—less than 90 minutes, if you don't count the end credits. Like the second half of a double bill in the 1940s, it doesn't overstay its welcome.

One of the ways it saves time is by stunningly perfunctory character development. There's hardly a line of dialogue that doesn't directly serve the plot in one way or another. Even Sam Neill's pontifications about those who would trifle with the mystery of life are in the movie only as punctuation, to separate the action scenes. In a summer when B-movie ideas like this have been blown up to gargantuan size and length with A-movie budgets, here is an action picture we actually wish was a little longer.

Part of its brevity is explained by the abrupt ending, which comes with little preparation and will have you racing to the dictionary to look up "deus ex machina." Trained by the interior tides and rhythms of most action movies, we get the ending when we expect the false crisis, followed by the false dawn, and then the real crisis and the real dawn. We can't believe the movie is really over, and when some flying pteranodons appear, we expect another action scene, but no—they're just flapping their way overseas to set up the next sequel.

The movie begins with a fourteen-year-old named Eric (Trevor Morgan) parasailing with his mother's boyfriend over the forbidden island of Isla Sorna, off the coast of Costa Rica. You will recall that this is the location of the doomed theme park in *The Lost World: Jurassic Park II.* The towboat disappears into a mist of fog and emerges sans crew, and the parasailers crash on the island. Cut to America, where two people (William H. Macy and Tea Leoni) offer a big bucks donation to the research of famous paleontologist Alan Grant (Sam Neill) if he will be their guide for a flight over the island.

They are in fact not just tourists; their secret is that they are Eric's parents, and they plan to land the plane on the island and rescue him. Along for the ride are Neill's gung ho assistant (Alessandro Nivola) and three other crew members, some of whom are quickly eaten by dinosaurs, although for a change the black character doesn't die first. The search for Eric consists mostly of the survivors walking through the forest shouting "Eric!" but the movie is ingenious in devising ways for prehistoric beasts to attack. There are some truly effective action sequences—one involving flying lizards and a suspension bridge, another involving an emergency rescue with the recycled parasail—that are as good as these things get.

I also liked the humor that's jimmied into the crevices of the plot. There are two nice gags involving the ringer on a cell phone, and a priceless exchange of dialogue between the fourteen-year-old and the expert paleontologist:

> Dr. Grant: This is T-Rex pee? How'd you get it?
> Eric: You don't want to know.

I am aware that *Jurassic Park III* is shorter, cheaper, and with fewer pretensions than its predecessors, and yet there was nothing I disliked about it, and a lot to admire in its lean, efficient storytelling. I can't praise it for its art, but I must not neglect its craft, and on that basis I recommend it.

Note: That last shot obviously means that the giant flying pteranodons are headed to civilization for Jurassic Park IV. *I am reminded of the 1982 movie* Q, *in which a flying reptile monster builds its nest atop the Chrysler Building and flies down to snack on stockbrokers. The movie was screened at Cannes, after which its proud producer, Samuel Z. Arkoff, hosted a gathering for film critics, at which I overheard the following conversation:*

> Rex Reed: Sam! I just saw your picture! What a surprise! All that dreck—and right in the middle of it, a great Method performance by Michael Moriarity!
> Arkoff: The dreck was my idea.

Just Visiting ★ ★ ★
PG-13, 88 m., 2001

Jean Reno (Thibault), Christina Applegate (Rosalind/Julia), Christian Clavier (André), Matthew Ross (Hunter), Tara Reid (Angelique), Bridgette Wilson-Sampras (Amber), John Aylward (Byron), George Plimpton (Dr. Brady), Malcolm McDowell (Wizard). Directed by Jean-Marie Poire and produced by Patrice Ledoux and Ricardo Mestres. Screenplay by Poire, Christian Clavier, and John Hughes.

A medieval sorcerer accidentally sends a French knight and his serf on a trip into the future—landing them in today's Chicago, where the elevated trains terrify them. But they grow to like the city, and when the sorcerer prepares to return them to the Middle Ages, the serf is against it: "I want to stay here, where I can eat doughnuts, and wear exciting men's fashions at rock-bottom prices."

Just Visiting, which tells their story, is one of those rare American remakes of a French film that preserves the flavor of the original and even improves upon it. The movie is a remake of *The Visitors*, or *Les Visiteurs* (1993), which was the top-grossing comedy in French history, but did only moderate business in America. Like the original, it's broad and swaggering, but somehow it plays better in English— maybe because the fish-out-of-water concept works better with French and American accents, instead of everybody speaking in subtitles.

The movie, directed by Jean-Marie Poire, wisely centers on its two original French stars, Jean Reno (of *Mission: Impossible* and *Godzilla*) and Christian Clavier. They look and sound the part; I can imagine the roles being assigned to Adam Sandler and David Spade, but I don't want to. Reno is Sir Thibault, a French knight who goes to Sussex to marry the beautiful Rosalind (Christina Applegate). His vassal André (Clavier) follows along, trotting obediently behind the cart and being whacked occasionally just to honor the class divide.

After a setup heavy on special effects and overacting, involving witches, cauldrons, and royal schemers, Thibault convinces a sorcerer (Malcolm McDowell) to jump them back a little in time, so they can get things right on a second try. The wizard, alas, miscalculates and sends them to modern Chicago, where the knight and serf are terrified by semis, awestruck by skyscrapers, and soon involved in the life of Thibault's great-great-great-great-great (I think) granddaughter Julia (Applegate again).

She's the heir to the family's old European fortune, founded all those years ago by Thibault, and the spitting image of his beloved Rosalind. But her boyfriend, the sneering

Hunter (Matthew Ross) wants her to sell the family's European estate, so he can get his claws on the money. Thibault and André understandably have difficulty convincing Chicagoans they are really from the twelfth century, but their behavior certainly seems authentic enough (in a restaurant, Thibault expects André, as his servant, to eat off the floor).

Thibault cannot actually fall in love with Julia, since she is his great, etc., granddaughter, but since she looks exactly like the woman he loved, he cares for her deeply, and tries to protect her from Hunter's schemes while schooling her in the ways of medieval gallantry. This involves a sword-fighting lesson in which they slice up refrigerators and Dumpsters, and a horsemanship adventure in which they actually ride their horses up the stairs, across an L platform, and onto the train.

André meanwhile falls in love with Angelique (Tara Reid), providing a counterpoint to the courtly idealism of his master. And every day is an adventure. Their first ride in a car, for example, is a terrifying experience. "Slower! Slower!" cries Thibault, as the car creeps at twenty miles per hour and both visitors hurl out the windows.

Is it only because the movie is in English that I like it more than the original? I hope I'm not that provincial. It strikes me that *Just Visiting* is brighter and sprightlier than *Les Visiteurs*, and the contrasts are funnier. Modern Europe is filled with Gothic and medieval piles, but in Chicago, when the visitors go looking for castles and turrets, they find them in the architecture of bars—where the regulars are always ready to drink with a man in armor, as long as he pays for his round.

There's something else too. *Just Visiting* isn't low and dumb like so many recent American comedies. It depends on the comedy of personality and situation, instead of treading meekly in the footsteps of the current gross-out manure-joke movies. Jean Reno, who usually plays a tough guy (remember him in *The Professional*?), plays Thibault more or less straight, taking his chivalric code seriously. Both he and Clavier try to appear truly baffled by what they see, instead of going straight for the gags.

Note: It must be said, all chauvinism aside, that the city of Chicago itself makes an impor-

tant contribution. John Hughes, who sets almost all of his movies here, is one of the movie's producers and cowriters, and he knows the town better than any other director (maybe it's a tie with Andrew Davis). Chicago locations have not been better used in any movie since Davis's Code of Silence and The Fugitive and Hughes's Ferris Bueller's Day Off, and they work not simply as backdrops but as dramatic settings. Given a knight on a horse in a city with elevated trains, it may seem inevitable that sooner or later he'd ride the horse onto the train, but it certainly looked like an inspired idea to me.

Juwanna Mann ★ ★

PG-13, 91 m., 2002

Miguel A. Nunez Jr. (Jamal/Juwanna Mann), Vivica A. Fox (Michelle Langford), Tommy Davidson (Puff Smokey Smoke), Kevin Pollak (Lorne Daniels), Ginuwine (Romeo), Kim Wayans (Latisha Jansen), Kimberly "Lil' Kim" Jones (Tina Parker). Directed by Jesse Vaughan and produced by Bill Gerber, James G. Robinson, and Steve Oedekerk. Screenplay by Bradley Allenstein.

Let us now consider predictability. Most of the time, I consider it an insult to the audience. We can sense when a movie is on autopilot, and we wonder, not unreasonably, why the filmmakers couldn't be bothered to try a little harder. Then a movie like Juwanna Mann comes along and is predictable to its very core, and in a funny way the predictability is part of the fun. The movie is in on the joke of its own recycling.

How predictable is it? It begins with a pro basketball star who is thrown out of the league (he gets so angry at a referee's call that he takes off all of his clothes and flashes the audience). He's faced with foreclosure, bankruptcy, and the loss of all his commercial endorsements, is fired by his manager, and has no skills except the ability to play basketball. In desperation, he dresses in drag and passes himself off as Juwanna Mann, a female player, and is soon a star of the women's pro basketball league.

With that information in mind, there are scenes we can all predict: (1) A date with an obnoxious man who doesn't know Juwanna is male. (2) Weird times in the shower. (3) A crush on a beautiful teammate who likes Juwanna as a friend but, of course, doesn't realize she's a man. (4) Unruly erections. (5) Ill-disciplined falsies. We can also predict that Juwanna will lead her team into the finals, become a big star, learn useful lessons about human nature, be faced with a crisis and exposure, and emerge as a better person, all of her problems solved, while the team wins the big game.

These predictable scenes are, I submit, inevitable. There is no way to make this movie without them—not as a comedy, anyway. So the pleasure, if any, must come from the performances, not the material. Up to a point, it does. Although Juwanna Mann is not a good movie, it isn't a painful experience, and Miguel A. Nunez Jr. is plausible as Juwanna, not because he is able to look like a woman, but because he is able to play a character who thinks he can look like a woman.

Vivica A. Fox plays Michelle, the teammate Juwanna falls in love with, and it is a challenging assignment, because almost all her dialogue needs to be taken two ways. Screenplay gimmicks like this are hard for actors, because if they are too sincere they look like chumps, and if they seem to be grinning sideways at the audience, they spoil the illusion. Fox finds the right tone and sticks to it; there is skilled professionalism at work, even in a rent-a-plot like this.

Since the entire movie is, of course, completely implausible, it seems unkind to single out specific examples of implausibility. But there's a difference between the implausibility of the basic gimmick (man passing as a woman) and the implausibility of plot details within the gimmick. The most obvious comes at the end, when Juwanna is exposed as a man. The movie deals with that exposure, but ignores another fact that almost every audience member will pick up on: If Juwanna's team played the season with an ineligible player, doesn't it have to forfeit all of its games?

We aren't supposed to ask questions like that, I suppose, but there's another glitch that stands out because the movie insists on it. Early in the film, Juwanna is informed that dunking is illegal in the women's league. Late in the film, she wins a game with a last-second dunk. Say what? Has everyone in the league forgotten the rules?

Such glitches would matter more, I suppose,

if the movie were serious. In a comedy, they're distractions, suggesting the filmmakers either weren't paying attention or didn't care. I can't recommend *Juwanna Mann,* and yet I admire the pluck of the actors, especially Nunez, Fox, and Tommy Davidson, as a spectacularly ineligible lothario, and I liked the way Kevin Pollak soldiers away as the manager who must be perpetually offended, astonished, or frustrated. *Juwanna Mann* is unnecessary, but not painful.

K

Kadosh ★ ★ ★
NO MPAA RATING, 110 m., 2000

Yael Abecassis (Rivka), Yoram Hattab (Meir),
Meital Barda (Malka), Uri Ran Klausner
(Yossef), Yussef Abu Warda (Rav Shimon),
Sami Hori (Yaakov), Lea Koenig (Elisheva).
Directed by Amos Gitai and produced by
Laurent Truchot, Michel Propper, and Amos
Gitai. Screenplay by Amos Gitai, Eliette
Abecassis, and Jacky Cukier.

Kadosh is an Israeli film about the ultraorthodox Jewish sect of Hassidim, where men make the decisions and women are seen, narrowly, as vessels for the production of more sons. It is a very angry film, and has caused much discussion in Israel and within American Jewish circles, where most share its anger. Tolerance is not the strong point of the Hassidim, and a Jewish friend of mine was much saddened when his family was spat upon in Jerusalem for mistakenly entering a place where they were not welcome.

The film takes place in Mea Shearim, an area of Jerusalem where life is regulated according to ancient and unwavering laws. It tells the stories of two sisters, one married and one single but in love with an unacceptable man. Rivka and her husband, Meir, have been married for ten years and still have no children, a fact that preys on the mind of Meir's father, a rabbi. "The only task of a daughter of Israel is bringing children into the world," he believes, and eventually he orders his son to divorce his wife and marry a younger woman who might give him children. Meir protests—he loves his wife—but eventually he obeys. (Rivka has learned that her husband is sterile, but cannot share this information because such tests are forbidden.)

The other sister, Malka, has been in love for years with a man named Yaakov (Sami Hori), who was once a member of the sect but had to leave it when he joined the Israeli army; his religion did not permit him to serve. There is great family pressure on her to marry another man, a religious zealot who cruises the streets with a loudspeaker attached to his car, exhorting his listeners at deafening volume to see things his way.

The film, directed by a longtime Israeli documentarian named Amos Gitai, sees the story largely through the eyes of the women, who sometimes share rebellious thoughts like naughty schoolgirls: Their men spend their days in the study of the Torah, they observe, but women are not allowed to read it—perhaps because they might not agree that it prescribes such a limited life for women. Although some marriages, like Rivka's, are happy, women are actually told that their primary function in life is to bear as many children as possible, to "help vanquish the secular movement"—which includes Jews whose observance does not mirror the strict ways of the sect.

The women are restive, but obedient. Rivka leaves her house and goes to live alone, sinking into solitude and depression. Malka marries the zealot, and her wedding night brings into cruel focus the definition of husbandly duties. Their mother does not agree with what has happened to them but dares not oppose her husband. The men spend their days closed off together in ceaseless study and debate, even over the details for brewing (or not brewing) tea on the Sabbath. (This particular discussion seems more interested in finding theological loopholes than in honoring the underlying ideas.)

As I watched the film, I was reminded of *Two Women,* an Iranian film I saw recently, in which a woman was given a brief taste of freedom before being yanked out of college and married to her father's choice of a mate. Extreme forms of belief in both films seem designed to rationalize a fear of sex and distrust of women. My own notion is: I would be more persuaded by religious laws that are harder on the enforcers than on those under their authority, but it never seems to work out that way.

It occurred to me, during *Kadosh,* that while the Hassidim are a sect, the men within it have essentially formed a cult—excluding women, suspicious of others, dressing in such a way that they cannot mix unnoticed with outsiders, denying their own natures and instincts in order to follow their leaders. Although I am sure happy lives can be led and happy marriages created within such boundaries—and I realize the story of *Kadosh* may be an extreme example, not typical—I left the film with the thought that if God in his infinite love cannot gather both sexes into his arms equally, then I would like to sit down with him and ask him, respectfully, what his problem is.

Kandahar ★ ★ ★ ½
NO MPAA RATING, 85 m., 2002

Nelofer Pazira (Nafas), Hassan Tantai (Tabib Sahid), Sadou Teymouri (Khak). Directed and produced by Mohsen Makhmalbaf. Screenplay by Makhmalbaf.

When she was a child, Nafas was taken to Canada, while her sister stayed behind in Afghanistan. Now Nafas has received a letter from her sister, who lost both legs after stepping on a land mine, and plans to kill herself during the final eclipse of the twentieth century. Nafas sets off on a desperate journey to smuggle herself from Iran into Afghanistan, to convince her sister to live. *Kandahar* follows that journey in a way that sheds an unforgiving light on the last days of the Taliban.

I saw the movie, by Iran's Mohsen Makhmalbaf, at Cannes 2001, where it was admired but seemed to have slim chances of a North American release. Of course, 9/11 changed that, and Kandahar became a familiar place name. The movie is especially accessible because most of it is in English—the language of the heroine, who keeps a record of her journey on a tape recorder, and also the language of one of the other major characters.

Nafas (Nelofer Pazira) is unable to get into Afghanistan by conventional means, perhaps because her family fled for political reasons. In Iran, she pays an itinerant trader, who travels between the two countries, to bring her in as one of his wives; she wears a burka, which covers her from head to toe, making the deception more possible. And as she sets out, we begin to realize that the journey, not the sister's fate, is the point of the film: Nafas is traveling back into the world where she was born.

Makhmalbaf and his cinematographer, Ebraham Ghafouri, show this desert land as beautiful but remote and forbidding. Roads are tracks from one flat horizon to another. Nafas bounces along in the back of a truck with other women, the burka amputating her personality. There are roadblocks, close calls, confusions, and eventually the merchant turns back, leaving her in the company of a boy of ten or twelve named Khak (Sadou Teymouri). With that terrible wisdom that children gain in times of trouble, he knows his way around the dangers and takes $50 to lead her to Kandahar. At one point they trek through a wilderness of sand dunes, and when he finds a ring on the finger of a skeleton he wants to sell it to her.

Nafas grows ill, and Khak takes her to a doctor. She stands on one side of a blanket, the doctor on the other, and he talks to her through a hole in the fabric. The Taliban forbids any more intimate contact between unmarried men and women; he can ask her to say "ah," and that's about it. But this doctor (Hassan Tantai) has a secret—a secret he reveals when he hears her English with its North American accent. Khak hangs around, hungry for any information he can sell, until the doctor bribes him with peanuts and sends him away.

Kandahar does not provide deeply drawn characters, memorable dialogue, or an exciting climax. Its traffic is in images. Who will ever forget the scene of a Red Cross helicopter flying over a refugee camp and dropping artificial legs by parachute, as one-legged men hobble on their crutches to try to catch them? The movie makes us wonder how any belief system could convince itself it was right to make so many people miserable, to deny the simple human pleasures of life. And yet the last century has been the record of such denial.

Khak, the boy, has been expelled from school. We see one of the Taliban schools. All of the students are boys, of course—women are not permitted to study. That may be no great loss. The boys rock back and forth while chanting the Koran. Not studying or discussing it, simply repeating it. Then they are drilled on the parts of a rifle. "Weapons are the only modern thing in Afghanistan," the doctor tells Nafas.

Kate & Leopold ★ ★ ★
PG-13, 118 m., 2001

Meg Ryan (Kate), Liev Schreiber (Stuart), Hugh Jackman (Leopold), Josh Stamberg (Bob), Bradley Whitford (J.J.), Philip Bosco (Otis), Bill Corsair (Morty). Directed by James Mangold and produced by Cathy Konrad. Screenplay by Mangold and Steven Rogers.

Kate & Leopold is a preposterous time-travel romance in which the third Duke of Albany leaves the New York of 1876 and arrives in the New York of Meg Ryan. Well, of course it's preposterous: Time travel involves so many paradoxes that it is wise, in a romantic comedy like this, to simply ignore them. The movie is not really about time travel anyway, but about elegant British manners versus American slobbiness. Like the heroine of one of those romance novels her best friend reads, our gal Meg is swept off her feet by a wealthy and titled English lord.

Ryan plays Kate, who works in market research and is responsible for promoting products of dubious value. She's been dating Stuart (Liev Schreiber), a half-loony inventor who discovers an opening in the matrix of time, jumps off the Brooklyn Bridge, finds himself in 1876—and returns with his own great-great-grandfather, Leopold, Duke of Albany (Hugh Jackman).

It is inevitable that Kate will overcome her lukewarm affection for Stuart and fall in love with the dashing Englishman (even though the first time she sees him in military costume, she thinks he's dressed as Sergeant Pepper). Meg Ryan does this sort of thing about as well as it can possibly be done, and after *Sleepless in Seattle* and *You've Got Mail,* here is another ingenious plot that teases us with the possibility that true love will fail, while winking that of course it will prevail.

Kate & Leopold wisely does not depend on the mechanics of the developing romance for its humor. Instead, it uses its fish-out-of-water plot to show Leopold as a proper, well-behaved English aristocrat, astonished by what he finds in modern Manhattan. He's struck not so much by the traffic and the skyscrapers as by the manners. Walking a dog, he's asked by a cop if he plans to scoop the poop, and draws himself to his full height to intone: "Are you suggesting, madam, there exists a law compelling gentlemen to lay hold of canine bowel movements?"

Both Leopold and his descendant Stuart are inventor types. Leopold, we learn, designed the Brooklyn Bridge and invented the elevator. Stuart not only discovered the portal in time, but had enough confidence in his calculations to jump off the bridge and trust that it would open for him. Why he lands on his feet instead of falling to his death in the 1876 river is a question the movie prudently ignores.

The movie, directed by James Mangold *(Heavy; Girl, Interrupted)* and written by Mangold and Steven Rogers, has some droll scenes after Kate enlists Leopold to appear in a TV commercial for Farmer's Bounty, a low-calorie spread. Leopold's accent and his sincere conviction are perfect, and the spot goes well until he actually tastes the product, and compares it to saddle soap or raw suet: "It's revolting!" Kate tries to calm him: "It's diet. It's *supposed* to taste awful."

One of the reasons the movie works is because we like the goodness of the characters; it's wise, I think, to let Schreiber get over his romantic disappointment as quickly as possible and become a coconspirator for love. (Apart from any other reason, Stuart knows that unless Albany returns to 1876 and starts a family, Stuart will never exist.) We know there will be scenes where Kate the practical and cynical girl is swept off her feet by old-fashioned romance, and there are: a candlelit rooftop dinner, and a moment when Leopold tucks her in, she asks him to stay, and he does, in full uniform.

I have here a precautionary message from Will Shank of Toronto, Ontario, who writes that before I review *Kate & Leopold* there are a couple of things I should know: "Prince Leopold, the Duke of Albany, was a hemophiliac and although he has been described as daring and high-spirited, would not have been foolish enough to participate in the dangerous stunts seen in the trailer. He was sickly all his life and his mother, Queen Victoria, expressed surprise that he lived long enough to be married and have a child. Also, Victoria and her children spoke German among themselves, not English. People who knew them related that when they did speak English, it was with a strong German accent."

Thanks, Will. The next time I meet James Mangold, I'll ask him why he didn't make *Kate & Leopold* the story of a hemophiliac with a German accent who was afraid to jump off bridges. Sounds like a movie we are all waiting to see.　　　　　　　　　　　　☞

Keeping the Faith ★ ★ ★
PG-13, 129 m., 2000

Ben Stiller (Jake), Edward Norton (Brian), Jenna Elfman (Anna), Anne Bancroft (Ruth), Eli Wallach (Rabbi Lewis), Ron Rifkin (Larry Friedman), Lisa Edelstein (Ali Decker), Milos Forman (Father Havel), Holland Taylor (Bonnie Rose), Rena Sofer (Rachel Rose). Directed by Edward Norton and produced by Hawk Koch, Norton, and Stuart Blumberg. Screenplay by Blumberg.

Edward Norton's *Keeping the Faith* is a profoundly secular movie about the love lives of a priest and a rabbi. It shares the universal Hollywood presumption that love should conquer all—that gratification of immediate emotional needs is more important than ancient values. Both the rabbi and the priest are in love with the same girl, and if only priests were allowed to marry, or if only Jews didn't mind a rabbi with a gentile wife, their problems would be over—except for the problem of which one the girl chooses.

We in the audience have been trained by a multitude of other movies to cheer for romance, especially when the girl is played by the sunny and lovable Jenna Elfman, and the boys are Rabbi Ben Stiller and Father Ed Norton. The movie does finally nod toward tradition at the end, with a loophole in the form of one brief dialogue exchange that is easily missed. But make no mistake: Both of these boys are ready to sleep with this girl no matter what their theology teaches.

The screenplay by Stuart Blumberg, of course, casts the story as a romantic comedy, not an ethical dilemma, and on that level I enjoyed it, especially since the dialogue makes the characters more thoughtful than we might expect. The story begins when all three characters are best friends as children. They go everywhere together, share everything, and then the parents of Anna (Elfman) move to California. Jake (Stiller) grows up to be a rabbi, Brian (Norton) grows up to be a priest, and they remain best friends whose church and synagogue even share development of a community center. Then Anna moves back to New York.

She's very successful. "I'm like a plumber except I fix leaky corporations," she explains. The three old friends go out together to dinner and the movies, and it's clear both guys are thunderstruck with love. But Jake is the one she likes, although she also has a conversation with Brian about the "sex thing" that, in his mind at least, contains faint echoes of invitation.

Written by a Jew and directed by a Catholic, the film has an evenhanded approach where possible. But there is one imbalance. The priest, with his vow of chastity, is not supposed to date or marry. The rabbi, who is not getting any younger and is still a bachelor, is under enormous pressure from his mother (Anne Bancroft) and his entire congregation to date and marry a Jewish woman. Indeed, his job depends on it. And since the mechanics of the screenplay require him to love only Anna, it follows that he is unable to find a Jewish woman he likes enough to marry.

This dilemma leads to a series of scenes in which romantic candidates are paraded before him like exhibits from a bachelor's nightmares. We meet Ali, the pushy physical fitness nut (Lisa Edelstein), and Rachel (Rena Sofer), the glamorous ABC correspondent, and lots of other available women, who all seem to crowd the lens and gush all over the film, with their mothers smiling and nodding behind them. We get the point, but we question it: Isn't it possible to write a movie in which Jake just plain loves Anna, period—without making every visible Jewish girl obnoxious? My guess is that if Anna had stayed in California, Jake would have been crawling through broken glass to date the ABC correspondent.

These are the kinds of thoughts that occur after the film. During the film, we're swept up in the story's need to find a happy ending. In conservative moral terms, the happiest ending, of course, would be: (1) priest remains celibate, offers up his sacrifice; (2) rabbi explains "two different worlds we come from," wishes Anna well, marries nice Jewish girl, and (3) Anna returns to California, where all things are possible. It is safe to say that no audience would accept this ending, however, as there is an emotional conservatism that runs much deeper in movie audiences than any other form of belief, and which teaches: If a movie shows us a boy and a girl who are really in love, there *must* be a happy ending.

What helps is that all of the major characters in the movie are good people—yes, even Jake's mother, who is played gently by Anne Bancroft as a woman willing to admit her mistakes and learn from them. And I like the way the filmmakers bring in older role models for the two young men. Jake turns to old Rabbi Lewis (Eli Wallach) and the wise Larry Friedman (Ron Rifkin), the head of his congregation. Brian turns to old Father Havel (Milos Forman), who confesses to having fallen in love, big time, at least every decade of his priesthood.

Why are love stories comedies and not tragedies? Because it is funny when we lose control of ourselves despite our best efforts to remain dignified. A man in love has stepped on an emotional banana peel. When a woman falls in love with an unavailable man, he *is* a banana peel.

Keep the River on Your Right ★ ★ ★
R, 110 m., 2001

A documentary directed and produced by David Shapiro and Laurie Gwen Shapiro.

In the mid-1950s, a New York artist and anthropologist named Tobias Schneebaum walked into the rain forests of Peru, planning to paint some pictures there. His geographical knowledge was limited to the advice: Keep the river on your right. A year later, he walked out of the jungle naked, covered with body paint, having found and lived with an Indian tribe.

At some point during that year, the tribe went on a raid, killed enemies, and ate them. Schneebaum joined them in consuming human flesh. "Didn't you try to stop them?" someone asks him in this documentary. It is the kind of question asked by a person who has never had to live with cannibals, on their terms.

Schneebaum is not the kind of man you

would immediately think of in connection with this adventure. Seventy-eight when the film was made, he is a homosexual aesthete who lectures on art and works as a tour guide on cruise ships. Yet his adventures were not limited to Peru, and in the extraordinary documentary *Keep the River on Your Right: A Modern Cannibal Tale,* he also revisits the jungles of New Guinea, where he lived with a tribe, took a male lover, and has a reunion with his old friend. Many years have passed, but the friend accepts him as warmly as if he'd been away for a week or two.

The visits to his old homes in New Guinea and Peru are not without hazards. Schneebaum isn't worried about jungle animals or diseases, but has more practical concerns on his mind, like breaking a hip: "If I slip on the mud, I've had it."

The movie is the work of a brother and sister, David Shapiro and Laurie Gwen Shapiro, who learned about Schneebaum and became determined to make a movie about him. It is a story he has been telling for years; he wrote a memoir about his adventures, and we see clips of him chatting about the book with Mike Douglas and Charlie Rose. He also, I imagine, gets good mileage out of his stories on those cruise ships, although he is not particularly eager to discuss cannibalism, and we sense pain that his dry, laconic style tries to mask. Asked how people taste, he answers shortly, "I don't remember." At another point, in another context, he observes: "I kind of died. Something I had that was made of me, and then it was gone after the Peruvian experience."

Can we speculate that he penetrated so close to the fault line of human existence that he lost the unspoken security we walk around with every day? Things may get bad for us, even hopeless, but we will not be naked in the jungle, face-to-face with life's oldest and most implacable code, eat or be eaten. Schneebaum doesn't strike us as the Indiana Jones sort. He didn't go into the jungle as a lark. Whatever happened there he prefers to describe in terms of its edges, its outside.

The sexuality he encountered in New Guinea is another matter, and there he cheers up. The men of the tribe he lived with have sex with both men and women and consider it natural. We sense this is not the kind of sex people go looking for in big Western cities, but more of a pastime and consolation among friends. There is a certain shy warmth in the reunion with his former lover, but subtly different on Schneebaum's side than on the other man's, because sex between men means something different to each of them.

Tobias Schneebaum could probably develop a stand-up act based on his adventures, but he is more of a muser and a wonderer. "You're there to study them, not to play with them," he says sharply at one point. I met him at the 2000 Toronto Film Festival, where in interview and question sessions he answered as if he were a teacher or a witness, not a celebrity. We get glimpses of his earlier life in Greenwich Village (former neighbor Norman Mailer remembers him as "our house homosexual— terrified of a dead mouse"), and learn something of his painting and his books.

But mostly we are struck by the man. *Keep the River on Your Right* could have been quite a different kind of film, but the Shapiros wisely focus on the mystery of this man, who was spectacularly ill-prepared for both of his jungle journeys, and apparently walked away from civilization prepared to rely on the kindness of strangers. Perhaps it was his very naïveté that shielded him. The cannibals obviously had nothing to fear from him. Today, we learn, they no longer practice cannibalism, and indeed are well on their way down the capitalist assembly line, shedding their culture and learning to eat fast food. Tobias Schneebaum was not only their first visitor from "civilization," but their most benign.

Note: The flywheels at the MPAA Ratings Board have given this sweet and innocent movie an R rating, explaining "mature thematic material." Yes, but the cannibalism is not seen, only discussed. How can this film and Freddy Got Fingered, *with Tom Green biting a newborn baby's umbilical cord in two, deserve the same rating?*

Kikujiro ★ ★ ½
PG-13, 116 m., 2000

Beat Takeshi (Kikujiro), Yusuke Sekiguchi (Masao), Kayoko Kishimoto (Kikujiro's Wife), Yuko Daike (Masao's Mother), Kazuko Yoshiyuki (Masao's Grandmother), Beat Kiyoshi (Man at Bus Stop), Great Gidayu (Biker/Fatso), Rakkyo Ide (Biker/Baldy). Directed by Takeshi Kitano and produced by Masayuki Mori and Takio Yoshida. Screenplay by Kitano.

The little boy lives with his grandmother, who leaves food for him before she goes to work. The summer days stretch long, and the streets are empty. He is lonely, and finds the address of his mother, who works far away. He wants to visit her. The grandmother has a friend who has a husband who is a low-level gangster. The gangster is assigned to take the kid to find the mother, and that's the setup for *Kikujiro,* which is a lot of things, although one of them is not a sweet comedy about a gangster and a kid.

The movie was made by Takeshi Kitano, currently Japan's most successful director, and he stars in it under the name he uses as an actor, Beat Takeshi. Kitano is a specialist in taut, spare crime dramas where periods of quiet and tension are punctuated by sharp bursts of violence. *Kikujiro* is the last sort of film you would expect him to make—even though he skews the material toward his hard-boiled style and away from the obvious opportunities for sentiment.

Kikujiro, known only as "Mister" to the little boy, is played by Kitano as a man who is willing to seem a clown, but keeps his thoughts to himself. His dialogue to the kid is not funny to the kid, but might be funny to a third party, and since there is none (except for the audience), it seems intended for self-amusement. Unlike *Gloria* or *Little Miss Marker,* this movie's kid doesn't have much of a personality; he pouts a lot, and looks at Mister as if wondering how long he will have to bear this cross.

The two of them are essentially broke for most of the movie, after Mister trusts the kid's ability to pick the winners at a bicycle race track. The kid guesses one race right and all the others wrong, and so the man and the boy are reduced to hitching to the remote city where the mother may live. This turns the movie into a road picture that develops slapstick notes, as when Mister tries to stop cars by lying down in the road or positioning nails to cause flat tires. (His efforts produce one puncture, which results in a great sight gag.)

Some of the adventures, like the kid's run-in with a child molester in a park, are fairly harrowing; the movie is rated only PG-13, but we can see why one paper mistakenly self-applied an R rating; scenes like this would be impossible in an American comedy, and it's all Kitano can do to defuse them enough to find comedy (very little, it is true) in them. Other scenes are funnier, including a road relationship with a couple of Hells Angels named "Baldy" and "Fatso," who despite their fearsome appearance are harmless. One extended sequence, when the man and boy are stranded at a remote bus stop, has a Chaplinesque quality.

If the movie finally doesn't work as well as it should, it may be because the material isn't a good fit for Kitano's hard-edged underlying style. Japanese audiences would know he is a movie tough guy (Clint Eastwood's Dirty Harry is our equivalent), and so they'd get the joke that he seems ineffectual and clueless. Western audiences, looking at the material with less of the context, are likely to find some scenes a little creepy, even though the cheerful music keeps trying to take the edge off. This same movie, remade shot-for-shot in America, wouldn't work at all, and only its foreign context blunts the bite of some scenes that are a little cruel or gratuitous.

Still, Takeshi Kitano is a fascinating filmmaker—a man with a distinctive style that's comfortable with long periods of inactivity. As an action director, he relishes the downtime, and keeps the action to a minimum; there is a relaxed rhythm, a willingness to let scenes grow at their own speed instead of being pumped out at top volume. I like the director and his style, but the material finally defeats him. You can't smile when you keep feeling sorry for the kid—who is not, after all, in on the joke.

Kingdom Come ★ ★
PG, 95 m., 2001

LL Cool J (Ray Bud Jr.), Jada Pinkett Smith (Charisse), Vivica A. Fox (Lucille), Loretta Devine (Marguerite), Anthony Anderson (Junior), Toni Braxton (Juanita), Cedric the Entertainer (Reverend Hooker), Whoopi Goldberg (Raynelle Slocumb), Darius McCrary (Royce). Directed by Doug McHenry and produced by Edward Bates and John Morrissey. Screenplay by David Dean Bottrell and Jessie Jones, based on their play *Dearly Departed.*

In an opening scene of *Kingdom Come,* Whoopi Goldberg's husband drops dead at the breakfast table. This triggers a funeral, and Raynelle Slocumb (Goldberg) welcomes her children, in-laws, and descendants to a disorganized family reunion in which three or four subplots jostle for attention.

The movie is based on the play *Dearly Departed,* much performed by local theater groups, and has been adapted by the playwrights, David Dean Bottrell and Jessie Jones. The director, Doug McHenry, also has a long list of credits; as a producer or director he's been involved with *New Jack City, House Party II, Jason's Lyric,* and *The Brothers.* Together, they've made a movie that has generated a terrific trailer, making the film look like a warmhearted comedy. But the movie doesn't match the trailer.

Somewhere along the line a curious disconnect has taken place between the Whoopi Goldberg character and the others. She doesn't seem like their mother, their relative, or even an inhabitant of the same social milieu as the other members of her family. She's more like a wise, detached oracle, and when she's given comedy lines, they just don't fit. Early on, for example, she declares that her late husband was "mean as a snake, and surly." Later she insists that "Mean and Surly" be engraved on his tombstone. But she doesn't seem to hear them or feel them; they're words for another character in another movie, and have no connection to how she, or her children, feel about the dearly departed. With those and certain other lines, it's as if she's quoting a stranger.

We meet the family members, played by an all-star cast that never seems to mesh. Raynelle's son Ray Bud Jr. (LL Cool J) is married to Lucille (Vivica A. Fox). She's a scold; he's a good guy trying to handle a drinking problem. Her daughter Charisse (Jada Pinkett Smith) is married to another Junior (Anthony Anderson), who cheats on her. She's over the top in most of her scenes, which aren't played to the scale of the other performances. Another daughter, Marguerite (Loretta Devine), has her hands full with her son Royce (Darius McCrary), who apparently plans to nap through life, and taunts his mother with his shiftlessness. Then there's rich Cousin Juanita (Toni Braxton), and the pious Reverend Hooker (Cedric the Entertainer), who must officiate at the funeral and keep the peace.

Reverend Hooker makes some unwise dietary choices shortly before the funeral begins and farts all the way through it, causing the congregation to break up at this solemn moment. This material is an example of the movie's approach, which is all over the map. Fart jokes have their place, I concede, when the Klump family is at the dinner table. They may even have their place at a funeral—but not one where Raynelle has so recently had a heart-to-heart with Ray Bud Jr. The film changes tone so quickly we get whiplash.

There are times when the movie plays like a pilot for a TV comedy. Each family unit is given a costume, speaking style, and lifestyle that seems self-contained, so that when they assemble it's like a collision involving separate sitcoms. Some of the humor is broad and bawdy, some is observational, some is whimsical, and sometimes the humor collapses into sentiment. The central problem is that the movie seems unsure whether the late Bud Slocumb was indeed mean and surly—and if he was, how it feels about it. Is his death a loss or a liberation?

The pieces are here for a better movie. The cast is capable. A rewrite or two might have helped. *Kingdom Come* has passably funny moments, but they don't connect; it might work on video for viewers who glance up at the screen from time to time. The more attention you pay to it, the less it's there.

The King Is Alive ★ ★ ★
R, 105 m., 2001

Jennifer Jason Leigh (Gina), Miles Anderson (Jack), Romane Bohringer (Catherine), David Bradley (Henry), David Calder (Charles), Bruce Davison (Ray), Brion James (Ashley), Peter Khubeke (Kanana), Vusi Kunene (Moses), Janet McTeer (Liz). Directed by Kristian Levring and produced by Patricia Kruijer and Vibeke Windelov. Screenplay by Anders Thomas Jensen and Levring, based on *King Lear* by William Shakespeare.

In the Namibian desert in southwest Africa, a tourist bus strays far off course and runs out of petrol. The passengers stumble into the blinding sun and find themselves at an abandoned German mining station, its only occupant an old African who surveys them impassively. Jack (Miles Anderson) is the only passenger with any desert experience. He lectures them: There are five things you need to survive in the desert, and in descending order of importance they are water, food, shelter, making yourself visible, and keeping up your spirits.

Well, there is food here (rusted cans of carrots), water (they can collect the morning dew), and old buildings. They tend a signal fire at night. Jack walks off in search of help. Those left behind consider a suggestion by Henry (David Bradley) that they rehearse a production of *King Lear* to keep their spirits up. *Lear* is not the first play one thinks of when spirits sink, but perhaps in this desolate landscape it is a better choice than *The Producers*.

We meet the tourists, without ever discovering what they were seeking in Namibia (they took the bus after their flight was canceled). Many seem more appropriate for a play by Beckett, and Ray and Liz (Bruce Davison and Janet McTeer) are a squabbling couple out of Albee (when Ray asks her what *King Lear* is about, she replies: "You don't have to worry, you know. Nobody has to fall in love and everybody gets to die in the end").

Hardly anybody dies in the end of the movie, but a lot of them have sex, which seems inspired less by pleasure than by the desire to annoy. There are moments of truth and despair, marital crises, denunciations, renunciations, false hopes, and raving madness. Henry writes out the roles for the play (chosen, we suspect, simply because he happened to know it by heart), there are rehearsals, and finally a performance of sorts. But although the movie's credits say "Based on *King Lear* by William Shakespeare," I was unable to sift through the cast finding specific characters who represented Cordelia, Regan, Kent, the Fool, etc. I think perhaps the play acts more as a mirror; like Lear, they are lost in the wilderness and no longer have faith in goodness.

The King Is Alive is the fourth of the Dogma 95 movies, so called because of a "vow of chastity" signed by the four Danish directors Kristian Levring (who directed this one), Thomas Vinterberg *(Celebration)*, Søren Kragh-Jacobsen *(Mifune)*, and Lars von Trier *(The Idiots)*. Dogma wanna-bes have been produced by Harmony Korine *(julien donkey-boy)*, and von Trier made a half-Dogma, half-musical *(Dancer in the Dark)*. What they have in common is a rough, immediate feel: The drama isn't too formed, the dialogue isn't tamed, the lighting and music are found on the set, the performances seem raw and improvisational.

In *The King Is Alive*, the Dogma approach helps the film look like what might have resulted if one of the characters had used a digital camera. It has the same relationship to a commercial film that their production of *King Lear* has to a conventional staging. It's built from raw materials, needs, and memories, instead of off-the-shelf parts from the movie store.

On one level, of course, we're aware of the artifice. It's an old dramatic formula to strand a group of characters somewhere and have them try to survive while conditions edge toward the primitive. Cross *Lord of the Flies* with *Flight of the Phoenix* and add *Lifeboat* and you have this film's second cousin. On another level, this kind of story gives great opportunities to actors, who can test their emotional range. But what does the audience get out of it?

I imagine many people would be actively hostile to *The King Is Alive*. It doesn't make the slightest effort to cater to conventional appetites. But the more you appreciate what they're trying to do, the more you like it. I saw it for the first time at Cannes in May 2000, and it stuck with me. It didn't fade in the memory. Ungainly, ill-formed, howling, and desperate, it was there and endured—while, of the more forgettable films, I could observe with Lear that nothing will come of nothing.

Kissing Jessica Stein ★ ★ ★
R, 94 m., 2002

Jennifer Westfeldt (Jessica Stein), Heather Juergensen (Helen Cooper), Scott Cohen (Josh Meyers), Tovah Feldshuh (Judy Stein), Jackie Hoffman (Joan), Michael Mastro (Martin), Carson Elrod (Sebastian), David Aaron Baker (Dan Stein). Directed by Charles Herman-Wurmfeld and produced by Eden Wurmfeld and Brad Zions. Screenplay by Heather Juergensen and Jennifer Westfeldt.

Same-sex romance, a controversial topic in movies millions now alive can still remember, is a lifestyle choice in *Kissing Jessica Stein*. Yes, a "choice"—although that word is non-PC in gay circles—since one of the two women in the movie is nominally straight, and the other so bisexual she pops into her art gallery office during an opening for a quickie with her boy toy. Helen (Heather Juergensen), the gallery manager, is a lesbian in about the same way she would be a vegetarian who has steak once in a while. Jessica (Jennifer Westfeldt), disillusioned after a series of blind dates with hopeless men, answers Helen's personals ad not because she is a woman but because she quotes the poet Rilke.

Jessica is above all a hopeless perfectionist. This places her in contrast with her mother (Tovah Feldshuh), whose idea of an eligible mate for her daughter is any single Jewish male between the ages of twenty and forty-five in good enough shape to accept a dinner invitation. Like many perfectionists, Jessica works as a copy editor and fact checker, finding writers' mistakes with the same zeal she applies to the imperfections of would-be husbands. In a funny montage, she goes through a series of disastrous dates, including one with a man whose word choices would make him a copy editor's nightmare (he uses the phrase "self-defecating").

Helen is more flexible, knowing, and wise. She seeks not perfection in a partner, but the mysteries of an intriguing personality. She finds it challenging that Jessica has never had a lesbian experience, and indeed approaches sex with the enthusiasm of a homeowner considering the intricacies of a grease trap. Jessica arrives at their first real date with an armload of how-to manuals, and makes such slow progress that Helen is driven all but mad by weeks of interrupted foreplay.

The movie makes of this situation not a sex comedy but more of an upscale sitcom in which the romantic partners happen both to be women. Jessica is fluttery and flighty, breathy and skittish; Helen is cool, grounded, and amused. Adding spice is Jessica's panic that anyone will find out about her new dating partner. Anyone like Josh (Scott Cohen), her boss at work and former boyfriend. Or Joan (Jackie Hoffman), her pregnant coworker. Or especially her mother, who brings single IBM executives to dinner as if they are the Missing Link.

There are a couple of serious episodes to give the story weight. One involves Jessica's reluctance to invite Helen to her brother's wedding, thus revealing to the family the sex of the mysterious "person" she has been dating. The other is a heart-to-heart talk between Jessica and her mother, during which Feldshuh takes an ordinary scene and makes it extraordinary by the way she delivers the simple, heartfelt dialogue.

What makes the movie a comedy is the way it avoids the more serious emotions involved. I reviewed a movie about a man who gives up sex for Lent, and received a reader's letter asking, hey, aren't Catholics supposed to give up extramarital sex all of the time? A theologically excellent question; I am reminded of the priest in *You Can Count on Me,* asked about adultery and reluctantly intoning "That . . . would . . . be . . . wrong."

The would-be lovers in *Kissing Jessica Stein* are not having sex, exactly, because of Jessica's skittish approach to the subject, but if they did, it would be a leisure activity like going to the movies. If it really meant anything to either one of them—if it meant as much as it does to the mother—the comedy would be more difficult, or in a different key. We can laugh because nothing really counts for anything. That's all right. But if Jessica Stein ever really gets kissed, it'll be another story. Right now she's like the grade-school girl at the spin-the-bottle party who changes the rules when the bottle points at her.

Kiss of the Dragon ★ ★ ★
R, 98 m., 2001

Jet Li (Liu Jian), Bridget Fonda (Jessica), Tcheky Karyo (Jean-Pierre Richard), Max Ryan (Lupo). Directed by Chris Nahon and produced by Luc Besson, Steve Chasman, Jet Li, and Happy Walters. Screenplay by Besson and Robert Mark Kamen.

There is a point early in *Kiss of the Dragon* when the Chinese cop played by Jet Li is being searched for weapons. Around his wrist they find a band with a lot of little needles stuck into it. This doesn't indicate that he does tailoring in his spare time. These are acupuncture needles, and he can cure or kill with one deftly inserted point.

The title of the movie refers to the ultimate use of a needle, which he describes as "highly illegal," as indeed it must be, altering the body's flow of blood so that it all rises to the head and bursts from every available orifice. I hate it when that happens. The Jet Li character is also master of the full array of the martial arts, and in this movie he needs them, since he is opposed by more or less every villain in Paris.

The plot has been described as hard to follow. It is simplicity itself, if all you want is a scorecard of the heroes and villains. It admittedly gets murky when it comes to motivation and logic, but never mind: In a movie where the physical actions border on the impossible, why expect the story to be reasonable?

Jet Li's character is apparently the most skilled law enforcement officer in China, brought to Paris to assist a high-level official in dealings that may involve some off-the-record drug traffic. The official is entertained by two hookers in a way that leaves him with his lust unslaked, and dead. Jet Li quickly determines that the mastermind behind the murder, the drug traffic, and much of the crime in modern France is Inspector Jean-Pierre Richard (Tcheky Karyo), a crooked cop with a limitless supply of henchmen.

That's all you're really told about the plot, and all you need to be told, since all else is action, except for some heartfelt scenes between Jet Li and Bridget Fonda, as Jessica, a farm girl from North Dakota whom the evil inspector has hooked on drugs and enslaved as a prostitute by separating her from the young daughter she loves.

Jet Li is one of the best-known martial arts stars, although you might pass him without noticing. He's compact, quiet, good-looking, not a show-off; the Alan Ladd of the genre. His action scenes involve a lot of physical skill (on his part, and also on the part of the editor) and the ingenious use of actual props that come to hand—a flying billiard ball, for example. There's a nice sequence involving a laundry chute and a hand grenade that's so effective only a churl would wonder why a place as expensive as the Hotel Bristol in Paris has an alarm system that doesn't notice a fiery explosion.

Fonda's scenes are mostly played out in evil-looking dens on grotty streets lined with hookers who look as if they were costumed for *Sweet Charity.* Their costumes look so good one wonders how her character gets work; she's grimy and beat-up most of the time, making it easier for us to believe she's an addict than a hooker. She is, however, effective as a desperate woman who finds unlikely friendship with this Chinese cop.

The movie looks great. The producer and coauthor of the screenplay is Luc Besson *(The Fifth Element, La Femme Nikita),* who loans his ace cameraman Thierry Arbogast to the director, Chris Nahon. They get a kind of gray-green, saturated *noir* feeling that's a perfect match for Tcheky Karyo's face—the face of a man whose next visit to the confessional, should he ever make it, will take days or weeks.

I like the movie on a simple physical level. There is no deeper meaning and no higher skill involved; just professional action, well staged and filmed with a certain stylistic elegance. Jet Li is the right star for the material, not too cocksure, not too flashy. His character isn't given a lot of motivation, but one key element is that he's never been in Paris before. He's a stranger in a strange land; that helps him bond with the Bridget Fonda character in a way that gives the movie what emotional center it needs.

A Knight's Tale ★ ★ ★
PG-13, 132 m., 2001

Heath Ledger (William), Rufus Sewell (Count Adhemar), Shannyn Sossamon (Jocelyn), Paul Bettany (Chaucer), Laura Fraser (Kate), Mark Addy (Roland), Alan Tudyk (Wat), Berenice Bejo (Christiana). Directed and produced by Brian Helgeland. Screenplay by Helgeland.

It is possible, I suppose, to object when the audience at a fifteenth-century jousting match begins to sing Queen's "We Will Rock You"

and follows it with the Wave. I laughed. I smiled, in fact, all through Brian Helgeland's *A Knight's Tale,* which tells the story of a low-born serf who impersonates a knight, becomes a jousting champion, and dares to court the daughter of a nobleman.

Some will say the movie breaks tradition by telling a medieval story with a sound track of classic rock. They might as well argue it breaks the rules by setting a 1970s rock opera in the Middle Ages. To them I advise: Who cares? A few days after seeing this movie, I saw Baz Luhrmann's *Moulin Rouge,* which was selected to open the Cannes Film Festival despite being set in 1900 and beginning with the hero singing "The Sound of Music." In the case of *A Knight's Tale,* Helgeland has pointed out that an orchestral score would be equally anachronistic, since orchestras hadn't been invented in the 1400s. For that matter, neither had movies.

The film stars Heath Ledger, said to be the next big thing on the Australian sex symbol front, as William, a servant to a knight. The knight is killed, and his servants will be eating parboiled hedgehogs unless someone comes up with an idea. Along happens a desperate and naked man who makes them an offer: "Clothe, feed, and shoe me, and I'll give you your patents!" *Brewer's Dictionary* teaches us that "letters patent" are documents signed by a sovereign, conferring such rights as a title of nobility. The man offering to forge them introduces himself as Chaucer (Paul Bettany), and indeed, *A Knight's Tale* is a very, very, *very* free adaptation of one of his *Canterbury Tales.*

With the forged patents and the dead knight's suit of armor to disguise him, William and his sidekicks Roland and Wat (Mark Addy and Alan Tudyk) put themselves through one of those standard movie training montages and are soon ready to enter a joust, which is the medieval version of golf, with your opponent as the ball. There are many fearsome jousting matches in the movie, all of them playing with perspective and camera angles so that the horses and their riders seem to thunder at high speed for thirty seconds down a course that would take about five, until one knight or the other unseats his opponent three times and takes the victory.

This is not handled with great seriousness but in the spirit of high fun, and there is the evil Count Adhemar (Rufus Sewell) as an opponent. Since the knights wear armor guarding their faces, it might seem hard to distinguish them, but since time immemorial the movies have solved this dilemma by giving good knights attractive facial armor, and bad knights ugly little asymmetrical slits to peer through. I imagine a bad knight going into the armor store and saying, "I want the ugliest facial mask in the place!" Darth Vader is the only villain in the movies with a cool face plate.

Anyway, there are lots of babes in jousting land, especially the lady Jocelyn (Shannyn Sossamon), whose father is the ruler (at a banquet after the first tournament, she dances with William as David Bowie sings "Golden Years"). There is also a cute blacksmithess named Kate (Laura Fraser), who must be good, as she has obviously not been kicked in the head much.

The movie is centered around a series of jousting matches, alternating with threats to unveil the secret of William's identity. Finally we arrive at the World Championships in London, alas without the movie supplying a definition of what in these pre-Columbian times is considered the "world." My guess is that the World Championship of Jousting is to England as the World Series is to North America. Another thing they have in common: Both events feature "The Boys Are Back in Town."

The movie has an innocence and charm that grows on you. It's a reminder of the days before films got so cynical and unrelentingly violent. *A Knight's Tale* is whimsical, silly, and romantic, and seeing it after *The Mummy Returns* is like taking Tums after eating the Mummy.

K-19: The Widowmaker ★ ★ ★
PG-13, 138 m., 2002

Harrison Ford (Captain Alexi Vostrikov), Liam Neeson (Captain Mikhail Polenin), Peter Sarsgaard (Vadim Radtchenko), Christian Camargo (Pavel Loktev), George Anton (Konstantin Poliansky), Shaun Benson (Leonid Pashinski), Dmitry Chepovetsky (Sergei Maximov). Directed by Kathryn Bigelow and produced by Bigelow, Edward S. Feldman, Chris Whitaker, and Joni Sighvatsson. Screenplay by Christopher Kyle.

Movies involving submarines have the logic of chess: The longer the game goes, the fewer the possible remaining moves. *K-19: The Widowmaker* joins a tradition that includes *Das Boot* and *The Hunt for Red October* and goes all the way back to *Run Silent, Run Deep*. The variables are always oxygen, water pressure, and the enemy. Can the men breathe, will the sub implode, will depth charges destroy it? The submarine *K-19* is not technically at war, so there are no depth charges, but the story involves a deadlier threat: Will the onboard reactor melt down, causing a nuclear explosion and possibly triggering a world war?

The movie is set in 1961, at the height of the cold war, and is loosely based on a real incident. A new Soviet nuclear sub is commissioned before it is shipshape, and sails on its first mission as a bucketful of problems waiting to happen. Many of the problems are known to its original captain, Mikhail Polenin (Liam Neeson). But when he insists after a test run that the submarine is not capable, he is joined on board by Captain Alexi Vostrikov (Harrison Ford), who outranks him and is married to the niece of a member of the Politboro.

Both men are competent naval officers, and Polenin does his best to work with Vostrikov; his men consider Polenin their captain but are persuaded to go along with the senior man, even after Vostrikov orders a dive that tests the ultimate limits of the sub's capabilities. (Such scenes, with rivets popping and the hull creaking, are obligatory in submarine movies.) Most of the big scenes take place in close quarters on the command desk, where dramatic lighting illuminates the faces and eyes of men who are waiting for the sub's shell to crack. By casting the two leading roles with authoritative actors, *K-19* adds another level of tension; if one were dominant and the other uncertain, there would be a clear dramatic path ahead, but since both Vostrikov and Polenin are inflexible, self-confident, and determined, their rivalry approaches a standoff.

The sub's mission is to demonstrate the Soviet Union's new nuclear submarine power to the spy planes of the Kennedy administration. The sub's voyage is shadowed by a U.S. destroyer, which is not unwelcome, since the purpose of this mission is to be seen. When there is an accident involving one of the onboard nuclear reactors, however, the game changes: If the reactor explodes and destroys the U.S. ship, will that event be read, in the resulting confusion, as an act of war? *K-19* could surface and put its men in lifeboats, but for Vostrikov the thought of the United States capturing the new technology is unthinkable. Therefore, the options are to repair the reactor or dive the boat to its destruction.

More problems. The *K-19*'s original reactor officer, an experienced man, has been fired for alcoholism and replaced with a recent naval academy graduate. This man, Vadim (Peter Sarsgaard), is not only inexperienced but scared to death, and he freezes when the accident occurs. As the reactor core overheats, the crew comes up with a jury-rigged quick fix— diverting the onboard water supply—but that involves men entering the sealed reactor compartment to weld pipes and make repairs. They should wear protective radiation suits, but alas, the captains are told, "the warehouse was out. They sent us chemical suits instead." Neeson: "We might as well wear raincoats."

The scenes involving the repair of the reactor are excruciating, and director Kathryn Bigelow creates a taut counterpoint between the men who take ten-minute shifts in the high-radiation zone, and the growing tension between the two captains. Footage involving radiation sickness is harrowing. A mutiny is not unthinkable. And meanwhile, in Moscow, *K-19*'s sudden radio silence inspires dark suspicions that the sub has been captured or given away by traitors.

The physical limitations of a submarine create technical difficulties for filmmakers—who can, after all, only move their cameras back and forth within the narrow tube. That claustrophobia also heightens the tension, and we get a sense of a small group of men working desperately together under the pressure of death. *K-19* draws out the suspense about as far as possible, and Bigelow, whose credits include *Point Break* and *Strange Days,* is an expert technician who never steps wrong and is skilled at exploiting the personal qualities of Ford and Neeson to add another level of uncertainty.

It is rare for a big-budget Hollywood production to be seen entirely through the eyes of foreigners, and rarer still for actors like Neeson and Ford to spend an entire role with Russian accents. There isn't even a token role for an American character, and the movie treats the

Soviets not as enemies but as characters we are expected to identify with; the same approach allowed us to care about the German U-boat crew in *Das Boot.*

Are Harrison Ford and Liam Neeson, both so recognizable, convincing as Russians? Convincing enough; we accept the accents after a few minutes, and get on with the story. The fact that both men seem unyielding is crucial, and the fact that Vostrikov may be putting political considerations above the lives of his men adds an additional dimension. There is one surprise in the movie, a decision having nothing to do with the reactor, that depends entirely on the ability of the characters to act convincingly under enormous pressure; casting stars of roughly equal weight helps it to work.

K-PAX ★ ★ ★
PG-13, 120 m., 2001

Kevin Spacey (Prot), Jeff Bridges (Dr. Mark Powell), Mary McCormack (Rachel Powell), Alfre Woodard (Claudia Villars), David Patrick Kelly (Howie), Melanee Murray (Bess), Saul Williams (Ernie), Peter Gerety (Sal), Celia Weston (Mrs. Archer), Ajay Naidu (Dr. Chakraborty). Directed by Iain Softley and produced by Lawrence Gordon, Lloyd Levin, and Robert F. Colesberry. Screenplay by Charles Leavitt, based on the novel by Gene Brewer.

If a visitor from another planet appeared among us in human form and told the truth about his origins, no doubt he would be treated like Prot, the hero of *K-PAX,* who finds himself locked in a closed ward of the Psychiatric Institute of Manhattan. He might not, however, be as lucky as Prot in his psychiatrist. "This is the most convincing delusional I've ever come across," says Dr. Mark Powell, and his voice toys with the notion that Prot might not be delusional.

Certainly the patient tells a good story. Played by Kevin Spacey, who has made a career out of being the smartest character in the movie, Prot describes his intergalactic travels, dismisses Einstein's theories about the speed of light, and amazes a group of astronomers in a scene that suggests, as it is intended to, Christ addressing the elders in the temple.

Jeff Bridges plays the shrink, and brings to the role exactly what is required, a weary workaholic who thinks he has seen everything, and is relieved to discover that he hasn't. His sessions with Prot turn into two-way experiences, with Prot offering advice and insights, and seeming intelligent and normal—all except for his impression that his home is 1,000 light-years away. There is also the matter of how he eats a banana. "K-PAX is a planet," he explains to his doctor, "but don't worry—I'm not going to leap out of your chest."

The movie doesn't force its parallel with Christ (who said he was the son of God at a time when, luckily for him, the Psychiatric Institute of Manhattan was not yet admitting patients). But the analogy is there, not least in Prot's relationships with his fellow mental patients; he quietly goes about trying to cure them. The movie populates its ward with the usual job lot of colorful eccentrics, who behave as if they have intensely studied *One Flew Over the Cuckoo's Nest.* The most intriguing, because she never speaks, is Bess (Melanee Murray).

The movie intercuts the psychiatric sessions with Prot and domestic scenes at home, where the doctor's wife, Rachel (Mary McCormack), frets that his mind is always on his work. Why must all men involved in great enterprises have wives who are obsessed with whether they come home for dinner on time?

Is it forbidden that the wife also become fascinated with the case and get involved?

No matter. The heart of the movie is in the Spacey performance, and knowing that less is more, he plays Prot absolutely matter-of-factly. *K-PAX* avoids an ending that invites tears, and supplies one that encourages speculation. Is Prot really from another planet? What happens to him at the end is not quite the answer it seems to be. And consider his range of vision, his versatile blood pressure, his tolerance for Thorazine, and the fact that he describes the intricate orbit of his planet to astronomers who have just discovered it. Against this we must balance the investigative road trip that Powell makes to New Mexico, which offers a persuasive answer and then snatches it away (perhaps Prot simply borrowed a human form).

A final answer is unprovable on the basis of what we're told, and I like it that way. I admired how the movie tantalized us with possibilities and allowed the doctor and patient to talk sensibly, if strangely, about the difference between the delusional and that which is simply very unlikely. Whether Prot is right or wrong about where he comes from is not as important as what he does with his conviction. ☞

L

La Cienaga ★ ★ ★

NO MPAA RATING, 103 m., 2001

Martin Adjemian (Gregorio), Diego Baenas (Joaquin), Leonora Balcarce (Veronica), Silvia Bayle (Mercedes), Sofia Bertolotto (Momi), Juan Cruz Bordeu (Jose), Graciela Borges (Mecha), Noelia Bravo Herrera (Agustina), Mercedes Moran (Tali), Daniel Valenzuela (Rafael), Andrea Lopez (Isabel). Directed by Lucrecia Martel and produced by Lita Stantic. Screenplay by Martel.

La Cienaga is a dank, humid meditation on rotting families. By its end we are glad to see the last of most of its characters, but we will not quickly forget them. The film opens in a crumbling vacation home on a rainy plateau in northern Argentina, and I suspect, although I am not sure, that it expresses the director's feelings about the current downturn in the country's fortunes. These are people who once were rich, and now squat in the ruins of their own lives.

The title translates as "the swamp." Not too hard to spot the symbolism. Thunder rumbles unceasingly on the sound track. It rains and rains. In every room circulating fans look back and forth for relief from the heat. The children find something they are good for: When you put your mouth right in front of the whirling blades and talk, your words get chopped up. Neat. I had forgotten that.

The opening shots show the mottled, exhausted bodies of the slack characters. They've flung themselves on deck chairs next to a stagnant pool. They drink. A woman stands up to carry some wine glasses, slips on the mossy surface, falls, and badly cuts herself. The others do not even look up. She lies in her own blood until her children raise the alarm and take her to a hospital. An alcoholic, she does not seem much interested in what has happened.

The name of the vacation home is La Mandragora ("the mandrake")—"a poisonous plant," the *Concise Oxford* explains, "with emetic and narcotic properties." It is said to shriek when it is plucked. Charming. The mother is named Mecha (Graciela Borges) and her husband is Gregorio (Martin Adjemian). They have four teenage children. In the nearby town of La Cienaga live her cousin Tali (Mercedes Moran), her husband, Rafael (Daniel Valenzuela), and their four younger children.

The older children go hunting in the swamp and kill cattle mired in the mud. One son is missing an eye. Of the younger children in town, one needs to be taken to the dentist because he has a tooth growing out of the roof of his mouth. Later, he cuts his leg. These are potentially cute kids, but not here, where every time they look at their parents they see what's in store for them.

Graciela Borges's performance as Mecha is the centerpiece of the movie. She hints darkly that the "native servants" are stealing the towels. Indeed, when the beautiful servant Isabel (Andrea Lopez) brings towels to stop the flow of blood after she falls, Mecha's first words are, "So that's where the towels went." She stays in bed all day, watching television, sipping wine, complaining, her cuts healing into scars.

Various adulteries have taken place, are taking place, will take place. Mecha's oldest daughter Momi (Sofia Bertolotto) thanks God in her nightly prayers for Isabel, and perhaps is in love with her. Whatever. There is talk by both Mecha and Tali about driving to nearby Bolivia to buy back-to-school supplies, since they are cheaper there. The implication is that Argentineans have fallen from the heights when they consider Bolivia a shopping destination.

This is the first film by writer-director Lucrecia Martel, who doesn't want to tell a story so much as re-create the experience of living in the same houses with these people. Her film is like everyday life in the way events do not always fit together, characters don't know what happens while they're offscreen, and crucial events, even a death, can go unobserved. It's better to know going in that you're not expected to be able to fit everything together, that you may lose track of some members of the large cast, that it's like attending a family reunion when it's not your family and your hosts are too drunk to introduce you around.

La Ciudad (The City) ★ ★ ★
NO MPAA RATING, 88 m., 2000

Bricks—Ricardo Cuevas (Man), Anthony Rivera (Boy), Joe Rigano (Contractor). *Home*—Cipriano Garcia (Young Man), Leticia Herrera (Young Woman). *The Puppeteer*—Jose Rabelo (Father), Stephanie Viruet (Daughter). *Seamstress*—Silvia Goiz (Seamstress), Rosa Caguana (Friend), Guillermina de Jesus (Friend). Directed by David Riker and produced by Riker and Paul S. Mezey. Screenplay by Riker.

Those who leave their native land and immigrate to another are often, almost by definition, the boldest and most capable, able to imagine a new life for themselves. Arriving in a new land without language or connections, they are likely to be shuttled into low-paying jobs and scorned by the lucky citizens who are already onboard. They earn their living by seizing opportunities.

Consider the puppeteer (Jose Rabelo), who is the third subject of David Riker's *La Ciudad (The City)*. He lives in a station wagon with his daughter (Stephanie Viruet). He supports them both by performing Punch and Judy shows for city kids, whose video games must make this entertainment look quaint. His daughter loves to read, is bright, wants to go to school. He tries everything to get her accepted. Every child is guaranteed a place in school, he has been told, but there is a hitch: He needs a receipt for rent or a telephone to show where he lives. And, of course, he lives in a car.

His story is one of four in *The City*, a direct, spare, touching film developed by Riker during six years of acting workshops with immigrants in New York City. His characters come from the Spanish-speaking lands to the south, have arrived in New York filled with hope, and now are exploited as cheap labor.

The first of his stories, *Bricks*, is about day laborers. They're hired a truckload at a time to be carted out to a work site, where they're promised $50 a day only to find out that is a theoretical sum and the job is piecework—fifteen cents for every brick they chip clean of mortar. A man (Ricardo Cuevas) wants to bring along his boy (Anthony Rivera). "This isn't a day-care center," growls the foreman. But if the man is to work, is the boy to wait alone on the streets? There is an accident at the construction site, and we see how expendable these day workers are considered to be.

The second story, named *Home*, is the most bittersweet because it suggests the possibility of hope, even love. A young man (Cipriano Garcia) arrives in the city from Mexico. He crashes a party and finds himself dancing with a woman (Leticia Herrera) who, wonder of wonders, is from his hometown. He confesses to her: "My whole life is in this bag I am carrying." She responds with sweet formality, "I invite you to my home." They have the promise of happiness. And then, in an O. Henry ending, the man's hand closes on air.

Seamstress, the final story, is about a woman (Silvia Goiz) who has left her village and country to earn money to buy medicine for a sick child. Now she works in a sweatshop where no wages have been paid for weeks—and when she asks for her pay, she is fired. The other workers listen silently and glance out of the corners of their eyes. They have no job security, and they need this work desperately; will they express solidarity with her?

The Italian neorealists Rossellini and De Sica believed that everyone could play at least one role in a movie—himself. The movie camera is an effortless recorder of authenticity (it does just as well when exposing the false), and in *The City* we sense in the faces and voices of the performers an experience shared at firsthand. Their stories may be fictional, but their knowledge of them is true. The film is in black and white, as it must be; these spare outlines would lose so much power in color. Riker does an interesting thing with his writing: He never quite closes a story. The open endings are a way of showing that these lives continue from one trouble to another, without happy endings.

I saw this film at its first public screening at the 1998 Toronto Film Festival. Finally it is making its way around the country, at venues like the Film Center of the Art Institute of Chicago. It is a film that would have great power for Spanish-speaking working people, who, of course, are not likely to find it at the Art Institute. Eventually, on television, it may find broader audiences. It gives faces to the faceless, and is not easily forgotten.

The Ladies Man ★
R, 84 m., 2000

Tim Meadows (Leon Phelps), Karyn Parsons (Julie), Billy Dee Williams (Lester), Tiffani Thiessen (Honey DeLune), Lee Evans (Barney), Will Ferrell (Lance), Julianne Moore (Bloopie). Directed by Reginald Hudlin and produced by Lorne Michaels. Screenplay by Tim Meadows, Dennis McNicholas, and Andrew Steele.

The Ladies Man is yet another desperately unfunny feature-length spin-off from *Saturday Night Live,* a TV show that would not survive on local access if it were as bad as most of the movies it inspires. There have been good *SNL* movies, like *Wayne's World, The Blues Brothers,* and *Stuart Saves His Family.* They all have one thing in common: *SNL* producer Lorne Michaels was not primarily responsible for them.

Michaels had nothing to do with *Stuart* and *Brothers.* Credit for the glories of the *Wayne's World* pictures, which he did produce, should arguably go to their directors and stars. Mike Myers went on to *Austin Powers.* Michaels went on to *Coneheads, Superstar, A Night at the Roxbury,* and now *The Ladies Man.*

If I were a Hollywood executive, I would automatically turn down any Michaels *SNL* project on the reasonable grounds that apart from the Mike Myers movies he has never made a good one. He doesn't even come close. His average star rating for the last four titles is 1.125. Just to put things in perspective, the last three Pauly Shore movies I reviewed scored 1.5.

The Ladies Man, directed by Reginald *(House Party)* Hudlin, stars Tim Meadows as Leon Phelps, a boundlessly enthusiastic seducer who seems stylistically and ideologically stuck in the sexist early 1970s. The character, with his disco suits and giant Afro, is funny on TV—but then so are most of the reoccurring *SNL* characters; that's why the show recycles them. At feature length, Leon loses his optimistic charm and slogs through a lamebrained formula story that doesn't understand him.

He plays a radio talk show host in Chicago (i.e., Toronto with CTA buses), who offers late-night advice to the sexually challenged. (To one lonely lady who can't seem to meet the right guy: "Take yo panties off and hang out at the bus station.") In real life he has extraordinary luck picking up girls, for reasons perhaps explained in one scene where he displays his equipment to a girl he's just met. We can't share the sight because he's standing on the other side of the bar, but from the way her face lights up while angelic music swells on the sound track, his pants obviously contain a spotlight and the Mormon Tabernacle Choir.

Leon gets into trouble for what he says on the radio, is fired, and lands briefly at a Christian station, where he tries to sound devout but finds the struggle is too much for him. Following him loyally is his producer Julie (Karyn Parsons), who likes him because she can see he's a nice guy inside. Tiffani Thiessen costars as one of Leon's admirers, Billy Dee Williams is the bartender and narrator, and Julianne Moore has an inexplicable scene as the lustful Bloopie the Clown.

There is a painfully bad sequence involving bets in a bar about who is willing to eat what; it exists *only* to get a merde-eating scene into the movie. Meanwhile, a posse of outraged husbands forms on the Internet and wants to hunt Leon down for seducing their wives. They know they're all looking for the same guy because he has a smiley face tattooed on his butt. At one point the outraged husbands have a song-and-dance scene. The movie makes the mistake of thinking it is funny *that* they sing and dance; next-level thinking would have suggested their song and dance be funny in itself.

All of the outraged husbands but one are white. Leon is black. The movie makes no point of this, for which we can be grateful, since lynch mobs are very hard to make amusing. Spike Lee's *Bamboozled* would have been funnier if this very movie, rather than a blackface minstrel show, had been offered as an example of black stereotypes marketed by white executives. While Lee's fictitious TV show could never conceivably be aired, *The Ladies Man* has been made and distributed and is in theaters as proof that Lee's pessimism is not exaggerated.

The Lady and the Duke ★ ★ ★
PG-13, 129 m., 2002

Lucy Russell (The Lady, Grace Elliott), Jean-Claude Dreyfus (Duke of Orleans), Francois

Marthouret (Dumouriez), Leonard Cobiant (Champcenetz), Caroline Morin (Nanon), Alain Libolt (Duc de Biron), Helena Dubiel (Madame Meyler). Directed by Eric Rohmer and produced by Francoise Etchegaray. Screenplay by Eric Rohmer, based on the memoir *Journal of My Life During the French Revolution* by Grace Elliott.

In the Paris of the mob, during the French Revolution, a patrician British lady supports the monarchy and defies the citizens' committees that rule the streets. She does this not in the kind of lamebrained action story we might fear, but with her intelligence and personality—outwitting the louts who come to search her bedroom, even as a wanted man cowers between her mattresses.

Eric Rohmer's *The Lady and the Duke* is an elegant story about an elegant woman, told in an elegant visual style. It moves too slowly for those with impaired attention spans, but is fascinating in its style and mannerisms. Like all of the films in the long career of Rohmer, it centers on men and women talking about differences of moral opinion.

At eighty-one, Rohmer has lost none of his zest and enthusiasm. The director, who runs up five flights of stairs to his office every morning, has devised a daring visual style in which the actors and foreground action are seen against artificial tableaux of Paris circa 1792. These are not "painted backdrops," but meticulously constructed perspective drawings that are digitally combined with the action in a way that is both artificial and intriguing.

His story is about a real woman, Grace Elliott (Lucy Russell), who told her story in a forgotten autobiography Rohmer found ten years ago. She was a woman uninhibited in her behavior and conservative in her politics, at one time the lover of the prince of Wales (later King George IV), then of Phillipe, the duke of Orleans (father of the future king Louis Phillipe). Leaving England for France and living in a Paris town house paid for by the duke (who remains her close friend even after their ardor has cooled), she refuses to leave France as the storm clouds of revolution gather, and survives those dangerous days even while making little secret of her monarchist loyalties.

She is stubbornly a woman of principle. She dislikes the man she hides between her mattresses, but faces down an unruly citizens' search committee after every single member crowds into her bedroom to gawk at a fine lady in her nightgown. After she gets away with it, her exhilaration is clear: She likes living on the edge, and later falsely obtains a pass allowing her to take another endangered aristocrat out of the city to her country house.

Her conversations with the duke of Orleans (attentive, courtly Jean-Claude Dreyfus) suggest why he and other men found her fascinating. She defends his cousin the king even while the duke is mealymouthed in explaining why it might benefit the nation for a few aristocrats to die; by siding with the mob, he hopes to save himself, and she is devastated when he breaks his promise to her and votes in favor of the king's execution.

Now consider the scene where Grace Elliott and a maid stand on a hillside outside Paris and use a spyglass to observe the execution of the king and his family, while distant cheering floats toward them on the wind. Everything they survey is a painted perspective drawing—the roads, streams, hills, trees, and the distant city. It doesn't look real, but it has a kind of heightened presence, and Rohmer's method allows the shot to exist at all. Other kinds of special effects could not compress so much information into seeable form.

Rohmer's movies are always about moral choices. His characters debate them, try to bargain with them, look for loopholes. But there is always clearly a correct way. Rohmer, one of the fathers of the New Wave, is Catholic in religion and conservative in politics, and here his heroine believes strongly in the divine right of kings and the need to risk your life, if necessary, for what you believe in. Lucy Russell, a British actress speaking proper French we imagine her character learned as a child, plays Grace Elliott as a woman of great confidence and verve. As a woman she must sit at home and wait for news; events are decided by men and reported to women. We sense her imagination placing her in the middle of the action, and we are struck by how much more clearly she sees the real issues than does the muddled duke.

The Lady and the Duke is the kind of movie one imagines could have been made in 1792. It centers its action in personal, everyday experience—an observant woman watches from the center of the maelstrom—and has time and attention for the conversational styles of an age when evenings were not spent stultified in front of the television. Watching it, we wonder if people did not live more keenly then. Certainly Grace Elliott was seldom bored.

Lagaan: Once Upon a Time in India
★ ★ ★ ½
PG, 225 m., 2002

Aamir Khan (Bhuvan), Gracy Singh (Gauri), Rachel Shelley (Elizabeth Russell), Paul Blackthorne (Captain Andrew Russell), Suhasini Mulay (Yashodamai), Kulbhushan Kharbanda (Rajah Puran Singh), Raghuvir Yadav (Bhura), Rajendra Gupta (Mukhiya), Yashpal Sharma (Lakha), Rajesh Vivek (Guran), Pradeep Rawat (Deva). Directed by Ashutosh Gowariker and produced by Aamir Khan. Screenplay by Kumar Dave, Sanjay Dayma, Gowariker, and K. P. Saxena.

Lagaan is an enormously entertaining movie, like nothing we've ever seen before, and yet completely familiar. Set in India in 1893, it combines sports with political intrigue, romance with evil scheming, musical numbers with low comedy and high drama, and is therefore soundly in the tradition of the entertainments produced by the Bombay film industry, "Bollywood," which is the world's largest.

I have seen only five or six Bollywood movies, one of them in Hyderabad, India, in 1999, where I climbed to the highest balcony and shivered in arctic air conditioning while watching a movie that was well over three hours long and included something for everyone. The most charming aspect of most Bollywood movies is their cheerful willingness to break into song and dance at the slightest pretext; the film I saw was about a romance between a rich boy and a poor girl, whose poverty did not prevent her from producing backup dancers whenever she needed them.

Lagaan is said to be the most ambitious, expensive, and successful Bollywood film ever made, and has been a box-office hit all over the world. Starring Aamir Khan, who is one of the top Indian heartthrobs, it was made with an eye to overseas audiences: If *Crouching Tiger, Hidden Dragon* could break out of the martial arts

ghetto and gross $150 million, then why not a Bollywood movie for non-Indians? It has succeeded in jumping its genre; it won an Academy Award nomination in 2002 as Best Foreign Film, and has been rolling up amazing per-screen averages in North American theaters.

All of which evades the possibility that most readers of this review have never seen a Bollywood movie and don't want to start now. That will be their loss. This film is like nothing they've seen before, with its startling landscapes, architecture, and locations, its exuberant colors, its sudden and joyous musical numbers right in the middle of dramatic scenes, and its melodramatic acting (teeth gnash, tears well, lips tremble, bosoms heave, fists clench). At the same time, it's a memory of the films we all grew up on, with clearly defined villains and heroes, a romantic triangle, and even a comic character who saves the day. *Lagaan* is a well-crafted, hugely entertaining epic that has the spice of a foreign culture.

The story takes place at the height of the Raj, England's government of occupation in India. In a remote province, the local British commander is Captain Russell (Paul Blackthorne), a lip-curling rotter with a racist streak, who insults the local maharajah to his face and thinks nothing of whipping a Hindu upstart. Even his fellow officers think he's over the top. He administers "lagaan," which is the annual tax the farmers must pay to their maharajah, and he to the British. It is a time of drought and hunger, and the farmers cannot pay.

Enter Bhuvan (Aamir Khan), a leader among his people, who confronts Russell and finds his weak point: The captain is obsessed by cricket, and believes it's a game that can never be mastered by Indians. Bhuvan says it is much like an ancient Indian game, and that Indians could excel at it. Russell makes Bhuvan a bet: The Brits and a village team will play a cricket match. If the Indians win, there will be no lagaan for three years. If the Brits win, lagaan will be tripled. The villagers think Bhuvan is insane, since a triple tax would destroy them, but he points out that since they cannot pay the current tax, they have nothing to lose.

Bhuvan assembles and starts to coach a local team. Elizabeth Russell (Rachel Shelley), the evil captain's sister, believes her brother's deal is unfair, and secretly sneaks out to the village to provide pointers on cricket. Her closeness to Bhuvan disturbs Gauri (Gracy Singh), a local woman who has believed since childhood that she and Bhuvan are fated to marry. There's another coil of the plot with the two-faced Lakha (Yashpal Sharma), who wants Gauri for himself, and acts as a spy for Russell because he feels that if Bhuvan loses face, he'll have a better chance with her.

We meet the members of the village team, an oddly assorted group that includes a low-caste fortune-teller named Guran (Rajesh Vivek), whose crippled arm allows him to throw a wicked curve ball. There is also Deva (Pradeep Rawat), whose service in the British army has fueled his contempt for his former masters. As training proceeds in the village and the British sneer from their regimental headquarters, the action is punctuated by much music.

The British hold dances, at which single young women who have come out from home hope to find an eligible young officer. (Elizabeth, dreaming about Bhuvan, is not much interested in the candidate selected for her.) And in the village music wells up spontaneously, most memorably when storm clouds promise an end to the long drought. In keeping with Bollywood tradition, the singing voices in these sequences are always dubbed (the voice-over artists are stars in their own right), as the camera plunges into joyous choreography with dancers, singers, and swirls of beautifully colored saris. Such dance sequences would be too contrived and illogical for sensible modern Hollywood, but we feel like we're getting away with something as we enjoy them.

Lagaan somehow succeeds in being suspenseful at the same time it's frivolous and obvious. The final cricket match (which we can follow even if we don't understand the game) is in the time-honored tradition of all sports movies, and yet the underlying issues are serious. And there is the intriguing question of whether the hero will end up with his childhood sweetheart, or cross color lines with the Victorian woman (this is hard to predict, since both women are seen in entirely positive terms).

As a backdrop to the action, there is India itself. It is a long time since I praised a movie for its landscapes; I recall *Dr. Zhivago* or *Lawrence of Arabia*, and indeed, like David Lean, director Ashutosh Gowariker is not shy about lingering on ancient forts and palaces, vast plains, and the birthday-cake architecture of the British Raj, so out of place and yet so serenely confident. Watching the film, we feel familiarity with the characters and the showdown, but the setting and the production style are fresh and exciting. Bollywood has always struck a bargain with its audience members, many of them poor: You get your money's worth. Leaving the film, I did not feel unsatisfied or vaguely shortchanged, as after many Hollywood films, but satisfied: I had seen a *movie*. ☞

Lakeboat ★ ★ ★
R, 98 m., 2001

Charles Durning (Skippy), Peter Falk (The Pierman), Denis Leary (The Fireman), Robert Forster (Joe Pitko), J. J. Johnston (Stan), Tony Mamet (Dale Katzman), Jack Wallace (Fred), George Wendt (First Mate Collins), Andy Garcia (Guigliani). Directed by Joe Mantegna and produced by Tony Mamet, Mantegna, and Morris Ruskin. Screenplay by David Mamet.

Lakeboat was the tenth play by David Mamet to be produced, but it feels like the wellspring. Here in the rough, awkward, poetic words of the crew members of a Lake Michigan ore boat, he finds the cadences that would sound through his work. The play was first produced in 1981, and three years later came *Glengarry Glen Ross*. Both draw from his early jobs, when as a college student he supported himself working on a lake steamer and as a real-estate salesman. Both are unusual because their young protagonists are not heroes, but witnesses. These plays are not about a young man coming of age, but about older men who have come of age. In *Lakeboat*, a veteran crew member, a thoughtful loner who spends all of his free time reading books, tells the young cook, "You got it made."

We sense that men like these taught the young Mamet how his characters would think and talk. They're not narrow proletarians but men confident of themselves and their jobs, and yet needful of the isolation and loneliness of long lake voyages. No one quotes Melville, who said a ship was his Yale and his Harvard, but his words must have been in Mamet's mind as he created Dale Katzman, a second-year graduate student from "a school outside Boston," who signs on as a cook and sails with the *Seaway Queen.*

Dale is played by Tony Mamet, David's brother. The music is by Bob Mamet, another brother. The screenplay adaptation is by David and the direction is by Joe Mantegna, who has appeared in countless Mamet plays. The key actors include two who have been with him from the beginning, Jack Wallace and J. J. Johnston, and others who show how the poignancy and rhythm of the material allows them living space inside the words: Robert Forster, Charles Durning, Peter Falk, George Wendt, Denis Leary, Andy Garcia. I once taught a class on Mamet's films. I wish I could have opened it with this one, because for Mamet it all starts here.

It is important to note that nothing "happens" in the film in conventional movie-plot terms. It is not about a storm, a mutiny, a personal conflict, an old grudge. There is some mystery about why the regular cook, Guigliani (Garcia), is missing on the voyage, but he makes a space for Dale to be hired, and when the ship sails there is nothing much to be done but get the ore to the other end. Denis Leary plays the fireman, who tells Dale: "I keep my eye on the gauges. I watch them constantly." Yes, and studies porno magazines, although why a man would sign on for a world without women and then yearn for them is a question Mamet asks just by creating the character.

Another crew member with theories about women is Fred, played by Jack Wallace in a performance of such crude sweetness you can hear echoes of those very first Mamet plays, when Wallace was onstage in church basements and rented storefronts. Like most limited men, Fred knows a few things very well, and repeats them often to give himself the air of an expert. He thinks he knows all about women (they like to be smacked around a little, so they can see that the guy really cares). Fred delivers a meditation on the use of the f-word that could be printed as an introduction to Mamet's plays.

If Fred's obsession is with women, Stan (J. J. Johnston) is fascinated and baffled by drink. Booze too is a companion, always there to un-

derline the good times and drown the bad ones, and Stan lectures Dale on drink the way Fred does on women. Both of them give extraordinarily bad advice, but not without having given their subjects a good deal of misguided thought.

The captain (Charles Durning) and first mate (George Wendt) are heavy-set men whose weight makes their movements into commitments. They have worked together a long time, long enough so that the skipper can ask the mate to make him a sandwich without giving offense. Without being sexual, their relationship seems domestic. They fiercely love their jobs.

It is the crew member Joe Pitko (Robert Forster) who is young Dale's mentor, the one he will remember with the most affection many years later. This is a working man who hungers for the life of the mind, and who leads two parallel lives, one in his work, the other in his books. There was perhaps a turning point in his life when he might have gone to school or tested some secret dream, but he took the safe bet of a regular paycheck and now finds himself working with men he cannot have nourishing conversations with. The college boy is a godsend. Pitko, in an unspoken way, gives his blessing to the fact that the boy may someday turn this summer of work into a story or a play. Pitko is not so narrow that he sees himself only as the subject for something the kid might write: He also sees himself as audience and critic.

The lakeboat sails on. Mantegna gives us just enough detail, enough exterior shots, so that we feel we're on a ship. All the rest is conversation and idleness. What do men think about on a long uneventful voyage? The routine of their work, the personalities of their crewmates, the certainty of their paychecks, the elusiveness of their dreams, the rhythms of their anecdotes, and sex. The lakeboat is a lot like life.

Lantana ★ ★ ★ ½
R, 121 m., 2002

Anthony LaPaglia (Leon Zat), Geoffrey Rush (John Sommers), Barbara Hershey (Dr. Valerie Sommers), Kerry Armstrong (Sonja Zat), Rachael Blake (Jane), Vince Colosimo (Nik),

Daniella Farinacci (Paula), Peter Phelps (Patrick). Directed by Ray Lawrence and produced by Jan Chapman. Screenplay by Andrew Bovell, based on the play *Speaking in Tongues.*

Lantana opens with a camera tracking through dense Australian shrubbery to discover the limbs of a dead woman. We are reminded of the opening of *Blue Velvet,* which pushed into lawn grass to suggest dark places hidden just out of view. Much of the movie will concern the identity of the dead woman, and how she died, but when the mystery is solved it turns out to be less an answer than a catalyst—the event that caused several lives to interlock.

Ray Lawrence's film is like Robert Altman's *Short Cuts* or Paul Thomas Anderson's *Magnolia* in the way it shows the lives of strangers joined by unsuspected connections. It discovers a web of emotional hope and betrayal. At its center is a cop named Leon Zat (Anthony LaPaglia) in the process of meltdown; he is cheating on his wife, he has chest pains, he beats a suspect beyond any need or reason, he is ferocious with his son, he collides with a man while jogging and explodes in anger.

Zat's wife, Sonja (Kerry Armstrong), worried about him, is seeing a psychiatrist named Valerie Sommers (Barbara Hershey). Valerie is married to John (Geoffrey Rush). A few years ago their daughter was killed. Valerie wrote a book as a way of dealing with the experience. John hides behind a stolid front. One of her clients (Peter Phelps) is a gay man who wants to talk about his married lover, and Valerie comes to suspect that the lover is, in fact, her own husband.

Other characters. Jane (Rachel Blake) is the separated housewife who is cheating with Leon. Her neighbors are the happily married Nik and Paula (Vince Colosimo and Daniella Farinacci). When Valerie's car is found abandoned and she is missing, murder is feared, and Leon is assigned to the case. He suspects her husband, John, and there is another suspect—Nik, the father of three, seen throwing a woman's shoe into the underbrush by Jane. When Leon arrives to question Jane it is significant, of course, that they were lovers.

This description no doubt makes the film seem like some kind of gimmicky puzzle. What's surprising is how easy it is to follow the plot, and how the coincidences don't get in the way. Lawrence's film, based on a play by Andrew Bovell, only seems to be a murder mystery. As it plays out, we're drawn into the everyday lives of these characters—their worries, their sorrows, the way they're locked into solitary sadness. Nik and Paula are the only happy couple, blessed with kids, happiness, and uncomplicated lives. When the evidence seems overwhelming against Nik, we can hardly believe it. Certainly Valerie's husband, or even an ominous dance instructor, might make better suspects.

Anthony LaPaglia makes his cop into a focus of pain: He cheats, takes no joy in cheating, is violent, takes no joy in violence, is shut inside himself. LaPaglia is so identified with American roles that *Lantana* comes as a little surprise, reminding us that he has an Australian background. The other actors, especially Hershey, Rush, and the two unhappy women in the cop's life (played by Armstrong and Blake) are so attentive to the nuances of their characters, so tender with their hurts, that maybe we shouldn't be surprised when the crime plot turns out to be a form of misdirection.

One particularly effective scene involves a conversation between LaPaglia and Rush. It comes at a point when LaPaglia clearly thinks the other man has murdered his wife, and the Rush character almost willfully says things that will not help his case. In another kind of movie, his dialogue could be cheating—deliberately misleading the audience. Here we sense it grows out of a disgust he feels that he is not a better man.

Lawrence and Bovell ground their stories in a lot of domestic details, involving children: the daughter Valerie and John lost; the sons Leon is alienated from; Nik and Paula's kids, who need baby-sitting and get earaches. After Jane reports her suspicions about the neighbors, she ends up minding the kids, and there is a wonderfully observed moment when the little one gets sick and the slightly older one knows just what medication is necessary.

Lantana is, we learn, the name of a South American plant that, transplanted to Sydney, prospered and became a nuisance. What is its connection to the film? Perhaps suspicion can also grow out of control, when people get out of the habit of assuming that others are good and mean well.

Lara Croft Tomb Raider ★ ★ ★
PG-13, 96 m., 2001

Angelina Jolie (Lara Croft), Daniel Craig (Alex Marrs), Leslie Phillips (Wilson), Mark Collie (Larson), Rachel Appleton (Young Lara), Chris Barrie (Hilary the Butler), Iain Glen (Manfred Powell), Julian Rhind-Tutt (Pimms), Jon Voight (Lord Croft). Directed by Simon West and produced by Colin Wilson, Lawrence Gordon, and Lloyd Levin. Screenplay by Patrick Massett, West, and John Zinman.

Lara Croft Tomb Raider elevates goofiness to an art form. Here is a movie so monumentally silly, yet so wondrous to look at, that only a churl could find fault. And please don't tell me it makes no sense. The last thing I want to see is a sensible movie about how the Illuminati will reunite the halves of the severed triangle in order to control time in the ruins of the ancient city that once rose in the meteor crater— if, and it's a big "if," the clue of the all-seeing eye inside the hidden clock can be used at the moment of planetary alignment that comes every 5,000 years, and if the tomb raiders are not destroyed by the many-armed Vishnu figure and the stone monkeys. The logic is exhausting enough even when it doesn't make sense.

This is, at last, a real popcorn movie. I have been hearing for weeks from fans of *The Mummy Returns* and *Pearl Harbor,* offended that I did not like those movies—no, not even as "popcorn movies." I responded that *The Mummy* was a good popcorn movie, but *The Mummy Returns* was a bad popcorn movie. It is my job to know these things. That *Pearl Harbor* is even discussed in those terms is depressing.

The plot of *Lara Croft Tomb Raider* exists as a support system for four special-effects sequences. Right away you can see that the movie is relatively advanced; *The Mummy Returns* had no plot and one special-effects sequence, which was 121 minutes long.

The film opens with Lara Croft doing desperate battle with a deadly robot, in what turns out to be an homage to the openings of the *Pink Panther* movies where Clouseau took on Kato. When the dust settles, we learn that she is Lady Lara Croft (Angelina Jolie), daughter of the tomb raider Lord Croft (Jon Voight), whose memorial stone sadly informs us, "Lost in the Field, 1985." Lady Lara lives in a vast country estate with a faithful butler and a private hacker and weapons system designer. Elaborate research-and-development and manufacturing facilities must be tucked away somewhere, but we don't see them.

Lara Croft is a major babe with a great set of ears. She hears a faint ticking under the stairs, demolishes the ancient paneling (with her bare hands, as I recall), and finds an old clock that conceals the all-seeing eye. This is the key to whatever it is the Illuminati plan to do with the lost city, etc., in their plan to control time, etc. Why they want to do this is never explained. A letter from her father is discovered sewn into the binding of an old edition of William Blake; "I knew you would figure out my clues," it says. And a good thing, too, since fate hangs in the balance while she plays his parlor games.

We now visit "Venice, Italy," where the Illuminati gather, and then there is an expedition to the frozen northern land where the ancient city awaits in a dead zone inside the crater created by the meteor that brought the key to time here to Earth—I think. Machines do not work in the dead zone, so Lara and the others have to use dogsleds. It is cold on the tundra, and everyone wears fur-lined parkas. Everyone but Lara, whose light gray designer cape sweeps behind her so that we can admire the tight matching sweater she is wearing, which clings tightly to those parts of her body which can be found a foot below and a little to the front of her great ears.

The inside of the city is an inspired accomplishment in art direction, set design, and special effects. A giant clockwork model of the universe revolves slowly above a pool of water, and is protected by great stone figures that no doubt have official names, although I think of them as the "crumbly creatures," because whenever you hit them with anything, they crumble. They're like the desert army in *The Mummy Returns* and the insect alien soldiers in *Starship Troopers*—they look fearsome, but they explode on contact, just like (come to think of it) targets in a video game.

Angelina Jolie makes a splendid Lara Croft, although to say she does a good job of playing the heroine of a video game is perhaps not the highest compliment. She looks great, is supple and athletic, doesn't overplay, and takes with great seriousness a plot that would have reduced a lesser woman to giggles. In real life she is a good actress. Lara Croft does not emerge as a person with a personality, and the other actors are also ciphers, but the movie wisely confuses us with a plot so impenetrable that we never think about their personalities at all.

Did I enjoy the movie? Yes. Is it up there with the *Indiana Jones* pictures? No, although its art direction and set design are (especially in the tomb with all the dead roots hanging down like tendrils). Was I filled with suspense? No. Since I had no idea what was going to happen, should happen, shouldn't happen, or what it meant if it did happen, I could hardly be expected to care. But did I grin with delight at the absurdity of it all? You betcha.

The Last Castle ★ ★ ★
R, 91 m., 2001

Robert Redford (General Irwin), James Gandolfini (Colonel Winter), Mark Ruffalo (Yates), Steve Burton (Captain Peretz), Delroy Lindo (General Wheeler), Paul Calderon (Dellwo), Samuel Ball (Duffy), Jeremy Childs (Cutbush), Clifton Collins Jr (Aguilar), George W. Scott (Thumper), Robin Wright (Daughter). Directed by Rod Lurie and produced by Robert Lawrence. Screenplay by David Scarpa and Graham Yost.

The Last Castle tells the story of a war hero who becomes the prisoner of a tin soldier. Robert Redford stars as General Irwin, much-decorated former Hanoi POW, hero of the Gulf and Bosnian campaigns, now sentenced to a military prison under the command of Colonel Winter (James Gandolfini), a sadistic sentimentalist who obsessively dotes on his collection of military memorabilia.

"They should have given him a medal instead of sending him to prison," Winter tells an underling, as he watches Irwin in the prison yard through the plate-glass window of his office. He admires Irwin, who was found guilty of disobeying a direct command (for heroic reasons, of course). Winter's infatuation is short-lived; he overhears the general telling the orderly, "Any man who has a collection like this has never set foot on a battlefield."

That does it. Winter's true nature emerges: He is a sadist who hides behind military law to run a reign of terror. The Redford character wants only to do his time and go home. But inevitably he finds himself in conflict with Winter, tells him he's "a disgrace to the uniform," and finds himself leading a clandestine uprising. "He's building a structure of loyalty," Winter frets. *The Last Castle*, directed by Rod Lurie *(The Contender)*, builds this bitter personal rivalry into a struggle for power that involves psychological strategy and armed conflict.

There are similarities to *Cool Hand Luke* and its battle of wills. The film does such a good job of creating its oppressive, claustrophobic prison atmosphere and peopling it with sharply defined characters that it grips us, and we shake away logical questions. Lurie shows again, as he did in *The Contender*, that he can tell a dramatic, involving story, even if later we're wondering about loopholes and lapses.

Redford and Gandolfini are two reasons the movie plays so well. Redford, because he does what's expected, as a calm, strong, unbreakable leader. Gandolfini, because he does what is not expected, and creates not simply a villain, but a portrait of a type that is so nuanced, so compelling, so instinctively right that we are looking at the performance of a career. This actor, who can be so disarmingly genial (see his scene-stealing in *The Mexican*), who can play bad guys we enjoy (see *The Sopranos*), here transforms his face and posture to make himself into a middle-aged boy, a hulking schoolyard bully. He does a lot with his mouth, making the lips thin and hurt, as if he is getting back for a lifetime of wounds and disappointments. Colonel Winter's childhood must have been hell.

The immediate experience of watching *The Last Castle* is strongly involving, and the action at the end is exciting. It's the kind of movie people tell you they saw last night and really liked. I really liked it last night too. It's only this morning that I'm having trouble with.

Standing back from the excitement of the

engagement, it occurs to me that the Irwin character, in his way, is no less a monster than Winter. Both men delight in manipulating those they can control; Irwin is simply better at masking his puppet-mastery in nobility. If Winter has been responsible for the injury and death of some of the men under his command, Irwin is responsible for more. If Winter is a disgrace to the uniform, so in a way is Irwin, who could achieve his objectives with less carnage than he does. Much of the plot hinges on a convenient character named General Wheeler (Delroy Lindo), who is wheeled on and off like a Shakespearean chorus. He trusts Irwin, despises Winter, yet makes his decisions entirely for the convenience of the plot. In the real world, he could have easily brought about a peaceful solution.

I was also surprised at the equipment unveiled in the later stages of the film. One of the delights of prison movies like *Stalag 17* and *The Great Escape* is the way the prisoners manufacture props or dig tunnels under the eyes of the guards. All of that ingenuity takes place offscreen in *The Last Castle,* and when we see what Irwin has secretly prepared, we're surprised that Winter could miss such large-scale activities.

There's also a plot thread left hanging. Irwin gets a bitter prison visit from his daughter (Robin Wright), who tells him, "You weren't a father at all." He wants to make peace, but she says it's too late. Fair enough—but this relationship is then dropped. So what was the purpose of the visit? To set up a quest for personal closure in later scenes that have been cut from the film? Or simply because the filmmakers felt that they should supply some family angst from the past because that's what all prison movies do?

Because of these lapses in story logic and character development, *The Last Castle* falls short of the film it could have been. It relies too much on a conflict between colorful characters and a thrilling finish. On those levels it works— I enjoyed watching this movie. It could have been more, could have been a triumph and a classic, instead of simply an effective entertainment. The performances by Redford and Gandolfini are there, ready to be used in the service of something better. ☞

Last Orders ★ ★ ★ ½
R, 109 m., 2002

Michael Caine (Jack), Tom Courtenay (Vic), David Hemmings (Lenny), Bob Hoskins (Ray), Helen Mirren (Amy), Ray Winstone (Vince), Laura Morelli (June). Directed by Fred Schepisi and produced by Elisabeth Robinson, Schepisi, and Gary Smith. Screenplay by Schepisi, based on the novel by Graham Swift.

Too many films about the dead involve mourning, and too few involve laughter. Yet at lucky funerals there is a desire to remember the good times. The most charismatic man I ever knew was Bob Zonka, an editor at the *Chicago Sun-Times,* and even five years after his death his friends gathered just to tell stories and laugh about them. Yes, he was infuriating in the way he treasured his bad habits, but it was all part of the package. There is the impulse to try to analyze the departed, figure out their motives, ask the questions they never answered, wonder what they were really thinking.

Last Orders, Fred Schepisi's new film, based on the Booker Prize–winning novel by Graham Swift, knows all about those stages in the process of grieving and celebration. It is about four old friends in London who, at one level, simply drank together for years at a pub called the Coach and Horses, and at another level came as close as people can to sharing each others' lives. Now one has died—the most enigmatic and problematical of the four— and the three survivors and the dead man's son gather in the pub with his ashes and set off on a journey to Margate, where he thought to retire. His wife does not make the journey but chooses to spend the day with their retarded daughter.

The three friends and the widow all have faces that evoke decades of memories for moviegoers. In a certain way, we have lived our lives with them, so it feels right to find them on this mission at the end.

Tom Courtenay electrified me in *Loneliness of the Long Distance Runner* when I was still in college. I had lunch with him in 1967 in London, and in a sense have just gotten up from that meal. David Hemmings was the photographer in *Blow-Up,* the movie everybody was talking about when I became a film critic. Michael Caine was one of the first stars I ever interviewed (about *Hurry, Sundown,* a film he had a hard time keeping a straight face about). Bob Hoskins joined the crowd later, with *The Long Good Friday,* walking onto the screen with the authority of a lifelong lease-holder. Helen Mirren I became aware of when I saw *Cal* at the 1984 Cannes festival. Ever since, she has been brave in her film choices, going her own way, so that her character's behavior here mirrors her career.

Because I share history and memories with these actors, it is easy to stand at the bar with their characters as they regard the urn of ashes. "So that's Jack, is it?" they say, looking at the container as if it might explode. Have you noticed that although people feel odd around a corpse, they sometimes have a little smile when looking at ashes, because the ashes so clearly are *not* the departed—who has left for other pastures, leaving behind this souvenir. Having scattered a few ashes myself, I find it more cheerful than putting someone into the ground. It's a way the dead have of telling the living to go outdoors to some nice place and remember them.

The fact that Jack wants his ashes to be scattered into the sea at Margate has a lot to do with his widow Amy's decision not to go along. It was there they met, as kids from London, gathering hops as a summer job. It was there that their daughter was conceived. And when June (Laura Morelli) was born retarded, Jack refused to deal with her—refused even to acknowledge her existence. All these years Amy (Mirren) has visited the daughter in an asylum once a week. The girl has never given the slightest sign of recognizing her mother, and so Amy is trapped between two great gulfs of disregard. That Jack would think Amy would want to retire to a place associated with these memories is—well, typical of the deep misunderstandings a marriage can engender and somehow accommodate.

Jack, we might as well say, is the character played by Michael Caine. It is no secret after the first scene of the film. We get to know him well, because Schepisi's flashback structure shows Jack as a young man at war, as a second-generation butcher, as a young man courting Amy, and as a jolly regular in the pub. The

other friends include benign Vic (Courtenay), an undertaker; Ray (Hoskins), who likes to play the ponies; and Lenny (Hemmings), once a boxer, now a portly greengrocer. The actors have logged time in pubs and know the form. Notice how Caine captures the look of a drinker late at night, with the saggy lower eyelids and the slight loosening of tension in the lips.

They all live and work in the same south London neighborhood, and are joined at the pub by Vince (Ray Winstone), who is Jack and Amy's son. It was Jack's wish that Vince join him in the family butcher business, but Vince instead became a car dealer, and turns up in a Mercedes to drive the pals and the ashes to Margate. Many old secrets are revealed in the course of the journey, but they are not really what the movie is about. The details are not as important as the act of memory itself.

A death in the family is a sudden interruption of the unconscious assumption that things will go on forever. There can be a certain exhilaration at this close contact with eternal truths; we were not aware at our births, so death is the only conscious contact we have with this mysterious journey. The final shot of Schepisi's movie finds a visual way to suggest the great silence that surrounds us. Another scene near the end puts it in human terms. On the day the friends go to scatter Jack's ashes, Amy pays her usual visit to June—to the daughter who was denied the gift of awareness; as Amy tells Ray, "Not once in fifty years did she ever give me a sign—not even a flicker—that she knew me." As we consider June's uncomprehending eyes and fixed smile, we think, death is not so bad. Not knowing we live, not knowing we die, that would be bad. Ashes are scattered in more ways than one in the film's closing scenes.

Note: Some reviews have complained about the Cockney accents. All of these actors can speak the Queen's English if they choose to. The Cockney is their gift to us in creating the world of their characters. You may miss a word or two, but you hear the music.

Last Resort ★ ★ ★
NO MPAA RATING, 76 m., 2001

Paddy Considine (Alfie), Dina Korzun (Tanya), Artiom Strelnikov (Artiom), Lindsay Honey

(Les). Directed by Pawel Pawlikowski and produced by Ruth Caleb. Screenplay by Pawlikowski and Rowan Joffe.

Tanya's fiancé was going to meet them in England, but he is not at the airport, the rat. The Russian woman with the small boy and the uncertain English tries to deal with British immigration officials, who are not unkind but have seen this scenario countless times before. She talks about her fiancé, she cites vague employment plans, and finally, in desperation, she requests political asylum.

Asylum is not really what she wants, but it's what she gets: asylum inside the British bureaucracy, which ships Tanya (Dina Korzun) and her son, Artiom (Artiom Strelnikov), to a bleak and crumbling seaside resort named Dreamland, where she's given some food coupons and a barren apartment, and told to wait for a decision that may take months, or years.

Tanya learns over the telephone that the fiancé is never going to show. But in making the call she has also made a crucial connection; using an unfamiliar phone card at a run-down seaside arcade, she meets its owner, Alfie (Paddy Considine). He is an enigma, a seemingly nice man who perhaps has a subtle romantic agenda, or perhaps simply feels sorry for her and wants to help. Having been betrayed by her fiancé, Tanya is not much interested in a new man. But Alfie doesn't push it.

The movie was directed for the BBC films division by Pawel Pawlikowski, who has a background in documentaries and does a good job of sketching in everyday life in the area, where the cold concrete and joblessness of a housing project has bred a generation of young outlaws. It's not clear whether the barbed wire is to keep people out, keep them in, or simply supply a concentration camp decor.

Young Artiom is an enterprising lad who makes friends with Alfie more quickly than his mother will, and is soon hanging out in the arcade, finding his niche in the Dreamland ecology. ("Mom, why can't we stay here with him?") His mother, desperately poor, fields a job offer from a pornographer named Les (Lindsay Honey) who wants to pay her to writhe on a bed for his Internet customers (he demonstrates with a teddy bear, in a scene balancing humor and the grotesque). Les is a

sleazeball but a realist, the heir to generations of Cockney enterprisers. He points out that Tanya at least will not have to see, or be touched by, any of her "clients," and that the money's not bad. Such employment would be a change; in Russia, Tanya was an illustrator of children's books.

It's intriguing the way Pawlikowski keeps his hand hidden for most of the movie. We can't guess where things are headed. The movie is not on a standard Hollywood romantic arc in which the happy ending would be Alfie and Tanya in each other's arms. That's only one of several possibilities, and economic factors affect everything. Dina Korzun's performance holds our interest because she bases every scene on the fact that her character is a stranger in a strange land with no money and a son to protect. *Last Resort* avoids all temptations to reduce that to merely the setup for a romantic comedy; it's the permanent condition of her life.

Some movies abandon their soul by solving everything with their endings. Life doesn't have endings, only stages. To pretend a character's problems can be solved is a cheat—in a realistic film, anyway (comedies, fantasies, and formulas are another matter). I like the way *Last Resort* ends, how it concludes its emotional journey without pretending the underlying story is over. You walk out of the theater curiously touched.

The Last September ★ ★
R, 104 m., 2000

Maggie Smith (Lady Myra), Michael Gambon (Sir Richard Naylor), Jane Birkin (Francie Montmorency), Fiona Shaw (Marda Norton), Lambert Wilson (Hugo Montmorency), David Tennant (Captain Gerald Colthurst), Richard Roxburgh (Daventry), Keeley Hawes (Lois Farquar), Gary Lydon (Peter Connolly). Directed by Deborah Warner and produced by Yvonne Thunder. Screenplay by John Banville, based on the novel by Elizabeth Bowen.

Years ago I visited one of the great country houses built by the Anglo-Irish in Ireland. It was Lissadell, the very one Yeats wrote about, its "great windows open to the south." The Gore-Booth family lived there; one of its daughters, Constance, Countess Markiewicz, was a leader in the Easter Rebellion of 1916, which marked the beginning of the Irish republic and the end for the Anglo-Irish. I went with an Irish friend whose family had grown up nearby. The tour was conducted by a distant relative of the family. As we left, my friend chortled all the way down the drive—that the gentry had so fallen that the son of a working-man could drop some coins in the collection pot near the door.

Deborah Warner's *The Last September* is set during the slow decline of the Anglo-Irish. It takes place in 1920 in county Cork, where Sir Richard Naylor and his wife, Lady Myra, pre-side over houseguests who uneasily try to enjoy themselves while the tide of Irish repub-licanism rises all around them. British Army troops patrol the roads and hedgerows, and Irish republicans raid police stations and pick off an occasional soldier. It is the time of the Troubles.

We meet the owners of the great house: pleasant and befuddled Sir Richard (Michael Gambon) and Lady Myra (Maggie Smith), a sharp and charming snob. She notices that her niece, Lois (Keeley Hawes), is sweet on Gerald Colthurst, a British captain (David Tennant), and warns her that, socially, the match won't do. It would be bad enough if the captain's parents were "in trade," but that at least would produce money; it is clear to Lady Myra that the suitor is too poor to afford thoughts of Lois.

Lois keeps her own thoughts to herself, and knows that Peter Connolly (Gary Lydon), a wanted Irish killer, is hiding in the ruined mill on their property. She brings him food, but he wants love, too, and she is not so sure about that—although she returns despite his roughness. Does she love either man? She is maddeningly vague about her feelings, and may simply be entertaining herself with their emotions.

Also visiting: Hugo and Francie Montmor-ency (Lambert Wilson and Jane Birkin), who have had to sell their place and become full-time guests, and Marda Norton (Fiona Shaw), a woman from London who is uncomfortably aware that she is approaching her sell-by date. She and Hugo were once lovers; she wouldn't marry him, Francie would, and now volumes go unspoken between them.

The weakness of the movie is that these characters are more important as types than as people. The two older women, Marda and Lady Myra, are the most vivid, the most sure of who they are. Hugo is an emasculated free-loader, and Captain Colthurst is a young man in love with infatuation. As for Connolly, the IRA man, he is a plot device.

The movie is based on a novel by Elizabeth Bowen, whose stories of London during the Blitz capture the time and place exactly. She grew up at Bowen's Court, a country house in county Cork, was a member of an Anglo-Irish family, and would have been twenty-one in 1920—about the same age as Lois. But if Bowen modeled Lois on herself, she did her-self no favor; Lois is bright and resourceful and likes attention, but is irresponsible and plays recklessly at a game that could lead to death.

The movie is elegantly mounted, and the house is represented in loving detail, although the opening scenes allow so much of the red-gold sunset to pour into the drawing room that we fear the conservatory is on fire. The tone is one of languid hedonism; life is pleas-ant for these people, who speak of themselves as Irish even though to the native Irish they are merely trespassers for the British empire. I'm not sure the movie should have pumped up the melodrama to get us more interested, but something might have helped.

The Last Waltz ★ ★ ★
PG, 117 m., 2002

Featuring The Band, Eric Clapton, Neil Diamond, Bob Dylan, Emmylou Harris, Joni Mitchell, Van Morrison, Robbie Robertson, The Staples, Muddy Waters, Ronnie Wood, Neil Young, and Martin Scorsese. A concert documentary directed by Martin Scorcese and produced by Robbie Robertson.

I wonder if the sadness comes across on the CD. The music probably sounds happy. But the performers, seen on-screen, seem curiously morose, exhausted, played out. Recently I was at a memorial concert for the late tenor sax man Spike Robinson, and the musicians—jazz and big-band veterans—were cheerful, filled with joy, happy to be there. Most of the musicians in *The Last Waltz* are, on average, twenty-five years younger than Spike's friends, but they drag themselves onstage like exhausted veterans of wrong wars.

The rock documentary was filmed by Martin Scorsese at a farewell concert given on Thanksgiving Day 1976 by The Band, which had been performing since 1960, in recent years as the backup band for Bob Dylan. "Sixteen years on the road is long enough," says Robbie Robertson, the group's leader. "Twenty years is unthinkable." There is a weight and gravity in his words that suggests he seriously doubts if he could survive four more years.

Drugs are possibly involved. Memoirs recalling the filming report that cocaine was everywhere backstage. The overall tenor of the documentary suggests survivors at the ends of their ropes. They dress in dark, cheerless clothes, hide behind beards, hats, and shades, pound out rote performances of old hits, don't seem to smile much at their music or each other. There is the whole pointless road warrior mystique, of hard-living men whose daily duty it is to play music and get wasted. They look tired of it.

Not all of them. The women (Joni Mitchell, Emmylou Harris) seem immune, although what Mitchell's song is about I have no clue, and Harris is filmed in another time and place. Visitors like the Staples Singers are open-faced and happy. Eric Clapton is in the right place and time. Muddy Waters is on sublime autopilot. Lawrence Ferlinghetti reads a bad poem, badly, but seems pleased to be reading it. Neil Diamond seems puzzled to find himself in this company, grateful to be invited.

But then look at the faces of Neil Young or Van Morrison. Study Robertson, whose face is kind and whose smile comes easily, but who does not project a feeling of celebration for the past or anticipation of the future. These are not musicians at the top of their art, but laborers on the last day of the job. Look in their eyes. Read their body language.

The Last Waltz has inexplicably been called the greatest rock documentary of all time. Certainly that would be *Woodstock*, which heralds the beginning of the era that The Band gathered to bury. Among 1970s contemporaries of

The Band, one senses joy in the various Rolling Stones documentaries, in Chuck Berry's *Hail! Hail! Rock and Roll*, and in concert films by the Temptations or Rod Stewart. Not here.

In *The Last Waltz*, we have musicians who seem to have bad memories. Who are hanging on. Scorsese's direction is mostly limited to close-ups and medium shots of performances; he ignores the audience. The movie was made at the end of a difficult period in his own life, and at a particularly hard time (the filming coincided with his work on *New York, New York*). This is not a record of serene men, filled with nostalgia, happy to be among friends.

At the end, Bob Dylan himself comes on. One senses little connection between Dylan and The Band. One also wonders what he was thinking as he chose that oversize white pimp hat, a hat so absurd that during his entire performance I could scarcely think of anything else. It is the haberdashery equivalent of an uplifted middle finger.

The music probably sounds fine on a CD. Certainly it is well rehearsed. But the overall sense of the film is of good riddance to a bad time. Even references to groupies inspire creases of pain on the faces of the rememberers: The sex must have been as bad as anything else. Watching this film, the viewer with mercy will be content to allow the musicians to embrace closure, and will not demand an encore. Yet I give it three stars? Yes, because the film is such a revealing document of a time.

Late Marriage ★ ★ ★
NO MPAA RATING, 100 m., 2002

Lior Louie Ashkenazi (Zaza), Ronit Elkabetz (Judith), Moni Moshonov (Yasha [Father]), Lili Kosashvili (Lily [Mother]), Sapir Kugman (Madona), Aya Steinovits Laor (Ilana). Directed by Dover Kosashvili and produced by Marek Rozenbaum and Edgard Tenembaum. Screenplay by Kosashvili.

When children are grown they must be set free to lead their own lives. Otherwise it's no longer a parent guiding a child, but one adult insisting on authority over another. Wise parents step back before they cross this line. Wise children rebel against parents who do not.

345

Late Marriage is about parents who insist on running the life of their thirty-two-year-old son, and a son who lets them. The characters deserve their misery.

The film is set in Israel, within a community of Jewish immigrants from the former Soviet republic of Georgia. Zaza at thirty-one has still not filled his obligation to marry and produce children. His parents have marched a parade of potential wives past him, without success. His secret is that he's in love with Judith, a divorcée from Morocco, four years older, with a daughter. His parents would never approve of Zaza marrying such a woman.

As the movie opens, Zaza and his family descend on the home of Ilana, a sulky seventeen-year-old who has been proposed as a prospective bride. There may be a difference in age and education, but at least she is single, childless, and arguably a virgin. In a scene of excruciating social comedy, the two families arrange themselves in the living room and discuss Zaza and Ilana as if they were this week's Tupperware specials. Then Ilana is produced and the would-be couple dispatched to her bedroom "to get to know one another."

"Is that a dress or a nightgown?" Zaza (Lior Louie Ashkenazi) asks her when they are alone. "What do you think?" asks Ilana (Aya Steinovits Laor). She shows him her portfolio and confides her desire to be a dress designer. She seems to be designing for the hostesses in an Havana hooker bar, circa 1959. "I want a rich man," she tells him. Obviously he will not do, but they fall on her bed and neck for a while until summoned back to the family council.

Zaza's parents find out about Judith (Ronit Elkabetz), the divorcée. They stake out her house and eventually break in upon the romantic couple, calling Judith a whore and demanding that the relationship end. Does Zaza stand up to his mother, Lily (Lili Kosashvili—the director's own mother)? No, he doesn't, and Judith sees this, and wisely drops him because there is no future for her.

The contest between arranged marriages and romantic love is being waged in novels and movies all over those parts of the world where parents select the spouses of their children. Art is on the side of romance, tradition on the side of the parents. Sometimes, as in

Mira Nair's wonderful *Monsoon Wedding*, set in Delhi, there is a happy medium when the arranged couple falls in love. But look at Rohinton Mistry's new novel, *Family Matters*, about a man who spends a lifetime of misery after having a widow foisted on him by a family that disapproves of the Christian woman from Goa he truly loves.

The most important sequence in *Late Marriage* is a refreshingly frank sex scene involving Zaza and Judith. We don't often see sex like this on the screen. The scene is not about passion, performance, or technique, but about (listen carefully) familiarity and affection. They know each other's bodies. They have a long history of lovemaking, and you can see how little movements and gestures are part of a shared physical history. Watching this scene, we realize that most sex scenes in the movies play like auditions.

Late Marriage is not a one-level film, and one of its most revealing moments shows the strong-minded mother expressing respect for the equally iron-willed Judith. These women understand each other, and the mother even realistically discusses the chances that her Zaza will defy her and choose the divorcée. The mother would, if forced to, actually accept that—but Zaza is too frightened of her to intuit that there is a crack in his mother's heart of stone.

I know couples whose marriage were arranged, and who are blissful. I know couples who married for love, and are miserable. I am not saying one way is right and another wrong. The message of *Late Marriage*, I think, is that when a marriage is decided by the parents crushing the will of the child, it is wrong for the child and unfair to the new spouse. I have more thoughts on this subject, but have just remembered this is not the advice column, so I will close with the best all-purpose advice I have heard on this subject: Never marry anyone you could not sit next to during a three-day bus trip.

Left Luggage ★ ★
NO MPAA RATING, 100 m., 2001

Laura Fraser (Chaja), Isabella Rossellini (Mrs. Kalman), Maximilian Schell (Chaja's

Father), Marianne Sagebrecht (Chaja's Mother), Jeroen Krabbe (Mr. Kalman), Adam Monty (Simcha), Chaim Topol (Mr. Apfelschnitt). Directed by Jeroen Krabbe and produced by Ate de Jong, Hans Pos, and Dave Schram. Screenplay by Edwin de Vries.

Left Luggage is one of those movies where the audience knows the message before the film begins and the characters are still learning it when the film ends. No matter how noble a film's sentiments, it's wearying to wait while elementary truths dawn gradually on slow learners. Add to this yet one more tiresome story in which the women possess all the wisdom and humanity and the men are cruel, stubborn, and crazed, and you have a long slog through a parched landscape.

The movie takes place in 1972 in Antwerp, where a young woman named Chaja (Laura Fraser) gets a job as a nanny for the Kalmans, a family of Hasidic Jews. Chaja is a Jew herself, but so indifferent to her identity that one of her best friends doesn't even realize she's Jewish. She finds the Hasidim, with their traditional black garments, strict observances, and unyielding patriarchy, absurd throwbacks. But she needs the money and takes the job, and soon bonds with Mrs. Kalman (Isabella Rossellini) and her children, especially a four-year-old named Simcha (Adam Monty).

Simcha has not started to speak. One reason for this may be the fierce tyranny with which Mr. Kalman (Jeroen Krabbe, the film's director) rules his family. He is strict, forbidding, and unforgiving, in accordance with the convention in which most movie fathers are deeply flawed repositories of character defects, while their wives are bubbling reservoirs of life, wit, and humanity. Gene Siskel called this the Bad Dad Syndrome, noting that we could go months at a time between films where a father was smart, gentle, and caring.

At home, Chaja's parents are stuck in their own pasts. Both her father and mother (Maximilian Schell and Marianne Sagebrecht) are Holocaust survivors whose lives are still governed by the experience. The mother compulsively bakes cakes and endlessly tries to feed them to everyone within sight. The father prowls Antwerp with a map and a shovel, try-

ing to find the spot where he buried two precious suitcases before being shipped off by the Nazis. "They're probably all moldy by now," his wife warns—and so is the labored plot device. Surely there is a more creative way to suggest a search for lost roots than to have poor Maximilian Schell up to his armpits in holes he is frantically digging in Antwerp's gardens and backyards.

Chaja becomes close with little Simcha, who eventually reveals that he can indeed speak. His first word is "quack." It is inspired by a toy duck he pushes along so that it quacks too. It goes without saying that the toy duck arouses the ire of Mr. Kalman, who wants to banish it from the house ("My son is saying 'quack, quack' when he should be asking the four questions for the Seder"). Later, when Chaja teaches little Simcha the four questions (remember, this is a child who was thought to be mute), the beast of a father criticizes a mistake and the kid pees in his pants. My notion is that a great many Hasidic fathers succeed in combining their religion with love and kindness for their children, and that this particular father is an example of melodramatic overkill crossed with gender bias.

Ah, but there's more. The Kalmans have succeeded in being the only family still resident in a building where the concierge is a vicious anti-Semite. This is no doubt a great convenience for the plot, since by stationing him at the door to hiss and swear at the Jews every time they enter or leave, the screenplay doesn't have to waste valuable screen time importing anti-Semites from elsewhere. And then there is a development at the end which, as tearjerking goes, is shameless.

In the midst of this contrivance, both Isabella Rossellini and Laura Fraser give solid and affecting performances, and Schell makes his character less of a caricature than he might have been. But the very last shot of the film, intended as uplifting, seems to solve nothing and to condemn the characters to continue to let the past destroy their present and future. With limitless possibilities for stories involving essentially these same characters, Krabbe and his writer, Edwin de Vries, are trapped by sentimentality and awkward contrivance.

Legally Blonde ★ ★ ★
PG-13, 96 m., 2001

Reese Witherspoon (Elle Woods), Luke Wilson (Emmett), Selma Blair (Vivian), Matthew Davis (Warner Huntington III), Victor Garber (Professor Callahan), Ali Larter (Brooke), Jennifer Coolidge (Paulette), Holland Taylor (Professor Stromwell). Directed by Robert Luketic and produced by Ric Kidney and Marc E. Platt. Screenplay by Kirsten Smith and Karen McCullah Lutz, based on the novel by Amanda Brown.

Legally Blonde is a featherweight comedy balanced between silliness and charm. It is impossible to dislike, although how much you like it may depend on your affection for Reese Witherspoon. She is so much the star of the movie that the other actors seem less like costars than like partners in an acting workshop, feeding her lines. They percolate; she bubbles.

Witherspoon plays Elle Woods, named perhaps for the magazine, perhaps because the word means "she" in French. Work on that pun a little more and you could name the movie *The Vengeance of Elle*, since Elle gets her revenge on the stuck-up snob who dumps her, and thus inspires a brilliant legal career.

We meet Elle as she basks in general approval as president of the Delta Nu house on a Los Angeles campus. She moves in a cloud of pink, dispensing advice on grooming, hair care, and accessorizing; she has a perfect grade point average in her major, which is fashion. She thinks Warner Huntington III (Matthew Davis) plans to propose to her, but actually he wants to break up. He plans to be a senator by the time he's thirty, he explains, and for that career path, "I need to marry a Jackie, not a Marilyn."

Outraged, Elle determines to follow Warner to Harvard Law School and shame him with her brilliance. And so she does, more or less, after being taken on as an intern by the famous Professor Callahan (Victor Garber) and assigned to help him in the case of a famous weight-loss consultant (Ali Larter) accused of murdering her much older husband. The defense hinges on such matters as whether a Delta Nu would sleep with a man who wears a thong, and the chemistry of perms.

Reese Witherspoon effortlessly animates this material with sunshine and quick wit. Despite the title and the implications in the ads, this is a movie about smart blondes, not dumb ones, and she is (I think) using her encyclopedic knowledge of fashion and grooming to disguise her penetrating intelligence. On the other hand, maybe not; maybe it's just second nature for her to win a client's confidence by visiting her in prison with Calvin Klein sheets, Clinique skin care products, and the latest issue of *Cosmo*.

I smiled a lot during the movie, laughed a few times, was amused by the logic of the court case. *Legally Blonde* is not a great movie (not comparable with *Clueless*, which it obviously wants to remind us of, or Witherspoon's own wonderful *Election*). But Witherspoon is a star, and the movie doesn't overstay its welcome. It also contains at least one line I predict will enter the repertory: Elle Woods is asked, "A spa? Isn't that kind of like your mother ship?"

The Legend of Bagger Vance ★ ★ ★ ½
PG-13, 127 m., 2000

Will Smith (Bagger Vance), Matt Damon (Rannulph Junuh), Charlize Theron (Adele Invergordon), Bruce McGill (Walter Hagen), Joel Gretsch (Bobby Jones), J. Michael Moncrief (Hardy Greaves), Peter Gerety (Neskaloosa), Lane Smith (Grantland Rice), Jack Lemmon (Old Hardy). Directed by Robert Redford and produced by Redford, Michael Nozik, and Jake Eberts. Screenplay by Jeremy Leven, based on the novel by Steven Pressfield.

Look how silky this movie is, and how completely in command of its tone. Robert Redford's *The Legend of Bagger Vance* could be a movie about prayer, music, or mathematics, because it is really about finding yourself at peace with the thing you do best. Most of the movie is about an epic golf tournament, but it is not a sports movie in any conventional sense. It is the first Zen movie about golf.

I watched it aware of what a delicate touch Redford brings to the material. It could have been punched up into clichés and easy thrills, but no: It handles a sports movie the way Billie Holiday handled a trashy song, by finding the love and pain beneath the story. Redford and his writer, Jeremy Leven, starting from a novel by Steven Pressfield, are very clear in their minds about what they want to do. They want to explain why it is possible to devote your life to the love of golf, and they want to hint that golf and life may have a lot in common.

I am not a golfer. It doesn't matter. Golf or any game is not about the rules or tools, but about how you conduct yourself. Civilized games make civilized societies. You look at the movie and you see that if athletes are not gentlemen and gentlewomen, there is no reason to watch them. Michael Jordon is a gentleman. Roger Clemens is not. You see how it works.

The Legend of Bagger Vance takes place in Savannah, Georgia, in the first years of the depression. A man builds a great golf course, goes broke, and shoots himself. His daughter Adele (Charlize Theron) faces ruin, but risks everything on a $10,000 tournament. She invites the two greatest golfers in the world: Bobby Jones (Joel Gretsch) and Walter Hagen (Bruce McGill). And she also invites Rannulph Junuh (Matt Damon), who was the greatest player in Savannah until he went off to World War I and something broke inside. He spent the 1920s drinking and playing poker.

Junuh doesn't much want to return to golf, which for him also means returning to civilization and to his own better nature. Three people encourage him. One is Adele. Before the war they were in love. One is a young boy named Hardy (J. Michael Moncrief) who dreams about golf. And one is Bagger Vance (Will Smith), a caddy who appears out of nowhere and assigns himself to the rehabilitation and education of Rannulph Junuh.

We have here the elements for a cruder movie. We can imagine how Jones and Hagen could be painted as hard-edged professionals, how the caddy could be sketched with broad strokes like some kind of an angel in a sitcom, how the little kid could be made insufferable and cute, how Adele and Junuh could fight and make up and fight, all according to the outlines they hand out in screenwriting class.

That's not how this movie goes. Nothing in it is pushed too far; it is a masterpiece of tact. Not even the outcome of the tournament is pumped up for effect; quietly, the movie suggests that how the tournament is won is more important than who wins it. As for the romance, it's in a minor key good for regret and tremulous hope; Charlize Theron's wise, sweet Adele handles Junuh like a man she wants to teach about tenderness.

Every actor makes the point, and then pauses, content. Matt Damon's Junuh is not a comeback hero but a man who seems surprised to be playing golf. Jones and Hagen are not the good cop and the bad cop. They're both good—sportsmen who love the game but don't talk a lot about it. Jones is handsome, a golden boy. Hagen is dark and has a gut and smokes all the time. Jones plays a beautiful game. Hagen is always getting into trouble and saving himself. Both of them are . . . having fun. Just having fun.

Will Smith could make Bagger Vance insufferable, but the part is written and played to make it more of a bemused commentary. He has theories about golf, and ways of handling his player, and advice, but it is all oblique and understated. No violins. Is he a real person or a spirit? You tell me. Oh, and the kid: He's necessary because he has to grow up and become an old man (Jack Lemmon) and tell the story, so that you can see that lessons were learned.

The photography by Michael Ballhaus makes the great course look green, limitless, and sad—sad that every shot must fall and every game must end. There is a dusk here that is heartbreaking, like the end of every perfect summer day. The spectators do not make spectacles of themselves, but seem to identify with the aspirations of the players. Hagen and Jones know each other well, and during the marathon tournament they watch Junuh carefully, and decide that he will do. Redford found the same feeling in *A River Runs Through It*, where the standards a man forms through his pastime give value to his whole life. Golf, Bagger tells Junuh, is "a game that can't be won, only played."

The Legend of Rita ★ ★ ★ ½
NO MPAA RATING, 101 m., 2001

Bibiana Beglau (Rita), Martin Wuttke (Hull), Nadja Uhl (Tatjana), Harald Schrott (Andi), Alexander Beyer (Jochen), Jenny Schily (Friederike), Mario Irrek (Klatte), Thomas Arnold (Gerngross). Directed by Volker

Schlondorff and produced by Arthur Hofer and Emmo Lempert. Screenplay by Wolfgang Kohlhasse and Schlondorff.

It's said that European films are about adults, Hollywood films about adolescents. For evidence, compare two recent films: *The Legend of Rita* and *Invisible Circus*. Both are about young women who become involved with German terrorist gangs. The German film is told through the eyes of a woman who tries to remain true to her principles while her world crumbles around her. The American film is told through the eyes of a kid sister, who seeks the truth of her older sister's death, and ends up sleeping with her boyfriend, etc. The German woman is motivated by political beliefs. The American woman is motivated by family sentiment, lust, and misguided idealism, in keeping with Hollywood's belief that women are driven more by sex than ideas, and that radicalism is a character flaw.

The Legend of Rita, directed by the gifted German Volker Schlondorff *(The Tin Drum),* won two acting prizes and the award as best European film at the 2000 Berlin Film Festival. It stars Bibiana Beglau as Rita, a West German who belongs to a left-wing terrorist group in the 1970s. The group robs banks, kills people, and inspires a dragnet after a jailbreak. The movie doesn't make it easy for us: Rita is not an innocent bystander, and kills a policeman herself. But this isn't a simplistic parable about her guilt or motivation; it's about the collapse of belief during the last decade of the Cold War. Schlondorff believes his audience may be grown-up enough to accept a story about a woman who is not a heroine. Imagine that.

The setup comes as Rita, who has been in Lebanon, attempts to enter East Germany with a revolver in her luggage. She is questioned by Hull (Martin Wuttke), an agent for Stasi, the East German secret police, and allowed to enter the country with the weapon but without her bullets. Later, because Hull (and Stasi, it is implied) sympathizes with her group's opposition to capitalism, she is offered a new identity.

Cutting her ties to her name, her past and everyone she knows, Rita becomes a cog of the working class. This is all right with her: She isn't a naive hobbyist but seriously believes in socialism. With a new name and identity, she goes to work in a textile factory and becomes friendly with a fellow worker named Tatjana (Nadja Uhl); their affection nudges toward a love affair, but when her identity is discovered, Hull yanks her into another life, this time running a summer camp for the children of factory workers. Here she falls in love with a man. But can she marry a man who doesn't know who she really is?

The movie isn't about love, unrequited or not. It's about believing in a cause after the cause abandons you. Here the intriguing figure is Hull, who is not the evil East German spy of countless other movies, but a bureaucrat with ideals who likes Rita and believes he is doing the right thing by protecting her. When the Berlin Wall collapses, there is an astonishing exchange between Hull and the general who is his superior. The general says West Germany demands the extradition of Rita and other terrorists.

"How did they know they were here?" asks Hull.

"They always knew," says the general.

"How did they find out?"

"From us, perhaps."

The Legend of Rita shows a lot of everyday East Germans, workers and bureaucrats, who seem unanimously disenchanted by the people's paradise. Rita's original cover story was that she moved to the East from Paris because of her ideals; not a single East German can believe that anyone from the West would voluntarily move to their country. In the last days of the East, as the wall is coming down, Rita makes a touching little speech in the factory cafeteria, saying the ideals of socialism were good, even if they were corrupted in practice. The East German workers look at her as if she's crazy.

The Legend of Rita doesn't adopt a simplistic political view. It's not propaganda for either side, but the story of how the division and reunification of Germany swept individual lives away indifferently in its tide. In 1976, Schlondorff and his wife, Margarethe von Trotta, made another strong film, *The Lost Honor of Katharina Blum,* set in West Germany. It was about an innocent bystander caught in the aftermath of raids by the Baader-Meinhof Gang, the same group Rita presumably belongs to. From West or East, from right or left, his stories have the same message: When the state's interests are at stake, individual rights and beliefs are irrelevant.

The Legend of Drunken Master ★ ★ ★ ½
R, 101 m., 2000

Jackie Chan (Wong Fei Hung), Ti Lung (Wong's Father), Anita Mui (Wong's Mother), Felix Wong (Tsang), Lau Ka Leung (Master Fu), Low Houi Kang (John), Chin Ka Lok (Fo Sang), Ho Sung Pak (Henry), Tsung Chi Kwong (Tso). Directed by Lau Ka Leung and produced by Eric Tsang, Edward Tang, and Barbie Tung. Screenplay by Tang, Tong Man Ming, and Yeun Chieh Chi.

Jackie Chan's *The Legend of Drunken Master* is quite simply amazing. It involves some of the most intricate, difficult, and joyfully executed action sequences I have ever seen. If you have any interest in seeing a Jackie Chan martial arts film, then this is the one to see. Filmed in 1994 but not given a wide North American release until now, it is considered by those who have seen most of Chan's seventy-plus films to be one of his two or three best.

When I did a seminar at the Hawaii Film Festival several years ago, comparing the physical comedy of Chan and Buster Keaton, martial arts fans brought in their bootleg Hong Kong laser discs of this film and told me that I had to see the final twenty-minute fight sequence. They were correct. Coming at the end of a film filled with jaw-dropping action scenes, this extended virtuoso effort sets some kind of benchmark: It may not be possible to film a better fight scene.

But before I describe it, some general comments:

1. Most of Jackie Chan's plots exist only as clotheslines on which to hang the action scenes. Characters are thin, the dubbed dialogue ranges from rudimentary to inane, and the climax comes not at the end of the story but during the outtakes, when we see Jackie *really* getting hit, burned, dropped, slammed, etc. The man seems to spend half of his life on a hospital stretcher or having fire extinguishers aimed at him.

2. At least half the running time consists of violence, but this is curiously innocent, harmless violence—not the brutal and ugly stuff of many Hollywood action pictures. There are villains and heroes—a fight needs two sides—but everyone on both sides is in superb physical condition, and seems to be fighting largely for the fun of it. Between the action, Jackie hams it up with broad humor. To rate this movie R is to be terminally clueless.

3. The pleasure of the fight sequences comes not in seeing people get hit, but in watching physical coordination and precise choreography. Chan himself routinely does little throwaway things like running up walls, leaping into train windows, and making tricky twist-and-jumps.

4. The whole point is that Chan and the other actors *actually do most of the stunts.* Yes, there are certain special effects, and camera angles and editing make it appear that things happen in a way they perhaps did not. But when Jackie Chan falls into a pit of burning coals in this movie, that is really Jackie Chan, and the coals are really burning, and Chan insisted on doing the stunt three times until he got it right (the third time was when he burned himself and got those nasty scars you can still see on his arm).

Chan was forty when *The Legend of Drunken Master* was made, and although he is still in superb shape, he is reaching the age when he might want to produce and direct these movies instead of starring in them. It is all rather academic, sadly, because computerized special effects have made the authenticity of his physical skills sort of obsolete. When you see bodies whirling in midair in *The Matrix,* you don't think about computers, you simply accept them. But what Chan does, he is more or less, one way or another, actually doing.

The movie's plot is nonsense about Jackie battling with ambassadorial thieves who would steal precious Chinese national treasure. The title comes from the notion that pretending to be drunk, or being just drunk enough (without being too drunk) can make one a better fighter. Chan gets some low physical humor out of drunk jokes during the action scenes (he seems able to lean over at impossible angles). The sets are elaborate, the photography is elegant, and at the end, in the twenty-minute sequence, Chan faces his own bodyguard (filling in after another actor was injured) in one

351

of the most remarkably sustained examples of martial arts choreography ever filmed. (I *think* the bodyguard is named Lo Wai Kwong, although the credits are confusing.)

Jackie Chan became a worldwide star because of word of mouth. Hollywood discovered him belatedly. There is a kind of innocence in his films, an exuberance, that can't be faked. Some people love Jackie; others have no interest in ever seeing his films because they think they know what they will see. The bottom line is: Chan deserves a place in movie history somewhere in the same hall of fame that also houses the other great physical performers who really did their stuff themselves: Buster Keaton, Douglas Fairbanks Sr., Fred Astaire, Gene Kelly, and, yes, Jackie Chan.

L'Humanite ★ ★ ★ ½
NO MPAA RATING, 148 m., 2000

Emmanuel Schotte (Pharaon De Winter), Severine Caneele (Domino), Philippe Tullier (Joseph), Ghislain Ghesquiere (Commandant), Ginette Allegre (Eliane). Directed by Bruno Dumont and produced by Rachid Bouchareb and Jean Brehat. Screenplay by Dumont.

Bruno Dumont's *L'Humanite* has the outer form of a police movie, but much more inside. It is not about a murder, but about the policeman in charge of the investigation. It asks us to empathize with the man's deepest feelings. I saw the film a week after *Shaft*. Both films are about cops driven to the edge of madness by a brutal crime. *Shaft* is about the story; *L'Humanite* is about the character.

It is not an easy film and is for those few moviegoers who approach a serious movie almost in the attitude of prayer. A great film, like a real prayer, is about the relationship of a man to his hopes and fate.

The man this time is named Pharaon De Winter. He is played by Emmanuel Schotte as a man so seized up with sadness and dismay that his face is a mask, animated by two hopeless eyes. He lives on a dull street in a bleak French town. Nothing much happens. He once had a woman and a child, and lost them. We know nothing else about them. He lives with his mother, who treats him like a boy. Domino (Severine Caneele) lives next door. She has an

intense physical relationship with her lover, Joseph, that gives her no soul satisfaction. It is impossible to guess if Joseph even knows what that is.

There is a scene where Pharaon walks in as they are making love, and regards them silently. Their lovemaking is not erotic or tender, but just a matter of plumbing arrangements. Domino sees him standing in the doorway. Later she asks him, "Get an eyeful?" He mumbles a lame excuse. She says something hurtful and leaves. Then she returns, touches him lightly, and says, "I'm sorry." When she leaves again, he pumps his fists in the air with joy.

Why? Because he loves her or wants her? It isn't that simple. He is like those children or animals who go mad from lack of touching and affection. His sadness as he watched them was not because he wanted sex, but because they were getting nothing out of it. His joy was because she touched him and indicated that she knew how he felt, and that she had hurt him.

He is a policeman, but he has no confidence or authority. The opening shots show him running in horror from a brutal murder scene, and falling inarticulate on the cold mud. He tells his chief how upset he is by the crime. He doesn't have the chops to be a cop. He watches a giant truck race dangerously through the narrow lanes of the little town, and then exchanges a sad shrug with the old lady across the street. His police car is right there, but he doesn't give chase.

His relationship with Domino and Joseph is agonizing. He goes along with them on their dates for sad reasons: He has nothing else to do, they have nothing to talk about with each other, he's no trouble. Because Joseph is the dominant personality, he enjoys flaunting the law in front of Pharaon, who is so cowed he can't or won't stop him. There's a scene with the three of them in a car, Joseph speeding and running stop signs and Pharaon impotently saying he shouldn't. Domino listens, neutral. And a scene where Joseph behaves piggishly to bystanders, and Pharaon is passive. The dynamic is: Joseph struts so that Domino can observe that he is more of a man than Pharaon the cop. Pharaon implodes with self-loathing.

The murder investigation continues, sending Pharaon to England and to an insane asylum. His efforts are not really crucial to the solution of the case. In a way, the rape and death of the girl at the beginning is connected with his feelings for Domino—because she offers him sex (in a friendly way) and he cannot separate her body from the memory of the victim in the field. The rapist has taken away Pharaon's ability to see women in a holy light.

The movie is long and seemingly slow. The actors' faces can be maddening. We wait for something to happen, and then realize, something *is* happening—*this* is happening. In the spiritual desert of a dead small town, murder causes this cop to question the purpose of his life. Eventually he goes a little mad (notice the way he sniffs at the possible drug dealer).

The film won the Grand Jury Prize at the 1999 Cannes Film Festival; Emmanuel Schotte won as Best Actor, and Severine Caneele shared the Best Actress Award. On stage, Schotte seemed as closed-off as in the film. Perhaps Bruno Dumont cast him the way Robert Bresson sometimes cast actors—as figures who did not need to "act" because they embodied what he wanted to communicate.

The Cannes awards were not popular. Well, the movie is not "popular." It is also not entirely successful, perhaps because Dumont tried for more than he could achieve, but I was moved to see how much he was trying. This is a film about a man whose life gives him no source of joy, and denies him the consolation of ignorance. He misses, and he knows he misses. He has the willingness of a saint, but not the gift. He would take the suffering of the world on his shoulders, but he is not man enough. The film is not perfect but the character outlives it, and you will not easily forget him.

Liam ★ ★ ★ ½
R, 90 m., 2001

Ian Hart (Dad), Claire Hackett (Mam), Anthony Borrows (Liam), Megan Burns (Teresa), David Hart (Con). Directed by Stephen Frears and produced by Colin McKeown and Martin Tempia. Screenplay by Jimmy McGovern.

Set among the Irish working people of Liverpool in the 1930s, Stephen Frears's *Liam* shows us a family where the children are terrified of sin and their parents of poverty. The first is more easily combated than the second; in two crucial personal transformations, the eight-year-old boy makes his first confession and communion, and his father joins the fascist brownshirts of Oswald Mosley. Both are obsessed with blame; the father blames the Jews for his unemployment and poverty, and his son blames—himself.

This is, says Charles Taylor of *Salon,* the movie that *Angela's Ashes* might have been, and he is correct: It is harder-edged, more unsparing, and when the father tells his wife, "We're skint," he is not making an announcement but accepting a doom. Broke and unemployed, he is expected to outfit little Liam (Anthony Borrows) in a nice new suit from the tailor shop for his first communion.

The way he sees it, to pay the Jewish tailor, he has to get funds from the Jewish pawnbroker, and when, on First Communion Sunday, the priest in his pulpit compliments the children on how well they are dressed, Dad (Ian Hart) stands up furious in his pew to cry out in the church: "Do you know how much it costs to dress the children, Father?" He then goes on to blame the Jews, although he might better blame the church itself for not welcoming the children of the poor in whatever clothes they have.

Times change. I was reminded of Ken Loach's *Raining Stones* (1994), in which it is the unemployed father who is determined that his girl have a nice communion dress, and the priest who tries to talk him out of it. That priest even goes on to make a tricky moral judgment that seems to owe more to situational ethics than to church doctrine; he is that rarity in the movies, a clergyman who is good, flexible, and sympathetic. The priest in *Liam* seems straight from the pages of James Joyce, terrifying the children with visions of hell and informing them that their sins drive the nails deeper into the hands of Christ, which may be more than you can handle when you are eight years old.

The film is built on strong performances, but two stand out. Little Anthony Borrows, short, stout, and always in earnest as Liam, has a stutter that makes it almost impossible for him to get the words out. Sometimes this works to his advantage: He takes a suit to the pawnshop instructed to get "seven and a tanner" but seizes up and gets nine and a tanner when another customer appeals to the good heart of the pawnbroker. During Liam's first confession, he literally cannot say a word until he hits upon a sudden inspiration that releases the flow.

What he wants to confess is that his sins have caused his mother to grow hair upon her body. This he knows from having accidentally seen her in her bath, and comparing her body with the hairless perfection of the art reproductions so thrillingly studied in secret by the boys at school. The priest, who is not a bad man but simply clueless about children, is able to relieve him of this great burden.

The other performance is by Ian Hart, a British actor you may not even recognize, although he has given a series of brilliant, self-effacing performances. He plays the kind of man who cannot bear the pain of seeming insufficient, and must blame somebody. We see him lining up with the other unemployed men outside a factory, hoping to be chosen by the foreman. We see him buying a pint of Guinness for the foreman as a bribe—and *still* being passed over, and spitting in the man's face. And we see how for him the attraction of fascism and anti-Semitism is that it removes the guilt from his shoulders; it is his form of absolution, and when he puts on his fascist shirt and marches out to join a rally, you get a vision of hate groups as clusters of the weak, clinging together to seek in the mob qualities they lack in themselves.

Two children have work: Con (David Hart), the older brother, brings home a paycheck but is at war with his father, and Teresa (Megan Burns) is a housemaid for a wealthy Jewish family, and gets bribes from the wife for keeping quiet about an affair she is having. There is a Jewish daughter, about Teresa's age, who wants to be friendly across the class divide. When Teresa is given some of her dresses, it's no problem that they're hand-me-downs; what breaks Teresa's heart is when she is asked by her mother to select one so the others can be pawned.

Some will find Dad's last big act in the movie too melodramatic. I think it follows from a certain logic, and leads to the very last shot, which is heartbreaking in its tenderness. The film as a whole suggests that Catholicism (in those days, in that society) came down more

heavily upon children than some of them could bear, and that children thus diminished in self-esteem might grow up to seek it in unsavory places. It suggests a connection, in some cases, between extreme guilt and low self-esteem in childhood and an adult attraction to the buck-passing solutions of racism, fascism, and even, as Dad's final big scene makes perfectly clear, terrorism.

L.I.E. ★ ★ ★
NC-17, 97 m., 2001

Brian Cox (Big John Harrigan), Paul Franklin Dano (Howie Blitzer), Billy Kay (Gary Terrio), Bruce Altman (Marty Blitzer), James Costa (Kevin Cole), Tony Donnelly (Brian), Walter Masterson (Scott). Directed by Michael Cuesta and produced by Rene Bastian, Linda Moran, and Michael Cuesta. Screenplay by Stephen M. Ryder, Michael Cuesta, and Gerald Cuesta.

Some pederasts are besotted by sentimentality, seeing their transgression through a misty-eyed desire to be understood. The popular arts usually paint them as monsters, and even a great novel like Michel Tournier's *The Ogre* goes straight for a link between the pederast's idealization of young men and the psychosexual impulses of Nazism. The most remarkable thing about *L.I.E.*, a drama about a fifteen-year-old boy and a middle-aged ex-marine, is that it sees both of its characters without turning them into caricatures. The man is helpless in the face of his compulsion, but he seeks only where he is possibly welcome.

The title is an abbreviation for the Long Island Expressway, and in the opening shot we see Howie (Paul Franklin Dano) hazardously balanced on one foot on a guard rail above the speeding traffic. In narration, he tells us the expressway "has taken a lot of people and I hope it doesn't get me." He lists some of the victims: "Harry Chapin, the director Alan Pakula, and my mother."

Howie lives with his father, who has taken a bimbo girlfriend with unseemly haste. He skips school, hangs out with the kinds of boys his mother would have warned him against, breaks into houses, deals uncertainly with the erotic feelings he has for his best friend, Gary (Billy Kay). Gary is actively gay, we learn, and hustles older guys for money, but he keeps that side of his life secret from his friends.

One of the houses they break into belongs to Big John Harrigan (Brian Cox, who played Hannibal Lecter in *Manhunter*). Big John, a client of Gary's, tracks Howie down, confronts him with proof of his crime, and offers him a choice between arrest and friendship. He does not quite require sex as part of the bargain, and perhaps Howie does not quite understand the nature of the older man; some of his naïveté is real, and some is deliberately chosen.

When Howie's father is arrested on fraud charges connected to his business, Howie ends up at Big John's home, and uncertainly begins to offer what he thinks is expected. Big John turns him away: "It's not about sex, Howie." Isn't it? We have a feeling that for Big John sex is an activity that takes place at the local parks where male hustlers do business, and Howie represents something more complex and, in a twisted way, idealistic.

Make no mistake: *L.I.E.* is not an apologia for pederasty. It does not argue in defense of Big John. But its director, Michael Cuesta, has the stubborn curiosity of an artist who won't settle for formulas but is intrigued by the secrets and mysteries of his characters. My guess is that for every actual sexual liaison of this sort, there are dozens or hundreds of ambiguous, unfulfilled, tentative "friendships." Many men can remember that when they were boys there were sometimes older men around who used friendship or mentoring as a metaphor for a vague, unexpressed yearning. This movie is balanced along that murky divide just as Howie is balanced above the expressway.

Brian Cox has been a superb actor in more than fifty movies, from *Braveheart* to *Rob Roy* to *Rushmore* to Shakespeare. His character here is macho to an extreme (his doorbell plays a patriotic march). He is a man's man in both meanings of the phrase. His achievement in *L.I.E.* is to remain just outside our comprehension: We do not approve of what he does, but he is just subtle enough so that we are sometimes not sure exactly what he's doing. The courts would judge this case in black and white, but the movie occupies the darker shades of gray.

The ending is a cheap shot. An inconclusive ending would have been better, and perhaps more honest. The movie and the ending have so little in common that it's as if the last scene is spliced in from a different film. Although *L.I.E.* is rated NC-17 as it is, one almost suspects that this ending replaces another one that was removed for one reason or another. That is the only plausible explanation.

Life and Debt ★ ★ ★
NO MPAA RATING, 86 m., 2001

A documentary directed and produced by Stephanie Black. Narration written by Jamaica Kincaid.

Most Americans have been bewildered by the antiglobalization protesters at recent meetings of the International Monetary Fund and the World Bank. Isn't free trade a good thing? Isn't a global economy great for everyone? What could the protesters possibly be objecting to?

Life and Debt, a documentary by Stephanie Black with a commentary written by Jamaica Kincaid, looks at the effect of the International Monetary Fund on the economy of Jamaica. The result, she argues, has been the destruction of Jamaican industry and agriculture, the end of Jamaica as a self-sufficient economic entity, and its conversion into a market for North American goods and a source of underpaid labor.

A harsh indictment, but the film is persuasive, showing how powdered milk from America (purchased from subsidized American dairy farmers and dumped at a loss), has destroyed the Jamaican fresh milk industry, and how even the one remaining market for Jamaican bananas—England—is threatened by the Chiquita–Dole–Del Monte forces, who think one Jamaican banana not sold by them is too many. Latin American banana workers earn $1 a day; Jamaicans can't live on that. Other markets reflect the same policies: Subsidized Idaho potatoes have bankrupted Jamaican potato farmers, McDonald's refuses to buy local meat, sweet Jamaican onions are underpriced by American onions sold at a loss, and so on.

One scheme to help the Jamaican economy, the film says, has been the establishment of "free zones," fenced-in manufacturing areas

355

where workers are paid $30 a week to assemble goods that arrive and leave by container ship without legally being on Jamaican soil. Labor unions are banned, working conditions are subhuman, strikers are forced back to work at gunpoint, and paychecks are taxed for health and retirement schemes that don't seem to exist. The Hanes clothing division of Chicago's Sara Lee company was one of the beneficiaries, until, the movie says, it pulled out to find even cheaper workers elsewhere.

The IMF ideally loans money that can be used to help local businesses, but as former Jamaican prime minister Michael Manley observes, it charges twice the world rate for interest and forbids the country from charging its own lenders less. An IMF-backed small business loan in Jamaica might carry 25 percent interest.

"You ask, whose interest is the IMF serving?" Manley says. "Ask—who set it up?" IMF policies can be changed only by an 80 percent vote. The United States, Japan, Germany, England, Canada, and Italy control more than 80 percent of the votes. The bottom line: Developing economies of the Third World are deliberately destroyed and turned into captive markets for the rich nations, while their once self-sufficient inhabitants become cheap labor, and local competition is penalized.

Are these charges true? I do not have the expertise to say. I only bring you the news that this documentary, which has played twice on PBS and is now in theaters, exists. If you're curious about why the demonstrators are so angry, this is why they're so angry.

Life as a House ★ ★ ½
R, 128 m., 2001

Kevin Kline (George), Kristin Scott Thomas (Robin), Hayden Christensen (Sam), Jena Malone (Alyssa), Mary Steenburgen (Coleen), Mike Weinberg (Adam), Scotty Leavenworth (Ryan), Ian Somerhalder (Josh), Jamey Sheridan (Peter), Sam Robards (David). Directed by Irwin Winkler and produced by Winkler and Rob Cowan. Screenplay by Mark Andrus.

Life as a House has much heart and not enough brain, and to the degree that you can put your centers of higher intelligence on hold, it works as a tragicomic weeper. Because it is slick and classy and good to look at, and the actors are well within their range of competence, you can enjoy the movie on a made-for-TV level, but you wish it had been smarter and tougher. It is a little deadening to realize, at about the twenty-five-minute mark, that the problems of every single major character will be resolved by the end.

Those characters include George (Kevin Kline), a model maker who has just been fired from his job at an architect's firm. Robin (Kristin Scott Thomas), his ex-wife, now trapped in a loveless marriage with the absentminded Peter (Jamey Sheridan). Sam (Hayden Christensen), George and Robin's angst-ridden, pierced, drug-using, and self-loathing son. Coleen (Mary Steenburgen), the next-door neighbor, and her daughter, Alyssa (Jena Malone). And Josh (Ian Somerhalder), Sam's friend and Alyssa's boyfriend, and a part-time pimp.

I cannot proceed further without informing you that very early in the movie (spoiler warning), George discovers he has about four months to live. For a time we assume he has Ali MacGraw's Disease (the sicker you get the better you look), but a specific diagnosis is revealed toward the end. George got a severance package when he was fired, and he determines to tear down the shack he lives in, build a new house, and win the love and respect of his son, all in one summer.

George's shack sits in a cul-de-sac high on a cliff overlooking the Pacific in Orange County, California. Owners of ocean frontage in that area will be interested to learn that with twenty-six weeks of severance pay as a model maker, George can afford to tear down his house and build another one. Some will be surprised he could even pay the taxes.

Any sentient being will be able to predict, after sizing up the characters and their establishing dialogue, that Sam will remove the hardware from his face and learn through hard work to become clean and sober and love his father. That Robin will want to share the experience with Sam (and her two young children by the second marriage), and will recall her early love for George. That Sam and Alyssa will become friends, and a little more. And that two unassigned characters of opposite genders are required by the laws of screenwriting to get together, even if one is a teenage pimp and the other a yuppie housewife.

But I am getting way too cynical. You have to approach *Life as a House* knowing that it has no interest in life as it is really lived or people as they really are, and offers lovable characters whose personality traits dictate their behavior, just like on TV. What is remarkable is how Kline and Thomas, in particular, are able to enrich their characters by sheer skill and depth of technique, so that we like them and care what happens to them. (Whether it is George and Robin we like or Kline and Thomas is beside the point—the characters and actors amount to the same thing.)

Some episodes in the movie seem especially contrived. One involves a character who discovers something astonishing and falls off the roof. In my experience, people on roofs tend to hold on while digesting astonishing discoveries. Another involves the comeuppance of a nasty neighbor (Sam Robards). The nature of his comeuppance is dictated by the Law of Character Economy, which decrees, I believe, that the purpose of concealing his identity in an earlier scene is to reveal it in a later one. There is also a scene involving Christmas lights that strains geography, plausibility, visibility, and special effects to the breaking point. It gets distracting when some scenes in a movie exist on a different plane of possibility than the others.

Hollywood has fallen on dark days, dumbing down many of its films to the point where the actors seem measurably brighter than their dialogue and decisions. The current *My First Mister* has surprisingly similar situations, more effectively handled. *Life as a House* is aimed at the audience that admired a movie like *Terms of Endearment* (1983), but exists, alas, on the level of its pale sequel, *The Evening Star* (1996). The scenes that play best are not the ones of high drama and tear-jerking intensity, but the moments of simple affection between Kline and Thomas. Those moments have truth, and they humble some of the other material.

Life or Something Like It ★
PG-13, 104 m., 2002

Angelina Jolie (Lanie Kerigan), Stockard Channing (Deborah Connors), Edward Burns (Pete), Melissa Errico (Andrea), Tony Shalhoub (Prophet Jack), Christian Kane (Cal Cooper), Gregory Itzin (Dennis), Lisa Thornhill (Gwen). Directed by Stephen Herek and produced by Kenneth Atchity, John Davis, Toby Jaffe, Arnon Milchan, and Chi-Li Wong. Screenplay by John Scott Shepherd and Dana Stevens.

Someone once said, live every day as if it will be your last.

Not just someone once said that. Everyone once said it, over and over again, although *Life or Something Like It* thinks it's a fresh insight. This is an ungainly movie, ill-fitting, with its elbows sticking out where the knees should be. To quote another ancient proverb, "A camel is a horse designed by a committee." *Life or Something Like It* is the movie designed by the camel.

The movie stars Angelina Jolie as Lanie Kerigan, a bubbly blond Seattle TV reporter whose ignorance of TV is equaled only by the movie's. I don't know how the filmmakers got their start, but they obviously didn't come up through television. Even a *viewer* knows more than this.

Example. Sexy Pete the cameraman (Edward Burns) wants to play a trick on Lanie, so he fiddles with her microphone during a stand-up report from the street, and her voice comes out like Mickey Mouse's squeak—like when you talk with helium in your mouth. Everybody laughs at her. Except, see, your voice comes out of your *body*, and when it goes through the air it sounds like your voice to the people standing around. When it goes into the microphone, it kind of *stays* inside there, and is recorded on videotape, which is not simultaneously played back live to a street crowd.

Lanie dreams of going to New York to work on *AM USA*, the network show. She gets her big invitation after attracting "national attention" by covering a strike and leading the workers in singing "Can't Get No Satisfaction" while she dances in front of them, during a tiny lapse in journalistic objectivity. Meanwhile, she is afraid she will die, because a mad street person named Prophet Jack has predicted the Seattle Mariners will win, there will be a hailstorm tomorrow morning, and Lanie will die next Thursday. They win, it hails, Lanie believes she will die.

This leads to a romantic crisis. She is engaged to Cal Cooper (Christian Kane), a pitcher with the Mariners. He's on the mound, he looks lovingly at her, she smiles encouragingly, he throws a pitch, the batter hits a home run, and she jumps up and applauds. If he sees that, she may not last until Thursday. Meanwhile, she apparently hates Pete the sexy cameraman, although when Cal is out of town and she thinks she's going to die, they make love, and *then* we find out, belatedly, they've made love before. The screenplay keeps doubling back to add overlooked info.

Cal comes back to town and she wants a heart-to-heart, but instead he takes her to the ballpark, where the friendly groundskeeper (who hangs around all night in every baseball movie for just such an opportunity) turns on the lights so Cal can throw her a few pitches. Is she moved by this loving gesture? Nope: "Your cure for my emotional crisis is batting practice?" This is the only turning-on-the-lights-in-the-empty-ballpark scene in history that ends unhappily.

Lanie and Pete the sexy cameraman become lovers, until Pete whipsaws overnight into an insulted, wounded man who is hurt because she wants to go to New York instead of stay in Seattle with him and his young son. This about-face exists *only* so they can break up so they can get back together again later. It also inspires a scene in the station's equipment room, where Jolie tests the theoretical limits of hysterical overacting.

Lanie's *AM USA* debut involves interviewing the network's biggest star, a Barbara Walters type (Stockard Channing), on the star's twenty-fifth anniversary. So earthshaking is this interview, the *AM USA* anchor breathlessly announces, "We welcome our viewers on the West Coast for this special live edition!" It's 7 A.M. in New York. That makes it 4 A.M. on the West Coast. If you lived in Seattle, would you set your alarm to 4 A.M. to see Barbara Walters plugging her network special?

Lanie begins the interview, pauses, and is silent for thirty seconds while deeply thinking. She finally asks, "Was it worth everything?" What? "Giving up marriage and children for a career?" Tears roll down Channing's cheeks. Pandemonium. Great interview. Network president wants to hire Lanie on the spot. Has never before heard anyone ask, "Was it worth it?" The question of whether a woman can have both a career and a family is controversial in *Life or Something Like It*—even when posed by Ms. Jolie, who successfully combines tomb-raiding with Billy Bob Thornton.

I want to close with the mystery of Lanie's father, who is always found stationed in an easy chair in his living room, where he receives visits from his daughters, who feel guilty because since Mom died they have not been able to communicate with Dad, who, apparently as a result, just sits there waiting for his daughters to come back and feel guilty some more. Eventually there's an uptick in his mood, and he admits he has always been proud of Lanie and will "call in sick" so he can watch Lanie on *AM USA*. Until then I thought he *was* sick. Maybe he's just tired because he's on the night shift, which is why he would be at work at 4 A.M.

Lilo & Stitch ★ ★ ★ ½
PG, 85 m., 2002

With the voices of: Daveigh Chase (Lilo), Chris Sanders (Stitch) Jason Scott Lee (David Kawena), Tia Carrere (Nani), Kevin McDonald (Pleakley), Ving Rhames (Cobra Bubbles), David Ogden Stiers (Jumba). Directed by Chris Sanders and Dean Deblois and produced by Clark Spencer. Screenplay by Sanders and Deblois.

Only a week ago I deplored the wretched *Scooby-Doo* as a blight on the nation's theaters. My fellow critics agreed. Checking the Websites that monitor reviews, I find that at Rotten-Tomatoes.com the movie scored a 26, at Meta-critic.com a 27. Passing grade is 60. The American public effortlessly shrugged off this warning cry and raced to the box office to throw away $57 million.

Now here comes a truly inspired animated feature named *Lilo & Stitch*. How will it do? It's one of the most charming feature-length cartoons of recent years, funny, sassy, startling, original, and with six songs by Elvis. It doesn't get sickeningly sweet at the end, it has as much stuff in it for grown-ups as for kids, and it has a bright offbeat look to it.

If *Scooby-Doo* grossed $57 million in its first weekend, then if there is justice in the world, *Lilo & Stitch* will gross $200 million. But there is not justice. There is a herd instinct. On Monday a man on an elevator asked me what I thought about *Scooby-Doo*. I said it was a very bad movie. "My kids want to see it," he said. Yes, I said, because they've heard of nothing else all week. But, I said, there is a *much better* animated family film opening this weekend, named *Lilo & Stitch*, that your kids are sure to like much more than *Scooby-Doo*, and you will enjoy it too. Take my word, I said; I do this for a living. Take the kids to *Lilo & Stitch*.

I could see from the man's eyes that he was rejecting my advice. How could I possibly be right when $57 million said I was wrong? How could human taste be a better barometer of movie quality than the success of a marketing campaign? Prediction: This weekend, more parents and their children will dutifully file into the idiotic wasteland of *Scooby-Doo* than will see the inspired delights of *Lilo & Stitch*.

That will be a shame. *Lilo & Stitch*, produced by the same Disney team that made *Mulan*, is a toothy fantasy about an alien monster that accidentally finds itself adopted as the pet of a little girl in Hawaii. The creature, named Stitch (voice by Chris Sanders), was produced by an illegal genetic mutation, and is so horrifyingly hostile that it's been locked up by its inventors. It escapes to Earth, is mistaken for a very strange dog, and adopted by Lilo (voice by Daveigh Chase), who essentially uses her innocence and the aloha spirit to confuse and even civilize the creature.

This all takes place against a cheerful background of pop-culture references, including scenes spoofing *Men in Black, Jaws,* and *Godzilla* (with Stitch first building a model of San Francisco, then destroying it). And the film firmly positions itself in Hawaii—both the Hawaii of tourist kitsch, and the Hawaii of the aloha spirit. The plot revolves around concepts of "ohana," or family, since Lilo is being raised by her big sister Nani (voice by Tia Carrere), who is disorganized and not always a perfect substitute mom, and is up against a disapproving social

worker named Cobra Bubbles (voice by Ving Rhames).

Nani works as a waitress in one of those "traditional" Hawaiian musical revues, where her boyfriend, David Kawena (Jason Scott Lee), is a fire dancer. Lilo takes Stitch to the show, and Stitch is much confused, especially after David sets the stage on fire, but even more confusing episodes are ahead, as the little girl teaches her alien pal how to be an Elvis imitator.

Lilo and Stitch, of course, have trouble communicating, since Lilo is very young and Stitch speaks no English, but the alien, who is a quick study, picks up some words and, more important, some concepts that challenge its existence as a destructive being. Lilo and Nani are learning, too, how to be a family and take care of each other, but the movie doesn't get all soppy at the end and is surprisingly unsentimental for a Disney animated feature. It keeps its edge and its comic zest all the way through, and although it arrives relatively unheralded, it's a jewel.

Note: I was far off in my prediction; Lilo & Stitch *opened like gangbusters and was a huge box-office success.*

Little Nicky ★ ★ ½
PG-13, 93 m., 2000

Adam Sandler (Nicky), Patricia Arquette (Valerie), Harvey Keitel (Satan), Rodney Dangerfield (Satan's Dad), Tommy "Tiny" Lister Jr. (Cassius), Rhys Ifans (Adrian), Quentin Tarantino (Blind Preacher), Robert Smigel (Bulldog), Ozzy Osbourne (Himself), Reese Witherspoon (Angel). Directed by Steven Brill and produced by Jack Giarraputo and Robert Simonds. Screenplay by Adam Sandler, Tim Herlihy, and Brill.

I've met Adam Sandler a couple of times and he's a nice guy, smart and personable. Considering what I've written about his movies, he could also be described as forgiving and tactful. What I cannot understand is why he has devoted his career to finding new kinds of obnoxious voices and the characters to go along with them.

Consider Nicky, the star of his new film, *Little Nicky*. Nicky may be the spawn of Satan, but his two brothers, Cassius (Tiny Lister) and Adrian (Rhys Ifans) are reasonably presentable.

Nicky, on the other hand, looks like the star of a low-rent road company version of *Richard III*, has a face twisted out of plumb (one of his brothers socked him in the head with a shovel), and speaks in yet another bizarre Sandler voice—sort of a mush-mouthed lisping whine.

Thinking back over the movie, I'm not sure why. Nicky is an intriguing comic character, whose appeal doesn't depend on how he talks or looks—Sandler's contributions, indeed, detract from the character. I try to imagine the movie with Nicky played as a more ordinary guy, and I think it would benefit (hundreds of millions of dollars of Sandler box-office grosses suggest I could be wrong).

Anthony Hopkins talks about how he needs to find a character's "mask" before he can play him. Many actors find it painful to play themselves, and are comfortable only after they find the right mask or persona to occupy. Is it that way with Sandler? I dunno, but for his next movie I suggest a mask that allows him to play an adult, instead of an infantile grotesque.

The movie surrounding Nicky is actually pretty good—the best Sandler movie to date. The premise: Satan (Harvey Keitel) has been on the job for 10,000 years and is thinking of retiring. The changes in Hell roil up Cassius and Adrian, who bolt for New York and freeze the gates of Hades behind them. Without fresh souls to feed on, Satan starts to disintegrate, literally. First an ear falls off, and then it's one thing after another until he's reduced to two hands holding his mouth. (It's Keitel's most piecemeal performance, ho, ho.)

Worried about his old man, Little Nicky is able to follow his brothers to Manhattan, where a talking bulldog named Beefy befriends him. Soon he is occupying an authentic New York–style hell (i.e., his roommate is an actor), but he meets a fetching young woman (Patricia Arquette) who somehow likes him, even though he occasionally blurts out disgusting things. His excuse: The devil made him do it.

The plot is populated with large numbers of stars in cameo roles: Rodney Dangerfield as Nicky's grandfather, Ozzy Osbourne as himself, Quentin Tarantino as a blind preacher, supplying yet another reminder that he should be directing movies, not infiltrating them. The best cameo is by Reese Witherspoon, as an angel with dubious genes, who talks like a

Valley Girl and knows God: "He's so smart!" she says. "Like—*Jeopardy!* smart!"

Newscasts chart the progress as Hell's ambassadors change New York. The city motto, "I Love NY," becomes "I love hookers," the drinking age is lowered to ten (setting up the obligatory projectile vomiting scene without which no Sandler movie is complete), and—my favorite—the Harlem Globetrotters start being called for traveling violations and technical fouls.

All of this is kinda fun, and some of it more than that. I can see how *Little Nicky* could have worked. It's just that Sandler, at the center, is a distraction; he steals scenes, and we want him to give them back. He's thirty-five now. I know you can play an adolescent all of your life (consider Jerry Lewis), but isn't it time for us to see the real Adam Sandler? When I met him, I thought to myself, this guy has movie star potential.

The Little Vampire ★ ★
PG, 97 m., 2000

Jonathan Lipnicki (Tony Thompson), Richard E. Grant (Frederick), Jim Carter (Rookery), Alice Krige (Freda), Rollo Weeks (Rudolph), John Wood (Lord McAshton), Pamela Gidley (Dottie Thompson), Tommy Hinkley (Bob Thompson), Anna Popplewell (Anna). Directed by Uli Edel and produced by Richard Claus. Screenplay by Karey Kirkpatrick and Larry Wilson, based on the novel by Angela Sommer-Bodenburg.

The Little Vampire is a dim-witted but visually intriguing movie about a kid from San Diego who moves to Scotland with his mom and dad and befriends a family of vampires. It is based on a popular children's book by the German author Angela Sommer-Bodenburg, but those cute round wire frames on the hero's glasses are a clue that the Harry Potter books are at least as much to blame.

As the film opens, young Tony (Jonathan Lipnicki) doesn't much like Scotland, where his dad (Tommy Hinkley) has moved to construct a golf course for Lord McAshton (John Wood). The local kids pick on him at school, they're isolated in the middle of nowhere, etc., and his parents are impatient with his nightly dreams of vampires.

Then one night things pick up when a bat flies into Tony's fireplace and turns into a boy named Rudolph (Rollo Weeks), who is lonely too, as what vampire boy would not be. Rudy takes Tony on a flight to visit a vampire family that has been in hibernation for 300 years, waiting for a comet to cross the Moon and send a beam of light to a magic amulet—of which, alas, Rudy's dad (Richard E. Grant) possesses only half.

Touring the neighborhood is a scabby vampire hunter named Rookery (Jim Carter), whose personal appearance and demeanor and his giant truck (with searchlights, drills, cages, neon crucifixes, etc.) suggest he should be paying royalties to the character of Snowplow Man (Chris Elliott) in *Snow Day*.

The movie is aimed at kids but filmed with an adult sensibility, which leads to peculiar scenes like the one where Rudy's vampire sister Anna (Anna Popplewell) presents him with a dead mouse, explains it is a charm to get him out of trouble, and adds: "If you ever need me, just whistle. You know how to whistle, don't you? Just whistle." Puckering your lips and blowing might be too risqué, I assume. (Miss Popplewell is refreshingly frank in comments about the film which she has posted on the Internet Movie Database: "My brother and sister, five and nine, both loved it and so did an audience full of children at the test screening. It is true that children above twelve may find it a little babyish.")

The movie has first-rate credits, from the director Uli Edel *(Last Exit to Brooklyn)* to the writers Karey Kirkpatrick *(James and the Giant Peach)* and Larry Wilson *(Beetlejuice)* to the cast (Lipnicki played the kid in *Jerry Maguire* and *Stuart Little*). The costumes are neat, the photography looks great—all the pieces are on hand, but they don't fit.

One problem is that the movie's saddled with too many elements. The vampires, we discover, want to become human again, and all of them but the father are vegetarians (lacto-ovo variety, if you were wondering). Fine, but then there's the complication of Lord McAshton's sinister plans, and the mumbo-jumbo about the comet and the beam of light and the amulet, and then the unwelcome periodic appearances of the spectacularly unfunny vampire hunter, and then Tony's problems in

communicating his amazing discoveries to his parents.

Occasionally there's a flash of wit to suggest what would have gone right. The vampire dad says, "We need darkness, dampness, and decay," and Tony, who misses southern California, replies, "Then you need our cellar." There's a herd of flying vampire cows that caught my attention. And a scene set atop a giant blimp that sounds James-and-the-Peachian notes. All the same, children over twelve may indeed find it babyish, and those under twelve may find it not babyish enough.

Live Nude Girls Unite! ★ ★ ★
NO MPAA RATING, 70 m., 2001

A documentary directed by Julia Query and Vicky Funari and produced by Query and John Montoya. Screenplay by Query and Funari.

This Union Maid was wise,
To the tricks of company spies.
She couldn't be fooled by company stools—
She'd always organize the guys.
—Old labor song

And not only the guys. When the strippers at the Lusty Lady, a San Francisco peep emporium, decided to organize themselves into a labor union, there were jolly news stories all over the country. People thought it was hilarious. This may be because in the popular mind strippers do not really work.

Opposing the strike, the management of the Lusty Lady argued that taking off your clothes in a peep show is not real labor so much as an enjoyable part-time job. The women putting in ten-hour shifts didn't see it that way—but their customers did. "What's your job?" one of the clients asks one of the girls. "I'm a stripper," she says. "I mean," he says, "how do you earn a living?"

There is the curious notion that strippers and prostitutes do what they do because they enjoy it. This is a fiction that is good for business. I am sure that some strippers and hookers do sometimes enjoy what they do, but not that they do it over and over, all day long, week after week, for a living. By way of illustration, it is possible to take pleasure in making a ham sandwich, but you might not want to work behind the counter at Mr. Submarine, especially when the customers always leave with the sandwiches.

When you think of strippers, you think of a stage, but the strippers at the Lusty Lady work in a small mirrored room. The clients enter little booths surrounding the room and put a quarter in a slot; a panel slides up and they can see the girls for fifteen seconds. Another quarter, another fifteen seconds. It's enough to bring back the silver dollar. The veteran girls make $20 an hour, and there are always two to four on duty, which makes you realize that the hardest job at the Lusty Lady belongs to the guy who collects the quarters.

Live Nude Girls Unite! is a documentary made by Julia Query, a stripper at the club, and Vicky Funari. It is an advertisement for the possibilities of the consumer digital video camera. It's not slick, it has some lapses, it sometimes looks like a home movie, but it's never boring. It follows some eighty strippers as they hire a lawyer, demand a contract, and threaten to strike. Query, Funari, and two other filmmakers simply took the camera along with them and shot whatever happened.

Miss Query is not your average stripper—but then no stripper ever is. She dropped out of graduate school, has worked as a dominatrix, and has a mother who is a famous public health advocate. The mother pilots a van around Manhattan handing out free condoms to hookers, and tells Barbara Walters in a *20/20* segment that her group facilitates 500,000 safe sex acts a year. "Peppermint?" Miss Walters asks, holding up one of the condoms.

When Julia turns up as a speaker and stand-up comic at the same conference where her mother is delivering a paper, the result is one of the more unusual mother-daughter arguments in movie history. Julia was raised to "do the right thing" and expects her mother to be proud of her as a union organizer, but the mother somehow cannot get around the stripping. This although Query tries to stir indignation about the club's discrimination against strippers who are not white (or, for that matter, white but not blond).

Julia is a disarmingly honest narrator. When she decided to earn money by stripping, she says, she was terrified by the thought of going

on the stage, because "I can't dance." The mirrored room at the Lusty Lady, which reminded her of an aquarium, seemed less of a challenge, especially since it has silver poles in it. The other girls use these for posing, but we gather Julia may need to grab one to keep from falling down. Still, she's a spirited Union Maid, and she and her sister organizers make labor history. She's the kind of woman Studs Terkel was born to interview.

The Lord of the Rings: The Fellowship of the Ring ★ ★ ★
PG-13, 178 m., 2001

Elijah Wood (Frodo Baggins), Ian McKellen (Gandalf the Grey), Viggo Mortensen (Aragorn, aka Strider), Sean Astin (Samwise "Sam" Gamgee), Liv Tyler (Arwen), Cate Blanchett (Galadriel), John Rhys-Davies (Gimli), Billy Boyd (Peregrin "Pippin" Took), Ian Holm (Bilbo Baggins), Christopher Lee (Saruman), Hugo Weaving (Elrond). Directed by Peter Jackson and produced by Jackson, Barrie M. Osborne, and Tim Sanders. Screenplay by Frances Walsh, Philippa Boyens, and Jackson, based on the novel *The Fellowship of the Ring* by J. R. R. Tolkien.

We invest hobbits with qualities that cannot be visualized. In my mind, they are good-hearted, bustling, chatty little creatures who live in twee houses or burrows, and dress like the merry men of Robin Hood—in smaller sizes, of course. They eat seven or eight times a day, like to take naps, have never been far from home, and have eyes that grow wide at the sounds of the night. They are like children grown up or grown old, and when they rise to an occasion it takes true heroism, for they are timid by nature and would rather avoid a fight.

Such notions about hobbits can be found in *The Lord of the Rings: The Fellowship of the Ring,* but the hobbits themselves have been pushed off center stage. If the books are about brave little creatures who enlist powerful men and wizards to help them in a dangerous crusade, the movie is about powerful men and wizards who embark on a dangerous crusade and take along the hobbits. That is not true of every scene or episode, but by the end *Fellowship* adds up to more of a sword-and-sorcery epic than a realization of the more naive and guileless vision of J. R. R. Tolkien.

The Ring Trilogy embodies the kind of innocence that belongs to an earlier, gentler time. The Hollywood that made *The Wizard of Oz* might have been equal to it. But *Fellowship* is a film that comes after *Gladiator* and *Matrix,* and it instinctively ramps up to the genre of the overwrought special-effects action picture. That it transcends this genre—that it is a well-crafted and sometimes stirring adventure—is to its credit. But a true visualization of Tolkien's Middle-Earth it is not.

Wondering if the trilogy could possibly be as action-packed as this film, I searched my memory for sustained action scenes and finally turned to the books themselves, which I had not read since the 1970s. The chapter "The Bridge of Khazad-Dum" provides the basis for perhaps the most sensational action scene in the film, in which Gandalf the wizard stands on an unstable rock bridge over a chasm, and must engage in a deadly swordfight with the monstrous Balrog. This is an exciting scene, done with state-of-the-art special effects and sound that shakes the theater. In the book, I was not surprised to discover, the entire scene requires less than 500 words.

Settling down with my book, the one-volume 1969 India paper edition, I read or skimmed for an hour or so. It was as I remembered it. The trilogy is mostly about leaving places, going places, being places, and going on to other places, all amid fearful portents and speculations. There are a great many mountains, valleys, streams, villages, caves, residences, grottos, bowers, fields, high roads, and low roads, and along them the hobbits and their larger companions travel while paying great attention to mealtimes. Landscapes are described with the faithful detail of a Victorian travel writer. The travelers meet strange and fascinating characters along the way, some of them friendly, some of them not, some of them of an order far above hobbits or even men. Sometimes they must fight to defend themselves or to keep possession of the ring, but mostly the trilogy is an unfolding, a quest, a journey, told in an elevated, archaic, romantic prose style that tests our capacity for the declarative voice.

Reading it, I remembered why I liked it in the first place. It was reassuring. You could tell by holding the book in your hands that there were many pages to go, many sights to see, many adventures to share. I cherished the way it paused for songs and poems, which the movie has no time for. Like *The Tale of Genji,* which some say is the first novel, *The Lord of the Rings* is not about a narrative arc or the growth of the characters, but about a long series of episodes in which the essential nature of the characters is demonstrated again and again (and again). The ring, which provides the purpose for the journey, serves Tolkien as the ideal MacGuffin, motivating an epic quest while mostly staying right there on a chain around Frodo Baggins's neck.

Peter Jackson, the New Zealand director who masterminded this film (and two more to follow, in a $300 million undertaking), has made a work for, and of, our times. It will be embraced, I suspect, by many *Rings* fans and take on aspects of a cult. It is a candidate for many Oscars. It is an awesome production in its daring and breadth, and there are small touches that are just right; the hobbits may not look like my idea of hobbits (may, indeed, look like full-sized humans made to seem smaller through visual trickery), but they have the right combination of twinkle and pluck in their gaze—especially Elijah Wood as Frodo and Ian Holm as the worried Bilbo.

Yet the taller characters seem to stand astride the little hobbit world and steal the story away. Galdalf the good wizard (Ian McKellen) and Saruman the treacherous wizard (Christopher Lee) and Aragorn (Viggo Mortensen), who is the warrior known as Strider, are so well seen and acted, so fearsome in battle, that we can't imagine the hobbits getting anywhere without them. The elf Arwen (Liv Tyler), the elf queen Galadriel (Cate Blanchett), and Arwen's father Elrond (Hugo Weaving) are not small like literary elves ("very tall they were," the book tells us), and here they tower like Norse gods and goddesses, accompanied by so much dramatic sound and lighting that it's a wonder they can think to speak, with all the distractions.

Jackson has used modern special effects to great purpose in several shots, especially one where a massive wall of water forms and reforms into wraiths of charging stallions. I like the way he handles crowds of Orcs in the big battle scenes, wisely knowing that in a film of this kind realism has to be tempered with a certain fanciful fudging. The film is remarkably well made. But it does go on, and on, and on—more vistas, more forests, more sounds in the night, more fearsome creatures, more prophecies, more visions, more dire warnings, more close calls, until we realize this sort of thing can continue indefinitely. "This tale grew in the telling," Tolkien tells us in the famous first words of his Foreword; it's as if Tolkien, and now Jackson, grew so fond of the journey they dreaded the destination.

That *The Fellowship of the Ring* doesn't match my imaginary vision of Middle-Earth is my problem, not yours. Perhaps it will look exactly as you think it should. But some may regret that the hobbits have been pushed out of the foreground and reduced to supporting characters. And the movie depends on action scenes much more than Tolkien did. In a statement last week, Tolkien's son Christopher, who is the "literary protector" of his father's works, said: "My own position is that *The Lord of the Rings* is peculiarly unsuitable for transformation into visual dramatic form." That is probably true, and Jackson, instead of transforming it, has transmuted it into a sword-and-sorcery epic in the modern style, containing many of the same characters and incidents. ☞

Loser ★ ★
PG-13, 97 m., 2000

Jason Biggs (Paul Tanneck), Mena Suvari (Dora Diamond), Greg Kinnear (Professor Edward Alcott), Dan Aykroyd (Paul's Father). Directed by Amy Heckerling and produced by Heckerling and Twink Caplan. Screenplay by Heckerling.

Love is blind, and movies about that blindness can be maddening. *Loser*, for example, is about Paul, a college student of almost surreal niceness, who falls in love with Dora, a college student who persists in the wrong romantic choice almost to the point of perversion. When a movie character does something against her best interests and beneath her intelligence, I get restless. When it's clear she is persisting

only because the plot requires her to, I grow unhappy. *Loser* is not a love story so much as an exercise in postponing the obvious.

Paul is played by Jason Biggs, the star of *American Pie*. Dora is played by Mena Suvari, the pom-pom girl who electrified Kevin Spacey's libido in *American Beauty*. Here he doesn't look as goofy and she looks grungier, like a college girl who dresses down as a lifestyle decision. They make a sweet couple, or would if she were not stupidly in love with Professor Alcott (Greg Kinnear), the arrogant prig who lets her do his typing, grade his papers, serve his tea, and share his bed, but values her about as much as a handy household appliance.

We buy the premise of the movie. He loves her but is a small-town boy who feels his case is hopeless. She likes him as a friend but is blind to his love because of her fantasies about the professor. He could expose the professor as a cruel fraud, but doesn't want to hurt her and figures he doesn't have a chance anyway. She is not so much blind to the professor's flaws as masochistically willing to endure them. We wait patiently for her to wake up and smell the coffee.

The movie is set in New York City, where Paul is categorized as a hick and even the lovely Dora is one of those "bridge and tunnel girls— they sleep around to avoid the commute." Paul gets a job in an animal hospital, Dora likes the animals (and a place where she can sleep over and avoid the commute). Paul's friends are keen amateur chemists who spike the drinks with date-rape drugs at their parties, which leads to a crisis when Dora nearly overdoses and the professor reveals how heartless he really is. Kinnear is wonderfully loathsome as the professor—and allowed to be as smart as he should be.

Watching this movie, I was reminded of *High Fidelity*, which has raised the bar for romantic comedies about twenty-somethings. The characters there were so accurately observed that we felt a stir of recognition. *Loser* wants to have that kind of perception, but doesn't trust itself. The movie, written and directed by Amy Heckerling (*Fast Times at Ridgemont High, Clueless*), has moments of truth, especially in the dialogue ("I love self-loathing complaint rock you can dance to," Dora tells Paul). But Dora is so obtuse in her inability to see through the professor and accept her love for Paul that eventually we grow impatient with her: She's sweet, smart, and cute, but she's simply not an interesting enough character to justify the wait while she figures things out.

Note: Ever since American Graffiti, *movies about kids in school have often ended with freeze frames telling us what happened to them later in life.* Loser's *bio notes are lame, and it is not encouraging when a college movie means "aid" but spells it "aide."*

Lost and Delirious ★ ★ ★ ½
NO MPAA RATING, 102 m., 2001

Piper Perabo (Paulie Oster), Jessica Pare (Victoria Moller), Mischa Barton (Mary Bradford ["Mouse"]), Jackie Burroughs (Fay Vaughn), Mimi Kuzyk (Eleanor Bannet), Graham Greene (Joe Menzies), Luke Kirby (Jake). Directed by Lea Pool and produced by Greg Dummett, Lorraine Richard, Louis-Philippe Rochon, and Richard Rochon. Screenplay by Judith Thompson, based on the novel *The Wives of Bath* by Susan Swan.

Lost and Delirious is a hymn to teenage idealism and hormones. It has been reviewed as a movie about steamy lesbian sex in a girls' boarding school, which is like reviewing Secretariat on the basis of what he does in the stable. The truest words in the movie are spoken by Paulie, the school rebel, when she says she is not a lesbian because her love rises above mere categories and exists as a transcendent ideal.

Indulge me while I tell you that as a teenager I was consumed by the novels of Thomas Wolfe. His autobiographical heroes were filled with a passion to devour life, to experience everything, to make love to every woman, read every book in the library. At night he could not sleep, but wandered the campus, "uttering wild goat cries to the moon."

I read every word Wolfe ever published. Today I find him unreadable—yes, even *Look Homeward, Angel* and *You Can't Go Home Again.* I have outlived that moment when all life seemed spread before me, all possibilities open to me, all achievements within my reach. Outlived it, but not forgotten it. *Lost and Delirious* stirred within me memories of that season in adolescence when the heart leaps up

in passionate idealism—and inevitably mingles it with sexual desire.

Yes, there is nudity in *Lost and Delirious,* and some intimate moments in the dorm room when the movie recalls the freedoms of the 1970s, before soft-core sex had been replaced by hard-core violence. The movie would be dishonest if it didn't provide us with visuals to match the libidos of its two young lovers—the heedless rebel girl Paulie (Piper Perabo) and the cautious rich kid Victoria (Jessica Pare), who is excited by her schoolgirl affair, but not brave enough to risk discovery; after all, her parents may not take her to Europe if they find out.

Paulie and Victoria represent two types familiar from everyone's high school—the type who acts out, and the type who wants to get all the right entries under her photo on the yearbook. At reunions years from now, Paulie will be the one they tell the stories about. Piper Perabo plays her with wonderful abandon and conviction, and Jessica Pare's "Tori" is sweet in her timidity. Perabo has scenes that would merely seem silly if she weren't able to invest them with such sincerity. The scene where she stalks into the library in her fencing gear, for example, and leaps onto a table to declare her love for Victoria. The scene where she challenges Victoria's new boyfriend to a duel. The scenes where she identifies with the wounded eagle she tends in the forest. The way she quotes great love poetry, promising, "I will make me a willow cabin at thy gate."

Their school is a vast, beautiful brick pile (actually Bishop's University in Lennoxville, Quebec). It seems to have only two faculty members: the headmistress and English teacher Fay Vaughn (Jackie Burroughs), who teaches Shakespeare's *Antony and Cleopatra* as if she sees herself as Cleopatra—or Antony. And the math teacher, Eleanor Bannet (Mimi Kuzyk). Paulie spots Bannet as a woman not quite brave enough to follow "to thine own self be true," and insolently calls her "Eleanor" in a classroom. Fay Vaughn, on the other hand, feeds into Paulie's hungers by being as romantic as she is—although Paulie doesn't always see that. Also on the staff is Joe Menzies (Graham Greene), a wise old gardener who acts as a Greek chorus, uttering wry epigrams.

The story is told through the eyes of a new

girl named "Mouse" (Mischa Barton), who is a little slow to catch on that her roommates are sapphic (the first time she sees them kissing, "I thought they were just practicing for boys"). In the immortal words of every high school movie—for Mouse, after this year, things will never be the same again. Of course, after every year, nothing is ever the same again for anyone, but when you're sixteen it seems to be all about you.

When I saw *Lost and Delirious* at Sundance, I wrote that it was one of the best crafted, most professional films at the festival. The director, Lea Pool, creates a lush, thoughtfully framed and composed film; her classical visual style lends gravitas to this romantic story. It seems important partly because the movie makes it look important, regarding it with respect instead of cutting it up into little emotional punch lines.

There is a temptation, I suppose, to try to stand above this material, to condescend to its eagerness and uncompromising idealism. To do that is to cave in to the cynicism that infects most modern films. This is a movie for those who sometimes, in the stillness of the sleepless night, are so filled with hope and longing that they feel like—well, like uttering wild goat cries to the moon. You know who you are. And if you know someone who says, "Let's go to *Scary Movie 2* instead," that person is not worthy to be your friend.

Note: The movie is being released "unrated," which means it is too poetic, idealistic, and health- fully erotic to fit into the sick categories of the flywheels at the MPAA. Mature teens are likely to find it inspirational and moving.

Lost Souls ★ ★
R, 102 m., 2000

Winona Ryder (Maya Larkin), Ben Chaplin (Peter Kelson), John Hurt (Father Lareaux), Sarah Wynter (Claire Van Owen), Elias Koteas (John Townsend), John Diehl (Henry Birdson), James Lancaster (Father Jeremy), Victor Slezak (Father Thomas), Philip Baker Hall (Father James), Alfre Woodard (Psychiatrist). Directed by Janusz Kaminski and produced by Meg Ryan and Nina R. Sadowsky. Screenplay by Pierce Gardner.

Lost Souls possesses the art and craft of a good movie, but not the story. For a thriller about demonic possession and the birth of the anti- christ, it's curiously flat. Strange, how a trashy Satanic movie like *End of Days* is filled with a fearful intensity, while this ambitious stab at the subject seems to lack all conviction. All through the movie I found myself thinking about how well it was photographed. Not a good sign.

Winona Ryder stars as Maya Larkin, a woman who was once possessed by the devil. Now she teaches children at a church school. One day her former exorcist squad summons her to the cell of a serial killer (John Diehl) who is also possessed. "He's in torment," Father Lareaux (John Hurt) tells her, "the way you were when I met you." The exorcism goes so badly that Hurt is hospitalized and the victim goes into a coma.

It is revealed during the exorcism that the devil will appear soon in human form. Ryder comes away with pages of numbers from the possessed man—long legal pads of figures. Smoking lots of cigarettes, she massages the encryption until she breaks it. As nearly as I could tell, looking over her shoulder, every number stood for a letter of the alphabet. When I was a kid I had a Lone Ranger Decoder Ring that could have saved her a lot of trouble.

What the message tells her is that Peter Kelson (Ben Chaplin), a best-selling author of true crime books, will be reborn on his thirty- third birthday as the antichrist. Maya tries to warn Peter, who at first thinks she's a nut and then, after a series of strange events and reve- lations, decides she may very well be right. There's lots of stuff about being born in incest, and blood types that don't match, and dreams in which he sees the letters XES. He's slow to catch on, he admits, when it's pointed out that XES is "sex" spelled backward. And that's not all. Those are also the Greek letters for 600, 60, and 6, a psychic tells him, and that spells 666— the mark of Satan.

These events and others are related in a downbeat, intense, gloomy narrative that seems better suited to a different kind of story. Even the shock moments are somewhat muted, as if the movie is reluctant to 'fess up to its thriller origins. The director is Janusz Kamin- ski, the Academy Award–winning cinematographer *(Schindler's List, Saving Private Ryan)*, and he and *his* cinematographer, Mauro Fiore, create a masterful look for the film—denatured blues and browns, filmed in shadow with lots of backlighting and a certain dreaminess around the edges.

The performers are convincing in the moment, even if the arc lets them down. Ryder, always able to suggest intelligence, also hints at the terrors of a child whose parents were murdered. Chaplin perhaps doesn't take his impending transformation urgently enough, but what would you do? The priests, including not only John Hurt with his sorrowful eyes but also Philip Baker Hall with his underpriced charm, are convincing as spiritual pros—when an exorcism team goes on assignment, the camera is low-angle to show the thick-soled, black business shoes beneath their cassocks.

Without revealing the ending, I will give it credit for being absolutely consistent with the logic of the material. No wedge-brained focus groups got their philistinic little hands on this material. But when it's all over, we're left without much to talk about in our next confession. What surprises me, in one Satanic movie after another, is how vulnerable Satan seems to be. He's terrific at grabbing control of minds and making his victims speak in foul tones, and he puts a lot of wear and tear on the priests, but in the end he's always defeated by lowly humans. Here's a being who once declared war on God, and is now facing Winona Ryder. What a comedown.

Love & Basketball ★ ★ ★

PG-13, 118 m., 2000

Sanaa Lathan (Monica Wright), Omar Epps (Quincy McCall), Alfre Woodard (Camille Wright), Dennis Haysbert (Zeke McCall), Debbi Morgan (Mona McCall), Harry J. Lennix (Nathan Wright), Kyla Pratt (Young Monica), Glenndon Chatman (Young Quincy), Jess Willard (Jamal), Chris Warren Jr. (Kelvin), Naykia Harris (Young Lena). Directed by Gina Prince-Bythewood and produced by Spike Lee and Sam Kitt. Screenplay by Prince-Bythewood.

Love & Basketball is about how you can either be in love or play basketball, but it's tricky to do both at the same time. It may be unique among sports movies in that it does *not* end with the Big Game. Instead, it's a thoughtful and touching story about two affluent black kids, a boy and a girl, who grow up loving each other, and the game.

Monica is a tomboy. Her parents and older sister despair of getting her to act like a girl. She'd rather shoot baskets. In 1981, when she's about twelve, her family moves into a new house in Baldwin Hills, a good Los Angeles neighborhood. Next door lives a star for the L.A. Clippers and his son, Quincy. The first time the kids meet, they play a pickup game. Monica goes for a score, Quincy pushes her, and she gets a little scar that will be on her right cheek for the rest of her life.

He likes her. "You wanna be my girl?" he asks. She wants to know what that means. "We can play ball and ride to school together and when you get mad I gotta buy you flowers." She doesn't like flowers, she says. But she kisses him (they count to five), and the next day he wants her to ride to school on the handlebars of his bike. She wants to ride her own bike. This will be the pattern of a lifetime.

Flash forward to 1988. Monica, now played by Sanaa Lathan, and Quincy (Omar Epps) are high school stars. They're not dating but they're friends, and when Quincy's parents (Dennis Haysbert and Debbi Morgan) start fighting, he slips out his bedroom window and sleeps on the floor of her room. In a sequence of surprising effectiveness, she takes the advice of her mom and sister to "do something" with her hair, and goes to a school dance with a blind date. Quincy is there too. They dance with their dates but they keep looking at each other. You know how it is.

They're both recruited by USC, and both turn into college basketball stars, although Monica, on the women's team, feels she's penalized for an aggression that would be rewarded on the men's team. Their romance has its ups and downs, and eventually they're both playing in the pros—he in America, she in Spain. The ending reunites them a little too neatly.

But these bare bones of the plot don't convey the movie's special appeal. Written and directed by first-timer Gina Prince-Bythewood (and produced by Spike Lee), it is a sports film seen mostly from the woman's point of view. It's honest and perceptive about love and sex, with no phony drama and a certain quiet maturity. And here's the most amazing thing: It considers sports in terms of career, training, motivation, and strategy. The Big Game scenes involve behavior and attitude, not scoring. The movie sees basketball as something the characters do as a skill and a living, not as an excuse for audience-pleasing jump shots at the buzzer.

Omar Epps is an accomplished actor, effective here if a little too old (twenty-seven) to be playing a high schooler. Sanaa Lathan is the discovery. This is her sixth movie (she was in the look-alike films *The Wood* and *The Best Man*) and her chance to flower, and she does, with a combination of tomboy stubbornness and womanly pride. She has some wonderful scenes with her mother (Alfre Woodard), a housewife who defends her choices in life against her daughter's half-formed feminist notions.

Epps has effective scenes, too, with his parents. His dad retires from pro ball and is socked with a paternity suit, and Quincy has to reevaluate how he feels about both parents in a couple of strong truth-telling scenes.

The movie is not as taut as it could have been, but I prefer its emotional perception to the pumped-up sports clichés I was sort of expecting. Like Robert Towne's *Personal Best*, it's about the pressures of being a star athlete— the whole life, not the game highlights. I'm not sure I quite believe the final shot, though. I think the girl suits up for the sequel.

Love & Sex ★ ★

NO MPAA RATING, 82 m., 2000

Famke Janssen (Kate Welles), Jon Favreau (Adam Levy), Noah Emmerich (Eric), Cheri Oteri (Mary), Ann Magnuson (Ms. Steinbacher). Directed by Valerie Breiman and produced by Timothy Scott Bogart, Martin J. Barab, Brad Wyman, and Darris Hatch. Screenplay by Breiman.

If *Love & Sex* contained nothing else, it would pass into memory for a pickup line that is either fatal or inspired—I am still trying to decide which: "You have those long E.T. fingers, like a tree frog." These words are spoken by

Adam, an artist, to Kate, a bimbo savant, on their first date. She fires back by telling him his head is too big. It will be like this for most of the movie: Love at first sight reduces itself to second thoughts and one-liners. If it weren't being released unrated, which translates to adults only, the movie might be fun for younger teenagers who want to be reassured that people in their thirties still behave like younger teenagers.

Kate is played by Famke Janssen, from *X-Men* and the Bond pic *GoldenEye,* who confesses she wears a size 11 shoe—a line usually reserved for the man in a movie like this. Adam is played by Jon Favreau, a versatile actor recently seen as the pit-bull lineman in *The Replacements.* Both of them show they can play characters a lot smarter than we associate them with. They don't play them, but they show they can.

Their dialogue examines the mechanics and technicalities of sex and love in the same way HBO's *Sex and the City* does, but at a reduced level of sophistication and self-knowledge. Kate and Adam may be chronologically adult, but they behave on dates the way they probably did in high school.

Kate is a magazine writer, recently fired by the editor of a women's magazine for writing an article about oral sex that presumed to describe it rather than snicker about it. Ironic, since in its own consideration of sex the movie also snickers and withdraws. She goes to an art opening with her current squeeze, a stand-up comic, and Adam falls in love with her from across the room. He red dogs her, and soon they're having dinner, exchanging insults, and sharing intimate moments, like passing gas in bed and having conversations like:

"When I look at you like this, it looks like you only have one eye."

"Thank you."

The film is told from Kate's point of view. It's a cautionary tale about love (which, she explains, we fall into because nothing feels better) and relationships, which, we gather, end because nothing feels worse. In an early sharing of confidences, they reveal how many sexual partners they've had. Adam has had two. Kate has had thirteen. My best guess is they're both lying, but never mind: Adam can't get over Kate's cheerful promiscuity. It becomes clear that his feelings are clouded and she intuits: "It's the thirteen guys, isn't it?" Then she starts dating a basketball player, just to make him jealous.

The thing is, nothing's at stake here. Adam and Kate don't have enough weight and complexity for us to care about them. They're pawns in the hands of writer-director Valerie Breiman, who hides them in a thicket of sitcom clutter. When they break up and he sends a drum-pounding midget to her office with an apologetic offering, we're not seeing Kate and Adam, but Lucy and Ricky. A movie like John Cusack's *High Fidelity* acts as a rebuke to *Love & Sex* by showing the real quirks and self-punishments of the romantically unsuccessful.

As for Favreau and Janssen, it would be unfair to say there's no chemistry between them, because that would blame the actors, when in fact the screenplay gives them little to have chemistry with, for, or about. The film seems shy of sexual intimacy and physical delight, and the lovers approach each other with all the perplexity of a jigsaw fanatic who has just discovered pieces are missing. In successful screen romance, there needs to be the sense that the partners are happy simply to be *there* with each other, that there is a physical yearning, and not simply the need to talk fast enough to stay ahead of the one-liners.

Love's Labour's Lost ★ ★ ½
PG, 95 m., 2000

Kenneth Branagh (Berowne), Alessandro Nivola (King), Nathan Lane (Costard), Adrian Lester (Dumaine), Matthew Lillard (Longaville), Natascha McElhone (Rosaline), Alicia Silverstone (Princess), Timothy Spall (Don Armado), Carmen Ejogo (Maria), Emily Mortimer (Katherine). Directed by Kenneth Branagh and produced by David Barron and Branagh. Screenplay by Branagh, based on the play by William Shakespeare.

Shakespeare supplies not so much the source of Kenneth Branagh's *Love's Labour's Lost* as the clothesline. Using the flimsy support of one of the least of the master's plots, Branagh strings together ten song-and-dance numbers in a musical that's more like a revue than an adaptation. After daring to film his great version of *Hamlet* using the entire, uncut original play

(the first time that had been done), Branagh here cuts and slashes through Shakespeare's text with an editorial machete.

What is left is winsome, charming, sweet, and slight. It's so escapist it escapes even from itself. The story pairs off four sets of lovers, supplies them with delightful songs and settings, and calls it a day. The cast is not especially known for being able to sing and dance (only the British Adrian Lester and the Broadway veteran Nathan Lane are pros in those departments), but that's part of the charm. Like Woody Allen's *Everyone Says I Love You*, this is one of those movies were real people are so seized with the need to break into song that a lack of talent can't stop them.

Not, in fact, that they are untalented. The songs here are well within the abilities of the cast to sing them, and indeed several of them were originally sung on the screen by Fred Astaire, whose vocal range was as modest as his footwork was unlimited. (Most of the songs have been recorded on albums by the British singer Peter Skellern, who can hit a note and the one below it and the one above it, and that's about it—and he makes them entertaining too.)

The plot: The king of Navarre (Alessandro Nivola) has declared that he and three of his comrades (Kenneth Branagh, Adrian Lester, Matthew Lillard) will withdraw from the world for three years of thought and study. During this time, they will reject all worldly pleasures, most particularly the company of women. No sooner do they make their vow and retire to their cloister than the princess of France (Alicia Silverstone) arrives for a visit, accompanied by three friends (Natascha McElhone, Carmen Ejogo, Emily Mortimer).

The men find it acutely poignant that they have sworn off the company of women (with a severe penalty for the first who succumbs). They search for loopholes. Perhaps if the ladies camp *outside* the palace walls, that won't count as a visit. Perhaps if the visit is a state occasion, it is not a social one . . .

All of these rationalizations collapse before the beauty of the women, and the eight men and women pair off into four couples so quickly it's like choosing sides for a softball game. Then we get the songs, some of them wonderfully well staged, as when "Cheek to

Cheek" (with its line "Heaven . . . I'm in heaven . . .") has them floating in midair beneath the stars painted on the underside of the dome of the king's library.

The eight starters are joined by low-comedy relief pitchers, in the tradition of all Shakespeare comedies. They include Timothy Spall as a Spaniard whose "I Get a Kick Out of You" is a charmer, and Nathan Lane (who does a nice slow-tempo "There's No Business Like Show Business"). Alicia Silverstone is the lead among the women, who playfully do a synchroswimming version of "Fancy Free," and Branagh gives himself the best male role, although not tilting the scales to an unseemly degree.

All is light and winning, and yet somehow empty. It's no excuse that the starting point was one of the weaker of Shakespeare's plays. *Love's Labour's Lost* is hardly ever performed on the stage and has never been previously filmed, and there is a reason for that: It's not about anything. In its original form, instead of the songs and dances we have dialogue that's like an idle exercise in brainy banter for Shakespeare.

It's like a warm-up for the real thing. It makes not the slightest difference which boy gets which girl, or why, and by starting the action in 1939 and providing World War II as a backdrop, Branagh has not enriched either the play or the war, but fit them together with an awkward join. There's not a song I wouldn't hear again with pleasure, or a clip that might not make me smile, but as a whole, it's not much. Like cotton candy, it's better as a concept than as an experience.

Loving Jezebel ★ ★ ½
R, 85 m., 2000

Hill Harper (Theodurus Melville), Laurel Holloman (Samantha), Lysa Aya Trenier (June), Gabe Parks (David), Nicole Ari Parker (Frances), David Moscow (Gabe), Phylicia Rashad (Alice Melville), Sandrine Holt (Mona). Directed by Kwyn Bader and produced by David Lancaster. Screenplay by Bader.

"I've spent my life," Theodurus Melville tells us, "loving other men's women." That would make him a Casanova, but the title of *Loving Jezebel* puts the blame on the women: A jezebel, we learn from a definition on the screen, is a woman who fools around with lots of men.

Either definition would set up a sex romp, I suppose, but this movie is not quite what you'd expect. Within its romantic comedy we find a character who is articulate and a little poignant, and we realize Theodurus doesn't so much seek out other men's women as have them, so to speak, thrust upon him.

That's because he knows how to listen to women, and meets many women whose men are intoxicated only by their own words. We're reminded of *The Tao of Steve,* and Steve's strategy for seduction: "Men and women both want to have sex, but women want to have sex fifteen minutes after us, so if you hold out for twenty, she'll be chasing you for five."

Theodurus is the son of an interracial marriage, whose romantic conquests range from blonde to Trinidadian, from a ballerina who looks perhaps Eurasian to one, who is, he says, and we can hear the savor in his voice, "Afro-Filipino-Bavarian." One of the movie's not incidental pleasures is what beautiful women Theodorus seems to attract.

The movie is narrated by Theodurus (Hill Harper), who explains that his lifelong dilemma began in first grade, when he was kissed by a girl and was blissful for thirty seconds, until he realized she kissed all the boys in the class. Flash forward to 1985, with Theodurus in college, where he yearns for the fragrant Frances (Nicole Ari Parker), who lays down the rules (no kissing, no sex, she's a virgin) and then turns out to like sex, has a boyfriend, and warns him, "You know I like to play the crowd."

Other women turn up, including Mona (Sandrine Holt) from Trinidad, and Samantha (Laurel Holloman), who mopes at the corner table in the café where he works, sipping cappuccino and writing, or trying to write, poetry. She has a husband named Gabe (David Moscow) who seems obtuse even for a chauvinist pig.

In a film filled with beautiful women, the distributors seem determined to overlook the most stunning. This is Lysa Aya Trenier, who plays June, a bartender and ballerina, who wonders if she will ever be able to dance well enough to become a prima. Trenier is one of those women who pop off the screen with stardom written all over her; whether she will become a successful actress I cannot predict, but she was born to be a Bond girl, and I mean that as a sincere compliment.

Strangely enough, her name is not included in the movie's press material, or on its official Website, or in the Internet Movie Database, and it is a measure of her unknown status that even Google, mightiest of the search engines, turns up absolutely no references to her. So anyone searching for her will be led, I assume, straight to this review, where all I can tell you is: I know why you're searching.

Hill Harper, seen before now on TV and in movie supporting roles *(He Got Game)*, is an engaging actor, able to sound absolutely convincing as he fast-talks his would-be conquests. No wonder he sounds smart; after graduating from Brown, he got graduate degrees in law and government from Harvard. He sounds like he knows what he's talking about even when he doesn't; I was fascinated by his theory about the egg-stealing activities of the bluebird (which I think he has confused with the cuckoo, although that doesn't slow him down).

The movie's problem is a fundamental lack of substance. None of the women are really developed in any depth except Samantha, so what we get is Theodorus as a tour guide through his romantic conquests and failures. He's like a guy paging through his college yearbook and telling us who he has, or would like to have, made love to: interesting for him, less interesting for us. Still, if the movie treats its women like pretty faces, at least it has good taste in pretty faces.

The Low Down ★ ★ ★
NO MPAA RATING, 96 m., 2001

Aidan Gillen (Frank), Kate Ashfield (Ruby), Dean Lennox Kelly (Mike), Tobias Menzies (John), Rupert Proctor (Terry), Samantha Power (Lisa), Dena Smiles (Susan), Maggie Lloyd Williams (Jean). Directed by Jamie Thraves and produced by John Stewart and Sally Llewellyn. Screenplay by Thraves.

You probably went through a time in your life like the one Frank is going through in *The Low Down.* I know I did. You may be going through it now. It passes. At the time, you hardly notice it. Later, you look back and wonder how you could have been so clueless. Frank is stuck. He should have quit his job, changed his apartment, and found a steady girl a long time ago, but he drifts in vagueness, unable to act. There are times when he may be terrified in social situations, but we can't be sure—and maybe he can't, either.

Frank (Aidan Gillen) works with Mike (Dean Lennox Kelly) and John (Tobias Menzies) in a London shop where they manufacture jokey props for TV shows and magic acts. He lives in a grotty walk-up above a hairdresser's and next door to a crack house. All night long junkies stand on the sidewalk beneath his window, shouting "Paul! Paul!" to their dealer. Frank knows he should move, but jokes about buying Paul a doorbell.

Thinking it is time to buy his own flat, he goes to a real-estate office and meets Ruby (Kate Ashfield). As they look at apartments together, they begin to like each other. The writer-director, Jamie Thraves, uses freeze-frames to show how they're struck with each other. A stylistic device like that leaps out because the movie is so low-key. It has no plot, no objective, no purpose other than to show a few days in the lives of a group of friends. They work, they gossip, they hang out, they go to parties, they sit on each other's beds and talk, and Frank and Ruby draw as close to each other as Frank can stand before he has to retreat. There is a subtle subplot about how he has stopped drinking, and starts again.

The British critics said the movie was about nothing. Depends on how you see it. I think it's about Frank's paralyzing inability to move, socially or any other way. The more you look at this guy, the more you realize he's trembling inside. Aidan Gillen is handsome in a Richard Gere–Timothy Hutton sort of way, and can be charming at first, but soon Ruby is looking at him strangely because he seems distant and tentative. He has a way of breaking dates, or turning up late; once he hides and watches her waiting for him.

The movie provides key scenes which are like tests. In one of them, he plays handball with a stranger he meets at the court, and then they have a drink together and it is possible that the other man wants to know if Frank is gay, and interested. I say "possible" because Frank is not receiving on that frequency. In another scene, he's in a pub with a friend at closing time, and an ugly drunk gets in Frank's face and Frank avoids a fight by meekly saying what the drunk wants to hear. A little later, when one of Frank's coworkers screws up by spilling paint on a prop, Frank attacks him violently for no real reason; the poor sap gets to stand in for the drunk, I guess.

Two other scenes intrigued me. Both involve encounters with a street woman who wants money. Frank gives the money both times. The second time, the woman offers her body in payment. Frank turns her down. But watch his body language. He takes her up to his flat, and when he goes into the bedroom to get the money, he straightens the cover on the bed, and runs his hand through his hair. Why? Because he doesn't really know if he will have sex with her or not. And, despite the fact that she's a junkie offering her body, she activates old habits and "manners" involving his uncertainty about women.

A movie like *The Low Down* gets better the more attention you pay. To say "nothing happens" is to be blind to everyday life, during which we wage titanic struggles with our programming. Someday a woman (or a man) will come along who can blast Frank out of his bunker. Someday he will give up the after-college job and find his real work. At the end of the film he at least moves to a different apartment. From time to time, he will remember Ruby, and wonder what went wrong—wonder, for a fleeting moment, if he had anything to do with it.

Lucky Break ★ ★ ★
PG-13, 107 m., 2002

James Nesbitt (Jimmy), Olivia Williams (Annabel), Timothy Spall (Cliff), Bill Nighy (Roger), Lennie James (Rudy), Christopher Plummer (Graham Mortimer). Directed by Peter Cattaneo and produced by Barnaby Thompson. Screenplay by Ronan Bennett.

Lucky Break is the new film by Peter Cattaneo, whose *The Full Monty* is the little British comedy that added a useful expression to the language. This movie is set in prison but uses much the same formula: A group of guys without much hope decide to band together and put on a show. This time they stage a musical comedy written by the prison warden, which means that instead of stripping they perform in costume. I am not sure if this is the half-monty, or no monty at all.

British prisons are no doubt depressing and violent places in real life, but in *Lucky Break,* the recent *Borstal Boy,* and the summer 2001 movie *Greenfingers,* they are not only benign places with benevolent governors, but also provide remarkable access to attractive young women. Jimmy (James Nesbitt), the hero of *Lucky Break,* finds abundant time to fall in love with Annabel, the prison anger-management counselor (Olivia Williams). Brendan Behan, the hero of the biopic *Borstal Boy,* has a youthful romance with Liz, the warden's daughter. And in *Greenfingers,* which is about a prize-winning team of prison gardeners, one of the green-thumbsmen falls in love with the daughter of a famous TV garden lady. Only in these movies is prison a great place for a wayward lad to go in order to meet the right girl.

Lucky Break stars James Nesbitt and Lennie James as Jimmy and Rudy, partners in an ill-conceived bank robbery that lands them both in prison. The prison governor (Christopher Plummer) is an amateur playwright who has written a musical based on the life of Admiral Nelson, whose statue provides a congenial resting place for pigeons in Trafalgar Square. The lads agree to join in a prison production of the musical after learning that the play will be staged in the old prison chapel—which they consider the ideal place from which to launch a prison break.

Much of the humor of the film comes from the production of *Nelson, the Musical,* with book and lyrics by the invaluable actor and comic writer Stephen Fry; we hear a lot of the songs, see enough of the scenes to get an idea of the awfulness, and hardly notice as the prison break segues into a movie about opening night and backstage romance.

I am not sure that the average prisoner has unlimited opportunities to spend time alone with beautiful young anger-management counselors, wardens' daughters, or assistant TV gardeners, but in *Lucky Break,* so generous is the private time that Jimmy and Annabel even share a candlelight dinner. To be sure, a can of sardines is all that's served, but it's the thought that counts.

The key supporting role is by Timothy Spall, sort of a plump British Steve Buscemi—a sad sack with a mournful face and the air of always trying to cheer himself up. What keeps him going is his love for his young son; this whole subplot is more serious and touching than the rest of the film, although it leads to a scene perhaps more depressing than a comedy should be asked to sustain.

The climax of the film, as in *The Full Monty*, is the long-awaited stage performance, which goes on as various subplots solve themselves, or not, backstage. There is not much here that comes as a blinding plot revelation, but the movie has a raffish charm and good-hearted characters, and like *The Full Monty* it makes good use of the desperation beneath the comedy.

Lucky Numbers ★ ★
R, 105 m., 2000

John Travolta (Russ Richards), Lisa Kudrow (Crystal Latroy), Tim Roth (Gig), Ed O'Neill (Dick Simmons), Michael Rapaport (Dale), Bill Pullman (Lakewood), Michael Moore (Walter), Daryl Mitchell (Chambers), Michael Weston (Larry). Directed by Nora Ephron and produced by Sean Daniel, Ephron, Jonathan D. Krane, and Andrew Lazar. Screenplay by Adam Resnick.

Lucky Numbers, starring John Travolta as a TV weatherman who tries to rig the lottery, tells too much story at not enough energy. It should have been cut back and cranked up. Instead, it keeps introducing new characters until the plot becomes a juggling act just when it should be a sprint. And there's another problem: Is it intended as a comedy, or not?

I ask because there are funny things in it, and then gruesome things, sad things and brutal things. Quentin Tarantino was able to cover that spread in *Pulp Fiction*. But Nora Ephron *(Sleepless in Seattle, You've Got Mail)* doesn't find a way. She has Travolta and Tim Roth from *Pulp Fiction*, but they didn't bring their notes.

Consider a scene involving Lisa Kudrow and

Michael Moore (yes, Michael Moore). Kudrow with the right material is one of the funniest actresses around; see her in *The Opposite of Sex* or *Romy and Michele's High School Reunion.* Here she plays a daffy model who draws the winning lottery numbers on TV. Moore is her sad-sack cousin, recruited to front as the purchaser of the winning number. He has asthma. When he won't tell her where the ticket is, she bounces on his chest until he has an asthma attack, and then won't give him his inhaler.

Up to a certain point this could be funny (it doesn't sound funny, but trust me). The movie takes it beyond that point, until we want to cringe. Ephron doesn't actually show the poor guy's tongue turning purple, but Kudrow can't make the payoff anything but pathetic, and neither could any other actress. When you add in the rest of the movie's violence, it looks like a black comedy that needed to go either blacker or funnier, instead of each approach undercutting the other.

Travolta and Kudrow work at a TV station managed by Ed O'Neill. Both men are having affairs with her, which makes her a two-way conduit of knowledge, among other things. Travolta is in debt because his snowmobile business is failing (it's the warmest winter in years). He and Kudrow plot with Tim Roth, the owner of a strip club, to rig the lottery, and the plan works, up to a point. But then so many characters want a cut of the action that, Travolta complains, he'll be back in debt again.

The movie has fun establishing the weatherman character as a big celebrity in the small pond of Harrisburg, Pennsylvania. He has a parking space with his name on it at Denny's, a private booth protected by a red velvet rope, and an omelet named after him. Travolta is wonderful at projecting a sunny joy in his own fame, but less successful later in the film as he goes into guilty meltdown.

The O'Neill character has his own agenda, but so do several other characters, including Roth, Dale the thug (Michael Rapaport), Lakewood the cop (Bill Pullman), Lakewood's partner Chambers (Daryl Mitchell), Larry the snowmobile salesman (Michael Weston), and a local numbers game operator. New characters are introduced as the story moves along, and the narrative gets expansive and gabby.

So much depends on tone in a movie. Either

you find the right one and stick with it, or you're in trouble (unless, like Tarantino, you really know what you're doing). If we're supposed to like these people, then there's a point beyond which they should not go in their villainy. If we're not, then the scenes where they're nice should have more irony. Kudrow figures out her own character and sticks with it successfully from beginning to end (apart from the unfortunate asphyxiation episode). I like the way she keeps glancing down at her body to be sure it still looks sexy.

Travolta as a person wants to be nice, and to be seen as nice, in every atom of his being, and that causes a tension the movie never resolves. He needs to be a little nastier. Instead of starting with a nice guy and getting him in trouble, it might have been a better idea to start with a tough guy and show him trying to be nice (Robert De Niro's character in *Meet the Parents* comes to mind).

By the end of the film, we're less entertained than relieved. Lots of stuff happened, and much of it might have been interesting in a different kind of film. Here we get the curious sense that the characters are racing around Harrisburg breathlessly trying to keep up with the plot. There is, however, good news. Travolta survived this experience with his sense of humor still intact. How can I be sure? He has announced he wants to make a sequel to *Battlefield Earth*.

Lumumba ★ ★ ★

NO MPAA RATING, 115 m., 2001

Eriq Ebouaney (Patrice Lumumba), Alex Descas (Joseph Mobutu), Theophile Moussa Sowie (Maurice Mpolo), Maka Kotto (Joseph Kasa Vubu), Dieudonne Kabongo (Godefroid Munungo), Pascal Nzonzi (Moise Tshombe), Andre Debaar (Walter J. Ganshof Van der Meersch), Cheik Doukoure (Joseph Okito). Directed by Raoul Peck and produced by Jacques Bidou. Screenplay by Peck and Pascal Bonitzer.

Why does the United States so often back the reactionary side in international disputes? Why do we fight against liberation movements and in favor of puppets who make things comfy for multinational corporations? Having built

a great democracy, why are we fearful of democracy elsewhere? Such thoughts occurred as I watched *Lumumba*, the story of how the United States conspired to bring about the death of the Congo's democratically elected Patrice Lumumba—and to sponsor in his place Joseph Mobutu, a dictator, murderer, and thief who continued for nearly four decades to enjoy American sponsorship.

Pondering the histories of the Congo and other troubled lands of recent decades, we're tempted to wonder if the world might not better reflect our ideals if we had not intervened in those countries. American foreign policy has consistently reflected not American ideals but American investment interests, and you can see that today in the rush toward Bush's insane missile shield. There is little evidence it will work, it will be obsolete even if it does, and yet as the largest peacetime public works project in American history it is a gold mine for the defense industries and their friends and investors.

Patrice Lumumba is a footnote to this larger story. Raoul Peck's film (a feature, not a documentary) begins with his assassinated body being dug up by Belgian soldiers so it can be hacked into smaller pieces and burned in oil drums. Lumumba's disfigured corpse begins the narration that runs through the film. He recalls his early days as a beer salesman, a trade that helps him develop a talent for speaking and leadership. As it happens, the beer he promotes has a rival owned by Joseph Kasa Vubu—who later becomes president while Lumumba is named prime minister and defense minister. It is Kasa Vubu who eventually orders the arrest that leads to Lumumba's murder.

In the 1950s, Lumumba becomes a leader of the Congolese National Movement. His abilities are spotted early by the Belgians, who after a century of inhuman despoliation of a once-prosperous land are fearful of powerful Africans. Lumumba is jailed, beaten, and then released to fly to Brussels for the conference granting the Congo its freedom. He takes office to find the armed forces still commanded by the white officers who tortured him, and when he tries to replace one of the most evil, he is targeted by the CIA, the Belgians, and the resident whites as a dangerous man, and his fate is sealed.

Most of the natural riches in the Congo are concentrated in Katanga Province, which declared independence from the mother country in a coup masterminded by the West. Lumumba's attempts to put down this rebellion got him tagged as a Communist, particularly when he considered asking the Russians to support the central government. Well, of course the opportunistic Russians would have been glad to oblige—but why did a democratic leader need help from the Russians to protect himself from the Western democracies?

The movie re-creates scenes that will be familiar, from another angle, to readers of Barbara Kingsolver's great novel, *The Poisonwood Bible*, which tells the story of an American missionary family that finds itself in the Congo at about the same time. Jailed by Kasa Vubu, Lumumba escapes and tries to flee with his family to a safe haven, but is captured and shot by a firing squad, without a trial.

We do not learn much about Lumumba the man. Eriq Ebouaney, a French actor whose family is from the Cameroons, plays Lumumba as a stubborn, fiery leader, good at speeches, but unskilled at strategy and diplomacy. Time and again, we see him making decisions that may be right but are dangerous to him personally. Although the narration is addressed to his wife, we learn little about her, his family, or his personal life; he is used primarily as a guide through the milestones of the Congo's brief two-month experiment with democracy.

Writer-director Raoul Peck has a longstanding interest in Lumumba, and made a documentary about him in 1991. He is a Haitian by birth, a onetime cultural minister there, and so knows firsthand how despotic regimes find sponsorship from Western capitals. His film is strong, bloody, and sad. He does not editorialize about Mobutu, except in one montage of shattering power. On his throne, guarded by soldiers with machine guns, Mobutu gives a speech on his country's second Independence Day. Mobutu asks for a moment of silence in Lumumba's memory, and as the moment begins, Peck cuts away to show the execution, burial, disinterment, dismemberment, and burning of Lumumba—and then back again to Mobutu's throne as the moment of silence ends.

The Luzhin Defence ★ ★ ½
PG-13, 108 m., 2001

John Turturro (Alexander Luzhin), Emily Watson (Natalia), Geraldine James (Vera), Stuart Wilson (Valentinov), Christopher Thompson (Jean de Stassard), Fabio Sartor (Turati), Peter Blythe (Ilya), Orla Brady (Anna). Directed by Marleen Gorris and produced by Stephen Evans, Philippe Gulz, and Caroline Wood. Screenplay by Petter Berry, based on the novel by Vladimir Nabokov.

"There is a pattern emerging!" cries the eccentric chess genius Alexander Luzhin. "I must keep track—every second!" To which the woman he loves can only reply, "It sounds like such a lonely battle." It is the 1920s in Italy, and they've met at a chess tournament, where Luzhin has the ability to become world champion, if his demons do not drive him mad. As anyone who has played chess knows, the game is utterly absorbing, driving out thoughts of anything else. The better you play, the deeper it becomes, until finally, among the very strongest players, it becomes an abyss. Some fall in. Where is Bobby Fischer?

The Luzhin Defence, based on a novella by Vladimir Nabokov, is about love, genius, and madness, but it is also about life among the wealthy emigrés of Europe in the years after World War I. They dress and move with elegance, their wealth preserving around them an illusion of the social order that was destroyed by the guns of August. They move from spa to spa, and although I am not sure where the movie is set, its villa looks as if it could be on the shore of Lake Como.

Here chess masters arrive from all over the world, as well as the debutante Natalia (Emily Watson) and her socially ambitious mother, Vera (Geraldine James). Alexander Luzhin (John Turturro) wanders in like a dreamer from another planet, absentminded, careless of his dress, in a world of his own. "That man is a genius," an onlooker whispers to Natalia. "He can accomplish anything he sets his mind to."

Well, perhaps. He sets his mind on Natalia. After having had no real conversation with her, he approaches her and announces, "I want you to be my wife. I implore you to agree." She doesn't turn him down as a madman, but asks for time to consider, and then agrees. She is won by his absolute simplicity and honesty. She is repelled by the corrupt marriage candidates sponsored by her mother. And something in her needs to protect Alexander.

The film follows a match between Luzhin and a grandmaster whose patience for chess is equaled only by his patience for Luzhin. But there is an evil presence on the premises: Valentinov (Stuart Wilson), who was the boy's chess teacher. The older man has never forgiven young Alexander for crushing him time and again at the board—emasculating him, ignoring him—and has tried for years on end to sabotage the dreamer's chess career. Now he turns up at the villa with more schemes. At one point, totally absorbed by a chess problem, Luzhin is driven away from the tournament by a chauffeur paid by Valentinov. Luzhin solves the problem and gets out of the car, belatedly noticing that he is stranded in the countryside.

The film is elegiac and sad, beautifully mounted, but not as compelling as it should be. It was directed by Marleen Gorris, whose *Antonia's Line* is what *Chocolat* wanted to be in its celebration of a female life-spirit. Here she captures Nabokov's elegance but not his passion. Perhaps we are never convinced by the bond between Alexander and Natalia. She pities him, she cares for him, she tries to protect him—but their relationship is so new we cannot understand the depth of her devotion, unless it involves madness too. And his love for her, after its first dramatic flourish in the marriage proposal, seems to recede into the clutter of his mind and its systems and patterns.

Turturro does something in his performance that demands more of an anchor than the film provides. He is floating in Luzhin's own interior monologue, entranced by the infinity of chess, and to the outer world seems childlike, innocent, incapable of protecting himself. At one point a doctor says he must stop playing to save his life. But it is never the Luzhins who are burnt out by chess. It is their opponents. The mad geniuses play on obsessively, while their opponents play at a level only high enough to understand how much higher there is to go. Turturro looks uncannily like Bobby Fischer, and I irreverently wish Gorris had abandoned Nabokov and his world and used Turturro in a movie about the match between Fischer and Spassky in Iceland in 1972. I see Bjork as Natalia.

M

Madadayo ★ ★ ★
NO MPAA RATING, 134 m., 2000

Tatsuo Matsumura (Hyakken Uchida), Kyoko Kagawa (Uchida's Wife), Hisashi Igawa (Takayama), George Tokoro (Amaki). Directed by Akira Kurosawa and produced by Hisao Kurosawa. Screenplay by Akira Kurosawa.

Made in 1993 when he was eighty-three, *Madadayo* is the last film by the Japanese master Akira Kurosawa, one of the greatest of all filmmakers, who died in 1998. And yet the very title of the film argued against death; "Madadayo" means "not yet!" That is the ritual cry that the film's old professor shouts out at the end of every one of his birthday parties, and it means that although death will come and may be near, life still goes on.

This is the kind of film we would all like to make, if we were very old and very serene. There were times when I felt uncannily as if Kurosawa were filming his own graceful decline into the night. It tells the story of the last two decades in the life of Hyakken Uchida, a writer and teacher who retires in the war years of the early 1940s. He was the kind of teacher who could inspire great respect and affection from his students, who venerate him and, as a group, help support him in his old age.

In Japan they have a tradition of "living national treasures"—people who because of their gifts and knowledge are treated like national monuments. Uchida is such a man, who has taught all his life and now finds that his books are selling well enough that he can move with his wife to a pretty little house, and sit in the entranceway: "That will be my study, and at the same time I will be the gatekeeper."

Kurosawa's career itself spanned some sixty years, and the titles of his films are spoken with awe by those who love them. Consider that the same man made *Rashomon, Yojimbo, Ikiru, The Seven Samurai, The Hidden Fortress, Red Beard, Throne of Blood, Kagemusha, Ran,* and twenty-five more. His movies have been filled with life and spectacle, but here, in *Madadayo,* he has made a film in the spirit of his near-contemporary Yasujiro Ozu, whose domestic dramas are among the most quietly observant and contemplative of all films.

Very little happens in *Madadayo*. The old man (Tatsuo Matsumura) and his wife (Kyoko Kagawa) are feted by his students on his sixtieth birthday, and go to live in the fine little house. The house is destroyed in an air raid. They move to a little hut, hardly more than a room and a half, and there the professor also sits in the doorway and writes. His students come to see him, and every year on his birthday they have the ritual party at which he downs a big glass of beer and cries out "not yet!"

The students conspire to find the professor a larger house. Then something very important happens. A cat named Nora wanders into their house, and the professor and his wife come to love it. Nora disappears. The professor is grief-stricken. Leaflets are circulated, and his students, now middle-aged businessmen, scour the neighborhood for Nora, without success. Then another cat walks into their house, and the wound is healed.

At the professor's seventy-seventh birthday dinner, we see that things have changed. The early events were held Japanese-style, with men only. Now women are present, too: wives, daughters, even grandchildren, in a Western-style banquet room. And still the cry is "not yet!"

Like Ozu, Kurosawa is content to let his camera rest and observe. We never quite learn what sorts of things the professor writes (the real Uchida was in fact a beloved essayist), but we know he must be a great man because his students love him so. We learn few intimate details about his life (not even, if I recall, his wife's first name). We see him mostly seated in his front door, as a stranger might.

Like his students, we are amused by his signs forbidding visitors and warning away those who would urinate on his wall. We learn about the burglar-proofing strategies in his first, larger, house: He leaves a door open, with a sign saying "Burglar's Entrance." Inside, signs indicate "Burglar's Passage," "Burglar's Recess Area," and "Burglar's Exit." He guesses right that burglars would prefer to operate in a house that grants them more anonymity.

The movie is as much about the students as

the professor, as much about gratitude and love as about aging. In an interview at the time of the film's release, Kurosawa said his movie is about "something very precious, which has been all but forgotten: the enviable world of warm hearts." He added, "I hope that all the people who have seen this picture will leave the theater feeling refreshed, with broad smiles on their faces."

Made ★ ★ ★
R, 95 m., 2001

Jon Favreau (Bobby), Vince Vaughn (Ricky), Peter Falk (Max), Famke Janssen (Jess), Sean "Puffy" Combs (Ruiz), Vincent Pastore (Jimmy), Dustin Diamond (Himself), Jennifer Bransford (Flight Attendant), Jenteal (Wendy), Faizon Love (Horrace). Directed and produced by Jon Favreau. Screenplay by Favreau.

There's a theory that American gangsters of the 1930s learned how to talk by studying Hollywood movies. Now comes *Made*, about two low-level modern gangsters who have possibly learned most of what they know about life by viewing *The Sopranos*. Bobby and Ricky (Jon Favreau and Vince Vaughn) have been best buddies since childhood, and played football at Hollywood High. Now they dream of success as professional boxers, while Bobby scrapes together a living as a personal manager—that is, he drives his girlfriend to her job as a stripper at bachelor parties.

They were made for each other: Bobby, the earnest, plodding, analytical seeker after success, and Ricky, the clueless instigator who can't involve himself in a situation without making it worse. There are some people with a gift for saying the wrong thing at the wrong time, and Ricky is one of them, talking when he should shut up, helpfully revealing secrets, blurting out the truth when a lie is desperately called for.

Made, a peculiarly entertaining comedy, revisits the rapport that Favreau and Vaughn had in *Swingers* (1996), and rotates it into a deadpan crime comedy. The movie was written, directed, and produced by Favreau, who plays Vaughn's straight man and loyal friend; think of Martin and Lewis. Vaughn gets many of the best moments, and knows just what to do with

them; his performance is a tricky balancing act since it depends entirely on tone—Ricky always has to be a little off-key.

The story. Bobby makes a lousy driver for his girlfriend, Jess (Famke Janssen, from *X-Men*). He's consumed by jealousy, and ends up getting in a fight with one of her clients. The wrong client. This lands him in trouble with his boss Max (Peter Falk), who books the strippers and has to pay eight grand in damages. Falk's character owes a little to some of the Cassavetes roles he's played; he operates out of an office that is meant to be impressive (and probably is, to the Rickys and Bobbys of the world). He has his thumbs in a lot of criminal pies, none of them very lucrative. He likes the sound of his own voice, and the way it coils through irrelevant details on its way to a triumphant, if murky, conclusion.

Max makes Ricky and Bobby an offer they can't, as they know from the movies, refuse. Actually, he makes Bobby the offer: Fly to New York and deliver a package. Bobby insists that Ricky come along because, well, Ricky always comes along. Ricky is like a faithful sidekick who would be lost without Bobby, since screwing up Bobby's plans is the only thing he does well.

They fly to New York. Jennifer Bransford is the flight attendant who deals severely with Ricky's belief that to sit in first class is to be king of the world. They meet a big, wide, tall, ominous driver (Vincent Pastore), who connects them, after many phone calls and mysterious trips to unlikely parts of town, with the crime boss Ruiz (Sean Combs). With Ruiz they have at last elevated themselves to a meaningful level in the crime hierarchy, and Ruiz does not look kindly on these two goofballs from the West Coast. We gather he considers Max essentially an elder version of the same species.

The movie is difficult to describe because it's not what happens that matters, it's how it happens and why. Mostly, it happens because Ricky exercises his genius for creating trouble where none need exist. He and Bobby are no more gangsters than they are boxers, and Combs (in an understated, convincing performance) has priceless reaction shots as he listens to their idea of how they should talk.

Comedies like *Made* are hard to make. It's easier when the payoffs are big, obvious laughs or intentional punch lines. Here we have a comedy of manners. The humor comes from the displacement between what any reasonable person would do, and what Ricky would do. Vaughn's work, in its own way, is masterful. Also thankless, because although to do what he does here is as hard as an acting assignment can be, it doesn't work unless it seems almost accidental. The proof of its quality is that it *does* work; another actor might take his dialogue and turn it to lead. And another director might not have the faith that Favreau has in his material. Maybe they made this movie together because no one else could understand how it could work. But they could, and it does.

Magnolia ★ ★ ★

R, 179 m., 2000

Jason Robards (Earl Partridge), Julianne Moore (Linda Partridge), Tom Cruise (Frank Mackey), Philip Seymour Hoffman (Phil Parma), John C. Reilly (Officer Kurring), Melora Walters (Claudia Gator), Jeremy Blackman (Stanley Spector), Michael Bowen (Rick Spector), William H. Macy (Donnie Smith), Philip Baker Hall (Jimmy Gator), Melinda Dillon (Rose Gator), April Grace (Reporter). Directed by Paul Thomas Anderson and produced by Joanne Sellar. Screenplay by Anderson.

Magnolia is operatic in its ambition, a great joyous leap into melodrama and coincidence, with ragged emotions, crimes and punishments, deathbed scenes, romantic dreams, generational turmoil, and celestial intervention, all scored to insistent music. It is not a timid film. Paul Thomas Anderson here joins Spike Jonze *(Being John Malkovich)*, David O. Russell *(Three Kings)*, and their master, Martin Scorsese *(Bringing Out the Dead)*, in beginning the new decade with an extroverted self-confidence that rejects the timid postmodernism of the 1990s. These are not movies that apologize for their exuberance or shield themselves with irony against suspicions of sincerity.

The movie is an interlocking series of episodes that take place during one day in Los Angeles, sometimes even at the same moment. Its characters are linked by blood, coincidence, and by the way their lives seem parallel. Themes emerge: the deaths of fathers, the resentments of children, the failure of early promise, the way all plans and ambitions can be undermined by sudden and astonishing events. Robert Altman's *Short Cuts* was also a group of interlinked Los Angeles stories, and both films illustrate former district attorney Vincent Bugliosi's observation in *Till Death Do Us Part* that personal connections in L.A. have a way of snaking around barriers of class, wealth, and geography.

The actors here are all swinging for the fences, heedless of image or self-protective restraint. Here are Tom Cruise as a loathsome stud, Jason Robards looking barely alive, William H. Macy as a pathetic loser, Melora Walters as a despairing daughter, Julianne Moore as an unloving wife, Michael Bowen as a browbeating father. Some of these people are melting down because of drugs or other reasons; a few, like a cop played by John C. Reilly and a nurse played by Philip Seymour Hoffman, are caregivers.

The film's opening sequence, narrated by an uncredited Ricky Jay, tells stories of incredible coincidences. One has become a legend of forensic lore; it's about the man who leaps off a roof and is struck by a fatal shotgun blast as he falls past a window before landing in a net that would have saved his life. The gun was fired by his mother, aiming at his father and missing. She didn't know the shotgun was loaded; the son had loaded it some weeks earlier, hoping that eventually one of his parents would shoot the other. All (allegedly) true.

This sequence suggests a Ricky Jay TV special, illustrating weird coincidences. But it is more than simply amusing. It sets up the theme of the film, which shows people earnestly and single-mindedly immersed in their lives, hopes, and values, as if their best-laid plans were not vulnerable to the chaotic interruptions of the universe. It's humbling to learn that existence doesn't revolve around us; worse to learn it revolves around nothing.

Many of the characters are involved in television, and their lives reflect on one another. Robards plays a dying tycoon who produces many shows. Philip Baker Hall, also dying, is a game show host. Cruise is Robards's son, the star of infomercials about how to seduce women; his macho hotel ballroom seminars could have been scripted by Andrew Dice Clay. Walters is Hall's daughter, who doesn't believe anything he says. Melinda Dillon is Hall's wife, who might have been happier without his compulsion for confession. Macy plays "former quiz kid Donnie Smith," now a drunk with a bad job in sales, who dreams that orthodontics could make him attractive to a burly bartender. Jeremy Blackman plays a bright young quiz kid on Hall's program. Bowen plays his father, a tyrant who drives him to excel.

The connections are like a game of psychological pickup sticks. Robards alienated Cruise, Hall alienated Dillon, Bowen is alienating Blackman. The power of TV has not spared Robards or Hall from death. Childhood success left Macy unprepared for life, and may be doing the same thing for Blackman. Both Hall and Robards have employees (a producer, a nurse) who love them more than their families do. Both Robards and Hall cheated on their wives. And around and around.

And there are other stories with their own connections. The cop, played by Reilly, is like a fireman rushing to scenes of emotional turmoil. His need to help is so great that he falls instantly in love with the pathetic drug user played by Walters; her need is more visible to him than her crime. Later, he encounters Macy in the middle of a ridiculous criminal situation brought about to finance braces for his teeth.

There are big scenes here for the actors. One comes as Cruise's cocky TV stud disintegrates in the face of cross-examination from a TV reporter (April Grace). He has another big scene at Robards's deathbed. Philip Baker Hall (a favorite actor of Anderson's since *Hard Eight*) also disintegrates on TV; he's unable to ask, instead of answer, questions. Julianne Moore's breakdown in a pharmacy is parallel to Walters's nervousness with the cop: Both women are trying to appear functional while their systems scream because of drugs.

All of these threads converge, in one way or another, upon an event there is no way for the audience to anticipate. This event is not "cheating," as some critics have argued, because the prologue fully prepares the way for it, as do some subtle references to Exodus. It works like the hand of God, reminding us of the absur-

dity of daring to plan. And yet plan we must, because we are human, and because sometimes our plans work out.

Magnolia is the kind of film I instinctively respond to. Leave logic at the door. Do not expect subdued taste and restraint but instead a kind of operatic ecstasy. At three hours it is even operatic in length, as its themes unfold, its characters strive against the dying of the light, and the great wheel of chance rolls on toward them.

The Majestic ★ ★ ★ ½
PG, 143 m., 2001

Jim Carrey (Peter Appleton/Luke Trimble), Martin Landau (Harry Trimble), Laurie Holden (Adele Stanton), Allen Garfield (Leo Kubelsky), David Ogden Stiers (Dr. Stanton), Bruce Campbell (Brett Armstrong/Roland), Amanda Detmer (Sandra Sinclair), Daniel von Bargen (FBI Agent Ellerby), Bob Balaban (Elvin Clyde), Brent Briscoe (Sheriff Coleman), Hal Holbrook (Johnston T. Doyle), Matt Wiens (Spencer Wyatt), James Whitmore (Stan Keller). Directed and produced by Frank Darabont. Screenplay by Darabont.

The Majestic is a proud, patriotic hymn to America, sung in a key that may make some viewers uncomfortable. At a time when our leaders are prepared to hold trials that bypass the American justice system, here is a film that unapologetically supports the Constitution and the Bill of Rights. It is set in the early 1950s, but the parallels with today are unmistakable and frightening.

Yet this is not a sober political picture. It's a sweet romantic comedy starring Jim Carrey, and it involves a case of mistaken identity and an attack of amnesia, those handy plot devices from time immemorial. It flies the flag in honor of our World War II heroes, and evokes nostalgia for small-town movie palaces and the people who run them. It makes us feel about as good as any movie made this year.

I imagine every single review of *The Majestic* will compare it to the works of Frank Capra, and that's as it should be. Frank Darabont has deliberately tried to make the kind of movie Capra made, about decent small-town folks standing up for traditional American values.

In an age of Rambo patriotism, it is good to be reminded of Capra patriotism—to remember that America is not just about fighting and winning, but about defending our freedoms. If we defeat the enemy at the cost of our own principles, who has won?

Darabont, the director of *The Shawshank Redemption* and *The Green Mile,* works on big canvases with lots of characters we can sympathize with. Carrey (who has never been better or more likable) plays Peter Appleton, a shallow, ambitious Hollywood scriptwriter who once, in college, attended a left-wing political meeting because he wanted to pick up a girl there. That wins him a place on the blacklist of the House Un-American Activities Committee, and he's subpoenaed to testify. No one believes he was a Communist (which was not against the law in any case), but to keep his job he is required to kowtow to the committee and "name names"—read a list of other Communists. Since he doesn't know any, the committee will helpfully supply it.

Depressed and confused (his current starlet girlfriend has dropped him like a hot potato), Peter drives north along the coast. His car plunges off a bridge, and he's discovered the next morning with no memory of who he is or how he got there. A kindly dog-walker (James Whitmore) takes him into the nearby town, where he looks kind of familiar to everyone. Finally old Harry Trimble (Martin Landau), who ran the local movie theater, blurts it out: This is his son Luke, lost in the war, now returned from the dead after nine years.

The town embraces Luke, and so does Adele Stanton (Laurie Holden), his onetime girlfriend. The town lost more than sixty of its young men in the war and has fallen into a depression. Somehow Luke's miraculous return inspires them to pick up the pieces and make a new start. Why, old Mr. Trimble even decides to reopen the Majestic Theater again.

The second act of the film involves Peter's gradual absorption in the identity of Luke. Darabont paints the town with a Capra palette: Everyone hangs out at the diner, there's a big-band dance down at the Point, Luke and Adele walk home down shady streets just like Jimmy Stewart and Donna Reed. Some, including Adele, have their doubts that this could really be Luke, but keep them to themselves.

Without getting into plot details, let me point out one moment when the screenplay by Michael Sloane does something exactly right. We know, because such stories require it, that sooner or later Peter's true identity will be discovered. In a routine formula picture, there would be a scene where Adele feels betrayed because she was deceived, and a giant misunderstanding would open up, based on the ancient Idiot Plot device in which no one says what they should obviously say.

Not here. In one of the movie's crucial turning points, Peter tells Adele the truth before he has to. Her reaction is based on true feelings, not misunderstandings. The movie plays fair with its plot, and with us. It even has townspeople raise the obvious questions about where Luke spent the past decade, and whether he's built another life. So we're on solid ground for the third act, in which Peter goes back to Los Angeles and testifies before the House committee.

The scenes of his testimony evoke memories of Gary Cooper, Jimmy Stewart, Spencer Tracy, and other Capra heroes standing up for traditional American beliefs ("That's the First Amendment, Mr. Chairman. It's what we're all about—if only we live up to it"). These scenes are also surprisingly funny (Peter defends himself against charges of subversion with the defense that he was feeling horny). Hal Holbrook is the committee chairman, Bob Balaban is the mean little inquisitor, and the committee evokes fears of communism as an excuse to shelve the Bill of Rights.

Darabont makes films long enough to sink into and move around in. *The Majestic* is not as long as *The Green Mile* (182 minutes), but at 143 minutes it's about the same length as *Shawshank*. It needs the time and uses it. It tells a full story with three acts, it introduces characters we get to know and care about, and it has something it passionately wants to say. When *The Majestic* went into production there could have been no hint of the tragedy of September 11, but the movie is uncannily appropriate right now. It expresses a faith that our traditional freedoms and systems are strong enough to withstand any threat, and that to doubt it is—well, un-American.

Malena ★ ★
R, 105 m., 2000

Monica Bellucci (Malena Scordia), Giuseppe Sulfaro (Renato Amoroso), Luciano Federico (Renato's Father), Matilde Piana (Renato's Mother), Pietro Notarianni (Professor Bonsignore). Directed by Giuseppe Tornatore and produced by Harvey Weinstein and Mario Cotone. Screenplay by Tornatore, based on a story by Luciano Vincenzoni.

Giuseppe Tornatore's *Malena* tells the story of a woman whose life is destroyed because she has the misfortune to be beautiful and have a great butt. The film tortuously tries to transform this theme in scenes of comedy, nostalgia, and bittersweet regret, but somehow we doubt its sincerity, maybe because the camera lingers so lovingly on the callipygian charms of the actress Monica Bellucci. There is nothing quite so awkward as a film that is one thing while it pretends to be another.

The setup scenes are like low-rent Fellini. In a small Italian town in 1940, a group of adolescent boys wait for the beautiful Malena to pass by. She is all they can imagine a woman could be, arousing their imaginations, and more, with her languorous swaying passage. Malena, who is a schoolteacher and of at least average intelligence, must be aware of her effect on the collective local male libido, but seems blissfully oblivious; her role is not so much dramatic as pictorial (a word I am using in the *Playboy* sense).

The story is told by Renato (Giuseppe Sulfaro), who as the movie opens is admitted to the local fraternity of girl-watchers. They use Malena as subject matter for their autoerotic pastimes, but for Renato she is more like a dream, like a heroine, like a woman he wants to protect from herself—with his bare hands, hopefully.

The story involves Malena's bad luck after her husband is called up by the army and her good name is sullied by local gossip. She's eventually reduced by wartime poverty to dating German soldiers. This descent in the world requires her to spend a great deal of time half-dressed before Tornatore's appreciative camera. She continues to shine brightly in

Renato's eyes, however, even after his field of knowledge is broadened when his father takes him to a bordello for the old "I give you the boy—give me back the man" routine.

Fellini's films often involve adolescents inflamed by women who embody their carnal desires. (See *Amarcord* and *8½.* Please.) But Fellini sees the humor that underlies sexual obsession, except (usually, but not always) in the eyes of the participants. *Malena* is a simpler story, in which a young man grows up transfixed by a woman, and essentially marries himself to the idea of her. It doesn't help that the movie's action grows steadily gloomier, leading to a public humiliation that seems wildly out of scale with what has gone before, and to an ending that is intended to move us much more deeply, alas, than it can.

The Man Who Cried ★ ★ ★
R, 97 m., 2001

Christina Ricci (Suzie), Cate Blanchett (Lola), John Turturro (Dante), Johnny Depp (Cesar), Harry Dean Stanton (Felix), Claudia Lander-Duke (Young Suzie), Oleg Yankovsky (Father), Danny Scheinman (Man in Suit). Directed by Sally Potter and produced by Christopher Sheppard. Screenplay by Potter.

Sally Potter makes movies about women who use art and artifice to escape from the roles society has assigned them. *Orlando* (1993) is about a character who lives for four centuries, first as a man, then as a woman. *The Tango Lesson* (1997) is about a British film director (Potter herself) who becomes a tango dancer. Now here is *The Man Who Cried,* about a little Jewish girl from Russia who becomes a little British girl and then a Parisian dancing girl and then a wartime refugee, and finally, once again, her father's daughter.

This is an amazingly ambitious movie, not so much because of the time and space it covers (a lot), but because Potter trusts us to follow her heroine through one damn thing after another. There is a moment when Suzie is on a bicycle, chasing Gypsy horsemen through the streets of Paris, and I thought: Yes, of course, realism at last—a woman in that situation *would* use a bicycle to chase a man on a horse.

By the time a ship is torpedoed near the end of the film, we're reflecting that most movies are too timid to offend the gods of plausibility.

Potter puts her money where her mouth is. If she personally, in her forties, can go to Argentina and become a tango dancer, then we can't complain about anything that happens to Suzie. Not that we'd want to. The story begins in Russia in 1927, when the girl's father determines to move the family to America. The girl and her father are separated, the girl is mislabeled by adults, and ends up being adopted by a well-meaning but grim British couple. When she sees Gypsies in the lanes of Britain, she is reminded of her own Jewish community in Russia.

Britain cannot hold a spirit like this. In Paris, Suzie is taken under the arm of a gold-digging showgirl named Lola (Cate Blanchett), who wants to marry well, and has her eyes on a famous opera singer named Dante (John Turturro). Suzie meanwhile falls for Cesar (Johnny Depp), the Gypsy on the white horse, and finds that he is a ride-on extra in Dante's current production. As the clouds of World War II gather, Dante reveals himself as a supporter of Mussolini and a hater of Gypsies and Jews, and Lola's appetite begins to fade.

Potter drenches her movies in bold, romantic music, and in wildly involved visuals. Her camera (here choreographed by the great European veteran Sacha Vierny) does not observe but joins. She loves rich images, unexpected whirls, camera movements that join unexpected elements. The music this time is mostly opera, evoking grand emotions that the action mirrors. *The Man Who Cried* is like an arthouse companion for *Moulin Rouge*.

Some of the actors are indulged, others reined in. Turturro's Dante is a character basking in his own glory, an ego with a voice, less an artist than a man who knows which way the wind is blowing. Blanchett uses a thick accent as a tart with a heart of pawned gold (consider the reach between this role and her Appalachian fortune-teller in *The Gift*). Depp more or less imports his soulful Gypsy from *Chocolat*, sensitive and moody. Christina Ricci's Suzie is at the still center, and very still herself; can a heroine ever have had less dialogue in a talking picture? And here is Harry Dean Stanton as the Parisian opera impresario. Yes, Harry Dean Stanton. Well, why not?—and with a scene where he takes a stand no matter what it costs him.

The Man Who Cried himself does not turn up until very late in the movie. He might once have cried for other reasons, but by then he is crying mostly for himself. He has paid a price for his decisions. As for Suzie, she ends up in Hollywood—and no, that is not giving away the ending. No doubt she grew old and became one of those strange women I would sometimes meet up in the Hollywood Hills, when David Bradley threw his dinner parties for the survivors of the silent era, or at Telluride, where they were the widows of legendary emigrés. Old women who told their stories and said, "But you'll never believe this."

The Man Who Wasn't There ★ ★ ★
R, 116 m., 2001

Billy Bob Thornton (Ed), Frances McDormand (Doris), Michael Badalucco (Frank), James Gandolfini (Big Dave), Katherine Borowitz (Ann Nirdlinger), Jon Polito (Creighton Tolliver), Scarlett Johansson (Birdy Abundas), Richard Jenkins (Walter Abundas), Tony Shalhoub (Freddy Riedenschneider), Adam Alexi-Malle (Carcanogues). Directed by Joel Coen and produced by Ethan Coen. Screenplay by Joel Coen and Ethan Coen.

The Coen brothers' *The Man Who Wasn't There* is shot in black and white, so elegant it reminds us of a 1940s station wagon—chrome, wood, leather, and steel all burnished to a contented glow. Its star performance by Billy Bob Thornton is a study in sad-eyed, mournful chain-smoking, the portrait of a man so trapped by life he wants to scream. The plot is one of those *film noir* twisters made of gin and adultery, where the right man is convicted of the wrong crime.

The look, feel, and ingenuity of this film are so lovingly modulated you wonder if anyone else could have done it better than the Coens. Probably not. And yet, and yet—for a movie about crime, it proceeds at such a leisurely pace. The first time I saw it, at Cannes, I emerged into the sunlight to find Michel Ciment, the influential French critic, who observed sadly, "A ninety-minute film that plays for two hours."

Now I have seen it again, and I admire its virtues so much I am about ready to forgive its flow. Yes, it has a deliberate step—but is that entirely a fault of the film, or is it forced by the personality of Ed Crane (Thornton), the small-town barber who narrates it? He is not a swift man, and we get the impression that the crucial decisions in his life—his job, his marriage—were made by default. He has the second chair in a two-barber shop, next to his talkative brother-in-law Frank (Michael Badalucco). He spends most of his waking hours cutting hair and smoking, the cigarette dangling from his lips as he leans over his clients. (This is exactly right; the movie remembers a time in America when everyone seemed to smoke all the time, and I cannot think of Darrel Martin, the barber on Main Street in Urbana, Illinois, without remembering the smoke that coiled from his Camel into my eyes during every haircut.)

Ed Crane has the expression of a man stunned speechless by something somebody else has just said. He is married to Doris (Frances McDormand), who is the bookkeeper down at Nirdlinger's Department Store. She works for Big Dave (James Gandolfini), and when Dave and his wife come over to dinner, Doris and Dave laugh at all the same things while Ed and Dave's wife stare into thin air. Ed thinks his wife may be having an affair. He handles this situation, as he handles most social situations, by smoking.

The story then involves developments I will not reveal—double and triple reverses in which two people die in unanticipated ways, at un-anticipated hands, and Doris ends up in jail. Ed mortgages the house to pay for the best lawyer in California, Freddy Riedenschneider (Tony Shalhoub), who is the defense attorney at two trials in the movie. Ed, who narrates the entire movie with deadpan objectivity, reports his summation for the jury: "He told them to look not at the facts, but at the meaning of the facts. Then he said the facts had no meaning."

The Coens have always had a way with dialogue. I like the way Ed's narration tells us everything we need to know about Ed while Ed seems to be sticking strictly to the facts. I like the way Freddy Riedenschneider tells Ed: "I'm an attorney. You're a barber. You don't know anything." And a conversation in Ed's car between Ed and Birdy Abundas (Scarlett Johansson), a teenage pianist he has taken an interest in. "You know what you are?" she asks him, after he insists she has talent. "You're an enthusiast!" Yes, and he is mostly enthusiastic not about Birdy's music but about Birdy, but too fearful to make the slightest admission of his feelings. She lacks all such inhibition, and when she attempts to demonstrate her grati-tude in an extremely direct way, all he can think of to say is, "Heavens to Betsy!"

Classic *film noir* specialized in bad luck and ironic turns of fate. A crime would be com-mitted flawlessly, and then the perp would be trapped by an inconsequential, unrelated de-tail. That's what happens here, but with the details moved laterally one position, so that you are obviously guilty—not of the crime you committed, but of the crime you didn't commit. *Film noir* is rarely about heroes, but about men of small stature, who are lured out of their timid routines by dreams of wealth or romance. Their sin is one of hubris: These little worms dare to dream of themselves as rich or happy. As the title hints, *The Man Who Wasn't There* pushes this one step further, into the realm of a man who scarcely exists apart from his transgressions. I kill, therefore I am. And he doesn't even kill who, or how, or when the world thinks he does (although there is a cer-tain justice when he receives his last shave).

Joel and Ethan Coen are, above all, stylists. The look and feel of their films is more impor-tant to them than the plots—which, in a way, is as it should be. Here Michel Ciment is right, and they have devised an efficient ninety-minute story and stretched it out with style. Style didn't used to take extra time in Holly-wood; it came with the territory. But *The Man Who Wasn't There* is so assured and perceptive in its style, so loving, so intensely right, that if you can receive on that frequency, the film is like a voluptuous feast. Yes, it might easily have been shorter. But then it would not have been this film, or necessarily a better one. If the Coens have taken two hours to do what hardly anyone else could do at all, isn't it churlish to ask why they didn't take less time to do what everyone can do?   ☞

A Map of the World ★ ★ ★ ½
R, 127 m., 2000

Sigourney Weaver (Alice Goodwin), Julianne
Moore (Theresa Collins), David Strathairn
(Howard Goodwin), Ron Lea (Dan Collins),
Arliss Howard (Paul Reverdy), Chloe Sevigny
(Carole Mackessy), Louise Fletcher (Nellie),
Sara Rue (Debbie), Aunjanue Ellis (Dyshett).
Directed by Scott Elliott and produced by
Kathleen Kennedy and Frank Marshall.
Screenplay by Peter Hedges and Polly Platt,
based on the novel by Jane Hamilton.

There is a pounding that starts inside the heads
of certain kinds of people when they're convinced they're right. They know in theory all
about being cool and diplomatic, but in practice a great righteous anger takes hold, and
they say exactly what they think in short and
cutting words. Later they cool off, dial down,
and vow to think before they speak, but then
the red demon rises again in fury against those
who are wrong or stupid—or seem at the moment to be.

Alice Goodwin, the Wisconsin farm woman
played by Sigourney Weaver in *A Map of the
World*, is a woman like that. She has never settled comfortably inside her own body. She is
not entirely reconciled to being the wife of her
husband, the mother of her children, the teacher
of her students. She is not even sure she belongs
on a farm. You sense she has inner reservations
about everything, they make her mad at herself, and sometimes she blurts out exactly what
she's thinking, even when she shouldn't be
thinking of it.

This trait leads to a courtroom scene of rare
fascination. We've seen a lot of courtrooms in
the movies, and almost always we know what
to expect. The witnesses will tell the truth or lie,
they will be effective or not, and suspense will
build if the film is skillful. *A Map of the World*
puts Alice Goodwin in the witness box, and she
says the wrong thing in the wrong way for reasons that seem right to her but nobody else.
She'd rather be self-righteous than acquitted.

This quality makes her a fascinating person, in one of the best performances Weaver
has given. We can't take our eyes off her. She is
not the plaything or the instrument of the
plot. She fights off the plot, indeed: The move-

ment of the film is toward truth and resolution,
but she hasn't read the script and is driven by
anger and a deep wronged stubbornness. She
begins to speak and we feel enormous suspense. We care for her. We don't want her to
damage her own case.

The plot involves her in a situation that depends on two unexpected developments, and
I don't feel like revealing either one. Neither
one is her fault, morally, but bad things happen all the same. She's smart enough to see
why she's not to blame for the first event, but
human enough to feel terrible about it anyway. And the second development is sort of a
combination of the first, plus her own big
mouth. Her family is terrified. Her husband
doesn't know what to make of her, and her
kids don't have the comfort of thinking of their
mom as an innocent in an unfair world, because she doesn't act like a victim—she acts
like a woman who plans to win the game in
the last quarter.

There are good performances all through
the movie, which was directed by Scott Elliott
and written by Peter Hedges and Polly Platt.
David Strathairn plays Howard, Alice Goodwin's husband, and Julianne Moore and Ron
Lea play their farm neighbors—just about their
only friends. When Alice spends time in prison,
she gets a hard time from an inmate (Aunjanue Ellis), who senses (correctly) that this
woman may have dug her own grave. And
there is a small but crucial role for Chloe Sevigny,
who in several recent movies *(Boys Don't Cry,
julien donkey-boy, American Psycho)* shows an
intriguing range. As for Julianne Moore, see
Stanley Kauffmann's praise in his *New Republic* review, where he finds her grief "a small
gem of truthful heartbreak."

The movie is not tidy. Like its heroine, it
doesn't follow the rules. It breaks into parts. It
seems to be a family story, and then turns into
a courtroom drama, and then into a prison
story, and there is intercutting with romantic
intrigue, and there aren't any of the comforting payoffs we get in genre fiction. I'm grateful for movies like this; *Being John Malkovich*
and *Three Kings*, so different in every other
way, resemble *A Map of the World* in being
free—in being capable of taking any turn at
any moment, without the need to follow tired
conventions. And in Sigourney Weaver, the

movie has a heroine who would be a lot happier if she weren't so smart. Now there's a switch.

Maryam ★ ★ ★ ½
NO MPAA RATING, 90 m., 2002

Mariam Parris (Mary/Maryam Armin), David Ackert (Ali Armin), Shaun Toub (Darius Armin), Shohreh Aghdashloo (Homa Armin), Maziyar Jobrani (Reza), Sabine Singh (Jill), Victor Jory (Jamie), Michael Blieden (Pete). Directed by Ramin Serry and produced by Shauna Lyon. Screenplay by Serry.

Girls just want to have fun, says Cyndi Lauper, and Maryam, a high school senior, is one of them. Yes, she's an honor student and anchors the news on the in-school TV program, but she also likes to hang out at the roller rink with her slacker boyfriend, and pot and booze are not unknown to her. In New Jersey in 1979, she is a typical teenage girl—until the Iran hostage crisis slaps her with an ethnic label that makes her an outsider at school and a rebel in her own home.

Maryam (Mariam Parris) is Iranian-American—or Persian, her father would say. Her parents immigrated from Iran before the fall of the shah, and settled comfortably into suburbia; her father is a doctor, her mother a warm, chatty neighbor, and Maryam (or "Mary," as she calls herself at school) doesn't think much about her Iranian or Muslim heritage. Then two things happen to force her to confront her history. The hostage crisis inspires knee-jerk hostility from her classmates (whose families also come from somewhere else), and her radical cousin Ali arrives from Tehran.

Ramin Serry's Maryam, a film that cares too deeply for its characters to simplify them, doesn't indulge in tired clichés about the generation gap. Maryam's home life is strict but not unreasonable. Her father doesn't want her to date, places great emphasis on her grades, doesn't know about her boyfriend. He is not a cruel or domineering man, and Maryam, to her credit, knows her parents love her. She's caught between trying to be a good daughter and a typical teenager, and has found a workable middle ground before Ali arrives.

With Ali comes a history of family tension she knows nothing about. Ali is an orphan, the son of Mary's uncle, and so he must be taken in. It is more complicated than that. Her father, we learn, turned his brother in to the shah's secret police; he felt he had no choice, but is consumed by guilt. The bloodstained backgammon board Ali brings as a "gift" is an ominous reminder of times past.

Ali is such an observant Muslim that he cannot touch his cousin Maryam, even to shake her hand. Pressed into service as a chaperone, he finds himself plunged into teenage culture that offends and attracts him. He calls Maryam a "whore" to her mother, but subtly flirts with her. More disturbing is his alliance with a campus radical, and his obsession with the deposed shah, who has just entered a New York hospital for cancer treatment. (Maryam's take on this: "He calls the U.S. the Great Satan. I mean, the guy could lighten up a little.")

Maryam was made before 9/11, and indeed I first saw it at the 2000 Hawaii Film Festival and invited it to my own Overlooked Film Festival in April 2001. It is, I learned, the somewhat autobiographical story of writer-director Ramin Serry, who grew up in Chicago and was made sharply aware of his Iranian heritage during the 1979 hostage crisis.

In the film, Maryam's neighbors put a yellow ribbon around the tree in their front yard, and discontinue their friendly chats and visits. Maryam's boyfriend drops her like a hot potato. She is deposed from her TV show (she suggests her newly arrived cousin might make a good interview; the other students prefer to cover a homecoming controversy). A brick comes through the front window. A public demonstration turns into shouts of "Iranians go home." Through all of this, the gifted actress Mariam Parris (British, but seamlessly playing American) finds the right notes: wounded, sad, angry, but more balanced than distraught.

Whatever hostility Serry felt in 1979 is no doubt much worse today for Arab-Americans, who have, like most immigrants since the Pilgrims, left a native land to seek the American dream. Strange how many Americans, themselves members of groups that were hated a few generations ago, now turn against newcomers. (I could hear the pain in my German-American father's voice as he recalled being yanked out of Lutheran school during World

War I and forbidden by his immigrant parents ever to speak German again.) *Maryam* is more timely now than ever.

Max Keeble's Big Move ★ ★
PG, 101 m., 2001

Zena Grey (Woodwind Girl), Alex D. Linz (Max Keeble), Larry Miller (Principal Jindraike), Justin Berfield (Caption Writer), Noel Fisher (Troy McGinty), Orlando Brown (Dobbs), P. J. Byrne (D. J./Young Executive), Robert Carradine (Don Keeble), Clifton Davis (Superintendent Knebworth). Directed by Tim Hill and produced by Mike Karz. Screenplay by Jonathan Bernstein, Mark Blackwell, and James Greer.

I sat down to write a review of *Max Keeble's Big Move* and found myself consumed by a certain indifference. It is the kind of movie one enjoys more at eight, or even twelve, than at sixteen and up. I am up. I stalled. I checked the Movie Answer Man's e-mail. I found a message from Brendan Staunton of London, who writes: "Don't you think that kids are a little, or perhaps even a lot, too wise in American movies—yes, even in serious ones? It's an understandable fault, I suppose, but I've never in my life come across the kind of kids you see in movies or TV dramas."

Brendan, I couldn't agree more. We have a touching faith in childhood wisdom in this country, matched only by our cynicism about adults. I am reminded of our poet e.e. cummings, who wrote "down they forgot as up they grew." The wise children in *The Sixth Sense* and *The Kid* know occult secrets hidden even from Bruce Willis. I imagine that K–6 teachers must go to these movies as a form of escapism, to see children totally unlike the real kids they teach every day.

Kids in comedies are especially clever. They see through adults in a wink, outsmart their opponents, plot to get what they want, and are cute, articulate, and never have pimples. Take Max Keeble (Alex D. Linz), for example. It is his first day of junior high school, and his hormones have recently started to send him messages which, when he sees Woodwind Girl (Zena Grey), he finds himself finally able to decode.

He likes junior high school, all except for those two obligatory characters in all junior high school movies, the bully and the obnoxious principal. The bully, named Troy McGinty (Noel Fisher), is taller, blond, and looks (as bullies always seem to look in these movies) like a twelve-year-old Gary Busey. The principal is named Principal Jindraike (Larry Miller) and looks (as principals always seem to look in these movies) like Larry Miller.

Max is beginning to make headway with Woodwind Girl, in his struggle against Troy, and in his campaign to prevent the principal's insane zeal to tear down an animal shelter and build a stadium. But then disaster strikes when his father (Robert Carradine) tells his mother (Nora Dunn) that they are moving in a week so he can take a new job. And just when she finally had the house decorated perfectly!

You will imagine that this is not the kind of movie that holds me spellbound. It explains why I am so grateful for a film like *Spy Kids*, that the entire family (including adults) can enjoy. This is more like an after-school Nickelodeon romp, with bright colors, broad jokes, lots of sight gags, characters landing in deep, wet puddles, and a plot assembled from off-the-shelf parts.

There's a tendency with these movies to spend money to conceal the lack of creativity. There is, for example, an ice-cream truck that at one point is hoisted aloft by a crane so that it can spill hundreds of gallons of melted ice cream over the villains, and we wonder if a funnier and more economical solution was not available.

Some moments are funny. I liked Larry Miller, who seemed to regard the movie's characters with about as much affection as I did, and makes schoolwide telecasts from his office with a U.S. Capitol photographic backdrop behind him, just like our lawmakers. And Alex D. Linz *(Home Alone 3)* is a talented young actor; I suspect this is a film about which he had private thoughts too, since anyone as smart as he is would not be much entertained by what he is made to do.

So, yes, Brendan Staunton, I agree that kids are a little, or perhaps even a lot, too wise in American movies. But you have to remember that when the movie is good enough, we forgive them. Look at *E.T.*, for example. And over here in America we are all enthralled by your

Harry Potter, who is a lot, or even a whole lot, too wise.

Maze ★ ★ ★
R, 97 m., 2001

Rob Morrow (Lyle Maze), Laura Linney (Callie), Craig Sheffer (Mike), Rose Gregorio (Lyle's Mother), Robert Hogan (Lyle's Father), Gia Carides (Julianne). Directed by Rob Morrow and produced by Paul Colichman, Mark R. Harris, Stephen P. Jarchow, and Morrow. Screenplay by Morrow and Bradley White.

Lyle Maze is a painter who has Tourette's syndrome and obsessive-compulsive disorder. His work should look like Jackson Pollock attacked a Mark Rothko, but no, his inner peace emerges when he's painting. He falls into a sort of reverie then, and "the house could burn down and I wouldn't notice." The rest of the time, there are problems; when he suddenly hurls paint into a model's eye, we sense it's happened before by his instant response: "Don't worry. It's nontoxic. Just wash it with water."

Maze (Rob Morrow) lives alone because, in his words, he's a "freak" and a normal relationship is impossible. His best friends are a doctor named Mike (Craig Sheffer) and Mike's girlfriend, Callie (Laura Linney). Mike is a do-gooder who does not believe humanitarianism begins at home, and leaves Callie for seven months to work as a volunteer doctor in Burundi. Callie is pregnant when he leaves, but Mike doesn't know, care, or notice, and that leaves best friend Maze to be her partner in the natural childbirth classes.

Maze and Callie are drawn toward each other, but Maze doesn't want to be disloyal to his best (only) friend. Callie, who knows Mike better, is more open. Maze experiments with a date: Julianne (Gia Carides) admires his work, but is less entranced when he throws wine at her during dinner.

Maze's OCD is a mild case, involving an obsession with the tongues of shoes and other harmless manifestations. His Tourette's doesn't involve the sudden shouting of obscenities, which is the widespread but limited view of the condition. He sometimes has sudden muscular spasms, or emits strange noises and pops (when that happens, we see a jerky worldview through a handheld video camera). He sees the humor in the situation; when Callie offers him a TV set, he asks her, "Have you ever seen an obsessive-compulsive with a remote control?"

The heart of the story is hard to resist, not least because Linney (the Oscar nominee from *You Can Count on Me*) is sweet and understanding, and Morrow has a shaggy appeal. It is a rite of passage required of all actors that they participate in at least one live childbirth scene, with somebody shouting "Push! Push!" but you have to hand it to the scene in *Maze*. It's original—a duet for screams and Tourette's.

There are small but telling scenes involving Maze's parents (Rose Gregorio and Robert Hogan). When the father needs a blood transfusion, he doesn't want his son's blood, even though his wife tells him what he should have long since known, that you can't "catch" nonorganic disorders. The father has always believed Maze could control his twitches if he wanted to. Morrow and Gregorio have a quiet scene together, son and mother sitting side by side on a bed, where one of her speeches unforgettably sums up her marriage.

The movie is Morrow's directorial debut, and he wrote the screenplay with Bradley White. The story arc is straight out of screenplay workshops, including setbacks that arrive right on time (an ultrasound test, a tantrum). The departure and return of Dr. Mike are so timely he must have had a copy of the script. There are several Idiot Plot moments when a simple line of dialogue ("He has Tourette's syndrome") would work wonders but is never said. And yet the movie has a sweetness and care that is touching.

Mean Machine ★ ★ ★
R, 98 m., 2002

Vinnie Jones (Danny Meehan), Jason Statham (Monk), David Kelly (Doc), David Hemmings (Prison Governor), Vas Blackwood (Massive), Jason Flemyng (Bob), Danny Dyer (Billy the Limpet), Robbie Gee (Trojan). Directed by Barry Skolnick and produced by Guy Ritchie. Screenplay by Tracy Keenan Wynn, Charlie Fletcher, Chris Baker, and Andrew Day.

The formula is familiar but enjoyable. A group of British tough guys are assembled for an enterprise that combines violence with humor, while cherishing their peculiar personalities and even finding goodness where none should grow. We've had prisoners winning a gardening competition, pot dealers helping little old ladies, and crooks leaving crime for life as real-estate agents. Now here is *Mean Machine*, about a corrupt British soccer champion, jailed for rigging an important match and ordered by the prison governor to coach the inmates' team. The big match will be against the guards' team.

If this premise rings a faint, far-off bell, you may be remembering Robert Aldrich's *The Longest Yard* (1974), with one of Burt Reynolds's best performances, that told the same story, more or less, in terms of American football. Barry Skolnick's *Mean Machine* is more than inspired by *The Longest Yard;* it's based on the same Tracy Keenan Wynn screenplay, and indeed *The Mean Machine* was even the original title of *The Longest Yard*.

The movie stars Vinnie Jones, a real-life footballer so tough he didn't even play for England; he played for Wales. According to the BBC Website, he was known for dirty football, just like Danny Meehan, his character in the film. You may recognize Jones's Fearless Fosdick features from *Lock, Stock and Two Smoking Barrels*, directed by Guy Ritchie, who produced this film. And he has appeared as a fearsome background presence in *Snatch, Gone in 60 Seconds*, and *Swordfish*. In his first lead role, he handles the dialogue like meat and potatoes, one line at a time, chewed carefully.

The deal: The prison governor (David Hemmings) has a gambling problem and is crazy about football. He orders his new celebrity prisoner to coach the team. This does not sit well with the head guard, who coaches the guards' team, but what can he say? Danny doesn't much want to enter the coaching profession, but the governor makes him a threat he can't ignore.

The most enjoyable passages are some of the most predictable, recycled out of countless other movies where a leader has to pick his men. Danny finds himself with the prison contraband retailer, Massive (Vas Blackwood), as his right-hand man, and a violent, feared con named Monk (Jason Statham) as his star player. He gets a lot of valuable prison lore and advice from the ancient convict Doc (David Kelly,

who you will remember from his naked scooter ride in *Waking Ned Devine*). Kelly has had a whole late flowering playing twinkly geezers, clouded only by the distressing tendency of his characters to end up in sentimental death scenes.

All leads up to the big match, which of course involves hard play and dirty tricks, and dovetails neatly with the governor's gambling problem. *Mean Machine* lacks the social satire of *The Longest Yard*, which was a true early 1970s film and therefore antiestablishment. It's interested only in the characters and the game. Guy Ritchie, who started out as such an innovator in *Lock, Stock, etc.*, seems to have headed directly for reliable generic conventions as a producer. But they *are* reliable, and have become conventions for a reason: They work. *Mean Machine* is what it is, and very nicely too.

Meet the Parents ★ ★ ★
PG-13, 108 m., 2000

Robert De Niro (Jack Byrnes), Ben Stiller (Greg Focker), Teri Polo (Pam Byrnes), Blythe Danner (Dina Byrnes), Nicole DeHuff (Debbie Byrnes), Jon Abrahams (Denny Byrnes), Owen Wilson (Kevin Rawley), Tom McCarthy (Bob Banks), Phyllis George (Linda Banks), Kali Rocha (Flight Attendant). Directed by Jay Roach and produced by Nancy Tenenbaum, Jane Rosenthal, Robert De Niro, and Roach. Screenplay by Jim Herzfeld and John Hamburg, based on a story by Greg Glienna.

Ben Stiller has a good line in embarrassment and chagrin. His chiseled face looks so earnest, so willing to please, and turns incredulous as the world conspires against him. In *There's Something About Mary* and again in *Meet the Parents*, he plays a young man who desperately wants to impress the girl he loves, and plunges into a series of humiliating miscalculations. He doesn't have anything hanging from his ear in this picture, but he acts as if he thinks he might.

In *There's Something About Mary*, Stiller played a character who managed to set a beloved dog afire. *Meet the Parents* is not a clone or imitation of *Mary*—it has its own original inspiration—but it does get Stiller into a lot of trouble over a beloved pet cat, and even funnier trouble over another cat, entirely imaginary, which he claims to have milked.

Why would a man claim to have milked a cat? The screenplay, by Jim Herzfeld and John Hamburg, gets a lot of its laughs out of the way Stiller's character tells thoughtless little social lies and then, when he's caught, improvises his way into bigger, outrageous lies. The development is like a comic pyramid: The base is a casual claim that he was raised on a farm. It is revealed he was actually raised in Detroit. Well, yes, he says, he was. Then why did he claim to have experience at milking? Well, he had a cat, which "birthed" thirty kittens, including one little fellow who could never get his turn at the table, and . . . by this time Stiller is demonstrating how he used his fingers on the mother cat's itsy-bitsy little nipple, and everyone in the room is regarding him as a madman.

In *Meet the Parents*, he plays the unfortunately named Greg Focker. That's not his real name; Focker is, Greg isn't. He is in love with a Chicago schoolteacher named Pam (Teri Polo), who takes him home to meet her parents on Long Island. Her dad, Jack, is played by Robert De Niro as the nightmare of every hopeful groom. He is a reasonable man, his reason operating like a steel vise to clamp down on every contradiction and improbability in Greg's conversation, and there is no shortage of them. He is also a man with a great love for his cat, which he has toilet-trained, but which, ominously, "has no outdoor survival skills."

What are the odds that Greg will let the cat outdoors? And that the cat will turn out to be better toilet-trained than Greg? *Meet the Parents* builds brilliantly on interlocking comic situations, until Greg has involved himself in a counterfeit cat, set the house afire, and flooded the lawn (where Pam's sister is about to be married) with an overflowing septic tank.

Pam's mom, Dina (Blythe Danner), understands that her husband can be hard on a young man. "Go easy on this one, Jack," she tells De Niro. "I think Pam really likes him." But Pam has really liked other young men—a lot of them, we gather. One that we meet is her ex-fiancé Kevin (Owen Wilson), a blond multimillionaire who, for the sister's wedding, has carved an altar out of a solid block of wood.

The thing with Kevin was "strictly physical," Pam assures Greg, who is far from assured by information like that.

Eventually it begins to appear, even to Greg, that he is a dangerous, lying maniac. The simplest situations conceal hidden traps. He is asked by Jack to say grace at dinner. "Greg is Jewish," Jack is told. "I'm sure Jews bless their food," Jack smiles, and Greg launches into a tortured prayer that segues, to his own horror, into lyrics from *Godspell*. (He has bad luck with lyrics; it is the wrong idea to chat with Jack about the various possible meanings of "Puff, the Magic Dragon.")

The De Niro character conceals secrets and sentimentalities. He loves his cat, he treasures the ashes of his dead mother, he is suspicious of anyone who wants to marry his daughter, and he has a wide range of double takes, frowns, lifted eyebrows, significant pauses, chilling asides, and subtle put-downs. He isn't a vulgarian, but a self-confident man who serenely enforces a set of standards that Greg violates, one by one, until finally everything has gone horribly wrong and Greg goes berserk—not in Pam's home, but at the airport, where he is pushed over the edge by a flight attendant (Kali Rocha) on autopilot.

Meet the Parents was directed by Jay Roach, who made the *Austin Powers* movies and here shows he can dial down from farce into a comedy of (bad) manners. His movie is funnier because it never tries too hard; De Niro, in particular, gets laughs by leaning back and waiting for them to come to him. And Stiller is like the target in a dunk-the-clown game, smiling while the world falls out from under him.

Memento ★ ★ ★
R, 113 m., 2001

Guy Pearce (Leonard), Carrie-Anne Moss (Natalie), Joe Pantoliano (Teddy), Mark Boone Junior (Burt), Stephen Tobolowsky (Sammy), Jorja Fox (Leonard's Wife), Harriet Harris (Mrs. Jankis). Directed by Christopher Nolan and produced by Jennifer Todd and Suzanne Todd. Screenplay by Christopher Nolan, based on the short story by Jonathan Nolan.

I have here a message from Vasudha Gandhi of

Queens Village, New York, about the movie *Memento:*

"Although I loved the film, I don't understand one key plot point. If the last thing the main character remembers is his wife dying, then how does he remember that he has short-term memory loss?"

Michael Cusumano of Philadelphia writes with the same query. They may have identified a hole big enough to drive the entire plot through. Perhaps a neurologist can provide a medical answer, but I prefer to believe that Leonard, the hero of the film, has a condition similar to Tom Hanks's "brain cloud" in *Joe vs. the Volcano*—Leonard suffers from a condition brought on by a screenplay that finds it necessary, and it's unkind of us to inquire too deeply.

Leonard is played by Guy Pearce, in a performance that is curiously moving, considering that by definition it has no emotional arc. He has witnessed the violent death of his wife, and is determined to avenge it. But he has had short-term memory loss ever since the death, and has to make copious notes—he even has memos tattooed to his body in order.

If Leonard keeps forgetting what has already happened, we in the audience suffer from the opposite condition. We begin at the end, and work our way back toward the beginning, because the story is told backward. Well, not exactly; it begins with a brilliant idea, a Polaroid photograph that fades instead of developing, but every individual scene plays with time running forward, and there are some lateral moves and flashbacks that illuminate, or confuse, the issue. Essentially, Leonard is adrift in time and experience, and therefore so are we.

The idea of a narrative told backward was famously used by Harold Pinter in the 1983 film *Betrayal*, based on his play. He told a story of adultery and betrayed friendship, beginning with the sad end and then working his way back through disenchantment to complications to happiness to speculation to innocence. His purpose was the opposite of the strategy used by writer-director Christopher Nolan in *Memento*. Pinter's subject was memory and regret, and the way adulteries often begin playfully and end miserably. There was irony in the way the characters grew happier in each scene, while the audience's knowledge of what was ahead for them deepened.

Nolan's device of telling his story backward, or sort of backward, is simply that—a device. It does not reflect the way Leonard thinks. He still operates in chronological time, and does not know he is in a time-reversed movie. The film's deep backward and abysm of time is for our entertainment and has nothing to do with his condition. It may actually make the movie too clever for its own good. I've seen it twice. The first time, I thought I'd need a second viewing to understand everything. The second time, I found that greater understanding helped on the plot level, but didn't enrich the viewing experience. Once is right for this movie. Confusion is the state we are intended to be in.

That said, *Memento* is a diabolical and absorbing experience, in which Pearce doggedly plays a low-rent Fugitive who patiently makes maps, jots notes, and explains over and over that he has to talk fast, because in a few minutes he'll start forgetting the conversation. A motel clerk takes advantage of his condition to charge him for two rooms at the same time, and cheerfully admits his fraud, pointing out Leonard will forget it. "Even if you get revenge, you're not going to remember it," he's told at one point, but his reply has a certain logic: "My wife deserves revenge whether or not I remember it."

One striking element of the film is a series of flashbacks to a case Leonard investigated when he worked for an insurance company. This involves a man named Sammy, who appears to have memory loss, although he seems otherwise just like good old Sammy. His wife, a diabetic, can't be sure he isn't faking his condition, and arranges a test I will not reveal. This story has relevance to Leonard's own plight, in an indirect way.

The other major characters are Natalie (Carrie-Anne Moss) and Teddy (Joe Pantoliano). Of Natalie, he has a Polaroid inscribed: "She has also lost someone. She will help you out of pity." Their relationship keeps starting over from the beginning. As for Teddy, his identity and role shifts mysteriously.

The purpose of the movie is not for us to solve the murder of the wife. ("I can't remember to forget you," he says of her.) If we leave the theater not sure exactly what happened, that's fair enough. The movie is more like a poignant exercise in which Leonard's residual code of honor pushes him through a fog of amnesia toward what he feels is his moral duty. The movie doesn't supply the usual payoff of a thriller (how can it?), but it's uncanny in evoking a state of mind. Maybe telling it backward is Nolan's way of forcing us to identify with the hero. Hey, we all just got here.   ☞

Me, Myself & Irene ★ ½

R, 116 m., 2000

Jim Carrey (Charlie/Hank), Renee Zellweger (Irene), Robert Forster (Colonel Partington), Chris Cooper (Lieutenant Gerke), Richard Jenkins (Agent Boshane), Daniel Green (Dickie Thurman), Anthony Anderson (Jamaal), Mongo Brownlee (Lee Harvey). Directed by Peter Farrelly and Bobby Farrelly and produced by the Farrellys and Bradley Thomas. Screenplay by the Farrellys and Mike Cerrone.

Me, Myself & Irene is a labored and sour comedy that rouses itself to create real humor, and then settles back glumly into an impenetrable plot and characters who keep repeating the same schtick, hoping maybe this time it will work. It stars Jim Carrey in a role that mires him in versions of the same gags, over and over. Renee Zellweger costars as a woman who stays at his side for no apparent reason except that the script requires her to.

The movie is by the Farrelly brothers, Peter and Bobby, whose *There's Something About Mary* still causes me to smile whenever I think about it, and whose *Kingpin* is a buried treasure. They worked with Carrey in *Dumb and Dumber,* which has some very big laughs in it, but this time their formula of scatology, sexuality, political incorrectness, and cheerful obscenity seems written by the numbers. The movie is as offensive as most of their work, which would be fine if it redeemed itself with humor. It doesn't. There is, for example, an extended passage making fun of an albino that is not funny at all, ever, in any part, but painfully drones on and on until the filmmakers cop out and make him the pal of the heroes.

Carrey plays a Rhode Island state trooper who puts up with shocking insults to his manhood and uniform and manages somehow to be a sunny Dr. Jeckyl, until he finally snaps and allows his Mr. Hyde to roam free. As the nice guy (named Charlie), he keeps smiling after his wife presents him with three black babies, fathered by a dwarf limo driver and Mensa member. He even keeps smiling when his neighbor allows his dog to defecate on his lawn, while the neighbor's wife steals his newspaper, and when the guys in the barbershop laugh at his attempts to enforce the law.

Years pass in this fashion. His wife runs off with the little genius. His sons stay with him, growing into enormous lads who are brilliant at school but use the MF-word as if it were punctuation (they learned it by watching Richard Pryor and Chris Rock videos). The movie must think all African-Americans are required by statute or genetics to repeat the word ceaselessly (it might have been funnier to have all three boys talk like Sam Donaldson).

After the evil side of his personality ("Hank") breaks free, Carrey starts kicking butt and taking no prisoners. Through twists unnecessary to describe, he hooks up with the perky, pretty Irene (Renee Zellweger), and they become fugitives from the law, pursued by the evil Lt. Gerke (Chris Cooper) for reasons that have something to do with environmental scandals, country clubs, bribery, and cover-ups; the plot is so murky we abandon curiosity and simply accept that Carrey and Zellweger are on the run, and the bad guys are chasing them.

The movie has defecation jokes, urination jokes, dildo jokes, flasher jokes, and a chicken that must be thoroughly annoyed by the dilemma it finds itself in. Not many of the jokes are very funny, and some seem plain desperate. I did laugh a lot during a sequence when Carrey tries to put a wounded cow out of its misery, but most of the time I sat quietly reflecting that the Farrelly brand of humor is a high-wire act; it involves great risks and is a triumph if they get to the other side, but ugly when they fail.

Carrey has a plastic face and body, and does remarkable things with his expressions. As Charlie he's all toothy grins and friendliness. As Hank, his face twists into an evil scowl, and his voice is electronically lowered into a more menacing register. Problem is, although it's sort of funny to see Charlie reacting to the insulting ways people treat him, it is rarely funny to see him transform himself into Hank, who then takes revenge. Hank is not really a comic character, and it's a miscalculation to allow him to dominate most of the movie.

Irene, the Zellweger character, has not been invented fresh with a specific comic purpose, but is simply a recycled version of the character she usually plays. Her job is to be loyal and sensible, lay down the law, pout, smile, and be shocked. It is a thankless task; she's like the on-screen representative of the audience.

The Farrellys are gifted and have made me laugh as loudly as anyone since the golden age of Mel Brooks. They have scored before and will no doubt score again. This time they go for broke, and get there.

Note: The film is dedicated to the late Gene Siskel, whose enthusiasm for Kingpin *came at a crucial time for the Farrellys, encouraging them to push ahead with* There's Something About Mary.

Me Myself I ★ ★ ★
R, 104 m., 2000

Rachel Griffiths (Pamela), David Roberts (Robert), Sandy Winton (Ben), Yael Stone (Stacey), Shaun Loseby (Douglas), Trent Sullivan (Rupert), Rebecca Frith (Terri), Felix Williamson (Geoff). Directed by Pip Karmel and produced by Fabien Liron. Screenplay by Karmel.

Consider now Rachel Griffiths. I first noticed her as the best friend with the infectious grin in *Muriel's Wedding*, the quirky Australian comedy. She was the lusty pig farmer's daughter who married the earnest student in *Jude*. In *Hilary and Jackie*, she played the sister of the doomed musician, and won an Oscar nomination. She was wonderful in two films that didn't find wide distribution: *My Son, the Fanatic*, where she played a hooker who forms a sincere friendship with a middle-aged Pakistani taxi driver in the British Midlands, and *Among Giants*, where she was a backpacking rock climber who signs up for the summer with a crew of British power pylon painters. That was the movie where, on a bet, she traversed all four walls of a pub with her toes on

the wainscoting, finding fingerholds where she could.

It is quite possible that Griffiths made all of these movies without coming to your attention, since none of them were big box-office winners, and a depressing number of moviegoers march off like sheep to the weekend's top-grossing hot-air balloon. She's been in one hit, *My Best Friend's Wedding*, but not so's you'd notice. I think she is one of the most intensely interesting actresses at work today, and in *Me Myself I* she does something that is almost impossible: She communicates her feelings to us through reaction shots while keeping them a secret from the other characters. That makes us conspirators.

Griffiths is not a surface beauty but a sexy tomboy with classically formed features, whose appeal shines out through the intelligence in her eyes and her wry mouth. You cannot imagine her as a passive object of affection. If Hollywood romances were about who women were rather than how they looked, she'd be one of the most desirable women in the movies. To the discerning, she is anyway.

Me Myself I is a fantasy as contrived and satisfactory as a soap opera. Griffiths plays Pamela, a professional magazine writer in her thirties who smokes too much and keeps up her spirits with self-help mantras ("I deserve the best and I accept the best"). Her idea of a date is to open a bottle of wine and look at photos of guys she dated fifteen years ago. "Why did I let you go?" she asks the photo of Robert (David Roberts). She's attracted to a crisis counselor named Ben (Sandy Winton), but finds out he is happily married, with children.

Should she have married Robert all those years ago? An unexplained supernatural transfer takes place, and she gets a chance to find out. She's hit by a car, and the other driver is—herself. After a switch, she finds herself living in an alternate universe in which she did marry Robert, and they have three children. This, of course, is all perfectly consistent with the latest theories in movie metaphysics; only the mechanism of the transfer remains cloudy.

Here is the key to the transformation scenes: Pamela knows she is a replacement for the "real" Pamela in this parallel world, and so do we, but everyone else fails to notice the substitution (except for Rupert, the youngest, who asks her bluntly, "When's Mommy gonna be home?"). There are scenes involving cooking dinner, managing the house, and copiloting for Rupert during his toilet duties. And a sex life with Robert that he finds surprising and delightful, since he and his original Pamela had cooled off considerably.

In this parallel universe, Ben is single, not married, and she takes the chance to have an affair with him, despite the complication that now she is married, not single. When she thinks Robert has been unfaithful, she is outraged, as much on behalf of the other Pamela as for herself, although in the new geometries of the universe-switch they are equally guilty, or innocent. This new Robert also has to be trained to accept an independent woman. When she announces that she needs a new computer and he says, "We'll see," she jolts him with: "I'm not asking your permission."

There are sweet scenes in the film, and touching ones. My favorite moments come when Pamela does subtle double takes when she realizes how her life is different now, and why. The plot is not remarkably intelligent, but Pamela (or Griffiths) is, and her reaction shots, her conspiratorial sharing of her thoughts with us, is where the movie has its life.

Rachel Griffiths's career is humming right along, if the criteria is that she stars in good roles in interesting movies, and is able to use her gifts and her intriguing personality. It could stand some improvement if the criteria is that she appears in big hits and makes $20 million a picture. The odds are she is too unique to ever make that much money; she isn't generic enough. And remember that the weekend box-office derby is usually won by the movie appealing to teenage boys. She doesn't play the kinds of women who are visible to them yet. All of this is beside the point for evolved moviegoers such as ourselves, who know a star when we see one.

Men in Black II ★ ½
PG-13, 88 m., 2002

Tommy Lee Jones (Kay), Will Smith (Jay), Rip Torn (Zed), Lara Flynn Boyle (Serleena), Johnny Knoxville (Scrad/Charlie), Rosario Dawson (Laura Vasquez), Tony Shalhoub (Jeebs), Patrick Warburton (Tee), (voice of) Tim Blaney (Frank). Directed by Barry Sonnenfeld and produced by Walter F. Parkes and Laurie MacDonald. Screenplay by Robert Gordon and Barry Fanaro, based on the Malibu Comic by Lowell Cunningham.

Some sequels continue a story. Others repeat it. *Men in Black II* creates a new threat for the MIB, but recycles the same premise, which is that mankind can defeat an alien invasion by assigning agents in Ray-Bans to shoot them into goo. This is a movie that fans of the original might enjoy in a diluted sort of way, but there is no need for it—except, of course, to take another haul at the box office, where the 1997 movie grossed nearly $600 million worldwide.

The astonishing success of the original *MIB* was partly because it was fun, partly because it was unexpected. We'd never seen anything like it, while with *MIB II* we've seen something exactly like it. In the original, Tommy Lee Jones played a no-nonsense veteran agent, Will Smith was his trainee, Rip Torn was their gruff boss, and makeup artist Rick Baker and a team of f/x wizards created a series of fanciful, grotesque aliens. Although the aliens had the technology for interplanetary travel, they were no match for the big guns of the *MIB*.

In *MIB II*, the guns are even bigger and the aliens are even slimier, although they do take sexy human form when one of them, Serleena, morphs into Lara Flynn Boyle. Another one, named Scrad (Johnny Knoxville), turns into a human who has a second neck with a smaller version of the same head, although that is not as amusing as you might hope.

The plot: The aliens are here to capture something, I'm not sure what, that will allow them to destroy Earth. The top MIB agent is now Jay (Smith), who needs the help of Kay (Jones), but Kay's memory has been erased by a "deneuralizer" and must be restored so that he can protect whatever it is the aliens want. Kay is currently working at the post office, which might have inspired more jokes than it does.

Smith and Jones fit comfortably in their roles and do what they can, but the movie doesn't give them much to work with. The biggest contribution is a dog named Frank (voice by Tim Blaney), whose role is much expanded from the first movie. Frank is human in everything but form, a tough-talking streetwise canine who keeps up a running commentary as the reunited MIB chase aliens through New York. One of the eyewitnesses they question is a pizza waitress named Laura, played by the beautiful Rosario Dawson, who Jay likes so much he forgets to deneuralize.

The special effects are good, but often pointless. As the movie throws strange aliens at us, we aren't much moved—more like mildly interested. There's a subway worm at the outset that eats most of a train without being anything more than an obvious special effect (we're looking at the technique, not the worm), and later there are other aliens who look more like doodles at a concept session than anything we can get much worked up about. There is, however, a very odd scene set in a train-station locker, which is occupied by a chanting mob of little creatures who worship the keyholder, and I would have liked to see more of them: What possible worldview do they have? If *Men in Black III* opens with the occupants of the locker, I will at least have hope for it.

Men of Honor ★ ★ ★
R, 128 m., 2000

Cuba Gooding Jr. (Carl Brashear), Robert De Niro (Billy Sunday), Charlize Theron (Gwen), Aunjanue Ellis (Jo), Hal Holbrook (Mister Pappy), David Keith (Captain Hartigan), Michael Rapaport (Snowhill), Powers Boothe (Captain Pullman). Directed by George Tillman Jr. and produced by Robert Teitel. Screenplay by Scott Marshall Smith.

Carl Brashear was quite a guy. A black sharecropper's son without a high school education, he signed up for the navy right after World War II. Harry Truman had integrated the services, but the navy was slow to change, and African-Americans were guided toward two job choices: They could become a cook or an officer's valet. Brashear (Cuba Gooding Jr.) wanted to be a diver. *Men of Honor* tells the story of how he became one despite everything, and then how he insisted on returning to active duty after losing a lower leg in an onboard accident.

The movie is an old-fashioned biopic, and I mean that as a compliment. It isn't pumped up with phony action scenes, but follows the curve of Brashear's life as it intersects with another man, Master Chief Billy Sunday (Robert De Niro), a redneck who at first hates Carl and then gradually changes his mind.

The most gripping scene in the movie is the reverse of the heroism in a lot of military movies. It isn't about thrills and explosions, but about tenacity, and most of it takes place within our own imaginations. To graduate from diving school, divers take a test where they have to assemble the pieces of a pump while working more or less in the dark, underwater. Brashear's test is rigged to make it almost impossible to pass. The water is so cold that long submersion could be fatal. Hour after hour, Brashear stays down there on the bottom.

De Niro's character is opposed to the idea of a black navy diver, but his master chief is first and foremost a diver, and if you love doing something enough, you come to respect others who do it well. The chief also comes from a dirt-farm background, and has another problem, alcoholism, which tests his marriage to the patient Gwen (Charlize Theron). There is also a good woman in Brashear's life: Jo (Aunjanue Ellis), the Harlem librarian who tutors him in reading when he has trouble with written exams.

The ugliest opponent of Brashear's dream is "Mister Pappy" (Hal Holbrook), the commanding officer of the group, who seems like a cross between Ahab and Queeg. "There may come a day when a colored diver graduates from this school," he thunders, "but it won't be while I'm here." I wonder if Mister Pappy needs to be such a nut job; surveying his realm from living quarters in a water tower, he is less a commanding officer than a refugee from the guys with the butterfly nets.

Cuba Gooding is the kind of actor who bubbles even when he's idling. That kind of energy wouldn't be appropriate here, and he dials down and delivers a strong, convincing performance. The secret of Carl Brashear's success is not complicated: He won't give up, he won't go away, and eventually his very presence shames navy men who cannot deny his ability.

The racism that permeated American life in the 1940s is shown in scenes like the one where all of the other navy trainees refuse to share a bunkhouse with Brashear—all except for one, Snowhill (Michael Rapaport), who stays. Snowhill's reason is not some noble liberal sentiment, but more simple and personal, and my guess is that this line, of all the dialogue in the movie, is the most likely to have been taken straight from real life. "I'm from Wisconsin," he explains.

This is the second feature by George Tillman Jr., whose *Soul Food* was a success in 1997. Here he depends on a strong story and solid performances and avoids unnecessary flash; the movie sells itself. But the screenplay betrays some evidence of knee-jerk front-office requirements. How else to explain the character of Gwen, the master chief's wife? She is simply unnecessary to the picture, and although Theron's performance is professional, it's beside the point.

Such details aren't important compared to the central strength of the film, which shows one American life, lived well and proudly. We glorify overpaid sports heroes and put them on postage stamps, but what about a man like Brashear, who wanted to serve his country and wouldn't take no for an answer?

Note: The R rating for this film, given because of salty talk by sailors, is inappropriate. This is an inspirational film for teenagers.

Metropolis ★ ★ ★ ★
PG-13, 107 m., 2002

With the voices of: Jamieson Price (Duke Red), Yuka Imoto (Tima), Kei Kobayashi (Kenichi), Kouki Okada (Rock), Toshio Furukawa (General), Dave Mallow (Pero), Scott Weinger (Atlas). Directed by Taro Rin and produced by Yutaka Maseba and Haruyo Kanesaku. Screenplay by Osamu Tezuka and Katsuhiro Otomo, based on Tezuka's comic book. Dubbed into English.

There's something about vast futuristic cities that stirs me. Perhaps they awaken memories of my twelfth year, when I sat in the basement on hot summer days and read through the lower reaches of science-fiction magazines: *Imagination, Other Worlds, Amazing.* On the covers, towering cities were linked by sky-bridges, and buses were cigar-shaped rockets. In the foreground a bug-eyed monster was attacking a screaming heroine in an aluminum brassiere. Even now, the image of a dirigible tethered to the top of the Empire State Building is more thrilling to me than the space shuttle, which is merely real.

Those visions are goofy and yet at the same time exhilarating. What I like about Tokyo is that it looks like a 1940s notion of a future city. I placed *Dark City* first on my list of the best films of 1998, loved *Blade Runner*'s visuals more than its story, liked the taxicabs in the sky in *The Fifth Element.* Now here is *Metropolis,* one of the best animated films I have ever seen, and the city in this movie is not simply a backdrop or a location, but one of those movie places that colonize our memory.

The Japanese anime is named after the 1926 Fritz Lang silent classic, and is based on a 1949 *manga* (comic book) by the late Osamu Tezuka, which incorporated Lang's images. The movie was directed by Taro Rin and written by the anime legend Katsuhiro Otomo, who directed *Akira* and wrote *Roujin Z.* It uses the Lang film as a springboard into a surprisingly thoughtful, ceaselessly exciting sci-fi story about a plot to use humanoids to take over the city. In the romance between Tima, the half-human heroine, and Kenichi, the detective's nephew who falls in love with her, the movie asks whether a machine can love. The answer is an interesting spin on *A.I.* and *Blade Runner,* because the debate goes on within Tima herself, between her human and robotic natures.

The film opens with astonishing visuals of the great city, which, like Lang's Metropolis, exists on several levels above- and belowground. We see the skyscraping Ziggurat, a complex of towers linked by bridges and braces. The building seems to be a symbol of progress, but actually masks a scheme by the evil Duke Red to wrest control of the city from elected officials. Deep inside Ziggurat is a throne suspended in a hall filled with giant computer chips; it is intended for Tima, a humanoid in the image of Duke Red's dead daughter, built for him by the insane Dr. Lawton. Tima's role will be to merge the power of computers and the imagination of the human brain into a force that will possess the city.

Rock, the adopted son of Duke Red, hates this plan and wants to destroy Tima. He is jealous that his father prefers this artificial girl to his son, and believes Duke Red himself should sit on the throne. Other characters include an elderly detective who arrives in the city to explore the mystery of Ziggurat; his nephew Kenichi becomes the hero.

The story is told with enormous energy; animation is more versatile than live action in making cataclysmic events comprehensible. Mob scenes at the beginning and explosions and destruction throughout have a clarity and force that live action would necessarily dissipate. The animation owes less to mainstream American animation than to the comic book or *manga* tradition of Japan, where both comics and animation are considered art forms worthy of adult attention.

In the figures of Tima and Kenichi, the movie follows the anime tradition of heroes who are childlike, have enormous eyes, seem innocent and threatened. The other characters have more realistic faces and proportions, and indeed resemble Marvel superheroes (the contrast between these characters' looks is unusual: Imagine Nancy visiting Spider-Man). The backgrounds and action sequences look like the anime version of big-budget Hollywood f/x thrillers.

The music, too, is Western. The introduction to the city is scored with Dixieland, Joe Primrose sings "St. James Infirmary" at one point, and the climactic scene is accompanied by Ray Charles singing "I Can't Stop Loving You" (the effect is a little like "We'll Meet Again" at the end of *Dr. Strangelove*).

The movie is so visually rich I want to see it again to look in the corners and appreciate the details. Like all the best Japanese anime, it pays attention to little things. There is a scene where an old man consults a book of occult lore. He opens it and starts to read. A page flips over. He flips it back in place. Considering that every action in an animated film requires thousands of drawings, a moment like the page flip might seem unnecessary, but all through the movie we get little touches like that. The filmmakers are not content with ordinary locations. Consider the Hotel Coconut, which seems to be a lobby with a desk clerk who checks guests into ancient luxury railway carriages.

Metropolis is not a simpleminded animated cartoon, but a surprisingly thoughtful and challenging adventure that looks into the nature of life and love, the role of workers, the rights (if any) of machines, the pain of a father's rejection, and the fascist zeal that lies behind Ziggurat. This is not a remake of the 1926 classic, but a wild elaboration. If you have never seen a Japanese anime, start here. If you love them, *Metropolis* proves you are right.

The Mexican ★ ★ ★
R, 123 m., 2001

Brad Pitt (Jerry Welbach), Julia Roberts (Samantha Barzel), James Gandolfini (Leroy), Bob Balaban (Nayman), J. K. Simmons (Ted), David Krumholtz (Beck), Richard Coca (Car Thief), Michael Cerveris (Frank), Gene Hackman (Margolese). Directed by Gore Verbinski and produced by Lawrence Bender and John Baldecchi. Screenplay by J. H. Wyman.

The Mexican stars Brad Pitt and Julia Roberts, and involves a quirky, offbeat relationship—but it's not between Brad and Julia, it's between Julia and James Gandolfini. I like it that way. Considering how badly Jerry and Samantha, the Brad and Julia characters, get along when they're together, a whole movie involving them would be a long, shrill slog. Gandolfini comes in from left field and provides a character with dimension and surprises, bringing out the best in Roberts. Their dialogue scenes are the best reason to see the movie.

The setup: The Mexican of the title is a priceless handgun that a Mafioso named Margolese (Gene Hackman) desires above all else. Margolese is in prison for complicated reasons, and Jerry, who was sort of responsible, has been trying to work off his debt (and stay alive) by running errands for Margolese's lieutenant, Nayman (Bob Balaban). But Jerry is unreliable because he's under the thumb of the demanding Samantha. His excuse for blowing an important assignment: "When you told me to pick up the thing at the thing, well, Samantha, she wanted the car to pick up some things."

Jerry gets one more chance: Go to Mexico, meet a man in a bar, pick up the handgun, and bring it back to America. Samantha blows her top: Jerry promised to take her to Vegas. Jerry explains that if he does not do the errand, he will be killed. Samantha is unmoved and throws his clothes out the window. Jerry leaves for Mexico. Samantha says she will never speak to him again. She leaves for Vegas, and is kidnapped by Leroy, the Gandolfini character.

That means Jerry and Samantha spend most of the movie apart, and that has drawn complaints from critics who would have preferred these two megastars to share lots of screen time. But Roberts, curiously, hardly ever makes love stories involving people her age. Maybe she has so much wattage all by herself that pairing her with an equivalent dude would blow the fuses. Most of her movies involve older men (Richard Gere in *Pretty Woman*), or unavailable men (Dr. Jekyll and Mr Hyde in *Mary Reilly*), or unacceptable men *(Runaway Bride)*, or make her the heroine of stories with less significant men *(Erin Brockovich, Notting Hill)*. She hardly ever goes knee-to-knee with a guy she's in love with.

Here Gandolfini (from *The Sopranos*) comes in as Leroy, a big bruiser who kidnaps her for reasons that start out simple and grow increasingly complicated as the plot unfolds. They're both talkers, and soon they're bathing each other in confessions and insights. She talks a lot about Jerry, who is guilty of "blame-shifting," etc., and he nods in sympathy and offers advice at least as sound as she could find in a women's magazine. Then, while they're sitting in a diner, he exchanges a look with a guy sitting at the counter, and she says, "You had a moment there. What was that about?" And then their psychobabble moves into sublime territory.

These scenes make the movie special. The screenplay, by J. H. Wyman, could have easily been one of those dreary road stories where the guy and the girl head south together on a rendezvous with steamy love scenes and lots of bloody chases. Instead, this movie is *about* something. Not something terrifically profound, to be sure, but at least it prefers style and wit to tired, old ideas.

Wyman and the director, Gore Verbinski, intercut the story with various versions of the legend of the Mexican. The movie goes to sepiatone as we learn why the handgun is so valued and legendary. None of these legends agree, which is part of the fun, and meanwhile the real Mexican in the movie runs rings

about Jerry, a character so brain-swoggled by Samantha that he can think of little else.

There are lots of things I like in *The Mexican*. Jerry's idiotic attempts to change English into Spanish by adding an "o" to the end of every word. And the way a supporting character keeps explaining, "I'm just trying to do my portion." And the way Samantha zeroes in on Leroy and sees right through his defenses. And the way the movie is amused by its plot, and keeps a wry distance from it, instead of breathlessly chasing it around the screen.

Pitt and Roberts are good, too—maybe better like this than if they were together. I don't see what purpose it serves to complain they don't have every scene together. Usually when $20 million stars are put into movies, we have to look at them every second so the producers can be sure they're getting their money's worth. *The Mexican* is more like a 1940s Warner Bros. picture where the stars get a breather while the supporting actors entertain us. If it had been a Pitt/Roberts two-hander, there wouldn't have been room for Gandolfini's wonderful character, and that would have been a shame.

Me You Them ★ ★ ★
PG-13, 107 m., 2001

Regina Case (Darlene), Lima Duarte (Osias), Stenio Garcia (Zezinho), Luiz Carlos Vasconcelos (Ciro), Nilda Spencer (Raquel). Directed by Andrucha Waddington and produced by Flavio R. Tambellini, Leonardo M. de Barros, Pedro B. de Hollanda, and Waddington. Screenplay by Elena Soarez.

Me You Them tells the story of a peasant woman who creates a happy home with three men— one a provider, one genial, one lustful—while producing children who hardly resemble their reputed father. The film has inspired the usual analysis in feminist terms, with some critics finding the woman strong and others finding her victimized. I don't think ideology has as much to do with it as poverty. In a poor and dusty backwater of Brazil, this woman and all three men find a pragmatic solution to their problems.

The movie could have been a dumb sex comedy, but cares too much for its characters, and is too intrigued by how this unlikely household came into being. It stars Regina Case, "the Oprah of Brazil," as Darlene, a strong country girl who isn't beautiful, but has an earth-mother energy that men are drawn helplessly toward. She has big teeth, she wipes her hands on her dress, she can work in the fields all day, and if she takes you to her bed, you'll have your work cut out for you.

The film opens with Darlene leaving her provincial town. Three years later she's back from the city, with a baby but no husband. She wants her grandmother to bless the child. But her grandmother is dead, and now she is bereft until Osias (Lima Duarte) offers her a deal: Marry him, and she can move into his house. "Tomorrow I'll give you an answer," she says, and her answer is yes.

Osias is not a prize. He raises goats. As a married man, he assigns Darlene to care for the goats while he swings in his hammock, listening to his portable radio. Soon another child arrives, curiously a good deal darker in hue than Osias. A local colonel may know something about this. And eventually another man drifts into Darlene's life. This is Zezinho (Stenio Garcia), Osias's cousin, who is easy-going, gets along with everybody, helps Darlene with the goats, and seems to sort of move in. Osias rationalizes this as providing a home for his cousin rather than thinking about the sexual implications, even though in due time another baby arrives, this one with blue eyes that Osias didn't supply.

Life continues peacefully, Osias listening to his radio and content to play the husband and father rather than to perform such duties in the flesh. Then down by the river Darlene encounters a sexy young man named Ciro (Luiz Carlos Vasconcelos), and feels passionate lust for the first time. When Ciro turns up at the compound, he doesn't like the arrangements, and wants Darlene to leave with him. Osias is possessive and angry, and it's up to Zezinho to explain the facts of life to him: Either they build another room for Ciro, or Darlene will leave, and then they will be lonely and sad.

Me You Them is "based on a true story," we are told, although movies should follow those words with the disclaimer, "as fictionalized according to our needs." It takes place in a remote Brazilian state of stark landscapes and scarce water, where it is usually autumn and the trees stand sad without their leaves. The director, Andrucha Waddington, has worked with cinematographer Breno Silveira to make this a place of dusty beauty, the reds, browns, and ochres fading into deep shadows. The key to the story is that these people so clearly seem to live here, to depend on this land, to have no place else to go. In a society with more movement and choice, the *Me You Them* household would lack what it has here: necessity.

It has been observed that Darlene essentially needs three men to give her one complete husband. One provides shelter, one provides companionship, one provides sex. This doesn't mean she exploits them; the movie also demonstrates that each man is given the opportunity to provide what is in his nature. That is why the household works. None of these men really wants the role of the other two. Even the jealousy of Osias is based more on pride of possession than pride of paternity; if the children are technically considered his, he is content not to have to rouse himself from his hammock to actually father them.

Me You Them, written by Elena Soarez, works because the story is sympathetic to the feelings of the characters, observes them as individuals, is not concerned with the sensational aspects of their household but in the gradual way practical matters work themselves out. In the end this is not a story about sex but about economics. The characters have probably never heard of Marx, but they find his formula useful: From each, according to his abilities; to each, according to his needs.

Michael Jordan at the Max ★ ★
NO MPAA RATING, 45 m., 2000

A documentary directed by Jim Stern and John Kempf and produced by John Kempf, Steve Kempf, and Stern.

It is awesome to see Michael Jordan on the five-story IMAX screen, and to hear the roar of the crowd in surround stereo. Any Jordan fan will enjoy *Michael Jordan at the Max* on that level. Unfortunately, that's the only level there is. As a documentary, the film plays like one of those packages NBC cobbles together before a semifinals round: game footage, talking heads, and a narrator who intones the usual mantras about His Airness.

We might as well get used to the idea that there will never be a real documentary about Michael Jordan—one made with the full tools of the filmmaker's art, with its own point of view and insights beneath the surface. *Michael Jordan at the Max*, like almost everything that has been filmed or written about Jordan, is essentially just a promotional film for Jordan as a product. It plays like a commercial for itself.

Jordan is a private man—so private, that although he talks about his dead father in this film, there is no mention of his mother, his wife, or his children. His mother is seen and heard once; his wife is (I think) glimpsed briefly. I didn't expect an intimate display of private matters, but in this film Jordan is a man who lives on the basketball court and evaporates otherwise, except when starring in commercials. The only time we see him not wearing a basketball uniform is when he's wearing a suit while walking into the dressing room.

Michael Jordan at the Max takes as its framework that remarkable final championship season, and there are moments from games we remember so well, against Indiana, Seattle, and Utah. But they aren't analytical or even very informative—just colorful shots of Michael scoring again and again (he misses two shots in the entire film). Sometimes you have to know the story to realize what you're seeing, as when we overhear Steve Kerr, during a time out, tell Michael that if he gets the ball he will not miss the shot—and then sinking his famous gamewinning two-pointer. The movie shows this, but doesn't underline it or explain it.

Jordan's career is commented on in interviews with Bob Greene, Phil Jackson, Bob Costas, Johnny "Red" Kerr, and others. The professional sportswriters who covered the games are not consulted. Not a word by the others seems spontaneous; the photography is flawless, like a studio portrait, and so are their comments, which sound (even if they aren't) scripted and rehearsed. I don't think we're seeing take one. Nobody ever fumbles, or pauses, or searches for a thought. They're all so sure what they want to say—and so is Jordan, interviewed in the United Center, his words so familiar they are like a politician's basic stump speech, perfected after many deliveries.

Season after season, Gene Siskel explained the Bulls to me (and anyone else who would listen). He was smarter on basketball than anyone else I've ever encountered. He noticed small things and drew lessons from them (why Dennis Rodman missed the first free throw, why Toni Kukoc was more willing to take a bad shot than a good one). He watched the games not only as a fan, but as an analyst. He was to fans as Jackson is to coaches.

That taste of real insight left me feeling empty after *Michael Jordan at the Max*, with its platitudes and the same familiar sentences of praise we've heard so many times before, about how hard Jordan practiced, and how fierce was his desire to win, and what a leader he was. Yes, yes, yes, but there was *strategy* at work too. Jordan outplayed his opponents on some nights. He outthought them on every night. By treating him like a god the movie diminishes the achievement of the man.

This movie has no curiosity about the way Jordan read the game and its players. It has the spirit of a promotional film. It's bright and colorful, and it makes it fun for us to revisit those cherished Bulls triumphs, but there is no bite. It's the official, authorized version. On the giant IMAX screen it has an undeniable impact, and as a Bulls fan I enjoyed it. But as a film critic I was disappointed: Shrink this to a videocassette, pop it into your VCR machine, and you might as well be looking at an NBA highlight reel.

Mifune ★ ★ ★
R, 99 m., 2000

Anders W. Berthelsen (Kresten), Iben Hjejle (Liva), Jesper Asholt (Rud, Kresten's Brother), Sofie Grabol (Claire, Kresten's Wife), Emil Tarding (Bjarke, Liva's Brother), Anders Hove (Gerner), Paprika Steen (Pernille), Mette Bratlann (Nina). Directed by Soren Kragh-Jacobsen and produced by Birgitte Hlad. Screenplay by Kragh-Jacobsen and Anders Thomas Jensen.

Mifune is the latest work with the imprimatur of Dogma '95, a group of Danish filmmakers who signed a cinematic "vow of chastity"—reserving poverty and obedience, apparently, for TV directors. Dogma films are encouraged to use natural light and sound, real locations, no props or music brought in from outside, hand-held cameras and "no directorial touches," as if the auteur theory was shamelessly immodest. Of the Dogma films I have seen *(The Idiots, Celebration)* and the Dogma wanna-be *julien donkey-boy, Mifune* is the most fun and the least dogmatic. With just a few more advances, like props, sets, lighting, music, and style, the Dogma crowd will be making real movies.

Only kidding. But in truth, Dogma '95 is as much publicity as conviction, and its films contain more, not less, directorial style. Like the American indie movement, they use small budgets and unsprung plots, but that's not a creed; it's a strategy for making a virtue of necessity. That the Dogma films have been good and interesting is encouraging, but a coincidence.

The story of *Mifune* breaks down no barriers but is in the tradition of offbeat romantic comedy, and one can imagine it being remade by Hollywood with Jeff Daniels as the hero, Martin Short as the retarded brother, and Angelina Jolie as the hooker. It is a "commercial" story, and all the more entertaining for being so, but Soren Kragh-Jacobsen's low-rent version has a freshness and spontaneity that the Hollywood version would probably lose. There's something about ground-level filmmaking that makes an audience feel a movie is getting away with something.

The story begins with the wedding of Kresten (Anders W. Berthelsen) and Claire (Sofie Grabol). If the eye contact between Kresten and Claire's sexy mother is any indication, this marriage might have soon grown very complicated, but Kresten's past catches up with him and dooms the marriage (not, luckily for Claire, before a wedding night that seems to set Guinness records). Kresten learns that his father has died, and he has avoided telling his wife and snotty in-laws about his family's ramshackle farm, his retarded brother, or his mother who hung herself on "one of the oldest trees in Denmark." ("He grew up," observes A. O. Scott, "in the Danish translation of a Tennessee Williams play.")

Kresten returns to the farm, which is a run-down shambles with water damage and animals making free use of the house, and finds his brother, Rud (Jesper Asholt), drinking under the table that bears the father's corpse. What to do? Rud cannot take care of himself, the farm is falling to pieces, and this is not the kind of situation he can bring Claire into. Desperate, Kresten hires a housekeeper named Liva, played by Iben Hjejle (she plays Laura, the lost love, in *High Fidelity*). Liva is desperate, too; we learn she was a hooker, is being pursued by an angry pimp, and receives alarming phone calls.

At this point in the story not even the most stringent application of Dogma vows can prevent the director and his audience from hurtling confidently toward the inevitable development in which Kresten and Liva fall in love and form a sort of instant family with Rud as honorary child. Dogma forbids genre conventions, but this story is made from the ground up of nothing else—and more power to it.

If the story is immensely satisfying in a traditional way, the style has its own delights. Kragh-Jacobsen feels free to meander. Every single scene doesn't have to pull its weight and move the plot marker to the next square. Asides and irrelevant excursions are allowed. Characters arrive at conclusions by a process we can follow on the screen, instead of signaling us that they are only following the script. And there is an earthiness to the unknown actors, especially Asholt as Rud, that grounds the story in the infinite mystery of real personalities.

Watching *Mifune* and the other Dogma films (except for *julien*, which is more of an exercise in video art), we're taught a lesson. It's not a new lesson; John Cassavetes taught it years ago and directors as various as Mike Leigh and Henry Jaglom demonstrate it. It has to do with the feel of a film, regardless of its budget or the faces in the cast. Some films feel free, and others seem caged. Some seem to happen while we watch, and others seem to know their own fates. Some satisfy by marching toward foregone conclusions, and others (while they may arrive at the same place) seem surprised and delighted by how they turn out.

Mifune is like a lesson in film watching. If you see enough films like this, you learn to be suspicious of high-gloss films that purr along mile after mile without any bumps. If a film like this were a car and it stalled, you could go under the hood with a wrench. When fancy films stall, you need a computer expert.

Minority Report ★ ★ ★ ★
PG-13, 145 m., 2002

Tom Cruise (John Anderton), Samantha Morton (Agatha [Precog]), Max von Sydow (Lamarr Burgess), Colin Farrell (Danny Witwer), Tim Blake Nelson (Gideon), Steve Harris (Jad), Neal McDonough (Officer Fletcher). Directed by Steven Spielberg and produced by Jan de Bont, Bonnie Curtis, Gerald R. Molen, and Walter F. Parkes. Screenplay by Scott Frank and Jon Cohen, based on a short story by Philip K. Dick.

At a time when movies think they have to choose between action and ideas, Steven Spielberg's *Minority Report* is a triumph—a film that works on our minds and our emotions. It is a thriller and a human story, a movie of ideas that's also a whodunit. Here is a master filmmaker at the top of his form, working with a star, Tom Cruise, who generates complex human feelings even while playing an action hero.

I complained earlier this summer of awkward joins between live action and CGI; I felt the action sequences in *Spider-Man* looked too cartoonish, and that *Star Wars: Episode II,* by using computer effects to separate the human actors from the sets and CGI characters, felt disconnected and sterile. Now here is Spielberg using every trick in the book and matching them without seams, so that no matter how he's achieving his effects, the focus is always on the story and the characters.

The movie turns out to be eerily prescient, using the term "precrime" to describe stopping crimes before they happen; how could Spielberg have known the government would be using the same term in the summer of 2002? In his film, inspired by, but much expanded from, a short story by Philip K. Dick, Tom Cruise is John Anderton, chief of the Department of Precrime in the District of Columbia, where there has not been a murder in six years. Soon, it appears, there will be a murder—committed by Anderton himself.

The year is 2054. Futuristic skyscrapers coexist with the famous Washington monuments and houses from the nineteenth century. Anderton presides over an operation controlling three "precogs," precognitive humans who drift in a flotation tank, their brain waves tapped by computers. They're able to pick up thoughts of premeditated murders and warn the cops, who swoop down and arrest the would-be perpetrators before the killings can take place.

Because this is Washington, any government operation that is high-profile and successful inspires jealousy. Anderton's superior, bureau director Burgess (Max von Sydow), takes pride in him, and shields him from bureaucrats like Danny Witwer (Colin Farrell) from the Justice Department. As the precrime strategy prepares to go national, Witwer seems to have doubts about its wisdom—or he is only jealous of its success?

Spielberg establishes these characters in a dazzling future world, created by art director Alex McDowell, that is so filled with details large and small that we stop trying to figure out everything and surrender with a sigh. Some of the details: a computer interface that floats in midair, manipulated by Cruise with the gestures of a symphony conductor; advertisements that crawl up the sides of walls and address you personally; cars that whisk around town on magnetic cushions; robotic "spiders" that can search a building in minutes by performing a retinal scan on everyone in it. *Blade Runner,* also inspired by a Dick story, shows a future world in decay; *Minority Report* offers a more optimistic preview.

The plot centers on a rare glitch in the visions of the precogs. Although "the precogs are never wrong," we're told, "sometimes . . . they disagree." The dissenting precog is said to have filed a minority report, and in the case of Anderton the report is crucial, because otherwise he seems a certain candidate for arrest as a precriminal. Of course, if you could outsmart the precog system, you would have committed the perfect crime.

Finding himself the hunted instead of the hunter, Anderton teams up with Agatha (Samantha Morton), one of the precogs, who seemed to be trying to warn him of his danger. Because she floats in a fluid tank, Agatha's muscles are weakened (have precogs any rights of their own?), and Anderton has to half-drag her as they flee from the precrime police. One virtuoso sequence shows her foreseeing the immediate future and advising Anderton about what to do to elude what the cops are going to do next. The choreography, timing, and wit of this sequence make it, all by itself, worth the price of admission.

But there are other stunning sequences. Consider a scene where the "spiders" search a rooming house, and Anderton tries to elude capture by immersing himself in a tub of ice water. This sequence begins with an overhead cross section of the apartment building and several of its inhabitants, and you would swear it has to be done with a computer, but no: This is an actual, physical set, and the elegant camera moves were elaborately choreographed. It's typical of Spielberg that, having devised this astonishing sequence, he propels it for dramatic purposes and doesn't simply exploit it to show off his cleverness. And watch the exquisite timing as one of the spiders, on its way out, senses something and pauses in midstep.

Tom Cruise's Anderton is an example of how a star's power can be used to add more dimension to a character than the screenplay might supply. He compels us to worry about him, and even in implausible action sequences (like falls from dizzying heights) he distracts us by making us care about the logic of the chase, not the possibility of the stunt.

Samantha Morton's character ("Agatha" is a nod to Miss Christie) has few words and seems exhausted and frightened most of the time, providing an eerie counterpoint for Anderton's man of action. There is poignance in her helplessness, and Spielberg shows it in a virtuoso two-shot, as she hangs over Anderton's shoulder while their eyes search desperately in opposite directions. This shot has genuine mystery. It has to do with the composition and lighting and timing and breathing, and like the entire movie, it furthers the cold, frightening hostility of the world Anderton finds himself in. The cinematographer, Janusz Kaminski, who has worked with Spielberg before (not least on *Schindler's List*), is able to get an effect that's powerful and yet bafflingly simple.

The plot I will avoid discussing in detail. It is as ingenious as any *film noir* screenplay, and plays far better than some. It's told with such clarity that we're always sure what Spielberg wants us to think, suspect, and know. And although there is a surprise at the end, there is no cheating: The crime story holds water.

American movies are in the midst of a transition period. Some directors place their trust in technology. Spielberg, who is a master of technology, trusts only story and character, and then uses everything else as a workman uses his tools. He makes *Minority Report with* the new technology; other directors seem to be trying to make their movies *from* it. This film is such a virtuoso high-wire act, daring so much, achieving it with such grace and skill. *Minority Report* reminds us why we go to the movies in the first place. ☞

Miss Congeniality ★ ★
PG-13, 110 m., 2000

Sandra Bullock (Gracie Hart), Benjamin Bratt (Eric Matthews), Michael Caine (Victor "Vic" Melling), William Shatner (Stan Fields), Jennifer Gareis (Miss New Jersey), Wendy Raquel Robinson (Miss California), Candice Bergen (Kathy), Heather Burns (Miss Rhode Island). Directed by Donald Petrie and produced by Sandra Bullock. Screenplay by Marc Lawrence, Katie Ford, and Caryn Lucas.

Something about Sandra Bullock strikes me the right way. She has a warmth that gets you smiling even when the material is weak—as it sometimes is, since she has uncertain luck in choosing projects. In *Miss Congeniality*, she makes her way through a screenplay that in other hands would have been a dreary sitcom mishmash, and her presence transforms it into a less dreary sitcom mishmash.

She has the producer's credit on the movie. That means she thought this project was a good fit. Since the material is tired and routine, what was she thinking of? Maybe she's not ambitious enough. Comedies will find her; she doesn't need to go looking for them. Stars with clout usually take on personal projects to break out of their typecasting, not to reinforce it.

In *Miss Congeniality*, Bullock plays another version of a familiar role for her, in which she begins the film looking unglamorous and then undergoes a transformation. Sometimes that happens in the eye of the beholder, as it did in *While You Were Sleeping*. This time, it happens because of a big-time beauty makeover. She starts as an FBI agent and ends up as a beauty contest finalist, and although churls may argue she's not convincing as a beauty queen, they are not of this Earth.

Before she grows up to become an FBI agent, she's a tomboy who can beat up the other kids at school. As an agent, she clomps around looking hearty and graceless, pounding on punching bags and running red lights on her way to Starbucks, until she's assigned to impersonate a contestant at a beauty pageant. As an undercover agent, she can help head off a rumored terrorist threat to the event.

Uh-huh. But there are some funny scenes as Michael Caine, a disgraced but still brilliant "beauty consultant," supervises her makeover and teaches her how to dress less like a model for L.L. Bean campwear. I saw this movie and Mel Gibson's *What Women Want* within a few days of each other, and in both stories the lead characters get a lot of mileage out of their unfamiliarity with feminine beauty products. Gibson has the edge on depilatories, but Bullock does a better job of not being able to walk like a woman.

The plot also involves Candice Bergen as the founder of the beauty pageant, and Benjamin Bratt as Bullock's FBI partner. No prizes for figuring out that Bergen is up to more than she seems, and that after Bullock's transformation the scales fall from Bratt's eyes and he realizes, gosh, she cleans up real well. Bullock's character has a thing she does where she snorts through her nose—kind of a genteel barnyard sound—and she even stops doing that after a while.

Miss Congeniality is harmless fun of a silly sort. It isn't bad so much as it lacks any ambition to be more than it so obviously is. I smiled during it, and enjoyed Bullock, but then again I got to see it for free, and I'm the guy who thinks *Speed 2* is a good movie, something even Bullock doesn't believe. Opening *Miss Congeniality* against more than a dozen big-name holiday releases is kind of suicidal. With that kind of competition, you gotta be more than congenial.

Mission: Impossible 2 ★ ★ ★
PG-13, 120 m., 2000

Tom Cruise (Ethan Hunt), Dougray Scott (Sean Ambrose), Thandie Newton (Nyah Hall), Richard Roxburgh (Hugh Stamp), John Polson (Billy Baird), Brendan Gleeson (McCloy), Rade Sherbedgia (Dr. Nekhorvich), Ving Rhames (Luther Stickell). Directed by John Woo and produced by Tom Cruise and Paula Wagner. Screenplay by Robert Towne, based on a story by Ronald D. Moore and Brannon Braga and the television series created by Bruce Geller.

If James Bond is still around at the end of the twenty-first century, he will look a lot like Ethan Hunt. The hero of the *Mission: Impossible* series is a 007 for our time.

That means: Sex is more of a surprise and a distraction than a lifestyle. Stunts and special effects don't interrupt the plot, but *are* the plot. The hero's interest in new consumer items runs more toward cybergadgets than sports cars. He isn't a patriot working for his government, but a hired gun working for a shadowy international agency. And he doesn't smoke, hardly drinks, and is in the physical condition of a triathlete.

The new Bond, in short, is a driven, overachieving professional—not the sort of gentleman sophisticate the British spy family used to cultivate. His small talk consists not of lascivious puns, but geekspeak. When he raises an eyebrow, it's probably not his, because he's a master of disguise and can hide behind plastic masks so realistic even his cinematographer doesn't know for sure.

The first *Mission: Impossible* (1996) had a plot no one understood. *Mission: Impossible 2* has a plot you don't need to understand. It's been cobbled together by the expert Hollywood script doctor Robert Towne out of elements of other movies, notably Hitchcock's *Notorious*, from which he takes the idea that the hero first falls in love with the heroine, then heartlessly assigns her to resume an old affair with an ex-lover in order to spy on his devious plans. In both films, the woman agrees to do this because she loves the hero. In *Notorious*, the hero loses respect for the woman after she does what he asks. The modern hero is too amoral to think of this.

Towne's contribution is quite skillful, especially if it's true, as I've heard, that he had to write around major f/x sequences that director John Woo had already written and fine-tuned. His strategy is to make Ethan Hunt (Tom Cruise) into a sympathetic yet one-dimensional character, so that motivation and emotion will not be a problem. He's a cousin of Clint Eastwood's Man With No Name—a hero defined not by his values but by his actions.

The villain remains in the Bond tradition: A megalomaniac who seeks power or wealth by holding the world ransom. In this case, he seeks control of a deadly virus, but the virus is what Hitchcock called a MacGuffin; it doesn't matter what it is, just so it's something everyone desires or fears. The movie wisely spends little time on the details, but is clever in the way it uses the virus to create time pressure: Twenty-four hours after you're exposed, you die, and that leads to a nicely timed showdown involving the hero, the woman he loves, the villain, the virus, and a ticking clock.

Thandie Newton plays the woman, and the most significant thing about her character is that she's still alive at the end, and apparently available for the sequel. The Bond girls have had a depressing mortality rate over the years, but remember that 007 was formed in the promiscuous 1960s, while Ethan Hunt lives in a time when even spies tend to stay with old relationships, maybe because it's so tiresome to start new ones.

Newton's character is unique in the way she plays a key role in the plot, taking her own initiative. Bond girls, even those with formidable fighting skills, were instruments of the plot; Newton's Nyah Hall not only lacks a name that is a pun, but shockingly makes a unilateral decision that influences the outcome of the movie. The playing field will be more level in the *M:I* battle of the sexes.

For Tom Cruise, the series is a franchise, like Mel Gibson's *Lethal Weapon* movies. *M:I3* is already on the drawing board, again with John Woo as director, and there's no reason the sequels can't continue as long as Cruise can still star in action scenes (or their computer-generated manifestations). This is good for Cruise. By more or less underwriting his box-office clout, it gives him the freedom to experiment with more offbeat choices like *Eyes Wide Shut* and *Magnolia*.

As for the movie itself: If the first movie was entertaining as sound, fury, and movement, this one is more evolved, more confident, more surefooted in the way it marries minimal character development to seamless action. It is a global movie, flying no flag, requiring little di-

alogue, featuring characters who are Pavlovian in their motivation. It's more efficient than the Bond pictures, but not as much pure fun. In this new century, I have a premonition we'll be seeing more efficiency and less fun in a lot of different areas. The trend started about the time college students decided management was sexier than literature.

Mission to Mars ★ ★ ½
PG, 113 m., 2000

Gary Sinise (Jim McConnell), Tim Robbins (Woody Blake), Don Cheadle (Luke Graham), Connie Nielsen (Terri Fisher), Jerry O'Connell (Phil Ohlmyer), Peter Outerbridge (Sergei Kirov), Kavan Smith (Nicholas Willis), Jill Teed (Renee Cote). Directed by Brian De Palma and produced by Tom Jacobson. Screenplay by Jim Thomas, John Thomas, Graham Yost, and Lowell Cannon.

Well, here it is, I guess, a science-fiction movie like the one I was wishing for in my review of *Pitch Black*. That film transported its characters to an alien planet in a three-star system and then had them chase each other around in the desert and be threatened by wicked bat-creatures. Why go to all the trouble of transporting humans millions of miles from Earth, only to mire them in tired generic conventions?

Mission to Mars is smarter and more original. It contains some ideas. It also has its flaws. It begins with an astronaut's backyard picnic so chirpy it could easily accommodate Chevy Chase. It contains conversations that drag on beyond all reason. It is quiet when quiet is not called for. It contains actions that deny common sense. And for long stretches the characters speak nothing but boilerplate.

And yet those stretches on autopilot surround three sequences of real vision, awakening the sense of wonder that is the goal of popular science fiction. The film involves a manned mission to Mars, which lands successfully and then encounters . . . something . . . that results in the death of three of the crew members, and loss of radio contact with the fourth (Don Cheadle).

A rescue mission is dispatched, led by co-pilots Tim Robbins and Gary Sinise, with Connie Nielsen as Robbins's wife and Jerry O'Connell as the fourth member. They run into a clump of tiny meteorites that puncture the hull and lead to a loss of air pressure. (It's here that the Sinise character defies logic by refusing, for no good reason, to put on his helmet and draw oxygen from his suit.) Then there's another crisis, which leads to a surprisingly taut and moving sequence in which the four characters attempt a tricky maneuver outside their ship and are faced with a life-or-death choice.

Arriving on the red planet, they find the survivor, hear his story, and then are led into a virtual reality version of a close encounter of the third kind. They learn the history of Mars, and the secret of life on Earth, and Sinise continues his journey in an unexpected way.

I am being deliberately vague here because one of the pleasures of a film like this is its visual and plot surprises. I like a little science in science fiction, and this film has a little. (The emphasis is on "little," however, and its animated re-creation of the evolution of species lost me when the dinosaurs evolved into bison—and besides, how would the makers of that animation know the outcome of the process?) The movie also has some intriguing ideas, and some of the spirit of *2001: A Space Odyssey.* Not a lot, but some. (It pays homage to Kubrick's film by giving us space suits and spaceship interiors that seem like a logical evolution of his designs.)

I watched the movie with pleasure that was frequently interrupted by frustration. The three key sequences are very well done. They are surrounded by sequences that are not—left adrift in lackluster dialogue and broad, easy character strokes. Why does the film amble so casually between its high points? Why is a meditative tone evoked when we have been given only perfunctory inspiration for it? Why is a crisis like the breached hull treated so deliberately, as if the characters are trying to slow down their actions to use up all the available time? And why, oh why, in a film where the special effects are sometimes awesome, are we given an alien being who looks like a refugee from a video game?

I can't recommend *Mission to Mars.* It misses too many of its marks. But it has extraordinary things in it. It's as if the director, the gifted Brian De Palma, rises to the occasions but the

screenplay gives him nothing much to do in between them. It was old Howard Hawks who supplied this definition of a good movie: "Three great scenes. No bad scenes." *Mission to Mars* gets only the first part right.

Miss Julie ★ ★ ★
R, 100 m., 2000

Saffron Burrows (Miss Julie), Peter Mullan (Jean), Maria Doyle Kennedy (Christine), Tam Dean Burn (Servant), Heathcote Williams (Servant), Eileen Walsh (Servant). Directed by Mike Figgis and produced by Figgis and Harriet Cruickshank. Screenplay by Helen Cooper, based on the play by August Strindberg.

Mike Figgis's *Leaving Las Vegas* was about a self-destructive man who pauses briefly for sex and kindness from a Vegas call girl on his way to the grave. Now Figgis has made *Miss Julie,* a film based on the Strindberg play about the daughter of a count and her footman—two people who use sex as their instrument of self-destruction. Both films are intense, erotic, and willful; the difference is that we pity and love the characters in the first, while Strindberg and Figgis allow only pity in the second.

It is Midsummer's Eve in the house of a wealthy Swedish count. In the kitchen, there's much cheerful toing-and-froing from the downstairs staff, while upstairs a party is under way. We meet Jean, the footman, played by Peter Mullan as a compact, self-assured man who polishes boots as if they were his enemies. His fiancée, Christine (Maria Doyle Kennedy), is a plump, jolly woman who not only knows her place, but approves of it.

Miss Julie walks down the stairs. Played by Saffron Burrows, she is several inches taller than Jean, and bold, the kind of woman who learned to handle men by first mastering horses. She's come for a little sport with the servants, or because she's bored with the aristocrats upstairs, or because she has noticed how Jean looks at her, or perhaps because her fiancé has left her. He left, we learn, because she was too headstrong. On the rebound, she is angry and reckless.

For the next hour and a half, Jean and Miss Julie will engage in a duel of wills. The movie is almost exactly as long as Strindberg's one-act play, which traps them in the same time and space, and calls their mutual bluff: Each wants to prove the other doesn't have the nerve to have sex. Intimacy between them, of course, is forbidden by all the codes that apply in this kitchen: the class system, religious beliefs, the separation of servant and master, Jean's engagement to Christine, and not least the fact that they do not like each other.

Their dislike is, however, an aphrodisiac, and so is the danger they place themselves in, because a servant and a mistress who have sex can never be accepted again by the society that contains them. They must leave—flee to Paris, perhaps—or find some other kind of escape. Ah, you say, but what if no one finds out? The whole point is that they themselves will know. They've been instructed by the class system to see themselves in a certain way, and sex would destroy that way of seeing.

Of course, their danger makes it all the more enticing, and the drama is a verbal duel in which words are foreplay. There is a lot of sadomasochism in their fencing. She at first wants him to grovel, and towers over him. Then he takes the upper hand and lashes her with harsh truths about herself. When they finally do have sex, it is not pleasurable but more like a mutual wounding: As you destroy me, I destroy you.

The actors are compelling. Mullan *(My Name Is Joe)* can be a hard man, roughened by his servant's life. Burrows *(The Loss of Sexual Innocence)* is a great beauty but, like Sigourney Weaver, another tall woman, possessed of angularity: She can be soft, and then all sharp corners. They talk, they fence, they dream, they are tender, they tease, they taunt, they dance closer and closer to the film's outcome, which, once you experience it, you know you saw coming right from the first.

Monkeybone ★ ½
PG-13, 87 m., 2001

Brendan Fraser (Stu Miley), Bridget Fonda (Julie McElroy), Whoopi Goldberg (Death), Chris Kattan (Organ Donor), David Foley (Herb), Giancarlo Esposito (Hypnos), John Turturro (Monkeybone's Voice), Rose McGowan (Kitty). Directed by Henry Selick and produced by Mark Radcliffe and Michael Barnathan. Screenplay by Sam Hamm.

A character played by Brendan Fraser spends half of *Monkeybone* on life support, and so does the movie. Both try to stay alive with injections of nightmare juice. The movie labors hard, the special effects are admirable, no expense has been spared, and yet the movie never takes off; it's a bright idea the filmmakers were unable to breathe into life.

Fraser plays a cartoonist named Stu Miley ("S. Miley"—ho, ho). He's created a character named Monkeybone, which has become enormously popular and might soon star on its own TV show—except that Stu is one of those unsullied artists who shies away from success. He flees a fancy reception with his girlfriend Julie (Bridget Fonda), but as they're driving away a giant plastic Monkeybone toy in the backseat suddenly inflates, causing a crash. Julie is unharmed, but Stu goes into a coma, with his sister negotiating with the hospital about how soon they can pull the plug.

The coma is, in fact, action-packed. In his mind, Stu has taken an escalator to Downtown, a nightmare dreamland nightclub ruled by Hypnos (Giancarlo Esposito); it's not far from Thanatopolis, ruled by Death (Whoopi Goldberg). Here Monkeybone is the emcee, and exit passes are hard to come by. That leads to a scheme by Monkeybone ("I'm tired of being a figment!") to occupy Stu's body and escape from Downtown.

Meanwhile, on Earth, Stu's time is drawing short and his sister has her hand on the plug. Julie scans a brain chart and intuits that Stu is trapped in a "nightmare loop." She thinks maybe an emergency injection of Nightmare Juice might scare him awake. Through a coincidental miracle of timing, Monkeybone leaves Downtown and possesses Stu's body just as the juice hits, so when he comes out of the coma and starts acting strangely, she blames it on the juice.

And so on. The plot is not exactly the issue here. *Monkeybone* was directed by Henry Selick, who also made *The Nightmare Before Christmas* and *James and the Giant Peach*. His ability to blend live action with makeup, special effects,

407

and computer effects is about as good as it gets—and he leans away from computers and in the direction of bizarre sets and makeup and stop-action animation, which gives his work an eerie third-dimensionality unmatched by slicker computer effects.

Here he achieves technical marvels, but the movie just doesn't deliver. The Monkeybone character doesn't earn its screen time; it's just a noxious pest. Brendan Fraser has been at home before in cartoon roles (*George of the Jungle, Dudley Do-Right*), but here he seems more like the victim of the joke than the perpetrator, and Bridget Fonda's girlfriend is earnest and plucky, but not funny (she has to look concerned about Stu all the time).

One sequence made me smile. It involves Chris Kattan, from *Saturday Night Live,* as an organ transplant donor snatched from the hospital in midoperation and lofted over the city by a hot air balloon, while spare parts fall from his incision and are greeted below by grateful dogs.

Downtown itself looks like the amusement park from (or in) hell, and there's a lot of *Beetlejuice* in the inspiration for the strange creatures, one-eyed and otherwise, who live there. But strangeness is not enough. There must also be humor, and characters who exist for some reason other than to look bizarre. That rule would include Whoopi Goldberg's Death, who is sadly underwritten, and played by Whoopi as if we're supposed to keep repeating: "Wow! Look! Death is being played by Whoopi Goldberg!" It is a truth too often forgotten that casting a famous actor in a weird cameo is the setup of the joke, not the punch line.

Monsoon Wedding ★ ★ ★ ½

R, 114 m., 2002

Naseeruddin Shah (Lalit Verma), Lillete Dubey (Pimmi Verma), Shefali Shetty (Ria Verma), Vasundhara Das (Aditi Verma), Parvin Dabas (Hemant Rai), Vijay Raaz (P. K. Dubey), Tilotama Shome (Alice), Rajat Kapoor (Tej Puri), Neha Dubey (Ayesha), Randeep Hooda (Rahul). Directed by Mira Nair and produced by Caroline Baron and Nair. Screenplay by Sabrina Dhawan.

Mira Nair's *Monsoon Wedding* is one of those joyous films that leaps over national boundaries and celebrates universal human nature. It could be the first Indian film to win big at the North American box office; like *Tampopo,* the Japanese noodle-shop romance, or *Crouching Tiger, Hidden Dragon,* which escaped the subtitled martial arts ghetto, it's the kind of film people tell their friends they ought to see.

The movie follows the events in the large Verma family of New Delhi, as their daughter Aditi prepares to marry Hemant, a computer programmer from Houston. He is an "NRI" (nonresident Indian), who has returned to meet the bride selected by his parents for an arranged marriage. Such marriages are an ancient tradition, but these are modern young people, and in the opening scene we see Aditi in a hurried exchange with her married lover, a TV host. She has agreed to the arranged marriage partly out of impatience with her lover's vague talk about someday divorcing his wife.

As in an Altman film, we plunge into the middle of an event and gradually figure out who everyone is—just as the members of the two families must. The key players are the parents of the bride, Lalit (Naseeruddin Shah) and Pimmi (Lillete Dubey). He worries about the weather, the happiness of his family, his duties as a host, and especially about the cost of everything. In charge of the festivities and apparently overcharging him is the wedding planner, P. K. Dubey (Vijay Raaz), who does not reassure Lalit with his use of such invaluable Indian English expressions as "exactly and approximately."

All of the characters speak English. Also Hindi and, in some cases, Punjabi, sometimes in the same sentence. The effect is delightful. We have the pleasure of seeing a foreign film and the convenience of understanding almost everything that's said. The spontaneous movement between languages, typical of modern middle-class Indians, reflects the mixture of characters: Some are returning from America or Australia and work with computers or on television, while others occupy ancient life patterns. One young family member wants to study creative writing in America, and a relative, no doubt aware of the current boom in English-language best-sellers about India, tells her, "Lots of money in writing."

The wedding creates a certain suspense:

What if the bride and groom do not like each other? They sneak off for quiet talks and find that they do like each other—at least, each other's looks and as much as they can learn in a few hours. Meanwhile, subterranean romances surround them. Aditi's pretty cousin Ayesha (Neha Dubey) makes no mystery of her attraction to Rahul (Randeep Hooda), the visitor from Australia; P. K. Dubey is thunderstruck by the beauty of the Verma's family maid, Alice (Tilotama Shome). And there is intrigue of a darker sort as Aditi's cousin observes a family friend who once assaulted her and now may have his eye on a young relative.

I have not even started on the groom's family. You will meet them at the wedding. What strikes you immediately about *Monsoon Wedding* is the quickness of the comedy, the deft way Nair moves between story lines, the brilliant colors of Declan Quinn's cinematography, and the way music is easily woven into the narrative. Nair, whose films include *Salaam Bombay!* and *Mississippi Masala*, says she wanted to make a Bollywood movie in her own way, and she has. "Bollywood" is the term for the Bombay film industry, the world's largest, which produces broad popular entertainments in which the characters are likely to start singing and dancing at any moment, in any context. There is a lot of singing and dancing in *Monsoon Wedding*, but all of it emerges in a logical way from the action, as it might in a Hollywood musical.

There are moments of truth in the romance between Aditi and Hemant, especially when they level with each other about their pasts. But the real heart-tugging moment, the moment audiences will love, is when P. K. Dubey falls to his knees before a heart made of marigolds, in a hopeless gesture of adoration before Alice. A harsher moment of truth comes when Aditi's father, who places loyalty to family above everything, breaks with tradition to do the right thing in a painful situation, no matter what.

The hope for *Monsoon Wedding* is that those who like it will drag their friends into the theater. There's such an unreasonable prejudice in this country against any film that is not exactly like every other film. People cheerfully attend assembly-line junk but are wary of movies that might give them new experiences or take them new places. *Monsoon Wedding*, which won the Golden Lion as the best film at Venice 2001, is the kind of film where you meet characters you have never been within 10,000 miles of, and feel like you know them at once.

Monster's Ball ★ ★ ★ ★
R, 111 m., 2002

Billy Bob Thornton (Hank Grotowski), Halle Berry (Leticia Musgrove), Heath Ledger (Sonny Grotowski), Peter Boyle (Buck Grotowski), Sean "Puffy" Combs (Lawrence Musgrove), Coronji Calhoun (Tyrell Musgrove). Directed by Marc Forster and produced by Lee Daniels. Screenplay by Milo Addica and Will Rokos.

Monster's Ball is about a black woman and a white man who find, for a time anyway, solace in each other for their pain. But their pain remains separate and so do they; this is not a message movie about interracial relationships, but the specific story of two desperate people whose lives are shaken by violent deaths, and how in the days right after that they turn to each other because there is no place else to turn. The movie has the complexity of great fiction, and requires our empathy as we interpret the decisions that are made—especially at the end, when the movie avoids an obligatory scene that would have been conventional and forces us to cut straight to the point.

Billy Bob Thornton and Halle Berry star as Hank and Leticia, in two performances that are so powerful because they observe the specific natures of these two characters and avoid the pitfalls of racial clichés. What a shock to find these two characters freed from the conventions of political correctness and allowed to be who they are: weak, flawed, needful, with good hearts tested by lifetimes of compromise. They live in a small Georgia town, circa 1990. She works the night shift in a diner, has a fat little son, and an ex-husband on Death Row. He works as a guard on Death Row, has a mean, racist father and a browbeaten son, and will be involved in her husband's execution. ("Monster's Ball" is an old English term for a condemned man's last night on Earth.)

At first Hank and Leticia do not realize the connection they have through the condemned man. For another movie that would be enough plot. We can imagine the scenes of discovery and revelation. How this movie handles that disclosure is one of its great strengths: how both characters deal with it (or don't deal with it) internally, so that the movie blessedly proceeds according to exactly who they are, what they need, what they must do, and the choices open to them.

The screenplay by Milo Addica and Will Rokos is subtle and observant; one is reminded of short fiction by Andre Dubus, William Trevor, Eudora Welty, Raymond Carver. It specifically does not tell "their" story, but focuses on two separate lives. The characters are given equal weight and have individual story arcs, which do not intersect but simply, inevitably, meet. There is an overlay of racism in the story; Hank's father, Buck (Peter Boyle), is a hateful racist, and Hank mirrors his attitudes. But the movie is not about redemption, not about how Hank overcomes his attitudes, but about how they fall away from him like a dead skin because his other feelings are so much more urgent. The movie, then, is not about overcoming prejudice, but sidestepping it because it comes to seem monstrously irrelevant.

Hank is an abused son and an abusive father. His old man, Buck, confined to a wheelchair and a stroller, still exercises an iron will over the family. All three generations live under his roof, and when Hank's son, Sonny (Heath Ledger), opts out of the family sickness, Buck's judgment is cruel: "He was weak." We do not learn much about Leticia's parents, but she is a bad mother, alternately smothering her son, Tyrell (Coronji Calhoun), with love, and screaming at him that he's a "fat little piggy." She drinks too much, has been served with an eviction notice, sees herself as a loser. She has no affection at all for Tyrell's father, Lawrence (Puffy Combs), on Death Row, and makes it clear during a visitation that she is there strictly for her son. There is no side story to paint Lawrence as a victim; "I'm a bad man," he tells Tyrell. "You're the best of me."

Leticia is all messed up. She sustains a loss that derails her, and it happens by coincidence that Hank is there when he can perform a service. This makes them visible to each other. It is safe to say that no one else in the community is visible, in terms of human need, to either one. Hank's shy, slow courtship is so

tentative it's like he's sleepwalking toward her. Her response is dictated by the fact that she has nowhere else to turn. They have a key conversation in which the bodies of both characters are tilted away from each other, as if fearful of being any closer. And notice another conversation, when she's been drinking, and she waves her hands and one hand keeps falling on Hank's lap; she doesn't seem to notice and, here is the point, he doesn't seem willing to.

Their intimate scenes are ordinary and simple, a contrast to Hank's cold, mercenary arrangement with a local hooker. The film's only flaw is the way Marc Forster allows his camera to linger on Halle Berry's half-clothed beauty; this story is not about sex appeal, and if the camera sees her that way we are pretty sure that Hank doesn't. What he sees, what she sees, is defined not by desire but by need.

Students of screenwriting should study the way the film handles the crucial passages at the end, when she discovers some drawings and understands their meaning. Here is where a lesser movie would have supplied an obligatory confrontation. Leticia never mentions the drawings to Hank. Why not? Because it is time to move on? Because she understands why he withheld information? Because she has no alternative? Because she senses that the drawings would not exist if the artist hated his subject? Because she is too tired and this is just one more nail on the cross? Because she forgives? What?

The movie cannot say. The characters have disappeared into the mysteries of the heart. *Monster's Ball* demonstrates that to explain all its mysteries, a movie would have to limit itself to mysteries that can be explained. As for myself, as Leticia rejoined Hank in the last shot of the movie, I was thinking about her as deeply and urgently as about any movie character I can remember. ☞

Monsters, Inc. ★ ★ ★
G, 86 m., 2001

With the voices of: Billy Crystal (Mike Wazowski), John Goodman ("Sulley" Sullivan), James Coburn (Henry J. Waternoose), Jennifer Tilly (Celia), Bonnie Hunt (Flint), Mary Gibbs (Boo), Steve Buscemi (Randall Boggs), Sam "Penguin" Black (George Sanderson). Directed by Peter

Docter and produced by Darla K. Anderson. Screenplay by Dan Gerson and Andrew Stanton. Art direction by Tia W. Kratter and Dominique Louis.

Kids and movie monsters have a lot in common. They feel conspicuous. They stand out in a crowd. They can't make small-talk with grown-ups. They are always stepping on stuff and breaking it. Anything that goes wrong is blamed on them. Now it turns out they share something else. Not only are kids scared of monsters, but according to *Monsters, Inc.*, monsters are scared of kids.

The new animated feature from Pixar reveals that it is true (as every child knows) that there are monsters in the bedroom closet, especially after the lights have been put out. What we did not realize is that the monsters are on assignment. A closet door, which by day leads to a closet, at night leads directly to Monstropolis, the world of monsters, which is powered by Scream Heat. The only reason monsters jump out of closets and scare kids is to collect their screams, which are to Monstropolis as power plants are to the rest of us.

As the movie opens, Monstropolis faces a crisis: Kids are getting too hard to scare, and there's a scream shortage. "Rolling blackouts" are predicted. A complete energy shutdown is a possibility. Responsibility falls on the broad shoulders of a big blue monster named Sulley (voice by John Goodman), who is the leading scream-producer. Sulley looks like a cross between a gorilla and a bear. His best pal, Mike Wazowski (voice by Billy Crystal), is a green eyeball with arms and legs. Sulley is brave and dedicated. Wazowski is phobic, frightened, and malingering. Together they cover the spectrum of work traits. The sexy Celia (voice by Jennifer Tilly) has a crush on Wazowski. What she sees in him is beyond me, although if there is anyone who can figure out how to have sex with a green eyeball, that would be Jennifer Tilly. I can imagine her brassy voice: "Blink! Blink!"

There must be villains, and this time they are Henry J. Waternoose (voice by James Coburn), who looks like a crab crossed with a cartoon of Boss Tweed, and Randall Boggs (voice by Steve Buscemi), a snaky schemer who wants to dethrone Sulley as the champion scream collector. Their competition grows

more urgent when a human child named Boo (voice by Mary Gibbs) goes where no human has gone before, through the closet door and into the monster world.

Monsters, Inc. follows the two *Toy Story* movies and *A Bug's Life* from Pixar, and once again shows off the studio's remarkable computer-aided animation, which creates an uncanny sense of dimension and movement. Monsters, like toys and bugs, come in every conceivable shape, size, and color, which must have been one of their attractions, and the movie is jolly to look at. And since the monsters are terrified of Boo, whose very name is a rebuke to their lifelong missions, there are screams and chases on both sides of the closet doors. ("There's nothing more toxic or deadly than a human child," Waternoose warns. "A single touch could kill you!")

Speaking of those doors—turns out they're manufactured in Monstropolis, to such exacting specifications that no one ever figures out they didn't come with the house. The most entertaining sequence in the movie is a roller-coaster chase scene involving hundreds of doors on an endless conveyor line that loops the loop at a breakneck speed.

Voice-over dubbing used to be what actors did instead of dinner theater. Now, with the multimillion-dollar grosses of the top animated films, it's a lucrative job that is finally getting the credit it deserves for the artistic skills necessary. Not everyone is a good looper, and stars like Goodman, Crystal, Coburn, Buscemi, and Bonnie Hunt bring a dimension to the film that both borrows from their screen personas and kids them. As for the invaluable Tilly, she has the only voice that has ever made me think simultaneously of Mae West and Slim Pickens.

The animation of Wazowski is interesting because the animators apparently had so little to work with. Instead of an expressive face and a lot of body language, they're given, as one of the leads of the picture—an eyeball. Luckily, the eyeball has an eyelid, or maybe it's a brow, and with this to work with the artists are able to supply him with all the facial expressions a monster would ever need—especially one without a face. It's a tour de force.

Monsters, Inc. is cheerful, high-energy fun, and like the other Pixar movies has a running supply of gags and references aimed at grown-ups (I liked the restaurant named Harry-hausen's, after the animation pioneer). I also enjoyed the sly way that the monster world mirrors our own, right down to production quotas and sales slogans. "We Scare," they assure us, "Because We Care."

The Mothman Prophecies ★ ★
PG-13, 119 m., 2002

Richard Gere (John Klein), Laura Linney (Sergeant Connie Parker), Will Patton (Gordon), Debra Messing (Mary Klein), Shane Callahan (Nat Griffin), Alan Bates (Alexander Leek), Nesbitt Blaisdell (Chief Josh Jarrett). Directed by Mark Pellington and produced by Gary W. Goldstein, Gary Lucchesi, and Tom Rosenberg. Screenplay by Richard Hatem, based on the novel by John A. Keel.

The Mothman Prophecies claims to be based on a true story, which sent me racing to the Web for a little research. And, yes, there is a belief among the folks in Point Pleasant, West Virginia, that a mothlike creature with red eyes can occasionally be glimpsed in the area. Some say he is a spirit evoked by a long-dead Indian chief. Others blame him for a deadly bridge collapse.

John A. Keel has written a book about Moth-man, and now here is this movie. The "true story" part involves the possible existence of Mothman; the human characters are, I believe, based not on facts but on an ancient tradition in horror movies, in which attractive people have unspeakable experiences.

Richard Gere stars as a *Washington Post* reporter named John Klein, who is so happily married (to Debra Messing) that when they agree to buy a new house, they decide to test the floor of a closet for lovemaking purposes, to the surprise of the real-estate agent who walks in on them. If there's one thing you demand in a real-estate agent, it's the good judgment to leave a closet door closed when he hears the unmistakable sounds of coitus coming from behind it. Furthermore: Richard Gere is fifty-three. He's in great shape, but to make love at fifty-three on the floor of a closet with a real-estate agent lurking about is, I submit, not based on a true story.

Then Klein and his wife are in a crash. "You didn't see it, did you?" she asks, and before she dies she draws a picture of a mothlike creature she saw flattened against the windshield. Unlike most windshield bugs, this creature has many forms and lives, as Klein discovers when his life takes a turn into the twilight zone. Driving, as he thinks, to Virginia, he ends up hundreds of miles away in West Virginia, and when he knocks on a door for help the frightened householder accuses Klein of having harassed him for three nights in a row.

Laura Linney plays Connie Parker, a local cop. She trusts Klein, and together they get involved in a strange series of events that culminate in a bridge collapse and a dramatic rescue of the sort that is always particularly annoying to me, because it displaces the focus of the movie. Is this a movie about the Mothman, or about a daring rescue after a bridge collapse? And since the Mothman presumably still exists, how does the happy end after the bridge collapse really settle the story? It's lazy for a movie to avoid solving one problem by trying to distract us with the solution to another.

The director is Mark Pellington *(Arlington Road)*, whose command of camera, pacing, and the overall effect is so good it deserves a better screenplay. The Mothman is singularly ineffective as a threat because it is only vaguely glimpsed, has no nature we can understand, doesn't operate under rules that the story can focus on, and seems to be involved in space-time shifts far beyond its presumed focus. There is also the problem that insects make unsatisfactory villains unless they are very big.

Richard Gere and Laura Linney have some nice scenes together. I like the way he takes a beat of indecision before propelling himself into an action. This is Linney's first movie since *You Can Count on Me,* which won her an Oscar nomination. I saw it again recently and was astonished by her performance. The melancholy lesson seems to be, if you make a small independent movie for very little money and are wonderful in it, you can look forward to being paid a lot of money to appear in a big-budget production in which the talent that got you there is scarcely required.

Moulin Rouge ★ ★ ★ ½
PG-13, 126 m., 2001

Nicole Kidman (Satine), Ewan McGregor (Christian), John Leguizamo (Toulouse-Lautrec), Jim Broadbent (Zidler), Richard Roxburgh (Duke of Monroth), Kylie Minogue (The Green Fairy), Christine Anu (Arabia), Natalie Jackson Mendoza (China Doll). Directed by Baz Luhrmann and produced by Fred Baron, Martin Brown, and Luhrmann. Screenplay by Luhrmann and Craig Pearce.

Like almost every American college boy who ever took a cut-rate flight to Paris, I went to the Moulin Rouge on my first night in town. I had a cheap standing-room ticket way in the back, and over the heads of the crowd, through a haze of smoke, I could vaguely see the dancing girls. The tragedy of the Moulin Rouge is that by the time you can afford a better seat, you've outgrown the show.

Moulin Rouge the movie is more like the Moulin Rouge of my adolescent fantasies than the real Moulin Rouge ever could be. It isn't about tired, decadent people, but about glorious romantics who believe in the glitz and the tinsel—who see the nightclub not as a shabby tourist trap but as a stage for their dreams. Even its villain is a love-struck duke who gnashes his way into the fantasy, content to play a starring role, however venal.

The film is constructed like the fevered snapshots created by your imagination before an anticipated erotic encounter. It doesn't depend on dialogue or situation but on the way you imagine a fantasy object first from one angle and then another. Satine, the heroine, is seen not so much in dramatic situations as in poses—in postcards for the yearning mind. The movie is about how we imagine its world. It is perfectly appropriate that it was filmed on sound stages in Australia; Paris has always existed best in the minds of its admirers.

The film stars Nicole Kidman as Satine, a star dancer who has a deadly secret; she is dying of tuberculosis. This is not a secret from the audience, which learns it early on, but from Christian (Ewan McGregor), the would-be writer who loves her. Toulouse-Lautrec (John Leguizamo), the dwarf artist, lives above Christian, and one day comes crashing through the ceiling of their flimsy tenement, sparking a friendship and collaboration: They will write a show to spotlight Satine's brilliance, as well as "truth, beauty, freedom, and love." (I was reminded of Gene Kelly and Donald O'Connor's motto in *Singin' in the Rain*: "Dignity. Always dignity.") The show must be financed; enter the venal Duke of Monroth (Richard Roxburgh), who wants to pay for the show and for Satine's favors. The ringmaster is Zidler (Jim Broadbent), impresario of the Moulin Rouge.

All of these characters are seen in terms of their own fantasies about themselves. Toulouse-Lautrec, for example, is flamboyant and romantic; Christian is lonely and lovelorn; Satine has a good heart and only seems to be a bad girl; Zidler pretends to be all business but is a softy; and the duke can be so easily duped because being duped is the essence of his role in life. Those who think they can buy affection are suckers; a wise man is content to rent it.

The movie has been directed by Baz Luhrmann, an Australian with a background in opera, whose two previous films were also experiments in exuberant excess. *Strictly Ballroom* made a ballroom competition into a flamboyant theatrical exercise, and his *William Shakespeare's Romeo + Juliet* updated the play into a contempo teenage rumble. He constructs *Moulin Rouge* with the melodrama of a nineteenth-century opera, the Technicolor brashness of a 1950s Hollywood musical, and the quick-cutting frenzy of a music video. Nothing is really "period" about the movie—it's like a costume revue taking place right now, with hit songs from the 1970s and 1980s (you will get the idea if I mention that Jim Broadbent sings "Like a Virgin").

I am often impatient with directors who use so many cuts that their films seem to have been fed through electric fans. For Luhrmann and this material, it is the right approach. He uses so many different setups and camera angles that some of the songs seem to be cut not on every word of the lyrics, but on every syllable. There's no breathing room. The whole movie is on the same manic pitch as O'Connor's "Make 'Em Laugh" number in *Singin' in the Rain*. Everything is screwed to a breakneck pitch, as if the characters have died and their lives are flashing before our eyes.

This means the actors do not create their

characters but embody them. Who is Satine? A leggy redhead who can look like a million in a nightclub costume, and then melt into a guy's arms. Who is Christian? A man who embodies longing with his eyes and sighs—whose very essence, whose entire being, is composed of need for Satine. With the duke, one is reminded of silent films in which the titles said "The Duke," and then he sneered at you.

The movie is all color and music, sound and motion, kinetic energy, broad strokes, operatic excess. While it might be most convenient to see it from the beginning, it hardly makes any difference; walk in at any moment and you'll quickly know who is good and bad, who is in love and why—and then all the rest is song, dance, spectacular production numbers, protestations of love, exhalations of regret, vows of revenge, and grand destructive gestures. It's like being trapped on an elevator with the circus.

Mr. Death: The Rise and Fall of Fred A. Leuchter Jr. ★ ★ ★ ★
PG-13, 96 m., 2000

A documentary directed by Errol Morris and produced by Michael Williams, David Collins, and Dorothy Aufiero.

The hangman has no friends. That truth, I think, is the key to understanding Fred A. Leuchter Jr., a man who built up a nice little business designing death-row machines, and then lost it when he became a star on the Holocaust denial circuit. Leuchter, the subject of Errol Morris's documentary *Mr. Death: The Rise and Fall of Fred A. Leuchter Jr.*, is a lonely man of limited insight who is grateful to be liked—even by Nazi apologists.

This is the seventh documentary by Morris, who combines dreamlike visual montages with music by Caleb Sampson to create a movie that is more reverie and meditation than reportage. Morris is drawn to subjects who try to control that which cannot be controlled—life and death. His heroes have included lion tamers, topiary gardeners, robot designers, wild turkey callers, autistics, death row inmates, pet cemetery owners, and Stephen Hawking, whose mind leaps through space and time while his body slumps in a chair.

Fred Leuchter, the son of a prison warden, stumbled into the death row business more or less by accident. An engineer by training, he found himself inspired by the need for more efficient and "humane" execution devices. He'd seen electric chairs that cooked their occupants without killing them, poison gas chambers that were a threat to the witnesses, gallows not correctly adjusted to break a neck. He went to work designing better chairs, trapdoors, and lethal injection machines, and soon (his trade not being commonplace) was being consulted by prisons all over America.

Despite his success in business, he was not, we gather, terrifically popular. How many women want to date a guy who can chat about the dangers of being accidentally electrocuted while standing in the pool of urine around a recently used electric chair? He does eventually marry a waitress he meets in a doughnut shop; indeed, given his habit of forty to sixty cups of coffee a day, he must have met a lot of waitresses. We hear her offscreen voice as she describes their brief marriage, and demurs at Fred's notion that their visit to Auschwitz was a honeymoon (she had to wait in a cold car, serving as a lookout for guards).

Leuchter's trip to Auschwitz was the turning point in his career. He was asked by Ernst Zundel, a neo-Nazi and Holocaust denier, to be an expert witness at his trial in Canada. Zundel financed Leuchter's 1988 trip to Auschwitz, during which he chopped off bits of brick and mortar in areas said to be gas chambers, and had them analyzed for cyanide residue. His conclusion: The chambers never contained gas. The "Leuchter Report" has since been widely quoted by those who deny the Holocaust took place.

There is a flaw in his science, however. The laboratory technician who tested the samples for Leuchter was later startled to discover the use being made of his findings. Cyanide would penetrate bricks only to the depth of a tenth of a human hair, he says. By breaking off large chunks and pulverizing them, Leuchter had diluted his sample by 100,000 times, not even taking into account the fifty years of weathering that had passed. To find cyanide would have been a miracle.

No matter; Leuchter became a favorite after-dinner speaker on the neo-Nazi circuit, and the camera observes how his face lights up and his whole body seems to lean into applause, how happy he is to shake hands with his new friends. Other people might shy away from the pariah status of a Holocaust denier. The hangman is already a pariah, and finds his friends where he can.

Just before *Mr. Death* was shown in a slightly different form at the 1999 Sundance Film Festival, a *New Yorker* article by Mark Singer wondered whether the film would create sympathy for Leuchter and his fellow deniers. After all, here was a man who lost his wife and his livelihood in the name of a scientific quest. My feeling is that no filmmaker can be responsible for those unwilling or unable to view his film intelligently; anyone who leaves *Mr. Death* in agreement with Leuchter deserves to join him on the loony fringe.

What's scary about the film is the way Leuchter is perfectly respectable up until the time the neo-Nazis get their hooks into him. Those who are appalled by the mass execution of human beings sometimes have no problem when the state executes them one at a time. You can even run for president after presiding over the busiest death row in U.S. history.

Early sequences in *Mr. Death* portray Leuchter as a humanitarian who protests that some electric chairs "cook the meat too much." He dreams of a "lethal injection machine" designed like a dentist's chair. The condemned could watch TV or listen to music while the poison works. What a lark. There is irony in the notion that many American states could lavish tax dollars on this man's inventions, only to put him out of work because of his unsavory connections. The ability of so many people to live comfortably with the idea of capital punishment is perhaps a clue to how so many Europeans were able to live with the idea of the Holocaust: Once you accept the notion that the state has the right to kill someone, and the right to define what is a capital crime, aren't you halfway there?

Like all of Errol Morris's films, *Mr. Death* provides us with no comfortable place to stand. We often leave his documentaries not sure if he liked his subjects or was ridiculing them. He doesn't make it easy for us with simple moral labels. Human beings, he argues, are fearsomely complex, and can get their minds around very strange ideas indeed. Sometimes it is possible to hate the sin and love the sinner. Poor Fred. What a dope, what a dupe, what a lonely, silly man.

Mr. Deeds ★ ½
PG-13, 96 m., 2002

Adam Sandler (Longfellow Deeds), Winona Ryder (Babe Bennett), John Turturro (Emilio), Steve Buscemi (Crazy Eyes), Jared Harris (Mac), Peter Gallagher (Chuck Cedar), Allen Covert (Marty), Conchata Ferrell (Jan), Roark Critchlow (William). Directed by Steven Brill and produced by Sidney Ganis and Jack Giarraputo. Screenplay by Tim Herlihy.

At one point during the long ordeal of *Mr. Deeds,* it is said of the Adam Sandler character, "He doesn't share our sense of ironic detachment." Is this a private joke by the writer? If there's one thing Sandler's Mr. Deeds has, it's ironic detachment. Like so many Sandler characters, he seems fundamentally insincere, to be aiming for the laugh even at serious moments. Since the 1936 Frank Capra film *Mr. Deeds Goes to Town* was above all sincere, we wonder how this project was chosen; did Adam Sandler look at Gary Cooper and see a role for himself?

He plays Longfellow Deeds, pizzeria owner in the hamlet of Mandrake Falls, New Hampshire. The pizzeria is one of those establishments required in all comedies about small towns, where every single character in town gathers every single day to provide an audience for the hero, crossed with a Greek chorus. Nobody does anything in Mandrake Falls except sit in the pizzeria and talk about Deeds. When he leaves town, they watch him on the TV.

Turns out Deeds is the distant relative of an elderly zillionaire who freezes to death in the very act of conquering Everest. Control of his media empire and a $40 billion fortune goes to Deeds, who is obviously too good-hearted and simpleminded to deserve it, so a corporate executive named Cedar (Peter Gallagher) conspires to push him aside. Meanwhile, when Deeds hits New York, a trash TV show makes him its favorite target, and producer Babe Bennett (Winona Ryder) goes undercover, convinces Deeds she loves him, and sets him up for humiliation. Then she discovers she loves him, too late.

Frank Capra played this story straight. But the 2002 film doesn't really believe in it, and breaks the mood with absurdly inappropriate "comedy" scenes. Consider a scene where Deeds meets his new butler Emilio (John Turturro). Emilio has a foot fetish. Deeds doubts Emilio will like his right foot, which is pitch black after a childhood bout of frostbite. The foot has no feeling, Deeds says, inviting Emilio to pound it with a fireplace poker. When Deeds doesn't flinch, Turturro actually punctures the foot with the point of the poker, at which point I listened attentively for sounds of laughter in the theater and heard none.

There's no chemistry between Deeds and Babe, but then how could there be, considering that their characters have no existence except as the puppets in scenes of plot manipulation. After Deeds grows disillusioned with her, there is a reconciliation inspired after she falls through the ice on a pond and he breaks through to save her using the black foot. In story conferences, do they discuss scenes like this and nod approvingly? Tell me, for I want to know.

The moral center of the story is curious. The media empire, we learn, controls enormous resources and employs 50,000 people. The evil Cedar wants to break it up. The good-hearted Deeds fights to keep it together so those 50,000 people won't be out of work. This is essentially a movie that wants to win our hearts with a populist hero who risks his entire fortune in order to ensure the survival of Time-AOL-Warner-Disney-Murdoch. What would Frank Capra have thought about the little guy bravely standing up for the monolith?

Of the many notes I took during the film, one deserves to be shared with you. There is a scene in the movie where Deeds, the fire chief in Mandrake Falls, becomes a hero during a Manhattan fire. He scales the side of a building and rescues a woman's cats, since she refuses to be rescued before them. One after another, the cats are thrown onto a fireman's net. Finally there is a cat that is on fire. The blazing feline is tossed from the window and bounces into a bucket of water, emerging wet but intact, ho, ho, and then Deeds and the heavy-set cat lady jump together and crash through the net, but

Deeds's fall is cushioned by the fat lady, who is also not harmed, ho, ho, giving us a heartrending happy ending.

That is not what I wrote in my notes. It is only the setup. What I noted was that in the woman's kitchen, nothing is seen to be on fire except for a box of Special K cereal. This is a species of product placement previously unthinkable. In product placement conferences, do they discuss scenes like this and nod approvingly? Tell me, for oh, how I want to know. ☞

Mulholland Dr. ★ ★ ★ ★
R, 146 m., 2001

Justin Theroux (Adam Kesher), Naomi Watts (Betty Elms), Laura Elena Harring (Rita), Ann Miller (Coco Lenoix), Dan Hedaya (Vincenzo Castigliani), Mark Pellegrino (Joe), Brian Beacock (Studio Singer), Robert Forster (Detective Harry McKnight), Michael J. Anderson (Mr. Roque). Directed by David Lynch and produced by Neal Edelstein, Joyce Eliason, Tony Krantz, Michael Polaire, Alain Sarde, and Mary Sweeney. Screenplay by Lynch.

David Lynch has been working toward *Mulholland Dr.* all of his career, and now that he's arrived there I forgive him *Wild at Heart* and even *Lost Highway*. At last his experiment doesn't shatter the test tubes. The movie is a surrealist dreamscape in the form of a Hollywood *film noir,* and the less sense it makes, the more we can't stop watching it.

It tells the story of . . . well, there's no way to finish that sentence. There are two characters named Betty and Rita whom the movie follows through mysterious plot loops, but by the end of the film we aren't even sure they're different characters, and Rita (an amnesiac who lifted the name from a *Gilda* poster) wonders if she's really Diane Selwyn, a name from a waitress's name tag.

Betty (Naomi Watts) is a perky blonde, Sandra Dee crossed with a Hitchcock heroine, who has arrived in town to stay in her absent Aunt Ruth's apartment and audition for the movies. Rita (Laura Elena Harring) is a voluptuous brunette who is about to be murdered when her limousine is front-ended by drag racers. She crawls out of the wreckage on Mulholland Drive, stumbles down the hill, and is taking a shower in the aunt's apartment when Betty arrives.

She doesn't remember anything, even her name. Betty decides to help her. As they try to piece her life back together, the movie introduces other characters. A movie director (Justin Theroux) is told to cast an actress in his movie or be murdered; a dwarf in a wheelchair (Michael J. Anderson) gives instructions by cell phone; two detectives turn up, speak standard TV cop show dialogue, and disappear; a landlady (Ann Miller—yes, Ann Miller) wonders who the other girl is in Aunt Ruth's apartment; Betty auditions; the two girls climb in through a bedroom window, Nancy Drew style; a rotting corpse materializes; and Betty and Rita have two lesbian love scenes so sexy you'd swear this was a 1970s movie, made when movie audiences liked sex. One of the scenes also contains the funniest example of pure logic in the history of sex scenes.

Having told you all of that, I've basically explained nothing. The movie is hypnotic; we're drawn along as if one thing leads to another—but nothing leads anywhere, and that's even before the characters start to fracture and recombine like flesh caught in a kaleidoscope. *Mulholland Dr.* isn't like *Memento*, where if you watch it closely enough you can hope to explain the mystery. There is no explanation. There may not even be a mystery.

There have been countless dream sequences in the movies, almost all of them conceived with Freudian literalism to show the characters having nightmares about the plot. *Mulholland Dr.* is all dream. There is nothing that is intended to be a waking moment. Like real dreams, it does not explain, does not complete its sequences, lingers over what it finds fascinating, dismisses unpromising plotlines. If you want an explanation for the last half-hour of the film, think of it as the dreamer rising slowly to consciousness as threads from the dream fight for space with recent memories from real life, and with fragments of other dreams—old ones and those still in development.

This works because Lynch is absolutely uncompromising. He takes what was frustrating in some of his earlier films, and instead of backing away from it, he charges right through.

Mulholland Dr. is said to have been assembled from scenes he shot for a 1999 ABC television pilot, but no network would air (or understand) this material, and Lynch knew it. He takes his financing where he can find it, and directs as fancy dictates. This movie doesn't feel incomplete because it could never be complete—closure is not a goal.

Laura Elena Harring and Naomi Watts take the risk of embodying Hollywood archetypes, and get away with it because they *are* archetypes. Not many actresses would be bold enough to name themselves after Rita Hayworth, but Harring does, because she can. Slinky and voluptuous in clinging gowns, all she has to do is stand there and she's the first good argument in fifty-five years for a *Gilda* remake. Naomi Watts is bright-eyed and bushy-tailed, a plucky girl detective. Like a dream, the movie shifts easily between tones; there's an audition where a girl singer performs "Sixteen Reasons" and "I Told Every Little Star," and the movie isn't satirizing *American Bandstand,* it's channeling it.

This is a movie to surrender yourself to. If you require logic, see something else. *Mulholland Dr.* works directly on the emotions, like music. Individual scenes play well by themselves, as they do in dreams, but they don't connect in a way that makes sense—again, like dreams. The way you know the movie is over is that it ends. And then you tell a friend, "I saw the weirdest movie last night." Just like you tell him you had the weirdest dream.

Note: See also my essay about a shot-by-shot analysis of Mulholland Dr. *in Boulder, Colorado.* ☞

The Mummy Returns ★ ★
PG-13, 121 m., 2001

Brendan Fraser (Rick O'Connell), Rachel Weisz (Evelyn), John Hannah (Jonathan Carnahan), Arnold Vosloo (Imhotep), Adewale Akinnuoye-Agbaje (Lock-Nah), Freddie Boath (Alex O'Connell), Oded Fehr (Ardeth Bay), Patricia Velasquez (Anck-Su-Namun), The Rock (Scorpion King). Directed by Stephen Sommer and produced by Sean Daniel and James Jacks. Screenplay by Sommer.

It is a curiosity of movie action that too much of it can be boring. Imagine yourself on a roller coaster for two hours. After the first ten minutes, the thrills subside. The mistake of *The Mummy Returns* is to abandon the characters, and to use the plot only as a clothesline for special effects and action sequences. If it were not for references to *The Mummy* (1999), this sequel would hardly have a plot at all.

Nine years have passed. Brendan Fraser is back again as Egyptologist Rick O'Connell, and Rachel Weisz, the librarian he met in the first film, is now his wife; they have an eight-year-old son named Alex (Freddie Boath). Also back are John Hannah as the twitty brother-in-law Jonathan, and Arnold Vosloo as the mummy Imhotep, whose name sounds more than ever like an ancient Egyptian chain of pancake houses. Oded Fehr is the worried sage Ardeth Bay, who begins sentences ominously with, "It is written that . . ." until Rick finally snaps, "Where is all this written?"

A good question, since much of the story involves a magical pyramid of which it is written, "No one who has seen it has ever returned alive." That logically leads us to wonder who told them about it. But logic applied to this movie will drive you mad. So will any attempt to summarize the plot, so I will be content with various observations:

1. The ads give The Rock, the WWF star, equal billing with Fraser. This is bait-and-switch. To call his appearance a "cameo" would be stretching it. He appears briefly at the beginning of the movie, is transmuted into a kind of transparent skeletal wraith, and disappears until the end of the film, when he comes back as the dreaded Scorpion King. I am not sure, at the end, if we see the real Rock, or merely his face, connected to computer-generated effects (his scorpion is blown up to giant size, which has the unfortunate effect of making him look more like a lobster tail than a scorpion). I continue to believe The Rock has an acting career ahead of him, and after seeing this movie I believe it is still ahead of him.

2. Alex, the kid, adds a lot to the movie by acting just like a kid. I particularly enjoyed it when he was kidnapped by a fearsome adversary of his parents, chained, and taken on a long journey, during which he drove his captor crazy by incessantly asking, "Are we there yet?"

3. The dialogue, "You have started a chain reaction that could bring about the next Apocalypse" is fascinating. Apparently we missed the first Apocalypse, which does not speak well for it.

4. I have written before of the ability of movie characters to outrun fireballs. In *The Mummy Returns,* there is a more amazing feat. If the rising sun touches little Alex while he is wearing the magical bracelet, he will die (it is written). But Rick, carrying Alex in his arms, is able to outrace the sunrise; we see the line of sunlight moving on the ground right behind them. It is written by Eratosthenes that Earth is about 25,000 miles around, and since there are twenty-four hours in a day, Rick was running approximately 1,041 miles an hour.

5. One of the big action sequences involves a battle between two vast armies, which stretch as far as computer-generated effects can see. One army is human. The other army is made of countless creatures named Anubis that look like giant savage dogs that stand upright and run on their hind legs (it is not done well, but one is surprised to find it done at all). These armies clash in bloody swordplay. Each dog-creature, as it is killed, reverts to the desert sand from whence it sprang. Finally all the creatures are destroyed, and we see the victors standing around feeling victorious and wishing that high-fives had been invented. And we notice that *not one single member* of the victorious army is dead or even wounded. Pathetic, that thousands of years of ancient curses and spells could engender such an incompetent army of dog-sand-creatures.

6. Several readers have argued with the rule in *Ebert's Little Movie Glossary* that teaches us: "No good movie has ever featured a hot-air balloon." To be sure, there are exceptions, but *The Mummy Returns* is not one of them. Its hot-air balloon looks like the ship that sailed to Winken, Blinken, and Nod.

7. At one point the action returns to London, and we see Tower Bridge, the dome of St. Paul's, and Big Ben clustered closely together in one shot. This is no doubt to make it easy for the geographically challenged. Perhaps adding a few snapshots from Madonna's wedding would not have been too much.

Murder by Numbers ★ ★ ★

R, 119 m., 2002

Sandra Bullock (Cassie Mayweather), Ryan Gosling (Richard Haywood), Michael Pitt (Justin Pendleton), Ben Chaplin (Sam Kennedy), Agnes Bruckner (Lisa), Chris Penn (Ray), R. D. Call (Rod), Tom Verica (Al Swanson). Directed by Barbet Schroeder and produced by Richard Crystal and Susan Hoffman. Screenplay by Tony Gayton.

Richard and Justin, the high school killers in *Murder by Numbers*, may not have heard of Leopold and Loeb, or seen Hitchcock's *Rope*, or studied any of the other fictional versions *(Compulsion, Swoon)* of the infamous murder pact between two brainy and amoral young men. But they're channeling it. *Murder by Numbers* crosses Leopold/Loeb with a police procedural, and adds an interesting touch: Instead of toying with the audience, it toys with the characters. We have information they desperately desire, and we watch them dueling in misdirection.

The movie stars Sandra Bullock as Cassie Mayweather, a veteran detective, experienced enough to trust her hunches and resist the obvious answers. Ben Chaplin is Sam Kennedy, her by-the-books partner, the kind of cop who gets an A for every step of his investigation, but ends up with the wrong conclusion. Paired against them are Richard Haywood and Justin Pendleton (Ryan Gosling, from *The Believer*, and Michael Pitt, from *Hedwig and the Angry Inch*). These are two brainy high school kids, fascinated, as Leopold and Loeb were, by the possibility of proving their superiority by committing the perfect murder.

Their plan: Pick a victim completely at random, so that there is no link between corpse and killers, and leave behind no clues. The film opens with the suggestion of a suicide pact between the two teenagers, who face each other, holding revolvers to their heads, in a crumbling Gothic building so improbably close to the edge of a seaside cliff that we intuit someone is going to be dangling over it by the end of the film.

Bullock's Cassie is the central character, a good cop but a damaged human being, whose past holds some kind of fearsome grip on her present. Cassie and Sam are assigned to a creepy case; the body of a middle-aged female has been found in a wooded area, and close analysis of clues (hair, strands from a rug) seem to lead back to a suspect. Sam is happy to follow the clues to their logical conclusion. Cassie isn't so sure, and a chance meeting with one of the young sociopaths leads to a suspicion: "Something's not right with that kid."

We learn a lot about police work in *Murder by Numbers*, and there's a kind of fascination in seeing the jigsaw puzzle fall into place, especially since the audience holds some (not all) of the key pieces. Many of the best scenes involve an intellectual and emotional duel between the two young men, who seem to have paused on the brink of becoming lovers and decided to sublimate that passion into an arrogant crime. Richard and Justin are smart— Justin smarter in an intellectual way, Richard better at manipulating others. The movie wisely reserves details of who did what in the killing, and why.

These are affluent kids with absent parents, who are their own worst enemies because their arrogance leads them to play games with the cops to show how smart they are. They'd be better off posing as vacant-headed slackers. It is Cassie's intuition that the boys are inviting her attention, are turned on by the nearness of capture. Meanwhile, of course, her partner and the brass at the station are eager for a quick solution. A janitor is the obvious suspect? Arrest the janitor.

The movie has been directed by the versatile Barbet Schroeder, who alternates between powerful personal films *(Our Lady of the Assassins)* and skillful thrillers *(Single White Female)*. When the two strands cross you get one-of-a-kind films like *Reversal of Fortune* and *Barfly*. After the semidocumentary freedom and scary Colombian locations of *Our Lady of the Assassins*, here's a movie that he directs as an exercise in craft—only occasionally letting his mordant humor peer through, as in an inexplicable scene where Cassie is bitten by a monkey.

Sandra Bullock does a good job here of working against her natural likeability, creating a character you'd like to like, and could like, if she weren't so sad, strange, and turned in upon herself. She throws herself into police work not so much because she's dedicated as

419

because she needs the distraction, needs to keep busy and be good to assure herself of her worth. As she draws the net closer, and runs into more danger and more official opposition, the movie more or less helplessly starts thinking to itself about that cliff above the sea, but at least the climax shows us that Bullock can stay in character no matter what.

The Musketeer ★ ★ ½

PG-13, 105 m., 2001

Justin Chambers (D'Artagnan), Tim Roth (Febre), Mena Suvari (Francesca), Catherine Deneuve (Queen of France), Stephen Rea (Cardinal Richelieu), Joachim Paul Assbock (Hessian), Jean-Pierre Castaldi (Planchet), Jeremy Clyde (Lord Buckingham), Patrick Dean (Febre's Man), Stefan Jurgens (Darcy), Jan Gregor Kremp (Athos). Directed by Peter Hyams and produced by Rudy Cohen and Moshe Diamant. Screenplay by Gene Quintano, based on the novel by Alexandre Dumas.

Peter Hyams's *The Musketeer* combines traditional swashbuckling with martial arts in a movie where the men wear plumes in their hats but pounce like crouching tigers and scheme like hidden dragons. No wonder; the choreography of the fight scenes is by Xin Xin Xiong—not a name on every tongue, I grant you, but he is one of the top action designers in Hong Kong.

The big-budget extravaganza, with sensational sets and battle scenes, is set in seventeenth-century France, where a Spanish invasion is feared and Cardinal Richelieu (Stephen Rea) has raised a private army while King Louis XIII's loyal musketeers are in disgrace. Then young D'Artagnan (Justin Chambers), who saw his parents murdered by the evil Febre (Tim Roth), rides to the rescue, jump-starts the musketeers, saves the queen, falls in love with the queen's comely dresser, and so on.

The history is not the point, and neither is the story. Both exist only to supply excuses for a series of action sequences, which steal the show to such an extent that if you like martial arts scenes you'll admire this movie, and if you don't, you won't.

Like Hong Kong fight movies, *The Musketeer* makes great use of handy props, folding them

into the action scenes. Nowhere is this more dramatic (or ludicrous, depending on your point of view) than in a final duel between D'Artagnan and Febre, which takes place in a warehouse stacked to the ceiling with shelves of big wine barrels. Of course to reach the barrels, you need ladders—*lots* of ladders, with the two fighters leaping from one to another, walking them across the floor, swinging through space clinging to them, and finally, incredibly, balancing one on a center beam and using it as a teeter-totter for their final showdown. This is harder than it looks.

Oh, and I forgot to mention what led up to that. D'Artagnan has freed all the imprisoned musketeers, who form an army to attack the castle where the queen (Catherine Deneuve) and the comely dresser (Mena Suvari, from *American Beauty* and *American Pie*) are being held prisoner by the vile Febre. After the queen drops a marble bust at his feet to attract his attention (lucky she didn't hit him on the head), D'Artagnan fires a rope to the top of the tower and climbs up, hand over hand, to rescue them—but then defenders lower their own ropes, and soon four or five fighters are swaying in big arcs back and forth high above the ground, holding on with one hand while swordfighting, which is harder than it looks.

An earlier chase sequence involves an attempt by Febre to capture the coach containing the queen and the comely dresser, where D'Artagnan single-handedly holds off the entire force, at one point leaping from the saddle of his galloping horse to the saddle of the horse in front (harder than it looks). And there is an early scene where D'Artagnan is able to support himself between two ceiling beams with pressure from his legs and one arm, while the free arm wields a sword. So much harder than it looks that it borders, I would hazard, on the impossible.

There are barrels in this movie. So many barrels they supply the leitmotiv, as they roll, thunder, spill, explode, and impede. At one point D'Artagnan actually balances on top of a barrel and rolls it beneath his feet while swordfighting. Harder than it looks.

Occasionally the action is interrupted by dialogue scenes, which are easier than they look. None of the drama in this movie would stretch Errol Flynn—or Errol Morris, for that matter. Tim Roth already holds the crown for the single best swashbuckling scene in modern film history (in *Rob Roy*). This time, where most of the action is special effects, stunts, rope-flies, and animation, he focuses on being hateful. I love it when the queen tells him, "You have no mercy in your heart" and he replies: "No mercy. No heart."

I cannot in strict accuracy recommend this film. It's such a jumble of action and motivation, ill-defined characters and action howlers. I am not even quite sure if Richelieu and Febre are on the same side, or if there are three or even four sides in the story. But the banquet scene is a marvel of art design. The action scenes are wonders to behold. And when Tim Roth vows vengeance on the man who blinded him, I, for one, believe him.

My Best Fiend ★ ★ ★
NO MPAA RATING, 95 m., 2000

A documentary directed by Werner Herzog and produced by Lucki Stipetic.

Werner Herzog made five films starring Klaus Kinski. Few other directors wanted to work with him more than once. Midway in their first film, *Aguirre, the Wrath of God* (1972), Kinski threatened to walk off the set, deep in the Amazon rain forest, and Herzog said he would shoot him dead if he did. Kinski claims in his autobiography that he had the gun, not Herzog. Herzog says that's a lie. Kinski describes Herzog in the book as a "nasty, sadistic, treacherous, cowardly creep." Herzog says in the film that Kinski knew his autobiography would not sell unless he said shocking things—so Herzog helped him look up vile words he could use in describing the director.

And so it goes on, almost a decade after Kinski's death, the unending love-hate relationship between the visionary German filmmaker and his muse and nemesis in five films. Herzog's new documentary, *My Best Fiend*, traces their history together. They had one of the most fruitful and troubled relationships of any director-actor team.

Together they made *Aguirre*, about a mad conquistador in the Peruvian jungle; *Fitzcarraldo* (1982), about a man who used block-and-tackle to pull a steamship from one Amazonian river system to another; *Nosferatu* (1979), inspired by Murnau's silent vampire classic; *Woyzeck* (1979), about a nineteenth-century army private who seems mad to others because he sees the world in his own alternative way; and *Cobra Verde* (1988), about a slave trader in Africa. All of their collaborations contain extraordinary images, but the sight in that one of Kinski running wild inside an army of naked, spear-carrying amazons may be the strangest.

Reviewing *Woyzeck*, I wrote: "It is almost impossible to imagine Kinski without Herzog; reflect that this 'unforgettable' actor made more than 170 films for other directors—and we can hardly remember a one." Consider, too, that their strange bond began long before Herzog stood behind a camera.

Herzog told me how they met. When he was twelve, he said, "I was playing in the courtyard of the building where we lived in Munich, and I looked up and saw this man striding past, and I knew at that moment that my destiny was to direct films and that he would be the actor." Kinski was known for his scorn of both films and acting, and claimed to choose projects entirely on the basis of how comfortable he would be on the location. Yet when Herzog summoned him to the rain forest for *Aguirre*, where he would have to march through the jungle wearing Spanish armor and end up on a sinking raft with gibbering monkeys, he accepted. Why? I asked him once, and he replied grimly: "It was my fate."

Herzog believes in shooting on location, arguing that specific places have a voodoo that penetrates the film. *Fitzcarraldo* could have been shot in comfort, not 900 miles up the Amazon, and with special effects and a model boat—but Herzog insisted on isolating his crew, and in hauling a real boat up a real hill. When engineers warned him the ropes would snap and cut everyone in two, he dismissed the engineers. That's all the more intriguing when you learn that Kinski was even more hated than Herzog on the location. In *My Best Fiend*, Herzog recalls that local Indians came to him with an offer to kill Kinski. "I needed Kinski for a few more shots, so I turned them down," he says. "I have always regretted that I lost that opportunity."

He learned early about Kinski's towering rages. The actor actually lived for several months in the same flat with Herzog's family, and once locked himself in the bathroom for two days, screaming all the while, and reducing the porcelain fixtures "to grains the size of sand." Only once, on *Aguirre,* was he able to fully contain his anger in his character—perhaps because Aguirre was as mad as Kinski—and there he gave one of the great performances in the cinema. Herzog revisits the original locations, recalling fights they had and showing the specific scenes that were shot just afterward.

There must have been good times, too, although Herzog shows only one of them—a happy day at the Telluride Film Festival. *My Best Fiend* suffers a little by not having footage to cover more of Herzog's sharpest memories (Les Blank's legendary documentary *Burden of Dreams,* shot on location during *Fitzcarraldo,* shows the two men at each other's throats). But as a meditation by a director on an actor, it is unique; most show biz docs involve the ritual exchange of compliments. *My Best Fiend* is about two men who both wanted to be dominant, who both had all the answers, who were inseparably bound together in love and hate, and who created extraordinary work— while all the time each resented the other's contribution.

My Big Fat Greek Wedding ★ ★ ★
PG, 95 m., 2002

Nia Vardalos (Toula Portokalos), John Corbett (Ian Miller), Lainie Kazan (Maria), Michael Constantine (Gus), Gia Carides (Nikki), Louis Mandylor (Nick), Joey Fatone (Angelo), Bruce Gray (Rodney Miller). Directed by Joel Zwick and produced by Gary Goetzman, Tom Hanks, and Rita Wilson. Screenplay by Nia Vardalos.

All the people in this movie look like they could be real people. The romance involves not impossibly attractive people, but a thirty-year-old woman who looks okay when she pulls herself out of her Frump Phase, and a vegetarian high school teacher who urgently needs the services of SuperCuts. Five minutes into the film, I relaxed, knowing it was set in the real world, and not in the Hollywood alternative universe where Julia Roberts can't get a date.

My Big Fat Greek Wedding is narrated by Toula Portokalos (Nia Vardalos), who, like all Greek women, she says, was put upon this Earth for three purposes: to marry a Greek man, to have Greek children, and to feed everyone until the day she dies. Toula is still single and works in the family restaurant (Dancing Zorbas), where, as she explains, she is *not* a waitress, but a "seating hostess." One day a guy with the spectacularly non-Greek name of Ian Miller (John Corbett) walks in, and she knows instinctively that marriage is thinkable.

The movie is warmhearted in the way a movie can be when it knows its people inside out. Watching it, I was reminded of Mira Nair's *Monsoon Wedding,* about an Indian wedding. Both cultures place great emphasis on enormous extended families, enormous extended weddings, and enormous extended wedding feasts. Nia Vardalos, who not only stars but based the screenplay on her own one-woman play, obviously has great affection for her big Greek family, and a little exasperation, too— as who wouldn't, with a father who walks around with a spray jar of Windex because he is convinced it will cure anything? Or a mother who explains, "When I was your age, we didn't *have* food."

Vardalos was an actress at Chicago's Second City when she wrote the play. The way the story goes, it was seen by Rita Wilson, a Greek-American herself, and she convinced her husband, Tom Hanks, that they had to produce it. So they did, making a small treasure of human comedy. The movie is set in Chicago but was filmed in Toronto—too bad, because the dating couple therefore doesn't have a chizbooger at Billy Goat's.

As the film opens, Toula the heroine is single at thirty and therefore a failure. Ian Miller causes her heart to leap up in love and desire, and Ian likes her too. Really likes her. This isn't one of those formula pictures where it looks like he's going to dump her. There's enough to worry about when the families meet. "No one in our family has ever gone out with a non-Greek," Toula warns him uneasily, and indeed her parents (Lainie Kazan and Michael Constantine) regard Ian like a lesser life form.

The movie is pretty straightforward: Ian and Toula meet, they date, they bashfully discover they like each other, the families uneasily coexist, the wedding becomes inevitable, and it takes place (when Ian's mother brings a bundt cake to the wedding, no one has the slightest idea what it is). One key shot shows the church with the bride's side jammed, and the groom's handful of WASP relatives making a pathetic show in their first four rows. Toula explains to Ian that she has twenty-seven first cousins, and at a prenuptial party, her dad even introduces some of them: "Nick, Nick, Nick, Nick, Nick, Nick, Nicky—and Gus."

The underlying story of *My Big Fat Greek Wedding* has been played out countless times as America's immigrants have intermarried. If the lovers have understanding (or at least reluctantly flexible) parents, love wins the day and the melting pot bubbles. This is nicely illustrated by Toula's father, Gus. He specializes in finding the Greek root for *any* word (even "kimono"), and delivers a toast in which he explains that "Miller" goes back to the Greek word for apple, and "Portokalos" is based on the Greek word for oranges, and so, he concludes triumphantly, "in the end, we're all fruits."

My Dog Skip ★ ★ ★
PG, 95 m., 2000

Frankie Muniz (Willie Morris), Diane Lane (Ellen Morris), Luke Wilson (Dink), Kevin Bacon (Jack Morris), Mark Beech (Army Buddy), Harry Connick Jr. (Narrator). Directed by Jay Russell and produced by Broderick Johnson and Andrew Kosove. Screenplay by Gail Gilchriest, based on the book by Willie Morris.

Don't trust any critic who writes about *My Dog Skip* without remembering his childhood dog. My dog was named Blackie. He was part cocker, part beagle, and he was my friend. The sweet thing about *My Dog Skip* is the way it understands the friendship between a kid and a dog. Dogs accomplish amazing things in the movies, but the best thing Skip does is look up at his master, eager to find out what they're gonna do next.

The movie is much elaborated from a memoir by Willie Morris, who grew up in Yazoo, on the Mississippi Delta, and went on to become the editor of *Harper's* magazine. Not everything

in the movie actually happened. Its embroideries remind me of Huck Finn's comment about Tom Sawyer: "He told the truth, mainly. There was things which he stretched, but mainly he told the truth."

It is probably not true, for example, that young Willie (Frankie Muniz) volunteered Skip to become an army para-puppy. Oh, I believe Willie (and Skip) saw a newsreel about the brave dogs in our fighting forces. And I believe that Willie trained Skip to become what the newsreel calls a "Yankee Doodle doggy." What I don't believe is that any kid would send his dog away to war. Let him serve on the home front.

The movie is set in the summer of 1942. Willie is a lonely child. He's no good at sports, he doesn't make friends easily, and he has a standoffish relationship with his dad (Kevin Bacon), who lost a leg in the Spanish Civil War, "and a piece of his heart." Will's mom (Diane Lane) tries to make her child happy, but look at that birthday party she throws, where all the guests are old folks, and one of them gives him a bow tie. Will's "older and only friend" is Dink (Luke Wilson), a high school sports star, who lives next door and goes off to war before he can teach Will the secrets of the curveball.

Mom decides Will needs a dog. Dad is against it. "He needs a friend," Mom says, snatching the cigar out of Dad's mouth and puffing on it herself, as a Freudian signal of her takeover. She gives the dog to Will, and Will's life is changed forever. With Skippy, he runs all over town, and the fields outside of town, and other kids want to be his friend because he has a dog.

This is some dog. It knows everybody in town, and makes a daily stop at the butcher shop for a slice of bologna. When Will makes several errors in a baseball game, Skip runs onto the field to help Will. When Will, distraught, slaps his dog, I found to my amazement that I recoiled with dismay. That's when I discovered how the movie had gotten to me. How I had shelved a movie critic's usual reserve and just started identifying with Will and Skip. I wasn't good at sports, either, and Blackie helped me make friends.

There's a subplot about moonshiners that isn't too convincing. I don't know why they'd need to hide their booze in a cemetery crypt, and I wasn't convinced when that led to a crisis for Skip at the end. But I did remember riding my bike all over the neighborhood once when Blackie ran away, calling out his name again and again as dusk fell, and the movie has that right.

Another subplot has to do with Dink, who comes back from the war in a different mood than when he left, and tells Will, "It isn't the dying that's scary—it's the killing." And there's a scene where Will sees a deer die before his eyes. We understand that in every childhood there are lessons burned into your memory. They shape you. In Willie Morris's case, they guided him out of Yazoo and to Oxford on a Rhodes scholarship, and then to New York and a literary career. But he never forgot Skip.

A movie like this falls outside ordinary critical language. Is it good or bad? Is there too much melodrama? I don't have any idea. It triggered too many thoughts of my own for me to have much attention left over for footnotes. I realize, for example, that the movie doesn't deal in any substantial way with the racial situation in Mississippi in 1942, and I know that Will's dad undergoes a rather miraculous transformation, and that Dink seems less like a neighbor than like a symbol of lost innocence. I know those things, but they don't seem relevant to the actual experience of this movie. If there was ever a day or even a minute when your dog was not your best but your only friend, you'll see what I mean.

My First Mister ★ ★ ★
R, 109 m., 2001

Leelee Sobieski (Jennifer), Albert Brooks (Randall), Carol Kane (Mrs. Benson), Michael McKean (Bob), Desmond Harrington (Randy), Mary Kay Place (Patty [Nurse]). Directed by Christine Lahti and produced by Mitchell Solomon, Sukee Chew, Anne Kurtzman, Carol Baum, and Jane Goldenring. Screenplay by Jill Franklyn.

Consider now Leelee Sobieski, who is nineteen years old and has been acting since she was twelve. My First Mister is the latest in a series of wonderful performances in a career so busy that earlier in 2001 she appeared in The Glass

House and Joy Ride. I did not much notice her in Deep Impact (1998) and wanted to avert my eyes from the entire movie during Jungle2-Jungle (1997). But in 1998, she came into her own as the heroine of A Soldier's Daughter Never Cries, based on the autobiographical story by Kaylie Jones, the daughter of the novelist James Jones. And in 1999, she found time to be Joan of Arc on TV, costar with Drew Barrymore in Never Been Kissed, and play a small role in Kubrick's Eyes Wide Shut.

A new star doesn't always explode. Sometimes she just . . . occurs to you. I was so involved in the story of A Soldier's Daughter Never Cries that my review said nothing specific about her performance, although in a sense the whole review was in praise of it. Only with The Glass House and Joy Ride, seen so close to each other, with the memory of My First Mister still warm from Sundance 2001, did it become inescapable that she is an important new talent, an actress who has arrived at the top without having to make a single teenage horror film or American Pie rip-off.

She usually plays intelligent, well-scrubbed characters, convincingly. Here she's Jennifer, smart but alienated—a pierced, tattooed Goth. Stomping around in zip-up boots, her chains clanking, she is the despair of a ditzy mother (Carol Kane) who thinks the answer to everything is getting dinner on the table on time. She has refused to go to college, has no job or boyfriend, is a loner wandering through the mall—and one day sees a man adjusting the window display at a men's clothing store. Something about his personal style, his manner of carrying himself, strikes her, and she drifts in to ask about a job.

This is Randall (Albert Brooks). "Hire you?" he says. "For every suit you sell, you're gonna send thirty customers fleeing out of the store." "Dress me," she says. He does. "I look like a Republican," she says. He's forty-nine; she's seventeen. It's odd how they become friends while tacitly sidestepping the idea of sex, although she does raise the subject once, so bluntly that he sprays his Sanka at a hip coffee shop.

The movie is not about sex, not about a Lolita, but about a friendship between two loners. He has her number. "Do you have a copy of The Bell Jar next to your bed?" he asks.

It's a good guess. "Who do you talk to? Who are your friends?" he asks. "You," she says.

These two characters are so particular and sympathetic that the whole movie could simply observe them. In a way, I wish it had. The film, directed by Christine Lahti from a screenplay by Jill Franklyn, is best in the first hour or more, when things seem to be happening spontaneously. I was a little disappointed when it narrowed down into more conventional channels, involving a crisis and a long-lost son. And a closing dinner scene, assembling the characters, seemed like a convenient plot device.

Still, Sobieski and Brooks stay true to their characters even as the movie gives them less room for spontaneity. Brooks is always able to enrich a role with specific, precise touches. Watch him straightening the stacks of magazines in his house, and listen to him tell a tattoo artist: "I want the smallest tattoo you have. Can you give me a dot, or a period?" Sobieski is wise to make Jennifer practical in the way she abandons her lifestyle: Instead of making it seem like a corny transformation, she makes it a pragmatic choice. It works for her, and when it stops working, she ditches it.

The bravest thing about the movie is the way it doesn't cave in to teenage multiplex demographics with another story about dumb adults and cool kids. *My First Mister* is about reaching out, about seeing the other person, about having something to say and being able to listen. So what if the ending is on autopilot? At least it's a flight worth taking.

Note: There is no earthly reason this movie is rated R. The flywheels at the MPAA have taken flight from the values of the world we inhabit.

The Mystic Masseur ★ ★ ★
PG, 117 m., 2002

Aasif Mandvi (Ganesh), Om Puri (Ramlogan), James Fox (Mr. Stewart), Sanjeev Bhaskar (Beharry), Ayesha Dharker (Leela), Jimi Mistry (Partap), Zohra Segal (Auntie), Sakina Jaffrey (Suruj Mooma). Directed by Ismail Merchant and produced by Nayeem Hafizka and Richard Hawley. Screenplay by Caryl Phillips, based on the novel by V. S. Naipaul.

The West Indies were a footnote to the British Empire, and the Indian community of Trinidad was a footnote to the footnote. After slavery was abolished and the Caribbean still needed cheap labor, thousands of Indians were brought from one corner of the empire to another to supply it. They formed an insular community, treasuring traditional Hindu customs, importing their dress styles and recipes, re-creating India far from home on an island where it seemed irrelevant to white colonial rulers and the black majority.

The great man produced by these exiles was V. S. Naipaul, the 2001 Nobel laureate for literature, whose father was a newspaperman with a great respect for books and ideas. *A House for Mr. Biswas* (1961) is Naipaul's novel about his father and his own childhood, and one of the best books of the century. But Naipaul's career began in 1957 with *The Mystic Masseur,* a novel casting a fond but dubious light on the Indian community of Trinidad. It is now the first of Naipaul's novels to be filmed, directed by Ismail Merchant, himself an Indian, usually the producing partner for director James Ivory.

The Mystic Masseur is a wry, affectionate delight, a human comedy about a man who thinks he has had greatness thrust upon him when in fact he has merely thrust himself in the general direction of greatness. It tells the story of Ganesh, a schoolteacher with an exaggerated awe for books, who is inspired by a dotty Englishman to write some of his own. Abandoning the city for a rural backwater, he begins to compose short philosophical tomes which, published by the local printer on a foot-powered flatbed press, give him a not-quite-deserved reputation for profundity.

If Ganesh allowed his success to go to his head, he would be insufferable. Instead, he is played by Aasif Mandvi as a man so sincere he really does believe in his mission. Does he have the power to cure with his touch and advise troubled people on their lives? Many think he does, and soon he has become married to the pretty daughter of a canny businessman, who runs taxis from the city to bring believers to Ganesh's rural retreat.

There is rich humor in the love-hate relationship many Indians have with their customs, which they leaven with a decided streak of practicality. In no area is this more true than marriage, as you can see in Mira Nair's wonderful comedy *Monsoon Wedding.* The events leading up to Ganesh's marriage to the beautiful Leela (Ayesha Dharker) are hilarious, as the ambitious businessman Ramlogan positions his daughter to capture the rising young star.

Played by the great Indian actor Om Puri with lip-smacking satisfaction, Ramlogan makes sure Ganesh appreciates Leela's dark-eyed charm, and then demonstrates her learning by producing a large wooden sign she has lettered, with a bright red punctuation mark after every word. "Leela know a lot of punctuation marks," he boasts proudly, and soon she has Ganesh within her parentheses. The wedding brings a showdown between the two men; custom dictates that the father-in-law must toss bills onto a plate as long as the new husband is still eating his kedgeree, and Ganesh, angered that Ramlogan has stiffed him with the wedding bill, dines slowly.

The humor in *The Mystic Masseur* is generated by Ganesh's good-hearted willingness to believe in his ideas and destiny, both of which are slight. Like a thrift shop Gandhi, he sits on his veranda writing pamphlets and advising supplicants on health, wealth, and marriage. Leela meanwhile quietly takes charge, managing the family business, as Ganesh becomes the best-known Indian on Trinidad. Eventually he forms the Hindu Association, collects some political power, and is elected to Parliament, which is the beginning of his end. Transplanted from his rural base to the capital, he finds his party outnumbered by Afro-Caribbeans and condescended to by the British governors; he has traded his stature for a meaningless title, and is correctly seen by other Indians as a stooge.

The masseur's public career has lasted only from 1943 to 1954. The mistake would be to assign too much significance to Ganesh. His lack of significance is the whole point. He rises to visibility as a homegrown guru, is co-opted by the British colonial government, and by the end of the film is a nonentity shipped safely out of sight to Oxford on a cultural exchange. Critics of the film have slighted Ganesh for being a pointless man leading a marginal life; they don't sense the anger and hurt seething just below the genial surface of the novel. The young Trinidadian Indian studying at Oxford, who meets Ganesh at the train station in the opening scene, surely represents Naipaul, observing the wreck of a man who loomed large in his childhood.

Movies are rarely about inconsequential characters. They favor characters who are sensational winners or losers. But Ganesh, one senses, is precisely the character Naipaul needed to express his feelings about being an Indian in Trinidad. He has written elsewhere about the peculiarity of being raised in an Indian community thousands of miles from "home," attempting to reflect a land none of its members had ever seen. The empire created generations of such displaced communities, not least the British exiles in India, sipping Earl Grey, reading the *Times,* and saluting "God Save the Queen" in blissful oblivion to the world around them.

Ganesh gets about as far as he could get, given the world he was born into, and he is such an innocent that many of his illusions persist. Shown around the Bodleian Library in Oxford by his young guide, the retired statesman looks at the walls of books, and says, "Boy, this the center of the world! Everything begin here, everything lead back to this place." Naipaul's whole career would be about his struggle with that theory.

N

National Lampoon's Van Wilder ★
R, 95 m., 2002

Ryan Reynolds (Van Wilder), Tara Reid (Gwen), Kal Penn (Taj), Tim Matheson (Vance Wilder Sr.), Kim Smith (Casey), Daniel Cosgrove (Richard Bagg), Tom Everett Scott (Elliot Grebb), Chris Owen (Timmy [the Jumper]). Directed by Walt Becker and produced by Peter Abrams, Robert L. Levy, Jonathon Komack Martin, and Andrew Panay. Screenplay by Brent Goldberg and David Wagner.

Watching *National Lampoon's Van Wilder,* I grew nostalgic for the lost innocence of a movie like *American Pie,* in which human semen found itself in a pie. In *NatLampVW,* dog semen is baked in a pastry. Is it only a matter of time until the heroes of teenage gross-out comedies are injecting turtle semen directly through their stomach walls?

National Lampoon's Van Wilder, a pale shadow of *National Lampoon's Animal House,* tells the story of Van Wilder (Ryan Reynolds), who has been the Biggest Man on Campus for seven glorious undergraduate years. He doesn't want to graduate, and why should he, since he has clout, fame, babes, and the adulation of the entire campus (except, of course, for the professor whose parking space he swipes, and the vile fraternity boy who is his sworn enemy).

Van Wilder is essentially a nice guy, which is a big risk for a movie like this to take; he raises funds for the swimming team, tries to restrain suicidal students, and throws legendary keg parties. Ryan Reynolds is, I suppose, the correct casting choice for Van Wilder, since the character is not a devious slacker but merely a permanent student. That makes him, alas, a little boring, and Reynolds (from ABC's *Two Guys and a Girl*) brings along no zing: He's a standard leading man when the movie cries out for a manic character actor. Jack Black in this role would have been a home run.

Is Van Wilder too good to be true? That's what Gwen (Tara Reid) wonders. She's a journalism student who wants to do an in-depth piece about Van for the campus paper. Of course she's the girlfriend of the vile frat boy, and of course her investigation inspires her to admire the real Van Wilder while deploring his public image. Tara Reid is remarkably attractive, as you may remember from *Josie and the Pussycats* and *American Pie 2,* but much of the time she simply seems to be imitating still photos of Renee Zellweger smiling.

That leaves, let's see, Kal Penn as Taj, the Indian-American student who lands the job as Van Wilder's assistant, and spends much of his time using a stereotyped accent while reciting lists of synonyms for oral sex. I cannot complain, since the hero's buddy in every movie in this genre is always a sex-crazed zealot, and at least this film uses nontraditional casting. (Casting directors face a catch-22: They cast a white guy, and everybody wants to know why he had to be white. So they cast an ethnic guy, and everybody complains about the negative stereotype. Maybe the way out is to cast the ethnic guy as the hero and the white guy as the horny doofus.)

The movie is a barfathon that takes full advantage of the apparent MPAA guidelines in which you can do pretty much anything with bodily functions except involve them in healthy sex. The movie contains semen, bare breasts and butts, epic flatulence, bizarre forms of masturbation, public nudity, projectile vomiting, and an extended scene of explosive defecation with sound effects that resemble the daily duties of the Port-a-Loo serviceman, in reverse. There are also graphic shots of enormous testicles, which are allowed under the *National Geographic* loophole since they belong to Van Wilder's pet bulldog. Presumably the MPAA would not permit this if it had reason to believe there were dogs in the audience.

"On a scale of 1 to 10 shots of bourbon needed to make a pledge ralph," writes Bob Patterson of the Website Delusions of Adequacy, "this film will get a very strong five from most college-age film fans who are not offended by vulgar humor. Older filmgoers who might be offended by such offerings are encouraged to do something that is physically impossible (i.e., lift yourself up by your bootstraps)."

Although this is obviously the review the movie deserves, I confess the rating scale baffles me. Is it better or worse if a film makes you ralph? Patterson implies that older filmgoers might be offended by vulgar humor. There is a flaw in this reasoning: It is not age but humor that is the variable. Laughter for me was such a physical impossibility during *National Lampoon's Van Wilder* that had I not been pledged to sit through the film, I would have lifted myself up by my bootstraps and fled.

The New Guy ★ ★
PG-13, 100 m., 2002

D. J. Qualls (Dizzy/Gil), Lyle Lovett (Bear Harrison), Eddie Griffin (Luther), Eliza Dushku (Danielle), Zooey Deschanel (Nora), Parry Shen (Glen), Laura Clifton (Emily). Directed by Ed Decter and produced by Mark Ciardi, Todd Garner, and Gordon Gray. Screenplay by David Kendall.

D. J. Qualls stars in *The New Guy* as a high school misfit who switches schools and gets a fresh start. At Rocky Creek, he was the target of cruel jokes almost daily (sample: being tied to a chair while wearing false breasts), but now, at Eastland High and with a new haircut, he is seen as a cool hero. "The point is," he explains with relief, "today nobody stuffed me in my locker or singed off my ass hairs."

The movie made from this material is quirkier than I would have expected, considering that the building blocks have been scavenged from the trash heap of earlier teenage comedies. Much of the credit goes to Qualls (from *Road Trip*), who not only plays the son of Lyle Lovett in this movie but looks biologically descended from him, no mean feat. He has a goofy grin and an offhand way with dialogue that make him much more likable than your usual teenage comedy hero.

Known at one school by his nickname Dizzy and at the other by his first name Gil, Dizzy/Gil does not approach the dating game with high expectations. Here's how he asks a popular girl out on a date: "Maybe sometime if you would like to drink coffee near me, I would pay." There is a school scandal at Rocky Creek when a librarian does something painful and embarrassing I cannot describe here to that part of his anatomy I cannot name, and he ends up in prison. (His condition or crime—I am not sure—is described as Tourette's syndrome, which is either a misdiagnosis, a

mispronunciation, or an example of Tourette's in action.)

Yes, prison. The movie begins with a direct-to-camera narration by Luther (Eddie Griffin), who is in prison for undisclosed reasons and is the narrator of this film for reasons even more deeply concealed. Perhaps my attention strayed, but I was unable to discern any connection between Luther and the other characters, and was baffled by how Dizzy/Gil was in prison whenever he needed to get advice from Luther, and then out again whenever it was necessary for him to rejoin the story in progress. Perhaps a subplot, or even a whole movie, is missing from the middle.

In any event, Dizzy/Gil is seen as a neat guy at the new school, especially after he unfurls a giant American flag at football practice and stands in front of it dressed as George C. Scott in *Patton* and delivers a speech so rousing that the team wins for the first time in five years. He also steals a horse and rides around on it more than is necessary.

The movie has all the shots you would expect in a movie of this sort: cheerleaders, football heroics, pratfalls. Some of them are cruel, as when a bully stuffs a midget in a trash can and rolls it downhill. Others are predictably vulgar, as when Dizzy snatches a surveillance camera from the wall and (aided by its extension cord of infinite length) uses it to send a live broadcast into every classroom of a hated teacher struggling with a particularly difficult bowel movement. Sometimes even verbal humor is attempted, as when a high school counselor (Illeana Douglas) tells our hero he is in denial, and helpfully explains, "Denial is not just a river in Egypt."

I don't know why this movie was made or who it was made for. It is, however, not assembly-line fodder, and seems occasionally to be the work of inmates who have escaped from the Hollywood High School Movie Asylum. It makes little sense, fails as often as it succeeds, and yet is not hateful and is sometimes quite cheerfully original. And D. J. Qualls is a kid you can't help but like—a statement I do not believe I have ever before made about the hero of a teenage vulgarian movie. ☞

The Next Best Thing ★
PG-13, 110 m., 2000

Rupert Everett (Robert), Madonna (Abbie), Benjamin Bratt (Ben), Michael Vartan (Kevin), Malcolm Stumpf (Sam), Neil Patrick Harris (David), Illeana Douglas (Elizabeth Ryder), Josef Sommer (Richard Whittaker), Lynn Redgrave (Helen Whittaker). Directed by John Schlesinger and produced by Tom Rosenberg, Leslie Dixon, and Linne Radmin. Screenplay by Thomas Ropelewski.

The Next Best Thing is a garage sale of gay issues, harnessed to a plot as exhausted as a junk man's horse. There are times when the characters don't know if they're living their lives or enacting edifying little dramas for an educational film. The screenplay's so evenhanded it has *no* likable characters, either gay or straight; after seeing this film, I wanted to move to Garry Shandling's world in *What Planet Are You From?* where nobody has sex.

Not that anybody has a lot of sex in this PG-13 film. The story hinges on a murky alcoholic night spent by Abbie (Madonna) and her gay best friend Robert (Rupert Everett). They were both in drunken blackouts, although of course by the next morning they're able to discuss their blackouts with wit and style, unlike your average person, who would be puking. Abbie gets pregnant and decides to have the baby, and Robert announces he will be a live-in father to the child, although he doesn't go so far as to become a husband to its mother.

Both Abbie and Robert are right up-to-date when it comes to sexual open-mindedness. Robert still dates, and Abbie's okay with that, although when Abbie meets a guy named Ben (Benjamin Bratt), Robert turns into a green-eyed monster. That's because Ben wants to marry Abbie and move to New York, and where would that leave Robert? If you think this movie, which begins as a sexual comedy, is going to end up as a stultifying docudrama about child custody, with big courtroom scenes before the obligatory stern black female judge, you are no more than ordinarily prescient.

The movie's problem is that it sees every side of all issues. It sides with Robert's need to be a father, and Benjamin's need to be a husband and lover, and Abbie's need to have a best friend, a husband, a lover, a son, and a lawyer. Luckily there is plenty of money for all of this, because Abbie is a yoga instructor and Robert is a gardener, and we know what piles of money you can make in those jobs, especially in the movies. I wish the film had scaled its lifestyles to the realities of service industry workers, instead of having the characters live in the kinds of places where they can dance around the living room to (I am not kidding) Fred Astaire's "Steppin' Out With My Baby" and have catered backyard birthday parties that I clock at $10,000, easy.

In describing the plot, I've deliberately left out two or three twists that had me stifling groans of disbelief. It's not that they're implausible; it's that they're not necessary. Any movie is bankrupt anyway when it depends on Perry Mason–style, last-minute, unexpected courtroom appearances to solve what should be an emotional choice.

Rupert Everett, "openly gay," as they say, must have had to grit his teeth to get through some of his scenes. Consider a sequence where, as Abbie's best friend, he is delegated to pick up her house keys after she breaks up with her early boyfriend, Kevin ("I want to date less complicated women," Kevin tells her). Kevin is a record producer, and we see him mixing the tracks for a rap group when Robert swishes in and pretends to be his ex-lover, while there are lots of yuks from the homophobic black rappers. Give the scene credit: At least it's not politically correct.

Madonna never emerges as a plausible human being in the movie; she's more like a spokesperson for a video on alternative parenting lifestyles. She begins the movie with a quasi-British accent, but by the halfway mark we get line readings like "we can be in each other's lifes" (a Brit, and indeed many an American, would say "lives").

This and other details should have been noticed by the director, John Schlesinger, whose career has included *Midnight Cowboy, Sunday Bloody Sunday, The Falcon and the Snowman, Madame Sousatzka,* and now . . . this?

Watching the movie, I asked myself why so many movies with homosexuals feel they need to be about homosexuality. Why can't a movie just get over it? I submit as evidence the magical film *Wonder Boys*, in which the homosexuality of the character played by Robert Downey Jr. is completely absorbed into the much larger notion of who he is as a person. Nobody staggers backward and gasps out that his character is gay, because of course he's gay and everybody has known that for a long time and, hey, some people *are* gay, y'know? Watching *The Next Best Thing*, we suspect that if sexuality were banned as a topic of conversation, Abbie and Robert would be reduced to trading yoga and gardening tips.

Nico and Dani ★ ★ ★

NO MPAA RATING, 90 m., 2001

Fernando Ramallo (Dani), Jordi Vilches (Nico), Marieta Orozco (Elena), Esther Nubiola (Berta), Chisco Amado (Julian), Ana Gracia (Sonia), Myriam Mezieres (Marianne). Directed by Cesc Gay and produced by Marta Esteban and Gerardo Herrero. Screenplay by Gay and Tomas Aragay, based on the play *Krampack* by Jordi Sanchez.

Nico and Dani considers ten days in the lives of two teenage Spanish boys, during which one finds that he is gay and the other finds that he is not. Oh, but it's a lot more complicated than that. Adolescence always is. The movie takes place at a Spanish beach resort; Dani's parents have gone on vacation, leaving him with a tutor and a cook in the daytime, but on his own at night. His best friend, Nico, comes from Barcelona to spend the week.

The boys are both seventeen, both virgins, both frank about their sexual aspirations but murky about the details. They meet two girls their own age—girls they met the previous summer, but a lot can change in a year when you're a teenager. Elena (Marieta Orozco) likes Nico (Jordi Vilches), and that leaves Berta (Esther Nubiola) and Dani (Fernando Ramallo) to pair off, until Dani realizes he'd rather pair off with Nico.

If this were an American teenage sex comedy . . . but don't get me started. Thanks to the MPAA's determination to steer American teenagers toward material that is immature and vulgar, this movie would never get made except with an R or NC-17 rating. Too bad, since an observant film like *Nico and Dani* could be useful to a confused teenager, suggesting that we all have to choose our own paths in life. Teenagers masturbate and worry about it, and this movie considers the subject in a healthy and helpful way, while the MPAA prefers jokes about despoiled apple pies.

Summer at the shore is casual and aimless. The two couples meet for drinks, go to parties and dances, and visit the beach, where Nico can show off his back flips. It gradually becomes clear that all four of them have concluded that these ten days of freedom are an opportunity to lose their virginity at last. Not all of them do, but the possibility is there.

Nico and Dani return to Dani's house after an evening with the girls, feeling the universal horniness of the teenage boy. They experiment. For Nico, it's a casual, meaningless experience, but for Dani it's more than that, and Nico becomes a little alarmed at Dani's urgency. They just don't share the same feelings.

Elena, meanwhile, has an agenda of her own, which Nico doesn't discover until a night when they meet to "do it," and she reveals—well, that Nico is expected to play a role but not make any long-range plans. That's okay with Nico, who like many teenage boys will agree to almost anything if his goal is in view.

The movie is more concerned with Dani. His English teacher, Sonia (Ana Gracia), has observed subtle signs of Dani's sexuality, and tries in a quiet way to let him know his feelings are not unique in all the world. She has a gay friend, Julian (Chisco Amado), and one night they all end up at Julian's for dinner, and Dani has too much to drink. Dani knows Julian is gay, and the next morning he makes a bold, if uncertain, pass; Julian knows Dani is underage, and so does Sonia—who warns Julian to keep his hands off. This episode ends inconclusively, like so much in life.

The movie, directed by Cesc Gay, reminds me of one of Eric Rohmer's movies about teenagers on summer vacation; it has the same lightness of feeling and delicacy of touch, although it's more directly concerned with sex than Rohmer would be. It has a plot—who will lose his or her virginity, and how?—but it's not *about* the plot. It isn't so stupid as to think the answer to Who and How is the whole point, since eventually all will lose their virginity, one way or another. American teenage movies tidy things up by pairing off the right couples at the end. In Europe they know that summers end and life goes on.

Nico and Dani is more concerned with values: with what is right and wrong, ethical or not. There's the night, for example, when the boys put Valium in the sangria they serve to the girls. Wrong, and dangerous. When Berta is half-unconscious, Dani begins to take advantage of her; the technical word is rape, although here it's more of a muddle, since Dani finds he's just not that interested in a girl. Spiking the drinks is immoral. So is the way Julian casually but unmistakably makes his life available to Dani. The movie trusts us to arrive at these conclusions, and doesn't add a lot of laborious plotting to pound home the message. We've all done things that we regret; with any luck we learned something from them. Next summer, Dani and Nico will know who they are, Elena will have moved on to another boy, and Berta—well, she's already told Nico, "Elena is Elena and I'm not. I'm me." It's the way she smiles when she says it that lets Nico know what that means.

Nine Queens ★ ★ ★
R, 114 m., 2002

Ricardo Darin (Marcos), Gaston Pauls (Juan), Leticia Bredice (Valeria), Tomas Fonzi (Federico), Ignasi Abadal (Gandolfo). Directed by Fabian Bielinsky and produced by Cecilia Bossi and Pablo Bossi. Screenplay by Bielinsky.

Fabian Bielinsky's *Nine Queens* is a con within a con within a con. There comes a time when we think we've gotten to the bottom, and then the floor gets pulled out again, and we fall for another level. Since nothing is as it seems (it doesn't even seem as it seems), watching the film is like observing a chess game in which all of the pieces are in plain view but one player has figured out a way to cheat. "David Mamet might kill for a script as good," Todd McCarthy writes in *Variety*. True, although Mamet might also reasonably claim to have inspired it; the setup owes something to his *House of Games*, although familiarity with that film will not help you figure out this one.

The film starts with *a seemingly* chance meeting. Indeed, almost everything in the film is "seemingly." A young would-be con man

named Juan (Gaston Pauls) is doing the $20 bill switch with a naive cashier—the switch I have never been able to figure out, where you end up with $39 while seemingly doing the cashier a favor. Juan succeeds. The cashier goes off duty. Juan is greedy, and tries the same trick on her replacement. The first cashier comes back with the manager, screaming that she was robbed. At this point Marcos (Ricardo Darin), a stranger in the store, flashes his gun, identifies himself as a cop, arrests the thief, and hauls him off.

Of course, Marcos is only seemingly a cop. He lectures Juan on the dangers of excessive greed and buys him breakfast, and then the two of them seemingly happen upon an opportunity to pull a big swindle involving the "nine queens," a rare sheet of stamps. This happens when Valeria (Leticia Bredice), seemingly Marcos's sister, berates him because one of his old criminal associates tried to con a client in the hotel where she seemingly works. The old con seemingly had a heart attack, and now the field is seemingly open for Marcos and Juan to bilk the seemingly rich and drunk Gandolfo (Ignasi Abadal).

Now before you think I've given away the game with all those "seeminglys," let me point out that they may only seemingly be seeminglys. They may in fact be as they seem. Or seemingly otherwise. As Juan and Marcos try to work out their scheme, which involves counterfeit stamps, we wonder if in fact the whole game may be a pigeon drop with Juan as the pigeon. But, no, the fake stamps are stolen, seemingly by complete strangers, requiring Marcos and Juan to try to con the owner of the *real* nine queens out of stamps they can sell Gandolfo. (Since they have no plans to really pay for these stamps, their profit would be the same in either case.)

And on and on, around and around, in an elegant and sly deadpan comedy set in modern Buenos Aires. A plot, however clever, is only the clockwork; what matters is what kind of time a movie tells. *Nine Queens* is blessed with a gallery of well-drawn character roles, including the alcoholic mark and his two bodyguards; the avaricious widow who owns the nine queens and her much younger bleached-blond boyfriend; and Valeria the sister, who opposes Marcos's seamy friends and life of crime, but might be willing to sleep with Gandolfo if she can share in the spoils.

Juan meanwhile falls for Valeria himself, and then there are perfectly timed hiccups in the plot where the characters (and we) apparently see through a deception, only to find that deeper reality explains everything—maybe. The story plays out in modern-day Buenos Aires, a city that looks sometimes Latin, sometimes American, sometimes Spanish, sometimes German, sometimes modern, sometimes ancient. Is it possible the city itself is pulling a con on its inhabitants, and that some underlying reality will deceive everyone? The ultimate joke of course would be if the Argentinean economy collapsed, so that everyone's gains, ill-gotten or not, would evaporate. But that is surely too much to hope for.

Note: Nine Queens *is like a South American version of* Stolen Summer, *the movie that won the contest sponsored by HBO, Miramax, and Matt Damon and Ben Affleck. According to* Variety, *some 350 screenplays were submitted in an Argentinean competition, Bielinsky's won, and he was given funds to film. It's illuminating that in both cases such competitions yielded more literate and interesting screenplays than the studios are usually able to find through their own best efforts.* ☞

The Ninth Gate ★ ★
R, 132 m., 2000

Johnny Depp (Dean Corso), Frank Langella (Boris Balkan), Lena Olin (Liana Telfer), Emmanuelle Seigner (The Girl), Barbara Jefford (Baroness Kessler), Jack Taylor (Victor Fargas), Jose Lopez Rodero (Ceniza Brothers), Toni Amoni (Liana's Bodyguard). Directed and produced by Roman Polanski. Screenplay by Enrique Urbizu, Polanski, and John Brownjohn, based on the novel *El Club Dumas* by Arturo Perez Reverte.

Roman Polanski's *The Ninth Gate,* a satanic thriller, opens with a spectacularly good title sequence and goes downhill from there—but slowly, so that all through the first hour there is reason for hope, and only gradually do we realize the movie isn't going to pay off. It has good things in it, and I kept hoping Polanski would take the plot by the neck and shake life

into it, but no. After the last scene, I underlined on my notepad: "What?"

The film stars Johnny Depp in a strong if ultimately unaimed performance, as Dean Corso, a rare-book dealer whose ethics are optional. He's hired by Boris Balkan (Frank Langella), a millionaire collector who owns a copy of *The Nine Gates of the Kingdom of the Shadows,* published in Venice in 1666 by one Aristide Torchia—who, legend has it, adapted the engravings from the work of Satan himself. Two other copies of the book survive, and Balkan wants Depp to track them down and compare the engravings.

Torchia was burned to death by the Inquisition, and indeed Andrew Telfer, one of the recent owners of the book, hangs himself in an early scene, after selling his copy to Balkan. Liana (Lena Olin), his widow, tries to appear indifferent, but has an unwholesome interest in getting the book back. Corso flies to Europe and meets the other two owners, a stately aristocrat (Jack Taylor) in Portugal and an elderly Parisian baroness (Barbara Jefford) in a wheelchair.

What's best about Corso's quest is the way he conducts it. Depp and Polanski bring a *film noir* feel to the film; we're reminded of Bogart pretending to be a rare-book buyer in *The Big Sleep.* As Corso moves from one bizarre millionaire collector to another, he narrowly avoids several threats on his life and realizes he's being followed by a young woman (Emmanuelle Seigner), whose purpose and identity remain obscure, although at one point she uses martial arts to save his life, and at another point we (but not he) see her fly.

The secret of the engravings in the three editions of the book will not be revealed here. Nor will various additional motives of Balkan, the Telfer widow, and the inexplicable young woman. Their stories are told with a meticulous attention to details, which are persuasive until we realize they are accumulating instead of adding up. If some of the engravings were indeed drawn by Satan, and if assembling them can evoke the Prince of Darkness, then that would be a threat, right? Or would it be a promise? And what happens at the end—that would be an unspeakably evil outcome, right? But why does it look somehow like a victory? And as for the woman—good or bad? Friend or foe? You tell me.

What's intriguing about the material is the way Polanski trusts its essential fascination, and doesn't go for cheesy special effects, as in the Schwarzenegger thriller *End of Days.* Satan need not show himself with external signs, but can work entirely within human nature, which is, after all, his drafting board. When Corso goes to visit the baroness in her wheelchair, I was reminded of Bogart's similar call on an elderly eccentric in *The Big Sleep,* and I relished a sequence where Corso calls on two booksellers, the twin Ceniza brothers, who in a neat f/x touch are played by one actor, Jose Lopez Rodero.

The movie does a good job of mirroring its deaths with situations from the Tarot deck, and making the Telfer widow (Olin) more sinister by (I think) inserting electronic undertones beneath her speech. I also liked the atmosphere evoked by the dialogue, which isn't too dumbed down, uses some of the jargon of the book trade, and allows us to follow Corso's process of deduction as he figures out what the engravings mean and what Balkan's true motives are. It's just that a film of such big themes should be about more than the fate of a few people; while at the end I didn't yearn for spectacular special effects, I did wish for spectacular information—something awesome, not just a fade to white.

No Man's Land ★ ★ ★ ½
R, 98 m., 2001

Branko Djuric (Chiki), Rene Bitorajac (Nino), Filip Sovagovic (Cera), Simon Callow (Soft), Katrin Cartlidge (Jane). Directed by Danis Tanovic and produced by Marc Baschet, Frederique Dumas-Zajdela, and Cedomir Kolar. Screenplay by Tanovic.

Set in the same place and about the same war, *No Man's Land* is like the grown-up version of *Behind Enemy Lines.* It's a bleakly funny parable that could be titled *Between Enemy Lines.* In Bosnia in 1993, Serbs and Bosnians find themselves trapped in the same trench. Anyone who sticks his head up gets shot. And when will that land mine explode?

The setup seems artificial until you reflect that things like this probably do happen in the confusion of war. As the film opens, a few Bosnian fighters are lost in a battlefield fog, and decide to wait until dawn to go farther. When the sun burns away the mist, they find themselves staring directly at Serbian troops. Some are killed. Chiki (Branko Djuric) falls into a trench and is spared.

Serbs come to inspect the trench. Chiki hides, and watches as they place one of his dead comrades onto a land mine as a booby trap. About to be discovered, he kills one Serb and wounds Nino (Rene Bitorajac). A stalemate is developing when the apparently dead man comes back to life. If he moves, the mine explodes and they're all dead.

And no, I haven't revealed too much of the plot because these are just the opening moves in a war game that eventually involves a UN observer (Simon Callow) and a cable news reporter (Katrin Cartlidge)—who assures, as the saying goes, that the whole world is watching. Untold thousands can die unremarked in a war, but when a situation like this develops, people are intrigued. Will the mine explode? How long can the poor guy lie on top of it? Will the two enemies kill each other?

The movie has been written and directed by Danis Tanovic, and it's a first feature that plays like a natural because the situation is so intriguing. Although the Serb and Bosnian debate who is right and wrong in their war, Tanovic's position is that the conflict has escalated into the arena of the absurd: There are so many grievances on both sides that revenge and redress are impossible, and the land mine symbolizes the unhappy situation Bosnia finds itself in. A movie like this helps illustrate the brilliance of the Truth and Reconciliation Commission in South Africa, which argued that it is wise to put the past at rest and start again in the morning.

No Man's Land has been compared to *Catch-22, M*A*S*H,* and *Waiting for Godot*—which means, I suppose, that it contains equal parts of irony and futility. There is something funny about characters stuck in the middle of a process; movement would solve everything (they'd all either live or die), but waiting is intolerable. Into this standoff comes Simon Callow's officious UN observer, appropriately named Soft, who must recite platitudes as if he believed them when the situation itself has underlined the absurdity of the whole "peace process."

The film is curiously beautiful. Knowing something about its story, I didn't expect that. I was visualizing characters and dialogue, and I got them, but Tanovic is also intrigued by the way this situation, by bringing the war to a halt, has allowed everyone to notice that it is being fought in—why, nature! A field. With growing things and a sky above. Dr. Johnson observed that the knowledge that one is about to be hanged concentrates the mind wonderfully. The knowledge that you are lying on your back on a land mine likewise, I imagine, inspires a fresh appreciation of clouds and birds and the deep blue sky.

No Such Thing ★

R, 111 m., 2002

Sarah Polley (Beatrice), Robert John Burke (Monster), Helen Mirren (TV Producer), Julie Christie (Doctor), Baltasar Kormakur (Dr. Artaud). Directed by Hal Hartley and produced by Fridrik Thor Fridriksson, Hartley, and Cecilia Kate Roque. Screenplay by Hartley.

Hal Hartley has always marched in the avant-garde, but this time he marches alone. Followers will have to be drafted. *No Such Thing* is inexplicable, shapeless, dull. It doesn't even rise to entertaining badness. Coming four years after his intriguing if unsuccessful *Henry Fool,* and filmed mostly on location in Iceland with Icelandic money, it suggests a film that was made primarily because he couldn't get anything else off the ground.

The film's original title was *Monster.* That this is a better title than *No Such Thing* is beyond debate. The story involves a monstrous beast who lives on an island off the Icelandic coast, and is immortal, short-tempered, and alcoholic. As the film opens the monster (Robert John Burke) has killed a TV news crew, which inspires a cynical New York network executive (Helen Mirren) to dispatch a young reporter (Sarah Polley) to interview him. Polley's fiancé was among the monster's victims.

Her plane crashes in the ocean, she is the sole survivor and therefore makes good news herself, and is nursed back to life by Julie Christie, in a role no more thankless than the others in this film. Since the filming, Julie Christie had a face-lift and Helen Mirren won an Oscar nomination. Life moves on.

We seek in vain for shreds of recognizable human motivation. By the time she meets the monster, Polley seems to have forgotten he killed her fiancé. By the time she returns with the monster to New York, the world seems to have forgotten. The monster wants to go to New York to enlist the services of Dr. Artaud (Baltasar Kormakur), a scientist who can destroy matter and therefore perhaps can bring an end to the misery of the immortal beast. We are praying that in the case of this movie, matter includes celluloid.

Elements of the movie seem not merely half-baked, but never to have seen the inside of an oven. Helen Mirren's TV news program and its cynical values are treated with the satirical insights of callow undergraduates who will be happy with a C-plus in film class. Characterizations are so shallow they consist only of mannerisms; Mirren chain-smokes cigarettes, Dr. Artaud chain-smokes cigars, the monster swigs from a bottle. At a social reception late in the film, Sarah Polley turns up in a leather bondage dress with a push-up bra. Why, oh why?

Hal Hartley, still only forty-two, has proudly marched to his own drummer since I first met him at Sundance 1990 with *The Unbelievable Truth,* a good film that introduced two of his favorite actors, Adrienne Shelly and Robert Burke (now Robert John Burke, as the monster). Since then his titles have included *Trust* (1991), *Simple Men* (1992), *Amateur* (1994), *Flirt* (1995), and *Henry Fool.* My star ratings have wavered around 2 or 2½, and my reviews have mostly expressed interest and hope—hope that he will define what he's looking for and share it with us.

Now I'm beginning to wonder how long the wait will be. A Hartley film can be analyzed and justified, and a review can try to mold the intractable material into a more comprehensible form. But why does Hartley make us do all the heavy lifting? Can he consider a film that is self-evident and forthcoming? One that doesn't require us to plunder the quarterly film magazines for deconstruction? I don't mind heavy lifting when a film is challenging or fun, like *Mulholland Drive*. But not when all the weight is in the packing materials.

In *No Such Thing* we have promising elements. The relationship between the monster and the TV reporter suggests *Beauty and the Beast* (more the Cocteau than the Disney version), but that vein is not mined, and the TV news satire is too callow to connect in any way with real targets. Many of the characters, like Dr. Artaud, seem like houseguests given a costume and appearing in the host's play just to be good sports. That gifted actors appear here show how desperate they are for challenging parts, and how willing to take chances. Hartley has let them down.

Not Another Teen Movie ★ ★
R, 82 m., 2001

Chyler Leigh (Janey Briggs), Chris Evans (Jake Wyler), Jaime Pressly (Priscilla), Mia Kirshner (Catherine Wyler), Eric Christian Olsen (Austin), Deon Richmond (Malik), Eric Jungmann (Ricky), Ron Lester (Reggie Ray). Directed by Joel Gallen and produced by Neal H. Moritz. Screenplay by Michael G. Bender, Adam Jay Epstein, Andrew Jacobson, Phil Beauman, and Buddy Johnson.

I suppose I should be grateful. After years of ridiculing teen movies, here's one that does it for me. It's like that soup that heats itself. *Not Another Teen Movie* assembles the clichés, obligatory scenes, and standard characters from three recent subgenres of the teen movie (prom, cheerleader, and tasteless sex) and cross-fertilizes them, if that is the word, with the John Hughes teenager movies of the 1980s. Of course, Hughes was a lot better than his recent imitators, but people who know that are likely to be in their thirties now and won't be going to *Not Another Teen Movie* anyway.

Who does that leave in the theater? The current audience for teen movies, I suppose. But if they're dumb enough to like them, why would they be smart enough to appreciate a satire? Maybe this will simply play for them like—just another teen movie.

Did I laugh during the movie? Yes, I did, a few times, although not as much as I did at the better teen movies like *American Pie* or *Scary*

Movie. I liked the way the characters pointed out the clichés they were inhabiting (although that was done first in *Scary Movie*). And the way that when the hero bets he can turn the plain girl into the prom queen, the black guy tells him, "You'll lose the bet, but learn valuable lessons." And the way the subtitles left spaces for the naughty bits in the scene with the nude foreign exchange student. And the awareness of the Slow Clap, a cliché that is rapidly getting to be a public nuisance.

It was good to see familiar faces from old movies, like Molly Ringwald, who offers some hard-learned advice, and John Vernon, who engages in some almost hallucinatory dialogue with a student in detention class. But it was not good to see yet still more wretched excess in the jokes about characters being sprayed with vast quantities of excrement. The movie does not understand that all fart jokes depend on context to be funny. And the opening sequence involving a vibrator is just plain embarrassing.

I have here a heartfelt message from a reader who urges me not to be so hard on stupid films, because they are "plenty smart enough for the average moviegoer." Yes, but one hopes being an average moviegoer is not the end of the road—that one starts as a below-average filmgoer, passes through average, and, guided by the labors of America's hardworking film critics, arrives in triumph at above average.

You will know you have reached that personal goal for yourself when it takes but a moment of thought to calculate that in the month of December, when the studios traditionally showcase Oscar candidates, when movies like *Harry Potter*, *Vanilla Sky*, and *Ocean's Eleven* are in theaters, when *Lord of the Rings*, *In the Bedroom*, and twenty-one other ambitious movies are circling for landings, to spend eighty-two minutes watching *Not Another Teen Movie* would be a reckless waste of your time, no matter how many decades you may have to burn.

Not One Less ★ ★ ★
G, 100 m., 2000

Wei Minzhi (Herself [Young Student]), Zhang Huike (Himself [Young Student]), Tian Zhenda

(Mayor Tian), Gao Enman (Teacher Gao), Feng Yuying (TV Receptionist), Li Fanfan (TV Host). Directed by Zhang Yimou and produced by Zhao Yu. Screenplay by Shi Xiangsheng.

Not One Less is not only about the poor in China's remote rural areas, but could be dedicated to them; we sense that Zhang Yimou, the director of such sophisticated films as *Raise the Red Lantern* and *Shanghai Triad,* is returning here to memories of the years from 1968 to 1978, when he worked as a rural laborer under the Cultural Revolution. His story is simple, unadorned, direct. Only the margins are complicated.

The actors are not professionals, but local people, playing characters with their own names. Wei Minzhi, a red-cheeked thirteen-year-old who usually looks very intent, stars as Wei, a substitute teacher, also very intent. The village's schoolmaster has been called away to his mother's deathbed, and Wei's assignment is to teach his grade school class.

To assist her in this task, she is supplied with one piece of chalk for every day the teacher will be away. And she gets strict instructions: Since the school's subsidy depends on its head count, she is to return the full class to the teacher—"not one less." Keeping all the students in class is more important than anything she teaches them, and indeed she isn't a lot more advanced than her students. This isn't one of those movies where the inspired teacher awakens the minds and spirits of her class; Wei copies lessons on the board and blocks the door.

These early scenes are interesting in the way they don't exploit the obvious angles of the story. This isn't a pumped-up melodrama or an inspirational tearjerker, but a matter-of-fact look at a poor, rural area where necessity is the mother of invention and everything else.

When one of her students, Zhang (Zhang Huike), runs away to look for work in the big city, Wei determines to follow him and bring him back. This is not an easy task. It involves buying a bus ticket, and that means raising the money for the ticket. Wei puts the whole class to work shifting bricks for a local factory to earn the funds. She eventually does get to the city, Jiangjiakou, and her encounters with bureaucracy there are a child's shadow of the heroine's problems in Zhang Yimou's famous film *The Story of Qui Ju* (1992).

The city scenes were not as compelling for me as the earlier ones, maybe because Wei's patience tried my own. She waits what seems like forever outside the gates of a TV studio, hoping to talk to the man in charge, and although her determination is admirable, it could have been suggested in less screen time. Once she does get on TV, there's a moment of absolute authenticity when the anchorwoman asks her a question, and Wei just stares dumbfounded at the camera.

For Chinese viewers, this film will play as a human drama (end titles mention how many children drop out of school in China every year). For Western viewers, there's almost equal interest at the edges of the screen, in the background, in the locations and incidental details that show daily life in today's China. One of the buried messages is the class divide that exists even today in the People's Republic, where TV bureaucrats live in a different world than thirteen-year-old rural schoolgirls. Zhang Yimou, whose films have sometimes landed him in trouble with the authorities, seems to have made a safe one this time. But in the margins he may be making comments of his own.

Note: Parents looking for intelligent films for children might consider Not One Less. *Like the Chinese film* King of Masks *and the Iranian film* Children of Heaven *(both available on video), it has subtitles, but none too difficult for a good young reader.*

Novocaine ★ ★ ★
R, 95 m., 2001

Steve Martin (Frank Sangster), Helena Bonham Carter (Susan Ivey), Laura Dern (Jean Noble), Elias Koteas (Harlan Sangster), Scott Caan (Duane Ivey), Keith David (Lunt), Lynne Thigpen (Pat), Kevin Bacon (Actor). Directed by David Atkins and produced by Paul Mones and Daniel M. Rosenberg. Screenplay by Atkins.

In the flat, too-calm tone of a man who still cannot understand why he was singled out for such bad luck, Steve Martin narrates *Novo-*

caine. It is the story of Dr. Frank Sangster, a dentist who wants only to do a good day's work at the side of his oral-retentive hygienist and fiancée, Jean Noble (Laura Dern). He is dutiful, stable, contented, and boring, until his chair is occupied one day by the pleading eyes and yearning body of Susan Ivey (Helena Bonham Carter). Soon he finds himself implicated in charges involving drugs, perjury, and murder. He got the wrong end of the lollipop.

His name, with its suggestions of blood and gangsters, is a harbinger of his fate. Frank is, in fact, not contented and boring at all, but a volcano of seething passion. Although he cannot admit it even to himself, he is driven to distraction by the blameless perfection of his fiancée, Jean, since if he could blame her for something, anything, he might like her a lot more.

Susan Ivey, on the other hand, is trouble right from the moment she asks for a prescription for Demerol. "Demerol?" he says knowingly. "I'm not that kind of dentist." He grudgingly fills out a prescription for five (5) pills, which after she has improved it on her way to the pharmacy becomes a prescription for fifty (50) pills. "She's just walked out the door," the druggist tells Frank; he waited too late to check on a prescription that seemed suspiciously large, even for a root canal.

If only Susan had taken the pills and kept going, life might still have been uneventful for Frank, with nothing more exciting to look forward to than the inevitable marriage to and divorce from Jean Noble. But Susan appears again in his office, her mind no doubt on the other controlled substances under his command, and soon they are discovering that modern dental chairs recline almost to the horizontal.

Novocaine is a screwball *film noir* with a lot of medium laughs and a few great big ones, written and directed by David Atkins. All I know about him for sure is that he wrote the screenplay for *Arizona Dream,* the only American film of the Yugoslavian mad genius Emir Kusturica. It was a comedy involving Johnny Depp as a fish warden in New York harbor, Jerry Lewis as an Arizona car dealer, and Faye Dunaway as a widow with an accordion-playing daughter and an eye for Depp. Most of these elements I think we can safely assign to Atkins, not Kusturica. Now in the director's chair, Atkins shows the same offbeat taste for crime, sex, comedy, and labyrinthine plotting.

What complicates *Novocaine* is not the triangle involving the dentist, his patient, and his oral hygienist, but the addition of two brothers, who form the movie's little herd of black sheep. Frank's brother Harlan (Elias Koteas) is a ne'er-do-well freeloader with an unpleasant habit of seeming willing to hang around forever until he sees cash. Susan's brother Duane (Scott Caan) is a violent psychopath who shares her appetite for drugs and far exceeds her capacity. By making the crucial mistake of lying to DEA agents at a time when the simple truth would have done just fine, Frank finds himself drawn into a web with these people that leads to a nightmare of murder, guilt, remorse, and confusion. He becomes a textbook illustration for Hitchcock's favorite character, The Innocent Man Wrongly Accused.

I have been vague about the details because the movie needs its surprises. You will gather that Frank and Susan are not among the dead. They find themselves, indeed, rather sweet on each other—to his surprise, because he thought he was happily engaged, and to hers, because she thought all she wanted was the drugs.

At just about that point when every comedy needs a little laughing gas, *Novocaine* gets a charge from a surprise appearance by Kevin Bacon, playing an actor who is following the police around to get insights for his starring role in a reality TV show. Bacon is playing not "himself," although that is what the reviews will say, but an actor he builds from the ground up as a type he must often have seen: an actor extremely, even obsessively, concerned that you understand he is not "just an actor," but in fact a person of rare intelligence and penetrating insight.

Novocaine is funny all the way through, and ingenious all the way through. I am not sure it plugs all its loopholes, but in a comedy, that's not such a problem. The key to the film is Helena Bonham Carter, whose passionate character is the engine that pulls the train. Martin is very funny by somehow being simultaneously terrified that he will be framed for murder and that his hair will get mussed.

The movie opens with X rays of the teeth of its stars, closes with bite marks as a clue, and uses root canals as its organizing symbol in more ways than one.

Nurse Betty ★ ★ ★
R, 112 m., 2000

Morgan Freeman (Charlie), Renee Zellweger (Betty), Chris Rock (Wesley), Greg Kinnear (Dr. David Ravell), Aaron Eckhart (Del), Tia Texada (Rosa), Crispin Glover (Roy), Pruitt Taylor Vince (Ballard). Directed by Neil LaBute and produced by Gail Mutrux and Steve Golin. Screenplay by John C. Richards and James Flamberg.

Neil LaBute's *Nurse Betty* is about two dreamers in love with their fantasies. One is a Kansas housewife. The other is a professional criminal. The housewife is in love with a doctor on a television soap opera. The criminal is in love with the housewife, whose husband he has killed. What is crucial is that both of these besotted romantics are invisible to the person they are in love with.

Morgan Freeman is Charlie, the killer, and Renee Zellweger is Betty, the housewife and waitress. Their lives connect because Del (Aaron Eckhart), Betty's worthless husband, tries to stiff Charlie on a drug deal. Charlie and Wesley (Chris Rock) turn up at his house, threaten him, scalp him, and kill him. Well, Charlie kills him only because Wesley scalps him—and then what you gonna do?

Betty witnesses the murder, but blanks it out of her memory. Her husband was a rat, she doesn't miss him, and in her mind his death frees her to drive out to Los Angeles to meet her "ex-fiancé," a doctor on a soap opera. Charlie and Wesley trail her, and in the course of their pursuit Charlie's mind also jumps the track. Under the influence of Betty's sweet smile in a photograph, he begins to idealize her—he speaks of her "grace"—and to see her as the bright angel of his lost hopes.

In Los Angeles, Betty meets George (Greg Kinnear), the actor who plays the doctor. She relates only to the character, and as she talks to "Dr. David Ravell" at a charity benefit, George and his friends think they're witnessing a brilliant method audition. Charlie and Wesley

meanwhile arrive in Los Angeles with Charlie increasingly bewitched by fantasies about Betty. When they started chasing her, she was an eyewitness to murder who was driving a car her husband had hidden their drugs in. Now Charlie thinks of her more as a person who would sympathize with his own broken ideals.

I'm spending so much time on the plot of *Nurse Betty* because I think it's possible to misread. When the film premiered at Cannes in May, some reviews didn't seem to understand that Betty and Charlie are parallel characters, both projecting their dreams on figures they've created in their own fantasies. Look at this movie inattentively, especially if you're looking for Hollywood formulas, and all you see is a mad woman pursued by some drug dealers—kind of a high-rent *Crazy in Alabama*. But it's more, deeper, and more touching than that. Zellweger plays Betty as an impossibly sweet, earnest, sincere, lovable, vulnerable woman—a "Doris Day type," as Charlie describes her. She has unwisely married Del, a vulgar louse who orders her around and eats her birthday cupcake. Her consolation is the daily soap opera about her fantasy lover, Dr. Ravell. When Charlie and Wesley turn up, nobody knows she's home. She glimpses the murder from the next room, and her response is to hit the rewind button for a crucial soap opera scene she's missed. A therapist tells the local sheriff (Pruitt Taylor Vince) she remembers nothing; she's in an "altered state—that allows a traumatized person to keep on functioning."

Betty heads west in the fatal Buick LeSabre with the drugs in the trunk, and outside a roadside bar she experiences a fantasy in which Dr. Ravell proposes marriage. Not long after, hot on her trail, Charlie pauses in the moonlight on the edge of the Grand Canyon and fantasizes dancing with Betty. Charlie has never met Betty and Betty has never met the "doctor"; both of their dream-figures are projections of their own needs and idealism.

Morgan Freeman has a tricky role. His Charlie is a mean guy, capable of killing but looking forward to retirement in Florida after one last "assignment." He has great affection for Wesley, a loose cannon, and tries to teach him lessons Wesley is not much capable of learning. Charlie has led a life of crime but has now gone soft under the influence of Betty, whose smile in a photo helps him to mourn his own lost innocence.

Betty is even further gone. Traumatized by the murder, she has no understanding that the soap opera is a TV show, and her first scene with Kinnear is brilliantly acted by both of them, as she cuts through his Hollywood cynicism with unshakable sincerity. Kinnear is deadly accurate in portraying an actor who has confused his ego with his training, and a scene where Betty is offered a role in the show is handled with cruel realism.

LaBute previously wrote and directed *In the Company of Men* and *Your Friends and Neighbors*, films with a deep, harsh cynicism. *Nurse Betty*, written by John C. Richards and James Flamberg, is a comedy undercut with dark tones and flashes of violence. Heading inexorably toward a tidy happy ending, LaBute sidesteps clichés like a broken-field runner. As for Charlie, his final scene, his only real scene with Betty, contains some of Freeman's best work. "I'm a garbageman of the human soul," he tells her, "but you're different." He is given an almost impossible assignment (heartfelt wistfulness in the midst of a gunfight) and pulls it off, remaining attentive even to the comic subtext.

Nurse Betty is one of those films where you don't know whether to laugh or cringe, and find yourself doing both. It's a challenge: How do we respond to this loaded material? Audiences lobotomized by one-level stories may find it stimulating, or confusing—it's up to them. Once you understand that Charlie and Betty are versions of the same idealistic delusions, that their stories are linked as mirror images, you've got the key.

Nutty Professor II: The Klumps ★ ★ ★
PG-13, 110 m., 2000

Eddie Murphy (Klumps/Lance Perkins/Buddy Love), Janet Jackson (Denise), Larry Miller (Dean Richmond), John Ales (Jason), Richard Gant (Denise's Father), Anna Maria Horsford (Denise's Mother),Melinda McGraw (Leanne Guilford), Jamal Mixon (Ernie Klump Jr.). Directed by Peter Segal and produced by Brian Grazer. Screenplay by Barry W. Blaustein, David Sheffield, Paul Weitz, and Chris Weitz, based on a story by Steve Oedekerk, Blaustein, and Sheffield.

My guess is, most of the reviews of *Nutty Professor II: The Klumps* will deliver perfunctory praise to the makeup and move on quickly to the comedy. But we're not talking garden-variety "makeup" here. We're talking about a rather astonishing creative collaboration between Eddie Murphy and makeup artist Rick Baker, with considerable help from director Peter Segal and cinematographer Dean Semler, to populate the movie with eight different characters, all played by Murphy, all convincing, each with its own personality. This is not just a stunt. It is some kind of brilliance.

Yes, it appears in a comedy of determined vulgarity. Yes, some of those long sessions of five hours in makeup were put at the service of scenes involving giant hamster sex and flammable farts. Yes, the story meanders. But yes, *Nutty II* is often very funny and never less than amazing when you consider the work and imagination that went into Murphy's creation of the Klump family (Sherman, Granny, Mama, Papa, Papa when he was younger, and Ernie) and two other characters, Lance Perkins and the diabolical alter ego Buddy Love.

Murphy has an uncanny gift for mimicry, for creating new characters out of thin air. That showed as early as *Saturday Night Live*, of course. In Steve Martin's underappreciated *Bowfinger* (1999), he plays two characters more or less without help from makeup: the movie superstar Kit Ramsey, who looks a lot like Murphy, and a doofus named Jiff, who looks a lot like Kit and is hired to play his double. This isn't simply a double role. Kit and Jiff are two different people, and Jiff is actually the funnier and more involving one; he was so abashed when he found out they wanted to put him in a movie that we couldn't help but like him.

The many Klumps played by Murphy in *Nutty II* are, of course, much broader characters, and yet Professor Sherman Klump, the family hero, also has that strain of sweetness: He is likable, vulnerable, and naive, and we can understand why his research assistant Denise (Janet Jackson) might want to marry him. We understand even better when he hires a Mexican band to stand under her window while he serenades her, although that touching scene is interrupted when Buddy Love takes over his personality.

Buddy Love is essentially Tourette's syndrome personified. Buddy appears without warning, taking over Sherman's personality, spewing insulting comments and embarrassing the professor in public. His nuisance value multiplies when Sherman tries a risky genetic split, externalizing Buddy but causing his own intelligence to start shrinking. One of the funniest twists in this movie is the way the tables are turned on Buddy. A strand of his DNA gets crossed with the genetic code of a dog, forcing Buddy to exhibit instinctual doggie behavior at all the most inconvenient moments. It's sort of wonderful when Sherman can distract his nemesis by forcing him to fetch.

Animal jokes have been obligatory in raunchy comedies since *There's Something About Mary*, and *Nutty II* builds to some kind of a crescendo as Dean Richmond (Larry Miller), Sherman's superior at the university, is assaulted by a giant hamster. How this happens and why is immaterial; what is important is the way it leads up to the line, "Do you think he'll call?"

Eddie Murphy has been a star since the 1970s, a movie star since *48 Hrs.* (1982). He started strong but has made more than his share of bad movies (*Vampire in Brooklyn* was perhaps the low point). In *Bowfinger* and *Nutty II*, he seems to be in a new flowering of his career. He seems more at ease with his comedy, willing to disappear inside characters, ready to find laughs with behavior and personality instead of forcing them with punch lines. Not only does he play eight different characters here, but he makes them distinct and (within the broad requirements of the story) plausible.

Sherman, of course, is the central character, a research professor who is brilliant, innocent, and fat. We like him and feel for him. Janet Jackson is warm and supportive as his girlfriend, and they have some touching moments together (borrowed from *Charley*) when his intelligence starts to dwindle and his genius to fade. In a movie so raucous, so scatological, so cheerfully offensive, it is a little surprising to find yourself actually caring for a character who is made mostly out of latex makeup, but there you have it.

O

O ★ ★ ★
R, 95 m., 2001

Mekhi Phifer (Odin James), Josh Hartnett
(Hugo Goulding), Julia Stiles (Desi Brable),
Elden Henson (Roger Rodriguez), Andrew
Keegan (Michael Casio), Rain Phoenix (Emily),
John Heard (Dean Brable), Anthony Johnson
(Dell), Martin Sheen (Coach Goulding).
Directed by Tim Blake Nelson and produced by
Daniel Fried, Eric Gitter, and Anthony Rhulen.
Screenplay by Brad Kaaya, based on the play
Othello by William Shakespeare.

Odin, the star basketball player at a private
school in the South, is the only African-
American student there. He dates the daughter of the dean, who may disapprove but keeps
his thoughts to himself because Odin (Mekhi
Phifer) is so useful to the school. Some reviews
of *O* have questioned the plausibility of these
details, but they are perfectly faithful to Shakespeare's *Othello*, the source of the movie: Othello
was the only Moor in Venice, Desdemona was
a senator's daughter, Othello's skill as a general
protected Venice against its enemies.

Odin James (whose initials, "O.J.," are surely
not a coincidence) is also, like Othello, too
easily made jealous—it is his fatal flaw. Desi
(Julia Stiles) loves him and is faithful to him,
but he cannot bring himself to trust her, and
that is his downfall. His supposed friend Hugo
(Josh Hartnett) plants the seeds of doubt, suggesting Desi is secretly sleeping with another
student, Michael (Andrew Keegan). And there
is an antique scarf that Odin gives to Desi and
that seems to become evidence of the cheating.

Again, all from Shakespeare, although the
movie creates Hugo's (Iago's) motivation. Hugo's
father is the basketball coach (Martin Sheen),
but dinnertime at their house is a grim and
silent affair, and when the coach says of Odin,
"I love him like my own son," look for Hugo's
reaction shot. It is sometimes forgotten that
Iago doesn't want Desdemona for himself. He
simply uses her as a way to bring about
Othello's downfall, correctly observing that
jealousy triggers his enemy's weakness. It is
Roderigo who was Desdemona's former lover
(here presented as Roger Rodriguez, and played

by Elden Henson as Hugo's gullible accomplice in treachery).

There have been and will be many modern
retreads of Shakespeare. *O* is close in spirit to
Baz Luhrmann's teen-gang version of *Romeo
and Juliet.* It isn't a line-by-line update of *Othello,*
but an attempt to reproduce the passion of the
original play, and for younger viewers new to
Shakespeare it would only enhance a reading
of the real thing. The film's misfortune, however, is that it was being made at the time of the
Columbine tragedy, and was immediately
deemed unreleasable by Miramax, which shelved
it for three years; Lions Gate is now the distribution company.

We have a peculiar inability in our country
to understand the contexts of things; when it
comes to art, we interpret troublesome works
in the most literal and simple-minded way. In
the aftermath of Columbine, Washington leg-
islators called on Hollywood to police itself,
and rumbled about possible national censorship. Miramax caved in by suppressing this
film. To suggest that *O* was part of the solution
and not part of the problem would have required a sophistication that our public officials
either lack, or are afraid to reveal for fear of
offending the bottom-feeders among their
constituents.

So now here is *O,* a good film for most of
the way, and then a powerful film at the end,
when, in the traditional Shakespearean manner,
all of the plot threads come together, the victims
are killed, the survivors mourn, and life goes
on. It is clearly established that Hugo is a psychopath, and that his allies are victims of that
high school disease that encourages the unpop-
ular to do anything in order to be accepted.
Those who think this film will inspire events
like Columbine should ask themselves how
often audiences want to be like the despised
villain.

Mekhi Phifer makes a strong, tortured Odin,
and delivers a final speech that in its heartbreaking anguish inspires our pity much as
Othello's does. Josh Hartnett showed here,
three years before *Pearl Harbor,* that he is capable of subtleties and complexities that epic
did not dream of. Julia Stiles, who is developing
into one of the best young actresses, adds this

modern Desdemona to her modern Ophelia in *Hamlet* (2000), and reminds us, too, of her interracial romance in *Save the Last Dance.*

True, some of the plot threads seem unlikely. Is it that easy to overhear and completely misunderstand crucial conversations? How much more use can a scarf be put to? But those are problems in Shakespeare, too—or perhaps simply plot mechanisms that allow the characters to arrive at their tragic destinations. And then there's the unexpected additional level, the suggestion that high school sports have become like a kind of warfare. What is insane in most American high schools is that sports are considered more important than study, generating heroism and resentment too powerful for most kids to cope with, and inspiring in their bitter backwash the kind of alienation we saw at Columbine.

O Brother, Where Art Thou? ★ ★ ½
PG-13, 103 m., 2000

George Clooney (Ulysses Everett McGill), John Turturro (Pete), Tim Blake Nelson (Delmar), Charles Durning (Pappy O'Daniel), John Goodman (Big Dan Teague), Michael Badalucco (George Babyface Nelson), Holly Hunter (Penny Wharvey), Stephen Root (Radio Station Man), Chris Thomas King (Tommy Johnson). Directed by Joel Coen and produced by Ethan Coen. Screenplay by Ethan Coen and Joel Coen, based upon *The Odyssey* by Homer.

The opening titles inform us that the Coen brothers' *O Brother, Where Art Thou?* is based on Homer's *The Odyssey.* The Coens claimed their *Fargo* was based on a true story, but later confided it wasn't; this time they confess they haven't actually read *The Odyssey.* Still, they've absorbed the spirit. Like its inspiration, this movie is one damn thing after another.

The film is a Homeric journey through Mississippi during the depression—or rather, through all of the images of that time and place that have been trickling down through pop culture ever since. There are even walk-ons for characters inspired by Babyface Nelson and the blues singer Robert Johnson, who speaks of a crossroads soul-selling rendezvous with the devil.

Bluegrass music is at the heart of the film, as it was of *Bonnie and Clyde,* and there are images of chain gangs, sharecropper cottages, cotton fields, populist politicians, river baptisms, hoboes on freight trains, patent medicines, 25-watt radio stations, and Klan rallies. The movie's title is lifted from Preston Sturges's 1941 comedy *Sullivan's Travels* (it was the uplifting movie the hero wanted to make to redeem himself), and from Homer we get a Cyclops, Sirens bathing on the rocks, a hero named Ulysses, and his wife, Penny, which is no doubt short for Penelope.

If these elements don't exactly add up, maybe they're not intended to. Homer's epic grew out of the tales of many storytellers who went before; their episodes were timed and intended for a night's recitation. Quite possibly no one before Homer saw the developing work as a whole. In the same spirit, *O Brother* contains sequences that are wonderful in themselves—lovely short films—but the movie never really shapes itself into a whole.

The opening shot shows three prisoners escaping from a chain gang. They are Ulysses Everett McGill (George Clooney), Pete (John Turturro), and Delmar (Tim Blake Nelson). From their peculiar conviction that they are invisible as they duck and run across an open field, we know the movie's soul is in farce and satire, although it touches other notes, too—it's an anthology of moods. Ulysses (played by Clooney as if Clark Gable were a patent medicine salesman) doesn't much want company on his escape, but since he is chained to the other two, he has no choice. He enlists them in his cause by telling them of hidden treasure.

What was *The Odyssey,* after all, but a road movie? *O Brother* follows its three heroes on an odyssey during which they intersect with a political campaign, become radio stars by accident, stumble upon a Klan meeting, and deal with Ulysses' wife, Penny (Holly Hunter), who is about to pack up with their seven daughters and marry a man who won't always be getting himself thrown into jail.

Hunter and Turturro are veterans of earlier Coen movies, and so is John Goodman, who plays a slick-talking Bible salesman. Charles Durning appears as a gubernatorial candidate with the populist jollity of Huey Long, and the story strands meet and separate as if the movie is happening mostly by chance and good luck—a nice feeling sometimes, although not one that inspires confidence that the narrative train has an engine.

The most effective sequence in the movie is the Klan rally (complete with a Klansman whose eye patch means he needs only one hole in his sheet). The choreography of the ceremony seems poised somewhere between Busby Berkeley and *Triumph of the Will,* and the Coens succeed in making it look ominous and ridiculous at the same time. (There are echoes here of *The Wizard of Oz.*)

Another sequence almost stops the show, it's so haunting in its self-contained way. It occurs when the escapees come across three women doing their laundry in a river. The Sirens, obviously. They sing "Didn't Leave Nobody but the Baby" while moving in a slightly slowed motion, and the effect is—well, what it's supposed to be, mesmerizing.

I also like the sequence of events beginning when the lads perform on the radio as the Soggy Mountain Boys. By now they have recruited a black partner, Tommy Johnson (Chris Thomas King), and later when the song becomes a hit they're called on to perform before an audience that is hostile to blacks in particular and escaped convicts in general. They wear false beards. Really false beards.

All of these scenes are wonderful in their different ways, and yet I left the movie uncertain and unsatisfied. I saw it a second time, admired the same parts, left with the same feeling. I do not demand that all movies have a story to pull us from beginning to end, and indeed one of the charms of *The Big Lebowski,* the Coens' previous film, is how its stoned hero loses track of the thread of his own life. But with *O Brother, Where Art Thou?* I had the sense of invention set adrift: of a series of bright ideas wondering why they had all been invited to the same film.

Ocean's Eleven ★ ★ ★
PG-13, 116 m., 2001

George Clooney (Danny Ocean), Brad Pitt (Rusty Ryan), Andy Garcia (Terry Benedict), Julia Roberts (Tess Ocean), Casey Affleck (Virgil Malloy), Scott Caan (Turk Malloy), Don Cheadle (Basher Tarr), Matt Damon (Linus Caldwell). Directed by Steven Soderbergh and produced by Jerry Weintraub. Screenplay by Ted Griffin.

Serious pianists sometimes pound out a little honky-tonk just for fun. That's like what Steven Soderbergh is doing in *Ocean's Eleven.* This is a standard genre picture, a remake of the 1960 Frank Sinatra caper, and Soderbergh, who usually aims higher, does it as a sort of lark. It's slick, all right: Directors this good don't usually handle material this routine. It has yearnings above its natural level, as if hoping to redeem itself and metamorphose into a really good movie.

The movie stars George Clooney, who can be powerfully impassive better than almost anybody, as Danny Ocean, fresh out of prison and eager for a new job. He's a smooth operator who, his parole board notes, figured in a dozen investigations where he was never charged. He contacts his old sidekick Rusty Ryan (Brad Pitt) with a scheme to steal millions from not one but three Las Vegas casinos. Amazingly, the movie specifies and shoots in real casinos (the Mirage, the MGM Grand, and the Bellagio) and incorporates the destruction of the Desert Inn.

Casing the job, Rusty sees the casino owner (Andy Garcia) with a woman he recognizes: Tess Ocean (Julia Roberts), Danny's ex-wife. "Tell me it isn't about her," Rusty begs Danny. Of course it is. Ocean wants to steal from his ex-wife's current lover *and* get her back again. They assemble a team, including Matt Damon, Don Cheadle, and Casey Affleck. I suppose there are eleven in all, although even during a long tracking shot I forgot to count.

The outlines of a caper movie are long and well established: The scary external shot of the impenetrable targets, the inside information, and voice-over as we see guards going about their work, the plan with the split-second timing. *Ocean's Eleven* even includes an elaborate full-scale mock-up of the strong room used by the three casinos, leading to such practical questions as (1) why does it need to be this elaborate? (2) how much did it cost? and (3) who contracted it for them, or did they knock it together themselves overnight?

The movie excels in its delivery of dialogue. The screenplay by Ted Griffin is elegantly epigrammatic, with dialogue that sounds like a cross between Noel Coward and a 1940s *noir* thriller.

Roberts: You're a thief and a liar.
Clooney: I only lied about being a thief.
R: You don't do that anymore?
C: Steal?
R: Lie.

They do this so well I was reminded of the classic exchanges between Bogart and Bacall. And notice, too, the conversation involving Clooney, Roberts, and Garcia, when the casino boss finds the ex-husband at Tess's table in the dining room. The two men, of course, despise each other, but are so smooth and cool we note it only in the precision of their timing and word choices, leading up to a final exchange in which Danny, leaving the table, says "Terry" in a way that uses the first name with inappropriate familiarity, and Terry responds, "Danny," on precisely the same note.

Brad Pitt has a nice dialogue passage too, when he's briefing the Matt Damon character. The jargon is all about strategy and entirely in modern terms, but listen to the music instead of the words and you realize it's a riff on Hamlet's instructions to the players.

As movie capers go, the specifics in *Ocean's Eleven* are not necessarily state of the art. I can think of more ingeniously executed plans, most recently in *The Score,* but then this is not a movie about suspense but about suavity. George Clooney and Julia Roberts deliberately evoke the elegance of stars like Cary Grant and Ingrid Bergman, Andy Garcia is as smooth, groomed, polished, and tailored as George Raft, and the movie blessedly ends not with a shoot-out but with a complicated plot finesse. I enjoyed it. It didn't shake me up and I wasn't much involved, but I liked it as a five-finger exercise. Now it's time for Soderbergh to get back to work.

Note: The 1960 Rat Pack version of Ocean's Eleven *was itself a remake. The original is* Bob le Flambeur, *a 1956 French film by Jean-Pierre Melville, now available on DVD in the Criterion Collection.* ☞

Once in the Life ★ ★
R, 111 m., 2000

Laurence Fishburne (20/20 Mike), Titus Welliver (Billy ["Torch"]), Eamonn Walker (Tony the Tiger), Dominic Chianese Jr. (Freddie Nine Lives), Michael Paul Chan (Buddha), Paul Calderon (Manny Rivera), Annabella Sciorra (Maxine), Gregory Hines (Ruffhouse). Directed by Laurence Fishburne and produced by David Bushell, Fishburne, and Helen Sugland. Screenplay by Fishburne.

Once in the Life tells the story of two half-brothers, one black, one white, one just out of prison, the other a heroin addict, who are in danger from a drug lord, and find themselves sharing a hideout with a man who may be their friend or their executioner. The key word here is "hideout." This is a film made from a play, and like many filmed plays it tried to cover its traces by limiting most of the action to one room, which we are not supposed to think of as the stage.

The play is by Laurence Fishburne, who also directs the film and stars as 20/20 Mike, an ex-con who says he has eyes in the back of his head—and apparently does. His half-brother, Billy (Titus Welliver), claims he has cleaned up from his habit, but may be lying. Mike and Billy have a lot of unresolved issues about their father. As for Tony the Tiger (Eamonn Walker), he and 20/20 became friends in prison. That's why 20/20 is asking for help now, not realizing that Tony is working for Manny (Paul Calderon), the drug lord whose henchman Freddie Nine Lives (Dominic Chianese Jr.) he has offended, and whose nephew he has killed.

These plot elements are standard stuff. Drugs themselves seem almost exhausted as a plot device for all but the most inventive movies; we've seen so many variations of their sale, use, trade, and theft, and the violence they inspire. But Fishburne's film and play aren't about drugs; they're the Maguffin, and the play is really about . . . well, the desired answers are "brothers" or "trust," but I'm afraid a better answer is "dialogue."

This is a film of words, especially once the three key characters hole up in a slum room that looks like the set decorator was given too much money. No abandoned room should look this atmospheric, unless it deliberately wants to resemble a stage set. In the room, the three go round and round, settling old scores, reopening old wounds, gradually learning the truth of the situation, and from time to time someone goes to the window and looks to see who's outside—an ancient device in movies based on plays. Among the people outside, or in other locations, are Ruffhouse (Gregory Hines), a spotter and enforcer (I think; his role is not very clear), and Annabella Sciorra as Maxine, Tony's threatened wife.

I imagine this material worked on the stage, where it was titled *Riff Raff* (it was produced at the Circle Repertory Company in lower Manhattan). But stage plays are about the voices and physical presence of the actors, and we supply the necessary reality. Movies have a tendency to be literal, no matter what the intention of their makers, and stylized dialogue and acting is hazardous—it calls attention to itself, and clangs. Consider, for example, a poem that Tony recites. It brings the movie to an awkward halt.

Fishburne is a powerful actor, and he has assembled a talented cast, but the movie remains an actor's exercise—too much dialogue, too much time in the room, too much happening offstage, or in the past, or in memory, or in imagination. Billy's meltdown provides a real-time reality check, but for most of the time we're waiting for the payoff, and when it comes, I'm afraid, it's not very satisfying.

The One ★ ½
PG-13, 87 m., 2001

Jet Li (Gabe, Yulaw, Lawless), Carla Gugino (T.K., Massie Walsh), Delroy Lindo (Roedecker), Jason Statham (Funsch), James Morrison (Aldrich), Dylan Bruno (Yates), Richard Steinmetz (D'Antoni). Directed by James Wong and produced by Glen Morgan and Steven Chasman. Screenplay by Morgan and Wong.

There is a vast question lurking at the center of *The One*, and the question is: Why? Assuming there are 124 universes and that you existed in all of them and could travel among them, why would you want to kill off the other 123 versions of you? This is, I submit, a good ques-

tion, but not one discussed in any depth by Yulaw (Jet Li), the villain of the film. Jet Li also plays the film's hero and one of its victims, but neither of them understandably knows the answer.

The film opens with a narration informing us that there are parallel universes, and that "a force exists who seeks to destroy the balance so that he can become—The One!" Apparently every time one of your other selves dies, his power is distributed among the survivors. If Yulaw kills 123 selves, he has the power of 124. Follow this logic far enough, and retirement homes would be filled with elderly geezers who have outlived their others and now have the strength of 124, meaning they can bend canes with their bare hands and produce mighty bowel movements with scornful ease.

What does Yulaw hope to accomplish with his power? He might, the narrator suggests, become God—and thus, if killed, might bring all of creation to an end. A guy like this, you don't want him getting in fights and taking chances. But the God theory is theologically unsound, because God works from the top down and didn't get where he is by knocking off the competition. Maybe Yulaw is just a megalomaniac who gets off on being able to beat up everyone in the room. Maybe one of the differences between a good martial arts movie and one that is merely technically competent is that in the good ones, the characters have a motivation, and in the others life is just a competitive sport.

Yulaw defeats Lawless, one of his other selves, fairly early in the film, and then zeroes in on Gabe, who is a Los Angeles County sheriff's deputy. Gabe knows nothing of the multiverses, but is, under the rules, as strong as half of the dead men, and so a good match for Yulaw. Meanwhile, Yulaw is pursued from his home universe by Roedecker (Delroy Lindo) and Funsch (Jason Statham), agents of the Multiverse Bureau of Investigations. His wife, woman, girlfriend, or sidekick in all of these worlds is played by Carla Gugino.

The possibilities with this plot are endless. Alas, the movie is interested only in fight scenes, and uses the latest in computer-generated effects to show the various Jet Li characters as they throw enemies into the air, dodge bullets, hold a motorcycle in each hand and slam them together against an opponent, etc. The final epic confrontation features Jet Li fighting himself. Both are wearing black jumpsuits at the start of the fight, but the evil Jet Li shows consideration for the audience by stripping down to a blue top, so we can tell him apart from the good Jet Li.

This titanic closing fight, by the way, may use cutting-edge effects, but has been written with slavish respect for ancient clichés. It begins with the venerable It's Only a Cat Scene, in which a cat startles a character (but not the audience) by leaping at the lens. Then the characters retire to a Steam and Flame Factory, one of those Identikit movie sets filled with machines that produce copious quantities of steam, flames, and sparks. Where do they have their fight? On a catwalk, of course. Does anyone end up clinging by his fingertips? Don't make me laugh.

The movie offers brainless high-tech action without interesting dialogue, characters, motivation, or texture. In other words, it's sure to be popular. Seeing a movie like this makes me feel bad that I applied such high standards to *Donnie Darko*, which also deals with logical paradoxes, and by comparison is a masterpiece. ☞

One Day in September ★ ★ ★
R, 92 m., 2001

A documentary featuring Ankie Spitzer, widow of Israeli fencing coach Andre Spitzer; terrorist Jamal Al Gashey; ITN News reporter Gerald Seymour; Alex Springer, son of Jacov Springer, Israeli and judge; and Gad Zabari, Israeli wrestler who escaped from the terrorists. Directed by Kevin Macdonald and produced by John Battsek and Arthur Cohn.

In September 1972, Palestinian terrorists invaded the athletes' quarters of the Munich Olympiad and took Israeli athletes hostage. By the following evening, eleven Israelis and five of the eight terrorists were dead. Kevin Macdonald's documentary *One Day in September* retells these events in the style of a thriller, which is a little unsettling. It's one thing to see a fictional re-creation of facts, such as the re-creation of the Cuban missile crisis in *Thirteen Days,* and another to see facts tarted up like fiction. Oh, it's exciting,

all right, but do we feel ennobled to be thus entertained?

Macdonald brings remarkable research to the film. He has managed to obtain interviews with most of the key figures who are still alive, including the one surviving terrorist, Jamal Al Gashey, now in hiding "in Africa" (the two other survivors were killed by Israeli assassination squads). He talks to an Israeli athlete who escaped, the son of another, and the widow of a third, to Israeli coaches and security experts, to German generals and policemen, to journalists who covered the event. His reporting is extraordinary, as he relentlessly builds up a case against the way the Germans and the International Olympic Committee handled the crisis.

Much is made of "German efficiency," Macdonald observes, but the Germans were so inefficient that they had no trained antiterrorist squad, no security around the compound, no contingency plans, not even effective communication (a police sniper and a helicopter pilot were shot by German police who had not been told where they were). In a development that would be funny if it were not so sad, the Germans stationed a 747 on an airport runway as a getaway plane for the terrorists, and staffed it with cops dressed as the plane's crew, but minutes before the plane was to be used, the cops took a vote, decided they were not competent to handle the assignment, and walked off the plane.

In a film filled with startling charges, the most shocking is that the three captured terrorists escaped from custody as part of a secret deal with the German government, which essentially wanted the whole matter to be over with. A German aircraft was hijacked by Palestinians, who demanded that the three prisoners be handed over, which they were, with "indecent haste." The film says the plane suspiciously contained only twelve passengers, none of them women or children; now Jamal Al Gashey confirms it was a setup.

As for the Olympic committee, at first it intended to continue the Games during the hostage crisis, and we see athletes of other nations training and relaxing within sight of the dorms where the Israelis were being held. After the Games were suspended, thousands watched the standoff as if it were a show, while the Germans continued to bungle (officers crept onto the roof of the building, but the scene was broadcast live on TV, and the terrorists, of course, were watching the news).

The death of the innocent athletes was an avoidable tragedy, we conclude. If the Israeli secret service had been able to stage a raid as they wanted, it's likely many lives would have been saved. The final bloodbath resulted more from German bumbling than from anything else.

Still, one wonders why newsreel shots of Hitler and reminders of the Nazi past are necessary in a film that has almost no time at all to explain who the Palestinians were or why they made such a desperate raid. The raid had nothing to do with the Nazi past, and the current Germans seemed like comic-opera buffoons from a Groucho Marx comedy. If the purpose of a documentary is to inform, it could be argued that audiences already know a great deal about Hitler but are not likely to learn much from a couple of perfunctory shots of Palestinian refugee camps.

One Day in September grips the attention and is exciting and involving. I recommend it on that basis—and also because of the new information it contains. I was disturbed, however, by Macdonald's pumped-up style, and by a tasteless conclusion in which images of action, bloodshed, and corpses are cut together into a montage and backed with rock music. What was he thinking of?

Note: When One Day in September *won the Academy Award in 2000, its producer, Arthur Cohn, held up the Oscar and boasted, "and I won this without showing it in a single theater!" The documentary community is still angry about that remark. Cohn exhibits his Oscar entries at screenings peopled largely by those on his invitation list, and to as few other people as possible. Under the Academy bylaws, only those who have seen all five docs can vote, and by limiting those who have seen his, Cohn shrinks the voting pool and improves his odds. Documentary groups and many individual filmmakers have protested this Oscar to the Academy.*

Onegin ★ ★ ½
NO MPAA RATING, 106 m., 2000

Ralph Fiennes (Evgeny Onegin), Liv Tyler (Tatyana Larin), Toby Stephens (Vladimir Lensky), Lena Headey (Olga Larin), Martin Donovan (Prince Nikitin), Irene Worth (Princess Alina). Directed by Martha Fiennes and produced by Simon Bosanquet and Ileen Maisel. Screenplay by Michael Ignatieff and Peter Ettedgui, based on the novel by Alexander Pushkin.

Onegin is a man bemused by his own worthlessness. He has been carefully prepared by his aristocratic nineteenth-century upbringing to be unnecessary—an outside man, hanging on, looking into the lives of others. Even when he's given the opportunity to play a role, after he inherits his uncle's estate, his response is to rent the land to his serfs. In another man, this would be seen as liberalism. In Evgeny Onegin, it is more like indifference.

Onegin is a leisurely, elegant, detached retelling of Pushkin's epic verse novel, with Ralph Fiennes as the hero. It is the kind of role once automatically assigned to Jeremy Irons. Both men look as if they have stayed up too late and not eaten their greens, but Irons in the grip of passion is able to seem lost and heedless, while Fiennes suggests it is heavy lifting, with few rewards. "I am not one who is made for love and marriage," his Onegin says soulfully.

As the film opens, Onegin is returning to inherit his uncle's estate outside St. Petersburg, after having lost his own fortune at the gambling tables. He is welcomed by receptions, teas, and balls, and embraced by his neighbor, Lensky (Toby Stephens). Lensky has a young bride named Olga (Lena Headey), and she has an older sister named Tatyana (Liv Tyler), who is a lone spirit and visits Onegin's estate to borrow books from his library.

Tyler has the assignment of suggesting passionate depths beneath a cool exterior, and succeeds: She is grave and silent, with an ethereal quality that is belied by her bold use of eye contact. Onegin probably falls in love with her the first time he sees her, but is not, of course, made for love, and shrugs off his real feelings in order to enter into a flirtation with Olga, who is safely married.

Tatyana's waters run deep. She declares herself in a passionate love letter to Onegin (the moment she saw his face, she knew her heart was his, etc.), but such passion only alarms him. "Any stranger might have stumbled into your life and aroused your romantic imagination," he tells her tactlessly. "I have no secret longing to be saved from myself." "You curse yourself!" she cries, rejected. The heartless Onegin continues his dalliance with Olga. This leads to a duel with Lensky. His heart is broken when he kills his friend; that will teach him to call a nineteenth-century Russian nobleman's wife "easy."

Onegin flees to exile (or Paris, which are synonymous). Six years pass. He returns to St. Petersburg and sees Tatyana again, at a ball. But now the tables are turned, in ironic revelations and belated discoveries, and Onegin pays the price for his heartlessness.

There is a cool, mannered elegance to the picture that I like, but it's dead at its center. There is no feeling that real feelings are at risk here. Liv Tyler seems sincere enough, but Fiennes withholds too well. And the direction, by his sister Martha Fiennes, is deliberate and detached when it should perhaps plunge into the story. The visuals are wonderful, but the drama is muted.

There is a tendency to embalm classics, but never was literature more tempestuous and heartfelt than in nineteenth-century Russia. Characters joyously leap from the pages of Pushkin, Dostoyevsky, and Tolstoy, wearing their hearts on their sleeves, torn between the French schoolmasters who taught them manners, and the land where they learned passion—inhaled it, absorbed it in the womb. I know *Eugene Onegin* is a masterpiece, but the story it tells is romantic melodrama, and requires some of the same soap-opera zest as David Lean's *Dr. Zhivago*. This film has the same problem as its hero: Its manners are so good it doesn't know what it really feels.

102 Dalmatians ★ ★ ½
G, 101 m., 2000

Glenn Close (Cruella De Vil), Alice Evans (Cloe), Ioan Gruffudd (Kevin), Tim McInnerny (Alonso), Gérard Depardieu (Monsieur Le Pelt), Tony Robinson (Cruella De Vil's Sidekick). Directed by Kevin Lima and produced by Edward S. Feldman. Screenplay by Kristen Buckley, Brian Regan, Bob Tzudiker, and Noni White, based on the novel by Dodie Smith.

Pavlov, you will recall, conditioned dogs to salivate at the ringing of a bell. It is only fitting that his namesake, a modern scientist in *102 Dalmatians,* is able to condition Cruella De Vil to feel affectionate when she sees a dog. As *102 Dalmatians* opens, the famous dognapper and fur enthusiast has been transformed into a dog lover by Dr. Pavlov's secret methods.

Released on probation, Cruella (Glenn Close) is assigned to a parole officer named Cloe (Alice Evans), who is a Dalmatian lover and doesn't believe Cruella has really been reformed. But Cruella seems to have turned over a new leaf, and even gets involved in the activities of a shelter for homeless animals run by Kevin (Ioan Gruffudd), who for his part has eyes for Cloe. Then, alas, a Pavlovian bell rings (it is no less than Big Ben) and Cruella reverts to type.

Such is the setup for *102 Dalmatians,* a movie in which it follows as the night the day that Cruella sooner or later goes back to her old dog-hating ways. While the 1996 live-action version of *101 Dalmatians* had the original animated film to supply much of its story, this sequel is an original, with new characters, most memorably Monsieur Le Pelt (Gérard Depardieu), a fur designer who wears a quasi-medieval costume influenced by Depardieu's other recent film, *Asterix.* There are also new dogs, including a puppy named Oddball who is depressed because it has been born with no spots.

The film is made with formidable resources, including Cruella's home with its secret fur-storage rooms and dungeons. The good characters are portrayed as plucky and cheerful, the evil ones gnash their teeth more than the dogs, and Cruella's hairstyle, half-black and half-silver, is in itself a wonder, as are her gowns, her nails, and her bizarre makeup (the character is so seriously kinky I have always wondered what an R-rated version might have to offer us). It is a movie made with style and energy.

And yet whether you like it or not depends largely, I think, on how you feel about the dogs. Oddball is cute, yes, but he and the other dogs suffer somewhat because they are—well, real. The Disney animal classics, including *Lady and the Tramp* and the animated *101 Dalmatians,* were able to make their dogs into stars; in a live-action movie, they're reduced to supporting characters. Smaller children aren't likely to understand Cruella and Le Pelt except as adults who are mean to dogs. There are some joys in chases and thrilling escapes, but taking the dogs out of the central roles leaves you with seriously weird humans and not enough puppy love.

Glenn Close does what can be done with the role. Indeed, she does more than can be done; Cruella is almost too big for a live-action film, and requires animation to fit her operatic scale. The Le Pelt character is not really necessary, and although Cloe and Kevin (and Cruella's timid servant Alonso) do what they can, the film itself doesn't really seem necessary, either.

Yet Cruella De Vil has possibilities. I wonder why movies like this stay so close to their origins. Wouldn't it be intriguing to lift Cruella entirely out of dog roles and put her back into animation as the star of a cartoon version of *Sunset Boulevard*? She's still big. It's live action that got small.

Note: I have here an urgent message from a dog lover urging me to emphasize in my review that Dalmatians are sensitive and demanding animals who require dedicated owners. The earlier Dalmatian films apparently inspired countless dog lovers to adopt Dalmatians they were not quite ready for, causing overbreeding and consequent homelessness; my correspondent will be happy to learn (1) the movie itself ends with a request that puppies be adopted only by owners prepared to be responsible and committed, and (2) if a movie hasn't yet driven you to acquire a Dalmatian, 102 Dalmatians *is unlikely to do the trick.*

One Night at McCool's ★ ★ ½
R, 93 m., 2001

Liv Tyler (Jewel Valentine), Matt Dillon (Randy), John Goodman (Detective Dehling), Paul Reiser (Lawyer Carl), Michael Douglas (Mr. Burmeister), Andrew Dice Clay (Utah/Mormon Brother), Reba McEntire (Carl's Psychiatrist), Richard Jenkins (Priest). Directed by Harald Zwart and produced by Michael Douglas and Allison Lyon Segan. Screenplay by Stan Seidel.

When a man tells a woman she's the one he's

been searching for, this is not a comment about the woman but about the man. The male mind, drenched in testosterone, sees what it needs to see. *One Night at McCool's,* a comedy about three men who fall for the same woman, shows how the wise woman can take advantage of this biological insight.

The movie stars Liv Tyler as Jewel Valentine, a woman who walks into a bar one night and walks out, so to speak, with the hearts of three men. Each one sees a different woman. For Randy the bartender (Matt Dillon), she's the sweet homemaker he has yearned for ever since his mother died and left him a house. For Carl the lawyer (Paul Reiser), she's a sexpot with great boobs and legs that go all the way up to here. When Dehling the detective (John Goodman) sees her a few days later, she's like an angel, backlit in soft focus, as if heaven has reincarnated his beloved dead wife.

Much of the humor of the case comes because when Jewel looks at Randy, Carl, and Dehling, she sees three patsys—men who can feed her almost insatiable desire for consumer goods. She may sorta like them. She isn't an evil woman; she's just the victim of her nature. She's like the Parker Posey character in *Best in Show* who considers herself "lucky to have been raised among catalogs."

Like movie sex bombs of the past, Tyler plays Jewel not as a scheming gold digger, but as an innocent, almost childlike creature who is delighted by baubles (and by DVD machines, which she has a thing for). At least, I think that's what she does. Like the audience, I have to reconstruct her from a composite picture made out of three sets of unreliable testimony. Perhaps there is a clue in the fact that the first time we see her, she's with a big, loud, obnoxious, leather-wearing, middle-aged hood named Utah (Andrew Dice Clay). On the other hand, perhaps Utah is a nicer guy, since we see him only through the eyes of his rivals.

We see everything in the movie through secondhand testimony. Like Kurosawa's *Rashomon,* the film has no objective reality; we depend on what people tell us. Jewel Valentine waltzes into each man's life and gets him to do more or less what she desires, and what she desires is highly specific and has to do with her relationship to the consumer lifestyle (to reveal more would be unfair). Each guy, of course, filters her behavior through the delusion that she really likes him. And each guy creates a negative, hostile mental portrait of the other two guys.

Each witness has someone to listen to him. Randy the bartender confides in Mr. Burmeister (Michael Douglas, buck-toothed and in urgent need of a barber). He's a hit man Randy wants to pay to set things straight. Carl the lawyer talks to his psychiatrist (Reba McEntire), who thinks the whole problem may be related to his relationship with his mother, and may be right. And Dehling the detective talks to his brother the priest (Richard Jenkins).

Jewel is not the only character who is seen in three different ways. Consider how Randy the bartender comes across as a hardworking, easygoing, nice guy in his own version, but appears to others as a slow-witted drunk and a letch.

The movie isn't only about three sets of testimony. Far from it. Jewel has a scam she's had a lot of luck with, and enlists Randy in helping her out—against his will, since he sees her as a sweet housewife. He can't imagine her as a criminal, and neither can the cop, who tortuously rewrites the evidence of his own eyes in order to make her into an innocent bystander who needs to be rescued by—well, Detective Dehling, of course.

One Night at McCool's doesn't quite work, but it has a lot of fun being a near miss. It misses, I think, because it is so busy with its crosscut structure and its interlocking stories that it never really gives us anyone to identify with—and in a comedy, we have to know where everybody stands in order to figure out what's funny, and how, and to whom. The same flaw has always bothered me about *Rashomon*—a masterpiece, yes, but one of conception rather than emotion.

We enjoy the puzzle in *McCool's*, and Tyler and her costars do a good job of seeming like different things to different people, but it's finally an exercise without an emotional engine to pull it, and we just don't care enough. Does it matter if we don't care about a comedy? Yes, I think, it does: Comedy needs victims, and when everybody is innocent in their own eyes, you don't know where to look while you're laughing.

On the Line ★

PG, 85 m., 2001

Lance Bass (Kevin Gibbons), Emmanuelle Chriqui (Abbey), Joey Fatone (Rod), GQ [Gregory Qaiyum] (Eric), James Bulliard (Randy), Richie Sambora (Mick Silver), Jerry Stiller (Nathan), Kristin Booth (Sam), Al Green (Himself). Directed by Eric Bross and produced by Wendy Thorlakson, Rich Hull, Peter Abrams, and Robert Levy. Screenplay by Eric Aronson and Paul Stanton.

Just when you think a dating movie can't conceivably involve more impossible coincidences and Idiot Plot situations, along comes another movie to prove you wrong. After *Serendipity*, here is *On the Line*, starring Lance Bass of 'N Sync in an agonizingly creaky movie that laboriously plods through a plot so contrived that the only thing real about it is its length. In both movies, a boy and a girl Meet Cute and instantly realize they are destined for each other, and then they plunge into a series of absurd contrivances designed to keep them apart.

Just once, could they meet and fall in love, and then the movie would be about their young lives together? I'm weary of romances about lovers who devote years to living far apart and barely missing chances to meet again. If this genre ever inspires a satire, it will end with the boy and girl sitting next to each other on an airplane—*still* not realizing they are together again, because by then they will be eighty, having spent sixty years missing each other by seconds.

Lance Bass plays Kevin Gibbons, a low-level Chicago ad executive who has no trouble with girls unless he really likes them. Then he freezes up and can't close the deal. One day on the el he meets Abbey (Emmanuelle Chriqui), who has a sunny smile and a warm personality, and can recite all of the American presidents, in order! So can Lance! Somewhere between Buchanan and Bush they realize they are meant for each other. But Kevin just *can't* ask for her phone number. And despite decades of feminist advances, all Abbey can do is smile helplessly and leave their future in his hands. They part with rueful smiles. No, make that Rueful Smiles.

Later, Kevin kicks himself and moans to his

roommates about the perfect girl who got away. These roommates include fellow 'N Sync-er Joey Fatone, as Rod, who sings in an open-mike saloon and specializes in kicking the amp; Eric (the comedian GQ), a devoted mope; and Randy (James Bulliard), the brains of the outfit. The four guys spend countless precious screen minutes hanging around their flat engaging in redundant dialogue while we desperately want the movie to *lose the roommates* and *bring back the girl!*

But no. Films for the teenage demographic are terrified of romance and intimacy between the sexes, and shyly specialize in boys plotting about girls and girls plotting about boys, with as few actual scenes between boys and girls as possible. So after Kevin papers the town with posters seeking the girl he met on the train, and dozens of calls flood in, the roommates divide up the calls and date the girls (not telling Kevin, of course).

Well, obviously, only the right girl would know she was not going out with Kevin. So when Eric dates Abbey and she knows he's not Kevin—*that's the girl!* Right? But no. Eric is dense to the point of perversity, and spends their date not saying the few obvious words that need to be said, while acting like a pig and giving Abbey the impression that Kevin planned this humiliation. This is the Idiot Plot gone berserk. One sentence—*one word!*—and all would be solved, but Eric and the screenplay contort themselves into grotesque evasions to avoid stating the crashingly obvious.

So of course Abbey is crushed, and so are we, because we realize we are in the grip of a power greater than ourselves—Hollywood's determination to make films at the level of remedial reading. No one involved in the making of this film is as stupid as the characters, so why do they think the audience is? Why not for once allow young lovers to be smart, curious, articulate, and quick?

It must be said that Lance Bass and Emmanuelle Chriqui have sweet chemistry together, in the few moments they are able to snatch away from the forces designed to separate them. Bass is likable (but then likability is the primary talent of 'N Sync), and Chriqui, from Montreal via *Snow Day* and *A.I.*, is warm and charming and has a great smile. I can imagine

a lovely love story involving these two actors. Too bad *On the Line* goes to such lengths to avoid making it. ☞

The Opportunists ★ ★ ★
R, 89 m., 2000

Christopher Walken (Victor Kelly), Peter McDonald (Michael Lawler), Cyndi Lauper (Sally Mahon), Vera Farmiga (Miriam Kelly), Donal Logue (Pat Duffy), Jose Zuniga (Jesus Del Toro), Tom Noonan (Mort Stein), Anne Pitoniak (Aunt Diedre), Olek Krupa (Ted Walikaki). Directed by Myles Connell and produced by John Lyons and Tim Perell. Screenplay by Connell.

Crime movies always seem to have neat endings. There's a chase or a shoot-out, a trial or a confession. *The Opportunists* is messier than that. It is less a matter of the big payoff than the daily struggle. In the movies, most safecrackers are egotistical geniuses who do it for the gratification. In life, I imagine they're more like Victor Kelly, and they're in it for the money. Not much money at that.

Kelly is played in *The Opportunists* by Christopher Walken, and it's one of his best performances. He's a guy who once screwed up big time, and now he's trying to keep his head down and stay on the straight and narrow. He's dutiful. He visits his Aunt Diedre, he brings her home from the geriatric hospital for a day out, and he tries his best with his daughter, Miriam. He has an auto repair shop, and is just scraping by.

Enter a visitor from Ireland, Michael Lawler (Peter McDonald), who says he is a cousin. He has heard all about the great master criminal Victor Kelly and wants to team up with him on a job. Victor is not interested, but gives the kid a cluttered mobile home to live in. Things take a turn for the worse. Victor's check bounces at the geriatric hospital, his aunt is about to be evicted, and from the way he says, "I had a setback at work," you can tell that setbacks are his way of life. It isn't long until he has agreed to join Michael and two neighbors (played by Donal Logue and Jose Zuniga) in going after a safe.

The structure of the movie is like a low-rent

version of the usual caper film. There is the obligatory rehearsal scene, but held while they're sitting on the living room floor. And the attempt to crack the safe itself is less cool than confused. When things do not go right, watch the way Christopher Walken's face absorbs and accepts the inevitable. He isn't even angry. It's more like he knew all along this thing would end badly. Instead of suspense and action, the movie links together a series of uh-oh moments, done with perfect pitch.

The sad thing is, there's a woman who loves him or could if he gave her a chance, and would have helped him out if he'd let her. That's Sally Mahon, played straight from the shoulder by Cyndi Lauper. But, no, Victor has to make the same mistakes. Meanwhile, Michael from Ireland is getting friendly with Victor's daughter (Vera Farmiga), and that may not end well, either.

It's here the movie resolutely refuses to fly on autopilot. We have seen more than a few crime movies and we expect things to happen in certain ways. They don't. Without getting into the details, I'll say that a criminal named Mort (Tom Noonan) supplies a kind of input that's refreshingly realistic, and that the aftermath of the safecracking job is not at all like Victor, or the police, expect it to be. The final notes of the movie are not tragic or triumphant, but kind of a quiet comeuppance.

The Opportunists was written and directed by Myles Connell, an Irishman who developed the project at the Sundance Institute, and you wonder if there's a touch of his character Michael Lawler in him—not the bad stuff, just the knowledge about neediness and the willingness to believe unlikely stories. Certainly he helps Walken create a touching character.

Walken has been so good for so long we take him for granted. Sometimes he plays weirdos and we smile because we know he'll sink his teeth into the role. But he is a gifted classical actor (the first time I saw him, he was in an O'Neill play), and here he understands Victor Kelly from the inside out. Victor is not a hero, not a wise guy, not a colorful character, but a working man who keeps repeating the same mistakes. There is a gentleness to the way the movie regards him. And a tact in the way Walken plays this sad and dignified character without ever feeling sorry for him.

Orange County ★ ★ ★
PG-13, 90 m., 2002

Colin Hanks (Shawn Brumder), Schuyler Fisk (Ashley), Catherine O'Hara (Cindy Beugler), Jack Black (Lance Brumder), John Lithgow (Bud Brumder), Kevin Kline (Marcus Skinner), Lily Tomlin (Guidance Counselor), Harold Ramis (Don Durkett). Directed by Jake Kasdan and produced by David Gale and Scott Rudin. Screenplay by Mike White.

Orange County has the form of a teenage movie, the spirit of an independent comedy, and the subversive zeal of Jack Black, whose grin is the least reassuring since Jack Nicholson. It's one of those movies like *Ghost World* and *Legally Blonde* where the description can't do justice to the experience. It will sound like the kind of movie that, if you are over seventeen, you don't usually go to see. But it isn't.

The movie is a launching pad for three members of Hollywood's next generation. The stars are Colin Hanks (son of Tom Hanks) and Schuyler Fisk (daughter of Sissy Spacek and Jack Fisk). The director is Jake Kasdan (son of Lawrence and Meg Kasdan). All have worked before, but this is one of those happy projects where everything seems to fall naturally into place.

Hanks plays Shawn Brumder, heedless and carefree teenage Orange County surfer—until one day he finds a novel half-buried in the sand. It's by Marcus Skinner, one of those authors who can strike a kid of the right age as a conduit to truth and beauty. Shawn casts aside his old surfer lifestyle (to the grief of his pot-brained buddy) and determines to get into Stanford and study at the feet of the great Skinner (Kevin Kline).

This should be a cinch, since his test scores are very high. But he's rejected by Stanford because the daffy high school counselor (Lily Tomlin) has sent in the wrong scores under his name. This disappointment is crushing to Shawn, less disturbing to the other members of his definitively dysfunctional family. His father, Bud (John Lithgow), is workaholic and distant, his mother, Cindy (Catherine O'Hara), is—well, Catherine O'Hara, and his brother, Lance (Jack Black), is a couch potato, although potatoes may be the one substance he doesn't abuse. There is also Ashley (Schuyler Fisk), his loyal girlfriend, who believes in him, supports him, and is, in a stunning breakthrough for the teenage comedy genre, a blonde who is as intelligent as he is, maybe more.

The movie was written by Mike White, who you may remember as the author and star of *Chuck and Buck* (2000). He has one of those sideways, sardonic, nerd-savant approaches, getting a lot of his laughs by the application of logic to situations where it is not usually encountered. His characters tend to take things literally; in this case, Lance, the Jack Black character, is usually so stoned that his tunnel vision gives him an extraordinary, if misguided, clarity. Lance loves Shawn, even though he doesn't see the point of ambition or achievement, and so he offers to drive him to Palo Alto so that he can personally confront the Stanford admissions counselor.

It's around this point that we see the strategy of *Orange County*. It wants to appear to be a formula teenage screenplay (sex and dope jokes, girlfriend who is almost alienated and then reunited, personal redemption at last possible moment after maximum contrived suspense). At the same time, it goes under and over this mark: under with gags that would distinguish a Farrelly brothers picture, and over with surprisingly touching attention to Shawn's personality changes, his hopes and dreams, and especially his support from the stalwart Ashley.

The movie's cast looks like a roll call from the comedy hall of fame. If you have Harold Ramis, Jane Adams, Garry Marshall, Chevy Chase, Ben Stiller, and Mike White himself in supporting roles, and Kevin Kline (unbilled) finding just the right balance between charming nobility and weary pomposity, you have a movie that can be undone only in the making. Jake Kasdan is still in his mid-twenties, but is sure-footed and has a nice skewed sense of comic timing; this movie is a world apart from his fine first feature, *Zero Effect* (1998), a Sherlockian web that could go on the puzzler shelf with *Memento* and *Mulholland Drive*. He has also directed a lot of episodic comedy on TV (*Freaks and Geeks, Grosse Pointe*).

I was in New York when the movie was previewed for the press, and heard some idle talk about how this movie was proof that if you had the right parents you could get hired in Hollywood. True, and not true. Certainly Kasdan, Hanks, and Fisk have connections. On the other hand, studios invest real money. If your father is a famous actor, you may be able to get hired as an intern or an assistant still photographer, or get an acting job in a TV series. If you're making a feature on your own, it's because somebody with money thought you were right for the job. In this case, somebody was right.

The Original Kings of Comedy ★ ★ ★
R, 117 m., 2000

With Steve Harvey, D. L. Hughley, Cedric the Entertainer, and Bernie Mac. A documentary directed by Spike Lee and produced by Lee, Walter Latham, and David M. Gale.

Could *Titanic* have been an African-American film? Not very likely, says the comedian Steve Harvey. What black band would have been so foolish as to remain on deck, playing "Nearer My God to Thee" while the icy waters rose around their knees? "Kool and the Gang would have been unplugged in no time," he says, during an early monologue in *The Original Kings of Comedy*. What would any sensible *Titanic* passenger do? Grabbing a small wooden table that's onstage, he upends it, climbs aboard, grabs a table napkin, and blows into it to make a sail.

Harvey is the emcee of Spike Lee's new concert film, which documents a Charlotte, North Carolina, stop on a concert tour called Kings of Comedy, which has become one of the top-grossing arena acts in the country. He and three other black stand-up comics pack houses with routines that all owe something, sometimes a lot, to Richard Pryor and Eddie Murphy, who have now achieved classic status.

The other three performers are D. L. Hughley, Cedric the Entertainer, and Bernie Mac, all different in style, all using material based on African-American life in America and black-white differences. Harvey is the smoothest of the performers, although the most aggressive toward the audience, picking targets in the front row for comments on their hair, clothes, and career prospects. Bernie Mac is the most hard-edged, and some of his material ventures away from comedy and into the wounds of real life.

He seems, at times, to be working directly from his autobiography, as when he says he's raising his sister's three kids ("she had some drug problems—you know how that is"). They're aged two, four, and six, he says, running down their problems and proclivities with a bluntness that seems to come not so much from comedy as from exhaustion. We wince a little as he describes the kids and wonder (since we don't know) if they're real, or fictional, or adapted for purposes of the act. No matter; his material skates close to the edge, as Pryor's did, and we realize what the poet meant when he said we laugh, that we may not cry.

Cedric the Entertainer is perceptive in pointing out the subtle fault lines between black and white culture, and does an extended riff on the difference between what a white person means by "hope" and a black person means by "wish." "Hope" here comes across as a bland and pious yearning for the best, while "wish" comes across more as an ultimatum or a dare. To hope someone is on time is to think positively for them; to wish they turn up on time is to yearn for them to get what's coming to them. It's hard to explain, but somehow Cedric's tone of voice does all the lifting.

D. L. Hughley does a very funny explanation of why black people are not enthusiastic bungee jumpers. His material is accessible and mainstream, as when he speculates that Jesus was black, just on the basis of his miracle at the wedding feast: Turning water into wine, he imagines Jesus explaining, "Normally, you know, I don't do this—but go on, keep the party goin'!"

Harvey comes on between every act and does a tightwire act with the audience's affection. There is a point beyond which you cannot kid an audience before it feels picked on, and there's tension in the way Harvey approaches that point and then smiles and releases the tension. He asks one young man in the front row what he does for a living. "Computer school," the guy says, and Harvey tells him that nothing about him seems to say "computer" or "school." This could turn bad, but Harvey is a master of timing and tone, and gets away with it.

The Original Kings of Comedy doesn't have

the theatrical subtext or, let it be said, the genius of Richard Pryor. But then again, Pryor went out for an hour or ninety minutes and just talked. These guys are working in a revue format. I got the feeling that Bernie Mac, working open-ended, free to improvise, would end up in some strange and fraught places, some funny, some just true.

Original Sin ★ ★ ★
R, 112 m., 2001

Antonio Banderas (Luis Durand), Angelina Jolie (Julia Russell), Thomas Jane (Walter Downs), Joan Pringle (Sarah), Allison Mackie (Augusta). Directed by Michael Cristofer and produced by Denise Di Novi, Kate Guinzburg, and Carol Lees. Screenplay by Cristofer, based on the novel *Waltz Into Darkness* by Cornell Woolrich.

The first shot on the screen is a close-up of Angelina Jolie's lips. And what lips they are, plump and pouting and almost bruised. Eventually we tear ourselves away from the sight and realize she's talking. She's telling the story of why she happens to be in a jail cell; these flashbacks will eventually reveal that she has been condemned to death by garroting—a nasty way to go, as the executioner turns a screw to tighten an iron collar around your neck.

This prologue undermines any romantic illusions as the story itself begins, circa 1900, introducing us to a wealthy Cuban coffee planter named Luis Durand (Antonio Banderas), who anticipates the arrival of a mail-order bride named Julia Russell (Jolie). Handsome and rich, he has never married ("Love is not for me. Love is for those people who believe in it"). His expectations for the bride are realistic: "She is not meant to be beautiful. She is meant to be kind, true, and young enough to bear children."

"You don't recognize me, do you?" Julia murmurs in a thrilling low register, as he finds her standing before him at the dock. He does not. This sultry vision is not the plain woman in the photograph he holds. She confesses she sent the wrong photo because she did not want a man who was attracted only to her beauty. He confesses too: He owns his plantation and is not simply a worker there. He didn't want to attract a gold digger. "Then we have something in common," she says. "Neither one of us can be trusted." Actually, he can.

Original Sin is based on the novel *Waltz Into Darkness,* by the famous *noir* writer Cornell Woolrich. Another of his books inspired Hitchcock's *Rear Window*—and indeed this one was earlier filmed as *Mississippi Mermaid* by Francois Truffaut in 1969 (Jean-Paul Belmondo and Catherine Deneuve played the roles). Like many good thrillers, it only really gets rolling after we think we've already seen through the plot. There are surprises on top of surprises, and I will tread carefully to preserve them.

The purpose of the movie is not really to tell its story, anyway, but to use it as an engine to pull Banderas and Jolie through scenes of lurid melodrama, dramatic ultimatums, and stunning revelations. Another purpose is to show off these two splendid human beings, and I am happy to report that there is even a certain amount of nudity—which you would expect with this passionate story, but then again you never know, now that studios are scurrying into the shelter of the PG-13 to hide from pruny congressmen.

Jolie continues to stalk through pictures entirely on her own terms. Her presence is like a dare-ya for a man. There's dialogue in this movie so overwrought it's almost literally unspeakable, and she survives it by biting it off contemptuously and spitting it out. She makes no effort to pretend to be a nice woman—not even at the first, when Luis believes her story. She's the kind of woman who looks a man in the eye and tells him what she wants and how soon she expects to get it. Banderas skillfully plays up to this quality, spaniel-eyed, lovestruck, so overwhelmed he will follow her literally anywhere.

The movie is not intended to be subtle. It is sweaty, candlelit melodrama, joyously trashy, and its photography wallows in sumptuous decadence. The ending is hilariously contrived and sensationally unlikely, as the movie audaciously shows an irrevocable action and then revokes it. I don't know whether to recommend *Original Sin* or not. It's an exuberant example of what it is—a bodice-ripping murder melodrama—and as that it gets a passing grade. Maybe if it had tried to be more it would have simply been watering the soup.

Orphans ★ ★ ½
NO MPAA RATING, 102 m., 2000

Gary Lewis (Thomas), Douglas Henshall (Michael), Rosemarie Stevenson (Sheila), Stephen McCole (John), Frank Gallagher (Tanga), Alex Norton (Hanson). Directed by Peter Mullan and produced by Frances Higson. Screenplay by Mullan.

How seriously does *Orphans* intend to be taken? On one hand it tells the gritty story of three Glasgow brothers and their handicapped sister in the twenty-four hours after their mother dies. On the other hand, it involves events that would be at home in a comedy of the absurd. When the sister's wheelchair topples a statue of the Virgin Mary and the damage is blamed on high winds that lifted the roof off a church, we have left the land of realism.

We have not, however, entered the land of boredom. *Orphans* is a film of great intensity and weird events, in which four suddenly parentless adults come unhinged in different ways. For Thomas, the oldest, the mother's death is an occasion for piety, and he spends the night with her coffin in the church and later tries to carry it on his back to the grave. For Michael, it's an occasion for boozing, a pub fight, and a spiral of confusion after he gets knifed. For John, the youngest, it provides a mission: to find and kill the man who stabbed Michael. And for Sheila, in the wheelchair, it leads to an act of defiance as she ventures out into the night alone.

The movie was written and directed by Peter Mullan. You may remember him as the title character in *My Name Is Joe,* Ken Loach's heartrending film about a recovering alcoholic in Glasgow. He won the Best Actor prize at Cannes for that role, and with *Orphans* focuses on at least two characters in urgent need of AA.

It's one of those sub–Eugene O'Neill family dramas in which a lifetime of confusion and anguish comes to a head during a family crisis. We see how each brother has hewn out his space in the family in reaction to the others, while the sister basically just wants out. The brothers Michael and John inhabit a world of hard characters and pub desperadoes (sample dialogue: "We'd cut your legs off for twenty

Silk Cut [cigarettes] and a rubber bone for his dog"). Thomas likes to see himself as older, wiser, saner, more religious, and yet he's the maddest of them all. And the movie staggers like its drunken characters from melodrama to revelation, from truth-telling to incredible situations, as when Michael finds himself used as a dart board by a pub owner.

How are we to take this? There are times when we want to laugh, as when Thomas tries to glue the shattered Virgin back together with hot wax candle drippings ("She's a total write-off," he observes morosely). We see the roof lifting off the church in a nice effects shot, but why? To show God's wrath, or simply bad weather conditions? It's a nice point when the funeral goes ahead inside the ruined church—but wouldn't the insurance company and public safety inspectors have something to say about that?

Maybe we're not supposed to ask such realistic questions, but we can't resist. Yet other moments seem as slice-of-life as anything in *My Name Is Joe*. My guess is that Mullan never decided what tone his film should aim for; he fell in love with individual sequences without asking how they fit together.

Note: Because of its Glasgow accents, the film has been subtitled. But we can understand most of what the characters say, and that leads to disconnections, since the subtitles are reluctant to use certain four-letter Anglo-Saxonisms we can clearly hear being uttered by the characters.

Osmosis Jones ★ ★ ★
PG-13, 98 m., 2001

Bill Murray (Frank), Elena Franklin (Shane), Molly Shannon (Mrs. Boyd), Chris Elliott (Bob), With the voices of: Chris Rock (Osmosis), Laurence Fishburne (Thrax), David Hyde Pierce (Drix), Brandy Norwood (Leah), William Shatner (The Mayor), Ron Howard (Tom Colonic). Directed by Peter Farrelly and Bobby Farrelly and produced by Bradley Thomas, Peter Farrelly, Bobby Farrelly, Zak Penn, and Dennis Edwards. Animation directed by Piet Kroon and Tom Sito. Screenplay by Marc Hyman.

Osmosis Jones is like the dark side of those animated educational films depicting the goings-on in the bowels. It takes us inside the human body for a tour of such uncharted neighborhoods as the Lower East Backside, and such useful organs as the Puke Button. These sights are depicted in colorful, gloppy, drippy animation, and then we switch to live action for the outside of the body in question, which belongs to a man named Frank (Bill Murray).

Frank follows the Ten-Second Rule, which teaches us that if food is dropped and stays on the ground less than ten seconds, it's still safe to eat. In the case of the hard-boiled egg in question, he might also have reflected that before the egg dropped, he had to pry it from the mouth of a monkey. The egg is crawling with germs, sending the inside of his body into emergency mode.

At the cellular level, we meet Osmosis Jones (voice by Chris Rock), a maverick cop, always being called into the chief's office for a lecture. In the first animated microbiological version of a buddy movie, he teams up with Drix (David Hyde Pierce), a timed-release cold capsule, to fight the viral invasion, which threatens to kill Frank after Thrax (Laurence Fishburne) introduces a new and deadly infection.

The live-action scenes, directed by Peter and Bobby Farrelly *(There's Something About Mary)*, use Bill Murray's seedy insouciance as a horrible object lesson in what can happen to you if you don't think all the time about germs. His second, potentially lethal, infection comes as he visits a science fair where his daughter, Shane (Elena Franklin), has an entry. Chatting with another entrant, he learns that the lad's experiment involves the cleansing of polluted oysters; assured that the oysters are cleansed, he eats one.

The inner, animated sequences, which occupy about two-thirds of the movie, were directed by Piet Kroon and Tom Sito. Imagine the journey through the human body undertaken by Dennis Quaid in *Innerspace* (1987) as if it were drawn by Matt Groening *(Life in Hell)* on acid, and you will have an approximation. I especially liked the way various parts of the body represented neighborhoods in the City of Frank (the stomach is the airport, with regular departures to the colon; the Mafia hangs out in the armpit; lawyers can be found in a hemorrhoid).

Inside Frank City, the mayor (William Shatner) tries to maintain the status quo in the face of campaigning by his opponent, Tom Colonic (Ron Howard), a "regular guy." Outside, the unshaven Frank embarrasses his spic-and-span daughter with his uncouth behavior, and mortally offends the science teacher (Molly Shannon) by throwing up on her after eating the wrong oyster. (I am reminded of Dr. Johnson observing to Mr. Boswell: "Sir, he was a brave man who ate the first oyster.") Back inside Frank, Osmosis Jones frets that he acted too quickly in pushing the Puke Button.

Who is the movie for? Despite my descriptions, it is nowhere near as gross as the usual effort, and steers clear of adventures in the genital areas. It was originally classified PG-13, but was upgraded to PG after some trims, and is likely to entertain kids, who seem to like jokes about anatomical plumbing. For adults, there is the exuberance of the animation and the energy of the whole movie, which is just plain clever.

The Others ★ ★ ½
PG-13, 104 m., 2001

Nicole Kidman (Grace), Christopher Eccleston (Charles), Fionnula Flanagan (Mrs. Mills), Elaine Cassidy (Lydia), Eric Sykes (Mr. Tuttle), Alakina Mann (Anne), James Bentley (Nicholas). Directed by Alejandro Amenabar and produced by Fernando Bovaira, Jose Luis Cuerda, and Park Sunmin. Screenplay by Amenabar.

The Others is a haunted house mystery—from which you assume, trained by recent movies, that it is filled with flashy special effects, violent shocks, bloodcurdling apparitions, undulating staircases, telescoping corridors, graves opening in the basement, doors that will not lock or will not open, and dialogue like, "There's something in this house! Something ... diabolic!"

You would be right about the dialogue. This is a haunted house movie, dark and atmospheric, but it's quiet and brooding. It has less in common with, say, *The House on Haunted Hill* than with *The Sixth Sense* or a story by Oliver Onions. It's not a freak show but a waiting game, in which an atmosphere of dread slowly envelops the characters—too slowly. Comparing this movie with *The Sixth Sense*, we feel a renewed admiration for the way

M. Night Shyamalan was able to maintain tension through little things that were happening, instead of (this film's strategy) big things that seem about to happen.

The film takes place in an isolated mansion on the island of Jersey off the French coast. In this house lives Grace (Nicole Kidman) and her two children, the tremulous Nicholas (James Bentley), and the cheeky Anne (Alakina Mann). To the house one day come three servants, who are responding, or say they are responding, to Grace's advertisement for domestic help. There are vacancies because the previous servants decamped in the middle of the night without a word of notice. The three new applicants have the advantage of being familiar with the house.

It is a sound tradition of British fiction that servants do not leave a house only to later return and be rehired (the sole exception is George Wellbeloved, Lord Emsworth's pig-keeper at Blandings Castle). But these are the days immediately after World War II, which claimed, or seems to have claimed, Grace's husband, and so perhaps help is hard to find. She hires them: Mrs. Mills (Fionnula Flanagan), the middle-aged Irish woman with the know-it-all nods, the young mute girl Lydia (Elaine Cassidy), and the gardener Mr. Tuttle (Eric Sykes), who is so ancient that for him planting a seed is an act of wild optimism.

There are odd rules in the house. Each of the fifty doors must be locked before another can be opened. The curtains must always be drawn. These measures are necessary because Anne and Nicholas are so allergic to the sunlight that they might die if exposed to it.

The events in the film are such that I must not describe them. Even a hint might give away the game. Of course they are elusive and mysterious, reported by some, not seen by others, explained first one way and then another. By the time we arrive at the line, "There's something in this house!" we are not only prepared to agree, but to suspect that in supernatural terms it's as crowded as the Smithsonian's attic.

The director, Alejandro Amenabar, has the patience to create a languorous, dreamy atmosphere, and Nicole Kidman succeeds in convincing us that she is a normal person in a disturbing situation and not just a standard-issue horror movie hysteric. But in drawing out his effects, Amenabar is a little too confident that style can substitute for substance. As our suspense was supposed to be building, our impatience was outstripping it. As Houdini said, or should have if he didn't, you can only listen to so much spectral knocking before you want to look under the table.   ☞

Otomo ★ ★ ★

NO MPAA RATING, 85 m., 2001

Isaach De Bankole (Otomo), Eva Mattes (Gisela), Hanno Friedrich (Heinz), Barnaby Metschurat (Rolf), Lara Kugler (Simone). Directed by Frieder Schlaich and produced by Thomas Lechner, Claudia Tronnier, and Irene van Alberti. Screenplay by Schlaich and Klaus Pohl.

On August 9, 1989, as a black man was stopped on a bridge in Stuttgart, Germany, for questioning, he knifed two officers to death and wounded three others before being shot dead himself. This man's name was Frederic Otomo. At about 6:15 that morning, he had been confronted on a subway train by a ticket inspector, who told him he had to get off at the next stop. The inspector got aggressive with Otomo, who headbutted him and fled from the train, setting up the manhunt that ended on the bridge.

Those facts are known. What happened between the two incidents is unknown, and inspires this film by Frieder Schlaich, who tries to imagine what went through Otomo's mind between the two confrontations. Along the way, Schlaich portrays a society in which some are racists who act cruelly toward the black man, and others, even strangers, go out of their way to help him.

Otomo, we learn, came from Liberia by way of the Cameroons, where his father fought for the Germans in World War II and was endangered as a German sympathizer. Technically, as one of the police officers observes, he may have had the right to German citizenship. But his only official papers are a temporary passport, not good enough to qualify him for a minimum-wage job he's turned away from at dawn. Before he's turned down, men make fun of his shoes—slippers they call "jungle creepers." Why is it assumed that the poor want to dress the way they must?

There is a moment on the subway line that the film interestingly leaves unclear. The inspector tells Otomo his ticket is only good for one zone, and he must get off. "You know it's a good ticket!" Otomo cries. Later, as the inspector and his woman partner sit in a police station to file a report, she looks at Otomo's ticket and holds it up to show it to the inspector. Why does she do this? I think it is because she notices the ticket is valid, although of course she doesn't mention that as her partner files his complaint.

Otomo (Isaach De Bankole) wanders through Stuttgart, avoiding police cars and helicopters (the scale of the manhunt seems a little large for the severity of his crime). In a restaurant, a waitress gives him food although he can only pay for coffee, and later when the police ask her if she has seen him, she says, "A nigger? Not in here." Using the word puts her on their side; lying for a man she doesn't know reveals, perhaps, an instinctive sympathy for the underdog.

On a river bank, Otomo is offered a flower by a little girl. This is a direct quote from *Frankenstein*, but the episode ends differently, with the girl's grandmother (Eva Mattes) taking him in and agreeing to lend him money to pay for a ride out of town. Why does she do this? Otomo is not talkative, says little to explain himself, yet somehow seems able to inspire sympathy. (Like Frankenstein's monster, he inspires fear on first sight from some, and is inarticulate in explaining himself.)

The movie's case for him is made, not by Otomo himself, but by the manager of the flophouse where he lives, who describes the lives of undocumented "guest workers" in simple terms: They are useful for undesirable jobs, but have no security and live constantly on the edge of destitution. "Is he violent?" a cop asks the manager. "Rather gentle," the manager says. "He'll talk to you for hours about the Bible."

The movie is about a man who reaches his snapping point. The ceremonial funerals for his police victims are contrasted with the three or four people who gather at his pauper's grave. The film doesn't believe the police deserved to die (or that the ticket inspector should have been assaulted), but then again it doesn't believe a society should so treat a man that this is what he comes to do.

Isaach De Bankole was seen most memorably in Jim Jarmusch's *Ghost Dog*, as the French-speaking African who carried on a long conversation with Forest Whitaker, the two speaking different languages. He also starred in *Chocolat*, Clair Denis's evocative 1988 film set in French West Africa. Eva Mattes was in many Fassbinder movies, including *Jailbait* (1972), made when she was seventeen. Now she plays a grandmother. "You old hippie!" her daughter calls her—needing to find a reason why her mother would befriend a desperate man.

Our Lady of the Assassins ★ ★ ★ ½
R, 98 m., 2001

German Jaramillo (Vallejo), Anderson Ballesteros (Alexis), Juan David Restrepo (Wilmar), Manuel Busquets (Alfonso), Wilmar Agudelo (Child Sniffing Glue), Juan Carlos Alvarez (4X4 Thief), Cenobia Cano (Alexis's Mother), Zulma Arango (Waitress). Directed by Barbet Schroeder and produced by Margaret Menegoz, Jaime Osorio Gomez, and Schroeder. Screenplay by Fernando Vallejo, based on his novel.

Vallejo is a writer who returns home to Colombia to die. By the end of Barbet Schroeder's *Our Lady of the Assassins*, he is almost the only person he knows who is still alive. His hometown is Medellín, company town of the cocaine industry, seen here as a cursed city of casual death, where machine gunners on motorcycles roam the streets settling gang feuds.

The writer knew this town thirty years ago, when it must have been a beautiful place. Now killings are common, bystanders look the other way, and in the movie (at least) the police seem absent. Vallejo (German Jaramillo) has arrived at a time in his life when he hardly seems to care: Did he come home half-expecting to find death before it found him?

A homosexual, he goes to a male brothel and meets Alexis (Anderson Ballesteros), a teenage boy. They spend the night. Not long after, Alexis moves into Vallejo's barren high-rise apartment. "There is no furniture," the boy observes. "There is a table, two chairs, a mattress," said Vallejo. "What else does one need?" A television and a boom box, Alexis explains. But soon the boom box goes over the

edge of the balcony; Vallejo is maddened by the music, as he is also annoyed by the ceaseless drumming of a neighbor, and by the musical tastes of a taxi driver who will not turn down the radio. Alexis, a gang member who is always armed, helpfully kills both the neighbor and the taxi driver. Vallejo is appalled and yet detached; the events in this city do not fully register—he is preoccupied by an inner agenda.

Our Lady of the Assassins, based on an autobiographical novel by the Colombian writer Fernando Vallejo, resonates also with Barbet Schroeder's own life; he was raised in Colombia, has worked mostly in the United States and France, at sixty is an extraordinary figure. "No other person in the film world can match his record of diversity," notes Stanley Kauffmann in his *New Republic* review. Schroeder's interests are astonishingly wide. He produces all the films of Eric Rohmer, whose work could not be more different than his own, and he has made movies about Charles Bukowski *(Barfly)*, the accused wife-killer Claus von Bulow *(Reversal of Fortune)*, and *Idi Amin Dada*, a doc about the dictator.

He made this Spanish-language film on the independent fringe, shooting on high-def video without permits, using guerrilla snatch-and-run video techniques, protected by bodyguards. Despite the danger involved in its production, the violence that weaves through all of its moments, and the documentary feel of the location photography in Medellín ("a city entirely without tourists," Schroeder notes), *Our Lady of the Assassins* is not a grim exercise in social realism. Vallejo's detachment sets the tone. He cannot easily be shocked or dismayed, because he's on the way out of life. He is saddened by the death of Alexis (the two grow genuinely close to each other), but that does not prevent him from finding another teenage lover, Wilmar (Juan David Restrepo). And when he discovers that Wilmar was Alexis's killer—well, Alexis killed Wilmar's brother, and what goes around comes around.

Can a man of sixty have a romantic relationship with a boy of sixteen? In a sane world, no. They would drive each other crazy. In a world where both expect to die in the immediate future, where plans are meaningless, where poverty of body and soul has left them starving in different ways, there is something to be said for sex, wine, music, and killing time in safety. And there is an agelessness in Vallejo, who has no family, no plans, no bourgeois preoccupations, and has simplified his life to a zen emptiness—he and these boys share the same cool disinterest in tomorrow. The morality of their arrangement, of course, is irrelevant in a city with no morality. (Every time a shipment of cocaine reaches the United States, the drug lords treat the people to a fireworks display.)

The film's title is appropriate. A desperate Catholicism flavors the doomed city. "He's happy it's Our Lady's day or I would have killed him," Alexis serenely observes after one violent episode. Drug deals take place in the cathedrals, and beggars fall on their knees to receive bakery handouts as if they are the Eucharist. Cocaine has brought billions to Colombia but little of it has trickled down; unlike a boomtown during the Gold Rush, Medellín does not share in the prosperity of its rich, but inherits only their depravity. A sign on a waste ground warns: NO DUMPING OF CORPSES.

Our Song ★ ★ ★
R, 96 m., 2001

Kerry Washington (Lanisha), Anna Simpson (Joycelyn), Melissa Martinez (Maria), D'Monroe (Terell), Kim Howard (Eleanor), The Jackie Robinson Steppers Marching Band (Themselves). Directed by Jim McKay and produced by McKay, Paul Mezey, and Diana E. Williams. Screenplay by McKay.

Three teenage girls, three possible futures. During a hot August in the Crown Heights section of Brooklyn, they hang out together, talk about boys and clothes, and attend band practice. One will get pregnant. One may drift away from these friends and find a new crowd. One may go back to school, even though the close local school has been closed (asbestos problems) and that means three hours on the bus every day. The theory is, their marching band may be sponsored for a trip to Alaska, a prospect that more or less brings conversation to a halt, since they are at a loss for opinions about Alaska one way or the other.

Our Song is the new movie by Jim McKay,

whose *Girls' Town* (1996) was also about adolescent girls making their plans. I admired that film, and like this one more, perhaps because the actors are closer to the ages of the characters and seem to inhabit their lives more easily. *Girls' Town* felt the need to have a plot. *Our Song*, like *George Washington*, has the courage to work without a net, aware that when you're a teenager your life is not a story so much as a million possible stories.

The movie stars Kerry Washington, Anna Simpson, and Melissa Martinez, all in their first roles, and it's impossible not to think a little of *Mystic Pizza*, which introduced Lili Taylor, Annabeth Gish, and Julia Roberts. I have a feeling we'll be seeing these newcomers again; indeed, Washington, who has a face the camera loves, has already made *Save the Last Dance* (as the white girl's new best friend) and *Lift* (a Sundance hit, where she plays a shoplifter).

In *Our Song*, Washington is Lanisha, with a divorced black father and Hispanic mother. She's a good student, has plans, lives in a neighborhood where dying young is a fact of life; she says she "sometimes thinks about being shot, like it would be okay." But then she snaps out of it and decides, "Today's a good day."

Anna Simpson plays Joycelyn, who has a job in retail and is beginning to bond with the other clerks at work. They begin to seem cooler to her than her old friends, and having a paycheck and money to spend seems cooler than going to school; she doesn't see yet that employment at that level is a life sentence.

Melissa Martinez plays Maria, whose boyfriend, Terell (D'Monroe), says he wants to break up. Her friends' theory: He's just trying to get out of buying her a birthday present. She discovers she is pregnant and tells her boyfriend. "I'll be around," Terell says, although he clearly prefers spending time on the streets with "my boys." Maria is realistic: "You barely act like you like me now." The sad truth is, she will probably have this baby and set the course of her life out of misplaced love for an indifferent boy who is already on his way to the exit door.

There is a counterpoint to her decision. Eleanor (Kim Howard), a young local girl with a baby, takes her child in her arms and jumps out of her project window. Friends and neighbors gather at a makeshift shrine of flowers and Polaroids, giving Eleanor the attention now that she needed yesterday.

The thread connecting the girls' lives is their marching band, the Jackie Robinson Steppers. It is a real band, something we don't have to be told after we see them. I learn that McKay got the idea for his film when he saw the Steppers in a parade, and began to wonder about the lives of some of its members. The band provides a focus, discipline, pride. It is very good. And the bandmaster provides a friendly but firm male presence for young people who often come from fatherless homes.

Interesting, the differences between this film and *Crazy/Beautiful*, another new film about young people about the same age. Both are good movies. *Crazy/Beautiful* has an established star (Kirsten Dunst), more plot, a more showy and entertaining sort of angst. It seems more sure of exactly what it wants to tell us. *Our Song* is not on the same fast track; it ambles, observes, meditates, has patience. Most audiences will connect more with *Crazy/Beautiful*, which does the lifting for them. *Our Song* requires us to look and listen to these girls, and make our own connections.

Example. Lanisha, the Kerry Washington character, has asthma. One day she starts to have an attack, and her friend takes her to the emergency room, where the receptionist of course exhibits the usual blindness toward a health crisis while demanding insurance forms, identification, and so on. In a different kind of film, this scene would have built up into a dramatic climax—*E.R.* lite. *Our Song* knows that things like this happen every day, that Lanisha will be frightened but will survive, that life goes on, that emergency rooms are more familiar to teenage girls from this neighborhood than to Kirsten Dunst's friends in Malibu.

Our Song is content with the rhythms of life, and so performs one of the noble functions of the movies, which is to give us the opportunity to empathize with characters not like ourselves.

Note: Because Our Song *deals with the daily reality of many girls under seventeen, it has been rated R by the MPAA, so that they can be prevented from learning from the movie's insights.*

P

Panic ★ ★ ★ ★
R, 88 m., 2001

William H. Macy (Alex), John Ritter (Josh Parks), Neve Campbell (Sarah), Donald Sutherland (Michael), Tracey Ullman (Martha), Barbara Bain (Deidre), David Dorfman (Sammy). Directed by Henry Bromell and produced by Andrew Lazar, Lori Miller, and Matt Cooper. Screenplay by Bromell.

"I've got two jobs. I run a small mail-order business out of the house. Lawn ornaments, kitchen geegaws, sexual aids—things like that."
"And the rest of the time?"
"I work for my father. I kill people."

The sad-eyed patient speaks calmly. His psychiatrist says, "You're kidding, right?" No, he is not kidding. He was raised in the family business. His father was a hit man, and he's a hit man too. Not even his wife knows; she believes the mail-order story. But now he's in his forties, has a young son he loves, and wants to stop murdering for a living.

It tells you something—it may even tell you enough—that the man, named Alex, is played by William H. Macy. This wonderful actor has a gift for edgy unhappiness, repressed resentment, and in *Panic* he speaks too calmly and moves too smoothly, as if afraid of trip wires and booby traps. He spent his childhood afraid to stand up to his father, and in a sense his childhood has never ended.

Henry Bromell's *Panic* seeps with melancholy, old wounds, repressed anger, lust. That it is also caustically funny and heartwarming is miraculous: How does it hit so many different notes and never strain? It has a relationship between Alex and his son, Sammy, that reminds us of *The Sixth Sense*, and one between Alex and the sexy young Sarah (Neve Campbell) that evokes *American Beauty*. And Alex himself, trying to keep everyone happy, trying to keep secrets, trying to separate the compartments of his life, has the desperation of the character Macy played in *Fargo*.

But this is not a movie assembled from spare parts. Bromell began as a writer (*North-*

ern Exposure, Chicago Hope), and this is a first film made with joy and with a writer's gift for character and dialogue. It involves a situation rich with irony and comic possibilities but isn't cynical about it; it's the kind of story that is funny when you hear about it from someone else, but not funny if it happens to you.

Alex was raised by his father, Michael (Donald Sutherland), to be a hit man. They started with squirrels and worked up from there. Alex didn't like killing squirrels, and in all of his killings since, it has been his father's finger pulling the trigger of Alex's tortured psyche. Alex is good at his job. But it makes him sick.

In the waiting room of his psychiatrist (John Ritter), he meets the patient of another doctor. This is Sarah, played by Neve Campbell as bright, cheeky, and with a gift for sharp observation. She has a complicated love life, is aware of her appeal, asks Alex if he's a guy in midlife crisis who thinks a sexy young girl might be just the ticket. In *American Beauty*, Kevin Spacey did indeed think that about the pom-pom girl, but Alex is looking not for sex but for approval, forgiveness, redemption; sex with Sarah would be less lust than rehab.

There are other important women in the picture. Tracey Ullman is Martha, Alex's wife, and Barbara Bain is Deidre, his mother. Martha has no idea how Alex really earns his living. Deidre knows all about everything, and when Alex confides that he wants out, she delivers a merciless lecture about how his father spent his whole life building up the family business, and Alex is an ungrateful child to destroy that dream. Yes, this is ironic, discussing murder in business terms, but it is so easy to separate success from morality. This could be any business in which the father insists that the son surrender his own dreams for the old man's.

Alex doesn't confide much in his wife; his secrets have built a wall. He loves her, but hopelessly, and he loves his son (David Dorfman, the little boy in *Bounce*). Their talks at bedtime are long and rich, and Sammy sees that something is deeply troubling his father: "Dad, are you all right?"

The movie takes these strands and weaves them into an emotional and logistical trap for

Alex. His relationship with Sarah, a complicated girl, creates more issues than it solves. His father assigns him to perform an execution that demonstrates the old man's inexorable power over his son. Flashbacks show Alex's anguish as a child, and there is also a flashback showing how he met his wife, and how he was attracted to her goofiness.

The elements of the movie stand on their own. The Neve Campbell character is not simply the younger woman in Alex's life, but creates plot space of her own, where Alex is a visitor. The parents, Michael and Deidre, have a relationship that depends on their son but excludes him. Alex and Sammy have a private bond. We come to see Alex as a desperate man running from one secret compartment to another, seeking a place where he can hide.

Macy is as easy to identify with as any actor working. He doesn't push it. As Alex, he approaches his problems doggedly, sometimes bravely, hoping for a reprieve. Sutherland makes the old hit man into a particularly unlikable person: There's something about the way he gobbles an outdoor meal, his hat askew, that sets our teeth on edge. Bain's mother in her cold confidence is even more hateful. Ullmann, that gifted character actress, creates a woman who knows her life is coming apart but doesn't know what her life is. Neve Campbell takes a tricky role and enriches it, brings it human dimension instead of being content with the "sexpot" assignment. And the little boy is heartbreaking, particularly in a conversation late in the movie. This is one of the year's best films.

Note: Panic was a success at Sundance 2000, but didn't get a major release after a test audience disliked it. I don't blame the test audience; this is not a look-alike movie. But the executives who believed the audience instead of their own eyes should be ashamed of themselves. Now the film has won a national release and, like Croupier, could be discovered by filmgoers who make up their own minds.

Panic Room ★ ★ ★
R, 112 m., 2002

Jodie Foster (Meg Altman), Kristen Stewart (Sarah Altman), Forest Whitaker (Burnham), Jared Leto (Junior), Dwight Yoakam (Raoul), Patrick Bauchau (Stephen), Ian Buchanan (Evan), Ann Magnuson (Lydia Lynch). Directed by David Fincher and produced by Cean Chaffin, Judy Hofflund, David Koepp, and Gavin Polone. Screenplay by Koepp.

As a critic I indulge myself by scoffing at loopholes in thrillers that could not exist without them. I guess I'm seeking the ideal of a thriller existing entirely in a world of physical and psychological plausibility. *Panic Room* is about as close as I'm likely to get. Yes, there are moments when I want to shout advice at the screen, but just as often the characters are ahead of me. They also ask the same questions I'm asking, of which the most heartfelt, in a thriller, is, "Why didn't *we* do that?"

The movie, directed by David Fincher and written by David Koepp, embraces realism almost as a challenge. The movie resembles a chess game: The board and all of the pieces are in full view, both sides know the rules, and the winner will simply be the better strategist. Once we sense *Panic Room* isn't going to cheat, it gathers in tension, because the characters are operating out of their own resources, and that makes them the players, not the pawns.

Jodie Foster and Forest Whitaker star, as the chessmasters. She's Meg, a rich woman, recently divorced, who is spending her first night in a big Manhattan brownstone with her teenage daughter, Sarah (Kristen Stewart). He's Burnham, a home invader lured by tales of millions hidden in the house by its former owner. The house includes a "panic room" on the third of four stories—a reinforced retreat with independent supplies of air, electricity, and water, which can be locked indefinitely to keep the occupants safe. Burnham's day job: "I spent the last twelve years of my life building rooms like this specifically to keep out people like us."

He's talking to his partners, Junior (Jared Leto) and Raoul (Dwight Yoakam). Junior brought Burnham and Raoul onto the job, and Burnham hates it that Raoul brought along a gun. Their plan is to get in, find the money, and get out. According to Junior's information, the house is empty. It is not, and soon Meg and Sarah are locked in the safe room, the three men are outside, and it looks like a stalemate except that neither side can afford to concede.

We already know the layout of the house. We got the tour when the real-estate agent showed the women through the rooms, and again in a vertiginous shot that begins in the upstairs bedroom, swoops down two floors, zooms into the keyhole, pulls back, and careens upstairs again. The shot combines physical and virtual camera moves, a reminder that Fincher *(Seven, The Game, Fight Club)* is a visual virtuoso. He's also a master of psychological gamesmanship, and most of the movie will bypass fancy camerawork for classical intercutting between the cats and the mice (who sometimes trade sides of the board).

I have deliberately not described much of the strategy itself. That would be cheating. Once you know what everyone wants and how the safe room works, the plot should be allowed to simply unfold. There is a neat twist in the fund of knowledge about the room; Burnham, who builds them, knows a lot more about how they work, their strengths and limitations, than Meg and Sarah, who start out basically knowing only how to run inside and lock the door.

The role of Meg was originally filled by Nicole Kidman. I learn from *Variety* that she had to drop out after a knee injury and was replaced by Foster. I have no idea if Foster is better or worse than Kidman would have been. I only know she is spellbinding. She has the gutsy, brainy resilience of a stubborn scrapper, and when all other resources fail her she can still think fast—and obliquely, like a chessmaster hiding one line of attack inside another.

The intruders are ill matched, which is the idea. Burnham has the knowledge, Junior has the plan, and Raoul has the gun. Once they are all inside the house and know the plan, therefore, Junior is not entirely necessary, unless the others are positively determined to split the loot three ways. On the other hand, Burnham hates violence, and Raoul is such a wild card he may shoot himself in the foot.

The end game in chess, for the student of the sport, is its most intriguing aspect. The loss of pieces has destroyed the initial symmetry and created a skewed board—unfamiliar terrain in which specialized pieces are required to do jobs for which they were not designed. There is less clutter; strategy must run deeper because there are fewer alternative lines. Sacrifices may be brilliant, or they may be blunders, or only apparent blunders. Every additional move limits the options, and the prospect of defeat, swift and unforeseen, hangs over the board. That is exactly the way *Panic Room* unfolds, right down to the detail that even at the end the same rules apply, and all the choices that were made earlier limit the choices that can be made now. ☞

Paradise Lost 2: Revelations ★ ★ ★
NO MPAA RATING, 2000

A documentary directed by Joe Berlinger and Bruce Sinofsky.

Three second-graders were brutally murdered on May 5, 1993, in West Memphis, Arkansas, and three young men are still in prison for the crimes, convicted in a climate that stereotyped them as members of a satanic cult.

The possibility that they are innocent gnaws at anyone who has seen *Paradise Lost: The Child Murders at Robin Hood Hills.* That 1996 documentary argued they were innocent, and implied that the father of one of the victims might have been involved. He even supplied a knife to the filmmakers that seemed to match the profile of the murder weapon, but DNA tests on bloodstains were botched.

When *Paradise Lost* played on HBO, it inspired a national movement to free the three prisoners—Damien Echols, now twenty-four, under sentence of death, and Jessie Misskelley, twenty-three, and Jason Baldwin, twenty-one, with life sentences. Now comes *Paradise Lost 2: Revelations,* a sequel that involves their appeals, and also features extraordinarily creepy footage of Mark Byers, the father under suspicion, whose wife has died in mysterious circumstances in the meantime.

The new documentary is directed like the first by Joe Berlinger and Bruce Sinofsky. There is unlikely to be anything else on TV more disturbing than this film. Watching it, you feel like an eyewitness to injustice.

Among new evidence introduced on appeal is the finding that human bite marks, found on one of the child's bodies, do not match the bites of the three defendants. The film points out that Mark Byers had his teeth extracted in 1997, four years after the murders, although on camera he places the extraction much earlier, and gives several contradictory reasons for it.

What does this prove? Not much to prosecution forensic experts, who testify the bite marks were caused by a belt.

Byers spends a lot of time on-camera (he accepted a payment for appearing in this film). He is described by Echols as "the fakest creature to ever walk on two legs," and that seems the simple truth: He has an odd way of speaking in rehearsed sound bites, avoiding eye contact while using lurid prose that sounds strikingly insincere. Visiting the murder scene, he stages a mock burial and cremation of the three defendants, saying, "There's your headmarker, you animal," and then pouring on charcoal lighter, chortling, "Now we're gonna have some fun," and lighting his cigar before dropping the match.

Did he do it? We hear a litany of his problems: a brain tumor, manic depression, bad checks, drug abuse, DUIs, hallucinations, blackouts, neighbors who got a restraining order after he spanked their child, and the death of his wife. Byers rants about those who accused him of her death and says she died in her sleep of natural causes. Later, possibly in a Freudian slip, he says, "after my wife was murdered."

The legal establishment in West Memphis seems wedded to their shaky case—dug in too deep to reconsider. Echols's new attorney claims the original defense was underfunded and incompetent, and indeed we find that one attorney was paid only $19 an hour, and the defense was limited to $1,000 for tests and research in a case dripping with forensic evidence.

Questions remain. If the victims were killed in the wooded area where they were found, why was there no blood at the scene? Can a confession by Misskelley be trusted? He has an IQ of 72, was questioned by police for twelve hours without a parent or attorney present, and then was tape-recorded only long enough to recite a statement, which he later retracted.

On June 17, 2000, the appeal was turned down by the same judge who officiated at the original trial. A federal habeus corpus motion is the defendants' last chance.

Near the end of the film, Byers takes a lie detector test and passes. The film notes that at the time he was on five mood-altering medications. The last shots show him singing "Amazing Grace," very badly.

Passion of Mind ★ ★

PG-13, 105 m., 2000

Demi Moore (Marie/Marty), Stellan Skarsgard (William), William Fichtner (Aaron), Sinead Cusack (Jessie), Peter Riegert (Dr. Peters), Joss Ackland (Dr. Langer), Gerry Bamman (Edward Youngerman), Julianne Nicholson (Kim). Directed by Alain Berliner and produced by Carole Scotta, Tom Rosenberg, and Ron Bass. Screenplay by Bass and David Field.

When Marie is asleep in France, Marty is awake in New York. When Marty is asleep in New York, Marie is awake in France. Both women are played by Demi Moore in Alain Berliner's *Passion of Mind,* a film that crosses the supernatural with "an interesting case of multiple personality," as one of her shrinks puts it. She has two shrinks. She needs them. She doesn't know which of her lives is real and which is the dream. Whenever she goes to sleep in one country, she wakes up in the other. Multiple personalities are bad enough, but at least she doesn't have eager kidneys; getting up in the middle of the night to go to the bathroom could lead to whiplash.

The movie uses its supernatural device to show Moore's characters living two contrasting lifestyles. In France, she leads a quiet life as a book reviewer and raises her two daughters. In New York, she's a powerful literary agent who dedicates her life to her career. In France, she meets William (Stellan Skarsgard). In New York, she meets Aaron (William Fichtner). They both love her. Each of her personalities, Marty and Marie, is aware of the other and remembers what happens in the other's life.

Like *Me Myself I,* the recent movie starring Rachel Griffiths, this movie is about a woman's choice between family and career. In the Griffiths film, a busy single writer is magically transported into a marriage with a husband and three kids. If she could have led both lives at once, as Marie/Marty does, I think she would have been okay with that. And as Marty and Marie trudge off to complain to their shrinks, I was wondering why it was so necessary to solve their dilemma. If you can live half of your life quietly in France and the other half in the fast lane of Manhattan, enjoy parenthood and yet escape the kids, and be in love with two great guys without (technically) cheating on either one—what's the problem? When you're not with the one you love, you love the one you're with. If it works, don't fix it.

Of course it doesn't work. If one of the worlds is real and the other is a dream, and if you cannot be in love with two men at once, then what happens if you commit to the dream man and lose the real one? This preys on the mind of Marie/Marty, who also dreads what could happen if the two worlds mix in some way. She won't let one guy spend the night, because "if someone were to be with me and wake me up, something bad might happen."

It is that very problem that the movie never quite solves logically. Forgive me for being literal. The time difference between New York and France is six hours. How does that fit into your sleep schedule? If she is awake until midnight in France, does that mean she's asleep all day in New York, and wakes up at six P.M.? Are there twenty-four hours in a day for both characters?

These questions are cheating. Forgive me for thinking of them. They obviously occurred to the screenwriters, Ron Bass and David Field, who just as obviously decided to ignore them. The movie is not about timetables but life choices, and to a degree it works. We see Marty/Marie pulled between two worlds, in love with her children, attracted to the two guys. The problem is, that's it. We master the situation in the first forty minutes, and then the wheels start spinning. What's needed is a way to take the story through some kind of U-turn.

Why not have the woman accept her situation, work with it, willfully experiment with her two lives, self-consciously engage with it? Don't make her a victim but a psychic explorer. Why, if we are dealing with a woman who is liberated half of the time from each

lifestyle, does the movie fall back on the tired formula that there is something wrong with her, and she must seek psychiatric help to cure it? The joy in *Me Myself I* is that the woman self-reliantly deals with the vast change in her life, instead of diagnosing herself as a case study.

Another difficulty in *Passion of Mind* is with the men. Stellan Skarsgard and William Fichtner bring more to the movie than is needed. These are complex actors with subtly disturbing undertones. They both play nice guys, but we can't quite believe them. We suspect secrets or hidden agendas. They smile, they're warm and pleasant and supportive, and we're wondering, what's their angle? For this particular story, it might have been better to cast actors who were more bland and one-dimensional, so that they could represent only what is needed (two nice guys) rather than veiled complications.

Demi Moore does what she can with a screenplay that doesn't seem confident about what to do with her. She is convincing as either woman, but not as both, if you see what I mean. She makes a wonderful mother in France and a convincing businessman in Manhattan, but when she is either one, we wonder where she puts the other one. The screenplay doesn't help her.

By the end of the film, which is unconvincingly neat, I was distracted by too many questions to care about the answers. The structure had upstaged the content. It wasn't about the heroine; it was about the screenplay. In *Me Myself I*, which has a much simpler premise (the woman goes from one life to another with an unexplained magical zap), there was room for a deeper and more human (and humorous) experience. First the heroine was one, then the other. In *Passion of Mind*, by being both, she is neither. Is her problem a split personality, or psychic jet lag?

The Patriot ★ ★ ★
R, 157 m., 2000

Mel Gibson (Benjamin Martin), Heath Ledger (Gabriel Martin), Joely Richardson (Charlotte Selton), Jason Isaacs (Colonel William Tavington), Chris Cooper (Colonel Harry Burwell), Tcheky Karyo (Jean Villeneuve), Rene Auberjonois (Reverend Oliver), Lisa Brenner (Anne Howard),

Tom Wilkinson (General Cornwallis). Directed
by Roland Emmerich and produced by Mark
Gordon and Gary Levinsohn. Screenplay by
Robert Rodat.

The Patriot is a fable arguing the futility of
pacifism, set against the backdrop of the Revolutionary War. It is rousing and entertaining
and you get your money's worth, but there
isn't an idea in it that will stand up to thoughtful scrutiny. The British are seen as gentlemanly
fops or sadistic monsters, and the Americans
come in two categories: brave or braver. Those
who have a serious interest in the period will
find it a cartoon; those raised on summer action pictures will find it more stimulating than
most.

Mel Gibson stars, in a powerful and effective performance, as a widower named Benjamin Martin with seven children. He saw
enough of battle in the French and Indian War,
and was frightened by what he learned about
himself. He counsels a treaty with King George.
Asked about his principles by an old comrade
in arms (Chris Cooper), he replies, "I'm a parent. I haven't got the luxury of principles." But
he gets some in a hurry after the monstrous
British Colonel Tavington (Jason Isaacs) arrests
Martin's eldest son, Gabriel (Heath Ledger),
and takes him away to be hanged, after first
shooting another of Martin's sons just for the
hell of it, and then burning down his house.

Since Martin had just been treating the
wounded of both sides in his home, this seems
excessive, and in the long run turns out to be
extremely unwise for the British, since Martin
goes on to more or less single-handedly mastermind their defeat. There must have been
many British officers less cruel—but none
would have served the screenplay's purpose,
which is to show Martin driven berserk by
grief, rage, and the need for revenge.

The following sequence is the film's most
disturbing. Martin and his sons hide in the
woods and ambush Tavington and his soldiers; eventually the battle comes down to
hand-to-hand fighting (Martin wielding a
tomahawk). Gabriel is freed, and the younger
adolescent boys get a taste for blood ("I'm
glad I killed them!" one of the tykes cries. "I'm
glad!"). The movie's scenes of carnage have

more impact than the multiple killings in a
film like *Shaft*, because they are personal, not
technical; individual soldiers, frightened and
ill-prepared, are fighting for their lives, while
in the modern action pictures most of the victims are pop-up arcade targets.

The big players in the war (George Washington, King George) are far offscreen, although
we do meet General Cornwallis (Tom Wilkinson), a British leader who counsels a "gentlemanly" conduct of the war and rebukes
Tavington for his brutality. Still, when the
Americans refuse to "fight fair" and adopt hit-
and-run guerrilla tactics against the British
(who march in orderly ranks into gunfire), he
bends enough to authorize the evil colonel to
take what steps are necessary to bring down
Martin (by now legendary as "the Ghost").

The movie's battle scenes come in two
flavors—harrowing and unlikely. Two battles
near the beginning of the film are conveniently
fought in open fields overlooked by the upper
windows of houses, so onlookers have excellent seats for the show and can supply a running narration. No doubt revolutionary battles
were fought right there in the pasture, but
would Benjamin Martin allow his kids to stand
in the windows, or tell them to hide in the
barn?

The "real" battles are grueling tests of men
and horses, as soldiers march into withering
fire and the survivors draw their swords or fix
their bayonets for blood-soaked combat in
close quarters. These battles seem anarchic
and pitiless, and respect the movie convention
that bitter rivals will sooner or later find themselves face-to-face. The scenes are well staged
by the director, Roland Emmerich, working
from a screenplay by Robert Rodat, the same
man who wrote *Saving Private Ryan*, with its
equally appalling battle scenes.

Hollywood movies are at pains these days to
provide a role for a heroic African-American
or two. A role for a black sailor was found in
the segregated U.S. Navy submarine corps in
U-571 (he was a mess orderly). Now we have a
black slave who fights beside white men (even
those who hate him) because General Washington has decreed freedom for all slaves who
fight for a year. Good enough, but why not go
all the way and give this character dialogue

and a real role to play, instead of demeaningly using him only to count down the months and days until his freedom? When the former slave finally gets two whole sentences in a row, at the end, he quotes Martin's son: "Gabriel said if we won the war, we could build a whole new world. We could get started right here with your home." Uh-huh. Why not get started with your own home?

The movie has light comic relief to ease the tension (Martin's handmade chairs keep collapsing beneath him), and a love story (Gabriel loves Anne, a plucky colonial girl who catches his eye with a patriotic speech). Anne's father is a deaf man who misunderstands things. When Gabriel asks permission to write Anne, the old man at first takes offense. Then he says, "Oh . . . *write* her! Of course you may." What did he think Gabriel had asked? Meanwhile, there's even female company for hard-bitten Benjamin Martin, who asks the sister of his dead wife, "May I sit here?" Her answer got laughs in the screening I attended: "It's a free country—or at least, it will be."

These passages and others (including The Dead Man Who Is Not Really Dead) have been trucked directly into *The Patriot* from the warehouse of timeless clichés. They betray the movie's lack of serious intentions. It basically wants to be a summer action movie with a historical gloss. At that, it succeeds. I enjoyed the strength and conviction of Gibson's performance, the sweep of the battle scenes, and the absurdity of the British caricatures. None of it has much to do with the historical reality of the Revolutionary War, but with such an enormous budget at risk, how could it?

Pay It Forward ★ ★ ½
PG-13, 122 m., 2000

Kevin Spacey (Eugene Simonet), Helen Hunt (Arlene McKinney), Haley Joel Osment (Trevor McKinney), Jay Mohr (Chris Chandler), James Caviezel (Jerry), Jon Bon Jovi (Ricki), Angie Dickinson (Grace). Directed by Mimi Leder and produced by Peter Abrams, Robert Levy, and Steven Reuther. Screenplay by Leslie Dixon.

Someone does you a good turn. You pass it on to three other people. They pass it on. And what a wonderful world this will be. That's the theory behind *Pay It Forward,* a movie that might have been more entertaining if it didn't believe it. It's a seductive theory, but in the real world altruism is less powerful than selfishness, greed, nepotism, xenophobia, tribalism, and paranoia. If you doubt me, take another look at the front pages.

Consider Las Vegas, the setting of the movie. If every person in trouble there paid it forward to three more people, there would be more Gamblers Anonymous members than gamblers. An intriguing premise, but not one that occurs to this movie—although Alcoholics Anonymous plays a supporting role, and paying it forward is, of course, the twelfth step.

The movie has its heart in the right place, but not its screenplay. It tells a story that audience members will *want* to like, but it doesn't tell it strongly and cleanly enough, it puts too many loops into the plot, and its ending is shamelessly soapy for the material. Two or three times during the film I was close to caving in and going with the flow, but the story lost the way and I was brought back up to the surface again.

Haley Joel Osment, the gifted young actor from *The Sixth Sense,* stars as Trevor, a resourceful latchkey kid whose father has disappeared and whose mother, Arlene (Helen Hunt), works two jobs as a Vegas cocktail waitress. She's a recovering alcoholic with a few relapses still to go. At school, Trevor is impressed by the grave, distant presence of his new teacher, Mr. Simonet (Kevin Spacey), whose face is scarred by burns.

Mr. Simonet doesn't want to win any popularity contests. "Do I strike you as someone falsely nice?" he asks Trevor. "No," the boy replies thoughtfully, "you're not even *really* all that nice." But Trevor responds to the lack of condescension in the teacher's manner: Mr. Simonet has standards, and applies them in the classroom. On the first day of school, he writes the year's assignment on the blackboard: "Think of an idea that could change the world."

Trevor thinks. Things happen in his life to help him think and guide his thinking, and before long his mother discovers that a homeless man (James Caviezel) is living in their garage. It was Trevor's idea to invite him in. Then he can pay it forward.

There are complications. One of Trevor's theories is that his mom and Mr. Simonet would both be a lot happier if they were dating each other. Mr. Simonet does not agree. Spacey does a wonderful job of suggesting the pain just beneath the surface of the character; the teacher's life is manageable only because he sticks to his routine. But Trevor plugs away, all but shoving the two adults toward each other. This is, unfortunately, the kind of self-propelling plot device that, once allowed into a movie, takes it over and dictates an obligatory series of events. Since it is self-evident that Trevor is right, we know with a sinking feeling that the screenplay must detour into tentative acceptance, hurt rejection, silly misunderstandings, angry retreats, confessions, tearful reconciliations, and resolutions, all in the usual order.

The movie intercuts between the predictable progress of the romance and the uncertain progress of Trevor's pay-it-forward scheme. We meet various supporting characters who get involved in paying it forward, and the time line is not always clear. The movie opens with one of those off-the-shelf hostage crisis scenes that ends with a criminal crashing into a reporter's car, and a stranger giving the reporter a new Jaguar. He's paying it forward. Then we flash back to "four months earlier" and Trevor's first day of school, but soon we're back to the present again, as the reporter tries to track down the pay-it-forward stories, and the lawyer who gave away the Jaguar tells why.

This leads to another flashback: When the lawyer's daughter had an asthma attack and was ignored in an emergency room, he explains, a gun-waving African-American stabbing victim forced a nurse to give the kid oxygen, and told him to pay it forward. It's an effective cameo, but it's awkward the way the movie cuts between scenes like that, Trevor's own setbacks, and the tentative romance.

With a cleaner story line, the basic idea could have been free to deliver. As it is, we get a better movie than we might have, because the performances are so good: Spacey as a vulnerable and wounded man; Hunt as a woman no less wounded in her own way; and Osment,

once again proving himself the equal of adult actors in the complexity and depth of his performance. I believed in them and cared for them. I wish the movie could have gotten out of their way.

Pearl Harbor ★ ½
PG-13, 183 m., 2001

Ben Affleck (Rafe McCawley), Josh Hartnett (Danny Walker), Kate Beckinsale (Evelyn Johnson), Cuba Gooding Jr. (Dorie Miller), William Lee Scott (Billy), Greg Zola (Anthony), Ewen Bremner (Red), Alec Baldwin (Doolittle), James King (Betty), Mako (Admiral Yamamoto). Directed by Michael Bay and produced by Bay and Jerry Bruckheimer. Screenplay by Randall Wallace.

Pearl Harbor is a two-hour movie squeezed into three hours, about how on December 7, 1941, the Japanese staged a surprise attack on an American love triangle. Its centerpiece is forty minutes of redundant special effects, surrounded by a love story of stunning banality. The film has been directed without grace, vision, or originality, and although you may walk out quoting lines of dialogue, it will not be because you admire them.

The filmmakers seem to have aimed the film at an audience that may not have heard of Pearl Harbor, or perhaps even of World War II. This is the *Our Weekly Reader* version. If you have the slightest knowledge of the events in the film, you will know more than it can tell you. There is no sense of history, strategy, or context; according to this movie, Japan attacked Pearl Harbor because America cut off its oil supply and they were down to an eighteen-month reserve. Would going to war restore the fuel sources? Did they perhaps also have imperialist designs? Movie doesn't say.

So shaky is the film's history that at the end, when Jimmy Doolittle's Tokyo raiders crash-land in China, they're shot at by Japanese patrols with only a murky throwaway explanation about the Sino-Japanese war already under way. I predict some viewers will leave the theater sincerely confused about why there were Japanese in China.

As for the movie's portrait of the Japanese

themselves, it is so oblique that Japanese audiences will find little to complain about apart from the fact that they play such a small role in their own raid. There are several scenes where the Japanese high command debates military tactics, but all of their dialogue is strictly expository; they state facts but do not emerge with personalities or passions. Only Admiral Yamamoto (Mako) is seen as an individual, and his dialogue seems to have been singled out with the hindsight of history. Congratulated on a brilliant raid, he demurs, "A brilliant man would find a way not to fight a war." And later, "I fear all we have done is to awaken a sleeping giant."

Do you imagine at any point the Japanese high command engaged in the 1941 Japanese equivalent of exchanging high-fives and shouting "Yes!" while pumping their fists in the air? Not in this movie, where the Japanese seem to have been melancholy even at the time about the regrettable need to play such a negative role in such a positive Hollywood film.

The American side of the story centers on two childhood friends from Tennessee with the standard-issue screenplay names Rafe McCawley (Ben Affleck) and Danny Walker (Josh Hartnett). They enter the Army Air Corps and both fall in love with the same nurse, Evelyn Johnson (Kate Beckinsale)—first Rafe falls for her, and then, after he is reported dead, Danny. Their first date is subtitled "Three Months Later" and ends with Danny, having apparently read the subtitle, telling Evelyn, "Don't let it be three months before I see you again, OK?" That gets almost as big a laugh as her line to Rafe, "I'm gonna give Danny my whole heart, but I don't think I'll ever look at another sunset without thinking of you."

That kind of bad laugh would have been sidestepped in a more literate screenplay, but our hopes are not high after an early newsreel report that the Germans are bombing "downtown London"—a difficult target, since although there is such a place as "central London," at no time in 2,000 years has London ever had anything described by anybody as a "downtown."

There is not a shred of conviction or chemistry in the love triangle, which results after Rafe returns alive to Hawaii shortly before the raid on Pearl Harbor and is angry at Evelyn for falling in love with Danny, inspiring her timeless line, "I didn't even know until the day you turned up alive—and then all this happened."

Evelyn is a hero in the aftermath of the raid, performing triage by using her lipstick to separate the wounded who should be treated from those left to die. In a pointless stylistic choice, director Michael Bay and cinematographer John Schwartzman shoot some of the hospital scenes in soft focus, some in sharp focus, some blurred. Why? I understand it's to obscure details deemed too gory for the PG-13 rating. (Why should the carnage at Pearl Harbor be toned down to PG-13 in the first place?) In the newsreel sequences, the movies fades in and out of black-and-white with almost amusing haste, while the newsreel announcer sounds not like a period voice but like a Top-40 DJ in an echo chamber.

The most involving material in the film comes at the end, when Jimmy Doolittle (Alec Baldwin) leads his famous raid on Tokyo, flying army bombers off the decks of navy carriers and hoping to crash-land in China. He and his men were heroes, and their story would make a good movie (and indeed has: *Thirty Seconds Over Tokyo*). Another hero in the movie is the African-American cook Dorie Miller (Cuba Gooding Jr.), who because of his race was not allowed to touch a gun in the racist prewar navy, but opens fire during the raid, shoots down two planes, and saves the life of his captain. Nice to see an African-American in the movie, but the almost total absence of Asians in 1941 Hawaii is inexplicable.

As for the raid itself, a little goes a long way. What is the point, really, of more than half an hour of planes bombing ships, of explosions and fireballs, of roars on the sound track and bodies flying through the air and people running away from fighters that are strafing them? How can it be entertaining or moving when it's simply about the most appalling slaughter? Why do the filmmakers think we want to see this, unrelieved by intelligence, viewpoint, or insight? It was a terrible, terrible day. Three thousand died in all. This is not a movie about them. It is an unremarkable action movie; Pearl Harbor supplies the subject, but not the inspiration.

The Perfect Storm ★ ★ ★ ½
PG-13, 129 m., 2000

George Clooney (Captain Billy Tyne), Mark Wahlberg (Bobby Shatford), Mary Elizabeth Mastrantonio (Linda Greenlaw), John C. Reilly (Murph), William Fichtner (Sully), Karen Allen (Melissa Brown), Allen Payne (Alfred Pierre), Diane Lane (Christina Cotter), John Hawkes (Bugsy), Cherry Jones (Edie Bailey). Directed by Wolfgang Petersen and produced by Paula Weinstein, Petersen, and Gail Katz. Screenplay by Bill Wittliff, based on the book by Sebastian Junger.

The Perfect Storm is a well-crafted example of the film of pure sensation. It is about ships tossed by a violent storm. The film doesn't have complex and involving characters, but they are not needed. It doesn't tell a sophisticated story, and doesn't need to; the main events are known to most of the audience before the movie begins. All depends on the storm. I do not mind admitting I was enthralled.

The movie, based on the best-seller by Sebastian Junger, is mostly about a fishing ship named the *Andrea Gail*, out of Gloucester, Massachusetts, which had the misfortune in 1991 of running into "the middle of the monster" when three great storm systems collided in the Atlantic. We learn about the economic pressures of the swordfishing industry, we meet the crew members and their women, we learn a little of their stories, and then the film is about the ship, the storm, and the people waiting in port for news. A parallel story, about a luxury sailboat in distress, cranks up the suspense even further.

The crew members of the *Andrea Gail* are a job lot of basic movie types. We count Captain Billy Tyne (George Clooney), whose pride has been stung because his catch has fallen behind this season. His crew includes Bobby Shatford (Mark Wahlberg), who is in love with divorced mom Diane Lane; Murph (John C. Reilly), whose seafaring life has led to a friendly but sad separation from his wife and son; Bugsy (John Hawkes), the sort of character who gets overlooked in crowds; Alfred Pierre (Allen Payne), a Jamaican who has ventured into northern waters for the paycheck; and a last-

minute addition, Sully (William Fichtner). He and Murph don't like each other. Why not? Jealousy over Murph's wife, the movie says. To provide the plot with some onboard conflict, is my guess.

These characters are not developed in the way that similar seafarers might be developed in a novel by Joseph Conrad or Herman Melville. We learn only their external signs and characteristics; we don't know or much care what makes them tick. That's not a fatal flaw to the film because *The Perfect Storm* is not about the people, but about the storm. When Conrad writes *Lord Jim* or Melville writes *Moby-Dick*, the stories are about the way men's characters interact with the sea and with their shipmates. They are novels about people.

If *The Perfect Storm* had taken that approach, there would be fewer characters and a lot more dialogue; it might be a better film and would certainly be a different one. Its director, Wolfgang Petersen, also made *Das Boot*, the submarine drama, that does develop the deeper human complexities of its characters—but that took so long that the original 210-minute cut was trimmed back to 145 more action-packed minutes for the first U.S. release. At 129 minutes, *The Perfect Storm* delivers the goods but little human insight.

The film's best scenes are more or less without dialogue, except for desperately shouted words. They are about men trapped in a maelstrom of overpowering forces. They respond heroically, because they must, but they are not heroes; their motivation is need. They have had a bad season, have made one risky last trip, have ventured beyond the familiar Grand Banks fishing grounds to the problematical Flemish Cap. Quentin, the salty old dog who sits at the bar and provides color commentary, gives us the background: "I was last there in '62. Lots of fish. Lots of weather."

They have good luck: a catch of 60,000 pounds of swordfish. Then bad luck: The ice machine breaks down. The catch will spoil unless they get it quickly back to port. There are reports of a gathering storm. Billy lists their choices: "Either we hang out here, or say the hell with it and drive right through." The crew votes to plow right through the storm and collect those paychecks. Of course, they don't understand how big the storm really is, and when another fishing boat skipper (Mary Elizabeth Mastrantonio) tries to tell them, their antenna has blown overboard.

The scenes at sea are intercut with scenes in the bar where most of the Gloucester fishing industry seems to drink; it is conveniently located right at the end of the dock (and Diane Lane conveniently lives right upstairs). This is about right; I do not doubt that the owners, retired sailors, wives, girlfriends, and drinking buddies all stand watch in a saloon during a storm, ordering rounds and eyeing the Weather Channel.

Even before the storm, there are terrific set pieces, as when Murph is yanked overboard by a fishing line, and two men dive in to save him (Sully, his enemy, is the first in the water). But the heart of the film is in the ordeal of two ships caught in the tempest. As the men of the *Andrea Gail* battle wearily against their fate, the skipper attempts to cut loose an anchor. He clings to a swaying beam while holding an acetylene torch; the wonder is that he doesn't burn a hole in himself in the attempt.

Even more exciting is the parallel plot involving a Coast Guard rescue of the sailboat. A passenger (Cherry Jones) pleads with its owner to seek safer waters, but he is a pigheaded millionaire yachtsman with no respect for nature ("This is *my* boat!"). A helicopter rescue is attempted, shown in amazing action footage, and then the tension escalates as the chopper tries to go on to the *Andrea Gail*, a midair refueling is attempted, and eventually men are risking their lives in what seems like a doomed struggle (at one point, a Guardsman who is safe goes back into the sea after a crew mate).

We know intellectually that we're viewing special effects. Tanks and wind machines are involved, and computer graphics and models. This is not important. The impetus of the story drives us forward, and by the end of the film I was wrung out. It's possible to criticize the sketchy characters, but pointless. The movie is about the appalling experience of fighting for your life in a small boat in a big storm. If that is what you want to see, you will see it done here about as well as it can be done.

The Piano Teacher ★ ★ ★ ½
NO MPAA RATING, 130 m., 2002

Isabelle Huppert (Erika Kohut), Benoit Magimel (Walter Klemmer), Annie Girardot (The Mother), Susanne Lothar (Mrs. Schober), Udo Samel (Dr. Blonskij), Anna Sigalevitch (Anna Schober), Cornelia Kondgen (Mme. Blonskij), Thomas Weinhappel (Baritone). Directed by Michael Haneke and produced by Viet Heiduschka. Screenplay by Haneke, based on the novel by Elfriede Jelinek.

There is a self-assurance in Isabelle Huppert that defies all explanation. I interviewed her in 1977, asking her how she got her start in the movies. She knocked on the door of a Paris studio, she said, and announced, "I am here." Was she kidding? I peered at her. I thought not.

In Michael Haneke's *The Piano Teacher*, which won three awards at Cannes 2001 (best actress, actor, and film), she plays a bold woman with a secret wound. She is Erika Kohut, fortyish, a respected instructor at a conservatory of music in Vienna. Demanding, severe, distant, unsmiling, she leads a secret life of self-mutilation. That she sleeps in the same bed with her domineering mother is no doubt a clue—but to what?

Erika is fascinated with the sexual weaknesses and tastes of men. There is a scene where she visits a porn shop in Vienna, creating an uncomfortable tension by her very presence. The male clients are presumably there to indulge their fantasies about women, but faced with a real one, they look away, disturbed or ashamed. If she were obviously a prostitute they could handle that, but she's apparently there to indulge her own tastes, and that takes all the fun out of it, for them. She returns their furtive glances with a shriveling gaze.

She has a handsome young student named Walter (Benoit Magimel). She notices him in a particular way. They have a clash of wills. He makes it clear he is interested in her. Not long after, in one of the school's rest rooms, they have a sexual encounter—all the more electrifying because while she shocks him with her brazen behavior, she refuses to actually have sex with him. She wants the upper hand.

What games does she want to play? A detailed and subtle plan of revenge against her mother is involved, and Walter, who is not really into sadomasochism, allows himself to be enlisted out of curiosity, or perhaps because he hopes she will yield to him at the end of the scenario. Does it work out that way? Some audience members will dislike the ending, but with a film like this any conventional ending would be a cop-out.

Most sexual relationships in the movies have a limited number of possible outcomes, but this one is a mystery. Another mystery is, what's wrong with Erika? She is not simply an adventuress, a sexual experimenter, a risk taker. Some buried pathology is at work. Walter's idle thoughts about an experienced older woman have turned into nightmares about experiences he doesn't even want to know about.

Huppert often plays repressed, closed-off, sexually alert women. At forty-seven, she looks curiously as she did at twenty-two; she is thin, with fine, freckled skin that does not seem to weather, and seems destined to be one of those women who was never really young and then never really ages. Many of her roles involve women it is not safe to scorn. Magimel won his best actor award for standing up to her force. He doesn't play the standard movie character we'd expect in this role (the immature twenty-something boy who flowers under the tutelage of an older woman). Instead, he's a capable, confident young man who thinks he has met hidden wildness and then finds it is madness.

The movie seems even more highly charged because it is wrapped in an elegant package. These are smart people. They talk about music as if they understand it, they duel with their minds as well as their bodies, and Haneke photographs them in two kinds of spaces: Sometimes they're in elegant, formal conservatory settings, and at other times in frankly vulgar places where quick release can be snatched from strangers. There is an old saying: Be careful what you ask for, because you might get it. *The Piano Teacher* has a more ominous lesson: Be especially careful with someone who has asked for you.

A Piece of Eden ★ ½
NO MPAA RATING, 112 m., 2000

Marc Grapey (Bob Tredici), Rebecca Harrell (Happy), Robert Breuler (Franco Tredici), Tyne Daly (Aunt Aurelia), Marshall Efron (Andres), Frederic Forrest (Paulo Tredici), Andreas Katsulas (Giuseppe Tredici), Jeff Puckett (Greg Tredici), Tristan Rogers (Victor Hardwick). Directed by John Hancock and produced by Hancock and Ken Kitsch. Screenplay by Dorothy Tristan.

A Piece of Eden is a good-hearted film with many virtues, although riveting entertainment value is not one of them. It's a family comedy that ambles down well-trodden paths toward a foregone conclusion, neither disturbing nor challenging the audience. It was filmed in and around LaPorte, Indiana; the only review I have seen so far comes from a Utah critic, Fawna Jones, who finds it predictable, and describes it quite accurately: "This a movie for those who generally stay away from the theater for fear of being offended and who like their movies to have happy endings."

Going to a movie so you won't be offended is like eating potato chips made with Olestra; you avoid the dangers of the real thing, but your insides fill up with synthetic runny stuff. Watching *A Piece of Eden*, I found myself wanting to be shocked, amazed, or even surprised. The most unexpected thing in the movie is a machine that shakes apple trees to make the apples fall off. That could have prevented a lot of heartbreak in *The Cider House Rules*.

The film opens in New York, where Bob Tredici (Marc Grapey) runs the struggling Television Publicity Bureau with his secretary, Happy (Rebecca Harrell). She's been late four out of the last five days, and even more ominously, has a psychological block that prevents her from pronouncing the word "publicity" correctly when she answers the phone. (She comes from a family of high-powered analysts, and thinks her block may be approach avoidance.)

Bob gets a call from northeast Indiana, where his family has run a fruit farm since time immemorial. His father, Franco (Robert Breuler), is dying. Bob has an unhappy relationship with the old man but returns home anyway, to learn that the patriarch has rallied enough to spend endless hours in a hospital bed in the living room, making life miserable for everyone with his salt-of-the-earth routine. Franco plans to leave the farm not to Bob but to a relative who has stayed behind in Indiana.

Bob has bright ideas for the farm, including using computers for cost control and starting a petting zoo. But he needs to appear more stable, less like a decadent Manhattanite, and so in desperation he imports Happy to pose as his wife. This leads to scenes that could exist only in a movie, as when they are assigned to bunk down in the barn, and he gets a glimpse of her silhouette through the sheet that hangs from the ceiling just as it did in *It Happened One Night* (1934).

The choices available to the story are limited and obvious. Either Bob will get the farm, or another happy solution will be found, since Fawna Jones is quite correct that this is not a film destined for an unhappy ending. There must also be a near disaster, and there is, when Bob holds an open house for the petting zoo concept and imports a friendly soap opera star (Tristan Rogers) as his celebrity guest. First no members of the public show up. Then they're swamped.

It must be said that the character of the father is a major pain in the netherlands. He is one of those blowhard bearded patriarchs so full of himself and so colorful in unconvincing ways that to have such a person as a parent would be enough to—well, inspire you to flee to New York and open a Television Publicity Bureau. His personality is so insufferable that when he has a change of heart, you don't believe it—you just figure, there goes Dad again, faking it for the evening news.

John Hancock, whose credits include the powerful *Bang the Drum Slowly* and the sweet *Prancer* (a much better family film also set in the same area), does indeed own a fruit farm near LaPorte, and no doubt *A Piece of Eden* flows from his experiences and memories, and those of his wife, the actress Dorothy Tristan, who wrote the screenplay. But the story line runs out of steam about four-fifths of the way through, and the closing scenes lack dramatic interest, dissolving in a haze of landscapes and blue skies and happily-ever-after music.

Pitch Black ★ ★
R, 107 m., 2000

Vin Diesel (Riddick), Radha Mitchell (Fry), Cole Hauser (Johns), Keith David (Imam), Lewis Fitz-Gerald (Paris), Claudia Black (Shazza), Rhiana Griffith (Jack). Directed by David Twohy and produced by Tom Engelman. Screenplay by Twohy and Jim and Ken Wheat.

No other movie opening thrills me more than a vast ship in interstellar space. The modern visual rules for these shots were set by Stanley Kubrick's *2001*, which used a detailed model moving slowly instead of a cheesy model moving fast. Kubrick had the good sense to know that sound does not travel in space, but *Star Wars*, with its deep bass rumbles, demonstrated that it certainly should. And then in the *Alien* and *Star Trek* pictures and in countless others, gigantic space cruisers aimed majestically at the stars, and I felt an inner delight that has its origins in those long-ago days when I devoured pulp space opera by Robert Heinlein and such forgotten masters as Murray Leinster and Eric Frank Russell.

My state of mind is best captured by a pulp mag that was defunct even before I started reading science fiction: *Thrilling Wonder Stories*, without doubt the best title in the history of magazines. I hope for strange and amazing adventures. Sometimes I am gratified. More often I am disappointed. *Pitch Black*, which begins in deep space and ends with a manhunt on a desert planet, falls somewhere in between: clever, done with skill, yet lacking in the cerebral imagination of the best science fiction. How sad it is that humans travel countless light years away from Earth, only to find themselves inhabiting the same tired generic conventions.

The movie begins during an interstellar mission, with the crew and a dangerous prisoner all in cryo-sleep. The ship collides with a cluster of tiny rock fragments, which penetrate the hull like BBs through cellophane. The captain and several other sleepers are terminally perforated, and Fry (Radha Mitchell) assumes command. The ship crash-lands on a planet that circles somehow within a three-star system, where at least one sun never seems to set, and the surviving crew members have to fight it out with the vicious and cunning prisoner, Riddick (Vin Diesel).

You may remember Diesel from *Saving Private Ryan,* where he was the hard-bitten Private Caparzo. He looks like a mean customer, and he is; he shares no fellow feeling with the other survivors, expresses no responsibility to them, does not consider himself in the same boat, and thinks only of escaping. Oh, and his eyes have a remarkable quality: He can see in the dark. Not a very useful ability on a planet with three suns and no night, right? (Hollow laugh.)

What disappointed me about *Pitch Black,* directed by David Twohy, is that it didn't do more with its alien world and less with its recycled human conflicts. I feel underwhelmed when humans land on another world and are so quickly reduced to jumping out from behind rocks at one another and playing hostage games. *Pitch Black* does have a nice look, all bleached blues and desert sands. And there are some promising story elements, one of which I am about to discuss, so you might want to set this review aside if you plan to see the movie.

The spoiler commences: Yes, night does fall on the planet, every once in a long while when all three suns are in eclipse. I am not sure what complex geometries of space and trajectory are necessary for a planet to exist in a three-star system and somehow manage to maintain any continuity of climate and temperature, but never mind: What is maybe more difficult to accept is that it would develop a life form that appears only in the dark. Since sunlight is the source of heat and energy, Darwinian principles would seem severely challenged by the task of evolving living things that hibernate for twenty-two years between eclipses. How does a thing that lives in the dark evolve in a planet where it is almost always daytime? This is not the kind of question you're supposed to ask about *Pitch Black,* but I'd rather have the answer than any forty-five minutes of this movie.

The story also poses the problem (less challenging from a Darwinian view, to be sure) of whether the Diesel character will cooperate with his species-mates or behave entirely like a selfish gene. Whether this happens or not I leave it to you to discover. By the end of the movie, however, I was wondering if the trip had been necessary; most of this movie's plot could be ported into a Western or a swashbuckler with little alteration. For Twohy, it's a step backward from *The Arrival* (1996), one of the smartest recent science-fiction films—one that really does develop suspense out of challenging ideas of alien conduct (space visitors are secretly warming the Earth to their comfort zone).

My suggestion for his next film: an expedition to the seas beneath the ice of Europe, where volcanic warmth may have allowed life to occur. Consider the physical properties of a life form that evolves under the tiny gravity of such a moon. It could be amorphous, tenuous, and enormous. In sailing a stellar sub through the seas of Io, you might be navigating not toward life, but . . . through it. What would a human crew do in such a situation? Not get into fights and start chasing each other through the sub, I hope.

Place Vendôme ★ ★ ★ ½
NO MPAA RATING, 105 m., 2000

Catherine Deneuve (Marianne), Jean-Pierre Bacri (Jean-Pierre), Emmanuelle Seigner (Nathalie), Jacques Dutronc (Battistelli), Bernard Fresson (Vincent Malivert), Francois Berleand (Eric Malivert), Laszlo Szabo (Charlie Rosen), Michael Culkin (De Beers Man). Directed by Nicole Garcia and produced by Christine Gozlan and Alain Sarde. Screenplay by Jacques Fieschi and Garcia.

She is an elegant beauty and a drunk. "The clinic is her second home," they whisper. "She's brought out for special occasions." Her husband owns one of the most famous jewelry shops in the world, on Place Vendôme in Paris, across from the Ritz. His secret is that the business is bankrupt. On one of the rare nights when she's at home instead of in rehab, he shows her where he has hidden five superb diamonds. Then he drives his car into the side of a lumber truck and kills himself.

Marianne Malivert, played by Catherine Deneuve, once knew something about the diamond trade herself. She met her husband while making a deal. But "I've forgotten all that," she says. At a business dinner with her husband before his death, she doesn't drink, but eventually she gets up, glides around the table, places a hand on his shoulder, and goes into another room—where he finds her draining leftover wine. "At least start with a new bottle," he says, handing her one. He accepts her alcoholism as a fact of life.

Place Vendôme begins as the portrait of a woman who has lost all interest and hope; when she sees her hungover face in a mirror, she recoils in disgust. After her husband's death, a curious thing happens. The name and reputation of the firm is worth something, even if its shelves are bare, and her brother-in-law wants to sell. But she thinks of those five diamonds, stops drinking, and begins to remember her old skills as a jeweler.

That's when the movie edges toward becoming a thriller. Not the kind of thriller with car chases, but a *film noir*, in which shady people appear from out of the past, and Marianne finds herself caught in a net of danger.

One of the pleasures of the movie is how it only gradually reveals the details of relationships. There is a bald man named Jean-Pierre (Jean-Pierre Bacri), for example, who is obsessed with Nathalie (Emmanuelle Seigner), a young woman who works in the store. Marianne knows Nathalie was her husband's mistress. Jean-Pierre is not a bad sort; he wants to help, and soon he is helping Marianne. He has information about Nathalie's associates, especially the handsome, aging, limping Battistelli (Jacques Dutronc), a veteran con man and jewel thief. How strange that Nathalie left Jean-Pierre for Battistelli. How even stranger that Marianne herself was once Battistelli's lover, years ago.

The movie, directed by the French actress Nicole Garcia, knows a lot about diamonds. Anyone who has purchased a wedding ring might be fascinated by the backstage details of the trade. The story takes Marianne's husband to London, for a confrontation with the De Beers cartel, and after his death it takes Marianne to the diamond bourse in Antwerp, which with its long wooden tables looks like a school cafeteria. She unwraps her little paper parcel on one of the tables and diamond buyers cluster around.

Of course the diamonds may be stolen. If they are, their owners will want them back. For that matter, the authorities may be more interested in Battistelli than the diamonds. Marianne is caught in the middle, all the time just one drink away from disaster.

Catherine Deneuve has been a movie star for a long time. She was twenty-one when she starred in *The Umbrellas of Cherbourg* (1964). In 1967, she made the great *Belle de Jour* with Bernard Fresson, who plays her husband in *Place Vendôme*. She is one of the world's great beauties, but has usually used her beauty for particular purposes in her roles, instead of simply trading on it. She is not just the blonde, and never the dumb one. Here, at fifty-six, she makes her Marianne look wonderful when she pulls herself together for the business meeting with her husband, and vague and shabby when she drinks. What is best is when she stops drinking and begins to think as a diamond merchant once again; we see not only craft in Marianne's eyes, but cautious joy—she is happy to be competent, to know what she's doing.

This human level is always there beneath the thriller elements. The screenplay takes care to bring the crime story and the personal histories together, so that even the crossed lines of romance work as plot points, not just sentiment. Watching the movie, we see it is not about diamonds, sex, or beauty, but about what a pleasure it is to get up in the morning and know you can do what needs to be done.

Planet of the Apes ★ ★ ½
PG-13, 110 m., 2001

Mark Wahlberg (Leo), Tim Roth (General Thade), Helena Bonham Carter (Ari), Kris Kristofferson (Karubi), Estella Warren (Daena), Paul Giamatti (Limbo), Michael Clarke Duncan (Attar), David Warner (Senator Sandar), Charlton Heston (Thade's Father). Directed by Tim Burton and produced by Richard D. Zanuck. Screenplay by William Broyles Jr., Lawrence Konner, and Mark D. Rosenthal, based on the novel by Pierre Boulle.

Tim Burton's *Planet of the Apes* wants to be all things to all men, and all apes. It's an action picture and a satire of an action picture. It's a comedy and then it gets serious. It's a social satire and then backs away from pushing that angle too far. It even has a weird interspecies romantic triangle in it. And it has a surprise ending that I loved.

The movie could have been more. It could have been a parable of men and animals, as daring as *Animal Farm*. It could have dealt in social commentary with a sting, and satire that hurt. It could have supported, or attacked, the animal rights movement. It could have dealt with the intriguing question of whether a man and a gorilla having sex is open-mindedness or bestiality (and, if bestiality, in both directions?). It could have, but it doesn't. It's a cautious movie, earning every letter and numeral of its PG-13 rating. Intellectually, it's science fiction for junior high school boys.

I expected more. I thought Burton would swing for the fence. He plays it too safe, defusing his momentum with little nudges to tell you he knows it's only a movie. The 1968 *Planet of the Apes* was made before irony became an insurance policy. It made jokes, but it took itself seriously. Burton's *Planet* has scenes that defy us to believe them (his hero survives two bumpy crash landings that look about as realistic as the effects in his *Mars Attacks!*). And it backs away from any kind of risky complexity in its relationships.

The key couple consists of Leo (Mark Wahlberg), who is the human hero, and Ari (Helena Bonham Carter), who is the Eleanor Roosevelt of the apes. They're attracted to each other but don't know what to do about it, and the screenplay gives them little help. Leo is also supposed to be linked romantically, I guess, with a curvy blond human named Daena (Estella Warren), but her role has been so abbreviated that basically all she does is follow along looking at Leo either significantly or winsomely, as circumstances warrant. At the end, he doesn't even bid her a proper farewell.

Leo, to be sure, is not one for effusive emotional outbursts. He's played by Wahlberg as a limited and narrow person with little imagination, who never seems very surprised by anything that happens to him—like, oh, to take a random example, crash-landing on a planet where the apes rule the humans. He's a space jockey type, trained in macho self-abnegation, who is great in a crisis but doesn't offer much in the way of conversation. His basic motivation seems to be to get himself off the planet,

and to hell with the friends he leaves behind; he's almost surly sometimes as he leads his little band through the wilderness.

The most "human" character in the movie is, in fact, the chimpanzee Ari, who believes all species were created equal, casts her lot with the outcast humans, and tells Leo, "You're sensitive—a welcome quality in a man." Helena Bonham Carter invests this character with warmth, personality, and distinctive body language; she has a way of moving that kids itself. There's also juice in a character named Limbo (Paul Giamatti), a scam artist who has a deal for everyone, and a lot of funny one-liners. That he sounds like a carnival pitchman should not be held against him.

The major ape characters include the fearsome General Thade (Tim Roth), his strong but occasionally thoughtful gorilla lieutenant Attar (Michael Clarke Duncan), and Senator Sandar (David Warner), who is a parliamentary leader and Ari's father. There's also a cameo for Charlton Heston, as a wise old ape who inevitably introduces a gun into the plot, and has a curmudgeonly exit line. Watching the apes is fun all during the movie, while watching the humans usually isn't; the movie works hard to bring the apes to life, but unwisely thinks the humans can take care of themselves.

It's interesting that several different simian species coexist in the planet's ape society. It may be a little hard to account for that, given the logic of the movie, although I will say no more. One major change between this film and the earlier one is that everyone—apes and humans—speak English. The movie explains why the apes speak English, but fudges on how they learned to speak at all.

The movie is great looking. Rick Baker's makeup is convincing even in the extreme close-ups, and his apes sparkle with personality and presence. The sets and locations give us a proper sense of alien awe, and there's one neat long shot of the ape city-mountain that looks, when you squint a little, like Xanadu from *Citizen Kane*. There are lines inviting laughs ("Extremism in the defense of apes is no vice") and others unwisely inviting groans ("If you show me the way out of here—I promise I'll show you something that will change your life forever"). And a priceless moment when Leo wants to stop the squabbling among his fugitive group of men and apes and barks: "Shut up! That goes for all species!"

Planet of the Apes is the kind of movie that you enjoy at times, admire at times, even really like at times, but is it necessary? Given how famous and familiar Franklin J. Schaffner's 1968 film is, Tim Burton had some kind of an obligation to either top it, or sidestep it. Instead, he pays homage. He calls this version a "reimaging," and so it is, but a reinvention might have been better. Burton's work can show a wild and crazed imagination, but here he seems reined in. He's made a film that's respectful to the original, and respectable in itself, but that's not enough. Ten years from now, it will be the 1968 version that people are still renting. ☞

Play It to the Bone ★ ½
R, 125 m., 2000

Antonio Banderas (Cesar Dominguez), Woody Harrelson (Vince Boudreau), Lolita Davidovich (Grace Pasi), Tom Sizemore (Joe Domino), Lucy Liu (Lia), Robert Wagner (Hank Goody), Richard Masur (Artie), Willie Garson (Cappie Caplan). Directed by Ron Shelton and produced by Stephen Chin. Screenplay by Shelton.

Play It to the Bone ends with a long, gruesome, brutal, bloody prizefight scene, which would be right at home in another movie but is a big miscalculation here, because it is between the two heroes of the story. We like them both. Therefore, we don't want either one to win, and we don't want either one to lose. What we basically want is for them to stop pounding one another. That isn't the way you want your audience to feel during a boxing movie.

The movie stars Antonio Banderas and Woody Harrelson as Cesar and Vince, a couple of has-been welterweights who get an emergency call from Las Vegas: Will they fight on the undercard before tonight's main event with Mike Tyson? Both slots have opened up after one of the scheduled fighters wiped himself out in a car crash and the other overdosed ("drugs are coming out of his ears"). Banderas and Harrelson are buddies and sparring partners who need a fresh start. The deal: They'll

split $100,000, and the winner gets a shot at the title.

The movie was written and directed by Ron Shelton, an expert on sports movies; he wrote and directed *Bull Durham, White Men Can't Jump* and *Cobb,* and wrote *Blue Chips.* One of his trademarks is expertise, and yet *Play It to the Bone* isn't an inside job on boxing but an assembly of ancient and familiar prizefight clichés (the corrupt promoter, the dubious contract, the ringside celebrities, the cut that may not stop bleeding, the "I coulda been a contender" scene). Even at that level it doesn't have enough of a boxing story to occupy the running time, and warms up with a prolonged and unnecessary road movie.

The setup: Neither fighter can afford air fare to Vegas. It doesn't occur to them to have the casino prepay their tickets. Instead, they convince Grace (Lolita Davidovich), who is Cesar's girlfriend, to drive them there in her vintage Oldsmobile convertible (all road movies involve classic cars, which drive down back roads with gas stations recycled from *The Grapes of Wrath*). When their credit card is rejected at a pit stop, they pick up Lia (Lucy Liu), a hitchhiker with funds.

The road trip involves many scenes intended to be colorful, including an obligatory fight between the two women. Shelton is good at comic conversation, but here the dialogue doesn't flow and sounds contrived, as when Cesar explains that he was once gay for a year, "but only exactly a year," because he was "trying all sorts of things." Vince, a Jesus freak, is shocked—but only, we sense, because the screenplay tells him he is. Both Cesar's sex life and Vince's spiritual visions are like first-draft ideas that don't flow convincingly from the characters. And what about Grace's motivation for the trip: Her hope of selling the rights to her gizmo inventions to high rollers? Uh, huh.

All leads up to the big fight, during which, as I've said, we want to hide our eyes. Shelton's approach is certainly novel: A match you want to stop before the fighters hit each other any more. It's bad enough that they're fighting, but why, in a silly comedy, did Shelton think he had to outdo *Raging Bull* in brutality? Vince and Cesar hammer each other until it is unlikely either fighter, in the real world, would still be conscious—or alive. It's a hideous spectacle, and we cringe because the movie doesn't know how odd it seems to cut from the bloodshed in the ring to the dialogue of the supporting players, who still think they're in a comedy.

The Pledge ★ ★ ★ ½
R, 124 m., 2001

Jack Nicholson (Detective Jerry Black), Sam Shepard (Eric Pollack), Mickey Rourke (Jim Olstand), Benicio Del Toro (Toby Jay Wadenah), Helen Mirren (Doctor), Robin Wright Penn (Lori), Vanessa Redgrave (Annalise Hansen), Aaron Eckhart (Stan Krolak). Directed by Sean Penn and produced by Michael Fitzgerald, Penn, and Elie Samaha. Screenplay by Jerzy Kromolowski and Mary Olson-Kromolowski, based on the book by Friedrich Durrenmatt.

Sean Penn's *The Pledge* begins as a police story and spirals down into madness. It provides Jack Nicholson with one of his best roles in recent years, as a retired cop who makes a promise and tries to keep it. Like their previous film together as director and actor, *The Crossing Guard* (1995), it isn't a simple revenge story but shows the desire for justice running out of control and becoming dangerous. The story has the elements of a crime thriller (cops, suspects, victims, clues) but finally it's a character study, and in Detective Jerry Black, Nicholson creates a character we follow into the darkness of his compulsion.

As the film opens, Jerry is retiring as a cop—a good cop—in Reno. He's from an earlier generation; you can see that by the way he looks for ashtrays in the offices of colleagues who don't smoke. News comes that the mutilated body of a young girl has been found. Jerry goes on the call (he wants to work out his last day), and eventually finds himself delivering the tragic news to the parents of the little girl.

This scene, staged by Penn on the turkey farm the parents operate, is amazing in its setting (Nicholson wading through thousands of turkey chicks) and its impact (holding a crucifix made by the murdered Ginny, he swears "by his soul's salvation" that he will find the

killer). This is the pledge of the movie's title, and eventually it obsesses him.

It appears at first that the killer has been found. Benicio Del Toro plays an Indian, obviously retarded, who was seen running away from the murder scene. Clues seem to link his pickup with the crime. A knife-edged detective (Aaron Eckhart) gets a confession out of him, with Jerry squirming behind the one-way glass and saying the Indian "doesn't understand the question." Then the Indian grabs a gun and shoots himself. Guilty, and dead. Case closed.

Jerry doesn't think so. His years as a cop tell him something is not right. In retirement, he continues to investigate the case, eventually finding that the dead Ginny had made friends with a "giant" she called "the Wizard." Who was this man? Was he the killer? Was he linked with other unsolved killings of young children?

Until this point, *The Pledge* has been a fairly standard, if well-done, police procedural. Now Penn, working from a novel by Friedrich Durrenmatt and screenplay by Jerzy Kromolowski and Mary Olson-Kromolowski, begins the film's descent into Jerry's obsession. He does a strange thing. He buys a gas station and convenience store halfway between two towns where he thinks the "wizard" might have committed crimes. Studying drawings by the dead Ginny, he thinks he knows what kind of vehicle the killer might have used. The store is a trap.

An unexpected thing happens. He meets a mother (Robin Wright Penn) and her young daughter, and they feel an instinctive sympathy which blossoms to his surprise into love. After a couple of divorces, Jerry discovers at last what a happy domestic life can be. We immediately realize that the daughter is a potential victim of the killer, if he is indeed still at large. We assume Jerry realizes this too. But surely he would not use this beautiful little girl as bait?

One problem with Jerry's quest is that he is the only person who believes in it. His former police colleagues think he's gone around the bend; even the chief (Sam Shepard), an old friend, looks sadly at Jerry's unhinged zeal. His gas station trap may be a long shot, or an inspiration, or simply proof he's losing touch with reality. The last third of the movie is where most police stories go on autopilot, with obligatory chases, stalkings, and confrontations. That's when *The Pledge* grows most compelling. Penn and Nicholson take risks with the material and the character, and elevate the movie to another, unanticipated, haunting level.

Sean Penn has been saying for years that he wants to quit acting and be a director. That would be a loss, because he is one of the finest actors alive (consider *Dead Man Walking*). What is clear from the three films he has directed (also including *The Indian Runner* in 1991) is that he has no interest in making ordinary films. He is fascinated by characters under stress. He is bored by the working out of obvious psychological processes.

The character of Jerry here is not merely a good cop, but a retired man, an older man, a man possessed by a fixed idea. He is able at one level to exude charm and stability (one reason the younger woman likes him is that he offers calm and strength after her violent marriage). But we sense deeper, darker currents, and issues he isn't fully aware of himself. By the end of *The Pledge*, the suspense hinges mostly on Jerry, and the solution of the crime is a sideshow. It is here that Nicholson's skill is most needed, and most appreciated: He has to show us a man who has embarked on a terrifying and lonely quest into the unknown places of his mind.

Pola X ★ ★ ★

NO MPAA RATING, 134 m., 2000

Guillaume Depardieu (Pierre), Katerina Golubeva (Isabelle), Catherine Deneuve (Marie), Delphine Chuillot (Lucie), Petruta Catana (Razerka), Mihaella Silaghi (The Child), Laurent Lucas (Thibault), Patachou (Margherite). Directed by Leos Carax and produced by Bruno Pesery. Screenplay by Carax, Lauren Sedofsky, and Jean-Pol Fargeau, based on the novel *Pierre* by Herman Melville.

It takes a raving lunatic to know one. Not that I have ever met Leos Carax, the director of *Pola X*, so that I can say for sure he's as tempestuous and impulsive as the subject of his film, but you aren't described as an "enfant terrible" at the age of thirty-nine without good reason. Certainly Pierre, his hero, is an inspired visionary, a youth inflamed by romantic fantasies, who sees himself as a great artist and is in love with reckless gestures.

The film is a reasonably close adaptation of Herman Melville's 1852 novel *Pierre*. Carax's title is an acronym of the French title, *Pierre, ou les Ambiguities,* and the X refers to the tenth draft of the screenplay. *Pierre* was written following Melville's *Moby-Dick,* and after the classical architecture of its prose, the next novel came as a shock with its lurid fevers. Melville wrote at white-hot speed, he said, as if in a dream, and for many years *Pierre* was unavailable in an uncensored version (an unexpurgated edition was published in the 1990s). Dealing as it does with Pierre's incestuous obsessions with a mother and a half-sister, it was not what admirers of the great white whale were expecting.

Carax sets his story in present-day France, although with the exception of a few cars, motorcycles, props, and street scenes its period could be the nineteenth century. He tells the story of Pierre (Guillaume Depardieu), a spoiled young aristocrat who has written a trendy best-selling novel and lives in a chateau with his mother, Marie (Catherine Deneuve). They are alarmingly close; they call each other "my brother" and "my sister," he lights two cigarettes and gives her one, he visits her nude in her bath, and so on. Deneuve is able to make scenes like these work because she can float above the carnal, in a realm where sex is a whim rather than a function.

Pierre is engaged to his cousin Lucie (Delphine Chuillot), who lives in a neighboring chalet and is an ethereal blond waif; his mother could no more be jealous of Lucie than if Pierre adopted a cute spaniel. Also on the scene, having recently returned from his labors on the Chicago Stock Exchange, is a dark-browed cousin, Thibault (Laurent Lucas), who in his satanic way resents that Pierre will take Lucie out of his grasp, and also perhaps that Lucie will take Pierre out of his grasp. He refers to them as "the three inseparables," but the other two lean toward separability.

There is a mystery woman (Katerina Golubeva), deep-eyed, long-haired, ragged, and wolflike, who shadows Pierre. The sight of her fills him with deep churnings and obscure dreams. One night as he is roaring through the woods on his motorcycle he surprises her lurking in the gloom, pursues her, and hears her story: "Believe me, Pierre, you are not an only child. I am your sister, Isabelle." In a long, long monologue (it is a stand-alone section in the novel), she tells her story. She is the love child of Pierre's father, was raised in the woods by an old man and woman, speaks simply in a high-pitched voice, is unsocialized and desperate.

Pierre is consumed by a manic need to throw away wealth and happiness, and share Isabelle's poverty and misery. "All my life I have waited for something that would push me beyond this," he says, waving a metaphorical arm to encompass Lucie, Marie, the chateau.

They will live together like brother and sister, he tells Isabelle. The world will think she's his wife. Turned away from fleabag hotels, they reside finally in a vast warehouse occupied by a group of terrorists, who breed their plots while a deathly conductor stands on a catwalk and conducts his orchestra in a mournful symphony for synthesizers, steel drums, and iron bars banged on with hammers.

Feverishly hunched beneath a blanket against the cold, he scribbles out his new novel, which will be great, which will be true, while the sound track itches with the sound of his pen scratching against the paper, like rats sharpening their nails on sandpaper. Meanwhile, he and Isabelle are not living together like most brothers and sisters, and there is a sex scene which would be shockingly graphic if we could quite see it.

Faithful readers will know I have an affection for raving lunatics, and am grateful for films that break free of the dismal bonds of formula to cartwheel into overwrought, passionate excess. This is a weakness, but I am protective of it. *Pola X* may not be successful and its closing passages may drift into the realm of the ludicrous, but "when it's over," as Stephen Holden so accurately wrote after it played in the New York Film Festival, "you'll know you've had an experience."

Guillaume Depardieu, Gérard's hulking blond son, makes a better Pierre than the wan

youth I pictured while reading the novel; he projects the sense of self-gratification that motivates Pierre—who is such an egotist that even throwing away his own life is an act of selfishness. Katerina Golubeva will wear on the nerves of some witnesses with her pitiful little-girl voice and her narcissistic way of hiding her face with her hair, but if anyone looks like she was raised in a hovel in the woods, she does. The cool elegance Deneuve brings to the opening scenes makes a useful contrast with the industrial anarchy of the conclusion, with those terrorist musicians pounding joylessly on their anvils. I would rather see one movie like this than a thousand *Bring It On*s.

Pollock ★ ★ ★ ★
R, 122 m., 2001

Ed Harris (Jackson Pollock), Marcia Gay Harden (Lee Krasner), Amy Madigan (Peggy Guggenheim), Jennifer Connelly (Ruth Klingman), Jeffrey Tambor (Clement Greenberg), Bud Cort (Howard Putzel), John Heard (Tony Smith), Val Kilmer (Willem de Kooning). Directed by Ed Harris and produced by Fred Berner, Harris, and John Kilik. Screenplay by Barbara Turner and Susan Emshwiller, based on the book *Jackson Pollock: An American Saga* by Steven Naifeh and Gregory White Smith.

Reporter from *Life* magazine: "How do you know when you're finished with a painting?"

Jackson Pollock: "How do you know when you're finished making love?"

Jackson Pollock was a great painter. He was also a miserable man who made everyone around him miserable a lot of the time. He was an alcoholic and manic-depressive, and he died in a drunken car crash that killed an innocent woman. What Ed Harris is able to show in *Pollock* is that when he was painting, he got a reprieve. He was also reasonably happy during those periods when he stopped drinking. Then the black cloud would descend again.

Pollock avoids the pitfall of making simplistic one-to-one connections between the artist's life and his paintings. This is not a movie about art but about work. It is about the physical labor of making paintings, and about the additional labor of everyday life, which is a burden for Pollock because of his tortured mind and hungover body. It is said that it takes more will for an alcoholic to get out of bed in the morning than for other people to go through the day, and there are times when Pollock simply stops, stuck, and stares into space. He didn't have de Kooning's luck and find sobriety.

Pollock is often depressed, but *Pollock* is not depressing. It contains all the hum and buzz of the postwar New York art world, the vibrant courage of Pollock's wife, Lee Krasner, the measured presence of the art critic Clement Greenberg (who more or less validated abstract expressionism), and the fun-loving energy of the millionaire art patron Peggy Guggenheim, who collected paintings and painters. It was a time when Pollack traded a painting to pay a $56 bill at a store, and found himself in *Life* magazine not long after. Things were on the move.

This is Ed Harris's movie. He started thinking about it fifteen years ago, after reading a book about Pollock. He commissioned the screenplay. He raised the money. He stars in it, and he directed it. He knew he looked a lot like Pollock (his father saw the book and thought the cover photo resembled his son). But his similarity to Pollock is not just superficial; he looks a little like Picasso, too, but is unlikely to find the same affinity. He seems to have made a deeper connection, to have felt an instinctive sympathy for this great, unhappy man.

The movie wears its period lightly. It gets rolling in postwar Greenwich Village. Everybody smokes all the time. Rents are cheap, but the first time Peggy Guggenheim visits Pollock's studio is almost the last: "I do not climb up five flights of stairs to nobody home!" Why did Pollock almost miss his first meeting with the famous patron? Some damn fool reason. He had a knack for screwing up, and it's arguable that his career would never have happened if Lee Krasner hadn't poked her head around his door one day.

Krasner (played by Marcia Gay Harden, evoking enormous sympathy and patience) comes calling because she wants to see his paintings. She passes her hand over them as if testing their temperature. She knows they are good. She senses that Pollock takes little initiative in personal matters, and takes charge of their re-

lationship, undressing while Pollock is still looking for his cigarettes. She goes in with her eyes open. She knows she's marrying a troubled man, but stands by him, and is repaid with a couple of happy years when they get a place in the country, and he doesn't drink. Then the troubles all start again—a bottle of beer, a fight, an upset table at Thanksgiving, and affairs with hero-worshipping girls like Ruth Klingman (Jennifer Connelly).

I don't know if Ed Harris knows how to paint, but I know he knows how to look like he's painting. There's a virtuoso scene where he paints a mural for Peggy's townhouse, utterly confident, fast and sure, in the flow. And others where we see the famous drip technique (and see that "anyone" could not do it). His judge and jury is the critic Clement Greenberg, played with judicious, plummy certainty by Jeffrey Tambor. He says what he thinks, praising early work and bringing Guggenheim around, then attacking later work even as the world embraces it ("pretentious muddiness").

Pollock is confident, insightful work—one of the best films of the year. Ed Harris is always a good actor but here seems possessed, as if he had a leap of empathy for Pollock. His direction is assured, economical, knows where it's going, and what it wants to do. No fancy visual gimmicks, just the look and feel of this world.

I first saw the movie at the Toronto Film Festival and a day later ran into the painter Julian Schnabel. I mentioned Pollock's suffering. "What happened to Jackson Pollock when he was painting," Schnabel said, "is, he was free." That's what Ed Harris communicates in the film. A man is miserable but he is given a gift. The gift lifts his misery while he employs it. It brings joy to himself and others. It creates space he can hide in, space he can breathe in, space he can escape to. He needs that space, and given his demons, painting is the only way he can find it.

Pootie Tang ½★
PG-13, 79 m., 2001

Lance Crouther (Pootie Tang), JB Smoove (Trucky), Jennifer Coolidge (Ireenie), Reg E. Cathey (Dirty Dee), Robert Vaughn (Dick

Lecter), Wanda Sykes (Biggie Shorty), Chris Rock (Pootie's Father/JB), Cathy Trien (Stacy), David Attel (Frank). Directed by Louis C.K. and produced by Cotty Chubb, David M. Gale, Ali LeRoi, Michael Rotenberg, Dave Becky, and Chris Rock. Screenplay by C.K.

Pootie Tang is not bad so much as inexplicable. You watch in puzzlement: How did this train wreck happen? How was this movie assembled out of such ill-fitting pieces? Who thought it was funny? Who thought it was finished? For that matter, was it finished? Take away the endless opening titles and end credits, and it's about seventy minutes long. The press notes say it comes "from the comedy laboratory of HBO's Emmy Award–winning *Chris Rock Show*." It's like one of those lab experiments where the room smells like swamp gas and all the mice are dead.

Lance Crouther stars as Pootie Tang, a folk hero who has gained enormous popularity even though nobody can understand a word he says. He crusades against the evil Lecter Corp., which sells cigarettes, booze, drugs, and fast food to kids. Pootie is a regular character on *The Chris Rock Show*, and has a following, but he's more suited to skits than to a feature film—or at least to this feature film, which is disorganized, senseless, and chaotic.

Characters appear and disappear without pattern. Pootie has funny scenes, as when he dodges bullets, and other scenes, as when a woman eats a pie off his face, that seem left in the movie by accident. His secret weapon is his daddy's belt, which he uses against criminals. His daddy (Chris Rock) gave it to him on his deathbed, after being mauled by a gorilla at the steel mill. When the belt is stolen by an evil woman named Ireenie (Jennifer Coolidge), he loses his powers, but is helped by a good woman named Biggie Shorty (Wanda Sykes, who provides more personality than the movie deserves).

Biggie Shorty is a hooker but spends most of her time boogying on street corners and encouraging Pootie Tang. She has a farm in Mississippi she loans Pootie, who, during his recuperation there, is encouraged by the white sheriff to date his daughter. This leads in the direction of a shotgun marriage, until the story

thread evaporates and Pootie ends up in bed with Biggie. There is another villain named Dirty Dee (Reg E. Cathey), who is very dirty, and a villain, Dick Lecter, played by Robert Vaughn as if he may have a touch of lockjaw. Bob Costas plays an interviewer on one of those dreadful assignments where the writers thought it was funny simply *that* he was in the movie, instead of giving him anything funny to do.

Material this silly might at least be mindless entertainment for children, but *Pootie Tang* for no good reason includes a lot of language it has no need for. The studios put enormous pressure on the MPAA to award PG-13 ratings to what once would have been R-rated material, and the MPAA obliges. Here is dialogue your MPAA rates PG-13: "You can't hurt a ho with a belt. They like it." Women are routinely described as bitches and slapped around a lot (so are men). I have no problem with street language in movies with a use for the language. But why use it gratuitously in a movie that has no need for it, with a lead character whose TV exposure will attract younger viewers? What's the point?

Anyway, I'm not so much indignant as confused. Audiences will come out scratching their heads. The movie is half-baked, a shabby job of work. There are flashes of good stuff: a music video in the closing titles, some good songs on the sound track, Lance Crouther heroically making Pootie Tang an intriguing character even though the movie gives him no help. This movie is not in a releasable condition.

Price of Glory ★ ★
PG-13, 118 m., 2000

Jimmy Smits (Arturo Ortega), Maria Del Mar (Rita Ortega), Jon Seda (Sonny Ortega), Clifton Collins Jr. (Jimmy Ortega), Ernesto Hernandez (Johnny Ortega), Ron Perlman (Nick Everson), Louis Mandylor (Davey Lane), Sal Lopez (Hector Salmon). Directed Carlos Avila and produced by Moctesuma Esparza, Robert Katz, and Arthur E. Friedman. Screenplay by Phil Berger.

Price of Glory made me feel like I was sitting in McDonald's watching some guy shout at his kids. You read the situation: Here's a man with problems of his own, who is projecting his troubles onto his children—because he thinks he can control them, and he knows he can't control himself. The world has him licked. The situation makes you feel sad and uncomfortable, but it's none of your business. You look away.

Price of Glory gives us two hours of that behavior, and it's a miscalculation so basic that it makes the movie painful when it wants, I guess, to be touching. Jimmy Smits plays Arturo Ortega, a Mexican-American father who was a boxer when he was young, was "brought along too fast" and beaten badly in a fight, and now leads a life obsessed with getting revenge through the lives of his three sons. He brings them up as boxers ("the Fighting Ortegas"), and tries to dominate their lives. But he does such a bad job of masterminding their careers that finally the sons and long-suffering wife see him less as a father than as their cross to bear. Even his rival, a boxing promoter who wants to handle the most promising son, comes across less as an enemy than as a man with more common sense than Arturo.

Smits is good in this performance—all too good. The movie is earnest and sincere, and an ordeal to watch, because there's no arc to his character, and learning and redemption are too little, too late. He's stuck. He keeps making the same mistakes over and over; he starts as tragic, and ends as a slow study. And he inflicts on his kids (and us) that tiresome strategy of the domineering parent who puts on an act of being reasonable, of "only wanting what's best" for his kids, when clearly his own issues are in charge. He even believes himself when he delivers his sanctimonious and self-serving speeches; the kids turn away, and we pity them.

The other arc in the film is that of a typical boxing movie. It opens with Arturo losing big in an early fight, and then we see him living in New Mexico with his wife, Rita (Maria Del Mar), who sees him clearly, loves him, but puts up with way too much. They have three kids, who are put in the ring at such young ages that we didn't know they made boxing gloves that tiny. (I don't even want to think about kids in the "Peewee Division.") He pushes them, browbeats them; even one kid's victory gets criticized because his style was wrong. We sense here a portrait of all parents who live through young children, pushing them onto the stage, forcing them into competitions they have no taste for, treating them not like kids but like puppets acting out the parents' fantasies.

Flash forward ten years and the kids are young men, but their father has learned nothing. They are Sonny (Jon Seda), Jimmy (Clifton Collins Jr.), and Johnny (Ernesto Hernandez). Sonny is the best boxer, but as the oldest he's the most driven to squirm from under his father's thumb. Jimmy is resentful and rebellious. Johnny has real promise, and as the youngest is most concerned with pleasing his dad. But the family by this point is twisted and distorted by years of Arturo's bullying, as Rita Ortega looks on helplessly.

Like many bullies, Arturo is filled with self-pity, and has a way of creating a family dynamic where guilt suppresses rage. Consider a scene where one of the boys proudly brings home the girlfriend he wants to marry and her parents, for dinner. Arturo behaves like such a jerk that we cringe. A family dinner quite like this could not exist anywhere outside a movie more concerned with making a point than drawing a convincing character.

The story's villain is a professional fight promoter named Nick Everson (Ron Perlman). With his deep-set eyes and burly physique, he's intimidating, and controls the bookings for big fights. I am sure there are people like him all through professional boxing, but what's amazing is that he comes as a surprise to Arturo, who wants to manage his sons himself. Everson has thugs working for him, but he and his men are not vicious, simply hardboiled. By the end of the film, Everson is looking reasonable compared to Arturo Ortega—even to Arturo himself.

The character scenes are intercut with standard scenes from boxing movies: training, strategy, talking about moves, early fights. None of this stuff is remarkable. What's peculiar is that the film doesn't build toward anything because even as the boxing careers flourish, the character of Arturo drags everything down. At the end there is a victory, and it means nothing—it's ashes, because Arturo has taken out the fun. He just never learns.

The Price of Milk ★ ★
PG-13, 89 m., 2001

Danielle Cormack (Lucinda), Karl Urban (Rob), Willa O'Neill (Drosophilia), Rangi Motu (Auntie), Michael Lawrence (Bernie). Directed by Harry Sinclair and produced by Fiona Copland. Screenplay by Sinclair.

Somewhere in New Zealand, a nation apparently inhabited by less than a dozen people, Lucinda and Rob run a dairy farm. So lonely is Rob that he knows all 175 of his cows by their names—or numbers ("Good morning, 47!"). So carnal is Lucinda that she surprises Rob at strange times and places with sudden, bold invitations to make love. So besotted is Rob that he produces a wedding ring and proposes. So fearful is Lucinda that she seeks advice to be sure that Rob really loves her. So realistic am I that I'm thinking—he'd better, since there is, so far, no other man in the movie.

Lucinda turns to her friend Drosophilia, who advises her to be absolutely sure of Rob's love by setting up a series of tests. In the first Lucinda goes bathing in a vat containing $1,500 worth of milk, spoiling it. Rob is angered, but so fetching is Lucinda's smile and so real her dismay that he plunges in with her, and so fervent are their ecstasies that the milk all but churns into butter right before our eyes.

We are thinking, meanwhile, that whatever else you can say for them, Lucinda, Rob, and Drosophilia are healthy-looking specimens, and look right at place on a farm. No wonder; they are played by Danielle Cormack, Karl Urban, and Willa O'Neill, who have all appeared on TV's *Xena* or *Hercules* (Cormack is the Amazon Ephiny). They were cast in *The Price of Milk* by its writer-director, Harry Sinclair—who, I learn from *Film Journal International*, "started out his project not with a story line, or a face in mind, but a bit of a Russian symphony by early-20th-century composer Anatol Liadov, accidentally heard over the radio while location-scouting. Sinclair was inspired by the music and the place, and themes appeared and fell into line for him."

If true, this would indicate Sinclair was scouting for locations before he knew what his story was about, which may explain the rather awkward tension between the cow farm and what is basically a fairy tale. He adds supernatural elements involving a Maori woman named Auntie (Rangi Motu). One day Lucinda runs straight into Auntie with her car, but Auntie is miraculously untouched, and disappears into the woods.

A few nights later, mysterious hands steal the quilt from Lucinda and Rob's bed, and Lucinda sees it soon after in Auntie's hands. Tracking her down to a cottage in the woods, she sees Auntie sleeping under a pile of dozens of quilts—all stolen for her, we learn, by her nephews (who are golfers, and practice putts between quilt raids). Lucinda demands her quilt back, and is given a series of demands by Auntie that *really* test Rob's love.

There is a place for whimsy and magic realism, and that place may not be on a cow farm in New Zealand. Or perhaps it is, but not with this story. I was never much convinced by the romantic chemistry between Rob and Lucinda, never believed in Drosophilia's jealous scheming, found Auntie tiresome, and was most intrigued by her golfing nephews, small though their roles may be. Imagine a golf movie involving six or seven Maoris on the pro Tour with a magic Auntie. Now there's a movie.

The Princess and the Warrior ★ ★ ★ ½
R, 130 m., 2001

Franka Potente (Sissi), Benno Furmann (Bodo), Joachim Krol (Walter), Marita Breuer (Sissi's Mother), Jurgen Tarrach (Schmatt), Lars Rudolph (Steini), Melchior Beslon (Otto). Directed by Tom Tykwer and produced by Stefan Arndt and Maria Kopf. Screenplay by Tykwer.

The positive but puzzled reviews for *A.I.* all agreed on one thing: The film was the work of an artist. I feel more positive and less puzzled about *The Princess and the Warrior*, which is also the work of an artist. Both titles are reminders that it is better to see an imperfect movie that lives and breathes than a perfect one that is merely a genre exercise.

The Princess and the Warrior is one astonishment after another. It uses coincidence with reckless abandon to argue that deep patterns in life connect some people. It uses thriller elements—not to thrill us, but to set up moral challenges for its characters. It is about a woman convinced she has met the one great love of her life, and a man convinced he is not that person. It is about a traffic accident, a bank robbery, an insane asylum, and it does not use any of those elements as they have been used before. Above all, it loves its characters too much to entrap them in a mediocre plot.

The movie was written and directed by Tom Tykwer, from Germany, who had international success with *Run, Lola, Run,* and now has made a deeper and more ambitious film. It stars Franka Potente, who played Lola (she was also the stewardess married to Johnny Depp in *Blow*). It uses the same kind of crazy looping energy as *Lola,* and is just as open to intersecting fates, but *Lola* was essentially about kinetic energy, and this is a film about the thin membranes that separate life and death, good and evil, success and failure, love and fear.

Potente plays Sissi, a nurse in the psychiatric hospital where she was born. She is much loved by her strange patients, and so shut off from the outside world that when she shares a secret erotic moment with one of them we sense they're performing a mutual service. Her costar is Benno Furmann, who plays Bodo—a bank robber, among other things.

They meet after Bodo unwittingly causes an accident that leaves Sissi pinned under a truck and choking on her own blood. He crawls under the truck to elude the police, sees that she is dying, and saves her life. I will not tell you how he does this, except to say that the scene, in its horror, its detail, its quiet observation, its reliance on the sound track to tell us what is happening, is overwhelming in its intensity.

It shows greatness—not just because of what I've referred to, but by something more, the detail that Tykwer adds *after* the scene seems to be over. Let us say, without giving too much away, that events have made Sissi acutely aware of the nature of each breath she takes. She has been looking into the eyes of this man who is saving her, and now she becomes aware that his breath is sweet and has sent a "peppermint sting" to her lungs.

Bodo accompanies her into an ambulance (it is his means of escape from the police—every action in this movie seems to have two purposes). She holds desperately to his hand, then passes out, and later finds she has nothing but the button from his coat. He has disappeared. She knows she must find him. It is their destiny. Here is another astonishing scene. She knows a patient at the asylum, a blind man, who like many blind people is acutely aware of his surroundings and may be psychic. She asks him to retrace the route of the man who saved her life.

While all of this is going on, we learn more about an elaborate bank burglary being planned by Bodo and his brother Walter (Joachim Krol), and eventually the lives of Sissi and Bodo cross—not once, not just as a "coincidence," but in a series of interlinking connections that take on a life of their own.

Tykwer uses the elements of genre in his film, but evades generic simplicities. He is using the conventions of a bank heist movie, not to make a bank heist movie, but to lay down a narrative map so that we can clearly see how the characters wander off of it—lose their way in the tangle of their lives and emotions. He looks at his characters a little harder than most directors; he isn't content with one level of writing to describe them, but needs many. Consider an opening sequence in which Bodo is working as a gravedigger and laborer at a funeral home, and is fired for—what would you guess? Do you have an idea? He is fired for crying.

The Princess and the Warrior is not perfect. It is a little too long, and takes us an extra lap around its ironic track. But it's so rich, how can we complain? Tykwer is thirty-six and this is his fourth feature. Like other directors of his generation, he's fascinated by narratives that play with time; like *Memento, Amores Perros,* and *One Night at McCool's,* his film is impatient with straight narratives and linear plots, and wants to filter events through more than one point of view. That's at the structural level. What's special about the film is at a deeper level, down where he engages with the souls of his characters.

The Princess Diaries ★ ½
G, 115 m., 2001

Julie Andrews (Queen Clarisse Renaldi), Anne Hathaway (Mia Thermopolis), Hector Elizondo (Joe), Heather Matarazzo (Lilly Moscovitz), Mandy Moore (Lana Thomas), Caroline Goodall (Mia's Mom, Helen), Robert Schwartzman (Michael Moscovitz), Erik Von Detten (Josh Bryant). Directed by Garry Marshall and produced by Whitney Houston, Debra Martin Chase, and Mario Iscovich. Screenplay by Gina Wendkos, based on the novel by Meg Cabot.

Haven't I seen this movie before? *The Princess Diaries* is a march through the swamp of recycled ugly duckling stories, with occasional pauses in the marsh of sitcom clichés and the bog of Idiot Plots. You recall the Idiot Plot. That's the plot that would be solved in an instant if anyone on the screen said what was obvious to the audience. A movie like this isn't entertainment. It's more like a party game that you lose if you say the secret word.

The film takes place in the present day, I guess, if through some kind of weird *Pleasantville* time warp the present day had the values and behavior of Andy Hardy movies. It is about a fifteen-year-old girl who doesn't realize she's really the princess of Genovia, which is "between France and Spain" and needs an heir from its royal bloodline if it is not to (a) go out of business, or (b) be taken over by the evil baron and baroness, I'm not sure which. Turns out that Mia Thermopolis (Anne Hathaway) is the daughter of the Prince of Genovia, but has never learned this fact, because her mother, Helen (Caroline Goodall), wanted to lead a normal life and thus left Genovia and her husband, never told Mia about her real father, and raised her normally—that is, in a San Francisco firehouse where she slides down the pole every morning.

The prince has come to an untimely end, and now his mother comes to recruit Mia to take up her royal duties. The mother is Queen Clarisse Renaldi, played by Julie Andrews as a nice woman with very, very, very good manners. The suspense involves: Will Mia accept the throne? And will she choose as her boyfriend the snobbish jerk Josh (Erik Von Detten) or the nice Michael (Robert Schwartzman), older brother of her best friend, Lilly (Heather Matarazzo)? And, for that matter, is there any possibility that Josh will dump a glamorous cheerleader (Mandy Moore) after he sees how Mia looks once she takes off her glasses and does something with her hair? Anyone who doesn't immediately know the answers to these questions either lives in a cave, or wrote this screenplay.

The words "why don't you do something about your hair" have inspired movie transformation scenes since time immemorial, but rarely has the transformation been more of a setup than here. Garry Marshall, the director, hasn't had the nerve to cast a real fifteen-year-old as Mia, but supplies us instead with Anne Hathaway, who is almost twenty-one years old, and is a classic beauty in the Daphne Zuniga tradition. We're expected to believe that this character gets so nervous in class that she throws up while trying to make a speech, and yet the rest of the time is as effortlessly verbal as a stand-up comedian.

One of the creaky problems thrown in the way of the plot is a "scandal" when Mia is photographed in what is not really a very scandalous situation at all, and so perhaps must renounce the throne. Queen Clarisse Renaldi seems reconciled to this. What do you think the chances are that the ruling family of a lucrative tax shelter—Monaco, for example—would abandon their principality because of a newspaper photo of the heir kissing a boy? In the interests of keeping the loot in the family, any heir—even Phoolan Devi, the late Bandit Queen of India—would be considered a viable candidate.

Garry Marshall made the wonderful *Pretty Woman*, but what was his thinking here? Some of the editing is plain sloppy. We are informed, for example, that when a kiss is magical, one of a girl's heels curls up off the floor. Cut to a heel curling up, but stuck to a strand of chewing gum. Whose heel? Whose gum? Nobody's. This is simply an isolated, self-contained shot. Later, at a dinner party, Marshall spends time establishing one of the guests as a drunk, but then the guest disappears without a payoff.

As *The Princess Diaries* creeps from one painfully obvious plot destination to another, we wait impatiently for the characters on-screen to arrive at what has long been clear to the audience. If the movie is determined to be this dim-witted, couldn't it at least move a little more quickly? The metronome is set too slow, as if everyone is acting and thinking in half-time. ☞

Proof of Life ★ ★ ½
R, 135 m., 2000

Meg Ryan (Alice Bowman), Russell Crowe (Terry Thorne), David Morse (Peter Bowman), David Caruso (Dino), Pamela Reed (Janis Bowman), Wolframio Benavides (Honcho). Directed and produced by Taylor Hackford. Screenplay by Tony Gilroy, based on an article "Adventures in the Ransom Trade" by William Prochnau and the book *The Long March to Freedom* by Thomas Hargrove.

Kidnapping is not a rare crime but a lucrative line of business in the Third World, according to *Proof of Life*, a movie that is best when it sticks closest to the tradecraft of a professional K&R man named Terry Thorne. K&R means "kidnap and ransom," we learn, and the specialty has grown along with the crime; somewhere in the world, businessmen are being snatched on an almost daily basis, making lots of work for Terry (Russell Crowe), who masterminds a helicopter snatch of a hostage in the opening sequence and makes his getaway clinging to the landing skips of the chopper.

Cut to Tecala, a fictional Latin American country where drugs are a major crop and a revolutionary movement has morphed into a professional kidnapping operation. We meet Peter and Alice Bowman (David Morse, Meg Ryan), an American couple going through a bad patch in their marriage, who are living in the country while Peter builds a dam. He thinks the dam will help the locals grow crops. She thinks it's window dressing for the oil company that employs him. They're hardly speaking to each other when she gets word he's been kidnapped.

Enter Terry Thorne, whose job is to negotiate the lowest possible ransom price and rescue the hostage. Exit Terry Thorne, when it's revealed that Bowman's employer didn't pay the premium on his K&R policy. Reenter Terry

Thorne, who returns to Tecala because something about Alice Bowman, some quiet unstated appeal with sexual undertones, has brought him back. He will risk his life for free, for the husband of the woman he doesn't know for sure he loves, although he has a strong hunch.

The movie, directed by Taylor Hackford, cuts between Thorne's K&R craft, Alice's guilt and emotional confusion, and the ordeal in the jungle by Peter, played by Morse as a hothead who talks back to the guys carrying the machine guns—not always prudent. Complications enter with Alice's sister-in-law (Pamela Reed); a fellow prisoner of Peter's (Gottfried John), who poses as a crazy missionary; and Thorne's old fighting partner Dino (David Caruso), who is in the country trying to rescue *another* kidnap victim.

The movie's kidnap lore, based on books and articles about professional K&R men, is intriguing. Crowe, as Terry, explains his work to Alice (and to us), and we learn why you never bring in local negotiators (on the take and maybe in on the snatch), why the opening asking price is way high, and how to demand proof the hostage is still alive. Meanwhile Terry and Alice carry on a buried flirtation in which both shyly acknowledge the chemistry between them with a kiss and eloquent body language. A more graphic sex scene was cut from the movie, reportedly because it reflected the real-life liaison between Crowe and Ryan; whether the movie would have been better with a more overt romance is an interesting question. Obviously Hackford preferred unreleased tension, and building toward his poignant final scene.

I found the movie absorbing in its details and persuasive in its performances, but the overall flight was somehow without lift. I wanted the tension wound tighter. The side relationships, with the sister-in-law and the missionary, were interesting in themselves but put the plot progress on hold. Crowe, Ryan, and Morse are everything the story asks for; her character is doubly interesting because the movie avoids the cliché of the grieving wife and shows a conflicted, sometimes angry woman who had a big fight with the husband just before he was snatched. Crowe's K&R man has a professional code, mostly (we gather) of his own enforcement, that inhibits his romantic feelings. Or is it that he gets off on playing the hero for unavailable women, and then nobly departing before they have the opportunity to choose him if they want to? Morse's role is more down to earth, as a captive who is mistreated but knows he can get away with a lot because he must remain alive to be of value.

I was interested all through the movie—interested, but not riveted. I cared, but not quite enough. I had sympathy with the characters, but in keeping at arm's length from each other they also kept a certain distance from me. Perhaps the screenplay should have been kept simmering until it was reduced a little, and its flavors made stronger.

Q

Queen of the Damned ★ ★
R, 101 m., 2002

Stuart Townsend (Lestat de Lioncourt), Aaliyah (Akasha), Marguerite Moreau (Jesse Reeves), Vincent Perez (Marius), Paul McGann (David Talbot), Lena Olin (Maharet), Christian Manon (Mael), Claudia Black (Pandora). Directed by Michael Rymer and produced by Jorge Saralegui. Screenplay by Scott Abbott and Michael Petroni, based on the novels *The Vampire Chronicles* by Anne Rice.

Vampires are always in pose mode, which tends to make vampire movies into comedies. The stark horror of *Nosferatu* has long since dribbled down into overwrought melodrama. The buried message of many scenes is: "Regard me well, for here I am, and I am thus." A lot of the dialogue is declamatory, and many sentences are versions of, "Together, we (will, can, must) (rule, change, destroy) the (world, our victims, the people in this bar)."

Queen of the Damned, based on Anne Rice's endless Vampire Chronicles, happily occupies this mode. It is happy to be goofy. *Interview With the Vampire,* Neil Jordan's glossy 1994 version of the earlier Rice novel, was more ambitious and anchored—even sad. This sequel, also about the vampire Lestat, is filled with characters who seem to have taken Gene Simmons as their role model.

The movie stars Stuart Townsend as Lestat, in the role played last time by Tom Cruise. The world got to be too much for him, Lestat explains, and so he withdrew from it and went to sleep 200 years ago. But then "the world didn't sound like the place I had left—but something different, better." Cut to a montage of musical groups, and Lestat pushes back the stone lid of his crypt and materializes during a rehearsal of a rock band. When they ask who he is, he smiles and casts centuries of tradition to the winds: "I am . . . the Vampire Lestat!"

Soon he's a rock god, the lead singer of a Goth band. Other characters emerge. We meet Jesse (Marguerite Moreau), researcher for a London vampire study institute. She likes to play with danger, and even cruises a vampire bar Lestat told her about. We meet the fey Marius (Vincent Perez), the older vampire who turned Lestat on, or out. And Maharet (Lena Olin), who I think is supposed to be a good vampire, or at least one who wishes the others would follow the rules. Along the way we are given vampire feeding lessons: "You must never take the last drop or it will draw you in and you die."

Most noticeably we meet Queen Akasha, the title character, played by Aaliyah, the singer who was killed in a 2001 air crash. She appears first as a statue in a phantasmagorical Egyptian cryptlike shrine, where Lestat plays his violin so fiercely that parts of her stone body seem to glow back into life. She "drank the world dry when she ruled Egypt," Marius tells Lestat. (Historical footnote: The first movie to make the queen of the Egyptians black also makes her a vampire. Is this progress?) Soon Akasha is alive all over, and has the hots for Lestat, making plans about how, together, they will rule the world.

Since this will be her only starring movie role, it's sad that her character has such a narrow emotional range. The Lestat-Akasha romance suffers by being conducted in declarative mode, with Akasha addressing her lover with the intimacy Queen Victoria would have lavished on her footman. Lestat digs her, though, because when he drinks her blood it makes him wild. Nothing good can come of this.

A more intriguing relationship is between Lestat and Marius, who seems to have a thing for him. Marius reappears in Lestat's life after so many centuries that Lestat comments on his outdated apparel. "How did you manage to slip through the fifties in red velvet?" he asks, forgetting that he slept through the 1950s himself and has probably not made much of a study of the decade's clothing styles. He welcomes Marius to Los Angeles and shows him the world from a perch on a painter's scaffold that hangs directly in front of Lestat's leather-clad crotch on a giant Sunset Boulevard outdoor advertisement. We get the feeling Marius would enjoy the view more if he turned around.

There is a showdown. Queen Akasha's subjects, fellow vampires, revolt against her tyrannical rule when she reveals her plans to rule, etc., the world, etc., together, etc., with Lestat.

The others hope to drink all of her blood, so that even if they die, she dies too. But Akasha is not without her defenses. All she has to do is point at enemies and they burst into flame, curl up into charred shadows of themselves, and float upward just like the wrapper from an Amaretti di Saronno cookie.

The movie doesn't reach the level of camp goofiness attained by films like *The Mummy Returns* and *Lara Croft: Tomb Raider,* perhaps because the filmmakers labor under the impression that Anne Rice's works must be treated respectfully. The key to a movie like this is to ask yourself, if these characters were not vampires, what would be interesting about them? The answer is, together they couldn't even rule the people in this bar.   ☞

Quills ★ ★ ★ ½
R, 123 m., 2000

Geoffrey Rush (Marquis de Sade), Kate Winslet (Madeleine), Joaquin Phoenix (Coulmier), Michael Caine (Royer-Collard), Billie Whitelaw (Madame LeClerc), Patrick Malahide (Delbene), Amelia Warner (Simone), Jane Menelaus (Renee Pelagie). Directed by Philip Kaufman and produced by Julia Chasman, Peter Kaufman, and Nick Wechsler. Screenplay by Doug Wright, based on his play.

Some are born evil, others choose evil, and some have evil thrust upon them. We are most inclined to forgive the members of the first category. The Marquis de Sade, for example, was hard-wired from birth as one of the most villainous of God's creatures. Although it is impossible to approve of him, it is possible to concede that he did what we are all enjoined to do: Taking the gifts and opportunities at hand, he achieved everything he possibly could. That his achievement is reprehensible does not entirely obscure the fact that his spirit was indomitable and his tenacity courageous. You know you've made your mark when "sadism" is named for you.

Philip Kaufman's *Quills* supplies us with a marquis toned down for popular consumption (you will not discover here that he thought an aristocrat like himself had the right to commit murder in search of pleasure). This marquis stands not so much for sexual license

as for freedom of artistic expression, and after he is locked up in an asylum and forbidden to write, he perseveres anyway, using his clothing, his skin, and the walls of his cell as surfaces, and his own blood and excrement in place of ink. A merciful deity would have supplied him with writer's block.

Kaufman's film, based on a play by Doug Wright, mostly takes place after the marquis (Geoffrey Rush) has once again gone too far, after the excesses of his writing and his life have exhausted the license and privilege granted to aristocracy. In 1801, at sixty-one, after twenty-seven years spent in various prisons, he is sealed up in the insane asylum at Charenton. There he finds a sympathetic friend in Father Coulmier (Joaquin Phoenix), a priest who thinks he should continue to write, perhaps to purge himself of his noxious fantasies.

The manuscripts are smuggled out of the asylum by Madeleine (Kate Winslet), and find a covert circulation before Napoleon assigns an administrator named Royer-Collard (Michael Caine) to crack down. The new man's sadistic measures bring out the best in de Sade, who mocks him, taunts him, outsmarts him, and remains indomitable almost to the moment of his death.

Kaufman has confided in interviews that Royer-Collard is inspired to some degree by Kenneth Starr. The type is familiar: the man fascinated by what he has forbidden himself to enjoy, savoring it vicariously through a victim he persecutes enviously. No one is quite so interested in sex as a puritan. The analogy with modern times breaks down, alas, if we seek a correspondence between de Sade and Clinton, whose milder transgressions would have flown quite beneath the marquis's radar.

Quills is not without humor in its telling of the horrendous last years of de Sade's life. There is, for example, the good cheer of Winslet's jolly, buxom laundry maid, who smuggles the manuscripts out of the prison. Father Coulmier is clearly stirred by her, but does not act, and we have the incongruity of the young, handsome man forbidden by religion from pursuing fruits which fall into the hands of the scabrous old letch.

Caine's Royer-Collard, on the other hand, is devoted to the pleasures of the flesh and keeps close watch on his too-young wife, Simone

(Amelia Warner), warning, "She is a rare bird and I intend to keep her caged." It is unmistakable that Royer-Collard is attracted to de Sade's sadism, and enjoys practicing it upon the man who gave it a name. If overt sinners are evil, how more contemptible are those who seek the same pleasures under the cover of hypocrisy. De Sade at least acknowledged his tastes.

Geoffrey Rush (the pianist from *Shine*) is a curious choice for de Sade; we might have imagined Willem Dafoe or Christopher Walken in the role, but Kaufman chooses not an actor associated with the bizarre but one associated with madness. De Sade is in the grasp of fixed ideas that sweep all sanity aside; unable to realize his fantasies in the asylum, he creates them through the written word, like a salesman or missionary determined to share his enthusiasm whether or not the world desires it. By the end, the words de Sade writes are indistinguishable, emotionally, from the pain he endures and invites by writing them.

Whether this film will please most audiences is a good question. It is more about the mind than the flesh, and de Sade's struggle is monomania to an excruciating extreme. Yet Kaufman *(The Right Stuff, The Unbearable Lightness of Being)* finds a tone that remains more entertaining than depressing, more absorbing than alarming. It was not much fun to be the marquis, but most of the time in this movie de Sade doesn't know that, and attacks each day with zest and curiosity. Those around him are inspired by a spirit so free, even if his tastes are inexplicable. There is a scene where he dictates a novel through a human chain of other prisoners, who seem more intrigued by his invention than repelled by his images. Audiences may have the same response; we do not share his tastes but we have a certain admiration for his obstinacy.

De Sade has been described as the ultimate extension of the libertarian ideal, but that is lunacy: He goes beyond ideology to madness. Still, he stands as an extreme illustration of the idea that society is best served if everybody behaves according to his own self-interests. And he gets the last laugh: In the face of Father Coulmier's liberal instinct to sympathize and Royer-Collard's conservative attempt to restrain, the marquis remains indomitably himself. It is in his nature. The message of *Quills* is perhaps that we are all expressions of our natures, and to live most successfully we must understand that. Good luck that hardly any of us are dealt such a bad hand as de Sade.

R

Ready to Rumble ★ ★
PG-13, 100 m., 2000

David Arquette (Gordie Boggs), Oliver Platt (Jimmy King), Scott Caan (Sean Dawkins), Bill Goldberg (Himself), Rose McGowan (Sasha), Diamond Dallas Page (Himself), Joe Pantoliano (Titus Sinclair), Martin Landau (Sal Bandini). Directed by Brian Robbins and produced by Bobby Newmyer and Jeffrey Silver. Screenplay by Steven Brill.

It must be a mixed blessing to be Michael Buffer. He is the man in the tuxedo famous for intoning, "Let's get . . . ready to RUMBLE?" before sporting events and, for all I know, weddings and bingo games. He is rich and famous, yes. But how many times a day/week/month/lifetime do you suppose he has to listen to people shouting Michael Buffer imitations into his ear? And is it discouraging that the excitement is over for him just as it's beginning for everyone else?

These thoughts ran through my mind during *Ready to Rumble*. Buffer appears in the movie and duly performs "Let's get ready to rumble," and so earnestly was I *not* ready to rumble that I wanted the camera to follow him out of the arena instead of staying for a three-cage fight to the death between Jimmy ("The King") King and Diamond Dallas Page.

It's not that I have anything against professional wrestling. I have a newfound respect for it after seeing the documentary *Beyond the Mat*, which establishes without a shadow of a doubt that when you are thrown out of the ring in a scripted fight with a prearranged winner, it nevertheless hurts when you hit the floor. I am in awe of wrestlers—not as athletes, but as masochists. They take a lickin' and keep on kickin'.

The problem with *Ready to Rumble* is that its hero is not a wrestler but an actor, Oliver Platt. Platt is a good comic actor and I have liked him in a lot of movies, but here he is not well used, and occupies a role that would have been better filled by a real wrestler. That is demonstrated every time Diamond Dallas Page is on the screen, playing himself with such ferocity that Platt seems to be playing Jimmy the King in a key heard only by himself.

The plot is easily summarized: *Dumb and Dumber Meet Dumbbell.* David Arquette and Scott Caan are Gordie and Sean, best pals in a Wyoming hamlet where watching the Monday night fights on cable brings the only joy into their lives as sanitation servicemen. By day they suction the contents out of Porta-Potties, and by night they hang out in the parking lot of the convenience store, lecturing callow youths on the glories of wrestling as America's finest sport.

They get tickets to The King's latest title defense, little realizing that the real kingmaker is Titus Sinclair (Joe Pantoliano), this movie's version of Vince McMahon. Titus has declared that The King will go down to Diamond Dallas, and by the end of the fight the loser has been kicked insensible by everyone on the card and banished from wrestling as a hopeless drunk.

When Gordie and Sean's tank truck overturns on the way home, creating a really nasty spill for the fire department to clean up, they take this as a sign that they must leave their town, find The King, and mastermind his comeback. Their plan involves enlisting the once-great, now aging Sal Bandini (Martin Landau) as a trainer. The King is not thrilled: "I don't need a trainer; I need a safe house!" He's right. Landau's scenes demonstrate that as an elderly wrestler he looks no more convincing than he did as a dying millionaire disco dancer in *B.A.P.S.* He's good in serious stuff (hint).

The movie is best when it deals with professional wrestling, and worst (which is most of the time) when it prefers a wheezy prefab plot to the possibilities of its subject. The machinations of a sexpot (Rose McGowan) are tired and predictable, and Platt, who might have done something with decent dialogue, is left on the sidelines while Arquette and Caan shout at each other in a forlorn attempt to reproduce the chemistry of Jim Carrey and Jeff Daniels in *Dumb and Dumber.* I gave that movie only two stars despite the fact that its dead parakeet scene caused me to laugh uncontrollably; now, after sitting through *Ready to Rumble*, with only the occasional grudging "ha!" I know better what a two-star movie looks like.

Recess: School's Out ★ ★ ½
G, 84 m., 2001

With the voices of: James Woods (Dr. Benedict), Andy Lawrence (T. J. Detweiler), Rickey D'Shon Collins (Vince), Jason Davis (Mikey), Ashley Johnson (Gretchen), Courtland Mead (Gus), Pam Segall (Ashley), Dabney Coleman (Principal Prickly), April Winchell (Miss Finster), Robert Goulet (Mikey's Singing Voice). Directed by Chuck Sheetz and produced by Stephen Swofford. Created by Paul Germain and Joe Ansolabehere. Screenplay by Jonathan Greenberg.

The highest school test scores in the world are recorded in Canada, Iceland, and Norway, according to the brilliant but twisted Dr. Benedict, villain of *Recess: School's Out*. And what else do those countries have in common? "It's snowing all the time." Benedict wants to be president, and part of his strategy is to raise U.S. test scores by using a secret green ray to nudge the moon into a different orbit, ending summer—and therefore summer vacation.

It's up to T. J. Detweiler, plucky grammar school kid, to save Earth, and summer vacation, in *Recess: School's Out*, a spin-off of the animated kids' TV program. He gets the responsibility because he's the only kid left behind when all the others board buses and roar off to summer camp. Meanwhile, Benedict moves his minions and their moon-moving equipment into the Third Street School, "back where it all began."

How so? In the 1960s, we learn, both Benedict and Principal Prickly were idealistic flower children. But then it rained on Benedict's dream, and he turned into the monster he is today. Prickly, on the other hand, simply grew old and lost his youthful enthusiasm in the day-to-day grind. As for Miss Finster, the draconian teacher, it's doubtful she was a child of the 1960s, although she retains some of the lingo (when she gets stuck trying to crawl through a basement window of the school, she cries out, "I'm stuck! Curse these bodacious hips of mine!").

Dr. Benedict, we learn, started out at Third Street School; his career prospered, and he was secretary of education before getting the boot because of his attempts to ban recess. In exile and isolation, his scheme escalated into an attack on the whole summer vacation, and there is a computer simulation of his dream, in which Earth enters a new ice age and the kids presumably all stay inside and study.

Recess is a Disney attempt to reach the same market that Nickelodeon taps with *Rug Rats*, and although it lacks the zany exuberance of *Rugrats in Paris* (2000), it's fast-footed and fun. *Rugrats in Paris* had charms for grown-ups, however, while *Recess: School's Out* seems aimed more directly at grade-schoolers. That makes the 1960s material problematical; do nine-year-olds really care about ancient history? Even if Myra, the fourteen-year-old "singing sensation," performs "Dancin' in the Streets" over the end titles?

The boom in animation has created a lot of voice-over work in Hollywood, and among the voices heard on *Recess* are Dabney Coleman as Principal Prickly, Andy Lawrence as T.J., and Robert Goulet as the singing voice of a character named Mikey (the song is "Green Tambourine," performed in a sequence made by animators who have obviously studied *Yellow Submarine* and the works of Peter Max).

The movie was directed by Chuck Sheetz, who has worked on shows like *King of the Hill* and *The Simpsons*. One of its charms is its defense of recess, which is, we learn, when all the real benefits of primary education take place. I recommend it for kids up to ten or eleven. Parents may find it amusing, but it doesn't have the two-track versatility of *Rugrats in Paris*, which worked for kids on one level and adults on another.

Red Planet ★ ★ ★
PG-13, 116 m., 2000

Val Kilmer (Gallagher), Carrie-Anne Moss (Bowman), Tom Sizemore (Burchenal), Benjamin Bratt (Santen), Simon Baker (Pettengill), Terence Stamp (Chantilas). Directed by Anthony Hoffman and produced by Mark Canton, Bruce Berman, and Jorge Saralegui. Screenplay by Chuck Pfarrer and Jonathan Lemkin.

Red Planet would have been a great 1950s science-fiction film. It embodies the kind of nuts-and-bolts sci-fi championed by John W. Campbell Jr. in his *Astounding* magazine—right down to the notion that a space mission would be staffed by research scientists, and although there would be a woman on board, she would not be the kind of woman depicted in an aluminum brassiere on the covers of his competitors. This is a film where much of the suspense involves the disappearance of algae.

The film has been sneered at in some quarters because it is not the kind of brainless, high-tech computerized effects extravaganza now in favor. I like its emphasis on situation and character. I've always been fascinated by zero-sum plots in which a task has to be finished within the available supplies of time, fuel, and oxygen.

Waiting for the screening to start, I was talking with a dive instructor about the challenge of diving inside glaciers. "Anytime you take away unobstructed access to the surface," he told me, "you're talking technical diving, and that makes you more of an astronaut than a diver." I thought of that during *Red Planet,* which is about four men who have essentially dived down to the surface of Mars, whose air is running out, and who do not have access to the spaceship circling above.

The movie takes place in 2025, when mankind has polluted Earth beyond the point of no return, and is seeking a new planet to colonize. Mars is bombarded with robot space probes carrying various strains of bioengineered algae. The Earth-born organisms seem to thrive, and green pastures spread on Mars. A space mission is launched with a crew of scientists who will investigate a curious thing. The algae seems to have disappeared. Really disappeared. It didn't simply die off, because that would have left withered remains. It seems to have . . . dematerialized.

This discovery takes place after a troubled voyage. The interplanetary ship, commanded by Bowman (Carrie-Anne Moss), has gone through a gamma ray storm, disabling a lot of its equipment. The Mars lander descends to the surface with Gallagher (Val Kilmer), Burchenal (Tom Sizemore), Santen (Benjamin Bratt), Pettengill (Simon Baker), and the scientist-philosopher Chantilas (Terence Stamp). It runs into trouble, too, has to jettison some of its equipment, and then there's a sensational landing scene. The lander is cocooned within huge, tough air bags so it can bounce to a soft landing. But when it bounces off a cliff, the ride gets rocky for the men inside.

Also along is AMEE, a robotic tracker and warrior that has, alas, not been programmed nearly carefully enough with Asimov's Three Laws of Robotics. The men are left with an incomplete landing module, and must depend on a supply station dropped by previous missions. And then . . .

Everything else should come as a surprise. What pleased me, however, was the nature of the situation they find on Mars. The movie's ads seem to suggest bug-eyed monsters of some sort, but the actual story developments are more ingenious and reasonable. John Campbell, who liked semiplausible scientific speculation in his stories, might have enjoyed the way *Red Planet* accounts for the disappearance of the algae. There is a scene—call it the fireworks scene—that in its own way is one of the more memorable encounters I've seen with extraterrestrial life forms.

The acting is serviceable. Most of it consists of functional observations and commands. Terence Stamp is given a brief opportunity to philosophize about the limitations of science, Val Kilmer is convincing as a competent space jockey with a mechanical and scientific background, and Carrie-Anne Moss, whose character Bowman is a nod to Dave Bowman from *2001,* is convincing as a no-nonsense pilot. But just like in 1950s sci-fi, the story's strong point isn't psychological depth or complex relationships, but brainy scientists trying to think their way out of a box that grows smaller every minute. To like that kind of story is to like this kind of movie.

Reindeer Games ★ ½

R, 98 m., 2000

Ben Affleck (Rudy), Charlize Theron (Ashley), Gary Sinise (Gabriel), Clarence Williams III (Merlin), James Frain (Nick), Dennis Farina (Jack Bangs), Isaac Hayes (Zook). Directed by John Frankenheimer and produced by Marty Katz, Bob Weinstein, and Chris Moore. Screenplay by Ehren Kruger.

Reindeer Games is the first all-Talking Killer picture. After the setup, it consists mostly of characters explaining their actions to one another. I wish I'd had a stopwatch to clock how many minutes are spent while one character holds a gun to another character's head and gabs. Charlize Theron and Gary Sinise between them explain so much they reminded me of Gertrude Stein's line about Ezra Pound: "He was a village explainer, excellent if you were a village, but if you were not, not."

Just a nudge, and the movie would fall over into self-parody, and maybe work better. But I fear it is essentially serious, or as serious as such goofiness can be. It opens in prison with cellmates Rudy (Ben Affleck) and Nick (James Frain). Both are about to be set free. Nick has engaged in a steamy correspondence with Ashley (Theron), one of those women who have long-distance romances with convicts. His cell wall is plastered with photos that make her look like a model for cosmetics ads.

But then (I am not giving away as much as it seems, or perhaps even what it seems) Nick is knifed in a prison brawl, and when Rudy walks out of prison and lays eyes on Ashley—well, what would you do? That's what he does. "I'm Nick," Rudy tells her. Soon they make wild and passionate love, which inevitably involves knocking things over and falling out of bed and continuing on the floor. You'd think if people were that much into sex, they'd pay more attention to what they were doing.

Then there's a major reality shift, and perhaps you'd better stop reading if you don't want to know that . . . Ashley's brother Gabriel (Gary Sinise) heads a gang of scummy gunrunners who think Rudy used to work in an Indian casino in upstate Michigan—because, of course, they think Rudy is Nick, and that's what Nick told Ashley about himself. Gabriel and his gang try to squeeze info about the casino's security setup out of Rudy, who says he isn't Nick, and then says he is Nick after all, and then says he isn't, and has so many reasons for each of his answers that Gabriel gets very confused, and keeps deciding to kill him, and deciding not to kill him, and deciding to kill him after all, until both characters seem stuck in a time loop.

There are other surprises, too, a lot of them, each with its explanation, usually accompanied by an explanation of the previous explanation, which now has to be re-explained in light of the new explanation. They all got a lot of 'splainin' to do.

The movie's weakness is mostly in its ludicrous screenplay by Ehren Kruger. The director, John Frankenheimer, is expert at moving the action along and doing what can be done with scenes that hardly anything can be done with. Ben Affleck and Charlize Theron soldier through changes of pace so absurd it takes superb control to keep straight faces. Theron's character looks soft and sweet sometimes, then hard and cruel other times, switching back and forth so often I commend her for not just passing a hand up and down in front of her face: smile, frown, smile, frown.

Perhaps the movie was originally intended to open at Christmas. That would explain the title and the sequence where the casino, which looks like a former Target store, is stuck up by five Santas. But nothing can explain the upbeat final scene, in which, after blood seeps into the Michigan snow, we get a fit of Robin Hood sentimentality. The moment to improve *Reindeer Games* was at the screenplay stage, by choosing another one.

Remember the Titans ★ ★ ★
PG, 113 m., 2000

Denzel Washington (Coach Boone), Will Patton (Coach Yoast), Wood Harris (Big Ju), Ryan Hurst (Bertier), Donald Faison (Petey), Craig Kirkwood (Rev), Ethan Suplee (Lewis Lastik), Kip Pardue (Sunshine). Directed by Boaz Yakin and produced by Jerry Bruckheimer and Chad Oman. Screenplay by Gregory Allen Howard.

Remember the Titans is a parable about racial harmony, yoked to the formula of a sports movie. Victories over racism and victories over opposing teams alternate so quickly that sometimes we're not sure if we're cheering for tolerance or touchdowns. Real life is never this simple, but then that's what the movies are for: to improve on life, and give it the illusion of form and purpose.

Denzel Washington and Will Patton are the stars, two football coaches, one black, one white, whose lives are linked for a season even though neither wants it that way. In 1971, a high school in Alexandria, Virginia, is integrated, and the board brings in Coach Boone (Washington) as the new head coach, replacing Coast Yoast (Patton), who is expected to become his assistant. Yoast understandably does not want to be demoted in the name of affirmative action. Boone doesn't like it either: He lost his own job in North Carolina, and "I can't do that to this man."

But Alexandria's black residents gather on Boone's lawn to cheer for the first black coach at the newly integrated high school, and Boone realizes he has a responsibility. So does Yoast: His white players say they won't play for a black coach, but Yoast doesn't want them to lose college scholarships, so he swallows his pride and agrees to be Boone's assistant, leading the whites back to practice.

All of this is said to be based on life, and no doubt largely is, but life was perhaps harder and more wounding than the film. *Remember the Titans* is not an activist 1970s picture, but more conciliatory in tone. It is more about football than race relations, and it wants us to leave the theater feeling not angry or motivated, but good.

We do. There are true and touching moments in the film, on top of its undeniable entertainment value. I was moved by a scene near the end where an injured white player, who once said he would not play with blacks, now only wants his black "brother" in the hospital room. And there is a delicate series of scenes in which the same white player breaks up with his girlfriend rather than break the bonds he's formed with teammates during an August training camp.

Those training camp scenes of course include the usual identifiable types (the fat kid, the long-haired Californian, the "Rev") who first clash, then bond. It's been seen before, but the director, Boaz Yakin *(Fresh)*, brings old situations to new life and carries us along in the current of a skilled popular entertainment. I like the way he shows Boone forcing the blacks and whites to get to know one another.

I admired the way his screenplay, by Gregory Allen Howard, doesn't make Boone noble and Yoast a racist, but shows them both as ambitious and skilled professionals. There are times when Boone treats his players more like marines than high school kids, and Yoast tells him so. And times when Yoast tries to comfort black players that Boone has chewed out, and Boone accuses him of coddling blacks as he would never coddle his fellow whites.

These scenes are tricky, and Washington and Patton find just the right notes to negotiate them. Washington is gifted at delivering big speeches without sounding portentous or seeming to strain. There's an early-morning training run that leads the players to the Gettysburg battlefield, and his remarks there place their experiences in a larger context.

Still, the story sweeps certain obvious questions under the rug.

(1) We see that the whites don't want to play with the blacks, and are afraid of losing their starting positions. But what about the blacks? Weren't they in a black high school last year? Aren't they losing their team too? Aren't some of them going to be replaced by white starters? The movie shows the whites as resentful and possessive but assumes the black players are grateful for the chance to leave their old school and integrate the other team. Maybe they are, and maybe they aren't. The movie doesn't say.

(2) Since there was certainly an all-black high school in town until this year, there must have been a black coach at that school. What happened to him? Did Coach Boone put him out of work too? That crowd of cheering blacks on Boone's front lawn—have they so quickly forgotten the team and coach they used to cheer?

In the real world such questions would be what the story was all about. But then we would have an entirely different kind of film. *Remember the Titans* has the outer form of a brave statement about the races in America, but the soul of a sports movie in which everything is settled by the obligatory last play in the last seconds of the championship game. Whether the Titans win or lose has nothing to do with the season they have played and what they were trying to prove. But it has everything to do with the movie's sleight of hand, in which we cheer the closing touchdown as if it is a victory over racism.

The movie is heartfelt, yes, and I was moved by it, but it plays safe. On the sound track we hear lyrics like, "I've seen fire and I've seen rain," and, "Ain't no mountain high enough," but not other lyrics that must also have been heard in Alexandria in 1971, such as, "We shall overcome."

The Replacements ★ ★
PG-13, 114 m., 2000

Keanu Reeves (Shane Falco), Gene Hackman (Jimmy McGinty), Brooke Langton (Annabelle Farrell), Orlando Jones (Clifford Franklin), Jon Favreau (Daniel Bateman), Rhys Ifans (Nigel Gruff), Faizon Love (Jamal Jackson), Michael "Bear" Taliferro (Andre Jackson). Directed by Howard Deutch and produced by Dylan Sellers. Screenplay by Vince McKewin.

The Replacements is a slaphappy entertainment painted in broad strokes, two coats thick. It's like a standard sports movie, but with every point made twice or three times—as if we'd never seen one before. And the musical score provides such painstaking instructions about how to feel during every scene, it's like the booklet that tells you how to unpack your computer.

Gene Hackman and Keanu Reeves star, and this is not a distinguished entry in their filmographies. As the movie opens, a football strike is under way, and the crusty old team owner (Jack Warden) has hired Jimmy McGinty (Gene Hackman) to coach the team. Hackman says he'll assemble a pickup team—but only if he can pick the players himself. His first choice is a kid named Shane Falco (Reeves), currently scraping gunk off the sides of boats, but known to McGinty as a promising quarterback.

Perhaps it will help to evoke the mood of the movie if we start with Falco's first scene. He is underwater, working on a boat, when he sees a football on the bottom. He swims down, grabs it, and *discovers it is a trophy—engraved with his own name!* No doubt he tossed it there during a time of despair. This is why they pay screenwriters so well, to think this stuff up. He throws an underwater pass. Just can't keep the kid down.

There is a convention, older than Shakespeare, that drama requires low characters to provide the broth through which the exalted characters swim. In *The Replacements*, Hackman and Reeves are the heroes, and most of the other characters are low comedy, includ-

ing a Welsh placekicker (Rhys Ifans) who chain-smokes, even while actually on the playing field, and other recruits including a sumo wrestler, a mad dog who attacks anything that is red, and a deaf lineman ("Look at it this way. He'll never be called offsides on an audible").

John Debney's musical score works on this material something like the alternate commentary track on a DVD. It comments on every scene. When Reeves talks, there is sometimes actually a violin beneath him, to lend additional nobility. Hackman gets resolute music. The team has a group of pom-pom cheerleaders who seem to have wandered in from a soft-core film of their own, and there is a scene where their lascivious choreography on the sidelines distracts the San Diego team so severely that our guys pull off a key play. Never before in the history of football movies have the cheerleaders had a larger role than the opposing team.

An even more curious role is given to John Madden and Pat Summerall, playing themselves as play-by-play announcers. It is not *that* hard in the movies to create the illusion that the announcers are actually in a real stadium looking at a real game. But it's too much for *The Replacements*, which stashes them in a booth with a couple of TV monitors and has them stand around awkwardly as if looking at a game. Sometimes they're not even looking in the same direction.

There are of course personal issues to be settled in the movie, and a romance between Falco and cute pom-pommer Annabelle Farrell (Brooke Langton). Also the nasty first-string quarterback from the regular season (Brett Cullen), who fancies Annabelle and hates Falco. And backstage politics involving whether the owner will respect his pledge to let the old coach call the shots.

The movie's approach to labor unions is casual, to say the least. Reeves and all of his teammates are scabs, but *The Replacements* can't be bothered with details like that, and indeed seems to think the regular players are the bad guys. The standard way the media handles such situations is to consider striking players as overpaid and selfish. Of course owners, sponsors, and the media, who dine off the players' brief careers, are more overpaid and more selfish, but that's the way the world turns.

The football footage is at least mostly comprehensible; director Howard Deutch tries to make sense of the plays, instead of opting for shapeless montages of colors and action, as Oliver Stone did in *Any Given Sunday*. But Stone's characters were conceived on a higher level—more complex, smarter, realistic—and his issues were more grown-up, compared to the slam-bam cheerleading that passes for thought here. It goes without saying that everything is settled in the last play in the last seconds of the last game of the season, and if you think *The Replacements* has the nerve to surprise you, you've got the wrong movie.

Requiem for a Dream ★ ★ ★ ½

NO MPAA RATING, 102 m., 2000

Ellen Burstyn (Sara Goldfarb), Jared Leto (Harry Goldfarb), Jennifer Connelly (Marion Silver), Marlon Wayans (Tyrone C. Love), Christopher McDonald (Tappy Tibbons), Louise Lasser (Ada), Keith David (Little John), Sean Gullette (Arnold the Shrink). Directed by Darren Aronofsky and produced by Eric Watson III and Palmer West. Screenplay by Aronofsky, based on the novel by Hubert Selby Jr.

Alcoholics or drug addicts feel wrong when they don't feel right. Eventually they feel very wrong, and *must* feel right, and at that point their lives spiral down into some sort of final chapter—recovery if they're lucky, hopelessness and death if they're not.

What is fascinating about *Requiem for a Dream*, the new film by Darren Aronofsky, is how well he portrays the mental states of his addicts. When they use, a window opens briefly into a world where everything is right. Then it slides shut, and life reduces itself to a search for the money and drugs to open it again. Nothing else is remotely as interesting.

Aronofsky is the director who made the hallucinatory π(1998), about a paranoid genius who seems on the brink of discovering the key to—well, God, or the stock market, or whatever else his tormentors imagine. That movie, made on a tiny budget, was astonishing in the way it suggested its hero's shifting prism of reality. Now, with greater resources, Aronofsky brings a new urgency to the drug movie by trying to reproduce, through his subjective camera, how his characters feel, or want to feel, or fear to feel.

As the movie opens, a housewife is chaining her television to the radiator. It's no use. Her son frees it and wheels it down the street to a pawn shop. This is a regular routine, we gather; anything in his mother's house is a potential source of funds for drug money. The son's girlfriend and best friend are both addicted too. So is the mother: to television and sugar. We recognize the actors, but barely. Sara Goldfarb (Ellen Burstyn) is fat and blowzy in her sloppy housedresses; if you've just seen her in the revived *Exorcist*, her appearance will come as a shock. Her son, Harry (Jared Leto), is gaunt and haunted; so is his girlfriend, Marion (Jennifer Connelly). His pal Tyrone is played by Marlon Wayans, who has lost all the energy and cockiness of his comic persona and is simply trying to survive in a reasonable manner. Tyrone suspects, correctly, that he's in trouble but Harry is in more.

Sara's life passes in modest retirement. She joins the other old ladies out front of their building, where they line up their lawn chairs in the sun. She's addicted to a game show whose host (Christopher McDonald) leads the audience in chanting, "We got a winner!" She's a sweet, naive woman who gets a junk phone call that misleads her into thinking she may be a potential guest on the show. She obsesses about wearing her favorite red dress, and gets diet pills from the doctor to help her lose weight.

She does lose weight, and also her mind. "The pills don't work so good anymore," she complains to the druggist, and then starts doubling up her usage. Her doctor isn't even paying attention when she complains dubiously about hallucinations (the refrigerator has started to threaten her). Meanwhile, Harry talks to Marion about the one big score that would "get us back on track." Tyrone can see that Harry is losing it, but Marion, under Harry's spell, has sex with a shrink (Sean Gullette, star of π) and is eventually selling herself for stag party gang-gropes.

Aronofsky is fascinated by the way in which the camera can be used to suggest how his characters see things. I've just finished a shot-by-shot analysis of Hitchcock's *The Birds* at the Virginia Film Festival; he does the same thing, showing us some things and denying us others so that we are first plunged into a subjective state and then yanked back to objectivity with a splash of cold reality.

Here Aronofsky uses extreme close-ups to show drugs acting on his characters. First we see the pills, or the fix, filling the screen, because that's all the characters can think about. Then the injection, swallowing, or sniffing—because *that* blots out the world. Then the pupils of their eyes dilating. All done with acute exaggeration of sounds.

These sequences are done in fast motion, to show how quickly the drugs take effect—and how disappointingly soon they fade. The in-between times edge toward desperation. Aronofsky cuts between the mother, a prisoner of her apartment and diet pills, and the other three. Early in the film, in a technique I haven't seen before, he uses a split screen in which the space on both sides is available to the other (Sara and Harry each have half the screen, but their movements enter into each other's halves). This is an effective way of showing them alone together. Later, in a virtuoso closing sequence, he cuts between all four major characters as they careen toward their final destinations.

Ellen Burstyn isn't afraid to play Sara Goldfarb flat-out as a collapsing ruin (Aronofsky has mercy on her by giving her some fantasy scenes where she appears on TV and we see that she is actually still a great-looking woman). Connelly, who is so much a sex symbol that she, too, could have disgraced herself in *Charlie's Angels,* has consistently gone for risky projects and this may be her riskiest; the movie is inspired by Hubert Selby Jr.'s lacerating novel, and in her own way Connelly goes as far as Jennifer Jason Leigh did in an equally courageous, quite different, film based on *Last Exit to Brooklyn,* another Selby novel. Leto and Wayans have a road trip together, heading for Florida, that is like a bleaker echo of Joe Buck and Ratso Rizzo's Florida odyssey in *Midnight Cowboy.* Leto's suppurating arm, punished by too many needles, is like a motif for his life.

The movie was given the worthless NC-17 rating by the MPAA; rejecting it, Artisan Enter-

tainment is asking theaters to enforce an adults-only policy. I can think of an exception: Anyone under seventeen who is thinking of experimenting with drugs might want to see this movie, which plays like a travelogue of hell.

Resident Evil ★
R, 100 m., 2002

Milla Jovovich (Alice/Janus Prospero/Marsha Thompson), Michelle Rodriguez (Rain Ocampo), Eric Mabius (Matt), James Purefoy (Spence Parks), Colin Salmon (James P. Shade), Marisol Nichols (Dana), Joseph May (Blue). Directed by Paul Anderson and produced by Anderson, Jeremy Bolt, Bernd Eichinger, and Samuel Hadida. Screenplay by Anderson.

Resident Evil is a zombie movie set in the twenty-first century and therefore reflects several advances over twentieth-century films. For example, in twentieth-century slasher movies, knife blades make a sharpening noise when being whisked through thin air. In the twenty-first century, large metallic objects make crashing noises just by being looked at.

The vast Umbrella Corporation, whose secret laboratory is the scene of the action, specializes in high-tech weapons and genetic cloning. It can turn a little DNA into a monster with a nine-foot tongue. Reminds me of the young man from Kent. You would think Umbrella could make a door that doesn't make a slamming noise when it closes, but its doors make slamming noises even when they're open. The narration tells us that Umbrella products are in "90 percent of American homes," so it finishes behind Morton salt.

The movie is *Dawn of the Dead* crossed with *John Carpenter's Ghosts of Mars,* with zombies not as ghoulish as the first and trains not as big as the second. The movie does however have Milla Jovovich and Michelle Rodriguez. According to the Internet Movie Database, Jovovich plays "Alice/Janus Prospero/Marsha Thompson," although I don't believe anybody ever calls her anything. I think some of those names come from the original video game. Rodriguez plays "Rain Ocampo," no relation to the Phoenix family. In pairing classical and literary references, the match of Alice and Janus

Prospero is certainly the best name combo since Huckleberry P. Jones/Pa Hercules was portrayed by Ugh-Fudge Bwana in *Forbidden Zone* (1980).

The plot: Vials of something that looks like toy coils of plastic DNA models are being delicately manipulated behind thick shields in an airtight chamber by remote-controlled robot hands; when one of the coils is dropped, the factory automatically seals its exits and gasses and drowns everyone inside. Umbrella practices zero tolerance. We learn that the factory, code named The Hive, is buried half a mile below the surface. Seven investigators go down to see what happened. Three are killed, but Alice/Janus Prospero/Marsha, Rain Ocampo, Matt, and Spence survive in order to be attacked for sixty minutes by the dead Hive employees, who have turned into zombies. Meanwhile, the monster with the nine-foot tongue is mutating. (Eventually, its tongue is nailed to the floor of a train car and it is dragged behind it on the third rail. I hate it when that happens.)

These zombies, like the *Dawn of the Dead* zombies, can be killed by shooting them, so there is a lot of zombie shooting, although not with the squishy green-goo effect of George Romero's 1978 film. The zombies are like vampires, since when one bites you it makes you a zombie. What I don't understand is why zombies are so graceless. They walk with the lurching shuffle of a drunk trying to skate through urped Slurpees to the men's room.

There is one neat effect when characters unwisely venture into a corridor and the door slams shut on them. Then a laser beam passes at head level, decapitating one. Another beam whizzes past at waist level, cutting the second in two while the others duck. A third laser pretends to be high but then switches to low, but the third character outsmarts it by jumping at the last minute. Then the fourth laser turns into a grid that dices its victim into pieces the size of a Big Mac. Since the grid is inescapable, what were the earlier lasers about? Does the corridor have a sense of humor?

Alice/Janus Prospero/Marsha Thompson and her colleagues are highly trained scientists, which leads to the following exchange when they stare at a pool of zombie blood on the floor.

Alice/J.P./M.T./Rain (I forget which): "It's coagulating!"
Matt/Spence (I forget which): "That's not possible!"
"Why not?!?"
"Because blood doesn't do that until you're dead!"

How does the blood on the floor know if you're dead? The answer to this question is so obvious I am surprised you would ask. Because it is zombie blood.

The characters have no small talk. Their dialogue consists of commands, explanations, exclamations, and ejaculations. Yes, an ejaculation can be dialogue. If you live long enough you may find that happening frequently.

Oh, and the film has a Digital Readout. The Hive is set to lock itself forever after sixty minutes have passed, so the characters are racing against time. In other words, after it shuts all of its doors and gasses and drowns everybody, it waits sixty minutes and *really* shuts its doors—big time. No wonder the steel doors make those slamming noises. In their imagination, they're practicing. Creative visualization, it's called. I became inspired, and visualized the theater doors slamming behind me.

Return to Me ★ ★ ★
PG, 115 m., 2000

David Duchovny (Bob Rueland), Minnie Driver (Grace Briggs), Carroll O'Connor (Marty O'Reilly), Robert Loggia (Angelo Pardipillo), Bonnie Hunt (Megan Dayton), James Belushi (Joe Dayton), David Alan Grier (Charlie Johnson), Joely Richardson (Elizabeth Rueland), Eddie Jones (Emmett McFadden). Directed by Bonnie Hunt and produced by Jennie Lew Tugend. Screenplay by Hunt and Don Lake.

Here's an old-fashioned love story so innocent, so naive, so sweet and sincere that you must leave your cynicism at the door or choose another movie. Bonnie Hunt's *Return to Me* could have been made in 1955, starring Doris Day and James Stewart. It has been made in 2000, starring Minnie Driver and David Duchovny, and I am happy that it has.

Duchovny stars as Bob, a Chicago architect

married to Elizabeth (Joely Richardson), who works at the Lincoln Park Zoo. Scenes establishing their happiness are intercut with hospital scenes involving Grace (Driver), who will die of heart disease unless she receives a transplant. To the surprise of nobody in the audience, Elizabeth dies in a tragic accident, and Grace is given her heart.

At the very moment when it starts beating in her chest, Bob, grieving at home, seems to sense it, as heartbeats on the sound track underline the segue. And a year later, Grace and Bob meet in the Old Town family-run restaurant where she works and lives. It is, for both of them, love at first sight, and their romance blossoms until she discovers something that Bob does not know—it is Elizabeth's heart beating in her chest.

Do not fear I have revealed too much of the story, because all of this is essentially setup, easily anticipated. What gives the movie its gentle charm is not the melodramatic story, but the warmth of the performances and the way the movie pokes merrily along, teasing us with rewards and disappointments.

The key element in the success, I think, is the illusion that Bob and Grace are truly in love. Duchovny and Driver (who has a gift for vulnerability) have an unforced chemistry that feels right. It is crucial in a story of this sort that we want the couple to be together—that we care about them. Otherwise we are simply looking at the puppet strings. I did like them, and felt protective toward them, and apprehensive as their inevitable problems approached.

The setting of the film is also old-fashioned, and a little too picturesque for my taste. Many of the scenes play in O'Reilly's Italian restaurant (actually the Twin Anchors), where the Irish and Italian branches of Grace's family offer such contradictory menu choices as chicken vesuvio and corned beef and cabbage. What is strangest about the restaurant is not the menu but the hours: O'Reilly's seems to close early every night so that the old cronies who run the place can sit around the back table, playing poker and holding desultory debates on the relative merits of Frank Sinatra, Dean Martin, and Vic Damone.

These stalwarts include Carroll O'Connor and Robert Loggia as, of course, the Irish and Italian patriarchs, O'Connor's accent a shade

too thick. The guys are all busybodies, peering through a back window into the rear garden where many of the key scenes take place, and playing matchmakers for all they're worth. A little trimming of their scenes wouldn't have hurt.

There is, however, a nice unforced feel to the home life of Grace's best friends, Megan and Joe Dayton, played by Hunt and James Belushi with a relaxed domesticity that makes their characters feel real, and not just helpers designed to speed a scene or two. The emphasis on the film is on friends and family, on a much-loved neighborhood woman who moves in a circle of people who want her to be happy.

Watching the film, I became aware that it lacked the gimmicks of many recent romances. It believes in love and fate, stuff like that. Its innocence is crucial to the plot, because much depends on Bob not seeing the scar on Grace's chest while their courtship moves along. In today's sex-happy movies, the secret would have been revealed when they slept together on their second date, but *Return to Me* convincingly lets them move slowly toward intimacy, so that Grace's delayed nudity creates effective tension.

No doubt this film will be disemboweled by cynics among the reviewers. It offers an easy target. It is almost an act of courage, the way it refuses to hedge its bets or cater to irony. It is what it is, without apology or compromise. It made me smile a lot. I have tried to describe it accurately, for the benefit of those who will like it, and those who will not. You know who you are.

Return to Never Land ★ ★ ★
G, 76 m., 2002

With the voices of: Blayne Weaver (Peter Pan), Harriet Owen (Jane), Corey Burton (Captain Hook), Jeff Bennett (Smee/Starkey and Wibbles), Kath Soucie (Wendy/Narrator), Andrew McDonough (Danny). An animated film directed by Robin Budd and Donovan Cook and produced by Christopher Chase and Dan Rounds. Screenplay by Carter Crocker and Temple Matthews.

The opening titles tell us this is "Peter Pan in Return to Never Land," and indeed, why can't an animated character be a movie star? Years have passed since the end of the first story—London is reeling under the Blitz—and Wendy has grown up, married, and produced a daughter, Jane. But Peter Pan, Tinker Bell, the Lost Boys, and Captain Hook all remain unchanged in Never Land.

During all of those years Hook has continued to search for his lost treasure, which was, he believes, stolen by Peter and hidden somewhere on the island. As the film opens, Jane indulges her mother's stories about fairies that can fly. She doesn't believe them, but is persuaded when kidnapped by Hook and his men—who fly in their pirate ship over London, luckily without engaging any antiaircraft batteries.

Hook believes Jane may be the key to finding the treasure—or at the least a way to pry the secret out of Peter. We can almost sympathize with his impatience. The original *Peter Pan* hurtled through its narrative, and then left him on hold for twenty-five years, gnashing his teeth and spinning his wheels. All the same, Never Land rules apply, and at one point Tinker Bell is grounded because, yes, Jane doesn't believe in fairies.

Of the voice-over talent, Corey Burton is almost inevitably the star, because he's assigned Captain Hook, one of those roles that sort of directs itself. Blayne Weaver is fine as Peter Pan, but it's interesting that none of the voice talents sing any of the movie's songs; they appear on the sound track as commentaries or parallels to the action.

Return to Never Land is a bright and energetic animated comedy, with all the slick polish we expect from Disney, but it's not much more. This one feels like it had a narrow escape from the direct-to-video market. It's not a major item like *Monsters, Inc.* and lacks the in-jokes and sly references that allow a movie like that to function on two levels. It's more of a Saturday afternoon stop for the kiddies—harmless, skillful, and aimed at grade-schoolers.

Riding in Cars with Boys ★ ★ ★
PG-13, 132 m., 2001

Drew Barrymore (Beverly Donofrio), Sara Gilbert (Tina), Steve Zahn (Raymond), Mika Boorem (Young Beverly), Brittany Murphy (Fay), Adam Garcia (Jason), Lorraine Bracco (Beverly's Mother), James Woods (Beverly's Father), Rosie Perez (Shirley). Directed by Penny Marshall and produced by James L. Brooks, Laurence Mark, Sara Colleton, Richard Sakai, and Julie Ansell. Screenplay by Morgan Upton Ward, based on the memoir by Beverly Donofrio.

"I'm twenty-two, and I still haven't accepted that this is my life," says Beverly Donofrio (Drew Barrymore), the heroine of *Riding in Cars with Boys*. She has a drunken and shiftless husband, a son from a teenage pregnancy, and a run-down house on a dead-end street in a section of town well known to the police. It doesn't help that her father is the chief of police.

Her problems all started not from riding in cars with boys, but from parking in cars with boys, and getting pregnant. Her wisdom in choosing the father didn't help. Ray (Steve Zahn) is an aimless slacker with a basically good heart, not too many smarts, and a life that's moving way too fast for him to keep up while he's using drugs and booze. His wife is manifestly smarter than he is, although not smart enough to avoid blaming her life on everyone but herself.

Riding in Cars with Boys is directed by Penny Marshall and based on a memoir by the real Beverly Donofrio (reportedly much revised by the screenwriters). It's a brave movie, in the way it centers on a mother who gets trapped in the wrong life, doesn't get out for a long time, takes her misery out on her son, and blames everything on her fate and bad luck. The movie traces a series of developments that dig her deeper into unhappiness. If only she hadn't gotten pregnant. If only the father hadn't been Ray. If only her parents had been easier to talk to. If only . . . well, if only she hadn't gone riding in cars with boys. The best way to avoid the problems of teenage pregnancy, as Beverly would be the first to tell you, is by not getting pregnant.

The movie is a showcase performance for Barrymore, who ages from fifteen to thirty-six, who doggedly plugs away trying to take classes and win college scholarships, who is heroic in her efforts to give her son, Jason, a right start in life, but whose fatal character flaw is that every time she looks at Jason she sees him as the reason for her misery. There's a key scene where Ray is supposed to baby-sit Jason while Beverly goes for a scholarship interview. Ray forgets. She has to take the kid along, and his presence possibly costs her the scholarship. "For me," Jason remembers later, "it's not how Ray let her down, it's about how my mere presence at the age of three crushed all of her dreams."

Steve Zahn's performance is crucial to the film. He has played dim bulbs before (*Joy Ride, Happy, Texas*), but usually for comic effect. Here he creates a character from the ground up, a dead-on accurate study of a man whose addiction to alcohol and drugs is simply too much for him to negotiate, so that he wakes up already defeated by the struggle ahead. How can you ask a man to do anything constructive when he's already exhausted by the task of feeding his system its daily fix? That he wants to do better, that he loves his son, that he knows his wife's resentment is justified, arouses our pity: He pays the price every second of his trembling existence for his shortcomings.

The movie opens with Jason as a young man, driving with his mother for a meeting with the father he barely remembers. She has written a book about her life, and needs his signature on a release form to protect the publishers against a lawsuit. This meeting will be one of the most painful scenes in the movie (underlined by the presence of Ray's second wife, played by Rosie Perez as the crown of thorns to top his other sufferings). What Jason sees clearly is that his mother is more concerned about her book than about how Jason will react to this sight of the broken, smelly, pathetic wreck that is his father.

Beverly has been a dutiful mother but not a wise one. No child can carry the burden of a parent's unhappiness, and a parent who demands that is practicing a form of abuse. Because the movie is honest enough to see that, *Riding in Cars with Boys* is brave—not the story of plucky Drew Barrymore struggling through poverty and divorce to become a best-selling author, but the story of a woman whose book, when it is published, will be small consolation.

Perhaps her unhappiness begins with *her* parents—the police chief (James Woods) and his wife (Lorraine Bracco). They are not bad

people but, like their daughter, they are more concerned with what is "right" than with how to parent with love. And the failing goes down to the third generation, in a remarkable scene where little Jason rats on his own mother. Desperate for money, she has allowed a neighbor to dry some weed in her oven, and (1) the kid actually tells his grandfather the cop, and (2) the cop actually arrests his own daughter. It's curious how by the end of the movie the mother is not only blaming the son, but the son the mother, and it's the stumblebum father who emerges with some credit for at least blaming himself.

A film like this is refreshing and startling in the way it cuts loose from formula and shows us confused lives we recognize. Hollywood tends to reduce stories like this to simplified redemption parables in which the noble woman emerges triumphant after a lifetime of surviving loser men. This movie is closer to the truth: A lot depends on what happens to you, and then a lot depends on how you let it affect you. Life has not been kind to Beverly, and Beverly has not been kind to life. Maybe there'll be another book in a few years where she sees how, in some ways, she can blame herself.

The Road to El Dorado ★ ★ ★
PG, 83 m., 2000

With the voices of: Kevin Kline (Tulio), Kenneth Branagh (Miguel), Rosie Perez (Chel), Armand Assante (Tzekel-Kan), Edward James Olmos (The Chief), Jim Cummings (Cortez), Frank Welker (Altivo), Elton John (Narrator). Directed by Eric "Bibo" Bergeron and Don Paul and produced by Bonne Radford and Brooke Breton. Screenplay by Ted Elliott and Terry Rossio.

There is a moment in *The Road to El Dorado* where the two heroes and their profoundly dubious horse are in a rowboat somewhere in the ocean off of Central America. It looks like the end. Then a sea bird appears, circles, and lands on their boat. This is a good omen. Land must be near. Then the bird drops dead. Bad sign. Then a shark leaps out of the sea and snaps up the bird in one gulp. Piling gag on top of gag is the strategy of the film, a bright and zesty animated comedy from DreamWorks.

In the studio's quest to compete with Disney in the feature-length animation sweepstakes, it's a worthy entry. It's not as quirky as *Antz* or as grown-up as *The Prince of Egypt,* but as silly fun it does nicely, and no wonder: Its directors are Disney veterans, and the sound track includes such effective cartoon voices as Kevin Kline, Kenneth Branagh, Armand Assante, Edward James Olmos, and the unsinkable Rosie Perez.

As the movie opens, the heroes, Tulio (Kline) and Miguel (Branagh), are gambling in a waterfront dive in Spain, 1519. They win a map to the treasures of El Dorado, before it's discovered that their dice are loaded and they beat a hasty retreat—pretending to duel with each other to confuse their pursuers. One thing leads to another, and they find themselves on board Cortez's ship as the explorer sails for South America. They're discovered, sentenced to flogging and enslavement, and escape with their horse in a rowboat, which brings us to the bird, the shark, and landfall at a point that corresponds exactly with the treasure map.

The Road to El Dorado doesn't have a hero; it's about supporting characters. In other hands, the story might have centered around Cortez, the explorer, whose ship catches up to Tulio and Miguel in the new land. But this is the story of two pals caught up in events beyond their comprehension, after the roly-poly local chief (voice by Edward James Olmos) mistakes them for gods. The plot then recycles Kipling's *The Man Who Would Be King:* One likes being a god, the other doesn't. Along the way, they get a sidekick of their own, Chel, a local woman. She's voiced by Perez, and looks like her too. She learns their secret—they aren't gods, only men, but likes them anyway, and decides she wants in on their team when the priest (Armand Assante) devises a monster to destroy them.

The movie has songs by Elton John, which may grow on me, but haven't yet, and some funny comedy sequences. The best may be the invention of the game of basketball, with a living ball—a round little creature who contributes his own moves to the game. More comedy comes as the friends realize the game is up, and try to sneak away with some gold of their own.

Freed of a towering central figure like Poc-

ahontas or Tarzan, *The Road to El Dorado* is liberated for goofiness. There are no serious themes lurking about, or uplifting lessons to learn—just a couple of con men in over their heads, their gal pal, and a horse that some of the time is smarter than the other three put together. (Since the horse doesn't speak, it's able to exploit the miming gifts of the animators.) This is not a landmark in the history of feature animation, but it's bright and has good energy and the kinds of witty asides that entertain the adults in the margins of the stuff for the kids.

Road to Perdition ★ ★ ★
R, 119 m., 2002

Tom Hanks (Michael Sullivan), Paul Newman (John Rooney), Tyler Hoechlin (Michael Sullivan Jr.), Jude Law (Maguire, aka The Reporter), Anthony LaPaglia (Al Capone), Daniel Craig (Connor Rooney), Stanley Tucci (Frank Nitti), Jennifer Jason Leigh (Annie Sullivan). Directed by Sam Mendes and produced by Mendes, Dean Zanuck, and Richard D. Zanuck. Screenplay by David Self, based on the graphic novel by Max Allan Collins and Richard Piers Rayner.

Road to Perdition is like a Greek tragedy, dealing out remorseless fates for all the characters. Some tragedies, like "Hamlet," are exhilarating, because we have little idea how quirks of character will bring about the final doom. But the impact of Greek tragedy seems muted to me, because it's preordained. Since *Road to Perdition* is in that tradition, it loses something. It has been compared to *The Godfather,* but *The Godfather* was about characters with free will, and here the characters seem to be performing actions already long since inscribed in the books of their lives.

Yet the movie has other strengths to compensate for the implacable progress of its plot. It is wonderfully acted. And no movie this year will be more praised for its cinematography; Conrad L. Hall's work seems certain to win the Academy Award. He creates a limbo of darkness, shadow, night, fearful faces half-seen, cold, and snow. His characters stand in downpours, the rain running off the brims of their fedoras and soaking the shoulders of their thick wool overcoats. Their feet must always be cold. The photography creates a visceral chill.

The story involves three sets of fathers and sons—two biological, the third emotional—and shows how the lives they lead make ordinary love between them impossible. Tom Hanks plays Michael Sullivan, an enforcer for a suburban branch of the Chicago mob, circa 1931. Tyler Hoechlin plays his son Michael Jr., a solemn-eyed twelve-year-old. After his brother, Peter, asks, "What does Dad do for a job?" Michael Jr. decides to find out for himself. One night he hides in a car, goes along for the ride, and sees a man killed. Not by his father, but what difference does it make?

Sullivan works for John Rooney (Paul Newman), the mob boss, who is trim and focused and uses few words. John's son Connor (Daniel Craig) is a member of the mob. Sullivan finds out that Connor has been stealing from his father, and that sets up the movie's emotional showdown, because Sullivan thinks of John like his own father, and John speaks of Sullivan as a son. "Your mother knows I love Mr. Rooney," Michael Sr. tells his son. "When we had nothing, he gave us a home."

Men who name their sons after themselves presumably hope the child will turn out a little like them. This is not the case with Michael Sr., who has made a pact with evil in order to support his wife (Jennifer Jason Leigh) and two boys in comfort. Unlike Rooney, he doesn't want his son in the business. The movie's plot asks whether it is possible for fathers to spare their sons from the costs of their sins. It also involves sons who feel they are not the favorite. "Did you like Peter better than me?" Michael Jr. asks his father, after his little brother has been killed. And later Sullivan goes to see Mr. Rooney, and cannot understand why Rooney would prefer his son Connor, who betrayed and stole from him, to his loyal employee who is "like a son."

The movie is directed by Sam Mendes, from a graphic novel by Max Allan Collins and Richard Piers Rayner, much revised by screenwriter David Self. This is only Mendes's second film, but recall that his first, *American Beauty,* won Oscars in 1999 for best picture, director, actor, screenplay—and cinematography, by Conrad Hall. Both films involve men in family situations of unbearable pain, although the first is a comedy (of sorts) and this one certainly is

not. Both involve a father who, by leading the life he chooses, betrays his family and even endangers them. Both involve men who hate their work.

The key relationships are between Hanks and Newman, and Hanks and Tyler Hoechlin, the newcomer who plays his son. Newman plays Mr. Rooney as a man who would prefer that as few people be harmed as necessary, but he has an implacable definition of "necessary." He is capable of colorful Corleone-style sayings, as when he declares that his mob will not get involved in labor unions: "What men do after work is what made us rich. No need to screw them at work." Against this benevolence we must set his trade in booze, gambling, and women, and his surgical willingness to amputate any associate who is causing difficulty.

The Hanks character sees the good side of Mr. Rooney so willfully that he almost cannot see the bad. Even after he discovers the worst, he feels wounded more than betrayed. He's a little naive, and it takes Rooney, in a speech Newman delivers with harsh clarity, to disabuse him. Called a murderer, Rooney says: "There are *only* murderers in this room, Michael. Open your eyes. This is the life we chose. The life we lead. And there is only one guarantee—none of us will see heaven."

Sullivan wants his son to see heaven, and that sets up their flight from Rooney justice. Father and son flee, pursued by a hit man (Jude Law) who supplements his income by selling photographs of the people he has killed. The plot all works out in an ending that may seem too neat, unless you reflect that in tragedy there is a place of honor for the *deus ex machina*—the god being lowered by the machinery of the plot into a scene that requires solution.

I mentioned the rain. This is a water-soaked picture, with melting snow on the streets and dampness in every room. That gives Conrad Hall the opportunity to develop and extend one of his most famous shots. In *In Cold Blood* (1967), he has a close-up of Robert Blake, as a convicted killer on the night of his death. He puts Blake near a window, and lights his face through the windowpane, as raindrops slide down the glass. The effect is of tears on his face. In *Road to Perdition,* the light shines through a rain-swept window onto a whole room that seems to weep.

After I saw *Road to Perdition*, I knew I admired it, but I didn't know if I liked it. I am still not sure. It is cold and holds us outside. Yes, there is the love of Hanks for his son, but how sadly he is forced to express it. The troubles of the mob seem caused because Rooney prefers family to good management, but Michael Sullivan's tragedy surely comes because he has put it the other way around—placing Rooney above his family. The movie shares with *The Godfather* the useful tactic of keeping the actual victims out of view. There are no civilians here, destroyed by mob activities. All of the characters, good and bad, are supplied from within the mob. But there is never the sense that any of these characters will tear loose, think laterally, break the chains of their fate. Choice, a luxury of the Corleones, is denied to the Sullivans and Rooneys, and choice or its absence is the difference between Sophocles and Shakespeare. I prefer Shakespeare.

Road Trip ★ ★
R, 91 m., 2000

Breckin Meyer (Josh), Seann William Scott (E.L.), Amy Smart (Beth), Paulo Costanzo (Rubin), D. J. Qualls (Kyle), Rachel Blanchard (Tiffany), Anthony Rapp (Jacob), Fred Ward (Earl Edwards). Directed by Todd Phillips and produced by Daniel Goldberg and Joe Medjuck. Screenplay by Todd Phillips and Scot Armstrong.

Road Trip is mellow and dirty, which is the wrong combination. It's sweet when it should be raunchy, or vice versa, and the result is a movie that seems uneasy with itself. It wants to be evil, really it does, but every so often its better nature takes over, and it throws sweetness right there in the middle of the dirty stuff and the nudity. We feel unkind, watching it. We'd enjoy the nudity more if it were ribald and cheerful, but it feels obligatory, as if the actresses were instructed to disrobe every five minutes in a movie that's only really interested in sex for commercial reasons.

Nude scenes should be inspired by the libido, not the box office. That's why I object to the phrase "gratuitous nudity." In a movie like this, the only nudity worth having is gratuitous. If it's there for reasons that are clankingly commercial, you feel sorry for the actresses, which is not the point.

The plot is a lamebrained contrivance about a frat boy named Josh (Breckin Meyer), who has been dating Tiffany (Rachel Blanchard of TV's *Clueless*) ever since high school. Now he's a student at Ithaca College, and she has decided she needs room to grow, or concentrate on her major, or something, and she enrolls at the University of Austin, which is not as far from Ithaca as you can get, but might as well be.

Josh and Tiff keep in touch by telephone, but Josh senses her attention waning, and then there's a period when she doesn't answer the phone. Josh meanwhile has been flirting with a campus sexpot named Beth (Amy Smart), and one night she seduces him and they make a video of themselves having sex, perhaps because they have seen the same thing done in *American Pie*, or perhaps because the makers of *Road Trip* are ripping off *American Pie*, which is probably more likely.

Josh has made a sweet video to send to Tiffany, but we get no points for foreseeing the obvious, which is that the wrong video gets mailed to Tiff, and so Josh and his friends, who lack airfare, have to make an emergency road trip to Austin to try to retrieve the video before Tiffany can see it. All of this is complicated by the presence of Jacob (Anthony Rapp), an unpleasant undergraduate whose minor seems to be in stalking.

Josh borrows a car that belongs to his geeky friend Kyle (D. J. Qualls), and takes along his friends Rubin (Paulo Costanzo) and E.L. (Seann William Scott), who is from *American Pie* and thus functions as a cross-cultural trivia bookmark. They have versions of the usual adventures along the way, including an awkward scene where these white boys try to convince the members of an African-American fraternity that they are members. This scene is as uncomfortable as comedy can be, because the humor in it is latently racist, and so the movie lets it remain latent, which means that all the characters, black and white, seem to be standing around self-consciously avoiding tasteless material. (The movie is bereft, unfortunately, of any alternative material.)

Whether Josh gets to the tape before Beth sees it, I will leave for you to determine. And yes, I said "determine" and not "decide," because to be honest with you I was confused. I thought she had seen it, and then it appeared that she had not, all because of a dream sequence that was either (a) incompetently presented, or (b) failed to engage what I fondly think of as my full intelligence.

On the way out of the movie, I met three teenage girls who asked me what I thought of it, and I requested their opinion: Didn't it seem like Beth had seen the video and then that she hadn't? The three girls agreed with me, and said they'd been confused, too, and together we figured out what had happened, which was useful, but not the sort of conversation you should be having. When a movie doesn't have a brain in its head, don't you agree it's kind of unfair to require thought on the part of the audience?

Full disclosure requires me to report that there were several moments in the movie when I did indeed laugh, and that the characters are likable when they are not being required to act dirty for the transient purposes of the screenplay. Those virtues are not enough to redeem the film, but they suggest that the cast should be regarded more as victims than perpetrators.

Rock Star ★ ★ ½
R, 110 m., 2001

Mark Wahlberg (Chris "Izzy" Coles), Jennifer Aniston (Emily Poule), Timothy Spall (Manager), Jamie Williams (Mason), Deborah Leydig (Marjorie), William Martin Brennan (Office Drone), Jason Flemyng (Bobby Beers). Directed by Stephen Herek and produced by Toby Jaffe and Robert Lawrence. Screenplay by John Stockwell.

Rock is a business like any other, and musicians are businessmen, and what goes on behind the scenes isn't always pretty. We know this, and we don't want to know this. *Rock Star* is a movie about a copy machine repairman who becomes the lead singer in a famous heavy metal band, and somehow with that premise it should be more fun than it is. (It doesn't even have a crucial moment where the new star saves the day with an emergency copier repair.) Instead, it's a morality play with

morose undertones, and for the second movie in a row (after *Planet of the Apes*) here is Mark Wahlberg looking like he doesn't enjoy being out front.

Wahlberg plays Chris "Izzy" Coles, a Pennsylvania copier repairman who sings in the church choir, loves and is loved by his parents and a loyal girlfriend, and leads a local tribute band named Blood Pollution. He idolizes the band Steel Dragon, and insists that his band do only their songs, and only in the exact way they perform them ("You're not nailing the squeal," he tells a guitarist during rehearsal). Eventually his fanaticism makes him such a nuisance that his own band fires him. Miraculously, the lead singer of Steel Dragon is in the process of being kicked out, and the band sees one of Izzy's tapes and hires him as a replacement singer.

This is all loosely inspired by fact. An Ohio office supply salesman named Tim "Ripper" Owens actually did replace Rob Halford, the lead singer in Judas Priest, after warming up as lead singer in a tribute band. Most of the film's other details are, I imagine, fiction— but they portray a world that must be more or less the same for many bands, involving the ordeal of touring, personality clashes, the danger of violence, unhappy relationships, omnipresent groupies, and managers who must be liars, thieves, drug counselors, and psychoanalysts to keep the show on the road.

The best parts of the movie are the early ones, as Izzy fights with his band, stands by his dream, and is supported by his girlfriend Emily (Jennifer Aniston), who at one point goes beyond the call of duty by piercing his nipple so he can wear a ring just like his idol Bobby Beers, the lead singer in Steel Dragon. One of the funniest scenes in the movie involves what appears to be a fight with a cop who breaks into Izzy's bedroom; I won't spoil the punch line.

The members of Steel Dragon are revealed, behind the scenes, to be cynical professionals who casually boot out Bobby Beers, see a tape of Izzy performing, fly him to L.A. for an audition, and hire him. Izzy brings Emily along ("We traded in the first-class ticket for two tourist tickets"), and indeed plans on keeping her by his side during the whole adventure. This is not the way the tour works, and Emily is banned from the band bus; she and the other wives and girlfriends trail behind in a stretch limousine, although an astrologer and a drag queen are allowed on the bus.

We follow Izzy's adventures as a lead singer; he falls down a flight of stairs on his first entrance, and makes a good impression by singing while blood runs down his forehead. Eventually we, and he, understand that he who can be hired can be fired. Timothy Spall anchors this section of the film with his observant, solid performance as the manager, who sees all, knows all, tolerates all until it affects the box office. Aware that Emily feels shut out while groupies cluster around the band, he counsels her to "build up a little tolerance to it, you know?"

Watching *Rock Star* was an instructive experience. Until the halfway mark I approved of it, and then slowly my enthusiasm faded. It stopped being an adventure and started being a parable. Instead of the life and energy in a movie like *Almost Famous*, set in roughly the same period, there was a glum disconsolance. I began to feel that Izzy lacked the imagination to turn the situation into fun, that his rigidity in insisting that Blood Pollution copy Steel Dragon note for note translated to a kind of paralyzing inflexibility. Where was the juice and joy? By the end of the film I conceded, yes, there are good performances and the period is well captured, but the movie didn't convince me of the feel and the flavor of its experiences.

Note: Rock Star began production with the title Metal God, which is incomparably better; at one point, it was called So You Wanna Be a Rock Star?—the inspiration, no doubt, of a ratings-crazed executive who thought it could attract all the Regis Philbin fans.

Rollerball ½★
PG-13, 98 m., 2002

Chris Klein (Jonathan Cross), Jean Reno (Alexi Petrovich), LL Cool J (Marcus Ridley), Rebecca Romijn-Stamos (Aurora), Naveen Andrews (Sanjay), Paul Heyman (Announcer). Directed by John McTiernan and produced by McTiernan, Charles Roven, and Beau St. Clair. Screenplay by William Harrison, Larry Ferguson, and John Pogue, based on the short story by Harrison.

Rollerball is an incoherent mess, a jumble of footage in search of plot, meaning, rhythm, and sense. There are bright colors and quick movement on the screen, which we can watch as a visual pattern that, in entertainment value, falls somewhere between a kaleidoscope and a lava lamp.

The movie stars Chris Klein, who shot to stardom, so to speak, in the *American Pie* movies and inhabits his violent action role as if struggling against the impulse to blurt out, "People, why can't we all just get along?" Klein is a nice kid. For this role, you need someone who has to shave three times a day.

The movie is set in 2005 in a Central Asian republic apparently somewhere between Uzbekistan and Mudville. Jean Reno plays Petrovich, owner of "the hottest sports start-up in the world," a Rollerball league that crowds both motorcycles and roller skaters on a figure-eight track that at times looks like Roller Derby crossed with demo derby, at other times like a cruddy video game. The sport involves catching a silver ball and throwing it at a big gong so that showers of sparks fly. One of the star players confesses she doesn't understand it, but so what: In the final game Petrovich suspends all rules, fouls, and penalties. This makes no difference that I could see.

Klein plays Jonathan Cross, an NHL draft pick who has to flee America in a hurry for the crime of racing suicidally down the hills of San Francisco flat on his back on what I think is a skateboard. His best friend is Marcus Ridley (LL Cool J), who convinces him to come to Podunkistan and sign for the big bucks. Jonathan is soon attracted to Aurora (Rebecca Romijn-Stamos, from *X-Men*).

"Your face isn't nearly as bad as you think," he compliments her. She has a scar over one eye, but is otherwise in great shape, as we can see because the locker rooms of the future are co-ed. Alas, the women athletes of the future still turn their backs to the camera at crucial moments, carry strategically placed towels, stand behind furniture, and in general follow the rules first established in 1950s nudist volleyball pictures.

I counted three games in the Rollerball season. The third is the championship. There is one road trip, to a rival team's Rollerball arena, which seems to have been prefabricated in the city dump. The games are announced by Paul Heyman, who keeps screaming, "What the hell is going on?" There is no one else in the booth with him. Yet when Aurora wants to show Jonathan that an injury was deliberate, she can call up instant replays from all the cameras on equipment thoughtfully provided in the locker room.

The funniest line in the movie belongs to Jean Reno, who bellows, "I'm this close to a North American cable deal!" North American cable carries Battling Bots, Iron Chefs, Howard Stern, and monster truck rallies. There isn't a person in the audience who couldn't get him that deal. Reno also has the second funniest line. After Jonathan engages in an all-night 120-mph motorcycle chase across the frozen steppes of Bankruptistan, while military planes drop armed Jeeps to chase him, and after he sees his best pal blown to bits *after* leaping across a suspension bridge that has been raised in the middle of the night for no apparent reason, Reno tells him, "Play well tonight."

Oh, and I almost forgot Aurora's breathless discovery after the suspicious death of one of the other players. "His chin strap was cut!" she whispers fiercely to Jonathan. Neither she nor he notices that Jonathan makes it a point never to fasten his own chin strap at any time during a game.

Someday this film may inspire a long, thoughtful book by John Wright, its editor. My guess is that something went dreadfully wrong early in the production. Maybe dysentery or mass hypnosis. And the director, John McTiernan *(Die Hard)*, was unable to supply Wright with the shots he needed to make sense of the story. I saw a Russian documentary once where half the shots were blurred and overexposed because the KGB attacked the negative with X rays. Maybe this movie was put through an MRI scan. Curiously, the signifiers have survived, but not the signified. Characters set up big revelations and then forget to make them. And the long, murky night sequence looks like it was shot, pointlessly, with the green-light NightShot feature on a consumer video camera.

One of the peculiarities of television of the future is a device titled "Instant Global Rating." This supplies a digital readout of how many viewers there are (except on North American cable systems, of course). Whenever something tremendously exciting happens during a game, the rating immediately goes up. This means that people who were not watching somehow sensed they had just missed something amazing, and responded by tuning in. When *Rollerball* finally does get a North American cable deal, I predict the ratings will work in reverse.

Romeo Must Die ★ ½
R, 110 m., 2000

Jet Li (Han Sing), Aaliyah (Trish O'Day), Isaiah Washington (Mac), Delroy Lindo (Isaak O'Day), DMX (Silk), D. B. Woodside (Colin), Anthony Anderson (Maurice), Henry O. (Ch'u Sing). Directed by Andrzej Bartkowiak and produced by Joel Silver and Jim Van Wyck. Screenplay by Mitchell Kapner, Eric Bernt, and John Jarrell.

Shakespeare has been manhandled in countless modern-dress retreads, and I was looking forward to *Romeo Must Die*, billed as a war between Chinese and African-American families, based on *Romeo and Juliet*. After *China Girl* (1987), which sets the story in New York's Little Italy and Chinatown, and *Romeo + Juliet* (1996), which has a war between modern gangsters in a kind of CalMex strip city, why not a martial arts version in Oakland?

Alas, the film borrows one premise from Shakespeare (the children of enemy families fall in love), and buries the rest of the story in a creaky plot and wheezy dialogue. Much is made of the presence of Jet Li, the Hong Kong martial arts star *(Lethal Weapon 4)*, but his scenes are so clearly computer-aided that his moves are about as impressive as Bugs Bunny doing the same things.

Li stars as Han Sing, once a cop, now taking the rap for a crime he didn't commit. He's in a Hong Kong prison as the movie opens. His brother is killed in Oakland after a fight at an African-American dance club, and Sing breaks out of prison to travel to America and avenge his brother. In Oakland, he meets Trish O'Day (Aaliyah, the singer) and they begin to fall in love while she helps him look into the death of his brother.

But what a coincidence! Her father, Isaak (Delroy Lindo), may know more about the death than he should, and soon the two lovers are in the middle of a war between Chinese and black organizations who are involved in a murky plot to buy up the waterfront for a new sports stadium. This real-estate project exists primarily as a clothesline on which to hang elaborate martial arts sequences, including one Jackie Chan–style football game where Jet Li hammers half a dozen black guys and scores a touchdown, all at once.

It is a failing of mine that I persist in bringing logic to movies where it is not wanted. During *Romeo Must Die*, I began to speculate about the methods used to buy up the waterfront. All of the property owners (of clubs, little shops, crab houses, etc.) are asked to sell, and when they refuse, they are variously murdered, torched, blown up, or have their faces stuck into vats of live crabs. Don't you think the press and the local authorities would notice this? Don't you imagine it would take the bloom off a stadium to know that dozens of victims were murdered to clear the land?

Never mind. The audience isn't in the theater for a film about property values, but to watch Jet Li and other martial arts warriors in action. *Romeo Must Die* has a lot of fight scenes, but key moments in them are so obviously special effects that they miss the point. When Jackie Chan does a stunt, it may look inelegant, but we know he's really doing it. Here Jet Li leaps six feet in the air and rotates clockwise while kicking three guys. It can't be done, we know it can't be done, we know he's not doing it, and so what's the point? In *The Matrix*, there's a reason the guy can fly.

There's a moment in Jackie Chan's *Rumble in the Bronx* when he uses grace and athletic ability to project his entire body through the swinging gate of a grocery cart, and we say, "Yes!" (pumping a fist into the air is optional). Here Jet Li tries the Chan practice of using whatever props come to hand, but the football game looks overrehearsed and a sequence with a fire hose is underwhelming (anybody can knock guys off their feet with a fire hose).

Closing Notes: Many windows are broken in the movie. Many people fall from great heights.

There are a lot of rap songs on the sound track, which distract from the action because their lyrics occupy the foreground and replace dialogue. Killers on motorcycles once again forget it is dangerous for them to chase cars at high speed, because if they get thrown off their bikes, it will hurt. The reliable Motorcycle Opaque Helmet Rule is observed (when you can't see the face of a character because the visor is down, chances are—gasp!—it's a woman). No great romantic chemistry is generated between the young lovers, and there is something odd about a martial arts warrior hiding behind a girl's bedroom door so her daddy won't catch him. Delroy Lindo projects competence, calm, and strength in every scene. This movie needs a screenplay.

The Rookie ★ ★
G, 129 m., 2002

Dennis Quaid (Jimmy), Rachel Griffiths (Lorri), Jay Hernandez ("Wack" Campos), Beth Grant (Olline), Brian Cox (Jim Sr.). Directed by John Lee Hancock and produced by Gordon Gray, Mark Ciardi, and Mark Johnson. Screenplay by Mike Rich.

The Rookie combines two reliable formulas: the Little Team That Goes to State and the Old-Timer Who Realizes His Youthful Dream. When two genres approach exhaustion, sometimes it works if they prop each other up. Not this time, not when we also get the Dad Who Can't Be Pleased However Hard His Son Tries, and the Wife Who Wants Her Husband to Have His Dream but Has a Family to Raise. The movie is so resolutely cobbled together out of older movies that it even uses a totally unnecessary prologue, just because it seems obligatory.

We begin in the wide open spaces of west Texas, where wildcat oil prospectors have a strike in the 1920s. The little town of Big Lake springs up, and in the shadow of one of the rickety old derricks a baseball diamond is scratched out of the dust. Supporting this enterprise, we're told, is St. Rita, "patron saint of hopeless causes." I thought that was St. Jude, but no, the two saints share the same billing. Certainly St. Rita is powerful enough to deal with baseball, but it would take both saints in harness to save this movie.

The story leaps forward in time to the recent past, as we follow a career navy officer (Brian Cox) who moves with his family from town to town while his son, little Jimmy, pounds his baseball mitt and is always getting yanked off his latest team just when it starts to win.

Now it's the present and the Little Leaguer has grown up into big Jimmy (Dennis Quaid), coach of the Big Lake High School baseball team. He's married to Lorri (Rachel Griffiths), they have an eight-year-old, and he has all but forgotten his teenage dream of pitching in the majors. By my calculations thirty years have passed, but his dad, Jim Sr., looks exactly the same age as he did when Jimmy was eight, except for some gray hair, of course. Brian Cox is one of those actors like Walter Matthau who has always been about the same age. I was so misled by the prologue I thought maybe Jim and Jim Sr. were connected in some way with the wildcatters and St. Rita, but apparently the entire laborious prologue is meant simply to establish that baseball was played in Big Lake before Jimmy and Lorri moved there.

All movies of this sort are huggable. They're about nice people, played by actors we like, striving for goals we can identify with. Dennis Quaid is just plain one of the nicest men in the movies, with that big goofy smile, but boy, can he look mean when he narrows his eyes and squints down over his shoulder from the pitching mound.

Faithful readers will know that I have a special regard for Rachel Griffiths, that most intelligent and sexy actress, but what a price she has had to pay for her stardom on HBO's *Six Feet Under*. Instead of starring roles in small, good movies (*My Son the Fanatic, Hilary and Jackie, Me Myself I*), she now gets the big bucks on TV, but her work schedule requires her to take supporting roles in movies that can be slotted into her free time. So here she plays the hero's faithful wife, stirring a pot and buttoning the little boy's shirt, her scenes basically limited to pillow talk, telephone conversations, sitting in the stands and, of course, presenting the hero with the choice of his dream or his family.

The high school team comes from such a small school that, as nearly as I can see, they have only nine members and no subs (Jimmy's eight-year-old is the batboy). It's captained by "Wack" Campos (Jay Hernandez), who is good in the standard role of coach's alter ego. Every single game in the movie, without exception, goes according to the obvious demands of the screenplay, but there is a surprise development when Jimmy pitches batting practice and they're amazed by the speed he still has on his fastball. They make him a deal: If they get to district finals or even state, Jimmy has to try out for the majors again. Is there anyone alive who can hear these lines and not predict what will happen between then and the end of the movie?

The Rookie is comforting, even soothing, to those who like the old songs best. It may confuse those who, because they like the characters, think it is good. It is not good. It is skillful. Learning the difference between good movies and skillful ones is an early step in becoming a moviegoer. *The Rookie* demonstrates that a skillful movie need not be good. It is also true that a good movie need not be skillful, but it takes a heap of moviegoing to figure that one out. And pray to St. Rita. ☞

A Room for Romeo Brass ★ ★ ★
R, 90 m., 2000

Andrew Shim (Romeo Brass), Ben Marshall (Gavin "Knocks" Woolley), Paddy Considine (Morell), Frank Harper (Joseph), James Higgins (Bill), Vicky McClure (Ladine), Bob Hoskins (Steven Laws). Directed by Shane Meadows and produced by George Faber and Charles Pattinson. Screenplay by Paul Fraser and Meadows.

In a small town near Nottingham, two young teenage friends live next door to each other, and get along like all teenage friends do—which is to say, weirdly, with long silences that have no reason, followed by business as usual.

Romeo Brass (Andrew Shim), the pudgy, optimistic son of a black mother and an absent white father, is not the lad to send to the fish and chips shop if you expect to find any chips left in the bag when he gets home. Gavin Woolley (Ben Marshall), nicknamed Knocks, limps from a back disorder, needs surgery, and has a father who would rather watch television than talk to members of his own family. Romeo and Knocks like each other but don't get carried away by it.

This is Ken Loach country, with its working-class characters from the Midlands, but then a little Mike Leigh creeps in. Knocks, whose limp singles him out, is picked on by some school bullies. Romeo, who was sort of the instigator, tries to help him, but then an adult stranger in a van leaps in and breaks it up. This is Morell (Paddy Considine), well named after a mushroom since he flourishes in the shady, damp spaces of his own mind. Coming to visit Romeo and his family, he puzzles them with a dramatic account of his battles between himself and an "unseen entity."

Romeo has a sister named Ladine (Vicky McClure), very attractive, stranded in this backwater, and Morell wants to date her. This is not a simple matter, since Morell is a very peculiar man, unpredictable, erratic, subject to quick shifts of mental weather. At one point Morell actually convinces Romeo to ask his sister out for him, and when Ladine does go on a date, it is more out of boredom and recklessness than any possible interest.

We have by now become familiar with the characters. We kind of understand why, after Knocks comes home from surgery, Romeo doesn't visit him. Embarrassments grow up between kids without any reason. Earlier we understood when Romeo didn't want to stay at home, and Knocks was happy to have him move into his room. Everybody knows everybody's business in this neighborhood; when Romeo's mother berates him for not going to see Knocks, Knocks can hear their argument through the thin walls separating their row houses.

Morell is the character who supplies unpredictability and the possibility of danger. And yet he is not simply a stalker or a psycho or any of the other easily categorizable things he might be in a more ordinary movie. He is different every time we see him, and sometimes surprises himself. He can be dangerous, and then suddenly disarm himself. The performance by Paddy Considine is a work of sullen and unpredictable craft; I was reminded of David Thewlis in Mike Leigh's *Naked*. The film's climax is logical, I suppose,

and yet utterly unanticipated—especially in the way it brings in violence through a marginal character.

A Room for Romeo Brass was directed by Shane Meadows, who made *TwentyFourSeven* (1998), the movie where Bob Hoskins started a boxing club for disadvantaged lads who were reduced to fighting in the streets. That film felt like it wanted to be a documentary, and here, too, Meadows seems fascinated by the happenings of everyday life. *Romeo Brass* is a better film, effortless in the way it insinuates itself into these families, touching in the way it shows how fiercely Romeo and Knocks are, despite everything, their own little men.

Rosetta ★ ★ ★ ½
R, 95 m., 2000

Emilie Dequenne (Rosetta), Fabrizio Rongione (Riquet), Anne Yernaux (Mother), Olivier Gourmet (Boss), Bernard Marbaix (Campgrounds Manager), Frederic Bodson (Head of Personnel), Florian Delain (Boss's Son), Christiane Dorval (First Saleswoman), Mireille Bailly (Second Saleswoman). Directed by Luc and Jean-Pierre Dardenne and produced by the Dardennes and Michele and Laurent Petin. Screenplay by the Dardennes.

At night before she goes to sleep, Rosetta has this conversation with herself: "Your name is Rosetta. My name is Rosetta. You found a job. I found a job. You've got a friend. I've got a friend. You have a normal life. I have a normal life. You won't fall in a rut. I won't fall in a rut. Good night. Good night."

This is a young woman determined to find a job at all costs. She is escaping from the world of her alcoholic mother, a tramp who lives in a ramshackle trailer and runs away near the beginning of the story, leaving her daughter to fend for herself. Rosetta sees an abyss yawning beneath her and will go to any length to avoid it.

Her story is told in a film that astonishingly won the Palme d'Or at the 1999 Cannes Film Festival, as well as the Best Actress prize for its star, Emilie Dequenne. The wins were surprising not because this is a bad film (in its uncompromising way it's a very good one), but because films like this—neorealist, without pedigree, downbeat, stylistically straightforward—do not often win at Cannes. *Variety*'s grudgingly positive review categorized it as "an extremely small European art movie from Belgium." Not just European but Belgian.

Rosetta opens with its heroine being fired, unjustly, we think, from a job. She smacks the boss, is chased by the police, returns home to her mother's trailer, and we get glimpses of her life as she sells old clothes for money, and sometimes buries things like a squirrel. She fishes in a filthy nearby stream—for food, not fun. She makes a friend of Riquet (Fabrizio Rongione), a kid about her age who has a job in a portable waffle stand (yes, Belgian waffles in a Belgian art movie). He likes her, is kind to her, and perhaps she likes him.

One vignette follows another. We discover that unlike almost every teenage girl in the world, she can't dance. That she has stomach pains, maybe from an ulcer. One day Riquet falls in the river while trying to retrieve her fishing line, and she waits a strangely long time before helping him to get out. Later she confesses she didn't want him out. If he had drowned, she could have gotten his job. After all, the local waffle king likes her, and she'd have a job already, had it not gone to his idiot son.

What happens next I will leave for you to discover. The film has an odd, subterranean power. It doesn't strive for our sympathy or make any effort to portray Rosetta as colorful, winning, or sympathetic. It's a film of economic determinism, the story of a young woman for whom employment equals happiness. Or so she thinks until she has employment, and is no happier, perhaps because that is something she has simply never learned to be.

Two other films prowled like ghosts in my memory as I watched *Rosetta*. One was Robert Bresson's *Mouchette* (1966), about a poor girl who is cruelly treated by a village. The other was Agnes Varda's *Vagabond* (1986), about a young woman alone on the road, gradually descending from backpacker to homeless person. These characters are Rosetta's spiritual sisters, sharing her proud disdain for society and her desperate need to be seen as part of it. She'll find a job. She'll get a friend. She'll have a normal life. She won't fall in a rut. Good night.

The Royal Tenenbaums ★ ★ ★ ½
R, 103 m., 2001

Gene Hackman (Royal Tenenbaum), Anjelica Huston (Etheline Tenenbaum), Ben Stiller (Chas Tenenbaum), Gwyneth Paltrow (Margot Helen Tenenbaum), Luke Wilson (Richie Tenenbaum), Owen Wilson (Eli Cash), Danny Glover (Henry Sherman), Bill Murray (Raleigh St. Clair), Seymour Cassel (Dusty), Kumar Pallana (Pagoda), Alec Baldwin (Narrator). Directed by Wes Anderson and produced by Anderson, Barry Mendel, and Scott Rudin. Screenplay by Anderson and Owen Wilson.

Wes Anderson's *The Royal Tenenbaums* exists on a knife edge between comedy and sadness. There are big laughs, and then quiet moments when we're touched. Sometimes we grin at the movie's deadpan audacity. The film doesn't want us to feel just one set of emotions. It's the story of a family that at times could have been created by P. G. Wodehouse, and at other times by John Irving. And it's proof that Wes Anderson and his writing partner, the actor Owen Wilson, have a gift of cockeyed genius.

The Tenenbaums occupy a big house in a kind of dreamy New York. It has enough rooms for each to hide and nurture a personality incompatible with the others. Royal Tenenbaum (Gene Hackman), the patriarch, left home abruptly some years before and has been living in a hotel, on credit, ever since. There was never actually a divorce. His wife, Etheline (Anjelica Huston), remains at home with their three children, who were all child prodigies and have grown into adult neurotics. There's Chas (Ben Stiller), who was a financial whiz as a kid; Margot (Gwyneth Paltrow), who was adopted and won a big prize for writing a school play; and Richie (Luke Wilson), once a tennis champion.

All three come with various partners, children, and friends. The most memorable are Raleigh St. Clair (Bill Murray), a bearded intellectual who has been married to Margot for years but does not begin to know her; Eli Cash (Owen Wilson), who lived across the street, became like a member of the family, and writes best-selling Westerns that get terrible reviews; Henry Sherman (Danny Glover), who was Etheline's accountant for ten years until they suddenly realized they were in love; and such satellites as Pagoda (Kumar Pallana), Royal's faithful servant (who once in India tried to murder Royal and then rescued him from . . . himself), and the bellboy Dusty (Seymour Cassel), who impersonates a doctor when Royal fakes a fatal illness.

Trying to understand the way this flywheel comedy tugs at the heartstrings, I reflected that eccentricity often masks deep loneliness. All the Tenenbaums are islands entire of themselves. Consider that Margot has been a secret smoker since she was thirteen. Why bother? Nobody else in the family cares, and when they discover her deception they hardly notice. Her secrecy was part of her own strategy to stand outside the family, to have something that was her own.

One of the pleasures of the movie is the way it keeps us a little uncertain about how we should be reacting. It's like a guy who seems to be putting you on, and then suddenly reveals himself as sincere, so you're stranded out there with an inappropriate smirk. You can see this quality on-screen in a lot of Owen Wilson's roles—in the half-kidding, half-serious way he finds out just how far he can push people.

The movie's strategy of doubling back on its own emotions works mostly through the dialogue. Consider a sort of brilliant dinner-table conversation where Royal tells the family he has cancer, they clearly don't believe him (or care), he says he wants to get to know them before he dies, the bitter Chas says he's not interested in that, and Royal pulls out all the stops by suggesting they visit their grandmother. Now watch how it works. Chas and Richie haven't seen her since they were six. Margot says piteously that she has never met her. Royal responds not with sympathy but with a slap at her adopted status: "She wasn't your real grandmother." See how his appeal turns on a dime into a cruel put-down?

Anderson's previous movies were *Bottle Rocket* (1996) and *Rushmore* (1998), both offbeat comedies, both about young people trying to outwit institutions. Anderson and the Wilson brothers met at the University of Texas, made their first film on a shoestring, have quickly developed careers, share a special talent. (That Owen Wilson could cowrite and star in this, and also star in the lugubrious *Behind Enemy Lines,* is

one of the year's curiosities.) Like the Farrelly brothers, but kinder and gentler, they follow a logical action to its outrageous conclusion.

Consider, for example, what happens after Royal gets bounced out of his latest hotel and moves back home. His wife doesn't want him and Chas despises him (for stealing from his safety deposit box), so Royal stealthily moves in with a hospital bed, intravenous tubes, private medical care, and Seymour Cassel shaking his head over the prognosis. When this strategy is unmasked, he announces he wants to get to know his grandkids better—wants to teach them to take chances. So he instructs Richie's kids in shoplifting, playing in traffic, and throwing things at taxicabs.

The Royal Tenenbaums is at heart profoundly silly and loving. That's why it made me think of Wodehouse. It stands in amazement as the Tenenbaums and their extended family unveil one strategy after another to get attention, carve out space, and find love. It doesn't mock their efforts, dysfunctional as they are, because it understands them—and sympathizes. ☞

Rugrats in Paris ★ ★ ★
G, 80 m., 2000

With the voices of: Susan Sarandon (Coco La Bouche), John Lithgow (Jean-Claude), Debbie Reynolds (Lulu Pickles), Tim Curry (Sumo Singer), Casey Kasem (Wedding DJ), E. G. Daily (Tommy Pickles), Christine Cavanaugh (Chuckie Finster), Kath Soucie (Phil, Lil, and Betty Deville). Directed by Stig Bergqvist and Paul Demeyer and produced by Arlene Klasky and Gabor Csupo. Screenplay by J. David Stem, David N. Weiss, Jill Gorey, Barbara Herndon, and Kate Boutilier.

Many members of the target audience for *Rugrats in Paris* cannot read, so I am dedicating this review to their parents, especially their moms. I know your secret. You watch *Rugrats* too. It supplies a time in the day when you and the kids can get together in front of the set and both laugh, often for different reasons. You don't make a habit of announcing you're a *Rugrats* fan, but when you get together with other moms and the Rugrats come up, you grin and say you hate to admit it, but you actually *like* the show.

You will like *Rugrats in Paris* too. I liked it. It's better than the 1998 *Rugrats* movie, funnier, weirder, with more stuff for adults to clue into. Or maybe kids also clue into this stuff. Today's real-life rugrats are so hip to the media that a lot of them will even get the *Godfather* satire that opens the movie. (My favorite moment: One of the kids finds a hobbyhorse head in his bed, and another says, "That's what you get for wiping your boogers on Cynthia.")

The original *Rugrats* satirized *2001, Jurassic Park, The Fugitive, Raiders of the Lost Ark,* and Busby Berkeley musicals. This one has fun not only with *The Godfather* but also with *King Kong, Godzilla, Little Indian, Big City, Lady and the Tramp,* and *101 Dalmatians.* It also pokes fun at Euroreptorland, a Japanese-owned theme park in Paris with giant reptiles that look a lot like *The Iron Giant.* (Not many of the kids will know that the artificial wave towering above the park is based on Katsushika Hokusai's famous drawing *The Great Wave* from 1831, but look it up on the Web with them and they'll want the T-shirt).

The plot. As the movie opens, little Chuckie Finster (voice by Christine Cavanaugh) is sad because his dad took him to a wedding where there was a dance all the kids were supposed to dance with their moms, but Chuckie's mom is dead. He thinks his dad ought to get married again. They check out the dating sites on the Web, and one candidate has all the right credentials except that she is not allowed to enter the state of Georgia. Then there's an emergency call from Paris: A raptor is malfunctioning at the theme park, and a friend of the Finsters, a raptor engineer, is summoned to Paris—and mistakenly thinks he was asked to bring along his family and friends.

That's a convenient way for the entire Rugrats crowd to be transported to France, where we meet Coco La Bouche (voice by Susan Sarandon), the witchy theme park executive, whose Japanese boss thinks she should be married and love kids, so she decides to marry Mr. Finster, forcibly if necessary, and adopt Chuckie.

The plot is just the excuse for the goofiness, including a dance line of sumo wrestlers, a thrilling trip to the Princess at the very top of the park, a love affair between a poodle and a mutt, and the Godzilla-style chase through the streets of Paris, with the kids running a giant raptor that scales the Eiffel Tower before finally arriving at Notre Dame Cathedral, where the wedding is in progress.

The graphic style of the movie will be familiar to anyone who watches the TV show. I like it. It's bright and quirky, with the oversized heads of the kids owing a little to Charles Schulz. The dialogue is direct and fundamental, geared to young values: "My dad is marrying a lady who doesn't like me or my wa-wa or any kids." His wa-wa, of course, is his stuffed pet. And there are the usual jokes about poo and pee and farts and stinky didies; as I observed in my *Rugrats* review, kids are fascinated with bodily excretions because they have so recently celebrated their own personal victories over them.

The point is, adults can attend this movie with a fair degree of pleasure. That's not always the case with movies for kids, as no parent needs to be reminded. There may even be some moms who insist that the kids *need* to see this movie. You know who you are.

Rules of Engagement ★ ★ ½
R, 123 m., 2000

Tommy Lee Jones (Colonel Hays Hodges), Samuel L. Jackson (Colonel Terry Childers), Guy Pearce (Major Mark Biggs), Philip Baker Hall (General Hodges), Bruce Greenwood (William Sokal), Blair Underwood (Captain Lee), Anne Archer (Mrs. Mourain), Mark Feuerstein (Captain Tom Chandler), Ben Kingsley (Ambassador Mourain). Directed by William Friedkin and produced by Richard D. Zanuck and Scott Rudin. Screenplay by Stephen Gaghan.

Rules of Engagement works splendidly as a courtroom thriller about military values, as long as you don't expect it to seriously consider those values. It's convincing on the surface, evasive beneath. I found myself involved in the story, and was pleased that for once I couldn't guess how a movie trial was going to turn out. Still, I expected the closing scenes to answer questions and close loopholes, and they evaded the questions and slipped through the loopholes.

The film centers on a relationship forged

throughout the adult lifetimes of two marine colonels, Hodges (Tommy Lee Jones) and Childers (Samuel L. Jackson). They fought side by side in Vietnam, where Childers saved Hodges's life by shooting an unarmed POW. That's against the rules of war, but understandable, in this story anyway, under the specific circumstances. Certainly Hodges is not complaining.

Years pass. Hodges, whose wounds make him unfit for action, gets a law degree and becomes a marine lawyer. He also gets a divorce and becomes a drunk. Childers, much decorated, is a textbook marine who is chosen to lead a rescue mission into Yemen when the U.S. embassy there comes under threat from angry demonstrators.

Exactly what happens at the embassy, and why, becomes the material of a court-martial, after Childers is accused of ordering his men to fire on a crowd of perhaps unarmed civilians, killing eighty-three of them. He convinces his old friend Hodges to represent him in the courtroom drama that occupies the second half of the film. Although the story marches confidently toward a debate about the ethical conduct of war, it trips over a villain who sidetracks the moral focus of the trial.

Remarkable, though, how well Jones, Jackson, and director William Friedkin are able to sustain interest and suspense even while saddled with an infuriating screenplay. Little is done to provide the characters with any lives outside their jobs, and yet I believed in them and cared about the outcome of the trial. If their work had been supported by a more thoughtful screenplay, this film might have really amounted to something.

Some of the lapses can't be discussed without revealing plot secrets. Here's one that can. Hodges makes a fact-finding visit to Yemen, and sees children who were victims of Childers's order to fire (the scene echoes one in *The Third Man*). He returns, drunk and enraged, and accuses Childers of lying to him. Childers punches him. Hodges fights back. They have a bitter brawl—two middle-aged men, gasping for breath—while we try not to wonder how a lame attorney can hold his own with a combat warrior. Finally, with his last strength, Hodges throws a pillow at Childers, and the two bloodied men start laughing. This works fine

as an illustration of an ancient movie cliché about a fight between friends, but what does it mean in the movie? That Hodges has forgotten the reason for his anger? That it was not valid?

Much depends, during the trial, on a missing tape that might show what really happened when the crowd was fired on. The tape is destroyed by the national security adviser (Bruce Greenwood), who tells an aide: "I don't want to watch this tape. I don't want to testify about it. I don't want it to exist." How do you get to be the national security adviser if you're dumb enough to say things like that out loud to a witness? And dumb enough, for that matter, to destroy this particular tape in the first place—when it might be more useful to the United States to show it?

Much is made in the movie of the marine esprit de corps, of protecting the lives of the men under your command, of following a warrior code. Yet one puzzling close-up of Childers's eyes during the Vietnam sequence supplies an undertow that influences our view of the character all through the movie: Is he acting as a good marine, or out of rage? This adds usefully to the suspense (movie stars are usually found innocent in courtroom dramas, but this time we can't be sure). But eventually we want more of an answer than we get.

One entire subplot is a missed opportunity. We see the U.S. ambassador (Ben Kingsley) and his wife and son as they're rescued by Childers. Later we hear his testimony in court, and then there's a scene between Hodges and the ambassador's wife (Anne Archer). Everything calls for a courtroom showdown involving either the ambassador or his wife, but there isn't one. Why set it up if you're not going to pay it off?

I ask these questions and yet admit that the movie involved me dramatically. Jones and Jackson work well together, bringing more conviction to many scenes than they really deserve. The fundamental problem with *Rules of Engagement*, I suspect, is that the filmmakers never clearly defined exactly what they believed about the issues they raised. Expert melodrama conceals their uncertainty up to a point, but at the end we have a film that attacks its central issue from all sides, and has a collision in the middle.

Running Free ★ ½
G, 82 m., 2000

Chase Moore (Young Richard), Jan Decleir (Boss Man), Maria Geelbooi (Nyka), Arie Verveen (Adult Richard), Graham Clarke (Mine Supervisor), Patrick Lyster (Officer). Directed by Sergei Bodrov and produced by Jean-Jacques Annaud. Screenplay by Jeanne Rosenberg, based on a story by Annaud and Rosenberg.

Running Free tells the life story of a horse in its own words. We do not find out much about horses in this process, alas, because the horse thinks and talks exactly like a young boy. The movie is another example, like Disney's *Dinosaur*, of a failure of nerve: Instead of challenging the audience to empathize with real animals, both movies supply them with the minds, vocabularies, and values of humans. What's the point?

As the film opens, the horse, later to be named Lucky, is born in the hold of a ship bound for German Southwest Africa, today's Namibia. It is 1911, and horses are needed to work in the mines. Lucky has to swim ashore while still a nursing colt. He glimpses daylight for the first time, and tells us, "I didn't see anything green in this desert land." Hello? Lucky has never seen anything green at all in his entire life.

But the movie keeps making that same mistake, breaking the logic of the point of view. Adopted by a young orphan stable boy named Richard (Chase Moore), Lucky finds himself in a stable of purebreds ruled by a stallion named Caesar. Lucky wants to make friends with the stallion's daughter, Beauty, but, "I was only the stable boy's horse. I wasn't good enough to play with his daughter." And when Lucky's long-missing mother turns up, Caesar attacks her, apparently in a fit of class prejudice, although you'd think a stallion would be intrigued by a new girl in town, despite her family connections.

Will the mother die from the attack? "I stayed with her all night, praying that she would survive," Lucky tells us. Praying? I wanted the movie to forget the story and explore this breakthrough in horse theology. I am weary of debates about whether our pets will be with us in heaven, and am eager to learn if trainers will be allowed into horse heaven.

The human characters in the movie are one-dimensional cartoons, including a town boss who speaks English with an Afrikaans accent, not likely in a German colony. His son is a little Fauntleroy with a telescope, which he uses to spy on Richard and Lucky. Soon all the Europeans evacuate the town after a bombing raid, which raises the curtain on World War I. The horses are left behind, and Lucky escapes to the mountains, where he finds a hidden lake. Returning to the town, he leads the other horses there, where at last they realize their birthright and Run Free.

Uh-huh. But there is not a twig of living vegetation in their desert hideout, and although I am assured by the movie's press materials that there are wild horses in Namibia to this day, I doubt they could forage for long in the barren wasteland shown in this film. What do they eat?

I ask because it is my responsibility: Of all the film critics reviewing this movie, I will arguably be the only one who has actually visited Swakopmund and Walvis Bay, on the Diamond Coast of the Namib Desert, and even ridden on the very train tracks to the capital, Windhoek, that the movie shows us. I am therefore acutely aware that race relations in the area in 1911 (and more recently) would scarcely have supported the friendship between Richard and Nyka (Maria Geelbooi), who plays the bushman girl who treats Lucky's snakebite. But then a movie that fudges about which side is which in World War I is unlikely to pause for such niceties.

I seem to be developing a rule about talking animals: They can talk if they're cartoons or Muppets, but not if they're real. This movie might have been more persuasive if the boy had told the story of the horse, instead of the horse telling the story of the boy. It's perfectly possible to make a good movie about an animal that does not speak, as Jean-Jacques Annaud, the producer of this film, proved with his 1989 film *The Bear*.

I also recall *The Black Stallion* (1979) and *White Fang* (1991). Since both of those splendid movies were cowritten by Jeanne Rosenberg, the author of *Running Free*, I can only guess that the talking horse was pressed upon her by executives who have no faith in the intelligence of today's audiences. Perhaps *Running Free* would appeal to younger children who really like horses, but see my review of *The Color of Paradise*, a film in release at the same time, for a glimpse of a truly inspired film for family audiences.

Rush Hour 2 ★ ½
PG-13, 120 m., 2001

Jackie Chan (Detective Inspector Lee), Chris Tucker (Detective James Carter), Chris Penn (Clive), Roselyn Sanchez (Isabella Molina), John Lone (Ricky Tan), Zhang Ziyi (Hu Li), Alan King (Steven Reign). Directed by Brett Ratner and produced by Roger Birnbaum, Jonathan Glickman, Arthur M. Sarkissian, and Jay Stern. Screenplay by Ross LaManna and Jeff Nathanson.

Rush Hour (1998) earned untold millions of dollars, inspiring this sequel. The first film was built on a comic relationship between Jackie Chan and Chris Tucker, as odd-couple cops from Hong Kong and Los Angeles. It was funny because hard work went into the screenplay and the stunts. It was not funny because Chris Tucker is funny whenever he opens his mouth—something he proves abundantly in *Rush Hour 2*, where his endless rants are like an anchor around the ankles of the humor.

Jackie Chan complained, I hear, that the Hollywood filmmakers didn't give him time to compose his usual elaborately choreographed stunts in *Rush Hour 2*, preferring shorter bursts of action. Too bad Brett Ratner, the director, didn't focus instead on shortening Tucker's dialogue scenes. Tucker plays an L.A. cop who, on the evidence of this movie, is a race-fixated motormouth who makes it a point of being as loud, offensive, and ignorant as he possibly can be.

There is a belief among some black comics that audiences find it funny when they launch extended insults against white people (see also Chris Rock's embarrassing outburst in *Jay and Silent Bob*). My feeling is that audiences of any race find such scenes awkward and unwelcome; I've never heard laughter during them, but I

have sensed an uncomfortable alertness in the theater. Accusing complete strangers of being racist is aggressive, hostile, and not funny, something Tucker demonstrates to a painful degree in this movie—where the filmmakers apparently lacked the nerve to request him to dial down.

There's one scene that really grated: The Tucker character finds himself in a Vegas casino. He throws a wad of money on a craps table and is given a stack of $500 chips. He is offended: It is racist for the casino to give him $500 chips instead of $1,000 chips, the dealer doesn't think a black man can afford $1,000 a throw, etc. He goes on and on in a shrill tirade against the dealer (an uncredited Saul Rubinek, I think). The dealer answers every verbal assault calmly and firmly. What's extraordinary about this scene is how we identify with the dealer, and how manifestly the Tucker character is acting like the seven-letter word for "jerk." Rubinek wins the exchange.

The movie begins with Tucker and Jackie Chan going to Hong Kong on vacation after their adventures in the previous movie. Soon they're involved in a new case: A bomb has gone off in the American embassy, killing two people. Their investigation leads first to the leader of a local crime triad (John Lone) and then to an American Mr. Big (Alan King). Sex appeal is supplied by Roselyn Sanchez, as an undercover agent, and Zhang Ziyi, from *Crouching Tiger, Hidden Dragon*, as a martial arts fighter.

Jackie Chan is amazing as usual in the action sequences, and Zhang Ziyi has hand-to-hand combat with Chris Tucker in a scene of great energy. There are the usual Chan-style stunts, including one where the heroes dangle above city streets on a flexible bamboo pole. And a couple of those moments, over in a flash, where Chan combines grace, ability, and timing (in one, he slips through a teller's cage, and in another he seems to walk up a scaffolding). Given Chan's so-so command of English, it's ingenious to construct a sequence that silences him with a grenade taped inside his mouth.

But Tucker's scenes finally wear us down. How can a movie allow him to be so obnoxious and make no acknowledgment that his behavior is aberrant? In a nightclub run by Hong Kong gangsters, he jumps on a table and shouts,

"Okay, all the triads and ugly women on one side, and all the fine women on the other." He is the quintessential Ugly American, and that's not funny. One rule all comedians should know, and some have to learn the hard way, is that *they* aren't funny—it's the material that gets the laughs. Another rule is that if you're the top dog on a movie set, everybody is going to pretend to laugh at everything you do, so anyone who tells you it's not that funny is trying to do you a favor. ☞

S

The Salton Sea ★ ★ ★
R, 103 m., 2002

Val Kilmer (Danny/Tom), Vincent D'Onofrio (Pooh-Bear), Adam Goldberg (Kujo), Luis Guzman (Quincy), Doug Hutchison (Morgan), Anthony LaPaglia (Garcetti), Glenn Plummer (Bobby), Peter Sarsgaard (Jimmy the Finn), Deborah Kara Unger (Colette). Directed by D. J. Caruso and produced by Ken Aguado, Frank Darabont, Eriq LaSalle, and Butch Robinson. Screenplay by Tony Gayton.

The Salton Sea is a low-life black comedy drawing inspiration from *Memento, Pulp Fiction,* and those trendy British thrillers about drug lads. It contains one element of startling originality: its bad guy, nicknamed Pooh-Bear and played by Vincent D'Onofrio in a great, weird, demented giggle of a performance; imagine a Batman villain cycled through the hallucinations of *Requiem for a Dream.*

The movie opens with what looks like a crash at the intersection of film and *noir:* Val Kilmer sits on the floor and plays a trumpet, surrounded by cash, photos, and flames. He narrates the film and makes a laundry list of biblical figures (Judas, the prodigal son) he can be compared with. As we learn about the murder of his wife and the destruction of his life, I was also reminded of Job.

Kilmer plays Danny Parker, also known as Tom Van Allen; his double identity spans a life in which he is both a jazz musician and a meth middleman, doing speed himself, inhabiting the dangerous world of speed freaks ("tweakers") and acting as an undercover agent for the cops. His life is so arduous we wonder, not for the first time, why people go to such extraordinary efforts to get and use the drugs that make them so unhappy. He doesn't use to get high, but to get from low back to bearable.

The plot involves the usual assortment of lowlifes, scum, killers, bodyguards, dealers, pathetic women, two-timing cops, and strung-out addicts, all employing Tarantinian dialogue about the flotsam of consumer society (you'd be surprised to learn what you might find under Bob Hope on eBay). Towering over them, like a bloated float in a nightmarish Thanksgiving parade, is Pooh-Bear, a drug dealer who lives in a fortified retreat in the desert and brags about the guy who shorted him $11 and got his head clamped in a vise while his brains were removed with a handsaw.

D'Onofrio is a gifted actor and his character performances have ranged from Orson Welles to Abbie Hoffman to the twisted killer with the bizarre murder devices in *The Cell.* Nothing he has done quite approaches Pooh-Bear, an overweight good ol' boy who uses his folksy accent to explain novel ways of punishing the disloyal, such as having their genitals eaten off by a rabid badger. He comes by his nickname because cocaine abuse has destroyed his nose, and he wears a little plastic job that makes him look like Pooh.

The Salton Sea is two movies fighting inside one screenplay. Val Kilmer's movie is about memory and revenge, and tenderness for the abused woman (Deborah Kara Unger) who lives across the hall in his fleabag hotel. Kilmer plays a fairly standard middleman between dealers who might kill him and cops who might betray him. But he sometimes visits a world that is essentially the second movie, a nightmarish comedy. Director D. J. Caruso and writer Tony Gayton *(Murder by Numbers)* introduce scenes with images so weird they're funny to begin with, and then funnier when they're explained. Consider Pooh-Bear's hobby of restaging the Kennedy assassination with pet pigeons in model cars. Note the little details like the pink pillbox hat. Then listen to his driver/bodyguard ask what "JFK" stands for.

On the basis of this film, meth addiction is such a debilitating illness that it's a wonder its victims have the energy for the strange things the screenplay puts them up to. We meet, for example, a dealer named Bobby (Glenn Plummer), whose girlfriend's writhing legs extend frantically from beneath the mattress he sits on, while he toys with a compressed-air spear gun. Bobby looks like a man who has earned that good night's sleep.

The Salton Sea is all pieces and no coherent whole. Maybe life on meth is like that. The plot does finally explain itself, like a dislocated shoulder popping back into place, but then the plot is off the shelf; only the characters and details set the movie aside from its stable-mates. I liked it because it was so endlessly, grotesquely, inventive: Watching it, I pictured Tarantino throwing a stick into a swamp, and the movie swimming out through the muck, retrieving it, and bringing it back with its tail wagging.

Save the Last Dance ★ ★ ★
PG-13, 112 m., 2001

Julia Stiles (Sara Johnson), Sean Patrick Thomas (Derek Reynolds), Terry Kinney (Roy), Kerry Washington (Chenille Reynolds), Fredro Starr (Malakai), Vince Green (Snookie), Bianca Lawson (Nikki), Marcello Robinson (Wonk). Directed by Thomas Carter and produced by Robert W. Cort and David Madden. Screenplay by Duane Adler and Cheryl Edwards.

Save the Last Dance begins with standard material but doesn't settle for it. The setup promises clichés, but the development is intelligent, the characters are more complicated than we expect, and the ending doesn't tie everything up in a predictable way. Above all, this is a movie where the characters ask the same questions we do: They're as smart about themselves as we are.

As the film opens, we meet Sara (Julia Stiles), a morose high school girl on a train. Flashbacks fill us in. She was a promising dancer with an audition at Julliard, but her mother was killed in an accident while driving to see her daughter dance. Now there's no money for school; Sara has lost her comfortable suburban existence and is coming to live with her father, Roy (Terry Kinney), a musician who lives in a walk-up flat in a gritty Chicago neighborhood. Roy is not unfriendly, but isn't the parent type.

The students at Sara's high school are mostly African-American, but as we notice this, we notice something else: The movie doesn't fall into ancient clichés about racial tension, the school is not painted as some kind of blackboard jungle, and the students are not electrified by the arrival of—gasp!—a white girl. They have more important things to think about.

Sara is befriended by a girl named Chenille

(Kerry Washington), who shows her how easy it is to get your bag stolen if you leave it untended. In class, she notices Derek (Sean Patrick Thomas), whose comments show he's smart. She's taken to a club on Friday night, dances with Derek (who turns out to be Chenille's brother), and starts to like him. Eventually it becomes a romance, but this is not your basic high school love story, and includes dialogue like, "We spend more time defending our relationship than actually having one."

Derek's best friend is Malakai (Fredro Starr). They've been in trouble together, and Malakai once pulled him out of a situation that could have destroyed his life. Malakai is a petty thief and a gang member; Derek is on a different track (he's just won a scholarship to Georgetown), but loyalty tugs at him when Malakai wants him to come along as backup at a potentially fatal encounter. Derek's choice, and the way the episode ends, may surprise you.

Meanwhile, Derek and Sara dance together—not just at the club, but in a deserted building where he shows her an urban style of dance, and learns of her passion for ballet. All of this is interesting because it is not simply presented as courtship, but as two young people seriously curious about dance. Their romance, when it develops, doesn't show that love is blind, but suggests that it sees very well indeed; the movie doesn't simple-mindedly applaud interracial relationships, and Sara gets bitterly criticized by Derek's sister Chenille: "You come and take one of the few decent men left after drugs, jail, and drive-bys." That overstates the case; there are lots of decent men left, but we understand how she feels.

Do you know who Julia Stiles is? She's one of the most talented of the emerging generation of actresses, although not yet a major star. Born in 1981, acting since she was eleven, she was Ethan Hawke's Ophelia in the modern-dress 2000 version of *Hamlet,* and plays the local teenager who inflames Alec Baldwin in David Mamet's *State and Main* (she was also Freddie Prinze Jr.'s squeeze in the less-than-brilliant *Down to You*). Here she is good in ways that may not be immediately apparent, as when she jockeys for personal space with her bohemian bachelor father, and likes the way she can talk with Derek (ever notice how many teenage lovers in the movies have nothing to say to each other except comments driven directly by the mechanics of the plot?).

Sean Patrick Thomas is good, too, especially in Derek's scenes with Malakai. We see the pull of loyalty struggling with the wisdom of common sense, as Malakai tries to convince him to head into trouble, and Derek fights between his instincts and his intelligence. The movie was directed by Thomas Carter (*Swing Kids, Metro*), who seems determined to let this be the story of these specific characters and not just an exercise in genre. The movie's awake. It surprises you. You can see Derek and Sara thinking. For them, romance is not the end of the story. Their lives are ahead of them. They're going to college. They have plans. Maybe they'll figure in each other's plans. They'll see. You need a lot of luck if you plan to spend your life with the first person you fall in love with in high school.

Saving Grace ★ ★
R, 93 m., 2000

Brenda Blethyn (Grace), Craig Ferguson (Matthew), Martin Clunes (Dr. Bamford), Tcheky Karyo (Jacques), Jamie Foreman (China MacFarlane), Bill Bailey (Vince), Valerie Edmond (Nicky), Tristan Sturrock (Harvey). Directed by Nigel Cole and produced by Mark Crowdy, Craig Ferguson, and Torsten Leschly. Screenplay by Crowdy and Ferguson.

When Grace's husband falls, jumps, or is pushed out of an airplane and qualifies for his closed-casket funeral, Grace discovers she's been living in a fool's paradise. She occupies a magnificent country home outside a picturesque Cornish village, she dotes on her garden, she heads local committees—and, she discovers, she is bankrupt and owes money she has no possible way of paying.

Her husband was a louse, something everyone in town seems to have known except for Grace (Brenda Blethyn). He was also a ladies' man with a mistress in London, and he spent all the money and borrowed more. Grace is appalled as the movers arrive to carry out the furniture: What is to become of her garden?

The gardener himself suggests the solution. His name is Matthew, played by Craig Ferguson, who also cowrote the movie, and he also works at the vicarage, where he has a few private marijuana plants under cultivation. They're not flourishing in the shade, alas, and he recruits Grace for advice. She suggests moving them into her greenhouse for better light and food, and, one thing leading to another as in such situations they inevitably do, before long Grace and Matthew are raising dope in wholesale quantities and may make enough money to pay the bills with lots left over.

Saving Grace sets this story in one of those villages that have been a staple of British (and Welsh, Scots, and Irish) comedies since time immemorial: villages in which P. G. Wodehouse novels would be considered realistic, where everyone knows one another, is nice, is an eccentric, plays a role, and winks at those kinds of sins that are harmless and fun. Such villages have had a renaissance in recent years. Think of *Local Hero, Waking Ned Devine, The Snapper, The Full Monty, The Englishman Who Went Up a Hill and Came Down a Mountain, Brassed Off, Circle of Friends, The Van,* and many more.

Do such places exist? I hope so. St. Isaacs, the village in Cornwall that provides the setting for *Saving Grace*, seems like the kind of place you might never want to leave, so friendly are the citizens and charming the aspect. The horrors of modern life have not penetrated here, and Grace only vaguely understands them when she ventures to London on her own to sell her marijuana harvest. For anyone who has ever ventured down Portobello Road in Notting Hill and sniffed the sweet scents on its breezes, there is a good laugh in the sight of middle-aged, respectable Grace trying to find customers. She is wearing a white summer suit—her idea of what is appropriate for a trip to London, but nobody's idea of how a pot dealer should dress.

The London scenes also provide us with a low-level drug dealer named Vince (Bill Bailey), who realizes he is in way over his head, and a higher-level drug dealer named Jacques (Tcheky Karyo), who wants to be menacing and fearful but is disarmed by Grace's naïveté (how do you threaten someone who is oblivious to threats?). When it turns out that Grace has a *lot* of very high-quality marijuana, Vince in particular wants out: "I have to go pick up my daughter from her flute lessons."

The setup of *Saving Grace* is fun, and Blethyn helps by being not just a helpless innocent but a smart woman who depended too much on her husband and now quickly learns to cope. The London dope scene is also amusing, although more might have been done with Jacques (he sometimes seems at a loss for words). But the film's ending decays into farce that is more or less routine; if it was funny to see one naked old man in *Waking Ned Devine*, how about several naked old ladies this time? We're left with a promising idea for a comedy, which arrives at some laughs but never finds its destination.

Saving Silverman ½★
PG-13, 90 m., 2001

Jason Biggs (Darren Silverman), Steve Zahn (Wayne Le Fessier), Jack Black (J. D. McNugent), Amanda Peet (Judith Snodgrass-Fessbeggler), Amanda Detmer (Sandy Perkus), R. Lee Ermey (Coach), Neil Diamond (Himself). Directed by Dennis Dugan and produced by Neal H. Moritz. Screenplay by Greg DePaul and Hank Nelken.

Saving Silverman is so bad in so many different ways that perhaps you should see it, as an example of the lowest slopes of the bell-shaped curve. This is the kind of movie that gives even its defenders fits of desperation.

Consider my friend James Berardinelli, the best of the Web-based critics. No doubt ten days of oxygen deprivation at the Sundance Film Festival helped inspire his three-star review, in which he reports optimistically, "*Saving Silverman* has its share of pratfalls and slapstick moments, but there's almost no flatulence." Here's a critical rule of thumb: You know you're in trouble when you're reduced to praising a movie for its absence of fart jokes, and have to add "almost."

The movie is a male-bonding comedy in which three friends since grade school, now allegedly in their early twenties but looking in two cases suspiciously weathered for anyone under a hard-living thirty-two, are threatened by a romance. Darren Silverman (Jason Biggs), Wayne Le Fessier (Steve Zahn), and J. D. McNugent (Jack Black) grew up together sharing a common passion for the works of Neil Diamond; their sidewalk band, the Diamonds, performs his songs and then passes the hat.

The band is broken up, alas, when Darren is captured by Judith Snodgrass-Fessbeggler (Amanda Peet), a blonde man-eater who immediately bans his friends and starts transforming him into a broken and tamed possession. "He's my puppet and I'm his puppet master!" she declares, proving that she is unfamiliar with the word *mistress*, which does not come as a surprise. In a movie so desperately in need of laughs, it's a mystery why the filmmakers didn't drag Ms. Snodgrass-Fessbeggler's parents onstage long enough to explain their decision to go with the hyphenated last name.

Wayne and J.D. concoct a desperate scheme to save Darren from marriage. They kidnap Judith, convince Darren she is dead, and arrange for him to meet the original love of his life, Sandy Perkus (Amanda Detmer), who is now studying to be a nun. She hasn't yet taken her vows, especially the one of chastity, and is a major babe in her form-fitting novice's habit.

I was going to write that the funniest character in the movie is the boys' former high school coach (R. Lee Ermey, a former marine drill sergeant). It would be more accurate to say the same character would be funny in another movie, but is stopped cold by this one, even though the screenplay tries (when the boys ask Coach what to do with the kidnapped Judith, he replies, "kill her").

The lads don't idolize Neil Diamond merely in theory, but in the flesh, as well. Yes, Diamond himself appears in the film, kids himself, and sings a couple of songs. As a career decision, this ranks somewhere between being a good sport and professional suicide. Perhaps he should have reflected that the director, Dennis Dugan, has directed two Adam Sandler movies (both, it must be said, better than this).

Saving Silverman is Jason Biggs's fourth appearance in a row in a dumb sex comedy (in descending order of quality, they are *American Pie, Boys and Girls,* and *Loser*). It is time for him to strike out in a new direction; the announcement that he will appear in *American Pie II* does not seem to promise that.

Steve Zahn and Jack Black are, in the right movies, splendid comedy actors; Zahn was wonderful in *Happy, Texas,* and Jack Black stole his scenes in *High Fidelity* and *Jesus' Son*. Here they have approximately the charm of Wilson, the soccer ball. Amanda Peet and Amanda Detmer do no harm, although Peet is too nice to play a woman this mean. Lee Ermey is on a planet of his own. As for Neil Diamond, *Saving Silverman* is his first appearance in a fiction film since *The Jazz Singer* (1980), and one can only marvel that he waited twenty years to appear in a second film, and found one even worse than his first one.

Say It Isn't So ★
R, 93 m., 2001

Chris Klein (Gilly Noble), Heather Graham (Jo Wingfield), Orlando Jones (Dig McCaffey), Sally Field (Valdine Wingfield), Richard Jenkins (Walter Wingfield), John Rothman (Larry), Jack Plotnick (Leon), Eddie Cibrian (Jack Mitchelson). Directed by James B. Rogers and produced by Bobby Farrelly, Peter Farrelly, and Bradley Thomas. Screenplay by Peter Gaulke and Gerry Swallow.

Comedy characters can't be successfully embarrassed for more than a few seconds at a time. Even then, it's best if they don't know what they've done wrong—if the joke's on them, and they don't get it. The "hair gel" scenes in *There's Something About Mary* are a classic example of embarrassment done right. *Say It Isn't So*, on the other hand, keeps a character embarrassed in scene after scene, until he becomes an . . . embarrassment. The movie doesn't understand that embarrassment comes in a sudden painful flush of realization; drag it out, and it's not embarrassment anymore, but public humiliation, which is a different condition, and not funny.

The movie stars Heather Graham and Chris Klein as Jo and Gilly, a hairdresser and a dogcatcher who fall deeply in love and then discover they are brother and sister. Jo flees town to marry a millionaire jerk. Gilly lingers behind in public disgrace until he discovers they are not related after all. But since Jo's family wants her to marry the rich guy, everybody conspires to keep Gilly away. The movie tries for a long-running gag based on the fact that everybody in town mocks Gilly because he

slept with his alleged sister. They even write rude remarks in the dust on his truck. This is not funny but merely repetitive.

The movie was produced by the Farrelly brothers, who in *There's Something About Mary* and *Kingpin* showed a finer understanding of the mechanics of comedy than they do here. *Say It Isn't So* was directed by James B. Rogers from a screenplay by Peter Gaulke and Gerry Swallow, who show they are students of Farrellyism but not yet graduates. They include obligatory elements like physical handicaps, sexual miscalculations, intestinal difficulties, and weird things done to animals, but few of the gags really work. They know the words but not the music.

Consider a scene in which Chris Klein, as Gilly, punches a cow and his arm becomes lodged in just that portion of the cow's anatomy where both Gilly and the cow would least hope to find it. I can understand intellectually that this could be funny. But to be funny, the character would have to have a great deal invested in *not* appearing like the kind of doofus who would pull such a stunt. Gilly has been established as such a simpleton he has nothing to lose. The cow scene is simply one more cross for him to bear. There is in the movie a legless pilot (Orlando Jones) who prides himself on his heroic aerial abilities. If he had gotten stuck in the cow and been pulled legless down the street—now that would have been funny. Tasteless, yes, and cruel. But not tiresome.

That leads us to another of the movie's miscalculations. Its characters are not smart enough to be properly embarrassed. To be Jo or Gilly is already to be beyond embarrassment, since they wake up already clueless. The genius of *There's Something About Mary* and *Kingpin* was that the characters played by Ben Stiller and Woody Harrelson were smart, clever, played the angles—and still got disgraced. To pick on Gilly and Jo is like shooting fish in a barrel.

Chris Klein's character seems like someone who never gets the joke, who keeps smiling bravely as if everyone can't be laughing at him. We feel sorry for him, which is fatal for a comedy. Better a sharp, edgy character who deserves his comeuppance. Heather Graham's Jo, whose principal character trait is a push-up bra, isn't really engaged by the plot at all, but is blown hither and yon by the winds of fate.

That leaves three characters who are funny a lot of the time: Jo's parents, Valdine and Walter Wingfield (Sally Field and Richard Jenkins), and Dig McCaffey (Orlando Jones), the legless pilot. Valdine is a scheming, money-grubbing con woman who conceals from Gilly the fact that she is not his mother, so that Jo can marry the millionaire. And Walter is her terminally ill husband, communicating through an electronic voice amplifier, who bears a grudge against almost everyone he can see. These characters have the necessary meanness of spirit, and Dig McCaffey is so improbable, as a Jimi Hendrix look-alike, that he gets laughs by sheer incongruity.

On the TV clips, they show the scene where Jo gets so excited while cutting Gilly's hair that she takes a slice out of his ear. Since you have seen this scene, I will use it as an example of comic miscalculation. We see her scissors cutting through the flesh as they amputate an upper slope of his earlobe. This is not funny. It is cringe-inducing. Better to choose an angle where you can't see the actual cut at all, and then have his entire ear spring loose. Go for the laugh with the idea, not the sight, of grievous injury. And instead of giving Gilly an operation to reattach the missing flesh, have him go through the entire movie without an ear (make a subtle joke by having him always present his good ear to the camera). There are sound comic principles at work here, which *Say It Isn't So* doesn't seem to understand.

Note: The end credits include the usual obligatory outtakes from the movie. These are unique in that they are clearly real and authentic, not scripted. They demonstrate what we have suspected: that real outtakes are rarely funny.

Scary Movie ★ ★ ★
R, 85 m., 2000

Carmen Electra (Drew), Dave Sheridan (Doofy), Frank B. Moore (Not Drew's Boyfriend), Keenen Ivory Wayans (Masked Killer), Cheri Oteri (Gail Hailstorm), Regina Hall (Brenda), Mark McConchie (Drew's Dad), Karen Kruper (Drew's Mom), Anna Faris (Cindy), Shawn Wayans (Ray). Directed by Keenen Ivory Wayans and produced by Eric L. Gold and Lee R. Mayes. Screenplay by Shawn Wayans, Marlon Wayans, Buddy Johnson, Phil Beauman, Jason Friedberg, and Aaron Seltzer.

I recently published a book about movies I hated, and people have been asking me which reviews are harder to write—those about great movies or those about terrible ones. The answer is, neither. The most unreviewable movies are those belonging to the spoof genre—movies like *Airplane!* and *The Naked Gun* and all the countless spin-offs and retreads of the same basic idea.

Scary Movie is a film in that tradition: a raucous, satirical attack on slasher movies, teenage horror movies, and *The Matrix*. I saw the movie, I laughed, I took notes, and now I am at a loss to write the review. All of the usual critical categories and strategies collapse in the face of a film like this.

Shall I discuss the plot? There is none, really—only a flimsy clothesline to link some of the gags. The characters? They are all types or targets, not people. The dialogue? You can't review the dialogue in the original movies (like *I Know What You Did Last Summer*) because it is mindlessly functional, serving only to advance the plot. How can you discuss the satire, except to observe it is more mindless? (Some of the dialogue, indeed, seems lifted bodily from the earlier films and rotated slightly in the direction of satire.)

Faced with a dilemma like this, the experienced critic falls back on a reliable ploy. He gives away some of the best jokes and punch lines. He's like a buddy who has just walked out of a movie and tells you the funny stuff before you walk in.

I am tempted. I fight the impulse to tell you that when a character is asked for the name of a favorite scary movie, the answer is "Kazaam." That some of the scenes take place at B.A. Corpse High School. That the teenagers in the movie are played mostly by actors in their late twenties and thirties—and that the movie comments on this. That the movie's virgin has a certificate to prove it. That the invaluable Carmen Electra plays a character not coincidentally named Drew.

The movie takes a shotgun approach to horror and slasher movies, but if it has a single target, that would be Kevin Williamson, screenwriter of *Scream* and coinventor of the self-aware slasher subgenre. There is a sense in which *Scary Movie* is doing the same sort of self-referential humor as *Scream,* since it is not only directed by Keenen Ivory Wayans, cowritten by Shawn and Marlon Wayans (among others), and starring several Wayanses, but makes fun of various Wayans trademarks, especially the obligatory homophobic jokes. (There's a scene involving a closeted jock who can make love to his girlfriend only when she's wearing football shoulder pads.)

The movie also features the wild exaggeration of stereotypical African-American behavior, which is another Wayans specialty. Consider the scene where Regina Hall plays a black woman at *Shakespeare in Love* who shouts, "That ain't no man!" when Gwyneth Paltrow is on the screen, videotapes the movie from her seat, and carries on a cell phone conversation. Funny, though; now that I've written about it, I realize this is not intended to be a satire of African-American behavior, but an attack on the behavior of countless moviegoers, and Wayans has simply used Regina Hall as an example of nontraditional casting. Or maybe not.

The bottom line in reviewing a movie like this is, does it work? Is it funny? Yes, it is. Not funny with the shocking impact of *Airplane!,* which had the advantage of breaking new ground. But also not a tired wheeze like some of the lesser and later Leslie Nielsen films. To get your money's worth, you need to be familiar with the various teenage horror franchises, but if you are, *Scary Movie* delivers the goods.

Note: The original title of Scary Movie *was* Scream If You Know What I Did Last Halloween. *The original title of* Scream *was* Scary Movie. *Still available:* I Still Know What You Did the Summer Before Last.

Scooby-Doo ★
PG, 87 m., 2002

Matthew Lillard (Norville "Shaggy" Rogers), Freddie Prinze Jr. (Fred Jones), Sarah Michelle Gellar (Daphne Blake), Linda Cardellini (Velma Dinkley), Rowan Atkinson (Mondavarious), Isla Fisher (Mary Jane), Andrew Bryniarski (Henchman). Directed by Raja Gosnell and produced by Charles Roven. Screenplay by James Gunn, based on characters created by Willam Hanna and Joseph Barbera.

I am not the person to review this movie. I have never seen the *Scooby-Doo* television program, and on the basis of the film I have no desire to start now. I feel no sympathy with any of the characters, I am unable to judge whether the live-action movie is a better idea than the all-cartoon TV approach, I am unable to generate the slightest interest in the plot, and I laughed not a single time, although I smiled more than once at the animated Scooby-Doo himself, an island of amusement in a wasteland of fecklessness.

What I can say, I think, is that a movie like this should in some sense be accessible to a nonfan like myself. I realize that every TV cartoon show has a cadre of fans that grew up with it, have seen every episode many times, and are alert to the nuances of the movie adaptation. But those people, however numerous they are, might perhaps find themselves going to a movie with people like myself—people who found, even at a very young age, that the world was filled with entertainment choices more stimulating than *Scooby-Doo.* If these people can't walk into the movie cold and understand it and get something out of it, then the movie has failed except as an in-joke.

As for myself, scrutinizing the screen helplessly for an angle of approach, one thing above all caught my attention: the director, Raja Gosnell, has a thing about big boobs. I say this not only because of the revealing low-cut costumes of such principals as Sarah Michelle Gellar, but also because of the number of busty extras and background players, who drift by in crowd scenes with what Russ Meyer used to call "cleavage cantilevered on the same principle that made the Sydney Opera House possible." Just as Woody Allen's *Hollywood Ending* is a comedy about a movie director who forges ahead even though he is blind, *Scooby-Doo* could have been a comedy about how a Russ Meyer clone copes with being assigned a live-action adaptation of a kiddie cartoon show.

I did like the dog. Scooby-Doo so thoroughly upstages the live actors that I cannot understand why Warner Bros. didn't just go ahead and make the whole movie animated. While Matthew Lillard, Sarah Michelle Gellar, and Linda Cardellini show pluck in trying to outlast the material, Freddie Prinze Jr. seems completely at a loss to account for his presence in the movie, and the squinchy-faced Rowan *(Mr. Bean)* Atkinson plays the villain as a private joke.

I pray, dear readers, that you not send me mail explaining the genius of *Scooby-Doo* and attacking me for being ill prepared to write this review. I have already turned myself in. Not only am I ill prepared to review the movie, but I venture to guess that anyone who is not literally a member of a *Scooby-Doo* fan club would be equally incapable. This movie exists in a closed universe, and the rest of us are aliens. The Internet was invented so that you can find someone else's review of *Scooby-Doo.* Start surfing.

The Score ★ ★ ★
R, 124 m., 2001

Robert De Niro (Nick Wells), Marlon Brando (Max Baron), Edward Norton (Jackie Teller/ Brian), Angela Bassett (Diane), Jamie Harrold (Stephen), Gary Farmer (Burt). Directed by Frank Oz and produced by Gary Foster, Lee Rich, and Peter Guber. Screenplay by Kario Salem, Lem Dobbs, and Scott Marshall Smith, based on a story by Daniel E. Taylor and Salem.

The Score is the best pure heist movie in recent years. It assembles three generations of great American actors and puts them to work on a break-in of awesome complexity, and has the patience to build real suspense instead of trying to substitute cheap thrills. Its climax is a sustained sequence involving three parallel lines of action, and we're reminded of the best heist movies of the past, like *Grand Slam* (1968), where everything depends on a meticulous and dangerous scenario.

The movie is above all an exercise of traditional craftsmanship. It is very hard to write and direct a screenplay like this, where there can't be loopholes, where the key scenes involve little dialogue and a lot of painstaking physical action, and where the plot surprises, when they come, have been prepared for and earned. Who would have guessed that Frank Oz, a onetime Muppeteer whose work has been mostly in comedy, could direct a *noir* caper that's so lean and involving?

The Score tells the kind of story that ex-plains itself as it goes along, so that by the end we more or less understand how the heist is supposed to work. For that reason, I won't describe specific details of the plot. The setup is another matter, developing characters who are convincing and colorful, as this genre goes, and putting them in relationships that flash with humor and a little mystery.

Robert De Niro stars as Nick Wells, who runs a jazz club in the old town of Montreal but is not, judging by his French, a native. His other job is as a specialist in break-ins, and the title sequence shows him trying to crack a safe in Boston. His rule: Never rob where you live. But now his old friend Max (Marlon Brando), a Montreal crime lord, comes to him with an offer. He knows of an invaluable antique in the Montreal Customs House, and of a way to steal it. The key to his plan: a contact named Jackie (Edward Norton), who is a janitor at the building. Jackie has become a coddled favorite there by pretending to be "Brian," whose speech and movement seem affected by some kind of brain damage.

These three performances are what they need to be and no more. It is a sign of professionalism when an actor can inhabit a genre instead of trying to transcend it. De Niro's Nick is taciturn, weary, ready to retire after the proverbial one last score. Norton is younger and hungrier, and a show-off who angers Nick by fooling him with the Brian performance. Brando's Max is a dialed-down Sidney Greenstreet character, large, wealthy, a little effeminate; his days of action are behind him, and now he moves other men on the chessboard of his schemes.

To these three characters the screenplay adds a fourth, but does not use her well. This is Diane (Angela Bassett), Nick's girlfriend, who flies into town for brief romantic meetings and is assigned the thankless task of saying yes, she'll marry him—but only if he promises he has retired from his life of crime. Diane is so sadly underwritten that Bassett, a good actress, seems walled in by her dialogue. The filmmakers should have eliminated the role, or found a real purpose for her; as a perfunctory love interest, Diane is a cliché.

There are, however, a couple of flashy supporting roles. When it's necessary to crack the security code used by the agency that guards the Customs House, Nick calls on a friend named Stephen (Jamie Harrold), who lives in a kind of cybernetic war room in his basement, and boasts he's the best: "Give me a KayPro 64 and a dial tone and I can do anything." (There's a running gag about Stephen's mother shouting downstairs to him—a nod to De Niro's character in *The King of Comedy*.) Another supporting role, quieter but necessary, is played by Gary Farmer, the big Canadian Indian actor, who is Nick's strong-arm man.

The dialogue has a nice hard humor to it. When Nick meets a man in the park who is going to sell him a secret, the man comes with another man. "Who's that?" asks Nick. "My cousin," the man says. "See that man reading the newspaper on the bench over there?" says Nick, nodding to the gigantic Farmer. "He's my cousin. So we both have family here."

Brick by brick, the screenplay assembles the pieces of the heist plan. Obligatory elements are respected. We learn that the Montreal Customs House is the most impenetrable building in Quebec, and maybe Canada. We go on a scouting expedition in a labyrinth of tunnels under the building. We're introduced to high-tech equipment, like miniature cameras and infrared detectors. We study the floor plan. We are alarmed by last-minute changes in plans, when the customs officials finally find out how valuable the treasure is and install motion sensors and three cameras. And then the caper itself unfolds, and of it I will say nothing, except that De Niro's character does incredibly difficult and ingenious things, and we are absorbed.

That's the point. That we sit in the theater in silent concentration, not restless, not stirring, involved in the suspense. Of course there are unanticipated developments. The risk of premature discovery. Twists and turns. But there is not a lot of violence, and the movie honorably avoids a cop-out ending of gunfights and chases. It is true to its story, and the story involves characters, not stunts and special effects. At the end, we feel *satisfied*. We aren't jazzed up by phony fireworks, but satiated by the fulfillment of this clockwork plot that has never cheated. *The Score* is not a great movie, but as a classic heist movie, it's solid professionalism.

The Scorpion King ★ ★ ½
PG-13, 94 m., 2002

The Rock (Mathayus), Steven Brand (Memnon), Michael Clarke Duncan (Balthazar), Kelly Hu (The Sorceress), Bernard Hill (Philos), Grant Heslov (Arpid), Peter Facinelli (Takmet), Ralf Moeller (Thorak). Directed by Chuck Russell and produced by Stephen Sommers, Sean Daniel, James Jacks, and Kevin Misher. Screenplay by Sommers, William Osborne, and David Hayter, based on a story by Sommers and Jonathan Hales.

"Where do you think you are going with my horse?"
"To Gomorrah. Nothing we can say will stop him."
—Dialogue in *The Scorpion King*

And a wise move, too, because *The Scorpion King* is set "thousands of years before the Pyramids," so property values in Gomorrah were a good value for anyone willing to buy and hold. Here is a movie that embraces its goofiness like a Get Out of Jail Free card. The plot is recycled out of previous recycling jobs, the special effects are bad enough that you can grin at them, and the dialogue sounds like the pre-Pyramidal desert warriors are channeling a Fox sitcom (the hero refers to his camel as "my ride").

The film stars The Rock, famous as a WWF wrestling star (Vince McMahon takes a producer's credit), and on the basis of this movie, he can definitely star in movies like this. This story takes place so long ago in prehistory that The Rock was a hero and had not yet turned into the villain of *The Mummy Returns* (2001), and we can clearly see his face and muscular physique—an improvement over the earlier film, in which his scenes mostly consisted of his face being attached to a scorpion so large it looked like a giant lobster. How gigantic was the lobster? It would take a buffalo to play the Turf.

The story: An evil Scorpion King named Memnon (Steven Brand) uses the talents of a sorceress (Kelly Hu) to map his battle plans, and has conquered most of his enemies. Then we meet three Arkadians, professional assassins who have been "trained for generations in the deadly art," which indicates their training began even before they were born. The Arkadian leader Mathayus, played by The Rock, is such a powerful man that early in the film he shoots a guy with an arrow and the force of the arrow sends the guy crashing through a wall and flying through the air. (No wonder he warns, "Don't touch the bow.")

How The Rock morphs from this character into the *Mummy Returns* character is a mystery to me, and, I am sure, to him. Along the trail Mathayus loses some allies and gains others, including a Nubian giant (Michael Clarke Duncan), a scientist who has invented gunpowder, a clever kid, and a wisecracking horse thief. The scene where they vow to kill the Scorpion King is especially impressive, as Mathayus intones, "As long as one of us still breathes, the sorcerer will die!" See if you can spot the logical loophole.*

Mathayus and his team invade the desert stronghold of Memnon, where the sorceress, who comes from or perhaps is the first in a long line of James Bond heroines, sets eyes on him and wonders why she's bothering with the scrawny king. Special effects send Mathayus and others catapulting into harems, falling from castle walls, and narrowly missing death by fire, scorpion, poisonous cobra, swordplay, arrows, explosion, and being buried up to the neck in the sand near colonies of fire ants. And that's not even counting the Valley of the Death, which inspires the neo-Mametian dialogue: "No one goes to the Valley of the Death. That's why it's called the Valley of the Death."

Of all the special effects in the movie, the most impressive are the ones that keep the breasts of the many nubile maidens covered to within one centimeter of the PG-13 guidelines. Kelly Hu, a beautiful woman who looks as if she is trying to remember the good things her agent told her would happen if she took this role, has especially clever long flowing hair, which cascades down over her breasts instead of up over her head even when she is descending a waterfall.

Did I enjoy this movie? Yeah, I did, although not quite enough to recommend it, because it tries too hard to be hyper and not hard enough to be clever. It is what it is, though, and is pretty good at it. Those who would dislike the movie are unlikely to attend it (does

anybody go to see The Rock in *The Scorpion King* by accident?). For its target audience, looking for a few laughs, martial arts and stuff that blows up real good, it will be exactly what they expected. It has high energy, the action never stops, the dialogue knows it's funny, and The Rock has the authority to play the role and the fortitude to keep a straight face. I expect him to become a durable action star. There's something about the way he eats those fire ants that lets you know he's thinking, "If I ever escape from this predicament, I'm gonna come back here and fix me up a real mess of fire ants, instead of just chewing on a few at a time."

Now see if you can spot the logical error in my question. ☞

Scotland, PA. ★ ★ ½
R, 102 m., 2002

James LeGros (Joe "Mac" McBeth), Maura Tierney (Pat McBeth), Christopher Walken (Lieutenant Ernie McDuff), Kevin Corrigan (Anthony "Banco" Banconi), James Rebhorn (Norm Duncan), Tom Guiry (Malcolm Duncan), Andy Dick (Hippie Jesse), Amy Smart (Hippie Stacy), Timothy "Speed" Levitch (Hippie Hector), Josh Pais (Doug McKenna), Geoff Dunsworth (Donald Duncan). Directed by Billy Morrissette and produced by Richard Shepard and Jonathan Stern. Screenplay by Morrissette, based on *Macbeth* by Shakespeare.

Scotland, PA. translates Shakespeare's *Macbeth* into a comedy set in a Pennsylvania fast-food burger stand, circa 1975. Lady Macbeth rubs unhappily at a grease burn on her hand, the three witches become three local hippies, and poor Duncan, the manager, isn't attacked with a knife but is pounded on the head with a skillet. If you know *Macbeth*, it's funny. Anyone who doesn't is going to think these people are acting mighty peculiar.

Like all good satire, this one is based on venom and loathing. I learn that Billy Morrissette, the writer-director, first began to think of burger stands in Macbethian terms while working in one some twenty years ago. He shared his thoughts with his girlfriend, Maura Tierney, who became his wife, and appropriately plays Lady Macbeth, a.k.a. Mrs. McBeth, in this movie.

The story: "Mac" McBeth (James LeGros) and his wife, Pat, slave unhappily in Duncan's, a fast-food outlet run by Norm Duncan (James Rebhorn). Mac lives with the dream that he will someday be manager. His current boss is Doug McKenna (Josh Pais), who is ripping off Duncan and pocketing receipts. The McBeths tell Duncan about the theft, expecting Mac will be named the new manager. But, no, Duncan picks his two sons, Malcolm (Tom Guiry) and Donald (Geoff Dunsworth) as his heirs.

This is not right, Pat McBeth hisses fiercely to her husband. Especially not after Mac has increased sales by introducing the concept of a drive-through line to Scotland, Pa. Pat badgers her husband to kill Duncan and buy the eatery from his indifferent sons. "We're not bad people, Mac," she argues. "We're just underachievers who have to make up for lost time."

Macbeth is Shakespeare's most violent play, and *Scotland, PA.* follows cheerfully in that tradition; after Duncan is pounded on the head, what finishes him off is a headfirst dive into the french-fry grease. The case is so suspicious that the local cops call in Lieutenant Ernie McDuff (Christopher Walken), who affects a kind of genial absentmindedness as a cover for his investigation. "This place really looks great," he tells the proud couple at the grand opening of their McBeth's. "Of course, the last time there was a dead body in the fryer."

Morrissette uses the Shakespeare parallels whenever he can (there is, of course, a ghost at McBeth's opening), and Tierney, in the juiciest role, actually evokes some of the power of the original Lady Macbeth, especially in the way she deals with the torment of her blistered hands. And James LeGros is as feckless and clueless as Shakespeare's Macbeth—easily led, easily deceived, easily disheartened.

The buried joke in many parodies is that events must happen because they did in the original. That works here to explain the remorseless procession of bloody and creepy events. We're expected to engage with the movie on two levels—as itself, and as a parallel to Shakespeare. While modern retellings of Shakespeare often work (as in the Michael Almereyda–Ethan Hawke *Hamlet* or Tim Blake Nelson's *O*), a parody is another matter; like an update, it deprives itself of the purpose of the original. It's even more complicated when

the maker of the parody doesn't despise the original, but clearly likes it. Morrissette hates fast food, not *Macbeth.*

I enjoyed the movie in a superficial way, while never sure what its purpose was. I have the curious suspicion that it will be enjoyed most by someone who knows absolutely nothing about Shakespeare, and can see it simply as the story of some very strange people who seem to be reading from the same secret script.

Scream 3 ★ ★
R, 116 m., 2000

Neve Campbell (Sidney Prescott), Courteney Cox Arquette (Gale Weathers), David Arquette (Dewey Riley), Parker Posey (Jennifer Jolie), Scott Foley (Roman Bridge), Deon Richmond (Tyson Fox), Patrick Dempsey (Detective Kincaid), Lance Henriksen (John Milton), Liev Schreiber (Cotton Weary), Jenny McCarthy (Sarah Darling), Patrick Warburton (Guard). Directed by Wes Craven and produced by Cathy Konrad, Kevin Williamson, and Marianne Maddalena. Screenplay by Ehren Kruger.

The difference between a trilogy and a sequel, we're told in *Scream 3*, is that sequels go on and on, while a trilogy has a beginning, a middle, and an end: "In a trilogy, nobody's safe. Even the hero can die in the final chapter." So explains one of the movie buffs in the third of this self-aware slasher series in which the characters know all the horror clichés and get trapped in them anyway.

The action this time moves the key surviving actors from the previous *Screams* to Hollywood, where a horror film named *Stab 3* is under way. There is a death, and then another: The killer is slashing the actors in the same order they die in the screenplay. But the third victim may be hard to predict: "There were three different versions of the script," an executive explains, "to keep the ending off the Internet. I don't know which version the killer read." No matter; the fax machine rings, and it's a call from the killer, transmitting revised script pages.

That problem of spoilers on the Net could inspire a slasher movie of its own (serial killer, under delusion he is Freddy Krueger, kills to prove a Web rumor site is wrong). In an attempt to keep Websites from revealing the movie's secrets, Miramax's Dimension division delayed screenings until the last possible moment, and even then banned many Web-based critics from attending (although the lads from Playboy.com were hunkered down happily in the row in front of me).

Anyone who would reveal the identity of the killer in *Scream 3* would in any event be the lowest form of life, since the secret is absolutely unguessable. Why? Because the identity is absolutely arbitrary. It could be anyone in the movie or (this would be a neat twist) none of the above. The characters are so thin they're transparent. They function primarily to scream, split up when they should stick together, go alone into basements and dark rooms, and make ironic references to horror clichés and earlier movies in the series. The director, Wes Craven, covered the self-aware horror genre splendidly in *Wes Craven's New Nightmare* (1994), and this is the lite version.

Some of it is fun. You can play spot-the-cameo with visiting celebs like Roger Corman, Kevin Smith, and Carrie Fisher (she's a studio archivist who explains, "I was up for Princess Leia, but you know who gets it—the one who sleeps with George Lucas"). And you can appreciate the logic behind Parker Posey's reasoning. She plays the actress hired to portray TV journalist Gale Weathers (Courteney Cox Arquette), and tells her, "Everywhere you go, I'm gonna follow you, so if he wants to kill you, you'll be there to be killed, and he won't need to kill me."

Scream 3 is essentially an interlacing of irony and gotcha! scenes. The monster in his (or her) fright mask can be anywhere at any time and jump into the frame at any moment. All we know for sure is that two or three scares will be false. (When will the characters in these movies learn that when victims are being "cut up into fish sticks," it is *not funny* to sneak up behind friends to scare them?)

Neve Campbell is back as the key character, a woman so traumatized she has changed her name, moved to Monterey, and works for a crisis hot line. The camera loves her. She could become a really big star and giggle at clips from this film at her AFI tribute. Also starring are David Arquette as a former deputy, now a would-be security guard who's still in love with

Gale Weathers; Scott Foley as the *Stab 3* director; Deon Richmond as a guy who knows all the movie conventions; Liev Schreiber as an ex-con talk show host; Patrick Dempsey as a cop; Lance Henriksen as a demented horror film director with old secrets; and Jenny McCarthy as an actress who does or does not get killed, but certainly wears a dress we will see again in *Playboy*'s annual "Sex in the Cinema" feature. Patrick Warburton, a rising action star, has a funny bit as a "professional celebrity guard" whose clients have "included Julia Roberts and Salman Rushdie."

My own feeling is relief that the series is at last ended. If *Scream* (1996) was like a funny joke, *Scream 2* (1997) was like somebody telling you, "Here's how I heard that joke," and *Scream 3* is like somebody who won't believe you've already heard it. What I will remember from the movie is that everyone uses cell phones constantly, which is convenient for the screenplay, since the characters can be anywhere and still call for help or threaten one another. Remember the 1980 horror movie named *Don't Answer the Phone*? If the *Scream 3* gang had taken that advice, there would have been no movie, just a lot of lonely characters scattered all over California, waiting for calls.

See Spot Run ★ ½
PG, 94 m., 2001

David Arquette (Gordon Smith), Michael Clarke Duncan (Agent Murdoch), Leslie Bibb (Stephanie), Joe Viterelli (Gino Valente), Angus T. Jones (James), Steven R. Schirripa (Arliss Santino), Anthony Anderson (Benny), Paul Sorvino (Sonny Talia). Directed by John Whitesell and produced by Robert Simonds, Tracey Trench, and Andrew Deane. Screenplay by George Gallo, Dan Baron, and Christian Faber, based on a story by Stuart Gibbs, Craig Titley, and Gallo.

See Spot Run is pitched at the same intellectual level as the earlier stories involving Spot, which I found so immensely involving in the first grade. There are a few refinements. The characters this time are named Gordon, Stephanie, and James, instead of Dick and Jane. And I don't recall the *Spot* books describing the hero rolling around in doggy poo, or a gangster getting his testicles bitten off, but times change. The gangster is named Sonny Talia, in a heroic act of restraint by the filmmakers, who could have named him Gino with no trouble at all.

The movie is a fairly desperate PG-rated comedy about a dog that has been highly trained for the FBI's canine corps. After it bites off one of Talia's indispensables, the mob boss (Paul Sorvino) orders a hit on the dog, which is hustled into a version of the witness protection program, only to accidentally end up in the possession of young James (Angus T. Jones) and his baby-sitting neighbor, Gordon (David Arquette), who has a crush on James's mother, Stephanie (Leslie Bibb).

This is all setup for a series of slapstick comedy ventures, in which Gordon is humiliated and besmeared while the dog races about proving it is the most intelligent mammal in the picture. The most excruciating sequence has Gordon shinnying up a gutter pipe, which collapses (as all movie gutter pipes always do), tearing off his underpants and depositing him in one of Spot's large, damp, and voluminous gifts to the ecology. When Gordon is thoroughly smeared with caca, what do you think the odds are that (1) the lawn sprinkler system comes on, and (2) the police arrive and demand an explanation?

Another long sequence involves the destruction of a pet store, as mobsters chase the dog and Gordon gets encased in a large ball of bubble wrap, which is inflated by helium, causing him to ... oh, never mind. And don't get me started on the scene where he lights the zebra fart.

Movies like this demonstrate that when it comes to stupidity and vulgarity, only the best will do for our children. There seems to be some kind of desperate downward trend in American taste, so that when we see a dog movie like this we think back nostalgically to the *Beethoven* dog pictures, which now represent a cultural high-water mark. Consider that there was a time in our society when children were entertained by the *Lassie* pictures, and you can see that the national taste is rapidly spiraling down to the level of a whoopee cushion.

And yes, of course, there are many jokes in *See Spot Run* involving the passing of gas and the placing of blame. Also a fight with two deaf women. Also an electrified dog collar that is activated by a TV channel changer, causing David Arquette to levitate while sparks fly out of his orifices. And a bus that slides over a cliff. And an FBI agent named "Cassavetes," which must be a masochistic in-joke by the filmmakers to remind themselves of how far they have fallen from their early ideals.

The one actor who emerges more or less unharmed is Michael Clarke Duncan, the gentle giant from *The Green Mile*, who is the dog's FBI handler and plays his scenes with the joy of a man whose stream of consciousness must run like this: *No matter how bad this movie is, at least it's better than working for the City of Chicago Department of Streets and Sanitation. I'm still wading through doggy do, but at least now I'm getting paid a movie star salary for doing it.*

Serendipity ★ ½
PG-13, 95 m., 2001

John Cusack (Jon Trager), Kate Beckinsale (Sara Thomas), Molly Shannon (Eve), Jeremy Piven (Dean Kansky), John Corbett (Lars Hammond), Bridget Moynahan (Halley Buchanan), Eugene Levy (Bloomingdale's Salesman). Directed by Peter Chelsom and produced by Simon Fields, Peter Abrams, and Robert L. Levy. Screenplay by Marc Klein.

"If we're meant to meet again, we will."

So says Sara Thomas to Jon Trager. This much has already happened: They have a Meet Cute while fighting over the same pair of cashmere gloves in Bloomingdale's. They feel, if not love, strong attraction at first sight. They go out for hot chocolate. They find out each is dating somebody else. They separate. They return—he for a scarf, she for a parcel. They meet again. He wants her phone number. But no. They must leave themselves in the hands of Fate.

Fate I have no problem with. Leaving themselves in the hands of this screenplay is another matter. It bounces them through so many amazing coincidences and serendipitous parallels and cosmic concordances that Fate is not merely knocking on the door, it has entered with a SWAT team and is banging their heads together and administering poppers.

Jon is played by John Cusack in what is either a bad career move or temporary insanity. Sara is played by Kate Beckinsale, who is a good actress, but not good enough to play this dumb. Jon and Sara have much in common; both are missing an "h." The movie puts them through dramatic and romantic situations so close to parody as to make no difference; one more turn of the screw and this could be a satire of *Sleepless in Seattle*.

Consider. They want to be together. They like each other better than the people they are dating. But they toy with their happiness by setting a series of tests. For example: She says they'll get on separate elevators in a hotel and see if they both push the same button. Odds are against it. They do, however, both push the same button—but do not meet because of a little boy who pushes all the other buttons on Cusack's elevator. I consider this God's way of telling them, "Don't tempt me."

Another test. Jon will write his telephone number on a $5 bill and it will go out in the world, and she will see if it comes back to her. A third test. Sara will write her number in a copy of a novel by Gabriel García Márquez, and if Jon finds it in a used bookstore, well, there you are. (Márquez is fond of coincidences, but *Serendipity* elevates magic realism into the realm of three-card monte.) Jon searches in countless bookstores, having never heard of Bibliofind or Alibris, where for enough money every used bookseller in the world would be happy to have a peek inside his copies of the volume.

Years pass—two or three in the movie, more in the theater. Both are engaged to others. Some smiles are generated by her fiancé, a New Age musician (John Corbett) who illustrates the principle that men who chose to wear their hair very long after about 1980 are afflicted by delusional convictions that they are cooler than anyone else. The plot risks bursting under the strain of its coincidences, as Sara and Jon fly to opposite coasts at the same time and engage in a series of Idiot Plot moves so extreme and wrongheaded that even other characters in the same scene should start shouting helpful suggestions.

By the time these two people finally get together (if they do—I don't want to give anything away) I was thinking of new tests. What

if she puts a personal ad in a paper and he has to guess which paper? How about dedicating a song to her, and trusting her to be listening to the radio at that moment, in that city? What about throwing a dart at a spinning world globe? I hope this movie never has a sequel, because Jon and Sara are destined to become the most boring married couple in history. For years to come, people at parties will be whispering, "See that couple over there? The Tragers? Jon and Sara? Whatever you do, don't ask them how they met." ☞

Series 7: The Contenders ★ ★ ½
R, 86 m., 2001

Brooke Smith (Dawn), Glenn Fitzgerald (Jeff), Marylouise Burke (Connie), Richard Venture (Franklin), Michael Kaycheck (Tony), Merritt Wever (Lindsay), Angelina Phillips (Doria), Nada Despotovich (Michelle). Directed by Daniel Minahan and produced by Jason Kliot, Katie Roumel, Christine Vachon, and Joana Vicente. Screenplay by Minahan.

Sometimes the most astonishing thing about a movie is hidden right in plain sight. *Series 7: The Contenders* is a satire on reality TV, taking the world of *Survivor* and *Temptation Island* to its logical extension with a TV show where the contestants kill one another. This is not a new idea; the movie is similar to *The Tenth Victim* (1965) and has also been compared to *Death Race 2000, Running Man, EDtv,* and *The Truman Show* in the way it uses actual lives as TV fodder. The classic short story *The Most Dangerous Game* is also lurking somewhere in its history.

No, it's not the idea that people will kill each other for entertainment that makes *Series 7* jolting. What the movie correctly perceives is that somewhere along the line we've lost all sense of shame in our society. It's not what people will do, but what they'll say—what they eagerly reveal about themselves—that *Series 7* assimilates without even being aware of it. The killing part is the satire, and we expect that to be exaggerated. The dialogue, I suspect, is not intended as satirical at all, but simply reflects the way people think these days. There are still many Americans who choose not to reveal every detail of their private lives the moment a camera is pointed at them, but they don't get on TV much.

Allow me a digression. I was watching *Jerry Springer* the other day, as I often do when I want to investigate the limits of the permissible, and there was a "guest" who was complaining that his girlfriend would not respect his fetish. He likes to vomit during sex. He even had the word for his specialty, but I've forgotten it; "nauseaphilia," no doubt. It was amazing that this guy would reveal his secret on television, but even more astonishing that the girlfriend would also appear, in order to testify how disgusting it was. Anyone so desperate for fame that they will put themselves in a position like that should think, deeply and urgently, about the positive aspects of anonymity.

But what do people say when they meet Springer guests? (1) "Ugh! That was disgusting! You are depraved!" or (2) "I saw you on *Springer.* How do you get on that show?" I suspect the answer is (2).

I make these observations because the characters in *Series 7* have no pride and no shame, and that's more interesting than their willingness to kill one another. The killing is just the gimmick—the satirical hook of the movie—but their willingness to appear on TV and explain the details of their fatal diseases, or allow the cameras to see their filthy hovels, is illuminating. It suggests that fame is the antidote for almost any misfortune.

The movie stars Brooke Smith, that wonderful actress from *Uncle Vanya on 42nd Street,* as Dawn, eight months pregnant, who explains that she must kill people and win the game for the sake of her unborn child. This is a twisted logic with a kind of beauty to it: She kills to defend life. Other contestants include a teenager (Merritt Wever) whose parents drive her to shoot-outs; an ER nurse (Marylouise Burke) whose bloody job and bloody TV role overlap; a father (Michael Kaycheck) with a wife and three kids (he wants to provide for his family); a guy who lurks in a trailer park (Richard Venture); and a testicular cancer victim (Glenn Fitzgerald), who may be in the game because he wants to die.

The Brooke Smith character is the best drawn and most clearly seen, and as she walks into a convenience store and starts blasting away, we notice the reactions of the bystanders.

They understand. They know this is only TV. They are not horrified but intrigued, and they're no doubt wondering, "Am I on now?" The overlap between this behavior and some of the actions during the San Diego school shooting recently are uncanny, and disturbing. The kid who went back into the school with the video camera was interviewed *about how much he had been interviewed.*

Real life has caught up with *Series 7* and overlapped it. The movie was filmed before the first airing of a *Survivor* episode, and must have seemed more radical in the screenplay stage than it does now. We observe that the writer-director, Daniel Minahan, has a good feel for the slick graphics and theme songs of this brand of TV, and knows how the bumpers and the teasers work. But the movie has one joke and tells it too often, for too long. It leaves you with time to think about television, celebrity, and shame. Remind me to tell you sometime about the *other* guests on that *Springer* episode.

Set Me Free ★ ★ ★

NO MPAA RATING, 94 m., 2000

Karine Vanasse (Hanna), Alexandre Merineau (Paul), Pascale Bussieres (The Mother), Miki Manojlovic (The Father), Charlotte Christeler (Laura), Nancy Huston (The Teacher), Monique Mercure (The Grandmother), Anne-Marie Cadieux (The Prostitute). Directed by Lea Pool and produced by Lorraine Richard. Screenplay by Pool.

It is not reassuring when your father tells you, "Books are our only true friends." Where does that leave you—or your mom, or your brother? And yet what he says may be worth hearing. Hanna, the heroine of *Set Me Free,* is a thirteen-year-old growing up in 1963 in Montreal. Her father is distant, disturbed, incapable of supporting his family, and blames everyone but himself. Her mother is meek and suicidal. It's up to Hanna to find her own way in life, and that's what she does, at the movies.

Art can be a great consolation when you are a lonely teenager. It speaks directly to you. You find the right movie, the right song, the right book, and you are not alone. Books and movies are not our only friends, but they help us find true friends, and tell them apart from the crowd.

One day in the rain, Hanna (Karine Vanasse) sneaks into a theater and sees Jean-Luc Godard's *My Life to Live* (1962), where even the title is significant. It stars Anna Karina as an independent woman in Paris who leaves her husband and works as a prostitute to support herself. She keeps a distance from her clients; cigarettes form a wall between her and the world, and there is a famous shot where, as a man embraces her, she sullenly blows out smoke.

Not the character you would choose as a role model for a thirteen-year-old girl. But Hanna is unhappy and confused. She has just had her first period and does not quite understand it. Her father is cold to her mother, her brother, and herself, but then turns on the charm. There is no money in the household; her father (Mike Manojlovic) calls himself a writer but has published nothing, her mother (Pascale Bussieres) works as a seamstress, and the pawnbroker knows the kids by name. In this confusion, Hanna finds encouragement in the independent woman of the movie, who holds herself aloof, who is self-contained, who lets no man hurt her.

In her life there is some happiness. She idolizes her schoolteacher (Nancy Huston), who looks a little like Anna Karina. She makes a close school friend named Laura, and they share their first kiss together. Does this mean they will grow up to be lesbians? Maybe, but probably not; what it probably means is that they are so young that kissing is a mysterious activity not yet directly wired to sex and gender, and Laura offers tenderness Hanna desperately requires.

In school, like all the students, she is called upon to stand up and give her life details. This leads to her admission that her parents are not married. Religion? "My father is Jewish, my mother is Catholic," she says. And which is she? "Judaism passes the religion through the mother, which would make me Catholic, but Catholicism passes through the father, which would make me Jewish," she says. "Myself, I don't care."

Her father is a refugee from the Holocaust, an intellectual. Their apartment is filled with books. Her mother fell for him the first time

she saw him, and got pregnant at sixteen with Paul, her brother. When her father found this out two years later, he decided to care for them, and soon Hanna was born. In a moment of revelation, Hanna's father tells her that he was married in Europe, and that although his wife may have died in the camps, he has no proof, and refuses to think of her as dead. Her mother also confides in Hanna. Despite their troubles, she will never leave her husband: "I need him."

Set Me Free is set in 1963, when the films of the French New Wave would have been influential in French-speaking Quebec. In some of its details, it resembles François Truffaut's *The 400 Blows*, which is about a young boy whose parents are unhappy, and who keeps a shrine to Balzac in his bedroom. Hanna's Balzac is Karina in *My Life to Live*. Leaning against a wall, smoking insolently, not giving a damn, Karina provides not a role model but a strategy. It is not only possible to stand aside from the pain of your life, it can even become a personal style.

The movie gets a little confused toward the end, I think, as its writer and director, Lea Pool, tries to settle things that could have been left unresolved. Hanna's tentative walk on the wild side is awkwardly handled. You walk out not quite satisfied. Later, when the movie settles in your mind, its central theme becomes clear. We grow by choosing those we admire, and pulling ourselves up on the hand they extend. For Hanna, the hands come from her teacher, from her friend, and from the woman in the movie she sees over and over. "I am responsible," says Karina in the movie. "I am responsible," says Hanna to herself. It is her life to live.

Sexy Beast ★ ★ ★ ½
R, 88 m., 2001

Ray Winstone (Gary "Gal" Dove), Ben Kingsley (Don "Malky" Logan), Ian McShane (Teddy Bass), Amanda Redman (Deedee Dove), Cavan Kendall (Aitch), Julianne White (Jackie), Alvaro Monje (Enrique), James Fox (Harry). Directed by Jonathan Glazer and produced by Jeremy Thomas. Screenplay by Louis Mellis and David Scinto.

Who would have guessed that the most savage mad-dog frothing gangster in recent movies would be played by—Ben Kingsley? Ben Kingsley, who was Gandhi, and the accountant in *Schindler's List,* and the publisher in *Betrayal,* and Dr. Watson in *Without a Clue?* Ben Kingsley, whose previous criminal was the financial wizard Meyer Lansky in *Bugsy?* Yes, Ben Kingsley. Or, as his character, Don Logan, says in *Sexy Beast,* "Yes! Yes! Yes! Yes! Yes."

Logan spits the words into the face of a retired London gangster named Dove. He's an inch away, spitting like a drill sergeant, his face red with anger, the veins throbbing on his forehead, his body coiled in rage. Dove (Ray Winstone), whose nickname is "Gal," lives in a villa on the Costa del Sol in Spain with his wife, Deedee (Amanda Redman), also retired, she from the porn business. He has no desire to return to London to assist in "one last job," a bank heist being masterminded by Logan's boss, Teddy (Ian McShane).

But you can't say no to Don Logan. This is what Dove says about him before he arrives in Spain, and when we meet him, we agree. Logan is dangerous not because he is tough, but because he is fearless and mad. You cannot intimidate a man who has no ordinary feelings. Logan is like a pit bull, hard-wired and untrainable. It's in his nature to please his master, and frighten people. He has a disconcerting habit of suddenly barking out absurdities; he has a lopsided flywheel.

Sexy Beast is in a tradition of movies about Cockney villains. It goes on the list with *The Long Good Friday* and *The Limey.* It loves its characters: Dove, the gangster gone soft; Logan, who is driven to impose his will on others; Teddy, who has a cockeyed plan to drill into a safe-deposit vault from the pool of the Turkish bath next to the bank; and Harry (James Fox), who owns the bank and thinks he is Teddy's lover when in fact he is simply the man who owns the bank.

The heist is absurd in its own way, once Dove gets to London and helps mastermind it. The burglars have total access to the Turkish bath, but it never occurs to them to drain the pool, and so they wear breathing gear while drilling through the walls of the vault next door. The vault predictably fills with water, leading to a wonderful moment when a crook opens a deposit box, finds a container inside, opens it expecting diamonds, and gets a surprise.

The movie opens on an ominous note. While Dove works on his suntan, a boulder bounces down the slope behind his villa, barely misses him, and lands in the pool. In the movie's second act, Don Logan is the boulder. Kingsley's performance has to be seen to be believed. He is angry, seductive, annoyed, wheedling, fed up, ominous, and out of his mind with frustration. I didn't know Kingsley had such notes inside him. Obviously, he can play anyone.

His best scene may be the one when Logan gets on the airplane to fly out of Spain, and the attendant asks him to put out his cigarette. Anyone who lights a cigarette on an airplane these days is asking for it, but Logan is begging for a fight. Notice the improvised lies with which he talks his way out of jail and possibly into a nice check from the airline.

Ray Winstone's work is as strong, but not as flashy. He can play monsters too: He was an abusive father in Gary Oldman's *Nil by Mouth* and Tim Roth's *The War Zone,* and it says something when those two actors cast him as their villain. His Dove is a gangster gone soft, fond of the good life, doting on his wife, able to intimidate civilians but frankly frightened of Logan.

The movie's humor is inseparable from its brutality. The crime boss Teddy (suave and vicious) offers to drive Dove to the airport after the bank job, and that leads to a series of unexpected developments—some jolting, others with deep irony. These are hard men. They could have the Sopranos for dinner, throw up, and have them again.

Shadow Magic ★ ★
PG, 115 m., 2001

Jared Harris (Raymond Wallace), Xia Yu (Liu Jinglun), Xing Yufei (Ling), Liu Peiqi (Master Ren), Lu Liping (Madame Ren), Wang Jingming (Old Liu), Li Yusheng (Lord Tan), Zhang Yukui (Lao Chang). Directed and produced by Ann Hu. Screenplay by Huang Dan, Tang Louyi, Kate Raisz, Bob McAndrew, and Ann Hu.

In Peking in 1902, an Englishman arrives with a hand-cranked projector and a box of the earliest silent movies. Ann Hu's *Shadow Magic* tells the story of how he overcomes tradition to build an audience for the new art form, makes a local disciple, films the people of China, and eventually shows his magic to the empress. It also tells the story of his disciple, a photographer's assistant who is engaged to marry a woman for money but is in love with the daughter of an opera star.

The Englishman, we learn, is based on a real person, although no one seems to have remembered his name (the film calls him Raymond Wallace). The China in the movie may be based on a real China, but it falls too easily into the forms of movie formulas. Watching the movie, I was reminded of a 1922 novel named *Kimono*, by John Paris, that did an extraordinary job of suggesting how *different* Japan seemed to a British visitor in the early years of the century. Surely China was as intimidating, yet the values and customs in this movie seem familiar to a modern Western viewer. The Englishman should be more of a stranger, and China should be more of a strange land.

Consider a scene late in the movie where Wallace (Jared Harris) and his friend Liu Jinglun (Xia Yu), a young photographer, show the new invention to the Dowager Empress. The screening goes well until there is a fire (film combusts easily in *Shadow Magic*, almost on cue), and the foreigner is condemned to death before the empress pardons him, smiling benevolently as she praises the new art form. Is this what would have happened? Surely to be admitted to the presence of the empress a century ago was fraught with more mystery and drama than the movie suggests, and perhaps the empress herself would have been less like good Queen Victoria, cheerfully hailing progress. The movie is more concerned with the story line (premiere-fire-threat-rescue) than with painting the time and place.

The character Liu Jinglun is painted as an ambitious young man who instantly perceives the wonder of the new invention, while almost everyone else (except, of course, the audiences) seems hostile or indifferent. History suggests it was not this way. Movies were eagerly embraced by the curious in all countries, and the opposition by Liu's possessive father seems contrived (he fears a threat to his photography studio). The romantic subplots involving Liu seem composed on autopilot: There is an arranged marriage with a tubby older widow,

which must be avoided if he's to fulfill his secret love for the beautiful young Ling (Xing Yufei).

What the movie does achieve is a lively sense of color and energy. As Wallace and Liu photograph local citizens, we're reminded of *The Star Maker*, a 1995 film by Giuseppe Tornatore (*Cinema Paradiso*) about an itinerant photographer who travels the back roads of Sicily, filming people. He pretends to be making Hollywood screen tests, but actually he is recording something much more precious— the faces of those people at that time.

Shadow Magic ends with some of the footage Raymond and Liu have shot, and that suggests a different kind of film that might have been made. Why not, instead of romantic intrigue and family quarrels in a mildly melodramatic plot, make more of an effort to reconstruct what it must have really been like for that nameless Englishman with his equipment? Why not emphasize the barriers of language, race, and custom, and tell us a little more about the intricacies of the earliest cameras and projectors? Why not trust the subject matter instead of shaping it all to fit a formula? I got the feeling all through *Shadow Magic* that the real story was offscreen.

Shadow of the Vampire ★ ★ ★ ½
R, 93 m., 2001

John Malkovich (F. W. Murnau), Willem Dafoe (Max Schreck), Cary Elwes (Fritz Wagner), Eddie Izzard (Gustav von Wangenheim), Udo Kier (Albin Grau), Catherine McCormack (Greta Schroeder), Ronan Vibert (Wolfgang Muller), Ingeborga Dapkunaite (Micheline). Directed by E. Elias Merhige and produced by Nicolas Cage and Jeff Levine. Screenplay by Steven Katz.

The best of all vampire movies is *Nosferatu*, made by F. W. Murnau in Germany in 1922. Its eerie power only increases with age. Watching it, we don't think about screenplays or special effects. We think: This movie believes in vampires. Max Schreck, the mysterious actor who played Court Orlock the vampire, is so persuasive we never think of the actor, only of the creature.

Shadow of the Vampire, a wicked new movie

about the making of *Nosferatu,* has an explanation for Schreck's performance: He really was a vampire. This is not a stretch. It is easier for me to believe Schreck was a vampire than that he was an actor. Examine any photograph of him in the role and decide for yourself. Consider the ratlike face, the feral teeth, the bat ears, the sunken eyes, the fingernail claws that seem to have grown in the tomb. Makeup? He makes the word irrelevant.

In *Shadow of the Vampire,* director E. Elias Merhige and his writer, Steven Katz, do two things at the same time. They make a vampire movie of their own, and they tell a backstage story about the measures that a director will take to realize his vision. Murnau is a man obsessed with his legacy; he lectures his crew on the struggle to create art, promising them, "Our poetry, our music, will have a context as certain as the grave." What they have no way of knowing is that some of them will go to the grave themselves in the service of his poetry. He's made a deal with Schreck: Perform in my movie, and you can dine on the blood of the leading lady.

John Malkovich plays Murnau as a theoretician who is utterly uninterested in human lives other than his own. His work justifies everything. Like other silent directors he has a flamboyant presence, stalking his sets with glasses pushed up on his forehead, making pronouncements, issuing orders, self-pitying about the fools he has to work with and the price he has to pay for his art. After we meet key members of the cast and crew in Berlin, the production moves to Czechoslovakia, where Schreck awaits. Murnau explains that the great actor is so dedicated to his craft that he lives in character the clock around, and must never be spoken to except as Count Orlock.

"Willem Dafoe is Max Schreck." I put quotes around that because it's not just a line for a movie ad but the truth: He embodies the Schreck of *Nosferatu* so uncannily that when real scenes from the silent classic are slipped into the frame, we don't notice much difference. But he is not simply Schreck—or not simply Schreck as the vampire. He is also a venomous and long-suffering creature with unruly appetites, and he angers Murnau by

prematurely dining on the cinematographer. Murnau shouts in rage that he *needs* the cinematographer, and now will have to go to Berlin and hire another one. He begs Schreck to keep his appetites in check until the final scene. Schreck muses aloud, "I do not think we need . . . the writer . . ." Scenes like this work as inside comedy, but they also have a practical side: The star is hungry, and because he is the star, he can make demands. This would not be the first time a star has eaten a writer alive.

The fragrant Catherine McCormack plays Greta, the actress whose throat Schreck's fangs will plunge into, for real, in the final scene. She, of course, does not understand this, and is a trouper, putting up with Schreck for the sake of art even though he reeks of decay. Concerned about her close-ups, intoxicated by the joy of stardom, she has no suspicions until, during her crucial scene, her eyes stray to the mirror—and Schreck, of course, is not reflected.

The movie does an uncanny job of recreating the visual feel of Murnau's film. There are shots that look the way moldy basements smell. This material doesn't lend itself to subtlety, and Malkovich and Dafoe chew their lines like characters who know they are always being observed (some directors do more acting on their sets than the actors do). The supporting cast is a curiously, intriguingly, mixed bag: Cary Elwes as Murnau's cinematographer Fritz Wagner (not the one who is eaten), Eddie Izzard as one of the actors, the legendary Udo Kier as the producer.

Vampires for some reason are funny as well as frightening. Maybe that's because the conditions of their lives are so absurd. Some of Anne Rice's vampires have a fairly entertaining time of it, but someone like Schreck, here, seems doomed to spend eternity in psychic and physical horror. There is a nice passage where he submits to a sort of interview from his colleagues, remaining "in character" while answering questions about vampirism. He doesn't make it sound like fun.

"Every horror film seems to become absurd after the passage of years," Pauline Kael wrote in her review of *Nosferatu,* "yet the horror remains." Here Merhige gives us scenes absurd and frightening at the same time, as when

Schreck catches a bat that flies into a room, and eats it. Or when Murnau, knowing all that he knows about Schreck, reassures his leading lady: "All you have to do is relax and, as they say, the vampire will do all the work."

Note: Ebert's review of Nosferatu *is at www.suntimes.com/ebert/greatmovies/.* ☞

Shaft ★ ★ ½
R, 98 m., 2000

Samuel L. Jackson (John Shaft), Vanessa Williams (Carmen), Jeffrey Wright (Peoples Hernandez), Christian Bale (Walter Wade), Busta Rhymes (Rasaan), Dan Hedaya (Jack Roselli), Toni Collette (Diane Palmieri), Richard Roundtree (Uncle John), Lee Tergesen (Luger). Directed by John Singleton and produced by Singleton and Scott Rudin. Screenplay by Singleton, Richard Price, and Shane Salerno.

John Singleton's *Shaft* is a blaxploitation film with a modern urban drama trapped inside. Or maybe it's the other way around. On the one hand, we have John Shaft telling a pickup, "It's my duty to please your booty." On the other hand, we have a scene between a rich kid and a drug dealer that's so well written and acted it's chilling.

At the center of the tug-of-war, pulled both ways and enjoying it, is Samuel L. Jackson, as a tough cop who throws his badge back at a judge (literally) and becomes a freelance vigilante. The story's broad outlines are familiar not only from early 1970s black exploitation movies, but also from the early *Dirty Harry* pictures, and when a top cop orders Shaft to get out of his precinct, it's like he's reciting dialogue from the classics.

The movie has the obligatory elements of black exploitation (big cars, drugs, cigars, guns, sleazy nightclubs, gold chains, racism, babes, black leather coats, expensive booze, crooked white cops). But a newer sensibility sneaks in, probably thanks to a screenplay primarily by Richard Price, who wrote *Clockers* and specializes in dialogue that allows the characters some poetry; I like lines like "It's Giuliani time!"

On top of reports that Singleton and Jackson had many disagreements on the set, there were stories that neither of them much liked the Price screenplay, maybe because it nailed the small moments but missed the broader Shaftian strokes. Whatever compromises were made, the result is a movie more interesting than it might have been: not just a retread of the old movie, but Shaft as more complicated than before, and with well-observed supporting characters.

Jackson is at the center of the action, "too black for the uniform, too blue for the brothers," wearing a wicked goatee that looks like it was designed by a comic book artist. He's a cop made angry when a rich man's son (Christian Bale) murders a black youth, gets an easy bail, and skips to Switzerland. As one of the first on the crime scene, Shaft believes that a waitress (Toni Collette) saw more than she admits. Two years pass, the rich kid returns to the country, Shaft nabs him, and then the plot involves his partner (Busta Rhymes), the drug kingpin (Jeffrey Wright), the sexy narcotics cop (Vanessa Williams), the larcenous cop (Dan Hedaya), and his partner Luger (Lee Tergesen). Always look twice at a cop named Luger.

The casting here makes for some interesting echoes. Hedaya, of course, played the crooked cop in *The Hurricane,* and Christian Bale had the title role in *American Psycho.* Toni Collette, who was the mother in *The Sixth Sense,* is a good choice for the waitress; there's always something a little edgy about her. There's another echo in Bale's hairstyle, which evokes uncanny memories of JFK Jr.

One modern thing about the movie is its low sexual quotient. Blaxploitation came along at a time when American movies were sexy, with lots of nudity and bedroom time. Modern action pictures seem prudish by comparison; like *Gone in 60 Seconds* and *Mission: Impossible 2,* this one prefers action to sex. Can it be that Hollywood's Friday night specials, which were aimed at teenage boys, have now lowered their sights to include a demographic group so young it thinks girls are creepy?

The most intriguing relationship in the movie is between Bale and Wright, as the rich kid and the drug dealer. There's a scene where Bale comes to Wright, hoping to pay for a hit. Wright is not much into murder for hire, but wants the kid's connections as a way to develop a more affluent clientele for his drugs.

The way they talk to each other, the words they choose, the attitudes they strike, the changes they go through, are as subtly menacing as scenes in a film by Lee or Scorsese. The movie doesn't give us stereotypes in these two familiar roles, but closely examined originals.

The John Shaft character is more mainstream, but Jackson has a way of bringing weight to his roles. He always looks like he means it. But there's a disconnect between the realism of the murder case and the fantasy of Shaft's career as an unleashed vigilante who leaves countless dead bodies behind him. Different scenes seem to occupy different levels of reality. Of course the movie ends with a gunfight and a chase scene. That goes without saying.

Is this a good movie? Not exactly; too much of it is on automatic pilot, as it must be, to satisfy the fans of the original *Shaft*. Is it better than I expected? Yes. There are flashes here of the talent that John Singleton has possessed ever since *Boyz N the Hood*, and strong acting, and efficient action. Jackson makes a commanding Shaft (and a supporting role by Richard Roundtree, the original Shaft, serves to pass the mantle). The movie is what it is, but more than it needs to be.

Shallow Hal ★ ★ ★
PG-13, 113 m., 2001

Gwyneth Paltrow (Rosemary Shanahan), Jack Black (Hal Larsen), Jason Alexander (Mauricio), Rene Kirby (Walt), Tony Robbins (Himself), Susan Ward (Jill), Joe Viterelli (Steve Shanahan), Jill Fitzgerald (Mrs. Shanahan). Directed by Bobby Farrelly and Peter Farrelly, produced by the Farrellys, Bradley Thomas, and Charles B. Wessler. Screenplay by Sean Moynihan and the Farrellys.

Shallow Hal is given words of wisdom at the deathbed of his father, who, under the influence of painkillers, is speaking from the deepest recesses of his being. "Hot young tail," his father says. "That's what it's all about." He makes Hal promise to date only beautiful woman, and to beware of falling in love—"that was the tragic mistake I made with your mother."

Hal (Jack Black) grows up to follow this counsel. He has no meaningful relationships with women because meaningful is not what he's looking for. With his running mate Mauricio (Jason Alexander from *Seinfeld*), whose spray-on hair looks like a felt hat, he prowls the bars. His life is a series of brief encounters, until one day he is trapped on an elevator with Tony Robbins, the self-help guru, who hypnotizes him and tells him to look inside the women he meets, for their inner beauty.

Soon after, Shallow Hal begins to have extraordinary success with women—not least with a nurse and ex–Peace Corps volunteer named Rosemary, who looks exactly like Gwyneth Paltrow, because that's the way Hal's mind is working these days. The movie plays with point-of-view shots to show us that Rosemary actually weighs about 300 pounds, but to Hal she's slender and—well, Gwyneth Paltrow.

At first Rosemary thinks his compliments are ironic insults, and is wounded. Then she realizes he's sincere, and really does think she's beautiful. This has never happened to her before. They begin an enchanted romance, to the consternation of Hal's friends, who can't understand why he's dating this fatso. Of course, if the Tony Robbins hypnosis ever wears off . . .

Shallow Hal, written with Sean Moynihan, is the new movie by the Farrelly brothers, Bobby and Peter. They specialize in skirmishes on the thin line between comedy and cruelty. *There's Something About Mary* had its paraplegic suitor, *Dumb and Dumber* had the little blind boy, *Me, Myself and Irene* was about a man with a Jekyll-and-Hyde personality, and so on. Whether we laugh or are offended depends on whether our lower or higher sensibilities are in command at the time. The Farrellys have a way of tickling the lower regions while sending the higher centers off on errands. Reader, I confess I have laughed.

Shallow Hal is often very funny, but it is also surprisingly moving at times. It contains characters to test us, especially Walt (Rene Kirby), who has spina bifida and an essentially immobile lower body. Kirby doesn't use a chair or braces, but lopes around on all fours, and is an expert skier, horseman, bicyclist, and acrobat. Because he is clearly handicapped, we think at first his scenes are in "bad taste"—but he doesn't think so; his zest for life allows us to see his inner beauty, and his sense of humor, too, as in a scene where he explains why he's putting on rubber gloves.

There's something about the Farrellys that isn't widely publicized—they're both sincerely involved in work with the mentally retarded. There is a sense that they're not simply laughing at their targets, but sometimes with them, or in sympathy with them. *Shallow Hal* has what look like fat jokes, as when a chair collapses under Rosemary, but the punch line is tilted toward empathy.

Now here's a heartfelt message from Valerie Hawkins of Homewood, Illinois, who writes: "Um, what am I missing, regarding *Shallow Hal*? The trailer prattles on about how Hal now sees only the inner beauty of a woman. No, he doesn't. When he looks at an overweight woman and instead sees her as a thin woman, that's not inner beauty. What he's seeing is a typical tall, thin professional model type—which in some ways is more insulting than if he saw her as she really is and instantly rejected her."

This is persuasive. Hal sees Gwyneth Paltrow, who doesn't spend a lot of time wearing the "fat suit" you've read about in the celeb columns. What if she wore the fat suit in every scene, and he thought she was beautiful because of the Robbins training? This would also be funny; *we* could see her as fat but *he* couldn't. At the same time, screams of rage would come from the producers, who didn't pay Paltrow untold millions to wear a fat suit.

Hawkins has a good argument from our point of view and hers, but not from Hal's, because he *does* literally see an idealized beauty. To be sure, it is exterior beauty, not interior, but how else to express his experience visually?

I think we know to accept the Farrellys' premise as filtered through the realities of the marketplace, in which you do not put Gwyneth Paltrow into a movie where she doesn't look like Gwyneth Paltrow. (John Travolta played an abominable snowman from space in *Battleship Earth,* and look how that went over.) By showing the idealized Gwyneth, the Farrellys set up the third act, in which Shallow Hal does indeed see Paltrow as fat, and has to deal with how he feels about that. If she had been fat all along in the movie's eye, how could his test be made clear visually? Early and late, we see Pal-

trow as Hal sees her, which is not an evasion but maybe the point.

Whether or not you accept the fat-thin argument, the movie offers a good time. It's very funny across the usual range of Farrelly gags, from the spray-on toupee to a woman with a long second toe to a man with a tail. Gwyneth Paltrow is truly touching. And Jack Black, in his first big-time starring role, struts through with the blissful confidence of a man who knows he was born for stardom, even though he doesn't look like your typical Gwyneth Paltrow boyfriend. He's not so thin, either.

Note: Only the most attentive audience members will catch the Farrellys' subtle reference to a famous poem by Emily Dickinson. ☞

Shanghai Noon ★ ★ ★
PG-13, 110 m., 2000

Jackie Chan (Chon Wang), Owen Wilson (Roy O'Bannon), Lucy Liu (Princess Pei Pei), Brandon Merrill (Indian Wife), Roger Yuan (Lo Fong), Xander Berkeley (Van Cleef), Walton Goggins (Wallace), P. Adrien Dorval (Blue). Directed by Tom Dey and produced by Roger Birnbaum, Gary Barber, and Jonathan Glickman. Screenplay by Alfred Gough and Miles Millar.

The best way to criticize a movie, Jean-Luc Godard once said, is to make another movie. In that spirit, *Shanghai Noon* is the answer to *Wild Wild West,* although I am not sure these are the kinds of movies Godard had in mind. Jackie Chan's new action comedy is a wink at Westerns, martial arts, and buddy movies— enriched by a goofy performance by Owen Wilson, who would steal the movie if Chan were not so clever at sharing it with him.

The plot in a paragraph: China, the Forbidden City, 1881. The princess (Lucy Liu) resents her fate and hates her chosen fiancé. Her teacher offers to help her escape to America. She is kidnapped and held for ransom in Nevada. The three best Imperial Guards are selected to rescue her. Jackie Chan goes along as a bag carrier for his uncle, who is their interpreter. In Nevada, Jackie teams up with a train robber named Roy O'Bannon (Wilson), and they rescue the princess with much help from an Indian maiden (Brandon Merrill).

The plot, of course, is only a clothesline for Jackie's martial arts sequences, Wilson's funny verbal riffs, and a lot of low humor. Material like this can be very bad. Here it is sort of wonderful, because of a light touch by director Tom Dey, who finds room both for Chan's effortless charm and for a droll performance by Owen Wilson, who, if this were a musical, would be a Beach Boy.

Wilson has been edging up on us. Most moviegoers don't know who he is. If you see everything, you'll remember him from *Bottle Rocket*, where he was engaging, and *Minus Man*, where he was profoundly disturbing. This movie will make him a star. He is too smart and versatile to be packaged within a narrow range (his career also includes writing credits on *Bottle Rocket* and *Rushmore*), but if he could do only what he does in *Shanghai Noon*, he could support himself with Adam Sandler roles.

His train robber is hard to describe; the character is funny because of his tone, not his dialogue or actions. He's a modern, laid-back, self-centered southern California dude with a Stetson and six-guns. Flirting with a passenger on the train he is robbing, he gets competitive: "I kinda like to do the talking." His comic timing is precise, as in a scene where he and Jackie Chan get into a weird drinking contest while sharing adjacent bathtubs in a bordello, and play a funny and utterly inexplicable word game.

Chan's character is named Chon Wang (say it out loud). As in his 1998 hit *Rush Hour*, he plays a man of limited vocabulary and much action; Chris Tucker in that film and Owen Wilson in this one are motormouths who cover for Chan's shaky English, which is no problem because his martial arts scenes are poetic. He's famous for using the props that come to hand in every fight, and here there is a sequence involving several things we didn't know could be done with evergreen trees.

Lucy Liu, as the princess, is not a damsel in distress, but brave and plucky, and stirred by the plight of her Chinese countrymen, who have been made indentured servants in a Nevada gold town. She doesn't want to return to China, but to stay in America—as a social worker or union organizer, I guess. Not so boldly portrayed is Brandon Merrill's Indian

woman, who is married to Jackie in a ceremony that nobody seems to take seriously and that the movie itself has clearly forgotten all about by the time the last shot comes around.

Her pairing with Jackie Chan does, however, create a funny echo of *A Man Called Horse,* and on the way out of the theater I was challenged by my fellow critic Sergio Mims to name all the other movie references. He claimed to have spotted, I think, twenty-four. My mind boggled.

What *Shanghai Noon* proves—and here's how it's a criticism of *Wild Wild West*—is that no matter how much effort is put into production values and special effects, a movie like this finally depends on dialogue and characters. *Wild Wild West,* which came out almost exactly one year earlier, had a top-drawer cast (Will Smith, Kevin Kline, Kenneth Branagh), but what were they given to do? Plow through dim-witted dialogue between ungainly f/x scenes. Here Wilson angles on-screen and starts riffing, and we laugh. And Jackie Chan, who does his own stunts, creates moments of physical comedy so pure it's no wonder he has been compared with Buster Keaton. If you see only one martial arts Western this year (and there is probably an excellent chance of that), this is the one.

The Shipping News ★ ★
R, 120 m., 2001

Kevin Spacey (Quoyle), Julianne Moore (Wavey), Judi Dench (Agnis), Cate Blanchett (Petal Bear), Rhys Ifans (Nutbeem), Peter Postlethwaite (Tert X. Card), Scott Glenn (Jack Buggit), Allysa Gainer (Bunny), Kaitlin Gainer (Bunny), Lauren Gainer (Bunny). Directed by Lasse Hallstrom and produced by Rob Cowan, Linda Goldstein, Knowlton, Leslie Holleran, and Irwin Winkler. Screenplay by Robert Nelson Jacobs, based on the novel by E. Annie Proulx.

If one person has told me to read *The Shipping News,* half a dozen have. One friend actually pressed a copy of E. Annie Proulx's novel into my hands. They cannot all be wrong. It won the Pulitzer Prize. It must be a wonderful book. But the movie made from it is relentlessly colorful and cute, until you wonder if the characters stayed up late inventing quirky dialogue and thinking of peculiar behavior they can cultivate.

The movie follows the experiences of Quoyle (Kevin Spacey), a meek ink-man for the *Poughkeepsie News,* as he marries Petal, the local tramp (Cate Blanchett), has a daughter named Bunny, cares for Bunny while Petal sluts around, and then raises her alone after Petal dies, not so really very tragically if you think about it. At about this time he finds a message on his answering machine from his father, informing him, "It's time for your mother and I to put an end to it." That these tragedies range in emotional value from ironic to funny gives you the temperature of the film.

Quoyle and Bunny might have lived on forever in Poughkeepsie, she washing the ink from his coveralls, if Aunt Agnis (Judi Dench) had not happened along with enough gumption to put them all in motion toward Quoyle Point, Newfoundland, where they move back into the family homestead, a frame house on a point so exposed on the rocky coast that cables anchor it against the wind. This house is so decrepit and open to the weather that only in the movies could it be rehabbed into a comfy home after, oh, about three scenes.

The movie's drift is clear: Sad sack and daughter move to eccentric, isolated town where local free spirits will introduce them to the joys of living. Quoyle gets a job on the local paper, the *Gammy Bird,* where arguments rage about sailing vessels versus oil tankers (the tankers have their defender), and the journalists, like all small-town journalists I have ever known, know way more about everything than they can use in the kinds of stories they have to write.

Quoyle meets Wavey (Julianne Moore), who runs the local day-care center, and soon—but you can fill in the blanks. What you may not anticipate are several macabre turns including close calls with death, a severed head, spontaneous resurrection, twelve-year-old grandfathers, and ancient secrets just waiting to be unearthed.

The movie makes good use of the magnificent locations, and abundant use of water; Quoyle is afraid of swimming after traumatic experiences with his father, and has to endure several wet ordeals, one of which I seriously doubt was survivable, and meanwhile even the movie itself seems damp a lot of the time. I liked the feeling of community in the town, the palpable sense of place. But, lord, the characters are tireless in their peculiarities; it's as if the movie took the most colorful folks in Lake Wobegone, dehydrated them, concentrated the granules, shipped them to Newfoundland, reconstituted them with Molson's, and issued them Canadian passports.

Kevin Spacey can effortlessly play the smartest man in every movie. He is not as interesting playing hapless. Julianne Moore is the earth mother, warm, funny, and troubled. Judi Dench is rock-solid dependable as Aunt Agnis. Cate Blanchett is amazingly unrecognizable as Petal, who reminds us of the disused word "hellion." The guys on the newspaper are terrific, especially dreamer Rhys Ifans and dour Peter Postlethwaite, and I liked Scott Glenn as the publisher who would rather go fishing.

All of that said, the film suffers from a severe case of obviously being a film. There is never the sense that Quoyle Point, or any place remotely like it, could exist outside this movie. Maybe this is Canadian magic realism. At the Toronto Film Festival I saw *Rare Birds,* also shot in Newfoundland, starring William Hurt as a restaurant owner and Molly Parker in the Julianne Moore role. It is invaluable as a comparison, because it demonstrates that you can make quite a good human comedy about oddball characters in Newfoundland without going off the deep end. ☞

Shower ★ ★ ★
PG-13, 92 m., 2000

Zhu Xu (Master Liu), Pu Cun Xin (Da Ming), Jiang Wu (Er Ming), He Zheng (He Bing), Zhang Jin Hao (Hu Bei Bei), Lao Lin (Li Ding), Lao Wu (Feng Shun). Directed by Zhang Yang and produced by Peter Loehr. Screenplay by Liu Fen Dou, Zhang Yang, Huo Xin, Diao Yi Nan, and Cai Xiang Jun.

The customers of the bathhouse in *Shower* hardly seem to spend any time anywhere else. The old men are there from morning to night, bathing, soaking, being rubbed, playing cards, and staging fights to the death with their pet crickets (one feeds his champion ant eggs; his opponent accuses him of using "steroids").

Master Liu has run this bathhouse since time immemorial and brushes off his son's suggestions that he retire: "I've done this all of my life and I like doing it!"

The son is Da Ming (Pu Cun Xin), a successful businessman who lives in a distant city, but has returned because of an alarming postcard he received from his retarded brother, Er Ming (Jiang Wu). The postcard seems to indicate that old Liu (Zhu Xu) is dead or dying, but in fact Liu is presiding, as he has for decades, over the closed world of the bathhouse, where steam and ancient customs wall out the changing ways of modern Beijing.

The relationship between Liu and his retarded son is a close one. They're like playmates, racing around the block and staging contests to see who can hold his breath the longest. Er Ming is proud when he's allowed to man the desk by the door, greeting clients, most of whom have presumably known him since he was a child.

But now Er Ming and Da Ming are both grown men, and Da Ming worries about what the future holds for his brother. The city wants to tear down the entire bathhouse district to make way for progress, and then what will happen to Liu, Er Ming, the customers, and the crickets?

Shower, written, directed, and edited by Zhang Yang, is a cozy and good-hearted comedy, not startlingly original but convincing in the way it shows the rhythms of the days and customs of the bathhouse, and how they gradually seduce the harassed and preoccupied visiting brother. Da Ming planned a visit of only a day or two, but in calls to his distant wife, he keeps putting off his return, and the screenplay shows him gradually beginning to care for the family business and its destiny. (A scene where father and son wrestle with plastic sheeting on the roof during a rainstorm is contrived, but effective all the same.)

The best thing in the movie, I think, is the affectionate and yet unsentimental way the father and the retarded son are seen. Yes, Er Ming is slow. But he has good qualities and strong feelings, and has found a niche in life that suits him. He knows all the customers and cares about them; he helps raise the alarm when Mrs. Zhang bursts in looking for her no-good husband.

And look how he rises to the occasion when another customer faces a crisis. This man loves to sing in the shower, and always sings "O Sole Mio." We gather two things about him: He knows only one song, and he can sing only in a shower. There is a crisis when he is pressed into service for a neighborhood talent show, and Er Ming instantly grasps the situation and solves it.

Many recent films from China have emphasized either its exotic past or the unsettled politics of its recent history. But after all, most of its citizens lead ordinary lives and share dreams and fears similar to ours. *Shower* is about everyday people, and although it has some contrived plot devices (including the looming deadline of the city's threat to the bathhouse), it is warm and observant, and its ending is surprisingly true to the material.

Show Me Love ★ ★ ★

NO MPAA RATING, 89 m., 2000

Alexandra Dahlstrom (Elin), Rebecca Liljeberg (Agnes), Erica Carlson (Jessica), Mathias Rust (Johan Hult), Stefan Horberg (Markus), Ralph Carlsson (Father Olof), Maria Hedborg (Mother Karin), Axel Widegren (Little Brother Oskar). Directed by Lukas Moodysson and produced by Lars Jonsson. Screenplay by Moodysson.

This is all I ask of a movie about teenagers: That they be as smart, as confused, as good-hearted, and as insecure as the kids I went to high school with. Such characters are so rare that when you encounter them in a movie like *Show Me Love*, they belong to a different species than the creatures in the weekly Hollywood teenager picture.

Show Me Love is set in Sweden, but could be set in any American small town where kids believe they are desperate outcasts in a cultural backwater. Elin (Alexandra Dahlstrom), one of the girls in the film, pages through a teen magazine and despairs when she finds that raves are "out." Her town is so behind the times that stuff is out before it even gets there. She is bored, bored, bored. She wants to be a model, but is even bored with that.

The movie is also about Agnes (Rebecca Liljeberg), who moved to the town more than a year ago but still has few friends; she's an outsider at school because students whisper she's a lesbian. They have no reason to think that, but they're right. She has a crush on Elin, and locks herself in her room to write her love letters on her computer. One day at a party, a girlfriend bets Elin she won't kiss Agnes, and she does, sending the wrong message to Agnes, who doesn't know about the bet.

This sounds, I know, like the setup for a sexcom, or maybe one of those Swedish romps of long ago (*Therese and Isabelle* comes to mind). What I haven't conveyed is the sweetness, tenderness, and naïveté of all of these scenes, in which both girls are essentially wandering cluelessly through half-understood life choices. What they find at the end of the film is not romance so much as self-knowledge and fortitude, and a disdain for "popularity."

The movie (which outgrossed *Titanic* to become the most successful film in Swedish history) is not a story of heroines and villains. Everyone in it is more or less on the same moral plane. It is not about distant and blockheaded parents (the parents express love and understanding, as best they can, and we sympathize with their attempts to make sense of adolescent despair). It isn't about any of the standard characters (the stupid principal, the class nerd, the social snob) who wander through most Hollywood teenage movies on autopilot. It's about these specific people and their lives.

The movie is funny, gentle, and true. It knows how teenagers can be cruel, and how sharply they can regret it. Early in the film, Agnes's mother throws her a birthday party (she doesn't want one), and it looks like only one guest is going to turn up—her best friend, who is in a wheelchair. Mad at her parents, mad at herself, Agnes lashes out at her friend ("I don't want to be friends with a palsied cripple who listens to the Back Street Boys!") and mocks her gift of perfume. Later, she apologizes. The friend in the wheelchair is not all that deeply upset about the insult, because she has read it, correctly, as more about Agnes than about herself. In most American teenage movies, there's not depth enough for such subtlety: An insult is an insult, without nuance.

The film is refreshing in the way it handles "sex," and I put the word in quotes because there is hardly any sex in the film. While American teenage films cheerfully supply shower scenes, T&A, and four-letter words, this one is released without an MPAA rating, no doubt because its honesty would upset audiences accustomed to a cinema of dirty jokes. Two of the truest moments in the movie occur when the two girls confess they have no sexual experience. The "lesbian" reveals that the kiss on a bet was the first time she has kissed a girl, and Elin, who has a reputation for promiscuity, confides she is a virgin.

Show Me Love is not really about sexuality. It's more about vegetating in a town that makes the girls feel trapped. And it sees that the fault is not in the town, but in the girls: Maybe their boredom is a pose. Maybe all teenagers, in every town, feel like nothing is happening in their lives, and they will never find love or be understood or do thrilling things. Maybe that's just human nature. In its quiet, intelligent, understated way, this film loves teenagers; most teen movies just use them.

Showtime ★ ★
PG-13, 95 m., 2002

Robert De Niro (Mitch), Eddie Murphy (Trey), Rene Russo (Chase Renzi), William Shatner (Himself), Frankie Faison (Captain Winship). Directed by Tom Dey and produced by Jane Rosenthal and Jorge Saralegui. Screenplay by Keith Sharon, Alfred Gough, and Miles Millar, based on a story by Saralegui.

The cop buddy comedy is such a familiar genre that a movie can parody it and occupy it at the same time. The characters in *Showtime* do it as a kind of straddle, starting out making fun of cop buddy clichés and ending up trapped in them. The movie's funny in the opening scenes and then forgets why it came to play.

We meet two cops: Mitch (Robert De Niro), who never had to choose between a red wire and a green wire, and Trey (Eddie Murphy), who is a cop but would rather play one on TV. You can guess from the casting that the movie will have energy and chemistry, and indeed while I watched it my strongest feeling was affection for the actors. They've been around so long, given so much, are so good at what they do. And Rene Russo, as the TV producer who teams them on a reality show, is great at stalking in high heels as if this is the first time she's ever done it without grinding a body part beneath them.

Mitch wants only to do his job. Trey is a hot dog who has learned more from TV than at the police academy. Making a drug bust, he knowledgeably tastes the white powder and finds it's cocaine. "What if it's cyanide?" Mitch asks (or anthrax, we're thinking). "There's a reason real cops don't taste drugs."

We meet Chase Renzi (Russo), TV producer with a problem: Her report on exploding flammable baby pajamas didn't pan out. She's electrified when she sees TV footage of Mitch getting angry with a TV cameraman and shooting his camera. The network sues. Mitch is threatened with suspension, just like in all the *Dirty Harry* movies, but offered an ultimatum: Star in a new reality show with Trey ("You do the show; they drop the suit").

Mitch grudgingly agrees, and some of the best scenes involve the callow Trey instructing the hard-edged Mitch in the art of acting (this is a flip of John Wayne tutoring James Caan in *El Dorado*). During these scenes we're seeing pure De Niro and Murphy, freed from effects and action, simply acting. They're good at it.

Enter a bad guy with a big gun. A gun so big we are surprised not by its power but by the fact that anyone can lift it. An expert testifies: "This gun is like the fifty-foot shark. We know it's there, but nobody has ever seen it." Most of the second half of the movie involves Mitch and Trey chasing down the gun and its owners, who use it in a series of daring robberies. This we have seen before. Oh yes.

The movie was directed by Tom Dey, whose only previous film was *Shanghai Noon* (2000), a buddy movie pairing a Chinese martial arts fighter and a train robber. I learn from the Internet Movie Database that he studied film at Brown University, the Centre des Etudes Critiques in Paris, and the American Film Institute. He probably knows what's wrong with this movie more than I do.

But making movies is an exercise in compromise no less appalling than the making of the "reality" TV show in *Showtime.* My guess: The screenplay ("by Keith Sharon, Alfred Gough, and Miles Millar, based on a story by Jorge Saralegui") was funnier and more satirical until the studio began to doubt the intelligence of the potential audience, and decided to shovel

in more action as insurance. As we all know, the first rule of action drama is that when a gun as legendary as a fifty-foot shark comes on-screen in the first act, somebody eventually finds a spent shell casing the size of a shot glass.

Note: Most of the computers in movies for several years have been Macintoshes, maybe because the Mac is the only computer that doesn't look like every other computer and therefore benefits from product placement. But this is the first movie in which an entire iMac commercial runs on TV in the background of a shot. ☞

Shrek ★ ★ ★ ★
PG, 90 m., 2001

With the voices of: Mike Myers (Shrek), Eddie Murphy (The Donkey), Cameron Diaz (Princess Fiona), John Lithgow (Lord Farquaad). Directed by Andrew Adamson and Vicky Jenson and produced by Aron Warner and John H. Williams. Screenplay by Ted Elliott, Terry Rossio, Joe Stillman, and Roger S. H. Schulman, based on the book by William Steig.

There is a moment in *Shrek* when the despicable Lord Farquaad has the Gingerbread Man tortured by dipping him into milk. This prepares us for another moment when Princess Fiona's singing voice is so piercing it causes jolly little bluebirds to explode; making the best of a bad situation, she fries their eggs. This is not your average family cartoon. *Shrek* is jolly and wicked, filled with sly in-jokes and yet somehow possessing a heart.

The movie has been so long in the making at DreamWorks that the late Chris Farley was originally intended to voice the jolly green ogre in the title role. All that work has paid off: The movie is an astonishing visual delight, with animation techniques that seem lifelike and fantastical, both at once. No animated being has ever moved, breathed, or had its skin crawl quite as convincingly as Shrek, and yet the movie doesn't look like a reprocessed version of the real world; it's all made up, right down to, or up to, Shrek's trumpet-shaped ears.

Shrek's voice is now performed by Mike Myers, with a voice that's an echo of his Fat Bastard (the Scotsman with a molasses brogue in *Austin Powers: The Spy Who Shagged Me*).

Shrek is an ogre who lives in a swamp surrounded by "Keep Out" and "Beware the Ogre!" signs. He wants only to be left alone, perhaps because he is not such an ogre after all but merely a lonely creature with an inferiority complex because of his ugliness. He is horrified when the solitude of his swamp is disturbed by a sudden invasion of cartoon creatures, who have been banished from Lord Farquaad's kingdom.

Many of these creatures bear a curious correspondence to Disney characters who are in the public domain: The Three Little Pigs turn up, along with the Three Bears, the Three Blind Mice, Tinkerbell, the Big Bad Wolf, and Pinocchio. Later, when Farquaad seeks a bride, the Magic Mirror gives him three choices: Cinderella, Snow White ("She lives with seven men, but she's not easy"), and Princess Fiona. He chooses the beauty who has not had the title role in a Disney animated feature. No doubt all of this, and a little dig at DisneyWorld, were inspired by feelings DreamWorks partner Jeffrey Katzenberg has nourished since his painful departure from Disney—but the elbow in the ribs is more playful than serious. (Farquaad is said to be inspired by Disney chief Michael Eisner, but I don't see a resemblance, and his short stature corresponds not to the tall Eisner but, well, to the diminutive Katzenberg.)

The plot involves Lord Farquaad's desire to wed the Princess Fiona, and his reluctance to slay the dragon that stands between her and would-be suitors. He hires Shrek to attempt the mission, which Shrek is happy to do, providing the loathsome fairy-tale creatures are banished and his swamp returned to its dismal solitude. On his mission, Shrek is joined by a donkey named The Donkey, whose running commentary, voiced by Eddie Murphy, provides some of the movie's best laughs. (The trick isn't that he talks, Shrek observes; "the trick is to get him to shut up.")

The expedition to the castle of the princess involves a suspension bridge above a flaming abyss, and the castle's interior is piled high with the bones of the dragon's previous contenders. When Shrek and The Donkey get inside, there are exuberant action scenes that whirl madly through interior spaces, and revelations about the dragon no one could have guessed. And all along the way, asides and puns,

in-jokes and contemporary references, and countless references to other movies.

Voice-overs for animated movies were once, except for the annual Disney classic, quickie jobs that actors took if they were out of work. Now they are starring roles with fat paychecks, and the ads for *Shrek* use big letters to trumpet the names of Myers, Murphy, Cameron Diaz (Fiona), and John Lithgow (Farquaad). Their vocal performances are nicely suited to the characters, although Myers's infatuation with his Scottish brogue reportedly had to be toned down. Murphy in particular has emerged as a star of the voice-over genre.

Much will be written about the movie's technical expertise, and indeed every summer seems to bring another breakthrough on the animation front. After the three-dimensional modeling and shading of *Toy Story*, the even more evolved *Toy Story 2, A Bug's Life,* and *Antz,* and the amazing effects in *Dinosaur, Shrek* unveils creatures who have been designed from the inside out, so that their skin, muscles, and fat move upon their bones instead of seeming like a single unit. They aren't "realistic," but they're curiously real. The artistry of the locations and setting is equally skilled—not lifelike, but beyond lifelike, in a merry, stylized way.

Still, all the craft in the world would not have made *Shrek* work if the story hadn't been fun and the ogre so lovable. Shrek is not handsome but he isn't as ugly as he thinks; he's a guy we want as our friend, and he doesn't frighten us but stirs our sympathy. He's so immensely likable that I suspect he may emerge as an enduring character, populating sequels and spin-offs. One movie cannot contain him.

Sidewalks of New York ★ ★ ★
R, 100 m., 2001

Edward Burns (Tommy Reilly), Heather Graham (Annie), Rosario Dawson (Maria Tedesco), Brittany Murphy (Ashley), David Krumholtz (Ben), Dennis Farina (Carpo), Stanley Tucci (Griffin), Aida Turturro (Shari). Directed by Edward Burns and produced by Margot Bridger, Burns, Cathy Schulman, and Rick Yorn. Screenplay by Burns.

I saw Edward Burns's *Sidewalks of New York* in

September 2001 at the Toronto Film Festival, and enjoyed its lighthearted story of seven lovers who readjust their romantic priorities. It was scheduled to open in a week or two, and I was baffled by Paramount's decision to put it back on the shelf for a couple of months, as if after September 11 no one could possibly contemplate attending a movie named *Sidewalks of New York*.

Now the movie has arrived, the story of lovers, would-be lovers, former lover, and adulterers from each of the city's boroughs, who seem totally preoccupied with themselves. This is as it should be. When you're in love, you think of no one but yourself. Even your thoughts of your loved one are about *your love*, because the idealized other person exists in your imagination. John Donne got this right.

The movie lives at the intersection between Woody Allen and *Sex and the City*. Like *The Brothers McMullen*, Burns's first film, it is about people who spend a lot of time analyzing their motives and measuring their happiness. The film is framed by interviews in which the lovers address the camera directly, talking about themselves and about love, and from their comments we learn one thing for sure: Lovers recycle ancient truisms that have little to do with how they will behave tomorrow, or later tonight.

Like Jacques Rivette's *Va Savoir*, another 2001 movie, the film begins with three couples, and then readjusts the pairings. It actually begins with three and a half couples, because Griffin (Stanley Tucci) is married to Annie (Heather Graham) and is having an affair with Ashley (Brittany Murphy). He is a dentist, Annie is a real-estate agent, and Ashley is a student at NYU. Judging by recent Manhattan comedies, these are the three most popular occupations in town, after police work and prostitution. Griffin fancies himself a seducer. "I think you have the look of the new millennium," he tells Ashley the first time he sees her. Anyone who considers this a compliment deserves Griffin.

Burns himself plays Tommy, who works for a show not unlike *Entertainment Tonight* (where Burns himself once worked). A love affair has ended, and he has moved out of his apartment and is living temporarily with his boss, Carpo (Dennis Farina), who plays the field and ad-

vises Tommy to do likewise. Carpo is the kind of man who believes seduction is all in the cologne. His advice: "A wife and children will drive you to an early grave."

Tommy meets Maria (Rosario Dawson), who teaches rich kids in a private school. She is divorced from Benjamin (David Krumholtz), who supports himself as a doorman while dreaming of a career in music. He cannot believe she left him. We cannot believe she married him. He is a needy whiner who spends way too much energy believing it is only a matter of time until they get back together again. First he seems obnoxious, then you feel a little sorry for him, then he wears down your pity and you figure he got what was coming to him.

Let's see. Griffin, the Tucci character, is having trouble deceiving two women at the same time, which is what he's doing. (A more honest man would merely cheat on his wife with his mistress, but Griffin's nature is such that he also cheats on his mistress with his wife.) His wife, Annie (Graham), shows an apartment to Tommy, and begins to think of her romantic life as still holding promise. His mistress, Ashley, attracts the attention of Benjamin, who continues to annoy his ex-wife, but begins to suspect there may be alternatives to spending his nights ringing her doorbell.

In the Jacques Rivette film, the characters are all French, and so conduct their intrigues while drawing on centuries of experience. Ed Burns's New Yorkers have grown up in a society of psychobabble, and carry around half-digested concepts of guilt, redemption, and finding your karma. The teacher Maria (Dawson) is more centered, because she is the only one who has a job that does not depend on being nice to rich people. (As a waitress, Ashley would also seem to qualify, but in New York waiters are always "really" something else.)

The movie is funny without being hilarious, touching but not tearful, and articulate in the way that Burns is articulate, by nibbling earnestly around an idea as if afraid that the core has seeds. Not a lot is at stake. We would not be surprised if in three years an emotional reassignment has taken place, and all of the new couples, like all of the old ones, have been thrown on the ash-heap of romantic history. Yet *Sidewalks of New York* finds the right note of seeking and optimism among the shoals of hope. It's spiced by a rotter (Tucci) whose self-justifications are ingenious. And by a cynic (Farina) whose advice is sometimes pretty good.

Signs and Wonders ★ ★ ★

NO MPAA RATING, 104 m., 2001

Stellan Skarsgard (Alec Fenton), Charlotte Rampling (Marjorie), Deborah Kara Unger (Katherine), Dimitris Katalifos (Andreas), Ashley Remy (Siri), Michael Cook (Marcus), Dave Simonds (Kent). Directed by Jonathan Nossiter and produced by Marin Karmitz. Screenplay by James Lasdun and Nossiter.

Signs and Wonders looks through the eyes of a manic-depressive as the world sends him messages and he hurries to answer them. It shows how exhausting it is to be constantly in the grip of exhilaration, insight, conviction, idealism, and excitement—while bombarded all the time with cosmic coincidences. Nobody in the movie calls this man a manic-depressive, but it's as clear as day—or as the bright yellow suit he turns up wearing one morning, convinced it symbolizes his new and improved psyche. As a drama about the ravages of mental illness, the movie works; too bad most of the critics read it only as a romantic soap opera in which the hero is an obsessive sap. They read the signs but miss the diagnosis.

The movie stars Stellan Skarsgard and Charlotte Rampling as Alec and Marjorie, a married American couple living in Athens. ("It doesn't bother to explain away their foreign accents," complains one critic, although 10 percent of all Americans are first-generation and millions have accents.) She works for the embassy; he has a murky job in finance, and is having an office affair with Katherine (Deborah Kara Unger). The affair has been proceeding satisfactorily for months or maybe years, we gather, until one day Alec, beset with guilt, walks out of his house and uses the phone booth across the street to call back home and confess everything to his wife.

This sudden, dramatic confession marks the start of his bipolar illness. He has become seized with the conviction that vast forces are sweeping through him. He can no longer live a lie. Walking his daughter to school, he joins in her game of counting manholes and clocking various signs and portents in the city streets. For her it's a child's game; for him it becomes an obsession.

Marjorie forgives Alec his affair. Some time later, on the ski slopes in another country, he meets Katherine again—coincidentally, he believes. This random, accidental meeting is for Alec a sign that they were meant to be together, and he leaves Marjorie a second time. Then there is a tense, painful conversation with Katherine, after he explains the significance of their meeting, and why it proved they were predestined to be together. "What if I set it up?" she asks, as a woman who would prefer to be loved for herself rather than as the outward sign of cosmic forces.

I don't think we can be sure if Katherine arranged the meeting or not, but Alec decides she did, and that sends him racing back to Marjorie. Having smashed his family once, and then, as she puts it, returned to smash it again, he has run out of goodwill on the home front—and besides, she's in love with another man. Now come the most fascinating passages in Skarsgard's performance, as his mania becomes more evident. He will baby-sit while she goes out with the other man. He deserves to suffer. He will do penance. Yes! Yes! At one point as she shouts at him, he replies: "I want you to be this angry with me! We need this!" About this time the yellow suit turns up.

The movie is maddeningly obscure about details that do not directly involve Alec. We meet Andreas (Dimitris Katalifos), the man Marjorie plans to marry. He is a left-wing journalist, was tortured by the colonels, has an archive of secrets in his flat about right-wing Greek conspiracies, is perhaps a little paranoid. The twice-jilted Katherine, who comes hunting Alec and assumes a false identity, is also deranged; Marjorie is the sane center of the film. By the end, we are not sure exactly how to explain what happens to Andreas, and the movie leaves a lot of other unanswered questions. Perhaps the answer is, the story spins away from Alec, who as his illness progresses can no longer keep all the connections and meanings in order.

Jonathan Nossiter, the director and cowriter, made the 1997 Sundance prize-winner *Sunday,* about a British actress, down on her luck, who meets a man who may be a famous director or may be a homeless derelict. It's a movie about how people can be who we want them to be. *Signs and Wonders* is about a man who knows what he wants from Marjorie and Katherine, but can't get them to play the roles. They can't keep up with his fevered brain, as he connects, disconnects, reconnects. "I am not a frivolous man!" he cries at one point, aware that unless his signs and wonders are real, he is frivolous indeed. I had a friend once who suffered from manic behavior, and he said, "You know what I used to pray for? Boredom."

Simon Magus ★ ★
NO MPAA RATING, 106 m., 2001

Noah Taylor (Simon), Stuart Townsend (Dovid), Sean McGinley (Hase), Embeth Davidtz (Leah), Amanda Ryan (Sarah), Rutger Hauer (Squire), Ian Holm (Sirius/Boris), Terence Rigby (Bratislav). Directed by Ben Hopkins and produced by Robert Jones. Screenplay by Hopkins.

If there's anything worse than a laborious fable with a moral, it's the laborious fable without the moral. The more I think about *Simon Magus*, the less I'm sure what it's trying to say. It leads us through a mystical tale about Jews, Poles, and an outcast who takes orders from Satan. Both groups would like to build the local railroad station, but the outcast, a mystic, has visions of these very tracks being used to take Jews to the death camps. Does that mean it doesn't matter who builds the station because the trains will still perform their tragic task? In that case, what's the story about except bleak irony?

The movie takes place in nineteenth-century Silesia, bordering Hungary and Austria. Some twenty Orthodox Jews have a small community near a larger gentile town. The new railroad, bypassing the town, has created hard times for everyone. A Jew named Dovid (Stuart Townsend) wants to build a station and some shops, which will help out the woman he loves, a widowed shopkeeper named Leah (Embeth Davidtz). A gentile named Hase (Sean McGinley) also wants to build the station. The land is controlled by the Squire (Rutger Hauer), a dreamy intellectual.

This would be a story about anti-Semitism

and real estate were it not for two other characters. Simon (Noah Taylor) is a Jew who is scorned by his own community because of his crazy ways. From time to time, as he makes his way through the gloomy mists of the town and forest, he is approached by Sirius (Ian Holm), who seems to be the devil. When Satan appears in a movie, I always look around for God, but rarely find him; it's usually up to the human characters to defeat the devil. In this case, Simon's visions of the death trains perhaps suggest that God is taking a century off.

The nonsupernatural side of the story involves the good Dovid and the bad Hase (a villain so obvious he lacks only a mustache to twirl). Both want the Squire to make his land available. The Squire, a lonely and bookish man, wants intellectual companionship—someone to read his poems and keep him company around the fire on long winter evenings. Dovid, a Talmudic scholar but not otherwise widely read, takes lessons from Sarah (Amanda Ryan), who is up on poetry. At one point, she and the Squire get into a literature-quoting contest.

Simon Magus creates a sinister subplot in which the evil Hase tries to trick Simon into taking a box with a Christian baby inside and hiding it in the rabbi's house so that a mob can discover it as proof that the Jews plan to eat it. Simon responds with intelligence that surprises us, but what good purpose does it do to resurrect this slander? Most people now alive would never hear of such ancient anti-Semitic calumnies were it not for movies opposing them. Does Ben Hopkins, the writer-director, imagine audiences nodding sagely as they learn that baby-eating was a myth spread by anti-Semites? Isn't it better to allow such lies to disappear into the mists of the past?

In any event, the story is resolved along standard melodramatic lines, and good (you will not be surprised to learn) triumphs. Yet still those death trains approach inexorably through Simon's visions. The papers are filled these days with stories of Polish villagers who rounded up their local Jews and burned them alive. What difference does it make who builds the train station?

Simpatico ★ ½
R, 106 m., 2000

Nick Nolte (Vinnie), Jeff Bridges (Carter),
Sharon Stone (Rosie), Catherine Keener
(Cecilia), Albert Finney (Simms), Shawn Hatosy
(Young Vinnie), Kimberly Williams (Young
Rosie), Liam Waite (Young Carter). Directed
by Matthew Warchus and produced by Dan
Lupovitz, Timm Oberwelland, and Jean-Francois
Fonlupt. Screenplay by Warchus and David
Nicholls, based on a play by Sam Shepard.

Simpatico is a long slog through perplexities
and complexities that disguise what this really
is: The kind of B-movie plot that used to clock
in at seventy-five minutes on the bottom half
of a double bill. It's based on a Sam Shepard
play, unseen by me. Since Shepard is a good
playwright, we're left with two possibilities:
(1) It has been awkwardly adapted, or (2) it
should have stayed in Shepard's desk drawer.

The plot involves a kind of exchange of personalities between Carter (Jeff Bridges), a rich
Kentucky racehorse breeder, and Vinnie (Nick
Nolte), a shabby layabout who has been black-
mailing him for years. They were once friends,
long ago when they were young, and involved
in a scheme to cheat at the track by switching
horses. Vinnie has some photos that Carter
would not want anyone to see, and that gives
him leverage. This time, he interrupts Carter
in the middle of negotiations to sell an expensive horse named Simpatico, demanding that
he fly to California to get him out of a fix.
Seems a supermarket cashier named Cecilia
(Catherine Keener) is accusing him of sexual
misconduct.

Oh, but it's a lot more complicated than
that, and neither Cecilia nor her relationship
with Vinnie is quite as described. Two other
figures from the past also enter: Rosie (Sharon
Stone), now Carter's boozy but colorful wife,
and Simms (Albert Finney), once a racing com-
missioner, now a tracer of bloodlines. Students of *noir* will know that the contemporary
story will stir up old ghosts.

Those who are not *noir* lovers won't be in
the dark for long, since director Matthew Warchus and his cowriter, David Nicholls, supply
flashbacks that incriminate some of the char-

acters (although not, in this day and age, seriously enough to inspire the vast heavings of this
leviathan plot). Nolte and Bridges are portrayed as young men by Shawn Hatosy and
Liam Waite, a casting decision that adds to the
murkiness, since Hatosy, who is supposed to
be young Nolte, looks more like young Bridges,
and Waite, who is supposed to be young
Bridges, looks like nobody else in the movie.
This theme is developed further, I suppose, as
Nolte and Bridges subtly start to resemble
each other.

It happens that I've just revisited a complicated *noir*, Roman Polanski's *Chinatown*, which
also involves sexual misconduct in the past
and blackmail in the present. One reason it
works so well is that the characters seem to
drive the plot: Things turn out the way they
do because the characters are who they are.
The plot of *Simpatico* is like a clockwork mechanism that would tick whether or not anyone
cared what time it was.

The 6th Day ★ ★ ★
PG-13, 124 m., 2000

Arnold Schwarzenegger (Adam Gibson), Tony
Goldwyn (Drucker), Robert Duvall (Dr. Weir),
Michael Rapaport (Hank), Sara Wynter (Talia),
Wendy Crewson (Natalie Gibson), Rodney
Rowland (Wile E. Coyote). Directed by Roger
Spottiswoode and produced by Jon Davison,
Mike Medavoy, and Arnold Schwarzenegger.
Screenplay by Cormac Wibberley and
Marianne Wibberley.

On the sixth day, God created man. And man
should leave it at that, according to laws that
have been passed in *The 6th Day*, Arnold
Schwarzenegger's new thriller. In the near future there's a RePet store in every mall that
will clone your dead pet for you, but human
cloning, although technically possible, has been
outlawed.

There is, however, a clandestine market in
human clones. Consider the case of Johnny
Phoenix, a pro quarterback who's paid $300
million a season but is brain-dead after a
game injury. "We have a lifetime contract
with a vegetable," one of the team owners
moans, before pulling the plug on Johnny's

life-support system ("Sorry, Johnny—you're gonna have to take one for the team"). Sad, yes, but whaddaya know: Soon Johnny is back out there quarterbacking again.

All of this is miles away from the life of Adam Gibson (Arnold Schwarzenegger), a helicopter pilot who with his buddy Hank (Michael Rapaport) airlifts rich skiers to the slopes. Adam has a happy home life with his wife, Natalie (Wendy Crewson), and daughter, marred only by the death of their pet dog Oliver. Should Adam have Oliver cloned at RePet? He doesn't think so. He thinks there's something wrong about overturning the fundamental process of life and death.

Adam's friend Hank has fewer scruples, and enjoys life with a computer-generated holographic Perfect Virtual Woman, who greets him after a long day: "I've recorded all your sports programs. Maybe we could watch them together. Or should I just take this dress off right now?" (There is an *SNL* skit there somewhere, about a hard-pressed man taking Viagra to keep up with the insatiable willingness of his Virtual Woman. Perhaps she could be adjusted to say, "Honey, tonight I only feel like a pineapple and pepperoni pizza, a six-pack, and watching you clean your guns.")

Cloning in *The 6th Day* has made great leaps forward since the days of the sheep named Dolly. The cloners don't start with a cloned fertilized egg. Instead, they grow "blanks"— assemblies of protoplasm floating in a nurturing fluid, ready to have the total mind and body information of adults plugged into them. Using a quick eye scan, the cloners can make a "syncording" of the contents of a pet's mind, so it will still recognize its owner and know all the same tricks. And the same thing is done illegally in the movie with humans, by a shadowy corporation run by Drucker (the handsomely reptilian Tony Goldwyn). Robert Duvall is the brilliant scientist for the corporation, but has his doubts.

This process sounds like the Soul Catcher that has been hypothesized by Arthur C. Clarke—the memory chip into which the contents of a human mind might be downloaded. My problem with both processes is that while the resulting clone or chip might know everything I know and remember every-

thing that ever happened to me and think of itself as me, I myself would still be over here in the old container. Immortality for my perfect clone leaves behind what I insist upon considering the real me—something the Goldwyn character has time to reflect on during a melodramatic dying scene.

Such details do not slow the evil corporation, fueled by the genius of Dr. Weir (Robert Duvall) and prodded by the seductive, ruthless Talia (Sara Wynter). They have a scheme to kill and clone Hank, Adam's friend, but by mistake they clone Adam instead, leaving the movie populated by two Arnold Schwarzeneggers who both think they're the real thing. Since that is how most Arnold Schwarzenegger movies feel, this is not as confusing as it sounds.

This much you know from the trailers. What happens next I will not say, although of course it involves meetings both astonished and poignant between the two Adams, whose wife is named Natalie and not Eve only through the superhuman resolve of the screenwriters.

The 6th Day is not in the same league with the great Schwarzenegger films like *Total Recall* and *Terminator 2*, but it's a well-crafted entertainment containing enough ideas to qualify it as science fiction and not just as a futurist thriller. Arnold once again gets mileage out of the contrast between his muscular presence and his everyman persona; at one point, he has dialogue that slyly pairs the two: "My little girl—I don't want to expose her to any graphic violence. She gets enough of that from the media."

Both Drucker and Talia have been cloned many times, causing us to wonder how much they enjoy starting over, and whether any regrets are left behind in the process. We'll never know: The discarded entities left behind in the cloning process have no way to complain. Instead of living forever through the genes you give to your children, you live forever through reproducing your own genes, which brings evolution to a dead stop, of course. Could you make a syncording of yourself as a child, grow up, clone the kid, and raise yourself as your own child? Speculations like these are inspired by *The 6th Day*, and are part of the fun.

The Skulls ★
PG-13, 107 m., 2000

Joshua Jackson (Luke McNamara), Paul Walker (Caleb Mandrake), Hill Harper (Will Beckford), Leslie Bibb (Chloe), Christopher McDonald (Martin Lombard), Steve Harris (Detective Sparrow), William Petersen (Ames Levritt), Craig T. Nelson (Litten Mandrake). Directed by Rob Cohen and produced by Neal H. Moritz and John Pogue. Screenplay by Pogue.

I would give a great deal to be able to see *The Skulls* on opening night in New Haven in a movie theater full of Yale students, with gales of laughter rolling at the screen. It isn't a comedy, but that won't stop anyone. *The Skulls* is one of the great howlers, a film that bears comparison, yes, with *The Greek Tycoon* or even *The Scarlet Letter*. It's so ludicrous in so many different ways it achieves a kind of forlorn grandeur. It's in a category by itself.

The movie claims to rip the lid off a secret campus society named the Skulls, which is obviously inspired by the Yale society known as Skull and Bones. The real Skull and Bones has existed for two centuries, and has counted presidents, tycoons, and CIA founders among its alumni. Membership was an honor—until now. After seeing this movie, members are likely to sneak out of the theater through the lavatory windows.

The story: Luke McNamara (Joshua Jackson) attends a university that is never mentioned by name (clues: It is in New Haven and has a lot of big Y's painted on its walls.). He is a townie, rides a bike, lost his father when he was one, is poor, works in the cafeteria. Yet he's tapped for membership in the Skulls because he is a star on the varsity rowing crew.

Luke's best friends are a black student journalist named Will Beckford (Hill Harper) and a rich girl named Chloe (Leslie Bibb). Luke secretly loves Chloe but keeps it a secret because "Chloe's parents own a private jet, and I've never even been in a jet." Another of Luke's friends is Caleb Mandrake (Paul Walker), whose father, Litten (Craig T. Nelson), is a Supreme Court candidate. With soap opera names like Caleb and Litten Mandrake (and Senator Ames Levritt), the film contains an enormous mystery, which is, why doesn't Chloe have a last name? I suggest Worsthorne-Waugh.

Luke is tapped for the Skulls. This involves racing around campus to answer lots of ringing pay phones, after which he and the other new pledges are drugged, pass out, and awaken in coffins, ready to be reborn in their new lives. They go through "revealing ceremonies" inside the Skulls' campus clubhouse, a Gothic monument so filled with vistas and arches and caverns and halls and pools and verandas that Dracula would have something along these lines if he could afford it.

Mel Brooks said it's good to be the king. It's better to be a Skull. Luke and his fellow tappees find $10,000 in their ATM accounts (later they get $100,000 checks). Beautiful women are supplied after an induction ceremony. They all get new sports cars. The Skulls insignia is branded on their wrists with a red-hot iron, but they get shiny new wristwatches to cover the scar. I'm thinking, how secret is a society when hookers are hired for the pledge class? Do they wear those watches in the shower? In this litigious age, is it safe to drug undergraduates into unconsciousness?

Each Skull is given a key to the clubhouse and a rule book. "There's a rule for all possible situations," they're told. I want that book. Rule One: Don't lose the rule book. Will, the journalist, steals Caleb's key and rule book and sneaks inside the clubhouse, and (I am now revealing certain plot secrets) is later found to have hanged himself. But was it really suicide? Luke thinks Caleb might know, and can ask him, because the Skulls have a bonding ceremony in which new members are assigned soul mates. You are locked in an iron cage with your soul mate and lowered into a pit in the floor, at which time you can ask him anything you want, and he has to answer truthfully, while the other Skulls listen to the words echoing through the crypt.

Many powerful adult men still take the Skulls very seriously. Not only Judge Litten Mandrake but Senator Ames Levritt (William Petersen), who are involved in a power struggle of their own. They put pressure on Luke to end his curiosity about Will's death. The following dialogue occurs, which will have the New Haven audience baying with joy:

"This is your preacceptance to the law school of your choice."

"I haven't even applied yet."

"Imagine that!"

Chloe is enlisted as Luke's sidekick for some Hardy Boys capers, but soon Luke is subjected to a forcible psychiatric examination at the campus health clinic (no laughter here), and bundled off to a mental hospital where, so far-reaching is the influence of the Skulls, he is kept in a zombie state with drugs while the senator and the judge struggle over his future. Oh, and there's a car chase scene. Oh, and a duel, in broad daylight, with all the Skulls watching, in an outdoor pavilion on the Skulls' lawn that includes a marble platform apparently designed specifically for duels.

The real Skull and Bones numbers among its alumni the two George Bushes. Of course, there's no connection between Skull and Bones and the fictional Skulls. Still, the next time George W. has a press conference, a reporter should ask to see under his wristwatch. Only kidding.

Slackers no stars
R, 87 m., 2002

Devon Sawa (Dave), Jason Schwartzman (Ethan), James King (Angela), Jason Segel (Sam), Michael C. Maronna (Jeff), Laura Prepon (Reanna), Mamie Van Doren (Mrs. Van Graaf). Directed by Dewey Nicks and produced by Neal H. Moritz and Erik Feig. Screenplay by David H. Steinberg.

Slackers is a dirty movie. Not a sexy, erotic, steamy, or even smutty movie, but a just plain dirty movie. It made me feel unclean, and I'm the guy who liked *There's Something About Mary* and both *American Pie* movies. Oh, and *Booty Call*. This film knows no shame.

Consider a scene where the heroine's roommate, interrupted while masturbating, continues even while a man she has never met is in the room. Consider a scene where the hero's roommate sings a duet with a sock puppet on his penis. Consider a scene where we cut away from the hero and the heroine to join two roommates just long enough for a loud fart, and then cut back to the main story again.

And consider a scene where Mamie Van Doren, who is seventy-one years old, plays a hooker in a hospital bed who bares her breasts so that the movie's horny creep can give them a sponge bath. On the day when I saw *Slackers,* there were many things I expected and even wanted to see in a movie, but I confess Mamie Van Doren's breasts were not among them.

The movie is an exhausted retread of the old campus romance gag where the pretty girl almost believes the lies of the reprehensible schemer, instead of trusting the nice guy who loves her. The only originality the movie brings to this formula is to make it incomprehensible, through the lurching incompetence of its story structure. Details are labored while the big picture remains unpainted.

Slackers should not be confused with Richard Linklater's *Slacker* (1991), a film that will be treasured long after this one has been turned into landfill. *Slackers* stars the previously blameless Devon Sawa *(SLC Punk! Final Destination)* and Jason Schwartzman *(Rushmore)* as rivals for the attention of the beautiful Angela (James King, who despite her name is definitely a girl). Schwartzman plays Ethan, campus geek; Sawa is Dave, a professional cheater and con man. Ethan obsesses over Angela and blackmails Sawa by threatening to expose his exam-cheating scheme. He demands that Dave "deliver" the girl to him.

This demand cannot be met for a number of reasons. One of them is that Ethan is comprehensively creepy (he not only has an Angela doll made from strands of her hair, but does things with it I will not tire you by describing). Another reason is that Angela falls for Dave. The plot requires Angela to temporarily be blinded to Ethan's repulsiveness and to believe his lies about Dave. These goals are met by making Angela remarkably dense, and even then we don't believe her.

Watching *Slackers,* I was appalled by the poverty of its imagination. There is even a scene where Ethan approaches a girl from behind, thinking she is Angela, and of course she turns around and it is not Angela, but a girl who wears braces and smiles at him so widely and for so long we can almost hear the assistant director instructing her to be sure the camera can see those braces.

But back to the dirt. There is a kind of one-upmanship now at work in Hollywood, inspired by the success of several gross-out comedies, to elevate smut into an art form. This is not an entirely futile endeavor; it can be done, and when it is done well, it can be funny. But most of the wanna-bes fail to understand one thing: It is funny when a character is offensive *despite* himself, but not funny when he is *deliberately* offensive. The classic "hair gel" scene involving Ben Stiller and Cameron Diaz in *There's Something About Mary* was funny because neither one had the slightest idea what was going on.

Knowing that this movie will be block-booked into countless multiplexes, pitying the audiences that stumble into it, I want to stand in line with those kids and whisper the names of other movies now in release: *Monster's Ball, Black Hawk Down, Gosford Park, The Royal Tenenbaums, A Beautiful Mind, The Count of Monte Cristo.* Or even *Orange County,* also about screwed-up college students, but in an intelligent and amusing way. There are a lot of good movies in theaters right now. Why waste two hours (which you can never get back) seeing a rotten one?

Small Time Crooks ★ ★ ★

PG, 95 m., 2000

Woody Allen (Ray Winkler), Tracey Ullman (Frenchy), Hugh Grant (David), Michael Rapaport (Denny), Tony Darrow (Tommy), Elaine May (May), Jon Lovitz (Benny), Elaine Stritch (Chi Chi Potter). Directed by Woody Allen and produced by Jean Doumanian.

Small Time Crooks is a flat-out comedy from Woody Allen, enhanced by a couple of plot U-turns that keep us from guessing where the plot is headed. Allen often plays two types of characters, intellectuals and dumbos, and this time he's at the freezing end of the IQ spectrum, as an ex-con and dishwasher with a plan to rob a bank. His wife, Frenchy (Tracey Ullman), is incredulous as he explains his scheme to rent a storefront and tunnel into the bank vault two stores down.

This looks a lot like the master plan in the Italian comedy *Big Deal on Madonna Street,* but in *Small Time Crooks* it's more of a false alarm. Ray and Frenchy open up a cookie store

as a front for the heist, the cookies take off big-time, the heist is hopelessly bungled, and then Frenchy's cousin May (Elaine May) blabs to a cop about the tunneling in the basement. This leads indirectly to a franchise operation, and within a year Ray and Frenchy are rich beyond his, if not her, wildest dreams.

The first act of the movie has a lot of fun with Ray and his low-life criminal friends, including Jon Lovitz as a guy who has put his kids through college by torching buildings, and Michael Rapaport as a tunnel digger who wears his miner's cap backward, baseball cap style, so the light points behind him. If this heist idea had been spun out to feature length, however, it might have grown old and felt like other caper movies. Allen has a twist up his sleeve.

As millionaires, the Winklers put the nouveau in riche. Frenchy lavishes a fortune on their new luxury apartment, where Ray rattles around unhappily (he refuses to look at one abstract painting because it depresses him). At a housewarming, Frenchy offers her guests crudites (pronounced "CRUDE-ites") and adds, "They say I have a flair for decoration. This rug lights up." Ray follows behind miserably: "Show them your collection of leather pigs."

Then David (Hugh Grant) enters their lives. He's a British art expert, suave, a flatterer, and Frenchy wants to hire him to train them in culture. He quickly sees that Frenchy has "outgrown" Ray, and might be ripe for the plucking. He whisks her off on a whirl of gallery shows, opening nights, charity benefits, and chic restaurants, while Ray miserably seeks consolation in the simpler things: Knicks games, junk food, and the comforting company of May.

I've heard Woody Allen accused of making the same movie over and over, which is simply not fair. His recent films include an enchanting musical *(Everyone Says I Love You),* a Felliniesque black-and-white social satire *(Celebrity),* and the goofiness of Sean Penn's second-best jazz guitarist in the world, in *Sweet and Lowdown.* Now comes this straight comedy, with its malaprop dialogue ("I require your agreeance on this") and its sneaky way of edging from an honest bank job to sins like flattery, pride, and embezzlement.

Allen plays a blue-collar version of his basic

persona, and has bracketed himself between two of the funniest women in America, Tracey Ullman, who is seen too rarely, and Elaine May, who is hardly seen in movies at all. The supporting cast is written more sharply than is often the case in comedies (where the star gets all the good lines), and there's a lesson lurking somewhere, about how money can't buy you happiness and may even cost you extra by losing it. Dumb as they (allegedly) are, the characters in *Small Time Crooks* are smarter, edgier, and more original than the dreary crowd in so many new comedies. The movie opened on the same day as *Road Trip*. Now there's a choice.

Smiling Fish and Goat on Fire ★ ★ ★
R, 90 m., 2000

Derick Martini (Chris Remi), Steven Martini (Tony Remi), Christa Miller (Kathy), Amy Hathaway (Alison), Bill Henderson (Clive Winter), Rosemarie Addeo (Anna), Heather Jae Marie (Nicole), Nicole Rae (Natalie), Wesley Thompson (Burt Winter). Directed by Kevin Jordan and produced by Derick Martini, Jordan, and Steven Martini. Screenplay by Derick Martini, Jordan, and Steven Martini.

The two brothers who are the heroes of Kevin Jordan's *Smiling Fish and Goat on Fire* are not Native Americans, but their grandmother was half-Indian, and she nicknamed them—Tony is Smiling Fish because he floats in the current, grinning, waiting for the world to drift his way. Chris is Goat on Fire because he wants to get everything exactly right. Chris is an accountant and Tony is an actor, which is the Los Angeles word for unemployed.

In their twenties, they live in the cozy bungalow left them by their parents (whose marriage had an L.A.-style entrance and exit; they met on the Universal tour and died in a traffic accident). Tony and Chris both have girlfriends, but we sense that one relationship is dying and the other looks ominous since the girl cries a lot during sex. And then their lives take a turn for the better with the introduction of two women, a six-year-old girl, a ninety-year-old man, and a chicken named Bob.

Chris (Derick Martini) meets Anna (Rosemarie Addeo), an Italian who works on movies as an animal wrangler. Bob is her chicken. Tony (Steven Martini) meets his postal carrier, Kathy (Christa Miller), who is from Wyoming and has moved to L.A. in hopes that her daughter, Nicole (Heather Jae Marie), will find work as a child actress. Kathy's heart is more or less stolen by Tony when he silences the squeaking wheel on her mail cart with olive oil.

Our hearts, meanwhile, are warmed by the introduction of a character named Clive (Bill Henderson), who is the ninety-year-old uncle of Chris's boss. The boss asks Chris to give Clive a ride to work, and Clive turns out to be a bottomless well of entertainment and wisdom for Chris and Tony, and for us.

He used to work as a sound boom man on African-American movies, Clive says. He met Rebecca, the love of his life, on a Paul Robeson picture. At work, he erects a tent over his cubicle, moves a friendly desk lamp under it, and listens to jazz. The character could steal the movie, but generously shares it with the stories of the brothers and their new loves, and leftover problems with the old loves.

Smiling Fish and Goat on Fire is one of those handmade movies that sneaks into festivals and wins friends. I saw it on the final weekend of the 1999 Toronto Film Festival, where Henderson (who is nowhere near ninety) got a standing ovation. Talking to the filmmakers, I learned that director Jordan and the Martini brothers, who cowrote the screenplay, were longtime friends, that the movie cost $40,000, and that it was shot in the brothers' actual house. (There is an echo here of the Sundance winner *The Brothers McMullen*, also shot in the director's home.)

Many other movies costing $40,000 (and less, and more) have gone to deserved oblivion, but *Smiling Fish and Goat on Fire* has a freshness and charm, a winning way with its not terrifically original material. The movie isn't really about a plot, but about developments in the lives of characters we like. When a standard plot element develops (a possible pregnancy, for example), the movie uses it not for a phony narrative crisis, but for understated human comedy. By not trying too hard, by not pushing for opportunities to manipulate, the movie sneaks up and makes friends.

The brothers Martini are effortlessly likable

and convincing in the film, which we feel is close to their personalities if not to the facts of their lives. As for Henderson, I hope casting directors see him here and use him. He has been in a lot of movies (he was the no-nonsense cook in *City Slickers*), but this movie suggests new ways he could be used; it gives him notes we want to hear again. And the way he evokes the lost world of the African-American film industry is like a film within the film; the way he evokes his love for Rebecca, glimpsed only in old photos, is surprisingly moving.

Snatch ★ ★
R, 103 m., 2001

Brad Pitt (One Punch Mickey), Andy Beckwith (Errol), Ewen Bremner (Mullet), Nikki and Teena Collins (Alex and Susi), Sorcha Cusack (Mum O'Neil), Benicio Del Toro (Franky Four Fingers), Sam Douglas (Rosebud), Mike Reid (Doug the Head), Austin Drage (Gypsy Kid), Dennis Farina (Avi). Directed by Guy Ritchie and produced by Matthew Vaughn. Screenplay by Ritchie.

In my review of *Lock, Stock and Two Smoking Barrels*, Guy Ritchie's 1999 film, I wrote: "In a time when movies follow formulas like zombies, it's alive." So what am I to say of *Snatch*, Ritchie's new film, which follows the *Lock, Stock* formula so slavishly it could be like a new arrangement of the same song?

Once again we descend into a London underworld that has less to do with English criminals than with Dick Tracy. Once again the characters have Runyonesque names (Franky Four Fingers, Bullet Tooth Tony, Boris the Blade, Jack the All-Seeing Eye). Once again the plot is complicated to a degree that seems perverse. Once again titles and narration are used to identify characters and underline developments.

There is one addition of considerable wit: In the previous film, some of the accents were impenetrable to non-British audiences, so this time, in the spirit of fair play, Ritchie has added a character played by Brad Pitt, who speaks a Gypsy dialect even the other characters in the movie can't understand. Pitt paradoxically has more success communicating in this mode than some of the others do with

languages we allegedly understand. He sounds like a combination of Adam Sandler and Professor Backwards.

Ritchie is a zany, high-energy director. He isn't interested in crime; he's interested in voltage. As an unfolding event, *Snatch* is fun to watch, even if no reasonable person could hope to understand the plot in one viewing. Ritchie is almost winking at us that the plot doesn't matter, that it's a clothesline for his pyrotechnics (if indeed pyrotechnics can employ clotheslines, but don't get me started).

The plot assembles its lowlifes in interlocking stories involving crooked boxing, stolen diamonds, and pigs. After Franky Four Fingers (Benicio Del Toro) steals a diamond in Antwerp and returns to London, a Russian named Boris the Blade (Rade Sherbedgia) and an American gangster named Avi (Dennis Farina) try to separate him from it—not easy, since it is in a case handcuffed to his wrist.

Meanwhile (somehow I don't think "meanwhile" quite says it), a boxer named Gorgeous George is knocked flat, and two shady promoters find themselves in hock to a crime czar. Desperate to find a winner, they recruit the Gypsy played by Pitt, who is a formidable bare-knuckle fighter that London gamblers won't recognize. Also, bodies are fed to pigs. Pitt's character and the Gypsy community where he lives are the most intriguing parts of the movie.

If this summary seems truncated, it's because an accurate description of this movie dialogue might read like the missing chapters from *Finnegans Wake*. Because the actors have cartoon faces, the action is often outrageous, and Ritchie has an aggressive camera style, the movie is not boring, but it doesn't build, and it doesn't arrive anywhere. It's hard to care much about any of the characters, because from moment to moment what happens to them seems controlled by chance. I mentioned the Marx Brothers in my review of *Lock, Stock*, and I thought of them again here, as strangely dressed weirdos occupy an anarchic nightmare.

I don't want Ritchie to "grow." I don't care if he returns to the kind of material that worked for him the first time around. I just want him to get organized, to find the through-line, to figure out why we would want to see the movie for more than its technique. I can't recommend *Snatch,* but I must report that no movie can be all bad that contains the following dialogue:

U.S. Customs Official: "Anything to declare?"

Avi (Dennis Farina): "Yeah. Don't go to England."

Note: I am not so crass as to mention in my review that Guy Ritchie and Madonna recently became man and wife. I save such biographical details for my footnotes, and would overlook them altogether except that it is blindingly clear to me that he should direct, and she should star in, a British remake of Guys and Dolls.

Snow Day ★ ½
PG, 90 m., 2000

Mark Webber (Hal Brandston), Zena Grey (Natalie Brandston), Schuyler Fisk (Lane Leonard), Emmanuelle Chriqui (Claire Bonner), David Paetkau (Chuck Wheeler), Chevy Chase (Tom Brandston), Chris Elliott (Snowplow Man), Jean Smart (Laura Brandston), Pam Grier (Tina). Directed by Chris Koch and produced by Julia Pistor and Albie Hecht. Screenplay by Will McRobb and Chris Viscardi.

Snow Day involves a very, very busy day in the life of an upstate New York teenager named Hal (Mark Webber), who is hopelessly in love with the unavailable school dreamboat, Claire (Emmanuelle Chriqui). He is, he believes, invisible to her, but that changes when a record snowfall forces the schools to close for a day, and gives him an opportunity to demonstrate what a unique and wonderful person he is—potentially, anyway.

The movie surrounds Hal with a large cast of supporting characters—too many probably for a two-hour movie, let alone this one that clocks at ninety minutes including end titles. There's his dad (Chevy Chase), a weatherman who resents having to wear silly costumes; and his mom (Jean Smart), a woman whose career keeps her so busy that she doesn't stop to smell the coffee, or enjoy the snow.

And, let's see, his kid sister, Natalie (Zena Grey), and his best female friend, Lane (Schuyler Fisk), and, of course Snowplow Man (Chris Elliott), whose hated plow clears the streets and thus makes it possible to go to school—not that these kids don't wander all over town on the snow day. In a film top-heavy with plot and character, Snowplow Man should have been the first to go; played by Elliott as a clone of a Texas Chainsaw gang member, he is rumored to have made the snow chains for his tires out of the braces of the kids he's run down.

The arc of the movie is familiar. Hal yearns for Claire and is advised on his campaign by Lane, the loyal gal pal who perhaps represents true love right there under his very nose, were he not too blind, of course, to see it. He has to struggle against a school wiseguy on a high-powered snowmobile, who claims Claire for his own, while his weatherman dad has to wear hula skirts on the air in a fight for ratings with the top-rated local weather jerk. There's also a hated school principal and a square DJ at the ice rink (he likes Al Martino) and the programming executive (Pam Grier) who makes Chevy wear the silly costumes.

One of the inspirations for *Snow Day* is the 1983 classic *A Christmas Story,* also narrated by the hero, also with a kooky dad, also with a dream (a BB gun rather than a girl). But that was a real story, a memory that went somewhere and evoked rich nostalgia. *Snow Day* is an uninspired assembly of characters and story lines that interrupt one another, until the battle against Snowplow Man takes over just when we're hoping he will disappear from the movie and set free the teenage romance trapped inside it.

Acting Observation: Chris Elliott comes from a rich comic heritage (his father is Bob of Bob and Ray), but where his dad treasured droll understatement, Chris froths with overacting. There's a scene toward the end where he's tied to a children-crossing sign and laughs maniacally, like a madman, for absolutely no reason. Why is this funny? He has gone mad? Always was mad? It is funny to hear him laugh? We look curiously at the screen, regarding behavior without purpose.

Observation Two: Chevy Chase has been in what can charitably be called more than his share of bad movies, but at least he knows how to deliver a laugh when he's given one. (When his career-driven wife makes a rare appearance at dinner, he asks his son to "call security.") After the screening of *Snow Day,* I overheard another critic saying she couldn't believe she wished there had been more Chevy Chase, and I knew how she felt.

Third Observation: Through a coincidence in bookings, *Snow Day* and *Holy Smoke*, opened on the same day, and both contain Pam Grier roles that inspire only the thought, what's Pam Grier doing in such a lousy role? A year ago, she was in another lousy teenage movie, *Jawbreaker*. Is this the payoff for her wonderful performance in *Jackie Brown* (1997)? What a thoughtless place is Hollywood, and what talent it must feel free to waste.

Snow Falling on Cedars ★ ★ ★ ½
PG-13, 130 m., 2000

Ethan Hawke (Ishmael Chambers), Youki Kudoh Hatsue Miyamoto), Anne Suzuki (Young Hatsue Imada), Rick Yune (Kazuo Miyamoto), Max Von Sydow (Nels Gudmundsson), James Rebhorn (Alvin Hooks), Sam Shepard (Ishmael's Father), James Cromwell (Judge Fielding), Richard Jenkins (Sheriff Art Moran). Directed by Scott Hicks and produced by Harry J. Ufland, Ron Bass, Kathleen Kennedy, and Frank Marshall. Screenplay by Bass and Hicks, based on the novel by David Guterson.

Snow Falling on Cedars is a rich, many-layered film about a high school romance and a murder trial a decade later. The young lovers are Ishmael Chambers (Ethan Hawke), son of the local newspaper editor in a small Pacific Northwest town, and Hatsue Miyamoto (Youki Kudoh), daughter of Japanese-Americans. They meet at the time of Pearl Harbor, when feeling runs high against local Asians. Ishmael's father (Sam Shepard) runs editorials thundering, "These people are our neighbors," but then the U.S. government seizes their property and trucks them off to internment camps, in a shameful chapter of American history. Ten years later, Ishmael is editor of the paper, covering a murder trial. The defendant is the man Hatsue married in the camp.

Told this way, the story seems like crime and romance, but *Snow Falling on Cedars* reveals itself with the complexity of a novel, holding its themes up to the light so that first one and then another aspect can be seen. The style is crucial to the subject. The story un-folds in flashbacks, overlapping dialogue, half-understood events, flashes of memory, all seen in a variety of visual styles: color, desaturated color, black and white, even a little grainy 16mm. The look and sound of the film are not just easy flashiness, but match the story, which depends on the many different ways that the same events can be seen.

Above all there is a sense of place. Director Scott Hicks and his cinematographer, Robert Richardson, use a wide-screen canvas to envelop the story in trees and snow, rain and lowering skies, wetness and shadows. Rarely has a place been so evoked as part of a narrative. We sense that these people *are* neighbors partly because the forest crowds them together.

In this community the Japanese-Americans work as fishermen and shepherds, farmers and small-business holders, and their teenagers dance to the same pop tunes as everybody else. Yes, the races keep to themselves: Ishmael's mother disapproves of her son's friendship with Hatsue, whose own mother warns her against white boys. But boys with girls in love will fall, as e. e. cummings so simply put it, and Ishmael and Hatsue have a hidey-hole, a green cavern in the roots of a big cedar tree, where they meet to feel happy with one another. He asks her to marry him, and perhaps, if it had not been for the overwhelming fact of the war, this would have been a high school romance with a happy ending.

It is not, and in the early 1950s Ishmael covers a trial at which Kazuo Miyamoto (Rick Yune) is tried for the murder of a local fisherman whose body was found in some nets. He seems to have been bashed with a fish hook. There was bad blood between Kazuo and the victim; they fought a week before the death, and there is old bitterness involving the title to some land that was confiscated during the internment. The courtroom scenes pit a duty-bound prosecutor (James Rebhorn) against a tall, Lincolnesque defense attorney (Max Von Sydow), foreign-born, American to the core.

The movie slowly reveals its connections and motivations, which take on greater importance because the trial may result in all the relationships shifting again. If the husband is guilty, perhaps the teenage lovers can be reunited. Ishmael wants that, but does Hatsue? His resentment at being rejected even colors his coverage of the trial and his thinking about the accused man. We know Hatsue married Kazuo in the camps under pressure from her parents; does she love him? Is he guilty?

The only weakness in the film is its treatment of Kazuo, who is not seen in three dimensions but primarily through Ishmael's eyes. He is the man, after all, who has shared his life with Hatsue, and if they were married in the camps, well, people Ishmael's color put them there. Imagine the same triangle involving Jews and Nazis and see how it feels. We sympathize with Ishmael. Would we sympathize with a Nazi?

Because the movie is centered on Ishmael's point of view, Kazou is the interloper, the thief of love, and now probably a killer as well. From Kazou's point of view, which we can only infer, his society has put him behind barbed wire, discriminated against him, and now is rushing to a prejudiced judgment, while its representative stands ready to snatch away his bride. The movie never really sees him clearly. It places him over there at the defense table, or in long shot, objectively. It doesn't need him as a fully fleshed person, because he functions as a symbol and obstacle.

This may, however, be a weakness the film has to accept in order to get where it is going, because we need fears and confusions to make it more than just a courtroom drama. If we knew Kazou better, we might have a better notion of whether he could kill someone, and that would not help the story. In most movie trials we make fairly good guesses about guilt and innocence, but here there is real doubt, which plays against the bittersweetness of lost love.

And then there is the care given to the opposing attorneys, who are seen as quite particular people, especially Von Sydow, as Nels Gudmundsson, whose hands shake and whose voice sometimes trembles with anger as he defends the principles that drew him to immigrate to this land. The summation to the jury is a set piece in countless movies; rarely have I seen one better acted.

Snow Falling on Cedars is Scott Hicks's first film since *Shine,* the 1996 story of the pianist seized with paralyzing doubts. In both films he sees his stories as a whole, circling to their centers instead of starting at the beginning and trekking through. This film, written by Ron Bass and Hicks from the novel by David Guterson, is unusually satisfying in the way it unfolds. We don't feel the time structure is a gimmick; we learn what we need to know for each scene.

Some of them are of particular power, as when the Japanese-Americans are ordered from their homes by local authorities, told to take no more than will fit in a suitcase, and driven away to the internment "centers." We have seen scenes like this in stories about the Holocaust, and in parables of the future in which America has become a totalitarian state. Not everyone in the audience will have known it actually happened here.

Solomon and Gaenor ★ ★
R, 100 m., 2000

Ioan Gruffudd (Solomon), Nia Roberts (Gaenor), Sue Jones Davies (Gwen), William Thomas (Idris), Mark Lewis Jones (Crad), Maureen Lipman (Rezl), David Horovitch (Isaac), Bethan Ellis Owen (Bronwen), Adam Jenkins (Thomas). Directed by Paul Morrison and produced by Sheryl Crown. Screenplay by Morrison.

In Wales in 1911, it was simply not realistic for a Welsh girl and a Jewish boy to think they could find a happy ending to their love story, unless they were prepared to leave their families and journey elsewhere—to London, say. But since this course is open to them, it is a little difficult to have our hearts broken by the tragedy of *Solomon and Gaenor,* the story of a boy and girl who, essentially, want to have sex more than they want to pay the consequences.

The movie takes place in a coal-mining valley of unrelieved dreariness, which the local chapel seems to mirror in its gray rigidity. Here the sweet-faced Gaenor (Nia Roberts) lives with her family, including a brutish brother. Over the hills in a larger town, a Jewish family, newly immigrated from Russia, runs a pawn shop and clothing business. Here the handsome Solomon (Ioan Gruffudd) works as a door-to-door salesman of dry goods. His family is religious and observant, but Solomon is not, and when his grandfather prays aloud, he asks his father to "stop the old fool's braying."

One day Solomon knocks on doors in the mining village, and when Gaenor opens one of the doors, both of them feel a thrumming of the loins. He makes a red dress for her and gives it as a present, and soon (on their third or fourth meeting after no conversations of consequence) they are in the hayloft.

Their romance is a sweet one; they walk in the fields, and she is entranced by the first boy she has met who speaks poetically and gently. He finds her tender and bewitching—and, of course, available. He lies about himself. His name is Sam Livingstone, he says, posing as a gentile. His father works for the railroads. He meets Gaenor's family for tea (the brother glowering suspiciously), but does not invite her to meet his family because his father is "away."

Sooner or later, as we know and they should, Gaenor will get pregnant. And what will happen then? How the movie handles this is its main contribution to the underlying Romeo and Juliet theme, and so I will not reveal it, except to say that anyone with common sense could have figured out a less tragic ending than Solomon does. I didn't know whether to weep for his fate or his gormlessness.

The technical credits are superb. The valley groans under heavy clouds and snowfall. The houses are dark caves. We can feel the wet and cold underfoot. The treatment of Solomon by Crad (Mark Lewis Jones), the brother, is convincing and not simply routine villainy. The scene in the chapel where Gaenor is denounced by her former fiancé is like a sudden slap in the face.

Ioan Gruffudd and Nia Roberts are convincing in their roles—and moving, up to a point, until we grow impatient with their lack of caution and foresight. Gaenor is not presented as an innocent virgin, but as a woman who perhaps should have been less thrilled by the red dress. Solomon lies to her but never actually says he plans to marry her, and when Gaenor's sister asks, "Has he asked you, then?" she says, "He needs me." It is a reply but not an answer.

I suppose the film intends to be a lament about the way we humans are intolerant of those outside our own group. Both of the families in the film would fiercely oppose a member marrying an outsider, as has been true of most groups in most times. Solomon is more to blame, by concealing his true identity, since he must know that there are few plausible futures for them. Still, it's possible that Gaenor would have slept with him even if she'd known the truth; certainly she has sex with him before knowing the answers to those questions any prudent woman would first want answers to.

The movie's ending wants to inspire tears, but I was dry-eyed, perhaps as a response to its morose labors. It is one thing to be the victim of fate, and it is another thing to go looking for fate and wrestle it to the ground. The genius of *Romeo and Juliet* is that we can understand, step by step, how and why the situation develops. With *Solomon & Gaenor*, it is hard to overlook the folly of the characters. Does it count as a tragedy when the characters get more or less what they were asking for?

Someone Like You ★ ★
PG-13, 97 m., 2001

Ashley Judd (Jane Goodale), Greg Kinnear (Ray), Hugh Jackman (Eddie), Ellen Barkin (Diane), Matthew Coyle (Kooky Staff Member), LeAnna Croom (Rebecca), Hugh Downs (Himself), Marisa Tomei (Liz). Directed by Tony Goldwyn and produced by Lynda Obst. Screenplay by Elizabeth Chandler, based on the novel *Animal Husbandry* by Laura Zigman.

Ashley Judd plays Jane, a woman with a theory, in *Someone Like You*. It is the Old Cow, New Cow theory, and she developed it after reading an article in the science section of the newspaper. According to the article, there is no way to get a bull to service the same cow twice. You can paint the old cow blue or spray it with perfume, but the bull's not fooled: Been there, done that. The theory says that men are like bulls, and that's why they are tirelessly motivated to move on from old conquests to new challenges.

This is not precisely a novel theory, although it has been stated in more appealing forms ("If you can't be with the one you love, love the one you're with"). If the theory is correct, it gets men off the hook for their swinish behavior, since we are hard-wired that way and cannot be blamed for millions of years of tunnel-vision evolution. But is it correct? Even about bulls? On the answer to this question depends Jane's future happiness, as well as ours while we are watching the movie.

In *Someone Like You,* Judd plays Jane Goodale, not the chimp lady but a staffer on a daytime talk show hosted by Ellen Barkin. Also on the staff are Ray (Greg Kinnear) and Eddie (Hugh Jackman). Ray is in a relationship. Eddie is a walking, talking example of the Old Cow, New Cow theory, introducing a new cow to his bedroom every night. Jane likes Ray, and Ray, despite his old cow at home, likes Jane, who is a new cow, and so they have an affair, but then she becomes an old cow and the previous old cow begins to look like a new cow again, and so they break up. Jane has meanwhile given up her apartment because she thought she was going to move in with Ray, and so she becomes Eddie's platonic roommate, clocking the cow traffic.

This is, you will have gathered, a pretty lame premise. The screenplay is based on *Animal Husbandry,* a novel by Laura Zigman, unread by me. As a movie, it knows little about men, women, or television shows, but has studied movie formulas so carefully that we can see each new twist and turn as it creeps ever so slowly into view. Will Ray return to Jane? Will she begin to like Eddie? Can Eddie settle for one cow? What about the identity of Ray's mysterious girlfriend? Students of my Law of Economy of Characters will know that movies are thrifty and have a use for all the characters they introduce, and so the solution to that mystery arrives long, long after we have figured it out.

For a movie about a TV show, this one doesn't know much about television. The whole denouement depends on us believing that this high-rated show would do a telephone interview with an anonymous magazine columnist who has become famous for the Old Cow, New Cow theory, and that Jane (who writes the column anonymously) would then decide to blow her cover, burst onto the set, and deliver an endless monologue about how much wiser she is now than she used to be. The chances of a production assistant standing in front of the star of a TV show and talking for several minutes are approximately zero, especially since, let's face it, she's babbling: Her speech reminded me of something in a barnyard. It's not a cow, although it's often found close to one.

Songcatcher ★ ★ ★
PG-13, 112 m., 2001

Janet McTeer (Dr. Lily Penleric), Emmy Rossum (Deladis Slocumb), Aidan Quinn (Tom Bledsoe), Pat Carroll (Viney Butler), Jane Adams (Elna Penleric), E. Katherine Kerr (Harriet Tolliver), David Patrick Kelly (Earl Gibbons), Greg Cook (Fate Honeycutt), Iris DeMent (Rose Gentry), Stephanie Roth (Alice Kincaid), Mike Harding (Reese Kincaid). Directed by Maggie Greenwald and produced by Richard Miller and Ellen Rigas-Venetis. Screenplay by Greenwald.

Songcatcher tells the story of a woman who goes into the mountains of Appalachia in 1907, and finds the people singing British ballads that are almost unchanged since they arrived two hundred years earlier. It is also a feminist parable transplanted to earlier times, revealing too much consciousness of modern values. I'm more comfortable with the women I find in Willa Cather's novels, who live at about the same time, who strive to be independent and to be taken seriously, and yet are entirely in and of their worlds. The characters in a serious historical story should not know what happens later.

If we accept *Songcatcher* as a contemporary parable in period costumes, however, there is much to enjoy—not least the sound of the songs themselves. "I have never been anywhere where the music is so much a part of life as it is here," says Dr. Lily Penleric (Janet McTeer), the musicologist, who has fled to the mountains in anger after being passed over for an academic appointment she clearly deserves. The people of these North Carolina hills would as soon sing as talk, and indeed there's a scene where Tom Bledsoe (Aidan Quinn) knocks a man down, and the man stands up and starts to sing.

Tom is a suspicious leader of these people, and doubts Dr. Penleric's motives. He thinks she wants to steal his people's songs. He is right, although she calls it collecting, and hauls heavy Edison equipment up the hillside so she can record the songs on wax cylinders and maybe sell them in stores. She considers this preserving their culture. "The only way to preserve our way of life up here," Tom tells her, "is to preserve your way of life—down there."

We meet the people of the settlement: Viney Butler (Pat Carroll), a Ma Joad type; Deladis Slocumb (Emmy Rossum), a young woman with a voice pure and true; Elna Penleric (Jane Adams), the professor's sister, who has come here to start a one-room school; and her fellow teacher and lover Harriet Tolliver (E. Katherine Kerr), who says she will flee if anyone ever discovers she is a lesbian. Then there's David Patrick Kelly as a coal company representative, who wants to strip mine the land. There are so many issues simmering here in the hollow that it's a wonder Jeff Greenfield doesn't materialize and hold a town meeting.

The movie has a good amount of sex for a drama about folk music collecting. The lesbians find a secluded glade in the woods, Dr. Penleric and Tom Bledsoe feel powerful urges, and there's a local philanderer named Reese Kincaid (Mike Harding) who cheats on his wife, Alice (Stephanie Roth). The most startling sex scene involves the musicologist and the mountain man; a piercing scream rents the air, and we see Dr. Penleric running through the woods tearing off her clothes before discovering Tom in a clearing and covering him passionately with kisses. The scream comes from a panther (at first I thought it was the noon whistle), and Lilly has been advised by Viney to flee from such an attack by throwing off her clothes to distract it; as a depiction of Victorian morality making the leap into modern lust, this scene will serve.

I liked the tone of the movie, and its spirit. I liked the lashings of melodrama in the midst of the music collecting. Most of all, I liked the songs, especially one sung by Iris DeMent as a woman who loses her home, and by young Emmy Rossum when she is urged to give the newcomer a sample of her singing voice. *Songcatcher* is perhaps too laden with messages for its own good, but it has many moments of musical beauty, and it's interesting to watch Janet McTeer as she starts with Lily Penleric as a cold, abstract academic, and allows her, little by little, to warm in the sun of these songs.

The Son's Room ★ ★ ★ ½
R, 99 m., 2002

Nanni Moretti (Giovanni), Laura Morante (Paola), Jasmine Trinca (Irene), Giuseppe Sanfelice (Andrea), Sofia Vigliar (Arianna), Silvio Orlando (Oscar), Claudia Della Seta (Raffaella), Stefano Accorsi (Tommaso). Directed by Nanni Moretti and produced by Angelo Barbagallo and Moretti. Screenplay by Moretti, Linda Ferri, and Heidrun Schleef.

The Son's Room follows an affluent Italian family through all the stages of grieving. When the teenage son dies in a diving accident, his parents and sister react with instinctive denial, followed by sorrow, anger, the disintegration of their own lives, the picking up of the pieces, and finally a form of acceptance. Because all of these stages are reflected in the clearly seen details of everyday life, the effect is very touching.

The film has been written and directed by Nanni Moretti, whose 1994 film *Caro Diario (Dear Diary)* was about his own death sentence: Based on fact, it related his feelings when he was diagnosed with cancer and told (mistakenly) that he had a year to live. That film was not quite successful, an uneasy truce between Woody Allen and Elisabeth Kübler-Ross, but *The Son's Room* has a relaxed tenderness and empathy. He got the idea for the story, he has said, when he learned that he and his wife were expecting a son.

Moretti stars as Giovanni, a psychiatrist whose patients rehearse the same problems hour after hour in his office. Can he help them? That's a question he eventually has to ask himself. At home, there is a problem when his son Andrea (Giuseppe Sanfelice) is accused of having stolen a fossil from the school science lab. He denies the charge. Giovanni and his wife, Paola (Laura Morante), get involved, visit the parents of his son's accuser. We see that this is a happy family; the sister Irene (Jasmine Trinca) is on a basketball team, the son studies Latin, and when the parents overhear a conversation indicating that Andrea smokes pot, they are not too concerned. There is a lovely scene where all four sing together during a car trip.

Then the accident takes place, and has the effect of sending mother, father, and daughter spinning into their own private corners. For the father, this means impatience with his clients, and resentment against one whose call on a Sunday derailed Giovanni's plans to go jogging with his son—thus freeing the boy to go diving, and indirectly leading to his death. Grieving mixes with pain as Giovanni imagines the way the day *should* have unfolded, with the two of them on a run, and the son still alive at the end.

We know from the fable of the appointment in Samarra that it is no use trying to outsmart fate, but it is human nature to try—and to torture ourselves when we fail. For Irene, the sister, grief and anger cause her to fight during a basketball game. For Giovanni, they lead to questions about his practice. And then . . . a letter arrives, from Arianna (Sofia Vigliar). It is addressed to the dead Andrea, whom she met for only one day. But somehow there was a connection between them, and she hopes to see him again.

The Son's Room uses this letter, and Arianna's eventual appearance, as its means of resolving the story. To explain how this is done would be unsatisfactory, because Moretti is more concerned with tones and nuances than plot points, and the gradual way Arianna becomes the instrument of acceptance is quietly touching. She represents life that must go on—just as Auden in his poem observes that although Icarus falls into the sea, farmers still plow their fields and dogs go on their doggy errands. Curious, how a late shot of people at dawn says so much by saying nothing at all.

The Son's Room won the Palme d'Or, or top prize, at Cannes. It was a popular choice—too popular, sniffed some, who objected to its mainstream style and frank sentimentality. Yes, but not all movies can be stark, difficult, and obscure. Sometimes in a quite ordinary way a director can reach out and touch us.

Sorority Boys ½★

R, 96 m., 2002

Barry Watson (Dave/Daisy), Harland Williams (Doofer/Roberta), Michael Rosenbaum (Adam/Adina), Melissa Sagemiller (Leah), Heather Matarazzo (Katie). Directed by Wallace Wolodarsky and produced by Larry Brezner and Walter Hamada. Screenplay by Joe Jarvis and Greg Coolidge.

One element of *Sorority Boys* is undeniably good, and that is the title. Pause by the poster on the way into the theater. That will be your high point. It has all you need for a brainless, autopilot, sitcom ripoff: a high concept that is right there in the title, easily grasped at the pitch meeting. The title suggests the poster art, the poster art gives you the movie, and story details can be sketched in by study of *Bosom Buddies, National Lampoon's Animal House,* and the shower scenes in any movie involving girls' dorms or sports teams.

What is unusual about *Sorority Boys* is how it caves in to the homophobia of the audience by not even *trying* to make its cross-dressing heroes look like halfway, even tenth-of-the-way, plausible girls. They look like college boys wearing cheap wigs and dresses they bought at Goodwill. They usually need a shave. One keeps his retro forward-thrusting sideburns and just combs a couple of locks of his wig forward to "cover" them. They look as feminine as the sailors wearing coconut brassieres in *South Pacific.*

Their absolute inability to pass as women leads to another curiosity about the movie, which is that all of the other characters are obviously mentally impaired. How else to explain fraternity brothers who don't recognize their own friends in drag? Sorority sisters who think these are real women and want to pledge them on first sight? A father who doesn't realize that's his *own son* he's trying to pick up?

I know. I'm being too literal. I should be a good sport and go along with the joke. But the joke is not funny. The movie is not funny. If it's this easy to get a screenplay filmed in Hollywood, why did they bother with that Project Greenlight contest? Why not ship all the entries directly to Larry Brezner and Walter Hamada, the producers of *Sorority Boys,* who must wear Santa suits to work?

The plot begins with three members of Kappa Omicron Kappa fraternity, who are thrown out of the KOK house for allegedly stealing party funds. Homeless and forlorn, they decide to pledge the Delta Omicron Gamma house after learning that the DOGs need new members. Dave (Barry Watson) becomes Daisy and is soon feeling chemistry with the DOG president, Leah (Melisa Sagemiller), who is supposed to be an intellectual feminist but can shower nude with him and not catch on he's a man.

Harland Williams and Michael Rosenbaum play the other two fugitive KOKs—roles that, should they become stars, will be invaluable as a source of clips at roasts in their honor. Among the DOGs is the invaluable Heather Matarazzo, who now has a lock on the geeky plain girl roles, even though she is in actual fact sweet and pretty. Just as Latina actresses have risen up in arms against Jennifer Connelly for taking the role of John Forbes Nash's El Salvadoran wife in *A Beautiful Mind,* so ugly girls should picket Heather Matarazzo.

Because the intelligence level of the characters must be low, very low, very very low, for the masquerade to work, the movie contains no wit, only labored gags involving falsies, lipstick, unruly erections, and straight guys who don't realize they're trying to pick up a man. (I imagine yokels in the audience responding with the Gradually Gathering Guffaw as they catch on. "Hey, Jethro! He don't know she's a guy! Haw! Haw! Haw!") The entire movie, times ten, lacks the humor of a single line in the Bob Gibson/Shel Silverstein song "Mendocino Desperados" ("She was a he, but what the hell, honey / Since you've already got my money...").

I'm curious about who would go to see this movie. Obviously moviegoers with a low opinion of their own taste. It's so obviously what it is that you would require a positive desire to throw away money in order to lose two hours of your life. *Sorority Boys* will be the worst movie playing in any multiplex in America this weekend, and, yes, I realize *Crossroads* is still out there.

South ★ ★ ★

NO MPAA RATING, 80 m., 1915 (rereleased 2000)

A documentary featuring Ernest Shackleton, Captain Frank Worsley, Captain Frank Wild, Captain L. Hussey, Lieutenant J. Shenbouse, Frank Hurley, and Tom Crean. Directed by Hurley.

The most astonishing fact about *South* is that it exists at all. This is a documentary filmed in 1915 of Sir Ernest Shackleton's doomed expedition to the South Pole—a venture ending with his ship, *Endurance,* trapped in ice that eventually destroyed it, while he and five men made an 800-mile journey through frigid seas (and then scaled a glacier!) to bring help. That the expedition was filmed and that the film survived the shipwreck is astonishing.

South, which has now been restored, is essentially a home movie shot very far from home. The cinematographer, Frank Hurley, was a crew member whose approach is essentially to point his camera and trust to the subtitles to explain what we see. "Sir Ernest Shackleton, Leader of the Expedition," we read, while Shackleton poses self-consciously for posterity. Another title explains that a sick dog is being given medicine while the others look on enviously, thinking it's being fed. We see the crew member Tom Crean with a litter of puppies born onboard. Later, "Sulky, the black leader dog, trains the pups in harness."

Watching these images, we are absorbed, as we often are with silent film, in a reverie that is a collaboration with the images. We note how surprisingly small the *Endurance* is. How its crew of less than thirty become anonymous figures, bundled beyond recognition in cloth and fur, as they trudge across limitless snow. How the ship seems to be the only thing of human manufacture in the ice world. How later it is joined by another, as Shackleton tests a "motor sledge" which he thought might take the place of dog teams, but which had the unfortunate drawback of needing to be pushed by men or pulled by dogs. (And what dogs! There are breathtaking shots of them pulling a sled through snow powder almost over their heads.)

Some of Hurley's shots speak for themselves. It becomes clear that the worst Antarctic winter ever recorded will prevent the ship from reaching the point where Shackleton wants to drop off men, dogs, and supplies. Hurley and his camera hang from the prow of the *Endurance* as the ship opens up sudden, jagged cracks in the quickly forming ice. We see countless crab seals migrating north, as a title tells us a dismal season is on the way. We see the men building ice pylons to lead back to the ship because, in the storms of the Antarctic night, it is possible to become lost forever just a few yards from safety. And we see an astonishing sight: The *Endurance* photographed in the middle of the polar night with the use of eighteen lightbulbs, which reflect off the ice on every line and mast to make it glitter like a ghost ship.

After the *Endurance* is locked in ice, the men use two-handed logger's saws to try to cut through. When the ship then backs up and tries to ram itself free, Hurley and his camera are positioned on the ice, dangerously close to the front of it, and we imagine them disappearing into a sudden fissure—but the ice holds, eventually breaking the rudder and then caving in the sides of the ship. The dogs are evacuated, skidding nervously to safety down a canvas chute. The camera watches as the *Endurance* tilts and dies, its masts toppling over.

There is, of course, no footage of the 800-mile journey in a small lifeboat that Shackleton completed to bring rescue (not a single man was lost from the expedition). But Hurley does show us the glacier they had to scale on South Georgia Island, in order to reach the inhabited far shore. And an albatross like the one that provided their first meal on land. They encountered "quaint birds and beasts," a subtitle tells us, and "these pictures were obtained with a good deal of time and effort"— an understatement.

There is probably too much natural history toward the end of the film; we see elephant seals while the fate of the stranded crew members hangs in abeyance. Finally all are united and cheered as they return to safety. The *Endurance* did not get anywhere near the South Pole, but the expedition did sail into legend— like Robert Falcon Scott's attempt in 1911–12, where he lost a race to the Pole to the Norwegian Roald Amundsen and died on the return, but far overshadowed the Norwegian's fame. Ironic, that the two most famous British South Pole explorers either failed to begin or died on the way back. (Kevin McCorry, a writer on polar expeditions, quotes Amundsen's laconic commentary, "Never underestimate the British habit of dying. The glory of self-sacrifice, the blessing of failure.")

The overwhelming impression left by *South,* however, is of the bravery of everyone who ventured to the Pole. These men did not have cargo planes to drop supplies, satellites to tell them their position, solar panels for heating and electricity, or even adequate clothing. But they had pluck, and Frank Hurley with his hand-cranked camera recorded them, still to be seen, specks of life and hope in an ice wilderness.

Space Cowboys ★ ★ ★
PG-13, 123 m., 2000

Clint Eastwood (Frank Corvin), Tommy Lee Jones (Hawk Hawkins), Donald Sutherland (Jerry O'Neil), James Garner (Tank Sullivan), Loren Dean (Ethan Glance), Marcia Gay Harden (Sara Holland), James Cromwell (Bob Gerson), William Devane (Eugene Davis). Directed by Clint Eastwood and produced by Andrew Lazar. Screenplay by Ken Kaufman and Howard A. Klausner.

The guys who had the original right stuff get a second chance in *Space Cowboys,* forty-two years after their air force experimental flights in the X-2 rocket plane were replaced by orbiting monkeys and something called "astronauts." When NASA desperately needs expertise that only grizzled veteran Frank Corvin (Clint Eastwood) can offer, he issues an ultimatum: His original team goes into space with him, or else.

"I can't fill up a space shuttle with geriatrics!" moans space program official Bob Gerson (James Cromwell). "The clock's ticking, Bob," says Frank, "and I'm only getting older."

Eastwood has been having fun with his age for years. In *Absolute Power* (1997), accused of being a cat burglar, he tells the cops: "Go down a rope in the middle of the night? If I could do that, I'd be the star of my AARP meetings." The joke is that Eastwood, lean and mean, doesn't seem ready for retirement. And the old air force buddies and rivals he gathers for the space flight aren't old enough for the remake of *Cocoon.* Tommy Lee Jones, like Eastwood, is a plausible action star and will be for years. James Garner and Donald Sutherland are bald and graying here, but don't qualify as codgers. "You sent up John Glenn!" Eastwood barks at the NASA functionary.

Like Eastwood's *Unforgiven,* about veteran Western tough guys, *Space Cowboys* tells a genre story where the heroes have come out of retirement for one last hurrah. As the film opens, a satellite from the former Soviet Union is falling toward Earth, and only an emergency mission can steer it back into orbit. The computer code on board is so ancient only one man can understand it—Eastwood, who wrote it in the first place. "How did American code get on board a Soviet satellite in the middle of the cold war?" Eastwood reasonably asks. The answer is obvious (they stole it), but there's another secret lurking in space that comes as a nasty surprise for the repair crew.

The gathering of the crew takes place in an ancient and obligatory way: The leader (Eastwood) visits each man in the place where life has taken him, and yanks him back into the past. Hawk Hawkins (Tommy Lee Jones) is a stunt pilot. Jerry O'Neil (Donald Sutherland) designs roller coasters. Tank Sullivan (James Garner) is a preacher. They all cave in to Eastwood's call—even though one of them, of course, is an old rival who still bears a grudge.

After the gathering comes a montage in which the men train and prepare—also obligatory in movies like this. Secret schemes are revealed. Love interest develops between Jones and Marcia Gay Harden, as a space agency functionary. We meet the gum-chewing mission director (William Devane). And there's one of those early scenes where a hero does something daring and tricky in practice, and we know with certainly that he will be required to do it again later in an emergency situation.

Great swatches of *Space Cowboys* are constructed, indeed, out of generic expectations. But the stuff in outer space is unexpected, the surprise waiting out there is genuine, and meanwhile there's the abundance of charm and screen presence from the four veteran actors. There is a reason Eastwood, Garner, Sutherland, and Jones have remained stars for so long, and the movie gives them all characteristic scenes. (Sutherland's ladies' man has a funny moment on the *Jay Leno* show—only a line of dialogue, but it has been well set up and gets a big laugh.)

Space Cowboys lacks the urgency of a movie like *The Right Stuff*—it's too secure within its traditional story structure to make much seem at risk—but with the structure come the tra-ditional pleasures, as well. The actors know where the laughs and thrills are, and respect them. Eastwood as director is as sure-handed as his mentors, Don Siegel and Sergio Leone. We leave the theater with grave doubts that the scene depicted in the final feel-good shot is even remotely possible, but what the hell; it makes us smile.

Spider-Man ★ ★ ½
PG-13, 121 m., 2002

Tobey Maguire (Spider-Man/Peter Parker), Willem Dafoe (Green Goblin/Norman Osborn), Kirsten Dunst (Mary Jane Watson), James Franco (Harry Osborn), Cliff Robertson (Ben Parker), Rosemary Harris (May Parker), J. K. Simmons (J. Jonah Jameson), Joe Manganiello (Flash Thompson). Directed by Sam Raimi and produced by Laura Ziskin, Ian Brice, and Avi Arad. Screenplay by David Koepp, based on the Marvel comic by Stan Lee and Steve Ditko.

Imagine *Superman* with a Clark Kent more charismatic than the Man of Steel, and you'll understand how *Spider-Man* goes wrong. Tobey Maguire is pitch-perfect as the socially retarded Peter Parker, but when he becomes Spider-Man, the film turns to action sequences that zip along like perfunctory cartoons. Not even during Spidey's first experimental outings do we feel that flesh and blood are contending with gravity. Spidey soars too quickly through the skies of Manhattan; he's as convincing as Mighty Mouse.

The appeal of the best sequences in the Superman and Batman movies is that they lend weight and importance to comic-book images. Within the ground rules set by each movie, they even have plausibility. As a reader of the Spider-Man comics, I admired the vertiginous frames showing Spidey dangling from terrifying heights. He had the powers of a spider and the instincts of a human being, but the movie is split between a plausible Peter Parker and an inconsequential superhero.

Consider a sequence early in the film, after Peter Parker is bitten by a mutant spider and discovers his new powers. His hand is sticky. He doesn't need glasses anymore. He was scrawny yesterday, but today he's got muscles. The movie shows him becoming aware of these facts, but insufficiently amazed (or frightened) by them. He learns how to spin and toss webbing, and finds that he can make enormous leaps. And then there's a scene where he's like a kid with a new toy, jumping from one rooftop to another, making giant leaps, whooping with joy.

Remember the first time you saw the characters defy gravity in *Crouching Tiger, Hidden Dragon.* They transcended gravity, but they didn't dismiss it: They seemed to possess weight, dimension, and presence. Spider-Man, as he leaps across the rooftops, is landing too lightly, rebounding too much like a bouncing ball. He looks like a video-game figure, not like a person having an amazing experience.

The other superbeing in the movie is the Green Goblin, who surfs the skies. He, too, looks like a drawing being moved quickly around a frame, instead of like a character who has mastered a daring form of locomotion. He's handicapped, also, by his face, which looks like a high-tech action figure with a mouth that doesn't move. I understand why it's immobile (we're looking at a mask), but I'm not persuaded; the movie could simply ordain that the Green Goblin's exterior shell has a face that's mobile, and the character would become more interesting. (True, Spider-Man has *no* mouth, and Peter Parker barely opens his—the words slip out through a reluctant slit.)

The film tells Spidey's origin story—who Peter Parker is, who Aunt May (Rosemary Harris) and Uncle Ben (Cliff Robertson) are, how Peter's an outcast at school, how he burns with unrequited love for Mary Jane Watson (Kirsten Dunst), how he peddles photos of Spider-Man to cigar-chomping editor J. Jonah Jameson (J. K. Simmons).

Peter Parker was crucial in the evolution of Marvel comics because he was fallible and had recognizable human traits. He was a nerd, a loner, socially inept, insecure, a poor kid being raised by relatives. Tobey Maguire gets all of that just right, and I enjoyed the way Dunst is able to modulate her gradually increasing interest in this loser who begins to seem attractive to her. I also liked the complexity of the villain, who in his Dr. Jekyll manifestation is brilliant tycoon Norman Osborn (Willem Dafoe) and in his Mr. Hyde persona is a cack-

ling psychopath. Osborn's son, Harry (James Franco), is a rich kid, embarrassed by his dad's wealth, who is Peter's best and only friend, and Norman is affectionate toward Peter even while their alter egos are deadly enemies. That works, and there's an effective scene where Osborn has a conversation with his invisible dark side.

The origin story is well told, and the characters will not disappoint anyone who values the original comic books. It's in the action scenes that things fall apart. Consider the scene where Spider-Man is given a cruel choice between saving Mary Jane or a cable car full of schoolkids. He tries to save both, so that everyone dangles from webbing that seems about to pull loose. The visuals here could have given an impression of the enormous weights and tensions involved, but instead the scene seems more like a bloodless storyboard of the idea. In other CGI scenes, Spidey swoops from great heights to street level and soars back up among the skyscrapers again with such dizzying speed that it seems less like a stunt than like a fast-forward version of a stunt.

I have one question about the Peter Parker character: Does the movie go too far with his extreme social paralysis? Peter tells Mary Jane he just wants to be friends. "Only a friend?" she repeats. "That's all I have to give," he says. How so? Impotent? Spidey-sense has skewed his sexual instincts? Afraid his hands will get stuck?

Spirit: Stallion of the Cimarron
★ ★ ★
G, 82 m., 2002

With the voices of: Matt Damon (Narrator), James Cromwell (Cavalry Colonel), Daniel Studi (Little Creek). Directed by Kelly Asbury and Lorna Cook and produced by Mireille Soria and Jeffrey Katzenberg. Screenplay by John Fusco.

The animals do not speak in *Spirit: Stallion of the Cimarron,* and I think that's important to the film's success. It elevates the story from a children's fantasy to one wider audiences can enjoy, because although the stallion's adventures are admittedly pumped-up melodrama, the hero is nevertheless a horse and not a human with four legs. There is a whole level of cuteness that the movie avoids, and a kind of narrative strength it gains in the process.

The latest release from DreamWorks tells the story of Spirit, a wild mustang stallion, who runs free on the great western plains before he ventures into the domain of man and is captured by U.S. Cavalry troops. They think they can tame him. They are wrong, although the gruff-voiced colonel (voice by James Cromwell) makes the stallion into a personal obsession.

Spirit does not want to be broken, shoed, or inducted into the army, and his salvation comes through Little Creek (voice by Daniel Studi), an Indian brave who helps him escape and rides him to freedom. The pursuit by the cavalry is one of several sequences in the film where animation frees chase scenes to run wild, as Spirit and his would-be captors careen down canyons and through towering rock walls, duck under obstacles and end up in a river.

Watching the film, I was reminded of Jack London's classic novel *White Fang*, so unfairly categorized as a children's story even though the book (and the excellent 1991 film) used the dog as a character in a parable for adults. White Fang and Spirit represent holdouts against the taming of the frontier; invaders want to possess them, but they do not see themselves as property.

All of which philosophy will no doubt come as news to the cheering kids I saw the movie with, who enjoyed it, I'm sure, on its most basic level, as a big, bold, colorful adventure about a wide-eyed horse with a stubborn streak. That Spirit does not talk (except for some minimal thoughts that we overhear on voice-over) doesn't mean he doesn't communicate, and the animators pay great attention to body language and facial expressions in scenes where Spirit is frightened of a blacksmith, in love with a mare, and the partner of the Indian brave (whom he accepts after a lengthy battle of wills).

There is also a scene of perfect wordless communication between Spirit and a small Indian child who fearlessly approaches the stallion at a time when he feels little but alarm about humans. The two creatures, one giant, one tiny, tentatively reach out to each other, and the child's absolute trust is somehow communicated to the horse. I remembered the great scene in *The Black Stallion* (1979) where the boy and the horse edge together from the far sides of the wide screen.

In the absence of much dialogue, the songs by Bryan Adams fill in some of the narrative gaps, and although some of them simply comment on the action (a practice I find annoying), they are in the spirit of the story. The film is short at eighty-two minutes, but surprisingly moving, and has a couple of really thrilling sequences, one involving a train wreck and the other a daring leap across a chasm. Uncluttered by comic supporting characters and cute sidekicks, *Spirit* is more pure and direct than most of the stories we see in animation—a fable I suspect younger viewers will strongly identify with.

Spy Game ★ ★ ½
R, 115 m., 2001

Robert Redford (Nathan Muir), Brad Pitt (Tom Bishop), Catherine McCormack (Elizabeth), Stephen Dillane (Charles). Directed by Tony Scott and produced by Marc Abraham and Douglas Wick. Screenplay by Michael Frost Beckner and David Arata.

Consider now two spy thrillers: *Spy Game*, with Robert Redford and Brad Pitt, which opened over Thanksgiving, and *The Tailor of Panama*, with Pierce Brosnan and Geoffrey Rush, which opened in March 2001. Both, curiously, star Catherine McCormack as the girl for whom a spy risks all, or seems to, or means to.

Spy Game, directed by Tony Scott, is all style and surface, a slick artifact made of quick cutting and the kind of rough glamour you find in fashion ads; rat-a-tat datelines identify the times and places. *The Tailor of Panama*, directed by John Boormann and based on the John Le Carre novel, moves more deliberately to set up its characters and explore their personalities. *Spy Game* substitutes mannerisms for human nature; there's no time, in a film where individual shots rarely last more than twenty seconds, for deeper attention. The cinematography in *The Tailor of Panama* goes not for surface flash but for tone and mood, for the feel of its locations.

Oddly, although both movies have about the same running times, the slower pace of

The Tailor of Panama makes it seem shorter than the fast-paced *Spy Game*. Scott's restless camera, with flashbacks and whooshes, resists our attention; it moves so fast that things don't seem to *matter* so much, and because it discourages contemplation, we don't develop a stake in the material. We see it less as a story than as an exercise.

That's not to say the film is without interest. It stars Robert Redford as a veteran CIA spymaster on his last day at work, and Brad Pitt as the young idealist he recruited after Vietnam. Now Pitt is in a Chinese prison, captured in the act of helping Catherine McCormack escape, and it's Redford who was responsible for her being there. The framework is twenty-four hours during which Redford must scheme, lie, and deceive in order to save Pitt, whom the agency plans to sacrifice; nothing must upset top-level trade talks between the United States and China.

As Redford is quizzed by his masters, flashbacks show him meeting Pitt in Vietnam and later using him in operations in Berlin, Beirut, and Hong Kong. Pitt meets McCormack in Beirut, where she is a nurse and something shadowy besides, and that's where they fall in love, although a movie this fast moving has no time for conversations and tenderness, and so we have to accept their relationship on faith. (These scenes span the years from about 1965 to about 1991, during which the characters look about the same.)

What saves *Spy Game* from death by style is the Redford performance, which uses every resource of his star persona to create a character from thin air. At the end of the movie we still know next to nothing about him (and so, his bosses realize, do they), but he embodies the values the movie is too impatient to establish, and so we sympathize with him, and there's a trickle-down effect: We sympathize with Pitt because Redford does, and we sympathize with McCormack because Pitt does. We have no feelings at all about any of the CIA bosses, and indeed by the end of the film do not even know if they are supposed to be right or wrong (they seem to be doing exactly what Redford taught Pitt to do).

In *The Tailor of Panama*, where Pierce Brosnan plays a veteran British spy, also nearing the end of his career, there is a completely different approach: The visual style serves the story instead of replacing it. We appreciate Brosnan's droll cynicism, his weakness for pleasure, and his appreciation of the way the local British source, a tailor played by Geoffrey Rush, has milked a lot of money out of very little information. There is time for an appreciation of the political realities involved, seen through the eyes of a local radical (Brendan Gleeson), and we reflect that *Spy Game* is so devoid of politics that it could play, just as it stands, in China—or Afghanistan, now that the theaters are open again. The Catherine McCormack character in *Tailor* is allowed to be sexy, devious, and complicated, qualities that women are not allowed in a Boy's Own story like *Spy Game*.

I sat attentively through *Spy Game*, admired Redford for the way he created a performance that sometimes consisted only of quick shots of his facial expressions, and understood that Pitt's character was conflicted and would have explained why if the screenplay allowed dialogue as long as a paragraph. I was reminded that Redford's earlier spy thriller, Sydney Pollack's *Three Days of the Condor* (1975), had at its heart his brief, sad relationship with Faye Dunaway; it was interested in *how* they cared for each other, while *Spy Game*'s Pitt/McCormack pairing is simply declared to exist.

The Tailor of Panama didn't do well at the box office. Maybe people thought it was about a tailor. *Spy Game* at least has a title that gets the idea across. It is not a bad movie, mind you; it's clever and shows great control of craft, but it doesn't care, and so it's hard for us to care about. To see it once is to plumb to the bottom of its mysteries and beyond.

Spy Kids ★ ★ ★ ½
PG, 90 m., 2001

Antonio Banderas (Gregorio Cortez), Alan Cumming (Fegan Floop), Carla Gugino (Ingrid Cortez), Teri Hatcher (Ms. Gradenko), Angela Lanza (Reporter), Daryl Sabara (Juni Cortez), Tony Shalhoub (Minion), Alexa Vega (Carmen Cortez), Cheech Marin (Uncle Felix). Directed by Robert Rodriguez and produced by Elizabeth Avellan and Rodriguez. Screenplay by Rodriguez.

Spy Kids is giddy with the joy of its invention. It's an exuberant, colorful extravaganza, wall-to-wall with wildly original sets and visual gimmicks, and smart enough to escape the kid's film category and play in the mainstream. You can imagine Robert Rodriguez, the writer and director, grinning as he dreamed up this stuff. And being amazed that his visual-effects team could get it all on film so brilliantly.

The movie begins with Antonio Banderas and Carla Gugino as Gregorio and Ingrid Cortez, spies who were once enemies but then fall in love and get married and have two great kids, Carmen (Alexa Vega) and Juni (Daryl Sabara). They retire from the spy business, but then an evil minion named Minion (Tony Shalhoub) kidnaps the parents, and it's up to the spy kids to rescue them and save the world from the threat of robo-kids and Thumb Monsters.

Minion works for the diabolical Fegan Floop (Alan Cumming), whose job as a kiddie-show host masks his scheme to rule the world. His operation, centered in a fantastical seaside castle, includes workers who are all thumbs, literally: thumbs for heads, arms, and legs. Floop runs a cloning operation to turn out exact robotic copies of the children of powerful people. They look like the originals except for eyes with an eerie glow. Their problem: The brains aren't up to speed. Floop's answer: the Third Brain, which Gregorio Cortez secretly took along with him when he left the spy service.

This sounds, I know, like a plot for eight-year-olds, but Rodriguez charges at the material as if he wants to blow Indiana Jones out of the water, and the movie is just one outrageous invention after another. My feeling is that a "family movie" fails if it doesn't entertain the parents, since they're the ones who have to buy the tickets. *Spy Kids* is so endlessly imaginative, so high-spirited, so extravagant with its inspirations, so filled with witty dialogue, that the more you like movies, the more you may like this one.

The plot. After the kidnapping, it's up to the kids to rescue their parents, with a little help from their Uncle Felix (Cheech Marin) and guidance from Ms. Gradenko (Teri Hatcher), who claims to be a friend of their mother's from the old spy days. The kids have repaired to a secret "safe house," which is a lot different inside than outside, and they utilize all sorts of spy gimmicks; some they understand, some they don't. What's neat is the way the kids don't act like kids: They go about their business seriously, and along the way little Juni gains the self-confidence he needs (at school, he was the target of bullies).

Rodriguez has always been in love with special effects (as in his vampire movie *From Dusk Till Dawn*), and here he combines computer-generated images with brightly colored sets that look like a riot in a paint box. The movie's props range from bubble gum that can be used as a tracking device to the parents' car, which doubles as a submarine. And there's great imagination in a scene where the kids commandeer a combination aircraft-speedboat-submarine with a plump fish design that looks like something Captain Nemo might have dreamed up.

With a movie so enchanting and cheerful, I want to resist sociological observations, but it should be noted that Rodriguez has made a mainstream family film in which most of the heroic roles are assigned to Hispanic characters (at one point, the Banderas character even jokes about all the Latinos on Floop's TV show). It should also be observed that he avoids disturbing violence, that the entire movie is in a cheerful kidding spirit, and that the stunts and skills exhibited by the kids look fun, not scary. The props, even the boat-plane-sub, look like extensions of their toys, not like adult inventions that have been scaled down.

Movies like *Spy Kids* are so rare. Families are often reduced to attending scatological dumber-and-dumbest movies like *See Spot Run*—movies that teach vulgarity as a value. *Spy Kids* is an intelligent, upbeat, happy movie that is not about the comedy of embarrassment, that does not have anybody rolling around in dog poop, that would rather find out what it can accomplish than what it can get away with. It's a treasure. ☞

Startup.com ★ ★ ★
R, 103 m., 2001

A documentary directed by Chris Hegedus and Jehane Noujaim and produced by D. A. Pennebaker.

It seemed like a great idea at the time. They'd build a place on-line where people could go to pay their parking tickets. *Startup.com* tells the story of two longtime friends who go into business together, create a Website, raise millions, and at one point are worth $12 million—apiece, I think, but it makes no difference, because by the end of their adventure they have lost everything. The movie's story arc is like *Charly* or *Awakenings*, in which the heroes start low, fly high, and crash.

The friends are named Kaleil Isaza Tuzman and Tom Herman. Their idea is so compelling that Tuzman quits a job at Goodman, Sachs to move to the Internet. The story starts in May 1999, when instant Web millionaires were a dime a dozen, and ends in January 2001. The documentary's last shots were filmed only three weeks before it premiered at Sundance, still wet from the lab. As an inside view of the bursting of the Internet bubble, *Startup.com* is definitive. We sense there were lots of stories more or less like this one.

To film this sort of doc, you need access. The movie has it. One codirector, Jehane Noujaim, was Tuzman's Harvard roommate. She's also the cinematographer, and her digital camera has access to startlingly private moments. The other director, Chris Hegedus, has worked on such insider docs as *The War Room,* the story of the Clinton campaign. She coproduced that one with D. A. Pennebaker, the legendary documentarian, who is also the producer this time.

When the film begins, the new company doesn't even have a name. They settle on gov-Works.com. Tuzman and Herman make the rounds of venture capitalists, and it's obvious that Tuzman is the expert pitcher, while Herman, more technically oriented, drives his partner crazy by bringing up bright ideas in meetings on the spur of the moment. Tuzman lectures him to stay on message. Dollar signs dance before their eyes. At one point in Boston they're offered $17 million but lose the deal when they can't get their lawyers on the phone.

Meanwhile, of course, there's the problem of actually writing the software. It would seem to me that paying parking tickets over the Internet would involve basic programming skills plus cosmetic packaging, but no, apparently it's rocket science: Eventually govWorks.com

has 200 employees working on the site, and still Tuzman despairs that it's not good enough to be released to the public.

Famous figures float in and out of view. The partners smile from the covers of business magazines. Former Atlanta mayor Maynard Jackson turns up as a consultant. Tuzman appears on TV sitting next to President Clinton, who chairs a summit meeting on the Internet. Meanwhile, Tuzman and Herman, under enormous pressure, go through girlfriends and beards. Herman grows his beard and shaves it off so many times that the filmmakers finally photograph him in front of the mirror with a razor, just to explain the continuity errors. And Tuzman's girlfriends complain that he pays them no attention: "Just a call is all I ask," one says. "A simple call saying you're thinking of me, you're busy, but you miss me. That would keep me going for two weeks." She disappears from the film; her replacement also finds Tuzman a moving target.

There are setbacks. The govWorks office is broken into. Files are stolen. But that's not as big a problem as the disappointing software, and then comes the dot.com meltdown that dries up funds just when the site is turning the corner. On the day govWorks was sold to a competitor, we learn, it landed the big New York City contract.

Noujaim's camera catches painfully intimate moments, as the two old friends argue, split, and Herman leaves the company; in an age-old security ritual, he is "escorted from the building" and guards are told not to readmit him. Today, I learn, Tuzman and Herman are back in business together. My guess is, they could make it this time. The Internet is fundamentally sound. The bubble had to burst to correct its crazy overvaluation. Now that sanity has returned, bright guys like Tuzman and Herman can find more opportunities. All they need is another great idea. And better software.

Star Wars: Episode II— Attack of the Clones ★ ★
PG, 124 m., 2002

Ewan McGregor (Obi-Wan Kenobi), Natalie Portman (Senator Padme Amidala), Hayden Christensen (Anakin Skywalker), Christopher

Lee (Count Dooku), Ian McDiarmid (Palpatine), (voice of) Frank Oz (Yoda), Samuel L. Jackson (Mace Windu), Pernilla August (Shmi Skywalker), Jack Thompson (Cliegg Lars), Temuera Morrison (Jango Fett), Jimmy Smits (Senator Bail Organa). Directed by George Lucas and produced by Rick McCallum. Screenplay by Lucas and Jonathan Hales.

It is not what's there on the screen that disappoints me, but what's not there. It is easy to hail the imaginative computer images that George Lucas brings to *Star Wars: Episode II—Attack of the Clones*. To marvel at his strange new aliens and towering cities and sights such as thousands of clones all marching in perfect ranks into a huge spaceship. To see the beginnings of the dark side in young Anakin Skywalker. All of those experiences are there to be cheered by fans of the *Star Wars* series, and for them this movie will affirm their faith.

But what about the agnostic viewer? The hopeful ticket-buyer walking in not as a cultist but as a moviegoer hoping for a great experience? Is this *Star Wars* critic-proof and scoff-resistant? Yes, probably, at the box office. But as someone who admired the freshness and energy of the earlier films, I was amazed, at the end of *Episode II*, to realize that I had not heard one line of quotable, memorable dialogue. And the images, however magnificently conceived, did not have the impact they deserved. I'll get to them in a moment.

The first hour of *Episode II* contains a sensational chase through the skyscraper canyons of a city, and assorted briefer shots of spaceships and planets. But most of that first hour consists of dialogue, as the characters establish plot points, update viewers on what has happened since *Episode I*, and debate the political crisis facing the Republic. They talk and talk and talk. And their talk is in a flat utilitarian style: They seem more like lawyers than the heroes of a romantic fantasy.

In the classic movie adventures that inspired *Star Wars*, dialogue was often colorful, energetic, witty, and memorable. The dialogue in *Episode II* exists primarily to advance the plot, provide necessary information, and give a little screen time to continuing characters who are back for a new episode. The only characters in this stretch

of the film who have inimitable personal styles are the beloved Yoda and the hated Jar Jar Binks, whose idiosyncrasies turned off audiences for *Phantom Menace*. Yes, Jar Jar's accent may be odd and his mannerisms irritating, but at least he's a unique individual and not a bland cipher. The other characters—Obi-Wan Kenobi, Padme Amidala, Anakin Skywalker—seem so strangely stiff and formal in their speech that an unwary viewer might be excused for thinking they were the clones, soon to be exposed.

Too much of the rest of the film is given over to a romance between Padme and Anakin in which they're incapable of uttering anything other than the most basic and weary romantic clichés, while regarding each other as if love was something to be endured rather than cherished. There is not a romantic word they exchange that has not long since been reduced to cliché. No, wait: Anakin tells Padme at one point: "I don't like the sand. It's coarse and rough and irritating—not like you. You're soft and smooth." I hadn't heard that before.

When it comes to the computer-generated images, I feel that I cannot entirely trust the screening experience I had. I could see that in conception many of these sequences were thrilling and inventive. I liked the planet of rain, and the vast coliseum in which the heroes battle strange alien beasts, and the towering Senate chamber, and the secret factory where clones were being manufactured.

But I felt like I had to lean with my eyes toward the screen in order to see what I was being shown. The images didn't pop out and smack me with delight, the way they did in earlier films. There was a certain fuzziness, an indistinctness that seemed to undermine their potential power.

Later I went on the Web to look at the trailers for the movie, and was startled to see how much brighter, crisper, and more colorful they seemed on my computer screen than in the theater. Although I know that video images are routinely timed to be brighter than movie images, I suspect another reason for this. *Episode II* was shot entirely on digital video. It is being projected in digital video on nineteen screens, but on some 3,000 others, audiences will see it as I did, transferred to film.

How it looks in digital projection I cannot

say, although I hope to get a chance to see it that way. I know Lucas believes it looks better than film, but then he has cast his lot with digital. My guess is that the film version of *Episode II* might jump more sharply from the screen in a small multiplex theater. But I saw it on the largest screen in Chicago, and my suspicion is, the density and saturation of the image was not adequate to imprint the image there in a forceful way.

Digital images contain less information than 35mm film images, and the more you test their limits, the more you see that. Not long ago I saw *Patton* shown in 70mm Dimension 150, and it was the most astonishing projection I had ever seen—absolute detail on a giant screen, which was 6,000 times larger than a frame of a 70mm film. That's what large-format film can do, but it's a standard Hollywood has abandoned (except for IMAX), and we are being asked to forget how good screen images can look—to accept the compromises. I am sure I will hear from countless fans who assure me that *Episode II* looks terrific, but it does not. At least, what I saw did not. It may look great in digital projection on multiplex-size screens, and I'm sure it will look great on DVD, but on a big screen it lacks the authority it needs.

I have to see the film again to do it justice. I'm sure I will greatly enjoy its visionary sequences on DVD; I like stuff like that. The dialogue is another matter. Perhaps because a movie like this opens everywhere in the world on the same day, the dialogue has to be dumbed down for easier dubbing or subtitling. Wit, poetry, and imagination are specific to the languages where they originate, and although translators can work wonders, sometimes you get the words but not the music. So it's safer to avoid the music.

But in a film with a built-in audience, why not go for the high notes? Why not allow the dialogue to be inventive, stylish, and expressive? There is a certain lifelessness in some of the acting, perhaps because the actors were often filmed in front of blue screens so their environments could be added later by computer. Actors speak more slowly than they might—flatly, factually, formally, as if reciting. Sometimes that reflects the ponderous load of the mythology they represent. At other times it

simply shows that what they have to say is banal. *Episode II—Attack of the Clones* is a technological exercise that lacks juice and delight. The title is more appropriate than it should be.

* * *

I did go back a few days later to see the movie digitally projected.

After seeing the new *Star Wars* movie projected on film, I wrote that the images had "a certain fuzziness, an indistinctness that seemed to undermine their potential power." But I knew the film had been shot on digital video, and that George Lucas believed it should preferably be seen, not on film, but projected digitally. Now I've been able to see the digital version, and Lucas is right: *Star Wars: Episode II—Attack of the Clones* is sharper, crisper, brighter, and punchier on digital than on film.

This will come as melancholy news, I suppose, to the vast majority of fans destined to see the movie through a standard film projector. Although an accurate count is hard to come by, there are apparently about 20 screens in America showing *Episode II* with a digital projector, and about 3,000 showing it on film. Lucas is so eager to promote his vision of the digital future that he is willing to penalize his audience, just to prove a point.

But he *does* prove the point. On Sunday I returned to Chicago's McClurg Court theater, where I had seen *Episode II* on film the previous Tuesday. On Wednesday, technicians from Boeing Digital Cinema swooped down on the theater to install a new Texas Instruments digital projector, and that's how I saw the film a second time—sitting in almost exactly the same seat.

Watching it on film, I wrote: "I felt like I had to lean with my eyes toward the screen in order to see what I was being shown." On digital, the images were bright and clear. Since the movie was being projected on film on another McClurg screen (both screenings were part of a charity benefit) I slipped upstairs, watched a scene on film, and then hurried downstairs to compare the same scene on video. The difference was dramatic: more detail, more depth, more clarity.

Readers familiar with my preference for film over video projection systems will wonder if I have switched parties. Not at all. It's to be expected that *Episode II* would look better on digital, because it was entirely filmed on digital. Therefore, the digitally projected version is generation one, and the film version is one generation further from the source. Lucas is right as far as a computer-aided special-effects movie like *Episode II* goes, but may be wrong for the vast majority of movies that depict the real world on celluloid.

It is important to understand that *Episode II* is essentially an animated film with humans added to it. This is the flip side of *Who Framed Roger Rabbit*, which was a live-action film with cartoon characters laid on top. Most of the non-human screen images in *Episode II*, and some of the characters (Yoda, Jar Jar Binks) are created entirely in computers. Even in scenes dominated by humans, the backgrounds and locations are often entirely computer-generated.

Whether this is an advance is debatable. I am receiving mail from readers who prefer the earlier *Star Wars* effects, using models, back projection, puppets, and the like. They also question *Spider-Man*, where Spidey's action sequences are animated using CGI, or Computer-Generated Imagery. David Soto of Santa Ana, California, writes: "I liked it, although I wanted to love it. One thing I noticed—for a second I had the impression I was watching a Power Rangers episode." He said CGI made everything "look so fast, so weightless, so unreal."

I agree. In *Episode II*, this is true of the most popular scene in the movie, where Yoda abandons his contemplative and sedentary lifestyle and springs into action. Yes, it's fun to see the surprise Yoda has up his sleeve, but in the scene itself he turns from a substantial, detailed, "realistic" character into a bouncing blob of Yodaness, moving too quickly to be perceived in any detail.

The debate about CGI versus traditional effects will be fueled by *Episode II* and *Spider-Man*. The debate about digital projection is just beginning. My feeling is that movies shot on digital look better projected on video, and that movies shot on film look better projected on film. Of course, every theater, every print, and every projector is different, so results may vary.

What I dislike about Lucas's approach is that he wants to change the entire world of film to suit his convenience. Because his movies are created largely on computers, it suits him to project them digitally. Because the *Star Wars*

franchise is so hugely profitable, he hopes he has the clout to swing the movie world behind him—especially since well-funded Boeing and Texas Instruments stand to make millions by grabbing the projection franchise away from film. A century of cinematic tradition may be shown to the exit by Head Usher Jar Jar, while Yoda consoles us with the Force. ☞

State and Main ★ ★ ★
R, 106 m., 2000

Alec Baldwin (Bob Barrenger), Charles Durning (Mayor George Bailey), Philip Seymour Hoffman (Joseph Turner White), William H. Macy (Walt Price), Patti LuPone (Sherry Bailey), Sarah Jessica Parker (Claire Wellesley), David Paymer (Marty Rossen), Rebecca Pidgeon (Ann Black), Clark Gregg (Doug Mackenie), Julia Stiles (Carla Taylor). Directed by David Mamet and produced by Sarah Green. Screenplay by Mamet.

"Marty, we got a new town. Waterford, Vermont." (Pause) "Where is it? That's where it is."

David Mamet has a playful side that's sometimes overlooked, since his plays often favor lowlifes and con men. He delights in using dialogue to provide quick, sideways insights into his characters, and in *State and Main* he's directed his first pure comedy, although of course there was a lot of humor in *Things Change* and his screenplay *Wag the Dog*.

This is a playful movie about a film company that arrives in Waterford, Vermont (explained above), after having to beat a quick retreat out of New Hampshire, allegedly because a town lacked an old mill that could be used as a location, but more directly because Bob Barrenger (Alec Baldwin), the movie's star, has a weakness for junior high school girls.

The lines above are spoken on the phone by Walt Price (William H. Macy), the director of the film within a film. Macy brings along some of the same frustration he used in *Fargo*, as the car salesman trying to conceal fatal evidence, but he's more of a diplomat here, using tact and lies to soothe the townspeople, coddle his temperamental stars, and coax rewrites out of his easily wounded screenwriter (Philip Seymour Hoffman). Of course, he denies that he lies: "It's not a lie. It's a gift for fiction."

Mamet knows, from having directed nine films and written thirty-one, how even the most sensible projects eventually seem to hinge on crucial but utterly absurd details. His characters obsess about "the old mill," and a shot where the camera will be required to enter a firehouse through a window, and whether the heroine will do a topless scene. These details are more important to Walt Price than anything else in his movie, because they are *today's* problems. The long view is quickly abandoned on location.

Mamet populates his film with a large cast of movie pros and townspeople. Charles Durning and Patti LuPone play the town mayor and his wife, who prepare a dinner for the visitors that would shame Martha Stewart. Sarah Jessica Parker plays the actress who unexpectedly refuses to bare her breasts (even though, as the Baldwin character observes, the nation could "draw them from memory"). David Paymer is the harried producer, instructed by the director to find more money even though there is no money to be found.

Hoffman and Rebecca Pidgeon, as the owner of a local bookstore, have a sweet side plot when they suddenly fall in love. She's engaged to be married, but so awestruck by the visiting screenwriter, and so touched when he turns to her for help and advice, that at one point she almost forgets the name of her fiancé (Clark Gregg) while trying to introduce him. Eventually the whole production waits while the writer and his new girl sit on a bench and try to solve screenplay problems. Meanwhile, Julia Stiles uses saucy comic timing in the other major subplot. She's the local teenager who catches the eye of Baldwin's lustful movie star. He'll have to move fast to seduce her before she seduces him.

Visitors from Hollywood are considered heaven-sent by some citizens in the small towns where movies are shot, and the spawn of the devil by others. While the fiancé tries to shake down the production company, the company tries to cover up details involving a scandalous car crash, and meanwhile the cinematographer tries to figure out how his camera can move through a priceless stained-glass window without breaking it, and the Macy

character learns that the old mill and many other buildings were the victims of "a spate of suspicious fires" back in 1960.

With a few adjustments, *State and Main* could be adapted for the stage, where it would play as a farce of the *Noises Off* variety. It's Mamet in a lighthearted mood, playing with dialogue, repeating phrases just because he likes them, and supplying us with a closing line that achieves, I think, a kind of greatness.

Steal This Movie ★ ★ ★
R, 111 m., 2000

Vincent D'Onofrio (Abbie Hoffman), Janeane Garofolo (Anita Hoffman), Jeanne Tripplehorn (Johanna Lawrenson), Kevin Pollak (Gerry Lefcourt), Donal Logue (Stew Albert), Kevin Corrigan (Jerry Rubin), Alan Van Sprang (David Glenn), Troy Garity (Tom Hayden). Directed by Robert Greenwald and produced by Greenwald and Jacobus Rose. Screenplay by Bruce Graham.

Abbie Hoffman inspired some of the zaniest footnotes of the Vietnam War era with improv performances mixing civil disobedience and anarchist street theater. Some of his stunts had a certain brilliance, as when he scattered dollar bills onto the floor of the New York Stock Exchange and the traders dropped scrambling to their knees.

Hoffman was the clown prince of the antiwar movement. While Tom Hayden sawed away seriously at the 1968 Democratic convention, Abbie was announcing plans to drop LSD into the Chicago water supply—a threat Mayor Richard J. Daley took seriously (I remember the Chicago police boats ominously guarding the filtration plant). When Hayden, Hoffman, and their fellow Chicago Seven members were hauled up before Judge Julius Hoffman, surely the last jurist in America who should have been chosen to preside, Hayden and his allies played it straight while Hoffman treated the event like a circus.

Abbie Hoffman's Yippies provided the linguistic link between Hippies and yuppies. *Steal This Movie* provides an untidy and frustrating but never boring look at his life and times. More than anyone else in recent American history, he was able to capture headlines and gain national attention just with the audacity of his imagination. When he announced that he and fellow Yippie Party members would levitate the Pentagon, he drew an enormous crowd—among them Norman Mailer, who confessed that although he doubted Hoffman could do it, he wanted to be there, just in case. Richard Nixon and J. Edgar Hoover didn't get the joke, but then that was the whole point.

The movie traces the trajectory of Hoffman (played by Vincent D'Onofrio) from the early 1960s, when he was a civil rights worker in the South, to the late 1970s, when he had gone underground as "Barry Freed" and was a respected environmental campaigner in upstate New York, fighting to save the St. Lawrence River. Along the way he married Anita Hoffman (Janeane Garofalo), started a family, then fled underground into hiding. His first family, under constant FBI surveillance, was able to meet with him from time to time, but meanwhile, as "Freed," he met and fell in love with Johanna Lawrenson (Jeanne Tripplehorn). That the two women got along fairly well and were able to share Hoffman may indicate their generosity—or maybe just that he was too much for any one woman to deal with.

That was certainly true as it became clear he was suffering from manic depression. His wild antics in the 1960s were matched by deep gloom in the 1970s, and his limitless energy and imagination might have fed from a disorder that was a boost in his earlier life, a crushing burden later (he died a suicide).

Steal This Movie has a title inspired by Hoffman's once famous *Steal This Book,* not a title popular with its publisher. It evokes a time when it was not theft to "rip off" something, because the capitalist pigs, etc., etc. The movie, written by Bruce Graham and directed by Robert Greenwald, has an enormous amount of material to cover, and does it fairly clumsily. Information enters the screen from too many directions. Subtitles treat the material like a documentary. Spoken narration treats it as memory. Actual newsreel footage coexists with reconstructions. This is distracting at first, but the movie smoothes out and finds its rhythm, and the closing passages are quite moving.

One element evoked by the movie is the symbolic role of the American flag during the period—a time which also inspired the hard-hat patriotism of "Joe" and the John Prine lyrics:

Your flag decal won't get you into heaven anymore.
It's already overcrowded from that dirty little war.

Abbie Hoffman is seen wearing an American flag shirt and getting in trouble for desecrating it; the movie cuts in footage of Roy Rogers and Dale Evans yodeling while wearing *their* flag shirts. Hoffman insisted that the flag represented all Americans, including those opposed to the war; he resisted efforts of the right to annex it as their exclusive ideological banner.

Vincent D'Onofrio has an interesting task playing the role, since Hoffman seems on autopilot much of the time. He is charismatic and has an instinctive grasp of the dramatic gesture, but can be infuriating on a one-to-one level; the women in his life sometimes wonder whether he really sees and hears them, and can understand what he puts them through. Both Garofalo and Tripplehorn are valuable to the film because they supply the eyes through which we see a man who couldn't clearly see himself.

The late 1960s were thought at the time to be a period of social revolution in America. National Guardsmen were on the campus, demonstrators patrolled the streets, Nixon and Hoover (as shown here) instigated illegal programs to befuddle and discredit their opponents. But the transition from Yippie to yuppie went smoothly for most members of the '60s generation, prosperity soothed the voices of change, and the populace is anesthetized once again. Abbie Hoffman was not a revolutionary but he played one on television. He was prophetic, leading the way for virtual reality: It's not what you are, it's what you say, and whether you say it on TV.

Stolen Summer ★ ★ ★
PG, 91 m., 2002

Aidan Quinn (Joe O'Malley), Bonnie Hunt (Margaret O'Malley), Adi Stein (Pete O'Malley), Kevin Pollak (Rabbi Jacobsen), Mike Weinberg (Danny Jacobsen), Lisa Dodson (Mrs. Jacobsen),

Brian Dennehy (Father Kelly), Eddie Kaye Thomas (Patrick O'Malley), Ryan Kelley (Seamus O'Malley). Directed by Pete Jones and produced by Ben Affleck, Matt Damon, and Chris Moore. Screenplay by Jones.

Gene Siskel proposed an acid test for a movie: Is this film as good as a documentary of the same people having lunch? At last, with *Stolen Summer,* we get a chance to decide for ourselves. The making of the film has been documented in the HBO series *Project Greenlight,* where we saw the actors and filmmakers having lunch, contract disputes, story conferences, personal vendettas, location emergencies, and even glimpses of hope.

Movies are collisions between egos and compromises. With some there are no survivors. *Stolen Summer* is a delightful surprise because despite all the backstage drama, this is a movie that tells stories that work—is charming, is moving, is funny, and looks professional. That last point is crucial, because as everyone knows, director Pete Jones and his screenplay were chosen in a contest sponsored by Miramax and actors Ben Affleck and Matt Damon. Miramax gave them a break with their screenplay *Good Will Hunting,* and they wanted to return the favor.

Stolen Summer takes place on the South Side of Chicago in the summer of 1976, when an earnest second-grader named Pete O'Malley (Adi Stein) listens in Catholic school and believes every word about working his way into heaven. Seeking advice from a slightly older brother about how to guarantee his passage to paradise, Pete is startled to learn that the Jews are not seeking to be saved through Jesus. So Pete sets up a free lemonade stand in front of the local synagogue, hoping to convert some Jews and pay for his passage.

There is already a link between Pete's family and that of Rabbi Jacobsen (Kevin Pollak). Pete's dad, Joe (Aidan Quinn), is a fireman who dashed into a burning home and rescued the Jacobsens' young son Danny (Mike Weinberg), who is about Pete's age. Pete has already met the rabbi and now becomes best friends with his son. Although Danny is not much interested in the theology involved, he joins Pete's "quest" to get them both into the Roman Catholic version of heaven. Is Pete's obsession

with church rules and heaven plausible for a second-grader? Having been there, done that, I can state that this was not an unknown stage for Catholic school kids to go through, and that I personally knelt in prayer on behalf of my Protestant playmates, which they found enormously entertaining.

The touchier question of "converting the Jews" is handled by the movie so tactfully that it is impossible not to be charmed. The key performance here is by Kevin Pollak, as a rabbi whose counterpoint to Pete's quest involves understated reaction shots and instinctive sympathy and humor. When the Jacobsens invite Pete over for lunch, he makes the sign of the cross, and when the rabbi asks why he's doing it (the unstated words are "at our table"), Pete explains solemnly, "It's like picking up the phone and being sure God is there." Earlier, during his first visit inside the synagogue, Pete is surprised to find no crucifix hanging from the ceiling, and confides to the rabbi: "Sometimes I think of climbing up and loosening the screws and letting him go."

The movie cuts between Pete's quest, which is admittedly a little cutesy, and the completely convincing marriage of his parents, Joe and Margaret (Bonnie Hunt). These are (I know) actors who grew up in Chicago neighborhoods and were raised (I believe) as Catholics, and they are pitch-perfect. Note the scene where Hunt is driving most of her eight kids to Mass and the troublesome Seamus is making too much noise in the backseat. Still driving, she reaches out to him and beckons him closer, saying, "Come closer . . . come on, come on, I'm not going to hit you," and then smacks him up alongside the head. Every once in a while a movie gives you a moment of absolute truth.

Danny has leukemia, which he explains solemnly to Pete, who is fascinated. Danny's mother is worried about her young son spending so much time with Pete, but the rabbi observes it may be Danny's last chance to act like a normal kid. The "quest" involves such tests as swimming out to a buoy in Lake Michigan, and while we doubt that, even in innocent 1976, second-graders were going to the beach by themselves, we understand the dramatic purpose.

The most fraught scenes in the movie involve the synagogue's decision to thank the O'Malley family after Joe risked his life to save Danny. They settle on a scholarship for Patrick, the oldest O'Malley boy, and the rabbi is startled when Joe turns it down in anger. Joe tells his wife: "It's about the Jews helping out some poor Roman Catholic family so they can go on TV and get free publicity." Is this anti-Semitism? No, I think it's tribalism, and Joe O'Malley would say the same thing about the Episcopalians, the Buddhists, or the Rotary Club. Bonnie Hunt's response is magnificent: If Joe doesn't let his son accept the scholarship, "So help me God, when you come home at night, the only thing colder than your dinner will be your bed."

Stolen Summer is a film combining broad sentiment with sharp observation, although usually not in the same scenes. I don't know if writer-director Jones came from a large Irish-American family on the South Side, but do I even need to ask? The movie even has Brian Dennehy, patron saint of the Chicago stage, as the parish priest. In a time when so many big-budget mainstream movies are witless and heartless, *Stolen Summer* proves that studios might do just about as well by holding a screenplay contest and filming the winner.

Storytelling ★ ★ ★ ½
R, 87 m., 2002

Fiction
Selma Blair (Vi), Leo Fitzpatrick (Marcus), Robert Wisdom (Mr. Scott).
Nonfiction
Mark Webber (Scooby), John Goodman (Marty), Julie Hagerty (Fern), Jonathan Osser (Mikey), Noah Fleiss (Brady), Lupe Ontiveros (Consuelo), Paul Giamatti (Toby). Directed by Todd Solondz and produced by Ted Hope and Christine Vachon. Screenpaly by Solondz.

For some artists, especially younger ones, the creative impulse is linked directly to the genitals: They create because they hope it makes them sexually attractive. This is a truth so obvious it is rarely mentioned in creative writing circles, although writers as various as Philip Roth, Thomas Wolfe, and Martin Amis have built their careers on it. *Storytelling*, the in-your-face new film by Todd Solondz, is a con-

fessional in which Solondz explores his own methods and motives, and tries to come clean.

The movie contains two stories. The first, *Fiction*, is about a college creative writing student (Selma Blair) whose boyfriend (Leo Fitzpatrick) has cerebral palsy. "You wanna hear my short story now?" he asks her immediately after sex, and it is clear he is trading on sex as a way to win an audience. Although he is the "cripple," that gives him an advantage in her politically correct cosmos, and he milks it. Later, when they've broken up, he observes sadly, "The kinkiness has gone. You've become kind."

She moves on to a one-night stand with her writing professor (Robert Wisdom), a forbidding black man whose tastes run toward rough rape fantasies. She goes looking for trouble, but finds she doesn't like it, and writes a tearful, defiant story about their encounter. When the other students tear it to shreds, she weeps, "But it's the truth!"

All three of these characters are using the pose of "writer" as a way to get sex, get their work read, or both, sometimes at the same time. *Nonfiction*, the longer second section of the film, opens with a would-be documentary filmmaker named Toby (Paul Giamatti) looking at the high school yearbook photo of a girl he now remembers yearningly. Calling her, he finds she is married and has a family, and immediately decides he is making a documentary about an American family and needs hers.

This family, the Livingstons, is Jewish, lives in the suburbs, and is a seething zone of resentment and rage. The father (John Goodman) presides over the dinner table like an enforcer; the mother (Julie Hagerty) is a twittering mass of reconciliation. Scooby (Mark Webber), the oldest son, smokes pot, is sullen, hides in his room. Brady (Noah Fleiss), the middle son, plays football and speculates that Scooby is a "homo." Mikey (Jonathan Osser), the youngest son, has earnest conversations with the El Salvadoran maid, Consuelo (Lupe Ontiveros). She hates the family and her job. Mikey wants to be nice to her but is clueless ("But Consuelo, even though you're poor, don't you have any hobbies or interests or anything?"). When he finds her weeping because her son has been executed for murder, he expresses polite regret before asking her to clean up some grape juice he has spilled. Later, he hypnotizes his father and instructs him to fire her.

Dinner conversation at the Livingstons' is fraught with hazards. When the Holocaust comes up, it is Scooby who observes that since it forced an ancestor to escape to America, "If it wasn't for Hitler, none of us would ever have been born." This gets him immediately banished from the table, a fate that hangs over every meal as the father angrily monitors the conversation.

Alert readers will have noticed that *Storytelling* seems to be working from a list of sensitive or taboo subjects: physical disability, race, rape, facile charges of racism, exploitation of the poor, the Holocaust, homosexuality. I will not reveal the identity of the character who goes into a coma and is apparently brain-dead; I will observe that this development cheers the editor of Toby's documentary, who tells him it's just what his film needs.

One character does attack Toby's documentary, telling him it's "glib and facile to make fun of these people." "I'm not making fun of them," Toby says. "I love them." Toby, of course, represents Solondz, whose two previous films (*Welcome to the Dollhouse* and *Happiness*) were attacked for making glib and facile fun of the characters. So has this one; Ed Gonzalez of *Slant* refers to Solondz's "cowardly apologias." In a Solondz film there's always a delicate line to be walked between social satire on the one hand and a geek show on the other.

I think Solondz is not cowardly but brave, and does his bourgeois-mugging in full view, instead of concealing it. We live in a time when many comedies mock middle-class American suburban life, but Solondz is one director who does it out in the open, to extremes, pushing the envelope, challenging us to decide what we think. And because his timing is so precise and his ear for dialogue so good, he sometimes tricks us into laughing before we have time to think, gee, we shouldn't be laughing at that.

I saw *Storytelling* at Cannes 2001 and wrote that I wanted to see it again before deciding what I thought about it. I saw it again, and still felt I had to see it again. I saw it a third time. By then I had moved beyond the immediate

shock of the material and was able to focus on what a well-made film it was; how concisely Solondz gets the effects he's after.

I was also forced to conclude that I might *never* know for sure what I thought about it—that it was a puzzle without an answer, a demonstration that there are some areas so fraught and sensitive that most people just hurry past them with their eyes averted. By not averting his eyes, Solondz forces us to consider the unthinkable, the unacceptable, the unmentionable. He should not be penalized for going further than the filmmakers who attack the same targets but have better manners—or less nerve.

Note: During the sex scene between the professor and his student, a bright red quadrangle obscures part of the screen. When I saw the movie at Cannes, the audience could see the two characters—graphically, but not in explicit pornographic detail. The MPAA refused to give the film an R rating because of that scene. Solondz refused to cut it, and used the red blocking as a way of underlining the MPAA's censorship. Good for him. And one more reminder that the MPAA and Jack Valenti oppose a workable adult rating for America. ☞

Such a Long Journey ★ ★ ★ ½
NO MPAA RATING, 113 m., 2000

Roshan Seth (Gustad Noble), Soni Razdan (Dilnavaz Noble), Om Puri (Ghulam), Naseeruddin Shah (Major Jimmy Bilimoria), Ranjit Chowdhry (Pavement Artist), Sam Dastor (Dinshawji), Kurush Deboo (Tehmul), Vrajesh Hirjee (Sohrab Noble). Directed by Sturla Gunnarsson and produced by Paul Stephens and Simon MacCorkindale. Screenplay by Sooni Taraporevala, based on the novel by Rohinton Mistry.

India is the closest we can come in today's world to the London of Dickens, with its poverty and wealth side by side, in a society teeming with benevolence and intrigue, eccentrics and thieves, the suspect and the saintly. *Such a Long Journey*, filmed on location in Bombay, is a film so rich in atmosphere it makes Western films look pale and underpopulated. It combines politics, religion, illness, and scheming in the story of one family in upheaval, and is very serious, and always amusing.

The story, set in 1971 at the time of the war between India and Pakistan, is based on the novel of the same name by Rohinton Mistry, an Indian now living in Toronto. I haven't read it, but I have read his latest novel, the magnificent *A Fine Balance*, which has the same ability to see how political issues impact the lives of the ordinary and the obscure. Mistry's novels have the droll irony of Dickens, as when a legless beggar and a beggarmaster turn out to be brothers, and the beggarmaster is so moved that he purchases the beggar a better cart to push himself around on.

Such a Long Journey takes place mostly in and around a large apartment complex, its courtyard, and the street, which the municipal authorities want to widen so that even more choking diesel fumes can cloud the air. We meet the hero, Gustad (Roshan Seth), in the process of defending the old concrete wall that protects his courtyard from the street, and later he strikes a bargain with an itinerant artist (Ranjit Chowdhry), who covers the wall with paintings from every conceivable religious tradition, with the thought that all of the groups represented will join in defending the wall.

A greater struggle is in store for Gustad. A Parsi whose family has fallen on hard times, he works in a bank and is asked by Major Jimmy (Naseeruddin Shah), a friend from long ago, to hide and launder some money. The go-between (Om Puri) implies these are official Indian government funds being secretly transferred to finance the war against Pakistan in Bangladesh. (The movie doesn't require us to know much about modern history in the subcontinent, since the story works entirely in terms of the personal lives of its characters.)

Gustad is a good and earnest man, who has adopted the local idiot as a kind of surrogate son, who is the unofficial mayor of his building, who is always on call to help his neighbors, who dotes on his little daughter, and bursts with pride that his son, Sohrab (Vrajesh Hirjee), has been accepted by the Indian Institute of Technology. Alas, Sohrad doesn't want to go to IIT; he hates engineering and

wants to be an artist, and Gustad implores him to reconsider.

Gustad's relationship with his wife has elements of an Indian *Honeymooners*. The kitchen is her turf, where she defiantly spends long hours in consultation with a neighbor woman whom Gustad considers to be a witch (i.e., she has a different set of superstitions than his own). Their marriage is strong when it needs to be, as when their daughter falls ill with malaria.

All of these stories are told against the backdrop of the others who live in the apartment complex, the street vendors outside, and those who are understood to have claims to portions of the courtyard or sidewalk. There is great poverty in India, but because it is so common it's more of a condition of life than a particular shame, and Gustad is on easy terms with the people who live in, as well as on, his street.

Roshan Seth is not a name well known in the West, but his face is familiar; he played Nehru in *Gandhi*, the heroine's father in *Mississippi Masala*, the father again in *My Beautiful Laundrette*, and it is only poetic justice that he starred in the film of Dickens's *Little Dorrit*. In this role (which won him a Canadian Genie as the year's best actor), he plays an everyman, an earnest, worried, funny character always skirting on the edge of disaster, exuberantly immersed in his life. The way he masterminds the defense of the precious wall is brilliant, but the way he deals with its fate is even more touching, because it is simply human.

The director, Sturla Gunnarsson, is Icelandic, suggesting the universality of this story; the writer, Sooni Taraporevala, also wrote *Mississippi Masala* and *Salaam Bombay*. Their film is interesting not simply in terms of its plot (the politics, the money), but because of the medium it moves through—the streets of Bombay. It suggests a society that has more poverty than ours, but is not necessarily poorer, because it has a richer texture of daily life. *American Beauty* could not be an Indian story; it would be too hard to imagine Indian city dwellers with that much time to brood and isolate.

Sugar & Spice ★ ★ ★
PG-13, 93 m., 2001

Marley Shelton (Diane Weston), James Marsden (Jack Bartlett), Mena Suvari (Kansas Hill), Marla Sokoloff (Lisa Janusch), Alexandra Holden (Fern Rogers), Rachel Blanchard (Hannah Wold), Sara Marsh (Lucy Whitman), Melissa George (Cleo Miller), Sean Young (Kansas's Mom). Directed by Francine McDougall and produced by Wendy Finerman. Screenplay by Mandy Nelson.

Sugar & Spice puts your average cheerleader movie to shame. It's sassy and satirical, closer in spirit to *But I'm a Cheerleader* than to *Bring It On*. With its shameless pop culture references, wicked satire, and a cheerleader with the hots for Conan O'Brien, it's more proof that not all movie teenagers have to be dumb. (All right, these cheerleaders *are* dumb—but in a smart movie.) I was surprised by the PG-13 rating; the movie is so in tune with its under-seventeen target audience that it's amazing the MPAA didn't slap it with an R.

The movie takes place at Lincoln High School, with a crepe-headed Honest Abe prancing on the sidelines. We meet the A-team of the cheerleader squad, who seem like a cross between Olympic gymnasts and the pom-pom girl who inflamed Kevin Spacey in *American Beauty*. No wonder: Mena Suvari, who played the pom-pom girl, turns up here as Kansas, a girl whose mom is in prison.

The team leader is Diane (Marley Shelton), a beauty who is stunned when Jack (James Marsden), the captain of the football team, announces at a school assembly that his platform for prom king includes taking her to the prom. They share a wet kiss on stage, and soon Diane is pregnant, which doesn't curtail her cheerleading.

Jack and Diane receive a frosty reception from their parents, but after the movie quotes what for it is scripture ("Papa Don't Preach") they move into a cheap apartment and Jack gets a job at Señor Guacamole. He's fired, there's a financial crisis, and then Diane comes up with an inspiration while watching a heist movie on TV: They can rob a bank!

They do research by watching other crime movies, including *Heat, Point Blank,* and *Reservoir Dogs*. Cleo (Melissa George), the team member with the crush on Conan, makes it more fun by fantasizing Conan's head on the bodies of actors. Hannah (Rachel Blanchard), who has strict churchgoing parents, is allowed to watch only G-rated movies, so she researches *The Apple Dumpling Gang*. Lucy (Sara Marsh), the brains of the outfit, fits it all together. And they rationalize the robbery by saying they can give some of the money to charity: We can buy "one of those starving little kids that Sally Struthers auctions."

The robbery plans include a visit to a local exterminator, who supplies them with guns and insists that his daughter Fern (Alexandra Holden) be allowed to join the cheerleader squad. Fern looks at first like a candidate for one of her dad's poisonous sprays, but cleans up real good. The robbery itself involves disguises: five pregnant Betty dolls and one Richard Nixon. I liked the way a witness, also a cheerleader, sees through the disguises when she observes an "illegal dismount."

The film's narrator is the outsider Lisa (Marla Sokoloff), who has a Bette Midler quality. One of the weirder scenes involves a trip by Kansas to visit her mother (Sean Young) in prison; she needs advice on robbing banks. And the running gag about Conan O'Brien is funny because the passion seems so out of scale with its inspiration. *Sugar & Spice* seems instinctively in sync with its cheerleaders, maybe because it was made by women: director Francine McDougall, writer Mandy Nelson, producer Wendy Finerman. It is not a great high school movie, like *Election*, but it's alive and risky and saucy.

The Sum of All Fears ★ ★ ★ ½
PG-13, 127 m., 2002

Ben Affleck (Jack Ryan), Morgan Freeman (Bill Cabot), James Cromwell (President Fowler), Liev Schreiber (John Clark), Alan Bates (Richard Dressler), Philip Baker Hall (Defense Secretary Becker), Bruce McGill (Security Adviser Revel), Jamie Harrold (Dillon), Ciaran Hinds (President Nemerov), Bridget Moynahan (Cathy Muller). Directed by Phil Alden Robinson and produced by Mace Neufeld. Screenplay by Paul Attanasio and Daniel Pyne, based on the novel by Tom Clancy.

Oh, for the innocent days when a movie like *The Sum of All Fears* could be enjoyed as a "thriller." In these dark times it is not a thriller but a confirmer, confirming our fears that the world is headed for disaster. The film is about the detonation of a nuclear device in an American city. No less an authority than Warren Buffett recently gave a speech in which he flatly stated that such an event was "inevitable." Movies like *Black Sunday* could exorcise our fears, but this one works instead to give them form.

To be sure, Tom Clancy's horrifying vision has been footnoted with the obligatory Hollywood happy ending, in which world war is averted and an attractive young couple pledge love while sitting on a blanket in the sunshine on the White House lawn. We can walk out smiling, unless we remember that much of Baltimore is radioactive rubble. Human nature is a wonderful thing. The reason the ending is happy is because we in the audience assume we'll be the two on the blanket, not the countless who've been vaporized.

The movie is based on another of Tom Clancy's fearfully factual stories about Jack Ryan, the CIA agent, this time a good deal younger than Harrison Ford's Ryan in *A Clear and Present Danger,* and played by Ben Affleck. It follows the ancient convention in which the hero goes everywhere important and personally performs most of the crucial actions, but it feels less contrived because Clancy has expertise about warfare and national security issues; the plot is a device to get us from one packet of information to another.

The story: In 1973, an Israeli airplane carrying a nuclear bomb crashes in Syria. Many years later, the unexploded bomb is dug up, goes on the black market, and is sold to a right-wing fanatic who has a theory: "Hitler was stupid. He fought America and Russia, instead of letting them fight one another." The fanatic's plan is to start a nuclear exchange between the superpowers, after which Aryan fascists would pick up the pieces.

The use of the neo-Nazis is politically correct: Best to invent villains who won't offend any audiences. This movie can play in Syria,

Saudi Arabia, and Iraq without getting walk-outs. It's more likely that if a bomb ever does go off in a big city, the perpetrators will be True Believers whose certainty about the next world gives them, they think, the right to kill us in this one.

In the film, Ryan becomes a sort of unofficial protégé of Bill Cabot (Morgan Freeman), a high-level CIA official and good guy who maintains a "back channel" into the Kremlin to avoid just such misunderstandings as occur. Ryan and Cabot fly to Moscow when a new president assumes power, and the new Soviet leader (Ciaran Hinds) is shown as a reasonable man who must take unreasonable actions (like invading Chechnya) to placate the militarists in his government.

America is being run by President Fowler (tall, Lincolnesque James Cromwell), who is surrounded by advisers cast with some of the most convincing character actors in the movies: Philip Baker Hall, Alan Bates, Bruce McGill, etc. Crucial scenes take place aboard *Air Force One* after Baltimore has been bombed, and we see the president and his cabinet not in cool analytical discussions but all shouting at once. Somehow I am reassured by the notion that our leaders might be really upset at such a time; anyone who can be dispassionate about nuclear war is probably able to countenance one.

There are some frightening special effects in the movie, which I will not describe, because their unexpected appearance has such an effect. There are also several parallel story lines, including one involving a particularly skilled dirty-tricks specialist named John Clark (Liev Schreiber) who I am glad to have on our side. There are also the usual frustrations in which the man with the truth can't get through because of bureaucracy.

Against these strengths are some weaknesses. I think Jack Ryan's one-man actions in post-bomb Baltimore are unlikely and way too well-timed. I doubt he would find evildoers still hanging around the scene of their crime. I am not sure all of the threads—identifying the plutonium, finding the shipping manifest and invoice, tracking down the guy who dug up the bomb—could take place with such gratifying precision. And I smile wearily at the necessity of supplying Jack with a girlfriend (Bridget

Moynahan), who exists only so that she can (1) be impatient when he is called away from dates on official business; (2) disbelieve his alibis; (3) be heroic; (4) be worried about him; (5) be smudged with blood and dirt; and (6) populate the happy ending. We are so aware of the character's function that we can hardly believe her as a person.

These details are not fatal to the film. Director Phil Alden Robinson and his writers, Paul Attanasio and Daniel Pyne, do a spellbinding job of cranking up the tension; they create a portrait of convincing realism, and then they add the other stuff because, well, if anybody ever makes a movie like this without the obligatory Hollywood softeners, audiences might flee the theater in despair. My own fear is that in the postapocalyptic future, *The Sum of All Fears* will be seen as touchingly optimistic.   ☞

Sunshine ★ ★ ★
R, 180 m., 2000

Ralph Fiennes (Ignatz, Adam, Ivan), Rosemary Harris (Valerie [Older]), Rachel Weisz (Greta), Jennifer Ehle (Valerie [Younger]), Molly Parker (Hannah), Deborah Unger (Carola), William Hurt (Andor Knorr), James Frain (Gustave [Younger]), John Neville (Gustave [Older]). Directed by Istvan Szabo and produced by Robert Lantos, Jonathan Debin, Andras Hamori, and Rainer Koelmel. Screenplay by Szabo and Israel Horovitz.

"One gang was as bad as another," says an old woman at the end of Istvan Szabo's *Sunshine.* In her long lifetime in Hungary she has lived under the emperor, the Nazis, and the Communists. And she watched as the West betrayed the 1956 uprising. She has seen some members of her Jewish family spend the century trying to accommodate themselves to the shifting winds of politics and society, and failing. She has seen other members fight against the prevailing tyrannies, only to find them replaced by new ones.

And she has witnessed the Holocaust bearing down over three generations—not as an aberration, a contagion spread by Hitler, but as the inexorable result of long years of anti-Semitism. We are reminded of the 1999 documentary *Last Days,* also about Holocaust victims in Hungary, which observes that the persecution of the Jews there began fairly late in the war, at a time when Hitler's thinly stretched resources were needed for tasks other than genocide.

But the Nazis had help. "Nice, ordinary Hungarian people did the dirty work," we learn, and there is even the possibility that some members of the Sonnenschein family, which the movie follows over three generations, would have helped had they not been Jewish and therefore ineligible. The movie shows family members determined to think of themselves as good Hungarians. The family name is changed to Sors to make it "more Hungarian," and Adam Sors, in the middle generation, converts to Catholicism, joins an officers' club, and wins a gold medal for fencing in the Olympics.

But assimilation is not the answer, as he learns when he remains too long in Hungary, believing a national hero like himself immune to anti-Semitism. There is a heartbreaking scene in a Nazi death camp where he tells an officer that he is a loyal Hungarian army officer, too—and a gold medalist. "Strip," the officer tells him, and soon his naked body has been crucified and sprayed with water until it forms a grotesque ice sculpture.

Szabo's epic tells the story of one family in one country, but it will do as a millennial record of a century in which one bright political idea after another promised to bring happiness and only enforced misery. The Sonnenschein family fortune is founded on "Sunshine," an invigorating tonic with a secret recipe. The film does not need to underline the symbolism that the formula for the tonic is lost as the century unfolds.

Ralph Fiennes plays the father, son, and grandson, each one rebuffed or repelled by a Hungary in agony. Ignatz Sonnenschein, whose story begins the film (with some flashbacks about his father), is a successful businessman who presides over a comfortable bourgeoisie home and thinks of standing for parliament. His brother Gustave (James Frain, and later John Neville) is disgusted he would support a corrupt regime, and Ignatz speaks hopefully of progressive elements in the regime and the emperor's openness to reform.

After the war, a Communist government gets in briefly, and Gustave joins it. Then the rise of the right ends that chapter, and he is placed under house arrest before fleeing to France. Meanwhile, Fiennes now plays Adam Sors, whose attention is focused on fencing; since the best fencers are in the officers' club, he takes lessons and converts to Catholicism so he can join it too. He doesn't take religion seriously; it's just a ticket you punch in order to fence.

His son Ivan (Fiennes again—uncanny in his ability to suggest the three different personalities) emerges after the war as a police officer under the new Communist regime. Ivan grows close to an idealist named Knorr (William Hurt), who believes in communism and wants to do a good job, and therefore is a threat to the government. This sequence, showing a weary Hungary being betrayed once again by a corrupt regime, is the most effective, because it pounds the message home: The people running the Communist government are more of the nice, ordinary Hungarians who helped with the Holocaust. The point isn't that Hungarians are any worse than anyone else—but that, alas, human nature is much the same everywhere, and more generous with lackeys than heroes.

At three hours *Sunshine* made some audience members restless when it premiered at the Toronto Film Festival, but this is a movie of substance and thrilling historical sweep, and its three hours allow Szabo to show the family's destiny forming and shifting under pressure. At every moment there is a choice between ethics and expediency; at no moment is the choice clear or easy. Many Holocaust stories (like *Jakob the Liar*) dramatize the tragedy as a simple case of good and evil. And so it was, but that lesson is obvious. The buried message of *Sunshine* is more complex.

It suggests, first, that some Jews were slow to scent the danger because they were seduced into thinking their personal status gave them immunity (so do we all). Second, that those who felt communism was the answer to fascism did not understand how all "isms" distrust democracy and appeal to bullies. Third, that the Holocaust is being mirrored today all over the world, as groups hate and murder each other on the basis of religion, color, and

nationality. The Sonnenschein family learned these lessons generation after generation during the century. So did we all. Not that human nature seems to have learned much as a result. Is there any reason to think fewer people will die in the twenty-first century than died in the twentieth, because they belong to a different tribe?

Sunshine State ★ ★ ★ ½
PG-13, 141 m., 2002

Edie Falco (Marly Temple), Angela Bassett (Desiree Perry), Jane Alexander (Delia Temple), Ralph Waite (Furman Temple), James McDaniel (Reggie Perry), Timothy Hutton (Jack Meadows), Mary Alice (Eunice Stokes), Bill Cobbs (Dr. Lloyd), Mary Steenburgen (Francine Pickney), Tom Wright (Flash Phillips), Alan King (Murray Silver). Directed by John Sayles and produced by Maggie Renzi. Screenplay by Sayles.

John Sayles's *Sunshine State* looks at first like the story of clashes between social and economic groups: between developers and small landowners, between black and white, between the powerful and their workers, between the Chamber of Commerce and local reality. It's set on a Florida resort island, long stuck in its ways, that has been targeted by a big development company. But this is not quite the story the setup seems to predict.

If the movie had been made twenty or thirty years ago, the whites would have been racists, the blacks victims, and the little businessmen would have struggled courageously to hold out against the developers. But things do change in our country, sometimes slowly for the better, and *Sunshine State* is set at a point in time when all of the players are a little more reconciled, a little less predictable, than they would have been. You can only defend a position so long before the needs of your own life begin to assert themselves.

The island, named Plantation Island, consists of Delrona Beach, a small community of retirees and retail stores, and Lincoln Beach, an enclave of prosperous African-Americans. Both groups have been targeted by a big land development company probably owned by a white-haired golfer named Murray Silver (Alan King), although he exists so far above the world of the little people that it's hard to be sure. The company wants to buy up everything and turn it into a high-rise "beach resort community."

That would doom the Sea-Vue Motel and restaurant, which is run by Marly Temple (Edie Falco, of *The Sopranos*). The motel was built by her parents, Furman and Delia (Ralph Waite and Jane Alexander), and is Furman's life work. But it is not Edie's dream. In a movie made twenty years ago, she would be fighting against the capitalist invaders, but, frankly, she *wants* to sell—and she even begins a little romance with Jack (Timothy Hutton), the architect sent in to size things up.

Over on the Lincoln Beach side, Eunice Stokes (Mary Alice) lives in her tidy white house with a sea view. When she bought this house, it represented a substantial dream for an ambitious black couple; today, it looks a little forlorn. For the first time in years, her daughter Desiree (Angela Bassett) has come to visit. Desiree got pregnant at fifteen with the Florida Flash (Tom Wright), a football hero, and was sent away because Eunice was too proud of her middle-class respectability to risk scandal. Desiree has prospered on TV in Boston and returns with an anesthetist husband.

The Florida Flash, meanwhile, has not prospered. He had an injury on his way to the Heisman Trophy and now sells used cars. Success seems to go wrong on this island; while Francine (Mary Steenburgen), the bubbly Chamber of Commerce pageant chairman, narrates a story of pirates and treasure, her husband tries to kill himself, although neither hanging nor a nail gun does the trick. He's got business difficulties.

Because we are so familiar with the conventional approach to a story like this, it takes time to catch on that Sayles is not repeating the old progressive line about the little guy against big capital. He has made a more observant, elegiac, sad movie, about how the dreams of the parents are not the dreams of the children.

Because Furman wanted a motel, Marly has to work long hours to run it. Because Eunice wanted respectability, Desiree had to run away from home. Because the Chamber of Commerce wants a pageant about "local history," Francine has to concoct one. (The island's real history mostly involves "mass murder, rape, and slavery," she observes, so they'll "Disney-fy it a little bit.") Even the outside predators are

not so bad. Timothy Hutton, as the architect, is not typecast as an uncaring pencil pusher who wants to bulldoze the beach, but as a wage earner who moves from one job to another, living in motels, without a family, always on assignment.

Sayles pulls another surprise. His characters are not unyielding. Consider the scene where Marly tells her father she's had it with the motel. Consider the scene where her mother, an Audubon Society stalwart, observes that there might be an angle in selling birdlands and giving the money to the society. Consider Eunice's need to reconsider her daughter's needs and behavior. Look at the daughter's difficulty in reconciling memories of the Florida Flash with the car salesman she sees before her. And consider how at the end of the film, fate and history turn out to play a greater role than any of the great plans.

Sayles's film moves among a large population of characters with grace, humor, and a forgiving irony. The performances by Angela Bassett, Edie Falco, and Mary Alice are at the heart of the story, and there are moments when other characters can illuminate themselves with one flash of dialogue, as Ralph Waite does one day in considering the future of the motel. Some of the characters seem to have drifted in from Altman Land, especially Mary Steenburgen's, whose narration of the pageant is a wildly irrelevant counterpoint to the island's reality. Others, like Tim Hutton's sad architect, seem to have much more power than they do. And what about Alan King and his golfing buddies? They show that if you have enough money and power, you don't need to get your hands dirty making more (others will do that for you), and you can be genial and philosophical—a sweet, colorful character, subsidized by the unhappiness of others.

Sunshine State is not a radical attack on racism and big business, not a defense of the environment, not a hymn in favor of small communities over conglomerates. It is about the next generation of those issues and the people they involve. Racism has faded to the point where Eunice's proud home on Lincoln Beach no longer makes the same statement. Big business is not monolithic but bumbling. The little motel is an eyesore. The young people who got out, like Desiree, have prospered. Those who stayed, like Marly, have been trapped. And the last scene of the film tells us, I think, that we should hesitate to embrace the future in this nation until we have sufficiently considered the past.

Super Troopers ★ ★ ½
R, 103 m., 2002

Jay Chandrasekhar (Thorny), Kevin Heffernan (Farva), Steve Lemme (Mac), Paul Soter (Foster), Erik Stolhanske (Rabbit), Brian Cox (Captain John O'Hagan), Daniel von Bargen (Chief Grady), Marisa Coughlan (Ursula), Lynda Carter (Governor Jessman). Directed by Jay Chandrasekhar and produced by Richard Perello. Screenplay by Broken Lizard (Jay Chandrasekhar, Kevin Heffernan, Steve Lemme, Paul Soter, and Erik Stolhanske).

Super Troopers plays like it was directed as a do-it-yourself project, following instructions that omitted a few steps, and yet the movie has an undeniable charm. Imagine a group of Vermont state troopers treating their job like an opportunity to stage real-life *Candid Camera* situations. Now imagine that all of the troopers have ambitions to be stand-up comics. And that they were inspired to get into the force by watching *Police Academy* movies. But that they are basically good guys. That kind of describes it.

The movie is set in Spurbury, Vermont, where there isn't enough crime to go around. That causes a bitter rivalry between the state troopers, led by Captain O'Hagan (Brian Cox), and the city police, led by Chief Grady (Daniel von Bargen). When a dead body turns up in a Winebago and drug smuggling seems to be involved, the two forces compete for clues, arrests, and especially for funds. The state police post, indeed, has been threatened with a complete shutdown by the budget-minded governor (Lynda Carter).

Perhaps because these may be the last weeks they can spend working together, or perhaps simply because they're fundamentally goofy, the troopers pass their days blowing the minds of people they stop on the highway.

Trooper: Do you know how fast you were going?

Terrified kid whose friends are stoned: Sixty-five?
Trooper: Sixty-three.

Other nice touches include (a) using the loudspeaker to instruct a driver to pull over after he has already pulled over, and (b) casually saying "meow" in the middle of a conversation with a curbed driver.

Captain O'Hagan is understandably distressed at the bizarre behavior of his men, and worried about the possible closing of the post. A drug bust would save the day, but his men seem fairly unfocused as they look into a promising case. "Are you suggesting," the local chief asks the troopers, "that a cartoon monkey is bringing drugs into our town?" Well, no, but it's a long story.

There's romantic intrigue when a sweet and sexy local cop named Ursula (Marisa Coughlan) starts to date a trooper named Foster (Paul Soter). This goes against the rules and undermines the rivalry, but may provide a solution to the drug mystery. Foster, however, is not too bright, as when he suggests that he and Ursula get into the backseat of the cruiser. He has forgotten that once you are in the backseat of a cruiser, someone else has to let you out.

During their sessions in local diners, which are long and frequent, the cops trade dialogue like members of a comedy troupe, which indeed they are. The name of their troupe is Broken Lizard, it shares credit for the screenplay, and the director is Jay Chandrasekhar. He also plays the trooper named Thorny. Vermonters find it obvious that he is of ethnic origin, but are baffled by the challenge of identifying his ethnic group, and there's a running gag as he remains poker-faced while people assume he's Mexican, Arabic, Indian or . . . something.

Broken Lizard, I learn, began as an undergraduate troupe at Colgate in 1989, raised $200,000 to make a movie named *Puddle Cruiser* and, instead of making a distribution deal, did a campus tour to show it. *Super Troopers* aims higher, and may spin off a Fox TV sitcom which, on the basis of this film, might work.

Super Troopers has kind of a revue feel. There is a plot, which somehow arrives at a conclusion, but the movie doesn't tell a story so much as move from one skit to another, with a laid-back charm that is more relaxed and self-confident than the manic laffaminit style of the *Police Academy* pictures. No movie is altogether uninspired that includes lines like, "Desperation is a stinky cologne." I can't quite recommend it—it's too patched together—but I almost can; it's the kind of movie that makes you want to like it.

The Sweetest Thing ★ ½
R, 84 m., 2002

Cameron Diaz (Christina), Christina Applegate (Courtney), Thomas Jane (Peter), Selma Blair (Jane), Jason Bateman (Roger), Parker Posey (Judy). Directed by Roger Kumble and produced by Cathy Konrad. Screenplay by Nancy M. Pimental.

I like Cameron Diaz. I just plain like her. She's able to convey bubble-brained zaniness about as well as anyone in the movies right now, and then she can switch gears and give you a scary dramatic performance in something like *Vanilla Sky*. She's a beauty, but apparently without vanity; how else to account for her appearance in *Being John Malkovich*, or her adventures in *There's Something About Mary*? I don't think she gets halfway enough praise for her talent.

Consider her in *The Sweetest Thing*. This is not a good movie. It's deep-sixed by a compulsion to catalog every bodily fluids gag in *There's Something About Mary* and devise a parallel clone-gag. It knows the words but not the music; while the Farrelly brothers got away with murder, *The Sweetest Thing* commits suicide.

And yet there were whole long stretches of it when I didn't much care how bad it was—at least, I wasn't brooding in anger about the film—because Cameron Diaz and her costars had thrown themselves into it with such heedless abandon. They don't walk the plank, they tap-dance.

The movie is about three girls who just wanna have fun. They hang out in clubs, they troll for cute guys, they dress like *Maxim* cover girls, they study paperback best-sellers on the rules of relationships, and frequently (this comes as no surprise), they end up weeping in each other's arms. Diaz's running mates, played by Christina Applegate and Selma Blair, are pals and confidantes, and a crisis for one is a crisis for all.

The movie's romance involves Diaz meeting Thomas Jane in a dance club; the chemistry is right but he doesn't quite accurately convey that the wedding he is attending on the weekend is his own. This leads to Diaz's ill-fated expedition into the wedding chapel, many misunderstandings, and the kind of Idiot Plot dialogue in which all problems could be instantly solved if the characters were not studiously avoiding stating the obvious.

The plot is merely the excuse, however, for an astonishing array of sex and body plumbing jokes, nearly all of which dream of hitting a home run like *There's Something About Mary*, but do not. Consider *Mary*'s scene where Diaz has what she thinks is gel in her hair. Funny—because she doesn't know what it really is, and we do. Now consider the scene in this movie where the girls go into a men's room and do not understand that in a men's room a hole in the wall is almost never merely an architectural detail. The payoff is sad, sticky, and depressing.

Or consider a scene where one of the roommates gets "stuck" while performing oral sex. This is intended as a rip-off of the "franks and beans" scene in *Mary*, but gets it all wrong. You simply cannot (I am pretty sure about this) get stuck in the way the movie suggests—no, not even if you've got piercings. More to the point, in *Mary* the victim is unseen, and we picture his dilemma. In *Sweetest Thing*, the victim is seen, sort of (careful framing preserves the R rating), and the image isn't funny. Then we get several dozen neighbors, all singing to inspire the girl to extricate herself; this might have looked good on the page, but it just plain doesn't work, especially not when embellished with the sobbing cop on the doorstep, the gay cop, and other flat notes.

More details. Sometimes it is funny when people do not know they may be consuming semen (as in *American Pie*) and sometimes it is not, as in the scene at the dry cleaners in this movie. How can you laugh when what you really want to do is hurl? And what about the scene in the ladies' room, where the other girls are curious about Applegate's boobs and she tells them she paid for them and invites them to have a feel, and they do, like shoppers at K-mart? Again, a funny concept. Again, destroyed by bad timing, bad framing, and overkill. Because the director, Roger Kumble, doesn't know how to set it up and pay it off with surgical precision, he simply has women pawing Applegate while the scene dies. An unfunny scene only grows worse by pounding in the concept as if we didn't get it.

So, as I say, I like Cameron Diaz. I like everyone in this movie (I must not neglect the invaluable Parker Posey, as a terrified bride). I like their energy. I like their willingness. I like the opening shot when Diaz comes sashaying up a San Francisco hill like a dancer from *In Living Color* who thinks she's still on the air. I like her mobile, comic face—she's smart in the way she plays dumb. But the movie I cannot like, because the movie doesn't know how to be liked. It doesn't even know how to be a movie.

Sweet November ★
PG-13, 114 m., 2001

Keanu Reeves (Nelson Moss), Charlize Theron (Sara Deever), Jason Isaacs (Chaz), Greg Germann (Vince), Liam Aiken (Abner). Directed by Pat O'Connor and produced by Deborah Aal, Erwin Stoff, Steven Reuther, and Elliott Kastner. Screenplay by Kurt Voelker.

Sweet November passes off pathological behavior as romantic bliss. It's about two sick and twisted people playing mind games and calling it love. I don't know who I disliked more intensely—Nelson, the abrupt, insulting ad man played by Keanu Reeves, or Sara, Charlize Theron's narcissistic martyr. Reeves at least has the grace to look intensely uncomfortable during several scenes, including one involving a bag full of goodies, which we will get to later.

The movie is a remake of a 1968 film starring Sandy Dennis and Anthony Newley and, if memory serves, the same bed in a San Francisco bay window. Both films have the same conceit, which only a movie producer could believe: A beautiful girl takes men to her bed for one month at a time, to try to help and improve them. "You live in a box, and I can lift the lid," she explains. Why a month? "It's long enough to be meaningful and short enough to stay out of trouble," Sara says—wrong on both counts.

Read no further if you do not already know that she has another reason for term limits.

She's dying. In the original movie the disease was described as "quite rare, but incurable." Here we get another clue, when Nelson opens Sara's medicine cabinet and finds, oh, I dunno, at a rough guess, 598 bottles of pills. The girl is obviously overmedicating. Give her a high colonic, send her to detox, and the movie is over.

Nelson is one of those insulting, conceited, impatient, coffee-drinking, cell phone–using, Jaguar-driving advertising executives that you find in only two places: the movies, and real life. His motto is, speed up and smell the coffee. Sara, on the other hand, acts like she has all the time in the world, even though (sob!) she does not. She sits on the hood of Nelson's car and commits other crimes against the male libido that a woman absolutely cannot get away with unless she looks exactly like Charlize Theron and insists on sleeping with you, and even then she's pushing it.

Nelson gradually learns to accept the gift of herself that she is offering. Actually, he accepts it quickly, the pig, but only gradually appreciates it. So warm, cheerful, perky, plucky, and seductive is Sara that Nelson, and the movie, completely forget for well over an hour that he has an apartment of his own and another girlfriend. By then the inexorable march of the rare but incurable disease is taking its toll, Sara has to go into the hospital, and Nelson finds out the Truth.

Will there be a scene where Sara, with a drip line plugged into every orifice, begs Nelson, "Get me out of here! Take me home!" Do bears eat gooseberries? Will there be a scene where Sara says, "Go away! I don't want you to see me like this!" Do iguanas like papayas? Will there be a scene where Sara's faithful gay friend (Jason Isaacs) bathes and comforts her? Yes, because it is a convention of movies like this that all sexy women have gay friends who materialize on demand to perform nursing and hygiene chores. (Advice to gay friend in next remake: Insist, "Unless I get two good scenes of my own, I've emptied my last bedpan.")

I almost forgot the scene involving the bag full of goodies. Keanu Reeves must have been phoning his agent between every take. The script requires him to climb in through Sara's window with a large bag that contains all of the presents he would ever want to give her, based on all the needs and desires she has ever expressed. I could get cheap laughs by listing the entire inventory of the bag, but that would be unfair. I will mention only one, the dishwashing machine. Logic may lead you to ask, "How can an automatic dishwasher fit inside a bag that Keanu Reeves can sling over his shoulder as he climbs through the window?" I would explain, but I hate it when movie reviews give everything away.

Swordfish ★ ★ ½
R, 97 m., 2001

John Travolta (Gabriel Shear), Hugh Jackman (Stanley Jobson), Halle Berry (Ginger), Don Cheadle (Agent A. D. Roberts), Vinnie Jones (Marco), Camryn Grimes (Holly Jobson), Sam Shepard (Senator Reisman), Zach Grenier (A. D. Joy). Directed by Dominic Sena and produced by Jonathan D. Krane and Joel Silver. Screenplay by Skip Woods.

Swordfish looks like the result of a nasty explosion down at the Plot Works. It's skillfully mounted and fitfully intriguing, but weaves such a tangled web that at the end I defy anyone in the audience to explain the exact loyalties and motives of the leading characters. There is one person in the movie who is definitely intended to be a hero, but are the villains really villains? Are they even themselves?

The movie stars Hugh Jackman as a brilliant computer hacker named Stanley, who just spent two years in the pen for the crime of hacking a program used by the FBI to snoop on everybody's e-mail. Now he lives in squalor in a house trailer and yearns for the company of his daughter, whose mother inhabits a drunken stupor.

Enter Ginger (Halle Berry), wearing a sexy little red dress, to recruit Stanley as a hacker for a secret project being masterminded by Gabriel Shear (John Travolta). Stanley demurs: He's been forbidden by the courts to touch a computer. She persists, cornering him in a lapdancery and giving him one minute (at gunpoint) to hack into a government computer. He succeeds, of course, and is offered $10 million to work for Gabriel, who is (a) a patriot protecting us from bad guys, (b) a bad guy, (c) a double agent pretending to be either a patriot

or a bad guy, (d) a freelance, (e) Ginger's lover, or (f) Ginger's target. His true identity is even cloudier than that, but I have said enough.

I will, however, discuss the puzzling role of Ginger, the Halle Berry character. She goes through the motions of being the pretty girl who seduces the hero into working for the secret organization. But this is strange, since Stanley shows little interest in her, and Ginger ostensibly belongs to Gabriel. This does not prevent a scene in which Halle Berry bares her breasts to tempt the untemptable Stanley. This scene came as a huge relief because I thought the movies, in their rush to the PG-13 rating, had forgotten about breasts. In the age of computerized sci-fi special effects, beautiful skin finishes a distant second at the box office. Once teenage boys wanted to see Emmanuelle undulating; now they want to see Keanu Reeves levitating.

Swordfish, to be sure, does have great effects. One involves a horrific explosion that seems frozen in time while the camera circles it. It's a great visual moment. Another involves a sequence in which a bus is lifted above the city by a helicopter. There's the obligatory scene in which passengers fall to their deaths out the back of the bus—not exploited as well as in Spielberg's *Jurassic Park 2,* but good enough.

For originality, the best scene is a quieter one. Stanley sits at his computer keyboard and looks at six or eight monitors, hacking away in syncopated rhythm to a song about "50,000 volts of (bleeping)." As he works he talks, his words fitting neatly into the music. The song and the action work nicely together, even if we doubt hackers use their keyboards for percussion.

Dominic Sena directed *Gone in 60 Seconds* last year and is getting better. He can't stop himself from including one absolutely gratuitous car chase, but he takes more time with the plot here, and makes good use of Halle Berry to atone for ignoring Angelina Jolie last summer. He also gets a juicy performance out of Travolta, who opens with a monologue that would have been at home in *Get Shorty,* and plays a character whose dialogue is weirdly persuasive. (He defends his violent actions in hard-boiled realpolitik terms.) I also liked Don Cheadle as an FBI agent who supplies one of the few characters in the movie you can count on to be more or less who he says he is.

I see that I have forgotten to even mention that the movie involves a bank robbery and a hostage crisis. Well, it's that kind of film. The robbery and the crisis weave in and out of the plot like motifs in a symphony; we remember them when they're on-screen, but the movie isn't really about them. It's more about pulling the rug out from under the audience every five minutes or so. There comes a time when you seriously think the characters should wear red or blue shirts to keep from passing to the other team

T

Taboo ★ ★ ★

NO MPAA RATING, 101 m., 2001

Beat Takeshi (Captain Toshizo Hijikata), Ryuhei Matsuda (Samurai Sozaburo Kano), Shinji Takeda (Lieutenant Soji Okita), Tadanobu Asano (Samurai Hyozo Tashiro), Koji Matoba (Samurai Heibei Sugano), Masa Tommies (Inspecteur Jo Yamazaki), Masato Ibu (Officer Koshitaro Ito), Uno Kanda (Geisha Nishikigi-Dayu). Directed by Nagisa Oshima and produced by Eiko Oshima, Shigehiro Nakagawa, and Kazuo Shimizu. Screenplay by Nagisa Oshima, based on novellas by Ryotaro Shiba.

Nagisa Oshima's *Taboo* tells a story set in the late samurai period, when a youth of unusual beauty is admitted into a training program for warriors, stirring lust among his comrades and even a superior officer. When the film premiered at Cannes in May 2000, the joke was that it would be retitled, "Not to ask, not to tell."

Homosexuality in the military is as old as armies, and was sometimes encouraged as a way of inspiring soldiers to bond; we gather that within the closed world of the Japanese samurai, it was acknowledged as a fact of life. The problem with Sozaburo Kano (Ryuhei Matsuda) is not that he is gay, but that he is so beautiful, so feminine, that he is a distraction and inspires jealousy. He seems fully aware of his appeal, and enhances it with a kind of smoldering passivity that dares the other men to start something.

The movie takes place in Kyoto around 1865, in the last days of traditional samurai. Threatened by new kinds of fighting, new channels of power, and the opening of the country to the West, the men of the Shinsen-gumi troop adhere all the more rigidly to the samurai code, even enforcing death as a punishment for severe violations. It is strange that a candidate as effeminate as Sozaburo would be one of two finalists chosen after sword-fighting auditions, but then again there is a look in the eye of Captain Hijikata (Beat Takeshi) that hints of hidden agendas.

When Beat Takeshi directs, it is under his real name of Takeshi Kitano. As director and star, he is known for violent macho thrillers, and so his casting here is provocative; imagine John Wayne in *Red River*, with a stirring beneath his chaps every time he looks at Montgomery Clift. Hijikata is not gay, but Sozaburo is beautiful enough to inspire a lonely man to relax his usual standards. A samurai clearly in love with Sozaburo is Tashiro (Tadanobu Asano), a brawny type who feels competitive because both men were recruited at the same time.

Is Sozaburo capable of fighting well enough to carry his weight in the samurai army? He turns out be the best of the young swordsmen, and when a superior orders him to carry out the execution of a disobedient samurai, he beheads the offender without a blink. The thing about Sozaburo, indeed, is that he hardly blinks at anything: Even while another samurai is having sex with him, he hardly seems to notice.

Is this a weakness of the film? Maybe so. Oshima, directing his first film in fourteen years, has found an actor with the physical attributes to play the character, and seems content to leave it at that; his camera regards Sozaburo as an object of beauty but hardly seems to engage him. It's as if the young samurai is a platonic ideal of androgynous perfection, and the movie is not about him but about his effect on the others.

Nagisa Oshima, born in 1932, was a rebel of the Japanese cinema in the 1960s and 1970s, and is most famous for *In the Realm of the Senses* (1976), the story of a love affair that turned into a sadomasochistic obsession, resulting during one sex scene in the hero's loss of that implement he might most require if he hoped to have another one. So great was the crush to attend that film's Cannes premiere that one critic was shoved through a plate-glass window, luckily escaping the hero's fate. Oshima in recent years has become a Japanese TV star, and this film was a surprise to those who assumed he had more or less retired from filmmaking.

Taboo is not an entirely successful film, but it isn't boring. There is a kind of understated humor in the way the senior samurai officers discuss their troublesome young recruit, and a melancholy in the way the samurais follow their code as they are ceasing to be relevant or useful. I am not even sure it was a mistake to have Sozaburo be so passive. If he were a more active, complex character, that would generate a wider range of issues, and he works better within the plot as a catalyst.

I am reminded of a story told by Donald Richie, the great writer on Japanese themes. *In the Realm of the Senses* was based on a true story of a woman who castrated her lover at his request. After serving a prison sentence, she was hired by a Tokyo tavern to appear nightly. At the given hour, she would descend a flight of stairs, walk across the room, and exit. The room would always be jammed, Richie reports. "There she goes!" the customers would say. The character of Sozaburo seems to serve something of the same function in this movie.

The Tailor of Panama ★ ★ ★ ½
R, 109 m., 2001

Pierce Brosnan (Andy Osnard), Geoffrey Rush (Harry Pendel), Jamie Lee Curtis (Louisa Pendel), Brendan Gleeson (Mickie Abraxas), Catherine McCormack (Francesca), Leonor Varela (Marta), Harold Pinter (Uncle Benny), Daniel Radcliffe (Mark Pendel), David Hayman (Luxmore). Directed and produced by John Boorman. Screenplay by Boorman, Andrew Davies, and John Le Carre, based on the novel by Le Carre.

"Welcome to Panama—Casablanca without heroes."

Not that Casablanca had many heroes. The statement is made by Harry Pendel, a tailor in Panama City, to Andy Osnard, a British spy who for his sins has been posted to this diplomatic dead end. The beauty of John Boorman's *The Tailor of Panama* is that the movie has no heroes, either. It's a cynical, droll story about two con men taking advantage of each other and getting away with it because the British and American governments are begging to be lied to. The casting of Pierce Brosnan as Osnard is the perfect touch: Here's a nasty real-world James Bond with no gadgets and no scruples.

The movie is based on the John Le Carre best-seller, showing that when the Cold War ended, its diplomatic gamesmanship continued as farce. In London, we meet Osnard as an amoral cutup in MI6, a gambler and ladies' man with a gift for embarrassing the agency. He's given a chance to redeem himself with the assignment to Panama, where nothing much is happening, although local mischief picks up considerably under his influence.

His strategy: Pick a member of Panama City's British community and use him as a source and conduit for information. He chooses Harry Pendel (Geoffrey Rush), whose firm, Braithwaite and Pendel, claims to be late of London's Saville Row. Actually, as Osnard finds out, there never was a Braithwaite, and Pendel learned to be a tailor while serving a prison term for arson. By threatening to blow Pendel's cover, Osnard gets him to cooperate in a scheme neither one of them quite admits to the other, in which Pendel will supply information which may be dubious, and Osnard will not scrutinize it too suspiciously.

Both men are pragmatists without ideals, although Pendel at least has an inspiration: the safety and security of his American wife (Jamie Lee Curtis) and their two children. That, and his firm, and his farm that is deeply in debt, are all that matter to him. "Where's your patriotism?" Osnard asks him at one point, and he replies: "I had it out in prison—without an anesthetic."

The movie plays as a joy for lovers of well-written, carefully crafted character thrillers. It has a lot of wry, twisted humor. It depends not on chases and killings, but on devious, greedy connivance in a world where everyone is looking out for himself. Its Panama City is still in shock after the Noriega years, and Pendel (who was the dictator's tailor—but then he's the tailor for everyone who can afford him) is well placed to know what's going on. His wife works for the director of the Panama Canal company, and in his tailor shop, which doubles as a club where gentlemen can drop in for a drink or a cigar, he overhears a great deal, although not as much as he tells Osnard he overhears.

He also has genuine contacts with the hidden side of Panama. His shop assistant, the scarred and fierce Marta (Leonor Varela), was a former member of the anti-Noriega underground. And so was his best friend, the shabby, hard-drinking Mickie Abraxas (Brendan Gleeson, from Boorman's *The General*). Both still hold their political ideals, Mickie loudly and defiantly, which inspires Pendel to invent a fictitious radical political movement, which Osnard believes in for reasons of his own.

Osnard, meanwhile, has his eye, and hands, on Francesca (Catherine McCormack), a sexy official in the British embassy, while feeding her boss (David Hayman) his colorful information. Secrets create a vacuum that only more secrets can fill, and soon Osnard is making demands on Pendel, whose wife presumably knows the secrets of the canal company—although not the secrets Pendel invents and passes along.

This round-robin of cynicism and deception takes place against a city of nightclubs and B-girl bars, residential areas and city streets lined with "laundromats" (banks), embassies and the cozy confines of Pendel's shop. Boorman and Le Carre (his executive producer) were wise to shoot the exteriors on location in Panama, where the tropical look makes the overheated schemes seem right at home.

Many thrillers are essentially machines to inject a shock into the audience every few minutes. *The Tailor of Panama* is a real movie, rich and atmospheric, savoring its disreputable characters and their human weaknesses. And there's room for genuine emotion, too, in the way Harry Pendel desperately holds onto the respectability he has conjured out of thin air. And in the way the stubborn, heedless Mickie Abraxas says what he thinks no matter what the risk. The movie is abundant in its gifts, a pleasure for those who like a story to unfold lovingly over a full arc, instead of coming in short, mindless bursts.

The Tao of Steve ★ ★ ★
PG-13, 90 m., 2000

Donal Logue (Dex), Greer Goodman (Syd), Kimo Wills (Dave), Ayelet Kaznelson (Beth), David Aaron Baker (Rick), Nina Jaroslaw (Maggie), John Hines (Ed), Selby Craig (Chris), Craig D. Lafayette (Matt). Directed by Jenniphr Goodman and produced by Anthony Bregman. Screenplay by Duncan North with Greer Goodman and Jenniphr Goodman.

"Men and women both want to have sex, but women want to have sex fifteen minutes after us, so if you hold out for twenty, she'll be chasing you for five."

This is the wisdom of Dex, the hero of *The Tao of Steve*, who seems to get a lot of sex, considering he is a fat, thirty-two-year-old grade school teacher who shares the rent with three roommates, wears only a bathrobe whenever he possibly can, and has a dog that can intercept whipped cream sprayed directly from the can.

Dex (Donal Logue) lives in Santa Fe, where at his college reunion he makes love with an old girlfriend in the stacks of the library, then returns her glowing to her husband. Other old girlfriends gossip behind his back: "I can't believe how much weight he's gained." And they confront him about it. "You were Elvis!" one says accusingly. "Yeah," he says. "Well, now I'm fat Elvis."

But Dex has no trouble getting girls, and is happy to offer advice to his friends, in long talks spiked with references to Thomas Aquinas and Steve McQueen. He likes the name "Steve." To him, it represents all that is cool in life—the smooth, the lithe, the brave. He rattles off names: "Steve McQueen, Steve McGarrett, Steve Austin." (The least cool name, in case you were wondering, is Stu.) Playing pool and drinking beers, he explains his seductive techniques to guys who are thinner but hornier. There are three rules:

1. Eliminate your desire ("Women can smell an agenda").
2. Be excellent in their presence (even if it's only at throwing a Frisbee).
3. Withdraw (this is illustrated by the twenty-minute strategy).

Like many Don Juans, including Don Juan himself, Dex spends more time talking about sex than experiencing it. Then he's blindsided by Syd (Greer Goodman), who is in town as a set designer for the Sante Fe Opera, and catches his eye and tugs at his heart. He likes her. He likes her so much he desires her, which is against the rules. He desires her so much he allows her to sense his desire, which leads to the shattering revelation that they have *already* had sex—years ago, in college—and she remembers it but he doesn't, which is not being cool like Steve.

The Tao of Steve is an easygoing but bright

comedy that focuses on Donal Logue's effortless charm (he won the Best Actor Award at Sundance). It creates the feeling of settling in comfortably with old friends, and no wonder: Greer Goodman is not only the costar but cowrote the screenplay with her sister, Jenniphr Goodman, who is the director. It contains the insight, common to all stories about theories of love, that these theories never work out in practice, and eventually Dex is just as needy as some poor jerk who doesn't have the benefit of his deep wisdom.

One of the things I like about the movie is the wit of its dialogue, the way sentences and conversations coil with confidence up to a conclusion that is totally unexpected. It's the same sort of verbal humor I'm enjoying right now in the novel I'm reading, *A Heartbreaking Work of Staggering Genius* by Dave Eggers. So much dialogue, in print and on the screen, is machined to serve the plot. You don't often get the impression the people are really talking. Logue and the other actors here have the kind of back-and-forth timing of friends who have been kidding around for a long time, who know each other's timing, who have created entertaining personas for themselves.

Of course, all stories like this eventually come down to *commitment,* a word that strikes a chill into the heart of any man who lives in a bathrobe and feeds his dog out of the whipped cream can. Dex has his theories about it ("Don Giovanni slept with 1,000 women because he was afraid he wouldn't be loved by one"), but in practice, as Syd helps him to understand, you sooner or later have to make your choice, or you end up counting flowers on the wall.

Note: If there is one suspicion I have about the film, it's that Donal Logue is not as fat as the character he plays. At Sundance, he didn't exactly look underfed, but he didn't have that tire around his middle, and my best guess is that's padding. That may help to explain why he refuses to take off his shirt in the movie. If it isn't, that may also explain it.

Tape ★ ★ ★ ½
R, 86 m., 2001

Ethan Hawke (Vince), Robert Sean Leonard (Johnny), Uma Thurman (Amy). Directed by Richard Linklater and produced by Gary Winick, Alexis Alexanian, and Anne Walker-McBay. Screenplay by Stephen Belber, based on his stage play.

Tape made me believe that its events could happen to real people more or less as they appear on the screen, and that is its most difficult accomplishment. To describe the movie makes it sound like an exercise in artifice: Three characters, one motel room, all talk, based on a stage play. But the writing, acting, and direction are so convincing that at some point I stopped thinking about the constraints and started thinking about the movie's freedoms: freedom from idiocy, first of all, since the characters are all smart and articulate, and testing one another's nerves and values. Freedom from big, gassy, meaningless events. Freedom from the tyranny of an overbearing sound track that wants to feel everything for us. Freedom from the expected.

For Ethan Hawke, Robert Sean Leonard, and Uma Thurman, making this movie must have been scary. They have nowhere to run. The motel room is small, and they can't hide from the camera. Small moments must be real because there's nothing to cover them up. Against that is the flexibility of shooting in high-def video, which allows Maryse Alberti's camera to turn and stare and advance and recoil, commanding the space. This is not one of those films on video where the handheld camera gawks like a nervous home movie. The movements of the actors and camera are thoughtfully blocked, and the result is the *feeling* of spontaneous shooting, rather than its jumpy, handheld reality.

The movie opens with Vince (Hawke) alone in the room, obviously preparing for something. He chugs beers, arranges the furniture, takes off his pants and shirt, and somehow lets us know with body language this is part of a strategy. There's a knock on the door and Johnny (Leonard) enters. They went to high school together a decade ago. Now Johnny is in town (Lansing, Michigan) to show his film in a film festival, and Vince is—what? Attending the festival? In town by a coincidence and heard Johnny was around? It's clear that Johnny, who tries to seem very happy to see his old friend, is not sure.

Conversation. Johnny is confident, balanced,

sound. Vince, who snorts some cocaine, is spacy, but not as spacy as he seems. He guides the conversation around to memories of Amy (Uma Thurman), who was Vince's first love. Vince and Amy never made love, however, and that still hurts Vince, although not as much as the fact that Johnny and Amy did make love, during a brief, meaningless fling at the end of senior year. Or—was it love?

Vince batters at Johnny like a prosecutor. Hawke is brilliant in these scenes, which seem loose but, in retrospect, are as controlled as a chess game. Watching his control of body and voice as he flings himself around the room, intimidating Johnny with his command of the space, we see both physical and verbal acting mastery. Johnny's self-possession fades, and he finally makes an admission. But is his admission to be believed? Is he a reliable witness to his own misconduct?

Amy knocks. A surprise to Johnny. And Johnny is a surprise to her. And now Vince's plan becomes clear, with the introduction of a tape that (a) belongs to Vince, (b) contains Johnny's memories, and (c) involves Amy's past. So who should the tape belong to? Who does the past belong to? Who gets to say what it means? Is what happened then as important as what happens now?

In a lesser film, the conflict would be between Vince and Johnny—two boys fighting over the same girl, as she looks dutifully back and forth like a spectator at a tennis match. But she is more than a match for them, and besides, this is a struggle of ethics, not gender. No one is clearly right or wrong. The same information, viewed through different prisms, shifts righteousness from one character to another.

The screenplay by Stephen Belber is based on his own play, which in superficial ways resembles the battle in Mamet's *Oleanna*. Both films are about how the same events can be interpreted differently through male and female eyes. But Mamet is angry and has a point of view—two points of view, really—while Belber's *subject* is points of view. And sneaking along underneath the argument about what happened on that long-ago night is the question of who has the right to make use of it now.

Richard Linklater, the director, has had quite a year. This film follows quickly on the heels of his *Waking Life,* and both films show a director using video instead of being used by it. In *Waking Life* he used video footage as a starting point for an animated film of startling innovation. In *Tape,* he uses video as a way to move intimately and freely through a three-way conversation. Neither film is dominated by its style; both are about their ideas, and the style is at the service of the ideas. For audiences they are stimulating; for other filmmakers, instruction manuals about how to use the tricky new tools.

The Taste of Others ★ ★ ★
NO MPAA RATING, 112 m., 2001

Jean-Pierre Bacri (Castella), Anne Alvaro (Clara), Christiane Millet (Angelique), Brigitte Catillon (Beatrice), Alain Chabat (Deschamps), Agnes Jaoui (Manie), Gérard Lanvin (Moreno), Anne Le Ny (Valerie). Directed by Agnes Jaoui and produced by Christian Berard and Charles Gassot. Screenplay by Jaoui and Jean-Pierre Bacri.

Finding out somebody has bad taste is like discovering he needs dental work. Things were fine until he opened his mouth. Of course, your good taste might be my bad taste, and vice versa. For example, I know there are people who don't go to foreign films, and I am patient with them, as I would be with a child: With luck, they may evolve into more interesting beings. And then they could think about the lessons of *The Taste of Others.*

This is a film about a busy industrialist named Castella (Jean-Pierre Bacri) who is blindsided by love and idealism. As the movie opens his life is affluent but uninspiring. He is surrounded by material comforts, all of them dictated by his wife, an interior decorator. She is the kind of woman who, when she says something loving and affectionate, he has to look up to see if she's talking to him or the dog.

Castella signs up for English lessons, but is impatient at the work required; he gets stuck on the pronunciation of "the." He asks the teacher if she doesn't have a "fun" way to learn English. She doesn't, so he fires her. That night, his wife drags him kicking and screaming to a local dramatic production, and he falls in love with the leading actress. This is, of course, the very same woman who was the English teacher, but at first he doesn't realize that, because now she is surrounded by the aura of Art.

He pursues the actress, named Clara (Anne Alvaro). She is fortyish, attractive but not beautiful, a member of the artsy-fartsy set in their provincial town. She, of course, is not attracted to Castella, who has crass tastes and materialistic values and has led the life of money rather than the life of the mind. But he persists. He sends her flowers. He turns up everywhere. When she doesn't like his dorky mustache, he shaves it off. The movie doesn't present this simply as a romantic infatuation, but goes the additional step: It sees that Castella is in love not only with Clara, but with what she represents: the life of the arts, of the theater, of ideas, of questioning things, of developing your own taste. We are reminded of Jack Nicholson in *As Good as It Gets*, when he tells Helen Hunt, "I love you because you make me want to be a better man."

Meanwhile, things are shaky on the home front. Castella sees a painting he likes, brings it home, and hangs it on the wall. Whether it's a good painting is beside the point: It is *his* painting. When his wife rejects it in horror, he says very quietly, "Angelique . . . I like this picture," and those are words she should listen to very carefully if she values their marriage.

There's a parallel relationship in the movie between Castella's bodyguard, Moreno (Gerard Lanvin), and the barmaid Manie (played by Agnes Jaoui, the film's director). Manie sells hashish as a sideline, and Moreno disapproves. This, too, is a matter of taste: Anyone who sells drugs is telling you something about themselves that you don't want to know more about. The difference is, you can stop selling drugs, but you may never be able to tell a good painting from a bad one, or know why the decor of a living room should not hurt the eyes. Castella continues his lonely quest, uneasily joining Clara and her bohemian friends in the café they frequent after performances of the play, and eventually—well, people evolve, and taste involves not only judging superficial things, but being able to see beneath them.

One of the delights of *The Taste of Others* is that it is so smart and wears its intelligence lightly. Films about taste are not often made by Hollywood, perhaps because it would so severely limit the box office to require the audience to have any. *The Taste of Others* will be all but impenetrable to anyone unable to appreciate what's going on under the dialogue, under the action, down there at the level where we instinctively make judgments based on taste, style, and judgment. It's not, of course, that there's a right or wrong about taste. It's more that your taste defines the kinds of people who want to share it with you. Here's a test: If, as your taste evolves over a lifetime, you find that it attracts more interesting friends, you're on the right track.

The Terrorist ★ ★ ★ ½
NO MPAA RATING, 95 m., 2000

Ayesha Dharkar (Malli), Parmeshwaran (Vasu), Vishnu Vardhan (Thyagu), Bhanu Prakash (Perumal), Vinshwa (Lotus). Directed by Santosh Sivan and produced by Jit Joshi and A. Sreekar Prasad. Screenplay by Sivan, Ravi Deshpande, and Vijay Deveshwar. In Tamil with English subtitles.

She is nineteen years old and a soldier in a revolutionary movement. Her brother has died for the cause, and she has killed for it. A volunteer is needed for a suicide mission. She steps forward, fiercely and silently, and is accepted. She will become a "thinking bomb," and after she places a garland of flowers around a politician's neck, she will blow them both to pieces.

The Terrorist does not name its time or place, or the politician, but it seems broadly inspired by the 1991 assassination of India's Rajiv Gandhi. It is not a political film, but a personal one. If you have ever wondered what kind of person volunteers to become a human bomb, and what they think about in the days before their death, this film wonders too.

And its director, Santosh Sivan, does something filmmakers find almost impossible. It follows this young woman without identifying with her mission. We do not want her to succeed. Films are such a first-person medium—they identify so strongly with their protagonists—that they generate sympathy even for evil: Did we want Hannibal Lecter to escape? Of course we did. And at the end of *The Day of the Jackal* (1973) we instinctively wanted the assassin to succeed, simply because we had been following him for two hours. Of course we think murder is wrong, but fiction tends to argue for its heroes. Consider *Crime and Punishment*.

In *The Terrorist*, we do not want the young girl, named Malli, to succeed. That's despite the way the movie paints her loyalty to her cause, and the possibility that her cause is right. The movie is quiet and persuasive as it shows Malli learning more about her life in what may be her last days than she ever knew before.

Played by Ayesha Dharkar, a young actress with expressive eyes and a beauty that is innate, not cosmetic, Malli doesn't talk much, and we sense that she has deep wounds; her brother's death in the same cause suggests a painful background. After she volunteers for the mission, she is passed along an underground network of conspirators to the farm where she will spend her final days. One of her guides is a boy of thirteen or fourteen named Lotus (Vinshwa), who leads her down the center of a shallow river and shows her where to step to avoid land mines and booby traps. He has guided many others this way, he says; they have all later been killed. When a truck blows up, he weeps: "There will be blood everywhere." No more than a child, he is traumatized by his life.

Also on the journey she meets a young soldier who is mortally wounded. In a scene of great delicacy, she cradles him on the forest floor, and he whispers that he has never been so close to a woman in his life. Nor, we sense, has she ever been so close to a man. Just as Sivan makes a movie that does not identify with its violent mission, so he creates a love scene that is not about sex, but communication, surcease, healing.

Eventually Malli arrives at a farm and is given a room of her own. We meet the farmer Vasu (Parmeshwaran) and his helper. These are characters to remind us of the gentle humor of the great Indian novelist R. K. Narayan. Their philosophy and religion is a part of their lives, and the farmer tells Malli: "A flower is the earth smiling." He always sets an extra place at dinner for his wife, who is in a coma and has not stirred for seven years. Malli sees the woman in the room next to her own, staring sightlessly at nothing.

Malli's terrorist contact and his sidekick rehearse her carefully, and select clothing that

will conceal the bomb strapped around her middle. They are narrow functionaries, telling her that news of her action will go out to all the world. It is unclear if the farmer knows of her mission (I think he doesn't). He argues for life, not in words so much as in how he conducts his own life.

Malli says little in the film. Sometimes the sound track uses the sound of quiet breathing, which places us inside her head. She regards herself in the mirror, and we intuit what she's thinking. Conversations she has with the farmer put her action in a new light, with new consequences. All leads up to an ending that is the right ending for this film, although few members of the audience will anticipate it.

There is no shortage of those prepared to sacrifice their lives to kill others and advance their cause. If we disagree with them, they are fanatics. If we agree, they are heroes. At least they are personally involved and prepared to pay with their lives, which in a sense is more ethical than killing by remote control at long distance and calling it "modern warfare."

But what do they think? How do they feel? I've often wondered what goes through the mind of a condemned prisoner, who knows the exact hour of his death. How much stranger it must seem to be your own willing executioner: to die voluntarily because an idea is bigger than yourself. In my mind, the self is the biggest of all ideas; without it, there are no ideas. Does Malli arrive at this conclusion?

The Third Miracle ★ ★ ★
R, 119 m., 2000

Ed Harris (Father Frank Shore), Anne Heche (Roxanne), Armin Mueller-Stahl (Archbishop Werner), Barbara Sukowa (Helen O'Regan), Ken James (Father Paul Panak), James Gallanders (Brother Gregory), Caterina Scorsone (Maria Witkowski), Michael Rispoli (John Leone). Directed by Agnieszka Holland and produced by Fred Fuchs, Steven Haft, and Elie Samaha. Screenplay by John Romano and Richard Vetere, based on the novel by Vetere.

Here is a rarity, a film about religion that is neither pious nor sensational, simply curious. No satanic possessions, no angelic choirs, no evil spirits, no lovers joined beyond the grave.

Just a man doing his job. The man is Father Frank Shore, and he is a postulator—a priest assigned to investigate the possibility that someone was a saint. If he is convinced, he goes before a church tribunal and argues the case against another priest whose job is popularly known as "the devil's advocate."

Ed Harris plays Frank Shore as a man with many doubts of his own. After deflating one popular candidate for sainthood, he became known as "the miracle killer," and in his dark moments he broods that he "destroyed the faith of an entire community." Now perhaps he will have to do it again. It is 1979, in a devout Chicago ethnic community, and a statue weeps blood every November. That is the month of the death of a woman named Helen O'Regan (Barbara Sukowa), who is credited with healing young Maria Witkowski, dying of lupus.

Was Helen indeed a saint? Is the statue weeping real blood? What blood type? Father Shore is far from an ideal priest. We first see him working in a soup kitchen, having left more mainstream duties in a crisis of faith. Maybe he doesn't believe in much of anything anymore—except that the case of Helen O'Regan deserves a clear and unprejudiced investigation.

Many a saint has made it onto holy cards with somewhat dubious credentials (Did Patrick really drive the snakes from Ireland? Did Christopher really carry Jesus on his shoulders?). But in recent centuries the church has become rigorous in recognizing miracles and canonizing saints—so rigorous that the American church has produced only three saints. In an age when many churches scorn science and ask members to simply believe, the Catholic Church retains the rather brave notion that religion really exists in the physical world, that miracles really happen and can be logically investigated.

The Third Miracle, directed by Agnieszka Holland, has been written by John Romano and Richard Vetere, and based on Vetere's novel. It has no scenes of Arnold Schwarzenegger trying to prevent Satan from impregnating a virgin with the Antichrist. Instead, it is about church politics, and about a priest who doubts himself more than his faith.

His life only grows more complicated when he meets Roxanne O'Regan (Anne Heche), the daughter of the dead candidate for sainthood. There is a delicate scene at her mother's grave, where she and the priest have joined over a bottle of vodka to celebrate Helen's birthday. Their dialogue does that dance two people perform when they seem to be talking objectively but are really flirting. Finally Roxanne asks Frank if he believes all the church stuff. He asks her why she wants to know. "Because I can tell you like this," she says, on exactly the right note of teasing and invitation.

Ah, but the infallible church is made of fallible men. Frank can harbor doubts and lusts and nevertheless think his job is worth doing. Up against him is the fleshy, contemptuous Archbishop Werner (Armin Mueller-Stahl), the devil's advocate, who thinks three saints are quite enough for America. And then there is the problem of Maria Witkowski (Caterina Scorsone), who may have been cured of lupus but now is on life support after drug abuse and prostitution. "God wasted a miracle!" her mother cries.

Agnieszka Holland is a director whose films embody a grave intelligence; her credits include *Europa, Europa,* about a Jewish boy who conceals his religion to survive the Holocaust; *The Secret Garden,* based on the classic about a girl adrift in a house full of family secrets; and *Washington Square,* Henry James's novel about an heiress who is courted for her money. She pays close attention to the emotional weather of her characters, and is helped here by Ed Harris, whose priest talks as if he has finally decided to say something he's been thinking about for a long time, and Anne Heche, whose Roxanne approaches sexuality like a loaded gun.

In *The Third Miracle* Holland is not much interested in getting us to believe in miracles, or in whether Father Frank is true to his vow of chastity. She is concerned more with the way institutions interact with the emotions of their members. People *need* to believe in miracles, which is why, paradoxically, they resent those who investigate them. Believers aren't interested in proof one way or the other: They want validation. The fact that the church has refused to recognize the appearances of the Virgin at Medjugorje has done nothing to discourage the crowds of faithful tourists. There is a temptation (literally) for the church to go along with popular fancy and endorse the enthusiasms of the faithful. But to applaud bogus saints would be an insult to the real ones.

As Father Shore and Archbishop Werner face each other across a table in a board room, they are like antagonists in any global corporation. They would like to introduce a miraculous new product, but must be sure it will not damage the stock of the company. By seeing the church as an earthly institution and its priests as men doing their best to remain logical in the face of popular ecstasy, *The Third Miracle* puts Hollywood's pop spirituality to shame.

Thirteen ★ ★ ★ ½
NO MPAA RATING, 87 m., 2000

Wilhamenia Dickens (Nina), Lillian Folley (Lillian), Don Semmens (Artist), Michael Aytes (Michael), Michael Jeffrey (Social Worker), Dawn Tinsley (Social Worker), David Scales (Lillian's Male Friend), Doug Washington (Nina's Uncle). Directed and produced by David D. Williams. Screenplay by Williams.

Summon if you will the sound of a voice telling a favorite story. The details are well known to the other listeners, but not to you. The story is about a young girl much loved and worried about. It has been rehearsed in other tellings, and shaped by memory so that it reflects the girl's personality as much as the events. The tone of that story is the tone of *Thirteen*.

The person telling the story is Lillian (Lillian Folley). The story is about her thirteen-year-old daughter, Nina (Wilhamenia Dickens). Nina is just at that age when talkative kids turn into brooding and unpredictable teenagers. One day Nina disappears from home, and there is a search for her. Neighbors, friends, and the police get involved, and then Nina turns up again.

The movie tells this story in a documentary style. It is fiction, but the actors are basically playing themselves. It was written, produced, directed, photographed, and edited by David D. Williams, a Virginia filmmaker, and the actors are his neighbors. Lillian is an old friend. Watching this movie is not like being confronted with the determination of a plot. It is like sitting in a rocking chair on the porch while Lillian tells the story once again, and everybody smiles, even Nina.

The film is not angry, experimental, or confrontational, and no more fits in the underground or "indie" categories as in the mainstream. That's because it exists in no tradition. It is unique, the expression of particular voices, a deep understanding of the characters, and an interest in who they are.

I saw *Thirteen* for the first time in 1998 at the Virginia Film Festival in Charlottesville. In 1999, I invited it to my first Overlooked Film Festival in Urbana, Illinois. In the spring of that year, David Williams won the Someone to Watch Award at the Independent Spirit Awards in Santa Monica, California—given by other independent filmmakers to a new voice they wanted to recognize. Every time I have seen the film with an audience, it has created its spell. We are freed of contrivance, and allowed into lives.

From Virginia I wrote:

Nina is not a talkative girl. She keeps to herself. One senses that her imagination is so populated that outsiders are not needed. One also senses that at some point in her life she put up a wall. Not one of those unscalable walls of mental illness, but a temporary wall, like you find around construction sites.

Nina and Lillian live within the rhythms of an extended African-American family, where telephone calls form a network to keep everyone updated on everyone else, right down to distant cousins and the relatives of ex-spouses. Neighbors and relatives are in and out of the house all day, and in times of emergency they turn up unbidden to see how they can help.

For Lillian, Nina is a fascinating case study. She observes her, speculates about her, reports on her activities. When Nina disappears there is a search—but *Thirteen* doesn't traffic in the false alarms of conventional cinema. We know all along where Nina has gone. And the manner of her return supplies the trigger that all moviegoers know: That moment when you stir and say to yourself that this is going to be a good film.

The movie contains a lot of humor, quiet and understated. Nina wants to buy a car. She is thirteen and cannot drive, but Lillian accepts her ambition as Nina works at every job she can find to make money. She's blunt and direct with her employers, isn't shy to apply for grown-up jobs, asks for a higher salary, studies car magazines. Boys aren't in the picture yet. She is a freestanding, self-contained original. There is no attempt to ingratiate her with the audience.

In real life, Wilhamenia came to Lillian as a foster child, and was later adopted. They do live together in the house we see. But the characters in the movie are not quite the same as the actors, and the director is the third collaborator, using them to reflect larger truths about relationships.

All of this provides an incomplete picture of the film, I know, but it doesn't reduce easily to description. David D. Williams earlier made a documentary about Lillian, a neighbor, and then began this film, which is fiction based on the facts of the two women's personalities. It's not exactly improvised, he said, there was an outline, but no written dialogue, and many of the moments occur spontaneously.

The result is one of the truest films I've seen about the ebb and flow of a real relationship. Not one pumped up by a plot and a crisis and resolution, but one in which time flows and small changes accumulate. It's not a question of coming to the conclusion, but of starting a new chapter. *Thirteen* focused my attention the way the films of Robert Bresson do, challenging me to look into Nina and guess what she was thinking, and what deeper feelings were manifesting themselves in her comings and goings and her dream of a car.

Thirteen Conversations About One Thing ★ ★ ★ ★
R, 102 m., 2002

Matthew McConaughey (Troy), John Turturro (Walker), Alan Arkin (Gene), Clea DuVall (Beatrice), Amy Irving (Patricia), Barbara Sukowa (Helen), William Wise (Wade). Directed by Jill Sprecher and produced by Beni Atoori and Gina Resnick. Screenplay by Jill and Karen Sprecher.

Happiness is the subject of *Thirteen Conversations About One Thing*. For that matter, happi-

ness is the subject of every conversation we ever have: the search for happiness, the envy of happiness, the loss of happiness, the guilt about undeserved happiness. The engine that drives the human personality is our desire to be happy instead of sad, entertained instead of bored, inspired instead of disillusioned, informed rather than ignorant. It is not an easy business.

Consider Troy (Matthew McConaughey), the prosecutor who has just won a big conviction. In the movie's opening scene, he's loud and obnoxious in a saloon, celebrating his victory. He spots a sad sack at the bar: Gene (Alan Arkin), who seems to be pessimistic about the possibility of happiness. Gene is a midlevel manager at an insurance company, has to fire someone, and decides to fire Wade, the happiest man in the department, since he can see the sunny side of anything.

Troy buys drinks for Gene. He wants everybody to be happy. Then he drives drunk, hits a pedestrian with his car, and believes he has killed her. As an assistant district attorney he knows how much trouble he's in, and instinctively leaves the scene. His problem becomes an all-consuming guilt, which spoils his ability to enjoy anything in life; he was cut in the accident, and keeps the wound open with a razor blade to punish himself.

The movie finds connections between people who think they are strangers, finding the answer to one person's problem in the question raised by another. We meet Walker (John Turturro), a sardonic college professor, who walks out on his wife (Amy Irving) and begins an affair with a woman (Barbara Sukowa). She realizes that the affair is hardly the point: Walker is going through the motions because he has been told, and believes, that this is how you find happiness. We also meet a house cleaner (Clea DuVall), who is good at her job but works for a client who can only criticize. She is injured for no reason at all, suffers great pain, does not deserve to.

The truth hidden below the surface of the story is a hard one: Nothing makes any sense. We do not get what we deserve. If we are lucky, we get more. If we are unlucky, we get less. Bad things happen to good people, and good things happen to bad people. That's the system. All of our philosophies are a futile attempt to explain it. Let me tell you a story. Not long ago I was in the middle of a cheerful conversation when I slipped on wet wax, landed hard and broke bones in my left shoulder. I was in a fool's paradise of happiness, you see, not realizing that I was working without a net—that in a second my happiness would be rudely interrupted.

I could have hit my head and been killed. Or landed better and not been injured. At best what we can hope for is a daily reprieve from all of the things that can go wrong. *Thirteen Conversations About One Thing* is relentless in the way it demonstrates how little we control our lives. We can choose actions, but we cannot plan outcomes. Follow, for example, the consequences of Alan Arkin's decision to fire the happy man, and then see what happens to Arkin, and then see what happens to the happy man. Or watch as the Matthew McConaughey character grants reality to something he only thinks he knows. Or see how the Turturro character, so obsessed with his personal timetable, so devoted to his daily and weekly routines, is able to arrange everything to his satisfaction—and then is not satisfied.

The movie is brilliant, really. It is philosophy illustrated through everyday events. Most movies operate as if their events are necessary—that B must follow A. *Thirteen Conversations* betrays B, A, and all the other letters as random possibilities.

The film was directed by Jill Sprecher, and written with her sister, Karen. It's their second, after *Clockwatchers* (1997), the lacerating, funny story about temporary workers in an office and their strategies to prove they exist in a world that is utterly indifferent to them. After these two movies, there aren't many filmmakers whose next film I anticipate more eagerly. They're onto something. They're using films to demonstrate something to us. Movies tell narratives, and the purpose of narrative is to arrange events in an order that seems to make sense and end correctly. The Sprechers are telling us if we believe in these narratives we're only fooling ourselves.

And yet, even so, there is a way to find happiness. That is to be curious about all of the interlocking events that add up to our lives. To notice connections. To be amused or perhaps frightened by the ways things work out. If the universe is indifferent, what a consolation that we are not.

Thirteen Days ★ ★ ★
PG-13, 135 m., 2001

Kevin Costner (Kenny O'Donnell), Bruce Greenwood (John F. Kennedy), Steven Culp (Robert Kennedy), Dylan Baker (Robert McNamara), Henry Strozier (Dean Rusk), Kevin Conway (General Curtis LeMay), Len Cariou (Dean Acheson). Directed by Roger Donaldson and produced by Marc Abraham, Peter O. Almond, Armyan Bernstein, Kevin Costner, and Kevin O'Donnell. Screenplay by David Self, based on a book by Ernest R. May and Philip D. Zelikow.

The 1962 Cuban missile crisis was the closest we've come to a world nuclear war. Khrushchev installed Russian missiles in Cuba, ninety miles from Florida and within striking distance of 80 million Americans. Kennedy told him to remove them, or else. As Russian ships with more missiles moved toward Cuba, a U.S. Navy blockade was set up to stop them. The world waited.

At the University of Illinois, I remember classes being suspended or ignored as we crowded around TV sets and the ships drew closer in the Atlantic. There was a real possibility that nuclear bombs might fall in the next hour. And then Walter Cronkite had the good news: The Russians had turned back. Secretary of State Dean Rusk famously said, "We went eyeball to eyeball, and I think the other fellow just blinked."

The most controversial assertion of Roger Donaldson's *Thirteen Days*, an intelligent new political thriller, is that the guys who blinked were not only the Russians, but also America's own military commanders—who backed down not from Soviet ships but from the White House. The Joint Chiefs of Staff and Air Force general Curtis LeMay are portrayed as rabid hawks itching for a fight. It's up to presidential adviser Kenny O'Donnell (Kevin Costner) and Secretary of Defense Robert McNamara (Dylan Baker) to face down the top brass, who are portrayed as boys eager to play with nuclear toys. "This is a setup," O'Donnell warns President Kennedy (Bruce Greenwood). If fighting breaks out at a low level, say with Castro shooting at an American spy plane, "the chiefs will force us to start shooting."

This version of events, the viewer should be aware, may owe more to the mechanics of screenwriting than to the annals of history. In a movie where the enemy (Khrushchev) is never seen, living and breathing antagonists are a convenience on the screen, and when McNamara and a trigger-happy admiral get into a shouting match it's possible to forget they're both supposed to be good guys. Yet the cold war mentality did engender military paranoia, generals like LeMay were eager to blast the commies, and Kennedy was seen by his detractors as a little soft. "Kennedy's father was one of the architects of Munich," grumbles Dean Acheson, Truman's secretary of state and an architect of the cold war. "Let's hope appeasement doesn't run in the family."

My own feeling is that serious students of the missile crisis will not go to this movie for additional scholarship, and that for the general public it will play, like Oliver Stone's *JFK*, as a parable: Things might not have happened exactly like this, but it sure did feel like they did. I am not even much bothered by the decision to tell the story through the eyes of Kenneth O'Donnell, who according to Kennedy scholars can barely be heard on White House tapes made during the crisis, and doesn't figure significantly in most histories of the event. He functions in the movie as a useful fly on the wall, a man free to be where the president isn't and think thoughts the president can't. (Full disclosure: O'Donnell's son Kevin, the Earthlink millionaire, is an investor in the company of *Thirteen Days* producer Armyan Bernstein.)

Costner plays O'Donnell as a White House jack of all trades, a close adviser whose office adjoins the Oval Office. He has deep roots with the Kennedys. He was Bobby's roommate at Harvard and Jack's campaign manager, he is an utterly loyal confidant, and in the movie he helps save civilization by sometimes taking matters into his own hands. When the Joint Chiefs are itching for an excuse to fight, he urges one pilot to "look through this thing to the other side"—code for asking him to lie to his superiors rather than trigger a war.

The movie's taut, flat style is appropriate for a story that is more about facts and speculation than about action. Kennedy and his advisers study high-altitude photos and intelli-gence reports, and wonder if Khrushchev's word can be trusted. Everything depends on what they decide. The movie shows men in unknotted ties and shirtsleeves, grasping coffee cups or whiskey glasses and trying to sound rational while they are at some level terrified. What the Kennedy team realizes, and hopes the other side realizes, is that the real danger is that someone will strike first out of fear of striking second.

The movie cuts to military scenes—air bases, ships at sea—but only for information, not for scenes that will settle the plot. In the White House, operatives like O'Donnell make quiet calls to their families, aware they may be saying good-bye forever, that the "evacuation plans" are meaningless except as morale boosters. As Kennedy, Bruce Greenwood is vaguely a look-alike and sound-alike, but like Anthony Hopkins in *Nixon*, he gradually takes on the persona of the character, and we believe him. Steven Culp makes a good Bobby Kennedy, sharp-edged and protective of his brother, and Dylan Baker's resemblance to McNamara is uncanny.

I call the movie a thriller, even though the outcome is known, because it plays like one. We may know that the world doesn't end, but the players in this drama don't, and it is easy to identify with them. They have so much more power than knowledge, and their hunches and guesses may be more useful than war game theories. Certainly past experience is not a guide, because no war will have started or ended like this one.

Donaldson and Costner have worked together before, on *No Way Out* (1987), about a staff member of the secretary of defense. That one was a more traditional thriller, with sex and murders; this time they find almost equal suspense in what's essentially a deadly chess game. In the long run, national defense consists of not blowing everything up in the name of national defense. Suppose nobody had blinked in 1962 and missiles had been fired. Today we would be missing most of the people of Cuba, Russia, and the U.S. Eastern Seaboard, and there'd be a lot of poison in the air. That would be our victory. Yes, Khrushchev was reckless to put the missiles in Cuba, and Kennedy was right to want them out. But it's a good thing somebody blinked.

13 Ghosts ★
R, 90 m., 2001

Tony Shalhoub (Arthur), Embeth Davidtz (Kalina), Matthew Lillard (Rafkin), Shannon Elizabeth (Kathy), Rah Digga (Maggie), J. R. Bourne (Ben Moss), F. Murray Abraham (Cyrus), Alec Roberts (Bobby). Directed by Steve Beck and produced by Gilbert Adler and Dan Cracchiolo. Screenplay by Neal Stevens and Richard D'Ovidio.

13 Ghosts is the loudest movie since *Armageddon*. Flash frames attack the eyeballs while the theater trembles with crashes, bangs, shatters, screams, rumbles, and roars. Forget about fighting the ghosts; they ought to attack the sub-woofer.

The experience of watching the film is literally painful. It hurts the eyes and ears. Aware that their story was thin, that their characters were constantly retracing the same ground and repeating the same words, that the choppy editing is visually incoherent, maybe the filmmakers thought if they turned up the volume the audience might be deceived into thinking something was happening.

When the action pauses long enough for us to see what's on the screen, we have to admire the art direction, special effects, costumes, and makeup. This is a movie that is all craft and little art. It mostly takes place inside a house that is one of the best-looking horror sets I've seen, and the twelve ghosts look like pages from *Heavy Metal*, brought to grotesque life. (The thirteenth ghost is, of course, the key to the mystery.)

The screenplay, inspired by the 1960 William Castle film of the same name but written in a zone all its own, involves dead Uncle Cyrus (F. Murray Abraham), whose research into the occult included a medieval manuscript allegedly dictated by the devil. He leaves his house to his nephew Arthur (Tony Shalhoub), whose wife has tragically died; Arthur moves in with his son, Bobby (Alec Roberts), his daughter, Kathy (Shannon Elizabeth), and Maggie the Nanny (Rah Digga). They're joined by a wisecracking ghostbuster named Rafkin (Matthew Lillard) and Kalina (Embeth Davidtz), a paranormal who knows a lot about Uncle Cyrus, his research, and how the house works.

And does it ever work. Exterior steel panels slide up and down, revealing glass container-cages inside that hold the twelve invisible ghosts, which Cyrus needed in order to ... oh, never mind. What intrigues me is that this house, its shrieks of terror, and its moving walls attract no attention at all from the neighbors, even late in the film when truly alarming things are happening. Maybe the neighbors read the screenplay.

The shatterproof glass cages, we learn, are engraved with "containment spells" that keep the ghosts inside. You can see the ghosts with special glasses, which the cast was issued; when they see them, we see them, usually in shots so maddeningly brief we don't get a good look. Our consolation, I guess, is that the cast has the glasses but we will have the Pause button when *13 Ghosts* comes out on DVD. The only button this movie needs more than Pause is Delete.

The house, Kalina explains, is really an infernal device: "We are in the middle of a machine designed by the devil and powered by the dead." Gears grind and levers smash up and down, looking really neat, and wheels turn within wheels as it's revealed that the purpose of this machine is to open the "Oculorus Infernum." When a character asks, "What's that?" the answer is not helpful: "It's Latin." Later we learn it is the Eye of Hell, and ... oh, never mind.

If there are twelve ghosts there must, I suppose, be twelve containment cages, and yet when little Bobby wanders off to the subterranean area with the cages, he gets lost, and his father, sister, the nanny, the psychic, and the ghostbuster wander endlessly up and down what must be the same few corridors, shouting "Bobby! Bobby?" so very, very, very many times that I wanted to cheer when Rafkin finally said what we had all been thinking: "Screw the kid! We gotta get out of this basement!"

The production is first-rate; the executives included Joel Silver and Robert Zemeckis. The physical look of the picture is splendid. The screenplay is dead on arrival. The noise level is torture. I hope *13 Ghosts* plays mostly at multiplexes, because it's the kind of movie you want to watch from the next theater.

Thomas and the Magic Railroad ★
G, 79 m., 2000

Alec Baldwin (Mr. Conductor), Peter Fonda (Burnett Stone), Mara Wilson (Lily), Russell Means (Billy Twofeathers), Didi Conn (Stacy), Michael E. Rodgers (Junior), Cody McMains (Patch), Edward Glen (Voice of Thomas). Directed by Britt Allcroft and produced by Allcroft and Phil Fehrle. Screenplay by Allcroft.

Very early in *Thomas and the Magic Railroad,* Thomas the Tank Engine and another locomotive are having a conversation. Their eyes roll and we hear their voices—but their mouths do not move. No, not at all. This is such an odd effect that I could think of little else during their conversation. In an era when animated dinosaurs roam the earth, ships climb 200-foot walls of water, and Eddie Murphy can play five people in the same scene, is it too much to ask a tank engine to move its lips while speaking?

I think not. Either their mouths should move or their eyes should not roll. Take your pick. I felt like a grinch as I arrived at this conclusion, for Thomas was a cute tank engine and he steamed through a fanciful model countryside that was, as these things go, nice to look at. I was still filled with goodwill toward Thomas and his movie. That was before I met Burnett Stone.

He is the character played by Peter Fonda, and he spends much of his time in a cave deep within Muffle Mountain with Lady, a tank engine he has been trying to repair for years, but without luck: "I've never been able to bring her to life," he complains. "To make her steam." Fonda is so depressed by this failure that he mopes through the entire role, stoop-shouldered, eyes downcast, step faltering, voice sad, as if he had taken the screenplay too literally ("Burnett is depressed because he cannot get Lady to run") and did not realize that, hey, this is a kiddie movie!

Other actors are likewise adrift in the film. A few years ago Alec Baldwin was delivering the electrifying monologue in *Glengarry Glen Ross.* Now he is Mr. Conductor, about twelve inches tall, materializing in a cloud of sparkle dust in a geranium basket. I do not blame him for taking a role in a children's movie, not

even a role twelve inches high. I do question his judgment in getting into this one.

Thomas and the Magic Railroad is an inept assembly of ill-matched plot points, meandering through a production that has attractive art direction (despite the immobile mouths). Many of the frames would make cheerful stills. Thomas and his fellow trains, even Evil Diesel, have a jolly energy to them, and I like the landscapes and trees and hamlets.

But what a lugubrious plot! What endless trips back and forth between the Isle of Sodor and the full-sized town of Shining Time! What inexplicable characters, such as Billy Twofeathers (Russell Means), who appear and disappear senselessly. What a slow, wordy, earnest enterprise this is, when it should be quick and sprightly.

That *Thomas and the Magic Railroad* made it into theaters at all is something of a mystery. This is a production with "straight to video" written all over it. Kids who like the Thomas books might—*might*—kinda like it. Especially younger kids. Real younger kids. Otherwise, no. Perhaps the success of the Harry Potter books has inspired hope that Thomas, also a British children's icon, will do some business. Not a chance. And in an age when even the cheapest Saturday morning cartoons find a way to make the lips move, what, oh what, was the reasoning behind Thomas's painted-on grin?

Thomas in Love ★ ★
NO MPAA RATING, 97 m., 2001

Benoit Verhaert (Thomas), Aylin Yay (Eva), Magali Pinglaut (Melodie), Micheline Hardy (Nathalie), Alexandre von Sivers (Insurance Agent), Frederic Topart (Psychologist), Serge Lariviere (Receptionist). Directed by Pierre-Paul Renders and produced by Diana Elbaum. Screenplay by Philippe Blasband.

Is this all the better it's going to get? *Thomas in Love* images a cyberfuture in which the hero lives sealed in his apartment, and his entire social life takes place through his computer screen. But the computer technology isn't wildly futuristic; it's a modest extension of today's on-line chat rooms, pay sex sites, and streaming video. The only big breakthrough is a virtual sex suit, kind of a cross between an EKG hookup and a vibrator, that allows two people to access each other's bodies via the Internet. They have about as much fun as a man operating a robot arm to tighten a radioactive screw.

More advanced virtual sex fantasies have been postulated by William Gibson and others (Arthur C. Clarke imagined a world in which reality was represented to dreamers by direct computer input to their brains). But Pierre-Paul Renders and Philippe Blasband, who directed and wrote *Thomas in Love*, aren't trying to envision a brave new cyberworld; their film is about today's on-line "communities," taken another few steps.

We read about couples who meet on the Internet, meet, sometimes marry, sometimes end up killing each other. The Japanese film *Haru* (1996) was about an e-mail relationship. My notion is, anyone who takes this kind of communication much more seriously than a pen-pal exchange should get a life. I think that's what this film thinks about Thomas.

To be fair, Thomas has special problems. He's agoraphobic, and hasn't stepped foot outside his apartment in eight years. All of his needs are serviced via the Net. Some are mundane (he can't get a vacuum cleaner repairman) and others advanced. His insurance company pays for a therapist who suggests on-line dating services; later, the insurance adjuster himself recommends more direct measures—an on-line prostitute.

We never see Thomas (his voice is by Benoit Verhaert). We only see what he sees—his computer screen. Into view swims his mother, who interrupts his sex with an animated cyberdoll. He begs his mother to call only once a week, but she calls constantly (don't they have a "block address" function in this future?). Through the dating service, he meets Melodie (Magali Pinglaut), a poet with a special interest in her own feet, who is a good sport and buys the cybersex suit. They try it out, but she decides it's "creepy" and she can't do it anymore; she wants to see him in the flesh.

His other on-line connection is with Eva (Aylin Yay), a convict whose sentence consists of providing on-line prostitution to the handicapped. She's crying the first time he visits her, and thinks that's what he wants—to have

sex while she cries. Not at all. She makes an interesting slip at one point, talking about how "she" could get in trouble—indicating that the Eva that Thomas sees may be an avatar and not the real Eva.

We sense a growing desperation in Thomas. None of this is working out. He is afraid to leave his apartment, but too miserable to stay there. And the vacuum cleaner still doesn't work. *Thomas in Love* has ominous ideas about the claustrophobic world of on-line living, and although I am always ready to have a faster Internet connection and more bells and whistles on my browser, I don't think I'd much enjoy having Thomas's system.

The movie itself isn't as interesting as the conversations you can have about it. It duplicates Thomas's miserable world so well we want to escape it as urgently as Thomas does. In *Lady in the Lake* (1946), Robert Montgomery experimented with a film in which the camera represents the hero; you never see him, you only see what he sees. It didn't really work, and neither does the virtual version. Our only consolation is that it's better to see what Thomas sees for ninety-seven minutes than to see Thomas. As the complaint rep for the vacuum cleaner company observes, "You don't look too well."

3,000 Miles to Graceland ★ ½
R, 125 m., 2001

Kurt Russell (Michael), Kevin Costner (Murphy), Courteney Cox (Cybil Waingrow), David Kaye (Jesse [Her Son]), Christian Slater (Hanson), Bokeem Woodbine (Franklin), Kevin Pollak (Marshall Damitry), David Arquette (Gus), Jon Lovitz (Jay Peterson), Ice-T (Hamilton). Directed by Demian Lichtenstein and produced by Elie Samaha, Lichtenstein, Richard Spero, Eric Manes, and Andrew Stevens. Screenplay by Richard Recco and Lichtenstein.

Here's a movie without an ounce of human kindness, a sour and mean-spirited enterprise so desperate to please it tries to be a yukky comedy and a hard-boiled action picture at the same time. It's about a gang that robs a casino while masquerading as Elvis impersonators. I was nostalgic for the recent *Sugar and Spice*, in which cheerleaders rob a bank while masquerading as five pregnant Betty dolls (plus one Richard Nixon).

The movie has a heavy-duty cast, with top billing shared by Kurt Russell and Kevin Costner. Russell once played Elvis, very well, on TV, and hits some of the right verbal notes here. Costner, the leader of the gang, chainsmokes and looks mean. His fellow criminals include Christian Slater, David Arquette, and Bokeem Woodbine, who is the black guy and therefore the first to die, following an ancient cliché this movie lacks the wit to rewrite.

The casino robbery involves a gory bloodbath, all gratuitous, all intercut with an Elvis revue on one of the show stages. Not intercut a little, but a lot, complete with dancing girls, until we see so much of the revue we prefer it to the shooting. (Looks like dozens of patrons are killed, but the movie of course forgets this carnage the minute it's over.) The gang makes off with the loot, there is the inevitable squabble over how to divvy it up, and then the movie's most intriguing and inexplicable relationship develops.

This is between Kurt Russell and Courteney Cox, who plays the mom of a bright young kid (David Kaye), and is stranded in the Last Chance Motel, one of those movie sets from a *Road Runner* cartoon. Cox's character is intriguing because we never understand her motivation, and inexplicable because she doesn't, either. She really does like Russell, I guess, and that explains why they're in the sack so quickly, but then the kid, who is about eight, creeps into the bedroom and steals Russell's wallet. The movie never questions the wisdom of showing the kid in the room while his mother is in bed with a stranger. One imagines that the filmmakers were so tickled by the plot point that the moral questions just didn't occur to them.

At a point later in the movie, the Cox character drives off in a car containing most of Russell's loot, while leaving her son behind with him. Would a mother do this? Some would, but most movies wouldn't consider them heroines. There is an "explanation" for her behavior, based on the fact that Russell, a bank robber she has known for about ten minutes, is obviously a good guy and likes the boy—but, come on.

The plot is standard double-reverse, post–*Reservoir Dogs* irony, done with a lot of style and a minimum of thought. It's about behavior patterns, not personalities. Everybody is defined by what they do. Or what they drive: As the film opens, Russell is in a 1957 red Cadillac, and Costner drives a Continental convertible of similar vintage, perhaps because they want to look like Elvis impersonators, more likely because all characters in movies like this drive 1950s cars because modern ones are too small and wimpy.

The cast stays top-drawer right down to the supporting roles. Kevin Pollak turns up as a federal marshal, Jon Lovitz is a money launderer, Ice-T is hired muscle. You guess they all liked the script. But the Russell and Costner characters are so burdened by the baggage of their roles that sometimes they just seem weary, and the energy mostly comes from Courteney Cox—and from the kid, who seems to be smarter than anyone else in the film, and about as experienced.

I will give *3,000 Miles to Graceland* credit for one thing, a terrific trailer. When a bad movie produces a great trailer, it's usually evidence that the raw materials were there for a good movie. I can imagine a blood-soaked caper movie involving Elvis disguises, a lonely tramp, and her bright-eyed son, but it isn't this one.

Time and Tide ★ ★ ★
R, 113 m., 2001

Nicholas Tse (Tyler), Wu Bai (Jack), Anthony Wong (Uncle Ji), Couto Remotigue (Miguel), Candy Lo (Ah Hui), Cathy Chui (Ah Jo). Directed and produced by Tsui Hark. Screenplay by Koan Hui and Hark.

I denounced *The Mummy Returns* for abandoning its characters and using its plot "only as a clothesline for special effects and action sequences." Now I recommend *Time and Tide*, which does exactly the same thing. But there is a difference. While both films rely on nonstop, wall-to-wall action, *Time and Tide* does a better job, and plugs its action and stunt sequences into the real world with everyday props, instead of relying on computers to generate vast and meaningless armies of special-effects creatures.

It's one thing to create an Egyptian-canine-sand warrior on your computer, multiply it by 1,000, and send the results into battle. It's another thing to show a man rappelling down the sides of the interior courtyard of a high-rise apartment building, with the camera following him in a vertiginous descent. In *The Mummy Returns,* you're thinking of the effects. In *Time and Tide,* you're thinking you've never seen anything like *that* before.

Time and Tide is by Tsui Hark, a master of the martial arts action genre, returning to his Hong Kong roots after a series of Hollywood-financed coproductions starring Jean-Claude Van Damme. To describe its plot would be futile. No sane moviegoer should expect to understand most of what happens from a narrative point of view, beyond the broadest outlines of who is more or less good, and who is more or less bad. In general terms, the hero, Tyler (Nicholas Tse), is trapped in a war between two drug cartels, while simultaneously tracking a lesbian policewoman named Ah Jo (Cathy Chui), who was made pregnant by Tyler during an evening neither one can quite remember. The situation is further complicated by Tyler's friendship with the older mercenary Jack (Wu Bai), who has returned from adventures in South America and has also impregnated a young woman.

That gives us two roughly parallel action strands, populated by characters who look confusingly similar at many moments because we get only glimpses of them surrounded by frenetic action. Does Tsui Hark know this? Yes, and I don't think it bothers him. This is the man whose command of his genre helped make Jet Li into a star, and whose range also encompassed the legendary fantasy *A Chinese Ghost Story.*

Time and Tide is essentially a hyperactive showcase for Tsui Hark's ability to pile one unbelievably complex action sequence on top of another. Characters slip down the sides of parking garages on fire hoses, they crash through plate-glass windows, they roll out of range of sprays of machine-gun fire, they are pulled down staircases by ankle chains, they engage in chases involving every conceivable mode of transportation, and there is a sequence near the end where Tyler assists Ah Jo in giving birth while she uses his gun to fire over his head at their attacking enemies.

Who is Tsui Hark (pronounced "Choy Huck")? After more than sixty features he is the Asian equivalent of Roger Corman, I learn from a *New York Times* profile by Dave Kehr. He was born in Vietnam in 1951 when it was under French rule, immigrated to Hong Kong at fifteen, later studied at Southern Methodist University in Dallas, and edited a newspaper in New York's Chinatown. "From the beginning," Kehr observed, "Mr. Tsui was always willing to go a little bit further than his colleagues." He was "an instinctive postmodernist for whom style was its own justification. [He] created a cinema meant to appeal to the eye, ear, and skin far more than to the brain."

Certainly my eyes, ears, and skin were more involved than my brain as I watched *Time and Tide,* and that explains why I liked it more than *The Mummy Returns,* even though both films could be described as mindless action adventures. With *The Mummy Returns* I was repeatedly reminded that one extravagant visual sequence after another was being tied together with the merest of plot threads, which even the actors treated in a semi-ironic fashion. With *Time and Tide,* the plot might be as tenuous, but the actors treated it with ferocious seriousness (whatever it was), and the presence of flesh-and-blood actors and stunt people created an urgency lacking in the obviously fabricated *Mummy* effects.

After that childbirth-and-gunfire sequence near the end, there's one in which the newborn infant, in a small wooden box, is thrown through the air to save its life. As matters of taste go, is that more defensible than the scene in *Freddy Got Fingered* where Tom Green whirls the newborn infant around his head by its umbilical cord, saving its life? Yes, I would say, it is (the modern film critic is forced into these philosophical choices). It is defensible because there is a difference between thinking, "This is the grossest moment I have ever seen in a movie," and, "Gee, I hope the kid survives!"

Time Code ★ ★ ★
R, 93 m., 2000

Stellan Skarsgard (Alex Green), Saffron Burrows (Emma), Salma Hayek (Rose), Jeanne Tripplehorn (Lauren Hathaway), Glenne Headly (Therapist), Holly Hunter (Executive), Danny

Huston (Randy), Kyle MacLachlan (Bunny Drysdale). Directed by Mike Figgis and produced by Figgis and Annie Stewart. Screenplay by Figgis.

I remember the gleam in Mike Figgis's eyes when he talked of filming *Leaving Las Vegas* in cheaper, faster 16mm instead of the standard 35mm. "We didn't have to get a permit from the city or rope off the streets," he said. "We just jumped out of the car, set up the camera, and started shooting." Yes, and made the best film of 1995. Now he's directed a production where they didn't even have to set up the camera.

Time Code was shot entirely with digital cameras, handheld, in real time. The screen is split into four segments, and each one is a single take about ninety-three minutes long. The stories are interrelated, and sometimes the characters in separate quadrants cross paths and are seen by more than one camera. This is not as confusing as it sounds, because Figgis increases the volume of the dialogue for the picture he wants us to focus on, and dials down on the other three.

What is the purpose of the experiment? Above all, to show it can be done. With *Leaving Las Vegas*, the camera strategy came second to the story, and was simply the best way to get it on the screen. In *Time Code*, the story is upstaged by the method, sometimes more, sometimes less, and a viewer not interested in the method is likely to be underwhelmed.

What Figgis demonstrates is that a theatrical film can be made with inexpensive, lightweight digital cameras, and that the picture quality is easily strong enough to transfer to 35mm. He also experiments with the notion of filming in real time, which has long fascinated directors. Hitchcock orchestrated *Rope* (1948) so that it appeared to be all one shot, and Godard famously said that the truth came at twenty-four frames per second, and every cut was a lie.

Apart from proving it can be done, however, what is the purpose of Figgis's experiment? The first films ever made were shot in one take. Just about everybody agrees that the introduction of editing was an improvement. To paraphrase Wilde's Lady Bracknell: To make a film in one unbroken shot may be regarded as a misfortune; to make it in four looks like carelessness. Figgis has put style and technique

in the foreground, and it upstages the performances in what is, after all, a perfunctory story.

When I go to an experimental film, I am in one mind-set. When I go to a mainstream feature, I am in another. If the film works, it carries me along with it. I lose track of the extraneous and am absorbed by the story. Anything that breaks this concentration is risky, and Figgis, with a four-way screen, breaks it deliberately. The film never happens to us. We are always conscious of watching it. The style isn't as annoying as it might sound, but it does no favors to the story.

Cinema semiologists speak of the "disjoined signifier," and by that they refer to the separation of the viewer from the signified—in this case, from the story. So there I've done it. Used the words "semiologists" and "disjoined signifier" in a review. My students will be proud of me. Most readers will have bailed out. My defense is that *Time Code* is not likely to attract anyone who doesn't know what semiology is—or, if it attracts them, will not satisfy them.

The story involves interlocking adulteries, told in four parallel stories that begin at 3 P.M. on November 19, 1999, on Sunset Boulevard in or near Book Soup and the office building on the corner. We meet a limousine lesbian, Lauren (Jeanne Tripplehorn), a cokehead who is in love with Rose (Salma Hayek) and eavesdrops on her with a paging device as she has quick and meaningless sex with an alcoholic film executive (Stellan Skarsgard). Other characters include the executive's wife (Saffron Burrows), an ad executive (Holly Hunter), a shrink (Glenne Headly), and others in and around the entertainment industry. There is pointed satire during a "creative meeting" (an oxymoron), and at the end passion bursts out. The action is interrupted by no less than three earthquakes, which must have required fancy timing in coordinating the cameras and actors.

There may be a story buried here somewhere, and even splendid performances. We could try to extract them on a second or third viewing, but why use a style that obscures them? If *Time Code* demonstrates that four unbroken stories can be told at the same time, it also demonstrates that the experiment need not be repeated.

Still, I recommend the film. Mike Figgis is a

man who lives and breathes the cinema (see his 1999 film *The Loss of Sexual Innocence* for an altogether more breathtaking and, yes, daring experiment in storytelling). While most filmmakers are content to plod their dreary way from one foregone conclusion to another, Figgis is out there on the edge, joyously pulling off cockamamie stunts like this one. I'm glad I saw the film. It challenged me. The actors were the coproducers and joined in the spirit of the enterprise, testing their own limits. *Time Code* has a place in the history of the movies. But now I want to see Figgis cut back to one camera (digital if he must), resume editing, and conduct experiments that are more likely to arouse my sense of awe than my sense of timing.

A Time for Drunken Horses ★ ★ ★

NO MPAA RATING, 80 m., 2000

Ayoub Ahmadi (Ayoub), Ameneh Ekhtiar-Dini (Ameneh), Mehdi Ekhtiar-Dini (Madi), Rojin Younessi (Rojin). Directed and produced by Bahman Ghobadi. Screenplay by Ghobadi.

A Time for Drunken Horses supplies faces to go with news stories about the Kurdish peoples of Iran, Iraq, and Turkey, people whose land to this day is protected against Saddam's air force by a no-fly zone enforced by the United States. Why Saddam or anyone else would feel threatened by these isolated and desperately poor people is an enigma, but the movie is not about politics. It is about survival.

In dialogue over some of the opening scenes, we meet three young Iranian Kurdish children: Ameneh, a teenage girl; Ayoub, her brother, who is about twelve; and Madi, their fifteen-year-old brother, a dwarf whose fiercely observant face surmounts a tiny and twisted body. They live with their father, who, Ameneh matter-of-factly reports, works as a smuggler, taking goods by mule into Iraq, where they fetch a better price.

The children work every day in a nearby town. They are child labor, put to work wrapping glasses for export, or staggering under heavy loads they carry around the marketplace. Their hand-to-mouth existence undercuts easy Western theories about child labor; they work to eat, and will be dead if they don't.

We see them in the back of a truck bringing them back to their village, and there is a shot that emotionally charges the whole film. Ayoub and Ameneh sit close together, both helping to hold little Madi. Ayoub caresses the hair of the little creature, and Ameneh gently kisses him. They love their crippled brother, who never speaks throughout the film, who must have regular injections of medicine, who needs an operation, who will probably die within the year even if he gets the operation.

The truck is stopped by guards and impounded. The three siblings struggle together through the snow, separated now from their father. Their existence is more desperate than ever. They become involved with mule trains that smuggle truck tires over the mountains to Iraq. The high mountain passes are so cold that the mules are given water laced with alcohol to keep them going—thus the title. Ameneh agrees to marry into a Kurdish family from across the mountains if they will pay for Madi's operation. What happens then I will not reveal.

The movie is brief, spare, and heartbreaking. It won the Camera d'Or, for best first film, at Cannes 2000. Some find it boring, but I suspect they are lacking in empathy (one Internet critic magnanimously concedes that the movie "might have contained some appeal" if "my life were pathetic enough"). *A Time for Drunken Horses* has the same kind of conviction as movies like *The Bicycle Thief, Salaam Bombay,* and *Pixote*—movies that look unblinkingly at desperate lives on the margin.

The larger message is perhaps in code. The Iranian cinema, agreed to be one of the most creative in the world today, often makes films about children so that politics seem beside the point, even if they are not. First-time filmmaker Bahman Ghobadi, who wrote and directed this film, may or may not have intended to do anything but tell his simple story, but the buried message argues for the rights of ethnic minorities in Iran, and everywhere.

His visual style is documentary. There is little doubt that most of what we see is actually happening, or does happen much as it is represented here. The sight of the mules with two big truck tires lashed to their backs has an intrinsically believable quality.

As for the children, Madi (Mehdi Ekhtiar-Dini) is obviously sadly malformed; there is a touching shot of his eyes peering out apprehensively from beneath the big hood of his coat as he rides in a mule's saddlebag. Ameneh is played by Ameneh Ekhtiar-Dini, who has the same last name as Madi, and is probably his sister; I learn from the notes that in general "the villagers play themselves." I have read about the Kurds being bombed, about the no-fly zone. All merely words, until I saw this movie. Now I will think of little Madi peering out to see what luck he can expect today.

The Time Machine ★ ½

PG-13, 96 m., 2002

Guy Pearce (Alexander Hartdegen), Jeremy Irons (Uber Morlock), Sienna Guillory (Emma), Samantha Mumba (Mara), Orlando Jones (Vox), Mark Addy (Dr. Philby). Directed by Simon Wells and produced by Walter F. Parkes and David Valdes. Screenplay by John Logan, based on the novel by H. G. Wells.

The Time Machine is a witless recycling of the H. G. Wells story from 1895, with the absurdity intact but the wonderment missing. It makes use of computer-aided graphics to create a future race of grubby underground beasties who, like the characters in *Battleship Earth,* have evolved beyond the need for bathing and fingernail clippers. Because this race, the Morlocks, is allegedly a Darwinian offshoot of humans, and because they are remarkably unattractive, they call into question the theory that over a long period of time a race grows more attractive through natural selection. They are obviously the result of 800,000 years of ugly brides.

The film stars Guy Pearce as Alexander Hartdegen, a brilliant mathematician who hopes to use Einstein's earliest theories to build a machine to travel through time. He is in love with the beautiful Emma (Sienna Guillory), but on the very night when he proposes marriage a tragedy happens, and he vows to travel back in time in his new machine and change the course of history.

The machine, which lacks so much as a seat belt, consists of whirling spheres encompassing a Victorian club chair. Convenient brass gauges spin to record the current date. Speed and direction are controlled by a joystick. The time machine has an uncanny ability to move in perfect synchronization with Earth, so that it always lands in the same geographical spot, despite the fact that in the future large chunks of the Moon (or all of it, according to the future race of Eloi) have fallen to Earth, which should have had some effect on the orbit. Since it would be inconvenient if a time machine materialized miles in the air or deep underground, this is just as well.

We will not discuss paradoxes of time travel here, since such discussion makes any time travel movie impossible. Let us discuss instead an unintended journey that Hartdegen makes to 8,000 centuries in the future, when Homo sapiens have split in two, into the Eloi and Morlocks. The Morlocks evolved underground in the dark ages after the Moon's fall, and attack on the surface by popping up through dusty sinkholes. They hunt the Eloi for food. The Eloi are an attractive race of brown-skinned people whose civilization seems modeled on paintings by Rousseau; their life is an idyll of leafy bowers, waterfalls, and elegant forest structures, but they are such fatalists about the Morlocks that instead of fighting them off they all but salt and pepper themselves.

Alexander meets a beautiful Eloi woman (Samantha Mumba) and her sturdy young brother, befriends them, and eventually journeys to the underworld to try to rescue her. This brings him into contact with the Uber Morlock, a chalk-faced Jeremy Irons, who did not learn his lesson after playing an evil Mage named Profion in *Dungeons & Dragons.*

In broad outline, this future world matches the one depicted in George Pal's 1960 film *The Time Machine,* although its blond, blue-eyed race of Eloi have been transformed into dusky sun people. One nevertheless tends to question romances between people who were born 800,000 years apart and have few conversations on subjects other than not being eaten. Convenient that when humankind was splitting into two different races, both its branches continued to speak English.

The Morlocks and much of their world have been created by undistinguished animation. The Morlock hunters are supposed to be able to leap great distances with fearsome speed, but the animation turns them into cartoonish characters whose movements defy even the laws of gravity governing bodies in motion. Their movements are not remotely plausible, and it's disconcerting to see that while the Eloi are utterly unable to evade them, Hartdegen, a professor who has scarcely left his laboratory for four years, is able to duck out of the way, bean them with big tree branches, etc.

Guy Pearce, as the hero, makes the mistake of trying to give a good and realistic performance. Irons at least knows what kind of movie he's in, and hams it up accordingly. Pearce seems thoughtful, introspective, quiet, morose. Surely the inventor of a time machine should have a few screws loose, and the glint in his eye should not be from tears. By the end of the movie, as he stands beside the beautiful Eloi woman and takes her hand, we are thinking not of their future together, but about how he got from the Morlock caverns to the top of that mountain ridge in time to watch an explosion that takes only a few seconds. A Morlock could cover that distance, but not a mathematician, unless he has discovered wormholes as well.   ☞

Time Out ★ ★ ★
PG-13, 132 m., 2002

Aurelien Recoing (Vincent), Karin Viard (Muriel), Serge Livrozet (Jean-Michel), Jean-Pierre Mangeot (Father), Monique Mangeot (Mother). Directed by Laurent Cantet and produced by Caroline Benjo. Screenplay by Robin Campillo and Cantet.

Vincent loses his job. He cannot bear to confess this to his wife and children, so he invents another one, and the fictional job takes up more of his time than his family does. It is hard work to spend all day producing the illusion of accomplishment out of thin air. Ask anyone from Enron. The film *Time Out* is about modern forms of work that exist only because we say they do. Those best-sellers about modern management techniques are hilarious because the only things that many managers actually manage are their techniques.

Free from his job, Vincent is seduced by the pleasure of getting in his car and just driving around. He lives in France, near the Swiss border, and one day he wanders into an office building in Switzerland, eavesdrops on some of the employees, picks up a brochure, and tells his relatives he works in a place like this. It's an agency associated with the United Nations, and as nearly as I can tell, its purpose is to train managers who can go to Africa and train managers. This is about right. The best way to get a job through a program designed to find you a job is to get a job with the program.

Vincent, played by the sad-eyed, sincere Aurelien Recoing, is not a con man so much as a pragmatist who realizes that since his job exists mostly in his mind anyway, he might as well eliminate the middleman, his employer. He begins taking long overnight trips, sleeping in his car, finding his breakfast at cold, lonely roadside diners at daybreak. He calls his wife frequently with progress reports: The meeting went well, the client needs more time, the project team is assembling tomorrow, he has a new assignment. Since he has not figured out how to live without money, he convinces friends and relatives to invest in his fictional company, and uses that money to live on.

You would think the movie would be about how this life of deception, these lonely weeks on the road, wear him down. Actually, he seems more worn out by the experience of interacting with his family during his visits at home. His wife, Muriel (Karin Viard), a schoolteacher, suspects that something is not quite convincing about this new job. What throws her off is that there was something not quite convincing about his old job too. Vincent's father is the kind of man who, because he can never be pleased, does not distinguish between one form of displeasure and another. Vincent's children are not much interested in their dad's work.

In his travels Vincent encounters Jean-Michel (Serge Livrozet), who spots him for a phony and might have a place in his organization for the right kind of phony. Jean-Michel imports fake brand-name items. What he does is not legal, but it does involve the sale and delivery of actual physical goods. He is more honest than those who simply exchange theoretical goods; Jean-Michel sells fake Guccis, Enron sells fake dollars.

Time Out is the second film by Laurent Cantet, whose first was *Human Resources* (2000), about a young man from a working-class family who goes off to college and returns as the human resources manager at the factory where his father has worked all of his life as a punch-press operator. One of the son's tasks is to lay off many employees, including his father. The father heartbreakingly returns to his machine even after being fired, because he cannot imagine his life without a job. Vincent in a way is worse off. His job is irrelevant to his life. I admire the closing scenes of the film, which seem to ask whether our civilization offers a cure for Vincent's complaint.

Time Regained ★ ★ ★ ½
NO MPAA RATING, 165 m., 2000

Catherine Deneuve (Odette de Crecy), Emmanuelle Béart (Gilberte), Vincent Perez (Morel), John Malkovich (Charlus), Pascal Greggory (Saint-Loup), Marie-France Pisier (Madame Verdurin), Christian Vadim (Bloch), Arielle Dombasle (Madame de Farcy), Marcello Mazzarella (The Narrator), Chiara Mastroianni (Albertine). Directed Raul Ruiz and produced by Paulo Branco. Screenplay by Gilles Taurand and Ruiz, based on the book by Marcel Proust.

There are times when memory is simply a tool, supplying needed information, and others when it is like a ghostly time machine, summoning the experiences of our past so sharply that we gasp with loss and regret. Marcel Proust's *Remembrance of Things Past* is a work of memory, fed by the legend of the dying novelist in his cork-lined room, tended by the faithful maid Celeste, revisiting the scenes of his past. The memories of his narrator are awakened by the taste and aroma of a madeleine, a kind of pastry he loved as a child; in middle age its taste opens the floodgates of memory.

His novel does not tell a story so much as circle the materials; our lives are not plotted, but happen to us. We are the slate upon which others write our story, and at the end we possess the book but are mystified by those who wrote it. Who were our parents, really, and those we loved? More than any other novelist, Proust gave his life to the examination of it, and "Proustian" evokes a reverie in which the past is more vivid than the insubstantial present. His novel is considered by many the greatest of the twentieth century—considered by

more, perhaps, than have actually read it, because its great length makes it one of those works often begun and rarely finished.

Today I sit down to write a review of *Time Regained,* the new film by Raul Ruiz, based on the last volume of Proust's novel but informed by all of them. I type my words in a study lounge of the Illini Union at the University of Illinois in Urbana. In a chair over there by the wall I was sitting on the day in 1963 when the news came that John F. Kennedy had been shot. Last night I attended my high school reunion, where in the faces of middle-aged men I saw grinning boys, and we called the women by their maiden names.

Afterward I parked my car near the corner of Washington and Maple, and walked in the midnight moonlight down the sidewalks of my youth, retracing my paper route—even today I know which houses took the *Courier.* The houses were all the same. I remembered who lived in them. I remembered the names of the dogs that used to greet me, and my own dog Blackie who came along, and an evergreen that brushed the sidewalk. I saw my parents on the porch in metal rocking chairs, smoking cigarettes in the dark, talking softly. Where my car was parked there was a light green 1954 Ford—mine. Those memories are what Proust's novel is about. Not his memories, mine. We have the same memories. Only the names and the places are different. We still bow in wonder toward the first loves of our adolescence. We do not miss them, do not wish ourselves to recapture them, do not regret the present but the past. The point is that they are gone, and soon all will be gone. Memories, their objects, ourselves.

I walk out of the Illini Union and down Green Street, past the Co-Ed theater, which is gone, where my father took me to get Cleo Moore's autograph, and past the Capital, which is gone, where I drank beer with Larry Woiwode before he became a novelist, and past the Turk's Head, which is gone, where Simon told me who Samuel Johnson was, and the Book Nook downstairs, which is gone, where I bought *Boswell's Life of Johnson.* All gone.

The movie opens with an old man in bed (Marcello Mazzarella), being brought tea by his maid. He looks through photographs, which trigger memories, as the furniture in the room rearranges itself for other times. The movie circles the memories. We meet the women who once so captivated him. Here is Gilberte (Emmanuelle Béart). He did not love her so much as learn from her that he could love. Here is her mother, Odette (Catherine Deneuve). And Albertine (Chiara Mastroianni), another, more troublesome, love; in life, Mastroianni is Deneuve's daughter, and the resemblance suggests Albertine's subterranean connection with Odette . . . and her mother. What does it mean? The photographs evoke but do not explain.

Here is Gilberte's eventual husband, Robert de Saint-Loup (Pascal Greggory). He is composed, intact, as a younger man, but then he goes into the trench warfare of World War I, and when he returns he is crazed by his memories, and talks while shoveling food into his mouth like an animal who wants to eat before larger animals steal his kill. And here is Baron de Charlus (John Malkovich), who plays the role of the slightly elevated, bemused observer—a man like the man we all have in our lives, who seems to stand outside and have a wider view. In my high school that was David Ogden Stiers. Yes, the actor who played Winchester on *M*A*S*H*. He has never attended a reunion, but is discussed every ten years by the rest of us, who recall in wonder that he always talked like that. He came to Urbana from Peoria. Where did he learn to talk like Winchester? Tall, confident, and twinkling, he would ask, "And what have we here?"

Time Regained does not tell a story and you will be disappointed if you go looking for one. It does not contain anything like all of *Remembrance of Things Past*, because the novel is too vast to be contained in a film. It is not about memories but memory. Yours, mine, Proust's. Memory makes us human. Without it, we would live trapped inside the moving dot of time as it slides through our lives. But to remember the past is to experience its loss. Never again will Blackie come with me on my paper route. The *Courier* is not published anymore. The cigarettes killed my parents. High school reunions really take it out of you.

Titan A.E. ★ ★ ★ ½
PG, 92 m., 2000

With the voices of: Matt Damon (Cale), Bill Pullman (Korso), John Leguizamo (Gune), Nathan Lane (Preed), Janeane Garofalo (Stith), Drew Barrymore (Akima), Ron Perlman (Professor Sam Tucker), Alex D. Linz (Young Cale). Directed by Don Bluth and Gary Goldman and produced by David Kirschner, Goldman, and Bluth. Screenplay by Ben Edlund, John August, and Joss Whedon, based on a story by Hans Bauer and Randall McCormick.

Here's the animated space adventure I've been hoping for—a film that uses the freedom of animation to visualize the strangeness of the universe in ways live action cannot duplicate, and then joins its vision to a rousing story. Don Bluth and Gary Goldman's *Titan A.E.* creates the kinds of feelings I had as a teenager, paging eagerly through Asimov and Heinlein. There are moments when it even stirs a little awe.

The movie is pure slam-bam space opera. Its stills could be transferred intact to the covers of old issues of *Amazing Stories*. Yet it has the largeness of spirit that good SF can generate: It isn't just action and warfare, but also a play of ideas. Some of its galactic visuals are beautiful in the same way photos by the Hubble Space Telescope are beautiful: They show a careless hand casting colors and energy across unimaginable expanses of space, using stars and planets as its paintbox.

As the film opens, in A.D. 3028, Earth has been destroyed by the evil race of Drej, who fear the intelligence of humans. Survivors flee on spaceships, one of them the gigantic *Titan*, which carries crucial information on board. That ship was designed by the hero's father, who apparently disappears along with the *Titan*.

When we first meet Cale (voice by Matt Damon), he's a "colony bum," working in a space dump floating between the stars, where conditions are harsh ("I wish they'd kill my food before they give it to me"). He's bitter and indifferent because he believes he has been abandoned by his father. Yet he holds the key to the future of Earth and mankind in the palm of his hand—literally, in the form of a genetically coded map that reveals the hiding place of *Titan*. Soon he's on a mission to find *Titan*, with partners including a beautiful girl named Akima (Drew Barrymore), who treasures Earth's heritage and collects artifacts of its past, like baseballs. The captain of their expedition is the grave, responsible Korso (Bill Pullman); Gune (John Leguizamo) is the navigator.

The main story involves their journey to find *Titan* before the Drej can capture or destroy it. This quest involves high and low comedy, an exciting chase scene, and then one of the most involving hunt sequences I've seen in any movie, animated or not—a cat-and-mouse game played out in the Ice Rings of Tigrin. These are massive structures of interstellar ice, which form a ring like a miniature galaxy. They offer some protection from the sensing devices of the Drej, but can tear a spaceship to pieces with their huge, jagged masses.

The Ice Rings sequence is a perfect example of what animation can do and live action cannot. The vast, frozen shards of ice are clear and ominous, with a convincing presence, and the sound track does a masterful job of adding a dimension. We know sound does not travel in space, but do not care, because the groanings and creakings of the ancient ice masses are like cries of despair, and somewhere within the frozen maze lies *Titan* with its precious cargo.

The movie is rambunctious in its action scenes, which owe more than a little to *Star Wars* (just as *Star Wars* owes more than a little to old pulp SF and Saturday serials). But it's not simpleminded. I liked a scene where the heroes are trying to sneak past a hostile and suspicious guard. They've constructed counterfeit uniforms. The guard leads them on, pretends to be fooled, and then laughs in their faces, telling them their uniforms are obviously constructed from bedspreads. "An intelligent guard!" says one of the good guys. "Didn't see that one coming."

The movie adds small details that evoke the wonder of the universe. At one point in the journey, the ship is followed by space sprites— energy beings that follow space vessels and mean good luck, as dolphins do at sea. We get a sense of space not merely as a fearsome void, but as a place big enough to include even

whimsy. And *Star Wars* is evoked again with the tradition that the human heroes have cartoonish sidekicks. Preed (voice by Nathan Lane) is a first mate who seems to have a genetic similarity to Jar Jar Binks in *The Phantom Menace*. Stith (Janeane Garofalo) is the weapons master who looks like an extremely callipygian kangaroo. The evil Drej are seen as crackling white-blue force fields, seemingly at one with their ships.

One test for any movie is when you forget it's a movie and simply surf along on the narrative. That can happen as easily with animation as live action, and it happens here.

I argue for animation because I believe it provides an additional dimension for film art; it frees filmmakers from the anchor of realism that's built into every live-action film, and allows them to visualize their imaginations. Animation need not be limited to family films and cheerful fantasies. The Japanese have known that for years, and *Titan A.E.* owes as large a debt to Japanese anime as to *Star Wars*.

The movie works as adventure, as the *Star Wars* pictures do (and as live-action SF films like *Starship Troopers* do not). It tells a story cleverly designed to explain more or less reasonably why Cale, in the words of the ancient SF cliché, "has the future of Earth in his hands!" There is a sense of wonder here.

Titus ★ ★ ★ ½
R, 165 m., 2000

Anthony Hopkins (Titus), Jessica Lange (Tamora), Alan Cumming (Saturninus), Harry Lennix (Aaron), Jonathan Rhys Meyers (Chiron), Angus Macfadyen (Lucius), Matthew Rhys (Demetrius), Colm Feore (Marcus), James Frain (Bassianus), Laura Fraser (Lavinia). Directed by Julie Taymor and produced by Jody Patton, Conchita Airoldi, and Taymor. Screenplay by Taymor, adapted from William Shakespeare's *Titus Andronicus*.

So bloodthirsty is Shakespeare's *Titus Andronicus* that critics like Harold Bloom believe it must be a parody—perhaps Shakespeare's attempt to settle the hash of Christopher Marlowe, whose plays were soaked in violence. Other readers, like the sainted Mark Van Doren, dismiss it out of hand. Inhuman and unfeeling, he called it, and "no tragedy at all if pity and terror are essential to the tragic experience." Certainly most agree it is the least of Shakespeare's tragedies, as well as the first.

But consider young Shakespeare near the beginning of his career, trying to upstage the star dramatists and attract attention to himself. Imagine him sitting down to write the equivalent of today's horror films. Just as Kevin Williamson's screenplays for *Scream* and *I Know What You Did Last Summer* use special effects and wild coincidence to mow down their casts, so does *Titus Andronicus* heap up the gore, and then wink to show the playwright is in on the joke.

Titus as *Scream 1593*? Bloom cites the scene where Titus is promised the return of his sons if he will send Saturninus his hand—only to find the hand returned with only the heads of his sons. Grief-stricken, Titus assigns tasks. He, with his remaining hand, will carry one of the heads. He asks his brother to take the other. That leaves the severed hand. At this point in the play his daughter, Lavinia, has no hands (or tongue) after being raped and mutilated by the emperor's sons, and so he instructs her, "Bear thou my hand, sweet wench, between thy teeth." Bloom invites scholars to read that line aloud without smiling, and says Shakespeare knew the play "was a howler, and expected the more discerning to wallow in it self-consciously."

That is exactly what Julie Taymor has done, in a brilliant and absurd film of *Titus Andronicus* that goes over the top, doubles back, and goes over the top again. The film is imperfect, but how can you make a perfect film of a play that flaunts its flaws so joyfully? Some critics have sniffed at its excesses and visual inventions—many of them the same dour enforcers who didn't like the biblical surprise in *Magnolia*. I have had enough good taste and restraint for a lifetime, and love it when a director has the courage to go for broke. God forbid we should ever get a devout and tasteful production of *Titus Andronicus*.

It cannot be a coincidence that the title role is played by Anthony Hopkins. Not when by Act 5 he is serving Tamora (Jessica Lange) meat pies made out of her sons, and smacking his lips in precisely the same way that Hannibal Lecter drooled over fava beans. *Titus Androni-*cus was no doubt Lecter's favorite Shakespeare play, opening as it does with Titus returning to Rome with the corpses of twenty-one of his sons and their four surviving brothers, and pausing in his victory speech only long enough to condemn the eldest son of Tamora, vanquished queen of the Goths, to be hacked limb from limb and the pieces thrown on a fire.

Titus is not the hero of the film because it has no hero. He is as vicious as the others, and when he notes that "Rome is a wilderness of tigers," he should have included himself. Hopkins plays him, like Hannibal Lecter, as a man pitiable, intelligent, and depraved, as he strides through a revenge story so gory that there seems a good chance no one will be left alive at the end.

Some of the contrivance is outrageous. Consider the scene where a hole in the forest floor gradually fills up with corpses, as Aaron the Moor (Harry Lennix), the play's grand schemer, unfolds a devious plan to defeat both Titus and Saturninus and seduce Tamora. This hole, of course, would be convenient on the stage, where it could be represented by a trap door, but in the woods, as Saturninus (Alan Cumming) apprehensively peers over the side, it takes on all the credibility of an Abbott and Costello setup. Or consider the scene late in the play where Titus breaks the neck of his own long-suffering daughter, as if losing her tongue and arms were not bad luck enough, and then pities the fates that made him do it.

Taymor is the director of the Broadway musical *The Lion King*, which is one of the most exhilarating experiences I have ever had in a theater. In her first film she again shows a command of costumes and staging, ritual and procession, archetypes and comic relief. She makes it clear in her opening shot (a modern boy waging a food fight with his plastic action figures) that she sees the connection between *Titus Andronicus* and the modern culture of violence in children's entertainment. *Titus* would make a video game, with the tattooed Tamora as Lara Croft.

Taymor's period is basically a fanciful version of ancient Rome, but in the mix she includes modern cars and tanks, loud speakers and popemobiles, newspapers and radio speeches. Like Richard Loncraine and Ian McKellen's

Richard III (1995), she sees the possibilities in fascist trappings as Saturninus seizes control of Rome and marries Tamora. There's a jazzy wedding orgy, crypto-Nazi costuming, and a scene staged in front of a vast modern structure made of arches, a reminder of the joke that fascist architecture looked like Mussolini ordered it over the phone.

She lavishes great energy on staging and photography. Like the makers of a cartoon, Taymor and her cinematographer, Luciano Tovoli, sometimes move the camera in time with music or sound effects; as the picture swoops or pulls away, so does Elliot Goldenthal's score. There are scenes of rigid choreography, as in the entry into Rome, where Titus's army marches like the little green soldiers in *Toy Story*. And other scenes where the movements are so voluptuous we are reminded of *Fellini Satyricon*.

Mark Van Doren was correct. There is no lesson to be learned from *Titus Andronicus*. It is a tragedy without a hero, without values, without a point, and therefore as modern as a horror exploitation film or a video game. It is not a catharsis, but a killing gallery where the characters speak in poetry. Freed of pious meaning, the actors bury themselves in technique and the opportunity of stylized melodrama. Anyone who doesn't enjoy this film for what it is must explain: How could it be other? This is the film Shakespeare's play deserves, and perhaps even a little more.

Together ★ ★ ★
R, 106 m., 2001

Lisa Lindgren (Elisabeth), Michael Nyqvist (Rolf), Gustav Hammarsten (Goran), Anja Lundkvist (Lena), Jessica Liedberg (Anna), Ola Norell (Lasse), Shanti Roney (Klas), Sam Kessel (Stefan), Emma Samuelsson (Eva), Henrik Lundstrom (Fredrik), Olle Sarri (Erik). Directed by Lukas Moodysson and produced by Lars Jonsson. Screenplay by Moodysson.

With the recent announcement by its exiled founder that The Body Shop is an empty shell of commercialism, the 1970s I suppose are now officially over. *Together*, a sly, satirical Swedish film, shows the decade coming apart as early as 1975. In a commune in Stockholm, a mixed bag of adults, some with children, try to live according to their ideals, while human nature does its best to force them toward compromise, corruption, and—worst of all—realism.

Watching the film awakened memories of the time: a mother protesting against the gender-coding of pink and blue children's blankets. Arguments about men doing the dishes. Denouncements of Pippi Longstocking as a materialist and capitalist. A child named Tet, after the North Vietnamese offensive. "Open relationships," which have a way of ending in no relationships at all. By the time the kids start picketing for the right to eat meat, we see their point.

Together is the latest film by Lukas Moodysson, a distinctive new Swedish director whose previous film, *Show Me Love* (1998), told the tender story of two misfit teenage girls who fall in love even though one is probably straight. He has an ability to hold opposing ideas of the same character at the same time, which makes his people more intriguing and convincing than movie characters who are assigned rigid descriptions.

In *Together*, for example, an abused wife comes to the commune with her two children, fleeing her alcoholic husband. When we see the husband, he creates a drunken scene after taking his kids to a Chinese restaurant, and gets arrested. But Moodysson doesn't leave it at that. He shows the husband at work as a plumber, and introduces a minor character— an older man who calls the plumber just because he is lonely. And eventually the plumber turns out to be more redeemable than some of the more righteous members of the commune.

That would include Lena (Anja Lundkvist), married to the commune's leader Goran (Gustaf Hammarsten). They practice an open marriage, which means she makes love to the doctrinaire Marxist Erik (Olle Sarri), and Goran sits uneasily in the kitchen trying to pretend he doesn't mind. One of the movie's great moments is when Goran finally, suddenly, unexpectedly shows he does mind after all.

The movie's best relationship is between two kids: Eva (Emma Samuelsson), the daughter of the alcoholic, and plump, fourteen-year-old Fredrik (Henrik Lundstrom), who lives across the street with uptight parents who hate the commune. The two nearsighted kids discover they have exactly the same eyeglass prescription, and that is an omen, binding them together in an alliance that rejects both the crazy socialism at her house and the rigid conservatism at his. Meeting in the commune's van or in each other's rooms, they form an innocent friendship of mutual support that perhaps shows man's natural state is in the middle and not at the extremes. (There is also the ability of children to turn anything to their own ends. Eva's brother Stephan and his playmate Tet have a game inspired by the Chilean dictator Pinochet, in which they pretend to torture each other with electrodes.)

Sex causes more trouble than it is worth in the commune. One of the marriages has broken up because the wife has decided, for philosophical reasons, to become a lesbian. A gay man attempts unsuccessfully to use pure logic to persuade a straight man to sleep with him. (True, the genitals know no gender, but their owner-operators are rarely as open-minded.) There is a scene where a woman washes the dishes while naked from the waist down, justifying her decision with a medical complaint that might lead even the most open-minded commune member to prefer that she not wash the dishes at all. And all the time there seems to be a powerful subterranean force operating to sort these radical experimenters back into conventional, stable twosomes.

It may be that *Together* only wants to remember a time. That it does with gentle, observant humor. If it has a message, it is that ideas imposed on human nature may be able to shape lives for a while, but in the long run we drift back toward more conventional choices. In the 1970s, hippies defiantly sprawled on the floor—in airports, movie theaters, classrooms, malls. Now they and their children (and grandchildren) have gone back to chairs again, which were invented, as it turns out, for excellent reasons.

Tomcats no stars
R, 92 m., 2001

Jerry O'Connell (Michael Delaney), Shannon Elizabeth (Natalie), Jake Busey (Kyle Brenner), Jaime Pressly (Tricia), Horatio Sanz (Steve), Shelby Stockton (Mistaken Bride), Heather Ankeny (New Girl), Joseph D. Reitman (Dave), David Ogden Stiers (Surgeon), Bill Maher (Carlos). Directed by Gregory Poirier and produced by Alan Riche, Tony Ludwig, and Paul Kurta. Screenplay by Poirier.

The men in *Tomcats* are surrounded by beautiful women, but they hate and fear them. That alone is enough to sink the film, since no reasonable person in the audience can understand why these guys are so weirdly twisted. But then the film humiliates the women, and we wince when it wants us to laugh. Here is a comedy positioned outside the normal range of human response.

The movie belongs to an old and tired movie tradition, in which guys are terrified that wedding bells may be breaking up that old gang of theirs (like *The Brothers*, an African-American version of the theme, but gentler and nicer). There is always one guy who is already (unhappily) married, one who is threatened with marriage, one who claims he will never marry, and then the hero, who wants to marry off the unmarriageable one to win a bet. This plot is engraved on a plaque in the men's room of the Old Writer's Retirement Home.

The twist this time: The guys all agree to pay into a mutual fund. The last one still single collects all the money. The fund quickly grows to nearly $500,000, so their fund must have bought hot tech stocks. (In the sequel, those same stocks—oh, never mind.)

The guy who vows never to marry is Kyle (Jake Busey). He likes to take his dates golfing and run over them with the cart. They bounce right up and keep smiling. The guy who wants to collect the money is Michael (Jerry O'Connell). He comes into a valuable piece of information: Kyle met one perfect woman, cruelly dumped her, and has always wondered if he made a mistake. Michael tracks down the woman, who is Natalie (Shannon Elizabeth), and enlists her in his scheme. She'll seduce and marry Kyle and get her revenge—oh, and she wants half the money too.

The complication, which is so obvious it nearly precedes the setup, is that Michael and Natalie fall for each other. This despite the fact that by going along with his plan she reveals herself as a shameless vixen. The movie then runs through an assembly line of routine situations, including bad jokes about S & M and a proctologist who suspects his wife is a lesbian, before arriving at a sequence of astonishing bad taste.

Read no further if through reckless wrong-headedness you plan to see this movie. What happens is that Kyle develops testicular cancer and has to have surgery to remove one of his testicle teammates. During recovery he develops a nostalgia for the missing sphere, and sends Michael on a mission to the hospital's Medical Waste Storage room to steal back the treasure.

Alas, through a series of mishaps, it bounces around the hospital like the quarry in a handball game before ending up on the cafeteria plate of the surgeon who has just removed it, and now eats it, with relish. The surgeon is played by that accomplished actor David Ogden Stiers, my high school classmate, who also does Shakespeare and probably finds it easier.

The movie has other distasteful scenes, including a bachelor party where the star performer starts with Ping-Pong balls and works up to footballs. If the details are gross, the movie's overall tone is even more offensive. All sex comedies have scenes in which characters are embarrassed, but I can't remember one in which women are so consistently and venomously humiliated, as if they were some kind of hateful plague. The guys in the movie don't even seem to enjoy sex, except as a way of keeping score.

Tomcats was written and directed by Gregory Poirier, who also wrote *See Spot Run* and thus pulls off the neat trick, within one month, of placing two titles on my list of the worst movies of the year. There is a bright spot. He used up all his doggy-do-do ideas in the first picture.

Too Much Sleep ★ ★ ★

NO MPAA RATING, 86 m., 2001

Marc Palmieri (Jack), Pasquale Gaeta (Eddie), Philip Galinsky (Andrew), Nicol Zanzarella (Kate), Judy Sabo Podinker (Judy), Peggy Lord Chilton (Mrs. Bruner). Directed by David Maquiling and produced by Jason Kliot and Joana Vicente. Screenplay by Maquiling.

David Maquiling's *Too Much Sleep* is rich and droll, and yet slight—a film of modest virtues,

content to be small, achieving what it intends. It tells the story of a twenty-four-year-old security guard who is separated from his gun through a scam while riding the bus. He can't go to the cops because the gun wasn't registered. So he spends the next few days trying to track down the gun himself.

This summary, however, completely fails to reflect the tone of the movie, which is a coming-of-age comedy about how there are a lot of seriously weird people in the world. Jack (Mark Palmieri) enlists the help of a deli owner named Eddie (Pasquale Gaeta), a know-it-all who has a theory about everything and is an endless source of advice fascinating primarily to himself. Eddie has connections with the cops, and comes up with a list of locals whose M.O. fits the scam on the bus, and Jack wanders from one suspect to another in a kind of disbelieving daze. During this process he comes of age to the extent possible in a few days—at the end of the movie, he is a little older and a little wiser, but not much.

Jack sleeps too much and rarely seems quite awake. He sleeps too much because he has nothing interesting to do. He still lives at home, in a bedroom filled with his possessions from high school, and during the long nights on the job he listens to self-help tapes about starting his own business (he should begin, he learns, "by choosing a name"). He lives in a bland, boring suburb, or so he thinks, but during his odyssey in search of the gun he discovers that it is populated by strange and wonderful people, easily as eccentric as anyone in a De Niro crime movie or an Australian comedy.

These people talk a lot. I especially enjoyed Mrs. Bruner (Peggy Lord Chilton), the mother of a guy Jack urgently wants to question. She chatters away about her son and her late husband, in a conversation where sunny memories suddenly turn cloudy, and her timing and daffy energy is so infectious the whole audience is chuckling, partly in disbelief. (This is her first movie credit; where did she come from? She's like the sister of the Swoozie Kurtz character in *True Stories*.)

I also liked Pasquale Gaeta as Eddie. Guys like this are fun because they are obviously con men, but verbal, entertaining, and ingratiating. Watch the way Eddie shamelessly flatters Mrs. Bruner and makes up facts about her son (whom he has never seen) while Jack is upstairs plundering the kid's room. Eddie is a natural, but why did he take on this job of being Jack's adviser and sidekick in the search for the gun? He hardly knows Jack, has to have their mutual connection described in detail, calls him by the wrong name, and yet is like a father to him.

I think Eddie gets involved in Jack's search because it's in his nature to stick his nose in. To make other people's business his own. To play the role of wise guy. To show how he has the inside info. This is, amazingly, only his second movie; where does David Maquiling, the writer-director, find these engaging naturals?

And who, for that matter, is Maquiling? I learn that he's a Filipino-American who based this seemingly all-American story on a legend from his native land, and that the Eddie character represents a shaman in the original version. Yes, but every culture has shamans, and *Too Much Sleep* has been so Americanized it seems like a road movie (all on city streets) that makes itself up as it goes along. Maquiling loves the specifics of dialogue. He has an ear for word choices, for how people pause for a second after uttering outrageous lies, and for the way the suburbs (his suburbs, at least) are not homogenized flatlands but breed people who go slightly mad in intriguing ways.

When I recommend a movie like this, there are always people who go to see it and challenge me: "What was *that* about?" Sometimes they send me their ticket stubs and demand a refund. They're not used to films this specific and unsprung. Others will cherish it as a treasure. Depends on what you're looking for. *Too Much Sleep* doesn't shake you by the throat with its desire to entertain. It doesn't *want* you to roll in the aisles. It would rather you smiled than laughed out loud. It is enormously amused by the way people invent themselves as characters, and allows itself to be entertained by their preposterous sublimity.

Topsy-Turvy ★ ★ ★ ★
R, 160 m., 2000

Allan Corduner (Arthur Sullivan), Jim Broadbent (William Schwenck Gilbert), Lesley Manville (Lucy Gilbert ["Kitty"]), Ron Cook (Richard D'Oyly Carte), Timothy Spall (Richard Temple), Wendy Nottingham (Helen Lenoir), Kevin McKidd (Durward Lely), Martin Savage (George Grossmith), Shirley Henderson (Leonora Braham), Alison Steadman (Madame Leon). Directed by Mike Leigh and produced by Simon Channing-Williams. Screenplay by Leigh.

Mike Leigh's *Topsy-Turvy* is the work of a man helplessly in love with the theater. In a gloriously entertaining period piece, he tells the story of the genesis, preparation, and presentation of a comic opera—Gilbert and Sullivan's *The Mikado*—celebrating all the dreaming and hard work, personality conflict and team spirit, inspiration and mundane detail of every theatrical presentation, however inspired or inept. Every production is completely different, and they are all exactly like this.

As the movie opens, Arthur Sullivan and William Schwenck Gilbert rule the London stage. Their comic operettas, produced by the famed impresario Richard D'Oyly Carte, have even paid for the construction of the Savoy Theater—where, alas, their latest collaboration, *Princess Ida,* has flopped so badly that even Gilbert's dentist tells him it went on too long.

Sullivan, the composer, has had enough. Newly knighted by the queen, he decides it is time to compose serious operas: "This work with Gilbert is quite simply killing me." He flees to Paris and a bordello, where D'Oyly Carte tracks him down and learns that there may never be another collaboration between Gilbert (Jim Broadbent) and Sullivan (Allan Corduner). When Sullivan returns to London, he has a meeting with Gilbert, tense and studiously polite, and rejects Gilbert's latest scenario, which is as silly as all of the others: "Oh, Gilbert! You and your world of Topsy-Turvy-dom!"

The two men are quite different. Sullivan is a womanizer and dandy, Gilbert a businessman with an eagle eye for theatrical detail. One day in the middle of the impasse, his wife, Kitty (Lesley Manville), drags him to London's newly opened Japan exhibition, where he observes a Kabuki performance, sips green tea, and buys a sword that his butler nails up over the door. Not long after, as he paces his study, the sword falls down, and inspiration strikes: Gilbert races to his desk to begin writing *The Mikado.*

The world of Gilbert and Sullivan is one of whimsical goofiness, presented with rigorous attention to detail. The fun is in the tension between absurd contrivance and meticulous delivery; consider the song "I Am the Very Model of a Modern Major-General" from *The Pirates of Penzance,* which is delivered with the discipline of a metronome, but at breakneck pace. The form itself is a poke in the eye for Victorian values: The plots and songs uphold the conventional while making it seem clearly mad.

Mike Leigh might seem to be the last of modern British directors to be attracted to the world of the Savoy operas. His films, which do not begin with finished screenplays but are "devised" by the director in collaboration with his actors, have always been about modern Britain—often about inarticulate, alienated, shy, hostile types, who are as psychologically awkward in his comedies as in his hard-edged work. His credits include *Life Is Sweet, Naked,* and *Secrets and Lies,* and nothing remotely in the same cosmos as Gilbert and Sullivan.

But think again. Leigh has worked as much in the theater as for film, and his films depend more than most on the theatrical disciplines of improvisation and rehearsal. In London his productions have often been in vest-pocket theaters where even details like printing the tickets and hiring the stagehands may not have escaped his attention. He is a man of the theater in every atom of his being, and that is why there is a direct connection between his work and Gilbert and Sullivan.

The earlier reaches of *Topsy-Turvy* resemble in broad outline other films about theater: a flop, a crisis, a vow to never work again, a sudden inspiration, a new start. All well done, but the film begins to glow when the decision is made to go ahead with *The Mikado.* This is not merely a film that goes backstage, but also one that goes into accounting ledgers, hiring practices, costume design, personnel problems, casting decisions, sex lives, and the endless detail work of rehearsal: Hours of work are needed to manufacture and perfect even a silly throwaway moment, so that it is thrown away with style and wit, instead of merely being misplaced.

My favorite scene is one in which Gilbert rehearses his actors in line readings. The actor George Grossmith (Martin Savage) expresses insufficient alarm, and Gilbert reminds him that his character is under sentence of death, "by something lingering. By either boiling oil or melted lead. Kindly bear that in mind." There is also much travail over the correct pronunciation of "corroborative."

Many of the cast members are veterans of earlier Leigh films, including the pear-shaped, pouty-lipped Timothy Spall, whose character blinks back tears as his big song seems doomed in dress rehearsal. Jim Broadbent makes a precise Gilbert, bluff and incisive, and Allan Corduner's Sullivan is a study in the partner who cannot admit that his greatness lies always in collaboration. Leigh's construction is canny as he follows big musical numbers like "Three Little Maids" from rehearsal through opening night, and the costumes and sets faithfully recreate the classic D'Oyly Carte Co. productions.

Not everyone is familiar with Gilbert and Sullivan. Do they need to be to enjoy *Topsy-Turvy*? No more, I suspect, than one needs to know all about Shakespeare to enjoy *Shakespeare in Love*—although with both films, the more you do know, the more you enjoy. The two films have been compared because both are British, both are about theatrical geniuses, both deal with theatrical lore. The difference is that *Shakespeare in Love* centers on a love story, and *Topsy-Turvy* is about love of the theater. Romantic love ages and matures. Love of the theater, it reminds us, is somehow always adolescent—heedless, passionate, guilty.

Tortilla Soup ★ ★ ★
PG-13, 100 m., 2001

Hector Elizondo (Martin Naranjo), Jacqueline Obradors (Carmen Naranjo), Tamara Mello (Maribel Naranjo), Elizabeth Pena (Leticia Naranjo), Paul Rodriguez (Orlando), Constance Marie (Yolanda), Nikolai Kinski (Andy), Raquel Welch (Hortensia), Jade Herrera (Eden). Directed by Maria Ripoll and produced by John Bard Manulis. Screenplay by Hui-Ling Wang, Ang Lee, James Schamus, Ramon Menendez, Tom Musca, and Vera Blasi.

There is a quality about Hector Elizondo that is immediately likable, but too often we have to glimpse it in supporting roles; we smile with recognition, and he's gone from the screen.

Now comes a starring role that could have been written for him—but wasn't, oddly enough. His Mexican-American patriarch in the wonderful *Tortilla Soup* was originally a Chinese patriarch in the differently wonderful *Eat Drink Man Woman* (1994). That movie, about a Chinese chef and his three daughters, was directed by Ang Lee, and when Samuel Goldwyn Jr. bought the U.S. distribution rights, he wisely bought the remake rights too.

Can a Chinese family be made into a Mexican-American family? Of course, and although six writers worked on the adaptation, for once too many cooks didn't spoil the broth. (One of the writers is Vera Blasi, who directed *Woman on Top*, the 2000 movie with Penelope Cruz as a Brazilian chef.) The underlying idea is universal: We meet a widower who is a great chef, but has entered into the autumn of his life depressed because he has lost his senses of taste and smell. He has to depend on his best friend, a Cuban chef named Thomas, to sample his dishes. Martin Naranjo (Elizondo) now cooks mostly for his family; he presides over a dinner table with his three grown daughters, who all still live at home: Leticia (Elizabeth Pena), a spinster schoolteacher who has abandoned Catholicism to become a born-again Jesus fan; Carmen (Jacqueline Obradors), who is successful in business but feels something is lacking; and Maribel (Tamara Mello), the youngest, with her streaked hair and hip look, who is going through the kind of mild rebellion that leads to boyfriends you can still bring home to dinner.

This father, his daughters, the men in their lives, and the widow (Raquel Welch) who wants to be in his are the ingredients for a warm human comedy that has no great, deep message but simply makes us feel good—especially since Hector Elizondo is so effortlessly able to make us worry and speculate about him, just as his daughters do. Mexican Americans are not often seen in middle-class domestic settings; Hollywood small-mindedly tends to relegate them, like African-Americans, to thrillers and crime movies. Here at last is a Mexican-American home with the kind of kitchen you'd see in *Gourmet* magazine. (The food on the screen was prepared by Mary Sue Milliken and Susan Feniger, the Too Hot Tamales from the Food Network.)

Martin Naranjo is a proud father, old-fashioned but not weird. He and his daughters have arrived at that subtle balancing point in life where he still considers himself taking care of them, but they are starting to think of themselves as taking care of him. He despairs that Leticia, his oldest, will ever get married, or even have sex. He fears that Carmen, the middle girl, has too much sex ("Don't treat me like a slut just because I've had sex in this decade," she tells him). And as for the youngest, the rebellious Maribel, who is this "Brazilian" boy she brings home to dinner? "The only white Brazilians I know," Martin tells him, "are Nazi war criminals." The Brazilian is played by Nikolai Kinski, son of Klaus (who qualifies at least as an honorary South American after *Aguirre* and *Fitzcarraldo*).

Leticia puts her faith in Jesus, and it is rewarded: One day she looks at the high school coach (Paul Rodriguez) in a certain way, and falls in love, and he is already halfway there. When she brings him home for dinner, that is the beginning of the seismic shift in the family's long routine—a shift that the sexy widow Hortensia (Raquel Welch) hopes will move in her favor, while Hortensia's daughter Yolanda (Constance Marie) smiles and keeps her thoughts to herself.

Tortilla Soup, directed by Maria Ripoll, is not a shot-by-shot remake of *Eat Drink Man Woman* by any means, although some plot points (like those involving the best friend Thomas) correspond. What the two films have most in common is their voluptuous food photography. What is it about great food in the movies that seems to stir audiences? Movies as different as *Babette's Feast, Like Water for Chocolate, Big Night, Soul Food,* and *What's Cooking?* (which featured four cuisines) elicit audible sighs from the audience, and Mexico of course has one of the world's great cuisines.

Tortilla Soup follows a familiar formula, in which the movie opens with everyone unmarried, and we suspect it will have to end with everyone happily paired off. But the movie is cast so well that the actors bring life to their predictable destinies, and Elizondo casts a kind of magical warm spell over them all. Watch his face during the scene where Leticia brings the coach home for dinner. How hard he tries to look stern, and how obviously he wants to fail.

Traffic ★ ★ ★ ★
R, 147 m., 2001

Michael Douglas (Robert Wakefield), Don
Cheadle (Montel Gordon), Benicio Del Toro
(Javier Rodriguez), Luis Guzman (Ray Castro),
Erika Christensen (Caroline Wakefield), Dennis
Quaid (Arnie Metzger), Catherine Zeta-Jones
(Helena Ayala), Steven Bauer (Carlos Ayala),
Albert Finney (Chief of Staff), James Brolin
(General Ralph Landry), Jacob Vargas (Manolo
Sanchez), Tomas Milian (General Arturo Salazar),
Miguel Ferrer (Eduardo Ruiz). Directed by
Steven Soderbergh and produced by Edward
Zwick, Marshall Herskovitz, and Laura Bickford.
Screenplay by Stephen Gaghan.

Our laws against illegal drugs function as a
price support system for the criminal drug industry. They do not stop drugs. Despite billions of dollars spent and a toll of death,
addiction, crime, corruption, and lives wasted
in prison, it is possible today for anyone who
wants drugs to get them. "For someone my
age," says a high school student in the new film
Traffic, "it's a lot easier to get drugs than it is to
get alcohol."

Who supports the drug law enforcement
industry? A good many honest and sincere
people, to be sure. Also politicians who may
know drug laws are futile, but don't have the
nerve to appear soft on the issue. And corrupt
lawmen, who find drugs a lucrative source of
bribes, kickbacks, and payoffs. And the drug
cartels themselves, since the laws make their
business so profitable. If the decriminalization of drugs were ever seriously considered in
this country, the opponents would include
not only high-minded public servants, but the
kingpins of the illegal drug industry.

These are the conclusions I draw from
Traffic, Steven Soderbergh's new film, which
traces the drug traffic in North America from
the bottom to the top of the supply chain.
They may not be your conclusions. Draw your
own. Soderbergh himself does not favor legal-
izing drugs, but believes addiction is a public
health problem, not a crime. Certainly drugs
breed crime—addicts steal because they must—
and a more rational policy would result in a
lower crime rate and a safer society.

The movie tells several parallel stories,
which sometimes link but usually do not. We
meet two Mexican drug enforcement cops.
Two San Diego DEA agents. A midlevel whole-
saler who imports drugs from Mexico. A high-
level drug millionaire who seems to be a
respectable businessman. A federal judge who
is appointed the U.S. drug czar. And his teenage
daughter, who becomes addicted to cocaine
and nearly destroys her life. We also meet a
Mexican general who has made it his goal to
destroy a drug cartel—but not for the reasons
he claims. And we see how cooperation between Mexican and American authorities is
compromised because key people on both
sides may be corrupt, and betray secrets.

The movie is inspired by a five-part *Masterpiece Theater* series named *Traffik*, which ran
ten years ago and traced the movement of
heroin from the poppy fields of Turkey to the
streets of Europe. The story in North America
is much the same, which is why adapting this
material was so depressingly easy. At every
level, the illegal drug business is about making
money. If there is anything more lucrative
than an addictive substance that is legal, like
alcohol or tobacco, it is one that is illegal, like
drugs—because the suppliers aren't taxed or
regulated and have no overhead for advertising, packaging, insurance, employee benefits,
or quality control. Drugs are produced by
subsistence-level peasants and move through
a distribution chain of street sellers; costs to the
end user are kept low to encourage addiction.

Soderbergh's film uses a levelheaded approach. It watches, it observes, it does not do
much editorializing. The hopelessness of antidrug measures is brought home through practical scenarios, not speeches and messages—
except for a few. One of the most heartfelt
comes from a black man who observes that at
any given moment in America, 100,000 white
people are driving through black neighborhoods looking for drugs, and a dealer who can
make $200 in two hours is hardly motivated to
seek other employment.

The key performance in the movie is by
Michael Douglas, as Robert Wakefield, an
Ohio judge tapped by the White House as the
nation's new drug czar. He holds all the usual
opinions, mouths all the standard platitudes,
shares all the naive assumptions—including
his belief that he can destroy one of the Mexi-

can cartels by cooperating with the Mexican authorities. This is true in theory, but in practice his information simply provides an advantage for one cartel over the other.

Wakefield is a good man. His daughter, Caroline (Erika Christensen), is an honor student. One night at a party with other teenagers, she tries cocaine and likes it, very much. We see how easily the drug is available to her, how quickly she gets hooked, how swiftly she falls through the safety nets of family and society. This is the social cost of addiction, and the rationale for passing laws against drugs—but we see that it happens *despite* the laws, and that without a profit motive drugs might not be so easily available in her circle.

In Mexico, we meet two hardworking cops in the drug wars, played by Benicio Del Toro and Jacob Vargas, who intercept a big drug shipment but then are themselves intercepted by troops commanded by an army general (Tomas Milian), who is sort of the J. Edgar Hoover of Mexican drug enforcement. In California, we meet a middleman (Miguel Ferrer) who imports and distributes drugs, and two federal agents (Don Cheadle and Luis Guzman) who are on his trail. And we meet the top executive for this operation, a respectable millionaire (Steven Bauer) and his socialite wife (Catherine Zeta-Jones), who has no idea where her money comes from.

Soderbergh's story, from a screenplay by Stephen Gaghan, cuts between these characters so smoothly that even a fairly complex scenario remains clear and charged with tension. Like Martin Scorsese's *GoodFellas, Traffic* is fascinating at one level simply because it shows how things work—how the drugs are marketed, how the laws are sidestepped. The problem is like a punching bag. You can hammer it all day and still it hangs there, impassive, unchanged.

The movie is powerful precisely because it doesn't preach. It is so restrained that at one moment—the judge's final speech—I wanted one more sentence, making a point, but the movie lets us supply that thought for ourselves. And the facts make their own argument: This war is not winnable on the present terms, and takes a greater toll in human lives than the drugs themselves. The drug war costs $19 billion a year, but scenes near the end of the film suggest that more addicts are helped by two free programs, Alcoholics Anonymous and Narcotics Anonymous, than by all the drug troops put together.

Training Day ★ ★ ★
R, 122 m., 2001

Denzel Washington (Alonzo Harris), Ethan Hawke (Jake Hoyt), Scott Glenn (Roger), Tom Berenger (Stan), Cliff Curtis (Smiley), Snoop Dogg (Sammy), Macy Gray (Sandman's Wife). Directed by Antoine Fuqua and produced by Jeffrey Silver and Bobby Newmeyer. Screenplay by David Ayer.

Training Day is an equal-opportunity police brutality picture, depicting a modern Los Angeles in which the black cop is slimier and more corrupt than anybody ever thought the white cops were. Alonzo Harris, played by Denzel Washington, makes Popeye Doyle look like Officer Friendly. So extreme is his mad dog behavior, indeed, that it shades over into humor: Washington seems to enjoy a performance that's over the top and down the other side.

He plays Alonzo as the meanest, baddest narcotics cop in the city—a dude who cruises the mean streets in his confiscated customized Monte Carlo, extracting tribute and accumulating graft like a medieval warlord shaking down his serfs. His pose is that the job must be done this way: If you don't intimidate the street, it will kill you. This is the lesson he's teaching Jake Hoyt (Ethan Hawke), a young cop who dreams of being promoted to the elite narc squad.

This is Jake's first day of training, and he's been placed in the hands of Alonzo for a taste of street reality. Jake's dream: Get a promotion so he can move his wife and child to a nicer house. This may not turn out to be a wise career move. Just as a warm-up, Alonzo forces him to smoke pot (it turns out to be laced with PCP): If you turn down gifts on the street, he's told, "You'll be dead." He watches as Alonzo stops two punks who are raping a girl, and then instead of arresting the rapists he thoroughly and competently beats them almost dead.

Dispensing street justice is what it's all about

625

Alonzo believes; the enemy lives outside the law, and you have to pursue him there. Jake hallucinates for a while because of the PCP, but surfaces to accompany Alonzo on a visit to an old and slimy colleague (Scott Glenn), on a raid on a drug dealer's house, on a visit to what seems to be Alonzo's secret second family, and to a restaurant rendezvous with what appears to be a circle of top cops who mastermind graft and payoffs. Along the way there's a sensational gun battle, although it doesn't draw enough attention to interrupt Alonzo's routine. I'm not saying all of these events in one day are impossible; in the real world, however, by the end of it both cops would be exhausted, and Alonzo would be shaking down a druggist for Ben-Gay.

Is Alonzo for real? Are the city and its cops really this evil? (I am asking about the movie, not life.) At first we wonder if Alonzo isn't putting on a show to test the rookie. The rookie thinks that, too—that if he yields to temptation, he'll be busted. That theory comes to an end when Jake is ordered to kill someone, or be framed for the murder anyway. And Alonzo isn't the exception to the rule: We can tell by the lunchtime summit that he's part of the ruling circle.

For Denzel Washington, *Training Day* is a rare villainous role; he doesn't look, sound, or move like his usual likable characters, and certainly there's no trace of the football coach from *Remember the Titans*. The movie, directed by Antoine Fuqua *(Bait)* and written by David Ayer *(The Fast and the Furious)*, keeps pushing him, and by the end it has pushed him right into pure fantasy. Alonzo, in the earlier scenes, seems extreme but perhaps believable; by the end, he's like a monster from a horror film, unkillable and implacable.

A lot of people are going to be leaving the theater as I did, wondering about the logic and plausibility of the last fifteen minutes. There are times when you're distracted from the action on the screen by the need to trace back through the plot and try to piece together how events could possibly have turned out this way. But Ayer's screenplay is ingenious in the way it plants clues and pays them off in unexpected ways; *Training Day* makes as much sense as movies like this usually can. It might

have been better if it had stayed closer to life, but it doesn't want to be.

For its kinetic energy and acting zeal, I enjoyed the movie. I like it when actors go for broke. Ethan Hawke is well cast as the cop who believes "we serve and protect" but has trouble accepting the logic of Alonzo's style of serving and protecting. And the supporting roles are well crafted, especially the retired cop played by Scott Glenn, who seems to be sitting on a whole other buried story. Aware as I was of its loopholes and excesses, the movie persuaded me to go along for the ride.

Of course, you can't watch the movie without thinking of the Rodney King and O.J. Simpson sagas, two sides of the same coin, both suggesting the Los Angeles police are not perfect. I found myself wondering what would have happened if the movie had flipped the races, with a rotten white cop showing a black rookie the ropes. Given the way the movie pays off, that might have been doable. But it would have involved flipping the itinerary of the street tours, too; instead of the black cop planting the white boy in the middle of hostile nonwhite environments, you'd have the white cop taking the black rookie to the white drug lords; gated mansions in *Traffic* come to mind. Not as much fun.

The Trial ★ ★ ★

NO MPAA RATING, 118 m., 1963 (rereleased 2000)

Anthony Perkins (Joseph K), Jeanne Moreau (Miss Burstner), Orson Welles (Advocate), Madeline Robinson (Mrs. Brubach), Elsa Martinelli (Hilda), Suzanne Flon (Miss Pittl), Akim Tamiroff (Bloch), Romy Schneider (Leni). Directed by Orson Welles and produced by Alexander Salkind. Screenplay by Welles, based on the novel by Franz Kafka.

I was once involved in a project to convince Orson Welles to record a commentary track for *Citizen Kane*. Seemed like a good idea, but not to the great one, who rumbled that he had made a great many films other than *Kane* and was tired of talking about it.

One he might have talked about was *The Trial* (1963), his version of the Kafka story about a man accused of—something, he know not what. It starred Anthony Perkins in his squirmy post-*Psycho* mode, it had a baroque visual style, and it was one of the few times, after *Kane*, when Welles was able to get his vision onto the screen intact. For years the negative of the film was thought to be lost, but then it was rediscovered and restored.

The world of the movie is like a nightmare, with its hero popping from one surrealistic situation to another. Water towers open into file rooms, a woman does laundry while through the door a trial is under way, and huge trunks are dragged across empty landscapes and then back again. The black-and-white photography shows Welles's love of shadows, extreme camera angles, and spectacular sets. He shot it mostly inside the Gare d'Orsay in Paris, which, after it closed as a train station and before it was reborn as a museum, offered vast spaces; the office where Perkins's character works consists of rows of desks and typists extending almost to infinity, like a similar scene in the silent film *The Crowd*.

Franz Kafka published his novel in Prague in 1925; it reflected his own paranoia, but it was prophetic, foreseeing Stalin's Gulag and Hitler's Holocaust, in which innocent people wake up one morning to discover they are guilty of being themselves. It is a tribute to his vision that the word "Kafkesque" has, like "catch-22," moved beyond the work to describe things we all see in the world.

Anthony Perkins is a good choice to play Joseph K, the bureaucrat who awakens to find strange men in his room, men who treat him as a suspect and yet give him no information. Perkins could turn in an instant from ingratiating smarminess to anger, from supplication to indignation, his voice barking out ultimatums and then suddenly going high-pitched and stuttery. And watch his body language as he goes into his confiding mode, hitching closer to other characters, buddy-style, looking forward to neat secrets.

The film follows his attempts to discover what he is charged with, and how he can defend himself. Every Freudian slip is used against him (he refers to a "pornograph player," and a man in a black suit carefully notes that down). He finds himself in a courtroom where the audience is cued by secret signs from the judge.

He petitions the court's official portrait painter, who claims he can fix cases and obtain a "provisional acquittal." And in the longest sequence, he visits the cavernous home of the Advocate, played by Welles as an ominous sybarite who spends much of his time in bed, smoking cigars and being tended by his mistress (Romy Schneider).

The Advocate has obscure powers in matters such as Joseph K is charged with, whatever they are. He has had a pathetic little man living in his maid's room for a long time, hoping for news on his case, kissing the Advocate's hand, falling to his knees. He would like Joseph to behave in the same way. The Advocate's home reaches out in all directions, like a loft, factory, and junk shop, illuminated by hundreds of guttering candles, decorated by portraits of judges, littered with so many bales of old legal papers that one shot looks like the closing scene in *Citizen Kane*. But neither here nor elsewhere can Joseph come to grips with his dilemma.

Perkins was one of those actors everyone thought was gay. He kept his sexuality private, and used his nervous style of speech and movement to suggest inner disconnects. From an article by Edward Guthmann in the *San Francisco Chronicle*, I learn that Welles confided to his friend Henry Jaglom that he knew Perkins was a homosexual, "and used that quality in Perkins to suggest another texture in Joseph K, a fear of exposure."

"The whole homosexuality thing—using Perkins that way—was incredible for that time," Jaglom told Guthmann. "It was intentional on Orson's part: He had these three gorgeous women (Jeanne Moreau, Romy Schneider, Elsa Martinelli) trying to seduce this guy, who was completely repressed and incapable of responding." That provides an additional key to the film, which could be interpreted as a nightmare in which women make demands Joseph is uninterested in meeting, while bureaucrats in black coats follow him everywhere with obscure threats of legal disaster.

But there is also another way of looking at *The Trial*, and that is to see it as autobiographical. After *Citizen Kane* (1941) and *The Magnificent Ambersons* (1942, a masterpiece with its ending hacked to pieces by the studio), Welles seldom found the freedom to make films when and how he desired. His life became a wandering from one place to another. Beautiful women rotated through his beds. He was reduced to a supplicant who begged financing from wealthy but maddening men. He was never able to find out exactly what crime he had committed that made him "unbankable" in Hollywood. Because Welles plays the Advocate, there is a tendency to think the character is inspired by him, but I can think of another suspect: Alexander Salkind, producer of *The Trial* and much later of the *Superman* movies, who like the Advocate, liked people to beg for money and power which, in fact, he did not always have.

Seen in this restored version (available on video from Milestone), *The Trial* is above all a visual achievement, an exuberant use of camera placement and movement and inventive lighting. Study the scene where the screaming girls chase Joseph K up the stairs to the painter's studio and peer at him through the slats of the walls, and you will see what Richard Lester saw before he filmed the screaming girls in *A Hard Day's Night* and had them peer at the Beatles through the slats of a railway luggage car.

The ending is problematical. Mushroom clouds are not Kafkaesque because they represent a final conclusion, and in Kafka's world nothing ever concludes. But then comes another ending: the voice of Orson Welles, speaking the end credits, placing his own claim on every frame of the film, and we wonder, is this his way of telling us *The Trial* is more than ordinarily personal? He was a man who made the greatest film ever made, and was never forgiven for it.

The Triumph of Love ★ ★ ★

PG-13, 107 m., 2002

Mira Sorvino (Princess/Phocion/Aspasie), Ben Kingsley (Hermocrates), Jay Rodan (Agis), Fiona Shaw (Leontine), Ignazio Oliva (Harlequin), Rachael Stirling (Hermidas/Corine), Luis Molteni (Dimas). Directed by Clare Peploe and produced by Bernardo Bertolucci. Screenplay by Peploe, Bertolucci, and Marilyn Goldin.

Mira Sorvino has a little teasing smile that is invaluable in *The Triumph of Love*, a movie where she plays a boy who does not look the slightest thing like a boy, but looks exactly like Mira Sorvino playing a boy with a teasing smile. The story, based on an eighteenth-century French play by Pierre Marivaux, is the sort of thing that inspired operas and Shakespeare comedies: It's all premise, no plausibility, and so what?

Sorvino plays a princess who goes for a stroll in the woods one day and happens upon the inspiring sight of a handsome young man named Agis (Jay Rodan) emerging naked from a swim. She knows she must have him. She also knows that he is the true possessor of her throne, that she is an usurper, and that her chances of meeting him are slim. That's because he lives as the virtual prisoner of a brother and sister, a philosopher named Hermocrates (Ben Kingsley) and a scientist named Leontine (Fiona Shaw.)

Hermocrates is a scholar of the sort who, in tales of this sort, spends much time in his study pondering over quaint and curious volumes of forgotten lore. He wears one of those skullcaps with stars and moons on it, and a long robe, and is obsessed, although not without method. His sister, past the second bloom of her youth, is ferociously dedicated to him, and together they raise the young Agis to think rationally of all things, and to avoid the distractions of women, sex, romance, and worldly things.

The scheme of the princess: She and her maid Hermidas (Rachael Stirling) will disguise themselves as young men, penetrate Hermocrates' enclave, and insinuate themselves into the good graces of the brother and sister. Then nature will take its course. This is the sort of plot, like *The Scorpion King*'s, that you either accept or do not accept; if it contained martial arts, skewerings, and explosions, no one would raise an eyebrow. Because it is elegant, mannered, and teasing, some audiences will not want to go along with the joke. Your choice.

The Triumph of Love, as a title, is literally true. Love does conquer Hermocrates, Leontine, and finally Agis. Of course it is not true love in the tiresome modern sense, but romantic love as a plot device. To win Agis, the cross-dressing princess must inveigle herself into the good graces of his guardians by seducing

Leontine and Hermocrates. The scene between Sorvino and Shaw is one of the most delightful in the movie, as the prim spinster allows herself reluctantly to believe that she might be irresistible—that this handsome youth might indeed have penetrated the compound hoping to seduce her. The director, Clare Peploe, stages this scene among trees and shrubbery, as the "boy" pursues the bashful sister from sun to shade to sun again.

Now comes the challenge of Hermocrates. Although there are possibilities in the notion that the philosopher might be attracted to a comely young lad, the movie departs from tradition and allows Hermocrates to see through the deception at once: He knows this visitor is a girl, accuses her of it, and is told she disguised herself as a boy only to gain access to his overwhelmingly attractive presence. Hermocrates insists she only wants access to Agis. "He is not the one my heart beats for," she says shyly, and watch Ben Kingsley's face as he understands the implications. Strange, how universal is the human notion that others should find us attractive.

Kingsley is the most versatile of actors, able to suggest, with a slant of the gaze, a cast of the mouth, emotional states that other actors could not achieve with cartwheels. There is a twinkle in his eye. He is as easily persuaded as his sister that this visitor loves him. But is it not cruel that the ripe young imposter deceives both the brother and sister, stealing their hearts as stepping-stones for her own? Not at all, because the ending, in admirable eighteenth-century style, tidies all loose ends, restores order to the kingdom, and allows everyone to live happily ever after, although it is in the nature of things that some will live happier than others.

Clare Peploe, the wife of the great Italian director Bernardo Bertolucci, was born in Tanzania, raised in Britain, educated at the Sorbonne and in Italy, began with her brother Mark as a writer on Antonioni's *Zabriskie Point*, and in addition to cowriting many of Bertolucci's films, has directed three of her own. The sleeper is *High Season* (1988), a comedy set on a Greek island and involving romance, art, spies, and a statue to the Unknown Tourist. If you know the John Huston movie *Beat the Devil* you will have seen its first cousin.

With this film, once again she shows a light-hearted playfulness.

Trixie ★ ★
R, 115 m., 2000

Emily Watson (Trixie Zurbo), Dermot Mulroney (Dex Lang), Nick Nolte (Senator Drummond Avery), Nathan Lane (Kirk Stans), Brittany Murphy (Ruby Pearli), Lesley Ann Warren (Dawn Sloane), Will Patton (Red Rafferty), Stephen Lang (Jacob Slotnick), Mark Acheson (Vince Deflore). Directed by Alan Rudolph and produced by Robert Altman. Screenplay by Rudolph, based on a story by Rudolph and John Binder.

Trixie has all the trappings and suits of woe of a comedy, but then it changes horses of a different color and turns into a thriller in the middle of the stream. That razes our expectations. It's not a success, but it's a closed mist, and kind of fun in its own ways and means.

I should warn you, however, that if you are not amused by cheerfully mangled language, you may think too much Trixie is not a treat. The movie stars Emily Watson as Trixie Zurbo, an undercover detective for a casino, who consistently and without flail commits a malappropriation every time she opens her mouth.

She gets her man "by hook or by ladder," she declares, and tells one bad guy he's a "Jekyll of all trades." Her sister is having a baby, "but I don't know if I'm gonna be an uncle or an aunt yet." She often finds herself "between a rock and the deep blue sea."

Trixie is hired on the overnight shift of the casino, which is located in a mountain area next to a scenic lake. She makes a pal of a lounge act (Nathan Lane). And she falls afoul of some local cheeseballs who are involved in the shade of influence peddling and real estate wheeler-stealing. That happens because Dex Lang (Dermot Mulroney) draws designs on her body. He works for a con man named Red Rafferty (Will Patton). Dex sneaks Trixie onto Red's boat for a little quality dock time, and they're on board when Red turns up with the crooked state senator Drummond Avery (Nick Nolte) and the senator's maintenance squeeze, Dawn Sloane (Lesley Ann Warren).

The plot is standard for anyone who has

read Ross MacDonald, or seen any movie involving gambling, real estate, and hook-or-by-crooked politicians. I guess the director, Alan Rudolph, intended *Trixie* as a *film noir* satire, but he's famous for the loose flywheels on his plots, and this one spins off in separated directions. First, the movie starts goofy and then gets more straight, which is perplexing. Second, Trixie as a character exists in a whirl of her own. Her typical shot involves looking into the camera and intonating lines like, "Either fish or get off the pot!"

Rudolph's characters exist at an angle from the reel world; when he works in a genre, he likes to avoid the genre's conventions, which sort of defeats its own purpose. With most genre movies, we know what's going to happen next but don't care. With Rudolph, we care what's going to happen next but don't know.

Nick Nolte fits easily into the Rudolph universe, and almost visibly expands with the freedom the director gives him. This is his third recent Rudolph film, after the unsuccessful *Breakfast of Champions* (1998) and the wonderful *Afterglow* (1997), in which Nolte, as a fix-it man, gave one of his best performances opposite the Oscar-nominated Julie Christie.

Nolte brings a poker-faced charm to dialogue other actors might find unsayable. At one point his senator orders everyone to "stop clowning around"—because "as a child my dad took me to the circus and a clown killed him." This line is delivered so offhandedly that it could be true, could be intended to be funny, could be a train of thought jumping the tracks, or could even be intended to intimidate by its sheer goofiness.

Emily Watson is a newcomer to Rudolph's films, but seems like a member of his repeatatory company. She is gifted at many diffident tones, but as Trixie, curiously, the character she reminds us of is the innocent in the totally different film *Breaking the Waves*. She has the same kind of wide-eyed innocence, the same straight-ahead approach to the world, the same heedlessness for danger. As Trixie puts it, she's able to "grab the bull by the tail and look him in the eye."

Does the movie work? Not on the whole. But individual scenes have a great comic zest. I like the way the confusion develops on board the boat. Later there is a nice scene where the senator is publicly humiliated at a private club when his privates get too much publicity. This is not the sort of movie you make it your business to see in a theater. But if you're ever surfing cable TV and come across it, you'll linger, unless you're entirely out of your rocker.

The Trumpet of the Swan ★ ½
G, 75 m., 2001

With the voices of: Dee Baker (Louie), Jason Alexander (Father), Mary Steenburgen (Mother), Reese Witherspoon (Serena), Seth Green (Boyd), Carol Burnett (Mrs. Hammerbotham), Joe Mantegna (Monty), Sam Gifaldi (Sam). An animated film directed by Richard Rich and produced by Lin Oliver. Screenplay by Judy Rothman Rofé, based on the novel by E. B. White.

The Trumpet of the Swan is an innocuous family feature that's too little, too late in the fast-moving world of feature animation. I would have found it slow going anyway, but seeing it not long after the triumph of *Shrek* made it seem even tamer and more flat. Maybe younger children will enjoy it at home on video, but older family members will find it thin.

The story is adapted from a 1970 E. B. White fable about a swan named Louie who is born without a voice. While his sisters, Ella and Billie, are trumpeter swans with magnificent calls, Louie paddles around in disconsolate silence. His father, desperate, raids a music store in Billings, Montana, and steals a trumpet, which Louie learns to play.

The young cygnet is a quick study. Encouraged by a local boy named Sam (voice by Sam Gifaldi), Louie enrolls in the local (human) school and learns to communicate by using a blackboard he straps around his neck. But his father's theft of the trumpet weighs upon him, and eventually he flies to Boston and appears in jazz clubs to raise cash to pay for the instrument.

There's more, involving his romance with the feathery Serena (voice by Reese Witherspoon), who in despair over Louie's absence waddles to the altar with the dastardly Boyd (Seth Green). Much is made of the buildup to the Serena-Boyd vows, but once they are interrupted by Louie's last-minute arrival, there are no further wedding scenes, leading thoughtful viewers to wonder whether Serena's nestful of eggs represents a little premarital feather-dusting. It wouldn't be the first time a bird fell for a trumpet player.

Turn It Up ★ ½
R, 83 m., 2000

Pras Michel (Diamond), Ja Rule (Gage), Tamala Jones (Nia), Vondie Curtis-Hall (Diamond's Father), Jason Stratham (Mr. B.), John Ralston (Mr. White). Directed by Robert Adetuyi and produced by Madonna and Guy Oseary. Screenplay by Ray "Cory" Daniels, Chris Hudson, Kelly Hilaire, and Adetuyi, based on *Ghetto Supastar,* the book and album by Prakazrel "Pras" Michel.

Turn It Up tells the story of a moral weakling who compromises his way through bloodbaths and drug deals while whining about his values. It's one of those movies where the more the characters demand respect, the less they deserve it. What's pathetic is that the movie halfway wants its hero to serve as a role model, but neither the hero nor the movie is prepared to walk the walk.

The rap singer Pras, of the Fugees, stars as Diamond, who dreams of becoming a superstar and spends hours in the studio, fine-tuning his tracks with small help from his cokehead mixer. Diamond's best friend is Gage (the rap singer Ja Rule), who finances the studio time by working as a runner for the drug dealer Mr. B (Jason Stratham). Diamond helps on deliveries, including one in the opening scene that leads to a shoot-out with a Chinese gang.

Dead bodies litter the screen, but there is not one word in the rest of the movie about whether Diamond and Gage are wanted by the police for questioning in the matter of perhaps a dozen deaths. By the end of the film, the two of them have killed, oh, I dunno, maybe six or eight other guys, but when we see the words "One Year Later" on-screen at the end, it is not to show Pras in prison but simply to share some sad nostalgia with him.

The movie is very seriously confused in its objectives, as if two or three story approaches are fighting for time on the same screen. Gage

is an uncomplicated character—a sniveling weakling with a big gun who murders in cold blood. Diamond is more of a puzzle. He is loyal to Gage, and yet demurs at some of his buddy's activities ("She's pregnant," he protests, when Gage wants to kill a cleaning woman who witnessed one of their massacres). He seems to accept Gage's lowlife atrocities as the price of getting his studio time paid for and not having to actually work for a living.

The stuff involving Gage, Mr. B, and the significantly named music executive Mr. White is standard drug-rap-ghetto-crime thriller material. But when Diamond's mother dies and his homeless, long-missing father (Vondie Curtis-Hall) turns up, another movie tries to get started. The father explains he abandoned his wife and son because he put his music first, and that was the start of his downfall. Now he sees his son doing the same thing. What he doesn't know is that Diamond has a pregnant girlfriend (Tamala Jones), and won't even give her his cell phone number because that's the first step on the long slide to enslavement by a woman.

Diamond's father listens to his demo tracks and abruptly drops a loud and clear message of music criticism into the movie: "Your music is too processed. You grew up on digitized music—you think that keyboard sample sounds like a real piano." Then his dad takes him to the American Conservatory of Music and plays classical music for him on a grand piano that apparently stands ready in a large empty space for the convenience of such visitors, and later tries to talk Diamond out of going along with Gage on a dangerous drug run.

Well, Diamond doesn't much want to go anyway. He keeps talking about how Gage should chill, and how he wants to get out of the drug and gun lifestyle, and how he loves his woman and wants to be a father to his unborn child, but he never really makes any of those hard decisions. It never occurs to him that he is living off of Gage's drug-soaked earnings—that his studio sessions are paid for by the exploitation of the very people he thinks his songs are about. He can't act on his qualms, I guess, because the movie needs him for the action scenes. *Turn It Up* says one thing and does another; Diamond frets and whines, while the movie lays on gunfire, torture, and bloodshed (the scene where Mr. B offers to run Gage's face through a meat slicer is memorable).

My guess is that Vondie Curtis-Hall had substantial input on his scenes, which have a different tone and sounder values than the rest of the movie. His advice to his son is good, and his performance is the best thing in the movie. But *Turn It Up* doesn't deserve it. Here is a film that goes out of its way to portray all the bad guys as white or Chinese, and doesn't have the nerve to point out that the heroes' worst enemies are themselves.

28 Days ★ ★ ★
PG-13, 103 m., 2000

Sandra Bullock (Gwen Cummings), Viggo Mortensen (Eddie Boone), Dominic West (Jasper), Elizabeth Perkins (Lily), Azura Skye (Andrea), Steve Buscemi (Cornell), Alan Tudyk (Gerhardt), Michael O'Malley (Oliver), Reni Santoni (Daniel). Directed by Betty Thomas and produced by Jenno Topping. Screenplay by Susannah Grant.

Every drunk considers himself a special case, unique, an exception to the rules. Odd, since for the practicing alcoholic, daily life is mostly unchanging, an attempt to negotiate daily responsibilities while drinking enough but not too much. When this attempt fails, as it often does, it results in events that the drunk thinks make him colorful. True variety comes only with sobriety. Plus, now he can remember it.

This is the lesson learned by Gwen Cummings, the character played by Sandra Bullock in *28 Days*. As the story opens, her life is either wild and crazy, or confused and sad, depending on where you stand. She parties all night with her boyfriend Jasper (Dominic West). After the clubs, the drinks, the designer drugs, they commence what may turn out to be sex, if they can stay awake long enough. Then a candle starts a fire, which they extinguish with champagne. What a ball.

In the morning, Gwen's day begins with a pass at the refrigerator so smooth and practiced she hardly seems to even open it while extracting a cold beer. Gwen is an accident waiting to happen—to herself, or innocent bystanders. Her victim is her sister Lily (Elizabeth Perkins). "Gwen, you make it impossible to love you," Lily says when she arrives late at the church for Lily's wedding. At the reception, Gwen delivers an insulting toast, knocks over the cake while dancing, steals a limousine to go buy another cake, and crashes it into a house. Not a good day.

Cut to Serenity Glen, where Gwen has been sentenced to twenty-eight days of rehab in lieu of jail time. The PA system makes a running commentary out of *M*A*S*H*-style announcements. The patients do a lot of peppy group singing (too much, if you ask me). "I don't have a health problem," Gwen protests. "I play Ultimate Frisbee twice a week." The patients include the usual cuckoo's nest of colorful characters, although they're a little more plausible than in most inmate populations. We meet Daniel (Reni Santoni), a doctor who pumped his own stomach to control his drinking, and wound up giving himself an emergency tracheotomy. Gerhardt (Alan Tudyk), prissy and critical, a dancer and coke addict. And Andrea (Azura Skye), Gwen's teenage roommate.

Gwen's counselor is Cornell, played by Steve Buscemi, who inspires a grin when we see him in a movie, because he's usually good for strange scenes and dialogue. Not this time; he plays the role straight, revealing toughness and a certain weary experience, as if all of Gwen's cherished kookiness is for him a very, very old joke. There's a nice scene where she says exactly the wrong things to him before discovering he's her counselor.

Another fellow patient is Eddie Boone (Viggo Mortensen), a baseball pitcher with a substance abuse problem. Of course they begin a tentative, unstated courtship. Of course Jasper, on weekend visits, misunderstands ("Where are all the celebrities?" he asks on his first arrival, looking around for Elizabeth Taylor). Of course there is a fight. This subplot is predictable, but made perceptive because Gwen and Eddie illustrate the lifeboat mentality in which sailors on the ship of rehab have only each other to cling to.

The movie was written by Susannah Grant, who also wrote Julia Roberts's hit film *Erin Brockovich*. I differed with *Erin* for the same reason I like *28 Days*: The tone of the central character. I found that Roberts, enormously likable though she is, upstaged the material in *Erin Brockovich* by unwise costume choices and scenes that were too obviously intended as showcases. Bullock brings a kind of ground-level vulnerability to *28 Days* that doesn't make her into a victim but simply into one more suitable case for treatment. Bullock, like Roberts, is likable, but in *28 Days* at least that's not the point.

Note: 28 Days is rated PG-13 and might be effective as a cautionary tale for teenagers.

Two Can Play That Game ★ ★ ½
R, 90 m., 2001

Vivica A. Fox (Shante Smith), Morris Chestnut (Keith), Anthony Anderson (Tony), Wendy Raquel Robinson (Karen), Gabrielle Union (Conny), Tamala Jones (Tracye), Mo'Nique (Diedre), Ray Wise (Bill Parker), Bobby Brown (Michael). Directed by Mark Brown and produced by Doug McHenry, Brown, and Paddy Cullen. Screenplay by Brown.

Two Can Play That Game reduces love to rules. At one point it even applies one of Newton's laws of motion to a cheating boyfriend: When one partner has negative energy, we learn, the other person has positive energy, or in any event no energy is lost in the transfer. That the film generates charm from this system is a tribute to the actors.

Vivica A. Fox stars in the film as Shante Smith, its heroine and narrator, who speaks directly to the audience as she talks us through the book of love. She's an ad executive, going with Keith (Morris Chestnut), a professional man with a roving eye. But then, of course, his eye is roving because it's spring, "breakup season," Shante explains. In the winter a man wants to cozy up at home, but the minute those spring outfits hit the streets, his imagination starts to roam.

Shante has three girlfriends, all with men and/or problems of their own: Diedre (Mo'Nique), Karen (Wendy Raquel Robinson), and Tracye (Tamala Jones). At their get-togethers, Shante is the theorist and lecturer, explaining the ways and weaknesses of men—but always confident of her own man, until one day she's shocked when he turns up at her favorite club with a hated rival, Conny (Gabrielle Union) on his arm. Since Keith knew she'd probably be there, this is war.

She fantasizes about flattening Conny with a right to the jaw, but decides on strategy instead, and initiates a ten-day plan designed to inspire any man to mend his ways and come crawling back for forgiveness. This plan includes letting herself be seen with an attractive man, not returning Keith's phone calls, and, on Day Seven, turning up unannounced at his house in full seduction mode, arousing him to the point of frenzy, and then walking out. (The girlfriends engage in some surprisingly crude talk about the results of this practice, with Diedre in particular doubting she could let a situation like that go to waste.) Keith is meanwhile advised by his worldly friend Tony (Anthony Anderson), who anticipates some of Shante's strategies and has some of his own.

The movie intercuts her battle plan with the adventures of her girlfriends, including Karen's inexplicable attraction for Big Mike (Bobby Brown), who when she meets him has a jheri curl and teeth that make Mortimer Snerd look reasonable. She pays for a complete makeover and extensive dental work, and they are blissful together until he catches sight of himself in a mirror and realizes he looks—well, like Bobby Brown.

Among the movie's pleasures is the fact that everybody on the screen is very good-looking, except for Big Mike before his dentistry. Vivica A. Fox, who has made her name in action movies, is so glamorous and bewitching here she may never again need to battle aliens or answer a booty call. Those who know about such things will probably be impressed by the clothes. Those who work for a living will be amused by how, in this movie as in most movies, the characters are given high-powered jobs and then never seem to work at them.

The movie does have charm and moments of humor, but what it doesn't have is romance. The Shante character is so analytical and calculating that life with her might be hell on Earth for poor Keith, even with all of Tony's advice. By Day Seven I was wondering if any man is worthy of (or deserves) such treatment.

And Shante doesn't just narrate a little from time to time; she must have half the dialogue in the movie, even interrupting love scenes to explain to the audience in great detail what is happening and why. What we basically have here is *Waiting to Inhale.*

Two Family House ★ ★ ★ ½

R, 104 m., 2000

Michael Rispoli (Buddy Visalo), Kelly Macdonald (Mary O'Neary), Katherine Narducci (Estelle Visalo), Kevin Conway (Jim O'Neary), Matt Servitto (Chipmunk), Michele Santopietro (Laura), Louis Guss (Donato), Rosemary DeAngelis (Marie). Directed by Raymond De Felitta and produced by Anne Harrison and Alan Klingenstein. Screenplay by De Felitta.

There really was an Uncle Buddy, and he really did finally open his own bar on Staten Island, and sing on Saturday nights to the customers. *Two Family House* vibrates with the energy of his presence. You can sense that real things are at risk, that Buddy really did finally break out of the jail of his life, that everyone in the old neighborhood thought he was insane, that only now can we look back and see that Buddy was a kind of hero.

As the movie opens, Buddy Visalo (Michael Rispoli) is in the navy and sings in a talent show. He's an Italian-American crooner, and Arthur Godfrey hears him and offers him an audition. But his fiancée, Estelle, won't let him go. She finds the idea "embarrassing," she says. Eventually Godfrey hires Julius LaRosa as his crooner, and it eats away inside Buddy that the job might have been his.

Estelle is played by Katherine Narducci, who like Rispoli is familiar from *The Sopranos.* Estelle is the kind of woman who grows taller by standing on the back of her husband's dreams. Buddy wants to open his own bar. "Serving drinks to a lot of bums?" Estelle sneers. "You want to turn me into a barmaid?" She wants them to stay back "where we belong, not making fools of ourselves, not having everybody laugh behind our backs." She would gladly send Buddy out into the world to a soul-crushing job for the rest of his life rather than let him take a chance.

Now this is where the story gets interesting,

and begins to accumulate the elements of family legend. Buddy buys a two-family house, planning to turn the downstairs into Buddy's Bar and rent the upstairs for income. He discovers he already has upstairs tenants: an Irish-American boozer named Jim O'Neary (Kevin Conway) and his considerably younger wife, named Mary (Kelly Macdonald), who is pregnant. There is an added detail: Her baby will be half-black. Who the father is we are not sure. Why the father is not Jim we can figure out just by looking at him: He is one of those drunks who give alcoholics a bad name.

Now all the pieces are in place for a story that must have been heard many times in many versions by Raymond De Felitta, Buddy's nephew, who wrote and directed this film. To some members of the family, Buddy was no doubt a lunatic loser. To others, who perhaps kept their opinions to themselves at family gatherings, he was a nice guy who was trying to do the right thing.

What with one thing and another, Buddy breaks loose from Estelle and decides to help this Mary O'Neary and her baby. Angelo, the guy who runs the bar down the street, thinks he's crazy: "You see that guy," he asks his regulars. "He threw his whole life away." But the narrator of the film, whose identity is revealed at the end, sees it differently: "It remains an undisputed fact that every man has one moment of total selflessness in his life."

What makes *Two Family House* such a touching and effective film is that every one of Buddy's decisions is made as a direct response to the situation in front of him. He is not particularly fond of African-Americans (indeed, knows almost none). He does not approve of adultery. At one point, after they have a fight, he evicts Mary, only to find her another place to live. He is no bleeding-heart liberal, but he confesses to her: "I thought it was kinda brave, keeping the kid." He helps her out because he is touched by her situation, and can see she is a good person. One night when he turns up late at her place, she thinks he's after sex, but "No, that ain't why—I just want to talk with someone."

I can imagine this movie as an uplifting parable, but it wouldn't be as convincing and it wouldn't have the moment-to-moment fascination of Buddy's journey. The movie's ideas and values are completely contained in its action. Nobody makes any big speeches. Buddy just does what a decent guy would do.

Michael Rispoli gets one of the roles of a lifetime. Buddy's the kind of guy we all know, who is unwilling to accept the hand that life (or his wife) had dealt him. His victory may be small in the great scheme of things, but it is satisfying. When everyone told him he was throwing his life away, did he dream that someday his nephew would make this movie, in which he comes across as, well, kind of a hero?

Two Family House opened in Chicago on the same day as *Pay It Forward,* which is a feel-good valentine for the audience. *Pay It Forward* is quite happy to have big speeches, little speeches, and earnest expressions of belief about its message, which is that if we do a good turn and someone "pays it forward" instead of paying it back, what a wonderful world this would be. *Two Family House* is about a guy doing someone a good turn when she needs it. It doesn't need the uplifting apparatus of *Pay It Forward.* It may not be as commercial, but I suspect it may strike deeper in the hearts of its viewers.

Two Women ★ ★ ★ ½
NO MPAA RATING, 96 m., 2000

Niki Karimi (Fereshteh), Marila Zare'i (Roya), Mohammad Reza Forutan (The Stalker). Directed by Tahmineh Milani. Screenplay by Milani.

She is a brilliant student who seems to be leading her own life in the Tehran of the early 1980s. Then the madness of men reaches out and swats her down. Her story is told in *Two Women,* an angry and heartbreaking film, made in Iran by a woman, about a patriarchal society that puts cruel limits on the freedom of women to lead independent lives.

Fereshteh is from a provincial town, and it is to her father's credit that he allows her to attend university, since he believes her proper place is at home, married, giving him grandchildren. In Tehran she excels in a "man's" field, sciences, and loves the heady freedom of books, classrooms, campus life, and her friends.

Perhaps it is her very air of freedom that attracts the strange young man on the motorbike, who begins to stalk her. Fereshteh's spirit has not been broken, and that both attracts and appalls him. He is an erotomaniac able to think of nothing but this woman. He makes advances bordering on assault. He sees her frequently with a young man, her cousin, and thinks it is her boyfriend. One day, after she has rejected his advances, the man on the motorbike speeds up and throws acid at the cousin.

There is a court case, but it is almost beside the point. She has disgraced her family. How? By being involved in a scandal that calls attention to her status as an independent woman. There is almost the thought that it must have been her own fault, to so inflame a man that he would make an acid attack. Fereshteh's father pulls her out of school, makes her return to their small town, and forces an arranged marriage with a man in his forties who is no worse than most of the men of his age and class in the town—which is to say, a man totally incapable of understanding her needs and rights.

Two Women deals in the details of daily life in postrevolutionary Iran: in the unspoken ways that a woman's duties, her clothing, her behavior, who she speaks to, what she says, all express her servitude in a male-dominated society. Her husband is a pathetic creature whose self-esteem seems to depend largely on his ability to limit and control her. When she behaves with any independence, he feels like a cowboy who has been thrown by his horse: His duty, obviously, is to beat and train her until she becomes a docile beast.

The movie expresses powerful currents in Iranian society. It was directed by Tahmineh Milani, whose films have made her a symbol of hope among feminists in Iran—although, really, why would one need to be a feminist to believe women should be as free as men? Her film steps carefully. It makes no overt or specific criticisms of Iranian laws or politics; it focuses on Fereshteh's life and plight, and we are left to draw our own larger conclusions.

I met Milani and her husband, Mohammed, an architect, at the Calcutta Film Festival in November 1999, and was struck by how hopeful she seemed about the currents of change in her homeland, which until a generation ago was one of the more progressive societies in the Middle East. And indeed, recent election results show an overwhelming sentiment for modernizing Iran once again, and moderating the stern rule of the fundamentalist clerics.

At every film festival I attend, I hear that the new Iranian cinema is the most exciting in the world. Films like this are evidence of it. So is a new Iranian children's film named *The Color of Paradise*, about a small blind boy, very bright, who is taken out of school and apprenticed to a blind carpenter—because the boy's father, a widower, feels a blind son will be a liability in the marriage market. These films tell very specific human stories, but their buried message is clear: They swim through the waters of a rigid patriarchy that fears change and distrusts women. The extra beat of anger, throbbing beneath the surface, gives them a transforming energy.

U

U-571 ★ ★
PG-13, 115 m., 2000

Matthew McConaughey (Tyler), Bill Paxton (Dahlgren), Harvey Keitel (Chief), Jon Bon Jovi (Emmett), David Keith (Coonan), Thomas Kretschmann (Wassner), Jake Weber (Hirsch), Jack Noseworthy (Wentz). Directed by Jonathan Mostow and produced by Dino De Laurentiis and Martha De Laurentiis. Screenplay by Mostow, Sam Montgomery, and David Ayer.

U-571 is a clever windup toy of a movie, almost a trailer for a video game. Compared to *Das Boot* or *The Hunt for Red October,* it's thin soup. The characters are perfunctory, the action is recycled straight out of standard submarine formulas, and there is one shot where a man is supposed to be drowning and you can just about see he's standing on the bottom of the studio water tank.

To some degree movies like this always work, at least on a dumb action level. The German destroyer is overhead dropping depth charges, and the crew waits in hushed suspense while the underwater explosions grow nearer. We're all sweating along with them. But hold on a minute. We saw the Nazis rolling the depth charges overboard, and they were evenly spaced. As the first ones explode at a distance, there are several seconds between each one. Then they get closer. And when the charges are right on top of the sub, they explode one right after another, like a string of firecrackers— dozens of them, as leaks spring and water gushes in and lights blink and the surround sound rocks the theater.

At a moment like this, I shouldn't be thinking about the special effects. But I am. They call attention to themselves. They say the filmmakers have made a conscious decision to abandon plausibility and put on a show for the kids. And make no mistake: This is a movie for action-oriented kids. *Das Boot* and *The Hunt for Red October* were about military professionals whose personalities were crucial to the plot. The story of *U-571* is the flimsiest excuse for a fabricated action payoff. Submarine service veterans in the audience are going to be laughing their heads off.

Matthew McConaughey stars as Tyler, an ambitious young man who thinks he's ready for his first command. Not so fast, says Captain Dahlgren (Bill Paxton). He didn't recommend his second-in-command because he thinks he's not ready yet: not prepared, for example, to sacrifice the lives of some men to save others, or the mission. This info is imparted at one of those obligatory movie dance parties at which all the navy guys look handsome in white dress uniform, just before they get an emergency call back to the boat.

The mission: A German U-boat is disabled in the mid-Atlantic. On board is the secret Enigma machine, used to cipher messages. The unbreakable Enigma code allows the Nazis to control the shipping lanes. The mission of Dahlgren, Tyler, and their men: Disguise their U.S. sub as a Nazi vessel, get to the other sub before the German rescuers can, impersonate Germans, capture the sub with a boarding party, grab Enigma, and sink the sub so the rescuers won't suspect what happened.

"But we're not marine fighting men," protests one of the sailors. "Neither is the other crew," says a marine on board, who has conveyed these instructions. "And I'll train your men." Uh-huh. In less than a week? There are no scenes of training, and I'm not sure what happened to the marine.

The details of the confrontation with the Nazi sub I will not reveal. Of course it goes without saying that Tyler gets a chance to take command and see if he has what it takes to sacrifice lives in order to save his men and his mission, etc. If you remember the vivid personalities of the sub crews in *Das Boot* and *Red October,* you're going to be keenly aware that no one in this movie seems like much of an individual. When they do have dialogue, it's functional, spare, and aimed at the plot. Even Harvey Keitel, as the Chief, is reduced to barking out declarative sentences.

The crew members seem awfully young, awfully green, awfully fearful, and so headstrong they border on mutiny. There's a scene where the (disguised) U.S. sub is checked out by a German reconnaissance plane, and a young sailor on the bridge panics. He's sure the plane is going to strafe them, and orders the man on the deck machine gun to fire at it. His superior officer orders the gunner to stand fast. The kid screams "Fire! Fire!" As the plane comes closer, the officer and the kid are both shouting their orders at the gunner. Without actually consulting navy regulations, my best guess is, that kid should be court-martialed.

You can enjoy *U-571* as a big, dumb war movie without a brain in its head. But that doesn't stop it from looking cheesy. Producers Dino and Martha De Laurentiis and director Jonathan Mostow *(Breakdown)* have counted on fast action to distract from the plausibility of most of the scenes at sea (especially shots of the raft boarding party). Inside the sub, they have the usual clichés: The sub dives to beyond its rated depth, metal plates creak, and bolt heads fire loose under the pressure.

U-571 can't be blamed for one story element that's standard in all sub movies: The subs can be hammered, battered, shelled, depth-bombed, and squeezed by pressure, and have leaks, fires, shattered gauges, ruptures, broken air hoses, weak batteries, and inoperable diesel engines—but in the heat of action, everything more or less somehow works. Better than the screenplay, anyway.

In case you're wondering, the German sub on display at the Museum of Science and Industry in Chicago is *U-505*, and it was boarded and captured not by submariners, but by sailors from the USS *Pillsbury,* part of the escort group of the carrier USS *Guadalcanal.* No Enigma machine was involved. That was in 1944. An Enigma machine was obtained on May 9, 1941, when HMS *Bulldog* captured *U-110.* On August 23, 1941, *U-570* was captured by HMS planes and ships, without Enigma. This fictional movie about a fictional U.S. submarine mission is followed by a mention in the end credits of those actual British missions. Oh, the British deciphered the Enigma code too. Come to think of it, they pretty much did everything in real life that the Americans do in this movie.

Unbreakable ★ ★ ★
PG-13, 107 m., 2000

Bruce Willis (David Dunne), Samuel L. Jackson (Elijah Price), Robin Wright (Megan Dunne), Spencer Treat Clark (Jeremy Dunne), John Patrick Amedori (Hostage Boy), Joe Perillo (Jenkins), Sean Oliver (Police Officer), Jose L. Rodriguez (Truck Driver). Directed by M. Night Shyamalan and produced by Barry Mendel, Sam Mercer, and Shyamalan. Screenplay by Shyamalan.

At the center of *Unbreakable* is a simple question: "How many days of your life have you been sick?" David Dunne, a security guard played by Bruce Willis, doesn't know the answer. He is barely speaking to his wife, Megan (Robin Wright), but like all men he figures she remembers his life better than he does. She tells him she can't remember him ever being sick, not even a day. They have this conversation shortly after he has been in a train wreck that killed everybody else on board, but left him without a scratch. Now isn't that strange.

The question originally came to him in an unsigned note. He finds the man who sent it. This is Elijah Price (Samuel L. Jackson), who runs a high-end comic-book store with a priceless stock of first editions. Elijah has been sick a lot of days in his life. He even had broken bones when he emerged from the womb. He has spent a long time looking for an unbreakable man, and his logic is plain: "If there is someone like me in the world, shouldn't there be someone at the other end of the spectrum?"

Unbreakable, the new film by M. Night Shyamalan, is in its own way as quietly intriguing as his *The Sixth Sense.* It doesn't involve special effects and stunts, much of it is puzzling and introspective, and most of the action takes place during conversations. If the earlier film seemed mysteriously low-key until an ending that came like an electric jolt, this one is more fascinating along the way, although the ending is not quite satisfactory. In both films Shyamalan trusts the audience to pay attention and makes use of Bruce Willis's everyman quality, so that we get drawn into the character instead of being distracted by the surface.

The Jackson character is not an everyman.

Far from it. He is quietly menacing, formidably intelligent, and uses a facade of sophistication and knowledge to conceal anger that runs deep: He is enraged that his bones break, that his body betrays him, that he was injured so often in grade school that the kids called him "Mr. Glass." Why does he want to find his opposite, an unbreakable man? The question lurks beneath every scene.

This story could have been simplified into a—well, into the plot of one of Elijah Price's old comic books. Shyamalan does a more interesting thing. He tells it with observant everyday realism; he's like Stephen King, dealing in the supernatural and yet alert to the same human details as mainstream writers. How interesting, for example, that the Robin Wright character is not simply one more bystander wife in a thriller, but a real woman in a marriage that seems to have run out of love. How interesting that when her husband is spared in a crash that kills everyone else, she bravely decides this may be their opportunity to try one last time to save the marriage. How interesting that David Dunne's relationship with his son is so strong, and that the boy is taken along for crucial scenes like the first meeting of David and Elijah.

In *Psycho*, Hitchcock made us think the story was about the Janet Leigh character, and then killed her off a third of the way into the film. No one gets killed early in *Unbreakable*, but Shyamalan is skilled at misdirection: He involves us in the private life of the comic dealer, in the job and marriage problems of the security guard, in stories of wives and mothers. The true subject of the film is well guarded, although always in plain view, and until the end we don't know what to hope for, or fear. In that way it's like *The Sixth Sense*.

There is a theory in Hollywood these days that audiences have shorter attention spans and must be distracted by nonstop comic-book action. Ironic that a movie about a student of comic-book universes would require attention and patience on the part of the audience. Moviegoers grateful for the slow unfolding of *The Sixth Sense* will like this one too.

The actors give performances you would expect in serious dramas. Jackson is not afraid to play a man it is hard to like—a bitter man, whose intelligence only adds irony to anger.

Willis, so often the centerpiece of brainless action movies, reminds us again that he can be a subtle actor, as muted and mysterious as actors we expect that sort of thing from—John Malkovich or William Hurt, for example. If this movie were about nothing else, it would be a full portrait of a man in crisis at work and at home.

I mentioned the ending. I was not quite sold on it. It seemed a little arbitrary, as if Shyamalan plucked it out of the air and tried to make it fit. To be sure, there are hints along the way about the direction the story may take, and maybe this movie, like *The Sixth Sense*, will play even better the second time—once you know where it's going. Even if the ending doesn't entirely succeed, it doesn't cheat, and it comes at the end of an uncommonly absorbing movie.

Under the Sand ★ ★ ★ ½
NO MPAA RATING, 95 m., 2001

Charlotte Rampling (Marie Drillon), Bruno Cremer (Jean Drillon), Jacques Nolot (Vincent), Alexandra Stewart (Amanda), Pierre Vernier (Gerard), Andree Tainsy (Suzanne). Directed by Francois Ozon and produced by Olivier Delbosc and Marc Missonnier. Screenplay by Ozon.

Her husband disappears and her mind refuses to process that fact. She dozed on the beach, she awoke, and he was gone. Did he drown? Was it an accident or suicide? Or did he simply decide to disappear? Her friends ask these questions, but Marie simply behaves as if he is still there.

She is not delusional. In some sense, in some part of her mind, she knows she will never see him alive again, and perhaps she even agrees with the police that he must have drowned. But that part of her mind is partitioned. Even when she dates other men, even when she sleeps with one, in a real sense her husband is still there, still with her. When she is in bed with another man, he looks on from the doorway, and they exchange a look, and they seem to be agreeing, silently, well, life goes on.

The thing is—it doesn't go on without him. It goes on with him, and she sees him and talks to him. This is not so strange. I know many people who talk about the departed in the present tense. I like it when they do that. When somebody dies, I cannot bring myself to take their telephone number out of my address book, because . . . you never know. Many people believe that their loved ones are with them in spirit. It is only when Marie refers to her husband, Jean, as if he is actually still present as a force in her life that her friends exchange glances.

Under the Sand is a movie of introspection and defiance. It stars Charlotte Rampling, the British actress, as the wife of a Frenchman (Bruno Cremer). We get some ideas about their marriage. Perhaps a reason why some men might commit suicide (a subtle hint about health), but not this man, we think. We do not learn everything there is to know about the marriage, but it could not have been very unhappy if Marie's mind refuses to allow it to end.

The movie has been written and directed by Francois Ozon. He is thirty-four, has made more than a dozen shorts and a few features. I saw his fifty-two-minute film *See the Sea* in 1997 and have not forgotten it. It is about a woman and her baby living in a seaside cottage; the husband is away. A woman drifter comes by and is befriended by the woman, and a sense of dread grows in us even though we can't put our finger on anything specific in the movie to explain it. There is separate tension growing in the woman, who is in some kind of crisis with the husband that the movie suggests without explaining.

Both of these Ozon films can do what few directors have mastered. They can make us feel exactly what the director intends, without overt or obvious cues. Our emotions are not caused by objective plot events, but well up from the very soul of the film. One of the hardest things for a director to do is to communicate the subjective feelings of a character who refuses to talk about those feelings—who, in Marie's case, does nothing out of the ordinary except to refuse "closure" on her husband's death.

That we are with Marie every step of her emotional journey is a tribute to Ozon, and to Rampling, who in some mysterious way has developed from a journeyman actress of the 1960s into this person capable of communicating the most subtle states with no apparent effort—she just gets on with it, and we are surprised how much we are touched.

Under the Sun ★ ★ ★ ½
NO MPAA RATING, 118 m., 2001

Rolf Lassgard (Olof), Helena Bergstrom (Ellen), Johan Widerberg (Erik), Gunilla Roor (Receptionist), Jonas Falk (Preacher), Linda Ulvaeus (Lena). Directed and produced by Colin Nutley. Screenplay by Nutley, based on the short story "The Little Farm" by H. E. Bates.

It takes more nerve to make a sincere film than an ironic one. Tell the story of a simple and good Swedish farmer, a hayseed who takes out a personals ad to find a wife, and you might be laughed out of town. Who in these days works a farm, has never slept with a woman, and has a heart of gold? *Under the Sun* is a "runny melodrama" with "melancholy mildew," according to Elvis Mitchell, who adds, "If you sit very still, you can probably hear the projectionist sobbing softly." Mitchell, from the *New York Times*, is a splendid critic, but the wrong one for *Under the Sun*, which transmits on a frequency inaudible to the hip. He's too cool for this job. Better to send someone like Andrew Sarris of the *New York Observer*, who finds it gentle, simple, sweet, and lyrical.

Movies like this are not for everyone, but arrive like private messages for their own particular audiences. Accustomed to fast-food films that appeal to the widest conceivable demographics, we're a little stunned by a film making the imaginative leap to the 1950s in rural Sweden—a land more alien to today's moviegoers than anything in *The Mummy Returns*.

I believe farmers like good, kind Olof (Rolf Lassgard) really existed there—a haystack of a man with an unruly shock of straw hair, who inherited the place from his parents, loves his livestock, and lacks any clue about how to meet a woman. I also believe in his younger friend Erik (Johan Widerberg), a country kid with a wild hunger fed by American movies, who drives a Ford convertible, has a ducktail, idolizes Elvis, talks like James Dean with a cigarette bobbing from his lips, and shamelessly uses Olof as a source for "loans" to feed his bets at the racetrack.

I do not believe, however, that very many classified ads for a "housekeeper" would produce in this rural backwoods a candidate like

Ellen (Helena Bergstrom), who appears in Olof's life like a wet dream. Blond, voluptuous, red lips, high heels—what business does she have on a farm? The plot eventually supplies an answer, but by the time the answer comes it is unnecessary, because Helena Bergstrom has already answered it in her own way. Hers is a sly and masterful performance, creating a character we are commanded to mistrust, and then turning her into a figure of such fascination and intrigue that by the halfway point we're burning with curiosity about her. What's her angle? Is she too good to be true?

Those are precisely the questions burning in the squirmy mind of Erik. He cannot believe that big, slow, illiterate Olof qualifies for this babe. Erik himself is a pig with women, mistreating his girlfriend of the moment (Linda Ulvaeus) with calculated cruelty. Erik is a player. He makes a move for Ellen, but we never feel it's fueled by lust. It's an autopilot response—he wants to see what happens. At a subterranean level, there is the possibility that Erik doesn't like women at all. (Erik's eventual fate is suggested in two words of dialogue that will sound loudly for students of nautical history.)

Under the Sun is based on a British short story, "The Little Farm" by H. E. Bates, whose work also inspired *Summertime* and *A Month by the Lake*. It has been transplanted to Sweden with no particular strain, since life on this farm is so simple it could be anywhere. What is not simple is the performance by Bergstrom, so carefully modulated that by the end we are hanging on every word and gesture, trying to solve the mystery of her motivation: Can she be as good—or as bad—as she seems? Undulating beneath both possibilities is the daydream shared by many men—that a dreamboat will come along and discover in them qualities concealed from the world at large and certainly invisible to other women. (The inaudible cry of many men is: Let me believe you find me more attractive and fascinating than I have any reason to believe that I am.)

There are two strands of suspense in *Under the Sun*—intrigues about Ellen's intentions regarding Olof and Erik. There is also the enormous question of the sexual future, if any, of this city woman and her farmer friend. He is a virgin, we learn, and so tremulous in the face of sex that he becomes motionless as a terrified

rabbit. The writer-director, Colin Nutley, who is married to Bergstrom, photographs her character with an unforced eroticism, having to do with bathing and changing and lingerie and getting sweaty, that makes it clear to us and to Olof that there is a sexual presence on the farm and something will have to be done about it. Eventually something is, in a scene that observes both how complicated sex can be, and how simple.

Two things surprised me about *Under the Sun*. I was surprised how involving this little story became—how much I cared for Olof, wondered about Ellen, despised Erik. And I was also surprised by how comforting and brave it made the life on the farm. There is something real about livestock and fields and big skies, and satisfying about doing a job of real work, and I could almost understand how this sexy, plump-lipped stranger could fall for it. Almost. Sometimes. And then, along with Erik and with Freud, I was maddened by the question: What does she want?

Unfaithful ★ ★ ★
R, 123 m., 2002

Diane Lane (Connie Sumner), Richard Gere (Edward Sumner), Olivier Martinez (Paul Martel), Erik Per Sullivan (Charlie Sumner), Myra Lucretia Taylor (Gloria), Michelle Monaghan (Lindsay), Chad Lowe (Bill Stone). Directed by Adrian Lyne and produced by Lyne and G. Mac Brown. Screenplay by Alvin Sargent and William Broyles Jr., based on the film by Claude Chabrol.

"The heart has its reasons," said the French philosopher Pascal, quoted by the American philosopher Woody Allen. It is a useful insight when no other reasons seem apparent. Connie Sumner's heart and other organs have their reasons for straying outside a happy marriage in *Unfaithful*, but the movie doesn't say what they are. This is not necessarily a bad thing, sparing us tortured Freudian explanations and labored plot points. It is almost always more interesting to observe behavior than to listen to reasons.

Connie (Diane Lane) and her husband, Edward (Richard Gere), live with their nine-year-old son, Charlie (Erik Per Sullivan), in one of those Westchester County houses that have a room for every mood. They are happy together, or at least the movie supplies us with no reasons why they are unhappy. One windy day she drives into New York, is literally blown down on top of a rare book dealer named Paul Martel (Olivier Martinez), and is invited upstairs for Band-Aids and a cup of tea. He occupies a large flat filled with shelves of books and art objects.

Martel is your average Calvin Klein model as a bibliophile. He has the Spanish looks, the French accent, the permanent three-day beard, and the strength to suspend a woman indefinitely in any position while making love. He is also cool in his seduction methods. Instead of making a crude pass, he asks her to accept a book as a gift from him, and directs her down an aisle to the last book on the end of the second shelf from the top, where he tells her what page to turn to, and then joins her in reciting the words there: "Be happy for this moment, for this moment is your life."

Does it occur to Connie that Martel planted that book for just such an occasion as this? No, because she likes to be treated in such a way, and soon she's on the phone with a transparent ruse to get up to his apartment again, where Martel overcomes her temporary stall in bed by commanding her: "Hit me!" That breaks the logjam, and soon they're involved in a passionate affair that involves arduous sex in his apartment and quick sex in rest rooms, movie theaters, and corridors. (The movie they go see is Tati's *Monsieur Hulot's Holiday,* which, despite its stature on my list of The Great Movies, fails to compete with furtive experiments that would no doubt have Hulot puffing furiously at his pipe.)

Edward senses that something is wrong. There are clues, but mostly he picks up on her mood, and eventually hires a man to shadow her. Discovering where Martel lives, he visits there one day, and what happens then I will not reveal. What does *not* happen then, I am happy to reveal, is that the movie doesn't turn into a standard thriller in which death stalks Westchester County and the wife and husband fear murder by each other, or by Martel.

That's what's intriguing about the film: Instead of pumping up the plot with recycled manufactured thrills, it's content to contemplate two reasonably sane adults who get themselves into an almost insoluble dilemma. *Unfaithful* contains, as all movies involving suburban families are required to contain, a scene where the parents sit proudly in the audience while their child performs bravely in a school play. But there are no detectives lurking in the shadows to arrest them, and no killers skulking in the parking lot with knives or tire irons. No, the meaning of the scene is simply, movingly, that these two people in desperate trouble are nevertheless able to smile at their son on the stage.

The movie was directed by Adrian Lyne, best known for higher-voltage films like *Fatal Attraction* and *Indecent Proposal.* This film is based on *La Femme Infidele* (1969) by Claude Chabrol, which itself is an update of *Madame Bovary.* Lyne's film is juicier and more passionate than Chabrol's, but both share the fairly daring idea of showing a plot that is entirely about illicit passion and its consequences in a happy marriage. Although cops turn up from time to time in *Unfaithful,* this is not a crime story, but a marital tragedy.

Richard Gere and Diane Lane are well suited to the roles, exuding a kind of serene materialism that seems happily settled in suburbia. It is all the more shocking when Lane revisits Martel's apartment because there is no suggestion that she is unhappy with Gere, starved for sex, or especially impulsive. She goes back up there because—well, because she wants to. He's quite a guy. On one visit he shows her *The Joy of Cooking* in Braille. And then his fingers brush hers as if he's reading *The Joy of Sex* on her skin.

Up at the Villa ★ ★ ★
PG-13, 115 m., 2000

Kristin Scott Thomas (Mary Panton), Sean Penn (Rowley Flint), Anne Bancroft (Princess San Ferdinando), James Fox (Sir Edgar Swift), Jeremy Davies (Karl Richter), Derek Jacobi ("Lucky" Leadbetter), Massimo Ghini (Beppino Leopardi), Dudley Sutton (Harold Atkinson). Directed by Philip Haas and produced by Geoff Stier. Screenplay by Belinda Haas from the novella by W. Somerset Maugham.

Does anyone read Somerset Maugham anymore? From the 1920s to the 1950s he was the most respected "popular" novelist in the world, or the most popular "respected" novelist (the praise was always tempered with quotation marks). He traveled the world to the haunts of British expatriates; his stories, whether set in Singapore or Italy, often dealt with the choice between prudent and passionate romance. He knew his characters; he had a deep knowledge of shallow people.

Philip Haas's *Up at the Villa* is based on Maugham's novella about a group of British expats in Florence, enjoying their last days of mannered sloth before the outbreak of World War II. It is not the same story that Franco Zeffirelli told in his 1999 movie *Tea With Mussolini*, but his characters and these characters would have known each other by name.

The villa of the title is occupied by a temporary guest, Mary Panton (Kristin Scott Thomas), a pretty widow in her mid-thirties. Her husband drank up and gambled away their money and himself. Now she depends on the kindness of friends. An old friend named Sir Edgar Swift (James Fox) has just journeyed over from Cannes to propose marriage to her. He is tall, slender, will not see sixty again, and has manners that make you want to sit very still. Soon he will be named governor of Bengal; Mary would become the first lady of British society in Calcutta. Mary's adviser on this possibility is the Principessa San Ferdinando (Anne Bancroft), who has a town house, thanks to a rich Italian husband, now dead, "so ugly he frightened the horses."

Sir Edgar's is an attractive offer to Mary. She asks time to think it over. She doesn't love Sir Edgar—but what, asks the princess, does love have to do with it? In a frank heart-to-heart, the princess explains that she married for security and took lovers for entertainment, although sex, she sighs, supplies you in old age with neither the fond memories nor the security of wealth. Once, says the princess (Bancroft delivering this confidence at the end of a virtuoso monologue as they walk in the garden), she made love recklessly for a single night with a risky young man, just for the fun of it.

At the princess's table in a restaurant that night, Mary is seated next to a brash, rich American named Rowley Flint (Sean Penn). He is married, separated, bold. He wants to spend the night with her. She likes him, but says no. He responds insolently, she slaps him and dumps him, and on the way home picks up a pathetic little unshaven violinist she saw in the restaurant. He is Karl Richter (Jeremy Davies), an Austrian refugee from Hitler. She takes pity on him and brings him into her bed, where, inspired by the princess's story, she gives him such a night to remember that she is still wearing her pearls in the morning.

Now the plot develops surprises. A hint or two: Mary turns to Rowley to help her out of a fix. The local Fascist Party chief (Massimo Ghini) threatens legal action against Rowley. Mary is prepared to betray a confidence of the princess to help Rowley. And then Sir Edgar returns for his answer. "I have some things I must tell you," she says, and the camera moves outside on the lawn and we see them through a window as they talk. In my notes I wrote: "She's got a lot of 'splaining to do."

This whole movie is about manners. There is sex and violence, but the movie is not about giving in to them; it's about carrying on as if they didn't exist—as if the part of you that was involved was a distant relation who will not be asked back again very soon. Kristin Scott Thomas is smashing, as Mary Panton would say. She is a woman with no financial means, who must decide between loveless security and insecure love. She has to jump fast; she will be thrown out of the villa and declared an enemy alien any day now. Yet . . . Mary has character. The whole movie leads up to, and savors, exactly what she tells Sir Edgar, and exactly what he tells her, and then, after they both think about what they have been told, what they tell each other. It is an exquisite verbal minuet; modern psychobabble would shred their conversational elegance like a madman with a machete.

It is not necessary to have manners to appreciate them, but you must at least understand why other people would want to have them. That is the case with the wild card in the cast, "Lucky" Leadbetter (Derek Jacobi), an old queen with his hair and beard dyed ginger. He looks so uncannily like the satanic dancing man in the nightclub scene in *La Dolce Vita* that I'll bet Jacobi showed the movie to his barber. "Lucky" is not essential to the story but knows all the characters and where, and why,

643

the skeletons are buried, and he will make all of this into a story someday. Like Maugham.

Urban Legends: Final Cut ★ ★
R, 94 m., 2000

Jennifer Morrison (Amy Mayfield), Matthew Davis (Travis/Trevor), Hart Bochner (Professor Solomon), Loretta Devine (Reese), Joseph Lawrence (Graham), Anson Mount (Toby), Eva Mendes (Vanessa), Jessica Cauffiel (Sandra), Marco Hofschneider (Simon), Anthony Anderson (Stan), Michael Bacall (Dirk). Directed by John Ottman and produced by Neal H. Moritz, Gina Matthews, and Richard Luke Rothschild. Screenplay by Paul Harris Boardman and Scott Derrickson.

Amy: *The winner is basically guaranteed a chance at directing in Hollywood.*
  Trevor: *Do you think that somebody would kill for that?*

You betcha. *Urban Legends: Final Cut* takes place at a film school where the best senior thesis film wins the Hitchcock Prize—a $15,000 stipend and a shot at the big time. As students start dropping like flies, it becomes clear that a mad slasher is on the loose, and eventually a kid figures out they were all involved in making the same film. Amy (Jennifer Morrison) screens the film, which is lousy, and then notices a splice before the end credits. "Did somebody change the credits on Travis's film?" his brother Trevor (Matthew Davis) asks. "No," she says portentously. "Somebody changed the film on Travis's credits."

Find out who stole the film and you'll have your killer, in a thriller that (like *Scream 3*) is about the making of a movie. The movie is set at the Orson Welles Film Center of Alpine University, so named although no mountains are ever seen (it was shot at Trent University in Peterborough, Ontario).

Some of these students should repeat freshman year. "You stole my (bleeping) genre!" shouts Toby, before walking off of Amy's film, blissfully unaware that although almost anything can be stolen from another movie, its

genre is in the public domain. Toby (Anson Mount) was going to be the director of photography. He's replaced by Simon (Marco Hofschneider), who is also none too canny in the ways of the film world. He walks onto a set just as the first assistant says, "Speed!" This is usually the word before "Action!" but Simon interrupts with a loud, "Excuse me!" Talking when the camera is rolling is usually reserved for the actors, something you want your D.P. to know.

Amy's idea for a film: A serial killer commits a series of crimes based on urban legends. This is what happened in the original *Urban Legend* (1998), but in *Final Cut* there aren't many urban legend killings because the filmmakers are killed instead. An exception: One girl wakes up in an ice-filled bathtub with her kidney missing, leading to a great line from the 911 operator. "I just woke up in an ice-filled bathtub!" the victim gasps. "Don't tell me—your kidney's gone," says the operator.

The film was directed by John Ottman, who also coedited and wrote the music. He has a good command of the genre, and carefully inserts the It's Only a Dream scene, the It's Only a Bird scene, the It's Only a Movie scene, and the Talking Killer scene. The killer has to talk a lot, because he needs to explain motives and rationales that are none too evident until he spells them out. This leads to an inventive comic riff on the basic Tarantinesque Mexican-standoff scene, in which there are more guns than are really practical.

Urban Legends: Final Cut has slick production credits and performances that are quite adequate given the (narrow) opportunities of the genre. It makes the fatal mistake, however, of believing there is still life in the wheezy serial-killer-on-campus formula, and spends way too much time playing horror sequences straight when laughs might have been more bearable. I don't know if you're tired of terrified girls racing through shadowy basements pursued by masked slashers while the sound track pulses with variations on the *Halloween* theme, but I am. Real tired. This time the killer wears a fencing mask, and at the end no one even thinks to say, "Touché!"

V

Vanilla Sky ★ ★ ★
R, 135 m., 2001

Tom Cruise (David Aames), Penelope Cruz (Sofia Serrano), Kurt Russell (Dr. Curtis McCabe), Cameron Diaz (Julie), Johnny Galecki (Peter), Jean Carol (Woman in New York), Jennifer Aspen (Nina), Zachary Lee (Joshua), Jason Lee (Brian). Directed by Cameron Crowe and produced by Tom Cruise and Paula Wagner. Screenplay by Crowe, based on a film by Alejandro Amenabar and Mateo Gil.

Think it all the way through, and Cameron Crowe's *Vanilla Sky* is a scrupulously moral picture. It tells the story of a man who has just about everything, thinks he can have it all, is given a means to have whatever he wants, and loses it because—well, maybe because he has a conscience. Or maybe not. Maybe just because life sucks. Or maybe he only thinks it does. This is the kind of movie you don't want to analyze until you've seen it two times.

I've seen it two times. I went to a second screening because after the first screening I thought I knew what had happened, but was nagged by the idea that certain things might not have happened the way I thought they had. Now that I've seen it twice, I think I understand it, or maybe not. Certainly it's entertaining as it rolls along, and there is wonderful chemistry of two quite different kinds between Tom Cruise and Cameron Diaz, on the one hand, and Tom Cruise and Penelope Cruz, on the other.

Vanilla Sky, like the 2001 pictures *Memento* and *Mulholland Dr.*, requires the audience to do some heavy lifting. It's got one of those plots that doubles back on itself like an Escher staircase. You get along splendidly one step at a time, but when you get to the top floor you find yourself on the bottom landing. If it's any consolation, its hero is as baffled as we are; it's not that he has memory loss, like the hero of *Memento,* but that in a certain sense he may have no real memory at all.

Cruise stars as David Aames, a thirty-three-year-old tycoon who inherited a publishing empire when his parents were killed in a car crash. His condo is like the Sharper Image catalog died and went to heaven. He has a sex buddy named Julie (Cameron Diaz) and he thinks they can sleep together and remain just friends, but as she eventually has to explain, "When you sleep with someone, your body makes a promise whether you do or not." At a party, he locks eyes with Sofia Serrano (Penelope Cruz), who arrives as the date of his friend Brian (Jason Lee) but ends up spending the night with him. Even though they don't have sex, it looks to me like their bodies are making promises to each other.

At this point the movie starts unveiling surprises that I should not reveal. A lot of surprises. Surprises on top of surprises. The movie is about these surprises, however, and so I must either end this review right now, or reveal some of them.

The End.

Okay, for those of us still in the room, and without revealing *too* much: Julie drives up just as David is leaving after his night with Sofia, offers him a lift, drives off a bridge in Central Park, kills herself, and lands him in front of "the best plastic surgeon in New York" with a horribly scarred face. This time thread is intercut with another one in which a psychiatrist (Kurt Russell) is interrogating David about a murder. He insists there was no murder. Maybe there was and maybe there wasn't, and maybe the victim was who we think it is, and maybe not.

Vanilla Sky has started as if it is about David's life and loves. It reveals an entirely different orientation (which I will not reveal even here in the room), and, to be fair, there is a full explanation. The only problem with the explanation is that it explains the *mechanism* of our confusion, rather than telling us for sure what actually happened.

That's why I went to see it a second time. In general, my second viewing was greatly helped by my first, and I was able to understand events more clearly. But there was one puzzling detail. At the second viewing, I noticed that the first words in the movie ("open your eyes") are unmistakably said in the voice of Sofia, the Penelope Cruz character. If the movie's explanation of this voice is correct, at that point in the movie David has not met Sofia, or heard her voice.

How can we account for her voice appearing before she does? There is a character in the movie who refers to a "splice." We are told where the splice takes place. But consider the source of this information—not the person supplying it, but the underlying source. Is the information reliable? Or does the splice take place, so to speak, before the movie begins? And in that case . . . but see the movie and ask the question for yourself.

Note: Early in the film, there's an astonishing shot of Tom Cruise absolutely alone in Times Square. You might assume, as I did, that computers were involved. Cameron Crowe told me the scene is not faked; the film got city permission to block off Times Square for three hours early on a Sunday morning. Just outside of camera range there are cops and barricades to hold back the traffic.

Va Savoir ★ ★ ★
PG-13, 150 m., 2001

Jeanne Balibar (Camille), Sergio Castillitto (Ugo), Marianne Basler (Sonia), Jacques Bonnaffe (Pierre), Helene de Fougerolles (Do), Bruno Todeschini (Arthur), Catherine Rouvel (Madame Desprez), Claude Berri (Autograph Librarian). Directed by Jacques Rivette and produced by Martine Marignac. Screenplay by Pascal Bonitzer, Christine Laurent, and Rivette.

One reason to see *Va Savoir* is to want to know these people. Art films can encourage escapism too. Some moviegoers like Julia Roberts and others like Jeanne Balibar, but we all have the same pipes and valves pumping away inside. Jeanne Balibar. A little like Audrey Hepburn, the way she wears those little sweaters tightly buttoned over her tummy. Skinny, lithe, confident. Jacques Rivette loves women helplessly. You can say all you want about what a great director he is, but you must remember that he founded the French New Wave along with Jean-Luc Godard, who said, "The history of cinema is boys photographing girls."

Rivette is seventy-three now, and *Va Savoir*, which translates as *Who Knows?* is the kind of film a young man might make if he were seventy-

three. It's a farce involving six characters who fall in love with one another in inconvenient and unforeseen combinations. Some of them are involved in the production of a play by Pirandello, who wrote farces about six people—a convenient number for onstage chaos. The action is a farce, with people being locked into rooms, stealing jewelry, cheating on their wives, and challenging each other to ridiculous duels. But the pacing is more leisurely—a farce in waltz time.

Clip and save: Camille (Jeanne Balibar), an actress, has been away from Paris for three years. She returns in a production being directed by Ugo (Sergio Castillitto), her new husband. Pierre (Jacques Bonnaffe) is her old boyfriend, now married to Sonia (Marianne Basler). Dominique (Helene de Fourgerolles), known as Do, is the daughter in a rich family with a famous library. Her half-brother Arthur (Bruno Todeschini) is a rotter who is having an affair with Sonia.

Now rotate everyone one position. Camille finds Pierre just where she knew she would find him, on a bench reading his morning paper. He is a creature of habit. Pierre finds he still loves Camille. Ugo is obsessed with finding a missing play by Goldoni, calls on the rich family and falls in love with Do. This happens while she is on a ladder in the library. No woman ever stands on a ladder in a library in the movies without getting kissed. Arthur goes through the motions of seducing Sonia because he wants to steal her jewels.

Now rotate everyone again. Camille eludes the trap Pierre has set for her. Sonia discovers Arthur's treachery and enlists Camille to steal back the jewelry. Ugo and Camille fight over the play, and Camille walks offstage before her bow on opening night. Ugo discovers Pierre is in love with Camille, and challenges him to a duel. Arthur . . . but you see how it goes.

All of these people are so sleek. In the manner of a certain class of French person, they know exactly who they are, what they stand for, how to behave, and what rules must not be violated even though all the others can be. Around and around they go, bemused, intrigued, as if they are adding elements to an emotional test tube, curious to see whether they will get a love potion or an explosion.

Jacques Rivette loves characters. His best-known films include *Celine and Julie Go Boating* (1974) and *La Belle Noiseuse* (1991). Both are twice as long as most movies, and consist of the minute and loving appreciation of beautiful young women—not their bodies, but their spirits, their amusement, their style. (Rivette also once made a version of *Joan of Arc*, a reminder that Godard finished his quote by adding, "The history of history is boys burning girls at the stake.")

Va Savoir is the kind of movie you settle into. It's supple and sophisticated, and it's not about much. It has no message and some will say it has no point. But it is a demonstration of grace and wit, it is photographed as a lesson in how to carry yourself, and it has such good manners as it leads us into such absurd situations. The duel has a kind of calm, insane genius to it.

Vertical Limit ★ ★ ★
PG-13, 126 m., 2000

Chris O'Donnell (Peter Garrett), Bill Paxton (Elliot Vaughn), Robin Tunney (Annie Garrett), Nicholas Lea (Tom McLaren), Scott Glenn (Montgomery Wick), Izabella Scorupco (Monique Aubertine), Temuera Morrison (Major Rasul), Stuart Wilson (Royce Garrett), Augie Davis (Aziz), Roshan Seth (Colonel Amir Salim). Directed by Martin Campbell and produced by Lloyd Phillips, Robert King, and Campbell. Screenplay by King and Terry Hayes.

Somebody, I think it was me, was observing the other day that Hollywood never really stopped making B pictures; they simply gave them $100 million budgets and marketed them as A pictures. *Vertical Limit* is an example: It's made from obvious formulas and pulp-novel conflicts, but strongly acted and well crafted. The movie may be compared with *The Perfect Storm*, another adventure about humans challenging the implacable forces of nature. One difference is that *Storm* portrays the egos and misjudgments of its characters honestly, and makes them pay for their mistakes, while *Vertical Limit* chugs happily toward one of those endings where everyone gets exactly what they deserve, in one way or another, except for a few expendable supporting characters.

It's a danger signal whenever a movie brings nitroglycerine into the plot. Nitro has appeared in good films like *The Wages of Fear* and *Sorcerer*, but even there it exhibits its most peculiar quality, which is that it invariably detonates precisely in synch with the requirements of the plot.

Vertical Limit introduces nitro into a situation where three climbers are trapped in an ice cave near the top of K-2. They are a venal millionaire ("This is a life statement for me"), an experienced guide, and the hero's sister. The hero gathers a group of six volunteers on a possibly suicidal rescue mission. They bring along nitro, and although I know that explosives are used from time to time on mountains to jar loose avalanches, the movie never explains how an uncontrollable nitro explosion has the potential to help the trapped victims more than harm them. The one scene where nitro is used as intended does nothing to answer the question.

The rest of the time, the nitro is necessary to endanger the rescue party, to provide suspense, to shock us with unintended explosions, and to dispose of minor characters so there won't be anything but speaking parts left for the climax. The nitro serves as evidence that *Vertical Limit* is not so much a sincere movie about the dangers and codes of mountain climbing as a thriller with lots of snow. At that, however, it is pretty good, and I can recommend the movie as a B adventure while wondering what kind of an A movie might have been made from similar material.

Chris O'Donnell stars as Peter Garrett, a *National Geographic* photographer. He and his sister Annie (Robin Tunney) are shown with their father in the opening title sequence, which ends with Peter cutting a rope that sends his father falling to his death but spares himself and Annie. Otherwise three lives might have, or would have, been lost. Peter and Annie disagree about this, although the legendary toeless mountaineer Montgomery Wick (Scott Glenn) tells Peter he did the right thing, and it follows as the night follows day that someone in the movie will reprise that final decision sooner or later.

Annie, a famous climber, is trapped on the mountain with the millionaire Elliot Vaughn (Bill Paxton) and Tom McLaren (Nicholas Lea), an ace guide. Vaughn owns an airline, and his dream is to stand on the summit of K-2 at the moment one of his inaugural flights zooms overhead. This involves an ascent in risky climbing weather, and a crucial error when McLaren thinks they should turn back and is overruled by the headstrong Vaughn.

Mountain climbing always inspires the same nightmare for me: I am falling from a great height, and cursing myself all the way down for being stupid enough to have climbed all the way up there voluntarily. I've seen climbing documentaries in which climbers do amazing things, although none quite so amazing as some of the stunts in *Vertical Limit*. The blend of stunt work and effects is seamless, and there's real suspense as they edge out of tight spots, even if occasionally we want to shout advice at the screen. (In one scene, a climber is hanging by an arm over the edge of a cliff, and another climber walks up to the edge, which is at a fearsome angle, while un-tethered. In another, a climber anchors her ice-ax *way* too close to the edge.)

One effective sequence shows the six rescuers being landed at 22,000 feet by a risky helicopter drop. Others show the suddenness with which things can go wrong. There are the absolute deadlines imposed by the reality of the mountain (after climbers dehydrate, they die). And strong performances, particularly by Glenn as the hard-bitten climber with a private agenda. *Vertical Limit* delivers with efficiency and craft, and there are times, when the characters are dangling over a drop of a mile, when we don't even mind how it's manipulating us.

The Vertical Ray of the Sun ★ ★ ★
NO MPAA RATING, 112 m., 2001

Tran Nu Yen-Khe (Lien), Nguyen Nhu Quynh (Suong), Le Khanh (Khanh), Ngo Quang Hai (Brother Hai), Tran Manh Cuong (Khanh's Husband Kien), Chu Ngoc Hung (Suong's Husband Quoc), Le Tuan Anh (Suong's Lover Tuan), Le Van Loc (Hai's Friend Loc). Directed by Tran Anh Hung, and produced by Christophe Rossignon. Screenplay by Tran.

The Vertical Ray of the Sun is beautiful, languorous, passive—it plays like background music for itself. Filmed in a Hanoi that looks more like an Asian love hotel than a city, it's a lush, sensuous work—the film equivalent of those old Mantovani albums with names like *Music for Lovers Only*. It tells the stories of three sisters, two married, one single, and although it contains adulteries in the present, rumors of adultery in the past, one or perhaps two pregnancies, and a hint of incestuous feelings, it would be fair to say that hardly anything happens.

Let me describe one shot. In the left foreground, a woman reclines on a bed. In the right background, a man looks out the window. It is raining. He is smoking. She lights a cigarette. For a time nothing happens except for the pleasure they take in silent companionship and smoking together. This time, passing in this intimacy without words, is a moment that says so much about their comfort in each other's company that we realize most movies are about people who are *doing* instead of *being*.

Little surprise that the director, Tran Anh Hung, grew up in Paris to love the work of Robert Bresson, that French master of films that were about the essence, not the adventures, of his characters. Tran was born in Vietnam, moved to France with his family at the age of six, and made the remarkable debut film *Scent of Green Papaya* in 1993 when he was still in his twenties. It was the love story of a simple servant girl and a sophisticated rich boy, and it was set in French-ruled Saigon—a Saigon created for the film, astonishingly, entirely on a Parisian sound stage. Then came a trip to Vietnam to film *Cyclo*, a rougher, more realistic story about street life in what had become Ho Chi Minh City. Now here is *Vertical Ray of the Sun*, filmed in Hanoi, but a Hanoi no more realistic than the Paris in MGM musicals like *An American in Paris*.

"I wanted my film to feel like a caress," Tran told Trevor Johnston of the *London Independent*. "It had to have a gentle smile floating through it, a sort of floating feeling." He wanted to find a style, he said, "which didn't present the drama as a series of emotional problems for the various couples." He has been so successful that his film may be maddening for those who expect conflict in their movies. The various couples do in fact have emotional problems, but they live in a sea of such emotional contentment that unhappiness is a wave that crests briefly and falls back, forgotten.

We meet three sisters. Lien, the youngest, is played by Tran Nu Yen-Khe, who is Tran's wife and was the star of *Green Papaya*. She still lives at home with her twin brother, Hai (Ngo Quang Hai). At times they chase each other around the house like children. At other times he awakens to find her in his bed because she "got lonely" in the night. "People think we are courting," she says with delight as they walk in the street. They talk about what he would do if she ever got married. This is emotional, not physical incest.

Their older sister Khanh (Le Khanh) is married to a novelist who says he is stuck on the ending of a novel that may not even have a beginning. She has, for me, the most luminous moment in the movie, in a close two-shot where she is filled with something she wants to say and then says it: She is pregnant. Do you know how a woman's lips look when she delays with delight, holding back happy news? The pause before she speaks is a moment of such beauty. The third sister is Suong (Nguyen Nhu Quynh), whose husband is obsessed with his photographs of rare plant species. Sometimes, she says, she thinks he cares more about his plants than about her. Actually, he also cares about another woman he lives with secretly on the island where he collects his specimens; they have a child. The nature of his life explains his long absences to both women, but Suong has a breathtaking scene where she tells him what she knows, how she knows it, and what she expects him to do about it.

The title, which can also be translated as *At the Height of Summer*, captures a season of heat and humidity when motion is to be avoided and the most luxurious time of the day is waking while it is still cool. The sisters meet to prepare meals, gossip, confess, and speculate. The men are more vaguely drawn. The film finds it so unnecessary to conclude and solve the characters' problems that after it's over you may not be able to remember if it did. It is not about incident, but about nostalgia for the slowness and peace of days past.

Here is Tran again, in the London interview: "My thoughts turned back to my childhood in Danang, remembering the time when I'd be waiting to fall asleep at night, my mind racing from one thing to another, nothing precise. The smell of fruit coming in through the window, a woman's voice singing on the radio. Everything was so vague. It was like a feeling of suspension. If I've ever experienced harmony in my life it was then. It was just a matter of translating that rhythm and that musicality into the new film."

Reading those words, I was reminded of a little-known but evocative film by Robert Altman named *Thieves Like Us* (1974) in which, in a small frame house in the summertime, on Sunday afternoon perhaps, the characters sit dozing in easy chairs, and from a distant room comes the sound of a song on the radio. On such warm and idle afternoons there is the possibility that lovemaking lies ahead, or perhaps it lies behind; it is too much to think about just now.

The Virgin Suicides ★ ★ ★ ½
R, 97 m., 2000

James Woods (Mr. Lisbon), Kathleen Turner (Mrs. Lisbon), Kirsten Dunst (Lux Lisbon), Josh Harnett (Trip Fontaine), Hanna Hall (Cecilia Lisbon), Chelsea Swain (Bonnie Lisbon), A. J. Cook (Mary Lisbon), Leslie Hayman (Therese Lisbon), Danny DeVito (Dr. Horniker). Directed by Sofia Coppola and produced by Francis Ford Coppola, Julie Costanzo, Dan Halsted, and Chris Hanley. Screenplay by Sofia Coppola, based on the novel by Jeffrey Eugenides.

It is not important how the Lisbon sisters looked. What is important is how the teenage boys in the neighborhood thought they looked. There is a time in the adolescent season of every boy when a particular girl seems to have materialized in his dreams with backlighting from heaven. Sofia Coppola's *The Virgin Suicides* is narrated by an adult who speaks for "we"—for all the boys in a Michigan suburban neighborhood twenty-five years ago, who loved and lusted after the Lisbon girls. We know from the title and the opening words that the girls killed themselves. Most of the reviews have focused on the girls. They miss the other subject—the gawky, insecure yearning of the boys.

The movie is as much about those guys,

"we," as about the Lisbon girls. About how Trip Fontaine (Josh Harnett), the leader of the pack, loses his baby fat and shoots up into a junior stud who is blindsided by sex and beauty, and dazzled by Lux Lisbon (Kirsten Dunst), who of the perfect Lisbon girls is the most perfect. In every class there is one couple that has sex while the others are still talking about it, and Trip and Lux make love on the night of the big dance. But that is not the point. The point is that she wakes up the next morning, alone, in the middle of the football field. And the point is that Trip, as the adult narrator, remembers not only that "she was the still point of the turning world then" and "most people never taste that kind of love" but also, "I liked her a lot. But out there on the football field, it was different."

Yes, it was. It was the end of adolescence and the beginning of a lifetime of compromises, disenchantments, and real things. First sex is ideal only in legend. In life it attaches plumbing, fluids, gropings, fumblings, and pain to what was only an hour ago a platonic ideal. Trip left Lux not because he was a pig, but because he was a boy, and broken with grief at the loss of his—their—dream. And when the Lisbon girls kill themselves, do not blame their deaths on their weird parents. Mourn for the passing of everyone you knew and everyone you were in the last summer before sex. Mourn for the idealism of inexperience.

The Virgin Suicides provides perfunctory reasons why the Lisbon girls might have been unhappy. Their mother (Kathleen Turner) is a hysteric so rattled by her daughters' blooming sexuality that she adds cloth to their prom dresses until they appear in "four identical sacks." Their father (James Woods) is the well-meaning but emasculated high school math teacher who ends up chatting about photosynthesis with his plants. These parents look gruesome to us. All parents look gruesome to kids, and all of their attempts at discipline seem unreasonable. The teenage years of the Lisbon girls are no better or worse than most teenage years. This is not the story of daughters driven to their deaths.

The story it most reminds me of, indeed, is *Picnic at Hanging Rock* (1975), about a party of young girls, not unlike the Lisbon sisters in appearance and sexual experience, who go for a school outing one day and disappear into the wilderness, never to be seen again. Were they captured? Killed in a fall? Trapped somehow? Bitten by snakes? Simply lost in the maze of nature? What happened to them is not the point. Their disappearance is the point. One moment they were smiling and bowing in their white dresses in the sun, and the next they were gone forever. The lack of any explanation is the whole point: For those left behind, they are preserved forever in the perfection they possessed when they were last seen.

The Virgin Suicides is Sofia Coppola's first film, based on the much-discussed novel by Jeffrey Eugenides. She has the courage to play it in a minor key. She doesn't hammer home ideas and interpretations. She is content with the air of mystery and loss that hangs in the air like bitter poignancy. Tolstoy said all happy families are the same. Yes, but he should have added, there are hardly any happy families.

To live in a family group with walls around it is unnatural for a species that evolved in tribes and villages. What would work itself out in the give-and-take of a community gets grotesque when allowed to fester in the hothouse of a single-family home. A mild-mannered teacher and a strong-willed woman turn into a paralyzed captive and a harridan. Their daughters see themselves as captives of these parents, who hysterically project their own failure upon the children. The worship the girls receive from the neighborhood boys confuses them: If they are perfect, why are they seen as such flawed and dangerous creatures? And then the reality of sex, too young, peels back the innocent idealism and reveals its secret engine, which is animal and brutal, lustful and contemptuous.

In a way, the Lisbon girls and the neighborhood boys never existed, except in their own adolescent imaginations. They were imaginary creatures, waiting for the dream to end through death or adulthood. "Cecilia was the first to go," the narrator tells us right at the beginning. We see her talking to a psychiatrist after she tries to slash her wrists. "You're not even old enough to know how hard life gets," he tells her. "Obviously, doctor," she says, "you've never been a thirteen-year-old girl."

No, but his profession and every adult life is to some degree a search for the happiness she does not even know she has.

The Visit ★ ★ ★
R, 107 m., 2001

Hill Harper (Alex Waters), Obba Babatunde (Tony Waters), Rae Dawn Chong (Felicia McDonald), Billy Dee Williams (Henry Waters), Marla Gibbs (Lois Waters), Phylicia Rashad (Dr. Coles), Talia Shire (Marilyn Coffey), David Clennon (Bill Brenner). Directed and produced by Jordan Walker-Pearlman. Screenplay by Walker-Pearlman, based on the play by Kosmond Russell.

The Visit tells the story of a thirty-two-year-old prison inmate, up for parole, dying of AIDS, trying to come to terms with his past. In a series of prison visits with his parents, his brother, a prison psychiatrist, and a woman who was his childhood friend, he moves slowly from anger to acceptance—he becomes a better person.

This outline sounds perhaps too pious to be absorbing, and the final scenes lay on the message a little thick. But *The Visit* contains some effective performances, not least from Hill Harper as Alex, the hero. I remembered him from *Loving Jezebel* and from a supporting role in *He Got Game*, but wasn't prepared for the depth here; this performance announcing Harper is to be taken seriously. Another surprise comes from Billy Dee Williams; we think of him as a traditional leading man, but here he is as a proud, angry, unyielding father—an authority figure who takes it as a personal affront that his son has gone wrong.

But has he gone wrong? Alex is doing twenty-five years for a rape he says he didn't commit. His mother (Marla Gibbs) believes him. His father remembers that Alex stole from them, lied to them, was a junkie and a thief, and thinks him capable of anything. Alex's brother Tony (Obba Babatunde), well dressed, successful, mirrors the father's attitudes; it diminishes them to have a prisoner in the family.

The movie doesn't crank up the volume with violence and jailhouse clichés, but focuses on this person and his possibilities for change. The key law enforcement officials are not sadistic guards or authoritarian wardens, but people who listen. Phylicia Rashad plays the psychiatrist, trying to lead him past denial into acceptance, and there are several scenes involving a parole board that are driven by insight, not the requirements of the drama. The board members, led by Talia Shire, discuss his case, express their doubts, get mad at one another, seem real.

Rae Dawn Chong plays Felicia, the old friend, who has her own demons; a former addict and a prostitute, she killed an abusive father, but now has her life together and visits Alex at the urging of Tony (it's perceptive of the movie to notice how reluctant family members often recruit volunteers to do their emotional heavy-lifting). Her story and other conversations trigger flashbacks and fantasies, in a story that has enormous empathy for this man at the end of a lost life. (The screenplay by director Jordan Walker-Pearlman is from a play by Kosmond Russell, based on his relationship with a brother in prison.)

Watching the movie, I was reminded of a powerful moment in *The Shawshank Redemption*, when the Morgan Freeman character, paroled as an old man, is asked if he has reformed. He says such words have no meaning. He is no longer the same person who committed the crime. He would give anything, he says, to grab that young punk he once was and shake some sense into him. *The Visit* is about the same process—the fact that the prisoner we see is not the same person who was convicted. If, that is, he is lucky enough to grow and change. The last act of *The Visit* hurries that process too much, but the journey is worth taking.

W

Waking Life ★ ★ ★ ★
R, 99 m., 2001

Featuring the voices and animated likenesses of Wiley Wiggins, Trevor Jack Brooks, Robert C. Solomon, Ethan Hawke, Julie Delpy, Charles Gunning, David Sosa, Alex Jones, Aklilu Gebrewald, Carol Dawson, Lisa Moore, Steve Fitch, Steven Prince, Adam Goldberg, Nicky Katt, David Martinez, Tiana Hux, Speed Levitch, Steven Soderbergh, and Richard Linklater. Directed by Richard Linklater and produced by Anne Walker-McBay, Tommy Pallotta, Palmer West, and Jonah Smith. Screenplay by Linklater and the cast members. Animation directed by Bob Sabiston.

Waking Life could not come at a better time. Opening in the sad and fearful days soon after September 11, it celebrates a series of articulate, intelligent characters who seek out the meaning of their existence and do not have the answers. At a time when madmen think they have the right to kill us because of what they think they know about an afterlife, which is by definition unknowable, those who don't know the answers are the only ones asking sane questions. True believers owe it to the rest of us to seek solutions that are reasonable in the visible world.

The movie is like a cold shower of bracing, clarifying ideas. We feel cleansed of boredom, indifference, futility, and the deadening tyranny of the mundane. The characters walk around passionately discussing ideas, theories, ultimate purposes—just as we've started doing again since the complacent routine of our society was shaken. When we were students we often spoke like this, but in adult life it is hard to find intelligent conversation. "What is my purpose?" is replaced by "What did the market do today?"

The movie is as exhilarating in its style and visuals as in its ideas—indeed, the two are interlocked. Richard Linklater and his collaborators have filmed a series of conversations, debates, rants, monologues, and speculations, and then animated their film using a new process that creates a shimmering, pulsating life on the screen: This movie seems alive, seems vibrating with urgency and excitement.

The animation is curiously realistic. A still from the film would look to you like a drawing. But go to www.wakinglifemovie.com and click on the clips to see how the sound and movement have an effect that is eerily lifelike. The most difficult thing for an animator may be to capture an unplanned, spontaneous movement that expresses personality. By filming real people and then animating them, *Waking Life* captures little moments of real life: a musician putting down her cigarette, a double-take, someone listening while eager to start talking again, a guy smiling as if to say, "I'm not really smiling." And the dialogue has the true ring of everyday life, perhaps because most of the actors helped create their own words: The movie doesn't sound like a script but like eavesdropping.

The film's hero, not given a name, is played by Wiley Wiggins as a young man who has returned to the town where once, years ago, a playmate's folding paper toy (we used to call them "cootie catchers") unfolded to show him the words, "dream is destiny." He seems to be in a dream, and complains that although he knows it's a dream, he can't awaken. He wanders from one person and place to another (something like the camera did in Linklater's first film, *Slackers*). He encounters theories, beliefs, sanity, nuttiness. People try to explain what they believe, but he is overwhelmed until finally he is able to see that the answer is—curiosity itself. To not have the answers is expected. To not ask questions is a crime against your own mind.

If I have made the movie sound somber and contemplative, I have been unfair to it. Few movies are more cheerful and alive. The people encountered by the dreamer in his journey are intoxicated by their ideas—deliriously verbal. We recognize some of them: Ethan Hawke and Julie Delpy, from Linklater's *Before Sunrise*, continue their conversation. Speed Levitch, the manic tour guide from the documentary *The Cruise*, is still on his guided tour of life. Other characters are long known to Linklater, including Robert C. Solomon, a philosopher at the University of Texas, who comes on-screen to say something Linklater remembers him saying in a lecture years ago, that existentialism offers more hope than predestination, because it gives us a reason to try to change things.

I have seen *Waking Life* three times now. I want to see it again—not to master it, or even to remember it better (I would not want to read the screenplay), but simply to experience all of these ideas, all of this passion, the very act of trying to figure things out. It must be depressing to believe that you have been supplied with all the answers, that you must believe them and that to question them is disloyal or a sin. Were we given minds in order to fear the questions? ☞

Waking the Dead ★ ★ ½
R, 105 m., 2000

Billy Crudup (Fielding Pierce), Jennifer Connelly (Sarah Williams), Janet McTeer (Caroline Pierce), Molly Parker (Juliet Beck), Sandra Oh (Kim), Hal Holbrook (Isaac Green), Lawrence Dane (Governor Kinosis), Paul Hipp (Danny Pierce). Directed by Keith Gordon and produced by Gordon, Stuart Kleinman, and Linda Reisman. Screenplay by Gordon and Robert Dillon, based on the novel by Scott Spencer.

There is a mystery in *Waking the Dead*, and at the end we are supplied with its answer, but I have seen the movie twice and do not know for sure what the answer is. There are two possibilities. Either would do. If it were a thriller or a ghost story, it wouldn't much matter, but the film has serious romantic and political themes, and in one way or another we really need to know, or it's all been a meaningless game.

The film begins in 1982, with a young politician named Fielding Pierce (Billy Crudup) who learns on the news that his friend Sarah Williams (Jennifer Connelly) has been killed by a car bomb attack in Minneapolis. She was working with a group of political activists opposed to U.S. actions in Chile. Fielding screams out in anguish, and we flash back to his first meeting with Sarah, in 1972, when she was his

brother's secretary. The brother publishes a magazine very like *Rolling Stone*. Fielding is in the Coast Guard to avoid service in Vietnam. Sarah is self-confident, outspoken, political.

The film, based on the novel by Scott Spencer, is a tug-of-war between Fielding's desire to work within the system and Sarah's conviction that it's rotten to the core. As they grow closer romantically, they grow further apart politically, until finally their love is like a sacrifice thrown on the bonfire of their ambitions. There comes a time at a fund-raising benefit when Sarah tells off a fat-cat who has written a column supporting the military junta in Chile. That is not good for Fielding's career.

The film does a lot of flashing back and forth between 1972, when Fielding's life is simple and idealistic, and 1982, when he is in the hands of Chicago political fixers. Hal Holbrook is assigned once again to the Hal Holbrook Role, which he has won so often it should be retired: He has to sit in the shadows of a boardroom or a private club, smoke a cigar, drink a brandy, and pull strings behind the scenes. He is the go-between for Fielding and Governor Kinosis (Lawrence Dane), who offers Fielding a shot at a safe congressional seat.

Fielding wants it. Sarah sees it as the selling of his soul. As the two of them ride the L together, Jennifer Connelly has a strong and bitter scene in which she explains exactly what he is doing and why it is wrong. They're drifting apart, and Fielding resents the presence in her life of a gimlet-eyed radical priest. We see her meeting with Chilean refugees. She leaves for Chile to bring some more out. Then she dies in the car bombing.

Or does she? The film toys with us, and with Fielding, who begins to imagine he sees Sarah here and there—on the street, in a crowd. There is one almost subliminal shot in which her face flashes on a TV screen, just as he turns away. Did he see it? Or was it in his imagination? Or did he not see it? And in that case, since we saw it, was it the first shot of the next story on the news, or a subtle hint that this movie has something in common with *Ghost*?

To speculate would be to give away the ending—which I can't do anyway, since I'm not sure of it. What I do know is that *Waking the Dead* has a good heart and some fine performances, but is too muddled at the story level to involve us emotionally. It's a sweet film. The relationship between Sarah and Fielding is a little deeper and more affectionate than we expect in plot-driven melodramas.

There are fuzzy spots; we never find out anything specific about Sarah's political activism, we never see the Chicago pols actually trying to influence Fielding in an inappropriate way, and we never know exactly what role the Catholic Church plays, except to lend its cinematic images and locations. I was amused when another critic pointed out that, to save money perhaps, the moviemakers show Fielding savoring his political victory all alone by himself.

Oscar nominee Janet McTeer plays Fielding's sister, in the kind of role every actress hopes she can escape from by getting an Oscar nomination. Paul Hipp plays his Jann Wennerish brother, who falls in love with a Korean hooker (Sandra Oh) he meets in a massage parlor, and tries to convince Fielding to pull strings so she can get her green card. This entire subplot should have been excised swiftly and mercilessly. And at the end, we are left with—what? When we invest emotional capital, we deserve a payoff.

A Walk to Remember ★ ★ ★
PG, 100 m., 2002

Mandy Moore (Jamie Sullivan), Shane West (Landon Carter), Daryl Hannah (Cynthia Carter), Peter Coyote (Reverend Sullivan), Lauren German (Belinda), Clayne Crawford (Dean). Directed by Adam Shankman and produced by Denise Di Novi and Hunt Lowry. Screenplay by Karen Janszen, based on the novel by Nicholas Sparks.

A Walk to Remember is a love story so sweet, sincere, and positive that it sneaks past the defenses built up in this age of irony. It tells the story of a romance between two eighteen-year-olds that is summarized when the boy tells the girl's doubtful father: "Jamie has faith in me. She makes me want to be different. Better." After all of the vulgar crudities of the typical modern teenage movie, here is one that looks closely, pays attention, sees that not all teenagers are as cretinous as Hollywood portrays them.

Mandy Moore, a natural beauty in both face and manner, stars as Jamie Sullivan, an outsider at school who is laughed at because she stands apart, has values, and always wears the same ratty blue sweater. Her father (Peter Coyote) is a local minister. Shane West plays Landon Carter, a senior boy who hangs with the popular crowd but is shaken when a stupid dare goes wrong and one of his friends is paralyzed in a diving accident. He dates a popular girl and joins in the laughter against Jamie. Then, as punishment for the prank, he is ordered by the principal to join the drama club: "You need to meet some new people."

Jamie's in the club. He begins to notice her in a new way. He asks her to help him rehearse for a role in a play. She treats him with level honesty. She isn't one of those losers who skulks around feeling put-upon; her self-esteem stands apart from the opinion of her peers. She's a smart, nice girl, a reminder that one of the pleasures of the movies is to meet good people.

The plot has revelations that I will not betray. Enough to focus on the way Jamie's serene example makes Landon into a nicer person—encourages him to become more sincere and serious to win her respect. There are setbacks along the way, as in a painful scene at school where she approaches him while he's with his old friends and says, "See you tonight," and he says, "In your dreams." When he turns up at her house, she is hurt and angry, and his excuses sound lame even to him.

The movie walks a fine line with the Peter Coyote character, whose church Landon attends. Movies have a way of stereotyping reactionary Bible-thumpers who are hostile to teen romance. There is a little of that here; Jamie is forbidden to date, for example, although there's more behind her father's decision than knee-jerk strictness. But when Landon goes to the Reverend Sullivan and asks him to have faith in him, the minister listens with an open mind.

Yes, the movie is corny at times. But corniness is all right at times. I forgave the movie its broad emotion because it earned it. It lays things on a little thick at the end, but by then it has paid its way. Director Adam Shankman and his writer, Karen Janszen, working from the novel by Nicholas Sparks, have an unforced trust in the material that redeems, even justifies, the broad strokes. They go wrong only three times: (1) The subplot involving the paralyzed boy should either have been dealt with or dropped. (2) It's tiresome to make the black teenager use "brother" in every sentence, as if he is not their peer but was ported in from another world. (3) As Kuleshov proved more than eighty years ago in a famous experiment, when an audience sees an impassive close-up it supplies the necessary emotion from the context. It can be fatal for an actor to try to "act" in a close-up, and Landon's little smile at the end is a distraction at a crucial moment.

Those are small flaws in a touching movie. The performances by Mandy Moore and Shane West are so quietly convincing we're reminded that many teenagers in movies seem to think like thirty-year-old stand-up comics. That Jamie and Landon base their romance on values and respect will blindside some viewers of the film, especially since the first five or ten minutes seem to be headed down a familiar teenage movie trail. *A Walk to Remember* is a small treasure.

The War Zone ★ ★ ★ ★
NO MPAA RATING, 99 m., 2000

Ray Winstone (Dad), Tilda Swinton (Mum), Lara Belmont (Jessie), Freddie Cunliffe (Tom), Colin J. Farrell (Nick), Aisling O'Sullivan (Carol), Kate Ashfield (Lucy). Directed by Tim Roth and produced by Sarah Radclyffe and Dixie Linder. Screenplay by Alexander Stuart, based on his novel *The War Zone*.

It must have been something like this in medieval times, families living in isolation, cut off from neighbors, forced indoors by the weather, their animal and sexual functions not always shielded from view. Tim Roth's *The War Zone*, brilliant and heartbreaking, takes place in the present but is timeless; most particularly it is cut off from the fix-it culture of psychobabble, which defines all the politically correct ways to consider incest. The movie is not about incest as an issue, but about incest as a blow to the heart and the soul—a real event, here, now, in a family that seems close and happy. Not a topic on a talk show.

The movie takes place in winter in Devon, which is wet and gray, the sky squeezing joy out of the day. The family has moved from London "to make a fresh start," the mother says. They live in a comfortable cottage, warm and sheltered, life centering around the big kitchen table. Mom (Tilda Swinton) is very pregnant. Dad (Ray Winstone) is bluff and cheery, extroverted, a good guy. Tom (Freddie Cunliffe) is a fifteen-year-old, silent and sad because he misses his friends in London. Jessie (Lara Belmont) is eighteen years old, ripe with beauty. This looks like a cheerful story.

Roth tells it obliquely, sensitive to the ways families keep secrets even from themselves. Early in the film the mother's time comes and the whole family rushes to the hospital; there's a car crash, but a happy ending, as they gather in the maternity ward with the newcomer, all of them cut and bruised, but survivors. Back at home, there is a comfort with the physical side of life. Mom nurses her child in kitchen scenes like renaissance paintings. Tom is comfortable with his sister's casual nudity while they have a heart-to-heart talk. Mum helps wash her men at the kitchen sink, Jessie dries her brother's hair in the laundry room, the family seems comfortable with one another.

Then Tom glimpses a disturbing part of a moment between his father and his sister. He challenges Jessie. She says nothing happened. Something did happen, and more will happen, including a scene of graphic hurtfulness. But this isn't a case of Tom discovering incest in his family and blowing the whistle. It's much more complicated. How does he feel about his sister and about her relationship with her new boyfriend, Nick? What about his father's eerie split personality, able to deny his behavior and see Tom's interference as an assault on their happy family? What about the mother's willingness not to know? What about his sister's denial? Does it spring from shame, fear, or a desire to shield Tom and her mother from the knowledge?

And what about a curious episode when Jessie and Tom visit London, and Jessie almost seems to have set up Tom to sleep with one of her friends—as what? Consolation? A bribe?

Revenge? The movie's refusal to declare exactly what the London episode means is admirable, because this is not a zero-sum accounting of good and evil, but a messy, elusive, painfully complex tragedy in which no one is driven by just one motive.

When Tom is accused of destroying the family and having a filthy mind, there is a sense in which he accepts this analysis. One critic of the film wrote that a "teenaged boy (from the big city, no less) would surely be more savvy—no matter how distraught—about the workings and potential resolutions of such a situation." Only in textbooks. When you're fifteen, what you learn in social studies and from talk shows is a lot different from how you confront your own family.

Incest is not unfamiliar as a subject for movies, but most incest stories are about characters simplified into monsters and victims. We know intellectually that most child abusers were abused children, but few films pause to reflect how that lifelong hurt reflects itself in real situations. The father here is both better and worse because of his own probably traumatic childhood. He must long ago have often promised himself that he would be different than his own father, that he would be a good dad—loving, kind, warm, cheerful—and so he is, all except for when he is not. When he's accused of evil, he explodes in anger—the anger of the father he is now and also the anger of the child he once was. For a moment his son is, in a sense, the abuser, making Dad feel guilty and shameful just as his own father must have, and tearing down all his efforts to be better, to be different.

Unsurprisingly, *The War Zone* affects viewers much more powerfully than a simple morality tale might. It is not simply about the evil of incest, but about its dynamic, about the way it plays upon guilt and shame and addresses old and secret wounds. The critic James Berardinelli says that when he saw the movie at the Toronto Film Festival, a viewer ran from the theater saying he couldn't take it anymore, and went looking to pull a fire alarm. Tim Roth was standing near the exit and intercepted him, becoming confessor for an emotional outpouring that the movie had inspired.

Roth is one of the best actors now working, and with this movie he reveals himself as a di-

rector of surprising gifts. I cannot imagine *The War Zone* being better directed by anyone else, even though Ingmar Bergman and Ken Loach come to mind. Roth and his actors, and Stuart's screenplay, understand these people and their situation down to the final nuance, and are willing to let silence, timing, and visuals reveal what dialogue would cheapen. Not many movies bring you to a dead halt of sorrow and empathy. This one does.

The Watcher ★ ★
R, 93 m., 2000

James Spader (Campbell), Marisa Tomei (Polly), Keanu Reeves (Griffin), Robert Cicchini (Mitch), Scott A. Martin (FBI Agent), Jenny McShane (Diana), Chris Ellis (Hollis), Joe Monaco (Policeman). Directed by Joe Charbanic and produced by Chris Eberts, Elliott Lewitt, and Jeff Rice. Screenplay by Darcy Meyers, David Elliot, and Clay Ayers.

The Watcher is about still another serial killer whose existence centers around staging elaborate scenarios for the cops. If these weirdos would just become screenwriters in the first place, think of the lives that could be saved. Keanu Reeves stars as Griffin, a murderer who follows an FBI agent named Campbell (James Spader) from Los Angeles to Chicago, complaining about the cold weather but explaining he had to move because "things didn't work out with your successor." Killing just wasn't the same without Campbell to bug.

According to a theory floated by Campbell's therapist (Marisa Tomei), the killer and the agent may need each other, or are they brothers neither one ever had. Freud would cringe. Griffin is indeed forever seeking Campbell's reaction; what the agent thinks is more important to him than what his victims think. Griffin spends relatively little time killing his victims, but must spend days preparing presentations for Campbell.

He sets puzzles, issues challenges, sends him FedEx packages with photos of the next victims, devises elaborate booby traps, and recklessly follows the agent (who does not know what he looks like) right onto elevators. Finally he sets up a face-to-face meeting in a cemetery. The psychology here is a little shaky. Although some serial killers may have issues with the law, most of them focus, I think, on their victims and not on some kind of surrogate authority figure.

The movie's structure is simple: Killer issues challenge, agent rises to bait, desperate citywide search leads to still more frustration. *The Watcher* devotes an inordinate amount of its running time to Chicago police cars with sirens screaming as they hurtle down streets and over bridges, never turning a corner without almost spinning out. There are also a lot of helicopters involved. At one point the killer is pinpointed "twenty miles north of the city," a map shows Lincolnwood, and the cops converge at first on the Wrigley Building, before relocating to an abandoned warehouse. I know you're not supposed to fret about local geography in a movie where a city is a backdrop and not a map, but aren't there a *lot* of people who know the Wrigley Building is not twenty miles north of the city? Maybe the helicopter pilots are disoriented; in the chase that opens the movie, they come whirling into town from Lake Michigan, which makes for a nice opening shot while not answering the puzzle of how many miles from shore they are usually stationed.

The actors cannot be faulted. They bring more to the story than it really deserves. Spader has his hands on an intriguing character; Agent Campbell's tragic history (shown in flashbacks) has led to migraines so bad that he injects himself with pain medication straight into the stomach muscle. Painkillers have made him start losing his way and forgetting stuff, he complains to Tomei, and a Chicago cop calls him "Captain Barbiturate," observing, "If his pupils don't dilate, we don't need him." Migraines literally cripple their victims, but Campbell has one of those considerate cases that never strike when he is saving lives or pursuing fugitives.

Spader's quiet exchanges with Tomei are effective, too, even if we know her character was put on earth to get into big trouble. Reeves, as the killer, has the fairly thankless task of saying only what the movie needs him to say; he's limited by the fact that his killer has no real dimension or personality apart from his function as a plot device. The final confrontation is an example: Is he more interested in revenge,

or in demonstrating the ingenuities of his booby-trapped scenario? It goes without saying, I guess, that the scene features hundreds of candles. Just once in a pervert killer movie, I wish they'd show a scene where he's pushing a cart through the Hallmark store, actually buying all those candles ("Do you have any that are unscented and aren't shaped, like, uh, little Hummel figures?").

Way of the Gun ★ ★ ½
R, 120 m., 2000

James Caan (Joe Sarno), Benicio Del Toro (Longbaugh), Ryan Phillippe (Parker), Juliette Lewis (Robin), Taye Diggs (Jeffers), Nicky Katt (Obecks), Scott Wilson (Mr. Chidduck). Directed by Christopher McQuarrie and produced by Kenneth Kokin. Screenplay by McQuarrie.

Way of the Gun is a wildly ambitious, heedlessly overplotted post-Tarantino bloodfest—the kind of movie that needs its own doggie bag. There's a good story buried somewhere in this melee, surrounded by such maddening excess that you want to take some home and feed it to undernourished stray movies.

The film is the directorial debut of Christopher McQuarrie, who won an Oscar for his screenplay for *The Usual Suspects*. He is a born director, and now what he needs to meet is a born editor. There are scenes here so fine, so unexpected, so filled with observation and nuance, that you can hardly believe the notes he's hitting. And then he'll cycle back for another round of *Wild Bunch* gunplay—not realizing that for Sam Peckinpah the shootout was the climax, not the punctuation.

Both of these McQuarrie films have loop-the-loop plots, unexpected reversals and revelations, and closing lines that call everything else into question—although not, I hasten to add, in the same way. Can this one really be only 120 minutes long? It has enough plot for a series. I'd love to see the prequel, in which these characters twist themselves into narrative pretzels just *setting up* all the stuff that pays off here.

Benicio Del Toro and Ryan Phillippe star as Mr. Longbaugh and Mr. Parker (the "mister" is a reminder of *Reservoir Dogs*). Having exhausted all their chances at normal lives (we doubt they tried very hard), they tell us in the narration that they "stepped off the path and went looking for the fortune we knew was ours." At a sperm bank, they overhear a conversation about a millionaire whose seed is being brought to term by a surrogate mother, who is always kept under armed guard. Their idea: Kidnap the mother and collect ransom.

The notion of kidnapping a (very) pregnant woman would provide complications enough for some directors, but not for McQuarrie, who hurtles into a labyrinth involving crisscrossing loyalties among the millionaire's current bodyguards, his shady employers, his long-time enforcers, the enforcer's old pal, and a gynecologist whose involvement in the case is more (and less) than professional.

The pregnant woman is played by Juliette Lewis, who is the movie's center of sanity. She is the only one who talks sense and understands more or less why everyone is doing everything—occasionally, so thick is the going, she'll simply explain things to the other cast members on a need-to-know basis. Mr. Longbaugh and Mr. Parker drive her into Mexico, the bodyguards (Taye Diggs and Nicky Katt) follow—and so does grizzled old Joe Sarno (James Caan), the suicidal but competent enforcer who is relied upon by the shady millionaire (Scott Wilson). It is a measure of McQuarrie's skill that the millionaire's wife plays a full and essential role in the movie while uttering a total of perhaps nine words.

Much of the movie consists of cat-and-mouse games, car chases, and shoot-outs. McQuarrie scatters fresh moments among the wearying routine of gunfire; shots of guys dashing into the frame with machine guns have become tiresome, but I liked the way Phillippe vaulted into a dry fountain that contained a nasty surprise. And the way the car chase slowed down to an elusive and tricky creep (I didn't believe it, but I liked it).

James Caan is very good here as the professional gunman who has seen it all. He's supposed to be on the same side as the bodyguards, but distrusts them, and tells one: "The only thing you can assume about a broken-down old man is that he is a survivor." McQuarrie gives Caan clipped lines of wisdom, and he has a wonderful scene with Del Toro in which he explains his functions and his plans.

He and Wilson have another nice scene—two old associates who trust each other only up to a point. Jeffers, the Taye Diggs bodyguard, meanwhile maintains cool competence while everything nevertheless goes wrong, and is only one of several characters who reveal an unexpected connection.

Up to a point, a twisting plot is entertaining. We enjoy being fooled and surprised. But we have to halfway believe these things could really happen—in a movie, anyway. McQuarrie reaches that point and sails past it like a ski jumper. We get worn down. At first you're surprised when you get the rug pulled out from under you. Eventually, if you're a quick study, you stop stepping on it.

As a video, viewed at less than full attention, *Way of the Gun* could nicely fill the gaps of a slow Saturday night. It's when you focus on it that you lose patience. McQuarrie pulls, pummels, and pushes us, makes his characters jump through hoops, and at the end produces carloads of "bag men" who have no other function than to pop up and be shot at (all other available targets have already been killed). Enough, already.

The Wedding Planner ★ ★
PG-13, 100 m., 2001

Jennifer Lopez (Mary Fiore), Matthew McConaughey (Steve Edison), Bridgette Wilson-Sampras (Fran Donelly), Justin Chambers (Massimo), Alex Rocco (Mary's Father), Erik Hyler (Dancer), Huntley Ritter (Tom). Directed by Adam Shankman and produced by Peter Abrams, Deborah Del Prete, Jennifer Gibgot, Robert L. Levy, and Gigi Pritzker. Screenplay by Pamela Falk and Michael Ellis.

Jennifer Lopez looks soulfully into the eyes of Matthew McConaughey, but is he looking back? One of the many problems of *The Wedding Planner* is that we can't tell and don't much care. When a plot depends on two people falling in love when they absolutely should not, we have to be able to believe at some level that they have been swept up by a destiny beyond their control. McConaughey seems less inflamed by his sudden new romance than resigned to it.

Lopez stars in the title role as Mary Fiore—yes, a wedding planner. With her walkie-talkie headset, cell phone, clipboard, spotters, and video crews, she's mission control as her clients walk down the aisle. Racing to an appointment, she meets Dr. Steve Edison (McConaughey) in one of the most absurd Meet Cutes in many a moon. Her Gucci heel gets stuck in a manhole cover, a garbage Dumpster rolls down a hill toward her, and Steve hurls her out of the way and, of course, lands on top of her; it's love at first full-body contact.

That night they have a perfect date, watching movies in the park. Mary has always been the wedding planner, never the bride (uh-huh—this is as convincing as Julia Roberts's old flame choosing another bride in *My Best Friend's Wedding*). Now she walks on air, until her current client, the millionairess Fran Donelly (Bridgette Wilson-Sampras), introduces Mary to the man Fran will marry, who is, of course, Dr. Steve Edison.

If Steve is engaged, why did he mislead Mary with that night of movies and soul talk? Because he is a dishonest louse, or, as the movie explains it, because he had no idea he would be thunderstruck by love. Since he is in love with Mary, the only sensible thing to do is call off his wedding to Fran and buy a season ticket to movies in the park. But the movie cannot abide common sense, and recycles decades of clichés about the wrong people getting married and the right ones making stupid decisions.

There are times when the movie's contrivance is agonizing. Consider all the plot mechanics involving Mary's Italian-American father (Alex Rocco) and his schemes to marry her off to Massimo, her childhood playmate from the old country (Calvin Klein model Justin Chambers, sounding as Italian as most people named Chambers). Consider how Mary spends her free time (on a Scrabble team) and how she accepts a proposal of marriage by spelling "OK" with Scrabble tiles when "Yes" would be more appropriate plus get her more points.

And consider a "comic" sequence so awkward and absurd it not only brings the movie to a halt but threatens to reverse its flow. While Mary and Steve wander in a sculpture garden, they accidentally knock over a statue, and the statue's male hardware gets broken off. Mary has some superglue in her purse, and they try to glue the frank and beans back in place, but alas, the broken part becomes stuck to Dr. Steve's palm. If he had gone through the rest of the movie like that it might have added some interest, but no: Mary also has some solvent in her purse. When you have seen Jennifer Lopez ungluing marble genitals from the hand of the man she loves, you have more or less seen everything.

A plot like this is so hopeless that only acting can redeem it. Lopez pulls her share of the load, looking genuinely smitten by this guy, and convincingly crushed when his secret is revealed. But McConaughey is not the right actor for this material. He seems stolid and workmanlike, when what you need is a guy with naughtier eyes: Ben Affleck, Steve Martin, William H. Macy, Alec Baldwin, Matt Dillon.

Bridgette Wilson-Sampras is, however, correctly cast as Fran, the rich bride-to-be. She's an Anna Nicole Smith type who gets the joke and avoids all the usual clichés involving the woman who gets left at the altar, perhaps because she realizes, as we do, that getting dumped by Dr. Steve is far from the worst thing that could happen to her. We sense midway in the movie that Mary and Fran could have more interesting conversations with each other than either one will have with Dr. Steve, and no matter which one marries him, we sense a future, five to eight years from now, after the divorce, when the two girls meet by chance at a spa (I see them at the Golden Door, perhaps, or Rancho La Puerta) and share a good laugh about the doc.

Wendigo ★ ★ ½
R, 91 m., 2002

Patricia Clarkson (Kim), Jake Weber (George), Erik Per Sullivan (Miles), John Speredakos (Otis), Christopher Wynkoop (Sheriff), Lloyd Oxendine (Elder), Brian Delate (Everett), Daniel Sherman (Billy). Directed by Larry Fessenden and produced by Jeffrey Levy-Hinte. Screenplay by Fessenden.

Wendigo is a good movie with an ending that doesn't work. While it was not working I felt a keen disappointment, because the rest of the movie works so well. The writer, director, and editor is Larry Fessenden, whose *Habit* (1997) was about a New York college student who found solace, and too much more, in the arms of a vampire. Now Fessenden goes into the Catskills to tell a story that will be compared to *The Blair Witch Project* when it should be compared to *The Innocents*.

The film builds considerable scariness, and does it in the details. Ordinary things happen in ominous ways. Kim and George (Patricia Clarkson and Jake Weber), a couple from New York, drive to the Catskills to spend a weekend in a friend's cottage, bringing along their young son, Miles (Erik Per Sullivan). Even before they arrive, there's trouble. They run into a deer on the road, and three hunters emerge from the woods and complain that the city people killed "their" deer—and worse, broke its antlers.

Two of the hunters seem like all-right guys. The third, named Otis (John Speredakos), is not. Holding a rifle that seems like a threat, he engages in macho name-calling with George, and the scene is seen mostly through the big-eyed point of view of little Miles, in the backseat. He says little, he does little, and the less he says and does, the more his fear becomes real to us. Fessenden is using an effective technique: Instead of scaring us, he scares the kid, and we get scared through empathy and osmosis.

Kim and George are not getting along too well, and that works to increase the tension. They're not fighting out loud, but you can feel the buried unhappiness, and Kim tells him: "You've got all this anger you carry around with you from work and I don't know where, and he feels it's directed at him." George tries to be nice to Miles, tries to take an interest, but he's not really listening, and kids notice that.

There are bullet holes in the cabin when they get to it. It's cold inside. Miles hears noises and sees things—or thinks he does. The next day at the general store, he is given a wooden figure by a man behind the counter who says it represents a Wendigo, an Indian spirit. His mother asks where he got the figure. "From the man," Miles says. "Nobody works here but me," says a woman behind another counter.

It doesn't sound as effective as it is. The effect is all in the direction, in Fessenden's control of mood. I watched in admiration as he created tension and fear out of thin air. When the boy and his father go sledding, an event takes place so abruptly that it almost happens to us. The way Fessenden handles the aftermath is just right, building suspense without forgetting logic.

The actors have an unforced, natural quality that looks easy but is hard to do. Look and listen at the conversation between Otis and the local sheriff (Christopher Wynkoop). Notice the way they both know what is being said and what is meant, and how they both know the other knows. And look at the way the scene involves us in what will happen next.

The buildup, which continues for most of the film, is very well done. Unfortunately, Fessenden felt compelled, I guess, to tilt over into the supernatural (or the hallucinatory) in a climax that feels false and rushed. Maybe he would have been better off dropping the Wendigo altogether, and basing the story simply on the scariness of a cottage in the woods in winter, and the ominous ways of Otis.

The ending doesn't work, as I've said, but most of the movie works so well I'm almost recommending it anyway—maybe not to everybody, but certainly to people with a curiosity about how a movie can go very right, and then step wrong. Fessenden has not made a perfect film, but he's a real filmmaker.

Wet Hot American Summer ★

R, 97 m., 2001

Janeane Garofalo (Beth), David Hyde Pierce (Henry), Michael Showalter (Coop/Alan Shemper), Marguerite Moreau (Katie), Paul Rudd (Andy), Christopher Meloni (Gene), Bradley Cooper (Ben), Michael Ian Black (McKinley), Ken Marino (Victor), Marisa Ryan (Abby). Directed by David Wain and produced by Howard Bernstein. Screenplay by Michael Showalter and David Wain.

Hello muddah,
Hello fadduh—
Here I am at *Wet Hot American Summah.*

Wow I hate it
Something fierce—
Except the astrophysicist David Hyde Pierce.

He lives in a
Cottage nearby
And boy can he make Janeane Garofolo sigh.

She's the director
Of Camp Firewood,
Which turns before our eyes into Camp Feel-
good.

She is funny
As she's hurrying
Through the camper's names, including David
Ben Gurion.

She dreams of bunking
David Hyde Pierce,
Who fears a falling Skylab will crush them first.

(Chorus)
Let me leave,
Oh muddah fadduh—
From this comic romp in Mother Nature . . .
Don't make me stay,
Oh muddah fadduh—
In this idiotic motion picture.

Every camper
And each counselor
Is horny, especially Michael Showalter.

He lusts after
Marguerite Moreau's bod,
But she prefers the lifeguard played by Paul
Rudd.

The camp cook,
Chris Meloni,
Goes berserk because he feels attacked by
phonies.

He talks to bean cans
And screams and moans
Periodically because of Post-Traumatic Anxiety
Syndrome.

(Chorus)
I want to escape,
Oh muddah fadduh—
Life's too short for cinematic torture.
Comedies like this,
Oh muddah fadduh—
Inspire in me the critic as a vulture.

Ben and McKinley
Achieve their fame
As campers whose love dare not speak its name.

Ken Marino
Doesn't go rafting
Prefering Marisa Ryan, who is zaftig.

Watch David Wain's
Direction falter,
Despite the help of cowriter Showalter.

They did The State,
On MTV,
And of the two that is the one you should see.

Thoughts of *Meatballs*
Cruelly hamper
Attempts by us to watch as happy campers.

Allan Sherman
Sang on the telly.
I stole from him, and he from Ponchielli.

We Were Soldiers ★ ★ ★ ½
R, 138 m., 2002

Mel Gibson (Hal Moore), Madeleine Stowe (Julie Moore), Sam Elliott (Sergeant Major Plumley), Greg Kinnear (Major Crandall), Chris Klein (Lieutenant Geoghegan), Don Duong (Ahn), Josh Daugherty (Ouelette), Barry Pepper (Joe Galloway), Keri Russell (Barbara Geoghegan). Directed by Randall Wallace and produced by Bruce Davey, Stephen McEveety, and Wallace. Screenplay by Wallace, based on the book by Joe Galloway and Hal Moore.

"I wonder what Custer was thinking," Lieutenant Colonel Hal Moore says, "when he realized he'd moved his men into slaughter." Sergeant Major Plumley, his right-hand man, replies, "Sir, Custer was a pussy." There you have the two emotional poles of *We Were Soldiers*, the story of the first major land battle in the Vietnam War, late in 1964. Moore (Mel Gibson) is a family man and a Harvard graduate who studied international relations. Plumley (Sam Elliott) is an army lifer, hard, brave, unsentimental. They are both about as good as battle leaders get. But by the end of that first battle, they realize they may be in the wrong war.

The reference to Custer is not coincidence. Moore leads the First Battalion of the Seventh Cavalry, Custer's regiment. "We will ride into battle and this will be our horse," Moore says, standing in front of a helicopter. Some 400 of his men ride into battle in the Ia Drang Valley, known as the Valley of Death, and are surrounded by some 2,000 North Vietnamese troops. Moore realizes it's an ambush, and indeed in the film's opening scenes he reads about just such a tactic used by the Vietnamese against the French a few years earlier.

We Were Soldiers, like Black Hawk Down, is a film in which the Americans do not automatically prevail in the style of traditional Hollywood war movies. Ia Drang cannot be called a defeat, since Moore's men fought bravely and well, suffering heavy casualties but killing even more Viet Cong. But it is not a victory; it's more the curtain-raiser of a war in which American troops were better trained and better equipped, but outnumbered, outmaneuvered, and finally outlasted.

For much of its length, the movie consists of battle scenes. They are not as lucid and easy to follow as the events in Black Hawk Down, but then the terrain is different, the canvas is larger, and there are no eyes in the sky to track troop movements. Director Randall Wallace (who wrote Braveheart and Pearl Harbor) does make the situation clear from moment to moment, as Moore and his North Vietnamese counterpart try to outsmart each other with theory and instinct.

Wallace cuts between the American troops, their wives back home on an army base, and a tunnel bunker where Ahn (Don Duong), the Viet Cong commander, plans strategy on a map. Both men are smart and intuitive. The enemy knows the terrain and has the advantage of surprise, but is surprised itself at the way the Americans improvise and rise to the occasion.

Black Hawk Down was criticized because the characters seemed hard to tell apart. We Were Soldiers doesn't have that problem; in the Hollywood tradition it identifies a few key players, casts them with stars, and follows their stories. In addition to the Gibson and Elliott characters, there are Major Crandall (Greg Kinnear), a helicopter pilot who flies into danger; the gung ho Lieutenant Geoghegan (Chris Klein); and Joe Galloway (Barry Pepper), a photojournalist who was a soldier's son, hitches a ride into battle, and finds himself fighting at the side of the others to save his life.

The key relationship is between Moore and

Plumley, and Gibson and Elliott depict it with quiet authority. They're portrayed as professional soldiers with experience from Korea. As they're preparing to ride into battle, Moore tells Plumley, "Better get yourself that M-16." The veteran replies: "By the time I need one, there'll be plenty of them lying on the ground." There are.

Events on the army base center around the lives of the soldiers' wives, including Julie Moore (Madeleine Stowe), who looks after their five children and is the de facto leader of the other spouses. We also meet Barbara Geoghegan (Keri Russell), who, because she is singled out, gives the audience a strong hint that the prognosis for her husband is not good.

Telegrams announcing deaths in battle are delivered by a Yellow Cab driver. Was the army so insensitive that even on a base they couldn't find an officer to deliver the news? That sets up a shameless scene later, when a Yellow Cab pulls up in front of a house and of course the wife inside assumes her husband is dead, only to find him in the cab. This scene is a reminder of Wallace's Pearl Harbor, in which the Ben Affleck character is reported shot down over the English Channel and makes a surprise return to Hawaii without calling ahead. Call me a romantic, but when your loved one thinks you're dead, give her a ring.

We Were Soldiers and Black Hawk Down both seem to replace patriotism with professionalism. This movie waves the flag more than the other (even the Viet Cong's Ahn looks at the Stars and Stripes with enigmatic thoughtfulness), but the narration tells us, "In the end, they fought for each other." This is an echo of Black Hawk Down's line, "It's about the men next to you. That's all it is."

Some will object, as they did with the earlier film, that the battle scenes consist of Americans killing waves of faceless nonwhite enemies. There is an attempt to give a face and a mind to the Viet Cong in the character of Ahn, but, significantly, he is not listed in the major credits and I had to call the studio to find out his name and the name of the actor who played him. Yet almost all war movies identify with one side or the other, and it's remarkable that We Were Soldiers includes a dedication not only to the Americans who fell at Ia Drang, but also to "the members of the

People's Army of North Vietnam who died in that place."

I was reminded of an experience fifteen years ago at the Hawaii Film Festival, when a delegation of North Vietnamese directors arrived with a group of their films about the war. An audience member noticed that the enemy was not only faceless, but was not even named: At no point did the movies refer to Americans. "That is true," said one of the directors. "We have been at war so long, first with the Chinese, then the French, then the Americans, that we just think in terms of the enemy."

Whatever It Takes ★ ½
PG-13, 92 m., 2000

Shane West (Ryan Woodman), Jodi Lyn O'Keefe (Ashley Grant), Marla Sokoloff (Maggie Carter), James Franco (Chris Campbell), Julia Sweeney (Ryan's Mom). Directed by David Hubbard and produced by Paul Schiff. Screenplay by Mark Schwahn, loosely based on Edmund Rostand's play *Cyrano de Bergerac*.

Whatever It Takes is still another movie arguing that the American teenager's IQ level hovers in the low 90s. It involves teenagers who have never existed, doing things no teenager has ever done, for reasons no teenager would understand. Of course, it's aimed at the teenage market. Maybe it's intended as escapism.

The screenplay is "loosely based on *Cyrano de Bergerac*," according to the credits. My guess is, it's based on the Cliff's Notes for *Cyrano*, studied only long enough to rip off the scene where Cyrano hides in the bushes and whispers lines for his friend to repeat to the beautiful Roxanne.

Cyrano in this version is the wonderfully named Ryan Woodman (Shane West), whose house is next door to Maggie (Marla Sokoloff). So close, indeed, that the balconies of their bedrooms almost touch, and they are in constant communication, although "only good friends." Ryan has a crush on Ashley (Jodi Lyn O'Keefe), the school sexpot. His best pal Chris (James Franco) warns him Ashley is beyond his grasp, but Ryan can dream.

If you know *Cyrano*, or have seen such splendid adaptations as Fred Schepisi's *Roxanne* (1987) with Steve Martin and Daryl Han-

nah, you can guess the key scene. Ryan talks Chris into going out with Maggie and then hides behind the scenery of a school play while prompting him with lines he knows Maggie will fall for. With Maggie neutralized, Ryan goes out with Ashley—who is a conceited, arrogant snob, of course, and will get her comeuppance in one of those cruel scenes reserved for stuck-up high school sexpots.

The film contains a funny scene, but it doesn't involve any of the leads. It's by Ryan's mom (Julia Sweeney), also the school nurse, who lectures the student body on safe sex, using a six-foot male reproductive organ as a visual aid. She is not Mrs. Woodman for nothing. As a responsible reporter I will also note that the film contains a nude shower scene, which observes all of the rules about nudity almost but not quite being shown.

And, let's see, there is a scene where Ashley gets drunk and throws up on her date, and a scene set in an old folks' home that makes use of enough flatulence to score a brief concerto. And a scene ripped off from *It's a Wonderful Life*, as the high school gym floor opens up during a dance to dunk the students in the swimming pool beneath. Forget about the situation inspired by *Cyrano:* Is there *anything* in this movie that isn't borrowed?

What Lies Beneath ★ ★
PG-13, 130 m., 2000

Michelle Pfeiffer (Claire Spencer), Harrison Ford (Norman Spencer), Katharine Towne (Caitlin Spencer), Miranda Otto (Mary Feur), James Remar (Warren Feur), Victoria Bidewell (Beatrice), Diana Scarwid (Jody), Joe Morton (Psychiatrist), Dennison Samaroo (Ph.D. Student No. 1). Directed by Robert Zemeckis and produced by Steve Starkey, Zemeckis, and Jack Rapke. Screenplay by Clark Gregg, based on the story by Sarah Kernochan and Gregg.

What Lies Beneath opens with an hour or so of standard thriller scare tactics, done effectively, and then plops into a morass of absurdity. Lacking a smarter screenplay, it milks the genuine skills of its actors and director for more than it deserves, and then runs off the rails in an ending more laughable than scary. Along the way, yes, there are some good moments.

Michelle Pfeiffer stars as Claire Spencer, the happily married wife of Dr. Norman Spencer (Harrison Ford), a scientist. They're renovating his old family house on the shores of a lake. A house that, when she is home alone, seems haunted—with doors that open by themselves, picture frames that keep falling over, a tub that fills itself, a dog that barks at invisible menaces, and a neighbor who has possibly murdered his wife.

Gruff, no-nonsense Dr. Spencer, of course, dismisses his wife's fears, and sends her to a psychiatrist. All of her early scenes are reasonable enough, even if the doors open themselves two or three times more than necessary. It's when we start to learn the motivation for the manifestations that we grow first restless, finally incredulous.

There's a bag of tricks that skillful horror directors use, and they're employed here by Robert Zemeckis *(Back to the Future, Forrest Gump)*, who has always wanted, he says, to make a suspense film—"perhaps the kind of film Hitchcock would have done in his day," according to one of his coproducers, Jack Rapke. Hitchcock would not, however, have done this film in his day or any other day, because Hitchcock would have insisted on rewrites to remove the supernatural and explain the action in terms of human psychology, however abnormal.

Zemeckis does quote Hitchcock; there's a scene where Pfeiffer spies on a neighbor with binoculars, and is shocked to see the neighbor spying back, and we are reminded of *Rear Window.* He also uses such dependable devices as harmless people who suddenly enter the frame and startle the heroine. And mirrors that suddenly reveal figures reflected in them. And shots where we are looking at a character in front of windows, and the camera slowly pans, causing us to expect a face to appear in the window.

All of these devices are used with journeyman thoroughness in *What Lies Beneath,* but they are only devices, and we know it. Late in the film, when the heroine walks close to the hand of a character who is assumed to be dead, the audience laughs, because it knows—or thinks it knows—that in a horror film no one is ever really dead on the first try. Such devices at least involve the physical world and the laws of nature as we understand them. What's hap-

pening in the supernatural scenes I leave you to decide; I think some of them are supposed to be real, others hallucinations, others seen in different ways by different characters.

Michelle Pfeiffer is very good in the movie; she is convincing and sympathetic, and avoids the most common problem for actors in horror films—she doesn't overreact. Her character remains self-contained and resourceful, and the sessions with the psychiatrist (Joe Morton) are masterpieces of people behaving reasonably in the face of Forces Beyond Their Comprehension. Harrison Ford is the most reliable of actors, capable of many things, here required to be Harrison Ford. The Law of Economy of Character Development requires that his husband be other than he seems, since he isn't needed as his wife's confidant and sidekick (Diana Scarwid's character fills that slot). As for the possibly wife-killing neighbor, I can forgive that red herring almost anything because it pays off in a flawless sight gag at a party.

I've tried to play fair and not give away plot elements. That's more than the ads have done. The trailer of this movie thoroughly demolishes the surprises; if you've seen the trailer, you know what the movie is about, and all of the suspense of the first hour is superfluous for you, including major character revelations. Don't directors get annoyed when they create suspense and the marketing sabotages their efforts?

The modern studio approach to trailers is copied from those marketing people who stand in the aisles of supermarkets, offering you a bite of sausage on a toothpick. When you taste it, you know everything there is to be known about the sausage except what it would be like to eat all of it. Same with the trailer for *What Lies Beneath.* I like the approach where you can smell the sausage but not taste it. You desire it just as much, but the actual experience is still ahead of you. Trailers that give us a smell and not a taste, that's what we need.

What Planet Are You From? ★
R, 100 m., 2000

Garry Shandling (Harold Anderson), Annette Bening (Susan Hart), Greg Kinnear (Perry Gordon), Ben Kingsley (Graydon), Linda Fiorentino (Helen Gordon), John Goodman

(Roland Jones), Caroline Aaron (Nadine Jones), Judy Greer (Rebecca). Directed by Mike Nichols and produced by Nichols, Garry Shandling, and Neil Machlis. Screenplay by Shandling, Michael Leeson, Ed Solomon, and Peter Tolan.

Here is the most uncomfortable movie of the new year, an exercise in feel-good smut. *What Planet Are You From?* starts out as a dirty comedy, but then abandons the comedy, followed by the dirt, and by the end is actually trying to be poignant. For that to work, we'd have to like the hero, and Garry Shandling makes that difficult. He begrudges every emotion, as if there's no more where that came from. That worked on TV's *Larry Sanders Show*—it's why his character was funny—but here he can't make the movie's U-turn into sentimentality.

He plays an alien from a distant planet, where the inhabitants have no emotions and no genitals. Possibly this goes hand in hand. He is outfitted with human reproductive equipment, given the name Harold Anderson, and sent to Earth to impregnate a human woman so that his race can conquer our planet. When Harold becomes aroused, a loud whirling noise emanates from his pants.

If I were a comedy writer I would deal with that alarming noise. I would assume that the other characters in the movie would find it extremely disturbing. I put it to my female readers: If you were on a date with a guy and every time he looked dreamy-eyed it sounded like an operating garbage disposal was secreted somewhere on his person, wouldn't you be thinking of ways to say you just wanted to be friends?

The lame joke in *What Planet Are You From?* is that women hear the noise, find it curious and ask about it, and Harold makes feeble attempts to explain it away, and of course the more aroused he becomes the louder it hums, and when his ardor cools the volume drops. You understand. If you find this even slightly funny, you'd better see this movie, since the device is never likely to be employed again.

On Earth, Harold gets a job in a bank with the lecherous Perry (Greg Kinnear), and soon he is romancing a woman named Susan (Annette Bening) and contemplating the possibility of sex with Perry's wife, Helen (Linda Fiorentino). Fiorentino, of course, starred in

the most unforgettable sexual put-down in recent movie history (in *The Last Seduction*, where she calls the bluff of a barroom braggart). There is a scene here with the same setup: She's sitting next to Harold in a bar, there is a humming from the nether regions of his wardrobe, etc., and I was wondering, is it too much to ask that the movie provide a hilarious homage? It was. Think of the lost possibilities.

Harold and Susan fly off to Vegas, get married, and have a honeymoon that consists of days of uninterrupted sex ("I had so many orgasms," she says, "that some are still stacked up and waiting to land"). Then she discovers Harold's only interest in her is as a breeder. She is crushed and angry, and the movie turns to cheap emotion during her pregnancy and inevitable live childbirth scene, after which Harold finds to his amazement that he may have emotions after all.

The film was directed by Mike Nichols, whose uneven career makes you wonder. Half of his films are good to great (his previous credit is *Primary Colors*) and the other half you're at a loss to account for. What went into the theory that *What Planet Are You From?* was filmable? Even if the screenplay by Garry Shandling and three other writers seemed promising on the page, why star Shandling in it? Why not an actor who projects joy of performance—why not Kinnear, for example?

Shandling's shtick is unavailability. His public persona is of a man unwilling to be in public. Words squeeze embarrassed from his lips as if he feels guilty to be talking. *Larry Sanders* used this presence brilliantly. But it depends on its limitations. If you're making a movie about a man who has a strange noise coming from his pants, you should cast an actor who looks different when it isn't.

What's Cooking? ★ ★ ★ ½
PG-13, 106 m., 2000

Alfre Woodard (Audrey Williams), Dennis Haysbert (Ronald Williams), Ann Weldon (Grace Williams), Mercedes Ruehl (Elizabeth Avila), Victor Rivers (Javier Avila), Douglas Spain (Anthony Avila), A. Martinez (Daniel), Lainie Kazan (Ruth Seeling), Maury Chaykin (Herb Seeling), Kyra Sedgwick (Rachel Seeling), Julianna Margulies (Carla), Estelle Harris

(Aunt Bea), Joan Chen (Trinh Nguyen), Will Yun Lee (Jimmy Nguyen), Kristy Wu (Jenny Nguyen), Jimmy Pham (Gary Nguyen), Brennan Louie (Joey Nguyen), Kieu Chinh (Grandma Nguyen). Directed by Gurinder Chadha and produced by Jeffrey Taylor. Screenplay by Paul Mayeda Berges and Chadha.

Thanksgiving is not a religious or patriotic holiday, and it's not hooked to any ethnic or national group: It's a national celebration of the fact that we have survived for another year, we eat turkey to observe that fact, and may, if we choose, thank the deity of our choice. We exchange no presents and send few cards. It's on a Thursday, a day not associated with any belief system. And it nods gratefully to American Indians, who have good reason to feel less than thrilled about the Fourth of July and Columbus Day.

What's Cooking? celebrates the holiday by telling interlocking stories about four American families, which are African-American, Jewish, Latino, and Vietnamese. They all serve turkey in one way or another, surrounded by traditional dishes from their groups; some are tired of turkey and try to disguise it, while an Americanized Vietnamese girl sees the chili paste going on and complains, "Why do you want to make the turkey taste like everything else we eat?"

These families have been brought together by the filmmaker Gurinder Chadha, an Indian woman of Punjabi ancestry and Kenyan roots, who grew up in London and is now married to Paul Mayeda Berges, a half-Japanese American. Doesn't it make you want to grin? She directed; they cowrote. All four of the stories involve the generation gap, as older family members cling to tradition and younger ones rebel. But because the stories are so skillfully threaded together, the movie doesn't feel like an exercise: Each of the stories stands on its own.

Generation gaps, of course, go down through more than one generation. Dennis Haysbert and Alfre Woodard play the parents of a college student who would rather be a radical than a professional, but another source of tension at the table is the presence of his mother, who casts a practiced eye over her daughter-in-law's menu, and is shocked that it lacks

macaroni and cheese, an obligatory item at every traditional African-American feast.

The Vietnamese family runs a video store. Grandma Nguyen (Kieu Chinh) is of course less assimilated than her family, but in the kitchen her eye misses nothing and her strong opinions are enforced almost telepathically. There's trouble because a younger sister has found a gun in her brother's room. Joan Chen plays the mother, a peacemaker in a family with a father who rules too sternly.

The Latino Thanksgiving starts uneasily when the kids are at the supermarket and run into their dad (Victor Rivers), who is separated from their mom (Mercedes Ruehl). They invite him to dinner without asking her; on the other hand, she hasn't told them she has invited her new boyfriend, a teacher.

The Jewish couple (Lainie Kazan and Maury Chaykin) greet their daughter (Kyra Sedgwick), her lover (Julianna Margulies), and Aunt Bea (Estelle Harris), one of those women who asks such tactless questions that you can't believe she's doing it by accident. The parents accept their daughter's lesbianism, but are at a loss to explain it (should they have sent her to that kibbutz?).

During this long day secrets will be revealed, hearts will be bared, old grudges settled, new ones started, pregnancies announced, forgiveness granted, and turkeys carved. And the melting pot will simmer a little, for example when a Latino girl brings home her Asian boyfriend (her brother tries to make him feel at home with a hearty conversation about Jackie Chan and Bruce Lee). If the Asian boy feels awkward at his girlfriend's table, he reflects that she is not welcome at all in his family's home. Or is she?

All that I've said reflects the design of the film. I've hardly even started to suggest the texture and pleasure. There are so many characters, so vividly drawn, with such humor and life, that a synopsis is impossible. What's strange is the spell the movie weaves. By its end, there is actually a sort of tingle of pleasure in seeing how this Thanksgiving ends, and how its stories are resolved. In recent years most Thanksgiving movies have been about families at war. Here are four families that have, in one way or another, started peace talks.

What's the Worst That Can Happen? ★

PG-13, 95 m., 2001

Martin Lawrence (Kevin Caffery), Danny DeVito (Max Fairbanks), John Leguizamo (Berger), Glenne Headly (Gloria), Carmen Ejogo (Amber Belhaven), Bernie Mac (Uncle Jack), Larry Miller (Earl Radburn), Nora Dunn (Lutetia Fairbanks). Directed by Sam Weisman and produced by Lawrence Turman, David Hoberman, Ashok Amritraj, and Wendy Dytman. Screenplay by Matthew Chapman, based on the novel by Donald E. Westlake.

What's the Worst That Can Happen? has too many characters, not enough plot, and a disconnect between the two stars' acting styles. Danny DeVito plays a crooked millionaire, Martin Lawrence plays a smart thief, and they seem to be in different pictures. DeVito as always is taut, sharp, perfectly timed. Lawrence could play in the same key (and does, in an early scene during an art auction), but at other times he bursts into body language that's intended as funny but plays more like the early symptoms of St. Vitus's dance.

There is an old comedy tradition in which the onlookers freeze while the star does his zany stuff. From Groucho Marx to Eddie Murphy to Robin Williams to Jim Carrey, there are scenes where the star does his shtick and the others wait for it to end, like extras in an opera. That only works in a movie that is about the star's shtick. *What's the Worst That Can Happen?* creates a world that plays by one set of comic rules (in which people pretend they're serious) and then Lawrence goes into mime and jive and odd wavings of his arms and verbal riffs, and maybe the people on the set were laughing but the audience doesn't, much.

The plot involves Lawrence as a clever thief named Kevin Caffery, who frequents auctions to find out what's worth stealing. At an art auction, he meets Amber Belhaven (Carmen Ejogo), who is in tears because she has to sell the painting her father left her; she needs money for the hotel bill. She has good reason to be in tears. The painting, described as a fine example of the Hudson River School, goes for $3,000; some members of the audience will be thinking that's at least $30,000 less than it's probably worth.

If Kevin is supplied with one love interest, Max Fairbanks (DeVito) has several, including his society wife (Nora Dunn), his adoring secretary (Glenne Headly), and Miss September. (When she disappears, Max's assistant, Earl (Larry Miller), observes there are "eleven more months where she came from.") Kevin also has a criminal sidekick named Berger (John Leguizamo), and then there is his getaway driver Uncle Jack (Bernie Mac), and a Boston cop (William Fichtner) who is played for some reason as a flamboyant dandy. If I tell you there are several other characters with significant roles, you will guess that much of the movie is taken up with entrances and exits.

The plot involves Kevin's attempt to burgle Max's luxurious shore estate, which is supposed to be empty but in fact contains Max and Miss September. After the cops are called, Max steals from Kevin a ring given him by Amber Belhaven, and most of the rest of the movie involves Kevin's determination to get it back, intercut with Max's troubles with judges, lawyers, and accountants.

The jokes and the plots are freely and all too sloppily adapted from a Dortmunder novel by Donald E. Westlake, who once told me he only really liked one of the movies made from his books *(The Grifters)*, and probably won't raise the count to two after this one. A comedy needs a strong narrative engine to pull the plot through to the end, and firm directorial discipline to keep the actors from trying to act funny instead of simply being funny. At some point, when a movie like this doesn't work, it stops being a comedy and becomes a documentary about actors trying to make the material work. When you have so many characters played by so many recognizable actors in a movie that runs only ninety-five minutes, you guess that at some point they just cut their losses and gave up.

Note: Again this summer, movies are jumping through hoops to get the PG-13 rating and the under-17 demographic. That's why the battle scenes were toned down and blurred in Pearl Harbor, *and no doubt it's why this movie steals one of the most famous closing lines in comedy history, and emasculates it. The Front Page ended with "The son of a bitch stole my watch!" This one ends with "Stop my lawyer! He stole my watch!" Not quite the same, you will agree.*

What Time Is It There? ★ ★ ★ ½
NO MPAA RATING, 116 m., 2002

Lee Kang-Sheng (Hsiao Kang), Chen Shiang-Chyi (Shiang-Chyi), Lu Yi-Ching (Mother), Miao Tien (Father), Cecilia Yip (Woman in Paris), Chen Chao-Jung (Man in Subway), Tsai Guei (Prostitute), Arthur Nauczyciel (Man in Phone Booth), David Ganansia (Man in Restaurant), Jean-Pierre Leaud (Man at Cemetery). Directed by Tsai Ming-Lian and produced by Bruno Pesery. Screenplay by Tsai and Yang Pi-Ying.

The reviewers of Tsai Ming-Lian's *What Time Is It There?* have compared it to the work of Yasujiro Ozu, Robert Bresson, Michelangelo Antonioni, Jacques Tati, and Buster Keaton. If none of these names stir admiration and longing in your soul, start with them, not with Tsai. Begin with Keaton and work your way backward on the list, opening yourself to the possibilities of silence, introspection, isolation, and loneliness in the movies. You will notice that the films grow less funny after Keaton and Tati; one of the enigmas about Tsai's work is that it is always funny and always sad, never just one or the other.

Tsai's hero, who indeed shares some of the single-minded self-absorption of the Keaton and Tati characters, is Hsiao Kang (Lee Kang-Sheng), a man who sells wristwatches from a display case on the sidewalks of Taipei. One day he sells a watch to Shiang-Chyi (Chen Shiang-Chyi—remember, family names come first in Chinese societies). He wants to sell her a watch from his case, but she insists on the watch from his wrist, which gives the time in two time zones, because she is flying to Paris.

Hsiao's home life is sad without redemption. In an early scene, we have seen his father, almost too exhausted to exhale the smoke from his cigarettes, die in a dark, lonely room. Hsiao's mother (Lu Yi-Ching) becomes convinced that her dead husband's soul has somehow been channeled into Fatty, the large white fish in a tank in the living room. Since Fatty is Hsiao's pet and only friend (he confides details of his life to the fish), this is doubly sad: Not only has the father died after bringing no

joy to his son's life, but now he has appropriated the fish. You see what I mean about humor and sadness coexisting, neither one conceding to the other.

The movie then develops into a story that seems to involve synchronicity, but actually involves our need for synchronicity. We need to believe that our little lives are in step with distant music, when synchronicity is simply the way coincidence indulges itself in wish fulfillment. The girl goes off to Paris. Hsiao, who has barely spoken to her, and then only about watches, is so struck by longing for her that he begins to reset watches to Paris time. First all of the watches in his display case. Then all of the watches and clocks available to him. Then even a gigantic clock on a building (the parallel to Harold Lloyd's most famous scene is inescapable).

Meanwhile, in Paris, Shiang-Chyi is also lonely. Does she even have a reason for being here? She wanders the streets and travels nowhere in particular on the Metro. Eventually all three lonely people—Hsiao, his mother, and Shiang-Chyi—look for release in sex. Sex is many things, and one of them is a way of reassuring yourself you are alive, that you retain the power to feel and cause feeling. Hsiao seeks out a prostitute, Shiang-Chyi experiments with another woman (who for her purposes could have been a man), and the mother masturbates while thinking of her dead husband.

These three acts take place at about the same time. Synchronicity? Or simply an indication that the loneliness clocks of the three characters started ticking at the same time, and so chime the hour simultaneously? There is another coincidence in the movie: Hsiao watches Truffaut's *The 400 Blows* on video—the scene where Jean-Pierre Leaud wanders the Paris streets because he is afraid to return home. And Shiang-Chyi visits a Paris cemetery where she talks to a strange man sitting on a gravestone. This man is Jean-Pierre Leaud forty-one years later. (It isn't mentioned in the movie, but I think this is the cemetery where Truffaut is buried. Is Leaud visiting the grave of the man who created his life-defining roles?)

What Time Is It There? is not easy. It haunts you, you can't forget it, you admire its conception, and are able to resolve some of the confusions you had while watching it. You realize it is very simple, really, even though at first you thought it was impenetrable. But can you recommend it to others? Does it depend on how advanced they are in their filmgoing? The critics don't seem to agree. Is it true that the movie "proceeds with all the speed of paint drying" *(Film Journal International)* or does Tsai create "shock waves of comedy, which both unleash a wave of euphoria in the audience and communicate the pleasure he gets from filmmaking" *(New York Times)*? Does "a sense of perseverance and comic acceptance trump any self-indulgent ennui" *(Salon)*, or do "emotionally disconnected characters . . . wade through their sterile Taipei surroundings hopelessly grasping for a piece of human comfort" *(Slant)*?

What happens, I think, is that the funny and sad poles of the story checkmate each other. Everything is funny. Everything is sad. There is nothing funnier than an unrequited love. Nothing sadder than an unrequited lover. Nothing tragic, really, about two people who have not connected when they only had two meaningless conversations. But nothing hopeful about two people so unconnected it doesn't matter what city they are in. When Hsiao resets all of the clocks, is that a grand gesture of romance or a pathetic fixation? Which is more depressing—that the mother thinks her husband's soul occupies the fish, or that the fish is her son's only confidant?

A movie that causes us to ask these kinds of questions deserves to be seen. A movie that thinks it knows the answer to them deserves to be pitied. Most movies do not know these questions exist.

What Women Want ★ ★ ★
PG-13, 110 m., 2000

Mel Gibson (Nick Marshall), Helen Hunt (Darcy Maguire), Marisa Tomei (Lola), Lauren Holly (Gigi), Mark Feuerstein (Morgan), Alan Alda (Dan Wanamaker), Valerie Perrine (Margo), Delta Burke (Eve). Directed by Nancy Meyers and produced by Susan Cartsonis, Bruce Davey, Gina Matthews, Nancy Meyers, and Matt Williams. Screenplay by Josh Goldsmith, Cathy Yuspa, and Diane Drake.

What women want is very simple: a man willing to listen when they're speaking to him. They also want a lot of other things, but that will do for starters. This we learn from *What Women Want*, a comedy about a man who is jolted by electricity and develops the ability to read women's minds.

You would assume that this ability would make him the world's greatest lover, since he would know precisely what to do and when to do it, and indeed the movie's hero does triumph in that area, although not without early discouragements. (Extreme detumescence can result when a man discovers that during the throes of passion his lover is asking herself, "Is Britney Spears on *Leno* tonight?")

Mel Gibson stars as Nick Marshall, an ad executive who thinks he's next in line for a top job at his Chicago agency. But his boss (Alan Alda) passes him over for Darcy Maguire (Helen Hunt), a hot steal from another agency. Nick declares war, at about the same time he develops the ability to read women's minds. His knack of stealing Darcy's best ideas is a dirty trick, but he's ambitious and shameless.

He is also a man who needs to listen to women more. We learn he was raised in Vegas as the pampered child of a showgirl, and has been doted on by admiring females ever since— including, recently, the sexy Lola (Marisa Tomei), who works in the coffee store he patronizes. At work, two assistants (Valerie Perrine and Delta Burke) approve categorically of everything he does, but mind reading reveals they never think about this. Many of the other women in the office, he is horrified to learn, pretend to like him but don't.

Because he feels chastened, and because he wants to win a valuable account, Nick starts a crash program to research being a woman. This leads him to experiment with lip gloss, eye shadow, pantyhose, and exfoliation, in scenes positioned somewhere between *Tootsie* and Arnold Schwarzenegger's *Junior*. Amazingly, given the opportunities, Gibson, king of the tush scenes, keeps his netherlands out of view during these adventures.

It's clear that Nick and Darcy will sooner or later fall in love, I suppose, and that's a cinematic first: Although Mel Gibson has been voted the World's Sexiest Man in one of those meaningless magazine-cover polls, this is his first romantic comedy. He and Hunt are not a match made in heaven, but that's one of the appeals as they edge closer together. Less appealing is the way he dumps poor Lola (Tomei), who really deserves better.

The movie, directed by Nancy Meyers, doesn't flow so much as leap from one good scene to another over the crevices of flat scenes in between. The movie is considerably slowed down by the unnecessary character of a suicidal file clerk, who does nothing of any interest until late in the movie, when Nick befriends her in a scene that serves no purpose except to delay us on our way to the happy climax which can be seen signaling eagerly from the next reel.

If the movie is imperfect, it's not boring and is often very funny, as in a solo dance that Nick does in his apartment to Sinatra singing "I Won't Dance." This is, we imagine, the way the Tom Cruise character in *Risky Business* might have ended some of his evenings if he had grown up to be Nick Marshall. I also liked the way Gibson handled the sex scene, where his look of joy and complete self-satisfaction at the end is equaled only by Jack Nicholson's famous Triumph T-shirt moment in *Five Easy Pieces*.

Note: The look and feel of the movie is just right. The set for the ad agency's office is inviting and seems lived in. Inspired by Chicago's nineteenth-century Monadnock Building, it looks plausible as an ad agency headquarters and allows sight lines that are important to the action. Great work by production designer Jon Hutman, art directors Gae Buckley and Tony Fanning, and set decorator Rosemary Brandenburg, and if you wonder why I list their names, you'll know when you see their work.

When Brendan Met Trudy ★ ★ ★

NO MPAA RATING, 95 m., 2001

Peter McDonald (Brendan), Flora Montgomery (Trudy), Marie Mullen (Mother), Pauline McLynn (Nuala), Don Wycherley (Niall), Maynard Eziashi (Edgar), Eileen Walsh (Siobhan), Barry Cassin (Headmaster). Directed by Kieron J. Walsh and produced by Lynda Myles. Screenplay by Roddy Doyle.

Roddy Doyle has written an original screenplay, and now we know his secret. He wrote the novels that became the rollicking Irish

comedies *The Commitments, The Snapper,* and *The Van,* and now here's *When Brendan Met Trudy.* If the title reminds you of *When Harry Met Sally,* that's because half the scenes in the movie are likely to remind you of other movies. Roddy Doyle's secret is, he's a movie fan. The kind of movie fan so fanatic that he creates a hero named Brendan who not only has a poster of Godard's *Breathless* in his office, but another one in his flat.

Brendan, played by Peter McDonald, is a sissy. He runs like a girl, with his arms held out rigidly at his sides, and he sings in the church choir, and he's so shy that when the choir members go into the pub for a pint after practice, he stands by himself at the bar. And there he's standing one night, a sitting duck, when Trudy accosts him. She's the kind of girl who can insult you, pick you up, get you to buy her a drink, keep you at arm's length, and tell you to sod off, simultaneously and charmingly.

Flora Montgomery is the actress. She's got one of those round, regular faces, pretty but frank, like your best friend's sister—the kind of girl you agree would make a great catch for some lucky bloke, but not, you add in an unspoken footnote, for yourself. Trudy doesn't leave Brendan with the free time for such sophistry, however, and soon he is in love with her and proving that he may run like a sissy but he makes love like that Jack Nicholson character with the "Triumph!" T-shirt.

All the same, Brendan has his misgivings. Trudy sneaks out at night, wearing a ski mask. And the TV news reports that young men have been castrated in Dublin by a mysterious masked predator. Could it be Trudy? One night she attempts to add a little spice to their sex by wearing her mask, and he is so terrified that she has to talk him down by confessing she is not a phantom castrator, but merely a thief.

This news comes as a shock to honest Brendan, a schoolteacher whose students openly mock him and whose only escape is going to the movies. Soon Trudy is going to the movies with him, and soon he is going on midnight raids with her, and the Doyle screenplay, directed by Kieron J. Walsh, casts many of their adventures in the form of classic movie scenes, sometimes even with the same dialogue. This is possible because when Brendan finds himself facedown in the gutter, his first thought is not to climb to his feet, but to imagine himself as William Holden in *Sunset Boulevard.*

The more movie references you recognize (from *Once Upon a Time in the West* to *The Producers*), the more you're likely to enjoy *When Brendan Met Trudy,* but the movie works whether you identify the scenes or not. It has that unwound Roddy Doyle humor; the laughs don't hit you over the head, but tickle you behind the knee. And there is, as usual, Doyle's great pleasure in kidding the Irish. At one point Brendan and Trudy visit a miniature Irish landscape, which includes an "Irish Famine Village," and it is so real, they agree "you can almost see them starving." The effect these miniature famine victims have upon Brendan's sex life, and how he deals with it, is making me smile again right now.

Where the Heart Is ★ ★ ½
PG-13, 121 m., 2000

Natalie Portman (Novalee Nation), Ashley Judd (Lexie Coop), James Frain (Forney), Stockard Channing (Sister Husband), Joan Cusack (Ruth Meyers), Jim Beaver (Clawhammer), Rodger Boyce (Harry the Policeman), Dylan Bruno (Willy Jack Pickens), Keith David (Moses Whitecotton), Sally Field (Mama Lil), Richard Jones (Mr. Sprock). Directed by Matt Williams and produced by Susan Cartsonis. Screenplay by Lowell Ganz and Babaloo Mandel, based on the novel by Billie Letts.

Remember that game in school where the teacher would write the first sentence of a story and then pass it around the class? Everybody would write a sentence, but the paper was folded so you could read only the last sentence before yours. *Where the Heart Is* has a screenplay like that, zigging and zagging and wildly careening from one melodramatic development to the next. What halfway holds it together are the performances, which are convincing and deserve a story with a touch more sanity.

The movie is based on a popular novel by Billie Letts, about a seventeen-year-old unwed mother named Novalee Nation (Natalie Portman), who is abandoned by her no-good boyfriend in a Wal-Mart in Sequoia, Oklahoma, and lives secretly in the store until she gives birth to her child, little Americus. The baby is delivered by the town's substitute librarian, Forney (James Frain), who has been following her, moonstruck, and breaks through the store's plate-glass window as she goes into labor. She finds a home locally with Sister Husband (Stockard Channing) and her partner, Mr. Sprock (Richard Jones).

Novalee is lucky to have landed in a town populated exclusively by character actors. Everyone in Sequoia, and indeed everyone in her life, is a salt-of-the-earth, good ol' eccentric, and that surely includes her new best friend Lexie Coop (Ashley Judd) who is always going and getting herself pregnant. When Novalee names her new baby Americus, Lexie is impressed. She names her kids after snacks: Praline, Baby Ruth . . .

The people in the movie are lovable and sympathetic, and if they live in a world of folksy fantasy, at least it looks like a good place to live. For example, Novalee makes a friend of Moses Whitecotton (Keith David), a photographer in the Wal-Mart, and soon she's exhibiting talent as a gifted photographer. But the characters have to negotiate the plot like runners through a minefield, as one weird and improbable situation after another comes up. At one point Novalee is about to be sucked up into the funnel cloud of a tornado, and clings upside down to the steps of the storm shelter with the fingertips of one hand while snatching little Americus as the child is about to be blown past her. Uh-huh.

There are times when you wonder, how self-aware *are* these people? Sister Husband is wonderfully played by Channing, who brings humanity and warmth to the character, but what's with her blessing before meals: ". . . and we ask forgiveness, Lord, for the fornication that Mr. Sprock and I have committed again this morning right here on this very kitchen table." Does she know that's funny? Or is she being sincere?

God has to forgive a lot of fornicating in this movie. Lexie, the Judd character, is forever taking up with the wrong man. She seems to be the town nurse, but has an imperfect understanding of birth control, not to mention abysmal taste in men (until at last she meets Ernie the Exterminator). Novalee's own unorthodox delivery gets on the TV news and attracts the attention of devout folks from as far away as Midnight, Mississippi, who travel to Sequoia, kidnap Americus, and abandon the infant in the crib of the local nativity scene. (The symbolism of this act is elusive; it could as easily be sacrilegious as disapproving.)

Novalee's first boyfriend, the father of her child, is the no-good would-be country singer Willy Jack Pickens (Dylan Bruno). After he abandons her, he's arrested while in the company of a fourteen-year-old hitchhiking thief, and is sent off to prison. When Novalee has the "Wal-Mart baby" and becomes a TV star, that fetches her lying mother, Mama Lil (Sally Field) from New Orleans. Meanwhile, the story follows later developments in Willy Jack's case, as he signs with a hard-boiled talent agent (Joan Cusack).

By now I'm ducking down in my seat to keep out of the line of fire of the plot. This movie is so heavy on incident, contrivance, coincidence, improbability, sudden reversals, and dizzying flash-forwards (sometimes years at a time) that it seems a wonder the characters don't crash into each other in the confusion. Melodramatic elements are slapped on top of one another like a hurry-up plaster-boarding job. The happy ending is so laboriously obvious that it's a little amazing, really, how Natalie Portman manages to find sweetness in it, for Novalee and for us.

Portman is quite an actress. I've been an admirer since her early work in *Beautiful Girls*. Here she's the calm eye of the storm, mightily aided by Ashley Judd, who brings a plausibility to Lexie that the character surely needs. James Frain, as the lonely librarian with a secret in his family, has to undergo a remarkable personality change, from skitterish neurotic to stable nice guy, but the movie is so busy he finds time to sneak off and do that. There is a core of truth to these three and their story, and real humanity in Channing's work as Sister Husband, but it would all mean a lot more if the screenplay had dialed down its manic inventions. And every time I looked at Portman or Judd, I was aware that whatever else Sequoia, Oklahoma, may lack, it obviously has makeup and hair facilities to rival Beverly Hills.

Where the Money Is ★ ★ ★
PG-13, 89 m., 2000

Paul Newman (Henry), Linda Fiorentino (Carol), Dermot Mulroney (Wayne), Susan Barnes (Mrs. Foster), Anne Pitoniak (Mrs. Tetlow), Bruce MacVittie (Karl), Irma St. Paul (Mrs. Galer), Michel Perron (Guard). Directed by Marek Kanievska and produced by Ridley Scott, Charles Weinstock, Chris Zarpas, and Christopher Dorr. Screenplay by E. Max Frye, Topper Lilien, and Carroll Cartwright.

Where the Money Is has a preposterous plot, but it's not about a plot; it's about acting. It's about how Paul Newman at seventy-five is still cool, sleek, and utterly self-confident, and about how Linda Fiorentino's low, calm voice sneaks in under his cover and challenges him in places he is glad to be reminded of. Watching these two working together is like watching a couple of thoroughbreds going around a track. You know they'll end up back where they started and you don't even have any money on the race, but look at that form.

Fiorentino plays a discontented nurse in a small town, married to the same guy (Dermot Mulroney) since high school. "We were king and queen of the prom, so it sort of made sense to get married," she tells Newman. "When did it stop making sense?" he asks. Newman can say a line like that to a woman and convince her it *never* made sense, even if she didn't know it until he asked the question.

I have given away a plot point by revealing that he speaks. In the opening scenes of the movie, he appears to be an old man paralyzed by a stroke. He can't move his body, he can't talk, he doesn't even look at anything. It's all an act: He's a veteran bank robber who has studied yoga in order to fake stroke symptoms, so he can be moved from prison to the retirement home, which he figures will be easier to escape from. Actually, it's not such a big point to reveal, since (a) we somehow intuit that Paul Newman wouldn't be starring in the movie if he didn't move or speak for ninety minutes, and (b) all the TV commercials and review clips show him moving and speaking.

The old crook, named Henry, is a good actor, and fools everybody except Carol, the nurse played by Fiorentino. She notices subtle clues, and tries to coax him out of his shell with a lap dance (she is dressed at the time, but in a nurse's uniform, which is always interesting). He resists. This is good yoga. She abandons sex for more direct methods, and he's forced to admit that he can indeed walk and talk. By later that night he's even dancing in the local tavern with Carol and her husband, Wayne.

Carol realizes that Henry is her ticket out of town. Either he still has a lot of money stashed away from all those bank jobs, or he can help her steal some more. Wayne finds this thinking seriously flawed, but eventually the three of them end up as partners in an armored car heist. The heist is as to the movie as Sinatra's cigarette and drink are to his song: superfluous, but it gives him something to do with his hands.

Newman you know all about. At his age he has such sex appeal that when the husband gets jealous, we believe it. He has that shucks, ma'am grin, and then you see in his eyes the look of a man who is still driving racing cars, and can find an opening at 160 mph. He counsels Wayne about an encounter with some dangerous men: "Be cool to these guys, right? Look them in the eye—but not like you're gonna remember their faces."

Fiorentino is a special case, an actress who in the wrong movie *(What Planet Are You From?)* seems clueless, and in the right one *(After Hours, The Last Seduction)* can make every scene be about what she's thinking she'd rather be doing. She is best employed playing a character who is the smartest person in the movie, which is the case this time.

As for the bank robber and his stroke: A lot of reviews are going to pair this movie with *Diamonds,* another 2000 movie involving a great movie star and a stroke. That one starred Kirk Douglas, who really did have a stroke, and has made a remarkable comeback. But the strokes in the two plots aren't the connection—after all, one is real and one is fake, and that's a big difference. The comparison should be between two aging but gifted stars looking for worthy projects.

Diamonds has a plot as dumb as a box of tofu. *Where the Money Is* has a plot marginally smarter, dialogue considerably smarter, and better opportunities for the human qualities of the actors to escape from the requirements of the story. After you see this movie, you want to see Paul Newman in another one. After you see *Diamonds,* you don't want to see another movie for a long time.

The Whole Nine Yards ★ ★ ★
R, 99 m., 2000

Bruce Willis (Jimmy Tudeski), Matthew Perry (Oz Oseransky), Rosanna Arquette (Sophie), Michael Clarke Duncan (Frankie Figs), Natasha Henstridge (Cynthi), Amanda Peet (Jill), Kevin Pollak (Yanni Gogolack), Harland Williams (Buffalo Steve). Directed by Jonathan Lynn and produced by David Willis and Allan Kaufman. Screenplay by Mitchell Kapner.

A subtle but unmistakable aura of jolliness sneaks from the screen during *The Whole Nine Yards,* and eventually we suspect that the actors are barely suppressing giggles. This is the kind of standard material everyone could do in lockstep, but you sense inner smiles, and you suspect the actors are enjoying themselves. George C. Scott said that a key element in any role was "the joy of performance"—the feeling that the actor is having a good time. This cast seems vastly amused.

Of course, I have no way of knowing if that was really the case. The actors may have hated one another and spent their evenings having anonymous pizzas delivered to each other's hotel rooms. All I can report is my subjective feeling. I know this is not the greatest comedy of all time, or even of the first seven weeks of the century, but I was entertained beyond all expectation.

One of the reasons for that is a perfect performance by Amanda Peet. I say it is perfect because it exactly matches what is required, and then adds a level of heedless glee. I do not write as a longtime fan: Amanda Peet has been in seventeen previous movies without inspiring any cartwheels, but this time, as an ambitious young woman named Jill who would like to kill people for a living, she is so disarmingly, infectiously funny that finally all she has to do is smile to get a laugh.

Jill's role model is Jimmy Tudeski (Bruce Willis), a professional hit man known as Jimmy the Tulip. As the film opens, he has moved in next door to a Montreal dentist named Oz Oseransky (Matthew Perry), whose French-Canadian wife, Sophie (Rosanna Arquette), smokes cigarettes and wishes he were dead. So insufferable is this woman that Jill, who is Oz's office receptionist, volunteers, "You'd be doing the world a favor if you just had her whacked."

Everybody is having everybody whacked in *The Whole Nine Yards.* Jimmy the Tulip is being sought by Yanni Gogolak (Kevin Pollak), a Chicago gangster, who wants him whacked. Sophie wants Oz to go to Chicago and rat on the Tulip so they can collect the finder's fee. Oz does not much want to do this, but flies to Chicago and is taken under the muscular arms of Yanni's henchman Frankie Figs (Michael Clarke Duncan, the big guy from *The Green Mile*), and ushered into the Gogolak presence. Every actor in the movie has at least one juicy scene, and Pollak has fun with his, combining an impenetrable accent with key words that are spat out like hot oysters.

There is more to the plot, all of which you will have to discover for yourself. What I can describe is the amusement the actors exude. Bruce Willis has played countless hit men. This one simply has to stand there and suggest the potential for painful action. "It's not important how many people I kill," he explains to Perry; "what's important is how I get along with the people who are still alive." Willis glows as absurdities revolve around him. One of those absurdities is Matthew Perry's dentist, who is always running into things, like glass doors and Michael Clarke Duncan. He falls in love with the Tulip's wife, Cynthia (Natasha Henstridge), who is being held captive by Gogolak—but there I go with the plot again.

I think you have to be observant during this film. There are some moments that are likely to be funny no matter what, but others depend on a certain momentum that gets going if you tune in to the underlying good humor. Here is a cast full of actors required to be silly while keeping a straight face, and somehow they have developed a faith that the screenplay is funny, and, of course, their belief makes it funny, and there you are.

And it would be worth renting the video just to study Amanda Peet's face and listen to

her voice during her early encounters with the Tulip. She makes it all look so easy we forget that what she accomplishes is just about impossible: She is funny because of her personality without resorting to a "funny personality." They don't teach that in acting school.

The Widow of St. Pierre ★ ★ ★
R, 112 m., 2001

Juliette Binoche (Madame La), Daniel Auteuil (Le Capitaine), Emir Kusturica (Neel Auguste), Michel Duchaussoy (Le Gouverneur), Philippe Magnan (President Venot), Christian Charmetant (Commissaire de la Marine), Philippe Du Janerand (Chef Douanier), Reynald Bouchard (Louis Olliver). Directed by Patrice Leconte and produced by Frederic Brillion and Gilles Legrand. Screenplay by Claude Faraldo.

A man gets drunk and commits a senseless murder. He is condemned to death by guillotine. But in the 1850s on a small French fishing island off the coast of Newfoundland, there is no guillotine, and no executioner. The guillotine can be shipped from France. But the island will have to find its own executioner, because superstitious ship's captains refuse to allow one on board.

Time passes, and a strange and touching thing happens. The murderer repents of his crime, and becomes a useful member of the community. He saves a woman's life. He works in a garden started by the wife of the captain of the local military. The judge who condemned him frets, "His popularity is a nuisance." An islander observes, "We committed a murderous brute and we're going to top a benefactor."

The Widow of St. Pierre is a beautiful and haunting film that tells this story, and then tells another subterranean story, about the seasons of a marriage. Le Capitaine (Daniel Auteuil) and his wife, referred to by everyone as Madame La (Juliette Binoche), are not only in love but in deep sympathy with each other. He understands her slightest emotional clues. "Madame La only likes desperate cases," someone says, and indeed she seems stirred by the plight of the prisoner. Stirred and . . . something else. The film is too intelligent and subtle to make obvious what the woman herself hardly suspects, but if we watch and listen closely we realize she is stirred in a sensual way by the prospect of a prisoner who has been condemned to die. Le Capitaine understands this and, because his wife is admirable and he loves her, he sympathizes with it.

The movie becomes not simply a drama about capital punishment, but a story about human psychology. Some audience members may not connect directly with the buried levels of obsession and attraction, but they'll sense them—sense something that makes the movie deeper and sadder than the plot alone can account for. Juliette Binoche, that wonderful actress, is the carrier of this subtlety, and the whole film resides in her face. Sad that most of those who saw her in *Chocolat* will never see, in this film, how much more she is capable of.

The Widow of St. Pierre is a title that carries extra weight. The French called a guillotine a "widow," and by the end of the film it has created two widows. And it has made a sympathetic character of the murderer, named Neel and played by the dark, burly Yugoslavian director Emir Kusturica. It accomplishes this not by soppy liberal piety, but by leading us to the same sort of empathy the islanders feel. Neel and a friend got drunk and murdered a man for no reason, and can hardly remember it. The friend is dead. Neel is prepared to die, but it becomes clear that death would redress nothing and solve nothing—and that Neel has changed so fundamentally that a different man would be going to the guillotine.

The director is Patrice Leconte, whose films unfailingly move me, and often (but not this time) make me smile. He is obsessed with obsession. He first fascinated me with *Monsieur Hire* (1989), based on a Simenon story about a little man who begins to spy on a beautiful woman whose window faces his. She knows he is looking, and plays her own game, until everything goes wrong. Then there was *The Hairdresser's Husband* (1990), about a man obsessed with hair and the women who cut it. Then *Ridicule* (1996), about a provincial landowner in the reign of Louis XVI, who wants to promote a drainage scheme at court and finds the king will favor only those who make him laugh. Then *The Girl on the Bridge* (1999), about a knife-thrower who recruits suicidal girls as targets for his act—because what do they have to lose?

The Widow of St. Pierre is unlike these others in tone. It is darker, angrier. And yet Leconte loves the humor of paradox, and some of it slips through, as in a scene where Madame La supplies Neel with a boat and advises him to escape to Newfoundland. He escapes, but returns, because he doesn't want to get anyone into trouble. When the guillotine finally arrives, he helps bring it ashore, because he doesn't want to cause work for others on his account. He impregnates a local girl and is allowed to marry, and the islanders develop an affection for him and begin to see the judge as an alien troublemaker from a France they believe "doesn't care about our cod island."

Now watch closely during the scene where Neel marries his pregnant bride. Madame La hides it well during the ceremony, but is distraught. "It's all right; I'm here," Le Capitaine tells her. What's all right? I think she loves Neel. It's not that she wants to be his lover; in the 1850s such a thought would probably not occur. It's that she is happy for him, and is marrying him and having his child vicariously. And Le Capitaine knows that, and loves her the more for it.

The movie is not even primarily about Neel, his crime, his sentence, and the difficulty of bringing about his death. That is the subplot. It is really about the captain and his wife. About two people with good hearts who live in an innocent, less self-aware time, and how the morality of the case and their deeper feelings about Neel all get mixed up together. Eventually Le Capitaine takes a stand, and everyone thinks it is based on politics and ethics, but if we have been paying attention we know better. It is based on his love for his wife, and the ethics are an afterthought.

Windtalkers ★ ★
R, 133 m., 2002

Nicolas Cage (Sergeant Joe Enders), Adam Beach (Private Ben Yahzee), Roger Willie (Private Charles Whitehorse), Christian Slater (Sergeant Peter "Ox" Henderson), Peter Stormare (Sergeant Eric "Gunny" Hjelmstad), Noah Emmerich (Corporal Charles "Chick" Rogers), Mark Ruffalo (Pappas), Brian Van Holt (Harrigan), Martin Henderson (Nellie). Directed by John Woo and produced by Terence Chang,

Tracie Graham, Alison Rosenzweig, and Woo. Screenplay by John Rice and Joe Batteer.

Windtalkers comes advertised as the saga of how Navajo Indians used their language to create an unbreakable code that helped win World War II in the Pacific. That's a fascinating, little-known story and might have made a good movie. Alas, the filmmakers have buried it beneath battlefield clichés, while centering the story on a white character played by Nicolas Cage. I was reminded of *Glory*, the story of heroic African-American troops in the Civil War, which was seen through the eyes of their white commanding officer. Why does Hollywood find it impossible to trust minority groups with their own stories?

The film stars Nicolas Cage as an Italian-American sergeant who is so gung ho his men look at him as if he's crazy. Maybe he is. After defending a position past the point of all reason, he survives bloody carnage, is patched up in Hawaii, and returns to action in a battle to take Saipan, a key stepping-stone in the Pacific war. In this battle he is assigned as the personal watchdog of Private Ben Yahzee (Adam Beach), an almost saintly Navajo. Sergeant Ox Henderson (Christian Slater) is paired with Private Charles Whitehorse (Roger Willie), another Indian. What the Navajos don't know is that the bodyguards have been ordered to kill them, if necessary, to keep them from falling into enemy hands. The code must be protected at all costs.

This is a chapter of history not widely known, and for that reason alone the film is useful. But the director, Hong Kong action expert John Woo, has less interest in the story than in the pyrotechnics, and we get way, way, way too much footage of bloody battle scenes, intercut with thin dialogue scenes that rely on exhausted formulas. We know almost without asking, for example, that one of the white soldiers will be a racist, that another will be a by-the-books commanding officer, that there will be a plucky nurse who believes in the Cage character, and a scene in which a Navajo saves the life of the man who hates him. Henderson and Whitehorse perform duets for the harmonica and Navajo flute, a nice idea, but their characters are so sketchy it doesn't mean much.

The battle sequences are where Woo's heart lies, and he is apparently trying to one-up *Saving Private Ryan*, *We Were Soldiers*, and the other new entries in the ultraviolent, unapologetically realistic battle film sweepstakes. Alas, the battles in *Windtalkers* play more like a video game. Although Woo is Asian, he treats the enemy Japanese troops as pop-up targets, a faceless horde of screaming maniacs who run headlong into withering fire. Although Americans take heavy casualties (there is a point at which we assume everyone in the movie will be killed), the death ratio is about thirty to one against the Japanese. Since they are defending dug-in positions and the Americans are often exposed, this seems unlikely.

The point of the movie is that the Navajos are able to use their code in order to radio information, call in strikes, and allow secret communication. In the real war, I imagine, this skill was most useful in long-range strategic radio communication. *Windtalkers* devotes minimal time to the code talkers, however, and when they do talk, it's to phone in coordinates for an air strike against big Japanese guns. Since these guns cannot be moved before airplanes arrive, a call in English would have had about the same effect. That Woo shows the Windtalkers in the heat of battle is explained, I think, because he wants to show everything in the heat of battle. The wisdom of assigning two precious code talkers to a small group of frontline soldiers in a deadly hand-to-hand fight situation seems questionable, considering there are only 400 Navajos in the Pacific theater.

The Indians are seen one-dimensionally as really nice guys. The only character of any depth is Cage's Sergeant Enders, who seems to hover between shell shock and hallucinatory flashbacks. There is a final scene between Enders and Yahzee, the Navajo, that reminded me of the male bonding in other Woo movies, in which you may have to shoot the other guy to prove how much you love him. But since the movie has labored to kill off all the supporting characters and spare only the stars, we are in the wrong kind of suspense: Instead of wondering which of these people will survive, we wonder which way the picture will jump in retailing war-movie formulas.

There is a way to make a good movie like *Windtalkers*, and that's to go the indie route. A low-budget Sundance-style picture would focus on the Navajo characters, their personalities and issues. The moment you decide to make *Windtalkers,* a big-budget action movie with a major star and lots of explosions, flying bodies and stuntmen, you give up any possibility that it can succeed on a human scale. The Navajo code talkers have waited a long time to have their story told. Too bad it appears here merely as a gimmick in an action picture.

With a Friend Like Harry ★ ★ ★
R, 117 m., 2001

Laurent Lucas (Michel), Sergi Lopez (Harry), Mathilde Seigner (Claire), Sophie Guillemin (Plum), Laurie Caminata (Sarah), Lorena Caminata (Iris), Victoire de Koster (Jeane). Directed by Dominik Moll and produced by Michel Saint-Jean. Screenplay by Gilles Marchand and Moll.

Michel uses the rest room of a highway oasis to splash some water on his face. He is addressed by a man who smiles too long and stands too close, and pauses as if expecting Michel to say something. Michel doesn't know what to say. The stranger introduces himself as Harry—an old school friend. Michel doesn't remember him, but Harry's memory is perfect. He remembers the girl they both dated, and quotes a poem Michel wrote for the school magazine.

When people make a closer study of us than we make of ourselves, we grow uneasy. They seem too needy. We want them to get a life. But Harry (Sergi Lopez) has an ingratiating way, and soon has inspired a dinner invitation. Michel (Laurent Lucas) and his wife, Claire (Mathilde Seigner), are on their way to their summer cottage with their noisy daughters. Harry and his girlfriend, Plum (Sophie Guillemin), come along.

We don't like this Harry. He sticks like glue. He insinuates. He makes offers and insists on them. He doesn't respect the distance strangers should keep from one another. He doesn't think of himself as a stranger. It's not wholesome. You can't put your finger on specific transgressions, but his whole style is a violation. He starts conversations Michel has no wish to join. "How do you like Plum?" Harry asks. "She's not brainy like Claire, but she has an animal intelligence that I like. Know what I

mean?" Michel doesn't want to know what he means.

With a Friend Like Harry, directed by Dominik Moll, works like a thriller, but we can't put our finger on exactly why we think so. Maybe it's only about an obnoxious pest. Yet Harry is admittedly helpful: Michel and Claire's old car has no air conditioning, and Harry presents them with a brand-new, bright red SUV. No obligation. He wants to. What are friends for?

Harry is a nickname for Satan. Is this Harry the devil? By using the name, the movie nudges us toward the possibility. On the other hand, maybe he's simply a pushy guy named Harry. Maybe the locus of evil is located elsewhere in the movie. Maybe Harry brings out the worst in people.

Movies like this are more intriguing than thrillers where the heroes and villains wear name tags. We know there's danger and possibly violence coming at some point, but we don't know why, or how, or even who will initiate it. Meanwhile, everyday horrors build up the tension. Michel and Claire's family cabin is rude and unfinished, almost a shack. "It needs a lot of work." Yes—but upstairs there is a brand-new bathroom with shocking pink tile. This is the gift of Michel's parents, who wanted to "surprise" them.

What do you do when someone surprises you with a gift that you consider a vulgar eyesore, and you're stuck with it? Are the people who give such gifts really so insensitive? Are their gifts acts of veiled hostility? A new SUV is at least something you want. A shocking pink bathroom is the wrong idea in a rustic country cabin. It might . . . well, it might almost be a gift to be rid of people who insist on such annoyances.

Sergi Lopez, who plays Harry, last appeared in *An Affair of Love,* the insidious French film about the couple who meet through the classifieds and spend one afternoon a week in a hotel room doing something that apparently no one else in the world wants to do, except for them. We never find out what it is. In that movie, before the situation grew complicated, his face bore the contentment of a man whose imaginary pockets are full.

Here he turns up the dial. He's bursting with confidences, reassurances, compliments, generosity. We realize with a shock that the most frightening outcome of the movie would be if it contained no surprises, no revelations, no quirky twist at the end. What would really be terrifying is if Harry is exactly as he seems, and the plot provides no escape for Michel and Claire, and they're stuck with their new friend. *With a Friend Like Harry,* you don't need enemies.

Woman on Top ★ ★ ½
R, 93 m., 2000

Penelope Cruz (Isabella Oliveira), Murilo Benicio (Toninho Oliveira), Harold Perrineau Jr. (Monica Jones), Mark Feuerstein (Cliff Lloyd), John DeLancie (Alex Reeves). Directed by Fina Torres and produced by Alan Poul. Screenplay by Vera Blasi.

Woman on Top is like one of those lightweight 1950s Universal romances, depending for its charm on the appeal of the actors, and supplying them with a story lighter than air. Even now, the formula seduces us for an hour or so before the movie sinks under the weight of its dim-wittedness. These characters in this story need to be smarter. And yet two of the leads, Penelope Cruz and Harold Perrineau Jr., are wonderful, and emerge untouched from the wreckage.

Cruz plays Isabella, a woman from the enchanted Brazilian state of Bahia, who is an artist with food (the character owes something to Tita, the heroine of *Like Water for Chocolate*). When she cooks, aromas waft from her pot and under the noses of men, and it is love at first bite. She falls for the macho hunk Toninho (Murilo Benicio), marries him, slaves in his restaurant, and is happy. There is one technicality. She was born with motion sickness. It doesn't affect her if she's in control. In a car, she must drive. She prefers the stairs to the elevator. And in bed, she has to be on top.

This drives Toninho crazy, and she catches him with another woman. "I'm a man!" he cries. "I have to be on top *sometimes!*" But in a rage she flies off to San Francisco and moves in with her best friend, Monica Jones, who is a transvestite played by Perrineau in a performance both funny and endearing. "Monica Jones" doesn't sound like the name of some-

one who grew up in Salvador, the capital of Bahia, but then this is one of those multinational movies where the ethnic flavor is suggested by speaking English with an accent.

Isabella's cooking soon wins her a show on local TV, with Monica as her sidekick, and Cruz is bewitching as she demonstrates how to inhale the soul of the pepper, and how to teach your fingers to salt without thinking. Cruz is bewitching all through the movie, but her beauty and charm have to pull a heavy train of clichés and inevitable developments—as when the national network execs want her to "look less ethnic," use Tabasco instead of real peppers, wear a low-cut dress, work under brighter lights, and "lose the freak" (Monica). Her American quasi-boyfriend (Mark Feuerstein) loves her cooking but sides with the suits, and what happens next will be predictable for all but those seeing their first motion picture.

Cruz is a Spanish star who was recently electrifying in Pedro Almodovar's *All About My Mother* and was indescribably sexy and funny in *Jamon, Jamon* (1992), which translates as "Ham, Ham" and which you should put at the top of the list of films you really should have seen. *Woman on Top* wants to combine the sexual freedom of Almodovar with the magical realism of *Like Water for Chocolate,* but succeeds in doing for its sources what the TV execs want to do to Isabella: going for the broad and dull commercial approach instead of the wicked inside curve.

And yet Cruz herself is lovable and charismatic, and we can just about believe it when she walks down the street with a dish she has cooked, and hundreds of men follow her like sheep. Perrineau is lovable, too; he plays Monica not as a stereotyped drag queen but as a character who would be believed by most of the audience as a woman if it were not for his entrance and the tip-offs in the dialogue. The performance is all the more impressive since Perrineau (the narrator of HBO's *Oz* and the man killed by the bear in *The Edge*) is not a professional transvestite but is simply playing a role—so well, he's invaluable in every scene he's in, and steals his share.

But the story is a slow slog toward the obvious. The evil TV execs are out of the Recycled Character Department. The Brazilian husband is a convenience, not a necessity. The American boyfriend is a dope. And the movie plays its story so very safely that it sidesteps all the comic and romantic possibilities in the Monica character. She's more like a mascot, when in a smarter movie she would have been the wild card. This is the kind of movie you sort of like, and yet even while you're liking it, you're thinking how much better these characters and this situation could have been with a little more imagination and daring. Starting with Isabella and Monica, what did they have to lose?

Wonder Boys ★ ★ ★ ★
R, 112 m., 2000

Michael Douglas (Grady Tripp), Tobey Maguire (James Leer), Frances McDormand (Sara Gaskell), Robert Downey Jr. (Terry Crabtree), Katie Holmes (Hannah Green), Richard Thomas (Walter Gaskell), Rip Torn (Q). Directed by Curtis Hanson and produced by Scott Rudin and Hanson. Screenplay by Steve Kloves, based upon the novel by Michael Chabon.

My father was an electrician at the University of Illinois. He never taught me a thing about electricity. "Every time I walk through the English building," he said, "I see the professors in their offices with their feet up on the desk, reading books and smoking their pipes. Now that's the life for you."

I thought I would be an English professor. Then I got into this game. Sometimes I am overwhelmed with a sense of loss: I remember myself walking across the snowy campus at dusk, a book bag thrown over my shoulder, on the way to the seminar room to drink coffee and talk about Cather or Faulkner. And I remember the endless weekends, driving around town in somebody's oversize American car, following rumors of parties. And the emotional and romantic confusion that played out at those parties, where everyone was too smart and too high and filled with themselves.

Wonder Boys is the most accurate movie about campus life I can remember. It is accurate, not because it captures intellectual debate or campus politics, but because it knows two things: (1) students come and go but the faculty actually lives there, and (2) many fac-

ulty members stay stuck in graduate student mode for decades. Michael Douglas plays a character like that. It is his best performance in years, muted, gentle, and wondering. He is a boy wonder long past his sell-by date, a fiftyish English professor named Grady Tripp who wrote a good novel seven years ago and now, everyone believes, has writer's block.

Wonder Boys follows him around a Pittsburgh campus in winter during a literary festival, as characters drift in and out of focus on his emotional viewfinder. His wife (we never see her) has just left him. His boss is Walter Gaskell (Richard Thomas), the head of the English department. Walter's wife, Sara (Frances McDormand), is the chancellor. Grady is having an affair with Sara. His New York editor, Crabtree (Robert Downey Jr.), is in town for the festival, and wonders where the new manuscript is. The famous writer "Q" (Rip Torn) is a visiting speaker. Two of Grady's students occupy his attention: James Leer (Tobey Maguire), who has written a novel and is moody and difficult and a pathological liar; and Hannah Green (Katie Holmes), who rents a room in Grady's house and would probably share his bed, although it has not come to that.

Because Grady is tired, depressed, and continuously stoned on pot, these characters all have more or less equal importance. That is, when he's looking at them they represent problems, and when they're absent, he can forget about them.

The movie is an unsprung screwball comedy, slowed down to real-life speed. Mishaps trip over one another in their eagerness to mess with Grady's mind. One thing leads to another. He goes to a party at the Gaskells' house and Sara tells him she is pregnant. He steps outside for a reefer, sees James standing in the dark with a gun, invites him in, and sneaks him upstairs to show him a secret closet where Walter Gaskell keeps his treasure (the suit Marilyn Monroe wore on her wedding day). Then the Gaskells' blind dog bites him and James shoots the dog dead.

At a certain velocity, this would be wacky. One of the wise decisions of *Wonder Boys* is to avoid that velocity. Grady plods around town in a pink bathrobe, trying to repair damage, tell the truth, give good advice, be a decent man, and keep his life from falling apart. The

679

brilliance of the movie can be seen in its details: (1) Hannah is brought onstage as an obvious love interest, but is a decoy; (2) Crabtree picks up a transvestite on the airplane, but dumps him for James, who is not exactly straight or gay (neither is Crabtree); (3) when the transvestite needs a ride, Grady says, "I'm your man" but their drive results not in sex but in truth-telling; and (4) Sara is not hysterical about being pregnant and is understanding, actually, about Grady's chaotic lifestyle.

So all the obvious payoffs are short-circuited. No mechanical sex scenes. No amazing revelation that the transvestite is not a woman (everyone in the movie clocks him instantly). No emotional show-offs. And the sex in the movie, gay and straight, is handled sanely, as a calming pastime after long and nutty evenings. (Notice how comfortable the Downey character is with his weaknesses of the flesh.)

Let me give one more example of how the movie uses observation instead of wheezy clichés. When Q, the writer, is giving his speech, he pontificates about piloting the boat of inspiration to the shore of achievement. James utters a loud, high-pitched giggle. In a lesser movie James would have continued, making some kind of angry and rebellious statement. Not in *Wonder Boys*, where James thinks Q is ludicrous, laughs rudely once, and then shuts up.

And listen to the dialogue. Grady has been working on his second novel so long it now runs well over 2,000 single-spaced pages. Hannah suggests tactfully that by including the "genealogies of everyone's horses, and their dental records," Grady's work "reads as if you didn't make any choices." The right line in a movie that does make choices. She also wonders if the book would have more shape if he hadn't been stoned when he wrote it. Yes, his brilliant first book was written on reefer, but then a lot of first novels are written long before they're actually put down on paper.

Wonder Boys is the first movie by Curtis Hanson since his *L.A. Confidential*. In a very different way, it is as accomplished. The screenplay by Steve Kloves, based on a novel by Michael Chabon, is European in its preference for character over plot. This is a funny and touching story that contains dead dogs, Monroe memorabilia, a stolen car, sex, adultery, pregnancy, guns, dope, and

cops, but it is not about any of those things. It is about people, and especially about trying to be a good teacher.

Could one weekend on a real campus possibly contain all of these events? Easily, given the tendency of writers to make themselves deliberately colorful. Grady knows exactly what he's doing. Of Hannah he observes: "She was a junkie for the printed word. Lucky for me, I manufactured her drug of choice."

Wonderland ★ ★ ★
R, 108 m., 2000

Gina McKee (Nadia), Molly Parker (Molly), Shirley Henderson (Debbie), John Simm (Eddie), Ian Hart (Dan), Kika Markham (Eileen), Jack Shepherd (Bill), Enzo Cilenti (Darren). Directed by Michael Winterbottom and produced by Michele Camarda and Andrew Eaton· Screenplay by Laurence Coriat.

Michael Winterbottom's *Wonderland* tells the story of three sisters in south London, each lonely in her own way, and of their husbands, parents, blind dates, neighbors, and children, all lonely too, during four rainy days in November. You seek in this movie for someone who is doing it right, who has found happiness, and all you come up with is the grown son who ran away from it all. Does that mean these people are unusual? Not at all. Most people are not terrifically happy most of the time. That's why, according to this movie, they invented booze, professional sports, television, hairdressing, and sex.

I saw the film at about the same time I took a fresh look at *Nashville* (1975), Robert Altman's film of interlocking lives. Altman has often ventured into these constructions, where you find out gradually how the characters are related; think also of his *Short Cuts* and *The Player*, and of two Paul Thomas Anderson films influenced by him, *Boogie Nights* and *Magnolia*. While most plots march from the beginning to the end of a film, these kinds of films move in circles, suggesting that life is not a story but a process. They're more true to life. Reality isn't a march toward a happy ending, but a long series of small and hopeful sideways moves toward dimly sensed goals.

Why do I feel touched by *Wonderland* and

other films like it? Because these films are about themselves and not about me. The real subject of most conventional films, especially the summer special-effects pictures, is me—how they make me feel, how they shock me, how they scare me, how I feel during the chase scenes. There is nothing to be discovered about human nature in them. A movie like *Wonderland,* on the other hand, is about them—about people I am not and will never be, but who are all around me in the city, and share this time and society. F/X pictures come out of the screen at me. Movies like *Wonderland* invite me into the screen with them. I am curious. I begin to care.

The sisters in *Wonderland* are Nadia (Gina McKee), Molly (Molly Parker), and Debbie (Shirley Henderson). Nadia works in a Soho café and answers singles ads. Molly is pregnant, and living with Eddie (John Simm), who sells small appliances, has very low self-esteem, and painfully rehearses how he will tell her he has quit his job. Debbie is a hairdresser, who has a young son by Dan (Ian Hart).

We also meet their parents: Eileen, their mother (Kika Markham), critical of everyone and everything, who steals out in the night to poison the neighbor's dog; and Bill (Jack Shepherd), who turns up hopefully at his daughters' places to help out, who is trapped in a loveless marriage, who does indeed find one moment of happiness. That comes when he locks himself out of the house and is invited in by a neighbor, the Caribbean woman across the street; they dance, sweetly, and it is clear there could be more, but he ducks out—he's broken, and doesn't have the nerve.

Dan has custody of his son for a weekend, long enough to give him object lessons in rage. He grows terrifyingly angry in traffic, takes the kid to a soccer game, which plays as violent mayhem, and eventually passes out at home, drunk. The boy is resourceful, riffles his dad's pants pockets for money, and disappears to a nearby funfair (it is Guy Hawkes's Day, celebrated in England with fireworks and the ritual burning of the traitor who tried to blow up Westminster). That leads to a panicked search for the missing boy, and a reunion at police headquarters; Dan is not a bad man, just a frustrated one, untidy with his emotions.

Life is made of moments like these. Eddie

quits his job without telling Molly, who doesn't see how they'll make ends meet with her pregnant. We know what she doesn't: That he hates his work, is terrified of social situations, tries painfully to rehearse how he will break the news to her, and flees rather than face her. Nadia has sex with a man she meets through the singles ads. He is very eager to have her leave his apartment once they've finished. Riding home, on the upper deck of a red London bus, she is surrounded by couples, and weeps. Franklyn (David Fahm), the son of the woman across the street, sits for hours in his room; his mom tells him he bottles everything up, and is like a total stranger. Later he and Nadia unexpectedly have a conversation that reveals much about their loneliness.

A movie like this is an act of attention. Winterbottom and screenwriter Laurence Coriat go out into their city and attend to how people live and how they feel. Like Studs Terkel in his books, they are listeners to ordinary lives. We watch not because we are "entertained" but because we begin as curious, end as sympathetic. The movie has no big point to make. If it did, it would be dishonest to itself.

World Traveler ★ ★
R, 104 m., 2002

Billy Crudup (Cal), Julianne Moore (Dulcie), Cleavant Derricks (Carl), David Keith (Richard), Mary McCormack (Margaret), James LeGros (Jack), Liane Balaban (Meg), Karen Allen (Delores). Directed by Bart Freundlich and produced by Tim Perell and Freundlich. Screenplay by Freundlich.

Cal drags a woman out of a bar to look at the stars and listen to his rants about the universe. She pulls loose and asks, "Do you get away with this crap because you look like that?" Later in the film two kids will ask him if he's a movie star. He's good-looking, in a morose, tormented way, but it's more than that; Cal is charismatic, and strangers are fascinated by his aura of doom and emptiness.

There is another new movie, *About a Boy,* with a hero who complains that he's a "blank." The dialogue is needed in *World Traveler.* Although others are fascinated by Cal's loneliness, his drinking, his lack of a plan, his superficial charm, he is a blank. Early in the film he walks out on his marriage, on the third birthday of his son. Taking the family station wagon, he drives west across the United States and into the emptiness of his soul.

Cal is played by Billy Crudup, one of the best actors in the movies, but there needs to be something *there* for an actor to play, and Cal is like a moony poet who embraces angst as its own reward. Throwing back Jack Daniels in the saloons of the night, he doesn't have a complaint so much as he celebrates one. When we discover that his own father walked out on Cal and his mother, that reads like an motivation but doesn't play like one. It seems too neat—the Creative Writing explanation for his misery.

The film, written and directed by Bart Freundlich, is a road picture, with Cal meeting and leaving a series of other lonely souls without ever achieving closure. It's as if he glimpses them through the windows of his passing car. There's a young hitchhiker who implies an offer of sex, which he doesn't accept. A construction worker named Carl (Cleavant Derricks), who wants friendship and thinks Cal offers it, but is mistaken. A high school classmate (James LeGros, bitingly effective), who provides us with evidence that Cal has been an emotional hit-and-run artist for a long time. Finally there is Dulcie (Julianne Moore), who is drunk and passed out in a bar.

Cal throws her over his shoulder and hauls her back to his motel room to save her from arrest. She involves him in her own madness. Both sense they're acting out interior dramas from obscure emotional needs, and there is a slo-mo scene on a carnival ride that plays like a parody of a good time. Nelson Algren advised, "Never sleep with a woman whose troubles are greater than your own," and Cal would be wise to heed him.

There are moments of sudden truth in the film; Freundlich, who also made *The Myth of Fingerprints* (1998), about an almost heroically depressed family at Thanksgiving, can create and write characters, even if he doesn't always know where to take them.

The construction buddy Carl and his wife (Mary McCormack) spring into focus with a few lines of dialogue. Cal persuades Carl, a recovering alcoholic, to get drunk with him and help him pick up two women in a bar. The next day Carl says his wife is angry at him, and brings her to life with one line of dialogue: "She's mad about the drinking—and the objectification of women." Later, drunk again, Cal meets Carl's wife, who says, "In all the years I've been married to Carl, I've never heard him talk about anyone the way he talks about you." She loves Carl, we see, so much she is moved that he has found a friend. But then Cal tries to make a pass, and the wife looks cold and level at him: "You're not his friend."

Cal isn't anybody's friend. Near the end of his journey, in the western mountains, he meets his father (David Keith). The role is thankless, but Keith does everything possible, and more, to keep the father from being as much a cipher as the son. One senses in *World Traveler* and in his earlier film that Freundlich bears a grievous but obscure complaint against fathers, and circles it obsessively, without making contact.

X

X-Men ★ ★ ½
PG-13, 96 m., 2000

Hugh Jackman (Logan/Wolverine), Patrick Stewart (Xavier), Ian McKellen (Magneto), Famke Janssen (Dr. Jean Grey), James Marsden (Cyclops), Halle Berry (Storm), Anna Paquin (Rogue), Tyler Mane (Sabretooth), Rebecca Romijn-Stamos (Mystique), Ray Park (Toad). Directed by Bryan Singer and produced by Lauren Shuler Donner and Ralph Winter. Screenplay by David Hayter, based on a story by Tom DeSanto and Singer.

The origin story is crucial to all superhero epics, from the gods of ancient Greece right down to Superman's parents. Next in importance is an explanation of superpowers: what they are, how they work. That's reasonable when there is one superhero, like Superman or the Crow, but in *X-Men*, with eight major characters and more in supporting roles, the movie gets top-heavy. At the halfway mark, it had just about finished introducing the characters.

That matches my experience of the *X-Men* comic books. The characters spent an inordinate amount of time accounting for themselves. Action spills across full pages as the heroes *splatt* and *kerrruuunch* each other, but the dialogue balloons are like little advertisements for themselves, as they describe their powers, limitations, and motivations.

Since the Marvel Comics empire hopes *X-Men* is the first entry in a franchise, it's understandable that the setups would play an important role in the first film. If only there were more to the payoff. The events that end the movie are sort of anticlimactic, and the special effects, while energetic, are not as persuasive as they might be (at one point an airplane clearly looks like a model, bouncing as it lands on water).

X-Men is at least not a manic editing frenzy for atrophied attention spans. It's restrained and introspective for a superhero epic, and fans of the comic books may like that. Graphic novels (as they sometimes deserve to be called) take themselves as seriously as the ones without pictures, and you can tell that here when the opening scene shows Jews being forced into death camps in Poland in 1944. One could argue that the Holocaust is not appropriate subject matter for an action movie based on a comic book, but having talked to some *X-Men* fans I believe that in their minds the stroy is as deep and portentous as, say, *Sophie's Choice.*

The Holocaust scene introduces Magneto (Ian McKellen) as a child; his mental powers twist iron gates out of shape. The narrator informs us that "evolution takes thousands and thousands of years," which is putting it mildly, and that we live in an age of great evolutionary leaps forward. Some of the X-Men develop paranormal powers that cannot be accounted for by the strictly physical mutations that form the basis of Darwinian theory; I get restless when real science is evoked in the name of pseudoscience, but hey, that's just me.

Magneto's opponent in *X-Men* is Xavier (Patrick Stewart), another mutant of the same generation. They aren't enemies so much as ideological opposites. Magneto, having seen the Holocaust, has a deep pessimism about human nature. Xavier, who runs a school for mutants in Westchester County, where it doubtless seems no stranger than the other private schools, hopes these new powers can be used for good. Bruce Davison plays the McCarthy-like senator who waves a list of "known mutants" during a congressional hearing and wants them all registered—no doubt for dire purposes. Magneto wants to counter by using a device that can convert world leaders to mutants. (The world leaders are conveniently meeting on an island near Ellis Island, so the Statue of Liberty can be a prop.)

How a machine could create a desired mutation within a generation is not much explored by the movie, which also eludes the question of why you would want to invest your enemies with your powers. No matter; Xavier, who can read minds, leads his good mutants in a battle to foil Magneto, and that's the plot, or most of it.

X-Men is arguably heavy on mutants; they have a way of coming onstage, doing their tricks, and disappearing. The leads are Wolverine (Hugh Jackman), whose fists sprout deadly blades; Cyclops (James Marsden), who wears a wraparound visor to control and aim his laserlike eyes; the prosaically named Dr. Jean Grey (Famke Janssen), who can move objects with her mind; Storm (Halle Berry in a platinum wig), who can control the weather; and Rogue (Anna Paquin), a teenager who is new to this stuff. I can't help wondering how a guy whose knuckles turn into switchblades gets to be the top-ranking superhero. If Storm can control, say, a tropical storm, she's obviously the most powerful, even if her feats here are limited to local climate control.

Magneto's team is not as colorful as the good guys, and includes Mystique (Rebecca Romijn-Stamos), who in the Japanese *anime* tradition can change her shape (as her cos-

tume tries to keep up), and Toad (Ray Park), who has a tongue that can whip out to great distances. Why is it that Xavier's team has impressive skills, while Magneto's team has specialties that would prove invaluable to a stripper?

I started out liking this movie, while waiting for something really interesting to happen. When nothing did, I still didn't dislike it; I assume the X-Men will further develop their personalities if there is a sequel, and maybe find time to get involved in a story. No doubt fans of the comics will understand subtle allusions and fine points of behavior; they should linger in the lobby after each screening to answer questions.

Y

The Yards ★ ★ ★
R, 115 m., 2000

Mark Wahlberg (Leo Handler), Joaquin Phoenix (Willie Gutierrez), Charlize Theron (Erica Stoltz), James Caan (Frank Olchin), Ellen Burstyn (Val Handler), Faye Dunaway (Kitty Olchin), Andrew Davoli (Raymond Price), Steve Lawrence (Arthur Mydanick), Tony Musante (Seymour Korman), Victor Argo (Paul Lazarides), Tomas Milian (Manuel Sequiera). Directed by James Gray and produced by Nick Wechsler, Paul Webster, and Kerry Orent. Screenplay by Gray and Matt Reeves.

There is a sad, tender quality in *The Yards* I couldn't put my finger on, until I learned that the director's father inspired one of the characters. The movie is set around the yards where the New York mass transit trains are made up and repaired. It is about a kid who gets out of jail, wants to do right, and gets in trouble again. And about his uncle, who works on both sides of the law. This uncle is not an evil man. When he breaks the law, it's because in his business those who do not break the law don't remain in business. The system was corrupt when he found it and will be corrupt when he leaves it. He has to make a living for his family.

It's that ambiguity that makes the film interesting. Most crime movies have a simplistic good vs. evil moral structure. When *The Godfather* came along, with its shades of morality within a shifting situation, it exposed most mob pictures as fairy tales. *The Yards* resembles *The Godfather* in the way it goes inside the structure of corruption, and shows how judges and elected officials work at arm's length with people they know are breaking the law. But it also resembles *Mean Streets*, the film about two childhood friends who get in over their heads.

Early in the film, Frank explains his business: "If it's on a train or a subway, we make it or we fix it." This process involves bribes, kickbacks, and theft. But Frank is a reasonable and measured man who operates within a system that everyone tacitly accepts, even the police. There's a way things are done, everybody gets taken care of, everybody's happy. I was intrigued by how the writer-director, James Gray, makes Frank not a villain but a hardworking guy who breaks the law, yes, but isn't a bad guy in the usual movie sense.

Then I learned that Frank was somewhat inspired by Gray's own father, who was involved in the same racketeering scandal that led to the 1986 suicide of Queens borough president Donald Manes, who stabbed himself when it was revealed he had taken payoffs. When your father is supposed to be the bad guy, you don't always see it that way. It gets complicated.

Complications are what *The Yards* is about. As the movie opens, Leo (Mark Wahlberg) has been released from prison, where he took the rap for his buddies on an auto theft charge. He was a stand-up guy, and is welcomed home at a party including his best friend Willie (Joaquin Phoenix). Leo's dad is dead. His mother, Val (Ellen Burstyn), has a sister, Kitty (Faye Dunaway), whose second husband is Uncle Frank. By her first marriage she has a daughter, Erica (Charlize Theron), who is dating Willie. So everyone is connected.

Leo goes to Uncle Frank looking for a job as a machinist. But that takes an apprenticeship, and Leo needs money; his mother has a heart condition. He seeks out Willie, who runs a crew for Frank, applying muscle in the yards. On his first night with Willie, everything goes wrong. A yardmaster is killed, and Leo beats up a cop. The cop fingers Leo, the only person he saw. "I didn't kill anyone," Leo tells Uncle Frank. "Then who did?" Leo shrugs in a way that lets Frank understand.

The movie is about how all of these relatives and friends deal with the tightening vise of the law. If Leo keeps quiet, he goes up for murder. If he talks, everyone goes down. Is Uncle Frank guilty? Yes, guilty of having a man like Willie on his payroll and using him for illegal purposes. But not guilty of murder. And there are shadings all around; a district police commander, offered a bribe to keep the cop from testifying, observes the cop was known for being free with his nightstick—a euphemism, we sense, for things left unsaid.

Mark Wahlberg, as Leo, doesn't pop out as

the "hero" of this film, but plays the character as withdrawn and sad. His mother is dying. His early promise died in prison. He doesn't have a higher education. There is a poignancy in the performance we don't often see in movies about organized crime; he isn't reckless or headstrong, but simply unlucky, and required to make desperate moral decisions.

The cast occupies the same uncertain terrain. Willie is played by Phoenix as a man who has to betray Leo or go down himself. He can't keep his mind on Erica when his world is coming down around him. Frank is in a painful dilemma: Leo is his wife's nephew, not some punk who can be taken care of. When family members gather, vast silences lurk outside their conversations because there is so much they know and cannot say.

The Yards is not exhilarating like some crime movies, or vibrant with energy like others. It exists in a morose middle ground, chosen by Gray, deliberately or not, because this is how his own memories feel. When indictments come down in political scandals, the defendants often say they were only trying to operate within the system. So they were. Their other choice was to find a new line of work. The system endures. If you don't take the payoff, someone else will. Fairly nice people can live in this shadowland. Sometimes things go wrong.

Yi Yi ★ ★ ★ ½

NO MPAA RATING, 173 m., 2001

Nien-Jen Wu (N.J.), Issey Ogata (Mr. Ota), Elaine Jin (Min-Min), Kelly Lee (Ting-Ting), Jonathan Chang (Yang-Yang), Yupang Chang (Fatty), Chen Xisheng (A-Di), Ke Suyun (Sherry Chang-Breitner), Adrian Lin (Lili), Tang Ruyun (Grandma), Michael Tao (Da-Da), Xiao Shushen (Xiao Yan), Xu Shuyuan (Lili's Mother), Zeng Xinyi (Yun-Yun). Directed by Edward Yang and produced by Kawai Shinya and Tsukeda Naoko. Screenplay by Yang.

"Daddy, I can't see what you see and you can't see what I see. How can we know more than half the truth?"

So asks little Yang-Yang, the eight-year-old boy in *Yi Yi,* a movie in which nobody knows more than half the truth, or is happy more than half the time. The movie is a portrait of three generations of a Taiwanese family, affluent and successful, but haunted by lost opportunities and doubts about the purpose of life. Only rarely is a film this observant and tender about the ups and downs of daily existence; I am reminded of *Terms of Endearment.*

The hero of the film is N.J., an electronics executive with a wife, a mother-in-law, an adolescent daughter, an eight-year-old son, and a life so busy that he is rushing through middle age without paying much attention to his happiness. He's stunned one day when he sees a woman in an elevator: "Is it really you?" It is. It is Sherry, his first love, the girl he might have married thirty years ago. Now she lives in Chicago with her husband, Rodney, an insurance executive, but she follows him fiercely to demand, "Why didn't you come that day? I waited and waited. I never got over it."

Why didn't he come? Why did he marry this woman instead of that one? It is a question raised in the first scene of the movie, at another wedding, where a hysterical woman apologizes to the mother of the groom: "It should have been me marrying your son today!" Perhaps, but as a character observes near the end of the film, if he had done things differently, everything might have turned out about the same.

The family lives in a luxury high-rise. We gradually get to know its members and even the neighbors (one couple fights all the time). The mother-in-law has a stroke, goes into a coma, and the family takes turns reading and talking to her. One day N.J. (Wu Nienjen) comes home to find his wife, Min-Min (Elaine Jin), weeping: "I have nothing to say to Mother. I tell her the same things every day. I have so little. How can it be so little? I live a blank. If I ended up like her one day . . ." Yes, but one day, if we live long enough, we all do. Talking to someone in a coma, N.J. observes, is like praying: You're not sure the other party can hear, and not sure you're sincere.

Little Yang-Yang (Jonathan Chang) is too young for such thoughts, and adopts a more positive approach. He takes a photo of the back of his father's head, since the father can't see it and therefore has no way of being sure it is there. And he takes photos of the mosquitoes on the landing outside the apartment, sneaking out of school to collect the prints at the photo shop (his teacher ridicules his "avant-garde art").

Meanwhile, N.J. is visited by memories of Sherry. Should he have married her? One of his few confidants and friends is a Japanese businessman, Mr. Ota (Issey Ogata); it is a measure of the worlds they live in that their conversations must be conducted in English, the only language they have in common. They sing in a karaoke bar, and then Mr. Ota quiets the room by playing sad classical music on the piano. Late one night, returning to a darkened office, N.J. telephones Sherry (Ke Suyun). She wonders if they should start all over with each other.

N.J.'s teenage daughter, Ting-Ting (Kelly Lee), is also considering cheating, with Fatty (Yupang Chang), her best friend's boyfriend. They actually check into a love hotel, but "it's not right," he says. That's the thing about life: You think about transgressions, but a tidal pull pushes you back toward what you know is right.

The point of *Yi Yi* is not to force people into romantic decisions. Many mainstream American films are impatient; in them, people meet, they feel desire, they act on it. If you step back a little from a movie like *3,000 Miles to Graceland,* you realize it is about stupid, selfish, violent monsters; the movie likes them and thinks it is a comedy. Our films have little time for thought, and our characters are often too superficial for their decisions to have any meaning—they're just plot points.

But the people in *Yi Yi* live considered lives. They feel committed to their families. Their vague romantic yearnings are more like background noise than calls to action. There are some scenes of adultery in the movie, involving characters I have not yet mentioned, but they come across as shabby and sad.

The movie is about the currents of life. But it's not solemn in a Bergmanesque way. N.J. and his family live in a riot of everyday activity; the grandmother in a coma is balanced by Yang-Yang dropping a water balloon on precisely the wrong person. Some scenes edge toward slapstick. Others show characters through the cold, hard windows of modern skyscrapers, bathed in icy fluorescence, their business devoid of any juice or heart.

There was a time when a film from Taiwan would have seemed foreign and unfamiliar—when Taiwan had a completely different culture from ours. The characters in *Yi Yi* live in a world that would be much the same in Toronto, London, Bombay, Sydney; in their economic class, in their jobs, culture is established by corporations, real estate, fast food, and the media, not by tradition. N.J. and Yang-Yang eat at McDonald's, and other characters meet in a Taipei restaurant named New York Bagels. Maybe the movie is not simply about knowing half of the truth, but about knowing the wrong half of the truth.

Note: Yi Yi is unrated; it is appropriate for mature audiences. It was named best film of the year by the National Society of Film Critics.

You Can Count on Me ★ ★ ★ ★
R, 109 m., 2000

Laura Linney (Sammy Prescott), Mark Ruffalo (Terry Prescott), Rory Culkin (Rudy), Matthew Broderick (Brian), Jon Tenney (Bob), J. Smith-Cameron (Mabel), Ken Lonergan (Priest). Directed by Ken Lonergan and produced by Barbara De Fina, John Hart, Larry Meistrich, and Jeff Sharp. Screenplay by Lonergan.

Sammy is a divorced mom, has an eight-year-old son, works as a loan officer at the bank, is making ends meet, dates a guy named Bob who doesn't excite her, and hates her new boss. Terry is her easy-come, easy-go brother, one of those charmers that drive you nuts because you love them but you can't count on them. *You Can Count on Me,* a film of great, tender truth, begins as they meet again after one of Terry's long, unexplained silences.

As the film opens, Terry (Mark Ruffalo) has left behind a girlfriend and come to visit Sammy (Laura Linney) in the little town of Scottsville, New York. She glows with happiness to see him; they raised each other after their parents died in an accident. Gradually her joy fades as she realizes he hasn't come home to stay, but just wants to borrow money. It's the same old story.

We meet Rudy (Rory Culkin), Sammy's

son, a good kid, close to his mother, suspicious of Terry at first, then growing crazy about him—because Rory aches for his absent father, and Terry does dadlike stuff, like taking him to a pool hall. Sammy is bitter about her ex-husband, won't talk to her son about him, has closed that chapter.

At the bank, the new manager is Brian (Matthew Broderick). He's one of those infuriating midlevel executives who has been promoted beyond his competence. The bank, like many other corporations, mistakes his tactlessness for tough managerial skills. Brian has no empathy and takes cover behind the regulations. "Is there anyone else who can pick your son up after school?" he asks Sammy, who gives up her lunch hour so she can slip out every afternoon and meet Rudy. It goes without saying that Brian's regard for the rules does not extend to himself, which is why he is willing to have an affair with Sammy even though he has a pregnant wife at home.

Sammy's personal life is limited. In a small town, there are few available men. Bob (Jon Tenney) is a nice enough guy, but forgets to call her for weeks at a time, and seems reluctant to commit—not that she thinks she wants to marry him anyway. One of the truest scenes in the movie comes when Sammy calls him one day to arrange a meeting for sex. Kind of like calling the plumber.

The situation in Scottsville is static when Terry comes to town. Because he's unpredictable and irresponsible, but good-hearted in his half-baked way, he acts as a catalyst. Yes, he forgets to meet Rudy after school. Yes, he ignores his commitments. Yes, it is irresponsible for him to take that eight-year-old kid to a pool hall. But when he lifts Rudy up to the table and Rudy takes a shot and sinks the ball, *this is what the kid needs!* He needs a guy in his life to take the place of the absent father he is so curious about.

Of course, Terry knows Rudy Sr., the ex-husband. They probably went to school together. He takes matters into his own hands and drives the kid to the house of his father, the louse, in a well-written scene where what happens is kind of inevitable.

The characters in *You Can Count on Me* have been freed from the formulas of fiction and set loose to live lives where they screw up, learn

from their mistakes, and bumble hopefully into the future. Ken Lonergan, the writer-director, is willing to leave things open. He shows possibilities without immediately sealing them with decisions. Laura Linney and Mark Ruffalo are open actors who give the impression of spontaneous notions; they are not programmed. We like them. We share their frustration. We despair of Terry even while we see he means well.

I admire the way Linney shows Sammy struggling with issues of right and wrong. Yes, she sleeps with the married bank manager—and with Bob. She doesn't feel right about it. She goes to her priest, played by Lonergan, the filmmaker. "What is the church's official position on fornication and adultery?" she asks, although she should have a good working knowledge of the answer. "Well," says the priest, wanting to be helpful, aware of situational ethics, "it's a sin . . ."

Yes. But after seeing the film I want you to ponder three possibilities. (1) The priest is quietly attracted to Sammy himself, although he would probably never act on his feelings. (2) Sammy's reason for sleeping with Brian, the bank manager, may have originated in passion, but includes a healthy component of office politics. (3) She may be coming around to the notion that Bob is not entirely unacceptable as a mate.

I call these possibilities because the movie does not seal them, or even take a position on them. They're serious matters, but the movie can be funny about them. Not funny like a comedy, but funny like at the office when some jerk makes enemies, and his enemies pounce. Then there are quiet little sarcastic asides around the watercooler, where you share your joy at the downfall of an ass. Such moments can be so enormously rewarding.

Beyond and beneath that is the rich human story of *You Can Count on Me*. I love the way Lonergan shows his characters in flow, pressed this way and that by emotional tides and practical considerations. This is not a movie about people solving things. This is a movie about people living day to day with their plans, fears, and desires. It's rare to get a good movie about the touchy adult relationship of a sister and brother. Rarer still for the director to be more fascinated by the process than the outcome. This is one of the best movies of the year.

Y Tu Mama Tambien ★ ★ ★ ★

NO MPAA RATING, 105 m., 2002

Maribel Verdu (Luisa Cortes), Gael Garcia Bernal (Julio Zapata), Diego Luna (Tenoch Iturbide). Directed by Alfonso Cuaron and produced by Alfonso Cuaron and Jorge Vergara. Screenplay by Alfonso Cuaron and Carlos Cuaron.

Y Tu Mama Tambien is described on its Website as a "teen drama," which is like describing *Moulin Rouge* as a musical. The description is technically true but sidesteps all of the reasons to see the movie. Yes, it's about two teenage boys and an impulsive journey with an older woman that involves sexual discoveries. But it is also about the two Mexicos. And it is about the fragility of life and the finality of death. Beneath the carefree road movie that the movie is happy to advertise is a more serious level—and below that, a dead serious level.

The movie, whose title translates as *"And Your Mama, Too,"* is another trumpet blast that there may be a New Mexican Cinema a-bornin'. Like *Amores Perros,* which also stars Gael Garcia Bernal, it is an exuberant exercise in interlocking stories. But these interlock not in space and time, but in what is revealed, what is concealed, and in the parallel world of poverty through which the rich characters move.

The surface is described in a flash: Two Mexican teenagers named Tenoch and Julio, one from a rich family, one middle class, are free for the summer when their girlfriends go to Europe. At a wedding they meet a cousin named Luisa, ten years older, who is sexy and playful. They suggest a weekend trip to the legendary beach named Heaven's Mouth. When her fiancé cheats on her, she unexpectedly agrees, and they set out together on a lark.

This level could have been conventional but is anything but, as directed by Alfonso Cuaron, who cowrote the screenplay with his brother Carlos. Luisa kids them about their sex lives in a lighthearted but tenacious way, until they have few secrets left, and at the same time she teases them with erotic possibilities. The movie is realistic about sex, which is to say, franker and healthier than the smutty evasions forced on American movies by the R rating. We feel a shock of recognition: This is what real people

do and how they do it, sexually, and the MPAA has perverted a generation of American movies into puerile, masturbatory snickering.

Whether Luisa will have sex with one or both of her new friends is not for me to reveal. More to the point is what she wants to teach them, which is that men and women learn to share sex as a treasure they must carry together without something spilling—that women are not prizes, conquests, or targets, but the other half of a precarious unity. This is news to the boys, who are obsessed with orgasms (needless to say, their own).

The progress of that story provides the surface arc of the movie. Next to it, in a kind of parallel world, is the Mexico they are driving through. They pass police checkpoints, see drug busts and traffic accidents, drive past shantytowns, and are stopped at a roadblock of flowers by villagers who demand a donation for their queen—a girl in bridal white, representing the Virgin. "You have a beautiful queen," Luisa tells them. Yes, but the roadblock is genteel extortion. The queen has a sizable court that quietly hints a donation is in order.

At times during this journey the sound track goes silent and we hear a narrator who comments from outside the action, pointing out the village where Tenoch's nanny was born, and left at thirteen to seek work. Or a stretch of road where, two years earlier, there was a deadly accident. The narration and the roadside images are a reminder that in Mexico and many other countries a prosperous economy has left an uneducated and penniless peasantry behind.

They arrive at the beach. They are greeted by a fisherman and his family, who have lived here for four generations, sell them fried fish, rent them a place to stay. This is an unspoiled paradise. (The narrator informs us the beach will be purchased for a tourist hotel, and the fisherman will abandon his way of life, go to the city in search of a job, and finally come back here to work as a janitor.) Here the sexual intrigues that have been developing all along will find their conclusion.

Beneath these two levels (the coming-of-age journey, the two Mexicos) is hidden a third. I will say nothing about it, except to observe there are only two shots in the entire movie

689

that reflect the inner reality of one of the characters. At the end, finally knowing everything, you think back through the film—or, as I was able to do, see it again.

Alfonso Cuaron is Mexican but his first two features were big-budget American films. I thought *Great Expectations* (1998), with Ethan Hawke, Gwyneth Paltrow, and Anne Bancroft, brought a freshness and visual excitement to the updated story. I liked *A Little Princess* (1995) even more. It is clear Cuaron is a gifted director, and here he does his best work to date. Why did he return to Mexico to make it? Because he has something to say about Mexico, obviously, and also because Jack Valenti and the MPAA have made it impossible for a movie like this to be produced in America. It is a perfect illustration of the need for a workable adult rating: too mature, thoughtful, and frank for the R, but not in any sense pornographic. Why do serious film people not rise up in rage and tear down the rating system that infantilizes their work?

The key performance is by Maribel Verdu, as Luisa. She is the engine that drives every scene she's in, as she teases, quizzes, analyzes, and lectures the boys, as if impatient with the task of turning them into beings fit to associate with an adult woman. In a sense she fills the standard role of the sexy older woman, so familiar from countless Hollywood comedies, but her character is so much more than that— wiser, sexier, more complex, happier, sadder. It is true, as some critics have observed, that *Y Tu Mama* is one of those movies where "after that summer, nothing would ever be the same again." Yes, but it redefines "nothing." ☞

Z

Zoolander ★
PG-13, 90 m., 2001

Ben Stiller (Derek Zoolander), Owen Wilson (Hansel), Christine Taylor (Matilda Jeffries), Will Ferrell (Jacobim Mugatu), Jerry Stiller (Maury Ballstein), Milla Jovovich (Katinka), David Pressman (Phil), Matt Levin (Archie). Directed by Ben Stiller and produced by Stuart Cornfeld, Scott Rudin, and Stiller. Screenplay by Drake Sather, Stiller, and John Hamburg, based on a story by Sather and Stiller.

There have been articles lately asking why the United States is so hated in some parts of the world. As this week's Exhibit A from Hollywood, I offer *Zoolander*, a comedy about a plot to assassinate the prime minister of Malaysia because of his opposition to child labor. You might want to read that sentence twice. The logic: Child labor is necessary to the economic health of the fashion industry, and so its opponents must be eliminated. Ben Stiller stars as Derek Zoolander, a moronic male model who is brainwashed to perform the murder.

Malaysia is a mostly Muslim country with a flag that looks a lot like ours: It has the red and white stripes of the American flag, and a blue field in the upper left corner, which instead of stars displays Islamic symbols, the star and crescent. Malaysia is home to the Petronas Towers of Kuala Lumpur, the world's tallest buildings. But you get the point. If the Malaysians made a comedy about the assassination of the president of the United States because of his opposition to slavery, it would seem approximately as funny to us as *Zoolander* would seem to them.

I realize I am getting all serious on you. Obviously, in times like these, we need a little escapism. "Hagrid," a critic at Ain't It Cool News, went to see *Zoolander* feeling "a comedy is just what I needed, and what I feel everybody needs at this time." His verdict? "It's a perfect film to help people forget everything for a few hours, and it's gonna be huge."

Well, you know, I wanted to forget, but the movie kept making me remember. I felt particularly uncomfortable during the scenes involving the prime minister, shown as an elderly Asian man who is brought to New York to attend a fashion show where he is targeted for assassination. I would give you his name, since he has a lot of screen time, but the movie's Website ignores him and the entry on the Internet Movie Database, which has room to list twenty-six actors, neglects to provide it. Those old Asian actors are just placeholders, I guess, and anyone could play the prime minister.

For that matter, any country could play Malaysia. In years past, movies invented fictional countries to make fun of. Groucho Marx once played Rufus T. Firefly, the dictator of Fredonia, and *The Mouse That Roared* was about the Duchy of Grand Fenwick. Didn't it strike *anybody* connected with this movie that it was in bad taste to name a real country with a real prime minister? A serious political drama would be one thing, but why take such an offensive shot in a silly comedy?

To some degree, *Zoolander* is a victim of bad timing, although I suspect I would have found the assassination angle equally tasteless before September 11. The movie is a satirical jab at the fashion industry, and there are points scored, and some good stuff involving Stiller and Owen Wilson, who play the world's two top male models—funny in itself. The best moments involve the extreme stupidity of the Stiller character. Shown a model of a literary center to be built in his honor, he sweeps it to the floor, exclaiming: "This is a center for ants! How can we teach children to read if they can't even fit inside the building?" Funny, yes, and I like the hand model whose hand is sealed inside a hyperbaric chamber to protect it.

I also admire the ruthlessness with which *Zoolander* points out that the fashion industry does indeed depend on child labor. The back-to-school clothes of American kids are largely made by Third World kids who don't go to school. In fact, the more you put yourself into the shoes (if he had any) of a Muslim twelve-year-old in a sport-shirt factory, the more you might understand why he resents rich Americans, and might be offended by a movie about the assassination of his prime minister (if he had the money to go to a movie). Kids like that don't grow up to think of America as fondly as the people who designed his flag.

Responding quickly to the tragedy of September 11, the makers of *Zoolander* did some last-minute editing. No, they didn't dub over the word "Malaysia" or edit around the assassination of the prime minister. What they did was digitally erase the World Trade Center from the New York skyline, so that audiences would not be reminded of the tragedy, as if we have forgotten. It's a good thing no scenes were shot in Kuala Lumpur, or they probably would have erased the Petronas Towers, to keep us from getting depressed or jealous or anything.

Note: This review, written soon after September 11, is more harsh than it would have been if that tragedy had not taken place. 🖝

The Best Films of 2001

1. *Monster's Ball*

With the subtlety and complexity of great fiction, this is a movie that introduces us to two of the most particular characters of the year. In Georgia, circa 1990, Billy Bob Thornton plays a guard on Death Row; he is an abused child and an abusive father, and all three generations of men live in the same household of seething resentment. Halle Berry plays an alcoholic mother, about to be evicted, aimless, distraught. The two characters have a connection: The man Thornton is executing is Berry's husband. But that isn't really the point. She no longer cares for the husband (Sean Combs), who tells his own son he is a bad man. She does care for their son, a sad, overweight boy she confuses with smothering love and sudden harsh discipline.

Berry and Thornton meet in the middle of the night, in the diner where she works. Soon a strange, shy, unspoken courtship begins. But *Monster's Ball* is not an exercise in interracial understanding; it is about these two specific characters, their need, their desperation. The movie pays full attention to both of them; each has a complete story arc, and the arcs do not intersect as in a conventional screenplay, but simply, inevitably, meet. The last scenes of Marc Forster's movie are breathtakingly good, as Berry makes a discovery, and then a decision, and the movie avoids any of the conventional payoffs we might have been expecting, requiring us to empathize with how and why she arrives at her next step.

2. *Black Hawk Down*

Ridley Scott's film does a brilliant job of taking the chaos of battle and showing, step by step, how a series of wrong decisions led to a defeat. The movie is set in Somalia in 1993, when U.S. troops were sent on a humanitarian mission to get food and relief to starving people. But the warlords who controlled the country were more concerned with their influence than with hunger, and met the Americans with armed resistance. On one disastrous day, eighteen Americans were killed and dozens injured in an ill-conceived raid.

Scott shows the raid from beginning to end: What assumptions it was based on, what went wrong, how mistakes multiplied, how relief could not reach the surrounded troops. The movie avoids gung ho war movie clichés and shows men who are wounded, tired, isolated, frightened, as the sun sets over their entrapment in hostile territory. Scott's achievement is to show both the mood and the logistics; we understand where the characters are, and why, and what they're up against.

3. *In the Bedroom*

Todd Field's directorial debut is, like *Monster's Ball,* about particular and complex characters. Sissy Spacek and Tom Wilkinson play a long-married couple whose son (Nick Stahl) wants to postpone graduate school because of his romance with a divorced mother in her thirties (Marisa Tomei). At first the film seems to be entirely about this family drama, but then there is an abrupt turn, and it becomes an intense character study—leading to revenge, and to the settling of long-unspoken tensions in the marriage. Like many of the best movies, this is not about what happens, but about why it happens and how the characters feel about it.

4. *Ghost World*

Terry Zwigoff's rich, droll comedy introduced us to a disaffected eighteen-year-old (Thora Birch) who feels stuck in a world of shallow phonies and makes her personal style into a rebuke. Idly answering a personals ad, she meets a pathetic loner in his forties (Steve Buscemi). At first she toys with him. Then, unexpectedly, she starts to like him, and he begins to realize there's something in the world beyond his collection of 78rpm records. Seymour and Enid both specialize in complex personal lifestyles that send messages no one is receiving. "I don't want to meet someone who shares my interests," Seymour observes. "I hate my interests." Why does Enid like him? "He's the exact opposite of all the things I hate."

5. *Mulholland Dr.*

The first film in David Lynch's quixotic, ironic style that I've liked—and I really liked it. A Hollywood dreamscape, involving the elements of *film noir* and backstage tarnished tinsel, plus sex, crime, and intrigue, all turned in upon itself like a Mobius strip; everything leads to everything else, but there is no beginning and no end. Every single scene is compelling and fascinating, so we're drawn in—but to what? Laura Harring and Naomi Watts play the two heroines. Or is there one heroine? Or is she a heroine?

6. *Waking Life*

Not only vibrantly entertaining, but the year's most significant film from a technical point of view. Richard Linklater's hero lands in some kind of posttraumatic fantasy that takes him floating through a series of wordy encounters with self-appointed gurus and motormouth philosophers. The film was shot in live-action digital video, then animated by a team of thirty artists who bring it to exciting life. A key point is that the animation was done on desktop Macintoshes, not million-dollar workstations, and yet the movie looked fully, competitively professional. *Waking Life* opens the world of theatrical animation to independent filmmakers.

7. *Innocence*

Paul Cox's lovely, sweet, sad, ineffably romantic story of a couple who met when they were teens, and find, when they meet again fifty years later, that the original passion is still there. Julia Blake and Charles Tingwell star, she married, he a widower, who have to face and deal with the fact of their love. The performances are astonishingly effective, and Cox's direction leads us not into a conventional love story but into deeper truths about life and memory.

8. *Wit*

This film, directed by Mike Nichols and starring Emma Thompson, represents both working at the height of their powers, and didn't play in theaters. It's an HBO production, dramatizing the high quality of many made-for-cable movies. Thompson plays a professor of English literature who was aloof for years and now finds, as she battles cancer, that she is pretty much alone in the world. Hospital routine heaps indignities on

a proud woman, who fights with every shred of her being not only for life but for self-respect.

9. *A Beautiful Mind*

Inspired by the story of John Forbes Nash Jr., a brilliant mathematician who won the Nobel Prize despite a lifelong battle with schizophrenia. Russell Crowe stars in another strong performance where he disappears into character (what an irony that he won the acting Oscar for *Gladiator* the year between *The Insider* and this film!). Jennifer Connelly plays the wife who stands beside him during what often seems a hopeless struggle. Directed by Ron Howard.

10. *Gosford Park*

A masterful assembly of time, place, and a large cast of characters, by the great Robert Altman. Some thirty speaking roles in an English country house, where during a shooting party there is a murder and many suspects. Begins with elements of an Agatha Christie whodunit, and deepens and broadens into comedy and class-conscious commentary. Perhaps only Altman, who loves large ensembles, could have taken such a large cast and made it clear who and what they were, and what they may (or may not) have done.

Special Jury Prize

At film festivals, the juries often award special prizes to films they want to call attention to. This year, as a jury of one, I am awarding my prize to ten extraordinary foreign films. At a time when Hollywood increasingly capitulates to the easy mark of the teenage action audience, subtitled films are a lifeline for more-demanding filmgoers. Alphabetically:

Amores Perros (Alejandro Gonzalez Inarritu) was the labyrinthine Mexican film where three stories, and a lot of dogs, meet at a fateful intersection. *Bread and Tulips* (Silvio Soldini) told the story of an Italian housewife (Licia Maglietta) who walks out of a cheerless marriage and into a romantic new life on the back streets of Venice. *Faithless* was Liv Ullmann's direction of Ingmar Bergman's screenplay about an aging film director who summons up the ghosts of his past and tries to make peace with them. *Fat Girl* (Catherine Breillat) was the painful, observant story of two sisters, one promiscuous and popular, the other chubby and resentful, heading for a shocking destiny. Banned in Ontario (why do censors have such a knack for targeting the best films?). *The Gleaners and I* was the year's best documentary, by Agnes Varda, who studies those who glean from society—the scavengers, the recyclers, and even herself, retrieving their stories with her camera.

Our Lady of the Assassins (Barbet Schroeder), filmed in considerable danger in Medellin, told the story of a Colombian writer who returns to his native city to die, he says, and begins liaisons with two young street kids trapped in the culture of murder. *The Princess and the Warrior,* Tom Tykwer's first film after *Run, Lola, Run,* once again starred the talented Franka Potente, as a woman convinced she has met her great love; involves a traffic accident, a bank robbery, and an insane asylum, using those elements in completely unexpected ways. *The Circle* (Jafar Panahi) is a daring, uncompromising Iranian film, showing that under current Iranian law, unattached women are made to feel like hunted animals; without a husband, father, or brother as an anchor, they circle in a world that gives them no place to rest. *Under the Sand* (Francois Ozon) stars Charlotte Rampling as a woman whose husband has disappeared, and who refuses to process that fact, drifting from denial into madness. *The Widow of St. Pierre* (Patrice Leconte) takes place on a French island off Quebec in the 1850s, where the governor (Daniel Auteuil) and his wife (Juliette Binoche) become personally involved in the life of a man condemned to death.

Eleventh Place

These eleven movies are equal in my affection with those listed above, and can be considered in a tie for eleventh place. Alphabetically:

The Crimson Rivers (Mathieu Kassovitz) lost its way at the end, but was an eerie and atmospheric thriller with the same savor as *The Silence of the Lambs* or *Seven. The Deep End* (Scott McGehee) starred Tilda Swinton as a mother who falls into a labyrinth of death, deception, and blackmail as she attempts to shield her son. *Endurance* (George Butler) was the astonishing documentary about Ernest Shackleton's doomed South Pole expedition, and incorporates film shot in Antarctica at the time. *Harry Potter and the Sorcerer's Stone* (Chris Columbus) was an

enchanting classic, red-blooded, dripping with atmosphere, surprisingly faithful to the novel. *Lantana* (Ray Lawrence) watches as interlocking lives are touched by infidelity and a mysterious disappearance; seems to be about murder, is more about loneliness and trust.

Lost and Delirious (Lea Pool) starred Piper Perabo and Jessica Pare in the story of adolescent crushes, schoolgirl idealism, and putting yourself to a test. Erotic, haunting. *The Majestic* (Frank Darabont) starred Jim Carrey as a troubled screenwriter who contracts amnesia and is mistaken for a war hero. A small-town love story, surrounded by a Frank Capra–style patriotic message. *Memento* (Christopher Nolan) starred Guy Pearce as a man with short-term memory loss who is trying to solve the mystery of his wife's murder. With the main thread of the story told backward, filmgoers debated the plot tirelessly. *Panic* (Henry Bromell) starred William H. Macy as a professional hitman who endures a midlife crisis and an unexpected friendship with a young woman (Neve Campbell). *Bully* was Larry Clark's fearlessly perceptive look at a culture of ignorance and violence among Florida teenagers; together, they commit a crime none could have contemplated alone. *Shrek* was a jolly, wicked animated comedy, filled with sly in-jokes and yet somehow possessing a heart.

Honorary Mention

There were a lot of other films I admired this year; the only reason they are not listed higher is that—well, other films were. They included:

A.I., Amelie, Atlantis, Baby Boy, Bread and Roses, Bridget Jones's Diary, The Center of the World, The Claim, The Day I Became a Woman, The Dish, Final Fantasy, Hearts in Atlantis, Heist, Joy Ride, The Legend of Rita, Liam, Lord of the Rings, Moulin Rouge, No Man's Land, The Pledge, The Royal Tenenbaums, Sexy Beast, Spy Kids, The Tailor of Panama, Tape, The Score, Under the Sun, and *Yi Yi.*

And recognition must also go to *Apocalypse Now Redux,* the restored and lengthened version of the 1979 Francis Ford Coppola classic. I preferred the unaltered version of the film, but seeing *Redux* on a big screen was a reminder of the days in cinema when giants walked the earth.

Two On-Ramps to *Mulholland Dr.*

Talking with David Lynch

I'd rather learn from one bird how to sing than teach ten thousand stars how not to dance.

                    —e.e. cummings

October 30, 2001—David Lynch's new movie, *Mulholland Dr.*, has driven its admirers into frenzies of explanation, as they attempt to disassemble his delicate web of dreams. They're like a cadre of code-breakers, peering at an Enigma machine, determined to make it reveal its secrets. The difference is that codes are meant to be broken, and movies are meant to be felt. If there is anything more futile than someone explaining the dream they had last night, it's someone explaining David Lynch's dream.

I have personally received at least two dozen explanations for the film—all persuasive, none in agreement. I am in awe of the effort that went into the explication by Bill Wyman, Max Garrone, and Andy Klein on Salon.com, who offered 4,900 words of close analysis, then posted a "revised and updated version" the next day, and have added another 8,250 words of Q&A from readers still puzzled despite this onslaught of information.

My own view, expressed in the first paragraph of my review: "The movie is a surrealist dreamscape in the form of a Hollywood *film noir,* and the less sense it makes, the more we can't stop watching it." I unwisely went on to say, "It tells the story of . . . well, there's no way to finish that sentence."

Readers have been finishing it for me ever since. I have been assured that two heroines are in fact one person, or perhaps four; that parts of the movie are not a dream; that all of the movie consists of the dying thoughts generated in the first scene; that the film is essentially Lynch's retelling of his earlier film *Lost Highway.* You are free to believe all of these things, but then you are also free to believe *Mulholland Dr.* is based on a novel by Jane Austen.

I am not against explaining films. But I think the effort is better spent on films that reward explanation—films that are intended to be understood, and can be better appreciated after close analysis. *Citizen Kane* is such a film, and so are *Vertigo, Persona, Pulp Fiction,* and, so help me, *Fight Club.* I have been through all of those films using the shot-at-a-time stop-action technique, in large rooms of movie lovers all contributing their insights to the process.

Although with a sinking feeling I realize *Mulholland Dr.* will probably be the subject of my annual Cinema Interruptus session at the University of Colorado in April *[it was],* I fear we will inspire more autobiography than enlightenment *[we did].* A film that defies rational analysis only encourages people to discover that it matches theories of their own. Or, as e.e. cummings also said, "For whatever we lose (like a you or a me), it's always ourselves that we find in the sea."

By reading the film as a dream from beginning to end, I am of course supplying my own explanation. But at least I am playing by a cardinal rule of criticism, which teaches us we must not bring to the film what it does not contain and insist that we have found it there. The film certainly supports a dream interpretation. But is that simply a cop-out, and am I too lazy to go to the heroic lengths of the Salon.com pick-and-shovel team?

I turn in uncertainty to the interview I did with David Lynch at Cannes last May. The transcript runs to 3,800 words. I find that I accosted Lynch with my dream theory in my first question, and that Lynch, who despite the wildman spirit of his films is a soft-spoken gentleman, did not disagree but did not agree, either:

RE: Is it sort of based on a dream . . . or resembling a dream?

DL: It's based on ideas that came along and joined themselves together and formed this story. And where these ideas come from, I don't know. But there is a dream. It's called the City of Dreams, Los Angeles, and there are so many things that are illusions and dreamlike there, and it's a city filled with desires—many times desires that are never satisfied. And so it's a desperate, sad place as well as a city of euphoria and success, and these things swim together.

In short, Lynch won't agree it is based on a dream, but is too nice to say it isn't. A little later, we got into the discussion of the two heroines:

RE: There's a convention, I suppose, that the dark brunette and the sunny blond represent two sides of the psyche; the one is the innocent girl from the country, the other is the dark city girl . . .

DL: . . . who's in trouble, right.

RE: . . . and we don't necessarily suspect they're gonna wind up as partners, helping each other and going out essentially on a Nancy Drew mission together, and instead of following through with the blond versus brunette archetype, it's almost as if they're part of the same person.

DL: Well, they're two different people but one relationship is a certain way and the other is another.

So there he had an opportunity to agree with me ("Yes! They're the same person!") and he flat out said they were different. Of course, if my dream theory is correct, they could be two different people in the dream and aspects of one person in the mind that dreams the dream.

We talked on and on, discussing Hollywood, discussing how he hit upon the idea for casting Ann Miller in the movie, discussing the man in the wheelchair in the room . . . but always, I think, as if the film's action was "real" when in fact at some level, dream or not, it clearly isn't.

But then there came a pause, and he lighted a cigarette. We were on the roof of the Hotel Carlton, the sea sparkling in the breeze, and it was a quiet, sunny day—an interruption from the ten days of madness at Cannes. And then Lynch, who at heart is a poet, said:

"To me, and I think for many people, the language of film is, or can be, abstract and nonlinear. Understanding it is intuitive. It becomes more like music. And because time is involved and things seem to happen in sequence, certain things are introduced and then others are introduced and then they come together just like in music, and knowing what has gone before makes them even greater. There are certain harmonics. If you just played that bunch of chords and notes, it wouldn't do it. But because of what's gone before, there's a greater thing happening now. Films can do these things and they can show emotions that are very abstract, and suddenly you catch it and it gets your heart. Or

it catches it in your mind and it starts . . . kinda zooming. Intuition is such a beautiful thing. It's a knowingness inside. And to me it's part of the language of cinema."

And right then and there, in that apparently abstract statement, I think he was flatly "explaining" his film. That it works more like music than like a novel. That when one sequence follows another it is colored by what went before but does not necessarily follow in a logical fashion. We know how futile it is to paraphrase music in words; only in grade school does music appreciation still involve interpreting the "story" of the music. The music speaks for itself in a language that cannot be translated into a spoken tongue.

Some movies work that way too. Not all, because film, as Pauline Kael pointed out, is the bastard art, and theater, fiction, politics, and philosophy are sometimes its parents. But some movies exist outside logical explanation. *Mulholland Dr.* is one of them. It shows emotions that are very abstract and suddenly you catch it and it gets your heart. When you leave the theater, it has given you a series of images cast in archetypal terms (The Dream City, The Blond, The Brunette, The Sitting Man, The Laughing Couple, Sex, The Monster, The Old Lady, Death, The Decaying Corpse) and instead of trying to line them up and make sense of them, we should shuffle them in the prism of our minds, making a kaleidoscope of flesh. The analysis of this movie may be a job, not for a critic or a logician, but for a student of the Tarot.

Lost on *Mulholland Dr.*

Boulder, Colorado, April 15, 2002—We have finally met defeat. A film has resisted our efforts to pound it into submission.

Every year I join some 1,000 students and townspeople here at the University of Colorado on a five-day, twelve-hour shot-by-shot trek through a film. Using the freeze-frame and slow-motion features of a DVD, we track down symbols, expose hidden messages, analyze visual strategies, expose special effects, and in general satisfy ourselves that we have extracted every fugitive scrap of meaning from the movie under discussion.

This year the target was David Lynch's *Mulholland Dr.* It is a film I greatly admire, and indeed it was on my Top 10 list for 2001. I still admire it, perhaps more than before. But I also find it more of a mystery. Here at the Conference on World Affairs, we gathered in Macky Auditorium every afternoon to look at the film together. We were sitting in the dark, so the voices were anonymous. Anyone in the hall could shout out "Stop!" and we would freeze-frame the film, and discuss what the shouter found intriguing. This process was named "Cinema Interruptus" by the late Professor Howard Higman, founder of the conference.

Because I've been doing this at Boulder for thirty years, the audience includes seasoned veterans. Not much eludes our collective mind and eye. We've looked at classics like *Citizen Kane, Vertigo,* and *The Third Man,* modern masterpieces like *Raging Bull, Silence of the Lambs,* and *Pulp Fiction,* foreign landmarks like *La Dolce Vita,* and *Persona,* and contentious films like *Fight Club*—last year's selection, a film I remained convinced, at the end of the week, consisted of two brilliant acts and a broken ending.

This year I chose *Mulholland Dr.* because I wanted to get to the bottom of its dream images and shifting realities. "The characters fracture and recombine like flesh caught in a kaleidoscope," I wrote in my original review. "*Mulholland Dr.* isn't like *Memento,* where if you watch it closely enough you can hope to explain the mystery." Analysis of the film ranges all the way from "it's all a dream" to a 6,000-word dissection on Salon.com that attempts to account for every scene (although even Salon, confronted with the movie's mysterious little blue box, admitted "We don't know about the box").

In my review, I wrote, "*Mulholland Dr.* is all dream. There is nothing that is intended to be a waking moment. Like real dreams, it does not explain, does not complete its sequences, lingers over what it finds fascinating, dismisses unpromising plotlines. If you want an explanation for the last half-hour of the film, think of it as the dreamer rising slowly to consciousness, as threads from the dream fight for space with recent memories from real life, and with fragments of other dreams—old ones and those still in development."

Did I still believe this at the end of the week? Yes, and definitely no. The last half-hour of the film does suggest a level of reality, although I still believe that real life and fragments of dream are interconnected. The more times you watch the film, the more the buried structure reveals itself. At the most basic level, I believe *Mulholland Dr.* involves a failed blond actress named Diane Selwyn, disappointed in love by a brunette woman, who hires a hit man to kill her. Neither Diane nor her lover looks the same at the reality level as at the dream level, although the blond actress is played all the way through by Naomi Watts.

Most of the movie involves Selwyn's dreams or nightmares, in which she appears as a chirpy young actress named Betty. Her brunette love in the dreams is a slinky forties-style sexpot named Rita (played by Laura Elena Herring). In the dreams, "Betty" and "Rita" (a name taken by the amnesiac sexpot from a Rita Hayworth movie poster) investigate Rita's missing identity, Nancy Drew–style, and become involved, at various levels of reality, with the casting and production of a movie. There is also material about gangsters who are dictating a casting choice to the film's director (Justin Theroux). There are scenes at which neither "Betty" nor "Rita" are present; there is a haunting performance in a nightclub; there is a monstrous homeless man (played by a woman) behind a diner where several crucial conversations take place; musical numbers are performed; a decomposing corpse makes an appearance; a man in a wheelchair wields great power; a cheery elderly couple turn up later reduced to cockroach-size, and there are two lesbian scenes of unusual frankness for today's Hollywood—perhaps because one is Diane Selwyn's erotic dream, and the other her masturbatory fantasy.

Well, yes, you're thinking, I've seen the movie, so tell me something new. But that, you see, is precisely what I was unable to do by the end of the week. Having trekked through *Mulholland Dr.* in great detail, I confess myself still outside looking in. I speak for many of my fellow Interrupti, whose interpretations ranged from "Her life is flashing before her eyes at the moment of death" to "It's a version of *The Odyssey,* with every character corresponding to a character in Greek mythology."

In short: *Mulholland Dr.* resists, defies, and finally defeats logical explanation. It is impossible to produce a consistent precis of the film that accounts for everything. And there is an admirable reason for this: Like a dream, it does not have to make sense.

And yet the movie still plays—like a movie. Every individual sequence is satisfactory and effective *in and of itself*.

It's just that they resist efforts to make them neatly add up. Often we seem to watch fragments of other movies, or threads of this one never completed. An early conversation between two detectives, for example, hits the familiar rhythm of a police procedural, but then the cops never turn up again. The first lesbian scene is moody and erotic (and contains the movie's best laugh), but later we suspect that both of the women in the scene may in fact be the same woman—that Betty is Diane's dream-self, and Rita is a Betty-fantasy replacing Diane's real-life partner, who is not as attractive.

In our shot-by-shot progress, we found many details I had not seen before. Consider the mysterious man in the wheelchair. He is played by Michael J. Anderson, who is forty-three inches tall. But is the man in the wheelchair a dwarf? Or is the body in the wheelchair a fake, with Anderson standing behind it, his face positioned atop the dummy's shirt collar? That's what someone suggested. We looked at it several times. Looks like it could be possible.

Something else we spotted: In a closing scene, as Diane reaches into a bureau drawer to take out a gun, there is a split-second glimpse of— the mysterious blue box. Earlier in the film, this box is introduced with a triangular blue key. In one of the "real" scenes, a hit man tells Diane that when she finds a blue key (not the same one), she will know the hit has taken place. Perhaps the blue box represents no secrets, but is simply a possession which Diane's dream combines with a blue key to symbolize the death she has paid for. And the monster behind the diner, who has the blue box in its paper bag, may be a displaced form of the decomposing corpse that Betty and Rita find in the dream, and that Diane imagines is the result of the hit? (Unless, of course, that is Diane's corpse.)

And so on. One clue to the movie may be the confusing number of blond actresses. Naomi Watts plays "Betty" and Diane, who look so different (Salon notes) that Watts deserves praise for creating such different appearances, Then there is a waitress in the diner, named Diane Selwyn, who is not played by Watts (although the dreamer may have transferred her own name to the waitress's name tag). And a singer in an audition scene who looks confusingly like Betty, but isn't.

I mention all these blonds not to explain them, but to remind us of a 1977 Luis Buñuel film named *That Obscure Object of Desire*, in which two different actresses interchangeably played the heroine, with no explanation, and without any of the other characters noticing. Buñuel was a surrealist, and Lynch's work has always suggested that he treasures him. Perhaps *Mulholland Dr.* can be seen as the first surrealist film of the twenty-first century.

I suspect the best way to appreciate *Mulholland Dr.* is simply to experience it as a series of scenes, each one with a power and consistency of its own, that do not "add up" to a logical plot summary, or cannot be reduced to an explanation—although various patterns and narratives form out of the mist and then evaporate. As we all staggered out at the end of our Boulder odyssey, that seemed to be the consensus—although I am still getting e-mails from people who have suddenly figured it all out.

Sight & Sound Best Film Poll

August 12, 2002—It is now, once again, as official as such things can be: *Citizen Kane*, directed by Orson Welles, is the greatest film of all time. So declare 108 movie directors and 145 movie critics from all over the world in the 2002 *Sight & Sound* poll to determine the best films ever made.

Sight & Sound, the magazine of the British Film Institute, has been conducting its poll every ten years since 1952. Because it is worldwide and reaches out to voters who are presumably experts, it is by far the most respected of the countless polls of great movies—the only one most serious movie people take seriously.

Citizen Kane routinely wins such polls, but of course all polls are a matter of apples and oranges, and it is instructive that even though it won, *Kane* was voted for by only 39 percent of the directors, and 32 percent of the critics. Altogether, the two groups nominated 885 different films, and somewhere in the world there are serious cineasts who believe William Castle's *The Tingler,* Radley Metzger's *The Opening of Misty Beethoven,* and Russ Meyer's *Faster, Pussycat! Kill! Kill!* belong on the list.

Because some great directors divided their support among several different titles, the magazine also compiled lists of great directors. Welles places first among both directors and critics, but it is interesting to find four names here that are not represented among the top ten films: Billy Wilder, Ingmar Berman, Jean-Luc Godard, and John Ford. Perhaps they diluted their chances by making too many good films.

Scrutinizing the lists uncovers countless trends. It is clear, for example, that the directors have lost interest in silent films, and include none of them among their favorites. The critics include two (*Sunrise* and *Battleship Potemkin*). Both groups have abandoned their long-standing affection for silent comedy, and neither Charlie Chaplin nor Buster Keaton made either list this time.

Only four films are on both lists (*Kane, The Godfather* and *The Godfather Part II,* 8½, and

Vertigo). The critics prefer Kubrick's *2001* but the directors like his *Dr. Strangelove*. Only the critics picked a musical (*Singin' in the Rain*), and neither group picked a single Western (Ford's *The Searchers* was fifth among the critics in 1992). In combining the votes for the first two *Godfather* films, the editors set themselves up for a controversy, because some participants voted for one and not the other.

It seems clear this time around that *Vertigo* has moved decisively into the lead as Hitchcock's most respected film. The critics put it in second place, just five votes behind first place, and the directors had it in a tie for sixth. Such Hitchcock titles as *Notorious, Rear Window,* and *Psycho* are often the choices of other polls, but with the serious crowd, *Vertigo,* Hitch's most autobiographical film, usually leads.

The moviegoer of some enthusiasm will have heard of most of the films on both lists, but a few titles are not widely known, probably including Renoir's *Le Règle du Jeu (Rules of the Game),* Ozu's *Tokyo Story,* and Murnau's *Sunrise,* a silent film by the German master, which shared the very first Academy Award.

What is fairly clear from both lists is that the critics and directors think great movies stopped being made circa 1980. The newest film on the directors' list is Scorsese's *Raging Bull* (1980), and the critics select nothing since The *Godfather Part II* (1974), which may have gotten in on the coattails of the 1972 film.

None of the most-heralded films of more recent decades made the cut. Not *Pulp Fiction,* with votes from three critics and four directors, or *Schindler's List* (one critic, one director) or *Fargo* (two critics) or von Trier's Dogma standard-bearer *Breaking the Waves* (four critics, one director) or Kieslowski's Three Colors trilogy, ignored by the directors, which got two critics' votes for *Blue,* one each for *White* and *Red,* and three for the trilogy as a whole.

Comparing the 2002 list to the 1992 list, it's as if time didn't stand still, exactly, but moved sideways. *Raging Bull, The Godfather,* and *2001* were also the newest films ten years ago. Now they are ten years older and nothing has come along since worthy of the *S&S* voters' attention.

When non-pro moviegoers are polled, the results are much more current. The Internet Movie Database, which is the most-used worldwide movie Website, polls its users and accumulates thousands of votes. Five of its top ten films were made since 1990: *Shawshank Redemption* (1994); *Lord of the Rings: The Fellowship of the Ring* (2001); *Schindler's List* (1993), and *Memento* (2000). The IMDb rates *The Godfather* first, *Citizen Kane* fifth.

What does this mean? Well, it might mean that if you have labored for a lifetime watching films and know a lot about them, you believe the cinema has gone to hell since about 1980. Or it may mean that the IMDb's voters are mostly voting on recent titles (they rate each film individually with a point system, instead of composing lists of ten), and *Citizen Kane* has done amazingly well. Or it might mean absolutely nothing at all. That's the thing about these polls.

Directors' Top Ten 2002 (108 directors)

1. *Citizen Kane* (Welles) 42 votes
2. *The Godfather* and *The Godfather Part II* (Coppola) 27 votes
3. *8½* (Fellini) 19 votes
4. *Lawrence of Arabia* (Lean) 15 votes
5. *Dr. Strangelove* (Kubrick) 14 votes
6. (tie) *Bicycle Thieves* (De Sica) 13 votes
6. *Raging Bull* (Scorsese) 13 votes
6. *Vertigo* (Hitchcock) 13 votes
9. (tie) *Rashomon* (Kurosawa) 11 votes*
9. *La Règle du Jeu* (Renoir) 12 votes
9. *Seven Samurai* (Kurosawa) 12 votes

*This appears to be a discrepancy. There should be a tie for ninth between *Le Règle du Jeu* and *Seven Samurai*, with *Rashomon* one vote shy. I have queried *Sight & Sound* without avail.

Critics' Top Ten 2002 (145 critics)

1. *Citizen Kane* (Welles) 46 votes
2. *Vertigo* (Hitchcock) 41 votes
3. *La Règle du Jeu* (Renoir) 30 votes
4. *The Godfather* and *The Godfather Part II* (Coppola) 23 votes

5. *Tokyo Story* (Ozu) 22 votes
6. *2001: A Space Odyssey* (Kubrick) 21 votes
7. (tie) *Battleship Potemkin* (Eisenstein) 19 votes
7. *Sunrise* (Murnau) 19 votes
9. *8½* (Fellini) 18 votes
10. *Singin' in the Rain* (Kelly, Donen) 17 votes

Directors' Top Ten Directors

1. Orson Welles
2. Federico Fellini
3. Akira Kurosawa
4. Francis Ford Coppola
5. Alfred Hitchcock
6. Stanley Kubrick
7. Billy Wilder
8. Ingmar Bergman
9. (tie) Martin Scorsese
9. David Lean
9. Jean Renoir

Critics' Top Ten Directors

1. Orson Welles
2. Alfred Hitchcock
3. Jean-Luc Godard
4. Jean Renoir
5. Stanley Kubrick
6. Akira Kurosawa
7. Federico Fellini
8. John Ford
9. Sergei Eisenstein
10. (tie) Francis Ford Coppola
10. Yasujiro Ozu

Votes of Ten Selected Directors

Bernardo Bertolucci (Italy): *La Règle du Jeu* (Renoir); *Sansho Dayu* (Mizoguchi); *Germany Year Zero* (Rossellini); *À Bout de Souffle* (Godard); *Stagecoach* (Ford); *Blue Velvet* (Lynch); *City Lights* (Chaplin); *Marnie* (Hitchcock); *Accattone* (Pasolini); *Touch of Evil* (Welles).

Roger Corman (United States): *Battleship Potemkin* (Eisenstein); *Citizen Kane* (Welles); *The Seventh Seal* (Bergman); *Lawrence of Arabia* (Lean); *The Godfather* (Coppola); *The Grapes of Wrath* (Ford); *Shane* (Stevens); *On the Waterfront* (Kazan); *Star Wars* (Lucas); *The Cabinet of Dr. Caligari* (Wiene).

Cameron Crowe (United States): *The Apartment* (Wilder); *La Règle du Jeu* (Renoir); *La Dolce Vita* (Fellini); *Manhattan* (Allen); *The*

Best Years of Our Lives (Wyler); *To Kill a Mockingbird* (Mulligan); *Harold and Maude* (Ashby); *Pulp Fiction* (Tarantino); *Quadrophenia* (Roddam); *Ninotchka* (Lubitsch).

Milos Forman (United States): *Amarcord* (Fellini); *American Graffiti* (Lucas); *Citizen Kane* (Welles); *City Lights* (Chaplin); *The Deer Hunter* (Cimino); *Les Enfants du Paradis* (Carné); *Giant* (Stevens); *The Godfather* (Coppola); *Miracle in Milan* (De Sica); *Raging Bull* (Scorsese).

Jim Jarmusch (United States): *L'Atalante* (Vigo); *Tokyo Story* (Ozu); *They Live by Night* (N. Ray); *Bob le Flambeur* (Melville); *Sunrise* (Murnau); *The Cameraman* (Sedgwick); *Mouchette* (Bresson); *Seven Samurai* (Kurosawa); *Broken Blossoms* (Griffith); *Rome, Open City* (Rossellini).

Norman Jewison (Canada): *Bicycle Thieves* (De Sica); *The Bridge on the River Kwai* (Lean); *Casablanca* (Curtiz); *Citizen Kane* (Welles); *City Lights* (Chaplin); *8½* (Fellini); *The 400 Blows* (Truffaut); *Gunga Din* (Stevens); *Rashomon* (Kurosawa); *The Wizard of Oz* (Fleming).

Mira Nair (India): *An Angel at My Table* (Campion); *The Battle of Algiers* (Pontecorvo); *Dekalog* (Kieslowski); *The Double Life of Véronique* (Kieslowski); *8½* (Fellini); *The Godfather* (Coppola); *In the Mood for Love* (Wong); *La Jetée* (Marker); *The Music Room* (S. Ray); *Pyaasa* (Dutt); *Raging Bull* (Scorsese); *Time of the Gypsies* (Kusturica).

Quentin Tarantino (United States): *The Good, the Bad, and the Ugly* (Leone); *Rio Bravo* (Hawks); *Taxi Driver* (Scorsese); *His Girl Friday* (Hawks); *Rolling Thunder* (Flynn); *They All Laughed* (Bogdanovich); *The Great Escape* (J. Sturges); *Carrie* (De Palma); *Coffy* (Hill); *Dazed and Confused* (Linklater); *Five Fingers of Death* (Chang); *Hi Diddle Diddle* (Stone).

Sidney Lumet (United States): *The Best Years of Our Lives* (Wyler); *Fanny and Alexander* (Bergman); *The Godfather* (Coppola); *The Grapes of Wrath* (Ford); *Intolerance* (Griffith); *The Passion of Joan of Arc* (Dreyer); *Ran* (Kurosawa); *Roma* (Fellini); *Singin' in the Rain* (Kelly, Donen); *2001: A Space Odyssey* (Kubrick).

John Waters (United States): *All That Heaven Allows* (Sirk); *Baby Doll* (Kazan); *Boom!* (Losey); *Brink of Life* (Bergman); *The Chelsea Girls* (Warhol); *8½* (Fellini); *Faster, Pussycat! Kill! Kill!* (Meyer); *La Maman et la putain* (Eustache); *The Tingler* (W. Castle); *The Wizard of Oz* (Fleming).

Votes of Ten Selected Critics

David Ansen *(Newsweek)*: *Chimes at Midnight* (Welles); *The Conformist* (Bertolucci); *Hope and Glory* (Boorman); *Jules et Jim* (Truffaut); *McCabe & Mrs. Miller* (Altman); *La Notte di San Lorenzo* (Tavianis); *La Règle du Jeu* (Renoir); *Sherlock Jr.* (Keaton); *The Third Man* (Reed); *Trouble in Paradise* (Lubitsch).

Michel Ciment (editor of *Positif*, France): *Barry Lyndon* (Kubrick); *L'Atalante* (Vigo); *La Règle du Jeu* (Renoir); *Madame de...* (Ophuls); *Sunrise* (Murnau); *The General* (Keaton); *The Travelling Players* (Angelopoulos); *Ugetsu Monogatari* (Mizoguchi); *White Heat* (Walsh); *Salvatore Giuliano* (Rosi).

David Denby *(New Yorker)*: *L'avventura* (Antonioni); *Citizen Kane* (Welles); *Dekalog* (Kieslowski); *The Godfather* and *The Godfather Part II* (Coppola); *Seven Samurai* (Kurosawa); *Sunrise* (Murnau); *La Règle du Jeu* (Renoir); *The Third Man* (Reed); *Weekend* (Godard); *Vertigo* (Hitchcock).

Roger Ebert *(Chicago Sun-Times)*: *Aguirre, Wrath of God* (Herzog); *Apocalypse Now* (Coppola); *Citizen Kane* (Welles); *Dekalog* (Kieslowski); *La Dolce Vita* (Fellini); *The General* (Keaton); *Raging Bull* (Scorsese); *2001: A Space Odyssey* (Kubrick); *Tokyo Story* (Ozu); *Vertigo* (Hitchcock).

Gilles Jacob (director, Cannes Film Festival): *L'Atalante* (Vigo); *Earth* (Dovzhenko); *The Empress Yang Kwei-Fei* (Mizoguchi); *Fanny and Alexander* (Bergman); *Ikiru* (Kurosawa); *The Last Laugh* (Murnau); *The Music Room* (S. Ray); *My Apprenticeship* (Donskoi); *Nanook of the North* (Flaherty); *Our Daily Bread* (Vidor).

Nick James (editor of *Sight & Sound*): *Andrei Roublev* (Tarkovsky); *L'Argent* (L'Herbier); *Barry Lyndon* (Kubrick); *Black Narcissus* (Powell, Pressburger); *The Conformist* (Bertolucci); *Hotel Terminus: Klaus Barbie, His Life and Times* (Ophuels); *A One and a Two...* (Yang); *Out of the Past* (Tourneur); *Singin' in the Rain* (Kelly, Donen); *Taxi Driver* (Scorsese).

Li Cheuk-To (Chairman of the Hong Kong Critics Guild): *Au Hazard Balthazar* (Bresson); *Floating Clouds* (Naruse); *The General* (Keaton); *Mirror* (Tarkovsky); *Pather Panchali* (S. Ray); *The Puppetmaster* (Hou); *Spring in a Small Town* (Fei); *Tabu* (Murnau); *Two or Three Things I Know about Her* (Godard); *Vertigo* (Hitchcock).

Todd McCarthy *(Variety): Trouble in Paradise* (Lubitsch); *The Scarlet Empress* (von Sternberg); *Le Crime de Monsieur Lange* (Renoir); *To Have and Have Not* (Hawks); *Notorious* (Hitchcock); *Tirez Sur le Pianiste* (Truffaut); *Lawrence of Arabia* (Lean); *Le Mépris* (Godard); *Chimes at Midnight* (Welles); *The Godfather Part II* (Coppola).

Jonathan Rosenbaum *(Chicago Reader): Les Vampires* (Feuillade); *M* (Lang); *The Story of the Late Chrysanthemums* (Mizoguchi); *Ivan the Terrible* (Eisenstein); *Gentlemen Prefer Blondes* (Hawks); *Last Year at Marienbad* (Resnais); *The House Is Black* (Farokhzad); *Gertrud* (Dreyer); *Playtime* (Tati); *When It Rains* (Burnett).

David Thomson *(London Independent): Blue Velvet* (Lynch); *Celine and Julie Go Boating* (Rivette); *Citizen Kane* (Welles); *The Conformist* (Bertolucci); *His Girl Friday* (Hawks); *A Man Escaped* (Bresson); *Pierrot le Fou* (Godard); *La Règle du Jeu* (Renoir); *That Obscure Object of Desire* (Buñuel); *Ugetsu Monogatari* (Mizoguchi).

Interviews

Robert Altman

December 18, 2001—"The saddest words," Robert Altman was saying, "are when somebody says they 'saw' my movie. That means they saw it once. That's not seeing it. I make movies that need to be seen three or four times. This movie, for example, needs to be seen once just to get the lay of the land. Then, when you know who everybody is and how they're related, you can go back and see all the things you didn't know were significant the first time."

He smiled that Altman smile, the one where he seems to be amused by the extent of the conspiracy against him. We were sitting in the dining room of the Shepperton Studios outside London one day last May while he was filming *Gosford Park*.

"Of course to make a movie my way is commercial suicide," he said. "A movie these days needs to be made so the audience can understand it immediately without thinking about it at all, or even being conscious that they're watching it. So I don't expect it to be commercially successful. Critically, it will be a success. And you know what? I am the producer, and frankly, my dear, I don't give a damn."

Altman always talks like this. Every movie is destined to fail. I don't know if he really believes it, but I think the bunker mentality is important to his work: He makes films without fear of the consequences, and that's why he works so much and is so prolific, while more timid directors hedge their bets and test the waters.

As I write, it is December and *Gosford Park* has gotten him named as the year's best director by the American Film Institute and the New York Film Critics Circle. So he is right and it is a critical success. It opens in January, and then we will see how it does commercially.

The movie is risky and audacious. Altman takes on the enormous challenge of a cast of thirty actors, almost all of them famous and recognizable, and assembles them in a British country house for a weekend party that is interrupted by murder.

"The murder is never solved," he chortled, which will surprise some viewers, who will think that it is. The country house murder is, of course, a staple of British crime fiction, supplying the plot for the longest-running play in history, Agatha Christie's *The Mousetrap*. But *Gosford Park* is Agatha and more. "It's *Ten Little Indians* meets *Rules of the Game*," he said, crossing classics by Christie and the French master Jean Renoir, whose film assembled the rich and their servants for a 1930s country weekend that erupts into class warfare.

In the Altman version, equal time is given to upstairs and downstairs. We meet the servants, led by the butler (Alan Bates), the first footman (Richard E. Grant), and the housekeeper (Helen Mirren), and including other cooks, maids, and the servants of the weekend guests. And we meet the lord of the manor (Michael Gambon), his sex-starved wife (Kristin Scott Thomas), her sharp-tongued aunt (Maggie Smith), and such guests as the Hollywood star Ivor Novello (Jeremy Northam) and his producer (Bob Balaban).

Altman's camera moves freely through the rooms, corridors, and staircases of the vast house; some audience members may want to know where it is so they can visit it, and will be disappointed to learn that a great deal of it is a set designed by Altman's son Steven ("When I die, Steve will be the hottest art director around").

I'd spent the morning watching Altman at work. He doesn't direct his actors so much as confide in them. At seventy-seven he has directed so long that it is like breathing to him, and there is a serenity on the set, as if all will go well because it must. He is deferred to, like a president or a symphony conductor, and has a certain quiet grandeur in his manner, as if long accustomed to power and attention.

There is a television hookup that allows him to look at an instant relay, and then replay, of what is going into the camera. At one point his cinematographer, Andrew Dunn, mentions a bad reflection on a doorknob. Does he want to check it out on TV? "Let me just talk about the film without looking at the screen," Altman says, impatient with technology, sure of what he wants.

At lunch, Altman refers to the life of a director who is always in production.

"We were out driving one day, looking for a location, I think, and it was time to go and have lunch. We went into a shopping center, and I suddenly realized there wasn't one single person there that would know who I was. We had stepped over into real life. We got lost. There was no assistant director around to do what I wanted him to do.

"I realized that if I stopped making movies, I would die, because my entire existence presupposes a movie in production. I don't remember the years when things happened, but I remember the movie I was directing when they happened. The movies are the eras of my life. In fact, the movies *are* life."

This is literally true. In the thirty-three years since his career as a feature director properly started, in 1968, he has made thirty-three movies—plus directing television *(Tanner '88)*, Broadway plays *(Come Back to the Five and Dime, Jimmy Dean, Jimmy Dean)*, and operas *(McTeague* for the Lyric of Chicago). He was in his forties when this act in his life started; before that, he did episodic TV, low-budget quickie features, and even industrial films. *M*A*S*H* in 1970 was his breakthrough, and since then perhaps no director has made more titles of the first rank, including *McCabe and Mrs. Miller, Nashville, The Player,* and *Short Cuts.*

His films tend to embody technical challenges: large casts (or one man alone in a room), interlocking plots, difficult locations, quirky subject matter. This time it is the decision to cast so many stars in the same picture.

"It's easy because most of them are British," he said. "They come to work. I've wondered sometimes why the British are such good actors, and I think maybe I know. It's their manners. They're taught as children to behave in a certain way, disguising their real feelings—so the British are all acting all the time, without knowing it."

With so many actors, so many overlapping lines, so many cues and such long shots, there are many things that can go wrong. Altman said he didn't care. "If it gets too perfect, it's false," he said. "I'm looking for mistakes. Shelley

Duvall's skirt got caught when she slammed a car door in *Three Women.* I said, Great! Leave it in! Oscar Wilde said that people basically die when they finally realize the only thing they don't regret are their mistakes. The saddest thing I can think of is an old person saying, 'But I did all the things they told me to do. Why did it turn out this way?'"

Altman rarely does what they tell him to do. He claims to always be looking for his next job, and likes to say, "I fiddle on the corner where the quarters are." I don't think he fiddles for quarters. I think his musical talent is whistling in the dark.

Halle Berry

January 31, 2002—I told Halle Berry this story. I was on the plane to Sundance. Sitting across the aisle was Michael Barker, honcho of Sony Classics. We were talking about Halle Berry's performance in *Monster's Ball.* Barker told me: "It is the best performance I have seen in a movie since Marlon Brando in *Last Tango in Paris.*"

"He said that?" said Berry, disbelievingly.

And it isn't even his picture, I said. And then he said, "My only worry is that not enough Academy voters will see it to find out how good it is."

On February 12, we will all find out. That's when the nominations are announced. Berry has already been nominated by the Screen Actors Guild, the American Film Institute, the Golden Globes, and countless critics' groups. But the movie goes into national release only on February 1, after "qualifying runs" in New York and Los Angeles.

I think it is the best film of the year, an exploration of two lonely and desperate people who reach out to each other to save their own lives. Berry stars with the great Billy Bob Thornton. She is a waitress in an all-night diner, drinks too much, has a troubled relationship with her chubby son. Thornton is a guard on Death Row, a racist, who executes Berry's former husband—although for a long time she doesn't know that.

It would be too simple to say they fall in love. Love is a luxury they cannot afford. It is clearer to say they need each other.

"They have the same amount of pain," Berry said. "It looks different, it is different, but it's the same, and they both need each other. They need the touch, the human connection. They're both dead inside, lonely souls. Dying a slow death. And when they meet each other it's like the kiss of life."

It's not an "interracial relationship" because they're not thinking about race, I said. That's far from their minds. He's gone through life parroting his father's racist line—he's an abused child and an abusive father—but racism falls away from him like a snake's dead skin.

"It supersedes color," she said. "Color is the issue for others but not for them."

For Berry, the movie is a crucial breakthrough. "Now other directors can see that I can do this," she said. She is a star who before *Monster's Ball* was not always taken seriously as an actress. It was clear she had great talent, but it was obscured by her beauty. Although *Monster's Ball* was shot on a limited budget and she was paid far less than her usual salary, she had to fight for the role—to convince director Marc Forster to look below the surface and see that she could play this waitress named Leticia.

"Marc didn't want me," she said, during a talk in Chicago. She was passing through town on her way to London, where she will be a Bond girl in the new 007 movie—a role on the other end of her career scale. "To his credit, he was so clear about who she was and how he saw her. And he just didn't see me as Leticia."

What did you do to persuade him?

"We had a lot of talks. I expressed my passion. I think I made him realize that my passion matched his own passion for the project. He almost didn't get to direct this film because he was new and some people didn't believe that he could do it. And so I asked him, please don't let me be a victim of the very thing that you yourself are fighting. Because you've never seen me do it, it doesn't mean that I can't. He took a chance."

Forster had made only one earlier movie, *Everything Put Together*, a 1999 Sundance entry unseen by me. Berry says she saw it, and although it was different from *Monster's Ball*, she liked the direction and the passion. Forster has a good feel for actors: "Never before have I worked with a director who said he would take however long it takes, to get where he wanted me to get to. Normally, it's like, that was great

but can you make it like two minutes shorter? Or, can you stand over there while you do it? He let us be, and that's never happened before; he just let those moments develop, and I thought that was really wonderful."

Being beautiful is an advantage in life, I said. But I suppose it can also be a disadvantage, in the sense that maybe he thought you were too good looking to be this sad and lonely.

"If he thought that, I remember telling him sad and lonely comes in all different kinds of packages, and most beautiful people are somewhat sad and lonely. They live somewhat of an isolated existence."

Berry got a lot of publicity on her previous picture, *Swordfish* (2001), for a scene in which she bared her breasts and received, it was reported, a $500,000 bonus for doing so—an amount far greater than her total salary for *Monster's Ball*, which has a good deal more nudity and sexuality.

I asked her about the disparity between the two films and she smiled.

"Well, the nudity in *Swordfish* was totally gratuitous," she said. "It didn't have to be there. I knew that when I read the script. I said, you know, guys, this doesn't have to be here. You would have the same movie without it. And (producer) Joel Silver said, yeah, I know, but I want it anyway.

"I took that as a challenge. I thought, there's a reason this is being presented to me. I now know what that reason was. It was because *Monster's Ball* was coming, and I would never have been able to even think about tackling a role like *Monster's Ball* had I not done *Swordfish* and got through that inhibition that was somewhat holding me back.

"With *Monster's Ball*, it's not even about sex, that scene; it's so unsexy and it's not about sexual titillation. It's about two people getting what they need—and that's the air to breathe. It's not a sexual thrill or sexual pleasure. Without that scene you don't understand why these people will be together; you understand after it why you want them to be together, why you root for them. And without that I don't think you would be able to make that big leap you have to make with their characters."

When you say it's not about sex, I said, there's another scene I found fascinating. You're a little bit drunk next to him on the couch, and you're waving your arms around and your hand keeps landing in his lap, and you don't notice it and either he doesn't notice it or he doesn't want to admit that he notices it. The audience notices it and it's funny because the two of you—your minds are elsewhere.

"Totally. And you know, that scene is the first time in the movie where they're really just people. Billy Bob's character isn't there with the issues of his father; she's not there with the issues of her dead husband or her son. They're there as just people being human, having a moment, and they naturally go where their hearts really want them to go."

What are your thoughts about the Oscars?

"I never really thought that in my lifetime my name would be synonymous with Oscar. I never believed I would get the opportunity to play a character that would be worthy, that would be seen in the way movies have to be seen to even be thought about for Oscar. If that should happen, that would be huge for me. Women of color don't often get roles that allow us to be in these categories, you know."

Although it's getting better. The casting is a little more color-blind than it was ten or certainly twenty years ago.

"It's slow but that's okay, because real evolution takes time. If it happened too quickly, I don't think I'd wanna hang my hat on it. I think it would disappear as fast as it came."

You got a lot of praise and honors for playing Dorothy Dandridge in that made-for-TV movie. The color line in movies essentially destroyed her.

"Part of it," Berry said, "is when she got nominated for that Oscar, after that Hollywood really didn't know what to do with her. She had nowhere to go and that eventually ate her alive. Hopefully, today—well, Angela Bassett got nominated a few years ago and it didn't eat her alive, so I know it's a new day. There are more opportunities for us."

One more comment about beauty, I said. Somebody asked me, isn't Halle Berry too beautiful to play an all-night waitress? I answered, If you want to see her not looking beautiful, check out a movie named *B.A.P.* where she has gold teeth and a hairdo that looks like it has things living in it.

Berry laughed. "I hear about *B.A.P.* all the time," she said. "Well, I'll tell you what. That came at a particular time in my life, right after the divorce. And it was either go to work in that movie, or hang myself with the shower curtain. So you know what? I'm glad I did it."

Peter Bogdanovich

April 23, 2002—It was the kind of story that made you willing to linger over the after-dinner coffee. "What do you know about the death of Thomas Ince?" Peter Bogdanovich asked me. I knew a little. Like everyone with a fascination for Hollywood gossip, I'd read Kenneth Anger's legendary book *Hollywood Babylon,* in which he speculates that Ince, the "Wizard of Westerns," died after drinking bootleg booze on William Randolph Hearst's yacht.

"Hearst made the bad mistake of trying to hush up the whole affair," Anger wrote. "The result was that the rumors kicked back on him: It was widely whispered that Hearst himself had killed Tom Ince when he caught the unfortunate Wizard in an intimate clinch with Marion Davies!" Davies was then Hearst's mistress.

"Orson Welles had a fascinating version of that story," Bogdanovich told me. "According to him, Willie was convinced Marion was having an affair with Charlie Chaplin. During a cruise on Hearst's yacht, Hearst was overcome with jealousy and took a shot at a man he thought was Chaplin. It was a case of mistaken identity, and Thomas Ince was killed. The true story of the death never came out. In fact, despite his fame at the time, the cause of Ince's death was never established, there was never an investigation, and no one on the yacht was ever questioned."

That sounds, I said, like a great idea for a movie.

"It does, doesn't it?" said Bogdanovich. "Orson Welles told me there was a version of the scandal in an early draft of the screenplay for *Citizen Kane* (the 1941 Welles film universally believed to be a thinly veiled version of Hearst's life). But he took the scene out of the movie. Orson said, 'I thought Hearst could have done it—but I didn't think Charlie Kane was a killer.'"

It happened that as Bogdanovich told me this story, we were aboard the *QE2,* crossing to Southampton on the 25th anniversary voyage of the Telluride Film Festival, in 1998. When Bogdanovich returned to New York there was a script waiting for him. It was an adaptation of Steven Peros's play about the very same scandal. Fate was sending him a message. No director is more steeped in Hearst/Welles/Kane/Hollywood lore than Bogdanovich, and now here is *The Cat's Meow,* his movie based on the long-ago rumors.

This is Peter Bogdanovich's first theatrical movie in eight years, a comeback for a man who like Welles had an early Hollywood triumph and then was exiled to the outer darkness of the unbankable. A film critic and magazine writer, Bogdanovich was only thirty-one when he made *The Last Picture Show* (1971), a masterpiece, and followed it with the huge hits *Paper Moon* and *What's Up, Doc?* Then somehow he lost his magic touch, and directed a string of flops.

Some of them were very good films, like *Saint Jack* (1979), with Ben Gazzara as a conniving Singapore pimp, and *Mask* (1985), with Eric Stoltz as a modern youth with Elephant Man's disease, and Cher as his mother. But most lost money, and although *Mask* did respectable business, Bogdanovich shot himself in the foot by holding a renegade press conference at Cannes to attack the studio's version of the film.

"How do you like that?" Bogdanovich was musing not long ago in Chicago, where he'd come to promote *The Cat's Meow.* "Cher wins the best actress award at Cannes, and I'm bad-mouthing my own film."

I met him for the first time in 1968, after he'd directed the low-budget thriller *Targets.* He was young and brash and filled with confidence. A few years later, at the height of his golden boy period, he bordered on the insufferable. Now he has mellowed, and says quietly, "I'm glad to be directing a film again." He's recognized on the street—but as an actor on *The Sopranos,* not as a director.

We talked about new movies. He said some audiences complained that *Moulin Rouge* was paced too quickly, but recalled what Frank Capra told him: "If you play something at normal speed, it'll seem slow. Faster equals normal, fast equals double." He used that rule when directing the screwball comedy *What's Up, Doc?* he said. "Barbra Streisand asked me, 'Can I have a moment here?' And I barked at her, 'No moments!'"

What did he think about all the "director's cuts" and other variant versions of movies?

"I can understand the desire to improve a film," he said. "I've added footage to *Last Picture Show* twice, and I still think it could be longer. Sometimes you are simply restoring damage. On *Texasville* (the sequel to *Picture Show*) I was forced to take out twenty-five minutes.

"My father was a painter. He wouldn't sign a painting until it was sold. Once a client bought a painting and asked him to come to his house to sign it. My father came over with his palate and went into the room with the painting, and when the client looked in half an hour later, he was busy repainting it."

It was unusual these days, I said, for a director to tour to promote his movies. Now journalists are summoned on junkets.

"Jimmy Stewart once told me," he said, "that if you're going to promote a picture, go to the town and say yes to all the appearances—at the theater, at city hall, at the radio station, wherever. What's the use of going if they don't know you're there?"

Paul Cox

September 2, 2001—Paul Cox is a hero of the cinema, a man who lives in seclusion in Melbourne, Australia, and turns out one extraordinary film after another. He doesn't use stars, ignores marketing advice, makes movies from his heart. In appearance he is like a poet or professor, always in a corduroy jacket, hair needing a trim, fiddling with his pipe. In his films he is a bold radical, often making stylistic experiments, but just as often doing something that is even more dangerous—making films about real and ordinary people.

Consider *Innocence.* This is one of the best films of the year. Indeed, Andrew Sarris calls it "the most powerfully emotional love story of the year" and "a film for the ages." I write that, and you think maybe you'd like to see it. Then I add that it's a love story involving two people in their late sixties, and you think maybe you wouldn't like to see it. But why not? Falling in love is easy at twenty. By old age it is a minefield, and anyone with the romantic imagination to risk it is daring and undefeated.

Innocence is about Claire and Andreas, who were in love when they were teenagers. Fifty years have passed, and now Andreas finds that Claire lives in the same city. He is a widower. She is married. He contacts her, and they find that the love and passion they felt then is still real—that no subsequent experience has touched their first love. Cox says he calls the film *Innocence* because after a first true love "you never love like that again in your life."

What his characters discover, he says, is that life and passion never die until we surrender them. But most people live on autopilot, and too many old people "live death and not life." For Andreas, it is easy: He sees Claire again, and loves her as much as ever. For Claire, it is harder, because for many years she has been in a marriage of habit, and she must consider leaving the husband she may not love but feels a commitment to, and a sympathy for.

The success of the film rests on the warmth and attractiveness of the characters, who are played by the luminous Julia Blake and gentle, lovable Charles "Bud" Tingwell. (Speaking of daring, what kind of courage do you think it takes to be a professional actor and insist on that "Bud"?) There are scenes of physical passion here (not graphic, but strong in feeling) that are so real, so romantic, it absolutely doesn't matter how old the actors are, because it is a boy and a girl who are kissing.

Cox himself is sixty-one, a filmmaker who was born in Holland, came to Australia on a scholarship, fell in love, immigrated, and has lived in Melbourne for some thirty-five years. His films are well loved but not widely known. He is championed by festivals like Telluride, which seek out the real directors and are uninterested in the nine-day wonders. The Chicago festival has championed him since the early days of *Lonely Hearts* (1981), *A Man of Flowers* (1984), and *My First Wife* (1985). When *Innocence* played in the Chicago festival last October, it was received with such enthusiasm and emotion that Cox was visibly moved. At Toronto 2000, the film placed third in the People's Choice balloting (since *Crouching Tiger, Hidden Dragon* was first, it is remarkable it placed at all).

And yet . . . Cox told me that when the film played at Telluride last year, he overheard two filmgoers deciding not to see it, because "it's about two old people making love."

"I know that when this film reaches an audience, it goes terribly well," Cox told me, in a Chicago coffee shop that had a corner where he could smoke his pipe. "I've seen it everywhere and we've had enormous response. Even when people see the trailer they're already moved by it. So I have no respect for people who are conditioned to accept only a certain formula. There was a little review in a Chicago paper today which is the typical cynical attitude of those people, accusing the film of being sentimental—which means the critic was unable to accept the theme, and incapable of opening himself to the film. It is not 'sentimental' at all."

The idea for the film came to him, Cox said, "from a photograph by Cartier-Bresson where there's an old couple walking hand in hand away from the camera. I always had this pinned on my wall. And I have a photograph of my own parents the last time I saw them together. They walked away from me holding hands. So all these things add up and then something happens. A little glimpse of light comes to you."

He is, he said, "one of those maniacs who really has to love the characters. Otherwise, I can't work with it. I can't do it. I have to love them passionately and madly. Otherwise there's no point."

Of humanity in general, he is less approving.

"I think of humanity or civilization as a pack of rats. I think together we're a very bad species. But individually people are very beautiful when you give them some time and some patience and some understanding. You'll find that people you think are absolute asses can blossom and suddenly become very human. In our so-called civilization people are not end products anymore. They're used by that civilization; they're consumed by that civilization. And so they have no option but to become rats. I don't trust people and I don't mix with many people. I live a very singular life, I can assure you."

Do you think of filmmaking more as a vocation than a career?

"I certainly don't look at it as a career. It's a curse. Sometimes it's a blessing. But it's made my life very difficult and very isolated."

To such a degree that you would have given it up in order just to have been happy?

"No, I can't give it up. The idea of happiness has always eluded me anyway. I mean, not that I can't be happy or see the joke of it all but . . . let's put it this way. I can't see what else I would have done. It just sort of happened. I never went out and said this is going to be my career. It happened."

What did you think you were going to do?

"I had no idea. I had a very difficult childhood and I escaped my family in Holland and got this scholarship to go to Melbourne University. I was born two or three weeks before the war started so the first five years of my life was nothing but bombs and destruction and everybody got killed and every time we approached our street, I was always happy that the house was still standing.

"My father never recovered from that. He was also a filmmaker and quite an interesting one. But he was very bitter so I had a difficult youth. I was glad to escape. I went to Australia and stayed there for a year and then went back to Europe, but I'd fallen in love, unfortunately, or fortunately, so that's why I went back to Australia as a migrant for the second time. And then I started my own little photographic studio and I taught at an art school there, and I made little movies on a Super 8 camera as a hobby.

"I still think now if you want to do anything seriously it must be a hobby, especially film. If you have it as a profession you automatically become an ass. Sorry. If you make it a profession then you have to compromise from morning till night and make a product you cannot possibly believe in.

"But as I was teaching, the school was suddenly given a grant to start a cinema department and there was nobody else to teach it. They didn't have money to employ another lecturer there. So overnight I became lecturer in charge of cinema. I knew very little about it, although I had learned something from my father, and up in the attic at home we had a lot of old film gear which I used to play with as a child. I used to sit there and stare at it. So in the process of teaching film, within six months I suddenly realized—God, this is spectacular!"

Harrison Ford

July 2, 2002—There is a new Jack Ryan movie this summer, but Harrison Ford is not starring in it. The character he played in *Clear and Pres-*

ent Danger and *Patriot Games* is played by Ben Affleck this time, and Ford is starring as Alexei Vostrikov, the captain of the Russian submarine in *K-19*. You suspect the submarine may be doomed when you consider the movie's subtitle: *The Widowmaker.*

I got some e-mails, I told him, from people saying they understand everything about Jack Ryan in the Tom Clancy thriller *The Sum of All Fears* except why he seems to be twenty-five years younger than he used to be.

Ford smiled, that slow, wide smile that screenwriters can use in place of dialogue.

"Younger, and cuter. If you ask Tom Clancy," he said, "and I'm not suggesting that you do . . ." Pause. "I was always too old for the role. So finally he has his way. I'm happy for everybody's success with the film."

You don't sound like you miss not having done it.

"No. I was presented with a situation in which I didn't want to engage, and so I passed on it."

So actually you were making *K-19* instead.

"It would have been one or the other."

Ford probably made the right choice. He plays a different kind of character, a captain with a Russian accent, a die-hard party-liner. And *K-19* is rare in that it's an American movie told entirely through the point of view of the Russian characters. "I can't think of another film that has done that," he says.

The submarine is the jewel in the Russian underwater fleet, a new nuclear-powered boat armed with nuclear missiles. Its captain is nominally Mikhail Polenin (Liam Neeson), but so crucial is the maiden voyage that the veteran Vostrikov is put on board as senior captain. Soon it becomes clear the sub was commissioned before it was shipshape, and when there's a nuclear reactor accident, disaster looms and the two captains are at each other's throats.

"The movie is based on a real event," Ford said. We were talking during a visit to Chicago, his hometown. "This submarine did exist, and was pushed into service before it was ready. The reactor cooling system failed, and men had to go into the reactor and expose themselves to radiation to fix it."

There were supposed to be radiation suits on board, but, the crew learns, there was a shortage, so the factory sent chemical hazard suits instead. Useless.

"They really thought they were going to have a fission event," Ford told me. "They were being closely shadowed by an American destroyer, and my character thought that if his ship blew up in a nuclear explosion in close proximity to an American ship, he could well be the instrument initiating World War III."

Ford said the movie is not a documentary—his character is a "literary construction"—but in St. Petersburg he met men who survived the cruise: "They were still very emotional, and that transferred to me as an obligation to get it right."

Ford's Russian accent is there in the role, but not thick. You forget about it after awhile, but at first, well, coming from Indiana Jones, it sounds unusual.

"I wanted people to hear it and say, 'Oh, this isn't going to be a typical Harrison Ford picture,'" he said. "Besides, I grew up at the movies thinking all Russians spoke with British accents, so this was a little different."

It is possible that Ford's movies have grossed more than those of any other actor in Hollywood history. If you add up the *Star Wars* pictures and the *Indiana Jones* pictures and all the others, it makes a nice pile. And now, he said, he and Steven Spielberg and George Lucas are talking about returning to Indiana Jones for a fourth episode.

"We've had story meetings, and a writer is assigned and scribbling away, and if we get a script we like, we've all held a slot in 2004. I'd love to do it again."

The Indy series has held up, he thinks, because "we complicated the character a little more every time we went back to him. And the ambition to make a good film never wavered; that has a lot to do with Steven taking the obligation of directing every time as well."

Ford is about to hit his sixtieth birthday, which worries him not at all: "The roles are just as interesting, maybe more interesting. Look at Sean Connery. He's only twelve years older than I am, even though he plays my father from time to time. So I think I've got at least twelve more years of useful shelf life."

Have you ever noticed, I said, how everybody in Los Angeles seems to claim you worked on their kitchen in the days when you were a carpenter?

The smile again. "If I did the amount of car-

pentry work that's credited to me, I would have had an eighty-year career as a carpenter. People say Harrison Ford worked on their kitchen and I say what I want to know is, why didn't he do a better job?"

Tom Hanks

July 2, 2002—So what was it like working with Paul Newman?

This is not the kind of question you learn at the Great Interviewers' School. To call it "basic" is a kindness. But any question can be redeemed by a good answer, and Tom Hanks has one.

"Once you get past the intimidation factor, it was a great experience."

You were intimidated by working with Paul Newman?

"Oh, landy! Yes, oh yes. You just can't have the history of going to the movies that I've had and not be. I remember going to see *Hud*. And *The Hustler*. And wasn't there a movie like *Apache*?"

Fort Apache, the Bronx?

"Not that one. There was one where he was a half-breed. I want to say *Honda*."

Hombre.

"*Hombre*! That was a big movie for me."

That was his H period, I said. *Hud, Hustler, Hombre.*

"Seeing those movies was a big time for me. So to be there on the set with him . . . number one, he's much taller than you think he's going to be. And number two, those eyes. The first take on the first day, I'm not thinking about my work, I'm thinking, Holy cow! I'm in a movie looking into Paul Newman's eyes. How did this happen?"

There's a theory, I say, that no one seems like a real movie star to you unless they were a star when you were still a kid growing up. If they come along after you're twenty-one or twenty-two, then they're just your contemporaries. But if you saw them in grade school . . .

"The theory is right," Hanks says. "Al Pacino in a room, I don't know what to say to Mr. Pacino. Sean Connery, when I first met him I believe I called him 'Commander.' There's just no way around it. I think it's like when you're a freshman in high school and the upperclassmen look like they're thirty-two years old, and it isn't until you get up there you realize, what was I thinking? We're all just a bunch of stupid kids."

But Tom Hanks was definitely in a movie with Paul Newman, the upperclassman: *Road to Perdition.* Hanks was in Chicago for the movie's world premiere, which filled the Chicago Theater. He stars in the movie as an enforcer for the Chicago mob, and Newman is the boss who treats him like his own son, up to a point—and then crosses him. In the movie, Hanks has two sons, Newman has a son, and then emotionally Hanks is Newman's son, so there are three sets of fathers and sons, and a lot of room for betrayal.

"One thing I wondered, reading the script," Hanks said, "is that you have to wonder, in a Catholic community in 1931, why they only have one or two children. You wonder if they don't feel a curse. Given their money and the theology, there should be six or seven, maybe eight, kids running around. Nope. It's just these tough, cold men. Do the women in town think they're cursed?"

The theme of tortured and disintegrating families is not new to the director, Sam Mendes, who won the Oscar in 1999 for his *American Beauty.* That one starred Kevin Spacey as a man whose family drives him a little nuts, and vice versa.

I talked to your son Colin Hanks a few months ago, I said, when he was starring in *Orange County.* So there's a son going into the family business, but *Road to Perdition* is about a father who does not want his son in the business. Did your own fatherhood inform what you do in the movie?

"I think there are periods of time when you're a father," he said, "when truly the only thing you have is regrets. All the wonderful qualities of your kids are mysteries to you and all you can see is the way you've scarred or burned or somehow neglected those kids. The feeling passes, but it's true. If you have omitted a moment, if you have bypassed a day, you'll never get it back."

This was your third movie filmed in Chicago, after *Nothing in Common* and *A League of Their Own.*

"And a little of *Sleepless in Seattle.* But this was the first time in the winter. It was so cold. We were doing a scene with real snow and fake snow and rain. You do that all night long and it's tough. That's why those coats are so big and heavy, and why the hats have such big brims.

They dress for the climate with a Depression-era Gortex sensibility."

Talk of Chicago reminds me of the box-office hit *My Big Fat Greek Wedding.* It began as a one-woman show by Nia Vardalos, a Second City actress who talked about being Greek and single at thirty. The movie was produced by Hanks and his Greek-American wife, the actress Rita Wilson.

"Nia put this show on and cobbled together the money for an ad the size of a postage stamp in the *Los Angeles Times,*" Hanks said, "and Rita said she had to go see the show. She came back saying it was hilarious and I had to see it. And we loved it and Nia had already been working on a screenplay, so we helped her turn it into a movie—and if you look at it proportionally, it is one of the most profitable movies of the year, because it cost X money to make, it's grossed four times X. If you look at it from the percentages—hey, it's right up there with *Gone With the Wind.*"

Majid Majidi

April 30, 2002—This man directs such gentle films to be an artist from the evil axis. Majid Majidi, from Iran, guards his words because he knows they may be scrutinized carefully both here and at home, but look at his movies and you can see his good heart. We sit in a Chicago hotel and talk about the cinema, and I sense that in his land there is more at stake than in Hollywood—that the risks are of a different order.

His new film, *Baran,* involves Afghan refugees in Iran and the role of women in a Muslim society, and yet it is, as nearly as it can be, nonpolitical. It is just about the people involved.

A construction boss employs Afghans illegally because they will work cheaply, and when one is injured the boss agrees to hire the man's son. An Iranian worker, who has the soft job of tea boy, is angered when the son, who is not strong, is given his job. The former tea boy makes things tough for the new one, until he discovers one day that the boy ... is a girl. Thus commences a love story that makes the problems of Romeo and Juliet look like a walk in the park.

Majidi is forty-three and started acting and directing when he was twenty-two. His *Children of Heaven* (1997) grossed more than $1 million in America, a record for an Iranian film. I showed it at my 2000 Overlooked Film Festival at the free family matinee, telling the bigger kids it was all right to read the subtitles to the smaller ones—but there was not a sound, because the images held them spellbound.

It tells the story of a boy who takes his sister's shoes to be mended and loses them through no fault of his own. The two are afraid to admit this to their parents, so they devise a deception. It is a film with the universality of Chaplin, and shows the two Tehrans, rich and poor.

In 1999, Majidi made *The Color of Paradise*, about a blind boy who is raised by his father after his mother dies. The boy is smart and quick, and excels at a school for the blind, but his father fears an imperfect child will hurt his own chances in the remarriage market. It is another deeply felt film. Now comes *Baran*.

One seeks messages in these works: Is there some buried commentary on Iranian society under the strict religious laws of recent years? Majidi thinks not. The stories are simply what they are. We talk about two kinds of censorship —censorship of the government over there, and of the box office over here, where a story like *Children of Heaven* could not be made because it lacks special effects, gags, quick pacing.

Majidi tells me through his interpreter: "I don't want to only tell their stories, not my stories. I also don't want to be part of a system where I can only work if it makes money. So it's like a purgatory."

It took him three years to finance *Children of Heaven*, he said: "The commercial investors told me that the film had no commercial potential. The government agencies had problems because they thought the film was too bitter and dark. They'd say, 'We're constructing a new society. Why do you want to project such a negative image of us, in which a pair of shoes make a family fall into despair?'

"They didn't understand that the pair of shoes was just the plot device. I wanted to make a film about the greatness of the spirits of two little kids and how they can go beyond their small world through their sacrifice and altruism."

Finally he found financing from an Iranian cultural organization for children. The irony is that people all over the world did want to see *Children of Heaven*, and it did make money.

In that film he had a character of a blind peddler, and in researching the blind he found the boarding school that's shown early in *The Color of Paradise*.

"There were two students standing in front of each other in kung-fu postures," he said, "but how can you attack someone you can't see? They were relying on the noise coming from their clothing. Looking around the school, I saw them managing, going through books, getting organized, you know, check their clothing, like any other students would do.

"I would go and visit them two or three times a week. And once on a school break I took three to the northern part of Iran, which is gorgeous. There are a lot of trees, a lot of birds flying by and making noises, and there's the Caspian Sea. These children had never experienced water. That trip became the basis of *The Color of Paradise*. When they were in the water they would pick up the petals and read them as if they were Braille."

Although *Baran* is not about children, the protagonists are adolescents, naive about the ways of the world. Through them it reflects on the millions of Afghans illegally in Iran.

"The protagonist is called Latif," Majidi said. "Latif in Farsi means gentle, but in the beginning he is anything but gentle. Baran, the girl's name, means rain, and could be like a shower that brings out his real core under all the roughness and toughness."

His decision to become an actor was made in opposition to his father: "I rehearsed with a small theater group, but I had to sneak out under the pretext of going to a remedial class. My father told us how hard he was working so I and my four brothers could make somebody of ourselves, become physicians, engineers. For several years I acted in a secret way. My mother knew, but I would bribe her by doing a lot of chores around the home. I got into the Department of Fine Arts, but I told my father that I was in the Department of Engineering. He gave candies and sweets to his colleagues to let them know how proud he was of me.

"Unfortunately, he died of a stroke right around the same time, and that gave me great guilt because of the lies that I had told. I remember going to his grave and apologizing to him, saying that I did this for my heart, and didn't mean to break his heart. I figured that he wanted me to be of some service. And I decided, okay, I can do that through acting.

When I made *Children of Heaven,* I did it for my father."

Steve Martin

November 11, 2001—Steve Martin is not a wild and crazy guy, but he plays one in the movies. Actually, he doesn't. People forget he applied that label in the first place as a bald-faced lie. It applied to the dorky Czechoslovakian brothers (Martin and Dan Aykroyd) on "Saturday Night Live," and they were so manifestly *not* wild and crazy guys.

If there is a single image everyone remembers of Steve Martin, it's of him on TV with an arrow stuck through his head. But he wasn't being a guy who was so wild and crazy he would stick an arrow through his head. He was playing a guy so white-breadlike he would do anything to look wild and crazy. What he actually plays in the movies is more of a worried and reckless guy. A guy who mopes and broods and then surprises himself by making love to the woman in his dentist's chair.

He came to Toronto last September with *Novocaine,* his new comedy, and we talked on the morning of the 8th, and on the 11th all hell broke loose and the movie's opening was put on hold along with everything else.

Steve Martin is someone I would have liked to talk with after September 11, because he'd have something to say. He fits in many categories, all of them uneasily, as if wondering if this is where he belongs. He published a novel last year that was touching and true, and he is an expert on modern art, and he is capable of hosting the Academy Awards and starring in a David Mamet movie and writing for *The New Yorker* and, no doubt, brooding a lot.

He tries to pick film roles, he says, that suit him. We were talking about the complexities of *Novocaine,* which combines screwball and caper elements with a portrait of a man lashing out at his own eagerness to compromise. He plays a dentist, engaged to his hygienist (Laura Dern), who is, Martin says, "The paper cutout of his dreams, the big-haired blond." Then a dangerous woman walks into his office—dangerous, because she inspires him to do crazy things: "It's not so much that he ran into the perfect person for him, but he ran into the person who tapped into his deeper need."

Dr. Frank Sangster, the dentist, is essentially a man who wants to keep the lid on, and the movie is about how he tries to dig himself out of trouble and only digs deeper. Martin plays him fairly straight.

"Sometimes I feel like I'm expected to do a certain kind of comedy," he said. "But the suit doesn't fit all the time, and even when it does, you're just doing the same thing. People *think* they want the wild stuff, but if you actually do it they're looking for a younger, fresher face. As a comedian, I have to work hard to find a new angle that's still within the realm of my own character and body. I'm older. I look different and I have to do movies that are appropriate for that. To do a movie where I'm still trying to act like I'm twenty-eight—that wouldn't be right."

It also wouldn't be interesting, and I sense that Martin is not looking to repeat himself. Consider such recent projects as the ingenious comedy *Bowfinger* (1999), which he wrote, where he plays a Poverty Row movie producer who dreams up a way to get a big star (Eddie Murphy) to appear in a movie without knowing it. Or Mamet's *The Spanish Prisoner* (1997), where he was the genial, trustworthy con artist in a plot so labyrinthine I'm not sure even he understood it. Or his phony faith healer in *Leap of Faith* (1992), who can't handle the possibility that miracles might be real. Or his producer of violent movies in *Grand Canyon* (1991), who is mugged and has a change of heart. Or his triumph in *L.A. Story,* also 1991, which he wrote, and which still inspires imitations every time people order complicated coffee. And back and back, through *My Blue Heaven, Parenthood, Dirty Rotten Scoundrels, Roxanne,* and the wonderful, underrated *Planes, Trains and Automobiles.*

With *Novocaine,* he said, he was "charmed by the screenplay. I had a lot of offers and this one was the one I kept going back to. It's got twists. I just love twists. It's a guy getting into a mess. I've been in messes, everybody's been in messes, and somewhere at the bottom there's a lie. The lies gets deeper and more complicated, and the thing about lying is trying to remember what you said and who you said it to."

The screenplay is by David Atkins, who wrote an overlooked, zany sleeper named *Arizona Dream* in 1993. It's Atkins's first movie as a director.

"I didn't know much about him," Martin said, "but I was struck by his complete authority. And I thought the script was kind of radical. And it had a great ending that was kooky as anything you've ever seen. Somebody said to me once, 'You always play extraordinary characters in ordinary circumstances. So what about playing an ordinary character in extraordinary circumstances?' I kinda liked that. Here's an ordinary guy who falls into a bottomless pit."

Martin published a novel, *Shopgirl*, last year that got enthusiastic reviews and made the bestseller lists. I admired it. It told the story of a rich, distant man who has an affair with a shopgirl who has complexities of her own, and is more about the negotiation of trust than about the mechanics of sex.

"I think the key thing in writing *Shopgirl*," he said, "was having a real story to tell and having experience to draw on—the age and time. I want to say wisdom. I only mean wisdom about a small thing."

Writing is a meditative, solitary activity, I said. It involves self-criticism and going back and throwing things away. Acting is thought to be more extroverted. Actors are supposed to want people to look at them; writers are supposed to want to put the book out there while they hide.

"I did find writing opposite to acting," he said. "The practice is very interior. You're staying at home. You're alone. Writing is more of an intellectual expression and acting is more of an emotional expression. There's emotion certainly in the book, but the emotion in the book is in sentence construction and your choice of words, and the emotion in acting is coming from the gut."

I get the sense, I said, that there's a whole life you live in your head—that your ideas, your thoughts, your art, exist apart from your career. Your career doesn't define your life the way it does with some actors.

"I think that's true. Boy, I find my life changing as I go. I'd do a movie and it'd be very, very public. And now I find that the retreat, the making of the thing and then putting it out there— it's a different thing. It's more in the mind. I don't consider myself an intellectual, although I get accused of it sometimes, since [a small smile] everything is relative in Hollywood, you know ..."

To be immersed in ideas and the arts and the world. I think that makes you an intellectual.

"I overthink everything. My greatest pleasure really is when I take my overthinking and just really focus it on a creative enterprise. That's where it pays off. There's a knot in your actual emotional life—we won't get into that—that does not pay off until you turn it into something creative."

John Sayles and Maggie Renzi

July 2, 2002—John Sayles has directed thirteen movies in the last twenty-two years, eleven of them produced by his wife, Maggie Renzi. They span a remarkable range of subject matter, from the sci-fi humor of *The Brother from Another Planet* to the baseball drama *Eight Men Out* to the coal miners of *Matewan* to the Irish folk tale *The Secret of Roan Inish* to the buried secrets of *Lone Star*. And find the link between *Passion Fish, Limbo, Return of the Secaucus Seven,* and *Men With Guns,* which he shot in Spanish in Latin America. And how do they connect with *Sunshine State,* his new film about a resort community in turmoil in Florida?

They do all have one thing in common: They were written, directed, and edited exactly as he thought they should be. He has no complaints about studio interference. He is the complete independent director, self starting, autonomous, one-stop shopping. His career is like a rebuke to directors who complain they can't get their dream films off the ground.

Sunshine State stars Edie Falco of *The Sopranos* and Oscar nominee Angela Bassett. It has, as usual, a cast of name actors willing to work for scale to film with Sayles: Jane Alexander, Ralph Waite, Timothy Hutton, Mary Alice, Mary Steenburgen, even Alan King. They'll get paid more if the movie makes money, and the funny thing is, Sayles's movies usually do make money, because he makes them for a reasonable cost.

The story involves a Florida island where Falco runs her father's motel and restaurant and hates every minute of it, and Mary Alice lives in a once-posh African-American beach town and meets her daughter (Bassett) for the first time since the girl got pregnant in her teens and was sent north to quiet the scandal. Now developers are circling the island like jackals, seeking to buy property to build new high-rises.

This is a textbook example of the kind of project that could not be financed within the studio system. For Sayles and Renzi, it was business as usual.

"We make them for less than anybody else does at our age and with our experience," Maggie Renzi tells me. We're sitting in their suite at the Chicago Ritz-Carlton. "We don't have to hit home runs."

She's small, sitting on the sofa next to John, his Lincolnesque face framed by the sideburns turning gray.

"What we do," Sayles says, "is come in saying: 'Here's the negotiation. We've made X number of movies; they've all come in on budget; they've all gotten a theatrical release, so you're gonna get up to the plate. It's not going to run away and cost more than we're telling you it's going to cost. Here's the screenplay; it'll be very close to this. It may be a little shorter, but I'm not gonna rewrite on the set, and the script is finished—which is, you know, rare these days.'"

His eyes are focused now on a standard-issue executive across an imaginary desk at a hypothetical studio.

"'Assume that you will know nobody in the cast. But we have been getting some really nice casting and there may be some good news for you as far as selling this. Are you interested?' And their answer is often no. But one thing is, it's a good quick no these days. We get our phone calls answered very quickly. Young film-makers can wander in the world for two years before somebody says, 'Well, we're still not quite sure.' They're waiting for them to get Sean Penn or whoever's hot, Vin Diesel. The executives want the big names even if they're wrong for the part," Sayles says.

He believes in getting the right actor. If they have a name, that's a bonus.

Maggie picks up. "We ask actors to work for us for scale, to live in the same kind of accommodation as everybody else, which is not a suite. We don't even give them a car, and they sure don't get a trailer. They get a holding area. And the ones who say 'no' should say 'no,' because they're not going to be happy. But the ones who say 'yes' have self-selected, so we get a group of actors who have a ball with each other."

"Who wanna be there," Sayles says.

"Who wanna be there," says Renzi. "And the same thing happened with Tom Bernard and Michael Barker at Sony Classics. They wanted this film with us in charge of it, with the result that they got. So there wasn't ever any arguing about it. I mean, we told them we were hoping to get Edie and Angela, and in very short order we got Edie and Angela. And after that . . ."

She's hot right now, Edie Falco is, I say.

"You know what?" Renzi says. "People love her; I mean, they just like the woman."

"They feel bad for her character on *The Sopranos*," Sayles says.

Your plots are all over the map, I say. Ireland, New Jersey, Alaska, Florida, Texas, South America, the coal mines, the big city, the baseball diamond, Louisiana . . . and you write them yourself, so it's not like you're buying stories from all over.

"I think about things and I start to see some kind of pattern, something that's happening in the world," Sayles says. "And then it just seems to coalesce. In one case, *Secret of Roan Inish*, it was something that Maggie had read when she was ten years old. As for Florida, this picture: I've been going to Florida since I was four years old. My mother's parents live there and I knew the Miami area before, during, and after the Cuban Revolution, and then branched out and saw different parts of the state. And then the last time I was out there, I was just blown away. It wasn't there anymore. It had changed so much. I started thinking, well, maybe that's what I should make the movie about."

Sunshine State surprised me, I said, by *not* doing the conventional things. In a conventional movie, it would have been about the battle of Edie Falco, the motel diner owner's daughter, against the encroachments of big business. But she's had it with running that damned diner.

"It's not her dream," Sayles said. "What was the dream for one generation doesn't necessarily mean that much to the next generation. You almost can't expect it to. For Ralph Waite's character (Edie's father, who built the motel), it was a huge deal for him to get out of the pulp mill. Out of all the generations of turpentine camp workers. Now he's a business owner, he belongs to the Chamber of Commerce. His daughter grew up with that, hated working there, and that's not her dream at all.

"And take Mary Alice's character. Angela Bassett's mother. She comes from that upper-middle black class who had cotillions and stuff, but there was also that feeling that they had to act well because the white people were watching and the black people were watching. Angela's from another generation. She doesn't share the ambition, or the fears."

I guess you feel that the developers are gonna come in and destroy the landscape and destroy the community, I said. Yet they're not painted as monolithic. They're kind of ineffectual, disorganized.

"The only guys who actually are powerful," Sayles said, "are those guys on the golf course."

He's talking about Alan King and three other old guys who play golf and philosophize and seem like genial duffers.

"There are a lot of earthlings," he said, "a lot of mere mortals, and there are a few guys who have that inside knowledge. Who know what the deal is. In *Chinatown* it was John Huston's character. In *Once Upon a Time in the West*, it was the guy who knew where the railroad was going. Here, it's them."

One interesting character, I said, is Tim Hutton's architect, who begins by appearing to be the outsider who's gonna come in and move everybody out, and ends up just being moved out himself. He's as powerless as his victims and next week he's gonna be someplace else.

"You get into the fact," Sayles said, "that this is a talented guy and he has something that he loves and believes in, but it's part of a larger system that has no morals. He's like a guy who wants to make good pictures but works for the studios."

So there isn't clear-cut good and evil here, I said.

"One of the most interesting ones for me," Renzi said, "is Jane Alexander (Edie's mother), who is a woman who still shows up at the Audubon meeting to protect the birds. But she considers that the land that her husband's motel is on is *already* blighted. To her, saving the motel is meaningless. She hates it. So what

I like to think is that she'll hold him up for all that money and write bigger checks than ever to the Nature Conservancy, Sierra Clubs, and whatever."

"But she's kinda given up on nature," Sayles said.

"Oh, she hasn't given up on nature!" Maggie says. "She goes every day to take care of the poor birds."

"But she realizes that it's a park," he says. "It's nature on a leash, and there may be some little raw pieces where she's gonna try to maintain the habitat ..."

"She's very sophisticated," she says.

"People are big and nature is small here," he says, "unlike Alaska, where nature is still big and people are still small."

"It's so like John," says Maggie, "to see the good side of the developers."

Steven Spielberg and Tom Cruise

June 16, 2002—After seeing Steven Spielberg's *Minority Report*, my mind was churning with amazement and curiosity. Talking to Spielberg and his star, Tom Cruise, I found myself not an interviewer but simply a moviegoer, talking the way you do when you walk out of a movie that blindsides you with its brilliance.

Our conversation jumped from subject to subject. We talked about technique, special effects, compositions, imagining the future, playing fair with the tradition of *film noir*. I sort my notes into the topics that interest me the most.

The Department of Precrime

Remarkable, that in the same week when the White House shuffled agencies into a new Department of Homeland Security, *Minority Report* is about a Department of Precrime in the District of Columbia. Fifty years in the future, three "precogs," people with the ability to foresee the future, float in a tank with their brains wired to computers, predicting crimes before they happen.

Spielberg: Today the only way to stop crimes is through intelligence and communication, but in our story the trio of precogs is psychically gifted, and we're able to use them to stop bad from happening. People are arrested and charged with being about to commit murder.

Film Noir and Whodunits

Spielberg: I had John Huston in my ear on *Minority Report*. I went back and looked at *The Maltese Falcon* and Hawks's *The Big Sleep* to see how some of those *film noir* mysteries were resolved. They didn't dot every "I" and cross every "T." They tried to keep you off-balance. They asked more questions than they could answer in those days.

RE: With your crime plot here, I think you play fair and answer all of the questions.

Spielberg: I went to Scott Frank for the screenplay. He wrote *Get Shorty* and *Out of Sight*. I gave him the original short story by Philip K. Dick and he said he didn't know anything about science fiction. I said, "Let me worry about the sci-fi element. Just write a terrific detective yarn. This taps into your strength. This is a murder mystery, a *film noir*, a whodunit."

Cruise: The idea of being able to predict a murder and stop it before it occurs—that's stunning. And the idea of devising a perfect crime to get around the precogs. That's great for the short story, but for a feature film it needed personal elements. You have to care about the people. That's what Scott Frank gave us.

The Future Is Now

For *2001: A Space Odyssey*, Stanley Kubrick famously consulted with industrial designers, futurists, and advertising people to try to visualize what the future world would look like. Spielberg does the same thing, imagining a world where ads recognize your retinal pattern, follow you around and speak to you.

Spielberg: I wanted all the toys to come true someday. I want there to be a transportation system that doesn't emit toxins into the atmosphere. And the newspaper that updates itself. At the same time, the city is not all skyscrapers with coils around them. In Washington, with its historical preservation rules, they're never going to change some neighborhoods, or the Mall, the Jefferson Memorial and the Lincoln Memorial. We mixed the old and the new.

The Ads That Talk to You

Spielberg: The Internet is watching us now. If they want to, they can see what sites you visit. In the future, television will be watching us, and customizing itself to what it knows about us. The thrilling thing is, that will make us feel we're part of the medium. The scary thing is, we'll lose our right to privacy. An ad will appear in the air around us, talking directly to us.

The Brilliant Two-Shot

In the film, the Cruise character liberates the most talented of the precogs, played by Samantha Morton, from the sensory deprivation tank, and drags her along with him in a desperate search for a killer who has outsmarted the pre-crime system, committed a perfect crime, and pinned it on Cruise.

Midway through this chase, there's a close-up of the two of them, Morton hanging on Cruise's shoulder, she looking left, he looking right, both of them exhausted and despairing. Spielberg holds the shot long enough for our eyes to look right, left, right, left, causing us to identify with their apprehension.

Spielberg: I'm glad you noticed that shot. They are basically at that point the same person—two heads from one heart.

RE: Who would have thought there would be another way to compose a two-shot?

Spielberg: I swear to you I discovered that shot through the viewfinder. I had them hug and suddenly I saw it through the viewfinder, and I asked Samantha to turn her head a little, for more profile, and I found this shot. I called Janusz Kaminski (the cinematographer) over and said, "Look at this thing! It's amazing!" And it was just there.

Cruise: It was Samantha's first day on the film and she came on like lightning out of a bottle, and Steven found that profile shot. It's one of my favorite shots in the movie. We were thinking we might use it on a poster at some point.

The Spiders

One of the tools of the movie's futuristic crime fighters are tiny robotic "spiders" that scurry around, clickety-click, finding every warm-blooded person in a house, leaping onto their faces and performing a retinal scan to identify them. When the spiders go looking for Cruise, it's a brilliant sequence using live action and the computer-generated spiders, which are absolutely convincing—unlike the somewhat awkwardly integrated CGI sequences in certain other summer movies.

To outsmart the spiders, Cruise immerses

himself in a bathtub filled with ice water, but a single bubble of air escapes from his nostril and a spider, about to leave the room, pauses with perfect timing, and goes back for another look.

Cruise: That air bubble was *not* a computer effect. Steven said, "I need one bubble to come out of this nostril," and I thought, forget about CGI, I can get a bubble to come out. The things an actor does.

Spielberg: I'm directing computer spiders now. Look what my life has come to. I've used ILM (Industrial Light and Magic) my entire career, but the spiders weren't ILM. The whole spider sequence was by a company called PDI, the guys who worked on *Shrek* for Dream-Works. There were only two animators and we spent many, many hours looking at variations. It was hard to get that little hesitation before the spider turns back again.

The Overhead Shot
Spielberg: Another shot I want to talk about is the overhead shot when the spiders first swarm into the tenement building. We're looking straight down into all those rooms, and the camera follows the spiders over to a girl's face, and to a guy sitting on the john—all these people in the building.

Now that *looks* like it must be a computer shot, but it isn't. That's a real, physical set. I tried to storyboard it, but it was so complicated, and finally Alex McDowell (the art director) suggested we try designing the shot on the computer. No set had been built yet. And we asked the computer, "How do we get this shot?" and the computer said, "You need a crane that goes in and out." There happens to be a TechnoCrane that telescopes in and out like a car aerial, and the computer told us where to put the crane, how to move it, how to get all the shots I wanted, all in one take. Then Alex built the set. So, no, there's not a single CGI shot in that sequence—but a computer told us how to do it!

Real Sets Versus Computer-Generated Sets
Spielberg: I really love George's *Star Wars: Episode II*. I thought it was operatic—George's most accomplished movie. But I don't think I'll ever go to computer-generated sets like he does. I think when you build a set in the 3-D world and actors walk onto that set, they get stimulated. They get ideas. Tom Cruise got

ideas about how to play (his character) John Anderton because we built his house with four walls and a ceiling—every aspect was real. He felt at home there and got ideas about Anderton's behavior. I'm sad for the day when sets will exist in cyberspace and not in real life.

Real Action Versus Spidey-Action
RE: I was surprised by how many e-mails I got after *Spider-Man* and *Episode II* from people who said, "Gee, I *like it* when they use models and miniatures and real sets and puppets." It may look real when done on a computer, but it looks real in a different way. There's something missing.

Spielberg: Sometimes on *Spider-Man*, which I quite liked, I enjoyed the CGI effects that made Spider-Man's flying look like a comic book and not like reality. It put me back in all the Spider-Man comics I read growing up. (Director) Sam Raimi was trying to get that comic art look, and what it requires is that you make the live-action scenes with Tobey Maguire look as much like comic art as the CGI swinging of Spider-Man. The trick is to get those values to meet in the middle.

The Computer Operating System
In the film, Cruise operates a computer by manipulating virtual images in midair.

Cruise: Steven called me over to his house and said, "I've been thinking of this idea I call 'scrubbing the image,'" and he showed it to me. He created this whole computer language so that he could physicalize it, free it from the keyboard. He gave the audience a visual way to discover it along with me. Of course, when we shot those scenes there were no images, just my hands, and he came up with the music and would just talk me through it when we were shooting.

The Psychic Chase
One virtuoso sequence shows Morton, as the precog, helping Cruise elude pursuit by foreseeing what the pursuers will do and telling him how to evade them.

Cruise: It's amazing the speed at which the ideas just come to him. He thought of that Psychic Chase, and started adding details. Those little touches like when there's a homeless man and she tells me to give him some money, and then she tells me to throw the coins on the floor, and then the man leans forward to pick them up and the cops trip over him.

Working with Tom Cruise

Spielberg and Cruise have been friends for twenty years, and have been looking for a project together for ten years.

Spielberg: I like to consider Tom my William Holden. He's going to be around until he's an old, old man, if he wants to continue acting. He'll be great-looking and he'll be heartfelt as he is now; he'll get better with age. He's not afraid to cry, to lose his temper, to become unglued. I think of him as a character actor. Look at his character in *Magnolia* and his Ron Kovic in *Born on the Fourth of July* and Jerry Maguire, and the vampire Lestat. Those are characters.

Tilda Swinton

August 13, 2001—Tilda Swinton. Unless you go to a lot of good but relatively obscure movies, you may not know who she is. Oh, and you might remember her as the stern cult leader who gave Leonardo DiCaprio a hard time in *The Beach*. Porcelain skin, widely spaced eyes, terrifyingly intelligent, don't mess with her. In Sally Potter's *Orlando*, she played a person who lived for 400 years, first as a woman, then as a man, and she is the only person alive of whom you could say that this was typecasting.

The Deep End is her breakthrough to the big time, a concept that leaves her completely disinterested. She is not in the success game, and makes movies only with people she has, or feels like she has, spent six years with around the kitchen table—not gabbing, you know, but really talking about things. She doesn't even think of herself as an actress, but as a "model" in the way Robert Bresson used the term—a focus for the material, a collaborator with the director, a person on whom we can project fantasies. She sees herself as artist's material, and once sat locked for two days in a box in London's Serpentine Gallery, for a piece which was no doubt about a box with a woman locked inside of it for two days. Those artists.

She uses the word "industrial" to describe the kinds of films she doesn't appear in. "Industrial" films are made by the Hollywood assembly line, like cars or toothpaste. They are products made by machines. Teenage sex comedies, science-fiction monsters, that sort of thing. Her kind of movie, she says, is "preindustrial," by which I think she means it is carved out of blocks of solid cinema by artisans using pocketknives.

She started in the 1980s with Derek Jarman, a British avant-garde outsider: "Those first movies were so exotic that they weren't really movies at all. We worked experimentally. Most of what we did was silent. We would make these Super 8 films that were being blown up to 35 a long time before Dogma was playing around with digital. It was a lab, really."

In *The Deep End*, directed by Scott McGehee and David Siegel, she plays a housewife who lives on the shore of Lake Tahoe with her three children. Her husband is an admiral, away at sea. Her seventeen-year-old son is new to his homosexuality, and under the spell of a hard-drinking thirty-year-old rotter. She can deal with the sexuality but not with the bad company, especially after the older man involves her son in a DUI situation. In the opening scene, she confronts him and demands that he stay away from her boy. He says he will do it for $5,000.

This leads to—well, it's a thriller. Stepping carefully, let's say it leads to trying to cover up evidence of what she thinks was a crime. And then to her meeting another man, a blackmailer. And then the plot tightens, gear within gear, in the Hitchcock style—he loved stories about innocent people who found themselves looking guilty. The plot is as unreasonable as Ashley Judd's dilemma in *Double Jeopardy,* but Tilda Swinton does an interesting thing. This actress who has played stylized conceptual roles in much of her work creates a performance of unforced, absolute believability. This is a real woman, and because it's happening to her, we think it's bad luck rather than impossible.

The film's critics, and there are a few, say the story is simply too implausible—that the plot tilts over into a distraction. Swinton says it may be impossible in life, but it's certainly "film possible."

"You know what I mean? When people ask, Why does she bury the body in shallow water? Well, because it had to happen that way; otherwise the film wouldn't happen. But then also because of the nightmare quality—you do something, and then you know it was a mistake. The thing about a nightmare is that not everything is surreal. It's that a lot of it is real as well. We wanted to make her as specific as she possibly could be to a particular class and situation. And also to disguise myself as closely as I could. My alien qualities were not being asked for this time."

Your alien qualities?

"I'm referring first to the fact that I'm alien to the place. I'm not an American. It was very important, very precise, that she had to be American. But by 'alien' I also mean—well, she doesn't live for 400 years. It meant a kind of realism I've not looked at very often."

If *The Deep End* makes Tilda Swinton into a star, that will not be part of her game plan: "I never committed myself to be an actor. I still haven't committed myself to be an actor. I don't really like the theater—isn't that shocking? I prefer going to the movies."

When she is not acting, she lives with her "sweetheart," a painter, and their twin children, on a farm so far north in Scotland "it is almost Scandinavia." She has two lives: working, and not working.

"I'm a registered schizophrenic."

You have to take a test?

"I've tested myself; it's true. It's a system. Four months filming, four months on the farm. It is genuinely a form of schizophrenia. There's almost nothing about my life when I am there and my life when I'm away that is similar. Let me tell you something. When I'm not working, you would not find me in a crowd. You wouldn't find me. You really wouldn't. It's a trick of the light. Now you see me, now you don't."

That's what Dolly Parton told me. She said, "Sweetie, if I took off this wig and these lashes and nails, and didn't push these up, I could be standing in line at the K-Mart and you wouldn't know who it was."

Swinton nodded. "We live so far out that we have to go to Inverness to see a film. I was standing in line behind some people who were talking over me, across me, to their friends, having just seen *The Beach*. I was standing there with my children and this conversation went on for a good seven minutes."

Nobody knew it was you.

"Absolutely nobody."

Even if it looked like Tilda Swinton they knew it couldn't be.

"But it probably didn't."

Essays

Iranian Filmmaker Arrested

August 30, 2001—A chill wind blew through the Iranian film world Thursday, with the news that the feminist filmmaker Tahmineh Milani has been arrested. Milani is a heroine of the New Iranian Cinema, which, despite the restrictive politics of the fundamentalist regime, has produced some of the best recent films on the world scene.

Milani was jailed on charges of slandering Iran's 1979 Islamic revolution, according to Reuter's. In her new film *The Hidden Half*, which played earlier this year in the Tehran Film Festival, she painted a positive portrait of rebels who mounted an armed uprising against the newly formed Islamic republic. The movie is based on a recent Iranian novel about a married woman who remembers a romantic affair with a rebel, Reuter's said.

Milani is the first filmmaker to be arrested in Iran in years. She was a standard-bearer of a move toward moderation in the country, where the ruling religious leaders have recently been rebuffed at the polls. "Hard-line courts until now spared artists," the news service said, so her arrest could be the harbinger of a wider crackdown.

Political prisoners are usually just names in the news, but Milani's arrest struck home because I met her in 1999 at the Calcutta Film Festival, and was struck by her forthright spirit. She and her husband, the architect Mohammed Nikbin, were there for the screening of her powerful film *Two Women*, about a woman whose father allows her to attend the university. There she attracts the attention of a stalker, who becomes obsessed with her and finally throws acid at the man he thinks is her boyfriend. He is actually her cousin.

The attack is not the point of the movie. It is about what happens then, as the woman is somehow blamed for having provoked this assault. Her father pulls her from school, makes her return to her small town, and forces her to marry a much older man who "accepts" her despite her "reputation."

It is said that bad times make good films.

Central European cinema blossomed under Soviet censorship. China has had a renaissance. Right now on the international festival circuit, Iran is the country with the best and most talked-about films. Many of them contain a political message in parable form, like Jafar Panahi's *The Circle*, which is about the difficulty of being a woman in Iran if you are independent of the protection of a husband, father, or brother. Others are children's films, like Majid Majidi's *The Color of Paradise*, about a blind boy who is smart and gifted, but rejected by his widowed father because he hurts the father's chances in the marriage market.

At the nightly gatherings of filmmakers at Calcutta, I found myself often at the same table with Milani, Nikbin, the Australian filmmaker Paul Cox, and the Canadian filmmaker Mitra Sen. As we talked about the situation in Iran, Milani and her husband were cautiously optimistic: At least she had been allowed to make her films, at least they had found distribution, at least she was allowed to visit film festivals. Now it appears that window may be closing.

Note: This story has a happy ending. Milani was released and I was able to invite her to my 2002 Overlooked Film Festival at the University of Illinois, where there was a reunion of the Calcutta group—Milani, Paul Cox, and Mitra Sen.

AFI Awards Nominations

Los Angeles, December 18, 2001—Despite all of the year-end pontifications of the film critics' associations, the most widely studied pre–Oscar Awards are the Golden Globes. They are also among the less respected—not quite down there with the Peoples' Choice Awards, but well below the National Society of Film Critics. No one is quite sure what qualifies the Hollywood Foreign Press Association to hand out prizes, but they sure throw a good party, and the TV special gets high ratings.

This year the American Film Institute throws down the gauntlet. The AFI, which, it is safe to say, is more respected that the HFPA, convened a panel in Los Angeles over the weekend to debate the year's films for fourteen hours over two days, and produced a list of nominees to be voted on by a cross section of 100 movie industry figures. Of course, this process will also produce a party (at the Beverly Hills Hotel) and a TV special, which when it airs on CBS January 5 will be the first in a long season of awards, leading up to the Oscars on March 24.

I was a member of the panel, along with producers, directors, writers, academics, and other critics, and as we debated the films for two days, I reflected that while I might not agree with all of the choices, I could see how they were arrived at, and none of the nominees got on the list because of studio clout, publicists' lobbying, or junket hospitality. The arguments were spirited at times, and unpredictable; you'd find a former studio head defending a little indie picture, or a film professor who loved a mainstream hit.

The nominees included several movies that hadn't even opened; they'd been previewed "for your consideration" and did indeed get considered—*A Beautiful Mind*, about a mathematician with schizophrenia; *Black Hawk Down*, about a disastrous U.S. military operation; *Monster's Ball*, about a romance based on desperation; the fantasy epic *The Lord of the Rings*; and *The Royal Tenenbaums*, about a very strange family. It was a received truth that 2001 was not a great year for the movies, but titles like those were proof it had a strong finish.

If there was a trend, it was toward films that questioned reality in one way or another, setting challenges to the audience to decide what was real, what happened, what it meant. Those titles included *A Beautiful Mind*, *Memento*, *Mulholland Dr.*, *The Business of Strangers*, *Vanilla Sky*, and *Waking Life*. The panel showed admirable open-mindedness in honoring relatively obscure films (*Ghost World*, *L.I.E.*), good work in commercial genre pictures (*Bandits*), and creativity in films that the marketplace didn't know what to make of (*A.I.*, *The Man Who Wasn't There*).

The ten nominees for best picture, in alphabetical order, are *A Beautiful Mind*, *Black Hawk Down*, *In the Bedroom*, *The Lord of the Rings: Fellowship of the Rings*, *The Man Who Wasn't There*, *Memento*, *Monster's Ball*, *Moulin Rouge*, *Mulholland Dr.*, and *Shrek*.

The four best actor (female) nominees:

Halle Berry, *Monster's Ball*; Stockard Channing, *The Business of Strangers*; Sissy Spacek, *In the Bedroom*; Naomi Watts, *Mulholland Dr.*

For best actor (male): Russell Crowe, *A Beautiful Mind*; Billy Bob Thornton, *The Man Who Wasn't There*; Denzel Washington, *Training Day*; Tom Wilkinson, *In the Bedroom*.

Best supporting actor (female): Cate Blanchett, *Bandits*; Jennifer Connelly, *A Beautiful Mind*; Cameron Diaz, *Vanilla Sky*; Frances O'Connor, *A.I.*

Best supporting actor (male): Steve Buscemi, *Ghost World*; Brian Cox, *L.I.E.*; Gene Hackman, *The Royal Tenenbaums*; Tony Shalhoub, *The Man Who Wasn't There*.

Best director: Robert Altman, *Gosford Park*; Todd Field, *In the Bedroom*; David Lynch, *Mulholland Dr.*; Ridley Scott, *Black Hawk Down*.

For awards in six other categories, visit www.afionline.org.

Nominating committee members were director Mimi Leder; writer-director Steven Zaillian; actress Marsha Mason; producers Michael Nesmith and Tom Pollock; academics Jeanine Basinger, Todd Boyd, Edward Branigan, and Vivian Sobchack; and critics Molly Haskell, Andrew Sarris, Richard Schickel, and myself.

The Mugging of *A Beautiful Mind*

March 1, 2002—Judging by the attacks against it, *A Beautiful Mind* is the most reprehensible film of the year. Amazing it was made, let alone nominated for an Academy Award. The mugging of this film is the most disturbing element of this year's Oscar season.

Ron Howard's film stars Russell Crowe as John Forbes Nash Jr., a schizophrenic who won the Nobel Prize for mathematics. We see him struggling with demons and fantasies, aided by a loyal wife (Jennifer Connelly). Like Nash, the audience is sometimes deluded about what's real in the story, and what is a phantasm.

The film is well written, directed, and acted. But the film's detractors see more, or less. They charge:

—Nash has been whitewashed; the film suppresses the facts that he fathered a child out of wedlock and refused to support it, was bisexual, and faced molestation charges after an incident in a public toilet.

—A book about Nash reports him making anti-Semitic comments. Joy Behar on *The View* said the movie should have included that behavior. Would she have preferred a movie about an anti-Semite who wins the Nobel?

—Russell Crowe, angry that the British Academy Awards telecast edited out four lines of poetry in his speech, pushed and shoved the director of the program.

—Press release: "Claiming that the film *A Beautiful Mind* distorts the life of John Nash, a coalition of 100 mental health advocacy groups issued a public statement today to Universal asking for an apology and retraction." The coalition is angry about a *USA Today* article reporting, "This brilliant mathematician stopped taking antipsychotic drugs in 1970 and slowly recovered over two decades."

My thoughts:

—The movie is caught in the controversy between those supporting drugs in the treatment of schizophrenia, and those interested in other approaches. The coalition is really disturbed not because the movie changed the facts, but because it didn't change them enough; in the film, Nash speaks of "newer medications" that in real life he was not taking, so they should be calling for an apology from *USA Today*, not the studio.

—A schizophrenic has a serious mental illness, yet Behar and others hold him to the standard of a healthy person. Who knows what he thought he was doing, or saying, during the episodes involving sex and anti-Semitism? In the film, he lives with imaginary characters for years. To say he should have "sought treatment" is to assume he was sane enough to do so, and to ignore his belief that medication would cloud his mathematical work.

—Crowe has a hot head, but he also has a point. Awards shows are inflated with endless gassy lists of people the winners want to thank. Crowe read four lines by Patrick Kavanaugh that directly express his humility as an artist. Cutting them made his speech pointless.

Are the attacks against *A Beautiful Mind* orchestrated? "I'm not going to reveal my sources," says the Web's Matt Drudge, whose report on the anti-Semitic remarks caused an uproar. His statement tips his hand: He didn't find out about the statements himself, but was told about them. Isn't he missing the real story—that someone came to him with a vested interest in hurting the film?

"If you are a responsible writer," says shell-shocked Universal chairman Stacey Snider, "you don't take statements out of context that someone made during a thirty-five-year battle with schizophrenia." True. *A Beautiful Mind* is a parable about triumph in the face of disaster, not a drive-by shooting.

Oscar Night 2002

March 25, 2002—Halle Berry and Denzel Washington were the radiant winners of the best acting awards Sunday night at the seventy-fourth Academy Awards. In Oscar's opening night at the Kodak Theater, it was the perfect Kodak moment.

A Beautiful Mind was named the year's best picture, and tied *The Lord of the Rings* in the overall Oscar count with four. But *Rings* wins were in the technical categories, while *Mind* cleaned up with big awards, including best picture, director Ron Howard, best supporting actress Jennifer Connelly, and its screenplay by Akiva Goldsman.

For Washington and Berry, it was not merely the first time two African-Americans had won the top acting prizes. It was the first time a black actress had ever won, and only the second time for a black actor. Some hailed it as the beginning of a new era, but it was more clearly the end of an old. Hollywood's long history of indifference to black talent was clearly repudiated. But it is important to acknowledge that Washington and Berry won because they deserved to, not because of symbolism or score-keeping.

Halle Berry brought the house down. That's the only way to describe it. As her name was read as best actress for *Monster's Ball*—the first African-American to win the category in seventy-four long years—waves of pure emotion and shouts of joy swept the hall, and Berry onstage dissolved in tears and cried out, "Oh, my God!" before an outpouring of one of the most emotional speeches in Oscar history:

"This moment is so much bigger than me," she cried. "This moment is for Dorothy Dandridge, Lena Horne, Diahann Carroll. It's for the women that stand beside me, Jada Pinkett, Angela Bassett, Vivica Fox, and for every nameless, faceless woman of color that now has a chance because this door tonight has been opened. I'm so honored! I'm so honored and I thank the Academy for choosing me to be the vessel."

There were many tears in the house, and much joy, and the award was perfectly timed for the night Sidney Poitier, the first African-American to win for best actor, was honored.

"Forty years I've been chasing Sidney," Denzel Washington said in his acceptance speech. "They finally give it to me, and what do they do? Give it to him the same night." Then, serious: "I'll always be following in your footsteps, Sidney."

Washington won for his change-of-pace performance in *Training Day*, as a vicious drug detective. He gave tribute to Antoine Fuqua, "a brilliant young African-American filmmaker," who guided him through the role so different from his usual more heroic characters.

Berry played a poor southern woman in *Monster's Ball*, a waitress in an all-night diner, whose life has so few options that she finally turns to a racist prison guard (Billy Bob Thornton), and he, equally lonely, to her, in a relationship that transforms them both. She was so nervous when she heard her name called, she said backstage, she almost fell on the stairs.

Barbra Streisand presented Robert Redford with his Oscar for lifetime achievement, and he spoke eloquently: "I've spent most of my life focused on the road ahead. But tonight I see in the rearview mirror something I've not thought about—history." He cited his personal work, "which is the most important to me," and said he also tried to give something back to the industry. That, of course, he said, was Sundance—the institute and the film festival, both bulwarks of independent film.

The evening's first real surprise: Jim Broadbent as best supporting actor, for *Iris*. He probably benefited from his even-more-demanding role as the nightclub impresario in the popular *Moulin Rouge*. In a subtle bow to this year's controversy over accuracy in biopics, he thanked the man he portrayed, Iris Murdoch's husband, John Bayley, for allowing him to play "and I am sure misrepresent" his life. Broadbent's closer: "Good luck, *Moulin Rouge!*"

Best supporting actress winner Jennifer Connelly "brought paper so I wouldn't forget," and read a speech of simple eloquence, ending with thanks to Alicia Nash, the character she played, "a true messenger of love."

Her award, the first, was the one most Oscar

prognosticators felt most confident about, on a night when, more than usual, the major races were too close to predict.

As expected in a year when two movies were sensational extravaganzas, *The Lord of the Rings* and *Moulin Rouge* shared Oscars in such categories as makeup *(Rings)*, costuming *(Moulin)*, art direction *(Moulin)*, and cinematography *(Rings)*—all categories that either film could have swept. Catherine Martin, who was co-winner of *Moulin Rouge*'s art direction and costuming Oscars, is the wife of director Baz Luhrman.

There was extra drama in the newly created best animated feature category this year, because of a face-off between archrivals Disney *(Monsters, Inc.)* and DreamWorks *(Shrek)*. Both had strong entries that grossed $500 million-plus worldwide, and like all animated features will keep on grossing for years. The third nominee, *Jimmy Neutron*, was out of the running, and there was widespread discontent that the innovative *Waking Life* and *Final Fantasy* were passed over.

The winner: *Shrek*, which was even reckoned to have a good chance at a nomination in the best picture category before the new animation category was initiated.

Julian Fellowes was a popular winner for best original screenplay, for *Gosford Park*. "I feel as if I'm in *A Star Is Born* and any moment Norman Maine is gonna come out and smack me in the mouth," he said. "My thanks to Robert Altman, who has given me the biggest break in the movies since Lana Turner walked into Schwab's."

Akiva Goldsman won the Oscar for best screenplay adaptation for *A Beautiful Mind*, despite controversy (unfounded, in my opinion) over details from the original book that he chose not to include. He made no mention of the critics of the film.

Although *Black Hawk Down* was passed over for best picture, the Academy had enough respect for it to nominate director Ridley Scott, and to acknowledge its extraordinary technical quality by voting Oscars for its editing (Pietro Scalia) and sound (Mike Minkler, Myron Nettinga, and Chris Munro). *Pearl Harbor*, a multi-million-dollar grosser that was dissed by the critics, picked up the Oscar for best sound editing (George Watters II and Christopher Boyes).

Randy Newman, the Susan Lucci of the Academy, finally won his first Oscar, after sixteen nominations. His "If I Didn't Have You," from *Monsters, Inc.*, ended his long drought. "I would like to thank the music branch," he said, "for giving me so many chances to be humiliated."

Major upset: The best foreign film Oscar went to Danis Tanovic's *No Man's Land,* from Bosnia and Herzegovina. *Amelie* from France was widely thought to be the front-runner, but there was much pre-Oscar buzz about the sheer quality of *No Man's Land,* which was about enemy soldiers trapped between the lines, one of them lying flat on his back on a land mine.

Sobering thought: Best actor nominee Denzel Washington helped introduce honorary Oscar winner Sidney Poitier. Poitier was the first African-American to win for best actor, thirty-nine years ago. No African-American actor, including Washington, had won since. The award served to heighten the suspense leading up to this year's best actor award.

The Poitier award was supported by a documentary directed by Kasi *(Eve's Bayou)* Lemmons, who asked leading figures in the African-American acting and directing community to speak personally about his influence on their lives and careers. It ended with a montage of them all saying simply, "thank you." Simply, but overpoweringly.

Poitier's acceptance speech was a model of emotion expressed in dignity. He recalled that when he arrived in Hollywood at twenty-two, "the odds against my standing here tonight fifty-three years later would not have fallen in my favor." He thanked by name the filmmakers who, by daring to cast a black man as the lead in a film, were "unafraid to have their art reflect their views, ethical and moral," and named them, including Joe Mankiewicz, Richard Brooks, Ralph Nelson, Darryl Zanuck, Stanley Kramer, the Mirisch brothers, Guy Green, and Norman Jewison. He closed: "I accept this award in memory of all the African-American actors and actresses who went before me in the difficult years, on whose shoulders I was privileged to stand, to see where I might go."

Unscripted moment backstage, after Poitier arrived in the print pressroom: A young black reporter from Montreal asked Poitier if he could simply touch his Oscar, Poitier nodded, and the reporter got his wish.

Another black reporter asked Poitier if he was "satisfied" with the rate of change.

"You can see as well as I can see," he said, "that there has been change." He mentioned Denzel Washington, Morgan Freeman, Wesley Snipes, Larry Fishburne. "We have lots and lots of African-American actors. When we didn't have *any* I appeared, not because I brought so much, but because the world was at a certain place."

The magical segment by Cirque du Soleil, linked to the visual-effects category, was representative of an overall show that seemed finally to have entered the twenty-first century. Laura Ziskind, the program's new producer, picked up the pace, put a zing and sometimes a bite in the writing of the intros, added visible backstage announcers (Donald Sutherland and Glenn Close), and replaced endless clip packages with snappy editing and relevant narration. You could even see the visual effects growing from drawing board to computer matrix to finished product.

The winner: *The Lord of the Rings* and Jim Rygiel, Randall William Cook, Richard Taylor, and Mark Stetson. It was well deserved; sequences like the fencing match on the crumbling stone bridge over the fiery cauldron were almost entirely created by the visual effects.

Another of Laura Ziskind's splendid ideas: The tribute to those who died during the year was handled with sound bites from their work, instead of a montage of still photos.

The category introductions were a hilarious leap above usual form—for example in the intro to the costume category by Ben Stiller and Owen Wilson, ad-libbing with an element of cutting truth (Wilson: "Stiller's *Zoolander* didn't get nominated! That was a shocker! I don't think the town has been so shocked since Scorsese got overlooked for *Raging Bull*.").

It was also interesting, and an improvement, how during the cinematography category, for example, we heard the cinematographers in voice-over describing their approach to their work.

The Academy loves surprises and got a big one with surprise guest Woody Allen, introducing a film about New York, assembled by Nora Ephron from great New York films *(Manhattan, Once Upon a Time in America, 42nd Street, New York, New York, On the Waterfront,*

Sweet Smell of Success, Saturday Night Fever). The message: Shoot your movies in New York.

Allen demonstrated he still has the knack for stand-up: "I'm working on a film about a foot fetishist who meets this beautiful and brilliant Harvard psychologist and falls in love with her footnotes."

Best documentary went to *Murder on a Sunday Morning,* an HBO documentary by French filmmakers Jean-Xavier de Lestrade and Denis Poncet, about a young African-American man's wrongful arrest because of racial profiling.

The short documentary winner was *Thoth,* by Sarah Kernochan and Lynn Appelle, a doc about a San Francisco street performer who performs operas in a language of his own—and performed on the red carpet for arriving guests.

The Jean Hersholt Humanitarian Award went to director and former Academy president Arthur Hiller, a leader in nontraditional casting—hiring minorities and the disabled in roles that were not specified for them in the screenplay.

The show began quickly on a thoughtful note and then a sensational one. First Tom Cruise introduced the theme of the evening—movies and what they mean to us—with the first of many head-on interviews with movie lovers, conducted by documentarian Errol Morris with his Interrotron technique (he is able to look directly through his camera at his subjects).

Then host Whoopi Goldberg descended from the ceiling dressed like a cross between a Moulin Rouge dancer and a nightmare by Cher. Her monologue faced 9/11, the topic overshadowing the night, and sidestepped it, talking of the great national tragedy we had overcome: "Mariah Carey is *already* making another film."

She worked the audience: "Here's the Smith family all seated together—Will, Jada, and Maggie." And she observed, "Security is tighter than a lot of the faces here tonight."

Whoopi's best unscripted one-liner: After a loud, passionate, girlish whoop echoed through the hall, she quipped: "Just wipe up when you're done."

The Kodak Theater on Hollywood Boulevard, Oscar's new home, inspired a festive street scene. Despite draconian security measures, movie fans surged against the sidewalk barricades and cheered the arrivals, and 400 lucky ones, cleared by security, were allowed in the grandstand. They included many regulars, including forty of the forty-one usual members of the yellow-shirted Bleacher Chat Club.

So many warnings were issued about potential traffic jams that most of the nominees arrived early. The red-carpet arrival shows ran out of guests half an hour before show time, because everyone was already inside except for late arrival Russell Crowe—and even he would have been on schedule in a routine year.

Independent Spirit Award Winners

Santa Monica, California, March 25, 2002—But first for something completely different. The 2002 Independent Spirit Awards, or Oscars Unchained, were handed out here under a big top on the beach. Oscar nominees such as Nicole Kidman, Ian McKellen, and Sissy Spacek rubbed shoulders with indie legends such as John Waters, Kasi Lemmons, and Steve Buscemi in a hip party atmosphere.

The nominees included small films fighting for recognition. The winners mostly tended to be closer to the mainstream. Christopher Nolan's *Memento,* the film told backward about a man seeking his wife's killer, dominated the afternoon with Indies for best film, best director (Nolan), best screenplay (Nolan), and best supporting female (Carrie-Anne Moss).

Other multiple winners included Todd Field's *In the Bedroom,* with Indies for best female lead (Spacek), best male lead (Tom Wilkinson), and best first feature. Terry Zwigoff's *Ghost World* won for best first screenplay (Daniel Clowes and Zwigoff) and best supporting male (Buscemi).

Other winners included Michael Polish's *Jackpot,* which won the John Cassavetes Award for best feature costing less than $500,000; Jean-Pierre Jeunet's *Amelie,* as best foreign film; Paul Franklin Dano of *L.I.E.* for best debut performance; Peter Deming of *Mulholland Dr.* for best cinematography; and Stacy Peralta's *Dogtown and Z-Boys* for best documentary.

In a hometown touch, *Dogtown,* a doc about the rise of skateboarding, was partly filmed on the very beachfront parking lot where the awards tent was pitched—and where skateboarding began its rise about twenty years ago.

There are three $20,000 prizes given during the day. The Motorola Producers Award went to Rene Bastian and Linda Moran, who made *Mar-*

tin *and Orloff* and *L.I.E.* The Turning Leaf Coastal Reserve Someone to Watch Award went to Debra Eisenstadt, director of *Daydream Believer*. And the DirectTV/Independent Film Channel Truer Than Fiction Award, for an emerging director of nonfiction features, went to Monteith McCollum, director of *Hybrid*.

The nominees included films that were obscure, difficult, and in some cases *(Lift)* still without distributors. But the winners tended toward more familiar titles, and there was some overlap with the Oscars. That may be because the nominees are chosen by a plugged-in committee headed by *New York Times* film critic Elvis Mitchell and including Sundance festival director Geoff Gilmore, while the entire membership of the Independent Feature Project West votes on the finalists—overlooking many films they might not have seen.

The Indie Spirits are famous for their irreverent acceptance speeches, and Saturday's tone was set by emcee John Waters, veteran director of cheerfully shocking camp exploitation films like *Pink Flamingos*. He suggested that winners augment their income by also starring in the porn films that rip off the titles of box-office hits. Buscemi, accepting his award for *Ghost World*, mused, "Maybe I should reconsider that offer for *Goat World*."

Sir Ben Kingsley, on hand to announce a supporting award, observed, "Without supporting actors, every film would be *Swimming to Cambodia*"—Spaulding Gray's one-man film. The openly gay Oscar nominee Sir Ian McKellen, introducing the best actor award, said he had come fresh from the first facial, manicure, and pedicure of his life: "I wanted to look my best for these actors."

And was Sissy Spacek serious, joking, or rehearsing for a down-home role when she advised independent filmmakers in her best Virginia twang, "It's not the size of the dog in the fight, but the size of the fight in the dog."

The Independent Feature Project West was founded more than twenty years ago in the living room of pioneering indie filmmakers Gregory Nava and Anna Thomas, to support independent films at a time when they were marginalized by the industry. In the years since, thanks to festivals like Sundance and cable channels like IFC and Bravo (which cosponsor and broadcast the awards), indie films have grown

in visibility and stature; indeed, as studio pictures tilt toward safe, mass-market product, the indies have taken up the slack in the mass "quality" market.

Funniest Movie Titles

May 13, 2002—The funniest movie title of all time is *The Incredibly Strange Creatures Who Stopped Living and Became Mixed-Up Zombies*.

That's the verdict of readers who responded to a recent Movie Answer Man discussion of funny movie titles. Reader Matt Sandler of New York started the discussion by nominating *Dracula: Dead and Loving It*. I asked for suggestions from experts Leonard Maltin *(Ski Lift to Death)* and Steve Friedman *(Sorority Babes in the Slimeball Bowl-O-Rama)*. My own candidate: the egotistical *God Is My Co-Pilot*.

Then the readers got in on the act. In addition to *The Incredibly Strange Creatures*, which was nominated by more than a dozen readers, here are some of the candidates:

Niki Wurster, Stuttgart, Germany: Carl Andersen's Austrian Z-grade flick titled, *I Was a Teenage Zabbadoing* (alternative title: *I Was a Teenage Zabbadoing and the Incredible Lusty Dust-Whip from Outer Space Conquers the Earth Versus the Three Psychedelic Stooges of Dr. Fun Helsing and Fighting Against Surf-Vampires and Sex-Nazis and Have Trouble with This Endless Titillation Title*).

Jada Genter, Conyers, Georgia: *In the Land of the Owl Turds*. Learned while playing the game Balderdash, and yes, we looked it up and it *does* exist.

(I didn't believe you, so I looked it up. It was directed by Harrod Blank, son of the great documentarian Les Blank.)

Bob Westal, Los Angeles: *The Ghost in the Invisible Bikini, Vampires on Bikini Beach, Dr. Goldfarb and the Bikini Machine*, and *Oh Dad, Poor Dad, Mama's Hung You in the Closet and I'm Feeling So Sad*.

Bob Terrill, Fort Collins, Colorado: *Mexican Wrestling Women vs. the Aztec Mummy*.

Itai Pines, San Jose, California: *Don't Tell Mom the Babysitter's Dead* and, more recently, *Dude, Where's My Car?* Both were funnier than the movies.

Richard Nikonovich-Kahn, Atlanta: *I Dismember Mama* is funnier than any of those you mentioned.

John Hobson, Bolingbrook, Illinois: *Rat Pfink a Boo Boo.*

Gilbert Hernandez, Lubbock, Texas: *976-EVIL.*

Rob Frye, Redlands, California: *Cannibal Women in the Avocado Jungle of Death,* a hometown favorite from J. F. Lawton, the man who went on to write *Pretty Woman* and *Under Siege.*

K. Jackson, Nacogdoches, Texas: What about John Astin and Frank Sinatra Jr. in *Pepper and his Wacky Taxi?*

Bob Koelle, Newark, Delaware: *Stuff Stephanie in the Incinerator,* which had the tag line, "Don't throw your love away. Burn it."

Peter Sobczynski, Chicago: *The Neverending Story II.*

(That reminds me of *The Other Side of the Mountain, Part 2,* which logically should have been titled *This Side of the Mountain.*)

David Vernon, Los Angeles: *Can Hieronymous Merkin Ever Forget Mercy Humppe and Find True Happiness, House 2: The Second Story.*

Brett Campbell, St. Catharines, Ontario: There's no funnier movie title than *Fat Guy Goes Nutzoid.*

Joe Nonneman, Maple Park, Illinois: *A Nymphoid Barbarian in Dinosaur Hell.*

Chris Galdieri, Arlington, Virginia: *Mars Needs Women.*

Erik Goodwyn, Cincinnati: *Surf Nazis Must Die, Attack of the 100-Foot Centerfold, Star Wars: Episode II—Attack of the Clones.*

In Memoriam

Sam Arkoff

Samuel Z. Arkoff, who in some ways invented modern Hollywood, died Sunday, September 16, 2001, of natural causes in a Burbank, California, hospital. The cofounder of American International Pictures and the godfather of the beach party and teenage werewolf movies was eighty-three.

When Arkoff and partner James H. Nicholson founded AIP in 1954, the major Hollywood studios were little interested in movies aimed at teenagers, or in the summer releasing season. AIP had surprising success with low-budget youth pictures, and took advantage of less competition in the summer to open double features with titles like *Muscle Beach Party* and *Invasion of the Saucer Men.*

In June 1975, eyeing a situation where AIP and other small indies controlled the summer, Universal released Steven Spielberg's *Jaws.* Its enormous success convinced the majors that there was gold to be mined in the summertime, and today the summer months dominate the box office. Ironically, the increased competition made it hard for AIP to survive; Nicholson left the company in 1972, and in 1979 Arkoff sold his shares and became an independent producer. He made his last film in 1985, but his legacy continues. What are the recent films *Godzilla, Independence Day, Armageddon,* and *The Mummy Returns* but Arkoff concepts with bigger budgets and better special effects?

It was said that Sam Arkoff produced more films by Hollywood's best directors and brightest stars than anyone else—and did it the hard way, *before* they were the best or the brightest. AIP films were directed by Francis Ford Coppola, Martin Scorsese, Brian De Palma, and Peter Bogdanovich, and featured early performances by such unknowns as Jack Nicholson, Robert De Niro, Charles Bronson, Barbara Hershey, Nick Nolte, and Peter Fonda—as well as making teen immortals out of Frankie Avalon and Annette Funicello.

Producer-director Roger Corman became AIP's favorite in-house moviemaker, making dozens of movies and serving as executive pro-

ducer for many more. He was praised by young filmmakers for giving them jobs, and cursed for the tiny budgets he allowed them. "Roger was born with cheap genes," Arkoff beamed, remembering an early Corman Western named *Five Guns West,* where Corman decided to save on the salaries of extras by "purchasing stock footage of a legion of Indians on the warpath, and splicing them around close-ups of the few actors actually hired for the picture."

In his 1992 autobiography, *Flying Through Hollywood by the Seat of My Pants,* Arkoff recalled that the AIP formula was straightforward. First they came up with the title. Then they came up with the poster. If both looked good, they made the movie.

Arkoff's first film was *The Beast With a Million Eyes,* in 1955. His films were rarely masterpieces, but they *sounded* like fun, and offered straightforward entertainment values. Even the titles made you smile: *The Ghost in the Invisible Bikini, Invasion of the Saucer Men, Beach Blanket Bingo, I Was a Teenage Werewolf, The Astounding She-Monster,* and *The Saga of the Viking Women and Their Voyage to the Waters of the Great Sea Serpent.*

Arkoff was a smart, jovial man who never took his movies too seriously. In the 1970s and early 1980s, one of the highlights of the Cannes Film Festival was a festive luncheon he and his wife, Hilda, threw for North American and British film critics at the ultraexpensive Eden Roc Restaurant of the Hotel du Cap d'Antibes, on the coast outside of town.

Unlike most events sponsored by Hollywood studios, Arkoff's featured no press releases, no publicity handouts, no interview opportunities, and only one speech. Arkoff, holding his trademark foot-long cigar, would stand up and say, "No business is discussed at this luncheon. The less said about some of my pictures the better. We're here to have a good time. Eat, drink, and enjoy yourselves." Then he would sit down again.

Critics jostled to get a seat within earshot of Arkoff, whose stories of low-budget movies and high-maintenance moviemakers became legend. One of his favorite stories, later repeated in the autobiography, involved working with the neurotic Hungarian actor Peter Lorre on *The Raven* (1963).

Lorre had the title role, but "sometimes found it hard to keep to the script while dressed like an oversize black bird with four-foot-long wings." So Lorre ad-libbed. He had a scene where Vincent Price told him his wife's body was buried in a crypt beneath the house. "Having seen the other Poe pictures, in which the coffin was *always* buried in a crypt beneath the house, Peter exclaimed, 'Where else?'"

After selling his stake in AIP, Arkoff became an independent producer, and threw one last luncheon in 1982 at the Hotel du Cap. It was after the screening of his new movie Q, about a prehistoric winged serpent that nests at the top of the Chrysler Building and swoops down to pick innocent victims off the streets of Manhattan.

Sam and Hilda stood by the door as always to greet their guests. One of the first was the critic Rex Reed.

"Sam!" said Reed. "What a surprise! Right in the middle of all that dreck, a magnificent Method performance by Michael Moriarty!"

Arkoff beamed with pride. "The dreck was my idea," he said.

Milton Berle

When Milton Berle died in March 2002, I began to prepare an obituary. Reading this interview from 1980, I realized that he had, in a sense, written his own.

Canada, March 16, 1980—"You wanna know what the difference is between a comic and a comedian?" Milton Berle was asking.

Yeah, I wanna know.

"A comic is a guy who says funny things." Berle drew on his cigar. "A comedian is a guy who says things funny."

Which are you?

"Depends on how I got up in the morning. There is only one comic situation, anyway. It comes in three steps. One, get the comic up in a tree. Two, throw rocks at him. Three, get him down out of the tree. Part 3 is the happy ending. Without the happy ending, it's not comedy. Aristotle."

Berle stretched out on a sofa. He was wearing a bathrobe and a two-day beard. This was in the

spring of 1980. He was on the set of *Off Your Rocker,* a comedy set in an old-folks home in Toronto. Berle, Lou Jacobi, and Red Buttons were playing the three old folks.

"Old? Have I got a story for you," says Berle. "They gave me an honorary Emmy for my three decades in television. I came on TV in 1949, so this is thirty years later. Have I got news for them. I was on TV for fifty years. In 1929, there was this outfit known as the United States Television Co. across from the Chez Paree in Chicago. They were experimenting. I did a show. It was in a room the size of a broom closet, filled with lights, and my lips came out looking as black as Theda Bara's. Twenty years later, I figure the medium is finally ready for me."

What was it like doing live television?

"What you saw was what you got."

Since it was live, you couldn't do it again?

"Since it was live, if you couldn't do it the first time, that was the show. If the backdrop fell over, you held it up with your hand and said, 'They're not making these things the way they used to.'"

So if you told a joke and it bombed, what did you do then?

"If it bombed? They had audiences in those days; to them, laughter was a foreign language. I had a whole list of things to say when a joke bombed."

Like what?

"Like what, he says. Like, 'Okay folks, here's another one you may not care for. There must be people out there—I hear breathing. Tap your canes when you want to laugh. Working this audience is like walking a gangplank without a ship. Did you come in here for entertainment or revenge? I feel like the captain of the *Titanic.* May I see your library cards? I've never been funnier, folks, and believe me, I sincerely regret it.'"

Live television—must have been a constant challenge.

"I sold a lot of sets. After I was on, my neighbor sold his set, my wife sold her set . . ."

I mean, did you work with a script, or . . .

"No cue cards, no TelePrompTers, just memory. My experience in vaudeville was a great boon to me. I got stuck, I could remember some old routine I did at the State-Lake in Chicago. I remember I played Chicago once in legit. *Adam and Eden,* I think it was called. People went out whistling the scenery.

"We were only sort of live, anyway. We were really live, but only to those places on the coaxial cable. We were live in New York, and we went out live to Chicago, but for the West Coast, we were on kinescopes, and they sent us out by train and we were on a week later.

"I remember how I got the nickname Uncle Miltie. My floor director in those days was Arthur Penn, who went on to become the famous movie director. He made *Bonnie and Clyde.* In those days, he would squat under the camera and give me signals so I knew how much time I had left. One day we had a new script girl. She timed the script, and made the mistake of allowing too much time for the laughs. With our scripts, allowing any time for the laughs was taking a risk.

"So I think the show is over and I'm standing there saying good-bye, and I look down at Penn, and he's holding up eight fingers. Eight fingers. That means I've got eight minutes to fill. And nothing to say. I started ad-libbing, doing old jokes from vaudeville. Finally I ran out of jokes. I started talking to the kids: 'Time to go to bed, kiddies! Uncle Miltie says goodnight!' The next day, they were calling me Uncle Miltie, and it stuck."

John Frankenheimer

To understand the special gift of John Frankenheimer, it is better to start with his stories instead of his movies. Yes, he made some of the most distinctive films of his time (and began and ended as one of the most gifted directors of drama on television), but the films were mostly serious, and Frankenheimer was a very funny man.

He had one story he loved to tell, about the earliest days of live drama on TV. He broke into the medium at the age of twenty-four, directing great actors twice or three times his age in a medium where, for better or worse, whatever was happening was what the viewers saw. Sets were changed while actors moved between them, sometimes but not always during commercial breaks.

He remembered a show where an outdoor scene was going to be shot on a very simple set—just a street lamp and a street sign and a wall—but fog would cover everything and make it look like a city. "When the scene began," Frankenheimer said, "there was no fog.

Where was the man with the fog machine? You could see the street lamp and the sign, but you could also clearly see in the background that the actors were standing in a TV studio.

"What did we do? What we always had to do on live TV. We just kept shooting. The scene ended, and we cut to an interior scene on the next set. Now that the actors were indoors, the fog machine finally started to work, filling the room with smoke."

He roared with laughter remembering that story, and had countless more. He was one of the youngest directors to come up through live TV drama, a medium that also birthed Arthur Penn and Sidney Lumet. TV took itself more seriously in those days, and shows like *Playhouse 90* presented high-quality work week after week. Frankenheimer directed some 152 TV plays in six years, including the famous original version of *Days of Wine and Roses,* with Cliff Robertson and Piper Laurie.

The reason you wanted to hear his stories, as well as watch his movies, is because you were witness to the great joy he took in making movies. He started young, worked fast, had good luck and high energy, and loved his craft. And that is the sensibility you find reflected in his films.

Frankenheimer's big-screen career took off in the early 1960s with an extraordinary series of successes, notably *Birdman of Alcatraz* (1962), with Burt Lancaster in an unexpected role; *The Manchurian Candidate* (1962), a classic thriller about brainwashing and assassination; *Seven Days in May* (1964), about the risk of a government coup; *The Train* (1964), about the Nazis' attempts to loot French art treasures; and *Seconds* (1966), with Rock Hudson in an intriguing story about changing identities.

Frankenheimer had a great enthusiasm for cars and racing, reflected in the big-screen epic *Grand Prix* (1966). Indeed, one time when I visited him at his home in the Malibu Colony, he led me solemnly into a room whose walls were lined with glass-fronted display cases filled with little model cars, mostly Ferraris. He showed me how the doors opened and closed, the hoods came up, the wheels turned, and how details like a gas-cap mounting distinguished one model from another. He had assembled and painted the cars himself, he said; watching his face, as the light bounced out from the display cases, I saw not a hobbyist but a dreamer for whom these perfect little cars represented an ideal world.

Frankenheimer's own world, which began in such sunshine, darkened from the later 1960s until 1980. He started drinking heavily, moved to Paris, took cooking classes ("for many people, being a chef and being a drunk amount to the same thing"), and had a series of films that didn't work. He stopped drinking, "one day at a time," in 1980: "It was either that or die." During this period he did direct one masterpiece, ironically about drinking: It was a film of Eugene O'Neill's *The Iceman Cometh* (1973) with great performances by Lee Marvin and Robert Ryan. Made for the short-lived American Film Theater subscription series, it disappeared from circulation, but recently the heirs of producer Ely Landau expressed hope that all the AFT films may be restored.

After he stopped drinking, Frankenheimer's career picked up again, notably with the knife-edged, weirdly funny *52 Pick-Up* (1986), one of the best of all the films of Elmore Leonard stories. *Year of the Gun* (1991) was a superior thriller starring Andrew McCarthy and Sharon Stone, in a key early role.

He made two other films in the 1990s (*Ronin*, 1998, with its astonishing Paris chase scene, and *Reindeer Games* in 2000), but he was at the top of his form in original television drama, the genre where he began. *George Wallace* (1997) starred Gary Sinise in an extraordinary portrait of the fall and repentance of the Alabama governor, and the well-reviewed *Path to War*, about Lyndon Johnson's escalation of the war in Vietnam, premiered in May. In recent years, he ruled made-for-cable films, winning four consecutive Emmys for his direction.

Although he never blamed his drinking on it, his personal life took a sad blow in 1968 with the assassination of Robert Kennedy. Frankenheimer was a close friend and media adviser to Kennedy, and RFK was staying at the director's house when he fought and won the crucial California primary. Frankenheimer drove Kennedy to the Ambassador Hotel for a victory speech, which was followed by the assassination.

Ironically, it was the 1963 assassination of John F. Kennedy that prompted Frank Sinatra, a producer of *The Manchurian Candidate*, to withdraw that film from release for many years, even though it contained perhaps Sinatra's best performance. It was rereleased in 1988, as powerful as ever and, sadly, even more timely.

News of Frankenheimer's death on Saturday, July 6, 2002, at seventy-two, came as a shock to those who remembered the tall, dynamic man, who seemed in vigorous health. Complications after back surgery led to a stroke. In a career that graced the second half of the twentieth century, he had his ups and downs, but the ups were glorious, and his joy in his craft was evident to anyone who met him.

Pauline Kael

Better than anyone else, Pauline Kael communicated the immediate, sensual, voluptuous experience of seeing a great movie. She was known for her harsh judgments, but it was in her praise that she stood alone as the most influential American film critic—maybe the most influential critic of any art form—of her time.

When she died Monday, September 3, 2001, her spirit and passion were still being echoed in the words of a generation of film critics she influenced. She changed the way we talk about the movies. Eyes flashing, hair tossing, talking back to the screen, she wrote not from theory or ideology but from her own personal feelings. *I Lost It at the Movies*, she said in the title of her first book, and the more you thought about those words, the more you understood the transformational power the movies can have for some people.

After earlier years spent in San Francisco, writing program notes, contributing to film magazines, broadcasting on the local public radio stations, Kael emerged nationally in the 1960s, just a few years in advance of what became known as the Film Generation. She praised the best of the new movies from Europe, but wasn't a sucker for "art films," some of which she found phony and pretentious. She had an eye out for native art, for the new winds in American cinema.

After false starts at *McCall's* and the *New Republic*, she settled in as the film critic of *The New Yorker* under William Shawn, and championed a new generation of American directors. She hailed *Bonnie and Clyde* when it was generally dismissed, and wrote decisive early articles on Martin Scorsese, Robert Altman, and Francis Ford Coppola—she spotted them all right out of the gate. Her long article on Scorsese's *Mean Streets* essentially launched his career. Week after week she bashed Hollywood frauds and stuck up for the directors with distinctive styles.

"Sometimes people don't really seem to draw a line between the movies that really enlarge their experience, and the movies that simply work them over," she said in 1975 in a lecture at the Arts Club of Chicago. "When a great movie like Altman's *McCabe and Mrs. Miller* comes along, one of the functions I felt as a critic was to discuss the ways in which the movie was new, and the wonderful things Altman was doing in it. But then when people are moved, and deeply moved, by trash like *The Trial of Billy Jack,* then perhaps the critic can help by explaining the ways in which trash can manipulate your responses, can work over your emotions in unworthy and dishonest ways."

She liked feelings in the movies better than ideas. She suspected message pictures, because she felt the best way to communicate messages was through the senses—through feeling, not preaching. She liked the way "Altman's movies are made up of moments that affect us in ways we can't fully understand—unconscious moments."

"Responsible artists," she said, "try to affect you sensually in a way that enlarges your experience. Altman, for example, has raised the sound track to a whole new level. He hears more perceptively than other directors. He hears Americans talking, and we talk more than any other nation in the world. When you come out of an Altman movie, you hear your environment in a new way.

"And sometimes directors can achieve a sensual affect that simply can't be explained. In Coppola's *Godfather II,* for example, after the scene where Robert De Niro, as the young Don Vito, kills the landlord, the extortionist, he walks down the street in such a way that the scene becomes incredibly moving and powerful—everyone I've talked to who has seen the movie was affected by that scene, and yet there's no way to explain why. I think Coppola got the power for that scene out of his own unconscious. I don't know if he could explain it, either."

In print she was a power, and in person she was a dynamo. I met her right at the beginning of my career as a film critic, at the 1967 New York Film Festival. She was open, friendly, and generous to me, and to many other new critics of that time—there was not a drop of snobbery in her—and I found myself invited along for the ride, crammed into booths in the back room of the Ginger Man, across from Lincoln Center, debating the films we'd just seen. There were late nights of talk in her apartment, and noisy dinners, and excited phone calls. And at screenings, where critics were not supposed to vocalize their feelings, there'd be Pauline's "Oh! Oh! Oh!" at something she detested. She wasn't expressing an opinion, but defending herself against a personal affront.

She gathered around her a salon of the new directors and writers. Wherever she went, she was surrounded. People loved to hear her talk. One night in the lobby bar of the Algonquin, she introduced me to a new director and his star: Brian De Palma and Robert De Niro. I'd never heard of them. She had. Another night, there was an Italian dinner with Pauline, De Palma, the writer Paul Schrader, and myself. Looking around the table, I realized Pauline was out of work (she'd been fired by *McCall's*), De Palma was broke after his first two indie films, and Schrader was a struggling screenwriter. I had a paycheck from the *Sun-Times,* so I grabbed the bill. Leaving the restaurant, Pauline was shaking with laughter. "You dope," she said, "Schrader just sold a screenplay for $450,000!"

Kael's reviews changed movie history. Her praise of Altman's *Nashville* was reprinted, word for word, in a double-truck ad in the *New York Times.* Her review of *Last Tango in Paris* helped open the way for a new sexual frankness in the movies.

She blasted the prudishness of Jack Valenti's new MPAA ratings system, saying: "The problem for younger moviegoers is that the rating system has meant that kids haven't been free to go to the best pictures unless their parents take them. How can they develop an appreciation for movies if all they're allowed to see are those dreadful, boring movies that are aimed at them? The best pictures are mostly those with the R ratings, and there have been pictures that got the R because of one forbidden word—when all you have to do is listen to kids talking today and you realize no four-letter word is going to come as news to them. In terms of the intelligence and invention that goes into them, the Saturday night shows on TV are a lot better than most G or PG movies."

While the MPAA wanted to protect kids in an artificially prolonged childhood, Pauline championed movies that would help them grow up. She lost it at the movies, and they should too.

She wrote some of the most merciless pans of her time, but she was best writing about what she loved. "The critic's power is mostly positive, not negative," she told me once. "We can't stop the expensive trash with the millions of dollars behind it, but what we can do is help a good little film get shown, and direct attention to the best new directors, the ones who are fresh and exciting. John Leonard said the other day that critics were lice on the body of art. But art would never reach the public without the critics. I don't feel like a louse."

Having fun with the sensual relationship she had with the movies, the titles of Kael's books continued the sexual connotation of *I Lost It at the Movies*. They included *Kiss Kiss Bang Bang, Going Steady, Deeper Into Movies, Reeling, When the Lights Go Down, Movie Love, Taking It All In, Hooked,* and *5001 Nights at the Movies*. Only *State of the Art* wasn't suggestive—maybe. She retired from *The New Yorker* in 1991, and in 1994 edited a vast collection of the best writing from all of her books. It was titled, suitably, *For Keeps*.

Rod Steiger

Rod Steiger, who lived with a laugh that filled a room and a depression that consumed a decade, died Tuesday, July 9, 2002. The actor, who played more than 100 roles over fifty-five years and won an Oscar and two nominations, was seventy-seven. The cause of death, pneumonia and kidney failure, would have disappointed him: "I want to die in front of the camera," he liked to say.

A runaway who lied about his age to get into the navy and saw action in the Pacific, Steiger drifted into acting after World War II, he said, "to meet girls." He was instrumental in the early days of the Method, which transformed modern screen acting; after studying under Lee Strasberg at the Actors Studio, he

made his first significant film in 1954. It was Elia Kazan's *On the Waterfront*, where he played opposite Marlon Brando in scenes that have become part of movie folklore; it was to Steiger that Brando delivered his immortal "I coulda been a contender." Steiger was nominated for Best Supporting Actor.

Legend has it that Steiger faithfully stood next to the camera to provide a sight-line for Brando's performance, but that Brando refused to stand in for Steiger's responses, which were delivered to an assistant director. The story has been much asserted and denied, but Steiger remained somehow in Brando's shadow. The two men had similar builds and bluster, but it was Brando who played *The Godfather*, which Steiger said he turned down. He did definitely turn down the title role in *Patton*, which won George C. Scott an Oscar, and later recalled: "I didn't want to make a film glorifying war. That was the biggest mistake in my career."

Steiger went from success to success in the 1950s, notably as Jud Fry, the ill-favored ranch hand who sang "Poor Jud Is Dead" in *Oklahoma!* (1955). The same year, he played a self-loathing Hollywood mogul in *The Big Knife*, and in 1959 starred in *Al Capone*, the first of several biographical roles.

Steiger starred in *Dr. Zhivago* in 1965, and then was nominated for the title role in *The Pawnbroker* (1965). Considered the frontrunner at the Oscars, he recalled that he was halfway out of his seat when Lee Marvin's name was called for *Cat Ballou*. But in 1967, Steiger won the Oscar, playing a southern police chief who learns to respect black northern police chief Sidney Poitier in *In the Heat of the Night*.

I spent the day before he won that Oscar with Steiger, on the set of a movie he was making named *The Illustrated Man*. Joking with fellow actor Robert Drivas, he talked about his timetable to make it to the ceremony:

"I got it all figured out. We're going first-class, first-class. We shoot here right up until 3:15, see, then a helicopter picks me up at 3:30 and we go right up into the sky like a great yellow bird and land at the studio at 3:45. That saves me an hour over driving. Then I shave at the studio, put on my tux, and Claire's there waiting. We get into that big, beautiful Mercedes-Benz custom limousine, and we arrive at Santa Monica Civic Auditorium, and, boy, that's what I mean when I say style."

He told Drivas he'd toyed with the idea of having the chopper drop him off in front of the Oscars, but, "I'm not so practiced at this business of pulling up in a limousine and everybody cheers. I only went to one Hollywood premiere. I figured everybody ought to go to one. That was my first and last premiere. We pulled up and stepped out. Unfortunately, the car in front of us contained Lassie, so we were upstaged. Upstaged, you hear me, boy? I learned a lot about the business in five seconds. 'Lassie, Lassie,' they were all screaming."

That was the Steiger people enjoyed in the 1960s: a raconteur, speaking in the dialect of his current character, filled with stories. A few years later, I found myself on the location of his movie *Waterloo,* in the Ukraine. He was depressed because his wife, the actress Claire Bloom, had left him and was currently living with the producer Hillard Elkins (or "Ellery Hilkins," as Steiger had it). And he was sick of the soup that was served monotonously every day.

"Borscht again!" Steiger said. "It's the goddamn staff of life on this location. Borscht for lunch. Borscht for dinner. I'm afraid to come down for breakfast. The role of Napoleon has always fascinated me. It is my hope that, when this picture is completed, the role of Napoleon will still fascinate me. But if Napoleon had to eat goddamn borscht every goddamn day, I wonder if Napoleon himself would have given a good goddamn."

He had other hits in the 1970s, following Napoleon with performances as Mussolini and the gangster Lucky Luciano. But in the 1980s, he said, a cloud of clinical depression settled over him, and although he continued to work, he was in misery.

There is a memory from that time, from a revival of *Oklahoma!* at a film festival in Dallas in 1983. The musical had been brilliantly restored, and the screening was a triumph. Later, well-wishers crowded up to congratulate Steiger, who smiled back but quietly observed, "They hate Jud Fry. Just hate him."

I encountered him again in 1991, on board a cruise ship as part of Dusty Cohl's Floating Film Festival. He was happily remarried to Paula Ellis, and in 1993 they would have his son, Michael; a daughter, Anna, had been born to Claire Bloom, and both children survive. There was a tribute to Steiger on the ship, and as he recalled his days of depression, he wept briefly—then broke the tension by saying that Paula had helped him through the worst times, and that they had asked the captain of the Holland-American ship to remarry them at sea.

A wedding ceremony was arranged, complete with cake, and Steiger was happy that day, although you felt life had grown fragile around him; he and Paula were later divorced, and at the time of his death he was married to Joan Benedict.

On the day before he won the Oscar in 1968, he said why it would be nice to win the Academy Award: "If I won, I'd get a crack at scripts I might otherwise not see. And that's what I want and need. I make enough money. But if you can get yourself into a certain position in this business, get your salary up to a certain level, win the awards, then you can get a wider choice of scripts, and you don't have to do the crap simply because there's nothing else available. I want to get myself into that position— I'm about there now, I think—and then work like hell."

Steiger continued to work almost until the end of his life, in good movies and bad, good roles and mediocre ones. I ran into him from time to time, and there was still the big laugh and the crooked grin, the feeling that the campaign continued. He did some of the best film acting of his time, and when the good roles were not there he soldiered on, a professional, perhaps finding in work deliverance from the demons that had haunted him.

Billy Wilder

Billy Wilder, cynic, wit, philosopher, genius, is dead at ninety-five. One of a handful of indisputably great directors, he died at home in Beverly Hills on March 27, 2001, reportedly of pneumonia.

Wilder was a beloved Hollywood presence almost until the end, alert, funny, sharp-tongued. As Hollywood converged on the Academy Awards last Sunday, a giant billboard looked down on the arriving cars, with a photo and a quote from Wilder: "The only rule in the movies is, there are no rules."

Honors rained upon Wilder, who was nominated for twenty-one Oscars and won six, was the first man to win three for one film *(Sunset Boulevard)*, added the Irving Thalberg Award for lifetime achievement, and when he was honored at a special Academy gala in 1999, beamed down on the assembled crowd and sighed, "These things are so boring."

When the American Film Institute selected the greatest 100 American films of all time, there were four Wilder films on the list, and when it picked the 100 greatest comedies, his *Some Like It Hot* placed first. In my new book *The Great Movies*, only Wilder has four titles among the 100 films.

More of a tribute is that his best films do not age or date, and retain the same fresh edge they had when new. Consider these titles to measure his achievement: *Sunset Boulevard, Some Like It Hot, The Apartment, Double Indemnity, The Lost Weekend, Stalag 17, The Seven Year Itch, Witness for the Prosecution, The Big Carnival* (also released as *Ace in the Hole*), *One, Two, Three, Irma La Douce, Sabrina, The Fortune Cookie,* and *The Private Life of Sherlock Holmes.*

His films were instrumental in creating the screen images of Jack Lemmon, who was in seven of his films, Walter Matthau, who was in three (all with Lemmon), Marilyn Monroe (whose most famous single pose was when the wind blew up her dress in *The Seven Year Itch*), William Holden (*Sunset Boulevard* made Hollywood take him seriously as an actor), Shirley MacLaine (*The Apartment* was a career watershed), and Audrey Hepburn *(Sabrina)*. He cowrote *Ninotchka* (1939), which was Garbo's last great role; *Sunset Boulevard* (1950) was Gloria Swanson's comeback and, essentially, her farewell; *One, Two, Three* (1961) was Jimmy Cagney's final leading role.

Born Samuel Wilder in an Austrian village in 1906, nicknamed "Billy" by a mother who adored things American, he was a newspaperman who gravitated toward the thriving film industry in Berlin, and left Hitler's Germany for America in 1933. Uncertain of his English ("I knew 100 words when I got off the boat") but with a sure hand for characters and construction, he teamed with Charles Brackett to write a series of successful 1930s films, became a director with *The Major and the Minor* (1942), and in the 1950s found a new writing partner, I. A. L. Diamond, who collaborated on most of his remaining projects. On the set of the Lemmon-Matthau starrer *The Front Page* (1974), I watched him quietly confer with Diamond in a corner of the set before every shot. "If I. A. L. Diamond had been a Black Muslim," Wilder confided to me, "his name would have been I. A. L. X."

Wilder's movies were famous for zingers, one-liners, and great closing lines. *Some Like It Hot* is said to have the greatest closing line in Hollywood history. After Jack Lemmon dresses in drag to escape murder by the mob, millionaire Joe E. Brown falls in love with him. "You don't understand, Osgood!" Lemmon tells him, "I'm a man!" Brown: "Well, nobody's perfect."

In *The Big Carnival (Ace in the Hole)*, about a man trapped in a cave, Kirk Douglas advises the man's wife to be photographed while praying. Jan Sterling: "I don't pray. Kneeling bags my nylons." Wilder's *Sunset Boulevard* screenplay with Brackett includes an anthology of classic lines. William Holden tells Gloria Swanson, as an aging silent star: "You used to be big." Swanson: "I *am* big. It's the *pictures* that got small." And at the end, after she has gone mad and murdered the Holden character, she regally descends the stairs to be arrested: "All right, Mr. DeMille, I'm ready for my close-up."

Wilder's pictures are timeless, I think, because they rarely stooped to easy sentimentality. He anticipated and helped invent the modern age of irony. There was a jaundiced view of human nature, a dubiousness about too much sincerity.

In life as in his art, Billy Wilder had a gift for tactlessness redeemed by humor. Only last Tuesday, I was talking with his good friend Wolfgang Puck, the chef who also comes from Austria. Wilder was a regular at Puck's restaurant Spago, where they usually spoke in German.

"One day," Puck said, "Tony Curtis comes in with some of his new paintings to hang on the walls for a little exhibition. I go over to Billy and ask him if he wants to see Tony's work. Of course Billy had a fabulous private art collection—Miro, Picasso, Matisse. He walks over and looks at one of Tony's paintings, and with Tony standing right there he says, 'Lousy actor, lousy painter.' Then he sees the look on Tony's face and he wants to apologize. 'I'm sorry,' he tells him. 'I thought I was speaking German.'"

Film Festivals

Telluride Film Festival

Telluride Report No. 1:
A Celebration of Film

Telluride, Colorado, September 1, 2001—Some sort of symbolic divide was crossed here Friday, on the opening night of the twenty-eighth Telluride Film Festival, when the Telluride Medal was presented to Colin Callender, head of HBO Films. Making the presentation, Telluride co-director Tom Luddy observed that much of the best work in American film these days is being produced on cable television. It is the simple truth.

Callender oversaw the production of Mike Nichols's *Wit,* an HBO film earlier this year with an Emma Thompson performance that would be leading the Oscar sweeps, if it had opened in theaters. To Telluride he brought Agnieszka Holland's *Shot in the Heart,* based on a book written by the brother of Gary *(The Executioner's Song)* Gilmore.

Focusing on the last week of the two-time killer's life, the movie stars Giovanni Ribisi as his quiet, tortured younger brother, and Elias Koteas as Gilmore. It takes place mostly in the form of death-row conversations and flashbacks to the tortured childhoods of all the Gilmore brothers (Sam Shepard and Amy Madigan play their parents). The movie is too dark and perhaps too ambitious for theatrical release; cable guarantees it an audience, and it is worth noting that *The Executioner's Song,* with its brilliant early Tommy Lee Jones performance, was also made for cable.

Telluride is a celebration of film, period—not just new theatrical films, but made-for-cable, classics, restorations, revivals, student films, whatever seems first rate. The guest programmer's name is always kept a secret, this year with better reason than usual, because it is Salman Rushdie, the novelist put under death sentence by the Iranian fundamentalists for his writings. He is here with a sampling of Indian films (including Satyajit Ray's little-known children's film *The Golden Fortress)* and another sampling of science fiction (including the silent *Metropolis* with live music by the Alloy Orches-

tra, and Andrei Tarkovsky's science-fiction epic *Solaris).*

The three Telluride Tributes this year are to Catherine Breillat, the French director who uses explicit sex in her work; Om Puri, the legendary Indian actor now becoming well known in the West with films like *My Son, the Fanatic;* and the British director Ken Russell, who made a torrent of passionate and sometimes over-wrought films in the 1960s through the 1980s *(Women in Love, The Devils, The Music Lovers)* and now claims he is reduced to making home movies on video.

When I first came to Telluride in 1980 the festival was shoehorned into four tiny venues—the jewel box Opera House, the little Nugget theater on Main Street, the Mason's Hall, and the Quonset hut community center—plus, of course, the free outdoor screenings. Since then the community center has disappeared, the high school gymnasium has been converted into the vast MAX theater (with the little Minnie nearby), the 800-seat Chuck Jones Cinema appeared in the Mountain Village at the top of the ski lift, and this year the grade school gym has become the 600-seat Galaxy, with eye-popping graphics that cross Copernicus with Jules Verne.

These temporary cinemas, which are state-of-the-art, are put up and taken down in a week; festival goers race from one to another, trying to juggle impossible schedules. On Saturday night, for example, do you want to go to the Om Puri tribute with the premiere of his new film *Mystic Masseur,* or to Harold Lloyd's silent classic *Speedy* with a live performance by the Alloy Orchestra, or the Cannes Prize–winning Eskimo drama *The Fast Runner,* or the new Dogma movie *Italian for Beginners,* or the twisted cop drama *Lantana,* with Anthony LaPaglia? Choose one of the above. (I chose *Speedy* because I knew I would never again be able to see it in 35mm with a live orchestra.)

My festival began on Friday night with *The Cat's Meow,* Peter Bogdanovich's best film of recent years, which is based on a persistent Hollywood legend that William Randolph Hearst shot and killed Hollywood executive Thomas Ince on his yacht, and had the incident hushed up. In Bogdanovich's version, based on a script and play by Steven Peros, Hearst (Edward Herrmann) thought his mistress Marion Davies (Kirsten Dunst) was having an affair with Charlie Chaplin (Eddie Izzard), and shot Ince (Cary Elwes) thinking he was Chaplin. One juicy scene shows gossip columnist Louella Parsons (Jennifer Tilly) as a witness who gets a lifetime contract as the price for her silence. Bogdanovich says he first heard the story from Orson Welles; the Ince death has never been satisfactorily explained.

In between the movies, there's brunch at a dude ranch, a feed on Main Street for all attendees, and the prospect of walking down Main Street and running into Faye Dunaway, Ken Burns, Milos Forman, or Catherine Keener. The town is also filled with a few hundred motorcycle club members, middle-aged, genial and despite their leathers extremely unlike Hells Angels. One told me they knew nothing about a film festival: "We bike up here for the mountain scenery and the burgers at the Floradora Saloon."

Telluride Report No. 2: Real Laughter

September 2, 2001—At last here is real humor, welling up from the heart and from human nature, instead of the crude physical comedy of the summer specials. In Ismail Merchant's *The Mystic Masseur* and Nicole Holofcener's *Lovely and Amazing*, the Telluride festival warmed the souls of its audiences and sent them blinking and smiling back into the mountain sunshine.

The two films are seemingly completely different. *The Mystic Masseur,* based on the novel by V. S. Naipaul, tells the story of a poor Indian boy in Trinidad, mesmerized by books, who lifts himself step by step out of poverty, growing into a pundit and a politician but not necessarily becoming happier along the way. *Lovely and Amazing* tells of a few weeks in the lives of a mother and her three daughters—two grown-up and white, one a precocious eight-year-old adopted African-American. What the films have in common is a deep sympathy for the hopes and frailties of their characters, and a close observation of how people behave in love, marriage, and their careers.

There are two kinds of laughter, the laughter of surprise and the laughter of recognition. The summer teenage specials get laughs by shocking us with surprises that are usually of a sexual or excretory nature. Movies like these two Telluride treasures are funny in a deeper and more rewarding way, because we recognize in the characters our own weaknesses and evasions, our own ambitions and dreams.

The Mystic Masseur is told by a narrator who is not far removed from Naipaul himself—a Trinidadian of Indian ancestry, now a student at Oxford, who welcomes a visiting island dignitary who turns out to be Ganesh, the very same writer and holy man who inspired him as a youth. Flashbacks tell the story of the visitor, who wanted to be an author, tried to support himself as a masseur, and found success only by putting on a turban and repackaging himself as a Hindu adviser and healer.

Aasif Mandvi is Ganesh the masseur, Ayesha Dharker *(The Terrorist)* is his long-suffering, plucky wife, and Om Puri is richly comic as the father-in-law who craftily arranges the marriage and then tries to get out of paying for the wedding. The film has an unfailing touch for the Trinidad flavor, and quietly makes a point about the world of the characters by showing almost only Indians until Ganesh becomes a politician and find himself afloat in Port of Spain with African-Caribbean and British colonial officials.

The film has the instinct for period and setting of all the Merchant-Ivory productions, but seems to have absorbed them into its very pores; it is rare to see a rags-to-riches story in which we are so intimately involved with the characters, so sympathetic to them, and led so easily to understand that riches may not always be a good trade for the happiness of youthful ambition.

Lovely and Amazing almost defies description. It is about relationships gently and comically observed, involving characters who are smart, sane, and artists of daily conversation. Often we laugh simply because of the way they express themselves, or because they are so clearly speaking as ordinary people, not plot-driven robots. Brenda Blethyn plays the mother, who has adopted a young, bright, observant, sassy African-American girl (Raven Goodwin). Her two grown daughters are an actress (Emily Mortimer) and an unhappily married "artist"

(Catherine Keener) who makes miniature chairs out of twigs.

The film includes adulteries, affairs, and a health crisis, but the screenplay, by director Nicole Holofcener, takes them for granted. It doesn't punch up the obvious confrontations and crises, but looks between the pages for the moments in which the characters are most human. Few of the expected denouements take place, and what replaces them are moments of sudden insight and empathy for the characters. In a film of so much richness, it is, well, lovely and amazing how its special angle on race in our society makes clear so much that is unsaid.

More movies still to come. At first when you arrive in Telluride you can hardly breathe because the air is so thin at this altitude. After seeing movies like these, you realize that you are breathing deeply again after the oxygen deprivation of Hollywood factory product.

Telluride Report No. 3: Lost Art

September 3, 2001—There is a scene in François Truffaut's *Fahrenheit 451* where a colony of book lovers pace slowly through the snow around a pond, reciting the books they have committed to memory. This is in a future where the printed word has been banned. At Telluride sometimes I feel that movie lovers are in the same position, now that the pressures of the marketplace have marginalized all but the most palatable of films.

We remember films that no longer exist, or that exist but are not seen. Though DVDs and tapes allow movies to have a long half-life in the home, they are not a preservation medium—and no one wants to pay for the storage of original 35mm prints. We are not talking only about old films. One morning, drinking coffee in line before a movie, I heard horror stories from Jeff Joseph, a Los Angeles collector of trailers and prints. *Croupier* (2000) was one of the biggest hits of the late, lamented Shooting Gallery series, but when Shooting Gallery went under, what happened to the prints? Joseph thinks only one print of *Croupier* may still exist.

At festivals we attend state-of-the-art screenings of wonderful new films, and then those films enter an impatient marketplace where they must perform well immediately, or die. There is no longer the time for a film to find its audience.

At a screening I sat next to Bingham Ray, an indie film pioneer who cofounded October Films and now heads United Artists, positioned as the specialty arm of MGM. He was mourning the brief windows of opportunity for unusual films. "A movie like *My Dinner With André* eventually found an enormous audience," he said, "but at first it was just ignored. Today the art houses are as impatient as the big multiplexes."

How does that impact on some of the best films I've seen at Telluride this year? Consider *Revolution #9*, Tim McCann's heartfelt film about a woman who gradually realizes her fiancé is schizophrenic. The movie doesn't have sensational or exploitative scenes; it's a closely observed character drama, starring Michael Risely and Adrienne Shelley in the leads, with glimpses of their families, friends, and mental health professionals. It is utterly absorbing, and contributes to the understanding of mental illness, but will it have time to find its audience?

Italian for Beginners is another popular film at the festival, the first Dogma 95 film directed by a woman—Lone Scherfig, who in her remarks poked gentle fun at the Dogma movement. Her film is all gentle fun, about a group of lonely people whose lives intersect in a hotel-sports-restaurant complex. Warm humor comes out of their peculiarities, and people here love it—but will people elsewhere have a chance to see it?

And what about *No Man's Land*, by Danis Tanovic, who finds Kafkaesque dark comedy in the war in Bosnia? The film was a hit at Cannes and again here, with its story of soldiers from both sides trapped between lines and discovering a big plot surprise. Will the word "Bosnia" turn off the short attention spans of moviegoers before they get to the news that the film is original and entertaining?

I've seen some other good films here that may have hooks to grab large audiences. One is Ray Lawrence's *Lantana*, from Australia, about unhappy marriages, scarcely happier adulteries, and a missing person. Anthony LaPaglia, Geoffrey Rush, and Barbara Hershey star, in a film whose intersecting characters reminded me of *Magnolia*.

Nine Queens, a sneak preview from Argentina, may be a sleeper. You have not heard of the director or the stars, and I can tell you next to nothing about the plot, except to say that it is about a sting within a sting within a sting, and then some

And audiences here love *Amelie,* which I wrote about from Cannes, where it was denied a berth in the official selection because it was "not serious," and then went on to become the most popular French film of the year. The most accessible film by the visual virtuoso Jean-Pierre Jeunet *(City of Lost Children),* it has a luminous performance by Audrey Tautou as a romantic innocent in Paris. Maybe it will be one of the two or three subtitled films every year that break out big in America.

The festival has one more day to go, and I will be there for the 8:30 A.M. screening of *The Fast Runner,* a three-hour film about Eskimos that won prizes at Cannes and has been generating amazed word-of-mouth ever since. Can American moviegoers envision themselves attending a three-hour film about Eskimos, however good, when disposable, brainless fodder is available in every multiplex? I am not holding my breath for the answer.

Toronto Film Festival
Toronto Report No. 1:
So Many Movies, So Little Time

Toronto, September 7, 2001—The Toronto Film Festival used to unfold grandly over ten days. Now it seems to run for a weekend, plus added attractions. The opening three days are so insanely front-loaded that critics go nuts trying to map out their schedules; they stand in the lobby of the Varsity, crossing screenings off their lists.

It's not such a problem for the public, because festivalgoers have made their choices weeks in advance, or sometimes had their choices made for them by ticket availability. But a critic can choose from several advance press screenings at the same time, and this year, more than ever before, the 500-pound gorillas have booked themselves Friday through Sunday.

If I were here representing a film I loved and wanted it to get fair attention, I would avoid the first weekend like a curse. Smaller films suffer because the Hollywood studios are here with their junket films; visiting journalists pad around the hotels like house pets, lapping up their five-minute sound bites. They've made a Faustian bargain with their editors: Let me go to Toronto, and I'll give you all the movie stars you want—as long as I can stay to see the art films.

A wiser course is the one mapped out by films like *Lovely and Amazing, Waking Life, Revolution #9,* and *Asoka,* which will slip into town midweek, when the frenzy has died and there's time to consider the films instead of processing them—time to discuss them over a cup of coffee instead of racing to get in line for the next screening. The closing Saturday of the festival is always fun for me, because the craziness is over and I can go shopping for a Vietnamese musical.

I suppose normal people find all of this incomprehensible. Every movie critic is asked incessantly, "How many movies do you see in a day?" (One answer: "For every movie I see, I get asked that question four times.") The notion of seeing three, four, or five movies back-to-back would not strike any reasonable person as a pleasure, and yet at a festival like Toronto, where there's a good chance they'll be interesting, we line up eagerly. It's not the movies we see that's the problem. It's the movies we're missing.

* * *

I have not been a Stephen King fan, and yet I approached *Hearts in Atlantis,* the Friday night Gala, with unusual anticipation. It was time for a new look at the best-selling author.

I had dinner two years ago in New York with Peter Mayer, who as chief of Viking-Penguin published many of the best books of recent decades, and I asked him who was the best living novelist. "Saul Bellow," he said. Then he said: "And the most overlooked is Stephen King. He sells millions of books, but doesn't get credit for being as good as he is. For the twentieth century, he's our Dickens."

Chastened, I decided to listen to the audiobook of King's *Hearts in Atlantis,* read by William Hurt, and found myself driving around the block because I didn't want to park the car until a chapter was over. I was humbled: King was better than I thought, or at least this book certainly was.

I went to the Scott Hicks film wondering if the movie could possibly capture the eerie, bittersweet tone of King's story (and of Hurt's great vocal performance, with its pauses and rushes and off-center emphasis, as if the story's narrator were puzzling it out as he remembered the story). I was not disappointed. I was also startled that the sets and locations looked so much as I had imagined them.

The movie is faithful to the events of the book and even more faithful to its mood—and with *Hearts in Atlantis* mood is more or less everything. A dispassionate synopsis of the story would seem to show it thin on plot and heavy on atmosphere. It involves a friendship between a boy named Bobby (Anton Yelchin) on the cusp of adolescence, and a boarder named Ted (Anthony Hopkins) who arrives with his possessions in paper bags and moves into the rooms upstairs. It quietly becomes clear that Ted has certain powers, that Bobby has tendencies in that direction, and that "low men" might come to town looking for the boarder.

It doesn't much matter who the low men are, or why they want Ted. Indeed, the book and movie skew slightly differently in what they lead us to believe about the men. The movie is not about that, although a lesser one would be. It's about friendship, and growing up, and Bobby's troubled relationship with his mom (Hope Davis), and about how his first kiss (with Mika Boorem) will be, as Ted tells him, the standard by which all future kisses will be judged.

Scott Hicks's *Shine* was one of the most celebrated Gala premieres of recent years. He has returned to Toronto for luck, no doubt, with this new film, and I think he will find it. He's rare among modern directors in choosing the wide screen and fully exploiting it; his interiors stay wide to emphasize rooms opening off of rooms, and mirrors reflecting the action back on itself. The film is gorgeous to look at. But its strength is in the mood, in the way Anthony Hopkins lazily smokes Chesterfields and nudges the kid into a richer adulthood without even seeming to think much about it.

* * *

On my Saturday calendar: George Christy's famous luncheon at the Four Seasons, which for years has gathered the top directors and stars for a menu invariably featuring Chicken Pot Pie à la Garth Drabinsky. George has been in hot water lately with Hollywood moralists who were shocked! shocked! to discover he follows approximately the same ethical guidelines as most other gossip columnists in the history of show business. Unlike some of them, George has brought more smiles than frowns into the world. Should be an interesting afternoon.

Toronto Report No. 2: Lunch with George

September 8, 2001—Seventy-five of his old friends turned up for lunch Saturday with George Christy. Many of them had logged ten years or more at his annual soiree at the Four Seasons, where the top stars and directors at the Toronto Film Festival mix with Canadian tycoons and political leaders. The routine was familiar, including the Chicken Pot Pie à la Garth Drabinsky, but there was one innovation: This was the first year George's after-dinner toast included the observation that since our last gathering he had been "screwed, stewed, and tattooed."

Christy is the embattled columnist for the *Hollywood Reporter*, on suspension after charges by a former *Reporter* writer that he accepted freebies such as limousines, meals, hotel rooms, and favors. He is also said to have entered the rolls of the Actors' Guild health benefits without having appeared in every picture that listed him in its credits. Such matters will be adjudged in the fullness of time by the appointed authorities, but in the meantime George is in exile.

It is a season for Hollywood moralists to be shocked! shocked! by practices that have been the industry standard for years. Recently Peter Bart, the powerful editor of *Variety*, was suspended. Among the charges was that he used politically incorrect language—another way of saying he talked exactly like every studio executive, editor, or journalist (or unsaintly human being) who came of age before 1980. Bart is now back at work, sentenced to take "sensitivity training." At Telluride, a *Variety* staffer expressed relief that Bart had survived, adding, "God help those poor kids if they make him coach a Little League team."

I found myself underwhelmed by both scandals, since they were essentially versions of Gotcha! aimed at people unwise enough to still observe the practices they learned in their youth. We move along. Until about 1980, I went on paid junkets, but then it began to seem wrong, and the paper agreed that it would pay. Times change. But do we expect gossip columnists to pick up their own tabs? Is nothing sacred? Or profane, in Bart's case?

In a sense, the consumer is protected by the practice of comping gossips: Since they never pick up the tab anywhere they go, you know they're not there for the free cocktail weenies. Christy's "The Great Life" column, sometimes assumed to refer to his own, included coverage of dinners, parties, openings, closings, weddings, dedications, premieres, festivals, funerals, awards, holidays, and coronations, all told in a rush of boldface names. It was what it was. Anyone assuming George paid for his own dinner at the Golden Globes was probably moving his lips as he read.

Characters like George Christy add a little color to an industry that has become terminally staid. He brings a flair to his act; we're grateful for the entertainment.

Let me tell you a story. On the night before the Academy Awards this year, Miramax threw the annual party at which its stars enact satirical scenes from the nominated films. On stage were actors like Ben Affleck, Geoffrey Rush, and Jennifer Tilly. The ballroom of the Beverly Wilshire was standing room only. By that I mean that Kevin Spacey was standing. Jennifer Connelly was standing. Gwyneth Paltrow was standing. Harvey Weinstein, the chief of Miramax, was standing. We were all standing because there weren't seats.

Only one person was seated. I plowed my way through the shoulder-to-shoulder mob, dodging trays of canapés that hungry stars lunged for with both hands. Then in the middle of the floor I came upon a table immaculately laid with a linen tablecloth and supplied with china and crystal. At this table was seated George Christy, attended by his own waiter, who was supplying him with choice crab legs and succulent jumbo shrimp.

The entire party was free for everybody. But George had raised the stakes. His private table was an expression of style, crossed with gamesmanship. Only a puritan or a prosecutor would fail to get the joke. The message was: Everyone in the room had turned up for the free feed, but George demanded to dine in a civilized manner.

Now back to the Four Seasons in Toronto on Saturday afternoon. At George's right hand sat Hilary Weston, the lieutenant governor of Ontario. At his left hand, Garth Drabinsky, whose stewardship of Cineplex Odeon has led to well-publicized legal trials. I was next to Garth, who told me, "George is going through hell." Maybe, I suggested, that was why he wanted Garth at his side—for moral support. "I sat next to him last year, before his troubles started," Drabinsky observed.

In the room were stars like Helena Bonham Carter, Laura Herring, and Arsinee Khanjian. Directors like Norman Jewison, Fred Schepisi, and Atom Egoyan. Four former directors of the festival and Piers Handling, its current head. Critics, columnists, tycoons, politicians, all regulars of what George calls "our pot pie family." And yes, reader, chicken pot pie was served, as it has been every year since Drabinsky said how much he admired it, except for the year of the unfortunate experiment with the chicken paella, which was dry.

George rose for his traditional toast, in which he thanked everyone involved plus various assistant pastry chefs not even visible. He told again the story of Drabinsky's passion for pot pie. He recalled the year that festival cofounder Dusty Cohl revealed he could not abide green peas—and how the kitchens of the Four Seasons had produced a pot pie for Dusty that contained no peas. He conceded he felt screwed, stewed, and tattooed by his recent travail, but said he was still standing, and happy to be joined by his friends. You have to admire a man who in the face of his troubles was still thanking the Four Seasons for the flower arrangements.

"Do you really like chicken pot pie?" I asked Drabinsky.

"Well . . ." he said. "Yes, I do. And I like the billing. Chicken Pot Pie à la Garth Drabinsky. If he changes the menu, he might name it after someone else."

George was accepting compliments for his speech. I asked him if Dusty really had a pea-free pie.

"I don't know what's the matter with that man," George sighed. "Those are fresh peas from the vine."

Toronto Report No. 3: Rohmer Unveils Historical Drama

September 9, 2001—One of the best films at this year's Toronto Film Festival is "too slow," another is a "chick flick," a third is "too weird," and a fourth is "too talky." People told me these things as they were leaving the theater.

1. "Too slow." That would be Eric Rohmer's *L'Anglaise et le Duc (The Lady and the Duke)*, the story of an aristocratic Scottish lady (Lucy Russell) who lives in Paris during the Revolution. Once the mistress of the future King George IV, now under the protection of the Duke of Orleans (Jean-Claude Dreyfus), she holds fiercely monarchist views and disdains the mob. The film, which uses digital effects to re-create the period, shows her concealing a wounded nobleman in her bed while a citizens' committee searches her house, standing up to the duke when he thinks hypocrisy will save his skin, and proudly facing a revolutionary tribunal. There is a scene in which her life depends on the contents of a letter in English that she possesses but has not opened, and when a translator is lacking, she reads it herself.

This movie, made in Rohmer's eighty-first year, is one of his most magnificent, an ambitious historical drama from a director better known for intensely observed moral tales of everyday life. Lucy Russell plays Grace Elliott as a woman who has not slept her way to the top so much as imposed herself there by sheer force of character. Unintimidated, unafraid, she is a fascination to Orleans, who is played by Dreyfus as a man who opposes free speech in the republic but admires it in his mistress. Like all of Rohmer's films, this one observes a moral dilemma in which some people act well and others badly; it has the visual beauty of an engraving, a pace that echoes the inexorable progress of the revolution, and the belief that it is less important whether you are Left or Right than whether you behave bravely in accord with your principles. Far from being too slow, it tells its story at a preordained pace; perhaps modern Hollywood product has trained some moviegoers to view too fast.

2. "The chick flick." I saw Nicole Holofcener's *Lovely and Amazing* at Telluride, where it was just about my favorite film. It stars Brenda Blethyn as the mother of three daughters. Michelle (Catherine Keener) is trapped in a loveless marriage and trapped, too, by her self-deception; she makes little chairs out of twigs, calls them her "art," and believes her husband steps on them deliberately. Elizabeth (Emily Mortimer) is a would-be actress who fills the house with stray dogs. And Annie (Raven Goodwin) is an adopted eight-year-old African-American, who in this emotional minefield of egos has the pluck to define her own space and defend it.

The movie sidesteps obvious climaxes and aims instead at the way the emotional mix shifts in the family. A lesser movie would have been preoccupied by the audition, the missing child, the health crisis, the unexpected injury. This one is about the way these women look for continuity and reconciliation, and try to find the emotional through-line in a crisis. Does that make it a "chick flick"? What an insult to women, and men. It doesn't condescend to women or close out men; it's too good for that. One of its treasures is the oblique way it handles the subject of the eight-year-old's race; the movie lives in a time when we have more or less gotten over the fact that someone else is of a different color and can move on to more interesting differences.

3. "Too weird." Not a useful observation, since it refers only to the values of the person speaking. The film is *From Hell*—an uncommonly creepy horror picture from the Hughes brothers, who star Johnny Depp as an opium-smoking, possibly psychic London detective on the trail of Jack the Ripper. I was expecting a Hammer horror film crossed with postmodern irony. What I got was an atmospheric reconstruction of the historical period, and a solution that is not a gimmick but a plausible hypothesis, based on clues that are in plain view.

Yes, the movie is gory. Hearts and livers are juggled like hamburger patties. The grisly nature of Jack's dismemberments is made perfectly clear. But isn't that at the heart of our fascination with Jack the Ripper, who has had a longer shelf life than any other serial killer? Depp and Robbie Coltrane, who plays his sergeant, shake loose from the clichés of the cop-buddy genre and submerge themselves in the story. Ian Holm plays one of those Victorian doctors besotted by mystical theories. "Too weird?" In a movie about Jack the Ripper? Why do so many moviegoers keep trying to push movies back into their boxes?

4. "Too talky." That would be Richard Linklater's *Waking Life*, the most visually alive movie of the year. Some moviegoers have the

wrong organs on duty. The critics of the Rohmer film were listening with their eyes, and those who find Linklater too talky are watching with their ears. The movie is a series of conversations about free will, dreams, existentialism, and the nature of reality, as its hero wanders through Austin, Texas, in a state between life and death. But that's only the story line. Look at this movie! Linklater shot it in live-action digital and then transformed it into shimmering, magical animation. He worked with Tommy Pallotta and Bob Sabiston, computer animation wizards who assigned separate artists to each major character, so that the movie interprets each scene according to the personalities involved.

The result is a film that dances and vibrates with life. I have never seen animation shapeshift in this way to mirror the elusive feel of a scene. The dialogue is no less engaging; the conversations are not empty exercises, but the quest of a hero trying to reason himself through that most perplexing experience—life. Since every word and idea of every conversation is expressed with clarity (there is no show-off obscurity), anyone who finds it too talky is not listening; in an age when too much dialogue is monosyllabic sound bites, are we forgetting how to listen?

Toronto Report No. 4: Mortality

"I was there before the beginning, young fellow. And now it's after the end."
—Mr. Bernstein in *Citizen Kane*

September 11, 2001—This is a meditation on mortality.

"I made a conscious decision to work all the time while I was growing up," Christina Ricci told me. "I didn't want people to see me in a movie and be shocked that I wasn't a kid anymore. I wanted to grow up on-screen."

We sat and talked late at night, this young woman of twenty-one whose wide, dark eyes I remembered from *The Addams Family* when she was eleven. And I thought about how the movies are a time machine that allow us to travel back and forth through the lives of actors, seeing them older today, younger tomorrow, as we reflect on our own inexorable movement through time.

The next day I went to see Josee Dayan's *Cet Amour-la,* starring Jeanne Moreau in a story about the last years of the novelist Marguerite Duras. At sixty-five, the famous writer attracts a handsome young man who comes to visit her, is mesmerized, moves in, and becomes her lover, secretary, and companion. He stays for sixteen years—until the end.

Jeanne Moreau is seventy-three. I remember her in *The Lovers, Jules and Jim, A Woman Is a Woman,* her full lips promising a wisdom that a college boy could barely imagine. I have seen her grow older on the screen. She was beautiful in her twenties, but those who are the real thing can look beautiful until the day they die, and here it is lovely how Moreau grins (and she grins a lot) and the wrinkles fade and we see the impudent spirit that fascinated Jim, and Jules.

I think she is fearless about her image because she doesn't obsess about her films; she told me once she never goes to see them, but acts because she enjoys the physical work itself: "Your job is to see them. My job is to make them."

The next movie I saw was Fred Schepisi's *Last Orders,* based on Graham Swift's novel about four men who set out to scatter the ashes of their friend. Flashbacks show happier days, and then reveal darker secrets.

The movie stars five actors of roughly the same generation: Michael Caine, Bob Hoskins, Tom Courtenay, David Hemmings, and Helen Mirren, and a younger one, Ray Winstone. Watching the older men on the screen was like a lesson on the passage of time. I had seen all of their first movies, and reviewed some of them.

Michael Caine has lost the sleek bad-boy look of *Alfie* and *The Ipcress File,* but seems settled forever into a comfortable middle age. Bob Hoskins always looks about the same. Helen Mirren still looks younger than her characters, although they are growing older.

But Tom Courtenay! I remembered him as the skinny rebel in *The Loneliness of the Long-Distance Runner* and the gawky dreamer of *Billy Liar.* I hadn't seen him much in the movies lately. Could this tall, benign, kindly looking man with the jowls and the paunch be—Tom Courtenay? And as for David Hemmings, whom I played darts with in London in 1967, whose *Blow-Up* I dissected a frame at a time two years ago at the Virginia Film Festival—I did not know who I was looking at until the final credits came up. Antonioni's swinging photographer has become an alderman.

The movie was uncommonly moving. But something was happening beneath it. Perhaps the Jeanne Moreau picture started me down this interior meditation on the gift that actors make when they let us watch them living their lives. I looked at Caine, and I thought, God, he just keeps plugging along in good pictures and bad, letting us get to know him as the best of company. Helen Mirren reminded me of her passionate earth-mother in the IRA drama *Cal*, and the fearless way she made her body available to Peter Greenaway in *The Cook, the Thief, His Wife and Her Lover*. Because she's done so many films and taken so many chances, I get a sense of her courage as an artist.

I felt love forming for these actors, and for all good actors. A good performance is a gift of the ego. A great performance is a gift of the spirit. Seeing dozens of performances during a lifetime of moviegoing allows us to know actors, in a certain way, better than people in our own lives. It is a civilizing process, because it allows us to observe mortality.

These thoughts occurred during *Last Orders*. Walking back to the hotel late at night I passed a sidewalk café, and sitting at a table was Richard Harris, white-haired and bearded. I remembered him in *This Sporting Life* and that I met him on the set of the first movie location I ever visited, *Camelot*.

He said he was waiting until the end of the screening of his new film, for a Q&A session. "It's called *My Kingdom*," he said. Tell me about your character, I said. "Think of King Lear in Liverpool," he said. "I will," I said.

As actors make their way from one end of life to another, we learn from them on their journey. The tragedy of Hamlet is that he has no answers. The tragedy of King Lear is that there are no answers.

Note: All of this was written late at night on Monday, September 10. After the news of the next morning, I was in a mood to scrap it. I return to it hours later and reflect that one of the reasons we go to movies is because the great ones help us treasure the gift of life. Artists are like priests. They share our mortality but are closer to the mysteries. Blow, winds, and crack your cheeks. We press on.

The Tragedy

I walked into a movie at 8:30 A.M. Tuesday, September 11, and walked out two hours later into a different world. The movie was a comedy about a wedding in India. Small human stories, little joys and heartbreaks, some music. It made me happy. I left the screening and was stopped by a woman who works with the festival; I've never learned her name, but we smile at each other every year.

"Something very bad has happened," she said. She told me what it was. I walked over to the coffee counter in the theater lobby. A crowd was watching the TV. You saw what I saw. We were all watching TV.

My wife and stepdaughter were in New York City. They had attended the Michael Jackson concert the night before. My heart began to pound. I walked as fast as I could back to the hotel.

I tried to call New York, but the lines were jammed. Also the lines to Chicago. I saw the phone light blinking. There was a message from my wife, Chaz, saying she and Sonia were safe. Thank God she got through. On the way to La-Guardia, they had seen the World Trade Center burning. At the airport, they ran into a woman Chaz knew, who had a car there, and who offered them a ride to her Long Island home. The airport was being evacuated, and the routes to Manhattan were closed. This woman saved them from standing on the street.

My story is like so many stories. Thousands of innocent victims are dead, but we think first about those we love.

What is new and frightening is that on Tuesday when the tragedy happened, we were all forced to think in these personal terms. The war was here.

This day was going to come sooner or later. In recent years, the United States has fought push-button wars thousands of miles from home. Today the war is no longer far away. The continental United States, which was not invaded during any of the wars of the twentieth century, has been stained by the blood of countless victims. We are weeping. The twenty-first century began today.

I sit in this Toronto hotel room, filled with sadness. It may be I know people who were helpless passengers when those planes went down. The tragedy of the collapsing World Trade towers is too sorrowful to contemplate.

One of my editors calls. Can I write something about the reaction in Toronto?

Yes, I can. The reaction here is the same as everywhere. We are stunned, we are in grief, and in the dark places of our hearts, we fear a time of anarchy and violence—an apocalypse on Earth—unless men learn to live together on a planet that has grown too small.

The phone rings. It is my wife. She and her daughter are safe in a hotel on Long Island. I advise them to rent a car right now, fill it with gas and wait until tomorrow to see what develops. They may have to drive back to Chicago. Who knows when the skies will be safe? I hear myself talking, and I feel like a character in one of those dumb end-of-the-world movies.

I hang up and watch the president on television. He is speaking on a pre-recorded tape, and there is something wrong with the tape. Fox News keeps stopping it, backing it up, starting it again. He backs away from the podium, approaches it, backs away again. I have seen so many movies I wonder if he is there at all. A few minutes later, of course they are interviewing Tom Clancy: He wrote the book.

I call the film festival office. All screenings and other events have been canceled for today; they are trying to decide about the rest of the festival. They tell me they are working with local hotels to find places for stranded guests, since the airports are shut down, and the border has been closed.

The border between the United States and Canada has been closed. That takes a moment to sink in.

How will I get home? Should I rent a car too? Thank God I have friends here. Me, me, me—and thousands dead. But that is what happened today. Now it is about us, and not just about them.

Toronto Report No. 5: An Antidote to Hate

September 13, 2001—Through the cloud of sadness which has enveloped the Toronto Film Festival since Tuesday, a few films have shone like beacons.

—*Atanarjuat (The Fast Runner)* is an astonishing epic film made by and about the Inuit

peoples of the Canadian Arctic, telling a story of a crime that ruptures the trust within a closely knit group, and how justice is achieved and healing begins. Director Zacharias Kunuk and his writer, Paul Apak Angilinq, collected oral versions of an Inuit legend from several elders, collated them into a story, submitted the story to the elders for suggestions, and then filmed it as a collaborative expression of the group's memory. The "fast runner" of the title is a man who must run naked through the snow and is presumed to be dead, but survives; the three-hour film was shot entirely on location, and shows the tenacity and creativity of a people making a home of a frigid wilderness.

—Tim Blake Nelson's *The Grey Zone* is about the "Sonderkommando"—work parties of Jewish prisoners in Nazi camps given special privileges in return for helping in the extermination process. Their own deaths are postponed four months, and with rumors of the Russian troops moving closer, there is the hope that they might be rescued in that time. Of course, they are condemned by their fellow Jews, and most are filled with self-loathing, but it is possible to understand why they would clutch at a thread of survival.

Two story lines intersect: One of the groups attempts a rebellion, at the same time that a young girl somehow survives the gas chamber and is hidden by her presumed executioners. The movie is less sentimental, more brutal than many Holocaust films, and pushes questions of situational ethics to the breaking point. Strong performances by Harvey Keitel, David Arquette, Steve Buscemi, Natasha Lyonne, and Mira Sorvino, none of them looking at all like themselves.

—Paul Cox's *The Diaries of Vaslav Nijinsky* is a haunting tone poem about the famous Polish-Russian dancer, told in his own words, in a narration read by Derek Jacobi. His diaries were written after a breakdown—when he felt he was mad not in his mind but in his heart. The soul of the film is in its extraordinary editing; Cox has assembled images realistic and abstract, symbolic and mundane, and Paul Grabowsky's sound track combines classical music and other sources to underline the thoughts of a man who trusted art as his defense against the void.

—Tim McCann's *Revolution #9* is a brave film starring Adrienne Shelley as the fiancée of a young man (Michael Risley) who begins to exhibit symptoms of mental illness, probably schizophrenia. The film is neither a horror show nor a docudrama, but a touching look at the way the woman's love makes her loyal even as she seems helpless to change the course of events. More realistic, tender, unsensational than most films about mental illness.

—Richard Linklater's *Waking Life* is particularly poignant after the events of September 11. It's about a young college graduate who wanders through Austin, Texas, as a seeker of truth, listening to advice, philosophy, wisdom, and foolishness—a torrent of words from vividly drawn and widely assorted characters. The film was shot as live action, and then digitally animated into a riotously creative feature. At a time when we seek answers, here is a film about—seeking answers.

—Jill Sprecher's *Thirteen Conversations About One Thing* is a film about happiness. The lives of its characters intersect in New York, in stories of careers, adultery, unemployment, the quest for love, the fear of death. One of the men in the film is singularly unlucky, and singularly sanguine about it; he sees the sunny side, and so he finds it, while those who plan and scheme find that life will not bend to their wills.

—Mira Nair's *Monsoon Wedding* shows the gathering of an extended Bombay family for an arranged marriage. It is a comedy and makes no deep discoveries about human nature, but it finds a way to be about love without being about sex, and there is a subplot involving the maid and the wedding planner, whose own surprise romance is amazingly touching. No matter where they're set, movies like this are universal, because all happy marriages, like all happy families, are the same.

—Fred Schepisi's *Last Orders* is as touching as any film in the festival, an elegiac story about a butcher who dies, and how his son and three of his friends make a journey to scatter his ashes, intercut with a conversation between one of his friends and the widow. Truths and secrets are revealed, alliances shift, the meaning of a life is revealed. The wonderful ensemble cast represents a generation of British actors: Michael Caine, Tom Courtenay, Bob Hoskins, Helen Mirren, David Hemmings and the younger Ray Winstone.

—Sturla Gunnarsson's *Rare Birds* is a sweetheart of a film, whimsical and touching, about a lonely restaurant owner (William Hurt) on a barren coast of Newfoundland. When sightings of a rare duck are reported, his business suddenly picks up, and so does his personal life, as Molly Parker wanders into it. He meets her through her brother-in-law (Andy Jones), a scuba-diving codger who dreams of marketing a "recreational submarine." By playing the character tenderly instead of going for obvious laughs, Hurt stays within the delicate fabric of the story.

—Nanni Moretti's *The Son's Room*, from Italy, which won the Palme d'Or at Cannes, tells a story of personal loss in a bright, perceptive way; we're reminded of *Ordinary People* or *Terms of Endearment*. The movie stars Moretti as a therapist, happily married, with two teenage children, whose life is shaken by an unexpected tragedy. The key to the film is in the way it sees and hears the specific responses of the survivors to their loss. Many of Moretti's earlier films, such as *Caro Diario* and *Aprile*, have placed him in the autobiographical foreground; here he steps back into a family unit and tells a story of surprising power.

There are other films I liked, and others still to see. A festival like this seems like an antidote to hate, because it brings together people and movies from all over the world, and we seek to understand others, instead of demonizing them.

Toronto Report No. 6: The Awards

September 16, 2001—A film turned down by the Cannes festival has won the AGF People's Choice Award at Toronto. Jean-Pierre Jeunet's *Amelie of Montmartre*, a dazzling comedy about a Paris waitress who interacts with the most unexpected people, was voted the most popular film at the twenty-sixth annual festival.

Toronto is technically not a competitive festival, although it has given birth to all sorts of associated prizes that are announced at the closing ceremonies just as if they were official. The People's Choice, the most important award, is a weighted ballot by the moviegoers themselves.

Amelie has been winning hearts ever since Cannes, where it played in the marketplace after festival officials rejected it for the main competition, sniffing that it was "not serious." Many critics said they liked it better than anything in the competition, and it went on to become the top-grossing film of the year in France.

The Inuit film *Atanarjuat (The Fast Runner)*, filmed on location north of the Arctic Circle, won the City of Toronto Award as best Canadian film. Winner of the Camera d'Or at Cannes, for best first feature, it was directed by Zacharias Kunuk from a screenplay compiled from age-old legends of the Arctic peoples. It's a three-hour epic, visually stunning, unmistakably authentic.

The International Critics' Prize went to Yamina Benguigui's *Inch'Allah Dimanche*, a French film about Algerian men separated from their families and brought to France. When a family

is reunited after many years, the husband is cruel to his wife.

The Volkswagen Discovery Award, voted by the press corps for best first film, went to CheeK's *Chicken Rice War*, from Singapore. It's a romantic comedy loosely inspired by *Romeo and Juliet* about feuding families in the chicken rice industry.

Inertia, by Sean Garrity, won the City TV Award for best Canadian first feature, for its story of "a tangled web of desire in Winnipeg."

The runners-up for the People's Choice Award were two Indian films by American-based directors: *Maya*, by Digvijay Singh, about a girl whose carefree childhood changes dramatically with adolescence, and *Monsoon Wedding*, by Mira Nair, about an extended family gathering in Bombay for a marriage.

Sundance Film Festival
Sundance Report No. 1:
Redford Opens Fifteenth Festival

Salt Lake City, Utah, January 11, 2002—Veterans of the Sundance Film Festival's opening nights make bets with first-timers that Geoffrey Gilmore, the festival's director, will walk onstage and use these exact words: "It is with great pleasure that I welcome you to this year's Sundance Film Festival." They always win. This year they lost. The lights went down, a spotlight picked out the podium, and there was—Robert Redford, the festival's founder, who usually avoids the limelight.

The applause was long and loud. Here is a mainstream Hollywood star who has won the affection of filmmaking outsiders with the single most useful contribution anyone has made to the independent film community. His Sundance Institute runs workshops for hopeful stage and screen projects. His Sundance Festival showcases indie films at the most important single festival in America. And the Sundance Channel, along with IFC, Bravo, HBO, and Showtime, provide cable outlets for films that can't always find screens in the nation's dumbed-down multiplexes.

This year, Redford observed, the institute is twenty years old and the festival is fifteen. "As Hollywood narrows its focus to younger audi-

ences, high-tech films, and special effects," he said, "moviegoers are starving for more diversity." The independent film movement fills the gap, acting as a "social barometer," especially after September 11.

The opening night film was an example, a Sundance project that began as a play, was performed onstage, then returned to the Sundance film workshop. *The Laramie Project* is a reconstruction of the murder of Matthew Shepard, the twenty-one-year-old gay college student who was kidnapped by two Laramie, Wyoming, men about his own age, driven out into the country, tied to a fence, tortured, and left to die.

To create the original play, Moises Kaufman and the Tectonic Theater Company went to Laramie, interviewed some 250 locals, and then wove their words into a play where they were portrayed by actors. The movie shows this process at work: Four filmmakers, moving around Laramie, talk to teachers, bartenders, mechanics, police officers, doctors, clergymen, parents, friends. It is significant that *The Laramie Project* was funded by HBO and will premiere on cable; at a time when Hollywood studios are shy of ambitious, risky projects, cable is stepping up to the plate.

At first the film's method is a little offsetting, because many of the actors are instantly recognizable as themselves. Here's Amy Madigan as the cop, Steve Buscemi as the mechanic, and Sandra Bullock, Christina Ricci, Laura Linney, Peter Fonda, Janeane Garofolo, Jeremy Davies. Then the material takes over.

Opening night is at Salt Lake City's huge Abravanel Hall, and then the festival moves up the hill to Park City, said to be already jammed this year with advance crews for the Winter Olympics. Before the screening, first-nighters mingle in the lobby, networking, exchanging pitches, and using the bane of every festival screening, their cell phones ("If it's for me," Redford said when a phone rang during his opening remarks, "tell them I'm speaking").

I ran into Joe Shumway, the mayor of Laramie, and Jo Ann B. Davis, executive director of the tourism board, and I thought to myself: Is it likely that a film about the murder of Matthew Shepard will boost tourism in Laramie? After seeing the film, I thought, well, it can't hurt. The film is not a shrill indictment of Laramie, but a sad portrait of two callow young men who, as they are portrayed in the film, were capable of committing a mindless act of cruelty without even thinking about it much.

Were they encouraged by a culture of hate? That is the easy answer, but the film isn't so predictable. It hears prejudice from many locals, but also finds citizens who are accepting and tolerant. It listens to local gays, some out, some not, and the phrase "live and let live" is skewed by a Laramie lesbian, who says, "In other words, don't tell me and I won't mind." One of the most eloquent characters is the local Catholic priest, who in a halting, sincere way provides the conscience for the film. It is typical of Laramie, as it would be probably of any small town, that the residents are shocked the crime was committed by locals, and would have been obscurely relieved if the killers had been outsiders, just passing through.

After the somber mood of *The Laramie Project,* the cold night air awaked the festival's latent spirit, which lies somewhere between a trade show and a carnival midway. People told each other about their screenings. John Malkovich, director of Friday night's Park City opener, *The Dancer Upstairs,* was there in his beret, with Lianne Halfon and Russell Smith; the three of them produced the wonderful *Ghost World.*

People promote their films in bizarre ways. I ran into Dan Gold and Judith Helfand, who made *Blue Vinyl,* a seriocomic documentary about vinyl in American society. They were handing out necklaces to promote their film. They got the idea when Helfand's parents had their house covered in vinyl siding. What's on each necklace? A piece of vinyl taken directly from her parents' house.

Now we all go up the hill, where Sundance is joined by unofficial satellite fests for refuseniks, like Slamdance and Slumdance. Helfand told me of the latest: Shmoozdance, a nightly party in Park City's Temple Har Shalom. Show your vinyl at the door.

Sundance Report No. 2: Festival Buzz Is All About *Gerry*

Park City, Utah, January 14, 2002—I walked out of the screening of *Gerry* and was pounced on by three women who had just seen the film.

"How would you describe it?" they said.

"It is easier to describe than any other film I have ever seen at Sundance," I said. "Two friends go for a hike in the desert and get lost."

"Not that kind of description! Would you say it was . . . existential?"

"Existential?"

"Like, we have to chose to live or die?"

"They do not have a choice to make. They're lost and they can't find their car. They have no water and no food."

"What I think," said one of the women, "is that it's like *Waiting for Godot,* except without the dialogue."

"It has dialogue," her friend said.

"But not serious dialogue."

"The dialogue in *Godot* is not serious," I said. "At least, it is not intended by the speakers to be serious."

"In *Godot,*" the women said, "they wait and wait and he never comes. In *Gerry,* they walk and walk and they never get anywhere."

"There you have it," I said, edging toward the sandwich counter.

My heart was sinking, because I knew that I was doomed to be asked about *Gerry* over and over and over during this Sundance festival. There is always a movie like this, a movie so simple that no one can believe it is that simple.

The movie stars Matt Damon and Casey Affleck, brother of Ben. It was written by them with the director, Gus Van Sant. Filmgoers will recall that Matt Damon and Ben Affleck, brother of Casey, wrote *Good Will Hunting,* which was directed by Van Sant.

The movie does indeed involve Damon and Affleck going for a walk on a desert trail, heedlessly leaving it, and getting themselves good and lost. They do not talk much. Their two longest conversations involve a dumb contestant on *Jeopardy* and Affleck's bad luck with a video game (he had just conquered Thebes, but then he needed twelve trained horses and only had eleven). The big action scene happens when one of the characters stands on top of a rock for a long time trying to decide whether to jump down to where the other character is.

I walked back into the Eccles Theater for the next movie, which was *Good Girl,* starring Jennifer Aniston, wife of Brad Pitt. I would not mention her marital status except that Brad came to the screening with his wife, and there was a media riot for fifteen minutes as photographers climbed on top of each other's inert bodies to get photographs of Brad and Jennifer, which, as you know, are in tragically short supply.

This melee was taking place in the lower right-hand corner of the vast auditorium. In the upper left-hand corner, in the back row, as far from the stars as possible, you would have found me sitting next to my friend Ken Turan, the film critic of the *Los Angeles Times,* who has single-handedly converted a dozen of his fellow critics, myself included, to the Timex Indiglo watch that lights up real bright in the dark when you want to know how long, oh, how long, dear Lord, a movie still has to play.

"Sundance is supposed to be the anti-Hollywood," I observed, "and all it takes is a couple of big stars to turn everybody into fans."

"What did you think of *Gerry*?" Turan asked. "Did you see it?"

"No."

"Well," I said, "it is the kind of movie it takes an experienced observer to appreciate. Someone who has seen a lot of movies and thought deeply about them. Someone who knows the work of Godard, Resnais, and Leone."

"Someone like us," Turan said.

"Exactly. The average viewer is going to be incapable of accepting it as only what it is. The story of two guys who go for a hike and get lost. Some woman in the lobby was insisting it was existential."

A woman in front of us turned around.

"Ted Field, the producer, walked out saying it was a load of pretentious crap," she said.

Not experienced enough, Turan and I agreed.

Sundance Report No. 3: *Our America* Is Affecting Tale

January 15, 2002—I have seen eleven films so far at this year's Sundance Film Festival, and the most affecting involves a couple of kids from a Chicago housing project who were given tape recorders by National Public Radio and asked to record the story of their lives.

Our America, by Ernest Dickerson, tells the story of LeAlan Jones (Brandon Hammond) and Lloyd Newman (Roderick Pannell), high school seniors who live near the Ida B. Wells housing project on the South Side. WBEZ producer David Isay (Josh Charles) gives them portable recorders and microphones, and they tell their stories with eloquence and stark honesty. "Soldiers who fought in Vietnam came back with shock syndrome," one observed. "We live in Vietnam."

The documentary wins praise and a Peabody Award (they are the youngest ever to win broadcasting's most important prize), but is attacked by some African-American leaders for painting a negative portrait. David Isay is stereotyped as a white man who exploited them by putting his ideas into their mouths. At first Jones and Newman are crushed, because they respect the teacher and talk show host who lead the charge, but then they decide they told the truth as they saw it, in their own words.

Then a tragedy occurs that captures national attention. Eric Morse, a five-year-old, is dropped from a fourteenth-story window of the Wells project by two boys, ten and eleven, who wanted him to steal candy for them. LeAlan and Lloyd go back to WBEZ and get backing to make a documentary about that, and they argue that the two boys (given ten-year sentences) were trying to scare the kid but not to kill him. The blame, they decide, lies "25 percent with the boys, 25 percent with their parents, 25 percent with the Wells project, and 25 percent with society."

Dickerson, the director, began as a cinematographer for Spike Lee and then directed such films as *Juice* and the TV movies *Strange Justice,* about Anita Hill, and *Blind Faith,* about a hate crime. This is his most eloquent work, an examination of a housing project that breeds crime and despair in its very bricks, and two young men (both now college students) who talked their way out of it.

This year's Sundance festival is so far not as strong as last year's extraordinary event, which premiered *In the Bedroom, Waking Life, The Believer, Memento, Deep End, Hedwig and the Angry Inch,* and *Lost and Delirious.* But some movies have been acclaimed, and the best buzz surrounds *Stolen Summer,* the film being documented in the current HBO series "Project Greenlight."

Stolen Summer was directed by Pete Jones, whose screenplay won a competition sponsored by Miramax, actors Matt Damon and Ben Affleck, and producer Chris Moore. Jones has become familiar to viewers of the TV series ("Sometimes I think I come across like a whiny weasel," he confessed while introducing his film). Weasel or not, he has directed a film with broad appeal, which begins with a large Chicago Irish-Catholic family (Aidan Quinn and Bonnie Hunt are the parents) and then follows their bright eight-year-old (Adi Stein) on his "quest."

The little boy, told by a nun he might not get into heaven, learns from a brother that St. Paul got into heaven by making converts to Christianity. So he sets up a lemonade stand outside the nearby synagogue, is tolerated by the bemused rabbi (Kevin Pollak), and then becomes close friends with the rabbi's son. The film begins as a comedy, then considers darker issues of prejudice and illness; it makes us smile, and then is surprisingly moving. Interesting that a screenplay chosen in a contest would be the audience favorite so far.

Mark Romanek's *One Hour Photo* is built on a haunting performance by Robin Williams, who reins in his stand-up instincts and creates a sad loner named Sy, who manages the photo developing department of a megastore. Over the years he has developed the photos of the Yorkin family, and fantasizes himself as their "Uncle Sy." He makes an unexpected discovery while developing pictures, at the same time the store manager discovers he may have been stealing prints, and the movie goes into an even darker place. In its portrait of lonely voyeurism that leads to violence, it deserves comparison with Michael Powell's horror classic, *Peeping Tom.*

Biggie and Tupac is the latest by guerrilla documentarian Nick Broomfield *(Kurt and Courtney, Heidi Fleiss: Hollywood Madam).* He investigates the murders of rap artists Tupac Shakur and Biggie Smalls, charging they were both murdered by off-duty Los Angeles police officers hired by Death Row Records CEO Suge Knight. This is a startling charge, but he backs it up persuasively, interviewing eyewitnesses and a former cop who resigned from the force after his own investigation was blocked. If nothing else, Broomfield proves that the LAPD bent over backward to avoid questioning the most obvious suspects.

The Dancer Upstairs is actor John Malkovich's directorial debut, starring Javier Bardem *(Before Night Falls)* as a lawyer turned cop assigned to investigate terrorism in a Latin American country. This sounds like a political thriller in the vein of Costa-Gavras (whose *State of Siege* is referenced in the film), but Malkovich is more intrigued by mood and tone than plot, and the great achievement of his film is to capture the way the cop's personality plays off others. Some said they couldn't understand the Spanish-accented English; they were listening for the words instead of the music.

Gus Van Sant's *Gerry,* which I wrote about yesterday, is the most puzzled-about film of the festival. Some hate it, some find it brilliant. It stars Matt Damon and Casey Affleck as two friends who get lost in the desert, and that's pretty much the entire plot. Antonioni and Kiarostami are evoked by its supporters. I found it bold, brave, and extreme—a challenge to the audience, more refreshing than an autopilot plot with lots of dialogue and intercuts with a search party.

As every year, I come out of the first weekend aware I have missed films everybody assures me are brilliant. I'm currently hot on the trail of *Real Women Have Curves* and *The Devil's Playground* (a doc about Amish teenagers). More later.

Sundance Report No. 4: Cable Channels Show Indie Strength

January 15, 2002—*The Laramie Project,* the opening-night film at Sundance this year, was an HBO made-for-cable movie. So is *Hysterical Blindness,* Mira Nair's new film starring Uma Thurman and Gena Rowlands. *Our America,* one of the hits of the dramatic competition, was made for Showtime. *Tadpole*, a buzz champ starring Sigourney Weaver, flies the flag of the Independent Film Channel's InDigEnt Films; Miramax has grabbed it for theatrical release. *Skins*, an American Indian drama, was backed by Starz Encore.

This year cable channels have stepped forward to claim a significant share of the action at Sundance and in the independent film world. *Laramie* and Nair's film are two of ten HBO films in the festival, seven of them documentaries. The Independent Film Channel is a major player here; among its 2002 entries are Victor Nunez's *Coastlines*, starring Timothy Olyphant as a returning prisoner, and Rebecca Miller's *Personal Velocity*, starring Kyra Sedgwick and Parker Posey in a story about domestic abuse. Richard Linklater's *Waking Life*, on my best ten list after its 2001 Sundance premiere, was a brilliant animation breakthrough backed by IFC.

"The studios these days are focusing on big-budget event movies, or concept comedies," says Colin Callender, head of HBO's moviemaking division. "The middle range is no longer the focus for them."

The trend has been building for years, as studios aim at megamillion-dollar special-effects movies and low-rent teenage sex comedies, and shy away from movies about recognizable people in plausible situations. If you are not a teenager, preferably a boy, you have to devote careful study to the openings at the multiplex to find a movie you might enjoy.

Some independent filmmakers work directly for cable. Others have their movies picked up for cable after they fail to find theatrical distribution. That doesn't mean they're weak movies; it means the mass-release multiplex pattern doesn't fit them.

Allison Anders's powerful *Things Behind the Sun* was a hit at Sundance last year. The story of a self-destructive rock musician who retraces her memories back to a childhood rape, it starred Kim Dickens in a great performance. Anders sold it to Showtime, where it found a large audience. Henry Bean's *The Believer*, which won last year's Grand Jury Prize here, failed to find a distributor because of its controversial subject matter. Ryan Gosling gave a brilliant performance as a tormented young self-hating Jew. It's also scheduled to play on Showtime.

On the other hand, said HBO's Callender, consider *Hedwig and the Angry Inch*, also a 2001 Sundance hit. It went out theatrically. "*Hedwig* grossed about $8 million," he said. "That's about 350,000 people who saw it. On HBO, it would have reached ten or fifteen times that number."

Attracted by artistic freedom and big audiences, talent from Hollywood's A list is no longer reluctant to work on cable. Consider *Wit*, also on my list of 2001's best films. It starred Emma Thompson in an Oscar-quality performance as an English professor dying of cancer. Mike Nichols was the director.

"Nichols and Thompson went into a room and rehearsed that role for a month," Callender said during a lunchtime interview at the Yarrow Inn, headquarters of the documentary screenings. "By the time shooting started, Emma had lived with the role for four or five months. A studio would have insisted a movie like that have a happy ending—a miracle cure or something. Not on cable."

HBO's forthcoming production of *Angels in America* is an indication that top stars no longer shy away from the small screen. The cast includes Al Pacino, Meryl Streep, Jeffrey Wright, and Emma Thompson. Why are they working for cable? Because any actor would kill to be in *Angels in America*, and no studio wanted to film it.

Ernest Dickerson's *Our America* got a standing ovation after its Sundance screening. It tells the story of two young black kids from the Chicago projects who were given tape recorders by NPR, made an audio documentary about their lives, and won a Peabody Award. Not multiplex material, but what a brilliant film. Showtime, which green-lighted it, also made Euzhan Palcy's powerful *The Killing Yard*, about the Attica massacre, with Alan Alda and Morris Chestnut.

Cable has a certain freedom from budgets that the studios don't share. Every studio picture is expected to make a profit, but "there is no direct connection," Callender said, "between the cost of a given project and the HBO balance sheet at the end of the year." Since HBO is funded by its subscribers, individual projects, if green-lighted, might get budgets from several hundred thousand dollars up to the $17 million range of John Frankenheimer's forthcoming

Vietnam film *The Path to War,* starring Alec Baldwin and Donald Sutherland.

Callender said ruefully that one thing bothers him about his cable movies: "The movie critics don't review them, because they're on TV, and the TV critics don't review them because they have a million shows to cover. But these are movies just as much as multiplex releases are movies—and many of them reach much larger audiences. All of the old definitions are beginning to break down."

Sundance Report No. 5: Plenty of Hits, No Home Runs

January 16, 2002—Good films but no great films. As the Sundance Film Festival heads into its final weekend, last year's exhilaration fades into a kind of contentment: We've enjoyed ourselves, we've seen films of originality and quality, but where is this year's equivalent of *Memento*? *The Deep End*? *In the Bedroom*? *Waking Life*?

Since my last roundup, the best film I've seen was wonderful because of its—I hesitate to say "old-fashioned values," but there you are. Maybe "traditional craftsmanship" is a better word. George Hickenlooper's *The Man from Elysian Fields* has sharply defined characters, dialogue of intelligence and wit, a fascinating premise, and keeps building through all three acts. It feels like work by Preston Sturges or Ernst Lubitsch; there is an elegance and confidence that trusts the audience.

The movie stars Andy Garcia as a struggling novelist who lives in Pasadena, on the other side of town from a legendary three-time Pulitzer Prize winner (James Coburn). He loves his wife (Julianna Margulies) and child, but can't confess to her he is broke. He meets a man named Luther Fox (Mick Jagger) who runs an escort service, and soon finds himself escorting the famous writer's much younger wife (Olivia Williams). The writer knows about this arrangement and enlists Garcia to help him with his latest novel.

The situation could fuel a one-level comedy, but *The Man from Elysian Fields* has many levels, involving love, trust, sexuality, art, and disenchantment. And the superb screenplay by Philip Jayson Lasker gives the Jagger character lines that perfectly suit his persona.

Garcia: "What does your agency provide?"
Jagger: "We make women happy."

Garcia: "Only women?"
Jagger: "Call me old-fashioned."

I also admired Chris Eyre's *Skins,* a drama about murder, vigilantism, alcoholism, and despair on the Pine Ridge Indian Reservation in South Dakota. Eric Schweig stars as a police officer whose beloved brother is dying from alcoholism. Investigating a murder, he gets more involved than he should, in a film that combines high drama with droll comedy and has an unforced feel for daily life on the reservation.

"These people are simply not visible to mainstream American society," Eyre told me after the screening. Indeed, few of the tourists who photograph themselves in front of Mount Rushmore every year will know, as everyone on Pine Ridge knows from birth, that the presidential effigies were carved out of a sacred mountain, and they overlook the site of the Massacre at Wounded Knee.

Eyre's first film was the much-loved *Smoke Signals,* the first feature made entirely by American Indians. *Skins* is as humorous and more engaging, with an undercurrent of violence. It has good prospects for breaking through to a wide audience.

Finn Taylor's *Cherish* stars Robin Tunney, who is on-screen almost every moment, as a woman arrested after being found drunk in a runaway car that killed a policeman. No one believes her story of a masked man who kidnapped her and put his foot on the accelerator. Awaiting trial, she is placed under house arrest and made to wear an ankle bracelet that limits her range to a run-down loft apartment.

The centerpiece of the film is her lonely existence there, her friendship with neighbors, and her odd relationship with the deputy (Tim Blake Nelson) who monitors the bracelet program. Then the film explodes into a thriller with elements of *Run, Lola, Run.* Tunney covers an enormous range, from despair to resourcefulness, from romance to fast-paced action.

Blue Vinyl, by Judith Helfand and Daniel B. Gold, is one of the fest's best documentaries, with a story that begins when Helfand's parents have their house re-sided with vinyl covering. Tracing the vinyl to its source, she discovers that the carcinogenic chemicals used in its manufacture have been responsible for decades of illness and death, and are particularly linked to a rare liver cancer, not so rare around the vinyl plants. In Venice, she covers the trial of fifty-one industry executives being tried for manslaughter for continuing to operate their plants after it was clear they were hazardous.

Helfand narrated the film herself. A film like this could adopt a morose, voice-of-doom approach, with cellos sawing away, but she is funny and irreverent, and the movie, despite its serious message, is surprisingly entertaining.

Philip Seymour Hoffman is the reigning sad sack of independent films, whose characters in movies like *Magnolia* live lives of grungy desperation. In Todd Louiso's *Love Liza*, he plays a man whose wife kills herself. Depressed, in a daze, he starts inhaling gasoline fumes and stumbles through many scenes in a stupor. Seeking an alibi for all the gas cans he fills at the corner station, he claims to be a model airplane enthusiast, and talks himself into a bizarre, befuddled adventure at a model plane and boat roundup—at one point swimming in the lake where model boats are whizzing past him. The movie brings Hoffman's loser character to its ultimate extreme.

These are all strong movies of the sort Sundance exists to celebrate. But we still wait for a director to knock one out of the park. As I write, there are four days left. Plenty of time.

Sundance Report No. 6: *Better Luck* Defies Stereotypes

January 17, 2002—The man in the audience was angry. "How could you," he asked the director, his voice trembling with sincerity, "despite your talented cast and great production values, make such a bleak, negative, amoral film? What kind of a portrait is this of Asian-Americans? Don't you have a responsibility to paint a more positive and helpful portrait of your community?"

Justin Lin, whose *Better Luck Tomorrow* had just played to an enthusiastic reception at the Sundance Film Festival, replied that he had made the film he wanted to make, the way he had wanted to make it. He felt it depicted a reality among teenagers of any race.

I usually don't speak during the Q&A sessions after screenings, but I couldn't restrain myself. I told the man I thought he was being condescending: "You would never make a comment like that to a white filmmaker."

I quoted Chris Eyre, the Native American filmmaker, who was on a panel with me that afternoon. "For 100 years," he said, "American Indians have played the same roles in movies—either savages or spiritual peoples who exist on some mystical plane. It is time to let us just simply be people."

The same could be said of Asian-American characters, who are often either martial arts practitioners, exotic sexual prizes, or winners of the spelling bee. Justin Lin's film tells the story of a posse of bright, ambitious Asian high school kids who live in an affluent suburb and have their sights set on Ivy League schools. The hero is a brain who captains an academic decathlon team. Because he wants his college application to look good, he also plays basketball, does community service, and belongs to half the clubs in school, in addition to getting high grades.

At the same time, he and his friends drift into criminal activity—at first selling cheat sheets, then dealing in drugs. Eventually they commit murder. He considers turning himself in to the police, but "I couldn't let one mistake get in the way of everything I'd worked for. I know the difference between right and wrong, but I guess in the end I really wanted to go to a good college."

Amoral, yes. Shockingly. He seems to exist in a world of achievement and ambition that operates entirely apart from moral values. Another audience member drew a parallel with Enron executives who apparently concealed the fact that their numbers didn't add up. Justin Lin said he senses a moral disconnect in some of today's teenagers and wanted to make a movie about it. His cast was all Asian-American because—well, why not?

For years filmmakers have tiptoed around the sensibilities of some ethnic groups, afraid to offend. Maybe the tiptoeing is the real offense. Until Indians, Asians, and African-Americans are shown with the same moral complexity as white characters, they are being shortchanged, stereotyped, closed off from the full range of human response. Some Italian-Americans were offended by *The Godfather*, but isn't it one of the best American movies of all time?

I thought about *Our America*, which played here three days ago. Ernest Dickerson's wonderful film, based on fact, tells the story of two black teenagers from a poverty-stricken Chicago housing project. Given tape recorders by an NPR station and asked to make a radio documentary of their lives, they produce a result so powerful that they become the youngest people ever to win a Peabody Award.

But they are attacked by power brokers within the black community. A school official and a talk show host say the portrait they painted was too negative—that a white producer must have put words in their mouths in order to show only the bad side of the Ida B. Wells project. The kids are shaken; they respect these black adults, and question themselves, but decide at last they told their own story in their own words.

Consider, in a different kind of film, Denzel Washington's astonishing performance in *Training Day*, where he plays a completely evil, vicious, corrupt cop. A negative portrait? Yes. Should he have shown the bright side, by playing a dedicated black cop? And denied us that performance? If there can be a corrupt white cop in the movies, why not a black one?

Morgan Freeman told me once that he liked to play villains in the movies because they were often the most interesting characters. His Oscar-nominated performance in *Street Smart* (1987), as a violent pimp, launched his starring career. But often producers preferred to have a white villain. James Woods, Tommy Lee Jones, and Christopher Walken got the juicy bad-guy roles, because Hollywood feared to portray blacks in a negative way.

That kind of thinking is an artistic straitjacket, exiling minority characters to a benevolent limbo. Denzel Washington may play a bad cop in *Training Day*, but he also represents a great black actor. In *Skins*, Chris Eyre shows alcoholism, poverty, and despair on an Indian reservation, but he also shows vibrant human characters both good and bad, in a real world. If Justin Lin had made *Better Luck Tomorrow* about white teenagers, no one would have batted an eye—and his cast of gifted young Asian-American actors would have been denied important roles.

One of the many qualities of the great film *Monster's Ball* is that it avoids stereotypes about black-white relationships and shows two characters who come together out of human need and desperation. Race is the last thing on their minds. That movie, and *Better Luck Tomorrow*, *Skins*, and *Our America*, are pointed in the right

direction, toward films that celebrate the full range of their characters without the emasculation of political correctness. If Justin Lin had a responsibility to "his community," it was to make the best film he possibly could.

Sundance Report No. 7: Robert Evans Is Still in the Picture

January 21, 2002—"If you could change one thing about your life," someone in the audience asked Robert Evans, "what would it be?"

"The second half," he said.

Everyone in the Sundance Film Festival audience knew exactly what he meant. We had just seen *The Kid Stays in the Picture*, a new documentary about the life of a producer who put together one of the most remarkable winning streaks in Hollywood history, and followed it with a losing streak that almost destroyed him.

Evans made the kinds of movies that would never have played at Sundance; it's ironic that he got into the festival with a documentary. As the boy wonder head of production at Paramount, he took the studio from last to first in annual ticket sales, dominating the late 1960s and 1970s with *The Godfather, Chinatown, Love Story, Rosemary's Baby, The Odd Couple, Black Sunday, Popeye,* and *Urban Cowboy.* And he married Ali MacGraw, his star in *Love Story.*

Then everything that had gone right started to go wrong. MacGraw left him for Steve McQueen. He had exited the studio job with a lucrative personal production deal when disaster struck. He was involved in a cocaine-purchasing sting set up by the DEA, rehabilitated himself with a series of public-service broadcasts, tried a comeback by producing a high-visibility flop (*The Cotton Club*) and then was linked by innuendo and gossip with the murder of a man obscurely involved in the film's financing.

Evans was never charged with anything. But to this day people vaguely remember the drug and murder stories, and at one point in the 1980s he was so depressed he committed himself to a mental hospital, afraid he would kill himself.

The Kid Stays in the Picture is narrated by Evans himself and based on his autobiography. It is a collage of film and TV clips, countless photographs, news headlines, and magazine covers, assembled by Brett Morgen and Nanette Burstein, whose documentary *On the Ropes* was an Oscar nominee two years ago. It is all told from Evans's point of view, but he includes so much of the sad side of his story that it feels balanced.

He was a man who seemed blessed with luck. A child actor, he had joined his brother in manufacturing women's clothes when he was spotted poolside at the Beverly Hills Hotel by Norma Shearer, and asked to play her husband, Irving Thalberg, in the Jimmy Cagney picture *Man of a Thousand Faces*. Then came the prize role of a bullfighter in *The Sun Also Rises*. Author Ernest Hemingway and actors Tyrone Power, Ava Gardner, and Eddie Albert sent studio head Darryl F. Zanuck a telegram saying the film would be a disaster with Evans. Zanuck flew to the Mexican location, took a look, and said, "The kid stays in the picture."

Evans's next film, *The Fiend Who Walked the West*, ended his acting career. But after being tapped to run Paramount by Charles Bludhorn, whose conglomerate Gulf and Western had inhaled the studio, he had more than a decade of success, and then a decade of disaster. Early on, he purchased the legendary home of Shearer and Thalberg. He sold it in the '80s, then realized he could not live without it; his pal Jack Nicholson flew to Monte Carlo and "got down on his knees" (perhaps Evans exaggerates slightly) to convince its new owner, a French millionaire, to sell it back.

Evans stood on the stage at Sundance, still trim and handsome at seventy-one, and answered the questions of filmmakers half or a third his age. Here was a room full of young people who dream of the kind of success he had. Did they find his life an object lesson? Probably not. At Sundance, they're still trying to change the first halves of their lives.

Sundance Report No. 8

January 21, 2002—From despair to victory, the South African documentary *Amandla!* has the widest range of emotion of any film at this year's Sundance. It follows the history of the struggle for freedom in terms of the movement's music—which was, as one singer observes, a weapon the apartheid government could not disarm.

Ten years in the making, it opens with footage of the exhumation of the remains of Vigisile Mini, a protest musician hanged by the government years earlier and put in a pauper's grave. It ends with Nelson Mandela joined onstage by musicians during an ecstatic rally after his release from prison.

The film, made by Lee Hirsch and Sherry Simpson, intercuts footage tracing the rise of apartheid after 1948 with a musical opposition that was like "cracks in the wall." The Sharpeville Massacre, the Soweto uprising, the jailing of Mandela and his ANC comrades, are paralleled by songs, from the uplifting "God Save Africa" to more pointed lyrics like "Watch Out Verwoerd" and "What Have We Done?"

Hugh Masekela, the jazz musician who spent from 1961 to 1990 in exile in America, smiles as he observes, "We lost the country in the first place, to an extent, because before we fight, we sing—so they knew where they were."

The movie is sorrowful and joyous; the music will no doubt inspire a CD to rival *Buena Vista Social Club*.

Amandla! (the word is an African National Congress power chant) won the Audience Award as favorite documentary at the closing awards ceremony, and was part of a surge of strong films during the closing days of the Sundance Festival. Others I admired:

—*Better Luck Tomorrow*, by Justin Lin, is about a group of bright Asian-American high school students who are on two tracks at once—to the Ivy League, and to prison. It is narrated by a gifted but amoral student who cynically signs up for high school activities to make his college application look better, while at the same time selling cheat sheets and dealing drugs. The movie's arc has echoes of Scorsese's *GoodFellas*, with its narrator describing a career that began as fun and darkened into a trap. This is an extraordinarily accomplished and thought-provoking film, a statement not just about its Asian-American characters, but about part of a whole generation that has been taught to value success above morality.

—Speaking of profits versus morality, consider *American Standoff*, a documentary about the long, bitter Teamsters strike against Overnite Transportation. Directed by Kristi Jacobson and produced by legendary documentarian Barbara Kopple, it shows the trucking company spending an estimated $100 million to avoid a contract that might have cost it a fraction of that amount. Overnite releases a video showing Teamsters violence against its trucks—gunshots, a brick through a window, a driver dead. Later a man comes forward to say he was paid $10,000 by Overnite to stage the violence.

—*Personal Velocity,* directed by Rebecca Miller, won the grand jury prize as the best feature in the festival. It is immediately, almost shockingly, intimate in its telling of the stories of three women. Kyra Sedgwick plays Delia, a high school slut who marries a wife-beater, escapes with her children, and tries to survive as a waitress. Parker Posey is Greta, a cookbook editor who attracts the attention of a novelist, threatening her safe but uneventful marriage. Fairuza Balk is Paula, who escapes death only by chance, has to deal with an unplanned pregnancy, and befriends a battered hitchhiker. Such stark descriptions do not even begin to hint at the complexities of the movie, which has such an observant eye that each segment has the depth of a full film.

—*Hysterical Blindness,* directed by Mira Nair, also has three great female performances. Uma Thurman and Juliette Lewis star as two working-class women who pick up guys in a nearby bar and deceive themselves that a one-night stand could lead to marriage. Meanwhile, Thurman's waitress mother, played by Gena Rowlands, finds the real thing with a widower (Ben Gazzara). Somebody told me they just couldn't picture Uma Thurman as a low-rent slut. This movie will make him a believer. Thurman and Lewis are right on the money, their dialogue an exercise in shallow desperation.

—*Real Women Have Curves,* directed by Patricia Cardoso, was a huge hit at the festival, winning the Audience Award as favorite feature, and a jury prize for acting for its two stars. It's a charmer, the story of a Mexican-American high school senior named Ana (America Ferrera), who wants to go to college but has a mother (the great Lupe Ontiveros) who insists she work in the storefront dress factory operated by another daughter. Ana, plump by conventional standards, lights up with warmth and personality; there is a scene toward the end where she invites all of the women in the little factory to accept their bodies, that had the audience laughing and applauding at the same time.

—One of the strangest films in the festival was *Secretary,* by Steven Shainberg, winner of the jury prize for originality. It starred Maggie Gyllenhaal as a neurotic young woman named Lee with the secret illness of self-mutilation.

She finds a job with a lawyer (James Spader), somehow senses they are on the same wavelength, and discovers her hidden tendencies toward sadomasochism. Given a role that in a sense is almost unplayable, Gyllenhaal uses an honesty and guilelessness that makes it work; Lee is strange, but we sense how her mind works.

—One of the festival's most absorbing discoveries was John Walters's *How to Draw a Bunny,* about an artist named Ray Johnson who produced thousands of works, was known and liked by almost everyone in the New York art world, never had a gallery show, and was found floating dead in Sag Harbor. He left clues leading his friends to conclude this death was not so much a suicide as a final artwork.

Sundance Report No. 9: The Winners

January 21, 2002—*Personal Velocity,* a film by Rebecca Miller telling the separate stories of three women, won the Grand Jury Prize for best feature film here Saturday night at the Sundance Film Festival.

Kyra Sedgwick, Parker Posey, and Fairuza Balk star in the stories, which Miller told the audience were intended to be told "as fast as the mind thinks." The film also won for best cinematography, by Ellen Kuras, and it was significant, in a year when cable outlets and digital video were in high profile here, that it was a production of the Independent Film Channel's all-digital InDigEnt division.

The grand prize for best documentary went to *Daughter from Danang,* by Gail Dolgin and Vincente Franco, which tells the story of a Vietnamese orphan, raised as a "100 percent American girl," who went back to her homeland to meet her birth mother and found that the reunion was far from a simple thing.

In addition to the jury prizes, Sundance polls its audiences to discover the films with the most popular support. The winner of the Audience Award for feature films was the HBO-produced *Real Women Have Curves,* a heartwarming film by Patricia Cardoso about a high-spirited Mexican-American teenager. Its costars, young America Ferrera and veteran Lupe Ontiveros, shared the jury prize for acting.

Among documentaries, the Audience Award winner was *Amandla!,* also an HBO production directed by Lee Hirsch, which traces the South

African freedom struggle through its music. *Amandla!* also won the Freedom of Expression Award sponsored by the Playboy Foundation.

Other special jury prizes included one to John Walters's *How to Draw a Bunny,* a documentary about the life and death of the private, shy, charming performance artist Ray Johnson, in the feature category, and in documentaries, to Lourdes Portillo's *Senorite Extraviada,* about an unsolved series of deaths of Mexican women near the American border.

A special jury prize for originality went to Steven Shainberg's *Secretary,* about a troubled young woman who discovers an unexpected penchant for sadomasochism. And one for ensemble acting went to the cast of Eric Eason's *Manito,* about a family from the Dominican Republic living in a dangerous Manhattan neighborhood. The jury award in Latin American cinema went to *The Trespasser,* by Beto Brant, a thriller about Brazilian corruption.

The Audience Award voting for World Cinema ended in a tie between Paul Greengrass's *Bloody Sunday,* about a clash in Belfast on January 30, 1972, between British soldiers and IRA backers and Gabriele Muccino's *The Last Kiss,* an Italian comedy about the interlocking lives of four couples.

The jury prize for best direction of a feature was won by Gary Winick's *Tadpole,* starring Sigourney Weaver and Aaron Stanford in the *Graduate*-like story of a preppie young man who falls in love with an older woman; it made headlines here by selling to Miramax for $5 million.

For best direction of a documentary, the jury honored *Sister Helen,* by Rob Fruchtman and Rebecca Cammisa, the story of an alcoholic mother of three, who, after the murder of a son and the drinking death of her husband, sobers up, becomes a Benedictine nun, and opens a halfway house in the Bronx.

The Waldo Salt Screenwriting Award went to Gordy Hoffman for *Love Liza,* which starred his younger brother Philip Seymour Hoffman as a man so depressed by the death of his wife that he falls into gas-sniffing and thence into a bewildering series of misadventures. Gordy Hoffman said the screenplay drew on his experiences as a Chicago taxi driver.

The jury prize for best documentary cinematography went to Dan B. Gold for *Blue Vinyl,* the story of how after director Judith Helfand's parents had their home covered with vinyl siding, she became curious about how vinyl byproducts cause cancer.

The best short film was *Gasline,* by Dave Silver, about the travails of a small gas station owner during the oil crisis.

Karlovy Vary Film Festival

Karlovy Vary, Czech Republic, July 15, 2002— The thirty-seventh Karlovy Vary Film Festival was like a trip back to the 1970s: There was no security, audiences were interested in difficult films, and everybody smoked all the time. As a member of the jury, I saw eighteen films, none of them Hollywood blockbusters, many of them frankly noncommercial, all of them made by directors with a personal idea they wanted to communicate. And I ate a lot of duck and dumplings.

Karlovy Vary, also known by its German name of Carlsbad, is an elaborately picturesque spa town in a steep valley about ninety minutes from Prague. Here since centuries past, Europeans have come to take the waters, which bubble up steaming hot from twelve springs and smell like they'd better be good for you.

The central part of the town consists of two miles of tall, ornate buildings facing each other across the river; mostly hotels and spas, they look imposing, but the walls of rock rise so close and steeply behind them that some are wider than they are deep. Visiting for the first time, the French architect Le Corbusier called the town "a procession of wedding cakes."

One end of the river parade is dominated by the Grand Hotel Pupp, a Victorian extravaganza. At the other is the towering Hotel Thermal, a Soviet-era skyscraper and conference center. Most of the movies were shown in the Thermal, in a vast hall with seats that were hard and straight; it was whispered that they were designed to keep delegates awake at party conferences.

But the Velvet Revolution brought a sudden

end to the Soviet control of Czechoslovakia, which then split into two republics. "I saw this town twenty years ago, under the Russians," a director told me, "and it was gray and run-down and forlorn. Now it is so beautiful again that it brings tears to my eyes. The buildings have all been painted cheerful colors, and the windows have flower boxes."

Karlovy Vary is one of the oldest film festivals, and one of the larger, with some 350 films this year. It is also one of the friendliest; ticket prices are low, and young people sleep in the parks and take advantage of a last-minute rush for free empty seats. There are stars here, although Sean Connery failed to turn up on closing night because of the flu. And retrospectives: Michael York came for *Cabaret*, and director John Boorman for *Deliverance*. But the emphasis is on the films themselves, and I saw audiences watch with interest during pictures so frankly difficult that the audiences would flee at certain other festivals I could name.

After growing accustomed in America to constant security checks, metal detectors, and bag searches, I was stunned to be able to walk anywhere in Karlovy Vary without challenge. There was a time when Americans were suspiciously scrutinized in these parts; now we come here to be ignored. Audiences walk into screenings and panel discussions with just an usher to eyeball them, like in the old, innocent days. So peaceful is the setting that on closing night Vaclav Havel, the beloved president of the Czech Republic, sat in the middle of the audience and later mixed with guests at a party at the Pupp. Instead of a phalanx of Secret Servicemen, he was accompanied only by his wife and by one tall guy with a close-cropped head who kept his arms crossed and wore an earpiece.

As a member of the jury, I am sworn to secrecy about our deliberations. But I can write about some of the principles we debated. I found on the jury a certain antagonism against mainstream Hollywood films, and although there were none in the competition, some of the eighteen contenders were criticized anyway for seeming too much like them. Films were attacked for being "too well made," and it was said you could "sense the crew behind the camera." Several jury members pre-ferred rougher, more authentic films. Ibolya Fekete, a director from Hungary, explained this feeling to me: "In the films of Eastern Europe, the world is not in order. In Hollywood films, the world is in order." The happy endings required on most Hollywood films, she said, force them to conclude with what is often a lie.

Night after night we debated the movies, in an old oak bar in the basement of the Pupp, which had been set aside for jury members and other VIPs. There was always a free buffet. In theory, the bar closed at midnight. In practice, the little band only started to play then. The jury was a collection of delightfully various people, led by Jean-Marc Barr, the actor and director who moves between France and America. (He showed two of his own films, one largely shot in India, the other in the downstate Illinois hamlet of Rankin.)

There was Jan Malir, the tall, always smiling Czech cinematographer *(Divided We Fall)*, also revealed to be a jazz pianist. And passionate Ibolya Fekete, who still doesn't trust e-mail because of the years when the Soviets tapped her phone and opened her mail. And Bibiana Beglau, the German actress, who won the Silver Bear at Berlin for her performance in Volker Schlondorff's *The Legend of Rita* (1999) and was so articulate about the profession of acting. And Kaynam Myong, the Korean producer, whose *Peppermint Candy* won the Special Jury Prize at Karlovy Vary in 2002; he did coin tricks and shared doubts about films that were too slick. And sly, smiling Assumpta Serna, the Spanish actress who starred in Pedro Almodovar's *Matador* but cried out: "I am sick of films that only play in festivals. That's why I moved to Los Angeles—to make movies people would see."

Very different people, but for some reason we liked one another, and on the closing night we did a spoof of the festival trailer and danced onstage to music, instead of filing up solemnly to be introduced. Our awards were fairly popular with the audience, although that is not the idea. No doubt we caused some disappointment. Maybe this story will convey the mood: David Mendes, a director from Brazil, was on the documentary jury and said he was approached by a filmmaker who was livid that his film had not taken a prize. "Why didn't you choose it?" he shouted. David replied: "Because we chose another film instead."

Karlovy Vary Winners

Year of the Devil, a Czech film in the spirit of *This Is Spinal Tap*, won the thirty-seventh Karlovy Vary Film Festival. Directed by Petr Zelenka, it stars popular singer Jaromir Nohavica in the lighthearted, sometimes harrowing story of a career beset by problems. It was a huge favorite, filled with music, and has export potential.

Nowhere in Africa won both the Special Jury Prize and the International Critics' Award. Directed by Caroline Link of Germany, it tells the story of a Jewish couple and their daughter, who flee Hitler and settle on a marginal farm in Kenya. It's remarkable how Link shows the three characters evolving separately in the new environment and avoids clichés while making a story of enormous popular appeal.

The Best Director Award went to Asghar Massombagi of Canada for *Khaled,* the story of a young half-Moroccan boy in Toronto who conceals the death of his mother because he fears being sent to a foster home. Ten-year-old Michael D'Ascenzo gives a touching performance as a smart, resourceful kid who gets into an insoluble situation.

Ugla Egilsdottir won the Best Actress Award for *The Seagull's Laughter,* from Iceland, a rich human comedy about a teenage girl who is competitive with a sexy local woman who returns to town after some years abroad.

William H. Macy won the Best Actor Award for *Focus,* the only American film in the official competition. In a story based on an Arthur Miller novel set during World War II, he plays an office manager who becomes the target of local anti-Semites. Although he is not Jewish, the experience opens his eyes to native racism.

Special Jury Mentions went to the Korean film *Let's Not Cry,* for its on-location cinematography in Uzbekistan, and to the screenplay of the Spanish film *The Smoking Room,* about a local revolt against no-smoking rules handed down to a Spanish firm by its American owners.

Questions for the Movie Answer Man

Almost Famous

Q. In the Ebert and Roeper review of the new *Almost Famous* DVD, Stillwater, the band in the movie, was referred to as "fictional." I'm from Michigan and remember the band vaguely. They were apparently quite real. I searched the Web, and at the *Michigan Daily* site found information about the real band (the photo shows how dead-on the casting was). So—was there a real band called Stillwater, upon which Cameron Crowe's characters in *Almost Famous* were based?

—Travis Charbeneau, Richmond, Virginia

A. Writer-director Cameron Crowe replies that you and the *Michigan Daily* have been deceived by a fictional band: "Your question man has dug up a bit of, shall we say, authentic fiction that originated from our Vinyl Films Website. The *Almost Famous* Stillwater from Troy, Missouri, is actually a composite of four or five bands I toured with back in the early 1970s—a little lynyrd skynyrd, a lot of the Allman Brothers, some Eagles, some Neil Young, and a large dose of Led Zeppelin. Many of the events in the movie, and some of the dialogue, actually happened while I was covering those bands. For example, when we showed *Almost Famous* to Robert Plant from Led Zeppelin last year, at the point Billy Crudup says, 'I never said I was a "golden god,"' Plant happily cried out, 'Well I did!' And he was right."

Amores Perros

Q. The Answer Man comment about sanitized Spanish translations prompts me to ask whether the title of *Amores Perros* has been sanitized for *English* consumption. I can't help wondering if the title could be translated more directly, as something like *Like a Mad Dog in Heat*, or even *Doggie Style*.

—Timothy Buchman, New York, New York

A. You're close. The title translates as *Love's a Bitch*.

Q. Regarding your Answer Man column reporting that the accurate Spanish translation of *Amores Perros* is *Love's a Bitch*. Sorry, but the correct translation is *Dog Love*. The word *bitch* is an American idiom. The Spanish word for a female dog is "perra" and wouldn't be used in the same slang way we use "bitch."

—Julio Gagne, Ventura, California

A. *Love's a Bitch* is the official international English title of the film, so apparently the filmmakers think that hits the right note. The Answer Man received several other translations from Spanish speakers. Among those that can be printed are *Love Doggie Style*. Of course any translation involves a certain degree of poetic license.

Anacronisms

Q. In recent movies about people in the past, many of the characters say "hey" as a form of greeting instead of "hi." This happened, for example, in *The Cider House Rules*, where it was way out of character.

—Diana Morley, Napa, California

A. And of course "hello" itself only came into use with the introduction of the telephone. Now that movies set in medieval times use songs by Queen on the sound track, this is perhaps only a technicality.

Animals

Q. Why do the movies always make the cats the bad guys, like in *Cats and Dogs*? Dogs are the ones that kill and maul kids and babies all the time. Cats only strike out in fear. Dogs are mean and vicious. Cats are polite. When they go to the bathroom they dig a hole and cover it up. Dogs leave it out so you can step in it and it stinks to high heaven. Cats are very clean. Dogs love stinky things. Male dogs have sex with each other, your arm, your leg, your coat—they are so dumb. Cats are very dignified and know who to have sex with. Cats stay beautiful all the time while dogs are ugly and get uglier.

—S. Cat Cole, Elmhurst, Illinois

A. The trainers for *Cats and Dogs* say the cats fought so much in their group scenes that they had to be filmed separately. Perhaps if you were a filmmaker and had to work all day with trained cats, you would understand why the movies seem fonder of dogs.

For another view, I turned to Jeff Wells, the Hollywood columnist for Reel.com, who had already informed me he hated *Cats and Dogs* with a passion beyond all reason. He responds: "This is the most virulently anticat movie I've ever seen. The filmmakers were obviously nursing a prejudice. I love dogs, but I've lived with and loved cats all my life. Ever notice how aggressive alpha-male dog lovers are sometimes hostile toward cats, but how cat lovers almost universally *never* say, 'I hate dogs?' Ever hear of a cat lover spinning a dog around by its tail? Truck drivers, overweight Sunday football fans who drink a lot of beer, CIA assassins, and *Cats and Dogs* producer Andrew Lazar—all fellows I have trouble relating to, and all (I'll be willing to wager) dog lovers with frosty attitudes toward felines. Cat lovers tend to be more sensitive, more reflective, more thoughtful, less brutish and overt."

A Beautiful Mind

Q. When I first saw *A Beautiful Mind,* I thought, like most other moviegoers and critics, that it was great, literate, moving, compelling—the best thing Ron Howard has ever done. Intrigued, I did some further research into Nash's life, and was discouraged by reading that the more unappealing aspects of his life were left out of the film. I feel this insults the audience's intelligence, keeping us from seeing the true man. This is a typical Hollywood move, thinking we would not think Nash's story inspiring and his achievements noble if we don't like him every second of the way. Now I see it as a shameless Oscar ploy, and an effort to jerk tears from us to make *Mind* more easily digestible. Can't we appreciate an antihero anymore?
—Gerry Miriello, Los Angeles, California

A. If the movie was great, literate, moving, and compelling until you learned more about Nash, then can we argue that it is still great, literate, moving, and compelling, but simply not as factual as you thought? Would it diminish *Gladiator* for you if you learned of its factual inaccuracies? Movies, even those "based on fact," weave fables and legends by picking and choosing from the available material. My feeling is that we go to books for facts, and to movies for feelings. John Forbes Nash is not an antihero but a man who struggled with a tragic mental illness, lived an imperfect life, and made an enormous contribution to human knowledge.

Q. Regarding the controversy over *A Beautiful Mind* changing some of the facts of John Forbes Nash's life: That I pretty much forgave, knowing that transferring a life to film is a messy affair, and not always truthful. But changing the ethnicity of a main character, a character who was pivotal in this man regaining his life, is more than an oversight. Alicia Nash is an El Salvadoran, and has been changed into a WASP named Alice in the movie. This provides a role for Jennifer Connolly and denies a role to a Latina actress. Hollywood filmmakers had a choice to make, and chose the easy route. In this case, they denied the role of a lifetime to a Latina, and also spit on any sense of allowing the world to know us in a different light, a positive light. Maybe if his wife had been a whore, a maid, or had left him in his darkest moment, they would have allowed a Latina to have the role, and probably would have accented the fact that she was Latina.
—Nancy De Los Santos, Los Angeles, California

A. My best guess: They went with the actress they wanted, and adjusted the character accordingly.

Q. Nancy De Los Santos of Los Angeles (who complained that *A Beautiful Mind* changed John Nash's El Salvadoran wife to a WASP and renamed her Alice) Fmust have seen a different version than I did. In the movie Nash's wife was named Alicia and her ethnicity was never addressed. I have seen photos of the real Alicia Nash, and she looks as much like Jennifer Connolly as John Nash looks like Russell Crowe. Viewers need to stop scrutinizing every detail of the movie to measure it against real life. It's a good film that gives us insights into the workings of the brain of a genius.
—Michael David Smith, Long Beach, California

A. You are correct about the name. The real Mrs. Nash, Alicia Larde, came with her parents to America as a child. At the same time, De Los Santos, producer of *The Bronze Screen*, a documentary about Latinos in Hollywood, makes an irrefutable point that Hollywood has been slow to cast Latinos in a wider range of roles, including many where they make perfect sense.

Behind Enemy Lines

Q. Here's a quote from Michael Medved's three-star review of *Behind Enemy Lines*: "Roger Ebert and other establishment critics have made fun of the movie because it held its world premiere on the USS *Carl Vinson*, the same massive aircraft carrier shown in the film. Sorry, Roger; that's a reason to admire the movie, not to scorn it."

—Paul West, Seattle, Washington

A. Apart from his quaint notion that the location of a movie's premiere is a reason to admire it, Medved deliberately misrepresents me. Here's what I actually wrote: "The premiere of *Behind Enemy Lines* was held aboard the aircraft carrier USS *Carl Vinson*. I wonder if it played as a comedy. Its hero is so reckless and its villains so incompetent that it's a showdown between a man begging to be shot, and an enemy that can't hit the side of a Bosnian barn."

I am clearly not making fun of the movie *because* of its Vinson premiere, but simply wondering if trained and combat-ready troops would find it as ridiculous as I did. Apparently some did. I received messages (not from the Vinson) ridiculing details in the film, such as (1) the decision of an admiral to personally lead an armed extraction; (2) the hero's stupid choice to travel by day instead of night; (3) decisions by both the hero and the U.S. admiral to deliberately disobey orders; (4) and the peculiarity that the helicopters that leave the carrier are not the same ones that return. One reader who was especially incensed: Lieutenant Jeffery "Perfect" Menna, USN, of China Lake, California, who says he is an F/A-18 Hornet pilot and considers it an insult that the movie refers to the Owen Wilson character as a pilot when he is a naval flight officer. He writes: "Please do not call NFOs/navigators pilots. They are not. It is an insult to all of us

who are pilots. NFO's have no training in how to fly an airplane. They only work the systems of the airplane and talk on the radio. It is like calling a nurse a doctor."

Q. I thought I was keeping up with current events, but I don't recall hearing that France had decided to rejoin NATO?

—John R. Quinsey, Dania Beach, Florida

A. I described the NATO superior in *Behind Enemy Lines* as a French admiral. France is a member of NATO but does not contribute troops. The character of Admiral Piquet has what sounds like a French name and accent, and I jumped to the wrong conclusion. The actor (Joaquim de Almeida) is Portuguese, but the movie doesn't say where the character is from.

B Pictures

Q. I was confused by your phrase, "especially the big-budget B pictures," since I was under the impression that B pictures are, or were, low-budget.

—Maria Carmicino, New York, New York

A. Hollywood is now making B-picture ideas and plots with A-picture budgets. Just because a movie costs $80 million doesn't mean it isn't a B picture at heart. Recent big-budget B pictures have included *The Mummy Returns, Pearl Harbor, Lara Croft Tomb Raider, Jurassic Park 3,* and *Rush Hour 2.*

Billy Wilder

Q. What amazes me about the late, great Billy Wilder is that his pictures hold up so well. Even those from forty or fifty years ago seem fresh and modern—fresher than a lot of the tired new films. What was his secret?

—Susan Lake, Urbana, Illinois

A. The director Cameron Crowe (*Almost Famous, Vanilla Sky*) was a close friend of Wilder's, and published *Conversations with Wilder,* a book-length dialogue with the great man that has a place of honor on my shelf next to Truffaut's *Hitchcock.* I asked Crowe what was distinctive about Billy Wilder's genius. His response:

"The question that comes up a lot between fans and filmmakers is, how did Wilder do it? Here's a sketch of his pattern. Wilder's movies always started with a premise, or 'the gag,' as he called it. Usually it was something he'd written down in a special notebook. One of his notes to himself was, 'A romantic comedy set against the St. Valentine's Day Massacre.' Then, working nine-to-five in a small office, Wilder and his writing partner would begin to fill out 'the gag' with characters and situations that would bring the concept to life. The job, said Wilder, was to hide the premise in the real-life behavior of those characters, or as he said, 'to sugarcoat that pill.' Within six months, the 'gag' would become *Some Like it Hot*. Another single line in that notebook was, 'The poor fellow who must sleep in the still-warm bed where lovers had been.' That premise became *The Apartment*. He never sat down in fifty-plus years of writing and directing. Always pacing, always moving. And when the script was being filmed, Wilder's great collaborator of his later years, I. A. L. Diamond, would stand with the document in hand, policing every line. For anybody musing about the possibility of movies being original and creative while still appealing to mainstream audiences, just look to Billy Wilder. When I asked him recently what happened to that special notebook, he shrugged. 'I believe it was lost in a fire, but I remember quite a bit of what was in that thing. One was *The Marx Brothers at the United Nations*,' he said. 'And the other, I cannot divulge to you because it will be my next picture.' He was ninety-three."

Black Hawk Down

Q. I recently read your review of *Black Hawk Down*. I have not seen the movie but wish to comment on your review. I have read Mark Bowden's book and have done research on the tragic events. My father is in the army and has personal knowledge of much of what went on that fateful day.

In your review you point out that the director, Ridley Scott, "cheats" by using aerial shots to show where troops are and what is happening. However, this is completely accurate. At the time, in the air above Mogadishu, was a Navy P-3 Orion "spy" plane providing aerial reconnaissance. There was a live feed from the P-3 to Task Force Ranger's J.O.C. command center where the commanders and operational people could see what was going on during

the operation. Ridley Scott wasn't cheating. It sounds like he is using the P-3 as a tool to show the audience what is going on during the operation. This is addressed in the first chapter of Mark Bowden's book. I just wanted to let you know the facts.

—Chris Negrete, Devon, Pennsylvania

A. Thanks for setting the record straight.

Boom Mikes

Q. I noticed the microphone overhead in the *A Beautiful Mind* movie, and toward the end it was almost blatant. Did they do this on purpose? Surely they could have deleted this from the film. It made it seem almost like an amateur film.

—Curtis Goodman, Carmel, Indiana

A. You have not been paying attention to the Answer Man, who has written about boom mikes again and again and again. One more time: When you repeatedly see a boom mike in a movie, 99.9 percent of the time it is *not* the fault of the film's director, but of the projectionist in your theater, who has framed the film incorrectly. Many films contain additional real estate above and below the frame, to allow the picture to bleed off the edge of the screen. A complaint to the theater manager may do the trick.

The Bourne Identity

Q. My name is Peter Donen and I was the visual-effects supervisor on *The Bourne Identity*. I just listened to your TV review of the film and am flattered by the attention you gave me, although it was probably unintentional. At the end of your reviews you both stated that you liked the film for the lack of visual effects in it. By this I take it to mean, the lack of *visible* visual effects. I strive very hard to have my work seamlessly integrate itself into the telling of the story and to make sure that the audience is unaware that any of the imagery has been manipulated. On this film I executed in excess of 150 visual-effects shots, which included miniatures, blue screen, wire removal, time manipulation, 3D character animation, and background replacement, for starters. I come from the school that says if I do my job well, my work will not be noticed by the audience.

—Peter Donen, Los Angeles, California

A. Richard Roeper said "no computer effects are as good as a well-shot movie in Paris . . ." and I agreed, "this movie is a convincing argument for really photographing real things happening on real locations." That isn't the same as saying there were no effects at all; I think we were contrasting it with the blue screen work in *Episode II*. But you make an excellent point, and your letter arrived just in time to assist me in the next reply.

Q. I saw *The Bourne Identity* last night. Question: If you are at the top of a stairwell several stories high and you want to fall to the bottom by using a corpse as your shield, how likely is it that (a) the corpse will sufficiently cushion your fall, and (b) while riding said corpse, you can shoot and kill a man at the halfway point in your descent?

—Steve Bailey, Jacksonville Beach, Florida

A. I don't think it's possible. Based on my expert ability to analyze a film, I'd guess it was done with visual effects.

The Cat's Meow

Q. Let's say that *The Cat's Meow* gets it right and that Hearst got away with the murder of Thomas Ince. If he had killed Chaplin, though, as he intended to, could he have pulled it off?

—Charles Wharton, Richmond, California

A. No. Leopold and Loeb would have had to move over as the Crime of the Century. *Citizen Kane* would never have been made. Buster Keaton would have gotten his due as the best silent comedian.

CGI

Q. Everyone in Hollywood thinks CGI is the end-all of special effects. The way it is being used in some movies is a big step back. I heard how much it cost to make *Spider-Man*, but I felt like I was watching a cartoon half the time. The "effect" is spoiled when I can effortlessly tell when it's a real person and when it's a computer image. This is why I hated Jar Jar Binks in *Star Wars*. I didn't for one second think there was something physically there. In the old *Star Wars*, you could tell there was a real being there. In *Blade II*, I'm watching a great fight sequence, then suddenly two flimsy

cartoon creatures jump around. The last great movie I saw that used it right was *The Matrix*.

—John Dingess, Nashville, Tennessee

A. Although CGI is supposed to render f/x scenes more realistic than the older techniques of models, backdrops, matte paintings, stuntmen, etc., sometimes they undercut themselves by being too slick to be true. There is a kind of weight and presence that we expect even in scenes we "know" are special effects, and we miss them when CGI gooses the action beyond a certain point.

Q. Did the Academy create the Best Animated Film category for such films as *Spider-Man* and *Star Wars Episode II: Attack of the Clones*? Do directors think the audience is so naive to believe there is no difference between Roger Rabbit and Jar Jar Binks? I love *Star Wars*, I just wish Mr. Lucas would go back to using models and puppets, they were at least three dimensional.

—Kellie Rheinschmidt, Madison, Wisconsin

A. I received lots of messages like yours, especially from people who resented the way Yoda was turned from a puppet who was a contemplative philosopher into an action figure animated with CGI. However, listen to *Star Wars* aficionado Justin Olson of La Crescenta, California, who writes: "Despite all the blustering about digital effects versus practical effects, the dirty little secret that no one wants you to know is that both *The Phantom Menace* and *Attack of the Clones* are *the* two biggest model (miniature) shows in the history of filmmaking. Hands down. Each of those great 2,000-plus CGI effects shots you say look better in DLP are in fact sometimes populated with dozens of practical miniatures, just like in the original trilogy of films. Please don't sully the names of hundreds of talented individuals who work very hard on these films in many new and time-honored ways. Some of these individuals are in fact the same people who worked on the original films."

Q. In the *Star Wars* series, didn't you find that the Trade Federation ambassador's appearance as a latex-and-blood being was far more satisfyingly real than his CGI self? I point this out because I was so shocked to see something besides a cartoon all of a sudden. The same can be said for some of the Jedi. The little CGI bug-people looked ridiculous by comparison. At least puppets and make-up f/x have to obey the laws of physics (sort of).

—Cary M. Babka, Elk Grove, California

A. I've been surprised by how much backlash there is against computer-generated figures in live-action movies. You're right that models and miniatures have more presence and heft.

Changing Lanes

Q. Amanda Peet has two short scenes in *Changing Lanes*, but the first is so powerful, so chilling in its way, that I think it deserves an Oscar nomination for Best Supporting Actress. Is it possible for such a small role to get nominated, and what is the smallest role to ever be nominated or win?

—Phineas Gage, Napa Valley, California

A. Everybody who has seen that movie re-members that amazing scene, where Peet dares her husband to cheat. Is it too brief for an Oscar nomination? Sometimes the Academy goes for impact rather than length. Beatrice Straight won in 1977 for *Network*, for a brief scene.

Q. In the last Answer Man, you discussed Amanda Peet's chances of an Academy nomination for her small role in *Changing Lanes* by referring to Beatrice Straight's win for *Network*. However, you neglected to mention Dame Judi Dench's win for Supporting Actress for *Shakespeare in Love*, during which she was on-screen for all of seven or eight minutes. At the time, this was considered the shortest amount of screen time for any Oscar winner. I'll have to rewatch *Network*, but I think Dench wins.

—Todd Restler, Ardsley, New York

A. Who had the shortest Oscar-winning performance? The AM turned to Tim Dirks, proprietor of the Greatest Films Website (www.filmsite.org), which has comprehensive info on hundreds of great American movies. His reply:

"Beatrice Straight as Louise Schumacher in *Network* (1976) appears in three scenes that equal about 7½ minutes of total screen time, with eight speeches totaling 260 words. Judi Dench as Queen Elizabeth in *Shakespeare in*

Love (1998) appears in four scenes that equal about ten minutes of total screen time, with fourteen speeches totaling 446 words. Verdict: The Best Supporting Actress Oscar-winner with less screen time *and* less dialogue is Beatrice Straight in *Network*."

Q. Didn't Ben Affleck's speech in *Changing Lanes* about the girl he stood next to on the beach and never spoke to remind you of a scene in *Citizen Kane*? I'm thinking of the one in which Kane's partner Mr. Bernstein is asked about whether "Rosebud" could be some long ago event in Kane's life, and he responds with a lovely story about a girl he saw for just a moment fifty years ago on a ferry and says that a month has not gone by since that he didn't think of her. I realize this is not actionable plagiarism, but the stealing of the idea spoiled the scene for me (though Affleck's flat-line delivery didn't help either).

—Tim Greaney, St. Louis, Missouri

A. An echo, not a steal. Besides, in literature, it's plagiarism; in cinema, it's homage.

Child Care Action Project

Q. Have you heard of the California project? "Child Care Action Project: Movie Analysis for Parents" (CAP) is the most insulting movie site on the Web. Their lust for demeaning a film solely on its content (violence, sex, profanity) is annoying. An example is their review of *Jurassic Park*, a film dear to my heart. They gave it an R rating in the Sex/Homosexuality department because there was "an inappropriate touch to a child from an adult." I wrote them back, saying that the film had no such scene. They told me they analyze every part of the film, including stuff parents and guardians wouldn't even recognize. To do that is perverted and wrong.

—Travis Denson, Yoakum, Texas

A. Later in your message you recommend www.screenit.com. I agree that ScreenIt is the most useful and sensible site on the Web for parents seeking sane advice about movies. It has no religious or political affiliation, but simply provides detailed information about the content of a movie, so that parents can make up their own minds.

At www.capalert.com, few films seem innocent. Disney's *Atlantis* contains "a tale of a homosexual kiss," "adults in underwear," and "female sensuality." *Planet of the Apes* includes "beatings by animals," "smoking what appears to be narcotics" (by apes), and an "offense to God—entire show built on evolution." It was with relief that I turned to the review of *The Princess Diaries*, which is pretty much sin-free, although CapAlert noted "kissing on school property during school hours" and "trashing of lunch that Mom made."

Q. Travis Denson wrote to you about the *Child Care Action Project* (www.capalert.com), and was wondering about the "inappropriate touch between an adult and child" that CAP warned about in *Jurassic Park*. I think the scene CAP was referring to was when the girl fell from the heating vent and a Raptor attempted to eat her. Alan Grant pulled her up to save her life and his hand touched her behind. I guess if a CAP staffer is ever attacked by a dinosaur they'd rather die than be touched inappropriately.
—Andrew Ricci, Manchester, New Hampshire

A. Being eaten by a Raptor ranks high on my list of inappropriate touching.

Chuck Jones
Q. Chuck Jones, legendary creator of Wile E. Coyote and the Road Runner and director of the best Bugs Bunny cartoons and other Warner Brothers classics, died on February 22. I was looking for your tribute, but nary a peep—or a beep! beep!
—Susan Lake, Urbana, Illinois

A. I have an excellent excuse: I was under full anesthetic on February 22. The news of Chuck Jones's death brought back happy memories of this warm man who gave such pleasure. I first met Chuck and his wife, Marian, as regulars at the Telluride Film Festival, where they were so beloved the festival's new Chuck Jones Cinema was dedicated to him. On Telluride's twenty-fifth anniversary crossing aboard the *QE2*, Chuck was an endlessly entertaining table companion, and his Q&A sessions delighted the passengers. His memories of life at the Warners cartoon factory resembles a cartoon, with the hated boss Leon Schlesinger playing the role of Elmer Fudd ("Leon never

did figure out," Chuck chuckled, "that his voice inspired the way Elmer spoke"). Unlike pro athletes who charge for their autographs, Chuck was delighted to do a quick sketch of Bugs or other characters for his fans. To know him was to know why the Tunes were Looney.

Citizen Kane
Q. I was listening to your commentary track on the *Citizen Kane* DVD where you identify Alan Ladd in the upper left corner of the frame during the postnewsreel sequence. It sure looks to me like it's Joseph Cotten there, sitting next to Erskine Sanford (neither of whom, of course, should be in that scene). When you get a chance, pop in the disc again and see for yourself. I believed the same thing you did for thirty-nine years, until last night and the miracle of digital freeze-frame and slow motion. And now someone just sent me the following excerpt from Peter Bogdanovich's book *This Is Orson Welles:*
Bogdanovich: Why did you do the projection-room scene in such darkness?
Welles: Because most of the actors play different parts later on. They're all doubling, except the head fellow. We didn't dare turn on the lights. . . . I used the whole Mercury cast, heavily disguised by darkness. . . . Everybody in the movie is in it.
PB: Not you too?
OW: Yes, I'm there. . . .
PB: Is it true that Alan Ladd's in there somewhere?
OW: Not in that one. He's the leading reporter when all of them gather at Xanadu at the end. And you can't miss him—it was his first movie part, and there he is, wearing his hat the way he wore it for thirty pictures afterward.
—Andy Klein, Santa Monica, California

A. As long as I can remember, it has been an item of folklore that Alan Ladd is in that scene. Jonathan Rosenbaum, critic of the *Chicago Reader* and a Welles expert, tells me, "I thought I recognized him in the projection room—at least on the new DVD, which makes that scene too bright." And Frank Brady's biography, *Citizen Welles*, says: "At 9:20 A.M., Welles crammed Richard Baer, Joseph Cotten, Gus Schilling, Erskine Sanford, William Alland, a then-unknown Alan Ladd, and others into a projection room at RKO . . ." So you are right about Cotten and Sanford, but am I wrong about Ladd?

I have looked carefully at the DVD, which has amazingly good image quality. You have shaken my confidence. The man I pointed out, who always looked like Alan Ladd, now looks like Joseph Cotten. Studying the scene even more closely, however, I think I see Alan Ladd in the very first shots after the newsreel ends—the man in a hat, lighting his pipe in the lower left corner. That would fit with the fact that his bit character also smokes a pipe and wears a hat in the last scene. Bogdanovich even quotes Welles on Ladd's "trademark pipe and hat" in his DVD commentary over the last scene. In saying Ladd was not in the first scene, however, I believe Welles had a memory lapse, and was wrong. Now it's your turn to pop in the disc and decide.

Classics

Q. I rented Kurosawa's *Ran* last November and watched it with my uncle, who fancies himself a film buff. He said he'd never heard of Kurosawa, so I felt incredibly jealous. There are a thousand films I'd give anything to see for the first time again, from *The Seven Samurai* to *Taxi Driver* and even something like *Road Warrior*. And I'd never seen anyone else watch Kurosawa for the first time. Then he went and ruined the experience for me by making kung fu movie noises throughout the film: "Waah Wooshaaw! Oh you have killed my master, now you will surely die!" I respect and love all film genres, especially kung fu, but not only has my uncle disrespected the master himself, but he also missed the whole quote; it's "You will die like the dog you are!" Anyway, my question is: Is what my uncle did a punishable offense?

—Gilbert Smith, Thoreau, New Mexico

A. His offense was making a public nuisance of himself, and for his punishment I suggest you reproduce this item and send it to everyone in his address book, so they will know they have a friend, relative, or business associate who has the aesthetic sensibility of Beavis and/or Butt-Head.

Q. I was wondering if you read Jeff Wells's column on Reel.com about *Citizen Kane.* I think he has a point, that it doesn't have the same power on today's audience like it did in the past. *Kane*'s reputation is so huge that I think many people who view the movie for the first time are disappointed. Indeed, it may be time for *Kane* to be retired as the greatest movie of the twentieth century, so another movie can have a shot at being Number 1 in the twenty-first century.

—Tony Wang, Calgary, Alberta

A. The thing about a movie like *Citizen Kane* is, you may be disappointed the first time, but as you watch it ten or twenty times, you grow progressively less disappointed as you are able to appreciate its riches. One might argue that the greatest films teach us to appreciate them, while lesser films simply cater to our desire for immediate gratification. Great films make audiences better; bad films make audiences worse. Any list of the "greatest films" is of course silly, but *Kane* amazes not only as an artistic triumph but as a technical breakthrough and a symbol of a director allowed to express his vision without second-guessing by mental midgets.

Q. After reading the review on your Great Movies site, I saw *The Bicycle Thief* last week. After seeing the film, I felt that something was wrong. This was caused by my presumption that the movie would end happily, with all the main characters contented. I guess to me the father character was not supposed to steal another man's bike. Or that if he did, he'd be repentant about it, and return the bike before being caught. Then gradually it dawned on me that perhaps one of the themes of the movie is human frailty. The scene where the child looks in terror at seeing his father steal a bike and thus getting caught for it seems to concede this. Even now, the child's facial expression during those moments, so full of despair and terror, haunts me with clarity. With this began my journey of empathy for the film. My question is, could *The Bicycle Thief* have been less great if it ended with a more "positive" ending: one where the father was indeed tempted to steal a bike, fought the temptation, and got blessed in return by the advent of a better-paying job?

—Robert Ong Tan, Taoyuan City, Taiwan

A. *The Bicycle Thief* was made in Italy immediately after the devastation of war, when filmgoers and filmmakers had seen too much suffering to accept facile solutions. But your "positive" ending would be the one chosen by modern Hollywood—plus an upbeat song over the end titles. In recent years happy endings have become obligatory for all mainstream films, to such a degree that for the intelligent moviegoer there is no real suspense. Now, post–9/11, I sense that some audiences will begin to replace the desire for escapism with a need for catharsis. I was asked by a friend at Toronto what film to watch in this season of hope and dread. I suggested Kieslowski's *Decalogue,* one hour a night for ten nights.

Concession Stands

Q. I admit, on most trips to the movies, I sneak in my food to avoid paying the prices at the concession stand. On one of my trips to an AMC theater, however, a friend of mine was halfway into eating a bag of chips as he entered the theater. He told the ticket usher that he was almost done with the chips and not to worry about it, but to our surprise, the employee said AMC allows customers to bring their own food. I did a double take when I heard this, but I'm left curious. Is this the policy of every AMC theater? Was this just the policy at the AMC theater I visited? Or was this just that employee's own policy? And if it is true that customers can bring their own food, how would AMC make any money?

—Ben Christie, Whitby, Ontario

A. Many AMC theaters do indeed have that policy, although they don't advertise it. There is a catch: Since theaters make most of their money at the concession stand (the studios get most of the admission price), if everyone brought their own food the theaters would go broke, or ticket prices would go to $20.

The Crimson Rivers

Q. You wrote in your review of *The Crimson Rivers* that "If the makers of the next Hannibal Lecter picture don't hire Mathieu Kassovitz to direct it, they're mad."

Word around the campfire is that Brett Rat-

ner, of the two *Rush Hour* movies, will helm *Red Dragon.* Can I get a collective *huh?*

—Paul West, Seattle, Washington

A. Huh? The Hannibal Lecter pictures depend above all on mood and tone, qualities a hammer-and-nails director like Brett Ratner hasn't demonstrated. Ratner pictures have recently grossed some $600 million, which makes him, by definition, a genius, but he has not yet revealed any hint of a personal style. His wham-bam hyperkinetic approach, which had Jackie Chan complaining that even the fight scenes were truncated, is alien to the creepy buildup of atmosphere and nuance required for Hannibal Lecter. I would suggest that producers Dino and Martha De Laurentiis screen both Lecter pictures, both *Rush Hour* pictures, and *The Crimson Rivers,* and ask themselves if they were out of their minds.

Critics

Q. If all writing on film is just one man's opinion, then why should we read any of it?

—Donny Wallace, Navasota, Texas

A. If this is just one man's question, why should I answer it?

Q. Does watching so many movies and having to critique them take the pleasure and escapism of the moviegoing experience away from you? Or does it make you appreciate it more when a good movie finally comes out?

—Lanford Beard, Birmingham, Alabama

A. Some critics, like my hero Dwight Macdonald, finally tired of the dreck and retired from reviewing. When I first got my job I thought five years was about as long as anyone could do it. But I have never tired of going to the movies, and even in a bad one you can see people trying and failing, which can be almost as interesting as seeing them trying and succeeding. When a truly great movie comes along, it cheers me up for weeks.

Q. I've seen ads for the movie *Frailty* that boast recommendations from directors like Sam Raimi and James Cameron. While these are preferable to quotes from the fictitious critic David Manning, can directors be considered as reliable as critics? Is the quality of a director's work any indicator of his or her tastes as a viewer?

—Lisa Tittle, Stanford, Wisconsin

A. Novelist Stephen King was also cited as a supporter of *Frailty.* These are all people with reputations to protect, and were under no pressure to endorse the movie, so we can assume they are sincere. And, yes, I think the quality of a director's work might be an indicator of his taste.

Q. You didn't acquit yourself very well in your article on *Amadeus.* You are presumably a film critic and quite evidently not a literary critic. Anyone who thinks Thomas Mann is not a great writer, worse still, that P. G. Wodehouse is, doesn't know much about literature.

—Franz Schulze, Department of Art, Lake Forest College, Illinois

A. The kind of person who thinks Mann a great writer and Wodehouse not a great writer is precisely the kind of person who would believe that professional credentials are necessary to make such judgments.

Q. On the DVD of David Lynch's *Blue Velvet,* one of the extras is the original Siskel and Ebert TV review. You didn't like it; Siskel did. Why did Lynch include this on his DVD? He also once advertised his movie *Lost Highway* as "Two Thumbs Down!"

—Joshua Hall, Kansas City, Missouri

A. David Lynch is a quiet, well-mannered man who has a certain Olympian detachment from critics.

Q. You've mentioned that the actor David Ogden Stiers is someone whom you have known for years. Do you ever have trouble suspending your disbelief when you "know" the person you are watching?

—Dave Jaycock, Victoria, British Columbia

A. I went to Urbana (Illinois) High School with Stiers. When I see him on the screen, I think "Hey! Dave Stiers!" But since I knew him when he was sixteen, he's changed enough so that it's not a big distraction.

Digital versus Real Movies

Q. In an ABCNEWS.com article, *The Digital Death of Film,* you are quoted as stating

that digital projection has yet to match the best that film can do. I'm a scanner technician (high-end digital color separation) at the National Geographic Society in Washington, D.C. While we (prepress division, magazine staff) deal here only with still images, it is our consensus that digital imagery, although rapidly improving, still has a long way to go to compare with film. It lacks the subtle, smooth transitions in the fine detail of film that allow for extreme magnification. While digital photography is good enough for many publications, we're not quite there yet.

—Peter Beck, Accokeek, Maryland

A. Thank you for words of sanity during the rush to throw away the celluloid heritage.

Q. I've read many complaints about the digital version of *Attack of the Clones.* I would imagine we're at the beginning of a new era, and imperfection is to be expected. Yes, at this time digital movies cannot match the quality and nuances of film. However, there are many advances to be made, The quality of the films 100 years ago wasn't up to standards of today, and the digital films twenty years from now will not likely bear much resemblance to today's. Give the technology a chance!

—Greg Weinstein, Augusta, Georgia

A. Oddly enough, however, the films of forty years ago, especially the 70mm films, were *better* than the standards of today. Meanwhile, a bombshell new research report by Credit Suisse/First Boston reports that digital is not yet ready for prime time, and gives high marks to a system it finds superior, easier to install, and much less expensive—none other than my longtime favorite, MaxiVision 48.

Q. Once again you're touting the greatness of MaxiVision. I am thoroughly convinced of its greatness, and have been waiting to see it ever since your original coverage. Digital projection seems to have made more headway, though. Can we really expect to see MaxiVision any time soon?

—Aaron Kucera, Dallas, Texas

A. You might be surprised. A bombshell research report just released by Credit Suisse/First Boston supports MaxiVision as preferable to digital projection, which is "not ready for prime time." The most unexpected finding of the report is that digital projection would *not* be cheaper than the current system of distributing prints, but, because of the financing costs, would be more expensive. Other bullet points: MaxiVision has dramatically better picture quality; its cost is around $10,000 a booth, as opposed to $100,000 to $150,000 for digital; it is backward compatible and can project all films ever made; and the current Texas Instruments digital system uses an inferior standard. The report praises the Kodak digital standard as superior, but criticizes Kodak for not supporting MaxiVision—which, because it uses film, dovetails with Kodak's dominance of the celluloid market. Since the much-heralded digital rollout of *Star Wars Episode II* was a nonevent, it's unlikely that exhibitors are prepared to make an enormous investment in digital projectors. If they want something new, affordable, and dramatically better, MaxiVision is the obvious choice.

Q. I read the Credit Suisse/First Boston report on digital projection versus MaxiVision. Interesting, and certainly well researched. While some of the financial concepts just barely made it through my gray matter, I did notice something that seemed off. There is a mention of the average life of the hardware used in projection. While I have little doubt that the electronics used for digital projection would need to be replaced/upgraded/supplanted every three years, I don't understand the number of seven years placed upon 35mm projection equipment. Many theaters have projectors with bodies that go back to the 1940s and 1950s. Lamphouses and audio gear may be upgraded, not a huge investment, but those old 35mm projectors just keep chugging along with only reasonable servicing.

Regarding the visual quality of digital: My son went to see *Clones* at a film venue and reported that it looked "soft." At 1.8k, it can't look anything but soft. As long as 1.8 is all that folks desire out of the theatrical experience, it certainly works, especially when the use of 24fps digital allows for ultrafast postproduction and multiple layers of digital efx. The only problem, as you've properly stated, is that the experience of cinema is gone.

I still haven't been able to create an acceptable film look using digital restoration in anything less than 4k—and that with emulsions from the 1950s and 1960s (Eastman 5248).

What the public doesn't seem to recognize and what the uneducated eye will not confirm unless the two are literally viewed side by side, is that current digital technology in the ultra-low-res of 1.8k looks like just so much mush when compared to a 35mm frame.

—Robert Harris, The Film Preserve

A. As the ranking genius of film restoration, you should know. I treasure your restorations of film classics from *Lawrence of Arabia* to *Vertigo*. What has happened, I think, is that executives who are only semiliterate in technical matters have been seduced by the magic word "digital" into embracing the idea of digital projection, and are too busy, lazy, or unprepared to do the necessary homework. The Credit Suisse/First Boston report essentially said the digital emperor has no clothes, by pointing out digital's shortcomings in quality, maintenance, and cost. The surprise was its endorsement of MaxiVision, and its conclusion that MaxiVision was a natural fit for Kodak.

Divine Secrets of the Ya-Ya Sisterhood

Q. Your review of *Divine Secrets of the Ya-Ya Sisterhood* was extremely harsh. I get the feeling you don't particularly like chick flicks. Why not simply admit they are not your cup of tea?

—Jane Holahan, Lancaster, Pennsylvania

A. I love chick flicks when they are not insulting to my intelligence. Of course, in that case they're not "chick flicks" but simply good movies. Here's an example. In the next month, a movie named *Lovely and Amazing* will be opening around the country. It is about a mother and her three daughters, and has the quality, depth, and originality I found missing in the inane *Ya-Ya*. To see it is to understand what I'm getting at.

Do-It-Yourself Commentary

Q. I'm the editor and webmaster of DVD-Verdict.com, a DVD review site. I have to say that your idea for a Web archive of homespun

DVD commentaries is one of the best ideas I've heard in a long time. For my first one, I'm tackling Renny Harlin's *Deep Blue Sea*, a film only I seemed to appreciate.

—Mike Jackson, Eugene, Oregon

A. I wrote a column in *Yahoo! Internet Life* magazine suggesting that movie fans record their own personal shot-by-shot DVD commentaries, and post them on the Web in the MP3 format (the column is at www.yil.com). Commentary tracks are recorded by directors, actors, critics, and scholars—why not by fans, who sometimes know more about a movie than anyone else?

Q. Your idea for do-it-yourself commentary tracks is brilliant. I plan to do some myself. You suggest that most commentary tracks are "inside jobs," but certainly there are a few that have been overtly critical of the film. Lem Dobbs's commentary for *The Limey* is very argumentative at times, Kevin Smith's commentary for *Mallrats* is deservedly self-deprecatory, and the commentary for the out-of-print Criterion Collection *Sid and Nancy* is scathingly critical of the liberties the filmmakers took with the life stories of the subjects. Do you have any favorite "critical" or "negative" DVD commentary tracks?

—Sean Duncan, Oxford, Ohio

A. You may have exhausted the list. I'd love to hear a commentary track by someone who hates a movie.

Q. Your *Yahoo! Internet Life* column is a little too quick in concluding that consumers should record MP3 commentaries to DVDs and trade them over the Web. I teach copyright law, and although I'm not altogether happy about where the law is headed these days, it seems at least possible that these MP3s could be considered unlawful derivative works by the holders of the copyrights in the original movies. In the language of the motion picture industry, that makes "critics and fans on the Web" into copyright thieves and pirates. This raises some interesting issues under the First Amendment, but I think this is the direction that recent court decisions take us.

—Professor Michael J. Madison, University of Pittsburgh School of Law

A. You're the expert, but wouldn't spoken freelance commentaries be protected in the same way as written commentaries? How are the copyright holders harmed? The original DVD must be purchased by both the commentator and those who want to listen to the commentary, and its copyrighted content is not being distributed.

Enough

Q. In your review of *Enough*, you wrote "The day when the evil husband is black and the self-defense instructor is white will not arrive in our lifetimes." *Enough* was certainly reprehensible on most levels, and I am not defending its honor—but would you not have reacted even more negatively toward it if the husband was black and those two characters were white (and the screenplay remained the same)? Wouldn't you have said that the movie reinforces a stereotype that black men are violent and the white heroine has to seek help from other whites to escape him? Wouldn't a movie like that be even more racist?

—Michael Lynderery, Toronto, Ontario

A. The movie was morally questionable no matter what the races involved. The color coding was simply another level of cynicism. My guess is the races could not be reversed without rewriting the screenplay, because without its politically correct camouflage the characters would have had to be individuals and not stereotypes. One of the accomplishments of *Monster's Ball* is that it transcends race by creating characters so specific they represent only themselves.

Q. Your review of Jennifer Lopez's *Enough* writes of the color coding of good and bad guys. The role of the villain Kingpin in the *Daredevil* movie is performed by Michael Clarke Duncan. In the comics, Kingpin was a big, fat white man who vaguely reminded me of Boss Hogg in the comics; do you feel the casting of a black actor in a traditionally white villain role indicates some change in Hollywood's current attitudes toward extreme political correctness?

—Chris Walsh, Vancouver, British Columbia

A. I hope so, although of course a comic

villain isn't a bad guy in the same sense as the villain in a serious action picture. Morgan Freeman often talks about his frustration at not being able to play villains (he wanted to play Hannibal Lecter) because producers are shy of showing African-Americans in a negative light. He observes: "The villain is often the best role in the movie."

E.T.'s Twentieth Anniversary

Q. What is your reaction to the rumored changes in the upcoming twentieth anniversary theatrical rerelease of Steven Spielberg's E.T.? I hear that E.T. himself has been replaced in some shots by a digital "update," that all shots of guns in adult hands will now be digitally "fixed" to show walkie-talkies instead, and that even certain lines of dialogue (particularly Elliott calling his brother "penis breath") will be relooped. Is there any veracity to these rumors? And if so, does this mean the original, already-classic version of E.T. will no longer be available to audiences perfectly capable of thinking for themselves?

—Aaron Reynolds, Houston, Texas

A. Marvin Levy, Spielberg's longtime spokesman, replies: "The rerelease of E.T. for the twentieth anniversary will have enhancements as well as some new footage and some relatively small changes. Years ago, Steven Spielberg said that he would take guns out of the scene where the authorities are chasing the boys and E.T. on their bikes if he ever had the chance to do it. Earlier, most likely at the time of the rerelease in 1985 or the first video release, he took out the line about 'going as a terrorist.' It was jarring in the eighties and would have been even more jarring today. The line about 'penis breath' must have been his choice now that he is a parent and E.T. should be as accessible as possible so that every parent could be comfortable seeing it with their family (he was not a parent when he made the film). There is a new scene in Elliott's house with E.T. in the bathtub. Most of the enhancements involve subtle changes in color or visual expressions of E.T. Most people will not notice the vast majority of them. Sound is also enhanced with new mastering. To call this overall a 'revision' of the film would be a gross

overstatement. We hope the final result will add to everyone's experience and enjoyment of E.T. while retaining the impact and integrity of the film first released in 1982."

My own reaction? It's Spielberg's film, and he can do what he wants with it (the original version will continue to be available). But he is rewriting history. "Penis breath" is a classic line, much beloved. As a parent he should know that kids have a direct way of expressing themselves about bodily parts and functions. Has the wonder kid become an old fogey? When I revisited E.T. for my Great Movies series, I watched it with grandchildren who were then about seven and five, and there was not a single shot to object to.

Fargo

Q. I played a role in the film Fargo and was disturbed recently to learn that someone died in Minnesota apparently while searching for the money Steve Buscemi buries in the roadside snow in the film! Is this tale, like the film, "based on a true story," or is it really true?

—Gary Houston, Chicago, Illinois

A. Yeah, you played the irate customer who didn't want to pay extra for the rustproofing. Fargo opens by saying it's based on a true story, but the Coen brothers reveal at the end that it's fiction. The story of the death is true. Reuters reports that a twenty-eight-year-old woman told police in Bismarck she had traveled to North Dakota from Tokyo to search for the buried treasure. She took a bus to Fargo, a taxi to Detroit Lakes, and then hitched a ride out of town, where her body was found. "We've narrowed it down to a couple of possibilities—either a prescription drug overdose or an exposure death," Detroit Lakes police chief Cal Keena told Reuters.

40 Days and 40 Nights

Q. Why has no reviewer pointed out that the idea of giving up sex for Lent, the basic premise of 40 Days and 40 Nights is akin to a Jew giving up pork only for a Jewish holy period? Don't religions that celebrate Lent also frown on sex outside marriage? Did I miss a recent papal decree?

—John McCauley, Arlington, Virginia

A. Here is the review by the U.S. Catholic Bishop's Office for Film and Broadcasting: "Crude romantic comedy about a young bachelor (Josh Hartnett) who swears off sex for Lent after his girlfriend (Vinessa Shaw) breaks up with him, but complications ensue as soon as he meets the girl of his dreams. Snickering at the Catholic Church's teaching on premarital sex, director Michael Lehmann's one-joke film exploits the holy season of Lent as a cynical pretext for abstinence. Misuse of the sacrament of penance, sexual encounters, recurring nudity, intermittent rough language, crass sexual expressions, and profanity. Rating: O—morally offensive."

Frailty

Q. (Spoiler alert: Reveals film secrets.) To me, it was quite obvious at the end of *Frailty* that Dad was actually on a real mission from God. Remember when Andy's character said that God would protect him, the cameras in the FBI agency all missed his face, and no one could even remember what he looked like.

—Anthony Galica, San Jose, California

A. Is Dad deluded into thinking an angel has ordered him to kill demons in human form, or did God really send him that message? And if God did, why would God have chosen as His instrument a father with two young sons who were irreparably harmed by the experience? I wrote in my review, "The movie contains one shot, sure to be debated, that suggests God's hand really is directing Dad's murders." It also contains subjective shots showing the sins of the people Dad kills. But are those shots trustworthy, or are they part of Dad's delusion? Is it not possible that even the FBI agent's transgressions, while true, are coincidental? The movie offers us a choice: Dad is deluded, or God has changed His methods, abandoned the notion of free will, and become a psychological child abuser. Under traditional Christian theology, I believe Dad should have refused the angel's instructions, because Thou Shalt Not Kill.

Q. I noticed that *Frailty*, a movie that most critics seem to like, isn't making much money. My question for you is, do you think a movie

can be *too* critically acclaimed? In other words, is it possible to see a four-star review and think, "Oh, that's an artsy movie. I don't want to see that."

—Grant Lankard, Indiana, Pennsylvania

A. Absolutely. One of the great mysteries is why people will cheerfully attend movies they expect to be bad, but approach good movies with great caution. This is an actual conversation I had years ago:

Reader: "We live near the Wilmette Theater, and it is showing *Cries and Whispers*. What can you tell us about that movie?"

Ebert: "I think it's the year's best film."

Reader: "Oh. That doesn't sound like anything we'd like to see."

Ghosts of Mars

Q. Upon reading your three-star review of *Ghosts of Mars*, I went with a date to see this film. *Ghosts of Mars* is a travesty, a film destined for the bottom of the direct-to-video release barrel. It is unoriginal (like the fifth film in the last two years set on Mars), unexciting (not one genuine scare or clever action sequence), badly written (they continue to shoot the bad guys despite the fact that they are more dangerous that way), and poorly acted (not one actor transcends the dialogue they were given). The only consolation I could offer anyone involved with the making of this film is that *Ghosts of Mars* will be easily forgotten. You said the film "delivered on its chosen level." What level was that? The bad movie level? If a film can receive a complimentary review and rating for simply setting its sights low, how can I know when a three-star movie is truly a good movie or a bad one with no ambitions?

—David Boostrom, St. Louis, Missouri

A. I would suggest ignoring the star ratings (which are relative, not absolute) and just reading the review. I believe my review of *Ghosts of Mars* accurately described the movie, and explained my reasons for liking it. Three stars for me means "recommended in the context of this review." A review is a personal, subjective opinion, not intended to predict your reaction, but I think you saw the same movie I described.

Godfather Ghost

Q. While watching the new *Godfather* DVD, I noticed a startling image. During Vito's funeral, Tessio comes over to tell Michael about the upcoming meeting. As Michael stands up, in the crook of his left armpit a half picture of a woman's face can be seen. Who is it? How did it get into the frame? My roommate says it's Kay, and since it's over his heart, it's symbolic of their love. That sounds like hogwash to me, but I don't have a better answer.

—Tony Bates, Norman, Oklahoma

A. Good gravy! I see her too. I owe an apology to Jeffrey Horowitz of Syosset, New York, who wrote earlier with the same sighting. I couldn't find the woman, and told him so. Now your description sent me back for a frame-by-frame creep through the sequence, and there she is, ghostly red against black, fading in and out. Is this a real ghost image, or only an optical illusion, like those Elvises people see on screen doors?

I asked director Francis Ford Coppola, who replies: "Gee, I know nothing about this. Will look, I guess. The funeral scene was shot really quickly, and I was disgruntled that they removed one day from its schedule. So nothing elaborate was done: we shot it as fast as we could."

Q. I looked at the mysterious face in the funeral scene of *The Godfather* last night, and I think I can explain it. Before Michael stands up, you can see a glare on the lens, but it is not discernible as a face because it is on a white background. When Michael shifts, so that his suit provides a dark contrast, the glare depicts the face of his mother, who in the scene immediately preceding is seated next to him. Presumably, the actors remained in place for the close-up shot of Michael. Coppola mentioned the shots were done in a hurry, and what we are seeing is a fluke of light, distortion, shadow, and lens peculiarity; the flared edge of the lens picks up the light from just out of the frame.

—Mike Spearns, St. John's, Newfoundland

A. Many readers wrote in with theories, but you hit the ghost on the head. After two AM readers spotted the face, I queried Francis Ford Coppola, and he requested Kim Aubry, producer of the *Godfather* DVDs and his VP of postproduction and technology, to look at the scene. Aubry writes: "Look closer, especially at the preceding shots. It's Morgana King (who is sitting next to Pacino) being reflected, probably by a filter in the matte box, explaining the orange hue. Look again even more closely. What is less explained: Why is she chewing gum at her husband's funeral?!? Francis and I just studied this little scene on the DVD, and her gum chewing was especially vexing to him and amusing to me. (Of course, she thought she was off camera.) We get so much bogus stuff that it was fun to check out a real one, and it turns out not to be an artistic trompe l'oeuil, but a *goof!* Love it!"

Gosford Park

Q. Regarding Robert Altman's *Gosford Park*, I note that Ivor Novello really did play the title character in both the 1932 version of *The Lodger* and the 1926 Hitchcock original, and really was a talented musician and composer. But was the 1932 *The Lodger* really a flop or was the Maggie Smith character just being catty?

—Chuck Huber, Goleta, California

A. It was very badly received, not least because Novello's voice was not suited to sound pictures.

Great Movies

Q. Answer Man, demand a recount! In *Entertainment Weekly*'s list of the "100 Greatest Film sound tracks ever," they have omitted Anton Karas's score to *The Third Man*!

—Matt Jaycox, Chicago, Illinois

A. That invalidates the entire list. They need to throw it out and start again.

Q. Stanley Kubrick's *2001: A Space Odyssey* is playing in New York at the Loews Astor Plaza but it's a virtual secret because Warners did little publicity or advertising. The film runs through next Thursday. It is a beautiful, apparently new 70mm print that looks gorgeous in one of the biggest cinemas in New York, but that cinema is mostly empty every show because nobody knows the film is there. What I deduce is that the film is playing because there was a contractual agreement to rerelease it in 2001 between Warners and Kubrick, who was known to be working on the rerelease before his death. The reason it is being dumped like this, one surmises, is because the current Warners regime has no enthusiasm for a full-blown rerelease. I feel a sense of personal outrage about this. *2001* inspired my very first movie review when I was a high-schooler way back in 1968, and I've been anticipating its 2001 rerelease literally since I've been a professional critic. But even if one isn't a fan of Kubrick or the movie, I think you have to agree that this showing of the film with no publicity is a shabby, criminal way to treat any important film. Worse than not rereleasing the film at all, it's an expression of contempt for film history and audiences who retain an interest in the cinematic past. For Warners to do this while it is raking in millions on *Harry Potter* is a sad commentary on the state of our film culture.

—Godfrey Cheshire, film critic, New York

A. I showed a new 70mm print of the film last April at my Overlooked Film Festival at the University of Illinois, where it sold out and received a standing ovation. I am convinced a proper rerelease would be a huge success. Disney reveres its classics, and is currently rereleasing *Beauty and the Beast* in IMAX screens. An IMAX release of *2001* would make perfect sense.

I forwarded your message to Jan Harlen, Kubrick's brother-in-law and coproducer of several of the later Kubrick films, and he responds that he intends to follow it up with Kubrick's friends and advisers in Los Angeles.

Q. In your Great Movie review of *Laura,* you write: "That *Laura* continues to weave a spell—and it does—is a tribute to style over sanity. No doubt the famous musical theme by David Raksin has something to do with it: The music lends a haunted, nostalgic, regretful cast to everything it plays under, and it plays under a lot." David Raksin's score came out of similarly somber tones. Struggling for days over a suitable theme. Raksin only found the infamous theme to the film after his marriage fell apart. That night, learning his wife had left him, he composed the classic music.

—Paul West, Seattle, Washington

A. Just on the basis of the music, I think he still loved her.

Q. Thanks to one of those DVD-mailing services, I recently viewed as much of the work of Keaton and Chaplin as possible. I was astonished by how much better Keaton is. He doesn't repeat gags, like Chaplin does. Chaplin acts out the same character. Keaton just is a character. When it comes to stunts and gags, Keaton is about three times as creative and daring. Chaplin has an edge over Keaton in one area, however—pathos. The Little Tramp tugs at the heart like Keaton's rocky expression can't. I would think in this age of postmodern irony that Keaton would be ten times as huge, with his acerbic roles, cynical wit, and gasp-inducing stunts skilled enough to out–Jackie Chan Jackie Chan.

—Luke Gibbs, Springfield, Missouri

A. You are not alone in preferring Keaton. Both men were geniuses, but Chaplin speaks to a more sentimental worldview, and Keaton seems fiercely modern. I'm preparing to teach a class on Keaton's films right now, and am astonished by his freshness. Most of his features are now available in good prints on DVD, although some buffs believe better prints have recently turned up in France.

Q. I am a nineteen-year-old film student at the University of Toronto. I have been an avid filmgoer since I can remember, but not until recently have I had the chance to experience films like *His Girl Friday* and *Vertigo.* My film class has rendered me completely infatuated with the classic films. I have never become so involved in the world of the characters as I was with Ozu's *Floating Weeds,* never so astonished by the power of film as I was during *Singin' in the Rain.* It makes me ill that a whole generation of teenagers will flock to junk and never experience film in its finest form.

—Ashton Lubman, Toronto, Ontario

A. Three of the four titles you mention are on-line in my Great Movies series, and *His Girl Friday* will eventually turn up there. I imagine everyone meanders through junk to begin with, and then the lucky ones see a film that jolts them into realizing how magical the medium can be. For me, that film was *Citizen Kane.* You mentioned Ozu. When you get to the point where you understand how good Ozu was, you have pretty much arrived at an understanding with the art of the cinema.

Q. I enjoyed your Great Movies essay on *In Cold Blood*. My only criticism is that I wonder how you could criticize the movie so much and still consider it a great movie.
—Steve Bailey, Jacksonville Beach, Florida

A. I criticized the narrator at the end . . . in much the same spirit that I singled out the psychiatrist and his superfluous explanation at the end of *Psycho*. Just because a movie is Great doesn't mean it's Perfect.

Q. In writing about *Lawrence of Arabia,* you said that seeing it on the big screen in 70mm "is on the shortlist of things that must be done during the lifetime of every lover of film." What else is on the list?
—Justin Weiss, Tokyo, Japan

A. Seeing a movie on the big screen of the Theater Lumiere at Cannes. Seeing a movie under the stars at Telluride. Seeing a Bollywood movie in a gigantic theater in India. Attending the first sneak preview of an enormous hit like *2001* or *The Godfather,* before anyone knows how good it is. Seeing a Buster Keaton movie with kids who don't even notice it's a silent film. Booking your own film festival. Seeing a movie in a really advanced high-quality projection system, like 30-fps Todd AO, 48-fps MaxiVision 48, or 60-fps Showscan. Going through a movie a shot at a time with an expert, like *Raging Bull* with editor Thelma Schoonmaker or *Bound for Glory* with cinematographer Haskell Wexler. Visiting the location of a Western starring John Wayne. Visiting the set of a movie being directed by Ingmar Bergman, Federico Fellini, Billy Wilder, Martin Scorsese, or Steven Spielberg. Getting a tour of Skywalker Ranch. Seeing *City Lights* projected in Piazza San Marco in Venice and then afterward seeing Charlie Chaplin wave to the crowd from a balcony. But I'm not answering your question, I'm writing my autobiography. You're too late for half of this stuff, but you have your own great moments ahead of you. It beats working for a living.

Hannibal

Q. I watched *Hannibal* on DVD last night, and when Clarice was searching the FBI's most wanted list, Osama Bin Laden's name and photo were prominent above those of Hannibal Lector. Was this a case of extreme divination on the part of the filmmaker? Or was this added for the DVD release?
—N. Nelson, Metaoroe, Louisiana

A. Osama Bin Laden would have been at the top of the real list at that time.

Harry Potter

Q. It's said no one ever went broke underestimating the intelligence of the American public. *Harry Potter and the Philosopher's Stone* is an excellent film up here in Canada, as was *The Madness of George III.* I wonder if the same can be said for the U.S. releases *Harry Potter and the Sorcerer's Stone* and *The Madness of King George.* The point, of course, is that these minor title details were changed for American audiences on the assumption they are too stupid to handle the concept of the philosopher's stone of alchemical fame, or to realize seeing George III doesn't mean you've missed parts I and II. Are these decisions made because the suits think I'm really dumb, or is it because they are?
—Brady Sylvester, Red Deer, Alberta

A. Let's say they think you're as dumb as they are when they make the decisions. The Harry Potter title change was made not by Warner Brothers but by the book publishers, Scholastic, who feared American readers might be scared off by the word "philosopher."

Q. In *Harry Potter,* when the stone is referred to, is the line "the sorcerer's stone" in all versions? Or is it referred to as the "philosopher's stone" in the UK, Canada, Australia, etc.?
—Jean Davis, Kansas City, Missouri

A. Director Chris Columbus says he shot two versions of the dialogue, one with "philosopher," the other with "sorcerer."

Q. A school district in North Dakota did not allow students to attend the premiere of *Harry Potter* in Fargo. They feel the portrayal of witchcraft would be in violation of the separation of church and state. I am very disappointed about the action being taken and I really feel for the kids.

—Sarah Adams, Fargo, North Dakota

A. Since this was to be an official class trip, I can understand the principle involved, and hope the school district applies the same standards to public prayers at football games, etc.

Heartbreakers

Q. I saw *Heartbreakers* on a recent airplane trip and was surprised to read in the credits that it was directed by David Mamet. In fact, I saw the movie twice on that trip, so I read Mamet's name four times in the credits (twice in the beginning, twice in the end). But the IMDb lists the director as David Mirkin. This doesn't seem to be just a case of misspelling, since I know that Mirkin is an established director in his own right. But which one directed *Heartbreakers*, Mamet or Mirkin? I did notice Mamet touches in the cast (such as the presence of Mamet favorite Ricky Jay) and the subject matter (con artists), but is it possible I was just seeing things when I saw Mamet credited as the director?

—Alexander Higle, Jamaica Plain, Massachusetts

A. You must have been. Jan Sirridge, vice president of nontheatrical sales at MGM, replies: "We never change the credits when editing our films for inflight exhibition. Just to confirm this, I had the video lab that duplicated all inflight exhibition cassettes check both masters and they have confirmed that David Mirkin is listed as the director."

Heist: Everyone Needs Money

Q. In your review of *Heist,* you say that the line, "Everyone needs money. That's why they call it money!" is one of the funniest lines that David Mamet has ever written. Why is it funny and how do you interpret it? I saw the film this weekend and heard the same line, yet I feel it just doesn't work.

—Rory L. Aronsky, Pembroke Pines, Florida

A. Ali Hirji of Edmonton agrees with you: "I personally do not understand what is so clever about this line, since it seems to have no meaning beyond its literal meaning." Why is it funny? As Louis Armstrong once said, "There

are some folks that, if they don't know, you can't tell 'em."

Q. Regarding your item about the line in David Mamet's *Heist,* "Everybody needs money! That's why they call it money!" I was wondering myself what was so funny about the line. You quoted Louis Armstrong but you didn't give us an answer as to why *you* thought it was so funny because, I guess, some of us are probably too dense to "get it." Could you please enlighten us anyway on why you think it's so funny? To me, the word has no meaning beyond its literal meaning.

—Binh Ha, Waterloo, Ontario

A. Of course it has no meaning beyond its literal meaning! That's why it's so funny! This is the question that will not go away. Juan-Jose Pichardo of Chicago also writes: "No, really, explain Mamet's money joke." I cannot explain it. I can only laugh at it, and quote Gene Siskel, who liked to say, "Two things are not debatable: Eroticism, and comedy. If you don't think it's sexy, or funny, there's no way I can change your mind."

Q. I was looking through the quotes section of the Internet Movie Database and ran across this exchange from *Me and My Pal* (1933):
Oliver: You know what a magnet is, don't you?
Stan: Sure, it's a thing that eats cheese.
I must not be as fluent in old movie/vaudeville jokes as I thought I was. "Magnet" sounds nothing like "mouse," so I'm stumped, unless it's just Stan Laurel being silly, I'm stumped.

—David Westhart, Philadelphia, Pennsylvania

A. Everybody likes magnets. That's why they call them magnets.

Q. Jeez, you really make us work! In a recent Answer Man, someone asked you to explain the Laurel and Hardy joke about a magnet being something that likes cheese. Your response was, "Everyone likes magnets. That's why they call them magnets." *What* were you referring to? I searched through recent AMs until I found the debate on the David Mamet line from *Heist* about how everybody needs money: "That's why they call it money." I laughed then, and laughed again today.

—Paul J. Marasa, Galesburg, Illinois

A. As many readers pointed out, including David E. Miller of Las Vegas, Howard Hoffman of Sterling, Virginia, and Edward Sullivan of San Francisco, Laurel and Hardy were making a play on *magnets* and *maggots*. Readers who don't think Mamet's line about money is funny continue to write me. I encourage them to write one another.

Q. Why are you being playfully difficult in refusing to point out what seems like a fairly obvious pun in David Mamet's *Heist* line, "Everybody needs money! That's why they call it money!" Say it aloud: "NEEDS money . . . call it Muh-NEED."
—Sean Traverse, Minneapolis, Minnesota

A. But . . . he says "Muh-KNEE."

Q. I recently watched the DVD of *Heist*, and while I had no problem with Mamet's "money" joke, I did have a problem with this joke Delroy Lindo told a would-be thug:
"Know why the chicken crossed the road? Because the road crossed the chicken."
What the hell does that mean? Does that mean the road angered the chicken and that the chicken crossed it out of spite?
—Drew McGary, New York

A. In a world . . . where chickens cross roads and roads cross chickens—it's payback time!

* * *

P.S. Faithful readers will recall several entries about a line in David Mamet's *Heist* that I said was the funniest he had ever written. Gene Hackman is a thief who wants to retire. Danny DeVito wants him to do one more job, for the money. Hackman says he doesn't like money. DeVito replies: "Everybody needs money! That's why they call it money!" (Earlier I quoted this as "likes" money, which is just as funny—but inaccurate, as Peter DeBruce of AOL Movies informs me.)

Many readers said they did not see anything funny about this line. I quoted Louis Armstrong: "There are some folks that, if they don't know, you can't tell 'em." More protest. I quoted Gene Siskel: "Comedy and eroticism are not debatable. Either it works for you or it doesn't." This also failed to satisfy many readers.

In desperation I sent the whole correspondence to David Mamet himself, and have received the following reply:

"Thank you for your update on the *Heist* controversy. A lot of people didn't even think World War One was funny. So it just shows to go you.

"Additionally, Clausewitz's *On War* was, it seems originally issued as a seriocomic 'memoire' of life in a garret. (Original title *Tales of a Garterbelt.*)

"I see where our beloved president has taken to speaking of 'terriers and barriffs.' Can he mean 'Braniffs'? Humor is where one finds it—George Dandin.

"With all best wishes,
"David."

Ice Age

Q. I was lucky enough to catch your *11th Hour* talk on PBS about a year ago and was affected by your thoughts on vegetarianism. I was therefore puzzled by your recent review of *Ice Age*, where you state, "Much of the serenity and order of nature depends on eating the neighbors."
—Jay Miller, Boulder, Colorado

A. Except in Boulder, where all living species dine on tofu, trail mix, and bottled water, human beings are the only voluntary vegetarians. All other species dine on their favorite foods without a moment's concern about how their favorite foods feel about that.

IMDb.com

Q. The Internet Movie Database has User Comments on every movie, and the first one is excerpted on the Details page for the movie. Is this another place where the studios have slimed their way to the top? You recently listed the Top Ten Rotten Movies from RottenTomatoes.com—ten titles with universal disapproval from all critics. Yet the first IMDb comments on each of these movies are nearly all fawning, and are mostly written by users who have contributed no other comments to IMDb. Are these plants by studio publicists? For example, *Down to You* is "The Best Teenage Romance Film I've Seen in Years." And check out the praise for *Battlefield Earth, Jawbreaker, 3 Strikes,* and *Lost Souls. Chill Factor* ("a great crowd pleasing movie . . .

the audience seemed to love it from beginning to end"), *Mod Squad* ("I thought it was one of the best movies I have ever seen"), *Bless the Child,* etc. Is there a new David Manning scandal brewing?

—Glenn Worthman, Mountain View, California

A. I turned for an answer to Col Needham, founder and managing director of this most useful of all Web movie sites. He responds: "We do not knowingly accept comments by studio publicists, though it is, of course, possible for such people to register from their private e-mail addresses and pose as ordinary users. We do try to address the problem by only allowing comments to be posted once a film has actually been released. This means that if there are any planted submissions, they will be drowned out by genuine comments from real IMDb users. Additionally, new policies have recently been implemented to ensure that the comment selected for the main page is representative of the general opinion expressed on the film by the users of our site, be that positive or negative. People are welcome to let us know at help@imdb.com of cases where the selected comment is out of balance with the prevailing opinion and we'll review the title and select a different comment, if appropriate. We'll look into Glenn's list; we had already changed one of the comments he noted via the normal review process."

Q. Sometimes I'll take a look at the Internet Movie Database (imdb.com) to see how people are reacting to a recent release. To my disbelief, people have rated *Lord of the Rings* the *best* movie of all time on IMDb's Top 250 list! I thought it was a good action/fantasy adventure but I wouldn't have even included it in my personal Top 100 list. After speaking with many people, I realize that most of those who consider it the best film are also fans of the books. I noticed the same reaction for *Harry Potter:* If the book is great, the movie must be great. Is it possible that movies in the future will simply be visualizations of a book? Will books in the future simply be "test script runs"? Will people rate movies based on how close the visuals and characters look and act like people think they are supposed to? I'm scared.

—Bruce M. Arnold, University of Arizona, Tucson, Arizona

A. Take it from me: *Lord of the Rings* isn't the best movie of all time. What's reflected is extreme enthusiasm by a lot of fans, who gave it a "10" on the IMDb poll although many of them, individually, might not rate it the best of all films.

The Independent

Q. The new movie *The Independent* is a spoof documentary about Morty Fineman, an exploitation filmmaker played by Jerry Stiller. At the end, the credits list hundreds of his titles—too fast to read them all. Where can I get the whole list?

—Ronnie Barzell, Los Angeles, California

A. "Morty Fineman" has his own Website at www.finemanfilms.com/. Among his 427 films: *Puberty County Line, Thongmonster, Ms. Kevorkian, Don't Pick at It, Saturday Night Fever Blister,* and the *Grounded Stewardesses* series.

Indiana Jones

Q. A recent story claims that a fourth *Indiana Jones* movie is in jeopardy because of Harrison Ford's age. Why is everybody so determined to have Ford play the role? Sean Connery retired his license to kill years ago, but even after forty years, the James Bond series is still going strong. Why? Quality of scripts and productions notwithstanding, it's the *role* that keeps a series going, not the actor. You didn't go see *Harrison Ford and the Temple of Doom.* Let another actor take over the fedora of Dr. Jones. After all, counting the TV series, four actors have played the role already. My suggestion: George Clooney. He's got the right build, looks, charm, and sense of humor to handle the role brilliantly! Remember, *Batman and Robin* wasn't his fault.

—Christopher M. Terry, Atlanta, Georgia

A. One problem may be that Harrison Ford, at fifty-nine, is understandably reluctant to agree he is too old to play Indy again. Sean Connery retired from Bond in 1971 *(Diamonds Are Forever),* at the age of forty-one, simply because he was tired of playing the character. He then gave it one more try in 1983 *(Never Say Never Again),* at fifty-three. Could he still play Bond today? Sure—brought out of retirement for one more crucial case. And Ford could still play Indy. It might require a certain suspension of disbelief, but then suspending disbelief is a specialty of fans of both the Bond and Indiana Jones movies.

Note: By mid-2002, Ford, Steven Spielberg, and George Lucas had agreed to move ahead with a fourth Indy pic.

Insomnia

Q. How does the screenwriter for *Insomnia* get away with saying in interviews that Nightmute, Alaska, is a fictional town? In reality it is a rural Yup'ik Eskimo village on the coast of southwestern Alaska. It is surrounded by rolling hills and tundra and sits on the coast. All of us out here in the Yukon-Kuskokwim Delta have been pretty put off by the fact that they took this name (probably because it sounded cool). We are not the Kenai peninsula out here. There aren't huge mountains and tall trees. I nearly fell off the couch when I heard "Nightmute" and saw that in Hollywood this very proud village is apparently full of white people, bears, mountains, and every other Alaskan stereotype.

—Tiffany Longan, Bethel, Alaska

A. Screenwriter Hillary Seitz replies: "It certainly wasn't my intention to put off the entire town of Nightmute, Alaska. When I went up to Alaska to do research for *Insomnia,* I was so intrigued and bewitched by both the people and scenery of this amazing part of the world, I shudder at the thought of giving offense. First, you shouldn't believe everything you read. I have never said Nightmute is a 'fictional town.' I tell interviewers that I did most of my research in Homer and Seward, but felt that 'Nightmute' had such a splendid poetic and thematic ring to it that I couldn't resist shuffling the geography around. This wasn't a case of my closing my eyes and randomly pointing at a map of Alaska. Poetic license is often taken for the overall effect of the piece; in many ways it is a compliment, not a slight."

In the Bedroom

Q. The blatant product placements, especially for Marlboro cigarettes, in *In the Bedroom* were so conspicuous, they distracted from the

movie. What can we, as movie viewers, do to voice our objections?

—Annette Osterlund, Boulder, Colorado

A. A full-page ad in the *New York Times,* previously turned down by *Variety,* made the same point. But Todd Field, who wrote and directed the film, says it contained no paid product placements. "Sissy Spacek's character smokes in the [Andre Dubus] short story," he told me. "I asked myself, why did she smoke? Should she continue to smoke? I projected how my own parents might behave. My father smoked for many years. If one of his children were killed, that is the first thing he would go back to. When people are grieving, they pick up old bad habits. No one notices, but Matt [the Tom Wilkinson character] nurses a soda at the beginning, when other people are drinking. After the death, he starts drinking, and his wife starts smoking." The *New York Times* ad by the antismoking group recommended that movies with smoking in them be rated R. "That's cultural. McCarthyism," Field said. "Does that mean *Casablanca* and *Lawrence of Arabia* should be rated R? And Groucho Marx?"

Q. Although the thriller elements of *In the Bedroom* left me flat, I found the characters and their relationships to be real, subtle, and profound. I felt, however, that Natalie, the Marisa Tomei character, despite her overtly sympathetic nature, was presented in a critical light—even misogynistic. The early conversation where Dr. Fowler explains to Jason the danger when a female lobster invites two male lobsters into the bedroom introduces this theme. The movie later closes the loop with Dr. Fowler remembering a photo showing a joyous Natalie in the arms of the menacing Richard Strout. I argued to my wife that Natalie at best was to blame for being attracted to psychopaths and for putting Frank in the line of danger, and at worst got off on the drama. My wife feels that I am reading too much into the movie and that this opinion is misogynistic itself.

—Paul Brodsky, Wayne, New Jersey

A. I don't think she got turned on by inspiring drama, but I did wonder what she saw in that guy in the first place. Still, some marriages begin well, with domestic abuse developing later. William Mapother's performance as Strout was strong and effective, and he has missed out on the general praise of the film's performances, I suspect, because audiences hated his character so much.

The Iron Ladies

Q. Your review of the Thai film *The Iron Ladies*, about the gay and transvestite volleyball team, knocked me out of my chair, not only because I was surprised that you had seen it, but also because you hit the nail on the head regarding "Coach Bee" as played by Siridhana Hongsophon. While watching the rather clichéd film I was simply transfixed by Ms. Hongsophon. Her acting simply put is one of the most "real" performances I have ever encountered. Indeed, I hesitate to write "acting" because she was so good that it almost seems a crime to call her an actress (I'm not sure if that's an insult to Ms. Hongsophon or the entire acting profession). It was quite refreshing to know that I am not the only person to notice that this film has quite a hidden gem in it.

—William Woods, Alhambra, California

A. Hongsophon's performance should be used as a benchmark at the Actors' Studio. I wrote in my review: "Her performance is so utterly without spin, style, or affect that it could be lifted intact from a documentary. She is utterly convincing as a volleyball coach. It's as if a real coach is being filmed with a hidden camera. There is no attempt to 'perform,' no awareness of punch lines, no artificial drama. Just a flat, straight-ahead, no-nonsense coaching job. It is either one of the most convincing performances I have ever seen, or no performance at all."

Iron Monkey

Q. In your review of *Iron Monkey* you write how one fight mirrors a similar scene in the recent *The Musketeer*. Anyone who has seen Jet Li's *Once Upon a Time in China* recalls an almost identical scene where king-fu fighters balance on ladders. It turns out the fight choreographer was the same for both films,

Xin Xin Xiong. So what's worse? Hollywood pilfering proven techniques from Asian cinemas, or people who work in Asian cinemas merely rehashing what they have already done?

—Matt Singer, Syracuse, New York

A. Once a stage choreographer composes a work, he is happy to see it performed by many different companies. Is this, in a sense, any different?

Jason X

Q. Before a recent showing of *Blade II*, I saw a trailer for the upcoming *Jason X*. Is this film *Jason Ten* or *Jason X*, as in the letter "x"? *Jason 10* makes no sense when there was no previous film entitled *Jason*.

—Tim Banach, Penn Yan, New York

A. The complete title explains everything: *Jason X: Friday the 13th, Part 10*. Yes, it's 400 years in the future, Earth is uninhabitable, but human colonists from outer space return to explore Camp Crystal Lake, and find a cryogenically frozen body wearing a hockey mask...

Jay and Silent Bob Strike Back

Q. I just got back from watching the movie *Jay and Silent Bob Strike Back*, and one thing that stood as a pillar of offense and ignorance was Chris Rock. As you know, he plays the part of a thoroughly racist movie director who continually slams his capable, undeserving white staff with racist comments and spews off unending streams of ethnic slurs. Is it just me, or is this entirely not funny? I noticed this same racist riff with Chris Tucker in *Rush Hour 2*, as did you in your review. Why not comment on it in your *J&SB* review? And what's with the current trend for these black so-called comics to insult whites incessantly in movies? I felt offended, and I don't get offended easily. Being Persian-American, I get a lot of flack from bigots anyway.

—Michael Shareghi, Thousand Oaks, California

A. I mentioned Rock's riff in my discussion of Tucker in *Rush Hour 2*, and didn't feel like repeating it. I am not a censor and believe all speech is protected, but I also reserve the right to be offended, and inane "comic" racist monologues are losing their charm. The sad thing in both cases is that the victims were in fact Chris Tucker and Chris Rock, whose characters come off looking like the butt of their own jokes. There is nothing more fatal for a comedian than to appear to be out of touch and off-key, and these performances were embarrassments.

Joy Ride

Q. I convinced my wife to go to *Joy Ride,* and found it a most enjoyable companion to *Duel.* However, the voice of the trucker, an integral element to the film's success, was not listed in the credits. My wife thought it was actor Clancy Brown *(The Hurricane, Shawshank Redemption)* and I thought it was Ted Levine *(Silence of the Lambs),* who was actually a costar with *Joy Ride*'s Walker in *Fast and the Furious.* Are either of us correct?
—Ed Vaira, San Diego, California

A. You are half right. Ted Levine does the voice, and Matthew Kimbrough plays the (only barely glimpsed) physical Rusty Nail.

Kate & Leopold

Q. In your review of *Kate & Leopold* you mention that Leopold is Stuart's great-great grandfather, but I couldn't recall any mention of that in the movie. Then I heard a rumor that the movie was moved from its December 21 release date to December 25 to allow for last-minute editing to remove a suggestion of incest. I heard this was due to some reviews that were critical of this. Is this true? How you feel about studios making changes to satisfy reviewers?
—Justin Hamaker, Paradise, California

A. Richard Roeper pointed out that Kate's relationship with Stuart was incestuous, since she was apparently his great-great grandmother. Director James Mangold decided to edit out the relevant references. I doubt he did this to "satisfy reviewers," but to head off an unintended controversy.

K-PAX

Q. I am obsessing over this new film, *K-PAX.* Do you remember the 1986 film, *Man Facing Southeast*? It was an Argentinean film, but, as I recall, based on a short story by Philip

K. Dick. Apparently, *K-PAX* is based on a novel of the early 1990s, by Gene Brewer. How can this be? The stories seem identical.
—Kaylie Jones, Southampton College, Long Island University

A. Many similar messages have come to the Answer Man, and Meinert Hansen of Montreal writes, "The trailer for *K-PAX* even has scenes identical to *Man Facing Southeast.*"

This is from Peter Henne's interview with Iain Softley, the director of *K-PAX,* in *Film Journal International:* "Told that the basic plot of *K-PAX* repeats the Argentine film *Man Facing Southeast,* directed by Eliseo Subiela, and recalls that of Terry Gilliam's *The Fisher King,* Softley isn't fazed. The fact that Bridges plays a man filled with compassion for another who is ostensibly, but not certainly, delusional in both films makes the resemblance especially strong. 'I don't think there are enough films like *The Fisher King,*' Softley counters. 'If it's similar to that genre, it's kind of an indication how unique it is. How many cop films, for example, are like each other, or gangster films, or romantic comedies? It seems to be the same kind of story. I don't think there are enough films of what could be classed as a modern fable, such as this.'"

K-PAX is based on a novel by Gene Brewer, published in 1995. Subiela's screenplay for *Man Facing Southwest* lists no sources, but Eric M. Van of Harvard notes on the IMDb that it is "clearly influenced by Philip K. Dick's autobiographical last novels *VALIS* and *The Transmigration of Timothy Archer,* and Subiela makes this explicit by naming the lead female character 'Beatriz Dick.'"

Of course Philip K. Dick himself toyed with the theory that we are all living in about A.D. 40 and imagining everything else, which was why one of *his* short stories turned out to contain the names of people he met later, and to be a detailed parallel of the Book of Acts, which he had never read (this story is told in Richard Linklater's new film *Waking Life*).

Q. I just saw *K-PAX* and then reread your review. How can you say that what happens to Kevin Spacey's character Prot at the end is "not quite what it seems to be"? Also in your review you state that "perhaps Prot simply borrowed a human form." If he had borrowed a human form and was from K-PAX, why did he wind up in a catatonic state at the end? Why didn't he just go back to K-PAX, which is the ending I would have preferred? This was a movie where I felt "warm and fuzzy" for three-quarters of the way through it and then it took a turn for the worse.

—Carol Minkel, Chicago, Illinois

A. Spoiler ahead. On the evidence in the movie, we cannot say for sure whether Prot was an alien, or simply insane. Both theories fit. If an alien, perhaps he occupied the dying human body of Robert Porter, and when he returned home, taking Bess, the shell of Porter's body was left in a catatonic state. If insane, Porter became catatonic because of his treatments, and Bess, the missing patient, simply escaped the grounds. Karen Rainey of Richardson, Texas, writes the AM: "The opening sequence, in which Prot appears out of thin air, was a dead giveaway to us that Prot was from another planet (and absolutely ruined the film for us)." But again the movie gives us the choice of believing Prot appeared from thin air, or only seemed to. In a crowded train terminal, the eye can be fooled.

Q. Forget the theory that *K-PAX* was borrowed from the Argentinean film *Man Facing Southeast*. The idea of a psychiatrist examining a patient who claims to be an alien dates back even further. *Ghidrah, the Three-Headed Monster* (1964) stars Akiko Wakabayashi as the princess of Salgina. Upon hearing a mysterious voice, she gains prophetic powers and claims to be a Martian (Venusian in the Japanese version). She is taken to a psychiatrist played by the late, great Takashi Shimura, who comes to the conclusion that there is nothing wrong with her, but he refuses to accept the notion that she is an alien.

—Brett Homenick, Spring Valley, California

A. Takashi Shimura starred in *Ikiru, The Seven Samurai, Hidden Fortress,* and *Kwaidan,* four of the greatest films of all time. I have to go with his diagnosis.

Lagaan: Once Upon a Time in India

Q. This year is a special one for us Indians as *Lagaan: Once Upon a Time in India* has been nominated in the Best Foreign Film category of the Academy Awards. Indians all over the world are ecstatic as a result. Though Indians have loved the film, I wonder how American audiences and critics will react.

—Yousuf Hussain, Farmington Hills, Michigan

A. Bollywood—the Bombay Hollywood— is the world's largest producer of films, but has never cracked the U.S. market. *Lagaan,* a film about how a cricket match helps settle a potentially bloody dispute over land and taxes, has been a worldwide hit, and is setting box office records in its U.S. engagements in theaters aimed at Indian moviegoers. Now it's been picked up by Sony Classics for American distribution. How will it go over? At the recent Floating Film Festival, conducted by Toronto Film Festival cofounder Dusty Cohl, it was the first film to ever win first prize both from the audience members and the critics' panel.

The Last Castle

Q. After the big battle in *The Last Castle,* when Redford and the men were standing in formation, where were the dozens of dead and wounded that should have been strewn all over the grounds?

—Art Rothstein, San Francisco, California

A. It would be inconvenient and counterproductive to show them, since the Redford character is the hero, and yet is responsible for the deaths of more men than the film's villain.

Q. When explaining why in my film *The Last Castle* we see none of the dead strewn in the prison yard after the film's climactic battle sequence, you wrote in the Answer Man that it would diminish Robert Redford's heroism to see that he was responsible for far more deaths than Gandolfini's character. The truth is this: There are no corpses because nobody was killed. We spent much of the movie establishing that the guards use rubber bullets and not live ones (at the very end of the battle, one of the guards switches to live ammo). Some men may have been wounded, but unless they were hit with direct shots to the temple (very hard to do with moving targets) they all would have survived.

—Rod Lurie, director, Pasadena, California

A. I knew about the rubber bullets, but what about the various explosions, fires, etc.? I

785

think many viewers, like the reader who asked that question, felt that some of the guards were using live ammo. It just felt that way.

Q. You mentioned in your review of *The Last Castle* that there were no bodies lying around after the battle. The director, Rod Lurie, wrote you to say there were no bodies because only rubber bullets were fired by the guards. This shows a lack of understanding about rubber bullets. They don't do their job if they don't put people down; they're designed to be incapacitating. The "reality" of the situation, in my mind, would have been prisoners lying unconscious.

—Anthony J. Hernandez, Denver, Colorado

A. I think the *real* reason we saw no bodies is because it would have marred the heroism of the Redford character to show him surrounded by his fallen comrades.

Letterboxing

Q. I hear talk of "ratio" and "format" all the time when people discuss releases on DVD. I am totally confused. Can you explain what "original aspect ratio" and all the other terms mean?

—Pete Pfister, Chicago, Illinois

A. All movies prior to 1954 were shot in the ratio of 1 to 1.33 (or 3 to 4.) Since then, most have been in varying widescreen ratios. True movie lovers insist on seeing each movie in the ratio it was originally shot in. In the case of widescreen movies, that means they must be "letterboxed" with black at the top and bottom of a TV screen, to allow you to see the full width. When a video says a widescreen movie has been "formatted to fit your screen," that is a misleading way of saying the sides have been cropped off to leave a 1–1.33 (or TV-shaped) image. Many DVDs have both versions, one on each side. That lets you make the decision.

Q. It is nice to see the networks HBO and NBC present their flagship shows *The Sopranos* and *E.R.* in letterbox format, but why won't they present films in their original aspect ratio? It seems that 99 percent of the classic films shown on the Turner Classic Movies channel are presented in widescreen format and I suspect that audience response has been

good (or the "all movies in their Original Aspect Ratio" policy would have ceased long ago). Why won't other networks follow suit and allow viewers to see films the way they were meant to be seen? If it's good enough for their Number 1 shows, it is good enough for the films that they broadcast as well!

—Michael Riesenbeck, Cincinnati, Ohio

A. They just don't care, and they think you're too stupid to notice. I got a chilling insight recently into the thinking at HBO. The network is one of the sponsors of the Grant Park Film Festival, the popular summer series of free outdoor screenings here in Chicago. I went to introduce *An American in Paris* and found that although the movie was shot in the 1-to-1.33 ratio (as were all films before 1954), it was being projected in a widescreen radio that had the effect of masking 20 percent of the image, and cutting off Gene Kelly's dancing feet. This was not merely a mistake—it was HBO policy! An HBO exec in New York, I was told, ordered the films to be shown in widescreen, "so people won't think we're showing television." This is one more pathetic example of the dumbing of America—to show the films in the wrong aspect ratio to placate the stupid, instead of in the right aspect ratio to reward the knowledgeable. I am happy to say that my complaints bore fruit, and the series will now show all films in their proper ratio. Wish I could say the same for HBO itself.

Q. Even though I'm not a big fan of the movie *The Mummy Returns*, I was appalled to find out that I could not rent a widescreen copy of that movie at either of my local rental chain stores. I can understand if some people would rather watch a third less of a movie's original picture just to fill their TV screen. What I can't understand is that these chains chose at a corporate level (or so I was told by the store managers when I complained) not to provide copies of *both* versions so those of us who want to watch the widescreen version have the choice to do so!

—Karl Englebright, Vancouver, Washington

A. I was actually told by a video chain spokesman that widescreen ("letterboxed") versions were not stocked in some stores because some customers complained, and the clerks did not have sufficient knowledge to explain the logic of letterboxing. My opinion is that (a) anyone who actually works in a video store and does not understand letterboxing has given up on life, and (b) any customer who prefers to have the sides of a movie hacked off should not be licensed to operate a video player.

Q. Regarding the new "special edition" of *Willy Wonka and the Chocolate Factory*—Warner Brothers has decided to sell *only* a pan-and-scan version of this film on DVD! I gave my original *Willy Wonka* DVD away to a relative and now I will be left with no *Willy Wonka* DVD as I won't come near one of these horrid new releases. I guess I'll have to find someone selling a copy of the old one.
—Frank Slove, Buffalo Grove, Illinois

A. *Willy Wonka* was originally released as a widescreen movie. The new Warner Brothers release has been "modified to fit your screen"—a sneaky way of saying, "we have chopped off the sides of the picture so what is left will be the same shape as a TV." Many movie lovers insist on seeing movies in their original aspect ratio (OAR, which in this case would mean letterboxing). Warners is experiencing a firestorm of criticism for their sliced-and-diced version, and a Warner Home Video spokesperson tells me: "It is in a full-frame format as research indicates that families prefer a full-frame presentation. We do recognize that there is an interest in a widescreen DVD edition and we are evaluating offering that version in the near future." What this overlooks is that many *Willy Wonka* fans are not children but adult DVD users who look with horror on the "full-frame format." ("Full-frame" is Orwellian double-speak for "lacking one third of the original frame.")

Q. Regarding widescreen DVDs: I work for Blockbuster and the company did indeed make the decision to stock only pan-and-scan DVDs for rent. Apparently, they would rather cater to the public's ignorance than try to educate them to the benefits of letterboxing. I have tried on numerous occasions to explain widescreen to customers, with some success. The visual example on the *Die Hard* DVD

changes a lot of minds. Some DVDs have both pan-and-scan and widescreen versions available and I have changed customers' minds by telling them to watch five minutes of one version and then five minutes of another. All it takes is a little effort to educate the customer.
—Toby Schmidt, Dayton, New Jersey

A. True, but Blockbuster has made a corporate decision that casts a pall over the emerging DVD market. The majority of DVD users want letterboxing, which is why most DVDs have been widescreen or offered both formats. Now Blockbuster has asked manufacturers to supply DVDs in the pan-and-scan format and does not carry letterboxed DVDs in many of its stores. This takes me back to a day years ago when I had one of the founders of Blockbuster in my home and was proudly showing off a letterboxed laser disc. To my disbelief, he did not understand the format and I had to explain it to him. He was a retailer, not a movie lover. The company follows in the same tradition.

The Lord of the Rings

Q. I saw *Lord of the Rings* this holiday season with my family and enjoyed it so much, I saw it again a few days later in Seattle with some friends. However, during the second showing, I noticed that subtitles appeared when the characters were speaking elfish. The first time I saw it, there were no subtitles and I remembered wondering what the heck they were saying. Do you know why there's a discrepancy?
—Steve Lazo, Redondo Beach, California

A. A New Line rep replies: "All prints of the movie are the same and there were subtitles on all prints." Assuming you were not hallucinating, the only explanation is that the film at the earlier screening was so badly framed that the subtitles were cut off.

The Man Who Wasn't There

Q. Yes, *The Man Who Wasn't There* is in beautiful black and white. But I hear it was shot in color, as USA Films wouldn't finance it any other way. They were afraid foreign markets wouldn't take it in black and white.
—Jeff Joseph, Los Angeles, California

A. It amazes me that there are people who

consider themselves moviegoers and do not appreciate the beauty of black and white.

Q. Regarding the discussion about how the Coen brothers filmed *The Man Who Wasn't There* in color and then converted it to black and white: On a recent *Charlie Rose* show, they said they chose to use color stock because few people film on b&w stock anymore, and film companies haven't made any significant advances with b&w film since the 1950's.

—Jeff Lanctot, Seattle, Washington

A. Here's elaboration from cinematographer Steven Poster: "The few b&w movies that get made today are almost always shot on color film stock. Sadly, there are few film laboratories that process b&w anymore. Another reason is that b&w film stocks have not been improved for over thirty years while color film stocks have been continuously improved. This allows for more versatile shooting if you use color films. Great improvements in sensitivity (film speed), texture (granularity), and dynamic range (number of steps of gray between the deepest shadow and the highest highlight) have been made. By shooting on color film and printing on several choices of b&w printing film stock, the cinematographer has more effective ways of creating different styles for b&w movies. Even European movies are done this way now. For example, Patrice Leconte's exquisite *The Girl on the Bridge* was filmed this way."

Q. I went to see *The Man Who Wasn't There*. Having seen the trailer and read some reviews, I assumed that the film was being shown entirely in black and white, although it had been filmed in color. To my surprise, the first reel of the film ran in color before abruptly switching to b&w at the beginning of the second reel. Are the Coens going for some sort of Wizard of Oz/Pleasantville effect, or is this a mistake?

—Matthew Long, Prince George, British Columbia

A. A mistake so big that if it had been a postage stamp instead of a movie, collectors would be fighting for it.

Q. A reader from British Columbia wrote to you saying that the first reel of *The Man Who Wasn't There* was in color when he saw it and you answered: "A mistake so big that if it had been a postage stamp instead of a movie, collectors would be fighting for it." Looks like it's not so rare. When I saw it in Toronto, the first two reels were in color. I thought it was by design and wondered why no reviews mentioned that.

—Serguei Oukladov, Toronto, Ontario

A. Parts of Canada apparently saw an unchecked print. Alun Evans of Seattle writes that the opening reel was in color in Vancouver when he saw it. Richard Carpenter of Toronto also reports on the black and white that wasn't there. USA films, which released the film in the United States, declined to offer an official statement, but I learned off the record that a glitch occurred at the developing labs. Audiences in the United States did not see the defective reel because it was caught before being shown to the public. Unfortunately, in Canada the glitch wasn't caught. The film was released in Canada by Odeon Films, a division of Alliance Atlantis.

Q. The wife in the Coen brothers' *The Man Who Wasn't There* works for a department store named Nirdlinger's. That is the surname of the man who is murdered in James M. Cain's novel *Double Indemnity*.

—John R. Simon, City of Salt Lake, Utah

A. Quite so. But in Billy Wilder's movie *Double Indemnity,* the name of the victim is changed to Diedrichson—and there is a character in the Coen brothers' movie named Diedrickson, which is so close I intuit a spelling error. Also, Freddy Riedenschneider, the movie's lawyer, may be related to Doc Riedenschneider, from *The Asphalt Jungle*. There is, however, nobody in the movie named Tenenbaum.

Memento
Q. With the new DVD release of *Memento*, which I feel is one of the all-time great movies, I was wondering if you can tell me in what sequence I would program my DVD player (using the Scene Selection option) to play the movie in a "normal" playing arc? Yes, I know it will lessen the effect of the movie,

but my best friend hates this movie in the director's current format, and I really want to help her understand and appreciate it.

—Bruce Lewis, Columbus, Ohio

A. The movie of course is told backward—the first scene is at the end, and the last scene is at the beginning. So you could use the chapter stops to show her the scenes in reverse order. My guess is that this would leave her exactly as confused as before. Whatever you do, don't let her see *Mulholland Dr.* Her ears might start to pop.

Q. An Answer Man reader wanted to know how to program his DVD to watch the scenes in *Memento* in chronological order. There is actually a hidden feature on the DVD that does this for you. On the main menu page the word "reversed" is marked out on one corner of the photograph. Click on this and it will take you to another menu that presents the scenes in chronological order. The movie is still compelling but I found myself more questioning of the logic afterward.

—Bruce Lewis, Columbus, Ohio

A. What is often overlooked is that while the color scenes are in reverse chronological order, the b&w scenes are in chronological order.

Minority Report

Q. In *Minority Report* there is a scene where Tom Cruise is on a train and a stranger, who is reading the newspaper, looks up at him in suspicion. This man seemed to resemble Cruise's directorial buddy Cameron Crowe, who on his last project, *Vanilla Sky,* had Spielberg make a cameo.

—Ryan Kirkby, Waterloo, Ontario

A. Cameron Crowe replies: "Okay, I admit it. It's me. Steven Spielberg came to the *Vanilla Sky* set one day to visit Tom Cruise, and I urged him to walk into the birthday sequence we were filming. He was a big hit, improvised dialogue, stayed a couple hours, and left threatening to put me into *Minority Report.* Months later, his costumer came to our office with an armful of bizarre, ill-fitting clothes, and told me I'd been cast as a futuristic bum. Mercifully, Spielberg later recast me as a businessman on the subway holding an interactive

USA Today. Excitedly chomping on an unlit cigar, he explained the *USA Today* would be alive with moving images, a newspaper from the future. He's a truly joyful director. Cameron Diaz, who was also visiting his set that day, plays a businesswoman talking on a cell phone right behind me. Diaz and Cruise gave me acting tips, which I promptly forgot. It's a great movie, one of Spielberg's very best. Not even my poor acting could hold him back."

Q. As a prosecutor, I loved the opening sequence of *Minority Report,* where Tom Cruise's precrime unit was able to apprehend the murder suspect moments before the foul deed was done. However, it should be noted that in nearly all U.S. jurisdictions, it is not considered "murder" when a spouse commits a homicide after discovering their partner in the act of adultery, or in flagrante delicto, as most courts put it. Of course, I think Spielberg did an excellent job of exploring a justice system where the courts were completely bypassed, foreclosing the raising of any defenses at trial. I think he should get this year's George Orwell Award for dark predictions that seem to have already come true. In *Minority Report,* murder suspects are given a direct ticket from the paddy wagon to the penitentiary—can anyone say Guantánamo Bay?

—Josh Smith, Augusta, Georgia

A. Seems to me the precrime department would want to stop a killing even if legally it isn't murder.

Q. In your review of Spielberg's *Minority Report* you noted the shot of Tom Cruise and Samantha Morgan looking over each others' shoulders in a moment of tension during a chase sequence. The composition of the shot appears to be a nod to the dual-faced Roman god Janus, whose power lay in the ability to foresee the future and recall the past simultaneously. A perfect flourish for a story throbbing with the pressures presented by "time."

—Christian Greco, Wellesley, Massachusetts

A. If the mask fits, wear it.

Miyazaki's Anime

Q. Why is it that Disney has been sitting on a completed version of Miyazaki's *Castle in the*

Sky for two years without releasing it? This movie could do at least as well on video/DVD as *Kiki's Delivery Service*, and yet it has languished on the shelf. Is Disney still so angry over *Princess Mononoke* that they are refusing to even attempt to realize gains on a project that is already paid for?

—Archer Sully, Boulder, Colorado

A. You are referring to Disney's purchase of the complete works of Studio Ghibli, the geniuses of Japanese anime, and its great director Hayao Miyazaki. His new *Spirited Away* is the biggest box-office hit in Japanese history. For a reply, I asked Drew McWeeny, an anime expert who writes as "Moriarity" for *Ain't It Cool News.* He responds:

"Disney's not angry over *Princess Mononoke*. Far from it. Their overall deal with Studio Ghibli has been all about bending over backward to please Miyazaki, following his wishes to the letter. Point in case: the release of the Ghibli titles on DVD in the United States has been held back in order to allow Japanese region-encoded discs to be released first, with enough lead time to prevent reverse exporting. In other words, Ghibli wants to be able to make some money in Japan without Disney's releases screwing it up. And Disney has taken the black eye in public perception and done exactly as Ghibli asked.

"Rest assured that when Disney finally does release the titles, they'll be done right. The dub track for *Laputa: Castle in the Sky* is exceptional, and with John Lasseter supervising, I'm sure *Spirited Away* will be, as well. Despite that, all of the Disney DVDs will be released with the original Japanese audio tracks (with English subtitles available as well as whatever English audio dub has been produced). Ghibli will actually be handling the authoring of all of the DVDs, so they'll be comparable to the Japanese releases both in content and quality."

Monster's Ball

Q. Angela Bassett was quoted in *Newsweek* as saying she turned down Halle Berry's role in *Monster's Ball* because she "wasn't going to be a prostitute on film" and "I couldn't do that because it's such a stereotype about black women and sexuality." I saw *Monster's Ball*

twice and felt that in no way were the sex scenes exploitative or pornographic.

—Matt Moreira, Brooklyn, New York

A. I agree. It is a great performance. An article in the July 1 *Los Angeles Times* covers the controversy, quoting some blacks who feel the role was demeaning, others who support Halle Berry. What we have here is an inability to see the role apart from the color of the character. Berry was playing a specific woman in a specific dramatic situation, and to expect that role and that woman to "speak" for black women in general is limiting. African-American actors deserve the freedom to play a wide range of roles, without being restricted to "positive" portrayals. The article notes that Denzel Washington, who won an Oscar for a character who was, frankly, vicious and evil, has been spared the criticism directed at Berry, whose character was not evil but simply desperate and grieving. If this sort of backlash gains ground, it could have a negative effect, making other African-American actresses hesitant to accept challenging, controversial roles.

Movie Ratings

Q. This puzzles me. A lot. How on earth can *Amélie* get an R rating? How can any sane human being think that this wonderful and uplifting movie can harm people under seventeen in any way? Actually, I think that if every living creature saw *Amélie*, there would be peace on earth. Can anyone at the MPAA give an explanation to this that makes sense to anyone? I live in Norway, where the movie received an 11-rating.

—Birger Vestmo, Trondheim, Norway ST

A. *Amelie,* the most popular film at this year's Cannes and Toronto Festivals, opens November 2. The ratings board has for some time cut loose from the commonsense values of the vast majority of Americans, and is making weird judgments apparently designed to placate Hollywood's critics from the extreme fringe. While penalizing thoughtful and mature movies with R ratings, they cheerfully give the green light of PG-13 to intentionally vulgar teenage films based on the nonsexual exchange of bodily wastes. In the case of *Amelie,* the MPAA objected to the chldbirth scene at the beginning, and the montage in which all of Paris seems to have an orgasm.

Q. What do you make of Blockbuster putting "Terrorist Themed" warning labels on certain films? This is obviously a very sensitive subject since September 11, but I feel this is just another ploy by Blockbuster to make themselves America's conscience, like they do with the edited-only versions of films they carry.

—Josh Korkowski, Minneapolis, Minnesota

A. Call me a cynic, but I believe those labels will only increase rentals of the titles they are applied to.

Q. I remember when *South Park: Bigger, Longer and Uncut* came out. I seem to remember that the earlier title of this film was *South Park: All Hell Breaks Loose*. This title was rejected by the MPAA on the basis of the word "Hell" in the title. I was wondering if this was true why they decided to allow the word "Hell" in the title of *From Hell*, the new movie with Johnny Depp? This would seem to be very contradictory.

—Russell Benz, Fargo, North Dakota

A. Richard Taylor, spokesman for the MPAA, says: "According to the Classification and Ratings Administration in Los Angeles, the word 'hell' was never part of the title of that film (at least never in any form when the ratings board was reviewing the film). Therefore, the simple answer to Mr. Benz's question is that the MPAA never rejected the use of the word 'hell' in the title of the film."

This statement is technically true in that it refers to the version submitted to the board. But the MPAA often makes *suggestions* before films are submitted. According to the Internet Movie Database, "In a clandestine rebellion against MPAA, who forced them to alter some of the film's content and its original title, Trey Parker and Matt Stone slipped the new title, *Bigger, Longer and Uncut* (adjectives that can describe a penis) as well as the film past the ratings board." And the Website The Censors quotes Parker: "Originally, our movie was called *South Park: All Hell Breaks Loose*. The MPAA said, You can't say 'hell' in the title." The site continues: "He and Stone's counter-

proposal for the title was an obvious penis joke, Parker said, but the MPAA approved it. 'They just didn't get it.'" This is also the story Parker and Stone told Jay Leno on the *Tonight Show*.

Q. I recently rented the film *Bully* by Larry Clark, and was played for a fool. On the box it was given an R rating, even though I knew it had been rated NC-17. Yet there was no disclaimer on the box stating that it had been altered from the original. I went home to watch it and sure enough, before the movie began there was a title screen explaining that the version I had rented was not the version the director intended to be seen! I was unable to return the film for a refund—nor would anyone else who made the same mistake! How could they market this film without a written disclaimer stating it had been altered, and why can't they carry the original "Director's Cut" as well?

—Kevin Young, Whitman, Massachusetts

A. You did not name the video store. If it was Blockbuster, the chain refuses to handle NC-17 movies, insisting that R-rated versions be supplied. Blockbuster thus dictates both format and content. Imagine the outcry if a bookstore stocked only the *Reader's Digest* condensed book versions of a novel, and quietly removed all the offensive parts.

Q. What is the difference between language and strong language?

—Alex Davidoff, Mohegan Lake, New York

A. You are referring to the descriptions the MPAA includes in its explanations of movie ratings.

Phuong Yokitis from the MPAA replies: "I want to note first that there is no list used by the Rating Board that would quantify when a movie receives a description of 'language' or 'strong language.' I can only say that if the language is at the upper end of the rating boundary, especially if the language is very plentiful, the Board would use 'strong.' As an example, in a PG-13 film, if the film contains a single use of one of the harsher sexually derived words, though only as an expletive, then the film might be given the description of 'brief strong language.'"

Q. Critics rarely discuss films among themselves afterward. However, *Mr. Deeds* had everyone jawing about the surprising amount of violence in the film, which is not only gratuitous but wholly inappropriate, considering what the film is about. And yet the MPAA's explanation for the PG-13 rating cites only "language, including sexual references, and some rear nudity." (Rear nudity! Nothing about Adam Sandler clobbering Allen Covert or Winona Ryder hitting a kid's head against a wooden banister or her brutal fight with Conchata Ferrell.) Go figure.

—Joe Baltake, film critic, *Sacramento Bee*

A. The reasoning of the MPAA should be turned over to the team that cracked Enigma.

Q. It is possible to search the MPAA database at mpaa.org for ratings of films, and the reason they were rated that way. A shocking experiment with their search engine, which may bolster your argument that the MPAA is completely insane, is to search for *Germinal*. The film is an adequate adaptation of the novel by Emile Zola starring Gérard Depardieu. It is remarkably free of cursing and nudity (unless you count a coal-smeared Gérard in the bathtub), and only contains minor violence by *Domestic Disturbance* standards. Stunned by its R rating, I wanted to know what it was the MPAA was trying to protect me from.

—Mark Hoofnagle, Charlottesville, Virginia

A. I looked it up. The MPAA informs us: *Rated R for intense depiction of suffering and class conflict.* I share your astonishment.

Q. I saw *Ghost World* based on your review. I, too, thought it brilliant. It is a must-see for every angst-ridden teen in American society today. But the MPAA has rated it unseeable (R for them), because of language that 99 percent of teens use or hear every day! My question: When will the MPAA film review idiots put gratuitous violence (generally rated PG-13) more in the scope of R-rated films? Some sex and four-letter words should not always give a film the taboo mark! Is there anything we can do to enlighten those dummies as to what teens should and shouldn't see?? Arrrgh.

—Eileen Kay, Boulder, Colorado

A. The MPAA system has lost touch with common sense, and arcane reasoning lies behind its ratings. For sane, sensible ratings information for parents, I recommend Screenit.com.

Mr. Deeds

Q. You cluelessly missed your own point by devoting a whole paragraph in your *Mr. Deeds* review to the Special K cereal cameo. Didn't you give Special K an *extra* product placement just by mentioning it in your review?

—Patrick Keys, Houston, Texas

A. Yes, but it's a funny thing. I think I missed the point. In a burning building, when the only thing on fire in the kitchen is a box of Special K, maybe the shot was intended as a satire of product placement.

Mulholland Dr.

Q. My wife and I watched *Mulholland Dr.* and returned home to read your four-star review. After discussing the movie for hours we determined the following:

1. It is a two-part movie, the first part being a dream that occurs after the attempted murder of "Camille"—the Betty character is entirely imagined and is a sort of alternate Diane character. The second part is a "cut-up" of Camille's life before she married the director Adam.

2. The most important (as well as metaphorical) part exists in the "Silencio" theater. Certainly it is open to many different interpretations.

3. The movie is, above all, a critique of the Hollywood system in which stars are created and used by the studios.

If it is nothing more than a confusing, nonsensical dream—as you seemed to think it was—then how could it merit four stars? I would like to see a deeper interpretation by you in a future column.

—Maxwell Heathcott, Chicago, Illinois

A. *Mulholland Dr.* goes on the list with *Fight Club, Memento,* and *The Usual Suspects* among recent movies that inspire detailed explanations. Yours does not contradict the facts, but can it be proven by them? I have received several other long explanations, also convincing, that differ. I believe my dream theory does not bring anything to the movie but uses only what can be found there (life is not like this movie, but dreams are). I did not find the dream "confused and nonsensical," but lucid, and with the clarity of a nightmare. I agree with your third point.

Q. Just saw *Mulholland Dr.* Aunt Ruth's apartment building looks familiar. Could it be the same one featured in *In a Lonely Place*, another terrific Hollywood *film noir?*

—Tim McDonald, Chicago, Illinois

A. A Universal Focus studio rep says David Lynch does not know whether the apartment used in *Mulholland Dr.* is the same one as in *In a Lonely Place*. If it is indeed the same place, Lynch was not aware of that and did not make the choice because of the earlier film.

Q. I just watched *Mulholland Dr.* last night on video and noticed something strange. During the scene where Rita (Laura Harring) takes off her robe, her crotch area is blurred. This is only for a second. Then as she approaches the bed, you can see a blurred rectangle in that area. No, I did not rent this from Blockbuster. What's the deal here? We are after all watching a Lynch film, I think we could be spared the "cover-up."

—John Reidy, Denver, Colorado

A. I just finished a weeklong shot-by-shot dissection of *Mulholland Dr.* at the University of Colorado at Boulder, where we did indeed notice the blurred areas. David Lynch made this statement: "We did that blurring for the DVD on purpose, as we know that pictures of Laura would be everywhere if we didn't." In other words, he feared fans would make still captures from the DVD and post them on-line. *Mulholland Dr.* thus joins *Eyes Wide Shut* and *Storytelling* among films where areas have been blocked out, either voluntarily or under MPAA pressure. If Lynch made this decision himself, I am less concerned than if it was forced upon him. But since the scene is intended as a detailed erotic fantasy (presumably in the mind of the dreaming Diane Selwyn), his decision may have undermined his purpose.

Q. In the newly released DVD of *Mulholland Dr.*, David Lynch gives ten clues to unwrapping the mystery of the movie. What do you make of the clues?

—Matt Warshauer, Evanston, Illinois

A. They are like those double acrostic clues that make perfect sense once you have solved the puzzle.

Q. Why was there no scene index on the *Mulholland Dr.* DVD?

—Kevin Montgomery, Otisco, Indiana

A. Director David Lynch believes that films are intended to be seen from beginning to end, and deliberately didn't provide chapter stops for *Mulholland Dr.* or *The Straight Story* because he didn't want you jumping around. There is also no director's commentary track on the *Mulholland Dr.* DVD, because he wants the film to speak for itself (and is famous for not supplying explanations). The helpful "berserker37" of West Chicago (a.k.a. Alan Pehl) has, however, provided do-it-yourself chapter stops, using the movie's time code, and you can find them at dvdtalk.com/forum.

Q. In *Mulholland Dr.*, the license plate on the limo is the same as the license plate on Steve Martin's Thunderbird in *LA Story*. Do you believe this to be a mere tribute to Martin?

—David Allen, Los Angeles, California

A. If you start looking for them, you'll see those California 2GATI23 plates in a lot of movies. They're the equivalent of the nonexistent "555" prefix on movie telephone numbers.

The New Guy

Q. I was watching *The New Guy* this weekend (D. J. Qualls is charming, what can I say), and during the Braveheart parody scene, I noticed an incredibly visible camera. There is a side shot of the students running toward the stadium, and at the far right side there is a camera and a cameraman. How can a major release movie have such an error? C'mon, I didn't expect a lot from a silly teen comedy, but this is just plain lazy.

—Dan MacRae, Regina, Saskatchewan

A. Something about the general tone of *The*

New Guy leads me to believe it was not made with fierce attention to detail.

Nine Queens

Q. In response to your mention of the con in *Nine Queens*, the way you "play" the twenties is you buy something that is, like, twenty-three cents. Give the clerk a $20 bill, absentmindedly take the change from the twenty while you are hunting for change, telling the clerk, "I know I have exact change." When you finally give the clerk the change, he will give you the twenty back and you hope forgot about the nineteen-plus dollars that he has already given you.
—Matthew Cleary, Miami, Florida

A. I can't wait to try this.

Ocean's Eleven

Q. During the end credits of *Ocean's Eleven* I noticed that it said "Introducing Julia Roberts." I thought that the word "introducing" is used when an actor stars in his or hers first film. Why is it used here?
—Sean O'Connell, Novato, California

A. Kinduva joke.

Q. You said Don Cheadle's name was omitted from the credits of *Ocean's Eleven* as a kind of "reverse-prestige thing." For what it's worth, Tom King of the *Wall Street Journal* has reported that after contentious salary and credit negotiations with the film's producers, a disgusted Mr. Cheadle voluntarily withdrew his name altogether from consideration for inclusion in the credits.
—Ben Bass, Chicago, Illinois

A. Thanks for setting the record straight.

The One

Q. How many universes are there in Jet Li's *The One*? And how many versions of his character are there? Your review suggests there are 124. But in the movie we are told he has killed Number 123 and is going after Number 124, which would make him Number 125.
—Susan Lake, Urbana, Illinois

A. Ah, but does the movie say he has *killed* 123 Jet Lis, or is *killing* Jet Li Number 123? Makes a big difference. The first way it's a run-

ning total, the second way it's a tracking number, and the bad Jet Li could be Number 1—or any other number. Critics are not in agreement. Mike Clark of *USA Today* agrees with me there are 124. Stephen Holden of the *New York Times* observes the villain has killed 123 and is going after the "remaining doppelganger"—thus, 125. Kirk Honeycutt of the *Hollywood Reporter* suggests 125, but a paragraph later writes of "one survivor out of the 123." A Columbia Pictures rep tells me: "As you watch the movie, the display behind Jet displays 123 total victims. The prisoner killed was the 123rd victim. Thus Yulaw and Gabe make up the 124th and 125th beings in the mutiverse, respectively, which consists of 125 parallel universes." The studio helpfully adds: "There may be other life waves in other alternate universes that exist."

On the Line

Q. Reading your review of the woeful *On the Line* reminded me of one of the film's many flaws: When Kevin and Abbey recite the presidents, I recited along with them, primarily to keep myself awake. Both of them conveniently left out Grover Cleveland's second term of office. It's one thing for two strangers to rattle off all the presidents, but for both of them to miss the same one . . . wow, that really is fate!
—Colin Boyd, Phoenix, Arizona

A. And not even a mention that he was one of baseball's winningest pitchers.

Oscars

Q. Jodie Foster recently said, "Winning the Oscar is no measure of performance. It's just bingo. You get five names that are thrown in a hat. One name is going to get pulled out and somebody goes, 'bingo!' You just wish it was your name." Three cheers for Jodie! Her comparison of an Academy Award to Bingo may not have been a wise career move, but at least she's telling the truth. In the Best Director category alone, I doubt anyone can list four American directors who have received Oscars who are better than these four who have not: Kubrick, Scorsese, Hitchcock, and Altman.
—William Swenson, Minneapolis, Minnesota

A. I agree. But because famous people are

involved and four out of five of them will lose, there is a certain fascination in the Oscars—especially when we feel strongly that one of the finalists should win. When Halle Berry won, somehow for me it was a lot more than Bingo.

The Others

Q. My wife and I saw *The Others* last night and we were surprised that a large number of people began laughing at the scary parts. I, meanwhile, was diligently suspending my disbelief. However, when we got to the scene where the little girl is wearing her communion dress and shows an aged face, I began to see what they were finding funny. Afterward, I asked several audience members why they laughed. They said that "nothing was happening." The latter sentiment echoes your comment, "As our suspense was supposed to be building, our impatience was outstripping it."
—Mike Geis, Grove City, Ohio

A. Horror movies require an existential age. We live in an age of irony. Therefore, we laugh at what we should dread. Movies like *The Others* are a challenge for audiences raised on special-effects freak shows; far from suspending their disbelief, they believe everything, and in *The Others* were brought to a dead halt because the movie did not tell them what to believe. And: If the movie seemed slow to us, think how slow it must have seemed to Freddy fans.

Panic Room

Q. In *Panic Room*, viewers are treated to another of those Hollywood creative moments: Jodie Foster on the toilet peeing. The camera pans tactfully away, leaving us with just the tinkle. My question: Did they use a bladder double?
—Neil Ferguson, Tempe, Arizona

A. Not Foster, not a double. You were probably hearing the work, in more than one sense, of a sound-effects editor.

Q. In your AM column responding to Neil Ferguson's question regarding the use of a "bladder double" in *Panic Room*, you stated: "You were probably hearing the work, in more than one sense, of a sound-effects editor."

Wouldn't that actually be the work of a Foley artist?
—Doug Dalrymple, Hanover, Pennsylvania

A. Quite right. Katz's *Film Encyclopedia* defines a Foley artist as "a member of the sound crew who, during the film's post-production creates certain sound effects heard on the effects track, particularly those made by people rather than machines or natural objects."

Foley artists get their name from Jack Foley (1891–1967), who began in silent pictures and at Universal in the early days of sound pioneered many of the same techniques used today to add sound effects to movies. It is doubtful, however, given the nature of movies in those days, that he ever created a tinkle.

Q. As I was watching the credits at the end of *Panic Room*, I noticed that three people were listed as "puppeteers." I can't for the life of me imagine a single scene in which puppeteers could possibly have been used in this movie.
—Phil Brown, San Francisco, California

A. Director David Fincher says they were used in creating the illusion of the broken collarbone on the husband (Patrick Bauchau) of the Jodie Foster character.

Q. You had an item about how the sound effect of peeing in *Panic Room* was created by a "Foley artist," a person who dubs in sound effects. I am fascinated by a sheer coincidence. I am a medical doctor and for your information, a Foley catheter is a soft plastic or rubber tube that is inserted into the bladder to drain the urine.
—Sean Chin, Malaysia

A. Another amazing coincidence: Frederic Eugene Basil Foley, who invented the catheter, and Jack Foley, who gave his name to Foley artists, were both born in 1891. I don't think I could handle it if they were twins.

Pauline Kael

Q. I can't help but wonder, upon the death of Pauline Kael, whether a movie critic can change the course of filmmaking, even a little. Kael would probably say no.
—Deborah Byron, Fresno, California

A. Some movie critics did change film history, but by making films, not writing about them. I'm thinking of the French New Wave and onetime critics like Godard and Truffaut. What they started in France in 1959 had a profound effect in America through the 1970s, until the studios cracked down. But can a critic change the course of filmmaking just by writing? No. What a critic can do, however, is change the course of filmgoing in individual cases, by nudging you away from the trash and encouraging you to honor your better instincts. Kael once said that criticism is the only news about movies; everything else is advertising.

Q. How did the Academy overlook Pauline Kael in their In Memorium tribute? True, she wasn't a producer, actor, director, or screenwriter, but is Hollywood's relationship with critics so poor that they cannot take a few seconds to remember a woman who made such a large contribution to both film and film reviewing?

—Ken Elliott, Ottawa, Ontario

A. Bruce Davis, executive director of the Academy, replies: "We didn't 'overlook' Pauline Kael. As much as we love (most) critics, we've always restricted the In Memoriam segments to filmmakers, and usually to Academy members. Even with that limitation, we always have to leave out an agonizing number of people each year who have made memorable contributions to the art form. This year's roster of painful omissions includes acting nominees Dorothy McGuire and Peggy Lee, the remarkable character actress Kathleen Freeman, and other master moviemakers such as animator Faith Hubley, cinematographer Piotr Sobocinski, makeup specialist John Chambers, and production designer Gary Wissner."

On the Oscarcast soon after Gene Siskel died, he was remembered by Whoopi Goldberg, but that was a decision by Goldberg and writer Bruce Vilanch, not the Academy. It is worth noting, sadly, that the AFI Awards in January included, in its almanac of the year's events in films, the scandal involving fake movie critic David Manning, but made no mention of Kael's death.

Planet of the Apes

Q. After sitting through *Planet of the Apes* I was compelled to go to several on-line forums that were discussing the ending. Many argued that the ending was great due to its "shock value" and "ambiguity." All will be revealed in the sequel, they say. I felt cheated by the ending. The twist at the end of a movie has to make sense in the context of the movie itself, not as a weak marketing ploy to attract potential customers for a sequel. I didn't appreciate watching a two-hour commercial for *Planet of the Apes 2.*

—Brian Thomsen, Schaumburg, Illinois

A. Spoiler warning! I liked the ending because it was such an ironic twist, and to the degree I tried to explain it to myself, I assumed that Leo Davidson, the Mark Wahlberg character, had been flipped into another space-time continuum by the electromagnetic storm. Then I found a convincing explanation by Josh Daniel, on Slate.com. He writes: "Before Davidson leaves the ape planet, there's a quick shot of Limbo, the orangutan slave trader, rummaging through his spaceship and slyly pocketing something. Evidently whatever he pockets contains the secret to space travel. (Maybe it's a manual: *Space Travel So Easy, a Chimp Could Do It.*) Thade, who's pointedly left alive at the end of the climactic battle, must have built a ship, flown into the time-warping electromagnetic storm, and landed on Earth at some point before Davidson returned. Then he led Earth's apes in a rebellion against humans, took over Earth, and had the monument built for him. Of course, back on their home planet, the apes don't even have simple motors yet. So, whatever Limbo takes from the spaceship allows them to, in Thade's lifetime, master physics, build computers, design space suits, test spacecraft, and send the general into space while he's still young enough to conquer Earth. Remember, we didn't say it was plausible."

Q. In the new *Planet of the Apes* movie, where did the horses come from? In the original, the ending tells us where the horses came from. By changing the "origin" of the Planet of the Apes in this version, they made the speaking of English by the apes reasonable but the presence of horses impossible.

—Cort Jensen, Missoula, Montana

A. Since only the apes are assumed to have landed on the planet from another world, the horses, along with all the other flora and fauna, obviously evolved there on their own.

Q. Regarding the ending of *Planet of the Apes,* I wanted to throw in a cent or two after reading the theory by Josh Daniel of Slate.com, as quoted in the Answer Man. Thade (or whoever) hardly needs to spend years developing a space program in order to go back into time. The craft that Mark Wahlberg uses at the end is not the one that he came on, but the one that the chimp arrived on during the climax. Wahlberg's original craft is still at the bottom of the lake. Assuming that there was another ape revolution that led to the freeing of Thade and assuming that the sunken craft was good ol' fashioned Detroit rolling stock, one could assume that Thade retrieved the craft from the lake. When the monkey ancestors passed on their knowledge to future generations, one might also assume that they passed on the knowledge of how to fly such a thing. That would be all that he needs to go back in time and create the events that would one day lead to the twist ending of the only semidisappointing Tim Burton film to date.

—Peter Sobczynski, Chicago, Illinois

A. Josh Daniel of Slate.com writes: "Quite a few readers in our Slate.com discussion forum pointed out that I'd made the ending too complicated. There's still Davidson's escape pod in the bottom of the pond. There also are, presumably, two other escape pods in the mother ship (in the beginning of the movie, they pointedly refer to the chimp's pod as Alpha, and Davidson goes after him in Delta, so that leaves two pods in between, I think). Davidson leaves Pericles, the pilot, on the ape planet, so Thade wouldn't have to learn to fly."

Spoiler warning: My own question is, how could Thade fly to Earth and achieve so much greatness that he was immortalized on the Mall in one ape lifetime? Presumably his biological clock remains unaffected by a time-warp. I think it's more likely that Wahlberg was hurtled into a *parallel* time-space continuum in which evolution favored a different branch of the family tree.

The Princess Diaries

Q. I attended *The Princess Diaries* last Saturday, and both myself and my companion absolutely loved this movie (and we are both grown men in our thirties). I can't begin to tell you how surprised and disappointed I was to see you give the movie one and a half stars. I will admit that *The Princess Diaries* was not a classic, but it was absolutely sweet and charming, and it was so wonderful to see Julie Andrews on the big screen again in a major role, which I thought she played extremely well. The audience I was with seemed to love the film too, even applauding at the end (which is very rare, especially the little girl in front of me who hugged her mother when Anne Hathaway's character decided that she would accept the throne). Any movie that can make a little girl hug her mother can't be all bad. I think "sweet" and "charming" are very underrated qualities for a movie to have, and in a year that has seen us subjected to *Freddy Got Fingered* and *Scary Movie 2,* "sweet" and "charming" are two adjectives that are welcome to see describing a film. I wish you would please reassess your view of this film.

—Gordon Parkhurst, Liverpool, New York

A. Sweet it is, charming it was not (to me). Perhaps I should have mentioned in the review (as I did in my *Dr. Dolittle 2* review) that smaller children were likely to enjoy it. Julie Andrews, who has done some great movie work, including the barbed comedies her husband, Blake Edwards, directed, seemed to play her role as an exercise in good manners. Didn't you think Anne Hathaway looked a little older than fifteen?

Queen of the Damned

Q. In your *Queen of the Damned* review you write of the vampires: "They burst into flame, curl up into charred shadows of themselves, and float upward just like the wrapper from an Amaretti di Saronno cookie." This sounds like a phenomenon that I've been trying to track down since I saw it in an old British movie: Partygoers placed their paper party hats on plates, lit them, and their ashes rose to the ceiling on the column of hot air. I've tried badgering every Brit I run across, but nothing. I've discovered that in the 1920s, the

S. S. Adams Co. (of Joy Buzzer fame) manufactured what they called "Table Balloons"
that performed the same feat. What shape/size/
type of paper is required? What technique of
lighting (if any) is necessary? I've ordered a
box of Amaretti cookies, and experiments will
commence. Is there a trick to lighting the
wrappers?
—Ben Truwe, Medford, Oregon

A. Yes. Roll the wrapper into a tube and
light the bottom.

Resident Evil

Q. In your review of *Resident Evil,* you
mention the corridor where lasers pass back
and forth as single lines, and are then followed
by a grid of lasers. You asked why the earlier
phases of the laser were necessary when the
final one would kill anything. I suppose, as
you theorized, that the corridor could have a
sense of humor, but I think it's more simple
than that. If it got them with the single laser
passing by it could stop, leaving larger pieces
of body.
—John Tucker, Abbeville, South Carolina

A. You think the computer running the
killer laser corridor, having drowned and
gassed everyone in the building, is worried
about *cleanup?*

Q. I just got back from watching the piece
of celluloid mediocrity known as *Resident Evil*
and I counted no less than seven of what I
like to refer to as "fake-out" jumps. You know,
the scene usually has dramatic music and
everyone is quiet and the character is usually
looking down a darkened hallway or is about
to pick up something from a presumed dead
body. If it deals with a dead body you *know*
that someone is getting an appendage grabbed
at the last moment (à la *What Lies Beneath*).
The other half of the time the "jump" is delivered by a cat or some other innocuous creature (à la take your pick of any horror movie
this side of *The Cabinet of Dr. Caligari*). These
things work great in the right places and I
myself have fallen prey to many a "fake-out"
instant. My question to you is: What has been
your greatest "fake-out" moment where you
actually jumped and felt the pang of fight or

flight, if even for a moment? What movie has
housed the most? I would think *RE* would be
in the running. Thanks in advance!!
—Patrick Coffey, Rosamond, California

A. I think maybe Carrie's comeback from
the grave.

Rewinding DVDs

Q. "Be Kind—Rewind!"
I've seen this label on rental DVD cases at
my local Blockbuster. I asked a person who
worked at Blockbuster why rewinding would
be necessary on DVDs, and was told, "DVDs
can be rewound so please rewind it." I asked
the manager and he told me, "DVDs can be
rewound like VHS." I e-mailed Blockbuster.
They told me, "Most DVD players have a
'Rewind' button. What it does is spin the DVD
the opposite direction from the Play mode.
It's similar to the rewind feature on a VCR." I
e-mailed them and told them they were wrong,
Blockbuster e-mailed me, "Sir, you are very
wrong, please don't contradict what we say, we
know more than you do about DVDs. Please
don't e-mail us regarding this topic again."
They were very rude. But I know that a DVD
cannot be rewound.
—Kun Sun Sweeley, Baltimore, Maryland

A. Your message first appeared on a Website devoted to "useless warnings." It sounded
like an urban legend to me, but when I contacted you, you replied: "This is true. I have
seen labels on DVDs at my local Blockbuster,
asking for the DVDs to be rewound. The post
that I wrote is true." I asked around, and
columnist/critic David Poland supplied the
likely explanation: The stickers double as
magnetic security tags. The tags for VHS ask
you to rewind. When they run out of DVD
tags, they just use the VHS tags. What that
doesn't explain are your phone conversations
and e-mails with Blockbuster. Is it possible the
chain has employees who don't know the first
thing about DVD? Judging from their clue-
lessness on letterboxing, I think it's a possibility.

The Rookie

Q. In your review of *The Rookie,* you complain it is too predictable and clichéd. Aren't
these things forgivable since they actually hap-

pened in real life, since the movie was based on a true story? It is a great story and I disagree with your critique.

—Brent Ecenbarger, Fort Wayne, Indiana

A. My *Sun-Times* review included this sentence, which a glitch kept out of the on-line version: "Yes, the movie is 'based on a true story,' but one of those true stories that seems based on a movie." Although the events really happened, they are so much the stuff of movie formulas that had they not really happened, it is possible the screenplay would have been turned down as too clichéd and predictable. Strange, but there you are.

Q. I read Ross Anthony's review of *The Rookie* (http://rossanthony.com/) and he claims the entire movie was shot on video (not film). I cannot find any facts to support that view.

—Herb Kane, criticdoctor.com

A. Anthony gives several reasons why he thinks *The Rookie* was shot on video, including jittery tracking shots, pastiness in long shots, and washed-out color. The print I saw looked superb. It may be Anthony saw it *projected* on video. For a verdict, I turned to Steven Poster, president of the American Society of Cinematographers, who responds: "The movie was shot Wide Screen Anamorphic, Panavision 'C' series lenses with Kodak 5277 Emulsion. Nothing but the best for my friend John Schwartzman. What Anthony might have seen is a digitally projected presentation at the El Capitian theater. And that would go to prove what you and I believe in our hearts; not only is film not dead, it doesn't even have a cold. I've seen the same kind of junky-looking presentations from digitally presented movies before. It's just not even close to film yet."

P.S.: Poster's guess was on the money. Ross Anthony writes me that he did indeed see the film projected digitally, has been discussing differences between film and video projection with Schwartzman, and will be writing about this experience.

The Royal Tenenbaums

Q. While looking at the cast list for *The Royal Tenenbaums*, I saw that the paramedic was played by a Brian Tenenbaum. I clicked on his credits and saw that he was also in *Rushmore* and *Bottle Rocket*—two other films directed by Wes Anderson and cowritten by Owen Wilson. Is there any connection between Brian and the story of the *Royal Tenenbaums*? Or did Wes Anderson just use his name?

—Adam Roberts, Atlanta, Georgia

A. Director Wes Anderson replies: "Brian Tenenbaum is a very good friend of mine and the three Wilson brothers. There is some inspiration for the character of Richie Tenenbaum (the tennis champion son in the movie is Brian, and he does come from a very tightly knit and interesting family from Savannah, Georgia), but the name Tenenbaum was really chosen just because I liked the sound of it. His sister is named Margot Tenenbaum, which is also the name of a character in the movie, and it is more difficult to come up with a reason why we would use someone's *full* name if they have nothing to do with the story, but then I suppose that's about all I have to say about that."

Rush Hour 2

Q. I think you misunderstood Chris Tucker's racial tirade in the casino, in *Rush Hour 2*. He was being obnoxious on purpose (and doing an excellent job), I agree, to distract everyone from Jackie Chan's attempt to get inside the room that had the counterfeit plates. Perhaps you were so put off you failed to notice.

—Ginny Shook, Palm Desert, California

A. In a movie like *Rush Hour 2*, the plot points are not—well, the point. A scene like Tucker's tirade is not necessary. There were countless other ways to distract attention, and some of them might have been funny, while his was not. Tucker could have invented some sort of odd, eccentric, or peculiar behavior that did not involve accusing an innocent person of racism. It left a bad feeling in the room. I think whole riff (black guy goes ballistic with allegedly funny charges of racism) is getting stale. Chris Rock does more or less the same thing in *Jay and Silent Bob*. It's time to move on.

Q. *Rush Hour 2* has just passed the $200 million mark, but why has no one noted that

this may be a first for a film with two non-Caucasians in the leads and with virtually no Caucasians at all in the cast? The two leads in the film are Chinese and African-American and the two females are Chinese and Latina. You have to go way down the list of credits to find anyone who isn't of color. I think this is quite an accomplishment, but no one, not even the releasing company, seems to have noticed.
—Joe Baltake, *Sacramento Bee*

A. I wish it had been *Eve's Bayou* and not *Rush Hour 2*, but I agree this is a noteworthy milestone.

The Scorpion King

Q. In your review of *The Scorpion King*, you address the line "As long as one of us still breathes, the sorcerer will die!" by saying "See if you can spot the logical loophole." I can't. Given that almost every other line in the movie has some logical flaw or another, I am willing to trust you on this. But for curiosity's sake, what exactly do you mean?
—Bruce Spence, New Brunswick, New Jersey

A. What happens if none of them still breathe?

September 11, 2001

Q. In your reviews, you've referred to the idea that we live in an ironic age—that in the last ten years we have tended to laugh at what we should fear (teenagers howling at *The Exorcist* comes to mind as an example) and mock what we should take seriously. Satirical enterprises like the *Onion* and the *Daily Show* have flourished in this kind of cultural environment, but now, along with the rest of us, they are faced with a phenomenon that my generation (I'm thirty) has never seen—a completely unmockable event. What does it mean? I would like to suggest to you that September 11, 2001, marks, along with many other brutal divides, the End of Irony. Irony, mockery, facetiousness . . . in the shadow of an event of such overwhelming sadness and seriousness, these are impossible reactions. Existential dread has returned, and the temper of the times will be reflected in the films that we see over the next decade. Austen is out; Dostoyevsky is in. Our filmmakers will have the opportunity and support to make it a time

of excellent, important, and compelling films. Cold comfort perhaps, but I'm looking forward to it nonetheless. What else can one do?
—James Ball, Osaka, Japan

A. Our filmmakers may want to make them, but if studio marketing remains driven and dictated by the immediate Friday night box-office results, and good films are given no chance to find audiences, most mainstream films will continue to be shallow and exploitable.

Q. To what extent do movies made prior to September 11, 2001, still remain relevant in our lives? We still look at movies made prior to December 7, 1941, such as *M* and *Citizen Kane*, and recognize them as the great films that they are, but I watched *Clerks*, one of my favorite films, earlier this evening, just to try to divert my mind from the current goings-on, and the petty complaints of a couple of my brethren (I'm from Monmouth County, New Jersey) seemed not funny anymore, but rather irrelevant in light of how our existence has changed since 8:58 A.M. Tuesday. I know that we will eventually be able to again appreciate the accomplishments produced by the better angels of our nature, but I wonder if we'll ever be able to again appreciate the small, silly, personal and political issues that seemed so large and overwhelming in the 1990s. I wonder what you think will become of the wonderful, if seemingly petty, movies of that decade.
—Thom Tolan, Norwalk, Connecticut

A. I am having less trouble these days with the small and the silly than with the grandiose and the heartless. There are some movies from the 1990s that seem almost prescient now. A few that come to mind are *Magnolia, Bringing Out the Dead, The Sweet Hereafter, Schindler's List*, and *Malcolm X*. But those films fought against irony, and to one degree or another paid the price.

I have just returned from the Toronto Film Festival, where two directors said things that continue to resonate. Norman Jewison told me, "The Hollywood studio movies of the last two years have been the worst in history. And you would not believe the crap that doesn't get made. I look at a screenplay and ask them if they're serious. And they are." And Paul Cox said, "A movie should not make you a more disgusting human being."

Q. Where does Hollywood go now? One of the comments made by a coworker after watching the towers go down was "this is real and not a movie." Are special-effects flicks doomed? I miss the movies of the 1970s that were more character-driven.
—Curt Chipman, Long Beach, California

A. Thrillers and disaster movies have played with fire for years now, titillating us with visions of apocalypse. Audiences found it fun to laugh at images of horror, because they could feel superior. Now the smiles fade, and we hunger for films that nourish hope.

Q. Here's an idea for a movie to be made in the year 2060: An epic about the attacks against the Twin Towers. Only let the three-hour film focus mainly on a love triangle stemming from a pair of friends as stock traders in New York and a young receptionist. When one of them is on a plane from Boston to Louisiana and another is busy with a client in the Twin Towers, the men are suddenly thrust in the middle of a terrible plot where there is chaos and tragedy, but we completely disregard the 5,000 citizens dead and instead concern ourselves with the love lives of three whining yuppies. Or, we could just look at *Pearl Harbor* and think about how horrible it is to trivialize such a tragedy on the screen.
—Derek Muller, Royal Oak, Michigan

A. A film can be made about the tragedy of September 11, but I believe it must be a small film, not an epic, it must be about individual humans, not special effects, and it should not have a happy ending but a somber and poignant one.

Q. Since September 11, one movie clip has been playing through my mind. It's from *Three Kings*, when the Mark Wahlberg character contacts his wife by cell phone when being held hostage. It underlines the depth of that movie under the guise of dark comedy.
—Mike Spearns, St. John's, Newfoundland

A. History repeats itself, first as farce, then as tragedy.

Q. I would like to hear your comments on the fact that Paul Crouch and his Trinity Broadcasting Network are using footage of the recent tragedies in New York and Washington in promos for their upcoming film, *Meggiddo: Omega Code 2*. This, to me, seems reprehensible.
—Fred Holliday, Washington, D.C.

A. It depends on how you look at it. Matthew Crouch, Paul's son and the film's producer, told the *Los Angeles Times:* "It was not God's breath that blew those planes off course and into those buildings, but when he knows that things like that are going to happen—because I believe God sees from the beginning to the end of all time—he positioned this film to be the answer for a question we didn't even know would be asked."

Serendipity

Q. In your review of *Serendipity* you say: "She says they'll get on separate elevators in a hotel and see if they both push the same button. Odds are about thirty to one against it." Assuming thirty possible floors to randomly choose from, the probability of each person picking a particular floor is itself $1/30$, but for both to simultaneously pick the same floor is actually $(1/30) * (1/30) = 1/900$. This makes things look even worse for the movie!
—Bobby Scurlock, Gainesville, Florida

A. You are . . . wrong! I thought you were right. I am easily intimidated by math questions. But Chris Knight, an editor at the *National Post* of Canada, saw your question and writes: "The odds of two people each choosing a predetermined floor (14, for example) is one in 900. However, the odds of two people choosing the same floor as the other is still one in thirty. —If I pick floor 1, you have a $1/30$ chance of picking the same floor, and if I pick floor 2 you have a $1/30$ chance of picking the same floor, and so on."

Shadow of the Vampire

Q. I went to see *Shadow of the Vampire* and thought it was fantastic. In such a situation I ask myself what, if anything, I didn't like about it. I was frustrated by the overly long opening credits when nothing was shown to entertain the viewer. It seemed like ten minutes of bizarre artwork being passed over the screen. I think directors should get rid of these epic continuous and pointless opening credits.

—Craig Nicholas, Petaluma, California

A. What? You didn't like *Vampire's* brilliant opening sequence, in which we seemed to pass through an endless series of magnificent Art Deco portals, evoking the great silent period in which the movie is set? I'm filing your complaint with the one from the guy who liked *The Third Man*, all except for the zither music.

Shallow Hal

Q. So let me get this straight about *Shallow Hal's* new girlfriend. She's fat, and the way to portray her inner beauty is that she is thin and stunningly beautiful on the inside. And the girls who are thin on the outside must be ugly on the inside and the best way to show it is to make their inner selves fat? Who decided clothes hangers were beautiful? Is your soul or spirit fat or thin? There are a bunch of ways this could have been visualized without fat equaling ugly.

—Melody Parish, Aurora, Colorado

A. I've received heartfelt messages both for and against the film. This is from Mike Parnell of Burgaw, North Carolina: "Being a person who is extremely large I could be offended by some of the images in the movie. The question I have is, why do moviegoers want people to have epiphanies where they get it all at once? I find myself struggling to get my mind around some of the stuff I face in my own life. It takes time for me to understand. Isn't the title enough to warn us that Hal is not going to be able to correct the bad instructions he got from his father (in a drug-induced haze) merely because of an encounter with Tony Robbins? I think it is good to see the growth of characters in a film."

Q. In your review of *Shallow Hal,* you write, "Only the most attentive audience members will catch the Farrellys' subtle reference to a famous poem by Emily Dickinson." Though I think I know her poetry, I must have missed the reference.

—Sara Jane Berman, East Williston, New York

A. When Shallow Hal's father dies, a fly buzzes.

Q. Amid all the howling and gnashing of teeth over how unfair *Shallow Hal* is to overweight women, would a male actor as unslender as Jack Black *ever* be cast as a serious love interest to Gwyneth Paltrow if she were playing a character like her model-thin self?

—Ward Wilson, Chicago, Illinois

A. No. Marlon Brando and Faye Dunaway did a bed scene in *Don Juan DeMarco*, but its highlight was Brando demonstrating how he could throw popcorn kernels into the air and catch them in his mouth.

The Shipping News

Q. Even though his hairline is receding, Kevin Spacey still has a perfectly fine head of hair. Why is it, then, that in *The Shipping News* he wears an obvious and distracting toupee? His character, Quoyle, does not strike me as the type of person who would be concerned about his hair in this manner. Since Mr. Spacey doesn't wear a hairpiece in his interviews to promote the movie, why would he wear a hairpiece in the movie itself?

—Larry MacInnis, Markham, Ontario

A. The movie doesn't intend to suggest Quoyle is wearing a hairpiece. It intends to suggest that's his hair. I didn't find it obvious or distracting. Of course, since you *know* that isn't Spacey's real hair, you have to give him a break. I knew it wasn't Billy Bob Thornton's real hair in *The Man Who Wasn't There*, but so what?

Showtime

Q. I just saw *Showtime* and noticed in the credits a person named De Niro (besides Robert). I was wondering if she was a relative or his wife.

—K. Oshima, Los Angeles, California

A. That's his daughter, Drena, playing Rene Russo's sidekick. She's been in fifteen movies.

Slow Clap

Q. Where did it begin—that priggish Slow Clap in the movies? Example: The sheepish star gives a heartfelt, unplanned speech. At first the audience is silent. Then one man (it's always a man), jaws clenched, claps his hands together—once. About two seconds later, he claps them together again. Around the room, others join in the slow clap, like the proverbial Chinese Water Torture. Eventually the whole sentimental group joins in full-fledged normal applause. When does this happen in real life? It's one of those "only in movies" devices, like the run-up-a-wall-turn-upside-down-and-windmill-kick-the-bad-guy-while-wearing-a-black-leather-trenchcoat scene.

—Jim Carey, Warrenville, Illinois

A. Your question moved me, and I was inspired by your bravery in asking it. Clap . . . clap . . .

Q. A recent Answer Man item asked about the origin of the Slow Clap. Like so many other movie conventions, I believe this came out of *Citizen Kane,* where Kane attempts to revive the applause for his wife's pitiful opera performance. In that scene, he begins clapping slowly and then with more fervor as he realizes that he is the only one doing so.

—Michael Richard, Pittsburgh, Pennsylvania

A. That's the earliest movie slow clap I can recall. As Steve Bailey of Jacksonville, Florida, points out, Kane clapping *after* everyone else reverses the modern practice of leading the applause.

Q. I wonder if the Slow Clap and the Gradually Gathering Guffaw are related? Or if they have ever both appeared in the same movie?

—Christopher Philippo, Troy, New York

A. Same movie? Only in the audience. Like during *Heist,* when after Danny DeVito's great line I went, "Haw!—pause—Haw!—pause — Haw!" And then, as the brilliance of the line sank in, I led the whole audience in a Slow Clap.

Spider-Man

Q. I am nine years old and in grade four. I saw *Spider-Man* on Friday. In your review, you write, "I have one question about the Peter Parker character: Does the movie go too far with his extreme social paralysis?" I know the answer to your question: Like his uncle told Peter, "Great power means great responsibility." Peter *has* to fight crime because he has superstrength. The Goblin tried to kill his Aunt

and his girlfriend to get at Peter. So, he can't have a girlfriend or her life will be in danger. I agree with most of your points about the movie but I will still tell my friends to go see it. My eleven-year-old sister, Emily, saw it also and she would tell her best friend, also Emily, to see it.

—James Stajov, Ontario

A. In the last paragraph of my review I floated various theories about why Peter told Mary Jane they could never have a relationship. You are the youngest of some 200 indignant readers who informed me that Peter is protecting Mary Jane, since he knows he will be a target for evildoers. I knew that. I was just trying to make a little joke, to bring some sunshine into my readers' days. Obviously, I failed miserably in my attempt at humor.

Q. With all the money and computers and expertise at their disposal, why can't Hollywood get superheroes right? You're right, the action sequences in *Spider-Man* are maddeningly devoid of physics. Don't they realize we want to see stunts that at least appear to be happening in the real world?

—Leon Lynn, Milwaukee, Wisconsin

A. Apparently we don't. I got countless e-mails from readers who like the special effects just as they are, some even arguing that since Spider-Man was a spider he should look as if he only weighed as much as a spider. I felt his motions in the f/x sequences were too quick, making him look more like a cartoon character than Peter Parker on a thread of webbing.

Q. I don't understand the difference between the first night a film is released and the second day it is out. I saw *Spider-Man* on opening night and then I saw it again the following night with a friend who couldn't go on Friday. The first night the crowd was pumped and cheered for everything. At the end everyone stood up and clapped and cheered. The next night, it was sold out again, but it was completely different. Jokes that got huge laughs on Friday got minimal to no laughs on Saturday.

—Craig Fields, Columbus, Ohio

A. Every audience has its own personality,

an impenetrable mystery that actors never tire of discussing.

Spy Kids

Q. I took my seven-year-old son to see *Spy Kids,* which he loved, so when the movie was released on VHS, we purchased a copy. Upon viewing the video, my son noticed one of his favorite parts was missing. It's the scene where Juni and Carmen are in scuba gear en route to the underwater entrance to Floop's Castle and the sleeping sharks are awakened by the change in water temperature when Juni "wets in his wetsuit." Why would they cut out such a scene?

—Shari Prenzler, Inez, Texas

A. I immediately suspected the insidious practice of some video outlets which silently "edit" films for "family viewing," deciding for themselves what is suitable. But, no, in this case the answer is more complicated. According to a spokesperson for Dimension Films, when *Spy Kids* was released on March 30, it contained only dialogue about the kid peeing in his wet suit. When it was rereleased in August, director Robert Rodriguez made some slight changes, including new footage actually indicating pee in the water. The video version is of the original March 30 version, which does not include that footage.

Star Wars: Episode II—Attack of the Clones

Q. I realized after seeing *Episode I* what was wrong with this new *Star Wars* series, despite its visual wonders: No Han Solo. The new series has no everyman, no skeptic. Who am I to relate to? Where am I up on that screen? We viewed the action in the first *Star Wars* trilogy through the eyes of the guy who didn't fit in, who was only in it for the money and "wasn't too sure about this 'force stuff.'" This new trilogy leaves a lot of viewers at the station.

—Dave Arnold, Sheridan, Oregon

A. You may be onto something. There were times during the first hour of *Episode II* when the discussions of Republic politics were so endless I felt like I was watching an intergalactic *McLaughlin Report.*

Q. I read your review of *Attack of the Clones* and also your update after you viewed the version in its digital form. I saw the film in digital form this morning. Throughout the film there were very obvious blurry pixelized images (where you could see the blocks that the computer uses to create an image). It was never more obvious than in the ending scene, and also whenever subtitles appeared on the screen. My companion kept remarking about how clear the film looked, but in my opinion if I can see pixels then the image is not "clear." It is obvious to me that you didn't see this: perhaps the movie I saw was being projected onto a larger screen than was initially intended? I do remember the screen being curved.

—Shanessa Jackson, Elyria, Ohio

A. If it was curved, it was almost certainly a widescreen from the golden age. I found the digital version of *AOTC* clearer than the film version, but have heard from many who disliked the digital projection.

George Hearn of San Jose, California, writes: "My main disappointment was the relatively low resolution it is shown in, which causes 'pixelization' (stars were replaced by square dots), and stationary objects were noticeably 'jagged.' I was unfortunate to have a seat fairly close to the screen; I will sit further back next time I see a DLP screening. To its credit, the image is bright, and by its nature free of dust scratches or grain. But in my opinion, in terms of resolution and detail it still has strides to make before equaling 35mm film."

And Daniel Switkin of Palo Alto writes: "I saw *AOTC* in digital. Although the image was completely flicker- and defect-free, and the sound was perfect, the resolution was dreadful. Pixels were clearly visible, and everything from subtitles to small details were much worse than film. Some digging on www.dlp.com reveals that the current digital projectors use a pathetic 1280x1024 resolution—the same as most seventeen-inch desktop LCD monitors! This is despite the fact that the Sony camera used to shoot the movie digitally operates at 1920x1080 resolution. How can we the audience tell the industry that these five-year-old digital projectors they're now just installing aren't good enough?"

I find it amusing that no one is complaining about fifty-year-old film projectors . . .

Q. I'm wondering why or how your criteria for evaluating the *Star Wars* movies has changed so drastically. You were one of the primary defenders of *Episode I*, but four years later you seem to be criticizing *Attack of the Clones* for the same reasons people criticized *Phantom Menace*. I'm confused how *Episode I* got a stellar 3.5 stars and *Episode II* got a deadly 2 stars.
—Harry Kallow, Cambridge, Massachusetts

A. I was deluged with messages asking how I could dislike *Two* when I liked *One*? My reviews are based on my immediate reaction to the film I have just seen. To skew them in order to make them "consistent" would be dishonest.

Q. Is it fair to disparage a film that is designed, essentially, for children by stating that it has failed to entertain and illuminate adults? Every review of *Episode II* that I've read seems to forget, or ignore, that the script, acting, themes, and visual design of the entire *Star Wars* saga are intended to be understood, and appreciated, first and foremost, by children. Of course the dialogue is somewhat trite to us—but a child, even an intelligent one, needs to understand what is going on at all times, and complex, witty dialogue won't necessarily help. As Lucas said recently: "The fans have grown up. The films haven't."
—Scott Spencer, Tokyo, Japan

A. I disagree that the *Star Wars* films are marketed primarily to children. The teenage demographic is the marketing bull's-eye. Movies like *Harry Potter* and *Spider-Man,* not to mention classics like *Ferris Bueller's Day Off, Raiders of the Lost Arc, E.T.,* and *Babe* are aimed at a similar audience, and sparkle with well-written dialogue.

Q. The fight scenes in *Attack of the Clones* would be slashed in half if only the light sabers had wrist straps: What little suspense there was hinged on a good guy losing his hold on his weapon. How come bad guys are scripted with firmer grips?
—Bill Stamets, Chicago, Illinois

A. Everytime I see one of those scenes I am reminded of Indiana Jones simply drawing his pistol and shooting the other guy dead.

Storytelling

Q. Regarding the Fiction section of Todd Solondz's film *Storytelling:* I read that in order to get the film made, Solondz had to guarantee an R rating for the final cut. When the MPAA objected to the scene in which Selma Blair has sex with her professor, Solondz refused to cut the scene and placed red quadrangles over the more graphic portions of the frame. I saw the film here in Paris where I am studying. I saw no bars of any kind and the figures were mostly shadowed. Bars hardly seem necessary. Did I see the uncensored version or were certain angles simply cut out to avoid bars entirely?
—Justin Canada, Dallas, Texas

A. I saw it uncensored at Cannes. You may not have thought bars were "necessary," but the MPAA did object to the scene. I credit Solondz for dramatizing this de facto censorship by blocking the targeted scenes with bright red oblongs, instead of meekly trimming them. The MPAA continues to deny America a workable adult rating.

Subtitles

Q. I was told that they're working on special subtitles that could be seen through the use of special glasses so deaf people could enjoy watching movies at a theater without distracting the hearing viewers. Is this logical in terms of cost, technology, and the cooperation of studios and theaters? Will it ever become a reality?
—Lindsay Drexler, Chicago, Illinois

A. I asked for help from Marca Bristo, president of Access Living in Chicago and chair of the National Council on Disability. She says you are referring to the Rear Window Captioning System, and steered me to the Website of the National Center for Accessible Media, which explains that the system "displays reversed captions on a light-emitting diode (LED) text display which is mounted in the rear of a theater. Patrons use transparent acrylic panels attached to their seats to reflect the captions so that they appear superimposed on or beneath the movie screen. The reflective panels are portable and adjustable, enabling the caption user to sit anywhere in the theater." For more info, go to http://ncam.wgbh.org/.

Q. I recently rented HBO's *Sex in the City* TV show on DVD. There is an alternate language track in Spanish. I noticed that the profanity, vulgarities, and slang in the English version are not in the Spanish version. This sanitizing causes it to lose its spice. I have noticed this on other alternative language DVDs as well. Why is this?

—Dwayne Williams, Orlando, Florida

A. As a general rule, Spanish subtitles are sanitized compared to original English dialogue, as a bow to the generally Catholic countries where their audiences originate.

The Sum of All Fears

Q. The neo-Nazi terrorists in the film version of *The Sum of All Fears* were radical Muslim terrorists in Tom Clancy's book, but as you noted in your review, the change was made in order to avoid offending people. What's your take on all this? Has the Muslim terrorist in movies gone the way of the Indian marauder?

—Stephen Athanson, Blue Ridge, Virginia

A. Mainstream Hollywood will not willingly offend any large group of ticket-buyers. Without the always-dependable Nazis, it would be left without stock villains, and would be forced to create good guys from scratch.

Q. I noticed at the beginning of *Sum of All Fears* that they are naming Russian diplomatic officials and "Elena Rhyzkov" is repeated a few times. Elena Rhyzkov is the name of the Russian scientist in *Sneakers* who catches Robert Redford. Not only that, but the actress who played Dr. Rhyzkov in *Sneakers* is the pregnant woman in that scene in *Sum of All Fears*. This can't just be an amazing coincidence, can it?

—Nathan Koob, Stillwater, Oklahoma

A. Probably not, considering both movies were directed by Phil Alden Robinson, and that actress Lee Garlington, who plays Rhyzkov, also appears in his films *Field of Dreams* and *In the Mood*.

Q. I noticed a time warp in *Sum of All Fears* that is driving me crazy. Why would the filmmakers detonate a nuclear bomb in 1993 in Baltimore when we know this did not happen in history? If the movie occurred in the near future, like most thrillers, then we could accept the possibility of a nuclear bomb in the United States (although I don't know how the film would explain Ryan's dip into the fountain of youth). But to show a horrific event from almost ten years ago that we know did not happen is like having the Germans attack Los Angeles during World War II. Did I miss something?

—Edward Rivera, New Orleans, Louisiana

A. The plane with the bomb on board crashes in 1973, so the attack on Baltimore would indeed seem to take place before the present day. Hard to explain. It is also rather difficult to understand why the Israelis would not have moved heaven and earth to investigate the crash scene and retrieve the bomb or any evidence of it.

Technical Matters

Q. In the full-page ad for the reissue of *Apocalypse Now Redux,* opening August 10 in many cities, in really tiny, tiny type, almost unreadable, is the credit: "Technicolor dye transfer prints." As far as I know, this is the first time the correct phrase "dye transfer" has been used in any advertisement of this type. So Technicolor is officially back. But you have to really squint to see the credit. All of the prints of the *Redux* version are indeed dye transfer, which is essentially a reworking of the old "3-strip" Technicolor. Instead of the chemical development of colors, color dyes are transferred to the film directly, resulting in the stunning "Technicolor" look of the forties and fifties: lush, gorgeous, bright, sharp, and vivid, with deep, rich, true blacks.

—Jeff Joseph, Los Angeles, California

A. And the film looks astonishingly good. What saddens me is that the movie industry is so shy about great-looking technology like dye transfer, 70mm, and the MaxiVision 48 system, and so eager to throw out film altogether and embrace inferior digital projection. People who talk about how good digital looks are like the guy who has to say he likes his new car, because he bought it.

Q. You've rightfully rallied against theaters that lower the foot-candles on their projectors in order to save on electrical costs. I've noticed that films are literally getting harder and harder to see at my local multiplex, and it's only after I rent the DVD that I can truly see what the director and cinematographer meant for me to see. What is the proper foot-candle level that projectors are supposed to emit, and if I complain about a noticeably dark picture, is it possible for the projectionist to change the projector without stopping the film? I want to make my dissatisfaction known at the multiplex, but I want to have enough information to know what I can reasonably expect the miserly theater managers to do.
—Jed Blaugrund, Sherman Oaks, California

A. It's a scandal that many theaters, while sparing no expense with their state-of-the-art refreshment stands, show noticeably dim pictures. You want to sound like an expert, so I consulted one. Steve Kraus owns the Lake Street Screening Room, where Chicago critics enjoy superb projection. He replies: "The brightness of a movie screen is measured in foot-Lamberts (a measure of light reflected off the screen, not foot-candles). The measurement is taken with the house lights off and projector running without film. The standard set by the Society of Motion Picture and Television Engineers is 16 fL +/- 2. There are several likely reasons why a theater may have a dim picture. Some hold off replacing the very expensive xenon bulb until it simply won't start, having racked up so many hours that the inside of the bulb has blackened and the picture has dimmed. In some cases the bulb may be misaligned. A small error can make a huge difference in brightness and sometimes unskilled persons may replace a bulb without knowing how to properly align the new one. In other cases the theater designers simply did not specify a sufficiently powerful lamphouse and power rectifier. In rare situations, depending on the particular equipment at that the-

ater, it may be possible to simply turn a knob to raise the brightness, but then only if they are not already at maximum, and it's simply not possible at all on many projection lamps without interrupting the show. Replacing an aging bulb and many of the alignment adjustments cannot be made while the show is under way, and depending on the projectionist, may require a visit from the service technician."

Q. Your review of *Monsters, Inc.* referred to "voice-over" actors "dubbing" or "looping" their lines. Nothing of the kind is involved. The voices for animated films are recorded beforehand, and the animation is drawn to match the voices.
—Justin Weiss, New York, New York

A. You took the words right out of my mouth.

Time Machine

Q. Feminist claptrap bores me, but what's up with your line about "ugly brides" in your *Time Machine* review? Let's accept your review's amusing premise that Morlocks are so ugly because they're the result of 800,000 years of evolution gone wrong. Wouldn't ugly Morlocks just as likely be the result of millennia of ugly husbands as of ugly brides?
—Irene Schneider, New York, New York

A. No, because evolutionary theory assumes men do most of the choosing and the strongest men get the bride they want. This has changed in recent years, however. Women look beneath surface beauty, and thanks to feminist claptrap they now do more of the choosing. Their tendency to avoid hunks and look for smart men who are good providers means that right now the human race looks about as good as it is ever going to look.

Q. You ask in your review why the Time Machine stays in one place rather than at a particular set of coordinates in space with Earth flying away from under it. It makes sense. The Time Machine is a physical device that creates a field in which funny things happen with time. Like most matter we see, it has been captured by Planet Earth and is carried with it. It is not immovable, it just does not move relative to Earth.

—Mark R. Leeper, Old Bridge, New Jersey

A. Okay, okay. So then what happens when it reappears in a space already occupied by another physical object?

Q. In your review of *The Time Machine*, accounting for the ugliness of the race of Morlocks, you write, "evolutionary theory assumes men do most of the choosing and the strongest men get the bride they want." Evolutionary theory predicts the opposite. Males invest little in offspring (other than sperm) so they are less choosy of their mates. Females have to be careful of their choices, because they invest more in each offspring, and their potential output of offspring is smaller than males. Therefore, the Morlocks in *The Time Machine* are more likely the result of ugly husbands than ugly brides. (Of course, the brides themselves would consider them to be beautiful.)

—David Seelig, Volen Center for Complex Systems, Brandeis University

A. I am sure you are right, especially that beauty is in the eye of the beholder. D. J. Trail of New York City informs me: "Judgments of attractiveness are species-centric, which is why chimpanzees do not find human females attractive. There is no such thing as objective attractiveness." I agree that Morlocks look sexy to other members of their gene pool, as do alligators, octupi, and boy bands. I am gratified that esteemed members of the academy are debating my evolutionary insights. Dan Jardine of Victoria, British Columbia, writes: "You will be happy to know that your theory that we are about as attractive as we are going to get, has some support in the scientific community. According to the *London Observer*, Professor Steve Jones told a Royal Society Edinburgh debate in February that human evolution is basically over, because modern medicine and the creature comforts of contemporary lifestyles assure that virtually all genes, and not just the 'fittest' ones, are making it through to the next generation."

Trailers

Q. Why do so many movie trailers use the the music from *The American President*? This evening there was a trailer for the new Mel Gibson movie and it was using the *American President* theme music. I have heard other movie trailers using that music as well. What gives?

—Gene Nimtz, St. Joseph, Michigan

A. For an answer, I turned to David J. Bondelevitch, a faculty member at the University of Southern California and an award-winning music editor. He replies:

"There is no simple answer. Most of the time the music for a trailer is chosen by the person who edits the trailer, or by a marketing person who supervises the editor. Since music is not necessarily their specialty, they often choose something fairly obvious. There is also a belief that people respond more to the familiar, so if music worked in an earlier trailer (especially for a film that had a huge opening weekend), then they think it will work for a similar trailer.

"You could also ask why all trailers use the same three voice-over artists. And why all trailers start with the words '*In a world . . . where . . .*'"

Q. Every time I see the trailer for *Changing Lanes*, I cringe. According to the trailer, the film stars "Academy Award nominee Samuel L. Jackson" and "Academy Award winner Ben Affleck." Now, since most folks can't even name the Oscar winners from last year, I'm willing to bet they have no idea what great performance Affleck won his Oscar for— which is what the studio wants, since Affleck won for Best Screenplay, not acting. This is a dubious practice, especially up against a mere "nominee" like Jackson, who should have a set of Oscars by now!

—Paul Castiglia, Huntington Station, New York

A. Technically, the trailer is correct. Ethically, it stands on shaky ground.

Undercover Brother

Q. While *Undercover Brother* is a very funny film, there is one problem that puzzles me. There's a running joke that black people don't like mayonnaise. While I agree that black people wouldn't be caught dead watching *Friends*, never in my life (and I've been black all my life) have I heard that black people don't eat mayonnaise. What are those jars of mayonnaise doing in my fridge?

—Sergio Mims, Chicago, Illinois

A. The movie argues that black people prefer hot sauce, leading me to wonder, what is the Undercover Brother's recipe for potato salad?

Waking Life

Q. Regarding your message questioning the R rating of my film *Waking Life*. Yeah, it's that one scene in the jail cell where the guy uses bad language, just enough f-words to get an R. Rumor has it they give you two or so, but I guess we'll never know because the MPAA is such a secret society/skull-and-bones kind of thing. It's a drag. Although I don't think the movie is for kids, I like the idea of a fifteen- or sixteen-year-old being able to go without all the hassle.

—Rick Linklater, director, Austin, Texas

A. The fundamental problem with the MPAA is that it avoids making any kind of commonsense evaluation of a film, and simply counts f-words and evaluates nudity. *Waking Life*, one of the most affirmative and challenging films I can imagine for smart teenagers, gets the R rating, while the thriller *Domestic Disturbance*, which shows a small child exposed to a murder, an incineration, and the beating of his mother (leading to a miscarriage and the beating of his father), after which the kid himself causes an electrocution, gets the PG-13—presumably because there is no nudity and the language stays below the cut-off point. What sane parent would prefer their teenager to see *Domestic Disturbance* rather than *Waking Life*?

Who Would Win?

Q. Who would win in a fight, William Wallace *(Braveheart)*, or Maximus *(Gladiator)*?

—Matt Maz, Tinley Park, Illinois

A. William Wallace.

Q. I read the question asked in the last Answer Man column about who would win in a fight between Maximus and William Wallace. I started thinking: Who would win in a fight between James Bond and Ethan Hunt?

—Jacob Barksdale, Birmingham, Alabama

A. Ethan Hunt.

Q. Who would win in a fight between Batman and Shaft (Richard Roundtree, not Samuel L. Jackson)?

—Duane Theriot, Baton Rouge, Louisiana

A. Which Batman? Jackson would beat them all. Roundtree would win against Keaton, lose to Kilmer, draw with Clooney.

Q. Who would win in a fight between the Ya-Ya Sisterhood and the Power Puff Girls?

—Peter Sobczynski, Chicago, Illinois

A. The Power Puff Girls would win if they attacked after the cocktail hour.

The Wizard of Oz

Q. Watching *The Wizard of Oz* the other day, I wondered: In Munchkinland, where does the Red Brick Road go?

—Ken A. Grant, South Bend, Indiana

A. The AM has dealt with this before, but now has a more authoritative answer. According to Oz expert James R. Whitcomb, "In L. Frank Baum's books, the Land of Oz was divided into four quadrants and each was designated a particular color: Quadling Country is red. Glinda the Good was the ruler of the Quadlings. As her bubble floats away from Munchkinland in the film, it appears to be following the Red Brick Road. Therefore, the road most likely leads back to her homeland, Quadling Country."

Y Tu Mama Tambien

Q. In *Y Tu Mama Tambien*, I can't figure out if the beach "Heaven's Mouth" really exists. The boatman, Chuy, mentions it, but I can't tell if this is an amazing coincidence, or if Tenoch sneakily asked him to label the beach as such for Luisa's benefit. I have seen the movie twice now and still am not sure.

—Andrea Pollack, Houston, Texas

A. Elisabeth English of IFC Films replies:

809

"The actual beach is on the west coast of Mexico and is located in Huatulco, Oaxaca."

Zoolander

Q. Shortly after seeing the mildly amusing *Zoolander*, I read your review. You wrote that it was in bad taste for the filmmakers to use Malaysia's prime minister as the target of the assassination attempt by the villains of the film. Three years ago, I read your review of *Wag the Dog*, which got your highest rating. In *Wag the Dog*, the U.S. government fabricates and leaks false information about an Albanian conflict, going as far as to accuse Albanians of smuggling bombs into the United States from Canada. Might not Albanian-Americans feel uncomfortable seeing a film spreading lies about their native country? Yet nowhere in your review do you mention that this film might be offensive to Albanians. Am I missing something? P.S.: No, I'm not Albanian.
—Ryan Lindahl, Toledo, Ohio

A. The day I begin believing that every review must be consistent with every other review is the day I go mad. I would justify this inconsistency, however, by arguing that *Wag the Dog*, a pointed and intelligent political satire written by David Mamet, criticized the kind of behavior that Ben Stiller's *Zoolander* uses for unnecessary and gratuitous throwaway comedy. I do not, by the way, plan to filter every movie for the next six months through the atrocity of the terrorist attack.

Q. I was disgusted to read your review of *Zoolander*, not because you hated it, but why you hated it. The events that have occurred in our nation are very tragic but should not be connected to the way you review a movie. The movie's job was to take people's minds off these events because it had nothing to do with them. Your review will be confusing in later years and not fair to this movie. It's the job of a critic to view movies without prejudice and not let their personal lives interfere.
—John Norton, Indianapolis, Indiana

A. You lost me right there at the end. My personal life does interfere, because it's *me* in the theater, just as it's you who allowed your personal life to interfere while you were reading my review. We are people who live in history, and cannot always leave it at the theater door. The movie would have been more effective in taking my mind off the tragic events if it hadn't made a joke out of the assassination of the prime minister of one of our Muslim allies. Now there is a big stink in Malaysia—completely unnecessary, because Stiller could have made up a fictitious country.

Ebert's Little Movie Glossary

These are contributions to my glossary project. Hundreds of entries were collected in *Ebert's Bigger Little Movie Glossary*, published in 1999. Contributions are always welcome.

* * *

Always Use the Valet Parkers. Anyone who walks through a parking garage will be physically assaulted.

—Stewart Glickman, Manhasset, New York

Big Wheel Keeps on Turnin'. Used in fantasy and medieval movies to portray bondage and torment, the Slave Wheel is simply a big wheel sticking out of the ground that prisoners are forced to push around and around. They never show what it actually does.

—Duff Mason, Kirkland, Washington

Busy Day on the Lot Rule. Whenever a Hollywood studio back lot is shown, the streets are clogged with extras in period uniforms. In the new movie *Showtime,* one shot shows soldiers in Jeeps, Little Bo Peep, and giant heads from Easter Island.

—R.E.

Cemetery Restraining Order. When a central character goes to a funeral at a cemetery, he or she must stay at least fifty feet away from the grave, preferably half-hidden behind a tree or another headstone.

—Zach Ralston, Los Angeles, California

Contents May Have Shifted During Handling Rule. Any time the hero hands somebody a bag or box containing the Maguffin, if the recipient fails to look inside the bag/box, the hero has pulled the old switcheroo and handed the other guy a bag/box full of lead weights/old newspapers/worthless junk, etc. See *The Score.*

—Mark Oristano, Dallas, Texas

Disbelief of Suspension. Almost every suspension bridge in the history of the movies has failed while the heroes were attempting to cross

it. Especially true when dinosaurs, raging rapids, or lava flows are involved.

—Paul West, Seattle, Washington

Extrasensory Singing. People who think they are singing alone can always sense it if someone is watching them.

—R.E.

The Geek Effect. The establishment authorities cannot crack a major investigation without the assistance of a group of antisocial nerds who specialize in and obsess over some archaic field of study.

—Doug Chase, Aurora, Illinois

The Healing Bathtub. When the female protagonist faces danger, a romantic crisis, an obstacle, or depression, she inevitably takes a bath, surrounded by countless candles. This can be seen in everything from *Panic Room* to *Don't Tell Mom the Babysitter's Dead.*

—Zach Rooker, Roachdale, Indiana

Just Here for the Ambience. Characters order full meals, talk for a few minutes, and then leave without eating any of the food or paying the bill.

—Gilbert Smith, Thoreau, New Mexico

Let Your Fingers Do the Ripping. No movie character in need of a telephone number ever carries a notepad or pen and must, therefore, always rip a page out of the phone book. Inexplicable Corollary: No movie character in search of a telephone number ever encounters a phone book from which the necessary page has been ripped out.

—Carol Pearsall, Seattle, Washington

Line Dead? Kill the Phone! A character realizes his phone has just gone dead and thinks, "I'll try pounding the receiver buttons repeatedly, while also shouting *Hello . . . ? Hello . . . ?* That should fix it."

—Scott Shepeck, Escanaba, Michigan

Listen! It Still Works! In postapocalyptic movies, the first working device from the past that people find always seems to be a music box. See *Waterworld,* where when the good guys finally make it to land and find the old hut with stuff inside, the little girl opens up—a music box.

—Scot Murphy, Highland Park, Illinois

Literati's Law of Averages. When any character in a movie is reading a book, the page he is reading always will be in the exact center of the book.

—Dennis Laycock, Columbus, Ohio

Most Undernoticed Overused Movie Dialogue. "You just don't get it, do ya?"

—Darrell Bowering, St. John's, Newfoundland

Mutations for the Entire Family. A movie mutant action hero will only mutate in ways that won't interfere with a PG-13 film rating. Example: Spider-Man shoots web out of his wrists. Real spiders shoot web out of their butts.

—David Garcia, Staten Island, New York

Mute Foreigners Rule. No one ever talks in foreign-language trailers, as if the marketing guys were hoping to hide the fact that the movie is actually spoken in a language other than English.

—Patricio López, Monterrey, Mexico

Nice Guy Bob. When a woman must choose between two men in a film, one of them will be dangerous, handsome, and bad for her. The other will be Nice Guy Bob. She always goes for the dangerous guy—instead of "settling" for NGB. The name comes from *You Can Count On Me,* where Laura Linney must pick between her shifty boss and N. G. Bob.

—Mike Phillips, Chicago, Illinois

The Other Weather Channel. Movies set at the present time continue to show characters asleep in front of TV sets with snow on the screen, although all channels now broadcast twenty-four hours a day.

—R.E.

Outright Accuser Riposte. When a tough character in a movie is asked, "Are you implying . . ." he always shoots back, "I'm not implying anything. I'm telling you!"

—Christopher W. Bruce, Salem, Massachusetts

Pocket Full of Rye. Movie alcoholics carry tiny pocket flasks holding only enough booze to make them crave more. Though the flask doesn't contain enough to satisfy himself, he always offers an offended sober person a drink.

—Don Howard, San Jose, California

San Francisco Chase Rule. In all chases in San Francisco, right before the hero's car reaches an intersection, two cars going in opposite directions will cross, showing how close he is to colliding. Also, at some point the car will be airborne.

—Gerardo Valero, Mexico City, Mexico

Self-Repairing Movie Cars. Heroes wreck cars that are magically restored in the next scene. In *Training Day,* Denzel Washington smashes up a bunch of parked cars, only to drive down the L.A. streets a couple of scenes later with nary a scratch on his own. Either Denzel has the fastest insurance adjuster and repairman on earth, he has a fleet of identical bad-guy cars, or his car is, in fact, self-repairing.

—Jeremy Roberts, New York, New York

This Door Could Have Been You. The villain swings at the hero and invariably misses, destroying a wall/door/column in the process. See *Matrix,* the *Jaws* character in James Bond movies, etc.

—Eduardo Vanegas, Mexico City, Mexico

Witness Protection Exception. Whenever a law enforcement officer tells a potential witness, "We can promise you protection," the witness replies, "Not from him, you can't."

—Gerardo Valero, Mexico City, Mexico

Reviews Appearing in All Editions of the *Movie Home Companion, Video Companion,* or *Movie Yearbook*

A

About a Boy, 2002, PG-13, ★★★½	2003
About Last Night . . . , 1986, R, ★★★★	1998
Above the Law, 1988, R, ★★★	1995
Above the Rim, 1994, R, ★★★	1995
Absence of Malice, 1981, PG, ★★★	1998
Absolute Power, 1997, R, ★★★½	1998
Accidental Tourist, The,	
1988, PG, ★★★★	1998
Accompanist, The, 1994, PG, ★★★½	1998
Accused, The, 1988, R, ★★★	1998
Ace Ventura: Pet Detective,	
1994, PG-13, ★	1998
Ace Ventura: When Nature Calls,	
1995, PG-13, ★½	1998
Addams Family, The, 1991, PG-13, ★★	1997
Addams Family Values,	
1993, PG-13, ★★★	1998
Addicted to Love, 1997, R, ★★	1998
Addiction, The, 1995, NR, ★★½	1997
Adjuster, The, 1992, R, ★★★	1998
Adventures of Baron Munchausen, The,	
1989, PG, ★★★	1998
Adventures of Ford Fairlane, The,	
1990, R, ★	1992
Adventures of Huck Finn, The,	
1993, PG, ★★★	1998
Adventures of Priscilla, Queen of the	
Desert, The, 1994, R, ★★½	1998
Adventures of Rocky & Bullwinkle, The,	
2000, PG, ★★★	2003
Adventures of Sebastian Cole, The,	
1999, R, ★★★	2002
Affair of Love, An, 2000, R, ★★★½	2003
Affair of the Necklace, The, 2001, R, ★★	2003
Affliction, 1999, R, ★★★★	2002
Afterglow, 1998, R, ★★★	2001
After Hours, 1985, R, ★★★★	1998
After Life, 1999, NR, ★★★★	2002
After the Rehearsal, 1984, R, ★★★★	1998
Against All Odds, 1984, R, ★★★	1998
Age of Innocence, The, 1993, PG, ★★★★	1998
Agnes Browne, 2000, R, ★★½	2003
Agnes of God, 1985, PG-13, ★	1989

A.I. Artificial Intelligence,	
2001, PG-13, ★★★	2003
Aimee & Jaguar, 2000, NR, ★★★	2003
Air Bud, 1997, PG, ★★★	2000
Air Bud 2: Golden Receiver, 1998, G, ★½	2001
Air Force One, 1997, R, ★★½	2000
Airplane!, 1980, PG, ★★★	1998
Airport, 1970, G, ★★	1996
Airport 1975, 1974, PG, ★★½	1996
Aladdin, 1992, G, ★★★	1998
Alan Smithee Film Burn Hollywood	
Burn, An, 1998, R, no stars	2001
Alaska, 1996, PG, ★★★	1999
Albino Alligator, 1997, R, ★★	2000
Alex in Wonderland, 1971, R, ★★★★	1998
Ali, 2001, R, ★★	2003
Alice, 1990, PG-13, ★★★	1998
Alice Doesn't Live Here Anymore,	
1974, PG, ★★★★	1998
Alien3, 1992, R, ★½	1997
Alien Nation, 1988, R, ★★	1994
Alien Resurrection, 1997, R, ★½	2000
Aliens, 1986, R, ★★★½	1998
Alive, 1993, R, ★★½	1997
All About My Mother, 1999, R, ★★★½	2002
All Dogs Go to Heaven, 1989, G, ★★★	1998
Allegro Non Tropo, 1977, NR, ★★★½	1995
Alligator, 1980, R, ★	1990
All Night Long, 1981, R, ★★	1986
All of Me, 1984, PG, ★★★½	1998
All the Little Animals, 1999, R, ★★★	2002
. . . All the Marbles, 1981, R, ★★	1986
All the President's Men,	
1976, PG, ★★★½	1998
All the Pretty Horses,	
2000, PG-13, ★★★½	2003
All the Right Moves, 1983, R, ★★★	1998
All the Vermeers in New York,	
1992, NR, ★★★	1998
Almost an Angel, 1990, PG, ★★½	1995
Almost Famous, 2000, R, ★★★★	2003
Along Came a Spider, 2001, R, ★★	2003
Altered States, 1980, R, ★★★½	1998

Note: The right-hand column is the year in which the review last appeared in *Roger Ebert's Movie Home Companion, Roger Ebert's Video Companion,* or *Roger Ebert's Movie Yearbook.*

815

Before the Rain, 1995, NR, ★★★★ — 1998
Behind Enemy Lines, 2001, PG-13, ★¹/₂ — 2003
Behind the Sun, 2002, PG-13, ★★ — 2003
Being John Malkovich, 1999, R, ★★★★ — 2002
Being There, 1980, PG, ★★★★ — 1998
Believer, The, 2002, R, ★★★ — 2003
Belle de Jour, 1967, R, ★★★★ — 1997
Belle Epoque, 1993, NR, ★★★¹/₂ — 1998
Beloved, 1998, R, ★★★¹/₂ — 2001
Benny and Joon, 1993, PG, ★★★ — 1998
Bent, 1997, NC-17, ★★ — 2000
Besieged, 1999, R, ★ — 2002
Best Boy, 1980, NR, ★★★★ — 1998
Best in Show, 2000, PG-13, ★★★¹/₂ — 2003
Best Laid Plans, 1999, R, ★ — 2002
Best Little Whorehouse in Texas, The, 1982, R, ★★ — 1991
Betrayal, 1983, R, ★★★★ — 1998
Betrayed, 1988, R, ★★ — 1993
Betsy's Wedding, 1990, R, ★★ — 1993
Beverly Hillbillies, The, 1993, PG, ¹/₂★ — 1995
Beverly Hills Cop, 1984, R, ★★¹/₂ — 1998
Beverly Hills Cop II, 1987, R, ★ — 1995
Beyond, The, 1998, NR, ¹/₂★ — 2001
Beyond Rangoon, 1995, R, ★★★ — 1998
Beyond Silence, 1998, PG-13, ★★★¹/₂ — 2001
Beyond the Limit, 1983, R, ★★¹/₂ — 1989
Beyond the Mat, 2000, R, ★★★ — 2003
Beyond Therapy, 1987, R, ★ — 1988
Beyond the Valley of the Dolls, 1970, NC-17, Stars N/A — 1997
Bicentennial Man, 1999, PG, ★★ — 2002
Big, 1988, PG, ★★★ — 1998
Big Bad Love, 2002, R, ★★ — 2003
Big Bang, The, 1990, R, ★★★ — 1995
Big Brawl, The, 1980, R, ★¹/₂ — 1986
Big Business, 1988, PG, ★★ — 1993
Big Chill, The, 1983, R, ★★¹/₂ — 1998
Big Daddy, 1999, PG-13, ★¹/₂ — 2002
Big Easy, The, 1987, R, ★★★★ — 1998
Big Eden, 2001, PG-13, ★★ — 2003
Big Fat Liar, 2002, PG, ★★★ — 2003
Big Foot, 1971, PG, ¹/₂★ — 1990
Big Hit, The, 1998, R, ★ — 2001
Big Kahuna, The, 2000, R, ★★★¹/₂ — 2003
Big Lebowski, The, 1998, R, ★★★ — 2001
Big Momma's House, 2000, PG-13, ★★ — 2003
Big One, The, 1998, PG-13, ★★★ — 2001
Big Red One, The, 1980, PG, ★★★ — 1996
Big Squeeze, The, 1996, R, ★ — 1999
Big Tease, The, 2000, R, ★★ — 2003

Big Town, The, 1987, R, ★★★¹/₂ — 1998
Big Trouble, 2002, PG-13, ★★¹/₂ — 2003
Bill & Ted's Bogus Journey, 1991, PG-13, ★★★ — 1998
Billy Bathgate, 1991, R, ★★ — 1993
Billy Elliot, 2000, R, ★★★ — 2003
Billy Jack, 1971, PG, ★★¹/₂ — 1993
Billy's Hollywood Screen Kiss, 1998, R, ★★ — 2001
Bird, 1988, R, ★★★¹/₂ — 1998
Birdcage, The, 1995, R, ★★★ — 1999
Bird on a Wire, 1990, PG-13, ★★¹/₂ — 1993
Birdy, 1985, R, ★★★★ — 1998
Birthday Girl, 2002, R, ★★ — 2003
Bitter Moon, 1994, R, ★★★ — 1998
Black and White, 2000, R, ★★★ — 2003
Black Cauldron, The, 1985, PG, ★★★¹/₂ — 1987
Black Hawk Down, 2002, R, ★★★★ — 2003
Black Marble, The, 1980, PG, ★★★¹/₂ — 1998
Black Rain (Japan), 1990, NR, ★★★¹/₂ — 1998
Black Rain (Michael Douglas), 1989, R, ★★ — 1993
Black Robe, 1991, R, ★★¹/₂ — 1994
Black Stallion, The, 1980, G, ★★★★ — 1998
Black Stallion Returns, The, 1983, PG, ★★¹/₂ — 1986
Black Widow, 1987, R, ★★¹/₂ — 1991
Blade, 1998, R, ★★★ — 2001
Blade II, 2002, R, ★★★¹/₂ — 2003
Blade Runner, 1982, R, ★★★ — 1998
Blade Runner: The Director's Cut, 1992, R, ★★★ — 1997
Blair Witch Project, The, 1999, R, ★★★★ — 2002
Blame It on Rio, 1984, R, ★ — 1987
Blast From the Past, 1999, PG-13, ★★★ — 2002
Blaze, 1989, R, ★★★¹/₂ — 1998
Blind Date, 1987, PG-13, ★★¹/₂ — 1988
Blink, 1994, R, ★★★¹/₂ — 1998
Bliss, 1997, R, ★★★¹/₂ — 1998
Blood and Wine, 1997, R, ★★★¹/₂ — 1998
Blood Guts Bullets and Octane, 1999, NR, ★★¹/₂ — 2002
Blood Simple, 1985, R, ★★★★ — 1998
Blood Simple: 2000 Director's Cut, 2000, R, ★★★★ — 2003
Blow, 2001, R, ★★¹/₂ — 2003
Blown Away, 1994, R, ★★ — 1996
Blow Out, 1981, R, ★★★★ — 1998
Blue, 1994, R, ★★★¹/₂ — 1998
Blue Angel, The, 2001, NR, ★★★¹/₂ — 2003

Blue Chips, 1994, PG-13, ★★★ 1998
Blue Collar, 1978, R, ★★★★ 1998
Blue Kite, The, 1994, NR, ★★★★ 1998
Blue Lagoon, The, 1980, R, ½★ 1991
Blues Brothers, The, 1980, R, ★★★ 1998
Blues Brothers 2000, 1998, PG-13, ★★ 2001
Blue Sky, 1994, PG-13, ★★★ 1998
Blue Steel, 1990, R, ★★★ 1998
Blue Streak, 1999, PG-13, ★★★ 2002
Blue Velvet, 1986, R, ★ 1998
Blume in Love, 1973, R, ★★★★ 1998
Blush, 1996, NR, ★★½ 1999
Bob Roberts, 1992, R, ★★★ 1998
Bodies, Rest and Motion, 1993, R, ★★ 1994
Body Double, 1984, R, ★★★½ 1998
Bodyguard, The, 1992, R, ★★★ 1998
Body of Evidence, 1993, R, ½★ 1994
Body Shots, 1999, R, ★★ 2002
Body Snatchers, 1994, R, ★★★★ 1998
Bogus, 1996, PG, ★★★ 1999
Boiler Room, 2000, R, ★★★½ 2003
Bolero, 1984, NR, ½★ 1993
Bone Collector, The, 1999, R, ★★ 2002
Bonfire of the Vanities, The,
 1990, R, ★★½ 1998
Boogie Nights, 1997, R, ★★★★ 2000
Book of Shadows: Blair Witch 2,
 2000, R, ★★ 2003
Boomerang, 1992, R, ★★★ 1998
Boost, The, 1988, R, ★★★½ 1998
Bootmen, 2000, R, ★½ 2003
Booty Call, 1997, R, ★★★ 1998
Bopha!, 1993, PG-13, ★★★½ 1998
Born on the Fourth of July,
 1989, R, ★★★★ 1998
Born Yesterday, 1993, PG, ★ 1994
Borrowers, The, 1998, PG, ★★★ 2001
Borstal Boy, 2002, NR, ★★ 2003
Bostonians, The, 1984, PG, ★★★ 1998
Bounce, 2000, PG-13, ★★★ 2003
Bound, 1996, R, ★★★★ 1999
Bound by Honor, 1993, R, ★★ 1994
Bounty, The, 1984, PG, ★★★★ 1998
Bourne Identity, The, 2002, PG-13, ★★★ 2003
Bowfinger, 1999, PG-13, ★★★½ 2002
Boxer, The, 1998, R, ★★★ 2001
Box of Moonlight, 1997, R, ★★★ 2000
Boyfriends and Girlfriends,
 1988, PG, ★★★ 1998
Boys, 1996, PG-13, ★★ 1999
Boys and Girls, 2000, PG-13, ★★ 2003

Boys Don't Cry, 1999, R, ★★★★ 2002
Boys on the Side, 1995, R, ★★★½ 1998
Boy Who Could Fly, The,
 1986, PG, ★★★ 1996
Boyz N the Hood, 1991, R, ★★★★ 1998
Brady Bunch Movie, The,
 1995, PG-13, ★★ 1997
Brainscan, 1994, R, ★★ 1995
Brainstorm, 1983, PG, ★★ 1986
Bram Stoker's Dracula, 1992, R, ★★★ 1998
Brandon Teena Story, The,
 1999, NR, ★★★ 2002
Brassed Off 1997, R, ★★★ 1998
Braveheart, 1995, R, ★★★½ 1998
Brazil, 1985, R, ★★ 1998
Bread and Roses, 2001, R, ★★★½ 2003
Bread and Tulips, 2001, PG-13, ★★★½ 2003
Breakdown, 1997, R, ★★★ 1998
Breakfast Club, The, 1985, R, ★★★ 1998
Breaking Away, 1979, PG, ★★★★ 1998
Breaking In, 1989, R, ★★★ 1995
Breaking the Waves, 1996, R, ★★★★ 1999
Breakin' 2-Electric Boogaloo,
 1984, PG, ★★★ 1995
Breathless, 1983, R, ★★½ 1989
Brewster's Millions, 1985, PG, ★ 1988
Bride of the Wind, 2001, R, ½★ 2003
Bridges of Madison County, The,
 1995, PG-13, ★★★½ 1998
Bridget Jones's Diary, 2001, R, ★★★½ 2003
Brief History of Time, A,
 1992, NR, ★★½ 1994
Bright Angel, 1991, R, ★★★½ 1998
Bright Lights, Big City, 1988, R, ★★★½ 1998
Brighton Beach Memoirs,
 1986, PG-13, ★★ 1989
Bringing Out the Dead,
 1999, R, ★★★★ 2002
Bring It On, 2000, PG-13, ★★ 2003
Bring Me the Head of Alfredo Garcia,
 1974, R, ★★★★ 1998
Broadcast News, 1987, R, ★★★★ 1998
Broadway Danny Rose,
 1984, PG, ★★★½ 1998
Brokedown Palace, 1999, PG-13, ★★★ 2002
Broken Arrow, 1996, R, ★★ 1999
Broken English, 1997, NR, ★★★ 2000
Broken Hearts Club, The,
 2000, R, ★★★ 2003
Broken Vessels, 1999, R, ★★★ 2002
Bronx Tale, A, 1993, R, ★★★★ 1998

Brother, 2001, R, ★★ | 2003
Brother from Another Planet, The,
 1984, PG, ★★★½ | 1998
Brotherhood of the Wolf, 2002, R, ★★★ | 2003
Brothers, The, 2001, R, ★★★ | 2003
Brother's Keeper, 1993, NR, ★★★★ | 1998
Brother's Kiss, A, 1997, R, ★★★ | 2000
Brothers McMullen, The, 1995, R, ★★★ | 1998
Brubaker, 1980, R, ★★½ | 1991
Buddy, 1997, PG, ★★ | 2000
Buddy Holly Story, The,
 1978, PG, ★★★½ | 1998
Buena Vista Social Club,
 1999, NR, ★★ | 2002
Buffalo '66, 1998, NR, ★★★ | 2001
Bug's Life, A, 1998, G, ★★★½ | 2001
Bugsy, 1991, R, ★★★★ | 1998
Bugsy Malone, 1976, G, ★★★½ | 1998
Bull Durham, 1988, R, ★★★½ | 1998
Bulletproof, 1996, R, ★★ | 1999
Bulletproof Heart, 1995, R, ★★★ | 1998
Bullets Over Broadway, 1994, R, ★★★½ | 1998
Bully, 2001, NR, ★★★★ | 2003
Bulworth, 1998, R, ★★★½ | 2001
'Burbs, The, 1989, PG, ★★ | 1992
Burden of Dreams, 1982, NR, ★★★★ | 1998
Burglar, 1987, R, ★ | 1989
Business of Strangers, The,
 2001, R, ★★★ | 2003
Buster, 1988, R, ★★★ | 1998
Buster and Billie, 1974, R, ★★★ | 1995
Butcher Boy, The, 1998, R, ★★½ | 2001
Butcher's Wife, The, 1991, PG-13, ★★½ | 1997
But I'm a Cheerleader, 2000, R, ★★★ | 2003
Butley, 1974, NR, ★★★★ | 1987
Butterfly, 2000, R, ★★★ | 2003
Butterfly Kiss, 1996, R, ★★ | 1999
Bye Bye Brazil, 1979, NR, ★★★★ | 1996
Bye Bye, Love, 1995, PG-13, ★★ | 1996

C

Cabaret, 1972, PG, ★★★½ | 1998
Cabaret Balkan, 1999, NR, ★★★★ | 2002
Cable Guy, The, 1996, PG-13, ★★ | 1999
Cactus, 1987, NR, ★★★ | 1998
Caddyshack, 1980, R, ★★½ | 1998
Cadillac Man, 1990, R, ★★ | 1994
California Split, 1974, R, ★★★★ | 1998
Caligula, 1980, NR, no stars | 1990
Camille Claudel, 1989, R, ★★★½ | 1998
Candyman, 1992, R, ★★★ | 1998

Candyman: Farewell to the Flesh,
 1995, R, ★★ | 1996
Cannery Row, 1982, PG, ★★½ | 1987
Cannonball Run, The, 1981, PG, ½★ | 1991
Cannonball Run II, 1984, PG, ½★ | 1988
Can't Hardly Wait, 1998, PG-13, ★½ | 2001
Cape Fear, 1991, R, ★★★ | 1998
Captain Corelli's Mandolin, 2001, R, ★★ | 2003
Career Girls, 1997, R, ★★★ | 2000
Carlito's Way, 1993, R, ★★★½ | 1998
Carmen (dance), 1983, R, ★★★★ | 1995
Carmen, 1984, PG, ★★★★ | 1998
Carnival of Souls, 1962, NR, ★★★ | 1997
Carrie, 1976, R, ★★★½ | 1998
Carried Away, 1996, R, ★★★ | 1999
Carrington, 1995, R, ★★★★ | 1998
Car Wash, 1976, PG, ★★★½ | 1995
Casablanca, 1942, NR, ★★★★ | 1997
Casino, 1995, R, ★★★★ | 1998
Casper, 1995, PG, ★★★ | 1998
Cast Away, 2000, PG-13, ★★★ | 2003
Castle, The, 1999, R, ★★★ | 2002
Casualties of War, 1989, R, ★★★ | 1998
Catfish in Black Bean Sauce,
 2000, PG-13, ★½ | 2003
Cat People, 1982, R, ★★★½ | 1998
Cats and Dogs, 2001, PG, ★★★ | 2003
Cats Don't Dance, 1997, G, ★★★ | 2000
Cat's Eye, 1985, PG-13, ★★★ | 1986
Cat's Meow, The, 2002, PG-13, ★★★ | 2003
Caught, 1996, R, ★★★ | 1999
Caught Up, 1998, R, ★★ | 2001
Caveman, 1981, PG, ★½ | 1986
Caveman's Valentine, The,
 2001, R, ★★★ | 2003
Cecil B. Demented, 2000, R, ★½ | 2003
Celebration, The, 1998, R, ★★★ | 2001
Celebrity, 1998, R, ★★½ | 2001
Celestial Clockwork, 1996, NR, ★★★ | 1999
Cell, The, 2000, R, ★★★★ | 2003
Celluloid Closet, The, 1995, NR, ★★★½ | 1999
Celtic Pride, 1996, PG-13, ★★ | 1999
Cement Garden, The, 1994, NR, ★★★ | 1998
Cemetery Club, The, 1992, PG-13, ★★★ | 1998
Center of the World, The,
 2001, NR, ★★★½ | 2003
Center Stage, 2000, PG-13, ★★★ | 2003
Central Station, 1998, R, ★★★ | 2001
Chain Reaction, 1996, PG-13, ★★½ | 1999
Chalk, 2000, NR, ★★★ | 2003
Chamber, The, 1996, R, ★★ | 1999

Chances Are, 1989, PG, ★★★½ — 1998
Changing Lanes, 2002, R, ★★★★ — 2003
Chaplin, 1993, PG-13, ★★ — 1994
Chapter Two, 1980, PG, ★★ — 1992
Character, 1998, R, ★★★½ — 2001
Chariots of Fire, 1981, PG, ★★★★ — 1998
Charlie's Angels, 2000, PG-13, ½★ — 2003
Charlotte Gray, 2002, PG-13, ★★ — 2003
Chase, The, 1994, PG-13, ★★½ — 1995
Chasing Amy, 1997, R, ★★★½ — 1998
Chattahoochee, 1990, R, ★★½ — 1992
Chef in Love, A, 1997, PG-13, ★★★ — 2000
Chelsea Walls, 2002, R, ★★★ — 2003
Cherish, 2002, R, ★★★ — 2003
Chicago Cab, 1998, R, ★★★ — 2001
Chicken Run, 2000, G, ★★★½ — 2003
Children of Heaven, 1999, PG, ★★★★ — 2002
Children of the Revolution, 1997, R, ★★ — 2000
Child's Play, 1988, R, ★★★ — 1998
Chill Factor, 1999, R, ★★ — 2002
China Moon, 1994, R, ★★★½ — 1998
China Syndrome, The, 1979, PG, ★★★★ — 1998
Chinatown, 1974, R, ★★★★ — 1998
Chocolat, 1989, PG-13, ★★★★ — 1998
Chocolat, 2000, PG-13, ★★★ — 2003
Choose Me, 1984, R, ★★★½ — 1998
Chopper, 2001, NR, ★★★ — 2003
Chorus Line, A, 1985, PG-13, ★★★½ — 1998
Christiane F., 1981, R, ★★★½ — 1998
Christine, 1983, R, ★★★ — 1998
Christmas Story, A, 1983, PG, ★★★ — 1998
Christopher Columbus: The Discovery, 1992, PG-13, ★ — 1994
Chuck & Buck, 2000, R, ★★★ — 2003
Chuck Berry Hail! Hail! Rock 'n' Roll, 1987, PG, ★★★★ — 1998
Chungking Express, 1996, PG-13, ★★★ — 1999
Cider House Rules, The, 1999, PG-13, ★★ — 2002
Cinderella, 1950, G, ★★★ — 1997
Cinema Paradiso, 1989, NR, ★★★½ — 1998
Cinema Paradiso: The New Version, 2002, R, ★★★½ — 2003
Circle, The, 2001, NR, ★★★½ — 2003
Circle of Friends, 1995, PG-13, ★★★½ — 1998
Citizen Kane, 1941, NR, ★★★★ — 1998
Citizen Ruth, 1997, R, ★★★ — 2000
City Hall, 1996, R, ★★½ — 1999
City Heat, 1984, PG, ½★ — 1991
City of Angels, 1998, PG-13, ★★★ — 2001
City of Hope, 1991, R, ★★★★ — 1998

City of Industry, 1997, R, ★½ — 2000
City of Joy, 1992, PG-13, ★★★ — 1995
City of Lost Children, 1995, R, ★★★ — 1998
City of Women, 1981, R, ★★½ — 1991
City Slickers, 1991, PG-13, ★★★½ — 1998
City Slickers II: The Legend of Curly's Gold, 1994, PG-13, ★★ — 1995
Civil Action, A, 1999, PG-13, ★★★½ — 2002
Claim, The, 2001, R, ★★★½ — 2003
Claire Dolan, 2000, NR, ★★★½ — 2003
Claire's Knee, 1971, PG, ★★★★ — 1998
Clan of the Cave Bear, 1985, R, ★½ — 1989
Clash of the Titans, 1981, PG, ★★★½ — 1998
Class Action, 1991, R, ★★★ — 1995
Class of 1984, The, 1982, R, ★★★½ — 1995
Class of 1999, 1990, R, ★★ — 1992
Clay Pigeons, 1998, R, ★★½ — 2001
Clean and Sober, 1988, R, ★★★½ — 1998
Clean, Shaven, 1995, NR, ★★★½ — 1998
Clerks, 1994, R, ★★★ — 1998
Client, The, 1994, PG-13, ★★½ — 1998
Cliffhanger, 1993, R, ★★★ — 1998
Clifford, 1994, PG, ½★ — 1995
Clockers, 1995, R, ★★★½ — 1998
Clockstoppers, 2002, PG, ★★½ — 2003
Clockwatchers, 1998, PG-13, ★★★½ — 2001
Close Encounters of the Third Kind: The Special Edition, 1980, PG, ★★★★ — 1998
Closer You Get, The, 2000, PG-13, ★★ — 2003
Closet, The, 2001, R, ★★½ — 2003
Close to Eden, 1992, NR, ★★★ — 1998
Clueless, 1995, PG-13, ★★★½ — 1998
Coal Miner's Daughter, 1980, PG, ★★★ — 1998
Cobb, 1994, R, ★★ — 1996
Coca-Cola Kid, The, 1985, NR, ★★★ — 1987
Cocktail, 1988, R, ★★ — 1993
Cocoon, 1985, PG-13, ★★★ — 1998
Cocoon: The Return, 1988, PG, ★★½ — 1997
Code of Silence, 1985, R, ★★★½ — 1998
Cold Comfort Farm, 1995, PG, ★★★ — 1999
Cold Fever, 1996, NR, ★★★ — 1999
Collateral Damage, 2002, R, ★★★ — 2003
Color of Money, The, 1986, R, ★★½ — 1998
Color of Night, 1994, R, ★½ — 1996
Color of Paradise, The, 2000, PG, ★★★½ — 2003
Color Purple, The, 1985, PG-13, ★★★★ — 1998
Colors, 1988, R, ★★★ — 1998
Coma, 1978, PG, ★★★ — 1995
Come Back to the 5 & Dime, Jimmy Dean, Jimmy Dean, 1982, PG, ★★★ — 1998

Cyborg, 1989, R, ★ — 1992
Cyrano de Bergerac, 1990, PG, ★★★¹/₂ — 1998

D

Dad, 1989, PG, ★★ — 1993
Daddy Nostalgia, 1991, PG, ★★★¹/₂ — 1998
Dadetown, 1996, NR, ★★ — 1998
Damage, 1993, R, ★★★★ — 1998
Dancer in the Dark, 2000, R, ★★★¹/₂ — 2003
Dances With Wolves,
 1990, PG-13, ★★★★ — 1998
Dance With a Stranger, 1985, R, ★★★★ — 1998
Dance With Me, 1998, PG, ★★★ — 2001
Dancing at Lughnasa, 1998, PG, ★★¹/₂ — 2001
Dangerous Beauty, 1998, R, ★★★¹/₂ — 2001
Dangerous Ground, 1997, R, ★★ — 1998
Dangerous Liaisons, 1988, R, ★★★ — 1998
Dangerous Lives of Altar Boys, The,
 2002, R, ★★¹/₂ — 2003
Dangerous Minds, 1995, R, ★¹/₂ — 1997
Daniel, 1983, R, ★★¹/₂ — 1987
Dante's Peak, 1997, PG-13, ★★¹/₂ — 1998
Dark Blue World, 2002, R, ★★ — 2003
Dark City, 1998, R, ★★★★ — 2001
Dark Crystal, The, 1982, PG, ★★¹/₂ — 1991
Dark Days, 2000, NR, ★★★¹/₂ — 2003
Dark Eyes, 1987, NR, ★★★¹/₂ — 1998
Dark Half, The, 1993, R, ★★ — 1994
Dark Obsession, 1991, NC-17, ★★★ — 1998
D.A.R.Y.L., 1985, PG, ★★★ — 1998
Date with an Angel, 1987, PG, ★ — 1989
Daughters of the Dust, 1992, NR, ★★★ — 1998
Dave, 1993, PG-13, ★★★¹/₂ — 1998
Dawn of the Dead, 1979, R, ★★★★ — 1998
Day After Trinity, The,
 1980, NR, ★★★★ — 1998
Day for Night, 1974, PG, ★★★★ — 1998
Day I Became a Woman, The,
 2001, NR, ★★★¹/₂ — 2003
Daylight, 1996, PG-13, ★★ — 1999
Day of the Dead, 1985, R, ★¹/₂ — 1992
Day of the Jackal, The, 1973, PG, ★★★★ — 1998
Days of Heaven, 1978, PG, ★★★★ — 1998
Days of Thunder, 1990, PG-13, ★★★ — 1998
Daytrippers, The, 1997, NR, ★★ — 2000
Dazed and Confused, 1993, R, ★★★ — 1998
D.C. Cab, 1983, R, ★★ — 1986
Dead, The, 1987, PG, ★★★ — 1998
Dead Again, 1991, R, ★★★★ — 1998
Dead Calm, 1989, R, ★★★ — 1998
Dead Man Walking, 1995, R, ★★★★ — 1999
Dead of Winter, 1987, PG-13, ★★¹/₂ — 1993

Dead Poets Society, 1989, PG, ★★ — 1998
Dead Pool, The, 1988, R, ★★★¹/₂ — 1998
Dead Presidents, 1995, R, ★★¹/₂ — 1998
Dead Ringers, 1988, R, ★★¹/₂ — 1993
Dead Zone, The, 1983, R, ★★★¹/₂ — 1998
Dear America: Letters Home from
 Vietnam, 1988, PG-13, ★★★★ — 1998
Dear God, 1996, PG, ★ — 1999
Death and the Maiden, 1995, R, ★★★ — 1998
Death in Venice, 1971, PG, ★★¹/₂ — 1994
Death to Smoochy, 2002, R, ¹/₂★ — 2003
Deathtrap, 1982, R, ★★★ — 1998
Death Wish, 1974, R, ★★★ — 1998
Death Wish 3, 1985, R, ★ — 1993
Death Wish II, 1982, R, no stars — 1993
Debut, The, 2002, NR, ★★★ — 2003
Deceived, 1991, PG-13, ★★ — 1993
Deceiver, 1998, R, ★★ — 2001
Deconstructing Harry, 1997, R, ★★★¹/₂ — 2000
Deep Blue Sea, 1999, R, ★★★ — 2002
Deep Cover, 1992, R, ★★★¹/₂ — 1998
Deep Crimson, 1998, NR, ★★★¹/₂ — 2001
Deep End, The, 2001, R, ★★★¹/₂ — 2003
Deep End of the Ocean, The,
 1999, PG-13, ★¹/₂ — 2002
Deep Impact, 1998, PG-13, ★★¹/₂ — 2001
Deep Rising, 1998, R, ★¹/₂ — 2001
Deer Hunter, The, 1978, R, ★★★★ — 1998
Defence of the Realm, 1987, PG, ★★★ — 1998
Defending Your Life, 1991, PG, ★★★¹/₂ — 1998
Deja Vu, 1998, PG-13, ★★★¹/₂ — 2001
Delta Force, The, 1985, R, ★★★ — 1998
Denise Calls Up, 1996, PG-13, ★★ — 1999
Dennis the Menace, 1993, PG, ★★¹/₂ — 1995
Desert Blue, 1999, R, ★★★ — 2002
Desert Hearts, 1985, R, ★★¹/₂ — 1988
Designated Mourner, The,
 1997, R, ★★★ — 2000
Desperado, 1995, R, ★★ — 1997
Desperate Hours, 1990, R, ★★ — 1992
Desperately Seeking Susan,
 1985, PG-13, ★★★ — 1998
Desperate Measures, 1998, R, ★★ — 2001
Destiny, 1999, NR, ★★¹/₂ — 2002
Deterrence, 2000, R, ★★★ — 2003
Deuce Bigalow: Male Gigolo,
 1999, R, ★¹/₂ — 2002
Devil in a Blue Dress, 1995, R, ★★★ — 1998
Devil's Advocate, 1997, R, ★★¹/₂ — 2000
Devil's Backbone, The, 2001, R, ★★★ — 2003
Devil's Own, The, 1997, R, ★★¹/₂ — 1998
Diabolique, 1955, NR, ★★★¹/₂ — 1999

Diabolique, 1995, R, ★★ — 1997
Diamond Men, 2002, NR, ★★★½ — 2003
Diamonds, 2000, PG-13, ★ — 2003
Diamonds Are Forever,
1971, PG, ★★★ — 1998
Diary of a Mad Housewife,
1970, R, ★★★ — 1996
Dice Rules, 1991, NC-17, no stars — 1992
Dick, 1999, PG-13, ★★★½ — 2002
Dick Tracy, 1990, PG, ★★★★ — 1998
Die Hard, 1988, R, ★★ — 1998
Die Hard 2: Die Harder,
1990, R, ★★★½ — 1998
Die Hard With a Vengeance,
1995, R, ★★★ — 1998
Different for Girls, 1997, R, ★★★ — 2000
Dim Sum, 1985, PG, ★★★ — 1998
Diner, 1982, R, ★★★½ — 1998
Dinner Rush, 2002, R, ★★★ — 2003
Dinosaur, 2000, PG, ★★★ — 2003
Dirty Dancing, 1987, PG-13, ★ — 1995
Dirty Harry, 1971, R, ★★★ — 1998
Dirty Rotten Scoundrels,
1988, PG, ★★★ — 1998
Disappearance of Garcia Lorca, The,
1997, R, ★★★ — 2000
Disclosure, 1994, R, ★★ — 1996
Discreet Charm of the Bourgeoisie, The,
1972, PG, ★★★★ — 1998
Dish, The, 2001, PG-13, ★★★½ — 2003
Disney's The Kid, 2000, PG, ★★★ — 2003
Distinguished Gentleman, The,
1992, R, ★★ — 1994
Disturbing Behavior, 1998, R, ★★ — 2001
Diva, 1981, R, ★★★★ — 1998
Divine Madness, 1980, R, ★★★½ — 1998
Divine Secrets of the Ya-Ya Sisterhood,
2002, PG-13, ★½ — 2003
D.O.A., 1988, R, ★★★ — 1998
Doc Hollywood, 1991, PG-13, ★★★ — 1998
Doctor, The, 1991, PG-13, ★★★½ — 1998
Doctor Dolittle, 1998, PG-13, ★★★ — 2001
Doctor Zhivago, 1965, PG-13, ★★★ — 1997
Dog Day Afternoon, 1975, R, ★★★½ — 1998
Dogfight, 1991, R, ★★★ — 1998
Dogma, 1999, R, ★★★½ — 2002
Dogs of War, The, 1981, R, ★★★ — 1988
Dogtown and Z-Boys,
2002, PG-13, ★★★ — 2003
Dolores Claiborne, 1995, R, ★★★ — 1998
Domestic Disturbance,
2001, PG-13, ★½ — 2003

Dominick and Eugene,
1988, PG-13, ★★★½ — 1998
Don Juan DeMarco, 1995, PG-13, ★★ — 1996
Donnie Brasco, 1997, R, ★★★½ — 1998
Donnie Darko, 2001, R, ★★½ — 2003
Don't Look Back, 1998, NR, ★★★ — 2001
Don't Say a Word, 2001, R, ★★½ — 2003
Doom Generation, The,
1995, NR, no stars — 1997
Doors, The, 1991, R, ★★½ — 1998
Do the Right Thing, 1989, R, ★★★★ — 1998
Double Jeopardy, 1999, R, ★★½ — 2002
Double Life of Veronique, The,
1991, NR, ★★★½ — 1998
Double Take, 2001, PG-13, ★ — 2003
Double Team, 1997, R, ★★ — 2000
Doug's 1st Movie, 1999, G, ★½ — 2002
Down and Out in Beverly Hills,
1986, R, ★★★★ — 1998
Down by Law, 1986, R, ★★★ — 1998
Down in the Delta, 1998, PG-13, ★★★½ — 2001
Down Periscope, 1996, PG-13, ★★★ — 1999
Down to Earth, 2001, PG-13, ★ — 2003
Dragnet, 1987, PG-13, ★★★ — 1998
Dragonheart, 1995, PG-13, ★★★ — 1999
Dragonslayer, 1981, PG, ★★★ — 1989
Dragon: The Bruce Lee Story,
1993, PG-13, ★★½ — 1995
Dr. Akagi, 1999, NR, ★★★ — 2002
Draughtsman's Contract, The,
1983, R, ★★★★ — 1998
Dr. Dolittle 2, 2001, PG, ★★★ — 2003
Dreamchild, 1985, PG, ★★★ — 1998
Dreamlife of Angels, The,
1999, R, ★★★½ — 2002
Dream Lover, 1994, R, ★★★ — 1998
Dreamscape, 1984, PG-13, ★★★ — 1989
Dream Team, The, 1989, PG-13, ★★ — 1993
Dream With the Fishes, 1997, R, ★★★ — 1998
Dressed to Kill, 1980, R, ★★★ — 1998
Dresser, The, 1984, PG, ★★★★ — 1998
Drifting Clouds, 1998, NR, ★★★½ — 2001
Drive, He Said, 1971, R, ★★★ — 1998
Drive Me Crazy, 1999, PG-13, ★★½ — 2002
Driven, 2001, PG-13, ★★½ — 2003
Driving Miss Daisy, 1989, PG, ★★★★ — 1998
Drop Dead Gorgeous, 1999, PG-13, ★★ — 2002
Drop Zone, 1994, R, ★★½ — 1997
Drowning by Numbers, 1991, NR, ★★ — 1995
Drowning Mona, 2000, PG-13, ★★ — 2003
Dr. Seuss' How the Grinch Stole
Christmas, 2000, PG, ★★ — 2003

Going All the Way, 1997, R, ★★★	2000
Golden Bowl, The, 2001, R, ★★★	2003
Golden Child, The, 1986, PG-13, ★★★	1998
Goldeneye, 1995, PG-13, ★★★	1998
Gone in 60 Seconds, 2000, PG-13, ★★	2003
Gone With the Wind, 1939, NR, ★★★★	1997
Good Burger, 1997, PG, ★★	2000
Goodbye Girl, The, 1977, PG, ★★★	1998
Goodbye, Lover, 1999, R, ★	2002
GoodFellas, 1990, R, ★★★★	1998
Good Housekeeping, 2002, R, ★★★	2003
Good Morning, Vietnam, 1988, R, ★★★★	1998
Good Mother, The, 1988, R, ★	1992
Good Son, The, 1993, R, ½★	1995
Good Will Hunting, 1997, R, ★★★	2000
Goofy Movie, A, 1995, G, ★★★	1998
Goonies, The, 1985, PG, ★★★	1998
Gordy, 1995, G, ★★	1996
Gorillas in the Mist, 1988, PG-13, ★★★	1998
Gorky Park, 1983, R, ★★★½	1998
Gosford Park, 2002, R, ★★★★	2003
Gossip, 2000, R, ★★	2003
Gotcha!, 1985, PG-13, ★★	1986
Go Tigers!, 2001, R, ★★★	2003
Governess, The, 1998, R, ★★★	2001
Goya in Bordeaux, 2000, R, ★★	2003
Grace of My Heart, 1996, R, ★★½	1999
Graduate, The, 1997, PG, ★★★	1998
Grand Canyon, 1992, R, ★★★★	1998
Grass, 2000, R, ★★	2003
Gravesend, 1997, R, ★★	2000
Grease, 1998, PG, ★★★	2001
Great Balls of Fire, 1989, PG-13, ★★	1994
Great Expectations, 1998, R, ★★★	2001
Great Gatsby, The, 1974, PG, ★★½	1998
Great Mouse Detective, The, 1986, G, ★★★	1996
Great Muppet Caper, The, 1981, G, ★★	1994
Great Santini, The, 1980, PG, ★★★★	1998
Greedy, 1994, PG-13, ★★	1995
Green Card, 1991, PG-13, ★★★	1998
Greenfingers, 2001, R, ★★	2003
Green Mile, The, 1999, R, ★★★½	2002
Green Room, The, 1978, PG, ★★★	1998
Gregory's Girl, 1982, PG, ★★★	1998
Gremlins, 1984, PG, ★★★	1998
Gremlins II, 1990, PG-13, ★★½	1995
Grey Fox, The, 1983, PG, ★★★½	1998
Greystoke, 1984, PG, ★★★	1998
Gridlock'd, 1997, R, ★★★	1998
Grifters, The, 1991, R, ★★★★	1998

Groove, 2000, R, ★★	2003
Gross Anatomy, 1989, PG-13, ★★★	1998
Grosse Pointe Blank, 1997, R, ★★½	1998
Groundhog Day, 1993, PG, ★★★	1998
Grumpier Old Men, 1995, PG-13, ★★	1997
Grumpy Old Men, 1993, PG-13, ★★	1997
Guantanamera, 1997, NR, ★★★	2000
Guardian, The, 1990, R, ★	1992
Guarding Tess, 1994, PG-13, ★★★½	1998
Guelwaar, 1994, NR, ★★★★	1998
Guilty as Sin, 1993, R, ★★★	1996
Guilty by Suspicion, 1991, PG-13, ★★★½	1998
Guimba the Tyrant, 1996, NR, ★★★	1999
Guinevere, 1999, R, ★★★½	2002
Gunmen, 1994, R, ★½	1995

H

Habit, 1997, NR, ★★★	1998
Hackers, 1995, PG-13, ★★★	1998
Hair, 1979, R, ★★★★	1998
Hairspray, 1988, PG, ★★★	1998
Half Moon Street, 1986, R, ★★★	1998
Halloween, 1978, R, ★★★★	1998
Halloween: H2O, 1998, R, ★★	2001
Halloween II, 1981, R, ★★	1993
Halloween III, 1982, R, ★½	1993
Hamlet, 1990, PG, ★★★½	1998
Hamlet, 1997, PG-13, ★★★★	1998
Hamlet, 2000, R, ★★★	2003
Handmaid's Tale, The, 1990, R, ★★	1995
Hanging Garden, The, 1998, R, ★★★	2001
Hanging Up, 2000, PG-13, ★★	2003
Hangin' With the Homeboys, 1991, R, ★★★	1998
Hannah and Her Sisters, 1985, PG-13, ★★★★	1998
Hannibal, 2001, R, ★★½	2003
Hans Christian Andersen's Thumbelina, 1994, G, ★★	1995
Happiness, 1998, NR, ★★★★	2001
Happy Accidents, 2001, R, ★★★	2003
Happy Gilmore, 1996, PG-13, ★½	1999
Happy, Texas, 1999, PG-13, ★★★	2002
Hardball, 2001, R, ★★½	2003
Hard Choices, 1986, NR, ★★★½	1998
Hardcore, 1979, R, ★★★★	1998
Hard Eight, 1997, R, ★★★½	1998
Hardly Working, 1981, R, no stars	1986
Hard Rain, 1998, R, ★	2001
Hard Way, The, 1991, R, ★★★½	1998
Harlan County, U.S.A., 1976, PG, ★★★★	1998

I

Jesus of Montreal, 1990, R, ★★★¹/₂ — 1998
Jesus' Son, 2000, R, ★★★¹/₂ — 2003
Jewel of the Nile, The, 1985, PG, ★★★ — 1998
JFK, 1991, R, ★★★★ — 1998
Jimmy Hollywood, 1994, R, ★★¹/₂ — 1997
Jimmy Neutron: Boy Genius, 2001, G, ★★★ — 2003
Jingle All the Way, 1996, PG, ★★¹/₂ — 1999
Joe Dirt, 2001, PG-13, ★¹/₂ — 2003
Joe Gould's Secret, 2000, R, ★★★¹/₂ — 2003
Joe Somebody, 2001, PG, ★¹/₂ — 2003
Joe the King, 1999, R, ★★ — 2002
Joe Vs. the Volcano, 1990, PG, ★★★¹/₂ — 1998
John Carpenter's Vampires, 1998, R, ★★ — 2001
Johnny Dangerously, 1984, PG-13, ★★ — 1993
Johnny Got His Gun, 1971, R, ★★★★ — 1998
Johnny Handsome, 1989, R, ★★★¹/₂ — 1998
Johnny Mnemonic, 1995, R, ★★ — 1996
John Q., 2002, PG-13, ★¹/₂ — 2003
johns, 1997, R, ★★★ — 1998
Jo Jo Dancer, Your Life Is Calling, 1986, R, ★★★ — 1998
Josh and S.A.M., 1993, PG-13, ★★ — 1995
Josie and the Pussycats, 2001, PG-13, ¹/₂★ — 2003
Journey of August King, The, 1996, PG-13, ★¹/₂ — 1999
Journey of Hope, 1990, NR, ★★¹/₂ — 1995
Journey of Natty Gann, The, 1985, PG, ★★★ — 1998
Joy Luck Club, The, 1993, R, ★★★★ — 1998
Joy Ride, 2001, R, ★★★¹/₂ — 2003
Jude, 1996, R, ★★★ — 1999
Judge Dredd, 1995, R, ★★ — 1996
Ju Dou, 1991, NR, ★★★¹/₂ — 1998
Juice, 1992, R, ★★★ — 1998
Julia, 1977, PG, ★★¹/₂ — 1988
Julia and Julia, 1988, R, ★★★ — 1998
julien donkey-boy, 1999, R, ★★★ — 2002
Jumanji, 1995, PG, ★¹/₂ — 1998
Jumpin' Jack Flash, 1986, PG-13, ★★ — 1990
Jump Tomorrow, 2001, PG, ★★★ — 2003
Jungle Fever, 1991, R, ★★★¹/₂ — 1998
Jungle 2 Jungle, 1997, PG, ★ — 1998
Junior, 1994, PG-13, ★★★¹/₂ — 1998
Junk Mail, 1998, NR, ★★★ — 2001
Jurassic Park, 1993, PG-13, ★★★ — 1998
Jurassic Park III, 2001, PG-13, ★★★ — 2003
Juror, The, 1996, R, ★★ — 1999
Just Between Friends, 1985, PG-13, ★¹/₂ — 1987
Just Cause, 1995, R, ★★ — 1997

Just Visiting, 2001, PG-13, ★★★ — 2003
Juwanna Mann, 2002, PG-13, ★★ — 2003

K

Kadosh, 2000, NR, ★★★ — 2003
Kafka, 1992, PG-13, ★★ — 1994
Kagemusha, 1980, PG, ★★★★ — 1998
Kalifornia, 1993, R, ★★★★ — 1998
Kama Sutra, 1997, NR, ★★ — 1998
Kandahar, 2002, NR, ★★★¹/₂ — 2003
Kansas City, 1996, R, ★★★ — 1999
Karate Kid, The, 1984, PG, ★★★★ — 1998
Karate Kid Part III, The, 1989, PG, ★¹/₂ — 1993
Kate & Leopold, 2001, PG-13, ★★★ — 2003
Kazaam, 1996, PG, ★¹/₂ — 1999
Keeping the Faith, 2000, PG-13, ★★★ — 2003
Keep the River on Your Right, 2001, R, ★★★ — 2003
Kerouac, 1985, NR, ★★¹/₂ — 1987
Kicked in the Head, 1997, R, ★¹/₂ — 2000
Kicking and Screaming, 1995, R, ★★★ — 1998
Kids, 1995, NR, ★★★¹/₂ — 1998
Kids in the Hall: Brain Candy, 1996, R, ★ — 1999
Kikujiro, 2000, PG-13, ★★¹/₂ — 2003
Killer: A Journal of Murder, 1996, R, ★★ — 1999
Killing Fields, The, 1984, R, ★★★★ — 1998
Killing Zoe, 1994, R, ★★¹/₂ — 1996
Kindergarten Cop, 1990, PG-13, ★★★ — 1998
King David, 1985, PG-13, ★ — 1987
Kingdom Come, 2001, PG, ★★ — 2003
King Is Alive, The, 2001, R, ★★★ — 2003
King Lear, 1972, PG, ★★★ — 1998
King of Comedy, The, 1983, PG, ★★★ — 1998
King of Marvin Gardens, The, 1972, R, ★★★ — 1998
King of Masks, The, 1999, NR, ★★★ — 2002
King of New York, 1990, R, ★★ — 1993
King of the Gypsies, 1978, R, ★★★ — 1998
King of the Hill, 1993, PG-13, ★★★★ — 1998
Kinjite: Forbidden Subjects, 1989, R, ★ — 1993
Kiss Before Dying, A, 1991, R, ★★★ — 1998
Kissed, 1997, NR, ★★★ — 1998
Kissing a Fool, 1998, R, ★ — 2001
Kissing Jessica Stein, 2002, R, ★★★ — 2003
Kiss Me, Guido, 1997, R, ★★ — 2000
Kiss of Death, 1995, R, ★★ — 1996
Kiss of the Dragon, 2001, R, ★★★ — 2003
Kiss of the Spider Woman, 1985, R, ★★★¹/₂ — 1998
Kiss or Kill, 1997, R, ★★★ — 2000
Kiss the Girls, 1997, R, ★★★¹/₂ — 2000

Klute, 1971, R, ★★★¹/₂	1998
Knight's Tale, A, 2001, PG-13, ★★★	2003
K-9, 1989, PG, ★★	1993
K-19: The Widowmaker,	
2002, PG-13, ★★★	2003
Kolya, 1997, PG-13, ★★★¹/₂	1998
Koyaanisqatsi, 1983, NR, ★★★	1998
K-PAX, 2001, PG-13, ★★★	2003
Krays, The, 1990, R, ★★★¹/₂	1998
Krippendorf's Tribe, 1998, PG-13, ★★	2001
K2, 1992, R, ★★	1994
Kundun, 1998, PG-13, ★★★	2001
Kung Fu Master, 1989, R, ★★★	1998
Kurt & Courtney, 1998, NR, ★★★	2001

L

La Bamba, 1987, PG-13, ★★★	1998
La Belle Noiseuse, 1992, NR, ★★★★	1998
La Cage aux Folles, 1979, R, ★★★★	1998
La Ceremonie, 1997, NR, ★★★	2000
La Cienaga, 2001, NR, ★★★	2003
La Ciudad (The City), 2000, NR, ★★★	2003
L.A. Confidential, 1997, R, ★★★★	2000
La Cucaracha, 1999, R, ★★★	2002
Ladies Man, The, 2000, R, ★	2003
Lady and the Duke, The,	
2002, PG-13, ★★★	2003
Ladybird, Ladybird, 1995, NR, ★★★★	1998
Lady in White, 1988, PG-13, ★★★	1995
Lady Sings the Blues, 1972, R, ★★★	1998
La Femme Nikita, 1991, R, ★★★	1998
Lagaan: Once Upon a Time in India,	
2002, PG, ★★★¹/₂	2003
Lair of the White Worm, The,	
1988, R, ★★	1991
Lakeboat, 2001, R, ★★★	2003
Lake Placid, 1999, R, ★	2002
La Lectrice, 1989, R, ★★★★	1998
Land and Freedom, 1995, NR, ★★★	1999
Land Before Time, The, 1988, G, ★★★	1996
Land Girls, The, 1998, R, ★★¹/₂	2001
Lantana, 2002, R, ★★★¹/₂	2003
Lara Croft Tomb Raider,	
2001, PG-13, ★★★	2003
Larger Than Life, 1996, PG, ★¹/₂	1999
Lassiter, 1984, R, ★★★	1995
Last Action Hero, The,	
1993, PG-13, ★★¹/₂	1995
Last Boy Scout, The, 1991, R, ★★★	1996
Last Castle, The, 2001, R, ★★★	2003
Last Dance, 1995, R, ★★¹/₂	1999
Last Days, The, 1999, NR, ★★★¹/₂	2002

Last Days of Chez Nous, The,	
1993, R, ★★★¹/₂	1998
Last Days of Disco, The,	
1998, R, ★★★¹/₂	2001
Last Detail, The, 1974, R, ★★★★	1998
Last Dragon, The, 1985, PG-13, ★★¹/₂	1991
Last Emperor, The, 1987, PG-13, ★★★★	1998
Last Exit to Brooklyn, 1990, R, ★★★¹/₂	1998
Last Flight of Noah's Ark, The,	
1980, G, ¹/₂★	1986
Last House on the Left, 1972, R, ★★★¹/₂	1998
Last Man Standing, 1996, R, ★	1999
Last Metro, The, 1980, NR, ★★★	1998
Last Night, 1999, R, ★★★	2002
Last of the Dogmen, 1995, PG, ★★★	1998
Last of the Mohicans, The,	
1992, R, ★★★	1998
Last Orders, 2002, R, ★★★¹/₂	2003
L.A. Story, 1991, PG-13, ★★★★	1998
Last Picture Show, The, 1971, R, ★★★★	1998
La Strada, 1954, NR, ★★★¹/₂	1997
Last Resort, 2001, NR, ★★★	2003
Last Seduction, The, 1994, NR, ★★★★	1998
Last September, The, 2000, R, ★★	2003
Last Starfighter, The, 1984, PG, ★★¹/₂	1991
Last Supper, The, 1995, R, ★★★	1999
Last Tango in Paris, 1972, X, ★★★★	1998
Last Temptation of Christ, The,	
1988, R, ★★★★	1998
Last Waltz, The, 2002, PG, ★★★	2003
Late for Dinner, 1991, PG, ★★¹/₂	1993
Late Marriage, 2002, NR, ★★★	2003
Late Show, The, 1977, PG, ★★★★	1998
Lawn Dogs, 1998, NR, ★¹/₂	2001
Lawrence of Arabia, 1962, PG, ★★★★	1997
Laws of Gravity, 1992, R, ★★★	1996
Leading Man, The, 1998, R, ★★★	2001
League of Their Own, A, 1992, PG, ★★★	1998
Lean on Me, 1989, PG-13, ★★¹/₂	1993
Leap of Faith, 1992, PG-13, ★★★	1998
Leave It to Beaver, 1997, PG, ★★★	2000
Leaving Las Vegas, 1995, R, ★★★★	1998
Leaving Normal, 1992, R, ★★¹/₂	1994
Left Luggage, 2001, NR, ★★	2003
Legally Blonde, 2001, PG-13, ★★★	2003
Legend, 1986, PG, ★★	1989
Legend of Bagger Vance, The,	
2000, PG-13, ★★★¹/₂	2003
Legend of Hell House, The,	
1973, PG, ★★★¹/₂	1995
Legend of 1900, The, 1999, R, ★★¹/₂	2002
Legend of Rita, The, 2001, NR, ★★★¹/₂	2003

Legend of the Drunken Master, The,
2000, R, ★★★¹/₂ — 2003

Legends of the Fall, 1995, R, ★★★ — 1998

Léolo, 1993, NR, ★★★★ — 1998

Les Miserables, 1998, PG-13, ★★¹/₂ — 2001

Less Than Zero, 1987, R, ★★★★ — 1998

Les Voleurs (The Thieves),
1996, R, ★★★¹/₂ — 1999

Lethal Weapon, 1987, R, ★★★★ — 1998

Lethal Weapon 2, 1989, R, ★★★¹/₂ — 1998

Lethal Weapon 3, 1992, R, ★★★ — 1998

Lethal Weapon 4, 1998, R, ★★ — 2001

Let Him Have It, 1992, R, ★★★¹/₂ — 1998

Let's Spend the Night Together,
1983, PG, ★★¹/₂ — 1994

Let's Talk About Sex, 1998, R, ★ — 2001

L'Humanite, 2000, NR, ★★★¹/₂ — 2003

Liam, 2001, R, ★★★¹/₂ — 2003

Lianna, 1983, R, ★★★¹/₂ — 1998

Liar Liar, 1997, PG-13, ★★★ — 1998

Liberty Heights, 1999, R, ★★★¹/₂ — 2002

Licence to Kill, 1989, PG-13, ★★★¹/₂ — 1998

L.I.E., 2001, NC-17, ★★★ — 2003

Life, 1999, R, ★★★ — 2002

Life and Debt, 2001, NR, ★★★ — 2003

Life as a House, 2001, R, ★★¹/₂ — 2003

Life Is Beautiful, 1998, PG-13, ★★★¹/₂ — 2001

Life Is Sweet, 1991, NR, ★★★★ — 1998

Life Less Ordinary, A, 1997, R, ★★ — 2000

Life or Something Like It, 2002, PG-13, ★ — 2003

Life Stinks, 1991, PG-13, ★★★ — 1998

Life With Mikey, 1993, PG, ★★ — 1995

Light It Up, 1999, R, ★★¹/₂ — 2002

Lightning Jack, 1994, PG-13, ★★ — 1995

Light of Day, 1987, PG-13, ★★★¹/₂ — 1998

Light Sleeper, 1992, R, ★★★★ — 1998

Like Father, Like Son, 1987, PG-13, ★ — 1991

Like Water for Chocolate,
1993, R, ★★★★ — 1998

Lilo & Stitch, 2002, PG, ★★★¹/₂ — 2003

Limbo, 1999, R, ★★★¹/₂ — 2002

Limey, The, 1999, R, ★★★ — 2002

Lion King, The, 1994, G, ★★★¹/₂ — 1998

Listen Up: The Lives of Quincy Jones,
1990, PG-13, ★★★¹/₂ — 1998

Little Big League, 1994, PG, ★★★¹/₂ — 1998

Little Big Man, 1971, PG, ★★★★ — 1998

Little Buddha, 1994, PG, ★★ — 1995

Little Darlings, 1980, R, ★★ — 1987

Little Dieter Needs to Fly,
1998, NR, ★★★¹/₂ — 2001

Little Dorrit, 1988, G, ★★★★ — 1998

Little Drummer Girl, 1984, R, ★★ — 1991

Little Indian Big City, 1995, PG, no stars — 1999

Little Man Tate, 1991, PG, ★★★¹/₂ — 1998

Little Men, 1998, PG, ★¹/₂ — 2001

Little Mermaid, The, 1989, G, ★★★★ — 1998

Little Nicky, 2000, PG-13, ★★¹/₂ — 2003

Little Nikita, 1988, PG, ★¹/₂ — 1991

Little Odessa, 1995, R, ★★ — 1996

Little Princess, A, 1995, G, ★★★¹/₂ — 1998

Little Vampire, The, 2000, PG, ★★ — 2003

Little Vera, 1989, R, ★★★ — 1996

Little Voice, 1998, R, ★★★ — 2001

Little Women, 1994, PG, ★★★¹/₂ — 1998

Live Flesh, 1998, R, ★★★¹/₂ — 2001

Live Nude Girls Unite!, 2001, NR, ★★★ — 2003

Living Daylights, The, 1987, PG, ★★ — 1994

Living Out Loud, 1998, R, ★★★¹/₂ — 2001

Local Hero, 1983, PG, ★★★★ — 1998

Lock, Stock and Two Smoking Barrels,
1999, R, ★★★ — 2002

Locusts, The, 1997, R, ★★¹/₂ — 2000

Lonely Guy, The, 1984, R, ★¹/₂ — 1995

Lonely Lady, The, 1983, R, ¹/₂★ — 1988

Lonely Passion of Judith Hearne, The,
1988, R, ★★★ — 1998

Lone Star, 1996, R, ★★★★ — 1999

Lone Wolf McQuade, 1983, PG, ★★★¹/₂ — 1995

Long Goodbye, The, 1973, R, ★★★ — 1996

Long Good Friday, The, 1982, R, ★★★★ — 1998

Long Kiss Goodnight, The,
1996, R, ★★¹/₂ — 1999

Longtime Companion,
1990, R, ★★★¹/₂ — 1998

Long Walk Home, The,
1991, PG, ★★★¹/₂ — 1998

Looking for Mr. Goodbar, 1977, R, ★★★ — 1998

Look Who's Talking, 1989, PG-13, ★★★ — 1998

Look Who's Talking Now, 1993, PG-13, ★ — 1995

Loose Cannons, 1990, R, ★ — 1992

Lord of Illusions, 1995, R, ★★★ — 1998

Lord of the Rings: The Fellowship of
the Ring, The, 2001, PG-13, ★★★ — 2003

Lords of Discipline, 1983, R, ★★ — 1991

Lorenzo's Oil, 1993, PG-13, ★★★★ — 1998

Loser, 2000, PG-13, ★★ — 2003

Losing Isaiah, 1995, R, ★★¹/₂ — 1997

Loss of Sexual Innonence, The,
1999, R, ★★★¹/₂ — 2002

Lost and Delirious, 2001, NR, ★★★¹/₂ — 2003

Lost & Found, 1999, PG-13, ★ — 2002

Lost Angels, 1989, R, ★★¹/₂ — 1992

Lost Boys, The, 1987, R, ★★¹/₂ — 1993

Lost Highway, 1997, R, ★★ — 1998
Lost in America, 1985, R, ★★★★ — 1998
Lost in Space, 1998, PG-13, ★½ — 2001
Lost in Yonkers, 1993, PG, ★★★ — 1998
Lost Souls, 2000, R, ★★ — 2003
Lost World: Jurassic Park, The,
  1997, PG-13, ★★ — 1998
Louie Bluie, 1985, NR, ★★★½ — 1996
Love Affair, 1994, PG-13, ★★★ — 1998
Love Always, 1997, R, ½★ — 2000
Love & Basketball, 2000, PG-13, ★★★ — 2003
Love and Death on Long Island,
  1998, PG-13, ★★★½ — 2001
Love and Human Remains,
  1995, NR, ★★½ — 1997
Love and Other Catastrophes,
  1997, R, ★★ — 2000
Love & Sex, 2000, NR, ★★ — 2003
Love Field, 1993, PG-13, ★★½ — 1997
Love Is the Devil, 1998, NR, ★★★½ — 2001
love jones, 1997, R, ★★★ — 1998
Love Letters, 1984, R, ★★★½ — 1998
Lover, The, 1992, R, ★★ — 1996
Lovers of the Artic Circle,
  1999, R, ★★★ — 2002
Lovers on the Bridge, The,
  1999, R, ★★★ — 2002
Love Serenade, 1997, R, ★★★ — 2000
Lovesick, 1983, PG, ★★★ — 1989
Love's Labour's Lost, 2000, PG, ★★½ — 2003
Love Story, 1970, PG, ★★★★ — 1998
Love Streams, 1984, PG-13, ★★★★ — 1998
Love! Valour! Compassion!,
  1997, R, ★★★ — 1998
Love Walked In, 1998, R, ★★ — 2001
Loving Jezebel, 2000, R, ★★½ — 2003
Low Down, The, 2001, NR, ★★★ — 2003
Lucas, 1985, PG-13, ★★★★ — 1998
Lucie Aubrac, 1999, R, ★★½ — 2002
Lucky Break, 2002, PG-13, ★★★ — 2003
Lucky Numbers, 2000, R, ★★ — 2003
Lumiere & Company, 1996, NR, ★★★ — 1999
Lumumba, 2001, NR, ★★★ — 2003
Lust in the Dust, 1985, R, ★★ — 1990
Luzhin Defence, The, 2001, PG-13, ★★½ — 2003

M

Maborosi, 1997, NR, ★★★★ — 1998
Mac, 1993, R, ★★★½ — 1998
Macbeth, 1972, R, ★★★★ — 1998
Madadayo, 2000, NR, ★★★ — 2003

Madame Bovary, 1991, NR, ★★★ — 1998
Madame Butterfly, 1996, NR, ★★★ — 1999
Madame Sousatzka, 1988, PG-13, ★★★★ — 1998
Mad City, 1997, PG-13, ★★½ — 2000
Mad Dog and Glory, 1993, R, ★★★½ — 1998
Mad Dog Time, 1996, R, no stars — 1999
Made, 2001, R, ★★★ — 2003
Made in America, 1993, PG-13, ★★★ — 1998
Madeline, 1998, PG, ★★★ — 2001
Mad Love, 1995, PG-13, ★★★ — 1998
Mad Max Beyond Thunderdome,
  1985, R, ★★★★ — 1998
Madness of King George, The,
  1995, NR, ★★★★ — 1998
Mafia!, 1998, PG-13, ★★ — 2001
Magnolia, 2000, R, ★★★★ — 2003
Majestic, The, 2001, PG, ★★★½ — 2003
Major Payne, 1995, PG-13, ★★★ — 1998
Making Love, 1982, R, ★★ — 1988
Making Mr. Right, 1987, PG-13, ★★★½ — 1998
Malcolm X, 1992, PG-13, ★★★★ — 1998
Malena, 2000, R, ★★ — 2003
Malice, 1993, R, ★★ — 1995
Mambo Kings, The, 1992, R, ★★★½ — 1998
Manchurian Candidate, The,
  1962, PG-13, ★★★★ — 1997
Mandela, 1997, NR, ★★★ — 2000
Manhattan, 1979, R, ★★★½ — 1998
Manhattan Murder Mystery,
  1993, PG, ★★★ — 1998
Manhattan Project, The,
  1986, PG-13, ★★★★ — 1998
Man in the Iron Mask, The,
  1998, PG-13, ★★½ — 2001
Man in the Moon, The,
  1991, PG-13, ★★★★ — 1998
Mannequin, 1987, PG, ½★ — 1990
Manny and Lo, 1996, R, ★★★½ — 1999
Man of Iron, 1980, NR, ★★★★ — 1998
Man of the Century, 1999, R, ★★★ — 2002
Manon of the Spring,
  1987, PG, ★★★★ — 1998
Man on the Moon, 1999, R, ★★★½ — 2002
Mansfield Park, 1999, PG-13, ★★★★ — 2002
Man Who Cried, The, 2001, R, ★★★ — 2003
Man Who Knew Too Little, The,
  1997, PG, ★ — 2000
Man Who Loved Women, The,
  1983, R, ★★ — 1988
Man Who Wasn't There, The,
  2001, R, ★★★ — 2003

Man Who Would Be King, The,
1975, PG, ★★★★ 1998
Man Without a Face, The,
1993, PG-13, ★★★ 1998
Man With Two Brains, The, 1983, R, ★★ 1995
Map of the Human Heart,
1993, R, ★★★★ 1998
Map of the World, A, 2000, R, ★★★½ 2003
Margaret's Museum, 1997, R, ★★★½ 1998
Marie, 1985, PG-13, ★★★ 1987
Marie Baie des Anges, 1998, R, ★ 2001
Marius and Jeannette, 1998, NR, ★★ 2001
Marriage of Maria Braun, The,
1979, R, ★★★★ 1998
Marrying Man, The, 1991, R, ★★★ 1995
Mars Attacks!, 1996, PG-13, ★★ 1999
Marvin's Room, 1997, PG-13, ★★★½ 1998
Maryam, 2002, NR, ★★★½ 2003
Mary Reilly, 1996, R, ★★★ 1998
Mary Shelley's Frankenstein,
1994, R, ★★½ 1997
M*A*S*H, 1970, R, ★★★★ 1998
Mask, 1985, PG-13, ★★★½ 1998
Mask, The, 1994, PG-13, ★★★ 1998
Mask of Zorro, The, 1998, PG-13, ★★★ 2001
Masquerade, 1988, R, ★★★ 1998
Masterminds, 1997, PG-13, ½★ 2000
Matchmaker, The, 1997, R, ★★★ 2000
Matilda, 1996, PG, ★★★ 1999
Matinee, 1993, PG, ★★★½ 1998
Matrix, The, 1999, R, ★★★ 2002
Maurice, 1987, R, ★★★ 1998
Maverick, 1994, PG, ★★★ 1998
Ma Vie en Rose, 1998, R, ★★★ 2001
Max Dugan Returns, 1983, PG, ★★½ 1986
Maxie, 1985, PG, ½★ 1987
Max Keeble's Big Move, 2001, PG, ★★ 2003
Maybe . . . Maybe Not, 1996, R, ★★★ 1999
May Fools, 1990, R, ★★★ 1998
Maze, 2001, R, ★★★ 2003
M. Butterfly, 1993, R, ★★½ 1995
McCabe and Mrs. Miller,
1971, R, ★★★★ 1998
Me and My Matchmaker, 1996, NR, ★★★ 1999
Mean Machine, 2002, R, ★★★ 2003
Mean Streets, 1974, R, ★★★★ 1998
Medicine Man, The, 1992, PG-13, ★½ 1994
Meeting Venus, 1991, PG-13, ★★★ 1995
Meet Joe Black, 1998, PG-13, ★★★ 2001
Meet the Deedles, 1998, PG, ★½ 2001
Meet the Parents, 2000, PG-13, ★★★ 2003

Melvin and Howard, 1980, R, ★★★½ 1998
Memento, 2001, R, ★★★ 2003
Memoirs of an Invisible Man,
1992, PG-13, ★★½ 1994
Memories of Me, 1988, PG-13, ★★★½ 1998
Memphis Belle, 1990, PG-13, ★★★ 1998
Me, Myself & Irene, 2000, R, ★½ 2003
Me Myself I, 2000, R, ★★★ 2003
Menace II Society, 1993, R, ★★★★ 1998
Men Don't Leave, 1990, PG-13, ★★ 1991
Men in Black, 1997, PG-13, ★★★ 1998
Men in Black II, 2002, PG-13, ★½ 2003
Men of Honor, 2000, R, ★★★ 2003
Men of Respect, 1991, R, ★ 1992
Men With Guns, 1998, R, ★★★★ 2001
Mephisto, 1981, NR, ★★★★ 1998
Mercury Rising, 1998, R, ★★ 2001
Mermaids, 1990, PG-13, ★★★ 1998
Merry Christmas, Mr. Lawrence,
1983, R, ★★½ 1991
Merry War, A, 1998, NR, ★★★ 2001
Message in a Bottle, 1999, PG-13, ★★ 2002
Messenger: The Story of Joan of Arc,
The, 1999, R, ★★ 2002
Meteor Man, The, 1993, PG, ★★½ 1995
Metro, 1997, R, ★★★ 1998
Metroland, 1999, NR, ★★★ 2002
Metropolis, 1926, NR, ★★★★ 1997
Metropolis, 2002, PG-13, ★★★★ 2003
Metropolitan, 1990, PG-13, ★★★½ 1998
Mexican, The, 2001, R, ★★★ 2003
Me You Them, 2001, PG-13, ★★★ 2003
Miami Blues, 1990, R, ★★ 1993
Miami Rhapsody, 1995, PG-13, ★★★ 1998
Michael, 1996, PG, ★★★ 1999
Michael Collins, 1996, R, ★★★ 1999
Michael Jordan at the Max,
2000, NR, ★★ 2003
Mickey Blue Eyes, 1999, PG-13, ★★ 2002
Micki & Maude, 1984, PG-13, ★★★★ 1998
Microcosmos, 1997, G, ★★★★ 1998
Midnight Clear, A, 1992, R, ★★★ 1998
Midnight Cowboy, 1969, R, ★★★ 1997
Midnight in the Garden of Good and
Evil, 1997, R, ★★½ 2000
Midnight Run, 1988, R, ★★★½ 1998
Midsummer Night's Sex Comedy, A,
1982, PG, ★★ 1997
Mifune, 2000, R, ★★★ 2003
Mighty, The, 1998, PG-13, ★★★ 2001
Mighty Aphrodite, 1995, R, ★★★½ 1998

Mighty Ducks, The, 1992, PG, ★★	1994	Moonlighting, 1982, PG, ★★★★	1998
Mighty Joe Young, 1998, PG, ★★★	2001	Moon Over Parador, 1988, PG-13, ★★	1993
Mighty Morphin Power Rangers™: The Movie, 1995, PG, ¹/₂★	1997	Moonstruck, 1987, PG, ★★★★	1998
Mighty Peking Man, 1999, NR, ★★★	2002	Morning After, The, 1986, R, ★★★	1996
Mighty Quinn, The, 1989, R, ★★★★	1998	Mortal Thoughts, 1991, R, ★★★	1998
Milagro Beanfield War, The, 1988, R, ★★¹/₂	1993	Moscow on the Hudson, 1984, R, ★★★★	1998
Miles From Home, 1988, R, ★★★	1998	Mosquito Coast, The, 1986, PG, ★★	1993
Milk Money, 1994, PG-13, ★	1996	Motel Hell, 1980, R, ★★★	1996
Miller's Crossing, 1990, R, ★★★	1998	Mother, 1997, PG-13, ★★★¹/₂	1998
Mimic, 1997, R, ★★★¹/₂	2000	Mother and the Whore, The, 1999, NR, ★★★★	2002
Minority Report, 2002, PG-13, ★★★★	2003	Mother Night, 1996, R, ★★¹/₂	1999
Minus Man, The, 1999, R, ★★★	2002	Mother's Day, 1980, R, no stars	1991
Miracle Mile, 1989, R, ★★★	1998	Mothman Prophecies, The, 2002, PG-13, ★★	2003
Miracle on 34th Street, 1994, PG, ★★★	1998	Moulin Rouge, 2001, PG-13, ★★★¹/₂	2003
Mirror Has Two Faces, The, 1996, PG-13, ★★★	1999	Mountains of the Moon, 1990, R, ★★★¹/₂	1998
Misery, 1990, R, ★★★	1998	Mouse Hunt, 1997, PG, ★★	2000
Mishima, 1985, R, ★★★★	1998	Mr. and Mrs. Bridge, 1991, PG-13, ★★★★	1998
Miss Congeniality, 2000, PG-13, ★★	2003	Mr. Baseball, 1992, PG-13, ★★★	1998
Miss Firecracker, 1989, PG, ★★★¹/₂	1998	Mr. Death: The Rise and Fall of Fred A. Leuchter Jr., 2000, PG-13, ★★★★	2003
Missing, 1982, R, ★★★	1998	Mr. Deeds, 2002, PG-13, ★¹/₂	2003
Mission, The, 1986, PG, ★★¹/₂	1993	Mr. Destiny, 1990, PG-13, ★★	1992
Mission Impossible, 1996, PG-13, ★★★	1999	Mr. Holland's Opus, 1996, PG, ★★★¹/₂	1999
Mission Impossible 2, 2000, PG-13, ★★★	2003	Mr. Jealousy, 1998, R, ★★¹/₂	2001
Mission to Mars, 2000, PG-13, ★★¹/₂	2003	Mr. Jones, 1993, R, ★★★	1998
Mississippi Burning, 1988, R, ★★★★	1998	Mr. Magoo, 1997, PG, ¹/₂★	2000
Mississippi Masala, 1992, R, ★★★¹/₂	1998	Mr. Mom, 1983, PG, ★★	1987
Miss Julie, 2000, R, ★★★	2003	Mr. Nice Guy, 1998, PG-13, ★★★	2001
Mister Johnson, 1991, PG-13, ★★★	1998	Mr. Saturday Night, 1992, R, ★★★	1995
Mo' Better Blues, 1990, R, ★★★	1998	Mrs. Brown, 1997, PG, ★★★¹/₂	2000
Moderns, The, 1988, NR, ★★★	1998	Mrs. Dalloway, 1998, PG-13, ★★★¹/₂	2001
Mod Squad, The, 1999, R, ★★	2002	Mrs. Doubtfire, 1993, PG-13, ★★¹/₂	1998
Mommie Dearest, 1981, PG, ★	1998	Mrs. Parker and the Vicious Circle, 1994, R, ★★★¹/₂	1998
Mona Lisa, 1986, R, ★★★★	1998	Mrs. Winterbourne, 1996, PG-13, ★★¹/₂	1999
Money Pit, The, 1986, PG-13, ★	1991	Mr. Wonderful, 1993, PG-13, ★¹/₂	1995
Money Talks, 1997, R, ★★★	2000	Much Ado About Nothing, 1993, PG-13, ★★★	1998
Money Train, 1995, R, ★¹/₂	1997		
Mon Homme, 1998, NR, ★★	2001	Mulan, 1998, G, ★★★¹/₂	2001
Monkeybone, 2001, PG-13, ★¹/₂	2003	Mulholland Dr., 2001, R, ★★★★	2003
Monkey Trouble, 1994, PG, ★★★	1998	Mulholland Falls, 1996, R, ★★★¹/₂	1999
Monsieur Hire, 1990, PG-13, ★★★★	1998	Multiplicity, 1996, PG-13, ★★¹/₂	1999
Monsignor, 1982, R, ★	1987	Mumford, 1999, R, ★★★¹/₂	2002
Monsoon Wedding, 2002, R, ★★★¹/₂	2003	Mummy, The, 1999, PG-13, ★★★	2002
Monster's Ball, 2002, R, ★★★★	2003	Mummy Returns, The, 2001, PG-13, ★★	2003
Monsters, Inc., 2001, G, ★★★	2003	Muppet Christmas Carol, The, 1992, G, ★★★	1998
Month by the Lake, A, 1995, PG, ★★★¹/₂	1998		
Monty Python's Meaning of Life, 1983, R, ★★¹/₂	1995	Muppet Movie, The, 1979, G, ★★★¹/₂	1998
Monument Ave., 1998, NR, ★★★	2001	Muppets from Space, 1999, G, ★★	2002

Muppets Take Manhattan, The, 1984, G, ★★★   1998

Muppet Treasure Island, 1996, G, ★★½   1999

Murder at 1600, 1997, R, ★★½   1998

Murder by Numbers, 2002, R, ★★★   2003

Murder in the First, 1995, R, ★★   1996

Murder on the Orient Express, 1974, PG, ★★★   1998

Muriel's Wedding, 1995, R, ★★★½   1998

Murphy's Romance, 1985, PG-13, ★★★   1998

Muse, The, 1999, PG-13, ★★★   2002

Music Box, 1990, PG-13, ★★   1993

Music Lovers, The, 1971, R, ★★   1993

Music of Chance, The, 1993, NR, ★★★   1998

Music of the Heart, 1999, PG, ★★★   2002

Musketeer, The, 2001, PG-13, ★★½   2003

My Beautiful Laundrette, 1986, R, ★★★   1998

My Best Fiend's Wedding, 1997, PG-13, ★★★   1998

My Best Friend, 2000, NR, ★★★   2003

My Big Fat Greek Wedding, 2002, PG, ★★★   2003

My Bodyguard, 1980, PG, ★★★½   1998

My Brilliant Career, 1980, NR, ★★★½   1998

My Cousin Vinny, 1992, R, ★★½   1998

My Dinner with André, 1981, NR, ★★★★   1998

My Dog Skip, 2000, PG, ★★★   2003

My Fair Lady, 1964, G, ★★★★   1997

My Family, 1995, R, ★★★★   1998

My Father's Glory, 1991, G, ★★★★   1998

My Father the Hero, 1994, PG, ★★   1995

My Favorite Martian, 1999, PG, ★★   2002

My Favorite Season, 1995, NR, ★★★   1999

My Favorite Year, 1982, PG, ★★★½   1998

My Fellow Americans, 1996, PG-13, ★★½   1999

My First Mister, 2001, R, ★★★   2003

My Giant, 1998, PG, ★★   2001

My Girl, 1991, PG, ★★★½   1998

My Girl 2, 1994, PG, ★★   1995

My Heroes Have Always Been Cowboys, 1991, PG, ★★   1992

My Left Foot, 1989, R, ★★★★   1998

My Life, 1993, PG-13, ★★½   1995

My Life So Far, 1999, PG-13, ★★★   2002

My Mother's Castle, 1991, PG, ★★★★   1998

My Name Is Joe, 1999, R, ★★★½   2002

My Own Private Idaho, 1991, R, ★★★½   1998

My Son the Fanatic, 1999, R, ★★★½   2002

My Stepmother Is an Alien, 1988, PG-13, ★★   1993

Mystery, Alaska, 1999, R, ★★½   2002

Mystery Men, 1999, PG-13, ★★   2002

Mystery Science Theater 3000: The Movie, 1996, PG-13, ★★★   1999

Mystery Train, 1990, R, ★★★½   1998

Mystic Masseur, The, 2002, PG, ★★★   2003

Mystic Pizza, 1988, R, ★★★½   1998

Myth of Fingerprints, The, 1997, R, ★½   2000

My Tutor, 1983, R, ★★★   1986

N

Nadine, 1987, PG, ★★½   1993

Naked, 1994, NR, ★★★★   1998

Naked Gun, The, 1988, PG-13, ★★★½   1998

Naked Gun 2½: The Smell of Fear, The, 1991, PG-13, ★★★   1998

Naked Gun 33⅓: The Final Insult, 1994, PG-13, ★★★   1998

Naked in New York, 1994, R, ★★★   1998

Naked Lunch, 1992, R, ★★½   1994

Name of the Rose, The, 1986, R, ★★½   1995

Narrow Margin, 1990, R, ★½   1992

Nashville, 1975, R, ★★★★   1998

Nasty Girl, The, 1991, PG-13, ★★½   1993

National Lampoon's Animal House, 1978, R, ★★★★   1998

National Lampoon's Christmas Vacation, 1989, PG-13, ★★   1995

National Lampoon's Loaded Weapon I, 1993, PG-13, ★   1994

National Lampoon's Van Wilder, 2002, R, ★   2003

Natural, The, 1984, PG, ★★   1995

Natural Born Killers, 1994, R, ★★★★   1998

Navy Seals, 1990, R, ★½   1992

Necessary Roughness, 1991, PG-13, ★★★   1996

Needful Things, 1993, R, ★½   1995

Negotiator, The, 1998, R, ★★★½   2001

Neighbors, 1981, R, ★★★   1996

Nell, 1994, PG-13, ★★★   1998

Nelly and Monsieur Arnaud, 1996, NR, ★★★½   1999

Nenette et Boni, 1997, NR, ★★★   2000

Net, The, 1995, PG-13, ★★★   1998

Network, 1976, R, ★★★★   1998

Never Been Kissed, 1999, PG-13, ★★★   2002

Neverending Story, The, 1984, PG, ★★★   1998

Never Say Never Again, 1983, PG, ★★★½   1998

New Age, The, 1994, R, ★★★½   1998

New Guy, The, 2002, PG-13, ★★   2003

New Jack City, 1991, R, ★★★½   1998

New Jersey Drive, 1995, R, ★★★ 1998
Newsies, 1992, PG, ★½ 1993
Newton Boys, The, 1998, PG-13, ★★ 2001
New York, New York, 1977, PG, ★★★ 1998
New York Stories, 1989, PG 1998
   Life Lessons, ★★★½
   Life Without Zoe, ★½
   Oedipus Wrecks, ★★
Next Best Thing, The, 2000, PG-13, ★ 2003
Niagara, Niagara, 1998, R, ★★★ 2001
Nick and Jane, 1997, R, ½★ 2000
Nico and Dani, 2001, NR, ★★★ 2003
Nico Icon, 1996, NR, ★★★ 1999
Night and the City, 1992, R, ★★ 1994
Night at the Roxbury, A, 1998, PG-13, ★ 2001
Night Falls on Manhattan, 1997, R, ★★★ 2000
Nightmare on Elm Street 3, A: Dream
   Warriors, 1987, R, ★½ 1990
Night of the Living Dead, 1990, R, ★ 1992
Night on Earth, 1992, R, ★★★ 1998
Nightwatch, 1998, R, ★★ 2001
Nil by Mouth, 1998, R, ★★★½ 2001
Nina Takes a Lover, 1995, R, ★★ 1997
9½ Weeks, 1985, R, ★★★½ 1998
Nine Months, 1995, PG-13, ★★ 1998
Nine Queens, 2002, R, ★★★ 2003
1984, 1984, R, ★★★½ 1998
Nine to Five, 1980, PG, ★★★ 1998
Ninth Gate, The, 2000, R, ★★ 2003
Nixon, 1995, R, ★★★★ 1998
Nobody's Fool, 1986, PG-13, ★★ 1991
Nobody's Fool, 1995, R, ★★★½ 1998
No Escape, 1994, R, ★★ 1995
No Looking Back, 1998, R, ★★ 2001
Nomads, 1985, R, ★½ 1987
No Man's Land, 1987, R, ★★★ 1998
No Man's Land, 2001, R, ★★★½ 2003
No Mercy, 1986, R, ★★★ 1996
Normal Life, 1996, R, ★★★½ 1999
Norma Rae, 1979, PG, ★★★ 1998
North, 1994, PG, no stars 1997
North Dallas Forty, 1979, R, ★★★½ 1998
Nosferatu, 1979, R, ★★★★ 1998
No Such Thing, 2002, R, ★ 2003
Not Another Teen Movie, 2001, R, ★★ 2003
Nothing But a Man, 1964, NR, ★★★½ 1997
Nothing in Common, 1986, PG, ★★½ 1988
Nothing to Lose, 1997, R, ★★ 2000
Not One Less, 2000, G, ★★★ 2003
Notting Hill, 1999, PG-13, ★★★ 2002
Not Without My Daughter,
   1990, PG-13, ★★★ 1998

Novocaine, 2001, R, ★★★ 2003
No Way Out, 1987, R, ★★★★ 1998
Nuns on the Run, 1990, PG-13, ★ 1993
Nurse Betty, 2000, R, ★★★ 2003
Nuts, 1987, R, ★★ 1993
Nutty Professor, The,
   1996, PG-13, ★★★ 1999
Nutty Professor II: The Klumps,
   2000, PG-13, ★★★ 2003

O

O, 2001, R, ★★★ 2003
Object of Beauty, The, 1991, R, ★★★½ 1998
Object of My Affection, The,
   1998, R, ★★ 2001
O Brother, Where Art Thou?,
   2000, PG-13, ★★½ 2003
Ocean's Eleven, 2001, PG-13, ★★★ 2003
October Sky, 1999, PG, ★★★½ 2002
Odd Couple II, The, 1998, PG-13, ★½ 2001
Off Beat, 1986, PG, ★★★½ 1995
Officer and a Gentleman, An,
   1982, R, ★★★★ 1998
Office Space, 1999, R, ★★★ 2002
Of Mice and Men, 1992, PG-13, ★★★½ 1998
Oh, God!, 1977, PG, ★★★½ 1998
Oh, God! Book II, 1980, PG, ★★ 1995
Oh, God! You Devil, 1984, PG, ★★★½ 1998
Old Gringo, 1989, R, ★★ 1993
Oleanna, 1994, NR, ★★ 1997
Oliver & Co., 1988, G, ★★★ 1998
Once Around, 1990, R, ★★★½ 1998
Once in the Life, 2000, R, ★★ 2003
Once Upon a Forest, 1993, G, ★★½ 1995
Once Upon a Time in America, 1984, R,
   ★—short version
   ★★★★—original version 1998
Once Upon a Time . . . When We Were
   Colored, 1996, PG, ★★★★ 1999
Once Were Warriors, 1995, R, ★★★½ 1998
One, The, 2001, PG-13, ★½ 2003
One Day in September, 2001, R, ★★★ 2003
One False Move, 1992, R, ★★★★ 1998
One Fine Day, 1996, PG, ★★ 1999
One Flew Over the Cuckoo's Nest,
   1975, R, ★★★ 1998
One from the Heart, 1982, PG, ★★ 1995
Onegin, 2000, NR, ★★½ 2003
One Good Cop, 1991, R, ★★ 1994
101 Dalmatians, 1961, G, ★★★ 1998
101 Dalmatians, 1996, G, ★★½ 1999
102 Dalmations, 2000, G, ★★½ 2003

Romy and Michele's High School
  Reunion, 1997, R, ★★★ 1998
Ronin, 1998, R, ★★★ 2001
Rookie, The, 2002, G, ★★ 2003
Rookie of the Year, 1993, PG, ★★★ 1996
Room for Romeo Brass, A, 2000, R, ★★★ 2003
Room with a View, A,
  1985, PG-13, ★★★★ 1998
Rosalie Goes Shopping, 1990, PG, ★★★ 1998
Rose, The, 1979, R, ★★★ 1998
Rosetta, 2000, R, ★★★½ 2003
Rosewood, 1997, R, ★★★½ 1998
Rough Magic, 1997, PG-13, ★★ 1998
Roujin-Z, 1996, PG-13, ★★★ 1999
Rounders, 1998, R, ★★★ 2001
'Round Midnight, 1986, R, ★★★★ 1998
Roxanne, 1987, PG, ★★★½ 1998
Royal Tenenbaums, The, 2001, R, ★★★½ 2003
Ruby, 1992, R, ★★ 1994
Ruby in Paradise, 1993, NR, ★★★★ 1998
Rudy, 1993, PG, ★★★½ 1998
Rudyard Kipling's Second Jungle Book:
  Mowgli and Baloo, 1997, PG, ★½ 2000
Rudyard Kipling's the Jungle Book,
  1994, PG, ★★★ 1998
Rugrats, 1998, G, ★★ 2001
Rugrats in Paris, 2000, G, ★★★ 2003
Rules of Engagement, 2000, R, ★★½ 2003
Runaway Bride, 1999, R, ★★ 2002
Runaway Train, 1985, R, ★★★★ 1998
Run Lola Run, 1999, R, ★★★ 2002
Running Free, 2000, G, ★½ 2003
Running on Empty, 1988, PG-13, ★★★★ 1998
Running Scared, 1986, R, ★★★ 1995
Run of the Country, The, 1995, R, ★★½ 1997
Rush, 1992, R, ★★★ 1996
Rush Hour, 1998, PG-13, ★★★ 2001
Rush Hour 2, 2001, PG-13, ★½ 2003
Rushmore, 1999, R, ★★½ 2002
Russia House, The, 1990, R, ★★ 1995
Ruthless People, 1986, R, ★★★½ 1998

S

Sabrina, 1995, PG, ★★★½ 1998
Safe, 1995, NR, ★★★ 1998
Safe Men, 1998, R, ★ 2001
Safe Passage, 1995, PG-13, ★★ 1996
Saint, The, 1997, PG-13, ★★ 1998
Saint Jack, 1979, R, ★★★★ 1998
Saint of Fort Washington, The,
  1994, R, ★★★ 1998
Salaam Bombay!, 1988, NR, ★★★★ 1998

Salton Sea, The, 2002, R, ★★★ 2003
Salvador, 1986, R, ★★★ 1996
Sammy and Rosie Get Laid,
  1987, R, ★★★½ 1998
Sandlot, The, 1993, PG, ★★★ 1998
Santa Clause, The, 1994, PG, ★★½ 1998
Santa Claus: The Movie, 1985, PG, ★★½ 1987
Santa Sangre, 1990, R, ★★★★ 1998
Sarafina!, 1992, PG-13, ★★ 1995
Saturday Night Fever, 1977, R, ★★★½ 1998
Savage Nights, 1994, NR, ★★½ 1995
Save the Last Dance, 2001, PG-13, ★★★ 2003
Saving Grace, 2000, R, ★★ 2003
Saving Private Ryan, 1998, R, ★★★★ 2001
Saving Silverman, 2001, PG-13, ½★ 2003
Savior, 1998, R, ★★★½ 2001
Say Amen, Somebody, 1983, G, ★★★★ 1998
Say Anything, 1989, PG-13, ★★★★ 1998
Say It Isn't So, 2001, R, ★ 2003
Scandal, 1989, R, ★★★★ 1998
Scarecrow, 1973, R, ★★★ 1998
Scarface, 1983, R, ★★★★ 1998
Scarlet Letter, The, 1995, R, ★½ 1997
Scary Movie, 2000, R, ★★★ 2003
Scene of the Crime, 1987, NR, ★★½ 1988
Scenes from a Mall, 1991, R, ★ 1995
Scenes from a Marriage, 1974, PG, ★★★★ 1998
Scent of a Woman, 1992, R, ★★★½ 1998
Scent of Green Papaya, The,
  1994, NR, ★★★★ 1998
Schindler's List, 1993, R, ★★★★ 1998
School Daze, 1988, R, ★★★½ 1998
School of Flesh, The, 1999, R, ★★★ 2002
School Ties, 1992, PG-13, ★★★ 1996
Scooby-Doo, 2002, PG, ★ 2003
Score, The, 2001, R, ★★★ 2003
Scorpion King, The, 2002, PG-13, ★★½ 2003
Scotland, PA., 2002, R, ★★½ 2003
Scout, The, 1994, PG-13, ★½ 1996
Scream, 1996, R, ★★★ 1999
Scream 2, 1997, R, ★★★ 2000
Scream 3, 2000, R, ★★ 2003
Screamers, 1996, R, ★★½ 1999
Scrooged, 1988, PG-13, ★ 1994
Sea of Love, 1989, R, ★★★ 1998
Searching for Bobby Fischer,
  1993, PG, ★★★★ 1998
Secret Agent, The, 1996, R, ★ 1999
Secret Garden, The, 1993, G, ★★★★ 1998
Secret Honor, 1984, NR, ★★★★ 1998
Secret of My Success, The,
  1987, PG-13, ★½ 1989

Singles, 1992, PG-13, ★★★	1998
Single White Female, 1992, R, ★★★	1996
Sirens, 1994, R, ★★★½	1998
Sister Act, 1992, PG, ★★½	1996
Sister Act 2: Back in the Habit, 1993, PG, ★★	1995
Sisters, 1973, R, ★★★	1998
Six Days, Seven Nights, 1998, PG-13, ★★½	2001
Sixteen Candles, 1984, PG, ★★★	1998
6th Day, The, 2000, PG-13, ★★★	2003
Sixth Man, The, 1997, PG-13, ★½	2000
Sixth Sense, The, 1999, PG-13, ★★★	2002
Skin Deep, 1989, R, ★★★	1998
Skulls, The, 2000, PG-13, ★	2003
Slacker, 1991, R, ★★★	1998
Slackers, 2002, R, no stars	2003
Slam, 1998, R, ★★½	2001
SlamNation, 1998, NR, ★★★	2001
Slappy and the Stinkers, 1998, PG, ★★	2001
Slaves of New York, 1989, R, ½★	1993
SLC Punk!, 1999, R, ★★★	2002
Sleeper, 1973, PG, ★★★½	1998
Sleeping with the Enemy, 1991, R, ★½	1994
Sleepless in Seattle, 1993, PG, ★★★	1998
Sleepy Hollow, 1999, R, ★★★½	2002
Sleuth, 1972, PG, ★★★★	1998
Sliding Doors, 1998, PG-13, ★★	2001
Sling Blade, 1996, R, ★★★½	1999
Slugger's Wife, The, 1985, PG-13, ★★	1986
Slums of Beverly Hills, 1998, R, ★★★	2001
Small Change, 1976, PG, ★★★★	1998
Small Soldiers, 1998, PG-13, ★★½	2001
Small Time Crooks, 2000, PG, ★★★	2003
Smash Palace, 1982, R, ★★★★	1998
Smiling Fish and Goat on Fire, 2000, R, ★★★	2003
Smilla's Sense of Snow, 1997, R, ★★★	1998
Smoke, 1995, R, ★★★	1998
Smoke Signals, 1998, PG-13, ★★★	2001
Smokey and the Bandit II, 1980, PG, ★	1986
Smooth Talk, 1986, PG-13, ★★★½	1998
Snake Eyes, 1998, R, ★	2001
Snapper, The, 1993, R, ★★★½	1998
Snatch, 2001, R, ★★	2003
Sneakers, 1992, PG-13, ★★½	1994
Sniper, 1993, R, ★★★	1996
Snow Day, 2000, PG, ★½	2003
Snow Falling on Cedars, 2000, PG-13, ★★★½	2003
Soapdish, 1991, PG-13, ★★★½	1998
So I Married an Axe Murderer, 1993, PG-13, ★★½	1995
Soldier of Orange, 1980, PG, ★★★½	1986
Soldier's Daughter Never Cries, A, 1998, R, ★★★½	2001
Soldier's Story, A, 1984, PG, ★★½	1993
Solomon and Gaenor, 2000, R, ★★	2003
Some Kind of Wonderful, 1987, PG-13, ★★★	1998
Some Mother's Son, 1996, R, ★★★	1999
Someone Like You, 2001, PG-13, ★★	2003
Someone to Watch Over Me, 1987, R, ★★	1992
Something to Talk About, 1995, R, ★★★½	1998
Something Wild, 1986, R, ★★★½	1998
Sometimes a Great Notion, 1971, PG, ★★★	1998
Somewhere in Time, 1980, PG, ★★	1988
Sommersby, 1993, PG-13, ★★	1994
Sonatine, 1998, R, ★★★½	2001
Songcatcher, 2001, PG-13, ★★★	2003
Songwriter, 1985, R, ★★★½	1996
Son-in-Law, 1993, PG-13, ★★	1995
Son's Room, The, 2002, R, ★★★½	2003
Sophie's Choice, 1982, R, ★★★★	1998
Sorority Boys, 2002, R, ½★	2003
Soul Food, 1997, R, ★★★½	2000
Soul Man, 1986, PG-13, ★	1989
Sounder, 1972, G, ★★★★	1998
Sour Grapes, 1998, R, no stars	2001
South, 2000, NR, ★★★	2003
South Central, 1992, R, ★★★	1996
Southern Comfort, 1981, R, ★★★	1996
South Park: Bigger, Longer and Uncut, 1999, R, ★★½	2002
Spaceballs, 1987, PG, ★★½	1991
Space Cowboys, 2000, PG-13, ★★★	2003
Space Jam, 1996, PG, ★★★½	1999
Spanish Prisoner, The, 1998, PG, ★★★½	2001
Spartacus, 1960, PG-13, ★★★	1997
Spawn, 1997, PG-13, ★★★½	2000
Special Effects Documentary, 1996, NR, ★★★	1999
Species, 1995, R, ★★	1997
Speechless, 1994, PG-13, ★★	1996
Speed, 1994, R, ★★★★	1997
Speed 2: Cruise Control, 1997, PG-13, ★★★½	2000
Sphere, 1998, PG-13, ★½	2001

Spice World, 1998, PG, ½★	2001
Spider-Man, 2002, PG-13, ★★	2003
Spider's Stratagem, The, 1973, PG, ★★★	1998
Spike of Bensonhurst, 1988, R, ★★★	1998
Spirit: Stallion of the Cimarron, 2002, G, ★★★	2003
Spitfire Grill, The, 1996, PG-13, ★★	1999
Splash, 1984, PG, ★½	1993
Spring Break, 1983, R, ★	1988
Sprung, 1997, R, ★½	2000
Spy Game, 2001, R, ★★½	2003
Spy Kids, 2001, PG, ★★★½	2003
Spy Who Loved Me, The, 1977, PG, ★★★½	1998
Stairway to Heaven, 1946, PG, ★★★★	1997
Stakeout, 1987, R, ★★★	1996
Stand and Deliver, 1988, PG-13, ★★½	1994
Stanley & Iris, 1990, PG-13, ★★½	1993
Stardust Memories, 1980, PG, ★★	1997
STAR 80, 1983, R, ★★★★	1998
Stargate, 1994, PG-13, ★	1997
Star Is Born, A, 1954 (1983), PG, ★★★★	1997
Star Kid, 1998, PG, ★★★	2001
Starmaker, The, 1996, R, ★★★	1999
Starman, 1984, PG, ★★★	1998
Star Maps, 1997, R, ★★	2000
Stars Fell on Henrietta, The, 1995, PG, ★★	1997
Starship Troopers, 1997, R, ★★	2000
Star Trek: First Contact, 1996, PG-13, ★★★½	1999
Star Trek: Generations, 1994, PG, ★★	1997
Star Trek: Insurrection, 1998, PG, ★★	2001
Star Trek: The Motion Picture, 1979, G, ★★★	1998
Star Trek II: The Wrath of Khan, 1982, PG, ★★★	1998
Star Trek III: The Search for Spock, 1984, PG, ★★★	1998
Star Trek IV: The Voyage Home, 1986, PG, ★★★½	1998
Star Trek V: The Final Frontier, 1989, PG, ★★	1997
Star Trek VI: The Undiscovered Country, 1991, PG, ★★★	1998
Startup.com, 2001, R, ★★★	2003
Star Wars, 1977, PG, ★★★★	1997
Star Wars Episode I: The Phantom Menace, 1999, PG, ★★★½	2002
Star Wars: Episode II—Attack of the Clones, 2002, PG, ★★	2003

Star Wars (Special Edition), PG, 1997, ★★★★	1998
State and Main, 2000, R, ★★★	2003
State of Grace, 1990, R, ★★★½	1998
Stay Hungry, 1976, R, ★★★	1996
Staying Alive, 1983, PG, ★	1994
Staying Together, 1989, R, ★★	1993
Stealing Beauty, 1996, R, ★★	1999
Steal This Movie, 2000, R, ★★★	2003
Steam: The Turkish Bath, 1999, NR, ★★★★	2002
Steel Magnolias, 1989, PG, ★★★	1998
Stella, 1990, PG-13, ★★★½	1998
St. Elmo's Fire, 1985, R, ★½	1987
Stepfather, The, 1987, R, ★★½	1994
Stephen King's Silver Bullet, 1985, R, ★★★	1988
Stepmom, 1998, PG-13, ★★	2001
Stepping Out, 1991, PG, ★★	1994
Stevie, 1981, NR, ★★★★	1998
Stigmata, 1999, R, ★★	2002
Still Crazy, 1999, R, ★★★	2002
Sting II, The, 1983, PG, ★★	1986
Stir Crazy, 1980, R, ★★	1987
Stir of Echoes, 1999, R, ★★★	2002
Stolen Summer, 2002, PG, ★★★	2003
Stonewall, 1996, NR, ★★½	1999
Stop Making Sense, 1984, NR, ★★★½	1998
Stop! Or My Mom Will Shoot, 1992, PG-13, ½★	1994
Stormy Monday, 1988, R, ★★★½	1998
Story of Qiu Ju, The, 1993, NR, ★★★½	1997
Story of Us, The, 1999, R, ★	2002
Story of Women, 1990, R, ★★½	1993
Storytelling, 2002, R, ★★★½	2003
Storyville, 1992, R, ★★★½	1998
Straight Out of Brooklyn, 1991, R, ★★★	1998
Straight Story, The, 1999, G, ★★★★	2002
Straight Talk, 1992, PG, ★★	1994
Straight Time, 1978, R, ★★★½	1998
Strange Days, 1995, R, ★★★★	1998
Stranger Among Us, A, 1992, PG-13, ★½	1994
Stranger than Paradise, 1984, R, ★★★★	1998
Strapless, 1990, R, ★★★	1998
Strawberry and Chocolate, 1995, R, ★★★½	1998
Streamers, 1984, R, ★★★★	1998
Streetcar Named Desire, A, 1951, PG, ★★★★	1997
Street Smart, 1987, R, ★★★	1998
Streets of Fire, 1984, PG, ★★★	1988

Taxi Driver, 1976, R, ★★★★ 1997

Taxi Driver: 20th Anniversary Edition,
1995, R, ★★★★ 1999

Taxing Woman, A, 1988, NR, ★★ 1992

Teachers, 1984, R, ★★ 1986

Teaching Mrs. Tingle, 1999, PG-13, ★½ 2002

Tea with Mussolini, 1999, PG, ★★½ 2002

Teenage Mutant Ninja Turtles,
1990, PG, ★★½ 1994

Teenage Mutant Ninja Turtles II: The
Secret of the Ooze, 1991, PG, ★ 1994

Teen Wolf Too, 1987, PG, ½★ 1989

Telling Lies in America,
1997, PG-13, ★★★ 2000

Tell Them Willie Boy Is Here,
1970, PG, ★★★½ 1996

Temptress Moon, 1997, R, ★★ 2000

10, 1979, R, ★★★★ 1998

Tender Mercies, 1983, PG, ★★★ 1998

10 Things I Hate About You,
1999, PG-13, ★★½ 2002

Tequila Sunrise, 1988, R, ★★½ 1994

Terminal Velocity, 1994, PG-13, ★★ 1996

Terminator 2: Judgment Day,
1991, R, ★★★½ 1998

Terms of Endearment, 1983, PG, ★★★★ 1998

Terrorist, The, 2000, NR, ★★★½ 2003

Terror Train, 1980, R, ★ 1986

Tess, 1980, PG, ★★★★ 1998

Testament, 1983, PG, ★★★★ 1998

Tetsuo II: Body Hammer,
1997, NR, ★★★ 2000

Tex, 1982, PG, ★★★★ 1998

Texas Chainsaw Massacre, The,
1974, R, ★★ 1995

Texasville, 1990, R, ★★★½ 1998

That Obscure Object of Desire,
1977, R, ★★★★ 1998

That Old Feeling, 1997, PG-13, ★ 1998

That's Dancing!, 1985, PG, ★★★ 1998

That's Entertainment!, 1974, G, ★★★★ 1998

That's Entertainment! III,
1994, G, ★★★½ 1998

That's the Way I Like It,
1999, PG-13, ★★★ 2002

That Thing You Do!, 1996, PG, ★★★ 1999

That Was Then . . . This Is Now,
1985, R, ★★ 1987

Thelma & Louise, 1991, R, ★★★½ 1998

Thelonious Monk: Straight, No Chaser,
1989, PG-13, ★★★½ 1998

Theory of Flight, The, 1999, R, ★★½ 2002

Theremin: An Electronic Odyssey,
1995, NR, ★★★½ 1998

Therese, 1987, NR, ★★★½ 1996

There's Something About Mary,
1998, R, ★★★ 2001

They Call Me Bruce, 1983, PG, ★★ 1986

They Shoot Horses, Don't They?,
1970, PG, ★★★★ 1998

Thief, 1981, R, ★★★½ 1996

Thief, The, 1998, R, ★★★ 2001

Thieves Like Us, 1974, R, ★★★½ 1998

Thin Blue Line, The, 1988, NR, ★★★½ 1998

Thing, The, 1982, R, ★★½ 1995

Things Change, 1988, PG, ★★★ 1998

Things to Do in Denver When You're
Dead, 1996, R, ★★½ 1999

Thin Line Between Love and Hate, A,
1996, R, ★★½ 1999

Thin Red Line, The, 1999, R, ★★★ 2002

Third Miracle, The, 2000, R, ★★★ 2003

Thirteen, 2000, NR, ★★★½ 2003

Thirteen Conversations About One
Thing, 2002, R, ★★★★ 2003

Thirteen Days, 2001, PG-13, ★★★ 2003

13 Ghosts, 2001, R, ★ 2003

13th Warrior, The, 1999, R, ★½ 2002

35 Up, 1992, NR, ★★★★ 1998

36 Fillette, 1989, NR, ★★★½ 1996

Thirty-two Short Films About Glenn
Gould, 1994, NR, ★★★★ 1998

This Boy's Life, 1993, R, ★★★½ 1998

This Is Elvis, 1981, PG, ★★★½ 1998

This Is My Father, 1999, R, ★★★ 2002

This Is My Life, 1992, PG-13, ★★★ 1996

This Is Spinal Tap, 1984, R, ★★★★ 1998

Thomas and the Magic Railroad,
2000, G, ★ 2003

Thomas Crown Affair, The,
1999, R, ★★½ 2002

Thomas in Love, 2001, NR, ★★ 2003

Thousand Acres, A, 1997, R, ★★ 2000

Three Kings, 1999, R, ★★★★ 2002

Three Lives and Only One Death,
1997, NR, ★★★ 2000

Three Men and a Baby, 1987, PG, ★★★ 1998

Three Men and a Little Lady,
1990, PG, ★★ 1994

Three Musketeers, The, 1993, PG, ★★ 1995

3 Ninjas Kick Back, 1994, PG, ★★½ 1995

Three of Hearts, 1993, R, ★★★ 1996

Three Seasons, 1999, PG-13, ★★★ 2002

Threesome, 1994, R, ★★★ 1996

3,000 Miles to Graceland, 2001, R, ★½   2003
Three to Tango, 1999, PG-13, ★   2002
3 Women, 1977, PG, ★★★★   1998
Throw Momma from the Train,
   1987, PG-13, ★★   1993
Thunderheart, 1992, R, ★★★½   1998
THX 1138, 1971, PG, ★★★   1998
Ticket to Heaven, 1981, R, ★★★½   1998
Tie Me Up! Tie Me Down!, 1990, NR, ★★   1993
Tiger's Tale, A, 1988, R, ★★   1989
Tightrope, 1984, R, ★★★½   1998
'Til There Was You, 1997, PG-13, ½★   1998
Tim Burton's Nightmare Before
   Christmas, 1993, PG, ★★★½   1998
Time and Tide, 2001, R, ★★★   2003
Time Bandits, 1981, PG, ★★★   1998
Time Code, 2000, R, ★★★   2003
Timecop, 1994, R, ★★   1997
Time for Drunken Horses, A,
   2000, NR, ★★★   2003
Time Machine, The, 2002, PG-13, ★½   2003
Time of Destiny, A, 1988, PG-13, ★★★½   1998
Time Out, 2002, PG-13, ★★★   2003
Time Regained, 2000, NR, ★★★½   2003
Times of Harvey Milk, The,
   1985, NR, ★★★½   1997
Tin Cup, 1996, R, ★★★   1999
Tin Drum, The, 1980, R, ★★   1988
Tin Men, 1987, R, ★★★   1998
Titan A.E., 2000, PG, ★★★½   2003
Titanic, 1997, PG-13, ★★★★   2000
Titus, 2000, R, ★★★½   2003
To Be or Not To Be, 1983, R, ★★★   1998
To Die For, 1995, R, ★★★½   1998
Together, 2001, R, ★★★   2003
To Gillian on Her 37th Birthday,
   1996, PG-13, ★★   1999
Tokyo Story, 1953, G, ★★★★   1997
To Live, 1994, NR, ★★★½   1998
To Live and Die in L.A., 1985, R, ★★★★   1998
Tom and Viv, 1995, PG-13, ★★½   1996
Tomcats, 2001, R, no stars   2003
Tommy, 1975, PG, ★★★   1998
Tomorrow Never Dies, 1997, PG-13, ★★★   2000
Too Beautiful for You, 1990, R, ★★★½   1998
Too Much Sleep, 2001, NR, ★★★   2003
Tootsie, 1982, PG, ★★★★   1998
Topaz, 1970, PG, ★★★½   1998
Top Gun, 1986, PG, ★★½   1998
Top Secret!, 1984, R, ★★★½   1998
Topsy-Turvy, 2000, R, ★★★★   2003
Torch Song Trilogy, 1988, R, ★★★½   1998

Tortilla Soup, 2001, PG-13, ★★★   2003
To Sleep With Anger, 1990, PG, ★★½   1993
Total Recall, 1990, R, ★★★½   1998
Toto le Heros, 1992, NR, ★★½   1994
Touch, 1997, R, ★★½   2000
Tough Enough, 1983, PG, ★★★   1986
Tough Guys Don't Dance, 1987, R, ★★½   1993
To Wong Foo, Thanks for Everything!
   Julie Newmar, 1995, PG-13, ★★½   1997
Toys, 1992, PG-13, ★★½   1994
Toy Story, 1995, G, ★★★½   1998
Toy Story 2, 1999, G, ★★★½   2002
Track 29, 1988, R, ★★★   1996
Trading Places, 1983, R, ★★★½   1998
Traffic, 2001, R, ★★★★   2003
Training Day, 2001, R, ★★★   2003
Trainspotting, 1996, R, ★★★   1998
Traveller, 1997, R, ★★★   2000
Trees Lounge, 1996, R, ★★★½   1999
Trekkies, 1999, PG, ★★★   2002
Trespass, 1992, R, ★★½   1994
Trial, The, 1994, NR, ★★½   1996
Trial, The, 2000, NR, ★★★★   2003
Trial and Error, 1997, PG-13, ★★★   1998
Tribute, 1981, PG, ★★★   1996
Trick, 1999, R, ★★   2002
Trippin', 1999, R, ★★½   2002
Trip to Bountiful, The, 1985, PG, ★★★½   1998
Triumph of Love, The, 2002, PG-13, ★★★   2003
Trixie, 2000, R, ★★   2003
Tron, 1982, PG, ★★★★   1998
Troop Beverly Hills, 1989, PG, ★★   1994
Trouble in Mind, 1985, R, ★★★★   1998
Troublesome Creek: A Midwestern,
   1997, NR, ★★★   2000
True Believer, 1989, R, ★★★   1996
True Colors, 1991, R, ★★   1994
True Confessions, 1981, R, ★★★   1996
True Crime, 1999, R, ★★★   2002
True Lies, 1994, R, ★★★   1998
True Love, 1989, R, ★★★   1996
True Romance, 1993, R, ★★★   1998
True Stories, 1986, PG-13, ★★★½   1998
Truly, Madly, Deeply, 1991, NR, ★★★   1998
Truman Show, The, 1998, PG, ★★★★   2001
Trumpet of the Swan, The, 2001, G, ★½   2003
Trust, 1991, R, ★★   1994
Truth About Cats and Dogs, The,
   1996, PG-13, ★★★½   1999
Truth or Dare, 1991, R, ★★★½   1998
Tucker: The Man and His Dream,
   1988, PG, ★★½   1993

W

Where the Boys Are, 1984, R, ½★	1987	Wild Wild West, 1999, PG-13, ★	2002
Where the Buffalo Roam, 1980, R, ★★	1991	Willard, 1971, PG, ★★	1991
Where the Day Takes You, 1992, R, ★★★	1996	William Shakespeare's A Midsummer	
Where the Green Ants Dream,		Night's Dream, 1999, PG-13, ★★★	2002
1985, NR, ★★★	1988	William Shakespeare's Romeo & Juliet,	
Where the Heart Is, 1990, R, ★½	1992	1996, PG-13, ★★	1999
Where the Heart Is, 2000, PG-13, ★★½	2003	Willie and Phil, 1980, R, ★★★	1996
Where the Money Is, 2000, PG-13, ★★★	2003	Willie Wonka and the Chocolate Factory,	
While You Were Sleeping,		1971, G, ★★★★	1998
1995, PG, ★★★	1998	Willow, 1988, PG, ★★½	1994
Whistle Blower, The, 1987, PG, ★★★½	1998	Wind, 1992, PG-13, ★★★	1998
White, 1994, R, ★★★½	1998	Windhorse, 1999, NR, ★★	2002
White Fang, 1991, PG, ★★★	1998	Windtalkers, 2002, R, ★★	2003
White Fang 2: Myth of the White Wolf,		Wing Commander, 1999, PG-13, ★	2002
1994, PG, ★★★	1998	Wings of Courage, 1996, G, ★★★	1999
White Hunter, Black Heart,		Wings of Desire, 1988, NR, ★★★★	1998
1990, PG, ★★★	1998	Wings of the Dove, The,	
White Man's Burden, 1995, R, ★★	1997	1997, R, ★★★½	2000
White Men Can't Jump, 1992, R, ★★★½	1998	Winslow Boy, The, 1999, G, ★★★½	2002
White Mischief, 1988, R, ★★★	1998	Winter Guest, The, 1998, R, ★★½	2001
White Nights, 1985, PG-13, ★★	1988	Winter of Our Dreams, 1983, R, ★★★	1998
White Palace, 1990, R, ★★★½	1998	Wired, 1989, R, ★½	1993
White Sands, 1992, R, ★★	1994	Wise Guys, 1986, R, ★★★½	1998
White Squall, 1996, PG-13, ★★★	1999	Wish You Were Here, 1987, R, ★★★½	1998
Who Framed Roger Rabbit,		Witches, The, 1990, PG, ★★★	1998
1988, PG, ★★★★	1998	Witches of Eastwick, The, 1987, R, ★★★½	1998
Whole Nine Yards, The, 2000, R, ★★★	2003	With a Friend Like Harry, 2001, R, ★★★	2003
Whole Wide World, The,		With Honors, 1994, PG-13, ★★½	1995
1997, PG, ★★★	1998	Withnail & I, 1987, R, ★★★★	1998
Whore, 1991, NC-17, ★★★	1996	Without a Trace, 1983, PG, ★★★½	1998
Who's the Man, 1993, R, ★★★	1998	Without Limits, 1998, PG-13, ★★★	2001
Why Do Fools Fall in Love, 1998, R, ★★	2001	Without You I'm Nothing, 1990, R, ★★★	1996
Wide Awake, 1998, PG, ★★	2001	Witness, 1985, R, ★★★★	1998
Wide Sargasso Sea, 1993, NC-17, ★★★½	1998	Wiz, The, 1978, G, ★★★	1998
Widow of St. Pierre, The,		Wizard, The, 1989, PG, ★	1992
2001, R, ★★★★	2003	Wolf, 1994, R, ★★★	1998
Widows' Peak, 1994, PG, ★★★½	1998	Woman on Top, 2000, R, ★★½	2003
Wife, The, 1997, R, ★★★	1998	Woman's Tale, A, 1992, PG-13, ★★★★	1998
Wild America, 1997, PG, ★★	1998	Woman Under the Influence, A,	
Wild at Heart, 1990, R, ★★½	1997	1974, R, ★★★★	1998
Wild Bill, 1995, R, ★★	1997	Wonder Boys, 2000, R, ★★★★	2003
Wild Bunch, The, 1969, R, ★★★★	1997	Wonderful Horrible Life of Leni	
Wildcats, 1985, R, ★½	1990	Riefenstahl, The, 1994, NR, ★★★½	1998
Wilde, 1998, R, ★★★½	2001	Wonderland, 2000, R, ★★★	2003
Wild Man Blues, 1998, PG, ★★★	2001	Woo, 1998, R, ★½	2001
Wild Orchid, 1990, R, ★	1994	Wood, The, 1999, R, ★★★	2002
Wild Orchid II: Two Shades of Blue,		Woodstock, 1969, R, ★★★★	1997
1992, R, ★★	1994	Working Girl, 1988, R, ★★★★	1996
Wild Reeds, 1995, NR, ★★★	1998	Working Girls, 1987, NR, ★★★	1998
Wild Things, 1998, R, ★★★	2001	World According to Garp, The,	
Wild West, 1993, NR, ★★	1995	1982, R, ★★★	1998

Index

A

Aaliyah: *Queen of the Damned,* 490; *Romeo Must Die,* 510

Aaron, Caroline: *What Planet Are You From?,* 664

Abadal, Ignasi: *Nine Queens,* 431

Abecassis, Yael: *Kadosh,* 317

Abedini, Hossein: *Baran,* 40

About a Boy, 1

Abraham, F. Murray: *Finding Forrester,* 214; *13 Ghosts,* 605

Abrahams, Jon: *Meet the Parents,* 389

Abrams, Abiola Wendy: *Jump Tomorrow,* 312

Accorsi, Stefano: *Son's Room, The,* 564Acevedo, Kirk: *Dinner Rush,* 160

Acheson, Mark: *Trixie,* 629

Ackert, David: *Maryam,* 386

Ackland, Joss: *Passion of Mind,* 465

Adams, Jane: *Anniversary Party, The,* 26; *Songcatcher,* 563

Adams, Jay: *Dogtown and Z-Boys,* 166

Adams, Joey Lauren: *Beautiful,* 45

Adams, Tacey: *Good Housekeeping,* 242

Adamson, Andrew: dir., *Shrek,* 547

Aday, Meat Loaf: *Focus,* 217

Addeo, Rosemarie: *Smiling Fish and Goat on Fire,* 557

Addy, Mark: *Down to Earth,* 170; *Flintstones in Viva Rock Vegas, The,* 216; *Knight's Tale, A,* 327; *Time Machine, The,* 612

Ade, Melyssa: *Jason X,* 301

Adebimpe, Tunde: *Jump Tomorrow,* 312

Adelstein, Paul: *Bedazzled,* 51

Adetuyi, Robert: dir., *Turn It Up,* 631

Adjemian, Martin: *La Cienaga,* 331

Adventures of Rocky & Bullwinkle, The, 2

Aernouts, Kenny: *Innocence,* 284

Affair of Love, An, 3

Affair of the Necklace, The, 4

Affleck, Ben: *Boiler Room,* 75; *Bounce,* 79; *Changing Lanes,* 109; *Jay and Silent Bob Strike Back,* 302; *Pearl Harbor,* 469;

Reindeer Games, 495; *Sum of All Fears, The,* 583

Affleck, Casey: *Drowning Mona,* 174; *Ocean's Eleven,* 443

Aghdashloo, Shohreh: *Maryam,* 386

Agnes Browne, 5

Agudelo, Wilmar: *Our Lady of the Assassins,* 459

Ahmadi, Ayoub: *Time for Drunken Horses, A,* 611

A.I. Artificial Intelligence, 6

Aiello, Danny: *Dinner Rush,* 160

Aiken, Liam: *I Dreamed of Africa,* 282; *Sweet November,* 590

Aimee & Jaguar, 7

Aitken, Isabella: *Big Tease, The,* 64

Akers, Michelle: *I Remember Me,* 291

Akhtar, Fatemeh Cheragh: *Day I Became a Woman, The,* 152

Akinnuoye-Agbaje, Adewale: *Bourne Identity, The,* 80; *Mummy Returns, The,* 417

Alajar, Gina: *Debut, The,* 153

Albers, Hans: *Blue Angel, The,* 73

Alda, Alan: *What Women Want,* 669

Ales, John: *Nutty Professor II: The Klumps,* 439

Alexander, Jane: *Sunshine State,* 586

Alexander, Jason: *Adventures of Rocky & Bullwinkle, The,* 2; *Shallow Hal,* 541; *Trumpet of the Swan, The,* 630

Alexi-Malle, Adam: *Man Who Wasn't There, The,* 383

Ali, 8

Alice, Mary: *Catfish in Black Bean Sauce,* 99; *Sunshine State,* 586

Allcroft, Britt: dir., *Thomas and the Magic Railroad,* 606

Allegre, Ginette: *L'Humanite,* 352

Allen, Douglas: *Diamond Men,* 158

Allen, Joan: *Contender, The,* 128

Allen, Karen: *In the Bedroom,* 286; *Perfect Storm, The,* 471; *World Traveler,* 681

Allen, Kevin: *Big Tease, The,* 64; dir., *Big Tease, The,* 64

Allen, Tessa: *Enough,* 191

Allen, Tim: *Big Trouble,* 64; *Joe Somebody,* 308

Allen, Woody: dir., *Company Man,* 128; *Curse of the Jade Scorpion, The,* 145; *Hollywood Ending,* 271; *Small Time Crooks,* 556; dir., *Curse of the Jade Scorpion, The,* 145; *Hollywood Ending,* 271; *Small Time Crooks,* 556

Allred, Corbin: *Diamonds,* 159

All the Pretty Horses, 10

Almani, Mariam Palvin: *Circle, The,* 120

Almela, Laura: *Amores Perros,* 22

Almereyda, Michael: dir., *Hamlet,* 251

Almost Famous, 11

Along Came a Spider, 12

Altman, Bruce: *L.I.E.,* 354

Altman, Robert: dir., *Dr. T and the Women,* 176; *Gosford Park,* 243

Alva, Tony: *Dogtown and Z-Boys,* 166

Alvarez, Juan Carlos: *Our Lady of the Assassins,* 459

Alvaro, Anne: *Taste of Others, The,* 597

Amado, Chisco: *Nico and Dani,* 430

Amati Girls, The, 14

Amedori, John Patrick: *Unbreakable,* 638

Amelie, 15

Amenabar, Alejandro: dir., *Others, The,* 457

American Movie, 16

American Outlaws, 17

American Pie 2, 18

American Psycho, 19

American Rhapsody, An, 20

America's Sweethearts, 21

Amoni, Toni: *Ninth Gate, The,* 432

Amores Perros, 22

Anderman, Maureen: *Final,* 211

Anderson, Anthony: *Big Momma's House,* 63; *Kingdom Come,* 323; *Me, Myself & Irene,* 392; *Romeo Must Die,* 510; *See Spot Run,* 532; *Two Can Play That Game,* 633; *Urban Legends: Final Cut,* 644

I

I Am Sam, 280

Ibu, Masato: *Taboo,* 593

Ice Age, 281

Ice Cube: *Ghosts of Mars,* 229

Ice-T: *3,000 Miles to Graceland,* 607

Ide, Rakkyo: *Kikujiro,* 322

I Dreamed of Africa, 282

Ifans, Rhys: *Human Nature,* 275; *Little Nicky,* 359; *Replacements, The,* 498; *Shipping News, The,* 543

Igawa, Hisashi: *Madadayo,* 377

Imoto, Yuka: *Metropolis,* 396

Importance of Being Earnest, The, 283

Inarritu, Alejandro Gonzalez: dir., *Amores Perros,* 22

Innocence, 284

Innushuk, Pakkak: *Fast Runner, The,* 203

Inoh, Shizuka: *8½ Women,* 183

Insomnia, 285

In the Bedroom, 286

In the Mood for Love, 288

Intimacy, 289

Invisible Circus, 290

Ipkarnak, Eugene: *Fast Runner, The,* 203

I Remember Me, 291

Iris, 292

Iron Ladies, The, 293

Iron Monkey, 293

Irons, Jeremy: *Dungeons & Dragons,* 178; *Time Machine, The,* 612

Ironside, Michael: *Crime and Punishment in Suburbia,* 136

Irrek, Mario: *Legend of Rita, The,* 349

Irving, Amy: *Thirteen Conversations About One Thing,* 602

Irwin, Dave: *Go Tigers!,* 246

Irwin, Steve: *Crocodile Hunter, The: Collision Course,* 139; *Dr. Dolittle 2,* 171

Irwin, Terri: *Crocodile Hunter, The: Collision Course,* 139

Isaac, Estelle: *Baise-Moi,* 35

Isaac, James: dir., *Jason X,* 301

Isaacs, Jason: *Patriot, The,* 466; *Sweet November,* 590

Iscove, Robert: dir., *Boys and Girls,* 81

Isn't She Great?, 294

Italian for Beginners, 296

It All Starts Today, 296

Itzin, Gregory: *Life or Something Like It,* 357

Iures, Marcel: *Hart's War,* 259

Ivalu, Madeline: *Fast Runner, The,* 203

Ivalu, Sylvia: *Fast Runner, The,* 203

Ivanek, Zeljko: *Hannibal,* 253

Ivans xtc., 298

Ivey, Dana: *Disney's The Kid,* 163

Ivory, James: dir., *Golden Bowl, The,* 240

Izzard, Eddie: *Cat's Meow, The,* 101; *Shadow of the Vampire,* 538

J

Jackie Robinson Steppers Marching Band, The: *Our Song,* 460

Jackman, Hugh: *Kate & Leopold,* 319; *Someone Like You,* 562; *Swordfish,* 591; *X-Men,* 683

Jackpot, 300

Jackson, Janet: *Nutty Professor II: The Klumps,* 439

Jackson, Jonathan: *Insomnia,* 285

Jackson, Joshua: *Gossip,* 245; *Skulls, The,* 554

Jackson, Peter: dir., *Lord of the Rings: The Fellowship of the Ring, The,* 362

Jackson, Samuel L.: *Caveman's Valentine, The,* 102; *Changing Lanes,* 109; *Rules of Engagement,* 516; *Shaft,* 540; *Star Wars: Episode II—Attack of the Clones,* 573; *Unbreakable,* 638

Jacobi, Derek: *Gladiator,* 235; *Gosford Park,* 243; *Up at the Villa,* 642

Jacobsen, Marit Pia: *Elling,* 185

Jaffrey, Madhur: *Cotton Mary,* 131

Jaffrey, Sakina: *Cotton Mary,* 131; *Mystic Masseur, The,* 425

James, Brion: *King Is Alive, The,* 324

James, Geraldine: *Luzhin Defence, The,* 375

James, Ken: *Third Miracle, The,* 599

James, Lennie: *Lucky Break,* 372

James, Raji: *East Is East,* 180

Jane, Thomas: *Original Sin,* 454; *Sweetest Thing, The,* 589

Jannings, Emil: *Blue Angel, The,* 73

Janssen, Famke: *Love & Sex,* 368; *Made,* 378; *X-Men,* 683

Jaoui, Agnes: *Taste of Others, The,* 597; dir., *Taste of Others, The,* 597

Jaramillo, German: *Our Lady of the Assassins,* 459

Jarmusch, Jim: dir., *Ghost Dog: The Way of the Samurai,* 228

Jaroslaw, Nina: *Tao of Steve, The,* 595

Jason X, 301

Jay, Ricky: *Heist,* 264

Jay and Silent Bob Strike Back, 302

Jean-Baptiste, Marianne: *Cell, The,* 104

Jefford, Barbara: *Ninth Gate, The,* 432

Jeffrey, Michael: *Thirteen,* 601

Jenkins, Adam: *Solomon and Gaenor,* 561

Jenkins, Richard: *Man Who Wasn't There, The,* 383; *Me, Myself & Irene,* 392; *One Night at McCool's,* 449; *Say It Isn't So,* 525; *Snow Falling on Cedars,* 560

Jenney, Lucinda: *Crazy/Beautiful,* 134

Jensen, Sara Indrio: *Italian for Beginners,* 296

Jenson, Vicky: dir., *Shrek,* 547

Jenteal: *Made,* 378

Jesus' Son, 303

Jeter, Michael: *Gift, The,* 231; *Jurassic Park III,* 312

Jeunet, Jean-Pierre: dir., *Amelie,* 15

Jewison, Norman: dir., *Hurricane, The,* 278

Jiang Wu: *Shower,* 544

Jimmy Neutron: Boy Genius, 305

Jin, Elaine: *Yi Yi,* 686

Jobrani, Maziyar: *Maryam,* 386

Joe Dirt, 305

Joe Gould's Secret, 306

Joe Somebody, 308

Johansson, Scarlett: *American Rhapsody, An,* 20; *Eight Legged Freaks,* 184; *Ghost World,* 229; *Man Who Wasn't There, The,* 383

John, Elton: *Road to El Dorado, The,* 504

John Q., 308

Johnson, A. J.: *Baby Boy,* 33

Johnson, Anthony: *O,* 441

Johnson, Ashley: *Recess: School's Out,* 494

Johnson, Edwin: *Chalk,* 108

Johnson, Melody: *Jason X,* 301

Johnston, J. J.: *Lakeboat,* 336

Johnston, Joe: dir., *Jurassic Park III,* 312

Johnston, Kristen: *Flintstones in Viva Rock Vegas, The,* 216

Jolie, Angelina: *Girl, Interrupted,* 233; *Gone in 60 Seconds,* 241;

Index

Rodriguez, Paul: *Crocodile Dundee in Los Angeles*, 138; *Tortilla Soup*, 622
Rodriguez, Robert: dir., *Spy Kids*, 571
Roebuck, Daniel: *Final Destination*, 212
Roeves, Maurice: *Beautiful Creatures*, 47
Rogers, James B.: dir., *Say It Isn't So*, 525
Rogers, J. B.: dir., *American Pie 2*, 18
Rogers, Michael E.: *Thomas and the Magic Railroad*, 606
Rogers, Tristan: *Piece of Eden, A*, 473
Rohmer, Eric: dir., *Lady and the Duke, The*, 333
Rollerball, 509
Romagnoli, Mario: *Fellini Satyricon*, 206
Romano, Ray: *Ice Age*, 281
Romeo Must Die, 510
Romijn-Stamos, Rebecca: *Rollerball*, 509; *X-Men*, 683
Roney, Shanti: *Together*, 618
Rongione, Fabrizio: *Rosetta*, 513
Rooker, Michael: *Here on Earth*, 265
Rookie, The, 511
Room for Romeo Brass, A, 512
Roor, Gunilla: *Under the Sun*, 640
Roos, Don: dir., *Bounce*, 79
Root, Stephen: *O Brother, Where Art Thou?*, 442
Rose, Bernard: dir., *Ivans xtc.*, 298
Rose, Gabrielle: *Five Senses, The*, 215
Rosebaum, Michael: *Sorority Boys*, 565
Rosenberg, Joseph: *I Am Sam*, 280
Rosetta, 513
Ross, Katharine: *Donnie Darko*, 167
Ross, Matt: *American Psycho*, 19
Ross, Matthew: *Just Visiting*, 313
Rossellini, Isabella: *Left Luggage*, 346
Rossum, Emmy: *Songcatcher*, 563
Roth, Hans: *Blue Angel, The*, 73
Roth, Joe: dir., *America's Sweethearts*, 21
Roth, Stephanie: *Songcatcher*, 563
Roth, Tim: *Lucky Numbers*, 373; *Musketeer, The*, 420; dir., *War Zone, The*, 655
Rothhaar, Will: *Hearts in Atlantis*, 262

Rothman, John: *Say It Isn't So*, 525
Roundtree, Richard: *Corky Romano*, 130; *Shaft*, 540
Rourke, Mickey: *Pledge, The*, 479
Rouse, Eddie: *George Washington*, 226
Routledge, Jordan: *East Is East*, 180
Rouvel, Catherine: *Va Savoir*, 646
Rowland, Rodney: *6th Day, The*, 552
Roxburgh, Richard: *Last September, The*, 343; *Mission: Impossible 2*, 404; *Moulin Rouge*, 413
Royal Tenenbaums, The, 514
Rubineck, Saul: *Contender, The*, 128
Rudd, Paul: *Wet Hot American Summer*, 660
Rudolph, Alan: dir., *Trixie*, 629
Rudolph, Lars: *Princess and the Warrior, The*, 485
Rudolph, Maya: *Chuck & Buck*, 118
Rue, Sara: *Map of the World, A*, 385
Ruehl, Mercedes: *Amati Girls, The*, 14; *What's Cooking?*, 665
Ruffalo, Mark: *Last Castle, The*, 340; *Windtalkers*, 675; *You Can Count on Me*, 687
Ruffini, Gene: *Jump Tomorrow*, 312
Rufus: *Amelie*, 15
Rugrats in Paris, 515
Ruiz, Raul: dir., *Time Regained*, 614
Rule, Ja: *Turn It Up*, 631
Rules of Engagement, 516
Rumi, Wentzle: *Dogtown and Z-Boys*, 166
Running Free, 518
Runyan, Tygh: *AntiTrust*, 28
Rush, Geoffrey: *Lantana*, 337; *Quills*, 491; *Tailor of Panama, The*, 594
Rush Hour 2, 519
Russell, Chuck: dir., *Scorpion King, The*, 529
Russell, Clive: *Emperor's New Clothes, The*, 186
Russell, Jay: dir., *My Dog Skip*, 423
Russell, Keri: *We Were Soldiers*, 661
Russell, Kurt: *3,000 Miles to Graceland*, 607; *Vanilla Sky*, 645
Russell, Lucy: *Lady and the Duke, The*, 333
Russell, Theresa: *Believer, The*, 55
Russo, Rene: *Adventures of Rocky*

& Bullwinkle, The*, 2; *Big Trouble*, 64; *Showtime*, 546
Rust, Mathias: *Show Me Love*, 545
Ryan, Amanda: *Simon Magus*, 551
Ryan, Eileen: *Eight Legged Freaks*, 184
Ryan, Marisa: *Wet Hot American Summer*, 660
Ryan, Max: *Kiss of the Dragon*, 326
Ryan, Meg: *Hanging Up*, 252; *Kate & Leopold*, 319; *Proof of Life*, 488
Rydell, Mark: *Hollywood Ending*, 271
Ryder, Lisa: *Jason X*, 301
Ryder, Winona: *Girl, Interrupted*, 233; *Lost Souls*, 366; *Mr. Deeds*, 415
Rylance, Mark: *Intimacy*, 289
Rymer, Michael: dir., *Queen of the Damned*, 490

S

Sabara, Daryl: *Spy Kids*, 571
Saboktakin, Elham: *Circle, The*, 120
Sackheim, Daniel: dir., *Glass House, The*, 237
Sagebrecht, Marianne: *Left Luggage*, 346
Sagemiller, Melissa: *Sorority Boys*, 565
Sai-kun Yam: *Iron Monkey*, 293
Saint, Eva Marie: *I Dreamed of Africa*, 282
Sakaguchi, Hironobu: dir., *Final Fantasy: The Spirits Within*, 213
Saldana, Zoe: *Center Stage*, 107; *Crossroads*, 140
Salinas, Jorge: *Amores Perros*, 22
Salles, Walter: dir., *Behind the Sun*, 54
Salmon, Colin: *Resident Evil*, 500
Salton Sea, The, 521
Samaroo, Dennison: *What Lies Beneath*, 663
Sambora, Richie: *On the Line*, 450
Samel, Udo: *Piano Teacher, The*, 472
Samuel, Marc: *Fat Girl*, 205
Samuelsson, Emma: *Together*, 618
Sanchez, Roselyn: *Rush Hour 2*, 519
Sand, Paul: *Chuck & Buck*, 118
Sanda, Dominique: *Crimson Rivers, The*, 137
Sanders, Chris: *Lilo & Stitch*, 358; dir., *Lilo & Stitch*, 358
Sanders, Jay O.: *Along Came a Spider*, 12

888